THE HANDBOOK OF

Strategic Public Relations and Integrated Marketing Communications

THE HANDBOOK OF

Strategic Public Relations and Integrated Marketing Communications

Second Edition

EDITED BY CLARKE L. CAYWOOD, Ph.D.

New York   Chicago   San Francisco   Lisbon   London
Madrid   Mexico City   Milan   New Delhi   San Juan
Seoul   Singapore   Sydney   Toronto

ABOUT THE AUTHOR/EDITOR

CLARKE L. CAYWOOD, Ph.D.

Clarke L. Caywood, Ph.D., is a full professor and member of the Integrated Marketing Communications Department in the Medill School of Journalism, Media, Integrated Marketing Communications at Northwestern University. He was one of 4 faculty members who initially created and designed the integrated marketing communications program. He is the first tenured professor of public relations to teach PR at Northwestern's Medill School of Journalism Media and Integrated Marketing Communications. Professor Caywood teaches graduate classes in public relations, marketing, social and business media, crisis management, communications management and marketing PR.

Dr. Caywood has published numerous articles and book chapters on public relations, advertising and marketing in business and political campaigns and has done research on values in contemporary advertising. Caywood is editor of the best-selling first and second editions of *The Handbook of Strategic Public Relations & Integrated Communications* (McGraw Hill).

He was named by *PRWeek* as one of the 100 most influential PR people of the twentieth century and one of the top 10 outstanding educators in 2000. He was named Educator of the Year by the Public Relations Society of America (PRSA) and awarded the PRSA Anvil prize. He was also named the Educator of the Year by the Sales and Marketing Executives of the Chicago area. He has served as vice president of marketing for start-up company eMarketWorld. He has worked for two past governors and the attorney general of the state of Wisconsin. He ran a number of state campaigns in Wisconsin and has served as a political expert for ABC-TV Channel 7 Chicago. Since 2004, he has spoken extensively to audiences in China and Chinese business leaders in the United States. Honored as an educator, he carried the Olympic Torch in Lijiang, China. He holds a number of honorary teaching posts with Chinese universities.

He is a member of the board of Aidmatrix.org, which is a global disaster relief organization using advanced supply chain solutions. He is also a member and former trustee of the A.W. Page Society. He is founding publisher and continues as publisher of the *Journal of Integrated Marketing Communications*. He is a member of the board of the *Journal of Interactive Advertising* (University of Texas–Austin), the new *Case Research Journal* (University of North Carolina–Chapel Hill) and the *Journal of Public Relations*. He is a member of the Public Relations Society of America, the American Academy of Advertising and the American Marketing Association.

Professor Caywood received his joint doctorate in business (management) and in journalism–mass communications (advertising and public relations) from the faculty of the University of Wisconsin–Madison. He also earned a Master of Science in Public Affairs in the first class of the Lyndon B. Johnson School of Public Affairs, University of Texas–Austin, and a Bachelor of Business Administration from the University of Wisconsin–Madison.

CONTENTS

Chapter 54

Chapter 55

A C K N O W L E D G M E N T S

It may not have taken a village, but it did take a relatively small community of people to produce this second edition of the *Handbook*.

Nearly 70 chapter authors were "cross nominated" by other professionals in the field as leaders in their fields, excellent writers and dedicated professionals. All of the authors were willing to share their knowledge with a new generation of public relations professionals, students and other managers. Many of the authors were personal and professional associates from the Arthur W. Page Society, my membership and service in the Public Relations Society of America and my work at Northwestern University as past chair of the Department of Integrated Marketing Communications (IMC) from 1994 to 2000 and also as director of the Graduate Program in Corporate Public Relations beginning in 1990. I owe most of these introductions initially to Ray Ewing, Professor Emeritus at Northwestern University, who first encouraged me to interview for a faculty position at Medill. We met during a program I managed on telecommunications in 1987 at Marquette University in Milwaukee.

The most important people were, of course, my "team" of editors and researchers. For this edition, Mary Caywood is the most important contributor. Her fluency in Spanish and French has given her an interest in grammar that makes her an excellent first-line copy editor. This is the third book she has helped me develop and edit. It was Mary's father, Professor J. Howard Westing at the University of Wisconsin–Madison, who inspired me to consider books based on the thoughts of other experts. While spending a lot of time in my early career standing in the shadow of great men and women in government, business and academics, I became persuaded that they had more than just spoken words to share. Mary has given me the discipline and diligence to complete the words of over 100 experts in three books that we have shared with thousands of readers.

Working with Mary was Sara Elizabeth Smith, an extraordinary young professional and scholar. Sara was the editor of the 21st edition of the *Journal of Integrated Marketing Communications* before she graduated with a degree in IMC in December 2010. With extraordinary business experience as well, she was the perfect recruit. I was fortunate to have the contributions of Sara, who also coauthored a chapter on the newer field of content management that she seems destined to lead.

Another contributor to the book, who authored a chapter on one of her areas of expertise and helped with the chapter editing process as well, was my daughter Emma Caywood. I thank Emma for taking the time to write this chapter while she was finishing her graduate degree. I also thank my son Graham Caywood, who was the research assistant to his boss, Scott McCallum at the Aidmatrix Foundation, for the case study in the chapter on NGOs. It would also be appropriate to recognize my son, Matt, who always has an intelligent and thoughtful comment to alleviate our writer's block or search for a new idea. I do not know how many public relations professors have a neuroscientist with a doctorate (Harvard, Cambridge and UCSF), a professional storyteller with a master's degree (Northwestern and Dominican) and a younger global NGO manager with a cognitive psychology degree (UCLA) advising them for free, but I find it useful and inspiring.

Always standing ready with the experience of the world-class publisher McGraw-Hill were Mary Glenn, Mary Therese Church and Peter McCurdy as our editorial contacts. They publish more books than even the faculty of the IMC program, so they know what to do and when it should be done. Mary Therese returned to graduate school and was replaced by her boss Mary Glenn, with the help of Peter McCurdy. We also wish to thank Richard Rothschild and his team from Print Matters. All have been terrific supporters of the book's authors, ideas and goals.

Academics sometimes speak of the "publish or perish" pressures of their jobs in research universities. Business leaders do not normally operate under these rules but, given the fact that many of the authors in this volume have published more than white papers and memoranda, PR professionals seem to have an appetite for cogently writing down their thoughts. I would like to thank my Northwestern colleagues in the Medill School of Journalism, Media, Integrated Marketing Communications, in Communications and in the Kellogg School of Management, who have inspired me during all these years that I have been a professor here. I would like to thank the exceptional students whom I have had the pleasure of teaching and learning from, while I have been privileged to enjoy the best part of being a professor: teaching in the classroom. Finally, I would like to thank the dean of Medill, John Lavine, for granting me a sabbatical so I could concentrate on completing this book. I hope that what I have learned from the 68 other writers will help me start new conversations with the new generation of students who are just entering this field and will be entering my classroom.

Clarke L. Caywood

F O R E W O R D

I am flattered that Clarke Caywood asked me to write a preface to this book, which covers essentially every facet of the communications business—a field I have worked in and loved for over a half century.

Shortly after I joined a fellow named Max Cooper, who had a small PR firm in Chicago, I made a cold phone call that led to the growth of our company. This call was made to Ray Kroc, who had a handful of restaurants nobody ever heard of—named McDonald's. Our first priority was to help them gain awareness—and thus sell franchises, which we accomplished through old-fashioned publicity techniques. As they, and we, grew, we had to deal with all the disciplines you will read about in this book.

When I started, the public relations business was in its infancy—and was a lot simpler than it is today. You could reach a huge percentage of the population with well-placed stories on television and in major newspapers and magazines.

Our goal was to get our clients mentioned, and as the cliché stated: "Just spell the name right."

Of course, there was no Internet back then, and communications were generally one way—but today, with millions of websites and web pages, anyone with an Internet connection and a point of view can potentially influence public opinion. In the world of phone cameras, citizen journalism and our global 24/7 news cycle, the PR-communications industry faces challenges I never dreamt about.

Invariably, after most of my speeches, I am approached by a young person in the audience, who laments the problem they have with their companies, in that their supervisor or management does not appreciate what they do or really does not understand their functions. They always ask me, "How can I convince them that what I do is meaningful to the success of the company?"

Most times I give them an answer that shocks them. I tell them to quit their job and go somewhere where the companies do understand and appreciate them.

Many of you who will read this book are already in the industry, and some are contemplating careers in this profession. I have never regretted going into it, as it has kept me engaged, because unless you are current, creative and curious (my three Cs), you will never succeed.

I would like to emphasize *curiosity*. My favorite trait, and lately, the common thread I have been hearing about, when determining why a CEO or even a president of the United States is successful, is "an insatiable curiosity." I am always happy when a grandchild of mine, or a youngster I meet, asks me a lot of questions!

The following pages will give you an outstanding background in just about every aspect of the communications business—but, in addition, don't forget to follow your "gut" feelings. When I hear someone say, "if it ain't broke, don't fix it," my blood begins to boil. Folks around my firm have always heard my constant mantra: "fix it *before* it breaks." We should all have the courage to change things before we have to.

Al Golin
Chairman, GolinHarris
April 28, 2011

1

INTRODUCTION TO PUBLIC RELATIONS AND INTEGRATED MARKETING COMMUNICATIONS

1 CHAPTER

TWENTY-FIRST CENTURY PUBLIC RELATIONS
The Strategic Stages of Integrated Marketing Communications

Clarke L. Caywood, Ph.D.
Professor and Past Chairman, Department of Integrated Marketing Communications
Medill School of Journalism, Media, Integrated Marketing Communications
Northwestern University

Since the last time I edited this book, public relations (PR) practitioners have continued their efforts to build strong leadership for businesses and other complex organizations. These continued efforts to integrate at several levels of business and society will create more integrated management processes, protecting and preserving the reputation of the organization and its stakeholders. In the past decade, public relations has moved beyond its self-defined role of building "relations" to integrating relationships between an organization and its publics.

DEFINITION

Public relations is the profitable integration of an organization's new and continuing relationship with stakeholders, including customers, by managing all communications contacts with the organization, which creates and protects the brand and the reputation of the organization.

After reading all the chapters in this second edition of the *Handbook*, the big idea that emerges is that PR provides management a leadership opportunity to integrate relationships both inside and outside their organization, using a wide range of management strategies and tactics, including communications. I was surprised to find that I only needed to modify my formal definition slightly since the first edition.

Out of all the functions of management, PR has the broadest reach, appealing to the greatest number of audiences or stakeholder groups and individuals. The chief executive officer (CEO) understands that the shareholder, employee and customer are all important stakeholders, although not the only ones. This book begins its section on stakeholders with a chapter on employees by Insidedge CEO, Keith Burton (Chapter 8), which makes this important point.

However, PR is still naturally focused on communications as its strategic advantage and knowledge base. Because of what we are presently calling social media, the field of communications has exploded. The social media chapter, written by part of the leadership team at Edelman, reinforces the concept that PR has gained the greatest ownership and understanding of the use of these applications. Reputation management is now under the wing of public relations, as demonstrated in the chapter by John Graham of Fleishman-Hillard (Chapter 25).

Although some teachers and practitioners continue to waiver between the fields being called *strategic communications* and *public relations*, I prefer not to begin to label all the sister fields of marketing, advertising, and human resources with the now overused descriptor of *strategy* or *strategic*.

Possibly the most confusing part of my working definition of PR is the word *profitable*. My defense is the effort to align PR with driving corporate and organizational goals rather than the use of a more narrow definition of PR, focusing only on the functions of PR. With my background in ethical political campaigns, government service, public television, business and academics, I know that the word *profit* has a special meaning in business. I have argued that the word *profitable* can be viewed as it appears in dictionary.com: "beneficial" or "useful." Using instead synonyms such as advantageous, valuable and helpful, the meaning for nonbusinesses such as nongovernmental organizations (NGOs) and other organizations may be clearer. Naturally, the link to profit reminds the reader of what they already know: profit is a financial term for the use of capital while profitable seems a bit less capitalistic.

The terms *new* and *continuing* are also prescient to the common marketing word *loyalty*. Perhaps loyalty is a more pithy representation of the idea, but new and continuing are dynamic. Finally, *relationship* is defined as a two-way interaction, obviously augmented by Web 2.0, which allows for the conversation to occur on the Internet. This idea continues to be defined by public relations.

GENERAL RELATIONSHIP INTEGRATION

Most of the authors in this field have the idea that integration is more than a simple (although useful) combination of the fields of advertising, promotions, direct marketing, events and marketing public relations. The growth of integrated marketing communications (IMC) as a practical field was based on the initial value of this useful combination of communication tactics into a more comprehensive strategy. However, what is still missing from the general teaching and understanding of IMC is a broader understanding of the importance of integration and why public relations is the ideal professional field to guide and lead in integration.

First, PR will lead corporations and other organizations on several levels, including the integration of relationships with various stakeholders, the integration of corporate and organizational structures, the integration with industry and competitive groups, and finally, the integration with society. The integration of complex organizations demonstrates the range of leadership that public relations professionals can offer, from a macro level of interaction with society to a more micro level with individual stakeholders. This range of relationship building and management is what is ultimately appealing to many professionals in the field, with a broader view of the ultimate role of individuals and organizations.

STAKEHOLDER RELATIONSHIP INTEGRATION

The first level of integration relies on the PR professional's intellectual and skill-based fostering of new relationships with valuable stakeholders to maintain and enhance the reputation of her organization. Stakeholders include individuals and organizations that have a stake in the failure or success of an organization.

As the name suggests, public relations manages relations with various publics. Rather than focusing on the important, but more narrow, relationship of marketing with customers, for example, public relations is expected to manage the corporation's or organization's relationships and reputation with many groups. More than other professions, public relations strengthens the outside–in perspective of an organization by managing relationships with many stakeholder groups inside and outside of the organizational boundaries. Borrowed from Chapter 7, with some modification from the energy industry, is a strong listing of stakeholders. In my experience, it is possible to double and triple the listings with specific names of stakeholder groups and individuals.

> Stakeholders
> > Employees
> > > Full-time

Part-time
Global
Contractors
Management and executives

Shareholders
Institutional
Individual investors

Government
Federal elected officials
State elected officials
Local elected officials
Staffs of elected officials

Non–U.S. Government
Elected officials
Regulators

Regulators
National, state, and local
Global

Traditional News Media
International
National
Local
Point-of-view journalists

Social Media, Blogging, Tweeting, Facebook
Industry bloggers
NGO bloggers
Fans
Employees
Competitors

Industry Associations
Integrated segment

Customers
Commercial
Retail
International

Retail Marketers of Your Product or Service
Company owned
Privately owned

Labor Unions
National
International

Local Community
Neighbors
Accident- or incident-affected residents

Nonprofits
International
National
Local

Nongovernmental Organizations
National, state and local
International
Relationship partners

MANAGEMENT FUNCTION INTEGRATION

Because public relations is responsible for stakeholders, this allows the practitioner to bring a tremendous asset to the boardroom. The second level of integration of PR is with other management functions, including marketing, finance, accounting, human resources and general management. PR also integrates with the legal profession.

The interaction of public relations practitioners with other managers will provide the men and women in the field the opportunity to assume a leadership role. A force driving this development is the downsizing of organizations, which has led to the expectation that all members of the organization are a part of a management team, rather than just staff. Because the lines between management and staff have blurred, projects must now be managed by qualified individuals, rather than by people with job titles or what used to be the necessary credentials. As you can see from Al Golin's preface, over the past decade public relations has earned a "place at the (management) table." Through the growth of management-level education of public relations professionals in universities, through professional societies, from corporate educational efforts and by means of individual commitments to learning, PR has become more managerial.

Public relations still offers its organizations the greatest experience and skill through the use of various communications-based strategies and tactics. Other management fields represented by the educational curriculum for the MBA in finance, management, marketing, human resources, production and accounting do not receive any serious level of communications knowledge or training. Although PR does not only use communications to accomplish its goals, the practitioners in this field have built their careers using, testing and recommending all forms of communications including written, oral and nonverbal. PR has used and refined all channels of communications, including advertising, speeches, press releases, Internet and intranet, direct mail, events and displays. According to most observers, PR has become the principal advocate of social media for management goals.

This level of PR integration also logically emerges out of the changes in the restructuring and design of organizations. Stress and demands on corporations and other complex organizations also force public relations professionals into a leadership role. In increasingly diversified corporate structures, where profit and management responsibilities have been given to strategic business units (SBUs) and separate profit centers, public relations must examine its role in all areas of management. The continued downsizing and leveling of the corporate hierarchy will force public relations managers to examine their roles in the management of divisions and at the corporate level.

As the chapters on the industries of oil, auto, and food and beverage show, the movement of power and responsibility away from the traditional headquarters toward the divisional level compels PR to examine its contribution to the marketing function, its ability to create relationships and drive employee communications as well as other diversified management issues at a more local level. For example, building relationships with the general media for a division president, strengthening specific trade press relationships for the products and services of the division, local community relations and other contacts must be moved from the corporate level to the SBU level.

Another integrated action might be to use zero-based planning and budgeting. This practice, long recognized in state and even federal governments, forces the managers to assume that last year's programs are not necessarily going to be supported in the forthcoming budget. Under financial pressures in public and private organizations in this second decade of the second millennium, the concept may find a more appreciative audience. Although it is dangerous to try to zero-base the entire budget too widely because organizational leaders may find it difficult to rethink all activities at once, the *selective* zero-basing of several programs can be productive. This challenge to the management team will permit fresh ideas, new strategies and new tactics to emerge.

Selectively using the traditional notion of zero-based planning and budgeting with selective programs can mentally challenge an organization's team not to think only incrementally. Although many organizations operate on a year-to-year basis, with budget increases or decreases of only 2 to 5 percent, such common instrumentalism does not provide a manager with the courage to totally re-examine the reason for the program, expenditure or objective. "Just because we did it last year," as the saying goes, does not mean the conditions of the market or environment are correct for the same program or tactic in the coming year. A fresh, zero-based view of the program gives permission to the management team to make new assumptions and use new developments to plan totally new programs.

For example, Dairy Management, Inc. (DMI), the largest national dairy food marketer for its farmer members, initiated, under the direction of its CEO Tom Gallagher, a "no sacred cows" planning effort to create a zero-based attitude among its managers and members. The effort was symbolized by an image of a dairy cow with a halo over its head within a circle with the international symbol of a diagonal bar meaning *no*. Used on printed planning materials, and naturally on the ever-present "corn seed" cap, the symbol sent the signal to the organization that the future might not necessarily look like the past for DMI. The very best communications professionals know how to use communications for strategic change to build new organizational policies and plans.

The ability of the PR professionals to integrate the communications, product and corporate branding strategies, and generate a unified message to investors increases the operational level role of PR in the C-suite. Again, the ability to manage current issues and anticipate future demands on corporate resources enables educated and well-trained public relations professionals to assume leadership roles.

INDUSTRY AND COMPETITIVE LEVEL INTEGRATION

The third level of integration also logically emerges from the changes in the restructuring and design of institutions. Where there are mergers and acquisitions, there are opportunities for the role of PR, as discussed by Joele Frank in Chapter 12.

In early 2011, CNN reported that, "global M&A has totaled $309.6 billion since January 1 (2011) according to data from Thomson Reuters. That's a 69% jump over the same period in 2009, and represents the busiest start since 2000." Globally, they reported that "the largest geographic gainer has been the Americas, up 97 percent year-over-year (including a 295% spike for U.S. M&A). European activity was up 90%, Asian activity up 1 percent, and both Africa and the Middle East experienced volume declines (–38% and –29%, respectively)."[1]

The merger of companies creates a constant redefinition of the boundaries of the industry, leadership in an industry sector and more. These mergers will force the restructuring of communications in many companies. More importantly, the dynamics of business and related sectors such as finance, health care, food, consulting, energy, entertainment and a long list of other subsectors to business will be radically changed.

The realignment of power within an industry sector, such as food and beverage, will send reverberations throughout the market. New stakeholder relationships will have to be defined without the previous players. The question of "who is on first" will be played out in the market, but also in the press. The addition or closing of merger-affected companies will affect all stakeholder groups, including local government, which will be affected by tax and employment changes. Some employees will be moved or let go and others will be newly hired. The press will have to find out who the new spokesperson is, and the spokesperson will have to develop new contacts. Experts and social media pundits will have to catch up on the change in leadership and policies. Industry associations, business conference planners and others will also have to adjust.

Industry integration has always been with us, but the driving forces of the economy, technology, regulation and the market will add another level of integration for public relations to manage, or at least direct, their response to the changes.

GLOBAL SOCIETAL INTEGRATION

Finally, public relations managers will lead their organizations' relationships with a more global society. With the micro relationship built with many stakeholder groups, the corporate and organizational public relations professional will guide the corporate values that permit organizations to operate at a macro, global level.

Again, the education and training of the PR professional may equip him or her to reflect the dynamics between the legal, political and social expectations of society, corporations and other organizations. After years of listening to, speaking to and building relationships with various publics and stakeholder groups, PR professionals have the experience to manage the corporate response to society and societal changes. PR has always advocated the importance of using local contacts to understand how to build relationships in richly varied cultures.

In a graduation speech to my students, Thomas Friedman, *New York Times* columnist and Pulitzer Prize–winning author, noted (from his series of books and revisions on a "flatter Earth") that the relationships have changed in the past decade from those between governments *or* companies to those between governments *and* companies.[2] Even more importantly, relationships have grown into those between individuals, governments and business in all combinations. Oprah Winfrey, in her last televised daytime show from Chicago, noted that she had visited 150 countries via her show. The global work of Bono and former presidents George Bush and Bill Clinton is a remarkable statement of the changing nature of the role of the individual and organizations' and society's need for strong communications and relationship building.[3] The work of Aidmatrix.org, reported in Chapter 18 by Ray Boyer and former Governor of Wisconsin, Scott McCallum, proves the importance of a global integration —in this case, using supply chain (logistics) software to raise nearly $2 billion in global aid each year.

The border-crossing role of public relations, in which the managers operate at the porous boundary of the organization, permits the PR professional to interact with a wide range of stakeholders, but it also creates an expectation that PR should be fully aware of the changing expectations of society and the matching of corporate purposes with societal goals. The ability of the PR professional to describe, explain and predict the societal pressures on the firm provides general management with a risk assessment and interpretation necessary to operate in a complex social setting. As Cornelius Pratt explains in Chapter 6 on ethics, having one more manager at the table with a vision of ethical and value-driven purpose and actions gives PR one more reason to be recognized for its leadership.

PR PROCESS INTEGRATION

Although the initial analysis of public relations above requires integration at various levels between stakeholders, business and society, the other powerful dimension of PR is the development of a more integrated process within PR itself. One of the fastest growing strategies associated with public relations and public relations communications tactics is integrated marketing communications (IMC). Pioneered by the faculty of the Department of Integrated Marketing Communications in Northwestern University's Medill School of Journalism, the field has flourished in the past 22 years in increasing practice and theoretical development. A definition of IMC was developed for a national study for industry at Northwestern:

> [IMC is a] concept of marketing communications planning that represents the added value of a comprehensive plan that evaluates the strategic roles of a variety of communications disciplines—general advertising, direct response, sales promotion and public relations—and combines these disciplines to provide clarity, consistency and maximum communication impact.[4]

IMC emerged out of an academic department that, for several decades, had been recognized as the number one advertising program in the country (and perhaps the world). The department's integration team was initially led by Professors Jack Scissors, Stanley Tannenbaum, Don E. Schultz and me. The department had also redefined public relations and direct marketing education with a strong managerial approach to traditional staff functions. One goal was to change the position of the new field from a service or staff function in organizations to a management function. Based on my MBA teaching and educational experience, the new curriculum included many of the core elements of an MBA curriculum. This unusual action in a traditional journalism school allowed us to position the PR and advertising students to "sit at the management table" with financial, organizational, marketing and general management knowledge skills.

The leadership of the school was again demonstrated when the faculty, administration and students integrated the existing power of the advertising, sales promotions, direct marketing and public relations courses and knowledge. The combination of the fields provided businesses and organizations that hired the graduate students, interacted with the faculty and read the research with a competitive advantage over the traditionally nonintegrated and functionally separate operations. Although the curriculum has fluxed from time to time under pressures of temporary market changes and changes in leadership, the field continues to fill an important void in business education. However, IMC has not been given as much attention from the academic community as it has from the practical professional community in PR, sales, marketing and advertising.

IMC proves that educators can take a new direction with the traditional elements of advertising, direct marketing and public relations education. The distinct elements provided corporations and other organizations with compelling reasons to re-examine their business processes. The reinvention and re-engineering of marketing, public relations and direct marketing as a more fully integrated process has offered public relations professionals the most significant opportunity for advancing the influence of the profession. As a number of authors have shown, IMC and integrated communications will permit PR to take the leadership role it deserves based on the range and depth of the field, its attention to multiple stakeholder groups, and its experience and strength using communications as an important management tool.

INTEGRATED MARKETING OR MARKETING COMMUNICATIONS?

Early in the creation of the discipline of IMC, I speculated on how long it would take for the word *integrated* to be dropped in favor of marketing communications (already used in business and business courses). It also became increasingly clear with the work of "relationship marketing" researchers that the term might gain favor.[5] Later, the even broader term *integrated marketing* began to gain momentum in the literature and references in the profession. The latter was recently explored by Kondo and Caywood to show that the movement in theory and research has moved toward the term *integrated marketing* several times more than the volume of research work and published thought on IMC suggested.[6] In other words, both integrated marketing and PR outpublish IMC. IMC was also outpublished by the concept of relationship marketing. Additionally, both the traditional fields of marketing and PR outflank and outpublish the still "thin blue line of IMC," challenging the more established intellectual and professional practice disciplines. As long as IMC was considered a marketing subfunction rather than a communications function, the term seemed to have an expected shorter shelf life. This book is one of the most successful publishing efforts in IMC to date. It has demonstrated the ability of integrated thinking to strengthen the communications function through stakeholder relationships. Without this perspective, it seems clear that the term *IMC* will fall into disuse, in favor of integrated marketing without more academic leadership.

More than 15 years ago, the use of the term *integrated communications* was an attempt I made to bridge the gap between academic communications, public relations and advertising by not using the "m" word (marketing). There was a healthy debate in the 1990s over the rapacious function of marketing taking over and subsuming the PR function in organizations, spearheaded by Professor Martha Lauzen, Ph.D.[7] Although there was some truth to it, its advocates' narrow definition of marketing communications as solely consumer oriented, and the still more narrow definition of marketing as being only consumer focused did not worry most business-oriented PR academics or practitioners. PR has thrived, as this book will show, with its wider agenda and growing powers.

For this edition of the *Handbook*, I have asked many of the authors to address their relationship with marketing, which has become more prominent since the previous edition. So, in keeping with some tradition and risk, we are using the descriptive phrase "Public Relations & Integrated Marketing & Communications." It still uses the transitory label of "integrated," but it assumes with more ampersands that public relations, marketing and communications must be integrated together in more than one combination.[8] Finally, on this seeming nuance, but useful distinction, which separates this book from others in public relations, I ask a somewhat obvious question that still might predict the future use of the hopefully unnecessary word *integrated* as the field matures. The question that will be answered time and time again in the book is, "What else would you want: a disintegrated management process?"

FINAL THOUGHTS

This book explores the power, depth and breadth of the field of public relations, with its sister fields of communications, integrated communications, integrated marketing communication and marketing, as a professional field of study and practice. PR is a highly applied discipline in the wide range of businesses and other organizations. The book's authors have recognized that, with their multigenerational perspectives, advanced education and broad experience, public relations does not operate in a vacuum.

In fact, the power of public relations is its ability to relate and develop productive relationships with other business functions and with multiple stakeholders. PR has not just been introduced to the notion of integration in the last decade, it has defined the concept and practice over many decades of leadership. If the future of public relations is *not* integrated, then the future will not be as bright as the authors predict in the following pages.

As the editor of this book, I promise you that all of the authors are individuals you would want to spend hours with, talking about the topics that they have generously summarized for this book. If you remember conversations about important subjects with your favorite teacher, professor, peer, boss or brightest friend, you will realize that these authors reflect the very highest levels of thought, trust and ability to recommend. If they were readily available, you would want to ask their opinions before making a decision.

My objective was to permit the "voice" of each author, as a leader in the field, to speak with his or her own point of view and style. Even with editing, the book tries to maintain the tone of each person's work and its details. Collectively, these chapters represent their willingness to share with you their experience and current thinking about how to manage, work and think—now and in the future. It is not their cumulative experience that makes these authors' ideas so powerful (although their total years of experience are significant); instead, it is the vitality and currency of their ideas that has permitted them to be successful during their entire careers, through change after change in the environment, market conditions and society.

To summarize, the book is organized around four key sections:

1. The first highlights the areas of professional practice in public relations that focus on specific stakeholder groups important to an organization. This area has been greatly expanded to show the importance of a stakeholder model in business and other organizations.

2. Many of chapters provide an extraordinary view of the practice of corporate communications and public relations in numerous specific businesses, nonprofit and government sectors including hospitality, technology, health care, consulting and many others. Again, this section has been broadened to give readers an even greater choice of topics relating to their targeted business or organization.

3. The book also includes several chapters related to research, law, career development and the history of the profession to provide students and professionals with a clear background to the field.

4. Finally, the book expanded the sections on how to create great communications with stories, speeches, virtual meetings and much more. All the chapters from the first edition have been substantially rewritten since 1997. The reader will find the wait worthwhile because so much has changed that empowers and redefines the professional and practical role of public relations.

This book was designed as both a professional project and a work of art and social science. The project dimensions were clear to the original publishers as we discussed the depth and breadth of the field and the range of experts necessary to define the field. The coordination of 70 authors on more than 50 topics was an intellectually stimulating challenge.

Based on an agreed structure for each chapter, the authors were asked to use their experience and knowledge of the field to produce chapters that (1) define their area of PR, (2) describe the strategic approach that their company and other organizations have taken to the field, (3) discuss and list tactics that have usefully implemented these strategies, (4) describe in one or more detailed case studies the best practices in public relations, and (5) discuss future trends relevant to their industry or area of expertise in PR. This format proves useful to the reader searching for specific ideas across industries. The organization of the book also provides a strong sense of the future from a wide range of authors and a wide selection of case examples illustrating the practice of PR.

The book also proves to be a resource for general knowledge about public relations. It is designed to serve the needs of the professional business book market, and it may be one of the longer entries in this category in 2012.

The first edition was, for a time, the third best-selling textbook in public relations. To all my colleagues who have encouraged me to design this book with two audiences in mind—the student and the professional—I appreciate their vote of confidence. At this point in my career, writing a typical textbook does not interest me. I believe the next generation of public relations professionals, management, marketing students and a host of others will find this book both instructive and helpful. Time and time again, the authors demonstrate their depth and breadth of knowledge about the field of PR. Seen as personal essays from individuals with experience and credentials, the chapters provide extraordinary insight to a wide range of organizations and PR practices. The authors are highly credible sources of information about their topics. In addition, many of the authors have relied on research from their organizations and others to document specific issues. The book serves as a source of personal insight, research and parallel discussion of key issues, industries and activities in public relations and management.

Without overpromising, I know that you will learn from the authors and enjoy their insightful perspectives on the field of integrated public relations now and throughout your career in the twenty-first century.

DISCUSSION QUESTIONS

1. Define public relations for a manager who is trying to decide if public relations could be of value to a new business that has innovative software.
2. What are the "stages" of the evolution of integration in public relations? What is the value of knowing in what stage your company might be?
3. Explain to an interviewer what you might bring to a company with knowledge of public relations.
4. What does the stakeholder concept bring to the discussion of the role of public relations in business and other organizations?

NOTES

1. Primack, Dan. "Gonna Be a Blockbuster? M&A Off to Best Start Since 2000." The Term Sheet: Fortune's Deals Blog Term Sheet. Fortune Finance: Hedge Funds, Markets, Mergers & Acquisitions, Private Equity, Venture Capital, Wall Street, Washington, finance.fortune.cnn.com/2011/02/04/gonna-be-a-blockbuster-ma-off-to-best-start-since-2000 (May 31, 2011).
2. Friedman, Thomas L. *The World Is Flat: a Brief History of the Twenty-First Century*. New York: Farrar, Straus and Giroux, 2006. Print.
3. Clinton, Bill. *Giving: How Each of Us Can Change the World*. New York: Knopf, 2007. Print.
4. Caywood, Clarke L., Don E. Schultz, and Paul Wang. 1991. *A Survey of Consumer Goods Manufacturers*. New York: American Association of Advertising Agencies, 1992.
5. Godson, Mark. *Relationship Marketing*. Oxford: Oxford UP, 2009. Print.
6. Kondo, Kimihiko, and Clarke L. Caywood. 2011. "IMC as an Innovation: Toward a Theory of Integrated Marketing Using Theoretical Propositions," Presented in June 2011 to the American Academy of Advertising 2011—Asia Pacific Conference, Brisbane Australia.
7. Lauzen, Martha M. "Public Relations Roles, Intraorganizational Power, and Encroachment." *Journal of Public Relations Research* 4.2 (1992): 61-80.
8. Tybout, Alice M., and Bobby J. Calder. 2010. *Kellogg on Marketing*. Hoboken, NJ: Wiley.

ADDITIONAL READING

Caywood, Clarke. 1995. "Integrated Marketing Campaigns." In *Integrated Marketing Communications Symposium*, edited by Ron Kaatz. Lincolnwood, IL: NTC Business Books.
Clinton, Bill. 2007. *Giving: How Each of Us Can Change the World*. New York: Knopf.

Lauzen, Martha M. "Public Relations Roles, Intraorganizational Power, and Encroachment." *Journal of Public Relations Research* 4.2 (1992): 61-80. Print.

Schultz, Don E., and Heidi Schultz. 2003. *IMC the Next Generation: Five Steps for Delivering Value and Measuring Returns Using Marketing Communication.* Boston: McGraw-Hill.

Thorson, Esther, and Jeri Moore. 1996. *Integrated Communication: Synergy of Persuasive Voices.* Mahwah, NJ: Lawrence Erlbaum Associates.

Tybout, Alice M., and Bobby J. Calder. 2010. *Kellogg on Marketing.* Hoboken, NJ: Wiley.

Vocus White Paper. Measuring the Marketing ROI on Public Relationships. www.vocus.com/codies/Marketing_ROI.pdf (Accessed 5/2/2011).

Wang, Paul. 1995. "Measuring ROI." In *Integrated Marketing Communications Symposium*, edited by Ron Kaatz. Lincolnwood, IL: NTC Business Books.

Weiner, Mark. "Beyond ROI." Institute for Public Relations. www.instituteforpr.org/2007/08/mark-weiner-beyond-roi/ (Sunday, August 19, 2007 at 12:45 pm).

2 CHAPTER

COMMUNICATIONS RESEARCH
Foundational Methods

Anders Gronstedt, Ph.D.
Chief Executive Officer
The Gronstedt Group

Clarke L. Caywood, Ph.D.
Professor and Past Chairman, Department of Integrated Marketing Communications
Medill School of Journalism, Media, Integrated Communications
Northwestern University

The public relations (PR) profession is under increasingly intense pressure to justify its existence and to demonstrate accountability. Nobody questions the need to have a sales, accounting or manufacturing department. The senior vice president of sales can show up for top management meetings with sales statistics. The vice president of manufacturing can bring productivity numbers, defect rates and cycle time reduction data. The chief financial officer can dazzle senior management with budget forecasts and cash flow analyses. However, most senior public relations or corporate communications directors do not have the hard data to demonstrate their value to the corporation. In the last decade, the percentage of respondents to the University of Southern California Annenberg General Accepted Practices (GAP) study who report directly and exclusively to the C-suite has increased to 42.5 percent, with 57.5 percent reporting to other officers. Among smaller companies, it is likely that the percentage reporting to the C-suite is much smaller.[1] Previously, it was thought that the small number (25 percent) of public relations or corporate communications managers in the United States who were also members of the senior management team may have kept public relations from helping make the decisions that have an actual impact on the organization.[2]

Demonstrating accountability through research is necessary not only to get behind closed doors but also to avoid being outplaced. Public relations has been a prime target for workforce reduction and elimination during the cost-cutting and downsizing mandates of the 1980s and 1990s. The good news is that in the first two decades of the twenty-first century, the growth of PR will be more than twice that of new and replacement work in advertising and promotions, according to the Bureau of Labor Statistics. In fact, PR is estimated to grow by 13 percent, while advertising promotions will decline by 1.7 percent. To put this category of advertising, marketing, promotions, PR and sales management in perspective, the employment size of sales management will continue to be six to seven times that of PR, and marketing management will be three times that of PR. PR will continue to present 27 percent more jobs than advertising and promotions and increase to 45 percent more by 2018.[3]

To reaffirm the central, strategic role of public relations or corporate communications, we need to be vigorous and persistent in systematically capturing and analyzing information from key stakeholders and in keeping the organization informed and focused on the stakeholders' needs. We need to be the organizational radar, taking soundings and providing early warnings to help the senior management team steer clear of public relations problems and charting the course to building a desired corporate reputation.

The focus of this chapter is on developing public relations strategy and objectives on the basis of insights from research and on using research to evaluate progress toward predetermined objectives. In survey after survey, public relations professionals rank measurement and accountability as the number one priority of the profession,[4] but few public relations managers "walk the walk" and "talk the talk." Most public relations research decisions are still based on gut feelings, speculation and hearsay. More than 50 percent of recently surveyed public relations managers rarely or never budget for research.[5] Experts in the industry recommend that at least 10 percent of the public relations budget should be allocated to research.

Lack of funding is the most frequently mentioned reason for not doing public relations research.[6] The more appropriate question is how anyone can afford *not* to do research. There are instances in which PR departments have tripled the outcomes of their efforts because of research-based planning and implementation.

Historically, the research most PR departments conducted was tactically rather than strategically oriented and was designed to legitimize decisions that had already been made rather than to gain new insights. In the words of the advertising luminary David Ogilvy, research is used like the drunkard uses the lamppost, for support rather than illumination. Because public relations is largely intangible, there is a strong tendency to focus the research on what is most tangible and easy to count, like the number of print publication clips about the company. Two-thirds of all public relations managers in one survey listed "count clips and broadcast placements" as the research approach of "first importance."[7] Such research is not exactly the fabric that strategy-building insights are built on. It is like a VP of sales citing "initiated sales calls" as the number one measure of success. Clip counting was a more important measure of success in the past when the number of media outlets was small and people still trusted media. Besides, there were few other research methods available in the 1950s and 1960s. Today, we have more sophisticated methods at our disposal. Chapter 3 will discuss online systems, but to know what questions and what data are needed for making decisions in management, public relations must take a leadership role in social science research or research that studies the response and action of consumers and other stakeholders to organizational messages, products and actions.

Public relations professionals frequently bemoan that senior managers "do not understand public relations" when, in fact, the real problem is that many PR professionals do not understand management. Our profession needs to develop tools and measures of accountability like our peers in other departments. When senior management asks, "What have you done for me lately," we need to have the hard data to support our answers.

One answer has been to change the educational definition of public relations. At Northwestern University's Medill School and the University of Colorado-Boulder's School of Journalism, the traditional journalistic curriculum was merged with advertising, promotions, direct mail marketing and public relations. Education and training in advertising and PR go back to the beginning of the 1900s when newspapers depended on advertising dollars and journalists often worked in PR after leaving the newspaper. By cross educating and training students, the focus on using communications as a strategic advantage is apparent.

By adding business courses in management, accounting, finance, statistics, marketing and communications research and marketing management, communications students are better equipped to address business and organizational challenges. The integrated model provides a superior knowledge of communications over the traditional approach of advertising or public relations, which taught the subjects separately in two different majors. The challenge would be that many small marketing communications agencies and smaller companies needed more professionals. After all, what marketing communications program would want to be considered "disintegrated?"

Historically, communications has not been a serious topic of study for schools of business, despite criticism by their own accrediting council.[8] In 1980 and 1983, the American Assembly of Collegiate Schools of Business held seminars on the teaching of business communication. In the 1980 seminar, three graduate programs were presented. These programs emphasized memorandum and report writing, visual aids and oral presentations. The graduate programs described at the 1983 seminar were much broader, emphasizing writing letters, memorandums and reports; oral presentations; interpersonal communication; interviewing; and organizational communication.

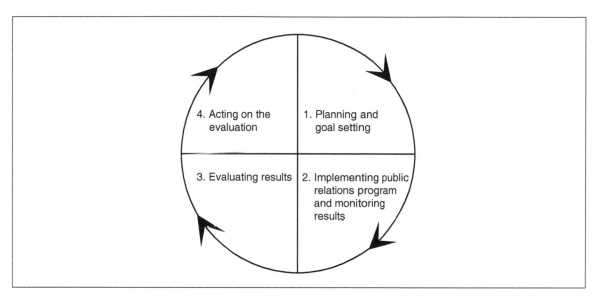

F I G U R E   2.1

The Role of Research in the Four Interactive Steps of Effective Public Relations Practice

RESEARCH
- ❑ How thorough and relevant was the research to overall planning and audience identification?
- ❑ Did the research reflect a clear need or opportunity?
- ❑ Was original or secondary research undertaken to achieve the desired results?
- ❑ How clearly was a baseline and/or process defined by which to gauge the program's success?

PLANNING
- ❑ Did the plan clearly define objectives?
- ❑ How well did the objectives support the organization's overall goals?
- ❑ Did the strategy reflect research findings and support objectives?
- ❑ How original was the strategy?
- ❑ How thorough was the plan?

EXECUTION
- ❑ How appropriate were the tactics to achieving objectives and executing strategy?
- ❑ How creative were the tactics?
- ❑ How well were the tactics implemented?
- ❑ How integrated were the various tools with one another?
- ❑ How efficient was the execution of tactics in relation to resources (personnel and budget)?

EVALUATION
- ❑ How successful was the organization in achieving its objectives?
- ❑ How thorough and relevant were analysis and quantification of results?
- ❑ Did the results clearly reflect original strategy and planning?
- ❑ How well did the team work together?
- ❑ Were there continuous opportunities for learning and program refinement?

F I G U R E   2.2

Silver Anvil

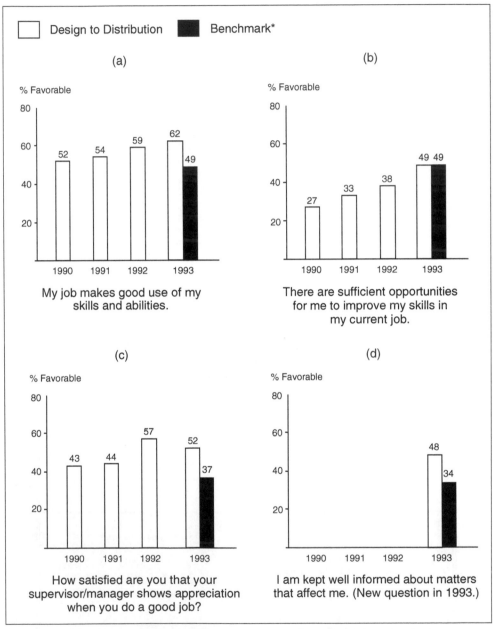

*The benchmark is an average from "Benchmark Club," which has survey data from 18 questions that have been given to 24 million employees in 46 countries.
Source: Design To Distribution's 1994 European Quality Award submission.

FIGURE 2.3

Design to Distribution Employee Satisfaction Compared with a Benchmark

Since then, the topics have become more strategic and complex, but the criticism of the master of business administration and executive master of business administration programs still stands that communications is not taught as a strategic tool or management advantage to the next generation of business managers (Figure 2.1).

Effective public relations should be practiced in four iterative steps, as illustrated in Figure 2.2: (1) research, (2) planning and goal setting, (3) implementation and monitoring and (4) evaluation and acting on the evaluation to make improvements. This approach is analogous to the continual improvement cycle of "plan–do–check–act" prescribed by W. Edwards Deming and other total quality management proponents. It is also similar to the Silver Anvil process for strategic public relations programs. The Silver Anvil process was refined by the chapter authors when Caywood was co-chair of the committee and Gronstedt was a consultant to the committee. New training standards for the 100 or more judges who evaluate the Silver Anvil awards for the Public Relations Society of America were developed, which included a more research-oriented process. In fact, of the maximum 40 points (10 points in each category), 30 points were specifically related to research methods, discussed in this chapter and in the next chapter (see Figure 2.3 from Silver Anvil). We will briefly describe these steps and then give examples of how they are applied to research different stakeholders.

RESEARCH

After 20 years of education and training in graduate, undergraduate, and professional education, the field acknowledges that research is a more critical part of the strategic process. The leadership of social science researchers in business, nongovernmental organizations (NGOs), education, and government has provided support for public relations practitioners to apply research to their PR programs.

The challenge to PR is to be able to use:

Secondary research: existing research perhaps collected for another purpose that can be applied to the current issue or program or
Primary research: newly developed, custom research directly inquiring about the questions and issues facing the organization

As we will discuss in greater detail, the first questions for the research- and planning-oriented PR professional, according to the Public Relations Society of America Silver Anvil standards are as follows:

1. How thorough and relevant was the research to overall planning and audience identification?

2. Did the research reflect a clear need or opportunity?

3. Was original or secondary research undertaken to achieve the desired results?

4. How clearly were a baseline and/or process defined by which to gauge the program's success?

As the questions suggest, the judges look for evidence that the program strategists in PR are precise in their understanding of the stakeholder or audience groups involved so that programs and messages will be carefully targeted. The research should be important and reflect a profitable or critical opportunity for the organization. Part of the business teaching is to set priorities, and careful research and planning will give the PR program a stronger justification. Finally, the initial research to understand the market, the audience and the challenge should rely on both primary and secondary data. It should also set a baseline or a clear level of previous support, performance or other metrics to allow the program to show progress with the new efforts.

PLANNING

Every carpenter knows that you save time, aggravation and money by measuring twice and cutting once. The same holds true for public relations and overall business planning. Research helps to frame issues, to identify key stakeholders and to set the objectives that the public relations program can be measured against.

Public relations research should support the planning of not only the PR programs but also the overall business strategy. Research can be used to redefine the organization's strategic direction in response to changing conditions in the environment. The researcher's involvement in strategic management processes ensures that public relations plans and objectives are aligned with overall business plans and objectives. In fact, one study indicated that 83 percent of public relations or corporate communications managers make no separation between corporate goals and public relations goals.[9]

To support the strategic management and strategic public relations planning processes, public relations professionals need to research the following issues.

WHAT ARE OUR MOST SIGNIFICANT STRENGTHS, WEAKNESSES, OPPORTUNITIES AND THREATS?

The first step in any planning is an environmental scan, in which the researcher is charting what is happening in the environment. One useful format is the strengths, weaknesses, opportunities and threats (SWOT) analysis, which analyzes the company's strengths and weaknesses in meeting the opportunities and threats in the external environment. The opportunities and threats have to be prioritized and strategies developed to leverage the company's strengths and address its weaknesses.

A less well-known but obvious application of SWOT is threats, opportunities, weaknesses and strengths (TOWS). The reason for the switch of the acronym is that an outside–in perspective is often more useful in PR and stakeholder work. Our experience has been that the planning process will focus initially on the internal strengths and weaknesses and spend too much time listing and talking about subjects familiar to the planners. By the time the planning exercise is coming to a close, the effort on the less known external threats and opportunities loses momentum. By starting with the external factors, the analysis illustrates the advantage of PR as an outside–in management process.

The environmental scan needs to be ongoing. By monitoring issues, opinions and corporate reputation over time, the researcher uncovers *dynamic complexity*,[10] that is, recurring processes of change that the organization can act on. In contrast, most research in the field today consists of the occasional "snapshot" survey with hundreds of variables that create *detailed complexity* without discerning any patterns. The research process needs to anticipate and prepare for events that are likely to affect the organization in the future, such as evolving debates over political issues or changes in customer preferences. Organizations that enter a communication process at an early stage are more likely to affirmatively manage issues.

One approach to make the environmental scan ongoing is to set up an *issues anticipation team* composed of employees from different parts of the organization who meet on a regular basis to discuss emerging issues that will affect the organization.[11]

WHO ARE OUR MOST IMPORTANT STAKEHOLDERS?

When the SWOT/TOWS analysis is completed, it is important to identify the key stakeholders and rank their relative importance to the organization. The stakeholders can first be ranked generically—customers, employees, investors and so forth. The next step is to identify the specific groups and individuals that have a stake in the organization's purpose. If at all possible, the stakeholders should be segmented on the basis of behavior. Examples of behavior segmentation among customers are nonusers, light users and heavy users. News reporters can be divided into categories on the basis of whether they have written negative stories about your organization, neutral stories, positive ones or no stories.

The development of relational database technology makes behavior segmentation manageable. Companies in the airline, hotel and mail order industries have massive amounts of individual consumer data, for instance. The relational database plays an important strategic role in public relations as well. The public relations department at Walmart, for instance, uses a database to track individual journalists. To build a stakeholder database, start with internal sources: the rolodex, the Christmas card mailing list, the billing list from the accounting department and so forth. Next, consider renting outside lists to enhance your database. The process of incorporating different databases with each other and deleting duplicates is called *merge or purge*.

The database can identify the "critical few," the small number of stakeholders that cause most problems or accomplishments. For instance, 80 percent of sales usually come from 20 percent of the customers. This phenomenon is called the *Pareto effect*, after the Italian economist Wilfredo Pareto who concluded that 80 percent of wealth was owned by 20 percent of the people. The Pareto effect is true for any stakeholder group. Most organizations will find, for instance, that 20 percent of all journalists account for 80 percent of the media coverage of the company, and 20 percent of all shareholders own 80 percent of the company. The critical few are, in most cases, the most cost-effective group to target with communications.

If behavioral data is not accessible, the segmentation can be based on demographic criteria such as sex, age, marital status, race, education, income or geographic region. Alternatively, segmentation can be based on psychographic criteria, such as opinion or lifestyle.

The researcher's responsibility goes beyond just defining a target audience by sterile behavioral or demographic data (which will probably tell you that the average audience member has one testicle and 2.2 children). They need to bring the target audience member to life by describing that person in qualitative terms. Celestial Seasonings, the herbal tea manufacturer, has even given its target customer a name, Tracy Jones. Tracy is a 35-year-old professional woman who enjoys relaxing in the evening with a soothing cup of herbal tea. During any meeting, employees will ask, "What would Tracy Jones say?" or "Would Tracy like that?"

WHAT ARE THE MOST IMPORTANT NEEDS OF EACH OF THE STAKEHOLDER GROUPS THAT OUR ORGANIZATION CAN ADDRESS?

For each prioritized stakeholder segment, the research must identify its most important needs. The critical questions to ask to identify these needs are as follows:

Customers: Why should I buy from company X?
Employees: Why should I work for company X?
Investment community: Why is company X a good long-term investment for me?
Regulators: How will changes in regulatory policies and practices which favor company X also provide benefit to customers or the general public?
Local communities and public at large: What makes company X an asset to my community and my country?

When the critical needs are identified, the public relations function needs to collaborate with the departments responsible for respective stakeholders to address these. Employee needs are addressed in collaboration with the human resource department, customer needs with marketing, and shareholder needs with the finance department. Thus, public relations research is supporting not only changed behavior by the stakeholder but also changed behavior by the organization.

WHAT ARE THE BEHAVIORAL AND COMMUNICATION OBJECTIVES?

On the basis of the stakeholder needs analysis, behavioral objectives should be developed for each targeted stakeholder group. The behavior objective for a consumer segment of "brand switchers" can be to turn them into loyal users, for employees it can be to recommend the company to a friend as a place to work, and for investors it can be to obtain the largest current shareholders to buy more shares in the company. When behavioral objectives for each stakeholder group are determined, communication objectives can be developed to support them.

WHAT IS THE PERSONAL MEDIA NETWORK OF A TYPICAL TARGET AUDIENCE MEMBER?

The final step of the planning process is to develop a media plan for each target group. Research plays an important role in identifying the *personal media network* of a target audience member. By mapping a typical day in the life of such a person, the researcher can identify *when*—during the year, month, week and day—and where the target audience member would be most receptive to your message. The advertising agency DDB calls these windows of opportunities media "apertures" (which is the opening in an optical instrument that limits the amount of light passing through). The agency has, for instance, found that people are more susceptible to home mortgage offers on Monday mornings, and the best media aperture to advertise diapers is right after the birth of a new baby. Sophisticated companies ask its most important stakeholders when and how they want to receive information to tailor the communication to each individual's need. New owners of a Lexus car, for instance, are asked how they want information from Lexus—if they like to get a call or a letter, if they want to be contacted at home or at work and so forth. The next issue is what combination of media vehicles can be used to communicate with the target audience at the times and places when it is ready to hear it. This *zero-based media approach*, where the media are selected from the target stakeholder's point of view, is dramatically different from traditional approaches where the planning team picks the tried-and-true media vehicles (like events and press releases) that have worked well in the past and that they are most comfortable with.

INSIDE–OUT VERSUS OUTSIDE–IN PLANNING

The approach just described is an outside–in approach to strategic public relations planning, which can be contrasted with the traditional inside–out planning model.[12]

The inside–out approach starts with the organization's objectives, which determine cognitive, attitude and action objectives. This model builds on an almost 100-year-old communication model of cognitive, affective, and behavioral response from the target audience, or "think–feel–do."[13] That is, communication will put information in the consumers' minds, change their attitudes and get them to act. There are endless variations of this learning hierarchy—"awareness–interest–desire–action" is one of the most commonly used. Every self-respecting research firm and public relations agency has its own in-house version of the model. There is only one little problem with this theory: the last 50 years of research indicate that the model is wrong!

The think–feel–do model is built on the assumption that communication is like injecting a hypodermic needle into someone; people will uncritically absorb messages, later develop a feel for them and eventually act on them. In reality, the different steps of the hierarchy might even be in conflict. United Color of Benetton's advertising, for instance, gets attention for reasons that make many consumers develop a negative attitude toward the brand; a different message focusing on an important product difference might be persuasive but fail to get the target audience's attention in today's cluttered media environment, as suggested by Patrick Jackson at the 1995 PRSA national conference. Another problem with the approach is that it treats the action as the culmination of the communication process, instead of treating it as the beginning of an ongoing relationship. The model does not address the issue of how communication can support a relationship with customers, employees, shareholders and other stakeholders, only how to attract new ones.

The traditional inside–out approach to public relations research is the product of a time when more than 90 percent of the U.S. population watched the three television networks and the rest of the world watched government-controlled TV stations. In today's world, people are actively seeking information they believe to be relevant. They are active, interactive and equal participants of an ongoing communication process rather than passive sponges. The role of the communicator is increasingly to make information available to stakeholders in a user-friendly way, rather than shoving it down their throats, and to support an ongoing relationship rather than transferring information. The purpose of communications is not necessarily to influence stakeholders but to add value to them.

Rather than focus the research on *what communication does to the stakeholder*, we need to focus on *what the stakeholder does with the communicated messages*. This is the focus of the outside–in or behavioral approach to research and planning. The outside–in approach begins with the key stakeholders' needs and then determines behavior objectives of the organization and the stakeholders. Research is essential in this process to determine what is the stakeholder's value, to monitor how well their needs are being met and to measure how their behaviors are changing.

DESIGNING THE RESEARCH STUDY

Several sources should be drawn on to answer the research questions. Every organization has internal sources of information such as records of customer service calls, market research and product performance data that need to be tapped. Most importantly, it has internal databases that can be used.

In addition, there are several external sources of information that can be tapped at low cost and with little effort. Trade and popular press and academic journals are readily available through computer (see Chapter 3 on online research methods). There are several syndicated research studies that companies can subscribe to.

Examples of such studies in the United States are Simmons, MRI and Nielsen for consumer information and media usage data and the Yankelovich Monitor and Roper Report for public opinion data. In addition, external databases can be purchased and overlaid onto the company's own database.

The analysis of existing information inside and outside the organization will determine what new research information is needed. The type of information that is needed and the budget and time frame determine the design of the research study. The most effective research design in most situations is a combination of qualitative and quantitative methods.

Qualitative methods like focus group interviews, in-depth interviews and observation are valuable to help determine the target audience, to frame the issues and to develop key messages. Box 2-1 briefly describes these methods. The aim of such research is to get insights into the hearts and minds of key stakeholders to formulate the PR strategy.

The strength of a qualitative interview is that the interviewer can probe the underpinnings of the interviewees' standpoints. That is important because most people are unable to describe or are unaware of their underlying feelings and motives. There are various creative questions that can be used in an in-depth interview or focus group to make it easier for people to talk about their feelings, like "If company X were an animal, what animal would it be?" or "If it were a country . . ." When Apple did focus group studies in preparation for the launch of its Macintosh, it found that people associated IBM with Big Brother, which sparked the idea of the famous 1984 commercial in which IBM was portrayed as author George Orwell's "Big Brother." Such questions require a lot of creativity to interpret. The continued higher "share of heart" of Apple's iPhone, iPad and Macs frustrates Microsoft and other competitors who have a

---

BOX 2-1 QUALITATIVE RESEARCH METHODS

Focus Group

A focus group is a group of 8 to 12 people in a roundtable discussion, led by a moderator (two moderators are preferred if resources allow). The discussion is typically video recorded and monitored by the client through a one-way mirror. Online focus groups can be held via phone and text chat. The participants are screened to create homogenous groups. For instance, one focus group might consist of people 45 years and older, another of people 30 to 44 years old and another of people younger than 30 years. The moderator(s) begins by asking easy and general questions about the topic, which get more and more specific as the discussion progresses. An important task for the moderator(s) is to avoid permitting a few individuals to dominate the discussion. The focus group is typically used in the early developmental stages of the planning process but can also be used to test and hone in on messages and creative message executions.

Ethnography (Observation)

Ethnography, developed initially by anthropologists, is based on extensive field observations. The researchers leave their offices and immerse themselves in the lives of the people being studied. By living and breathing the lives of consumers, employees or whoever forms the focus of the study, the researcher will experience the problem from their perspective. The researcher can either observe people or act in the role of the people under study. Mystery shopping is a common application of ethnography in marketing research, where researchers will act as customers and report their experiences.

In-depth Interview

Personal in-depth interviews offer many of the advantages of a focus group without the negative side effect of someone dominating the discussion. This format allows the researcher to use a questioning technique called *laddering*, in which the interviewer asks "why" several times to discover underlying feelings and motives. Another situation that calls for personal in-depth interviews is when the subjects are opinion leaders and experts who are difficult to recruit to a focus group. In a crisis, when the researcher only has a few hours to obtain information, it can be valuable to do a *soft sounding*, that is, in-depth interviews with a handful of opinion leaders over the phone.

relatively high "share of mind" with Apple but cannot grab the soul of the consumer. Paying attention to continuing research seems to keep Apple ahead of their competitors with their communications and business strategies.

After insights have been developed, it is important to use quantitative survey research to verify the insights and to obtain baseline data to measure progress. By repeating the survey after a public relations program, a researcher can measure the effect. The most commonly used quantitative, verification-oriented methods—telephone, mail and mall-intercept surveys—are described in Box 2-2.

The advantage of the survey is that the results reflect the general population from which the sample is drawn. The logic is much the same as drawing a blood sample. You do not need to drain your entire body of blood to determine your blood type. Similarly, a small random sample of people can represent a larger population. The key is that the sample must be randomly selected. Every individual in the population should have the same probability of being selected. The margin of *random sampling error* can be calculated mathematically on the basis of the sample size and some other factors. The results of a survey might, for example, have a 95 percent chance of having a margin of error of ±3 percent. It is important to keep in mind that there will also be *systematic errors* resulting from factors such as biased questions and poorly trained interviewers, which cannot be calculated.

Most questions in a quantitative survey are closed-ended. The answer alternatives can be dichotomous (yes–no), determinant ("pick one from the list"), frequency of occurrence ("how many bottles do you drink a

---

BOX 2-2 QUANTITATIVE RESEARCH METHODS

Telephone Survey

The telephone survey is by far the most commonly used research method in public relations. It is a quick, inexpensive and convenient way to reach people. With today's computer technology, the results can be tabulated immediately after the interviews are completed. The drawbacks are that the survey needs to be relatively short and the interviewer cannot show visuals. Rasmussen Reports (www.rasmussenreports.com) is one organization that uses telephone survey with random digit dialing to research national samples of respondents in polling across the United States. They can take advantage of the time zone changes and evening calling. Random digit dialing allows the company to find respondents by asking them to respond if they fit a specific profile and answer on the phone by pushing a button. The dialing is done automatically to reach the right sample and sample size. By the next morning or earlier, the company can deliver a full report on what a sample of consumers, voters and decision makers think and do about a critical topic.

Omnibus Study

A less expensive approach to telephone surveying is to piggyback some questions on a research company's omnibus poll.

Mail and E-mail Surveys

So-called self-administered e-mail and even mailed surveys are inexpensive but usually take a lot of time and have a low response rate. Survey Monkey is one online research tool that is free at beginner levels and low cost for more advanced analysis. Zoomerang is another online tool. The low response rate makes the findings less reliable because the people who responded might not be representative of the population at large. Another drawback is that people frequently give more superficial answers than in personal and telephone interviews.

Mall-Intercept Study

When the population is hard to reach by phone or mail or the budget is limited, people can be intercepted in a convenient public area. Employees can be surveyed in the lunchroom, doctors can be surveyed at a trade show and children can be surveyed at a shopping center.[11] Caution should be used in analyzing results of such surveys because the sample is not random. Everyone in the population does not have the same probability of being selected. Some employees don't go to the lunchroom and some parents never take their children to the mall.

BOX 2-3 COMPARISON OF QUALITATIVE AND QUANTITATIVE RESEARCH METHODS

Qualitative, Discovery-Based Methods:		Quantitative, Verification-Based Methods:
Discovering new insights	⟷	Verifying the insights
Small number of purposefully selected participants	⟷	Large number of randomly selected participants
Emphasizes *learning* from people	⟷	Emphasizes *studying* people
Emerging and creative survey design	⟷	Fixed and rigid survey design
Creative skills are important in analyzing results	⟷	*Analytical* skills are important in analyzing results

---

day?") or scale (good, fair or poor?). Such forced choices make quantitative analysis possible. It is common to include a few open-ended questions as well, thus combining quantitative and qualitative analysis.

Quantitative research delivers hard data. It is rigid and formulaic and does not leave as much room for subjective interpretations as qualitative methods do. However, if the quantitative survey is not grounded in qualitative research, it is likely to generate useless statistical artifacts. It is important to recognize that qualitative and quantitative research play different roles and can complement each other. Qualitative research stresses depth rather than breadth and offers insights instead of numbers. Quantitative research, with a larger randomly selected sample, is important to verify the insights and measure what number of people hold certain attitudes and behaviors. The main differences between qualitative and quantitative methods are summarized in Box 2-3.

Unfortunately, many researchers marry a particular research method and apply it to every situation, much like the carpenter who only has a hammer and thinks any problem can be fixed with a nail. Instead, it is important to use a combination of methods for each problem to "triangulate" findings. This is a metaphorical expression borrowed from the navigation technique by which an unknown point can be located by establishing the intersection of three vectors. In social science research, triangulation is the cross-checking of data and interpretations using multiple methods and sources.

In the case of the Silver Anvil awards, the judges will have reviewed each step above for the following questions:

- Did the plan clearly define objectives?
- How well did the objectives support the organization's overall goals?
- Did the strategy reflect research findings and support objectives?
- How original was the strategy?
- How thorough was the plan?

It is clear from the attention we have paid to the planning stages that we believe this step is crucial to the success of any PR effort. However, the Silver Anvil awards only 10 points, or 25 percent of the points, to planning. As we illustrate throughout the book, the implementation and the post-program evaluation are also critical.

IMPLEMENTATION AND MONITORING

When a strategy has been developed and the public relations plan is implemented, research plays an important role in monitoring its effectiveness and making adjustments. Telephone surveys and well-planned e-mail surveys of the targeted audiences and analyses of media coverage are quick ways to get an indication of how things are going. Questions from the Silver Anvil evaluations include the following:

- How appropriate were the tactics to achieving objectives and executing strategy?
- How creative were the tactics?
- How well were the tactics implemented?
- How integrated were the various tools with one another?
- How efficient was the execution of tactics in relation to resources (personnel and budget)?

EVALUATION

After a public relations program is implemented, the effect should be measured against predetermined objectives. If this sounds like a truism, consider that more than 70 percent of the winners in the most prestigious American public relations award, the Public Relations Society of America's Silver Anvil, did not measure how well the campaign met predetermined goals.[14]

Quantitative methods are most commonly used to evaluate public relations programs because they are replicable; that is, the same question can be asked at a later time to measure change. However, qualitative evaluations, like focus groups, are appropriate as well to identify improvements. The evaluation is not complete without measuring changes in behavior. Customer loyalty can be measured with recency, frequency, amount, retention and longevity of purchases and lifetime customer value. Employee, shareholder and customer loyalty can be measured with annual defection and retention rates and "half-life," the time it takes for half a class of entering customers, employees, or shareholders to leave the company.

Benchmarking is key to putting the evaluation in perspective. The evaluation of public relations programs can be benchmarked against other units in the same company, industry averages or companies that are "best in class." Figure 2.3 shows examples of benchmarking in the area of employee relations from one of the 1994 winners of the European Quality Award, Design to Distribution, Ltd.

With all this said, it is important to acknowledge the limitations of public relations evaluations. There is a fundamental difficulty inherent in establishing cause-and-effect relationships between public relations programs and such bottom-line outcomes as increased sales, lower employee turnover, higher earnings per share and more favorable legislative decisions. These outcomes are the results of a host of complex interactions, only a few of which are under the control of the public relations department or even a particular company. Public relations research will never be as precise a science as finance and manufacturing. The CFO can calculate return on investments in minute detail on the basis of different assumptions of interest rates. The VP of operations can measure defect levels with the accuracy of a thousandth of a percentage point. Public relations is different. Many aspects of public relations effects cannot be measured at all.

Consider the case of a company that is faced with an environmental accident and whose public relations department has prepared a crisis communication plan, conducted crisis simulation training with the senior managers and developed strong relationships with environmental groups that are supporting the company in the crisis. You do not measure the benefits of such actions any more than you measure the benefits of putting on your pants in the morning. It is simply not possible to measure the outcome of every action by the PR department. That does not make it less important. Even total quality management guru Edwards W. Deming argued that it is wrong to suppose that only what is measured can be managed.[15]

ACTING ON FINDINGS

It is important to make research *actionable* and share it widely in the organization. Most public relations research gets relegated to the bookshelf when it is done. Information that is collected but not properly disseminated throughout the organization and acted on is one of the largest sources of waste in any company. Approaches to making research findings "come alive" in a presentation include narrative description, role playing, video recorded interviews and quotes. Tailoring a research presentation to different audiences is another key to making it actionable. Senior management needs an overall picture to develop strategy, and salaried employees need to know what they can do to improve stakeholder satisfaction. Yet another important factor in making research actionable is to present the research information in a timely fashion. One case in point is the Eurobarometer, a telephone survey conducted every day in 15 European countries. The telephone interviewers are online with a central computer that tabulates last night's results every day, allowing the EU Commission to track Europeans' opinions on a daily basis.

One of the problems with public relations research is that the people who learn most about the stakeholders under study are the researchers, who typically are outsiders. To make the research truly actionable, the researcher needs to be a member of the public relations project team rather than someone who is called on an as-needed basis to deliver statistical pronouncements from on high. Public relations staffs should look at advertising agencies for inspiration. They have thrown out the old research departments and replaced them with account planners. The planners use qualitative research methods to immerse themselves in the lives of the customers and translate consumer insights to the creative team. The planner works with the account team during the entire period an advertising campaign is under development to keep it focused on the final customer.

The most sophisticated companies involve all managers in firsthand interaction with stakeholders. For instance, Federal Express' managing directors and above are required to spend one day each month out in the field with a salesperson. Xerox offers a similar example of a formal program to make managers interact with customers. The top 25 managers at Xerox spend one day every five weeks taking customer complaint calls and following through until the complaints are resolved. These top managers are also assigned a few clients each, to whom they are responsible for sales and service. Another example of such personal contacts is the telephone systems manufacturer Ericsson. Its Great Britain subsidiary matches employees at all levels with a counterpart at its major client, British Telecom (BT). For instance, each Ericsson secretary is responsible for keeping in touch with an assigned secretary at BT, each engineer is responsible for a particular engineer at BT, and Ericsson's public relations director keeps in touch with the public relations director at BT. Ericsson finds that such personal communication is important to develop partnership with clients.

Human beings learn best through firsthand experience. A Xerox manager who takes customer complaint calls and who is selling copy machines to clients on a regular basis can relate to clients in a unique way. When all communications professionals and other managers know their various stakeholders firsthand, instead of just as a set of demographic variables, communication with them is greatly improved.

Finally, the judges in the Silver Anvil will judge the overall excellence of a PR program by judging for 10 points (25 percent) the use of research by the practitioners to understand what worked and what did not work in the execution of the original research, planning and implementation of the PR effort. The questions that round out the research-oriented PR program planning and execution are evaluative. In this case, the questions can be summative or asked at the end of the program to see what we can "sum up" to say about the success or failure of the effort. Other evaluation questions asked earlier were formative or useful during the project to change the process when it seemed that the program was not working as planned. In that case, it would be pointless to continue a course of action if the response by the market or audience was not favorable. In summary, the questions asked in this latter stage but anticipating how to improve for the next program were as follows:

- How successful was the organization in achieving its objectives?

- How thorough and relevant were analysis and quantification of results?

- Did the results clearly reflect original strategy and planning?

- How well did the team work together?

- Were there continuous opportunities for learning and program refinement?

CASE STUDIES

One of the challenges of research in public relations is that it addresses such a variety of audiences. The following examples show how the research process has been applied to different stakeholders.

CUSTOMER SATISFACTION AT XEROX

Customers are the *raison d'être* of any organization, including nonprofits for whom the customers are students, patients, inmates or beneficiaries of charitable support. The customer needs to be put on a pedestal above every other stakeholder. Without customers, there would not be any other stakeholders. Surely, the customer focus needs to be balanced by the needs of other stakeholders. The stakes of the noncustomer stakeholders have never been higher, as evidenced during the last decade by the rise of business litigation, demise of employee morale, confrontations by interest groups and shareholder activism. However, the focus on the customer still needs to pervade the organization.

Customer information is gathered by several functions in the organization—the marketing department researches customer needs, the salesforce obtains feedback from prospective customers, research and development (R&D) anticipates future needs, customer service obtains feedback from dissatisfied customers, the managers obtain information from customer visits and the quality department gathers customer satisfaction information. Surprisingly, few companies have a systematic process to compile all this customer information and share it with everyone in the organization.

A case in point showing how information from customer surveys is shared broadly in the organization is Xerox's Customer Satisfaction Measurement System. Xerox mails out a customer satisfaction survey to 55,000 customers every month! The survey asks customers to rate Xerox's equipment, sales, service and customer administration performance. The survey results are sent to the customer relations representatives at the geographical sales district, who will make a call to every customer who has identified any dissatisfaction. It is also shared with the design and manufacturing departments for corrective actions.

Such sharing of research information so that people in the entire organization can add value to stakeholders is an important task of the communications function. Public relations and marketing have a unique role in setting up and running a customer database to capture information about individual customers and make the information available to the entire company. The role of the communication or public relations function is increasingly to manage such an integrated two-way process of communication between the stakeholders and the organization as a whole.

PR has a particular responsibility for dissatisfied customers, who might turn into hostile publics if they are not treated appropriately. Many companies encourage customers and other stakeholders to call a toll-free number with complaints and concerns. This is unique information that needs to be shared broadly in the organization. Federal Express communications managers obtain reports regularly about what concerns and complaints have been expressed by hotline callers. Celestial Seasonings has headsets by the copy and fax machines in its headquarters so that any employee can listen in on conversations between customer service representatives and customers (who have been informed that calls might be monitored). The Eastman Chemical Company has a 24-hour hotline for citizens to voice concerns about environmental issues or anything else on their minds. Special customer advocates follow up and resolve complaints. Eastman's goal is to respond to 90 percent of the complaints with an acknowledgment to the customer within 24 hours and to have 90 percent of complaints resolved within 30 days.

ONLINE SURVEYS AND TOWN HALL MEETINGS AT FEDERAL EXPRESS

Federal Express is an example of a company that is zealous about keeping in touch with employees. The company has a separate employee communication department of equal size and status as the public relations and marketing communication departments. FedEx's employees fill out online employee satisfaction forms every third month. A *leadership index* is calculated on the basis of the survey. Eight of the ten items on the survey measure managers' communication activities with employees. All managers present their results to their employees and develop action plans together with their work groups to improve areas in which the managers' scores are low. If a manager's leadership index is below a certain level, he or she receives support to become a better leader and communicator. If the scores are below the accepted level for two consecutive years, the manager will be reassigned to a nonmanagement position.

To create a dialogue between employees and senior management, Federal Express has regularly occurring television call-in shows on its internal satellite television network so that any employee can pick up the phone and speak live on the air to the company's founder and CEO, Fred Smith. The calls are not screened. The programs serve as corporate town hall meetings where problems get resolved on the spot. As a typical example, a customer service representative called in to tell her CEO that she did not know how to respond to a particular customer request. Smith suggested a response and told her that one of his colleagues would send out a memo the following day to all customer service representatives worldwide, explaining how to respond to the particular request.

THE INITIAL PUBLIC OFFERING OF A SWEDISH STEEL COMPANY

Investor relations research played a key role in the initial public offering by the Swedish government-owned steel manufacturer, SSAB, both in the strategic planning stage and during the campaign. Initially, a telephone survey was conducted using a random sample of 1,200 people from the general public. The survey asked about perceptions of different approaches to savings and privatization, knowledge about the privatization of SSAB and how much the respondents were willing to invest in its stocks. Later in the planning stage, focus groups were used to test messages and specific advertising approaches. The participants were asked if they understood, had interest and had trust in the company and the offering.

The campaign consisted of advertising and information pamphlets that were mailed to the clients of one of Sweden's largest banks and distributed at the bank's branch offices. During the campaign, a telephone survey of the general public was conducted every third day to monitor progress. The survey asked about awareness of the campaign and intention to sign up to buy stock. Branch managers of 80 randomly selected bank offices that handled the applications were interviewed as well. The bank offices were asked how many applications they had received and how many they expected. These ongoing studies saved the company hundreds of thousands of dollars because the studies suggested that it could pull some of the ads that were planned. The studies predicted that 130,000 people would apply to obtain the 67,000 available stock option packages; in reality, 118,000 people applied.

Two telephone surveys were conducted after the public offering, one with the general public and one with the new shareholders. The studies identified improvement opportunities for the next time the government decided to privatize a company.

TAKING THE PULSE OF MEMBERS OF A PROFESSIONAL ASSOCIATION

Members are a key stakeholder of any association. An example of an association that conducts membership research is the Swedish Association for Certified Accountants. Every three months, in preparation for the association's board meeting, it commissions a telephone interview with 100 members. It is conducted during two evenings by five interviewers, and a report is prepared the following day. The survey addresses different issues every time. One of the studies, for instance, focused on the association's two membership publications. Over half of the respondents found that the publications needed improvement. The survey contained open-ended questions about what kinds of improvements the publications needed. The report listed the responses and discussed some of the most frequently mentioned suggestions.

The case shows that research does not have to be elaborate and time and cost consuming. A telephone survey with a combination of quantitative and qualitative questions asked of a hundred members over the course of a few days can help keep the board focused on the members' needs.

CUSTOMER SATISFACTION SURVEY OF STATE LEGISLATURES

The Eastman Chemical Company, a Tennessee-based chemical manufacturer, has a company-wide index called *key result areas* (KRA) that measures how well the company is achieving its mission of "creating superior value for customers, employees, investors, suppliers, and publics." Examples of how this measure applies to public affairs are the KRA score for the percent of bills in the Tennessee state legislature for which Eastman has lobbied successfully and the KRA score for the dollar value of these bills. In addition, the company has a KRA score based on a customer satisfaction survey of the Tennessee legislators in which they are asked about the service that the government relations department is providing them and how well the Eastman Chemical Company performs as a corporate citizen. Another example of a public affairs KRA score is the company's philanthropy; Eastman tracks the time it takes for recipients to obtain contributions.

A POWER PLANT MEASURES TRUST IN THE COMMUNITY

An example of community relations research is a series of studies by a Swedish nuclear power plant, Forsmark. The community stakeholders are of paramount importance to the nuclear industry. The U.S. power industry's ignorance of the local community is a big reason no nuclear power plant has been approved in this country for the last 25 years.

The Swedish power plant's management conducts a survey of local communities every year. The results are tabulated separately for the "inner circle" of people living close to the power plant and an "outer circle" of people living further away. It shows that the increase of trust is particularly strong among the important inner circle community. The survey, moreover, asks how much trust people have in the information the power plant provides. The findings suggest that the inner circle of neighbors who receive a regular newsletter have more trust in the information from the power plant. A second study is conducted with opinion leaders in the entire country of Sweden. The opinion leaders were corporate executives, editorial page writers, city council members and union leaders. The findings guide the power plant's public affairs strategy.

RESEARCH TO OBTAIN PUBLICITY

Research information can have news value and as such can be used for publicity purposes. An example of an organization that skillfully used polling to obtain publicity is the Swedish Employers Confederation. It wanted to move the focus of debate from short-term economic cycles to long-term economic trends. To accomplish this goal, it surveyed business executives in each of Sweden's 24 regions and publicized the research in a book. The study showed distinct differences among the regions, and generated much regional and local press coverage. The news media in every region wanted to know how their region stacked up against the rest of the country. In addition, the employees and the members of the association obtained copies of the book and became more informed ambassadors of the organization.

Caution is called for in interpreting studies designed for publicity purposes. Many such studies are designed to purposely skew the results with leading questions, skewed sample frames and biased interpretations of results.

RESEARCHING INTERNAL CLIENTS

The public relations or corporate communications department serves *internal clients* such as human resource, finance and marketing departments, by offering counsel and by communicating with the internal clients'

BOX 2-4 HOW TO JUDGE THE EFFECTIVENESS OF A WEBSITE

Ease of use or navigability
Key messages conveyed
Interactivity
Content
Integration with other communication programs
Number of names that are captured

stakeholders (employees of the HR department, investors of the finance department, and customers of the marketing department). It is important to do research on these internal clients on an ongoing basis as well. This research is typically more informal and qualitative than the external stakeholder research. The senior communications managers at Eastman Chemical Company, for instance, meet once a year with all the senior managers to discuss what their communications needs are and what opportunities for improvement exist. They also determine how well the service provided by the communications department is adding value to the company.

Another example is AT&T's PR department, which has established a standard client satisfaction survey for general managers. The survey asks how important the managers find different communications tasks to be and how well they find that the public relations departments perform them. The questions deal with the overall quality of the public relations counsel, the quality of the public relations professionals and the quality of the communications service they offer to external stakeholders. The questionnaire also asks if the public relations function is worth its cost, if the overall service meets the general managers' expectations and if public relations gives AT&T a competitive advantage. Aggregate topline results of the survey are distributed to all communications professionals in the company every three months, broken down by business units.

MEDIA RESEARCH

Despite some of the methods offered for discussion in Chapter 3, the traditional tallying of press clippings and broadcast placements is still the prevailing method of evaluating mass media coverage. Occasionally, PR professionals will compare what equivalent advertising space would cost. These are quick and dirty ways of measuring publicity that can be extremely misleading. There are easy ways to "get more ink"—set your plant on fire or kidnap your CEO, for example. The clip-counting approach assumes that more is better, when in fact the objective sometimes is to minimize the amount of press coverage.

Instead of simply counting the clips, public relations professionals are increasingly relying on content analysis. In the most simple format, the researcher distinguishes articles and television broadcasts that are negative, neutral and positive to the client company. A more sophisticated form of content analysis measures the rate of articles in which the company was mentioned with its key message. Studies by one research firm show that of all articles a particular company is mentioned in, on average, 30 percent of articles are positive, 6 percent are negative and 29 percent contain key messages.[16] These figures can be used as a benchmark. Other variables to consider in a content analysis are as follows:

Audience of the publication
Quality of the publication (Is it *Fortune* or *Entertainment Magazine*?)
Prominence of the company in the story (Is the company the main feature or just mentioned in passing along with other companies in the same industry?)
Prominence of the article in the publication (Is it on the first page or hidden by the obituaries and birth announcements at the end of the paper or three levels down in the site?)
Visual presentation (Was there a favorable photo or graph?)
Spokesperson (Who gets quoted? What percentage of the CEO's quotes contain key messages?)

PR or research firms have developed scorecards on which articles are rated on these criteria.

In addition, PR has borrowed tools from advertising to measure cost. One way to compare the cost of different forms of mass media publicity and to compare publicity with advertising is cost per thousand. Cost per thousand is the cost of producing press release, video news release and press conference of whatever publicity vehicle is used, divided by the audience number of each publication or program where it was featured and multiplied by a thousand.

These examples of media analysis are important because they show which messages are getting through and which are not, which media outlets and which reporters are favorable and which are unfavorable and why, which spokespeople are most successful at getting the key messages across and which approaches are most cost effective. Keep in mind, however, that they are limited to the output of mass media relations. The true test of public relation's value comes from measuring the actual impact it had on the target audience.

HOW TO SELECT AND WORK WITH RESEARCH FIRMS

Most PR research is conducted by outside firms. The choice of firm and the relationship with it are key success factors in public relations research. As with any professional service, it is not a straight transactional process in which the supplier delivers a product that is consumed by the client. The research is coproduced by the research firm and the client, so the success of the research depends as much on the client as on the research firm. Instead of shopping for lowest bids, it is important to evaluate the research firm's ability to be a good partner and add value to the research process. You should have enough knowledge of research to be able to understand what the agency is offering and when its methods need to be challenged. For example, during the first two weeks of a 10-week summer internship on northwestern integrated marketing communications, a student challenged the sampling method of a research company working for her summer employer (a large technology company). She was able to persuade her summer employer to dismiss the agency and hire a more scientific research firm to be sure the data was representative of the consumer.

Research firms come in all shapes and forms, ranging from full-service companies with in-house telephone interview and focus group facilities to smaller consultants who contract out most of the work. The following is a list of specific considerations in hiring a research firm:

Do you need a full-service firm that will contract for an entire project or just specialized firms that can do focus group interviews, field interviews or data tabulation?

If you choose a full-service firm, will the particular firm you are considering select the combination of methods that best suits your needs or will they want to use particular methods that they have more expertise in or make more money on?

Do you want to use a research firm that has developed a standardized method for researching a particular area, like content analysis of mass media coverage or advertising testing?

Does the firm have any experience in your industry or with the particular group of stakeholders you will research?

Will the firm provide a list of clients for whom it has provided similar service? What experiences did these past clients have with the firm?

Two directories of research firms in the United States are *The Green Book,* published by the American Marketing Association, New York Chapter, and *The Blue Book*, published by the American Association for Public Opinion Research, Ann Arbor, Michigan.

When the firm is selected, it is important to develop a written research plan detailing the responsibilities of the research firm and the client during every step of the research process. The plan should include a time frame and budget.

Most larger public relations agencies have their own research departments. Some agency clients feel that the agency researchers represent a conflict of interest. These clients do not find it appropriate for public relations agencies to evaluate their own performance. Instead, they turn to independent research firms that do not have any vested interest in the outcome of the research. The agencies, on the other hand, argue that the only way they can make research an integral part of the public relations process is to have their own in-house research department. The agency researchers assert that the emphasis of their research is on identifying areas of improvement and building continual learning into the research process rather than on judging the quality of the agency.

RESEARCH TO SUPPORT INTEGRATED COMMUNICATIONS

Public relations cannot be managed independently from the rest of the business. The most powerful messages transmitted to stakeholders are not the annual report and brochures that the public relations department has direct control over but the product or service offerings, the financial performance of the firm and the environmental impact of its plants. We will now broaden the scope to describe how to set up an integrated communications research process that focuses not only on the communications functions but also on how the entire business communicates with key stakeholders. The first step is to evaluate and improve the communication process with an integrated

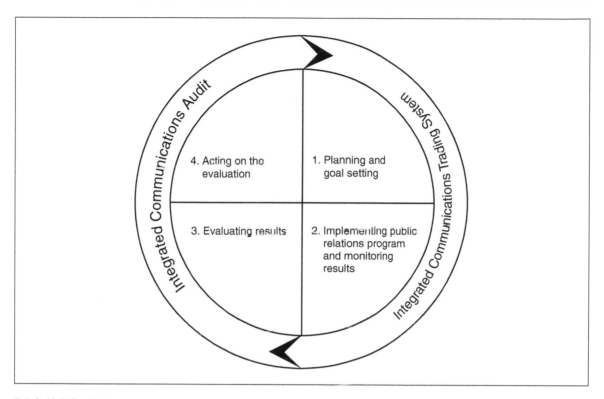

F I G U R E   2.4

Integrated Communications Research Added to the Stages of Effective Public Relations

communications audit. The next step is to set up a tracking system of integrated communications indicators. As illustrated in Figure 2.4, these are the strategic research components of effective PR.

INTEGRATED COMMUNICATIONS AUDIT

An audit is a good starting point to determine the extent to which communications are integrated. Unlike traditional marketing and public relations research, which focus on the outcome of the communications process such as attitude and behavior changes among stakeholders, an integrated communications audit is designed to focus on the process leading up to the results.

One approach to an integrated communications audit has been developed at the University of Colorado at Boulder, as a class project in its master's program in integrated marketing communications.[17] This audit has three parts: (1) interviews with managers in marketing communications as well as in other functions to find out if there is a consensus on objectives and key messages (there hardly ever is!); (2) content analysis of communications materials such as advertising, annual reports, and brochures to find out how well integrated the messages are; and (3) review of existing stakeholder research and "mystery shopper" exercises where the researchers act in the role of customers who try to obtain refunds for merchandise, call and ask questions and so forth.

The integrated communications audit can be conducted by an outside consultant or internally by senior management. The advantage of outsiders is that they bring a fresh perspective and can be more candid in their analysis. However, consider these advantages of an internal audit by top management:

The company's own managers, not an outsider, obtain the long-term benefit of the intimate knowledge of the organization that the audit process provides. It is a morale booster for employees to see that top management cares. It is not just an academic exercise. Senior management is committed to implementing suggestions.

Sometimes the term *audit* is intimidating. Other terms like *assessment* or *review* can be used. Procter & Gamble calls its quality management audits *visits*. Whatever term is used, the audit is an opportunity to identify weaknesses that need improvement, as well as the best practices that can be duplicated throughout the organization. The audit should lead to an action plan to improve the integration and quality of the communications.

In one of the University of Colorado's audits of a large beverage company, the product and marketing service managers were asked to identify the marketing communications objective for the company's major brand on which they were all working. Ten different objectives were mentioned, ranging from "top quality" to "fun in the sun" and "refreshing." When all of the advertising and merchandising materials for the previous 12 months were analyzed, the student audit team found that less than one-third executed the communications objective that was stated in the marketing plan.[18]

INTEGRATED COMMUNICATIONS TRACKING SYSTEM

Integrated communications calls for an integrated research system with key indicators that are linked to each other and monitored. The first steps in establishing an integrated communications research process are to define a single overall communication goal for the entire organization and to identify key stakeholders. Consider the case of AT&T. Its overall communication goal, or brand objective as the company put it, was to build the perception among stakeholders that AT&T was "the most helpful company." This objective was further defined as "offering the most helpful service, innovations that enhance people's lives, and being a company worthy of trust." Its priority stakeholders were customers, its own employees and the investment community.

The next step is to identify the communications programs that have the biggest leverage on the goal. The theory of leverage suggests that small, well-focused processes can cause large-scale improvements if they are in the right place. In the case of AT&T, its PR staff identified four communications programs, or brand programs, which its corporate communications focused around

1. Producing innovations that enhance people's capabilities
2. Being a leader in protecting the environment
3. Being a superior employer
4. Improving education in America

These are the leverage points that AT&T found to have the largest impact on its overall objective to be perceived as a "helpful" company.

The third step is to establish a comprehensive measurement process to track stakeholders' perceptions of the communication goal and the key messages on an ongoing basis. Such a measurement process helps to give all communication functions a shared understanding about the progress toward strengthening the corporate communication objective. Each measurement is plotted on a chart. By tracking processes of change, the research is used as a tool to direct long-term efforts.

After measurements are identified, it is important to link the items together in a system. Figure 2.5 summarizes the system of measurements at AT&T. It depicts the *process–result* or *means–end* relationships between the measurements. It can be described the following way. The senior VP or corporate communications at AT&T is accountable for the perceptions of AT&T as the "most helpful company" among its three priority stakeholder groups: customers, investors and employees. That is her *end*, illustrated on top of Figure 2.5 by the charts for each of its priority stakeholder groups. Her *means* to achieve this end are the four key messages, the brand programs. For the manager of the innovation brand program, the perception of AT&T as an innovative company among the prioritized stakeholders is the *end*, and the advertising campaign at the time, entitled "You Will," is one of the *means*. For the advertising manager of the "You Will" campaign, the *end* is how well the campaign changes stakeholders' perceptions of AT&T as an innovative company, and the *means* are the recall and recognition scores of the ad campaign. In this fashion, means become the ends for the next level of management, which in turn has to develop means to accomplish its ends. The process itself of setting up such a system facilitates important discussions between departments about how their processes relate to each other.

Such indicators are much better predictors of future success than financial information. Financial indices are lagging indicators that do not say anything about the future. Today's accounting practices are an anachronism, focusing on cost rather than value, precision rather than relevance, past rather than future and material assets rather than relationships. The traditional controller, who focuses only on finance and accounting, needs to be replaced by a *relationship equity controller*. The new job responsibility of the controller involves controlling, monitoring and auditing the relationship equity. The controller is the proactive custodian of corporate reputation and relationships with key stakeholders—the assets that matter above all others in the postindustrial corporation.

THE CENTRAL ROLE OF RESEARCH IN THE FUTURE OF PR

American managers often complain that it is lonely at the top. That is probably because the people at the top have lost touch with the company and its stakeholders. The public relations or corporate communications function has a unique role in keeping senior management in touch with the external environment through research. They are the eyes and ears of senior management to the external and internal environment, the early warning system of emerging crises and opportunities. They use research to support overall strategic management planning as well as the planning of the public relations function itself.

The public relations or corporate communications managers of the future have not only a finger on the pulse of their stakeholders but also an intravenous tube connected to the stakeholders inserted into them. They track the perceptions of their key stakeholders and internal clients, and they leave their offices to go out to the field to live and breathe the lives of the stakeholders. They use research to systematically measure progress toward predetermined objectives, to identify areas of improvement and to demonstrate accountability. This systematic use of research is the only way we can learn from experiences and grow as a profession. Most public relations programs have consequences that are neither immediate nor unambiguous. We cannot possibly learn from experiences if we never experience the consequences of our actions. By building on research in the public

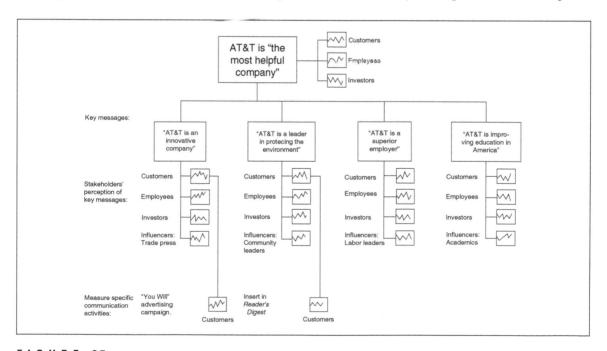

FIGURE 2.5

An Example of AT&T's Integrated Tracking System of Leading Communication Indicators

relations process through continual cycles of planning, monitoring, evaluating and acting on finds, we are building organizational learning, institutional memory and continual improvements.

ACKNOWLEDGMENT

Special thanks are due to Per Hörnsten and Arne Modig, who provided all of the European case studies for this chapter. A warm thanks also for the valuable help from Professors Clarke Caywood, Frank Durham and Bill Celis.

DISCUSSION QUESTIONS

1. What are the four steps to a research-based planning model for public relations? Describe each step briefly.
2. If your company does not have any survey data on a new product or new service idea, what research methods might you begin with to collect information? Describe more than one method.
3. Discuss the value of understanding statistics in conducting PR and marketing research. Give two examples of how knowing statistics can help secure the very best information about the prospective buyer and the nature of the product or service.
4. Why should a company bother to conduct research after the project is done?

NOTES

1. GAP VI
2. Lacey, T. Alan, and Benjamin Wright. 2009. "Occupational employment projections to 2018." Monthly Labor Review 132, no. 11: 82-123. Business Source Elite, EBSCOhost (accessed November 7, 2011).
3. T. Alan Lacey and Benjamin Wright, "Occupational Employment Projections to 2018".
4. Walter Barlow, "Establishing Public Relations Objectives and Assessing Public Relations Results" (New York: The Institute for Public Relations Research and Education, 1993). 1995 "Survey on Measurement and Accountability, Results of a Poll of Public Relations Professionals," conducted by Schenkein/Sherman Public Relations and PR News, "demand for measurement/accountability" was ranked as the top issue in public relations by 44 percent of the respondents. In a 1992 survey by the Counselor's Academy of the Public Relations Society of America, "demand for measurement/accountability" was named the top industry challenge by 70 percent of the respondents.
5. Schenkein/Sherman *Public Relations and PR News*, "Survey on Measurement and Accountability."
6. Ibid.
7. Ibid.
8. AASCB reports on need for communications in MBA programs.
9. Walter Barlow, "Establishing Public Relations Objectives and Assessing Public Relations Results," New York: The Institute for Public Relations Research and Education, 1993.
10. P. M. Senge, *The Fifth Discipline: The Art and Practice of the Learning Organization* (New York: Doubleday/Currency, 1990), p. 71.
11. Don E. Schultz and Beth E. Barnes, *Strategic Advertising Campaigns, 4th ed.* (Lincolnwood, IL: NTC Publishing Group, 1995).
12. Ivan L. Preston, "The Association Model of the Advertising Communication Process," *Journal of Advertising* 11, no. 2 (1982): 3–15.
13. David M. Dozier and William P. Ehling, "Evaluation of Public Relations Programs: What the Literature Tells Us About Their Effects," in *Excellence in Public Relations and Communication Management*, James E. Grunig, ed. (Hillsdale, NJ: Erlbaum, 1992), pp. 159–184.

14. Rick Fisher, "Control Construct Design in Evaluating Campaigns," *Public Relations Review* 21, no. 1 (Spring 1995): 45–58.

15. For instance, see the foreword to *Fourth Generation Management* by Brian Joiner (New York: McGraw-Hill, 1994).

16. Ibid.

17. Thomas R. Duncan and Sandra E. Moriarty, *Driving Brand Value* (Burr Ridge, IL: Irwin, 1997).

18. Ibid.

ADDITIONAL READING

Fisher, Rick. 1995. "Control Construct Design in Evaluating Campaigns." *Public Relations Review*.

Grunig, James E. 1992. *Excellence in Public Relations and Communication Management*. Hillsdale, NJ: L. Erlbaum Associates.

Lindenmann, Walter K. 1995. *A Brief Look at Public Relations Research at Ketchum*. New York: Ketchum Public Relations.

Preston, Ivan L. 1982. "The Association Model of the Advertising Communication Process," *Journal of Advertising* 11(2): 3–15.

Stacks, Don W. Primer of Public Relations Research. New York, NY: Guilford, 2011. Print.

Stacks, Don W., and David Michaelson. "*A Practitioner's Guide to Public Relations Research, Measurement and Evaluation*." New York, NY: Business Expert, 2010. Print.

3
C H A P T E R

COMMUNICATIONS RESEARCH
Dynamic Digital Methods

Clarke L. Caywood, Ph.D.
Professor and Past Chairman, Department of Integrated Marketing Communications
Medill School of Journalism, Media, Integrated Communications
Northwestern University

In the second decade of the 21st century, there are more ways to measure messages than ever before and more work for analysts and public relations professionals. This chapter shows that we need continually advancing software innovations to carry out these tasks. The preceding chapter on research is crucial for an understanding of the importance of social science and rigorous research for decision making regarding an organization's communications and organizational goals. Naturally, the research reported in this *Handbook*, in a number of chapters relevant to specific stakeholders or to specific industries, depends on web-based methods and services. In this chapter, we address the rapidly growing industry that supports public relations, integrated marketing communications and management with carefully created software to aid in the thorough analysis of the now-digitized traditional media, social media and other internal data that are used in strategic decision making. Also, the methods detailed in this chapter depend nearly 100 percent on the ability of public relations (PR) professionals to access information that is now on the public web or, in some cases, paid subscription services of news, business, policy and social content.

Starting with one of the best sources for best practices, we can see the impact of digital message delivery and message analysis. One of the useful professional practices of public relations and other marketing associations is the use of the annual global, although too often U.S.-exclusive, competitions of professional work. One of the best known is the Silver Anvil Awards[1] program of the Public Relations Society of America (PRSA. org). This program receives hundreds of entries each year from companies, PR agencies, nonprofit organizations and government organizations in its emphasis on research. The categories of the competition include research, planning, execution and evaluation.

Each category is equally valued and the judges are to determine how well the program was *researched*, *planned*, *executed* and *evaluated*. What is remarkable about both the competition and the entries is that all the sections, in one way or another, must contain some research, and all

SILVER ANVIL JUDGING POINTS

Total, 40
Research, 10
Planning, 10
Execution, 10
Execution, 10

are given equal possible points. Obviously, the *research* section is judged heavily on how well the team of professionals was able to identify and document a need and the public or audience that needed to be served. The *planning* section is also replete with references to research through which the plans may be refined and approved, based on the research findings' meeting the goals of the organization. The third section, called *execution*, which may be the least research-oriented section by most advanced organizations, is dedicated to continuous or formative research that measures each action step by step for corrections. Rather than wait until the project is done, it is important to periodically self-correct. Finally, the competition teaches a strong lesson that is often overlooked—*evaluating* the outcomes of the program. Too often, the team moves on to the next project. Naturally, to avoid future mistakes, more and more organizations are sending post-program surveys or other measures to get feedback that can help improve future contact with the customer or stakeholder.

For example, a recent contact with an automobile dealer provided the opportunity to complete a 20-item survey. The brand of the car, the service of the dealer and the particular business contact was compelling enough for me to spend eight minutes completing the survey online. In another case, for a nationwide survey by Erdos and Morgan on policy issues, there were more than 600 choices to make on a printed or optional follow-up online survey. In addition to imparting a certain pride to the recipient about being asked about extremely complex social issues, the research organization offered a $10 contribution to one of three policy foundations. Listed were Doctors without Borders, USA, the American Red Cross, and the Intrepid Fallen Heroes Foundation. In modern marketing and PR, consumers are willing to share their opinions and time if they believe the research will help them to receive superior personal service in the future. However, in the latter case, the online survey was a critical part of the offer and part of the ease and convenience.

From the PR programs created in 2010 and judged in 2011 for the Silver Anvils, evidence of even more concrete use of social media and the need to evaluate social media was presented. More intensive metrics follow.

SILVER ANVIL CASE 1

In an award-winning program, Johnson & Johnson teamed with the Healthy Mothers, Healthy Babies Coalition; Voxiva; CTIA and Hill & Knowlton to create an emerging media-based program entitled "text4baby: Going Mobile with Pregnancy Education."

"The description of the program begins with startling research and the rationale for the program. Each year, 500,000 American babies are born prematurely, and 28,000 die before their first birthday. Medical experts agree that awareness of proper prenatal care can help a mother deliver a healthy baby. text4baby makes receiving this information easy by delivering it directly to mobile devices where it's more likely to be read. The strategy relied on generating free coverage with a local radio public service announcement campaign featuring pro bono celebrity spokesperson, Sherri Shepherd, and securing a media partnership while building national and local partners. Following the campaign, text4baby achieved more than 650 placements, resulting in 75 million impressions and driving more than 134,000 subscribers."

One of the values of devoting our attention to using social media has been the increased ease of measuring outcomes, loyalty and follow-up actions. Although the data is still often reported in more traditional terms of placements, impressions and even subscribers, the numbers are accentuated by the ease of access in a wired world.

SILVER ANVIL CASE 2

Another example of an award winner seemed at first "slurp" to be a bit less important, but even social policy and politics can be fun and informative. The campaign was managed by Jamey Peters, senior vice president at Ketchum, for their client and called "7-Eleven Unites America with Purple Slurpees" campaign.

"Within moments of a President Obama press conference, when asked if he would hold a "Slurpee Summit" as a means for his first meeting with new Republican leaders, "Slurpee Summit" began trending high on Twitter. The Slurpee brand embodies having fun and connecting people. Riffing on the notion that America is divided into conservative "Red States" and liberal "Blue States," a new Slurpee flavor was created mixing the red and blue flavors together, and "Purple for the People" was born.

Overall, the Slurpee Unity Tour visited 13 cities over a two-week period, driving press coverage on the local and national levels. On the social media front, fans of the Slurpee Facebook page increased from 1.5 million to more than 2 million in a two-week period, and Slurpee was aligned positively with the terms *bipartisanship* and *unity* in 95 percent of the Slurpee Summit and overall campaign coverage.

SILVER ANVIL CASE 3

Alissa Blate, executive vice president and global consumer marketing practice leader at MWW Group developed for her client Volkswagen: "Volkswagen GTI Becomes the World's First Car Launched Exclusively on a Mobile Device" campaign.

"In 2009, Volkswagen challenged its partners to develop a campaign for the 2010 GTI that would be as powerful, stylish, and innovative as the car itself—all without paid media coverage or support of any kind. The resulting campaign made the GTI the first car in the world to be launched on an iPhone and used a mobile gaming strategy to reach the 25- to 40-year-old technophile male target. The results included an 800 percent return on investment, \$2 million in media value, the ranking of number 1 "app" in 36 countries, and a more than 80 percent increase in leads, quotes and test drives. Eighty-five cars were sold as a direct result of the effort."

Again, there are increasing opportunities with social media and digital communications to report data, although the question always remains in this and other competitions as to what was actually learned by the agency and client. It may be a cliché about data management but, as a profession, we are clearly richer in data from online research, if not actual information.

A research development in the last decade that has increasingly shown up in the Silver Anvil reports has provided communication, business, marketing and political researchers with a brand new bag of research tools. The newer research methods follow two developments: first is the well-established tradition of legal research of published case law, law journals and opinions being searchable via dedicated computer terminals and lines; second is the advanced development of artificial intelligence and graphic display of data for tracking traditional and social media all over the world.

As early as the 1980s, law schools, such as the University of Wisconsin School of Law, were testing grounds for law students and a few doctoral students in business and communications. Law schools, and later journalism schools (I requested Lexis-Nexis for my students when I arrived at the Medill School in 1989), were fertile fields for educating the next generation of law students and "curbside lawyers" (those who know a particular area of law for research, lobbying or reporting) on the value of nearly immediate computer access to the latest in jurisprudence. During those years, after spending part of a day searching for cases concerned with First Amendment issues of political and corporate advertising, users were notified at the end of the session that "more decisions and articles had been entered" during the several hours they were using the dedicated terminal.

Lexis-Nexis and Westlaw turbocharged the professional work of attorneys, paralegals and other policy researchers in the 1970s. Instead of "ticking through the card file" at the library or searching the indices of beautiful but heavy, leather-bound law books, researchers could use automated key words to find the full text of articles. I did some experimentation on searching using key words on an IBM 360 with punch cards and punch tape to search abstracts by student authors with faculty at the University of Wisconsin-Madison business school in 1968, and again at the Lyndon B. Johnson School of Public Affairs in 1971. The ability to search full text (rather than just abstracts) opened a new world of opportunities for researchers and decision makers. Although the vocabulary at the time of a text's being written might be a limitation, if those words became out of date during later search times, the searchers' insight and ability to broaden the search could overcome the limitations. For example, early journalism references to environmental issues with the letter *E* (E-day) might not contain the more contemporary terms *green*, *sustainability* or *eco*. More importantly, however, the researcher could uncover the thinking of far more authors and articles than a hand- and eye-directed hard copy search of articles and other resources would allow. The pattern was being set to search for sources other than traditional library or national journalistic outlets. For example, rather than being limited to searching *The New York Times*, a researcher might be able to find equally compelling ideas and information in blogs, on Twitter or in highly specialized subscription trade and professional press outlets. A modern Google or Bing search might generate more than 2 million hits on any number of key words. Critics of search note that most searches are often just two to three words. These searches demonstrate a lack of refinement that a more careful word choice or a longer string of words would generate.

However, the more refined search methods increase the likelihood that the researcher or manager will find the story, article, idea or quote that they are looking to find. There are increasingly automated or robotic search methods that are more similar to continuous "advanced searches" in university libraries or on Bing or Google. The paid services are either available for more publications, or more directed subscription publications and social media sites. More importantly, for analysis and decision making, the searches are enhanced by the vivid graphic display of the key words. The searches tell the subscriber whether the words in the context of an article are positive or negative, which authors are quoting your press release or the CEO's comments and dozens of other metrics.

The benefit to business over the past decade has been proven in part by the rapid growth of this novel industry of media tracking and analysis. Dozens of small and larger software-based companies have continuously refined their systems to create new reports, design easier-to-read charts and graphs and include more and more messages from both traditional media and newer social media from individuals, organizations and corporations.

The following examples are designed to illustrate to the reader some of the current systems. We can say without equivocation that newer, more powerful and comprehensive systems than anything developed at the time of this book's publication will be available when you read this section of the chapter. Nevertheless, as with any technology, each new innovation or improvement needs to be tested, considered and applied for the set of issues each manager faces. Although many readers could have waited to learn to use the Internet until searches were as rapid as they are today, or dozens of other improvements to web software were made, the value of testing the present developments were useful at the time. We believe that a constant testing of newer technologies and software are part of the manager's job to be ready for the next advance that may prove even more powerful and useful. Although it is useful for each younger generation to test and use new technologies, there are no barriers to having older managers test the same systems and use their experience to make judgments on the value of the systems to their work.

Obviously, at the time of this writing, the ability to conduct a simple Google search does not seem to be a breakthrough for research. However, the technological gift of search has opened, for public relations and marketing alike, the ability to track, analyze and use more data for decision making than at any time in history.

CASE: THE CASE OF THE STUDENT WHO WISHED SHE HAD A DIGITAL SYSTEM

For many decades, junior public relations assistants created the early morning news summary and review. One particular student with this task was compelled to arrive at the *Chicago Tribune* headquarters each workday at approximately 5 AM. Her job was to create a paste-up of summaries of news relevant to the Tribune Company and the publishing businesses it owned, including the *Los Angeles Times*. Whatever stories, news and results were generated from the end of business the previous day, including overnight, were to be identified, selected, cut and copied. The sources were usually other newspapers, wire services like the Associated Press or United Press International and Reuters (a form of digital media). The process involved some decision making by the assistant to know what issues were most relevant and what the interests of the management team were.

Now, the process is much more automated. With daily report-generating features, the software is able to collect, in seconds and minutes, the overnight news from markets that are open in other corners of the world. The articles can be inserted into a "newsletter" framework with links to the full article. In addition, the articles can be analyzed nearly instantaneously and compared with the stories of the previous day, week, month or year on the same subject, from the same or different authors, in the same or other media outlets and so forth. While the young assistant learned a great deal about news and the industry, today that assistant can spend more time helping to interpret the stories, trends and statistical reports.

"What work that you do today will be replaced by software?" asked Jim Carey, a Northwestern University colleague, when speaking to a group of Johnson Controls communications managers. As the first example suggests, the mechanical tasks of tracking news and court decisions have been replaced with rapid digital search tools. The real advantage of the new systems is not just convenience of labor, but providing insights for decision making.

First, with various search software readily available to the online user, it seemingly became possible to find out what others were saying about your company, your program, your brand and your CEO with a key word search on Google. One challenge facing the use of Google for a search is that Google and most of the free search engines do not have access to subscription news services in highly specialized industries or issues areas. Therefore, although search engines give the users a sense of confidence that they can find out all there is to know about a topic (often overwhelming), some of the more commercial and costly services provide specific access to specific media. Some of the services offer custom features to change the mix of media tracked on a real-time basis. For example, Attensity360, formerly Biz360, will allow the user to search only regional newspapers or specific files of groups of business magazines. Although this seems to be in contradiction to the idea that a broad search may produce a previously unread item about the company or issue, the wide search also costs a lot of time. There must be a trade-off to have the very best quality of information versus just a large quantity of information. For even more detailed answers, the research methods summarized in the previous chapter on research (surveys, focus groups and polls) are still critical to gather information about very specific questions and about relatively unknown subjects.

The biggest breakthrough has been the ability to conduct extremely large-scale searches for businesses and other organizations.

CASE: HARLEY-DAVIDSON'S 100TH BIRTHDAY AND 1 BILLION GREETINGS

In 2003, the well-known motorcycle brand, Harley-Davidson, celebrated its 100th anniversary. During that year, the company had what the old PR metrics simply called "mentions" (references to the company in print, video or radio) of over one billion! For those of us who used to count mentions for politicians in the 1960s and 1970s, the task is formidable, perhaps impossible, from a resource point of view. However, with the new software developed over the past decade and being refined each day, not only did the software count the number of mentions at levels beyond reasonable human capability, but it told the company how many of the articles (and which ones) were more favorable or more negative than others.

CASE: THE AIRLINE, THE REPORTER AND THE ANGRY CEO

Stereotypically, some CEOs of companies will explode about "unfair reporting" and threaten to cancel all advertising to a newspaper over an unfavorable mention of their company. As a century of experience has taught PR professionals and journalists, the threat is usually an empty one because the reporting function and the business function of newspapers have typically been separate. In fact, the dangerous threat may even generate another raft of articles about the company's cancelling the ads and opposing freedom of speech. In the case of the angry CEO, although it may have been only a rumor that the CEO might have threatened to act in this manner, the marketing and PR researcher acted instead to prove a point using new tracking software.

For instance, a major airline company was fighting for its public reputation after facing bankruptcy, several changes in top leadership and continually rising fuel costs. An analysis by a service vendor applying software that read articles by various journalists provided useful results. The analysis showed, as management expected, that a major newspaper reporter was not using complete information about the situation. A comparison with other journalists' writing on the same issue showed that they were using more government, industry and company data to provide more insights about the airline.

Based on the careful analysis of key writers in the industry, the airline company's PR professionals approached the journalist to discuss his stories. Although the reporter was naturally reluctant and defensive, he "took the meeting." However, the meeting started out on the wrong foot. The journalist did not like the implication that he was not using information for his stories whereas other reporters did. He charged that the analysis was just the bias of the company's reading their ideas into the stories. When the PR professionals explained that the analysis was done by a computer and was based on scientific methods, the reporter backed off somewhat and the meeting ended.

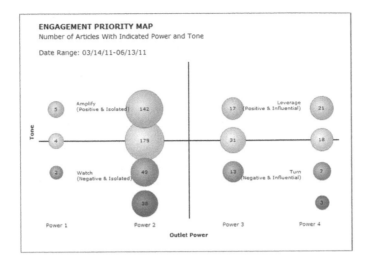

F I G U R E   3.1

Public Relay Engagement Priority Map

Nevertheless, in a repeat analysis completed over the next three weeks, the analysts noted that the targeted reporter had begun to use more data and research from third parties including the company itself. In 2005, I told this story to my colleagues in the Medill School of Journalism, Media, Integrated Marketing Communications as a way to manage reporting from both the publishers' and editors' perspectives. More recently, in 2011, the Medill School held a program in which a publisher spoke of using such systems to improve their reporters' work. This publisher was at least open to the idea but had not considered using the tracking systems to improve the work of writers and editors, but only to match stories to the interests of the customers (readers).

In the same way, it is possible to track and analyze what is being said on television. On most remote controls, the "CC" stands for closed caption, which allows concurrent live broadcasts and previously edited shows to provide a written version of the broadcast on a word-by-word basis. The system has been very useful for the hearing impaired and for those just learning English as a second language.

Imagine how useful this can be for a company or organization facing a crisis. Within just a few minutes of an interview on live television where the conversation is critical (or favorable) about the company, a manager in the firm can be watching the interview, seeing the text of what was said and analyzing the tone of the comments via his computer. The Public Relay Priority Map (Figure 3.1) illustrates the range of decision variables, including media power and tone, that can be tracked by comprehensive systems.

CASE: NBA STARS ON TELEVISION FOR THE WRONG REASONS

According to Tim Andree, former head of PR for the National Basketball Association (NBA), and now CEO of Dentsu America, the NBA found the closed-captioning tracking method very helpful in their high-profile, televised world of professional sports. A particularly sensitive crisis involving Kobe Bryant in 2003 was carefully tracked and, to the degree possible, managed from the NBA's perspective. At least the number of surprises would be reduced. It is also possible to track radio with voice recognition. Some of these systems have been around for decades based on technology available to the military and intelligence community, according to conversations with the Wisconsin Issues Network membership in the late 1980s.

Imagine being able to read, hear and see on your personal digital assistant (PDA) or laptop what was said about your company, product or CEO on the media just 15 seconds after it was released. The NBA subscribed to a service that fit their televised business. When a player created a personal crisis that could damage the reputation of the NBA, it was imperative that the communications manager and leaders of the NBA have immediate access to broadcast materials from all over the United States and the world. Knowing precisely what was being said and shown allowed the NBA to respond more accurately and with the correct tone.

The media and social media tracking systems that PR, marketing, political analysts and research professionals use are part of an important shift in management of communications, and the response of how companies, individuals and organizations measure their public image, brand acceptance, messages and actions.

The value of these sometimes expensive systems (depending on the level of customization) gives the PR professional access to the opinions, ideas, or comparisons of important reporters, quoted sources or thought leaders with their own blog or Twitter sites. With the dramatic increase in the number of "published" voices on the global web, it has become impossible for any national or global organization to manually track its coverage. However, digital changes have allowed for a significant growth in measuring PR and marketing:

1. Digitization of most information (on the web). With digitization comes standardized access to written documents, news, blogs, book, Tweets and the full content of published materials.

2. An increasing proliferation of information due to easy distribution on the web.

3. Nearly zero cost of entry to publishing today, as compared with traditional ink on paper or broadcast costs.

4. Almost instantaneous ability to track messages without the delay of printing, distribution or elite circulation outlets.

5. The nearly instantaneous spread of information from source to source regarding the company, individual or topic via the web, as information is shared or repurposed.

CASE: FOOD INDUSTRY AND UNFAIR ACCUSATIONS

In a similar case, dealing with agriculture and chemistry, a company found its products and name on a list of negatively targeted companies in Africa. Using the services of Evolve24 now part of Maritzresearch.com, the company gathered intelligence that suggested its products would be listed with other more risky genetically modified organisms (GMOs) as undesirable in some nations on that continent. By receiving advance notification from the service spotted in normally obscure publications and information sources, they were able to "get ahead" of the issue and prevent an undeserved crisis.

CASE: BANK OF AMERICA SHOWING PR SELLS SERVICES

What if you were any company, but in this case Bank of America, wanting to know if a marketing campaign with or without a PR program was more effective. The bank conducted a field experiment to test the idea in two similar cities, Phoenix, Arizona and Austin, Texas. Their goal was to see if the idea was profitable enough to "roll out" in their other markets. In one city, they offered a home mortgage financial product that was creatively designed to appeal to the Hispanic family market. In one market, the IMC plan was designed and launched with a marketing PR program of interviews in the Hispanic media about the product, events in the community, sponsorships, and other efforts to associate the bank's work and services with that of the targeted consumer group. In the other test city, the same exact advertising campaign was launched, but without the PR effort. In this case, logically, the customers in the city with the combination of PR and advertising were more likely to purchase the mortgage product. To provide more precise reporting data, they were able to track the press coverage in specialty publications to show the impact of the PR effort. For a national roll out, the use of the tracking systems would be even more crucial. Academics are always trying to get companies to test their marketing solutions. The tracking systems and this example are encouraging signs that marketers are willing to experiment more rather than take large and expensive leaps of faith that a marketing idea will work.

CASE: DELL COMPUTER TRACKING THE CEO

How can Dell track the C-suite to see if they are "on message?" The tracking service used by Dell communications professionals allowed them to almost instantly track and measure the speeches and interviews given by the top management team. Many of the managers were frequently on the road for the company to proselytize the company's goals and products. The executives had agreed to "stay on message," no matter how repetitive that might be for them, to be sure to reinforce the company goals. It was not unusual for the more senior executives, including the top executives, to vary their remarks. In the past, the only witness might be a single aide with the executive or someone catching the local TV, radio or newspaper interview. With immediate tracking systems, the communications professional was able to talk to the executive before the next interview to remind him to stay on message. According to the PR professional, this was a mixed blessing because the manager sometimes found the immediate feedback irritating. Imagine if the PR manager could contact the executive mid-interview by text message or even an urgent or quiet phone call as the interview was being conducted.

All of these examples illustrate the importance of operating in a new media environment. New companies with new software and service ideas are constantly being created. The principles of the companies cited here and listed in the readings section of the chapter are examples of the rapidly changing research function in PR and IMC.

Compared with my early days of research using legal systems, there is now an amazingly large range of concepts that can be measured. The following list of new metrics is only illustrative, but shows how far the field has progressed from the days of counting the number of column inches and comparing that earned space with the cost of a purchased advertising space.

NEW ENTERPRISE SOFTWARE FOR MEDIA TRACKING AND DECISION MAKING

There are several new software-based solutions for public relations and marketing managers. The wave of software development and the digitization of traditional communications (newspapers, magazines, television and radio) and newer social media (blogs, Twitter, Websites, Facebook, etc.) have allowed millions of words to be analyzed like millions of financial data points. A communications manager in the research and pharmaceutical company Genentech reported on her ability to present reports with "charts and graphs like the financial experts." Because of these skills and tools, she was invited into the company board meetings more often with real-time data and answers to questions in easily understood formats. In the constant search of public relations professionals for "harder" evidence of their success, the software providers have given PR a strong empirical lift. For example, the systems can:

- Compare reporting on your company or CEO by several reporters from all over the globe, and report which reporters (among dozens or even hundreds) were more negative, positive or neutral in their comments.

- Track and analyze what experts (from government, think tanks like MITRE, universities, competitors, etc.) are saying about specific aspects of your services or products. The information can be used to determine which ideas and messages may be misunderstood or resonate with experts for future message development and distribution. Some experts may need more and some less information, based on the analysis.

- Rate the articles by how well the company message was carried, from positive to negative, by media outlets' importance (your judgment), by frequency, and by proximity to important decisions announced in the company. This can help make future decisions of resource allocations.

- Stories not yet printed in traditional media can be tracked in advance of their printed release on the web to give the PR department and management a "heads-up" about possible questions the next day.

Although reporters can be evaluated, the risks are perhaps still too great (see Case: The Airline, the Reporter, and the Angry CEO) to rate or rank reporters in any public source, or even in private. It may be useful to analyze their stories on more journalistic issues such as quotes, use of data, timeliness of information and

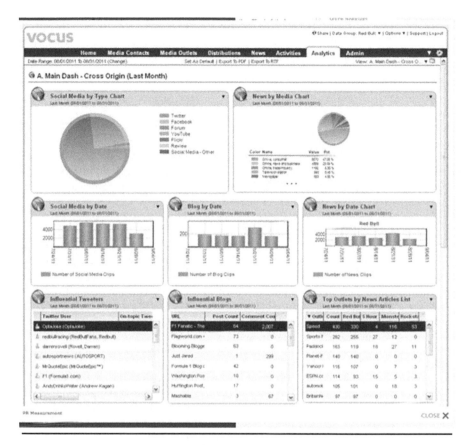

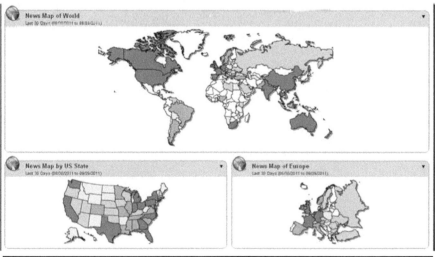

Vocus

more. This does not suggest that someone won't try to rank the journalists and end up in hot water for doing so (see case study on the reporter on page 41).

To service the advertising side of an integrated program, it is possible to test the effectiveness of news stories being released before an ad to measure the contribution of PR to marketing (see Case: Bank of America Showing PR Sells Services).

Comparison of "share of mind" or the amount of coverage (mentions of the brand, leaders and inventions) in the media can help determine the relative amount of attention you're being given in thousands or even hundreds of stories. Companies, such as Vocus and Radian6, provide comprehensive data of a wide range of metrics. Each firm has its own strengths.

It is possible to even examine "zero mindshare" as evidence of meeting your goal of *not* being mentioned in a series of articles attacking an industry. It can have negative repercussions if it shows that your competitors or opposition stakeholders are getting press whereas you are not quoted when you need to be.

Trends over time can be easily tracked to show progress or changes in business or policy climates.

Vocus On-Demand Software provides many services. They initially found a market in simply providing information from media to PR professionals. They also found that the PR departments' limited budgets were not enough to build their businesses on. However, the list of their clients is impressive. Their specialty is to demonstrate the value to the business goals of tracking and analysis in the boardroom and C-suite. As the industry developed and competed, the business model also changed to allow the supplier to provide higher margin and profitable consulting services to interpret and modify the system. This was helpful in creating a new job category for PR professionals sometimes working out of their home full-time (Figure 3.2).

Each service, in its own way, contributed to building this new industry that supports PR. For example, Vocus emphasized its experience and knowledge of public affairs, and Evolve24 developed more dedicated predictive modeling from the data. For a presentation to Johnson Controls in Milwaukee, Wisconsin, the company Public Relay provided images to show the audience how to segment influentials and use data to plan (Figure 3.1). The combination of images from the various enterprise software companies in this industry was a topic of great interest to the worldwide communications team of the $40 billion global energy and technology company. For a test of one system in a graduate class at Northwestern University, the students applied the system to tracking the White House initiative, *Let's Move!*, on childhood obesity and the corporate response to the effort.

Similarly, the Biz360 (now Attensity) system was used to analyze the public interest and fear over artificial sweeteners and sugar for Coca-Cola. The company managers were surprised that (according to the data) the public was not as concerned as the Coke managers over the issue of artificial sweeteners. According to the tracking of current social media and traditional media, the dominant issue and criticism of the industry was still over using fattening sugars in the product. Several other graduate practicum consulting projects were completed using the then Biz360 system, including a project for Harley-Davidson motorcycles. Based on the community of riders and

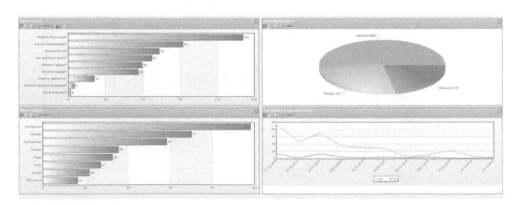

F I G U R E   3.3

Whirlpool Positive Theme Example

```
┌─────────────────────────────────────────────────────────────┐
│  Exhibit A: Commercial Software Packages                    │
│  Attensity (formerly Biz360)                                │
│  http://www.attensity360.com                                │
│  Cymfony                                                    │
│  http://www.cymfony.com                                     │
│  Public Relay                                               │
│  http://www.publicrelay.com                                 │
│  Radian 6                                                   │
│  http://www.radian6.com                                     │
│  Vocus                                                      │
│  http://www.vocus.com/content/index.asp                     │
│  Cision                                                     │
│  http://www.cision.com                                      │
│  Strategy One                                               │
│  http://www.competitiveinsights.net                         │
│  Evolve24                                                   │
│  http://www.maritzresearch.com                              │
└─────────────────────────────────────────────────────────────┘
```

F I G U R E   3.4

Commercial Software Packages (selected December 2011)

analysis of their blogs, the use of this software uncovered an opportunity to encourage women to ride Harley-Davidson bikes.

At "shoot-outs" around the country for PR professional audiences, I have talked about the issues raised in this chapter. Panels of experts from the companies would also explain the superior qualities of their software for the audience. Although relatively smaller and anonymous companies can perhaps rely on library-based searches with some discipline, the trend is clearly toward visible brands such as Whirlpool (Figure 3.3). Companies in high-risk industries selling to children, the elderly, the disabled, and other relatively protected stakeholder groups will find the use of such systems as "insurance" to protect their reputations and stay with or even ahead of the marketplace. The alternative to not tracking trends, customer buzz, and the impact of the companies own social media is not an acceptable management risk today (Figure 3.4).

There are many more new ways to "slice and dice" the data that software developers are creating every day. Many of the reports were simply too time consuming to count or analyze without the new software. This still begs the question of whether the data is just more data, or whether it is useful information for decision making. Radian6, for example, grew from social media to a comprehensive system for searching social media (Figure 3.5a and b).

GROWING SOCIAL MEDIA TRACKING AND ANALYSIS

A newer form of research has taken hold from the social media explosion. These highly specific metrics exist to allow social media users to evaluate their positioning in the social media ecosystem. Most of the applications seem dedicated to watching your social media presence compared with that of others. It can be done at an individual level of Twitter (e.g., my handle is IMCprof) or for a corporation or organization. The charts included in the inserts are engaging and certainly stimulate discussion on several levels:

1. Are we achieving the goals we set for using this particular social media? Who is following us? Are they our target audience? Do we have a critical mass of followers on any of the social media to justify our time updating the site? Are we cited on other sites?

2. How do we compare on our level of influence with other similar sites? What metrics are useful to compare our sites to those of other competitors or thought leaders?

FIGURE   3.5

Radian6 Summary Dashboard of Social Media

3. What can we do to improve our social media profile to meet our business goals? How are our social media incorporated into our integrated marketing communications and marketing plan? Do the sites continue to support our changing business goals?

4. Which social media measurement systems should be subscribed to? Many are currently free when they are launched. However, premium services (with a charge) will undoubtedly be made available at some time. Which services are worth our time? Which ones can answer our questions of influence, expertise and other considerations?

Naturally, all of these questions about the metric services will change rapidly as the metric sites change just as rapidly in response to the market and the need to monetize the sites for the inventors and investors. The

Exhibit B: Social Media Metrics
Crimson Hexagon http://www.crimsonhexagon.com **Klout** http://beta.klout.com/home **PeerIndex** http://www.peerindex.net **Tweet Topic Explorer** http://tweettopicexplorer.neoformix.com **WiseWindows** http://www.wisewindow.com

FIGURE 3.6

Social Media Metrics (selected December 2011)

lesson is still to experiment with the new sites to "stick your toe in the water to test the temperature" as they used to say in the pre–digital thermometer world (Figure 3.6).

As an aside, it initially seemed unfortunate to me that the whole realm of media known as social media may have been mislabeled for business and complex organizations. Naturally, social media, including Facebook and Twitter, started as media to facilitate the discussion among friends, associates and even initially unknown individuals at a very informal level. In fact, the word *social* may have explained to a high degree the original objection of business managers to allowing Twitter, Facebook, and blogs to be on a corporate IT system. Why would a company or serious organization condone something seemingly frivolous called social media? For example, for a period of time, employees developing messaging strategies to talk about Dow Chemical were forced to operate at their home or local coffee shop to access Twitter, YouTube or Facebook, which initially were not allowed in the corporate system. This changed. Business managers have learned that *social* has a relationship-building meaning for corporate stakeholders. Objections from professional colleagues seemed to have subsided as the term was redefined to mean communications leading to relationship building. It did not overtly make business relationships necessarily social, and business will have to live with it. PR practitioners will have to continue to define social media in more modern terms to outlive the initial meaning. On the other hand, it can also send the message that businesses must engage in more personal, authentic relationships with stakeholders and others interested in the success or failure of your organization—just like a friend should. Perhaps the word *social* has more value than we might have suspected.

A short list of software applications may help illustrate the value of social media metrics. Again, like the more formal and custom commercial systems discussed above, these applications may disappear overnight or be absorbed by other applications. The same lesson that we have learned over and over again using technology for business or education is that the value must be in incorporating each new software or application as part of our professional growth. Although a particular tool may not survive the market or may be outflanked by a new app within weeks of its launch, the value is in the testing and thinking about the metrics.

EXAMPLE: GOOGLE NEW METRICS

Just before this chapter was to be sent to the publisher, Softpedia reported that Google made news in the research of trends and search with the announcement of a product called Google Correlate. The metric tool will facilitate the work of researchers trying to find trends in their search data. "Tools that provide access to search data, such as Google Trends or Google Insights for Search, weren't designed with this type of research in mind," Matt Mohebbi, a software engineer at Google, explained. "Those systems allow you to enter a search term and see the trend; but researchers told us they want to enter the trend of some real-world activity and see which search terms best match that trend," he wrote.[2]

EXAMPLE: KLOUT

In mid-2011, Klout.com, still labeled beta for a test version, permitted users to compare their Twitter site to other dimensions, which were naturally graphically presented. The details in the following section are revealing for the user of the application to explain how the app can be relied on for making decisions.

Klout Score (edited and quoted from their website) describes true reach, amplification and network.

"The Klout Score is the measurement of your overall online influence. The scores range from 1 to 100, with higher scores representing a wider and stronger sphere of influence. Klout uses more than 35 variables on Facebook and Twitter to measure True Reach, Amplification Probability and Network Score.

"True Reach is the size of your engaged audience and is based on those of your followers and friends who actively listen and react to your messages.

"Amplification Score is the likelihood that your messages will generate actions (retweets, @messages, likes and comments) and is on a scale of 1 to 100.

"Network Score indicates how influential your engaged audience is and is also on a scale from 1 to 100. The Klout Score is highly correlated to clicks, comments and retweets."[3]

"We believe that influence is the ability to drive people to action; action might be defined as a reply, a retweet, a comment or a click. We perform significant testing to ensure that the average click-through rate on links shared is highly correlated with a person's Klout Score. The more than 25 variables used to generate scores for each of these categories are normalized across the whole data set and run through our analytics engine. After the first pass of analytics, we apply a specific weight to each data point. We then run the factors through our machine-learning analysis and calculate the final Klout Score. The final Klout Score is a representation of how successful a person is at engaging their audience and how big an impact their messages have on people."

TRUE REACH

"True Reach is the size of your engaged audience. We eliminate inactive and spam accounts, and only include accounts that you influence. To do this, we calculate influence for each individual relationship, taking into account factors such as whether an individual has shared or acted upon your content and the likelihood that they saw it.

"True Reach is broken into the following subcategories:

- Reach

- Are your tweets interesting and informative enough to build an audience?

- How far has your content been spread across Twitter?

- Are people adding you to lists and are those lists being followed?

- Demand

- How many people did you have to follow to build your count of followers?

- How often are your follows reciprocated?

"Factors measured: followers, mutual follows, friends, total retweets, unique commenters, unique likers, follower/follow ratio, followed back percentage, @ mention count, list count and list followers count."[3]

AMPLIFICATION PROBABILITY

"Amplification Probability is the likelihood that your content will be acted upon. How often do your messages generate retweets or spark a conversation? The ability to create content that compels others to respond and high-velocity content that spreads into networks beyond your own is a key component of influence.

"Amplification Ability is a composite of the following subcategories:

- Engagement

- How diverse is the group that @ messages you?

- Are you broadcasting or participating in conversations?

- Velocity

- How likely are you to be retweeted?

- Do a lot of people retweet you or is it always the same few followers?

- Activity

- Are you tweeting too little or too much for your audience?

- Are your tweets effective in generating new followers, retweets and @ replies?

"Factors measured: unique retweeters, unique messages retweeted, likes per post, comments per post follower retweet percentage, unique @ senders, follower mention percentage, inbound messages per outbound message, update count."

NETWORK INFLUENCE

"Network Influence is the influence level of your engaged audience. Engagement is measured based on actions such as retweets, @messages, follows, lists, comments, and likes. Each time a person performs one of these actions, it is a testament to the authority and the quality of your content. Capturing the attention of influencers is no easy task, and those who are able to do so are typically creating spectacular content. Network Score looks at the Klout Score of each person who interacts with you to determine:

- How influential are the people who @ message you?

- How influential are the people who retweet you?

- How influential are the people who follow you?

- How influential are the people who list you?

- How influential are the people who follow the lists you are on?

"Factors measured: list inclusions, follower/follow ratio, followed back percentage, unique senders, unique retweeters, unique commenters, unique likers, influence of followers, influence of retweeters and mentioners, influence of friends, influence of likers, and commenters"[4]

Another popular service is PeerIndex's scoring, which uses five metrics explained in greater detail on their website (Figure 3.7).

1. "Authority is the measure of trust; how much can you rely on that person's recommendations and opinion on a given topic.

2. "Related to benchmark authority is topic resonance. This is a measurement of how your actions within a topic interest community resonate with the community. Again, what goes on in the community is more important than your single action.

3. "Audience is an indication of your reach. It is not simply determined by the number of people who follow you, but instead is measured according to the number of people who listen and are receptive to what you are saying.

FIGURE 3.7

PeerIndex

4. "Activity is the measure of how much you do that is related to the topic area. Being too active will lead people to stop listening to you; and if you are too inactive, people will never know to listen to you. The Activity Score takes into account this behavior.

5. "Realness is a metric that indicates the likelihood that the profile is of a real person, rather than a spambot or Twitter feed. A score higher than 50 means that we think this account is of a real person; a score lower than 50 means that it is less likely to be a real person."[4]

Tweet Topic Explorer is not a highly complex site, but it does offer an intricate visual image of your Twitter site and other sites (Figure 3.8). It shows words most commonly used from recent Tweets on a specified Twitter site. The globes are larger depending on the frequency of word use; the words are grouped as they are used in the Tweet. The globe can be clicked on to show the specific Tweet in a right-hand column. If I were Tweeting on a corporate website, I would occasionally use this software to gather an image of my work and the work of competitors' sites. One simple question would be to illustrate if the Twitter site is "on message." And, what are the messages of other Twitter sites? Tweet Topic Explorer is simple, but powerful and visually very revealing. This idea may well be legally incorporated into other more comprehensive models.

Other software like OneStat.com (free for the basic service) can be used for a wide range of purposes such as:

1. Summary

2. Page views

3. Visits

4. Most visited pages

5. Referrer

6. Geography

7. Technology

8. Statistics

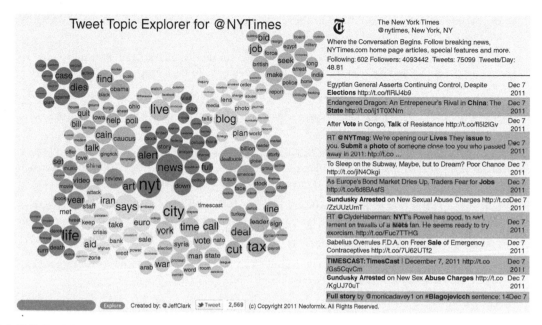

FIGURE 3.8

Tweet Topic Explorer Key Words

9. The Charts

10. Tools.

The reader will want to audit the existing systems when they need to measure success in either more direct PR and marketing terms or more general tracking such as page visits. Some additional reading is available at the end of this chapter.

CONCLUSION: THE FUTURE OF GRAPHICAL CONTENT TRACKING AND ANALYSIS RESEARCH

Early PR math merely counted clips (number of printed articles) that mentioned the name of the client, CEO or product, whether the articles were positive or negative or used information from the company. Added to the formula was an odd metric that estimated the size of the article to give a comparative figure of what that much space would have cost, if the space had been purchased based on a rate card as advertising. This rough metric has been both accepted and rejected by professionals in the field.

This has and will change the future of public relations and its related fields such as public affairs, public information, marketing communications, advertising, promotions and database marketing. We have begun an age of using words, issues and ideas as digital sources of information—not just data.

Some of the trends may include:

1. Most PR professionals and PR-educated students will be trained to use data systems.

2. PR will increasingly come under the same accountability pressures as marketing and other disciplines.

3. There may be confusion over which commercial platforms to use.

4. Increasing risks to industry and nongovernmental organizations (NGOs) from their actions will compel them to use tracking and analytical systems.

5. There will be an increasing liability for not having full service metrics and information as "required by law" (e.g., Sarbanes-Oxley, NYSE Rules. See Chapter 23 on Corporate Governance).

6. Software will take over some of your work. You will need to literally work around the clock.

7. The global economy and policy issues will make it necessary to use tracking to make money and decisions while you sleep.

8. For PR or other fields, accessible databases will more richly capture measurements of risk communications, issues management, competitive threats, financial fragility, government involvement, new industries, new sources (scripts) and repetition of your key messages.

9. Software experts and academics will invent more high-tech applications including risk- and issue-predictive metrics, return on investment analyses, photo and brand image analysis and mobile uses.

10. There will be viable visual media analysis (not just text).

11. The tracking and analysis systems will be linked to short-term and long-term consumer relationship management systems for better service.

12. The decline in the value and credibility of traditional media (Web 2.0 and 3.0 expansion) will increase the need for more comprehensive digital PR measurement.

For nearly a century, the unfair assumption has existed that public relations, marketing communications and even marketing professionals are not strong analytical managers. Too often, students and professionals have run away from the numbers rather than reached for the numbers. To overcome this disparaging view of PR and marketing, the last decade has provided the next generation of communications professionals with tools to give management more proof of effect than in the past.

DISCUSSION QUESTIONS

1. What is the argument for PR to be more driven by "the numbers?"
2. What budget do you need to begin to use online metrics for PR?
3. What are some of the questions that you would like to answer for your management team about your company's coverage in the global press? Can you create a demonstration of media metrics on a company or your own social media?

NOTES

1. "Free PR Webinar: Inside This Year's Silver Anvil Award Judging | PRSA." Public Relations Resources & PR Tools for Communications Professionals: Public Relations Society of America (PRSA). Web. 15 Nov. 2011. <http://www.prsa.org/learning/freewebinars>.
2. Parfeni, Lucian. "Dig Through Millions of Search Trends with Google Correlate - Softpedia." Latest News - Softpedia. Web. 15 Nov. 2011. <http://news.softpedia.com/news/Dig-Through-Millions-of-Search-Trends-with-Google-Correlate-202439.shtml>.
3. "Understanding the Influence Metric: What Is the Klout Score?" Klout | The Standard for Influence. Web. 15 Nov. 2011. <http://klout.com/corp/kscore>.
4. "Rankings - PeerIndex." Understand Your Online Social Capital - PeerIndex. Web. 08 Nov. 2011. <http://www.peerindex.net/help/scores>.

ADDITIONAL READING

Blanchard, Olivier. 2011. *Social Media ROI: Managing and Measuring Social Media Efforts in Your Organization.* Indianapolis, IN: Que.

Delahaye, Paine Katie. 2011. *Measure What Matters: Online Tools for Understanding Customers, Social Media, Engagement, and Key Relationships.* Hoboken, NJ: John Wiley & Sons.

Lovett, John. 2011. *Social Media Metrics Secrets.* Hoboken, NJ: John Wiley & Sons.

Sterne, Jim. 2010. *Social Media Metrics: How to Measure and Optimize Your Marketing Investment.* Hoboken, NJ: John Wiley & Sons.

4

C H A P T E R

PUBLIC RELATIONS LAW

Karla K. Gower
Professor, Department of Advertising and Public Relations
Director, Plank Center for Leadership in Public Relations
The University of Alabama

Today's business climate is wrought with legal pitfalls to which public relations (PR) practitioners, marketers and other managers working with the public can unwittingly expose their organizations. Although cases of corporate malfeasance such as the Enron and Waste Management (www.forbes.com/2002/07/25/accounting tracker.html) financial scandals of 2001 and 2002, and the more recent Goldman Sachs, Facebook, and other financial challenges (www.forbes.com/2010/05/12/financial-scandals-goldman-personal-finance-scandals.html) tend to generate the biggest headlines, most legal issues arise as a result of negligence or inadvertence rather than actual wrongdoing. Regardless of the cause, however, lawsuits and violations of regulations are costly for companies. The obvious expenses are monetary in the form of fines, but the reputation of an organization can take a real hit from legal issues. Lawsuits also often wind through the courts for years, requiring hundreds, if not thousands, of hours of personnel time with a subsequent loss in productivity.

Nike, Inc., the multinational athletic equipment marketer, found out just how costly lawsuits could be when allegations of sweatshop conditions in its overseas factories began to surface in the mass media in the 1990s. At the time, Nike had revenues of $2 billion with 5,300 employees worldwide, but nearly all of its products were manufactured by independent contractors, at first in Japan and later in China, Thailand and Indonesia. Soon, reports detailing poor working conditions in those overseas factories started to appear, alleging that workers received less than the local minimum wage; were required to work overtime; were subjected to verbal, physical and sexual abuse; and were exposed to toxic chemicals without adequate safety equipment. Because of the reports, Nike faced increased media scrutiny in the United States.

By 1997, the allegations had made the mainstream. Students on university campuses around the country protested Nike's treatment of workers overseas. New Jersey schoolchildren staged an anti-Nike play on Broadway. And 40 members of Congress signed letters calling for Nike to improve the conditions in its Asian factories. Until then, Nike had essentially ignored its detractors, remaining silent in the face of mounting opposition, but now it launched a public relations campaign that included issuing news releases and writing letters to editors and university presidents, among other tactics. In addition, Nike purchased a full-page ad in leading newspapers to publicize a report prepared by GoodWorks International, which found no evidence of unsafe working conditions in Nike's overseas factories. Nike repeatedly stressed that the allegations were not true and that, in any event, the responsibility for the factories belonged to the subcontractors. In October 1997, a Nike spokeswoman accused workers' rights groups of being behind the protests and of "using publicity stunts to promote mistruths and distortions for their own purposes."

One month later, an employee leaked the results of an Ernst & Young internal audit of Nike's overseas facilities to the media. Although Nike had been publicly claiming that it required its subcontractors to certify compliance with applicable government regulations regarding occupational health and safety by signing a Memorandum of Understanding and that its Code of Conduct protected the rights of workers, the audit cited evidence of widespread health and safety concerns in a Vietnamese factory. Even more damaging to Nike's reputation was that it had had the internal report for 11 months but had not released the findings to the public or changed its message.

The result was a 70 percent drop in profits in the first quarter of 1998. Suddenly, Nike's strategic response to the "sweatshop" allegations changed dramatically. On May 12, 1998, Nike CEO Phil Knight gave a speech at the National Press Club Conference in Washington, D.C., in which he apologized for Nike's practices and vowed to change the company's corporate culture.

A month before Knight's speech, however, activist Marc Kasky had brought a lawsuit in California claiming that Nike had violated the state's false advertising statute in its PR campaign by publishing false and misleading statements (www.corpwatch.org/article.php?id=3448). Essentially, Kasky argued that given the information contained in the Ernst & Young internal audit, Nike had misrepresented its labor practices in its letters and news releases when it said that its Memorandum of Understanding certified compliance with government regulations.

The heart of the complaint began with a section titled "Nike's Ubiquitous and Successful Promotional Schemes," in which Nike's extensive advertising budget and its numerous contracts with athletes and universities were set out. Nike was painted as the corporate bully whose revenues amounted to billions of dollars a year, who spent a billion to promote its products, and whose officers made millions a year. Yet, it willingly and knowingly underpaid its workers, 80 percent of whom were young women between the ages of 18 and 25 years, required them to work overtime without compensation and exposed these young women of child-bearing age to harmful toxins.

Nike immediately brought a motion to dismiss the lawsuit, arguing that the speech in question was not subject to the California false advertising law because it did not amount to commercial speech. It was, rather, noncommercial corporate speech and therefore protected by the First Amendment.

What might be termed public relations speech differs from other communication in that it gives a voice to corporations and is often for a commercial purpose. As a result, public relations speech comes under two different First Amendment categories of speech: corporate (noncommercial) and commercial. Corporate speech is speech by corporations about political and social issues. Commercial speech, on the other hand, is speech more directly related to the promotion of a product or service and has been defined by the U.S. Supreme Court as either speech that does no more than propose a commercial transaction or speech motivated by profit.

The commercial speech doctrine dates from the 1942 Supreme Court decision of *Valentine v. Chrestensen* (supreme.justia.com/us/316/52/). Chrestensen had attempted to get around a New York City ordinance banning leaflets on city streets by putting a protest of the ordinance on the back of his leaflet advertising tours of his submarine. The Court quickly disposed of the case saying that "purely commercial advertising" had no First Amendment protection. At the time, advertising was seen simply as a business activity, not as a form of speech.

In the 1960s and 1970s, however, the Court began to whittle away at the commercial speech doctrine, and commercial speech came to be recognized as serving a valuable function in society in its own right. In *Virginia State Board of Pharmacy v. Virginia Citizens Consumer Council* (supreme.justia.com/us/425/748/), for example, the Court in 1976 held that "advertising, however tasteless and excessive it sometimes may seem, is nonetheless dissemination of information as to who is producing and selling what product, for what reason, and at what price." Although the Court acknowledged that such information is "a matter of public interest," the Court was not prepared to give commercial speech the same protection it gives political or noncommercial speech.

The Court considers commercial speech "hardier" than noncommercial speech because it is "the offspring of economic self-interest" and is, therefore, not "particularly susceptible to being crushed by overbroad regulation." It is also more readily verifiable because commercial speech is usually about products and services over which the speaker has control and intimate knowledge. Commercial speech is also a planned activity rather than something expressed in the midst of a public debate. Thus, the Court does not fear the potential chilling effect of government regulation on commercial speech.

Today, the Court uses a four-part test to determine when government restrictions of commercial speech are permissible. Under the test, courts must consider each of the following:

1. Whether the commercial speech is worthy of First Amendment protection. The speech must be accurate and for a lawful product or service.

2. Whether the government has a substantial interest for regulating the speech. Usually, courts consider the government to have a substantial interest in protecting the health, safety, morals and aesthetics of the public.

3. Whether the regulation in question directly advances the government's interest. For example, if the government wishes to curtail gambling, it must show that banning advertisements about casinos would stop people from gambling.

4. Whether the regulation is no broader than necessary to realize that interest. The government must show that its restriction does not restrict more commercial speech than it needs to or that there is a reasonable fit between the regulation and the government interest.

CORPORATE SPEECH AND THE INCREASING ROLE OF PR IN SPEECH LAW

At around the same time as the Court was recognizing the contributions that commercial speech made to society, it was also recognizing corporate speech. The Supreme Court first granted corporations a First Amendment right to speak in the 1976 case, *First National Bank v. Bellotti* (supreme.justia.com/us/435/765). First National Bank challenged a Massachusetts law that prohibited corporations from making contributions or expenditures to influence or affect a vote on a political issue unless that issue directly affected them. The bank wanted to communicate to voters its position on a proposed constitutional amendment regarding personal income tax. The Supreme Court held that such speech deserved protection because it provided information that was vital to the public debate. Since then, the Court has continued to uphold the right of corporations to voice their positions on political and social issues of the day because they have important contributions to make to the debates.

However, not everyone believes that speech rights ought to be extended to corporations. Critics of corporate speech rights focus on the pervasive influence of corporations. They argue that corporations have such wealth and power that their voices could drown out the speech of individuals and distort the discourse on public policy issues. This argument can be seen clearly in the debates surrounding campaign financing. Spending limits have been placed on corporations at both the federal and state levels to prevent the "buying" of candidates through campaign contributions since the early twentieth century. The most recent effort was the 2002 Bipartisan Campaign Reform Act, also known as the McCain–Feingold Act. The Act regulated the raising and spending of "soft money" (money given to political parties rather than to particular candidates) and prohibited corporations and unions from using their general treasury funds during elections for issue ads regarding federal candidates.

In March 2010, however, the Supreme Court declared "virtually all limits on expenditures by corporations in political campaigns unconstitutional," as one mass media law scholar described it. The case, *Citizens United v. Federal Election Commission* (supreme.justia.com/us/558/08-205/opinion.html), involved a movie that criticized Hillary Rodham Clinton, who was seeking the Democratic presidential nomination at the time. The movie was released within 30 days of a primary, violating the Bipartisan Campaign Reform Act. Justice Kennedy in his opinion said the Court's decision reaffirmed the principle that "the Government may not suppress political speech on the basis of the speaker's corporate identity."

However, deciding whether a corporation's speech is on a political or social issue and therefore protected or commercial and therefore potentially subject to greater regulation is not always easy. In 1983, the Supreme Court said in *Bolger v. Youngs Drugs* (supreme.justia.com/us/463/60/case.html) that it relies on a "common sense" distinction to draw the line between the two. Youngs Drugs, a condom manufacturer, challenged a prohibition that prevented it from using the U.S. Postal Service to send a direct mail piece to potential consumers because contraceptive information cannot be sent unsolicited through the mail. A pamphlet in the package provided information on sexually transmitted diseases and how to prevent them. One of the prevention methods was the use of condoms during sex. Youngs Drugs' name appeared only at the end of the pamphlet, although the company acknowledged at trial that the pamphlet was an advertisement. The Court held that because the pamphlet was an advertisement, was motivated by profit and contained a product reference it was commercial speech.

It was this question of how best to describe Nike's speech that was facing the California courts in the *Kasky v. Nike* case. Should it be considered commercial speech and thus subject to the false advertising statute as Kasky was arguing? Or was it really noncommercial speech by a corporation on an issue of political or social importance as Nike claimed?

The trial and appeals courts both agreed with Nike and dismissed the lawsuit. The speech in question, the Court of Appeal held, served to promote a favorable corporate image through news releases and letters. Therefore, the speech did not fit within two of the three characteristics of commercial speech enunciated by the Court in *Bolger v. Youngs Drugs*—advertising format and product reference. Instead the court held, "they were part of a public dialogue on a matter of public concern: the perceived evils or benefits of labor practices associated with economic globalization."

The Supreme Court of California, however, saw things differently (www.law.com/regionals/ca/opinions/may/s087859.shtml). It held, in a four-to-three decision, that "because the messages in question were directed by a commercial speaker to a commercial audience, and because they made representations of fact about the speaker's own business operations for the purpose of promoting sales of its products," the messages were commercial speech and subject to the state law. The court acknowledged that the U.S. Supreme Court does not prohibit corporations from speaking out on issues of public importance, but "when a business enterprise, to promote and defend its sales and profits, makes factual representations about its own products or its own operations, it must speak truthfully."

Nike was free, the court noted, to address the issue of economic globalization and overseas labor conditions in the abstract and that speech would be fully protected. However, Nike was not entitled to discuss its own labor practices without being accurate. The speech in question was readily verifiable by Nike, and the false advertising regulations were unlikely to deter Nike from speaking in the future.

The dissenting judges disagreed, being particularly troubled that the majority had virtually handicapped one side in a public debate. Nike's critics were free to make whatever allegations they wanted to about the company and their speech was fully protected by the First Amendment. However, Nike could not freely engage in the debate and defend itself without ensuring that all of its statements were completely accurate and not misleading.

When Nike appealed the California decision to the U.S. Supreme Court, several media outlets, such as *The New York Times*, CNN and CBS; major corporations, such as Bank of America, Microsoft and Pfizer; and the Public Relations Society of America filed *amicus curiae* (friends of the court) briefs in support of Nike's position. The primary argument put forth in the briefs was that classifying Nike's speech as commercial would make corporations reluctant to speak on issues for fear that their materials might contain an inadvertent error or that their statements might be perceived as misleading. The result, it was feared, would be less corporate information at a time when greater corporate transparency and openness were being urged.

The Supreme Court ultimately decided not to hear the case and sent it back for trial (www.oyez.org/cases/2000-2009/2002/2002_02_575?sort=ideology). Before trial, however, Nike and Kasky settled the lawsuit, with Nike agreeing to contribute $1.5 million to the Washington, D.C.–based Fair Labor Association, which means the California decision stands as is.

IMPLICATIONS FOR PR PRACTICE: INTEGRATION WITH ADVERTISING

Many public relations professionals voiced disappointment at the position taken by the Public Relations Society of America in its brief before the Court, arguing that public relations professionals ought not to be advocating the right of a corporation to lie, that good and ethical public relations promotes truthfulness. However, such a position misses the point of the legal issues at stake. *Kasky v. Nike* was not about the right of a corporation to lie. It was about the extent to which a corporation is entitled to First Amendment protection for its speech, especially for what might be termed PR speech, and ultimately about a corporation's ability to defend itself in the court of public opinion.

Complete accuracy should always be the goal, but even accurate statements can be misleading. Noncommercial speech statements that are inaccurate and/or misleading will not result in liability unless made with the intention to deceive or with knowledge of their falsity. Commercial speech statements, on the other hand, that are inaccurate and/or misleading will result in liability if they were made even negligently or sometimes, as in the case of California, even if the communicator took precautions to prevent errors and mistakes.

The case also has implications for strategic integrated communication. It suggests that courts may well view such integration as proof that the speech is commercial and thus subject it to greater scrutiny.

REGULATING PUBLIC RELATIONS SPEECH

Public relations practitioners need to be careful about how and what they communicate on behalf of their clients not just because of potential lawsuits. Public relations speech is also regulated by many federal and state agencies. The primary regulatory bodies at the federal level are the Federal Trade Commission (FTC) and the Securities and Exchange Commission (SEC).

FEDERAL TRADE COMMISSION

Although the FTC is concerned with protecting consumers from deceptive advertising, the agency takes a broad view of "advertising" and looks at the totality of a campaign. The FTC defines deceptive advertising as a material representation, omission or practice that is likely to mislead a reasonable consumer.

Likely to Mislead: The advertisement does not have to actually mislead or cause deception so long as it appears likely to do so. A deceptive statement may mislead expressly, such as "Using Listerine prevents colds," or by implication. Omission of important or material information can also make an ad deceptive.

Reasonable Consumer: The FTC considers the advertisement from the perspective of a reasonable consumer. The test is whether the consumer's interpretation or reaction to the ad is reasonable. When ads are targeted to a specific audience, such as the elderly, then the test will be how a reasonable member of that group reacts.

Material Representation or Omission: A material misrepresentation is one that is likely to affect a consumer's decision to purchase the product or service. Express claims about the attributes of a product are always considered material.

Substantiation: In determining whether there has been a material misrepresentation, the FTC looks to see whether advertisers have a reasonable basis for their claims and whether they can substantiate those claims with scientific studies. Substantiation applies to PR materials that may include claims from independent studies.

Testimonials and Endorsements: Product endorsements include infomercials that often feature celebrities and "man on the street" testimonials. The FTC has defined an endorsement or testimonial as an ad that consumers are likely to believe reflects the opinion, belief and experience of someone other than the company. Celebrity or expert endorsers must be actual users of the product at the time of the endorsement.

Only real customers can give a testimonial, and it must reflect their actual experience. In advertisements for the weight-loss supplement Xenadrine EFX, customers testified about how much weight they had lost using the product. What they failed to say though was that they had engaged in a rigorous diet and exercise program at the same time and had been paid for their testimonial.

The FTC has extended its concern about misleading testimonials to blogs and tweets. Individuals who make an endorsement via social media "must disclose the material connections they share with the seller of the product or service," according to the 2009 guidelines. In April 2010, Ann Taylor Loft was one of the first companies to be investigated by the FTC for potentially violating the new rules. The company had invited bloggers to preview its summer 2010 collection and offered a "special gift" to those who did. The FTC found that the company had in fact told bloggers to disclose their connection and therefore should not be held responsible for

INSIDER TRADING

The SEC also prohibits insider trading. An insider is anyone who has material information that is unavailable to the general public. An insider who buys or sells shares in the company before the material information is made public has engaged in insider trading. Insiders include directors, officers, employees and agents of the company, as well as those who have acquired such information through their positions, such as accountants, lawyers, consultants and public relations professionals.

The best known of the recent insider trading scandals involved Martha Stewart. The SEC alleged that Stewart had sold her shares in ImClone Systems, Inc., a biopharmaceutical firm, in December 2001, after being told by her broker that ImClone's CEO had sold his. At the time, ImClone was awaiting approval from the Food and Drug Administration on an experimental cancer drug. The CEO's actions regarding his stock in the company suggested that the Food and Drug Administration was going to reject ImClone's application. Stewart was not actually convicted of insider trading; she was convicted of lying about the incident to investigators. She was, however, sued civilly by the SEC for insider trading. In August 2006, she agreed to a five-year ban on serving as a director of any public company and paid a fine of $195,081.

The ban on insider trading reflects the concept of fiduciary duty. Those who manage a corporation and their advisors owe a duty to the shareholders to act at all times in the best interests of the corporation. Using nonpublic material information to trade a corporation's shares, or telling a few select people who trade on it, without first disclosing that information to the public constitutes a breach of that fiduciary duty.

the actions of those who failed to do so. Legacy Learning Systems, Inc. was not so fortunate. The FTC hit the company with a $250,000 fine in 2011 for fake product reviews it obtained from bloggers on behalf of its clients.

Defenses. The basic defense against any false advertising complaint is truth, that is, proving that whatever is said about the product is true. The burden is on the government to prove that the ad is deceptive or misleading. However, as was seen in the Nike case, "truth," especially in PR materials, can be problematic.

SECURITIES AND EXCHANGE COMMISSION

The SEC oversees the financial markets and grew out of the stock market crash that triggered the Great Depression. The purpose of the SEC is to ensure a level playing field for all investors by requiring truthful, complete and timely disclosure to the public of information about publicly traded companies that could be important to an investor's decision to buy, sell or hold securities.

The Securities Exchange Act of 1934. The Securities Exchange Act of 1934 applies to publicly traded stock (The Securities Act of 1933 regulates initial public offerings). The Act's purposes are to ensure full disclosure of timely and pertinent information and to prevent any deception or manipulation of prices. As a result, the SEC requires reports to be filed periodically detailing a company's financial state, its future plans and other information that could affect an investor's decision regarding that company's securities.

Annual Reports. Companies are required to file with the SEC a Form 10-K annually. In it, a company discloses specific information about its financial status and direction. Form 10-K creates the basis of the annual report that must be given to shareholders no less than 15 days before the company's annual meeting. Public relations professionals are often involved in writing the narrative portion of annual reports, including the letter to the shareholders from the president/CEO and, as a result, need to be aware of the SEC rules regarding content to avoid liability. In recent years, the SEC has encouraged the writing of annual reports in plain English so that all shareholders, and not just the financially savvy, can understand them.

Disclosure. The SEC requires timely, accurate and widespread disclosure of material facts that may affect an individual's decision to buy, sell or hold a particular stock. In the past, the SEC required such disclosure via traditional news media. Thus, it was standard practice to issue releases to wire services like the Associated Press and Reuters. Even with the advent of the Internet, the SEC still required distribution services such as Business Wire and PR Newswire to send releases to the wires 15 minutes before posting the releases to their own websites. But in 2008, in recognition of the almost universal availability of the Internet, the SEC changed its guidelines, permitting corporations to announce earnings via their own websites rather than having to issue a news release.

Sarbanes-Oxley. After the spate of announcements about corporate wrongdoing among the likes of Enron, WorldCom, Tyco and HealthSouth in late 2001 and early 2002, Congress enacted the Sarbanes-Oxley Act that summer. The purpose of the Act is to make corporations more accountable and transparent regarding their finances. Companies must now file "on a rapid and current basis" and in plain English, material changes in their financial and operating conditions.

IMPACT OF SOCIAL MEDIA ON PR LAW

As is the case with the FTC, the SEC has broadened its perspective on corporate communication, moving into the realm of social media. In 2008, the SEC acknowledged that corporate blogs could serve to disclose material nonpublic information. That's the good news. The bad news is that social media can also be used to violate SEC rules. As one blogger wrote, "Investment firms without a strict policy about personal use of Twitter, blogs, Facebook and LinkedIn should beware. The feds may determine that social media use is the financial firms' responsibility."

Investment firms are not the only companies that need to be cognizant of the legal pitfalls involving social media and employees. All organizations need a policy on employees' use of social media at work, for work and personally. For example, employees who comment favorably about their company or its products and services may be deemed an endorser by the FTC and be required to disclose their relationship to the company. Employees also need to be educated on how their social media interactions may impact the company's reputation; how to avoid disclosure of trade secrets; and how not to discriminate, harass or violate the privacy of others.

Although in a recent study, 54 percent of companies said they denied employees the right to use social media at work, such bans can lead to low morale and are difficult to enforce. A better approach is to acknowledge that employees are going to interact on social media sites and have a policy in place that allows for use while protecting the organization as much as possible. Social media policies should include, at a minimum, a prohibition on the disclosure of confidential information and trade secrets; a requirement that employees disclose their relationship if they discuss any aspect of the company online and include a disclaimer that the views expressed do not necessarily represent those of the company; a prohibition on the use of logos and other trademarked properties of the organization without its consent; and a requirement that all postings respect defamation, privacy, harassment and copyright laws among others.

DEFAMATION

Defamation is an action brought by individuals to redress injuries to their reputation caused by false statements made about them. A defamatory statement is one that holds a person up to public hatred, ridicule or scorn. Libel refers to written defamatory statements, while slander is used for spoken defamatory statements.

The plaintiffs in a libel action include individuals, corporations (both for-profit and not-for-profit) and, in some states, unincorporated groups, such as labor unions, political action groups and trade associations. Governments at any level—federal, state, county, municipal—and government agencies cannot sue for libel. Plaintiffs must prove that:

- People would know the statement was about them.

- The statement defamed them, which means it caused others to think less of them and was false.

- They suffered injury as a result of the statement.

- The defendant was at fault in publishing the libel. Publication for the purposes of libel means simply that one person in addition to the writer saw or heard the material. Calling your boss an embezzler in an e-mail to your friend constitutes publication. The level of fault to be established depends on which of three categories the plaintiff falls into: public official, public figure or private person.

Any person elected to government office is a public official for the purposes of libel law, as is a wide range of other government employees. The term includes those who have, or appear to the public to have, substantial responsibility for or control over the conduct of government affairs. A public official for the purposes of libel holds a position that invites public scrutiny. Often, the position is one that involves policymaking decisions.

The second category of plaintiff is a public figure. Public figures are either individuals who have assumed roles of special prominence in the affairs of society and have pervasive power and influence or individuals who voluntarily thrust themselves into the vortex of a public controversy to affect the outcome. The latter individuals are public figures only for defamatory statements related to the controversy in question.

Public officials and public figures have to prove actual malice. Actual malice in this sense means that the defendant knew the statement was false or recklessly disregarded the truth and published it anyway. The Supreme Court established the actual malice standard to make it difficult for public officials and public figures to win libel suits because the Court wanted to encourage open discussion of their actions. Such individuals expect to be commented on and have the ability to defend themselves in the media. Private persons, on the other hand, are more vulnerable to injury.

Corporations, even large ones, are not automatically considered public figures despite their size and name recognition. It depends on the circumstances of the case.

Plaintiffs, including corporations, who do not fit into either the public official or public figure categories are private persons, and it is up to each state to determine the level of fault private persons have to prove. Negligence is the most common level of fault required.

Defenses to Libel Suits. At the end of the plaintiff's case, the burden shifts to the defendant to establish a defense. Ensuring that the information is true before it is published is the best protection against libel actions. Having materials approved before their release helps reduce the threat of defamation suits as well because an individual cannot claim to have been libeled if he authorized the story.

One possible defense for businesses is a common law privilege for messages of mutual interest. At common law, companies have a qualified privilege to share information essential to the conduct of their business with others. Communications made in the ordinary course of business would be considered subject to a qualified privilege, provided they were made in good faith, bear a reasonable relation to the business purpose and are made without malice.

Libel and Public Relations. Although the actual malice standard has reduced the fear of libel suits among journalists, public relations professionals are wise to review their copy for potentially libelous statements. Negative reviews, memos outlining the cause of an employee's termination or blog posts disparaging a competitor may result in lawsuits. In such cases, the individual defamed would most likely be a private person and only have to prove that the defendant was negligent in publishing the libel.

In advising a client whether to seek legal assistance because it has been defamed, public relations professionals should consider the nature of the allegations, who made the statements, how much damage has been done to the client's reputation and to what extent the client can counter those allegations publicly.

One problem with suing for libel is that the lawsuit may generate headlines and stay in the news longer than the original slight itself. A corporation also needs to be careful that it does not lose in the court of public opinion by bringing a libel action. A libel suit brought by McDonald's against British activists backfired on the company when it was framed in the media as a fight between David and Goliath. McDonald's won in court but lost the public image battle.

INVASION OF PRIVACY

Perhaps even more problematic for public relations practitioners is the legal concept of privacy. Privacy is either the right to be left alone or the right to control information about one's personal life.

Right to Be Left Alone. Appropriation occurs when an individual's name or likeness is used for commercial exploitation or purpose without consent. Celebrities sue for appropriation because others are making a profit on their name or likeness. Private individuals tend to sue because their privacy has been invaded.

Typically, appropriation suits involve the use of someone's photograph in an ad. Social media and the ease with which digitized images can be manipulated have widened the scope of format and increased the potential for appropriation suits. An ad on a bus shelter in Australia showed a young Asian girl making a funny face. The ad was for a cell phone company that was promoting unlimited calls to friends. The copy implied that the girl was not someone you would want to be friends with. Someone blogged about the photo and the ad, and within days and half a world away, the girl was shocked to see herself. It was a photo from her Facebook page, taken without her consent or knowledge and cropped to remove her friends, taking the shot out of context.

Photos of celebrities are showing up on websites endorsing products without their knowledge. Dr. Oz, who began his TV career on the *Oprah Show*, has been linked to several weight-loss and health supplements without his express consent. In these cases, the companies know the celebrities would not endorse the products, but also know the endorsement will carry weight.

Consent is a defense to an appropriation claim. Because public relations professionals and photographers usually obtain consent from their subjects, most appropriation actions result from attempts to revoke the consent or from allegations that the use went beyond what was consented to.

Informational Privacy. Informational privacy is the ability of "individuals, groups, or institutions to determine for themselves when, how and to what extent information about themselves is communicated to others." Digital technology has greatly increased the ability of marketers, governments and criminals to collect and disseminate private information about all of us. Medical, financial and criminal justice records are perhaps the most vulnerable to such dissemination, but at the same time, are the most protected by law. Medical information, for example, is protected by the Health Insurance Portability and Accountability Act, which regulates the use and disclosure of protected health information by health providers, plans and employers.

However, search engines and social networks, with their ease of information sharing, are the new battlegrounds in informational privacy cases. A 2011 Adweek/Harris Poll revealed that three-quarters of the 2,124 U.S. adults surveyed agreed that online companies such as Google and Facebook know and control too much information about us. From the information, marketers can build digital dossiers on an individual's likes, dislikes, preferences and behaviors, among other things. Much of that information can be used to better market to that person. However, it can also be used for price and policy discrimination and for denying an individual employment.

Privacy and Public Relations. PR practitioners should take care to guard the privacy of others. A signed release should be obtained from individuals when their photographs are taken for use in PR materials, and employees should always be asked before information about them is used.

NEGLIGENCE

Negligence is conduct that falls below the standard established by law for the protection of others against unreasonable risk of harm. The legal standard is the conduct of a reasonable person acting prudently and with due care under the circumstances. In the case of professionals, the question becomes, what would a reasonable public relations professional, acting prudently and with due care, have done in similar circumstances.

A plaintiff in a lawsuit alleging negligence must prove that:

- The defendant owed him or her a legal duty of care. Everyone has a duty or an obligation not to harm others. Essentially, the courts look at what a reasonable and prudent person would have done in the situation. In professional negligence cases, professionals have a duty to act with the same care and skill normally possessed by members of that profession.

- The defendant breached that duty. If the defendant's behavior was something less than what a reasonable person would have done in the circumstances, a court may consider the defendant to have breached the duty of care to the plaintiff.

- The plaintiff was injured as a result of the defendant's actions or omissions. To determine whether the defendant's actions or omissions were the actual cause of the plaintiff's injury, the courts apply the "but-for" test; that is, the defendant's actions are the actual cause of the plaintiff's injuries if those injuries would not have occurred but for those actions. The defendant's actions must also be the proximate cause of the injury. It may be that although the defendant's actions were the actual cause of the plaintiff's injury, there was no way the defendant could have foreseen that the plaintiff would be injured and therefore the actions were not the proximate cause.

Defenses to Negligence. Defendants will argue that the plaintiffs either contributed to their own injury or willingly assumed the risk that they might get hurt.

Negligence and Public Relations. Special events hold the greatest threat for negligence claims against public relations practitioners, but there is also the possibility that a public relations agency could be sued for professional negligence. Staying abreast of developments in the field and communicating openly and honestly with clients helps reduce the risk of such lawsuits. Professional liability insurance should also be purchased in addition to a general liability policy.

PRODUCT LIABILITY

Product liability occurs when consumers are injured or harmed by defective products. As with all lawsuits against companies, product liability cases carry monetary and reputational risks. Toyota's accelerator problem is but one example. Public relations professionals should be involved in the corporate strategic planning of any recalls.

Public relations professionals also need to remind companies of their ethical responsibilities to their stakeholders. Failure to implement full and immediate recalls can have serious repercussions for the public. Thus product liability cases involve not only an understanding of the legal issues, but also the ethical responsibilities of companies.

INTELLECTUAL PROPERTY

The legal concept of intellectual property includes copyright, trademarks and patents.

Copyright. Copyright protects "original works of authorship" and is governed by the federal Copyright Act. The term *original works* includes books, music, plays, photos, films and architecture, among other works. Because copyright is meant to protect creativity and originality, facts are not subject to copyright protection. Similarly, copyright does not protect ideas themselves, only their expression once fixed in a tangible medium. Disks, CDs and websites are considered tangible media for purposes of copyright. Registration of the work with the Copyright Office, although not required, is recommended because certain legal remedies depend on registration.

Ownership. Copyright belongs initially to the author or authors of the original work. Usually, the author is the one who creates the work, except when a work is made in the regular course of employment or when it is contracted to be made. In those cases, the employer or contractor is considered the author. Most freelance photographers and public relations firms retain ownership of the copyright in the work they do and grant consent to their use. Any transfer of ownership must be in writing.

Owner's Rights. The Copyright Act gives the copyright owner the exclusive right to reproduce the work, prepare derivative works, distribute copies and perform and display the work publicly.

Duration of the Protection. Copyright protection lasts for the life of the author plus 70 years if the work was created after 1978. A copyright owned by a corporation lasts for 95 years from the date of publication or 120 years from the date of creation, whichever is shorter. Works created before 1978 vary in the length of the protection. When a copyright term expires, the work enters the public domain and may be used freely by anyone.

Infringement of Owner's Rights. Infringement of copyright occurs whenever somebody exercises one of the copyright owner's rights without permission. Infringement need not be intentional. For example, copying or downloading images or text from a website may well be an infringement of copyright. To prove infringement, the plaintiff need merely prove ownership and that the defendant infringed one of the rights. Although registration of the copyright is no longer required under U.S. law, registration of the work with the Copyright Office is required before a plaintiff can sue for copyright infringement. Whether the work is registered, the copyright notice ©, plus the date and the owner's name, should be added to all publicly distributed copies of the work to serve as notice that the work is under copyright. If proper notice appears on all copies, defendants cannot claim they did not know the work was protected by copyright. To avoid copyright infringement, permission to use another's work should always be obtained.

Remedies for infringement include an injunction, impoundment and possible destruction of the articles, actual damages plus any profits made by the defendant and costs of the lawsuit.

Limitations on Owner's Rights. Although the copyright owner is entitled to exclusive rights with respect to the work, those rights are subject to several limitations. One of the most controversial limitations is the doctrine of fair use.

The Copyright Act provides that the fair use of copyrighted material for such purposes as criticism, comment, news reporting, teaching, scholarship or research is not an infringement of copyright. In determining whether the use is fair, the courts consider four factors: the purpose and character of the use, including whether the use is of a commercial nature or is for nonprofit educational purposes; the nature of the work; the amount and substantiality of the portion of the work used; and the effect of the use on the potential market value of the work.

Trademarks. Trademark law governs the use of brand names and other words or symbols associated with a product or service. It can be seen as protecting the goodwill or reputation of a company. A company that passes itself off as affiliated with another company deceives the public and deprives the real company of profits. The federal Trademark Act, known as the Lanham Act, prohibits businesses from using someone else's mark in connection with any goods or services. The Act also prevents a business from falsely describing or representing its own goods and services or another person's goods or services.

A trademark serves to identify tangible products. A service mark, on the other hand, is used to identify and distinguish the services of companies. A trade or service mark can be any word, symbol, design or color, provided it is in use as an identifier of the product, it is distinctive and it is not confusingly similar to someone else's trademark.

Registration. Like copyright, there is no registration requirement for trademark protection. Once a logo is used on an organization's letterhead, for example, the logo is a trademark. But also like copyright, there are certain advantages to registering the mark. Registration is evidence of the first use of the trademark by the company, it permits the owner to sue in federal court for infringement, and the registration symbol ® serves as notice to others of a claim of ownership. If the trademark is not registered, the owner may use the symbol ™ or ˢᴹ.

Infringement. Actions for trademark infringement arise when the use of a mark causes confusion among consumers. Lanham Act remedies for infringement include injunctive relief and a right of action for damages.

Duration. Registration of a trademark lasts 10 years but can be renewed indefinitely. Trademark rights can be lost only through dilution, infringement or abandonment. Trademark rights are abandoned if the mark's use is discontinued with no intent of using it again. Dilution occurs when the mark is used as a generic term, meaning that many people have infringed the trademark rights by using the mark. As a result, the mark loses its distinctiveness and its rights.

Many companies work hard to protect their rights from infringement and dilution. To those who do not understand trademark law, the actions of these companies often appear overly aggressive. Public relations professionals need to be aware of this potential for backlash and can play a key role in educating the public on the proper use of a trademark and on why the company may need to be aggressive in defending that use.

Patents. Patent law applies to inventions. Although most public relations practitioners will not deal with patents unless they work in a pharmaceutical or research-oriented industry, it is important to understand the differences among copyright, trademark and patent law. All three comprise the law of intellectual property and protect different aspects of it. Copyright protects the expression of ideas; trademark protects the good name of a company; and patent law protects inventions. A patent grants an inventor the right to make, use or sell an invention to the exclusion of all others for a period of 20 years from the date of application. Once the patent expires, the invention enters the public domain and anyone may use it.

WHAT THE FUTURE HOLDS

The relationship between public relations and advertising will continue to evolve and the line between the two blur with the expansion of new social media channels that are changing the way individuals receive information and interact with companies. One-way media outlets, the traditional venues of advertising, will still play a role, but their influence is decreasing in a world where information sharing, not control, is king. At the same time, transparency and ethics will take on increased importance. Companies that interact with their consumers openly and honestly will be rewarded, whereas companies that seek to mislead and deceive or just not be transparent will soon find themselves attacked online and in the courts.

Facebook's user "likes" are an example of how the landscape of public relations, advertising and the law is changing. When a user "likes" a brand page, that "like" is turned into an advertisement with the user's name and image that goes around the network. RSVPs to advertised concerts and sporting events also become shared "ads" as they show up on friends' news feeds. Companies naturally love these free endorsements. But are they legal? The law requires consent for the use of a person's name and likeness in advertising. As one advertising attorney mused, "Does disclosure in the terms of service and the use of the service constitute sufficient consent?" And what if the user is a minor? Although Facebook users must be at least 13 years old, according to Consumer Reports, 7.5 million Facebook users in the United States are not, and another 14.4 million are between the ages of 13 and 17. Parents in California and New York have filed lawsuits against Facebook for failing to obtain their consent for the use of their child's image. One complaint alleges "Facebook, Inc. has regularly and repeatedly used the names and/or likenesses of plaintiff . . . for the commercial purpose of marketing, advertising, selling, and soliciting the purchase of goods and services" (lexnimbus.com/?p=109).

Such lawsuits are only going to increase as individuals and marketers clash over what constitutes privacy in "the age of transparency," as one blogger described it. But public relations, with its emphasis on relationships and trust, can help manage that tension by insisting on transparency, honesty and ethical behavior.

DISCUSSION QUESTIONS

1. The California Supreme Court in *Kasky v. Nike* set out a limited purpose test for determining whether speech is commercial and therefore subject to increased scrutiny and regulation. The test called for the consideration of three elements:

   - Is the speaker engaged in commercial enterprises?
   - Is the intended audience actual or potential consumers or individuals, such as journalists, who are likely to repeat the message to consumers?
   - Does the content of the message involve statements of fact about the business operations, products or services of the speaker and made for the purpose of promoting sales of the speaker's products or services?
   - Did Nike's speech satisfy the test for commercial speech? Under what circumstances would a corporation's speech be considered noncommercial for the purposes of this test?

2. Consider the increased integration of public relations, advertising and marketing. What are the potential legal ramifications of that integration?

3. One legal scholar argues that the phrase "corporate media spending" is more accurate than "corporate speech" because corporations cannot "speak." The only thing they can do is spend money to have someone speak on their behalf. Do you agree that corporations do not have a voice and that therefore they should not be granted First Amendment protection in the same way that an individual is?

4. Regulatory agencies such as the FTC and SEC are increasingly examining social media channels for potential violations of their rules, looking beyond official corporate actions to those of employees. How can companies protect themselves from their own employees? Is banning social media use at work the way to go? What role might public relations practitioners play in helping companies resolve the issue?

5. The law has long protected an individual's privacy from the intrusion of others. How are social networks changing our expectations of privacy? In an age of transparency, where can we or should we draw the privacy line?

ADDITIONAL READING

Gower, K. K. 2008. *Legal and Ethical Considerations for Public Relations*. 2nd ed. Long Grove, IL: Waveland Press.

Kerr, R. L. 2010. "Naturalizing the artificial citizen: Repeating Lochner's error in *Citizens United v. Federal Election Commission.*" *Communication Law and Policy*, 15, 311–362.

Regulating public relations. In *Communication and the Law*, edited by W. W. Hopkins. Northport, AL: Vision Press.

Walsh, F. 2007. *An Introduction to the Law of Public Relations and Advertising: Legal Principles and Current Practices.* 3rd ed. Dubuque, IA: Kendall/Hunt Publishing.

5 CHAPTER

A BRIEF HISTORY OF PUBLIC RELATIONS
The Unseen Power

Scott M. Cutlip, Fellow, PRSA
Dean Emeritus, College of Journalism and Mass Communication
University of Georgia

Brent Baker
Rear Admiral (Ret) and Former Chief of Information
U.S. Navy
Dean Emeritus, College of Communication
Boston University

The way to get at the nature of an institution, as anything else that is alive, is to see how it has grown.

—A. G. Keller

EARLY HISTORY OF PUBLIC RELATIONS

Modern public relations, today an essential management function in enterprises around the world, large and small, got its start in the United States in the sense that we describe it today. Public relations has evolved in response to the growth of democratic freedoms and free markets. Efforts go back to antiquity; only the tools, the degree of specialization, the breadth of knowledge required of counselors and the costs and intensity of effort have escalated in the twentieth century. Public relations truly began when men came to live together in tribal camps. To function, civilization requires communication, conciliation, cooperation and consensus on common interests.

As far back as 1800 BC, Persian farmers were being instructed through bulletins how to deal with field mice and how to harvest their crops. Much of the literature and art of antiquity was designed to build support for kings, priests and other spiritual and secular leaders. Virgil's *Georgics* was written to get urban dwellers to return to the land so that they could produce food for a growing Rome. Rudimentary elements of public relations can be found in ancient India and in the English kings' Lords Chancellor, the keepers of the king's conscience and his intermediaries with the people. The concept of propaganda, now a major element of international public relations, was born in the Catholic Church in the seventeenth century when the church set up its *Congregation de Propaganda* to propagate the faith. The world's communication networks today are flooded with the propaganda of countries and causes.

Today, the function of public relations counseling is an essential element in management's dealing with a global economy and its competition for markets, the causes that cross national borders and the nation states' efforts to achieve their political objectives in a volatile and interdependent world. The function's increased use has been compelled by today's instant global communication, the growth of free markets and the spread of democracy and conflict around the globe. Truly, Marshall McLuhan's "global village" has come to pass and, with it, the need for specialists in public opinion and communication to deal with a highly competitive and somewhat chaotic world in transition to the twenty-first century.

To understand how this function and its supporting corps of practitioners have evolved in democratic societies, one must comprehend the forces in the world that have coerced and compelled its development. I hold that a professional practice must be informed by its history. Surely, we will be better able to deal with today and tomorrow if we understand our yesterdays. Experience will teach us if we are wise enough to learn its lessons. A concise history of public relations follows with the hope that it will be instructional to today's practitioners.

The use of publicity, puffery, and press agentry to promote causes, to tout land ventures and to raise funds is older than the nation itself. American talent for hype can be traced back to the first settlements on the Atlantic Coast in the sixteenth century.

The need for foreign governments to explain themselves and to promote trade and tourism in the United States became apparent after the Spanish–American War caused the United States to shed its isolationism and to move onto the world stage. These needs intensified through the twentieth century as nations grew more interdependent and a fiercely competitive world economy, ethnic wars and nationalism emerged in the wake of the Cold War. These needs are being met by a growing corps of public relations professionals in the United States specializing in the representation of foreign governments. These men and women serve variously the roles of promoters, propagandists and lobbyists. There has been a similar exponential growth in the number of professionals employed in government information services around the world.

HYPE FOR THE COLONIES

The exaggerated claims that today often characterize publicity began with Sir Walter Raleigh's ill-fated effort to settle Roanoke Island off the Virginia coast. When Captain Arthur Barlowe returned to England in 1584 from that desolate, swampy area, he reported to Raleigh that "the soile is the most plentiful, sweete, fruitful, and wholesome of all the worlde . . . they have those Okes that we have, but farre greater and better . . . the highest and reddest Cedars of the world and a great abundance of Pine or Pitch Trees." He even described the Indians as "most gentle, loving, and faithful, void of all guile or treason."

Even more glowing was the description of Raleigh's "lieutenant governor." Writing from Virginia is 1585, Ralph Lane trumpeted that the mainland had "the goodliest (s)oyle under the cope of heaven," and that "what commodities soever" France, Spain, Italy or the East produced, "these parts doe abound with the growth of them all . . ."

Contrary to the accounts of bold settlers eagerly flocking to the newly discovered America given in grade school histories, it would seem that many came from Europe to the new land in response to exaggerated publicity claims. Historian Hugh Lefler observes, "The glorified advertising of every colony was the chief means of procuring money and men. The degree of success varied considerably from time to time and from place to place."[1]

Although it is not possible to assess the effectiveness of this promotional material, Lefler wrote that a tract published by a layman, Robert Johnson, entitled "Nova Brittania: Offering Most Excellent Fruites by Planting in Virginia," published in 1609, did produce "a great increase in investments in the Company and in the number of people migrating to Virginia." Virginia's early promotional efforts were matched in varying degrees by the later colonies of the South Atlantic region. The promotion of Maryland began in 1622 with the Charles I edition of the "Charter of Maryland." Another tract, "Objections Answered Concerning Maryland," was published in 1662. In Lefler's opinion, Carolina's publicity did not match Virginia in the variety of appeals or in media used. "There were no poems or officially inspired sermons, few broadsides, and only a minimum of prospectuses."

Georgia's promotion of its colony for the poor and the outcast was most intensive because Lord Oglethorpe's venture was a philanthropic one. Because of its dependence on charity and Parliamentary appropriations, the Georgia Colony mounted an intensive, broadscale campaign of promotion and persuasion unmatched by any other colony. In one scholar's opinion, the trustees' promotional activities paralleled many of today's promotions. Like many a propaganda campaign since, the high, unrealistic expectations created by Georgia's unprecedented public relations turned to bitter disillusionment. Up and down the Atlantic Coast, disappointment set in. In the exaggerated publicity hype of the new American colonial settlements on the Atlantic Coast, there is a basic lesson many practitioners have yet to learn: building false hopes in hyping a product, a service or a candidate's message inevitably leads to disappointment, with the ultimate loss paid by the sponsor. No glowing accounts sent back to England from the malarial swamps of Jamestown and Savannah could alter the reality that would lead to hardship and heartache on the part of our intrepid forebears.

The first known systematic effort to raise funds on this continent was that sponsored by Harvard College in 1641 when the infant institution sent a trio of preachers to England on a "begging mission." Once the preachers got to England, they found what fundraisers know today—they needed a brochure making their case. In response to this request came *New England's First Fruits*, written in Massachusetts but printed in London in 1643, the first of countless public relations pamphlets and brochures.

SAMUEL ADAMS BRINGS ON A REVOLUTION

The use of public relations skills to shape the course and impact of government is older that the U.S. government itself. The tools and techniques of persuasive communication have long been used in the nation's political struggles. Political public relations practice dates back to the nation's prerevolution years, when a small and resourceful band of propagandists fed the fires of revolt, from 1763 to 1776, which brought the birth of the world's oldest constitutional government. These revolutionaries were among the first to demonstrate the power of an organized, articulate minority, carrying the day against the unorganized, apathetic majority of citizens. The small band of Whig propagandists was no match for Samuel Adams and his daring band. Little wonder Philip Davidson thought, "The influence of the propagandists was out of all proportion of their number."

Today's public relations practice has been shaped far more than most practitioners realize by the innovations in mobilizing public opinion developed by Adams and his cohort. In fomenting revolt against Great Britain, the revolutionaries developed and demonstrated the power of these techniques:

1. The necessity of organization, such as The Committees of Correspondence, to implement actions made possible by a propaganda campaign.

2. The use of symbols, such as the Liberty Tree, that are easily recognizable and arouse emotions.

3. The use of slogans, notably "Taxation without representation is tyranny," that compress complex issues in easy-to-remember stereotypes.

4. Staged events, for example, the Boston Tea Party, that catch public attention and thus crystallize public opinion.

5. The importance of getting your story to the public first so that your interpretation of events is the one accepted. An example is "The Horrid Boston Massacre" pamphlet that was spread swiftly throughout the colonies.

6. The necessity of a sustained, saturation campaign using these techniques through all available media to penetrate the public mind with a new conviction.

"GREATEST PUBLIC RELATIONS WORK EVER DONE"

The power of propaganda to mobilize public opinion was heavily relied on in the history-making campaign that won ratification of the U.S. Constitution in 1787 to 1788. This campaign, ranking alongside the propaganda campaign for independence in shaping the United States, was praised by the late historian Allan Nevins as "the greatest work ever done in America in the field on public relations." Surely, it was the most important one in U.S. history. The burden of the campaign to win quick ratification of the new Constitution, drafted in secrecy in Philadelphia in 1787, was carried by the *Federalist Papers*, which, like the Declaration of Independence, were written as propaganda documents. The papers were the work of Alexander Hamilton, James Madison and John Jay. A contemporary damned them as "the frankest, baldest, and boldest propaganda ever penned." The Hamilton-led campaign was strongly opposed by the Antifederalist forces, led by Virginia's Richard Henry Lee. In historian Frederick Jackson Main's opinion, at the outset, public opinion seemed to favor the Antifederalists, who argued that America had just fought a war to throw off the shackles of a strong central government and should not return to such.

Historian Robert Rutland saw this political contest as "the seedtime of American politics." He puts this battle for public support in perspective:

> The political ordeal that produced the Constitution in 1787 and brought about its ratification in 1788 was unique in human history. Never before had the representatives of a whole nation discussed, planned and implemented a new form of government in such a manner and in such a short time. In little more than a year, Americans established a political network that enlightened Europeans viewed with skepticism.

Surely, this was the most important public relations campaign ever done.

JACKSON AND KENDALL RESHAPE AMERICA'S DEMOCRACY

The presidential election of 1828, in which war hero Andrew Jackson decisively defeated President John Quincy Adams, marked a watershed in American politics by bringing a shift in political power from the "Eastern Establishment" to the nation's expanding frontier, an enlargement of the presidency and the genesis of the nation's second two-party political system. In these accomplishments, President Jackson had significant assistance from Amos Kendall, an astute political strategist and skilled publicist. Kendall served as Jackson's adviser for his two terms, devising his political strategy, publicizing his views and actions and providing accurate assessments of prevailing public opinion. Kendall performed all the work that now requires a large White House public relations staff.

His work was significant. A biographer, Robert V. Remini, sees Jackson as a great democrat who changed "the pure republican character" of the political system as originally established by the Founding Fathers by insisting on greater representation of the people and a greater responsiveness to their will.

Kendall played a decisive role in the first great public relations battle between big business and government—the Jackson–Biddle War that brought the end of the United States Bank, a contest that changed America's banking system forever. Directing the propaganda campaign for Nicholas Biddle's Bank of the United States was Mathew St. Clair Clarke, perhaps the first publicist to be employed by big business. The battle over the bank was fully joined in July 1832, when Congress passed a bill rechartering the bank as of 1836, a move that had been requested by Biddle but that would prove a blunder.

Congress passed the reauthorization bill, but President Jackson, at Kendall's strong urging, decided to veto the bill and directed his aide to write the veto message. The only complete draft of Jackson's veto message in the Library of Congress is in Kendall's handwriting. Jackson's veto was upheld.

One of the by-products of the Biddle–Jackson political struggle was in the buildup of Davy Crockett, financed by Biddle and promoted by the Bank's publicists in a futile effort to counter Jackson's popularity along the Western Frontier. They portrayed Crockett as a "real frontiersman" who boasted that he wore "no collar labelled 'My Dog—Andrew Jackson.'" Clarke and Whig Party publicists went to great lengths to create the public image of Crockett as the bold, coonskin-capped frontier democrat with a lusty pioneer spirit. When Crockett was defeated in his bid to be re-elected to Congress, he told his constituents they could go to hell and he went off to die in the Battle of the Alamo. Such shirt stuffing we see in today's celebrity world.

PRESS AGENTRY AND ADVERTISING IN THE NINETEENTH CENTURY

Led by the American railroads in their effort to sell land and lure settlers to the West, press agentry, promotion and advertising flowered in the nineteenth century. These fields, which often meld into one another, have the common purpose of attracting the public's attention for an entertainment, product or service. Today the world is stuffed with the cascading messages of the press agent, promoter and advertiser. The commercial value of publicity to sell books, circuses, stage shows and patent medicines, discovered early in the nineteenth century, was put to wide and imaginative use. As early as 1809, Washington Irving used press agent gimmickry to promote his *Knickerbocker's History of New York*.

The circus—a fabulous development of the nineteenth century—did much to stimulate the growth of press agentry and display advertising. Today's patterns of promotion and press agentry in the world of show business were the innovations of Phineas Taylor Barnum, the greatest showman and press agent of all time, "The Prince of Humbug." One writer termed him ". . . the first great advertising genius and the greatest publicity exploiter the world has ever seen." Barnum once remarked, "Advertising is like learning: a little is a dangerous thing." Although he had no equal in dreaming up newsmaking stunts, Barnum employed a staff of press agents. Barnum was the first to use display advertising on a large scale to promote his circus.

The practice of press agentry became more pervasive as the businesses of book publishing, travelling theater productions, resorts and professional sports developed in the last century. Near the end of 1898, *The Fourth Estate*, a newspaper trade journal, reported,

> Press agents have become a necessary adjunct to nearly all commercial enterprises. It was not so long ago when those energetic purveyors of publicity were confined in their efforts to the circus, theatrical, and operatic fields . . . . But business methods have changed materially during the last few years. Advertising and plenty of it is now essential to the success of almost any undertaking that depends on a large public patronage.

Advertising and product promotion, today intertwined under the umbrella of marketing, have their roots in the post–Civil War industrialization in the United States. With the introduction of mass production methods, more and more businesses needed regional and national distribution of their mass-produced soaps, foods and other products. For example, to break down a person's fear about meat that was slaughtered weeks earlier and far away, the meat packer Swift turned to advertising. By 1879, advertising revenue in newspapers totaled $21 million. The advertising agency was born at the end of the Civil War and became a vital part of the great expansion of industry and business that took place after the war and before the turn of the century. The oldest agency, J. Walter Thompson, was started in 1864, and N. W. Ayer & Son was founded in 1869. In March of 1877, Albert Frank opened a two-man agency in lower Manhattan. These agencies survive to this day, but other agencies started in those years have long since disappeared.

The railroads used publicity, tours and advertising to the hilt to lure settlers west to buy land, and they provided settlements that would bring passenger and freight traffic to their lines. Charles Russell Lowell, who was employed as a publicist for the Burlington Railroad in the 1850s, wrote a friend in 1859: "We are beginning to find that he who buildeth a railroad west of the Mississippi must also find a population and build up business. We wish to blow as loud a trumpet as the merits of our position warrant," a sound principle for today's practitioner. Historian J. Valerie Fifer has concluded, "Together the transport, tourist and information industries played a crucial role in Western development. All brought new settlement and investment into the West, demanded a new awareness of the environment, helped to define the new word, '*transcontinental*,' and stimulated the growth of a new spirit of American nationalism." The legacies of the promoter and advertiser are many and significant.

THE ERA OF "THE PUBLIC BE DAMNED"

The final two decades of the nineteenth century brought the beginnings of today's public relations practice in the United States. Contemporary public relations, as a practice and as a management concept, was to emerge from the melée of opposing forces in this period of the nation's growth both in business and in politics. Eric Goldman, in his brief history, *Two-Way Street*, observed, "Shouldering aside agriculture, large-scale commerce and industry became dominant over the life of the nation. Big Business was committed to the doctrine that the less the public knew about its operations, the more efficient and profitable . . . operations would be." It was a day of business arrogance toward employee and citizen alike, a day when railroad magnate E. H. Harriman would boast, "I don't want anything on this railroad that I cannot control," a day when Marshall Field made $600 an hour each day while his clerks earned a maximum of $12 dollars a week.

It was truly the era of "The Public Be Damned," epitomized in the memorable phrase of William Henry Vanderbilt, owner of the New York Central Railroad. He was reported to have made the remark to a Chicago freelance reporter in an 1882 interview. Vanderbilt vehemently denied making the remark, but it did not matter whether he did or did not. It summarized the contempt of Big Business for the public interest and thus stuck.

These industrialists, who were ruthlessly exploiting the nation's resources and their laborers, thought nothing beyond purchase for their selfish ends. They also knew the power of publicity as it had been demonstrated by the railroads. Buccaneer Jim Fisk employed a publicity man, George Crouch, to plant stories when he was trying to corner the gold market. Publicity was heavily used in the brawling insurance field. A Mutual Life Insurance Company historian describing this period wrote,

> To facilitate the labors of the sales force, the Mutual Life, like all similar institutions, endeavored to establish in the public mind not only its name, but also a favorable impression of its operations. Its chief vehicles of advertising were the insurance press and pamphlet literature. In the former the Company not only inserted bona fide advertisements, but it also paid editors to run its message as news articles or editorials. For the campaign against Jacob L. Greene of the Connecticut Mutual, the Mutual, along with the Equitable and New York Life, hired the services of C. C. Hine, editor of the *Insurance Monitor*, Stephen English of the *Insurance Times* and Charles J. (Dollar a Line) Smith of the *Insurance Record*. The editor of the *Insurance Monitor* had a fixed price for his Connecticut Mutual extras of $50 a thousand and boasted that he sold them "by the ton."

This obvious purchase of editorial content in these trade journals was expensive and had its risks. These mercenaries were for hire to all sides. The use of paid ads as news matter continued in public relations practice well into the twentieth century. Mutual was one of the first to use this shady practice. It established a "species of a literary bureau" in 1888 under the direction of Charles J. Smith. Another large firm that was buying news space in this period was the Standard Oil Company of Ohio.

In James Playsted Wood's history *The Story of Advertising*, he writes, "Part of this impulse and impetus behind the force which burst into the eruption of advertising in the United States in the 1890s sprang from England. Much of this came from Thomas Lipton, a canny Scotsman with a great flair for publicity and a strong belief in advertising of all kinds. The world-renowned merchant used every publicity and advertising trick his innovative mind could dream up." His racing for yachting's American Cup was one of these.

There also came a realization to businessmen whose innovations were bringing rapid-fire changes in living to America's frontier. For example, the National Biscuit Company revolutionized marketing at the turn of the century when it took the cracker out of the grocer's barrel and put it in a sanitary package. The N. W. Ayer advertising agency had the National Biscuit account. Ayer's executives soon realized that advertising alone could not get the public to buy the Uneeda Biscuit in the sanitary package. They learned a fundamental of public relations—change requires long-term education. Ayer used the homier word *biscuit* instead of the old-fashioned word *cracker* and introduced the use of symbols with the little boy in the yellow slicker. However, it found the campaign needed publicity. Ayer developed a publicity department to supplement its advertising campaigns for the National Biscuit and the Standard Oil Companies. The agency found that "it was compelled to prepare publicity material as part of its regular work and also prepare news releases," according to its historian, Ralph W. Hower. The Ayer agency was the first to establish a publicity department in 1919.[2]

THE BEGINNINGS IN POLITICS AND GOVERNMENT

The modern political campaign, employing the talents of campaign consultants, publicists, pollsters, electronic mail experts, video producers and writers, had its genesis in the last two decades of the nineteenth century. The employment of publicists by the federal government also got its start in those years. The political campaigns fashioned by Amos Kendall and Martin Van Buren in the 1820s and 1830s changed little until 1880.

The Republican Party, which had dominated the nation's elections since the Civil War by waving "The Bloody Shirt," got a rude jolt in the Rutherford B. Hayes–Samuel Tilden squeaker of 1876. As a result, both parties laid out systematic efforts to win in 1880. Such plans were given impetus by improved printing presses, reduced cost of paper and a growing awareness of the power of newspaper publicity.

The epochal 1896 campaign set the pattern for national presidential campaigns for the next 50 years, save for the innovation of radio in the 1928 campaign. This dramatic, hard-fought campaign between the conservative William McKinley and the populist William Jennings Bryan brought a marked increase in publicity and campaign management. The first step for both parties was to move the center of their campaign operations to Chicago, both sides realizing that the West would be a crucial battleground in this time of intense political and economic unrest. McKinley's front-porch campaign was implemented by large staffs in his hometown of Canton, Ohio, as well as in New York and Chicago. It overlooked no detail and spared no expense. Bryan, on the other hand, possessing a rare oratorical talent and having little money, was forced to rely on cross-country tours that would take him to as many voters as money and time permitted. Thus was born "the campaign train," last used by President Harry Truman in 1948 so effectively.

Republican Campaign Chairman Charles G. Dawes hired Perry Heath, a Cincinnati reporter, to direct the Chicago-based Bureau of Publications and Printing early in July. The bureau started sending out news releases, canned editorials and editorial reprints in large numbers. More than 275 pamphlets and leaflets, a series of posters, sheets of cartoons, and other campaign materials were produced at a furious pace over the next four months. These were being sent to newspapers and GOP workers in carload lots. The scope of Heath's output can be seen in the total of $469,079 spent for printing—in a day when printing was inexpensive.

Another important innovation in the Chicago headquarters was the organization of specially staffed bureaus to mobilize special-interest groups on McKinley's behalf. Pamphlets were printed in German, French, Italian, Spanish, Swedish, Norwegian, Finnish, Dutch and Hebrew in an effort to influence the tidal wave of immigrants who had come to the United States during the past two decades. Also created were a Colored Department, a Women's Department (although women could not vote) and a German Department. Bicycling had become a popular pastime in the 1890s, so Dawes also set up a department for Wheelmen to woo bicyclists. No special-interest group was overlooked. Dawes also used a rudimentary public opinion poll to assess the electorate.

The Bryan campaign, by contrast, was pinched for money and not well organized. Campaigning by train was his only recourse. According to Bryan's figures, he traveled 18,009 miles in his whistle-stop campaign. This was no match for the intensive and expensive McKinley campaign, and McKinley won easily. The result of the Republicans' massive publicity campaign can be seen in the fact that two million more voters voted Republican than had done so in any previous election.

This power of publicity did not go unnoticed in the executive branch of the federal government. Among the first of the bureaucrats to see the need for publicity was Major John Wesley Powell, explorer of the Colorado River and architect of the U.S. Geological Survey. Named to head the new agency by President James A. Garfield, Powell moved quickly to expand its size and concept. To build support in Congress and in the scientific community, Powell hired W. A. Croffut, an experienced journalist and editor who knew the ways of Washington. Two years later, in 1884, Powell set up a division of publications with John C. Filling as editor.

The Department of Agriculture led the way among the executive agencies in developing public relations as a tool of administration and education. In 1889, Jeremiah Rusk of Wisconsin was named secretary of agriculture by incoming President Benjamin Harrison. Rusk, after observing that some 40,000 letters of inquiry reached the department during the first 10 months of 1889, decided that the public must get out agricultural information more promptly and in more readable form. Rusk ordered the development of farm bulletins to disseminate information in plain language. This work was first carried on in Rusk's office; in 1890, he established a Division of Records and Editing to increase the output of agricultural information. "Tama" Jim Wilson, appointed secretary by President McKinley in 1897, made many innovations in the department's expanding public information effort at the turn of the century.

Thus was born a large and effective public relations–education organization that would make American agriculture the envy of the world through the work of the nation's Land Grant colleges and county agents in the twentieth century.

THE SEEDBED YEARS OF PUBLIC RELATIONS

The force setting the stage for the emergence of the pioneer public relations agencies in the early 1900s in the United States was the exploitive and bold development of industry, railroads, utilities and banking in America's post–Civil War years. In 25 breathtaking years from 1875 to 1900, America doubled its population, moved its people into cities, developed mass production and spanned the nation with rail and wire communications, which, in turn, brought a news forum of national press associations and popular magazines. With what Vernon Parrington termed "A Huge Buccaneering Orgy" came large concentrations of wealth. By 1900, one-tenth of the population owned nine-tenths of the wealth. The rise of powerful monopolies, concentrations of wealth and power, and the roughshod tactics of The Robber Barons would inevitably bring a strong wave of protest and demands for reforms by government. Out of this melée of opposing political forces would come the infant vocation of public relations.

The muckraking journalists—David Graham Phillips, Lincoln Steffens, Upton Sinclair, Ida Tarbell and others—were the catalysts that brought the popular revolt that manifested itself in political reforms championed by President Theodore Roosevelt—a master of publicity in his own right. Roosevelt forced the large corporations and railroads to adopt defensive publicity measures to defend themselves in the public forum. As Cutlip, Center and Broom record, "Long accustomed to a veil of secrecy, business leaders felt the urge to speak out but did not know how. Their first instinct was to turn to their lawyers [long used to 'fix' legislatures] and their advertising men."[3] When this did not prove effective, they came to see the need for newspapermen who had access to the nation's newspapers and muckraking magazines.

The first agency, the Publicity Bureau, was organized in 1904 in Boston by George V. S. Michaelis, Herbert Small and Thomas Marvin, all former newspapermen. Its first client was Harvard University, which agreed to pay $200 a month for publicity services. Two years later, President Eliot quit paying, saying the prestige of having Harvard as a client was "pay enough." The bureau agreed and continued to serve Harvard, along with the competing Massachusetts Institute of Technology, the Fore River Shipyard and the American Telephone Company.

As the waves of the Progressive Revolt began rising around Capitol Hill, it became apparent that conventional lobbying and legislative fixing would not prove adequate in a time when, in Theodore Roosevelt's words, there was "a condition of excitement and irritation in the public mind. . . ." The first Washington newsman to sense this was William Wolf Smith, who opened a "publicity business" in the Capital in 1902. Later Congressional testimony asserted, "He used to solicit press-agent employment from anybody who had business before Congress . . . and the whole press-agent business sprung up from that." The third agency started was that of Parker & Lee. George F. Parker, veteran newsman and political publicist for President Grover Cleveland, had directed publicity for the Democrats' 1904 losing presidential campaign. He was assisted by a young New York journalist, Ivy Lee, who would go on to define this emerging vocation. After the campaign, they opened a publicity bureau at 20 Broad St., New York City. In 1906, Lee landed the Pennsylvania Railroad account and two years later left the firm to work full-time for the Pennsy. The firm folded in 1913 when Parker took a full-time public relations job with the Protestant Episcopal Church.

Hamilton Wright was the first practitioner to see the need for American interests to explain themselves abroad and an equal need for foreign nations to make their case before America's public opinion. His son and his grandson, both named Hamilton Wright, would follow in the elder Wright's footsteps in building a public relations agency that specialized in the representation of foreign governments and institutions. The stakes involved in this representation are high and often crucial for Israel, seeking to maintain its support by the United States, or for South Africa, seeking aid and investment to shore up its new democratic government. Hamilton Wright was engaged by sugar interests to encourage support for and investment in the United States' newly acquired Philippine Islands. He also trumpeted the blessings of America's occupation of the Philippines with the encouragement of Major General Leonard Wood, who commanded the occupation forces. Wright's Philippine promotion culminated with the publication of a book, *A Handbook of the Philippines*, which is still in circulation.

Wright formally opened his office in 1908 on his return from the Philippines. His strong advocacy of the expansion of U.S. trade across the Pacific led to his being chosen editor-in-chief of the *Pacific International Exposition*, a position he held from 1915 to 1917. After completion of the exposition and a series of Latin

American trips to promote travel in the Caribbean nations, Wright opened a publicity office in New York City later in 1917. The agency was closed by the third Hamilton Wright in the late 1960s. Wright was the first of a growing army of practitioners who represent foreign nations and interests in this country. As of August 1994, there were 735 primary registrants (usually lobbying firms) representing 1,350 foreign principals and 3,400 short-form registrants (individuals).

The fifth firm to be started in this century's first decade was opened by Pendleton Dudley in 1909 on Wall Street. Dudley, a reporter for *The Wall Street Journal*, did so at the urging of his friend, Ivy Lee. The Dudley name disappeared from the public relations marquee in November 1988 when his successor firm, DAY, purchased by Ogilvy and Mather in 1983, was renamed Ogilvy & Mather Public Relations.

The last known agency started in this period was that of Thomas Reed Shipp in 1914 in Washington, moving into the vacuum created when William Wolff Smith decided to quit and go to law school. Shipp had served his public relations apprenticeship under two masters, Theodore Roosevelt and Gifford Pinchot, who had made conservation a household word in the United States in the early 1900s. The Theodore Roosevelt–Pinchot campaign to promote conservation of our forests and create our national parks was one of the innovative public relations efforts of this period, later widely copied. Their campaign drew the first of many efforts by Congress to halt or hamstring public relations in the executive branch of the federal government. This emerging vocation was given a national boost in 1914 when John D. Rockefeller, Jr., appointed Ivy Lee as his personal advisor.

WORLD WAR I BRINGS LARGE-SCALE PROPAGANDA

When America entered World War I in April 1917, public opinion was far from united. Soon after the United States declared war, President Woodrow Wilson, acting on the advice of Josephus Daniels, Raleigh publisher and Secretary of the Navy, created the Committee on Public Information (CPI) to mobilize supportive public opinion at home and to make known our peace aims abroad. He appointed George Creel, a crusading journalist, to head the committee, and because of Creel's strong personality, the CPI became known as the Creel Committee. The formal committee seldom met Creel's deputy, Carl Byoir, then 28 years old, the one who kept the store and the projects moving. In 1930, Byoir founded the public relations firm, which was the nation's largest until the 1960s.

Although early public relations emerged largely as a defensive measure on the part of big business, Creel converted it into a mighty offensive weapon, building a patriotic fervor for "the war to make the world safe for democracy" that ultimately led to public disillusionment and the corrosion of the word *propaganda*. The Liberty Loan drives were promoted by Guy Emerson, later a pioneer in bank public relations and John Price Jones, who led the way in organized fundraising after the war. During World War I, Ivy Lee directed public relations for the American Red Cross, which raised $273,239,768 in two war drives, an unprecedented sum. When the war started, the Red Cross had a membership of 486,000; when it ended, membership had zoomed to nearly nineteen million. Also coming to a successful close in this decade were the well-organized drives for women's suffrage and prohibition, both adopted in 1920. Little wonder that in the years after the war, there emerged an overly optimistic belief in the power of propaganda, then the common term, or in today's terms, the power of public relations.

THE PUBLICITY BOOM OF THE 1920s

The needs of World War I had brought about expansion of the nation's industrial capacity, new inventions, and new ways of producing mass consumer products. By war's end, there was an acute shortage of consumer goods and a need for experts in advertising, marketing, public relations and fundraising. Many war veterans, who had been schooled in these skills in the war, found a ready market for their talents in the 1920s.

Leo Rosten observed that there was a heightened consciousness of the importance of "a good press." The Creel Committee had been particularly influential in spreading the gospel of the magic of publicity.

Ivy Lee, who had pioneered the practice in the early 1900s, left his work with the American Red Cross and returned to New York to greatly enlarge his agency, now titled Ivy Lee & Associates. In 1919, Lee hired Thomas J. Ross, just back from the Army. Ross would assume leadership of the firm after Lee died of a brain tumor in 1934. Edward L. Bernays, who died in March 1995, opened the nation's eighth agency in 1919. Bernays had been a Broadway press agent before the war and in 1918 worked for the Creel Committee's New York office. Early in this period, Bernays began promoting the term *public relations counsel* and in 1923 wrote a landmark book *Crystallizing Public Opinion*, which for the first time defined the function as a two-way street, asserting that it was the job of the counsel to interpret the public to the institution as well as interpret the institution to the public, a concept that took decades to be fully understood and accepted by management.

Other agencies quickly followed those of Lee and Bernays. John Price Jones, who had learned the art of fundraising in World War I's Liberty Bond drives, opened a firm in November 1919 "to give counsel and service in organization and publicity to business houses, institutions of public, semi-public and private character, and to meet the demand for highly specialized knowledge in these fields." Jones would make his mark in fundraising more than in public relations. Harry Bruno and Richard Blythe, wartime fliers, formed a publicity agency in 1923. Their firm gained national prominence when they handled Charles A. Lindbergh's historic flight across the Atlantic in May 1927. Bruno, demonstrating one of the important tasks of public relations—gaining acceptance of change—did much to speed acceptance of commercial aviation. In 1926, William Baldwin III opened an agency "to serve corporate and civic clients." His firm folded in 1957 when he retired.

In 1927, John W. Hill, experienced in business writing, opened an office in Cleveland with Republic Steel and a bank as his first two clients. He later took in Don Knowlton as a partner in the Cleveland office. In 1933, Hill moved to New York to take a position with the American Iron and Steel Institute. A year or so later, he formed Hill & Knowlton, Inc., which in time would become one of the giant agencies. Don Knowlton had no role in the New York firm. Public relations growth from these uncertain early years was dramatically demonstrated when Hill & Knowlton, Inc., was sold in 1980 to J. Walter Thompson for $28 million. Both are now "profit centers" in the conglomerate WPP Group based in London.

The Booming Twenties (1919–1929) brought a boom in public relations agencies and in corporate recognition. Terms like *public relations counsel*, *specialized knowledge*, and *the power of public opinion* became common parlance. The advertising field grew even faster than public relations.

The first major corporate recognition of this new vocation came when Walter S. Gifford, president of American Telephone & Telegraph, hired his Harvard classmate Arthur W. Page in 1927 as vice president of public relations. In accepting the new position, Page made it clear that he would come in at the policymaking level, not as a publicist. Over the next 20 years, Page built probably the most sophisticated corporate public relations program this nation has seen. He was an innovator; for example, he was the first in public relations to use opinion research as a guide in communicating with the public. Today the Arthur W. Page Society keeps Page's credo alive: "All business in a democratic country begins with public permission and exists by public approval."

However, the 1920s ended on a sour note for this new vocation when Congress investigated the propaganda of Samuel Insull's creation, The National Electric Light Association. The Federal Trade Commission probers found that the National Electric Light Association, since 1922, had been carrying on a campaign of misinformation and bribery of educators. As Bernays noted, "The new profession received a bad name from which it did not free itself for years."

There were also significant advances in public relations in the 1920s. The National Publicity Council for Welfare Services was organized in 1922 by Evart G. Routzahn and Mary Swain Routzahn of the Russell Sage Foundation. In 1918, the National Lutheran Council started an extensive church publicity program. Later that same year, the Knights of Columbus, a Catholic organization, set up a publicity bureau. The first of many professional associations that would, in time, bring increased competence to the craft began to grow in numbers in this period. The Financial Advertisers Association, a bank group started in 1915, and the American College Publicity Association, organized in 1917, came alive in the 1920s. The New York–based National Association of Publicity Directors and the American Public Relations Council, started on the West Coast by pioneer Rex F. Harlow, were started in the late 1930s and early 1940s and formed the foundation stones for the 1947 emergence of the Public Relations Society of America.

FRANKLIN ROOSEVELT AND WORLD WAR II

The Great Depression, which set in after the historic Stock Market Crash of 1929, and World War II, would bring substantial expansion of the practice and its concepts. President Franklin D. Roosevelt, a consummate practitioner who had been tutored in public relations by Louis McHenry Howe since 1912, would lead the way. He was elected president four times against the strong opposition of most American newspapers by using his strong leadership and taking his message to the people on the nation's front pages and on radio. FDR's success in winning public support spurred the efforts of the conservative forces, particularly big business, to develop programs to counter his appeals. To bring the United States out of the Depression, President Roosevelt initiated several action agencies—the Agricultural Adjustment Administration, the Civilian Conservation Corps and the Works Project Administration—that required extensive publicity to gain cooperation and acceptance. Thus, the public information function in the federal government was greatly enlarged in FDR's administration.

The years 1932 to 1945 brought a tool that is today sine qua non in the practice of effective public relations—the scientific public opinion poll. The Roper and Gallup polls, born in the mid-1930s, gained great respect in predicting the outcome of the 1936 presidential election. This same election brought the demise of the unscientific *Liberty Digest* straw poll based on persons with telephones, a rare commodity in the Depression. In 1934, the first minority firm opened in Philadelphia when Joseph Varney Baker quit his job as city editor of the *Philadelphia Tribune* to provide counsel to the Pennsylvania Railroad.

This era also brought Whitaker & Baxter, the forerunner of today's army of campaign specialists who dominate the American political process. In 1933, Clem Whitaker and Leone Baxter, who later became his wife, opened an office in San Francisco to manage political campaigns. California, with its weak political party structure and its heavy reliance on initiatives and referendums to legislate, provided the propitious climate for this new specialty. From 1935 through 1958, the firm managed 80 political campaigns and won all but six. Today, political public relations is a major segment of the practice.

Just as World War I gave great impetus to the growth of public relations by demonstrating its efficacy and schooling hundreds in its techniques, so did World War II, but on a much larger scale. It is estimated that some 100,000 persons served in information posts—information was then the government euphemism for public relations. (Today public affairs is used generally in government.) In June 1943, President Roosevelt created, by executive order, the Office of War Information (OWI) and appointed newsman Elmer Davis as its director. The OWI set the pace for a great expansion of the practice in the armed forces, in industry and in allied fields. The OWI developed many new techniques of communication and trained many more practitioners than did the Creel Committee. Public relations in government and in the armed forces comprises large segments of the practice. The U.S. Information Agency, created in the postwar Cold War, is the successor to the OWI and employs some 10,000 persons to tell America's story around the world. The war also brought advertising to the fore as a major tool of public relations. The War Advertising Council, organized in 1942, combined the efforts of industry and government to get urgent war messages, such as the need for rationing, to the public. Today, advertising is heavily used as a major public relations tool.

THE POSTWAR BOOM

The greatest expansion of domestic public relations practice the field has known came between 1945 and 1980. Expanding world trade and political conflict spread the vocation around the world. Advances in communication and jet travel brought the closest contacts in the history of civilization. The same ecological forces that were operating in the United States to compel public relations' growth were now operating on a world scale. The advent of television as a powerful national and international medium—the most powerful communications medium man has known—brought vast new public relations opportunities and problems to institutions and their executives. The impact of television, now magnified by satellite communication, is beyond calculation, beyond accurate measurement. One example: in the United States, it has demonstrably changed the nation's political process by weakening the party system and by requiring that candidates raise millions of dollars from special interests to be spent on meaningless TV sound bites.

These and like developments of the postwar decades of the late 1940s, 1950s and 1960s brought rapid expansion, increased stability and increased management acceptance. This era saw the number of practitioners pass the 100,000 mark. Today it is estimated that more than 150,000 practitioners serve business, education, government, health and other fields. This period also saw the foundations for professionalism put in place by strong professional associations. In this period, the Public Relations Society of America initiated its accreditation program. These advances were undergirded by an increased number of strong educational programs in the nation's colleges and universities. Both these developments were spurred by more books and journals devoted to the practice. Today, public relations has an accepted body of knowledge and the most comprehensive bibliography of any field of mass communication to guide its growing body of researchers. The 1945 to 1965 period was given impetus by these developments:[4]

1. Steady growth in the number of programs in industries, institutions, social agencies, government bureaus and trade associations. Already-established programs tended to mature and to move beyond publicity.

2. Stabilization in the number of independent counseling firms, especially in the communication hubs of New York, Washington, Chicago and Los Angeles.

3. A tremendous spurt in the number of books, articles and journals devoted to the practice and its philosophy, problems and techniques. The literature is voluminous.

4. Organization of new associations for practitioners and redirection or consolidation of those already established. Many of these are now mature.

5. Growth in the number of college courses and students and in the breadth and depth of the courses. Increased support for collegiate preparation from practitioners and great acceptance of young graduates in the job market.

6. Internationalization of the practice and its standards, reflected in the formation of the International Public Relations Association in 1955.

THE GLOBALIZATION OF PUBLIC RELATIONS

With the advent of the Information Age and its globe-girdling communications and with world strife creating a more volatile public opinion environment, public relations practice grew more complex as it spread around the world. John Naisbett, keen student of society's trends, sets the beginnings of today's information society in 1956 and 1957. In 1956, the Russian Sputnik brought the world satellite communication. In 1957, the number of white-collar, high-technology jobs outnumbered industrial workers for the first time in U.S. history. From the mid-1960s, a time of turmoil in the United States and the Cold War, the public relations function increased markedly in importance and difficulty for executive officers. CEOs and their staffs faced a world made small and interdependent by the computer and the satellite. International trade, the turbulence of politics at home and abroad, and the resultant increased importance of public affairs forced management to take the public relations counselor more seriously. Although this new age of global public relations had its roots in earlier decades, as Naisbett observed, it really took off in the mid-1960s. Naisbett observed that, by the 1980s, the output of information was accelerating by some 40 percent annually. Surely, computer technology is to this Age what the assembly line production was to the Industrial Age at the dawn of this century. Advances in computer technology are moving at almost an exponential rate.

How these technological advances have changed the ways of doing business abroad was succinctly stated by Frank Popoff, then president of Dow Chemical Company, to the 1989 graduating class of Alma College:

Twenty years ago people talked in terms of air travel shrinking space and time, making it possible to move among nations and continents in hours instead of days. Today, with the advent of telecommunications, business people in Japan, Europe, and Midland, Michigan, can meet simultaneously without leaving their offices.

. . . Once people talked about industrialization, about nations developing the machinery and the skills to manufacture and distribute products on a large scale at affordable cost. In the mid-1990s, we talked about globalization, about the world as a global community where nations and people can share one economy, one environment, one technology and, at least in commerce, one language.

International public relations had its substantial beginnings in the wake of World War II. Today, the global market offers a challenging frontier for young persons with ability and a sense of adventure. As indicated at the outset of this chapter, the accelerating forces of interdependence, transportation and communication contribute to the intense battles for political support and market share that face organizations at home and abroad. International public relations emerged in the 1950s, primarily as a marketing tool in Europe and Latin America. Most firms emphasized product publicity in these early years; the large extractive companies, understandably, were more concerned with public relations in the broad sense, born of fear of expropriation.

These substantial beginnings of international practice are reflected in the birth of the International Public Relations Association (IPRA), which brought about a developing esprit and exchanges of information among the world's practitioners. This association had its genesis in 1949 when a group of Dutch industrialists invited some 20 public relations men from Western Europe and the United States to the Netherlands to discuss informally their common interests. Out of this group's spirited shoptalk came a provisional committee to study the feasibility of an international association. The committee was organized in 1950 with Odd Medbo of Scandinavian Airlines as chairman and Tim Traverse-Healy, a London counselor, as secretary. The organizing group found wide support, but getting international agreement took time. IPRA was finally organized at a meeting in London in 1955, with Sir Tom Fife Clark, able director of Britain's Central Office of Information, as president. This is an association of individual members, not a superstructure over the national public relations associations that now circle the globe. IPRA's biennial conferences and its publications have contributed substantially to the advancement of the practice worldwide.

A MAJOR FACTOR: GOVERNMENTS

Governments, too, employ thousands of practitioners to win world support for their foreign policy goals, to promote tourism and to establish a nation's identity in the world community. Much of today's world newsflow is provided by governments and their public relations departments. As I wrote in *The Unseen Power: Public Relations,*

> The need for foreign governments to explain themselves and to promote trade, tourism and political support in the United States increased after the turn of the century when America shed its isolation and became a world power in the wake of the Spanish–American War. These needs have grown over the course of the twentieth century as nations grew more economically and politically interdependent in today's fiercely competitive world economy. Today, with the United States as the world's sole Super Power, caught in a highly competitive global economy and one torn by ethnic and religious wars, the demands for U.S. political and economic support are many and intense. This has led to a boom in public relations representing foreign governments, and enterprises pushing their claims in the halls of Congress and in the public opinion arena.[5]

For example, a powerful Iraq invades its smaller neighbor Kuwait to gain control of its rich oil supply. Kuwait's monarchs retain a U.S. public relations agency, Hill and Knowlton, Inc., to build public support in the United States for U.S. intervention to rescue Kuwait's kingdom and its oil.

In 1994, there were 4,135 persons or firms registered under the Foreign Agents Act with the Department of Justice. This Act had its origins in 1938 in the wake of Congressional hearings on Ivy Lee's serving I.G. Farben and, through it, the Nazi government and Carl Byoir & Associates' representation of the German Railroads Tourist Bureau. On March 20, 1934, a resolution was passed by the House of Representative to provide appointment of a special committee to investigate the extent of Nazi propaganda in the United States. Representative John McCormack of Massachusetts, later to be Speaker, was appointed chairman of this committee. The Ivy Lee & T.J. Ross and the Carl Byoir firms were caught in the crossfire of the committee's concern for "dangerous propaganda of foreign origin." This led, ultimately, to passage of the Foreign Agents Registration Act of 1938. Senator J. William Fulbright revisited this issue with a series of Senate hearings in 1963. Fulbright argued that the 1938 law was being skirted. The Hamilton Wright Organization, Selvage & Lee (now Manning, Selvage & Lee), Julius Klein and Harry Klemfuss were brought before this Senate committee. The Wright agency took most of the beating, which became one of the factors that led to its closing in the late

1960s. Senators Fulbright and Bourke Hickenlooper introduced and got passed a bill strengthening the Act and moving its enforcement from the Department of State to the Department of Justice.

Public relations around our fast-shrinking world offers great opportunities for the expansion of public relations agencies here and abroad and for young persons entering this field in an exciting time. Public relations is being adapted to the needs of business firms, nonprofit institutions and nations of the world at breathtaking rate. In ever-growing numbers, as Dow's President Popoff indicated, U.S. companies are operating abroad through subsidiaries, branches, distributorship and in partnership with local and multinational corporations. Firms doing business across national boundaries and in different cultures find public relations more imperative than at home. Corporations abroad have to buck the onus of absentee ownership, avert the threat of expropriation, combat the ethnic and religious hatreds of centuries and deal sensitively with the cultures of other peoples.

In meeting these problems, there is increasing reliance on international public relations agencies and public relations firms in foreign markets. Take just one example of doing business in today's interdependent, shrunken world: the far-flung operation of International Telephone and Telegraph Corporation, a diversified, worldwide industrial firm with 200 affiliates in 67 countries and 236,000 employees. It must transact its business in 12 languages and in widely varying cultures. The International Telephone and Telegraph Corporation employs more than 100 professionals to meet these formidable tasks. Growth of international trade had caused several U.S. public relations agencies to develop worldwide services.

U.S. AGENCIES EXPAND OVERSEAS

Showing the courage and vision that led to his building Hill & Knowlton, Inc., into what for a time was the largest U.S. public relations firm, John Hill was first to see the burgeoning opportunities for international public relations. In September 1956, he established Hill & Knowlton International. He announced that the firm would have headquarters in The Hague, Netherlands and offices in Dusseldorf, Germany, and would include the facilities of experienced nationals in Great Britain, France, Belgium, Holland, Sweden, Australia, New Zealand, Canada, Mexico and Latin America. Hill chose an ally from his battles for Little Steel, J. Carlisle McDonald, as director of the new firm and its senior consultant in Europe, with offices in Paris. This was a bold, pioneering move on Hill's part, one that lost money during its first several years but eventually became profitable.[6]

Other agencies, in time, followed suit: Ruder & Finn, which in the 1960s represented Iran; Edelman International; Harry Bruno & Associates; and Burson-Marsteller, Inc. These agencies, which began developing overseas branches in the 1960s, saw, in Sylvan M. Barnet, Jr.'s view, a shift in emphasis from marketing to nonmarketing problems in the world economy. Barnet, long active in international practice, summarized the following:

1. A new emphasis on nonmarketing problems.

2. The marked impact of the worldwide consumerism movement.

3. The development of new government–industry relationships.

4. The development of financial public relations as it is known in the United States.

5. The centralization in multinational public relations practice.

6. The movement to upgrade the public relations function within the corporate structure.

The globalization of public relations has been accompanied by the merger of advertising and public relations agencies on a global scale. WPP Group, P.L.C., the London-based advertising–public relations holding company, owns Hill & Knowlton, Inc., J. Walter Thompson, and Ogilvy & Mather—the latter two WPP's biggest advertising agencies. After years when its survival seemed threatened by bloated debt, WPP had its best year in 1994. Saatchi & Saatchi, P.L.C., also London-based, is another of the world's largest advertising and marketing conglomerates. It was also having a good year in 1994 after some lean ones.

Burson-Marsteller, Inc. is owned by Young and Rubicam, a major advertising agency. This merger of public relations and advertising agencies on a mega basis is a hotly debated issue among professionals.

AN EXAMPLE: BURSON-MARSTELLER, INC.

To demonstrate how this international practice has grown, let's take the operations of Burson-Marsteller, Inc. around the world as illustrative.

Approximately half of Burson-Marsteller's $200 million annual fee income is realized from operations outside the United States, and overseas growth is at a greater rate than its domestic business. Burson-Marsteller was one of the first public relations firms to make a major commitment overseas. Although Burson-Marsteller established its first European office in 1961, its first office outside the United States was opened in Toronto in 1959. Burson-Marsteller entered the Asian market with offices in Hong Kong and Singapore in 1973, the Latin American market in 1978, and the Australian market in 1980.

Today, Burson-Marsteller operates 67 wholly owned offices and 71 affiliate offices in 98 countries across six continents. The company has four divisions by geographic region: Asia Pacific, Europe/Middle East/Africa, Latin America and the United States.[7] Abroad, Burson-Marsteller is managed and staffed by local nationals. Today, almost all Burson-Marsteller non-U.S. offices are managed by non-U.S. nationals, some who began their public relations careers with Burson-Marsteller as many as 25 years ago.

Thus, international public relations, which began in the sixteenth and seventeenth centuries as colonial hype to lure settlers to the new land of America, at the end of this twentieth century has reached global dimensions and billions of dollars in agency business. Similarly, since the first U.S. agency, the Publicity Bureau founded in 1900, U.S. public relations has grown in like dimensions. It is now a vocation employing some 150,000 practitioners in agencies, corporations, government, colleges and universities, health services and non-profit enterprises. As a new century dawns, the need for public relations in successful enterprises becomes clearer, and as the need grows, so do its opportunities.

A MODERN HISTORY OF THE OFFICE OF THE PRESS SECRETARY IN THE U.S. WHITE HOUSE

Note from Editor, Clarke Caywood: Professor Scott Cutlip, author of the first portion of this chapter, passed away in 2000. Since he was an authority on the history of this field, we knew that we wanted to use his chapter from the first edition of the Handbook. We only made a very few updates. As a former student of Professor Cutlip, I am aware that much of his career at the University of Wisconsin-Madison was dedicated to educating public affairs officers. So, I am sure he would approve of the addition of a history of the press office function in the American White House that follows. This next section on the history of public relations was prepared by Rear Admiral Brent Baker (also see his Chapter 14 on Government Public Information).

Beginning in the 1900s, officials in the U.S. Department of Agriculture began to institutionalize the governmental public relations or public affairs function. The U.S. Department of Agriculture operated a press bureau in the Division of Forestry, which upset some pro–timber company congressmen. The other federal government "early adopters" of public relations (then called publicity) included the Commerce and Interior Departments. The U.S. Congress (legislative branch) has always been skeptical about the executive branch's use of public relations or publicity people to inform the public. In 1913, Congress passed the Deficiency Appropriations Act, which stated, "No money appropriated by any act shall be used for compensation of any publicity expert unless specifically appropriated for that purpose." The Congress traditionally fears that the president will use the government's public relations machine for political propaganda. In the U.S. government, the President sets the leadership example as the Public Relations Commander in Chief. The major U.S. steps in the evolution of governmental public relations came during World War I and World War II.

President Woodrow Wilson (1913–1921) created the CPI on April 13, 1917, with newspaperman George Creel as head. The CPI was involved in the World War I mobilization of public opinion before there was any commercial radio or television. The CPI produced films and had a speakers' bureau of 75,000 speakers called "Minute Men." The CPI organized Victory Loan campaigns and War Expositions. Out of the CPI came the first American business and public awareness of the power of propaganda. Many who worked in the CPI, such as

Edward L. Bernays and Carl Byoir, left the government to apply their public relations "lessons learned" to the commercial world.

Herbert Hoover (1929–1933) was best known for being President at the beginning of the Great Depression. What is not well known is that he was a pioneer in integrating public relations (publicity) into the government during World War I. At that time, he was head of both the American Food Administration and the Commission for Relief of Belgium. He was responsible for voluntary food conservation by Americans and distribution of food in war-torn Europe. He used extensive publicity to gain cooperation of the public at home and abroad. Hoover then served Presidents Harding and Coolidge as Secretary of Commerce for seven years (1921–1928). In his department, he built a public relations–publicity team, composed of ex-newspaper people. His organization included personal publicity assistants in his front office (whom he paid for out of his own pocket), a centralized press office, a large department printing operation, and publicity officers in each of his departments' bureaus and domestic and foreign branch offices. He considered his target audiences as (1) business industry, (2) press and radio, (3) Congress, (4) various civil groups and (5) the general public. Hoover even used an "outside" publicity firm to promote Commerce Department conferences, such as a 1921 "Unemployment Conference."[8]

James L. McCamy, in his 1939 study of "Government Publicity," wrote, "Administration publicity in the contemporary scope is generally said to have reached its maturity in the Department of Commerce under the secretaryship of Mr. Hoover, who became President, some say, on the foundation of a reputation which was not damaged in any way by the Department of Commerce press agents."[9]

Hoover, an engineer by trade, stated in 1923, "With the growth of specialization in business, contact with the ultimate consumer or purchaser has become more and more complex. Buyer and seller no longer have the personal relationship that prevailed in generations passed. Public relations—publicity and advertising—has become an exact science."[10]

President Franklin D. Roosevelt (1933–1945) established the government's OWI in 1942. The OWI was under Elmer Davis, a radio broadcaster. In selecting a radio broadcaster (rather than a newspaperman) as head of the OWI, the president was acknowledging the growing power and electronic speed of radio news. Wartime radio news, with the voices such as CBS's Edward R. Murrow, changed journalism to a more timely, action oriented and brief oral style. Roosevelt became the first American president to use radio successfully in his "fireside chats" to communicate with the public. The OWI was involved in a full range of domestic and overseas propaganda efforts building on the foundation of the CPI's techniques. Congress quickly stopped appropriating money for the OWI in 1945, worried that Presidents Roosevelt and Truman were using the OWI resources to promote themselves.

To illustrate how compliant the American press was with Roosevelt, we need only cite how the press ignored his lack of personal mobility. When his polio struck, he got around in a wheelchair and wore heavy metal leg braces. He usually held press conferences seated behind his desk to hide his disability. The press self-censored and never published photographs of President Roosevelt that showed his disability and portrayed him as a vigorous striding leader. Although most newspaper publishers hated Roosevelt, the working journalists loved him. He called them by their first names and joked with them.

In her book *No Ordinary Time,* historian Doris Kearns Goodwin described a typical Roosevelt press conference, when the half-dozen members of the White House press corps lined up before Roosevelt's oval office desk. The wire service reporters lined up in front, then the reporters from the *New York Times* and other Washington papers, then the radio reporters and out-of-town newspapers. For seven years, this scene repeated itself twice a week. Roosevelt was "in charge" and was always friendly and exuded warmth. He usually received excellent press coverage. Goodwin wrote, "Once when a correspondent narrowly missed getting on Roosevelt's train, the president covered for him by writing his copy until he could catch up. Another time, when the mother of a bachelor correspondent died, Eleanor Roosevelt attended the funeral services, and then she and the president invited him for their Sunday family supper of scrambled eggs."[11]

During World War II, many American journalists served in military uniform. One of the most famous was Andy Rooney who served in the Army for four years as a correspondent for the military newspaper *Stars and Stripes.* Tom Brokaw wrote a forward to Rooney's book *My War*, which described Rooney as "a sergeant armed with a Jeep, a typewriter, and a writing style that many years later made him the star commentator of *60 Minutes.*"[12] He held that position until his retirement in 2011. After World War II, there was the demobilization of the military, including those with public relations or journalism experience leaving the military. The

Navy, like the other military services, was trying to hold its greatly downsized postwar public relations organization together. In January 1946, amid the demobilization, the Navy sent a message to all ships and stations asking officers of all grades, regular and reserve, qualified for public information duties to apply for a new "special duty public information" designator. The Navy specifically called for "reserve officers having backgrounds of public relations, newspaper work, advertising, radio or writing experience or graduates in journalism, or regulars with inclination or aptitude for public information work." In 1947, the Secretary of the Navy designated the first 40 Navy Special Duty (Public Information) officers. In 1948, the Navy established the enlisted "journalist" rating. During World War II, enlisted journalists were called "enlisted naval correspondents." In 1950, the Navy's Office of Public Relations name was changed to Office of Information.[13]

President Harry S. Truman (1945–1953) was not the communicator that President Roosevelt was, but he understood the importance of public relations. He observed, "You hear about the powers of the President. In the long run, his powers are great but he must know to make people get along together." When the Korean War came along, the federal government had fully integrated the public relations function into its organization, and there was no need for creation of a separate OWI. The Korean War (1950–1953) was still a radio and newspaper war, not a television war.

Dwight D. Eisenhower (1953–1961) was the father of America's interstate highway system. He noted, "We must mobilize public opinion to support and enforce highway safety." Shaping public opinion was now a recognized government function. The "golden age" of television emerged in the mid-1950s and 1960s, and government public relations adapted to this powerful new medium. Government radio studios and news briefing rooms were rewired to accommodate television. The old radio and film offices of government information operations became "radio–TV–film" sections.

During the Vietnam War (1961–1973), there was a gradual American shift to television as the dominant American mass communications medium. The war began with television news using film cameras and ended with the emergence of the new videotape technology. Television satellites were not yet operational, so film and videotape went via aircraft to the United States. The television cameras brought the dramatic images of war into American homes, and the government was forced to react to those images.[14]

President John F. Kennedy (1961–1963) was the first president to capitalize on the use of television. For the first time, presidential news conferences were carried "live" on TV. White House Press Secretary Pierre Salinger recalled that a huge cry of protest went up from the newspaper and magazine correspondents, when he announced that President Kennedy's press conferences would be open to live television. He recalled, "The TV debates had been such a big plus for him that he would be missing a golden opportunity if he did not use his easy mastery of the medium. He also felt, as did I, that television would be the ideal vehicle for going directly to the American people, and over the heads of the nation's editorial writers, who were universally opposed to a Democratic administration."[15]

President Lyndon B. Johnson (1963–1969) was obsessed with leaks in the media. He had three televisions in his oval office tuned to ABC, CBS and NBC. He also had three press wire services machines running all the time in his office. However, he had a poor relationship with the media because of his lies and deceptions about the facts in the Vietnam War. The term *credibility gap* was originally used by the press in association with President Johnson's deceptions in handling the March 1965 escalation of American involvement in the Vietnam War. He went through four press secretaries (Pierre Salinger, George Reedy, Bill Moyers and George Christian). Government public affairs professionals believe it was Johnson's lies and disinformation that turned the news media covering government into a more and more cynical group. The press no longer respected government spokespersons. The news media rightly distrusted information the government released and at the same time wrongly assumed that government critics were without any bias.

It was out of the troubled 1960s decade that CBS launched a new news magazine program called *60 Minutes* on September 24, 1968.[16] The other TV networks soon followed with their own versions of television magazines. To government leaders and their public affairs staffs, *60 Minutes* represented a difficult new challenge. It was produced by Don Hewitt and featured correspondents like Mike Wallace, who engaged in "advocacy journalism." That is, *60 Minutes* was presenting stories from a point of view—mostly a negative and irreverent challenge for all traditional American institutions, including the military. Later, during the Reagan administration, Defense Secretary Caspar Weinberger directed his public affairs staff to refuse to cooperate with the program. The downside of that "opt-out" policy was that the government critics on *60 Minutes* often had no response from the military, and the segment would end with the correspondent saying, "We tried to get the Pentagon to come on this program, but they refused to comment." This left the viewers with the negative perception that something must be wrong. The lesson learned is that you may not like a news program or a reporter, but its best to anticipate the critical issues and deal with them as best you can in an honest, forthright manner.

President Richard M. Nixon (1969–1974) hated the news media and that was reflected in his obsession with secrecy and paranoid fear of news leaks. He was also terrible on television. Aside from the end of the Vietnam War, public affairs officials remember his administration in the light of three main events: first, the June 1971 public affairs crisis surrounding the leak and the *New York Times'* publication of the 7,000-page classified Vietnam history, called the *Pentagon Papers*.[17] In short, the government tried to stop the *New York Times* from publishing the papers by going to federal court. Nixon lost the case because the government could not prove that the publication of the papers harmed national security. The second event was during the 1971 India–Pakistan War with the leak of classified information to columnist Jack Anderson by a Navy Yeoman. Anderson published the fact that President Nixon and his national security team had "tilted to Pakistan, which was different from the public policy of remaining neutral." Nixon then tried to prosecute Anderson but failed.[18] The third was the Watergate Scandal, which not only forced Nixon to resign but also continued to deepen the hostile atmosphere between the federal government and the news media.[19]

President Gerald Ford (1974–1977) realized he was following in the wake of the Watergate scandal. The government had a credibility gap with the public and the media. At his swearing in, he said, "I believe that truth is the glue that holds government together, not only our government but civilization itself. That bond, although stained, is unbroken at home and abroad. In all my public and private acts as your President, I expect to follow my instincts of openness and candor with full confidence that honesty is always the best policy in the end."[20] Within an hour of his swearing in, Ford went to the White House press room where he told reporters, "We will have an open . . . and candid administration."[21] However, his weaknesses, from a public affairs perspective, were as follows: First, he was terrible on television. As James A, Baker, III, explained, "He was not television friendly at a time when television had become the nation's window on politics."[22] Second, he failed to prepare the public and the media for the most dramatic and emotional decisions in the first days of his administration. With no warning, he pardoned President Nixon (his own press secretary, Jerry terHorst, resigned over the decision) and then he granted conditional amnesty for Vietnam War draft dodgers and deserters. In his defense, he did what he felt was right over the long haul, and there is little a public affairs plan could do to ease the resulting emotional atmosphere. President Ford's chief asset was his devotion to the truth. David Gergen, who served in the White House for four administrations (Nixon, Ford, Reagan and Clinton), said that in his 30 years of experience, "every White House—save one—has on occasion willfully misled or lied to the press." The one exception he said was the Ford White House.[23]

President Jimmy Carter (1977–1981) had a poor relationship with the news media and the public. He seemed stiff and ill at ease on television. In 2010, Carter released parts of his White House Diaries, with his reflections. It included this reflection on his media relations. He wrote,

> Another of my failures as president—one that I did recognize while in office—was my inability to form a mutually respectful relationship with key news media . . . . My frequent mentions of this issue in my diary indicate that I was aware of the problem my entire term. I made efforts to solve it with regular news conferences and evening sessions in our private White House quarters with influential media owners, editors and reporters. Rereading my diary all these years later, I have been somewhat surprised by the vehemence of my critical feelings toward specific members of the White House press corps. I am sure my disapproval was evident to those with whom I was seeking reconciliation—hardly a productive approach.[24]

The one positive Carter story was the 1978 signing of the Camp David Accords (Peace Treaty between Egypt and Israel). However, 1979 saw the Iranian radical students take over the U.S. Embassy and capture 51 hostages. Then, there was Carter's failed hostage rescue attempt. In 1979, Carter was presented with a series of public opinion polls, which indicated the public for the first time in history felt that the present was worse than the past and the future would be worse than the present. Public affairs officers remember his administration as a time of reaction to foreign and domestic events, which the government did not seem to be able to control. Carter came into office declaring "human rights" as the linchpin of his foreign affairs program. Ironically, his push for human rights restricted his foreign policy when facing countries like China, the Soviet Union and Iran.

During the Carter years, television entered into a new global broadcasting era. In December 1979, the first RCA communications satellite (SATCOM I) was launched. Cable television was now able to grow into a national network. Government public affairs staffs reacted to the June 1, 1980, launch of CNN, the first all-news cable television channel.[25] The news cycle, which had been tied to the evening broadcast television networks' newscasts and morning newspaper publishing cycles, had suddenly changed to the news-never-stops 24 hours a day, 7 days a week CNN news cycle. CNN was cynically called the "Chicken Noodle" network by the broadcast networks. CNN was initially blocked by broadcasters from becoming a member of the White House Press Corps but was finally admitted.

President Ronald Reagan (1981–1989) was known as the great communicator. He was good on television and a natural public speaker. About his "formula" for speeches, Reagan said, "I usually start with a joke or story to catch the audience's attention, then I tell them what I'm going to tell them, I tell them, and then I tell them what I just told them."[26] The American economy recovered, and by the 1984 Olympics in Los Angeles, it was clear that Americans had regained their national pride and had an optimistic view of the present and future. Citizens also began to regain confidence and trust in their government. Public affairs officers felt good about their jobs. David Gergen, Reagan's White House Communications Director, said the key to the president's good media relations was simple, "He treated reporters with respect and they returned it. That was critical."[27]

Some claim that Reagan's public relations success was because of White House "handlers" like Mike Deaver, who was a former public relations professional. It was Deaver who suggested in 1982 that during the State of the Union speech, the White House place individuals who had done extraordinary things in the balcony sitting with Mrs. Reagan and then work them into the president's speech. Television cameras would then pan to the balcony as congressional members applauded. Presidents after Reagan continued this practice, which is now a tradition. In his book, *Different Drummer*, Deaver said it was a "myth" to suggest that Reagan's popularity was due to his "handlers." Deaver continued, "I can assure you it was Reagan who had the gift for connecting with people, not me or any of the rest of us."[28]

During the Reagan administration, there was one major government–media crisis. It involved the U.S. military invasion of the island nation of Grenada on October 25, 1983. On the evening before the invasion, Bill Plant of CBS News asked White House Press Secretary Larry Speakes about Cuban reports that an invasion of Grenada was imminent. The National Security staff told Speakes, "There was nothing to it." Speakes then told CBS, "That's preposterous!" So, Speakes unknowingly lied to CBS, and was later asked if he would resign. He did not resign and wrote a memorandum to the White House Chief of Staff saying, "I was given virtually no information regarding the Grenada action, either before or after. What I was given yesterday was grossly misleading. In today's briefing my credibility was called into serious question. I can take that. That's what I am paid to do. Most seriously, the Reagan administration was accused of lying or deliberately misleading the *public. This cannot stand.*" Just like reporters, government spokesman depend on their "sources" for information. Unfortunately, most senior public affairs officers can tell their own stories of being misled by their "inside" government sources.

On the day of the Grenada invasion, there were 325 members of the media on the nearby island of Barbados who wanted to land with the U.S. troops. However, they were denied access to the invasion and battle, which lasted 60 hours. During the combat, 19 Americans were killed and 115 wounded. There was hell to pay as the media screamed in bold headlines that even in war the American public must be informed of what their troops are doing. This was a low point in U.S. government–media relations. What inflamed the media was the fact that President Reagan and Defense Secretary Caspar Weinberger defended the decision to exclude the media, saying they needed secrecy and total surprise to rescue American medical students on the island. Public opinion polls at the time showed that the public supported the government's decision to bar the media from the Grenada invasion.

Because of the loud and continuing media outcry over being excluded from Grenada, General John W. Vessey Jr., U.S. Army, Chairman of the Joint Chiefs of Staff, appointed a "panel" headed by retired Army Major General Winant "Si" Sidle to review how the military and media should cooperate in future combat operations. Sidle was well respected by the media and had been Chief of Information at the U.S. Military Assistance Command, Vietnam, during the Vietnam War and also had been Army Chief of Public Affairs before he retired.

The panel consisted of retired newsmen, representatives from colleges of communications or journalism and military public affairs officers.[29] (Originally, the panel was to have active news media representatives, but the news media leaders declared that it was "inappropriate" for the active media to be part of a government panel.)

In 1984, the panel met and presented its recommendations to the Defense Secretary. In short, the panel said that the news media should be allowed to accompany troops in combat, if they followed certain guidelines, including protecting operational security and troop safety. If the military could not initially accommodate many media during combat operations, the panel recommended that the Pentagon establish a permanent National Media Pool. The panel report concluded, "The appropriate media role in relation to government has been summarized aptly as being neither that of a lap dog nor an attack dog but rather, a watch dog. Mutual antagonism and distrust are not in the best interests of the media, the military, or the American people." Defense Secretary Weinberger approved the recommendations.

The news media leaders reacted with some misgivings and strong statements saying that any media pool should only "last a short time," and "open coverage" of combat operations was still desired. However, news media leaders agreed to the Pentagon news pool. The Pentagon pool was initially limited to 12 members, representing a cross section of the media (print, radio, TV, wire services, etc.). The Washington News Bureau Chiefs picked pool members.

During the Reagan years, newspapers were losing readers as more Americans turned to television for their news. Newspaper subscriptions were in decline as they still are today. On September 15, 1982, Gannett launched the first newspaper designed for television viewers, *USA Today*. Critics of *USA Today* called it the "McPaper" because of its fast paced delivery with short stories and a splash of color photos and graphics. The McPaper was a huge success, and it was not long until all newspapers adapted to the *USA Today's* design and style.[30]

President George H.W. Bush (1989–1993) took office inheriting the good will of the public and media, which President Reagan created. However, Bush was not Reagan. He looked stiff and uncomfortable on television. The Bush administration's public affairs reputation was largely based on how it handled the press during two major combat operations.

On December 20, 1989, Bush ordered the U.S. Armed Forces to invade Panama to depose and capture the dictator Manuel Noriega. A Pentagon media pool of American journalists was flown to Panama to cover the combat operations. However, the pool was kept at the U.S. military headquarters in the Panama Canal Zone and not allowed to cover combat operations until 17 hours after the invasion had begun. This was a clear violation of the Pentagon's Sidle Panel promise to allow the media pool into initial combat operations. This resulted in an outcry from media leaders. Finally, Pentagon spokesman Pete Williams (now an NBC correspondent) apologized and blamed the Panama military headquarters and himself, citing "incompetence." The message the media received in Panama was that in future combat operations, the government would always try to control the information flow.

On January 16, 1992, Bush ordered the start of the Gulf War (Desert Storm). The Gulf War accented the vital role of CNN as the only global news network allowed to remain in Baghdad during the war. Only CNN was able to air 24/7 live reports from Baghdad and the other battlefields. There was a downside to having CNN reporters in Baghdad during the war. CNN's Peter Arnett became a prisoner of Iraqi government "handlers." Arnett recalled that when he asked his handler what the rules would be, the Iraqi replied in perfect English, "No logistic information, no military information, no travel without permission." Arnett then asked, "What the hell would be left?" His handler replied, "No comment."[31]

During the January–February 1992 coalition bombing of Baghdad, Arnett was taken to two bombed-out sites by his handlers. First was what the Iraqis claimed was a Baby Milk Factory. There was a sign propped up against a fence, which proclaimed in English and Arabic, "Baby Milk Factory." The Iraqi message was that America and its allies were attacking innocent babies. The Pentagon spokesman reacted saying the site was really a plant for making chemical weapons. Later, Arnett was taken by handlers to what the Iraqis claimed was a civilian bomb shelter. The Pentagon spokesman reacted, saying it was a command and control center. The Pentagon spokesman pointed out that the bunker roof was painted with camouflage, and a tall chain link and barbed wire fence was installed around the bunker, and there was only one gate limiting access.

CNN's own book, *War in the Gulf*, stated,

> Still trying to win the propaganda war, Saddam allowed CNN correspondent Peter Arnett to walk around
> a badly battered Baghdad neighborhood. A well dressed woman, her face contorted in rage, ran up to

the camera and, shaking her finger, screamed in English: "We are human beings!" CNN ran the emotional scene along with an image of another woman; an Israeli, face streaked with blood, being borne on a stretcher out of rubble caused by a [Iraqi] Scud attack on Tel Aviv. A week later, CNN showed the outraged Baghdad woman again, this time to identify her as not just another passerby but an assistant to Deputy Foreign Minister Niazar Hamdoon, a former Iraqi ambassador to the United States. Another bit of staged TV had boomeranged on Saddam.[32]

CNN began to put a disclaimer on its Baghdad reports, citing the fact that the CNN coverage was "controlled" by the Iraqi government. CNN reporters were also all over the battle zone and in the Middle East, sending reports 24/7. For example, a CNN reporter was on the air live at the end of a runway, when coalition aircraft took off to bomb enemy positions. Pentagon public affairs officers complained to CNN that this gave the Iraqis advance warning that the planes were coming. CNN became the prime war information source used by all major American, allied and enemy leaders to get their messages and propaganda out to CNN's global audience. This CNN war coverage resulted in discussions by government and journalism leaders about how media technology (CNN) was driving international politics.[33]

Government public affairs efforts during the 1992 Gulf War adhered to controlling the large number of 1,500 news media in the war zone by keeping them in small media pools, escorted by public affairs officers. Some media reports were also "security reviewed" by public affairs officers. This resulted in media complaints about the government censoring and over controlling the media.[34]

President Bill Clinton (1993–2001) took office and quickly made some policy blunders on health care reform and taking on the issue of gays in the military. Clinton acknowledged that his compromise "Don't ask—don't tell" military policy pleased very few people. The president knew he was in trouble and called in former White House Communication Director David Gergen (a Republican) to help him. Gergen assisted with both policy and communications advice. Clinton had a major problem with his moral compass. On the positive side, he knew the political issues and was a formidable public speaker and campaigner. Clinton was usually good on television, until he was caught in a lie about an affair with a White House intern. Over time, the news media became distrustful of Clinton, and it was clear that the President had trouble taking responsibility for his actions. By 1998, Clinton had lost his moral authority. Thus, Clinton's actions resulted in the old cynical media attitudes about government's lying taking hold again.[35]

By the end of the twentieth century, the Internet (particularly the web) was becoming an emerging interactive public multimedia channel. Americans were logging on the net from both office and home computers. Lawrence Grossman, former President of NBC News and former President of the Public Broadcasting System (PBS), said in his 1995 book, *The Electronic Republic,*

> This is the first generation of citizens who can see, hear, and judge their own political leaders simultaneously and instantaneously. It is also the first generation of political leaders who can address the entire population and receive instant feedback about what people think and want. Interactive telecommunication [Internet] increasingly gives ordinary citizens immediate access to the major political decisions that affect their lives and property.[36]

Government public affairs officers were experimenting on how to use this emerging Internet medium. On January 13, 1994, Vice President Al Gore held the first White House "online conference." It was broadcasted by C-SPAN television, and the electronic "hosts" were U.S News Online (an online service of *U.S. News & World Report* magazine) and CompuServe. In the mid-1990s, government agencies (.gov) began building their own websites. Using the same web technology, the government agencies also built internal networks called Intranets used to track issues, to assign tasks and to disseminate internal information in multimedia formats.

In 1996, three CNN competitors were launched. First in summer 1996, MSNBC was launched with lots of technical glitter in the studio—it was a partnership of Microsoft and NBC. Then, on October 7, 1996, Fox News launched on cable. The Fox News' motto was "Fair and Balanced—We report—You decide." Owner Rupert Murdoch and head of Fox News Roger Ailes declared that Fox News was a counter to the "liberal" media. It was not long before Fox News became the "most watched" American cable news channel and the outlet for conservative Republican views.[29] Now, government public affairs staffs had to accommodate the three cable news networks and Internet outlets. Little noticed at the time, the first Arab cable news network, Al Jazeera, was launched in 1996, headquartered in Qatar. Now, the Middle East states had an Arab satellite news voice, which would later cause propaganda problems for the George W. Bush administration.

President George W. Bush (2001–2009) was the first Commander-in-Chief to be forced by the September 11, 2001, terrorist attack on New York's World Trade Center to fight a global war on terrorism. Initially, the Congress, the American news media, and the public provided enthusiastic and uncritical support for his administration. The media appeared to be in a "cheerleading role," which made most American journalists feel uncomfortable.

Bush's first press secretary, Ari Fleischer, who served from 2001 to 2003, noted the changes in the media environment facing public affairs officers. He said,

> The [broadcasting] networks have been losing viewers for years, and their remaining viewers are typically older. Cable news shows, especially those on Fox, are cutting deeply into territory that used to be the exclusive domain of the broadcast networks. As newspapers lose readers, younger Americans especially are turning to the Internet and to bloggers. The media is fracturing into more choices and more diversity. . . . The immediacy of the Internet and cable news has changed the way all White House reporters do their jobs.[37]

President Bush initiated the wars in Afghanistan and Iraq, and there was a natural government desire to control all war and homeland security information. On October 7, 2001, Al Jazeera cameras were in Afghanistan providing coverage of the first American attacks on the Al Qaeda training camps. The Arab news channel gave extensive airtime to America's enemies, including the Taliban, Al Qaeda (Osama bin Laden), and later Iraqi spokesmen. When the American-led coalition forces attacked Afghanistan and Iraq, the American government believed that the Al Jazeera coverage was biased against the coalition. Ironically, the Arab states believed the Al Jazeera coverage was biased against the Taliban, Al Qaeda, and Iraq.

For the first time since World War II and the Cold War, the American government was involved in a hot international propaganda war in 2001. It was clear that the United States had a major problem with Muslim public opinion around the world. Muslims viewed the Bush administration as the bad guys. In late 2001, the White House announced that a new global communications office was established, under the State Department, with branch offices in London and Pakistan. The State Department's "Public Diplomacy" program was expanded. Public diplomacy is a State Department term for their overseas information and cultural exchange efforts. American news media ran reports that America was losing the "propaganda war." In Iraq and Afghanistan, the U.S. military began "information operations," which involved placing information in foreign media news stories. Some of the foreign reporters were paid to place the stories in their outlets.

On February 19, 2002, the ugly issue of the government's using "disinformation" during wartime operations arose in *The New York Times*. The paper revealed that the Pentagon had created an Office of Strategic Influence (OSI). Its mission, according to *The New York Times*, was to develop and to distribute news items containing disinformation to foreign media. This was described as part of a new military "Information Operations" initiative to influence foreign public opinion. It was also discovered that the OSI had contracted with "outside" firms to contact and supply information to the foreign media. Defenders of the OSI said that the problem was that enemy propaganda was being published and aired by the foreign media and that OSI would be providing the truth, not disinformation to the foreign media. There followed a drumbeat of media criticism that such a disinformation program would upset allies and spread rumors and false information.

Pentagon reporters expressed concern that this OSI program would confuse people and impact the military's public affairs program. In the Pentagon, many public affairs officers, including the Assistant Secretary of Defense (Public Affairs), Victoria Clark, were deeply concerned that overseas information operations or disinformation operations would adversely affect their relations with the mainstream media. Things got so hot that the White House Press Secretary, Ari Fleischer, said at the February 25, 2002, news briefing that President Bush had not been aware of the new office in the Pentagon and that he learned about it via the media. Fleischer said, "The president would be troubled by any office that does not as a matter of public policy disseminate the truth and the facts." Finally, on February 26, 2002, Defense Secretary Donald Rumsfeld announced that the OSI had been closed.[38]

On March 19, 2003, President Bush ordered the second War in Iraq (Operation Iraqi Freedom) to begin. This was as much an information or propaganda war as it was a combat war. In Operation Iraqi Freedom, the news media were "embedded" with the troops to cover combat operations. This was considered a great improvement (by both the public affairs officers and the media) over the use of media pools in the 1991 Gulf War. One of the main reasons President Bush cited for going to war in Iraq was that Saddam Hussein had weapons of mass destruction or chemical and biological weapons. When the war ended and no weapons of mass destruction were found, the Bush administration claimed that an intelligence failure was to blame, but public and media confidence was lost. Also, as the violence continued in Iraq, Americans by a 2-to-1 ratio said they disapproved of the way the President was handling Iraq in 2006.

The second Bush press secretary was Scott McClellan. He served from 2003 to 2006. McClellan is controversial because in 2005 he misled the press denying that a leak that deliberately blew the cover of Valerie Plame (a covert CIA official) came from the White House. Plame was the wife of former Ambassador Joseph Wilson, who was a vocal critic of President Bush's decision to go to war against Iraq in 2003. The "outing" of Plame (by an unnamed source) was said to be a White House punishment aimed at Wilson. The second reason McClellan is controversial is that he wrote a "kiss and tell" book, published in 2008. In the book *What Happened*, he outlined how he was deceived by White House officials including Lewis "Scooter" Libby, the Vice President's chief of staff, Karl Rove, Bush's political advisor, and Andy Card, Bush's chief of staff.[39] McClellan wrote, "Washington has become the home of the permanent campaign. A game of endless politicking based on the manipulation of shades of truth, partial truths, twisting the truth and spin." He said he worked in "a culture of deception" and the media were also to blame because they wanted "conflict" and "scandal." Unlike most "kiss and tell" books, McClellan recommended a solution to the problems. For example, he suggested a White House reorganization with a new "deputy chief of staff for governing," who would make sure the president is committed to a "high level of openness and forthrightness, and transcending partisanship to achieve unity." That position, he said, would have "an assistant to focus on transparency."[40]

President Barack Obama (2009–present) inherited the worst economic recession since the Great Depression. He was a great communicator during the 2008 presidential campaign, but his critics said that once in the White House, he did not use his communications skills to sell his programs and policy. Timothy Egan, writing at the midpoint in Obama's first term said, "One of the mystifying paradoxes of Obama is how this gifted writer, this eloquent communicator, has not been able to come up with a simple, overarching governing frame." In 2009, Obama's communications director Dan Pfeiffer believed the White House did not have a clear strategic plan to merge the political and communications operations. He claimed Obama underused his cabinet in getting his messages out, and the White House had failed to coordinate their messages with Democrats in Congress and Democratic pundits on cable and in print. The Democrats had control of Congress when Obama took office but lost control of the House in the midterm 2010 elections. Pfeiffer explained the loss of strategic focus, saying, "It's easier to be strategic and laser-focused on a presidential campaign, as complicated and hard as it is, compared to government."[41]

In 2010, Robert Gibbs, White House Press Secretary, believed that the media were in an Internet "transition" and this would result in a fundamental change in the way future administrations deal with the news. He said that the classic press briefing would soon (in 5 or 10 years) be a thing of the past because a lot has changed in the way the government is covered. However, he said what has not changed is the need for "message delivery." Gibbs viewed his briefings as not so much driving the message but as a chance to comment on the daily media and Internet chatter, in his words, "like a televised version of newspaper's corrections and clarifications." He claimed the media are in his briefing to "cover the fight, whether or not the persons using facts that can be backed up." Often Gibbs would tell the media, "Wait that's not right!" Gibbs concluded, "I read people on the Internet who say I give long answers. Blah, blah, blah. That's the point. It's my time. I can take something and broaden it to discuss what I think needs to be contextualized."[42]

Obama's communication team believed that they were living in a "hyper-partisan world" and the media were partly responsibly with cable "political media" and critics (including congressional members) getting on television because to say the most outrageous things.

In summary, the government integration of the public relations or public affairs function began in earnest in the 1920s and expanded greatly with the wartime work of the CPI and the OWI. Today, the U.S. government is engaged in a global war on terrorism and is one of the world's largest government employers of public information or public affairs personnel with more than 12,000 practitioners. State and local governments have also had to build a large public relations or public affairs organizations. Today's 24/7 news flow and dynamic mix of mainstream media and digital social media have added to the government's communication challenge.

DICUSSION QUESTIONS

1. Discuss the professional challenges facing newspaper reporters moving from news to public relations in the beginning of the twentieth century.
2. Discuss the challenges facing news reporters changing from network, newspaper, magazine and other print journalism to social media reporting in the twenty-first century. How are the challenges similar to or different from those in the last century?
3. On the basis of the history of the American colonies, how might public relations help the states to establish their communications message and the confidence of citizens today?
4. Propaganda has a negative connotation. Does government use propaganda today? Do corporations use propaganda?
5. How are government officials more like journalists? Where do both professionals receive their information?
6. Discuss the decision by the Congress to not allow "public relations" to be funded in the U.S. government. Is the law realistic? How is it violated in "spirit?"
7. What role does the press secretary to the U.S. President fulfill? Describe a situation in which the press secretary seems to be deliberately not given information so he or she does not have to lie.
8. Write a one-page memo to the President of the United States on how the office of the Press Secretary and related public relations functions can be organized.

NOTES

1. This account of Colonial hype is taken from my book, *Public Relations History, 17th to 20th century* (Hillside, NJ: Lawrence Erlbaum Associates, Inc., 1995).
2. For a history of the Ayer agency, see Ralph M. Hower, *The History of an Advertising Agency* (Cambridge, MA: Harvard University Press, 1939).
3. Scott M. Cutlip, Allen H. Center, and Glen M. Broom, *Effective Public Relations, 7th ed.* (Englewood Cliffs, NJ: Prentice Hall, 1994).
4. Ibid.
5. Scott M. Cutlip, *The Unseen Power: Public Relations, a History* (Hillside, NJ: Lawrence Erlbaum Associates, Inc., 1994).
6. The story of Hill's pioneering venture is told in the John W. Hill papers, Mass Communications History Center, State Historical Society of Wisconsin, Madison.
7. http://en.wikipedia.org/wiki/Burson-Marsteller, (accessed 12/15/10).
8. Brent Baker, "Herbert Hoover's Engineering of Public Opinion: Federal Government Public Relations, 1921–1928," unpublished masters degree thesis, University of Wisconsin, 1971.
9. Baker, p. 2.
10. Baker, p. 154.
11. Doris Kearns Goodwin, *No Ordinary Time* (New York: Simon and Schuster, 1994), 26–27. Also see Myra MacPherson, *All Governments Lie!* (New York: Scribner, 2006), 89.
12. Andy Rooney, *My War* (New York: Public Affairs, 1994), xii.
13. Ed Castillo, L., Captain, USN (Ret), "U.S. Navy Public Affairs, Part I—The First Hundred Years (1861–1961)," unpublished manuscript, U.S. Navy Public Affairs Alumni Association, Alexandra, VA, 2007, 66–68. Also, see Navy Public Affairs Alumni Association website under history button, http://www.usnpaaa.org.
14. Dan Rather, *The Camera Never Blinks* (New York: William Morrow and Company, Inc., 1977), 205.
15. Pierre Salinger, *P.S. A Memoir* (New York: St. Martin's Press, 1995), 94–95.
16. Don Hewitt, *Tell Me A Story: Fifty Years and 60 Minutes in Television* (New York: Public Affairs, 2001); and Richard Campbell, *60 Minutes and the News* (Urbana: University of Illinois Press, 1991). For a Reagan White House press secretary's view of *60 Minutes*, see Marlin Fitzwater, *Call the Briefing* (New York: Times Books, 1995), 222–223.

17. David Rudenstine, *The Day the Presses Stopped: A History of the Pentagon Papers Case* (Berkeley: University of California Press, 1996).

18. Mark Feldstein, *Poisoning The Press: Richard Nixon, Jack Anderson, and the Rise of Washington's Scandal Culture* (New York: Farrar, Straus and Giroux, 2010), 155–198.

19. Carl Bernstein and Bob Woodward, *All the President's Men* (New York: Simon and Schuster, 1974).

20. Jerald. F. terHorst, *Gerald Ford and the Future of the Presidency* (New York: The Third Press, 1974), 188.

21. Jerald F. terHorst, *Gerald Ford and the Future of the Presidency* (New York: The Third Press, 1974), 188.

22. James A. Baker, III, *Work Hard, Study . . . and Keep Out of Politics* (New York: G.P. Putnam's Sons, 2006), 44–45.

23. David Gergen, *Eyewitness To Power* (New York: Simon and Schuster, 2000), 140.

24. Jimmy Carter, *White House Diary* (New York: Farrar, Straus and Giroux, 2010), 529.

25. Ted Turner, *Call Me Ted* (New York: Grand Central Publishing, 2008); and Reese Schonfeld, *Me and Ted Against the World: The Unauthorized Story of the Founding of CNN* (New York: Cliff Street, Harper Collins, 2001).

26. Ronald Reagan, *An American Life* (New York: Simon and Schuster, 1990), 247.

27. Gergen, p. 185.

28. Michael Deaver, *A Different Drummer* (New York: HarperCollins, 2001), 5.

29. The author, then a public affairs Captain in the Navy, was the Navy member of the Sidle Panel. Before the panel, news media representatives claimed there was no problem with "live" TV aired from the battlefield because history and past reporting from the battlefield demonstrated that the press could keep secrets. The author disagreed. The February 8, 1984, *New York Times*, "Naval Aide Questions Press" (p. A4), reported, "Captain Brent Baker the Navy's Assistant Chief of Information for Operations said those [past] practices evolved before new technology made it possible for broadcast correspondents to sent material directly to their networks or stations, using satellites and other equipment that are not subject to military control. He said the networks had asked to send a plane to Grenada carrying a ground station and other equipment needed for live battlefield broadcasts." Thus, the information on the Sidle Panel is based on the author's personal observations.

30. Peter Prichard, *The Making of McPaper* (New York: Andrew, McMeel & Parker, 1987).

31. Peter Arnett, *Live From The Battlefield* (New York: Simon and Schuster, 1994), 378.

32. Thomas B. Allen, Clifton F. Berry, and Norman Polmar, *CNN: War In The Gulf* Nashville, TN: (Turner Publishing Inc., 1991), 159.

33. Johanna Neuman, *Lights, Camera, War: Is Media Technology Driving International Politics?* (New York: St. Martin's Press, 1996).

34. The author was Navy Chief of Information during Desert Storm and had full access to the raw CNN satellite feed during the war in his Pentagon office. The press view of the Gulf War is outlined in two books: John R. Macarthur, *Second Front: Censorship and Propaganda In The Gulf War* (New York: Hill and Wang, 1992); and Smith Hedrick, *The Media And The Gulf War* (Washington, DC: Seven Locks Press, 1992).

35. Gergen, pp. 251–242.

36. Larry K. Grossman, *The Electronic Republic* (New York: Viking Penguin, 1995), 4.

37. Ari Fleischer, *Taking Heat: The President, The Press, and My Years in the White House* (New York: William Morris, 2005), xii.

38. David Dadge, *Casualty of War* (Amherst, New York: Prometheus Books, 2004), 144.

39. In a federal special prosecutor investigation into the Plame leak, Lewis "Scooter" Libby was brought before a grand jury. Libby was inducted for perjury, obstruction of justice, and making false statements. He resigned his White House position. He then went to trial and was convicted. In June 2007, he was sentenced to thirty months in prison. (It later came out that Deputy Secretary of State Richard Armitage told the special prosecutor that he has been the source of the leak.) Just before he left office, President Bush used his executive powers to commute Libby's sentence, meaning his conviction stood, but he would not serve any prison time.

40. McClellan, Scott. *What Happened: inside the Bush White House and Washington's Culture of Deception.* New York: Public Affairs, 2008. Print. pp. xiii and 1–2, 316.
41. Timothy Egan, "A Big Idea," *New York Times* (December 7, 2010): A22; and Richard Wolffe, *Revival: The Struggle for Survival Inside the Obama White House* (New York: Crown Publishing, 2010), 197–199.
42. Timothy Egan, "A Big Idea," *New York Times* (December 7, 2010): A22; and Wolffe, Richard, *Revival: The Struggle for Survival Inside the Obama White House* (New York: Crown Publishing, 2010), 199.

ADDITIONAL READING

Abrams, Floyd. 2005. *Speaking Freely Trials of the First Amendment.* Prince Frederick, MD: RB Large Print.
Baker, Brent. 1992. "Decisions at the Speed of TV Satellites," *Vital Speeches of the Day* 58(19): 581–583.
Baker, Brent. 1977. "Leakology: The War of Words," *U.S. Naval Institute Proceedings* 103/7/893, 43–49.
Cutlip, Scott M. 1995. *Public Relations History: From the 17th to the 20th Century: The Antecedents.* Hillsdale, NJ: Erlbaum.
Cutlip, Scott M. 1994. *The Unseen Power: Public Relations, a History.* Hillsdale, NJ: Erlbaum Associates.
Cutlip, Scott M., Allen H. Center, and Glen M. Broom. 1994. *Effective Public Relations.* Englewood Cliffs, NJ: Prentice-Hall.
Hill, John W., papers. Madison, WI: Mass Communications History Center, State Historical Society of Wisconsin.
Hower, Ralph M. 1939. *The History of an Advertising Agency; N.W. Ayer & Son at Work, 1869–1939.* Cambridge, MA: Harvard University Press.
Reedy, George E. 1970. *The Twilight of the Presidency.* New York: World Pub.
Stephanopoulos, George. 1999. *All Too Human: A Political Education.* Boston: Little, Brown.
Woodward, Bob. 2010. *Obama's Wars.* New York: Simon and Schuster.

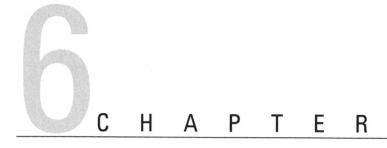

6

C H A P T E R

ETHICS
Grounding the Promotional Strategies of China's Tobacco Industry in Ethics

Cornelius B. Pratt, Ph.D., APR
Professor, Department of Strategic Communication
Temple University

> *At the state level, ethics should become a part of the public policy, and in particular of the state industrial policy. How? Our answer is through the integration of the ethical infrastructure into state's industrial policy.*
>
> —Choi and Digol 2010, pp. 229–230

> *. . . the Chinese government has a policy conflict between the economic interests of the tobacco industry and the health concerns of its people.*
>
> —Hu et al. 2006, p. i37

> *Although some progress has been made in the past decade, China still faces a long path to true tobacco control.*
>
> —Yang 2008, p. 31

An important element in national economic development and growth in the twenty-first century is a nation's imposing ethical standards on and integrating an ethical infrastructure into its industrial policy (Choi and Digol 2010). Another is institutionalizing international ethical standards and practices and compliance regimes in multinational corporations' supply chains in the Chinese economy (Krueger 2008). The rationale for both those elements is obvious: ethics is an important consideration in conducting business in China, in fostering best practices, and in boosting trade flows among nations (Brand and Slater 2003; Choi and Digol 2010; Robertson et al. 2008; Wei 1999). Ethics is also a determinant of foreign investment in China (Liu and Pearson 2010). Such a crucial role of ethics in a nation's business environment justifies three overarching arguments presented in this chapter.

First, to the degree that China, the world's largest producer and consumer of tobacco products, is increasingly directing its attention to smoking and amplifying the form and content of its measures to control it, this chapter argues that China's modest accomplishments in the tobacco wars are attributable partly to the tobacco industry's marketing communications strategies and tactics. These strategies and tactics, although beneficial to the industry and to the country, are largely bereft of ethics, exacerbating a public health menace in the world's most populous nation.

Second, the industry is taking appropriate measures to respond head-on to the outcomes of its high production–sale–consumption capacity by restructuring the China National Tobacco Company (CNTC). It is reducing the number of cigarette brands, and restricting the activities of global tobacco companies such as British American Tobacco and Philip Morris International in China. This chapter argues that such actions are inadequate and calls for major changes in the State Tobacco Monopoly Administration (STMA)–CNTC structural and administrative relationships.

Third, ethical issues are raised because of a duality of efforts regarding this industry in China. China's tobacco industry publicly acknowledges health concerns over its products, while at the same time uses marketing communications and organizational restructuring to circumvent public health initiatives and stricter government regulations, which should be the industry's societal responsibilities. One example of this is the industry's funding of elementary schools or sponsoring of athletes to competitive events as its contributions to the social good, a policy that raises far-reaching ethical issues that also have implications for a comprehensive public policy. The ideal policy, this chapter argues, should focus on grounding corporate normative conduct in the universals of four ethical theories: utilitarianism, deontology, virtue ethics, and egoism. Those ethical universals should also provide the framework for illuminating normative corporate practices such as the participation of citizens and civil society organizations in developing policy and in planning and implementing antismoking campaigns. The overarching significance of this chapter, then, lies in its raising new questions and in its providing policy directions that might serve as a global template for countries considering their own comprehensive policies on the effects of tobacco use on their national well-being.

This chapter is organized into six sections: (a) the importance of this topic, in light of the high levels of production and use of tobacco in China; (b) the tobacco industry's panoply of marketing communications; (c) an overview of the two government agencies in the forefront of regulating and marketing tobacco; (d) the ethical issues of tobacco marketing communications and regulation; (e) the theories of ethics; and (f) the directions for the future (values-driven, public policymaking proposals).

IMPORTANCE OF THIS TOPIC

The People's Republic of China, the world's second-largest economy and a major engine in the growth of the global economy, is in the throes of a paradox in which two sets of centrifugal, efferent forces are variously influencing its well-being economically, politically and clinically. One set of forces is coalescing in strengthening China in at least two ways as a formidable partner (and voice) in increasingly complex world affairs. First, it is an economic leader and an industrializing powerhouse whose double-digit growth in its gross domestic product makes it the world's fastest-growing economy. As such, it is at once ameliorating the global impact of a worldwide macroeconomic crisis and encouraging a rethinking of the "benefit mix" of having a government keep a tight rein on political activity while at once loosening its grip on a controlled economy and providing a fillip to a free-market economy. China's growing economic prominence and its market-authoritarian model are more appealing to the developing world and to middle-sized, non-Western economies than is the United States' market-democratic model (Halper 2010). Many observers think that China's economic clout is reshaping the world order so much that it is shrinking the West and making it less relevant in world affairs (Dobson 2009; Halper 2010).

Second, it is a political leader whose growing participation, strategic assertiveness, palpable confidence, and surging influence in world affairs have accorded it a veritable presence, an enhanced stature and an equally endearing attribute on the global stage.

The other set of forces, however, has created a national market with five ignominious distinctions. First, that market produces 1.7 trillion cigarettes (Hu et al. 2006; Tong et al. 2008), sells approximately that many and consumes approximately 30 percent of the world's cigarettes annually—the world's largest on all counts. And that market has 350 million active smokers (Smith and Zheng 2010) and 540 million passive smokers—both also the world's largest, in sheer numbers.

Second, in China, smoking accounts for 800,000 to an estimated one million deaths each year from diseases such as chronic obstructive pulmonary disease (a combination of chronic bronchitis and emphysema), lung cancer and pulmonary tuberculosis. That number is expected to increase to 2.2 million by 2020 at current rates of use (Abdullah et al. 2010; Gajalakshmi et al. 2000; Gu et al. 2009; Hu 2008; Zhu et al. 2004; Zhang and Cai 2003). The recent decline of more than 10 percent in male smoking prevalence "will not be sufficient to counteract approximately 26 million cardiovascular disease events and nine million cardiovascular deaths added by deleterious trends in systolic blood pressure, total cholesterol, diabetes, and body mass index" (Moran et al. 2010, p. 248).

Third, despite a decline of more than 10 percent in male smoking prevalence since the mid-1980s, China's tobacco market still indicates a "high consumption of tobacco use [that] appears very serious" (Yang 2008, p. 31). In males and females ages 15 and older, the prevalence rates are 57.4 percent (down from 63 percent in 1996) and 2.6 percent, respectively (Wanli 2010; Yang 2008). These statistics are broadly consistent with those of a national survey of nearly 140,000 respondents 18 years of age or older who reported that 52.4 percent of males and 3.4 percent of females were active smokers (Shi et al. 2008). For males, the ever-smoking rate has remained constant at approximately 66 percent since 1996 (Yang 2008; Tobacco Control Office 2010); and at least 49 percent of nonsmokers (mostly women) were being exposed to passive smoking at home or at work (Moran et al. 2010). Among adolescents, however, smoking prevalence is increasing: there are 80,000 new smokers per day (Zhang and Cai 2003), resulting in nine million adolescent smokers aged 15 to 19 and accounting for 18 percent of all boys and 0.28 percent of all girls in the country (Grenard et al. 2006). As Moran et al. (2010) note, an aggressive program that reduces active smoking in Chinese men to 20 percent prevalence in 2020 and 10 percent prevalence in 2030 would counteract adverse trends in other risk factors by preventing cardiovascular events and 2.9 to 5.7 million total deaths over two decades.

Fourth, the unique structure of China's tobacco industry, a state monopoly in its entirety whose center-piece is the nation's largest tobacco-producing company, the CNTC, established in 1982, enables the industry to serve as a national economic engine through offering employment opportunities and contributing to the nation's wealth through paying taxes. The CNTC is responsible to the STMA, which was established in 1984 to set and provide oversight for the nation's overall tobacco-control policy, "beginning with the allocation of tobacco production quotas among the provinces, pricing of tobacco leaf, production of cigarettes and international trade" (Tong et al. 2008, p. 213).

Finally, its provision of incomes to 60 million people and its accounting of between nearly 7 percent and 7.38 percent of the state's total revenue from taxes and profits (Chao 2009; Lee and Jiang 2008) are the world's largest. Among the top 100 tax-paying enterprises in China in 2004, 35 were from the tobacco industry, and those companies accounted for 35 percent of the total taxes paid by the top 100 (Zhong 2006).

Consequently, to improve public health through both reducing the outcomes of tobacco use and preventing its use, China, like other countries, has taken several measures to reduce demand for tobacco. For example, Article 19 of the Law of the People's Republic of China on Tobacco Monopoly 1991, prohibits the advertising of tobacco products from broadcasting stations, television stations, newspapers or periodicals. Similarly, Article 18 of the Advertisement Law 1994, bans direct tobacco advertisement on movies, radio and television; in magazines and newspapers; and in public venues such as waiting rooms, movie theaters, stadiums, gymnasiums and conference halls. Since 1994, about 100 cities have passed laws banning tobacco smoking in some public places and, since 2005, foreign cigarette companies have been banned from establishing joint manufacturing ventures in China (Kenkel et al. 2009). Other governmental measures include curtailing product sale; signing the World Health Organization (WHO) Framework Convention on Tobacco Control (FCTC) on November 10, 2003, ratifying it on August 28, 2005 and implementing it on January 9, 2006; requiring warning labels and health alerts on cigarette cartons; and increasing cigarette tax in May 2009, the first such increase since 2001. From the nongovernmental perspective, media advocacy is being used as an important component of China's tobacco-control programs (Liu et al. 2010). Yet, such measures have had limited overall effects on tobacco use, a situation summarized in this chapter's third epigraph and underscored by the importance of the focus of this analysis. One reason for such limitation can be illustrated as a prisoner's dilemma, in which the government and the industry (two parties) have chosen to cooperate and to gain some benefit from adhering to an agreement or to a rule on tobacco restrictions. The industry, in its attempt to support the government's antitobacco efforts, abides by restrictions on tobacco advertising and is forced to reduce tobacco sales, both of which undercut revenues from reduced tobacco sales and threaten the funding of national programs. That Hobson's choice has implications for public policymaking, a subject that will be addressed in a subsequent section of this chapter.

Another reason for the ineffectiveness of government's advertising laws is that China still suffers from a lack of political will and of coherence in implementing such laws in a uniform and timely manner throughout the country (Choukroune 2009). Thus, advertising attempts to persuade people to consume a harmful product such as tobacco, making today's advertisers act like ancient Greek sophists who used illogical methods of persuasion to create more illusion than the reality of truth (Cohan 2001).

IMPLEMENTING THE TOBACCO INDUSTRY'S PANOPLY OF MARKETING COMMUNICATIONS

Worldwide, there is an onslaught on the tobacco industry's manufacturing, marketing and placing (that is, distribution) practices, based largely on the premise that tobacco use is a leading cause of preventable death and disability among adults. There is also a growing governmental interest to curtail the commercial activities of the industry through antismoking and public information campaigns and research support. More recently, Article 13 of WHO FCTC stipulated the ban of all forms of tobacco advertising, promotion and sponsorship in accordance with each country's constitutional principles. Worldwide, only 26 countries, covering 8.8 percent of the world's population, have such bans. China has a partial ban. Yet, it has been argued that a comprehensive ban on all tobacco advertising, promotion and sponsorship could decrease tobacco consumption by about 7 percent, independent of the interventions of other tobacco controls. It has also been argued that partial bans have little or no effect because the tobacco industry will merely move its business to places where advertising is permitted (Saffer 2000; World Health Organization 2009). Cast against that backdrop, then, the industry has been exploring ingenuous ways to promote and market its products and to expand its sales, in the face of the central government's efforts to curtail tobacco use pari passu. That has meant circumventing advertising laws to market its products (Li and Yong 2009). Countries with effective tobacco-control policies and harm-reduction strategies employ a mix of marketing communication approaches (DeRuiter and Faulkner 2006; Laugesen et al. 2000; The World Bank 1999) to reduce the demand for and the use and supply of tobacco. Therefore, in its response to the onslaught of governmental, news media, and other nongovernmental organizations, the tobacco industry is drawing on key strengths of marketing communications, which target large and small audiences through a "process of planning, executing and evaluating unified messages that create stakeholder relationships and build brand recognition" (Stuart et al. 2007, p. 14).

Examples of the myriad marketing tactics used by China's tobacco companies to connect brand images to common values and lifestyles of Chinese women particularly are as follows, with message type in parentheses:

- Relate smoking to the notions of "beauty," "independence," "fashion," "slim," and "charm" (false association and attribution)

- Advertise cigarettes as "mild," "light," "low tar" and "low harm" (manipulation)

- Use attractive and novel designs on package (product packaging)

- Develop products with fruit favors and menthol taste to attract women (manipulation)

- Sponsor public events that target women (cause-related marketing)

- Use media and corporate activities to roll out new products that target women (product placement, publicity, market segmentation)

- Contribute to charitable causes (e.g., the Hope Project that helped build schools in poor regions) to publicize a corporate brand (hybrid message, event sponsorship, third-party endorsement)

- Use outdoor advertising (e.g., billboards) to persuade women to smoke (tobacco billboards and transit advertising)

- Disseminate the "smoking culture" through the Internet (electronic and social media, relationship and viral marketing)

- Place smoking women on television and movie screens (indoor advertising)

- Engage thousands of retailers in advertising efforts (hand-distributed advertisements, personal selling, point-of-purchase and co-op advertising, brand relationship, direct marketing; Tobacco Control Office 2010)

The preceding advertising practices are enabled by constantly shifting domestic institutional conditions that are but one factor that makes Chinese advertising a fluid, fascinating playground for its practitioners (Wang 2003).

USE OF SOCIAL MEDIA

Such media include broader nontraditional communication outlets such as product and point-of-purchase encounters. For example, some employees of British American Tobacco, a key marketer in China, promote their company on Facebook by posting photographs of British American Tobacco events, products and promotional items and moderating discussion fora (Freeman and Chapman 2010). Some of the employees on Facebook were from countries that are signatories to the WHO FCTC. Thus, such circumvention of an article of the WHO FCTC weakens the industry's argument that "voluntary codes and self-regulation are sufficient. However, voluntary restrictions are ineffective because there is no force of law and ultimately the industry fails to comply with its own voluntary regulations" (World Health Organization 2009, p. 52). Both those outcomes explain in part the modest outcomes of China's antismoking programs.

PRODUCT-CONTENT OBFUSCATION

The second form of marketing practice of China's tobacco industry emanates from its administrative structure which leaves the government with an antinomy regarding fervently marketing tobacco strictly as a business proposition while simultaneously attempting to reduce its consumption because of the growing impact of smoking-attributable illness and mortality. In other words, how can a dominant industry, a state monopoly, ensure that product standards are properly sensitive to consumer welfare? One strategy is downplaying the health effects of smoking in China (Wright and Katz 2007). Another is engaging in product-content obfuscation, by which the consumer is given the impression that brand selection can reduce health risks associated with product use. Thus, advertising labels such as "light," "mild," and "low tar" are as clinically misleading as they are communicatively deceptive. An analysis of urine samples of adult male smokers in Shanghai, China indicated that Chinese low-tar cigarettes do not deliver lower doses of nicotine and carcinogens compared with regular cigarettes; it is unlikely that there would be any reduction in harm from smoking them, yet the CNTC continues to market them as "less harmful" (Gan et al. 2010). Consequently, the government is clamping down on such practices by requiring that cigarette packages not contain misleading messages (e.g., "healthy," "curative effect," "safe") on the effects of cigarette use and that those on the quality of cigarettes (e.g., "low-tar") also be avoided ("The People's," 2011).

CNTC's promotion of low-tar cigarettes as "less harmful" and "fruit-flavored" is tantamount to a violation of WHO FCTC and a dissemination of deceptive, misleading advertising. And such misleading advertising seems persuasive: In a survey of 212 female smokers in Kunming, Yunnan Province, approximately 60 percent of them said they regularly bought "low-tar" cigarettes (Tobacco marketing lures Chinese women 2010) possibly because they thought the effects were zero to negligible. Gao (2008) suggests that "advertisers and their agencies must suspend their own assumptions about deceptive advertising, take a fresh look at the commonly used advertising techniques in the West, and readily adjust their advertising claims in China when necessary" (p. 174).

SPONSORSHIPS AND CAUSE-RELATED MARKETING

Another promotional practice, albeit limited to rural areas, is using sponsorships and cause-related marketing to fund programs and activities of more than 70 schools the industry has dubbed "Tobacco Hope Schools." Some examples: Liaoning Tobacco Trade Hope Elementary School, Panhe Tobacco Elementary School, Qinghai Tobacco Hope Elementary School, Sichuan Tobacco Hope School, Sinan County Gold Leaf Hope Elementary School, and Zunyi Tobacco Hope School. A sign at one of those schools reads: "Genius comes from hard work. Tobacco helps you to be successful." At another: "Talents are brewed by intelligence; tobacco helps you grow up and become accomplished." Engraved on a stone at a Hope school are the following: "Determine to contribute to society. Tobacco helps you to be successful." Advertising to children is potentially harmful. Such a marketing approach, which exposes children to words such as "genius," "tobacco," and "successful," all in the same breath, takes full advantage of sponsorship as a key ingredient of potentially credible, seemingly socially responsible communications. Such sponsorship is not limited to schools, however, as the industry has occasionally sought to sponsor noneducational and civic events. For example, on May 7, 2009, the Shanghai Tobacco (Group) Corporation donated $29 million to the Shanghai Municipal Government to help it build a China pavilion at the May–October 2010 World Expo in Shanghai. That donation was eventually returned to the corporation at the insistence of civic organizations intent on restricting the industry's burgeoning influence in China.

HYPED ADVERTISING MESSAGES

The theme of the May 31 World No-Tobacco Day 2010 was "Protect women from tobacco marketing and smoke," which called world attention to the industry's attempts to encourage women to smoke and sought to make men more aware of their responsibility to avoid smoking around the women with whom they lived and worked. In China, as noted earlier, women are the targets of vigorous advertising campaigns that associate smoking with fashion, beauty and freedom, all a throwback to cigarettes as torches of freedom in early twentieth century United States, where women, as a group, participated in a New York City parade during which they lighted and smoked cigarettes for the first time in public. Thereafter, for U.S. women, smoking became de rigueur on the streets and in pubs, restaurants and movie theaters. However, the impact of tobacco advertising on Chinese women has been constrained by social and cultural forces that celebrate masculine social preferences and discourage those of women.

NONDISCLOSURE

Finally, the industry withholds information on the full panoply of health risks and consequences associated with the use of its product (Kenkel and Chen 2000), and engages largely in what Habermas (1984, 1987) describes as strategic action in preference to communicative action. Communicative action thrives in linguistic media, for example, advertising, publicity and promotion, that are *not* necessarily used solely for transmitting information to exert influence, that is, coercion or manipulation (as in strategic action), but for knowing and reaching an understanding of the health and financial risks of smoking through full-disclosure language and social interaction. Health communication on tobacco use is receiver-centered whenever the message engages the receiver through rationally motivated agreement, that is, free and open dialogue, but not if it is achieved through withholding information or engaging in outright deception. Habermas is neither silent on nor oblivious to the importance of assessing communication conditions or processes. He proffers strategic action as a measure of success and operational effectiveness. Because of the strategic features of such assessment, for example, influence, control, deception and manipulation, it is not the preferred method for reaching an understanding of a sensitive health-behavior issue: smoking and its dire implications for public health.

Implementing a tobacco-sales promotion is much more than transmitting information from CNTC to its customers; rather, it enables at least two parties (CNTC and its customers) to interact in a mediated environment and to reach an understanding. The importance of this distinction is borne out by the process–outcome dichotomy in social–scientific contexts. Marketing communications, as a process, can be used to reach a mutual understanding with the smoking public, an understanding that engenders convictions (e.g., beliefs and attitudes) as precursors for behavior modification through rational, truthful communication. The point here is to ensure a mutual understanding of the act of smoking and its public consequences by using clear, everyday language to make them intelligible, enabling the smoking public to make an informed assessment and to reach a well-thought-out decision.

THE CHINA NATIONAL TOBACCO COMPANY AND THE STATE TOBACCO MONOPOLY ADMINISTRATION

Since its founding in 1982, the CNTC has been a state-owned enterprise (SOE) that has been cooperating with the Ministry of Health in controlling the health consequences of smoking. It is, therefore, a contradiction in terms for CNTC to undermine its own programs even as it seeks ways to enhance and strengthen its commercial mission, which generates an annual profit of $14 billion. In 2003, it contributed 7.38 percent of the government's total revenue (Lee and Jiang 2008). The government allows the tobacco industry to be self-regulated by having voluntary agreements on certain stipulations concerning the advertisement of tobacco, developing its role in education systems and contributing to policymaking for market regulation. To conclude that the government does not capitalize on this organizational structure is an understatement. The number of smokers is direct evidence of how the government allows people to be influenced by enforcing tobacco regulations selectively. The government profits from tobacco sale by not regulating and enforcing strictly. That in itself is a marketing tactic because it enhances the industry's communication strategy of perpetuating the social norms of socializing through cigarette smoking and of offering a carton of cigarettes as a common expression of gratitude.

In evaluating the industry, it must be noted that the largest manufacturer and consumer market are both ensconced in one political entity: China. It owns a majority of the market shares and has the world's largest smoking population. It does not have a national law or regulation that bans smoking in public places; however, there is a hodgepodge of similar provisions such as (a) "1991 Detailed Implementation Rules for the Public Place Hygiene Management Regulation," which banned smoking in 13 public places, including libraries, sports arenas, museums, shops, bookstores and waiting rooms for public transportation (Office of the Leading Small Group for Implementing the Framework Convention on Tobacco Control 2007, p. 13); (b) "Tobacco Monopoly Law of the People's Republic of China," which states that "the state and society shall strengthen the publicity and education of the health hazards of smoking, and prohibit or restrict smoking in public transport and public places" (Office of the Leading Small Group for Implementing the Framework Convention on Tobacco Control 2007, pp. 9–10); and (c) an article in the "Law on the Protection of Minors of the People's Republic of China," which bans smoking in primary and middle-school rooms, in kindergarten and childcare centers and in rooms where minors congregate. In 1997, several government ministries enacted regulations that banned smoking in waiting rooms and in public transportation. Local regulations ban smoking in some places such as medical centers, cinemas and theaters and music and exhibition halls. But such bans do not apply to workplaces. The murky regulatory landscape is compounded by the absence of a monolithic central government and by the devolution of administrative powers on "provincial and local governments setting their own priorities and strategies and exercising different types of intervention" (Dobson 2009, p. 19).

Because the country has 31 provinces and thousands of municipalities, counties, townships and villages, the workings of these disparate institutions are neither aided by a free, unfettered news media system nor by an independent judiciary that can critique local action—or inaction. Loyalty to the STMA in Beijing is, therefore, fraught with risks at local levels.

And, more recently, China signed on November 10, 2003, the WHO FCTC, an international treaty, which, among other provisions, recognizes "the need to develop appropriate mechanisms to address the long-term social and economic implications of successful tobacco demand reduction strategies" (World Health Organization 2005, p. 2); to be alert to any efforts by the tobacco industry to undermine or subvert tobacco-control efforts; and to be cognizant of the industry's activities that have a negative impact on tobacco-control policies. Granted, beginning January 2011, smoking will be banned in indoor public spaces such as workplaces and public transportation vehicles. On May 31, 2010, China's Ministry of Health became the first of the government's departments to ban indoor smoking in its building, a move that was hailed as a step in the right direction by antismoking advocates. But that is the essence of the government's action toward controlling an industry whose $14 billion annual profit is being met with a measly $3 million investment of antismoking campaigns by the Ministry of Health.

ETHICAL ISSUES IN TOBACCO MARKETING COMMUNICATIONS AND REGULATION

Business ethics in China leaves a lot to be desired. Chinese executives accept questionable negotiation strategies more than do their Canadian counterparts (Ma 2010). Chinese information technology professionals do not have a well-developed sense of ethical reasoning, tend to be amoral and make impulsive decisions (Davison et al. 2009), consistent with Ten Bos and Willmott's (2001) arguments that challenge the dominance of rational assumptions in business ethics and assert that emotion is an important source of morality. A study of Chinese executives' perceptions of the role of guanxi and ethics in their business operations indicated three clusters: (a) unethical profit-seekers who are most likely to break the law or exploit regulatory loopholes for profit; (b) antigovernance executives who resist government regulations and prefer to do business within their own social networks; and (c) apathetic executives who are least likely to profit through illegal means and place friendships ahead of profits (Chan et al. 2002). To the degree that most (69 percent) survey respondents fall into the first two clusters indicates the minuscule importance of ethical practices among Chinese business executives. Little wonder, then, that China's younger business executives have been advocating changes in that country's business ethics, but have had little success (Sardy et al. 2010; Wu 1999).

Ethical issues are embedded in two related areas of China's tobacco industry: (a) the marketing practices of the industry itself and (b) the administrative structure for regulating smoking and the advertising and marketing of tobacco products.

MARKETING PRACTICES

Within a decade of manufacturing the first cigarette in the mid-nineteenth century—that manufacturing had been preceded by the use of nonmanufactured tobacco among the Chinese before the first millennium—concerns, now common knowledge, had been raised about its health impact (Gajalakshmi et al. 2000). Several measures have been taken to not only limit tobacco consumption in China but in much of the world.

China's advertising laws do not comprehensively restrict tobacco advertisements and sponsorships. On December 12, 2009, the School of Law at Tsinghua University hosted a mock hearing on the merits and demerits of a comprehensive ban on tobacco advertising and industry sponsorship. Antismoking activists called for laws that instituted such bans, noting that there were no laws on indirect advertising. Tobacco industry representatives, however, argued that because tobacco was a legal product, prohibitions of its advertising and sponsorship were unjustifiable. Business representatives argued that tobacco industry sponsorship reflected the industry's social responsibility and that it should not be restricted. Such diverse views partly explain the central government's failure to limit the industry's marketing and advertising techniques and raises ethical questions about the protection of citizens and the conflict of interest in the control structure of the industry.

ADMINISTRATIVE STRUCTURE

Cigarette production and marketing in China were decentralized through the early 1980s; they were managed largely by provincial and local governments. In January 1982, China's central government instituted a unified, centralized, and vertical management structure for tobacco production and distribution by establishing the CNTC, subsumed under the administration of the Ministry of Economics and Trade (the Ministry of Industry and Information Technology now administers the CNTC). In January 1984, the STMA was established as a monopoly to serve as a conduit between the central government and those at the provincial, district and county levels (Figure 6.1). STMA oversees the CNTC, the largest single manufacturer of tobacco products in the world. STMA delegates to the CNTC full authority to (a) allocate quotas for tobacco leaf production to each province; (b) procure tobacco leaf, for which it has monopoly; (c) transport and store tobacco leaf; and (d) produce and market cigarettes. Private or public companies and individuals cannot purchase tobacco leaf without CNTC's approval and retailers are required to have its approval before selling cigarettes.

STMA controls tobacco leaf production, and the procuring, pricing and marketing of cigarettes. It is also responsible for developing government policy and enforcing regulations, such as those governing warnings on packages. It does not involve health departments in policymaking, keeping that role to itself and the government departments it nominates. The STMA issued regulations on cigarette package labeling that took effect in January 2009. The warnings on packaging fall well short of the requirements. According to Article 11

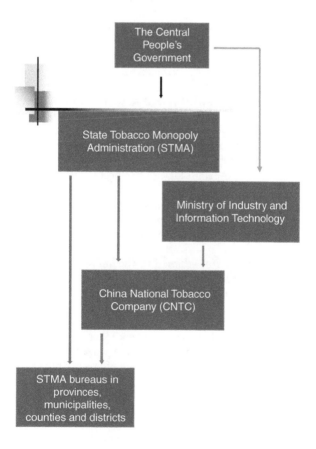

FIGURE 6.1

Administrative Structure for China's Tobacco Management

of the WHO FCTC, endorsed by China, warning signs should cover 50 percent of the display area; Chinese regulations require only 30 percent, and the warnings are in tiny characters, again, in defiance of WHO FCTC guidelines. And those health warnings should describe in specific terms the harm that results from tobacco use; however, China's warnings merely state that "Smoking harms your health," and "Quitting smoking early helps reduce the risk."

On China's adherence to the terms of Article 11, Yang Gonghuan, director of China's National Office of Tobacco Control, said, "By issuing domestic regulations on cigarette package labeling that flaunted Article 11, the State Tobacco Monopoly Administration hampered the best way for the public to learn about the harm caused by tobacco. The Administration's strategy of dodging price increases also blunts the effect of tobacco tax increases by the Ministry of Finance" (Cui 2010, p. 251). A reason for the foot-dragging is the economic significance of tobacco (Hu et al. 2006), particularly in the remote, poorer sections of the country, where, in Yunnan province, for example, the government depends on tobacco sales for more than 50 percent of its revenues (Wright and Katz 2007) and for financing infrastructural projects.

ETHICAL THEORIES

On May 12, 2008, the Wenchuan earthquake struck China's Sichuan province, killing nearly 70,000 people and injuring nearly 400,000. That disaster served as a beachhead for the tobacco industry's sponsoring schools and positioning itself as a caring, all-around socially responsible corporate citizen. Among the first responders to the earthquake site were tobacco companies, which quickly rebuilt schools and named the first rebuilt school the Sichuan Tobacco Hope Elementary School, which also serves as one of the many educational centers of Chinese restoration. Associating that type of philanthropic act with both a cause and with public perception of the tobacco industry is a time-honored tactic for enhancing both organizational reputation and a corporation's standing in communities. But such an act raises key normative questions within the context of the universals of classical ethical theories.

First, from a utilitarian (that is, macro-teleological) standpoint, to whom does the greatest benefit of cigarette consumption and largess accrue? Does it go to the user of a tobacco product or to the municipal and provincial governments or to the nation in general? Does tobacco use promote the good of society? Such questions should have been raised during corporate deliberations on taking creative risks by, say, dubbing schools as "Tobacco Hope Schools" and in using a mantra that associates genius with the tobacco industry.

From a deontological (that is, macro-deontological) perspective, whose duty or obligation is being fulfilled and by whose rules, laws, principles or maxims? Are product appeals to smoking as beautiful and endearing considered morally appropriate, quite apart from the consequences of such appeals? The industry has a fiduciary responsibility to its key investor, the government of the People's Republic of China, based on the universal maxim that a commercial enterprise is in the business of manufacturing and selling a product and of making a profit.

From the notion of (organizational) virtue ethics, does the industry demonstrate universal traits (or character) such as integrity, courage, temperance, compassion, honesty and justice against which our evaluation of its practices leads us to conclude that the institution's disposition to the community is morally defective or morally upright?

Elementary school children's educational experiences are being supported by direct gifts from tobacco sale. The same school children are being primed early in life to be benevolent, to gravitate toward an institution whose disposition is associated with an action that is as helpful as it is destructive to the welfare of the very young.

An organizational disposition to be benevolent? In a time of crisis, China's tobacco industry rescued victims of the Wenchuan earthquake rubble and rebuilt schools. These same children, some of whose parents were addicted to nicotine, could become adults also addicted to cigarettes and then their children would go to the same schools in which their parents were enrolled, only to reinvigorate the vicious cycle.

Can the conduct of the industry be morally justified on grounds of universal ethical egoism (or the self-interest criterion), in which the industry's best interest dominates the ethical decision-making process? To the degree that the industry continues to seek ways to downplay the clinical effects of its product and to parlay the economic benefits of its product line, its business rationale, ultimately, points to organizational, not national, interest.

Situation ethics or ethical relativism, although neither a classical ethical theory nor an ethical universal, can be used to justify the government's response to a major health challenge. Christians and colleagues (1993) write, "Ethical relativism is the belief that because moral judgments vary across cultures and historical periods, all moral systems are equally good, even if they are antithetical" (p. 59). That is a long-standing issue that threatens organizational or business ethics. A challenge to classical ethical theory is the endearing appeal of moral relativism couched within the frameworks of cultural diversity and of cultural relativism. The tobacco industry's marketing practices, for example, the sponsorship of civic and societal events as gift exchanges, could be culturally justified, making such cultural relativism appropriately decoupled from universal ethics.

Two cultural influences on Chinese managers' decision-making processes are Confucianism and folk wisdom. Confucian teachings emphasize propriety or reason (*li*), family, emotions, relationships (or *guanxi*), harmony and trust (Chan 2008; Ho and Redfern 2010; Romar 2002; Zhu 2009). Chinese managers' thinking and behavior reflect traditional values of Chinese folk wisdom, in which are embedded Confucian values (Szeto 2010). To the degree that these traditional values (e.g., Confucianism's human virtues) underpin Western classical theories (e.g., virtue ethics), Chinese managers have a wide arsenal of ethics repertoire from which they can draw complementary insights in making sound ethical business decisions.

FUTURE DIRECTIONS: PROPOSALS FOR PUBLIC POLICYMAKING ON TOBACCO CONTROL

China's first national forum on tobacco-control strategy, The National Conference on Tobacco Control Policy Development in China in the 21st Century, held in 2002 in response to China's leading the world in cigarette production and consumption, called for an aggressive tobacco-control policy to stem the upsurge in smoking-attributable mortality. Moran and colleagues (2010) iterated that call: "We projected that an aggressive tobacco control policy—lowering active smoking prevalence to 20 percent by 2020 and 10 percent by 2030—would produce a reduction in total mortality in Chinese men despite adverse trends in other risk factors" (p. 248). China earned "The Dirty Ashtray Award" during the third session of the WHO FCTC conference in South Africa in 2008 for "attempting to make a mockery of Article 11 guidelines including preferring beautiful cigarette packages over the health of its citizens" (Grasping at Straws? 2010). That was a clear indication that some in the global community did not think China was taking serious measures to rein in a public health epidemic.

The complex interplay of distal and proximal psychosocial issues, cultural factors, socioeconomic, family and personal factors that influence tobacco use and smoking initiation among adolescents in China (Arpawong et al. 2010; Grenard et al. 2006; Guo et al. 2007) and the nation's high smoking rate further substantiate the call for an aggressive tobacco-control policy, an appropriate action for which this chapter argues.

As noted in a preceding paragraph, smoking prevalence rates are still high, despite a more than 10 percent decline among male smokers. Such rates vary by gender, occupational groups, and by educational accomplishment, despite the country's implementing tobacco-control policies, restricting multinational companies' marketing practices in China, banning smoking in public places and restricting smoking at home (Abdullah et al. 2010; Hu et al. 2006; Yang 2008; Yang et al. 2001), and despite decades of efforts to control tobacco use. The prevalence rates among Chinese men is 57%; among women, 3%; among factory workers, 71%; among those without any formal education, 72% and among the college-educated, 54%.

In Poland, a local nongovernmental organization, the Health Promotion Foundation, used lobbying, advocacy, media relations and nationwide campaigns to help reduce tobacco use and its clinical effects (Malinowska-Sempruch et al. 2006). In China, two such organizations, the Chinese Association on Tobacco Control, a Beijing-based group, and the ThinkTank Research Center for Health Developments, are making inroads into a market protected, as it were, by an industry–government "firewall."

By implementing the following six tobacco-control proposals for values-driven public policymaking, China can more effectively manage a looming health issue conflated with economics, enforce requirements of WHO FCTC, and by extension, respond comprehensively to the determined health needs of the entire nation vis-à-vis smoking. The proposals are to (a) restructure the tobacco industry and privatize the manufacturing and distribution of tobacco products in a manner that obviates the palpable conflicts of interest in developing and implementing national tobacco-control policies; (b) develop rigorous legislation on smoking, ban smoking in all indoor public places nationwide and develop stringent enforcement mechanisms embedded in a national legislation on tobacco control; (c) require China's full and timely compliance with WHO FCTC and publicize compliance with all articles of WHO FCTC; (d) clarify the authority of the Ministry of Health and significantly increase its current minuscule annual budget of $3 million for antismoking campaigns, ensuring it to be commensurate with the $14 billion annual profit of the tobacco industry and designate the ministry as the point agency for national tobacco-control efforts; (e) craft community-based, antismoking campaigns that are, ultimately, broadly participatory and are cognizant of and sensitive to the multifactorial dimensions of tobacco use in China; and (f) ground public policymaking on tobacco-risk reduction in ethical universals. Each such proposal will now be described.

RESTRUCTURE THE TOBACCO INDUSTRY

The authority of the agencies responsible for tobacco production and distribution must be clearly delineated from that of the agencies charged with tobacco control. Lu (2009) noted that a challenge of business ethics in China "lies in improving the managerial economy, working on problems related to governance, and to the separation of ownership from management" (p. 459).

Fifteen government agencies are involved directly in tobacco control in China, an involvement that, from the perspective of nongovernmental organizations, is both a strength and a limitation of the country's tobacco-control efforts. From the perspective of China's antismoking observers, the immanent conflict of interest in the STMA-CNTC partnership has raised mammoth questions on the effectiveness of both agencies in at once producing tobacco products and controlling and preventing their use.

Sandford (2003) bemoans the regulation and performance of tobacco products, arguing that such regulation should be the responsibility of health authorities and observing the tobacco industry's dominance in a strictly anathematic context—that is, as detrimental to public health: "The tobacco industry dominates the process of tobacco and tobacco products standard setting to advance its political and commercial needs, therefore pre-empting the passage of regulatory policies that would indeed protect the health of the public" (p. 11). That notion is iterated by Wu Yiqun, Deputy Director of ThinkTank Research Center for Health Developments, a grassroots antismoking group: "The nation needs a tobacco-control institution that is independent from tobacco industry involvement and intervention. The tobacco industry should be cut off from politics and government" (Juan 2009). The Ministry of Health, whose bailiwick is the nation's health, should be in the forefront of attempts to control smoking, not the Ministry of Industry and Information Technology now responsible for implementing tobacco-health initiatives, particularly China's compliance with the WHO FCTC, a role that includes many ministries, including the Ministry of Health. The argument here, then, is for a functional, administrative separation between the government as an overseer and the government as an implementing agency. The organization of state institutions, argues Hsueh (2011), accounts for the state's capacity to exert central authority over an industry and to influence regulations and the way the state enforces them. The CNTC should, therefore, play no role in enforcing governmental injunction. In essence, there should be palpable separation of powers, roles and responsibilities, and enforcement mechanisms of government directives should be forceful and free of being commingled with implementation.

Related to the administrative structure is the question of the appropriateness of the Ministry of Industry and Information Technology in playing a leading role in tobacco use and public health, a responsibility that should fall squarely with the Ministry of Health. It is argued here that tobacco use is a lightning rod for government policy and public concern only because of its impact and deleterious effect on public health, a responsibility of health ministries worldwide. The Ministry of Health should play the lead role, particularly in ensuring the nation's compliance with WHO FCTC.

Finally, the CNTC should be privatized and its market further transformed from largely central to a full-blown market economy. The industry should be sold to private investors who will assume business risks, even as the government continues to close small manufacturing plants while guaranteeing employment to current employees. China has demonstrated to the world that it can liberalize economically without surrendering to liberal politics or engaging in ideological compromise and that its industry serves "as the world's largest billboard advertisement for the new alternative of 'going capitalist and staying autocratic'" (Halper 2010, p. 32). After all, the Chinese government is building on Communist Party leader Deng Xiaoping's initiatives by deploying what Hsueh (2011) describes as liberation two-step—a shift from universal control at the aggregate level across all industries to selective control by sector, employing a bifurcated strategy by which it deliberately controls state-industry relations and enforces economic regulations even as it liberalizes the economy at the aggregate level.

STMA's operational authority and responsibilities should be devolved on the Ministry of Industry and Information Technology. Some top Chinese officials have expressed the notion that within five to six years, the Chinese tobacco monopoly will be decentralized and privatized (Hu 2007). Granted, SOEs financed by state-controlled financial institutions dominate China's largely state-planned economy. However, the unique merit of this argument for privatization is based on its potential to ensure that the government's tobacco-oversight program (which will now be under the portfolio of the Ministry of Industry and Information Technology) will no longer be commingled with a product that does not have any known clinically redeeming value. The government can then focus on public health, collaborating with several agencies and civil society groups that have a stake in the nation's well-being.

However, privatizing an SOE is not without its challenges and social consequences, as indicated in the experiences of post-communist Russia and of the former Eastern Europe. In Poland, for example, the ability of stakeholders to negotiate appropriate legal recognition before the privatization of SOEs freed the stage from insider–outsider conflicts over stock ownership (Woodruff 2004). In Russia, however, the absence of negotiation and of effective post-privatization regulation set the stage for fraught relationships; for long-running legal conflicts among interest groups over property rights; and for privatization that was motivated, not by economic or management reasons, but by the greed of the old Soviet ruling class, the *nomenklatura*, who sought to take advantage of an evolving privatization (Berdnikova and Liamin 2002; Goldman 2004; Theft of the Century 2002; Woodruff 2004). Consequently, Russians are critical of privatization, which they see as an aggrandizement of wealth and power for the elite (Debardeleben 1999).

Privatization, if managed strategically, can have at least two major benefits: improve performance of the privatized enterprises and provide citizens a stake in a nation's transformation process (The World Bank 1996). In Russia and in former central and eastern Europe, privatization has had positive effects on social services, incentives, human capital, productivity and on efficiency through competition (Frydman et al. 1998; Perevalov et al. 2000; Pohl et al. 1997). In the case of China, it will also be a welcome opportunity to rid its administrative system of an incestuous relationship between two government agencies whose actions are demonstrably inimical to the well-being of their citizens. But there is the far-fetched possibility that a privatized CNTC could merely shift a negative public perception from a government-run agency to the private sector.

However, China is not new to such restructuring. Since the 1970s, it managed effectively the de-collectivization of the rural economy and the growth of private and quasiprivate enterprises. It has, since the 1990s, also closed inefficient SOEs and improved the performance of others and transformed state planning into a market-driven regime. The STMA, for example, decreased the number of regional tobacco companies from 185 in 2001 to 62 in 2004 and domestic cigarette brands from 1,049 in 2001 to 370 in 2004. Inarguably, if privatized, industry prices are likely to fall, as a consequence of moving from monopoly to competition, and, ceteris paribus, could result in higher output and more smoking. Therefore, significant regulatory oversight is essential.

PASS LEGISLATION ON TOBACCO PROMOTION AND ON SMOKING IN ALL INDOOR PUBLIC PLACES

China will be well served by legislation similar to the U.S. Family Smoking Prevention and Tobacco Control Act, which was signed into law on June 22, 2009—a bold step toward placing stricter limits on tobacco advertising, marketing and promotional practices. A similar legislation will have two possible effects on China's tobacco industry. First, it would reduce significantly the incidence of smoking among adolescents by eliminating persuasive communications and inducements to smoke. Second, in the short term, it would increase significantly tobacco industry's profits from savings that accrue from not spending vast sums on advertising and promotion.

Seventeen WHO FCTC signatories have comprehensive smoke-free policies that provide effective protection from secondhand smoke. Such countries tend to have strong enforcement provisions. Smoking bans in China are being instituted gradually. Only one central government agency, the Ministry of Health, on January 9, 2011, began banning indoor smoking in all medical centers and administrative facilities. Such a piecemeal effort, although encouraging, robs the nation of the momentum to reduce the prevalence of tobacco use. Article 8 of the WHO FCTC stipulates that all members "shall adopt and implement in areas of existing national jurisdiction . . . measures, providing for protection from exposure to tobacco smoke in indoor workplaces, public transport, indoor public places, and, as appropriate, other public places" (World Health Organization 2005, p. 8). Such an implementation in China should come with strong enforcement mechanisms. A report by the Tobacco Control Office (2010) calls for protecting women and banning tobacco advertising, noting that female smokers tend to suffer additional ailments: early aging, menstrual disorders, low estrogen levels, osteoporosis, coronary disease and breast cancer.

REQUIRE TIMELY COMPLIANCE WITH WHO FCTC

The extent of the smoking epidemic in some nations requires that they be allowed more lead time than others for developing tobacco-control policies. In 2007, more than one year after China's signing of the WHO FCTC, the government established the Implementation Coordination Mechanism to encourage the country's compliance with the expectations of that convention. The enactment by the General Administration of Quality Supervision, Inspection and Quarantine and the STMA of *The Provision on Cigarette Packaging, Labeling and Marketing in the People's Republic of China*, which took effect on January 1, 2009, has done little to rein in unethical advertising or marketing practices or to stop the tobacco industry from interfering with tobacco regulation—a conflict of interest (Lv et al. 2011). A significant gap, therefore, still exists between requirements of FCTC and the current state of affairs in China. Further delay in implementing WHO FCTC guidelines can mean more premature deaths and lost opportunities for maintaining vital public health. Increases in tobacco price and tax (Article 6 of the WHO FCTC), for example, can be promptly implemented in light of the finding that most tobacco-control leaders consider that approach an independently effective intervention (Ali and Koplan 2010). Publicizing the nation's efforts toward accomplishing compliance will serve as a reminder to citizens about the nation's commitment to fulfilling the terms of the convention.

CLARIFY THE AUTHORITY OF THE MINISTRY OF HEALTH AND INCREASE ITS OPERATIONAL BUDGET

The Ministry of Health should be *the* government agency that has full (not partial, not ad hoc) oversight for the nation's public health. It, of course, should collaborate with several other government agencies (e.g., the China Center for Disease Control and Prevention) and similar bureaus in fulfilling its mission, for which it competes with the likes of the Ministry of Industry and Technology.

The budgets of the ministry and of the National Office of Tobacco Control are minuscule for the size and complexity of their complementary responsibilities. That for the latter agency is 0.5 percent of the total budget for disease control and prevention. Conducting national antismoking campaigns requires an investment that is commensurate with the financial strength of the smoking-promoting agency: the tobacco industry. To the extent that public awareness of the dangers of smoking and of the manipulative activities of the industry seems lost on a good many Chinese, particularly those in rural areas, the public's susceptibility to the industry's marketing practices requires urgent public education on the subject.

IMPLEMENT COMMUNITY-DRIVEN, ANTISMOKING CAMPAIGNS

China faces an enormous challenge in modifying smoking-related social norms and in persuading smokers to stop smoking (e.g., Yang et al. 2001; Zhu et al. 2004). Such campaigns must ordinarily be participatory, which means that everyday citizens and civil society groups such as the Chinese Association on Tobacco Control and the ThinkTank Research Center for Health Developments will participate fully in conceiving, implementing and evaluating all campaigns. The value of such community involvement is important in ensuring the salience, relevance and acceptance of messages.

The industry is not short on spin. An example is the case of billboards with the message "Ai Wo Chung Hua," which, prima facie, translates into a public admission of patriotism (an endearing trope to love one's country): "I Love China," which fundamentally is a pun on the country's commitment to implementing the WHO FCTC, in light of the general knowledge that "Chung Hua" on a billboard is a subtle reference to a high-priced cigarette marketed by the Shanghai Tobacco (Group) Corporation. And that the same billboards also have the standard health notice, "Smoking can damage your health," raises questions about the subtext of the real message, namely, that it is an advertisement for Chung Hua cigarettes. Public awareness of the broad spectrum of tobacco issues—and their subtleties—is a fundamental criterion for message reception, acceptance and compliance.

The importance of community engagement is accentuated by geographical differences in the health consequences of tobacco use in China. In one study, 55 percent of Chinese nonsmokers and 69 percent of Chinese smokers believed that cigarettes did them "little or no harm" and about the same numbers believed that passive smoking did little or no harm to their health (Kenkel and Chen 2000). Smoking rates were still high even among Chinese male respondents who were aware of smoking's health hazards. The dissemination of information about the health risks of smoking has been shown to decrease demand for tobacco products in many middle-income and low-income countries.

A clearly defined public for antismoking campaigns in China is the adolescent public. Effective smoking cessation and prevention programs must understand that adolescents are a key public for reducing tobacco use in China (Chen et al. 2006). Also, such programs must incorporate Chinese adolescents' self-reporting of attributes for smoking such as curiosity (experimenting with tobacco products), social image (appearing cool, tough, confident and attractive to the opposite sex), social belonging (strengthening group membership and social relationships), and coping (calming down when stressed; Guo et al. 2010). Such incorporation is consistent with the view that rather than devoting resources to increasing public awareness of the details of tobacco risk, it is important to better understand the unique blend of normalizing impulses already militating against tobacco control in China and to integrate those impulses into new smoking-cessation techniques and to provide greater access to well-proven techniques such as quitting clinics and hotline-based counseling (Kohrman 2004). Additionally, such campaigns need to be segmented in a manner responsive to the elderly who derive substantial benefits from quitting smoking even after the age of 65 years (Lam et al. 2007).

GROUND PUBLIC POLICYMAKING ON TOBACCO IN ETHICAL UNIVERSALS

The notion of ethics advanced in this chapter acknowledges two realities: (a) differences in ethics, values and ideologies across China (Sardy et al. 2010), where social and corporate cultural values affect ethical attitudes and choices (Krueger and Ding 2009; Lam and Shi 2008; Lan et al. 2009; Whitcomb et al. 1998); and (b) debates on the presence or absence of "common morality," universal morality, universally shared values, or universally shared ethical principles (Beauchamp 2003; Turner 2003; Macklin 1998, 1999; Marshall and Koenig 2004; Veatch 2003). The position adopted here is that although it is fruitful to distinguish between universality and particularity, there are expectations, supreme moral principles and values that are broadly universal across societies and appeal to the nations' public policymaking on tobacco use. Veatch (2003) enunciates that position:

The core idea of a common morality is that all humans—at least all morally serious humans—have a pretheoretical awareness of certain moral norms. The claim is that normal humans intuit or in some other way know that there is something wrong with things like lying or breaking promises or killing people" (p. 189).

Some of the universally shared insights are health security, human rights, institutional integrity, truth telling and the principles of doing no harm, avoiding killing and respecting autonomy, all of which are at once relevant to analyzing marketing practices of China's tobacco industry within the contexts of classical ethical theories. To the degree that China's health security is threatened by its tobacco industry, that some of the latter's marketing communications practices leave much to be desired and that the Chinese are consistently deserving of the right to breathe clean air, a tobacco-control policy should be grounded in such universal ethical values in tandem with local practices that are not antithetical to the direction of that policy. Younger generation Chinese executives are receptive to Western management concepts, which tend to promote pragmatic approaches and openness (Ko 1998), making the universals both meaningful and instructive as Chinese business managers share ethical values with their counterparts in other world regions. U.S. and Chinese business executives, for example, believe equally in the positive relationship between ethics and conduct; on some issues, the Chinese reported a much stronger belief than do U.S. business executives that positive ethical practices are rewarded by more business and profit (Baglione and Zimmener 2007).

The questions that should be raised, then, are those consistent with the theoretical directions of this chapter—from utilitarianism to egoism—and focused on ethical universals such as human rights, national health security and institutional integrity.

SUMMARY AND CONCLUSION

Effective tobacco control requires a broad mix of complementary interventions anchored in policymaking. No intervention, in itself, can address the complexities of tobacco marketing and use. This chapter, therefore, underscores the need for novel, aggressive approaches to developing and implementing a tobacco-control policy in a high-use tobacco country, one that requires an overhaul of the administrative structure (and relationships) of key agencies in that economy. But more than that, it argues that privatizing the industry can disentangle the government from a sordid conflict of interest: manufacturing and selling through marketing communications a clinically harmful product while simultaneously self-regulating. Public policymaking that is based on the six public policymaking proposals will enable China to serve as a model in tobacco control and regulatory enforcement. The financial and human capital of China's rising economy is more than adequate for it to deliver on a promise that is inarguably attainable and whose beneficial effects on the nation can be far-reaching. Such a policy, if well grounded in ethical universals, for example, truth telling, compassion, institutional integrity and human rights, will enable the country to not only strengthen its place as an economic powerhouse but to also provide smoking-cessation programs and other tobacco-related health services that its citizens deserve urgently.

DISCUSSION QUESTIONS

1. Assume that a newly privatized CNTC has requested that you consult with it on how its staff and contractors can maximize their use of social media as an antismoking business tool. What specific social media–appropriate tactics will you propose?
2. If you were to advocate the application of classical ethical theories to everyday practices of a health-related government agency, say, China's Ministry of Health, what key elements of those theories would you emphasize and why?
3. Propose at least two values-driven proposals as complements to those presented in this chapter. Justify each.
4. Identify the limits of the administrative restructuring of the relationships between the CNTC and the STMA in addressing conflict-of-interest issues identified in this chapter.
5. Jürgen Habermas uses the modifier *strategic*, as in strategic action, in contradistinction to how communication practitioners generally use *strategic*, as in strategic communication. In practical terms, is there really a contradiction in terms here? Why or why not?
6. Apply arguments presented in this chapter to distinguish ethics per se from applied ethics.
7. This chapter identifies some actions that China's regulatory agencies have taken so far in response to the country's tobacco industry overreaching in its marketing communications. What additional actions would you recommend?

REFERENCES

Abdullah, S. A., T., Yang, J. Beard. 2010. "Predictors of women's attitudes toward World Health Organization Framework Convention on Tobacco Control policies in urban China." *Journal of Women's Health*, 19, 903–909.

Ali, M. K., J. P. Koplan. 2010. "Promoting health through tobacco taxation." *The Journal of the American Medical Association*, 303, 357–358. doi:10.1001/jama.2010.23.

Arpawong, T. E., P. Sun, M. C.-C. Chang, P. Gallaher, P. Zengchang, Q. Guo, C. A. Johnson, J. Unger. 2010. "Family and personal protective factors moderate the effects of adversity and negative disposition on smoking among Chinese adolescents." *Substance Use & Misuse*, 45, 1367–1387.

Baglione, S., T. Zimmener. 2007. "Ethics, values, and leadership beliefs and practices: An empirical study of U.S. and Chinese business executives." *Chinese Management Studies,* 1, 111–125.

Beauchamp, T. L. 2003. "A defense of the common morality." *Kennedy Institute of Ethics Journal*, 13, 259–274.

Berdnikova, T. B., M. A. Liamin. 2002. "Social consequences of privatization." *Sociological Research*, 41, 49–54.

Brand, V., A. Slater. 2003. "Using a qualitative approach to gain insights into the business ethics experiences of Australian managers in China." *Journal of Business Ethics*, 45(3), 167–182.

Chan, G. K. Y. 2008. "The relevance and value of Confucianism in contemporary business ethics." *Journal of Business Ethics,* 77, 347–360.

Chan, R. Y. K., L. T. W. Cheng, R. W. F. Szeto. 2002. "The dynamics of guanxi and ethics for Chinese executives." *Journal of Business Ethics*, 41, 327–336.

Chao, M. 2009. Make cigarettes less affordable. *China Daily*. Retrieved from http://www.chinadaily.com.cn/bizchina/2009-08/12/content_8560954.htm (August 12, 2009).

Chen, X., X. Fang, X. Li, B. Stanton, D. Lin. 2006. "Stay away from tobacco: A pilot trial of a school-based adolescent smoking prevention program in Beijing, China." *Nicotine & Tobacco Research*, 8, 227–237.

Choi, C. J., D. Digol. 2010. "Ethical infrastructure: A new requirement of the state's industrial policy." *Journal of Public Affairs*, 10, 225–232.

Choukroune, L. 2009. "'Harmonious' norms for global marketing the Chinese way." *Journal of Business Ethics*, 88(Suppl. 3), 411–432.

Christians, C. G., J. P. Ferré, P. M. Fackler. 1993. *Good News: Social Ethics and the Press*. New York: Oxford University Press.

Cohan, J. A. 2001. "Towards a new paradigm in the ethics of women's advertising." *Journal of Business Ethics*, 33, 323–337.

Cui, W. 2010. "China wrestles with tobacco control." *Bulletin of the World Health Organization*, 88, 251–252. doi:10.2471/BLT.10.040410.

Debardeleben, J. 1999. "Attitudes towards privatization in Russia." *Europe–Asia Studies*, 51, 447–465.

DeRuiter, W., G. Faulkner. 2006. "Tobacco harm reduction strategies: The case for physical activity." *Nicotine & Tobacco Research*, 8, 157–168.

Dobson, W. 2009. *Gravity Shift: How Asia's New Economic Powerhouses Will Shape the Twenty-first Century*. Toronto: University of Toronto Press.

Freeman, B., S. Chapman. 2010. "British American Tobacco on Facebook: Undermining article 13 of the global World Health Organization Framework Convention Framework Convention on Tobacco Control." *Tobacco Control*, 19(3), e1–e9. doi:10.1136/tc.2009.032847.

Frydman, R., C. Gray, M. Hessel, A. Rapaczynski. 1998. *When Does Privatization Work? The Impact of Private Ownership on Corporate Performance in the Transition Economies*. Economic Research Reports. No. 98–32. New York: C.V. Starr Center for Applied Economics, New York University.

Gajalakshmi, C. K., P. Jha, K. Ranson, S. Nguyen. 2000. "Global patterns of smoking-attributable mortality." In *Tobacco Control in Developing Countries*, edited by P. Jha, F. J. Chaloupka, 11–39. New York: Oxford University Press.

Gan, Q., W. Lu, J. Xu, X. Li, M., Goniewicz, N. L. Benowitz, S. A. Glantz. 2010. "Chinese 'low-tar' cigarettes do not deliver lower levels of nicotine and carcinogens." *Tobacco Control*. 19, 374–379. Advance online publication. doi:10.1136/tc.2009.033092.

Gao, Z. 2008. "Controlling deceptive advertising in China: An overview." *Journal of Public Policy and Marketing*, 27, 165–177.

Glynn, T., J. R. Seffrin, O. W. Brawley, N. Grey, H. Ross. 2010. "The globalization of tobacco use: 21 challenges for the 21st century." *CA: A Cancer Journal for Clinicians*, 60, 50–61. doi:10.3322/caac.20052.

Grasping at Straws? 2010. *Global Times*. Retrieved from http://www.globaltimes.cn/www/english/metro-beijing/community/events/2010-06/538302_2.html (June 3, 2010).

Goldman, M. I. 2004. *The Piratization of Russia: Russian Reform Goes Awry*. New York: Routledge.

Grenard, J. L., Q., Guo, G. K. Jasuja, J. B. Unger, C.-P. Chou, P. E. Gallaher, P. Sun, P., Palmer, C. A. Johnson, 2006. "Influences affecting adolescent smoking behavior in China." *Nicotine & Tobacco Research*, 8, 245–255.

Gu, D., T. N. Kelly, X. Wu, J. Chen, J. M. Samet, J.-F. Huang, M. Zhu, J. Chen, C.-S. Chen, X. Duan, M. J. Klag, J. He. 2009. "Mortality attributable to smoking in China." *The New England Journal of Medicine*, 360, 150–159.

Guo, Q., C. A. Johnson, J. B. Unger, L. Lee, B. Xie, C.-P. Chou, P. H. Palmer, P. Sun, P. Gallaher, M. Pentz. 2007. "Utility of the theory of reasoned action and theory of planned behavior for predicting Chinese adolescent smoking." *Addictive Behaviors*, 32, 1066–1081.

Guo, Q., J. B. Unger, S. P. Azen, C. Li, D. Spruijt-Metz, P. H. Palmer, C.-P. Chou, L. Lee, P. Sun, C. A. Johnson. 2010. "Cognitive attributions for smoking among adolescents in China." *Addictive Behaviors*, 35, 95–101.

Habermas, J. 1984. *The Theory of Communicative Action: Reason and the Rationalization of Society*, Vol. 1 (T. McCarthy, transl.). Boston: Beacon Press (Original work published 1981).

Habermas, J. 1987. *The Theory of Communicative Action: Lifeworld and System: A Critique of Functionalist Reason*, vol. 2 (T. McCarthy, transl.). Boston: Beacon Press. (Original work published 1981).

Halper, S. 2010. *The Beijing Consensus: How China's Authoritarian Model Will Dominate the Twenty-first Century*. New York: Basic Books.

Ho, C., K. A. Redfern. 2010. "Consideration of the role of guanxi in the ethical judgments of Chinese managers." *Journal of Business Ethics*, 96, 207–221.

Hsueh, R. 2011. *China's Regulatory State: A New Strategy for Globalization*. Ithaca, NY: Cornell University Press.

Hu, T.-W., Z. Mao, M. Ong, E. Tong, M. Tao, H. Jiang, K. Hammond, K. R. Smith, J. de Beyer, A. Yurekli. 2006. "China at the crossroads: The economics of tobacco and health." *Tobacco Control*, 15 (Suppl. 1), i37–i41. doi:10.1136/tc.2005.014621.

Hu, T. 2007. "The role of government in tobacco leaf production in China: National and local interventions." *International Journal of Public Policy*, 2, 235–248.

Hu, T. 2008. Introduction. In *Series on Contemporary China*: Vol. 12. *Tobacco Control Policy Analysis in China: Economics and Health*, edited by T. Hu, 1–9. Singapore: World Scientific.

Ip, P. K. 2009. "Is Confucianism good for business ethics in China?" *Journal of Business Ethics*, 88, 463–476.

Juan, S. 2009. Efforts to extinguish smoking hampered. *China Daily*. Retrieved from http://www.chinadaily.com.cn/china/2009-08/11/content_8552332.htm (August 11, 2009).

Kenkel, D., L. Chen. 2000. Consumer information and tobacco use. In *Tobacco Control in Developing Countries*, edited by Jha P., F. J. Chaloupka, 177–214. New York: Oxford University Press.

Kenkel, D., D. R. Lillard, F. Liu. 2009. "An analysis of life-course smoking behavior in China." *Health Economics*, 18, S147–S156.

Ko, E. 1998. "Lessons in leadership." *Asian Business*, 34(2), 53–56.

Kohrman, M. 2004. "Should I quit? Tobacco, fraught identity, and the risks of governmentality in urban China." *Urban Anthropology*, 33, 211–245.

Krueger, D. A. 2008. "The ethics of global supply chains in China—convergences of East and West." *Journal of Business Ethics*, 79, 113–120.

Krueger, D. A., B. Ding. 2009. "Ethical analysis and challenges of two international firms in China." *Journal of Business Ethics*, 89, 167–182.

Lam, T. H., Z. B. Li, S. Y. Ho, W. M. Chan, K. S. Ho, M. K. Tham, B. J. Cowling, C. M. Schooling, G. M. Leung. 2007. "Smoking, quitting and mortality in an elderly cohort of 56,000 Hong Kong Chinese." *Tobacco Control*, 16, 182–189. doi:10.1136/tc.2006.019505.

Lam, K.-C., G. Shi. 2008. "Factors affecting ethical attitudes in mainland China and Hong Kong." *Journal of Business Ethics*, 77, 463–479.

Lan, G., Z. Ma, J. Cao, H. Zhang. 2009. "A comparison of personal values of Chinese accounting practitioners and students." *Journal of Business Ethics*, 88, 59–76.

Laugesen, M., M. Scollo, D. Sweanor, S. Shiffman, J. Gitchell, K. Barnsley, M. Jacobs, G. A. Giovino, S. A. Glantz, R. A. Daynard, G. N. Connolly, J. R. Difranza. 2000. "World's best practice in tobacco control." *Tobacco Control*, 9, 228–236.

Lee, A. H., Y. Jiang. 2008. Tobacco control programs in China. In *Series on Contemporary China*, edited by T. Hu, Vol. 12. *Tobacco Control Policy Analysis in China: Economics and Health*, 33–55. Singapore: World Scientific.

Li, L., H.-H. Yong. 2009. "Tobacco advertising on the street in Kunming, China." *Tobacco Control*, 18, 63. doi:10.1136/tc.2008.027433.

Liu, Y., L. Jiang, H. Xiao, Q. Liu, B. Li, W. Xu. 2010. "Newspaper coverage about smoking in leading Chinese newspapers in past nine years." *Tobacco Control*, 19, 345–346. Advanced online publication. doi:10.1136/tc.2009.034793.

Liu, Y., C. Pearson. 2010. "An empirical study of the determinants of foreign investment in China: A Western Australian perspective." *Journal of Asia-Pacific Business*, 11, 99–120.

Lu, X. 2009. "A Chinese perspective: Business ethics in China now and in the future." *Journal of Business Ethics*, 86, 451–461.

Lv, J., M. Su, Z. Hong, T. Zhang, X. Huang, B. Wang, L. Li. 2011. "Implementation of the WHO Framework Convention on Tobacco Control in mainland China." *Tobacco Control*, 20, 309–314.

Ma, Z. 2010. "The SINS in business negotiations: Explore the cross-cultural differences in business ethics between Canada and China." *Journal of Business Ethics*, 91, 123–135.

Malinowska-Sempruch, K., R. Bonnell, J. Hoover. 2006. "Civil society—a leader in HIV prevention and tobacco control." *Drug and Alcohol Review*, 25, 625–632.

Macklin, R. 1998. "Ethical relativism in a multicultural society." *Kennedy Institute of Ethics Journal*, 8, 1–22.

Macklin, R. 1999. *Against Relativism: Cultural Diversity and the Search for Ethical Universals in Medicine.* New York: Oxford University Press.

Marshall, P., B. Koenig. 2004. "Accounting for culture in a globalized bioethics." *Journal of Law, Medicine & Ethics*, 32, 252–266.

Moran, A., D. Gu, D. Zhao, P. Coxson, Y. C. Wang, C-S. Chen, J. Liu, J. Cheng, K. Bibbins-Domingo, Y.-M. Shen, J. He, L. Goldman. 2010. "Future cardiovascular disease in China: Markov model and risk factor scenario projections from the Coronary Heart Disease Policy Model–China." *Circulation: Cardiovascular Quality and Outcomes*, 3, 243–252.

Office of the Leading Small Group for Implementing the Framework Convention on Tobacco Control. 2007. *2007 China Tobacco Control Report*. Beijing: Ministry of Health.

The People's Republic of China's regulations on cigarette packaging. 2008. Retrieved from http://www.tobaccochina.com/law/nation/wu/20084/20084153948_297463.shtml (April 16, 2008).

Perevalov, Y., I. Gimadii, V. Dobrodei. 2000. "Does privatization improve performance of industrial enterprises? Empirical evidence from Russia." *Post-Communist Economics*, 12, 337–363.

Pohl, G., R. E. Anderson, S. Claessens, S. Djankov. 1997. *Privatization and Restructuring In Central and Eastern Europe.* World Bank Technical Paper No. 368, Finance, Private Sector, and Infrastructure Network. Washington, DC: The World Bank.

Robertson, C. J., B. J. Olson, K. M. Gilley, Y. Bao. 2008. "A cross-cultural comparison of ethical orientations and willingness to sacrifice ethical standards: China versus Peru." *Journal of Business Ethics*, 81, 413–425.

Romar, E. J. 2002. "Virtue is good business: Confucianism as a practical business ethic." *Journal of Business Ethics*, 38, 119–131.

Saffer, H. 2000. Tobacco advertising and promotion. In *Tobacco Control In Developing Countries*, edited by Jha P., F. J. Chaloupka, 215–236. New York: Oxford University Press.

Sandford, A. 2003. "Government action to reduce smoking." *Respirology*, 8, 7–16.

Shi, J., M. Liu, Q. Zhang, M. Lu, H. Quan. 2008. "Male and female adult population health status in China: A cross-sectional national survey." *BMC Pubic Health*, 8, 277. doi:10.1186/1471-2458-8-277.

Smith, Jr. S. C., Z.-J. Zheng. 2010. "The impending cardiovascular pandemic in China." *Circulation: Cardiovascular Quality and Outcomes*, 3, 226–227.

Stuart, B. E., M. S. Sarow, L. P. Stuart. 2007, *Integrated business communication in a global marketplace.* Hoboken, NJ: John Wiley.

Szeto, R. W. F. 2010. "Chinese folk wisdom: Implications for guarding against unethical practices by Chinese managers." *Journal of Public Affairs*, 10, 173–185.

Ten Bos, R., H. Willmott. 2001. "Towards a post-dualistic business ethics: Interweaving reason and emotion in working life." *Journal of Management Studies*, 38, 769–793.

Theft of the Century: Privatization and the Looting of Russia (2002, January/February). *Multinational Monitor*, 23–28.

Tobacco Control Office, China Center for Disease Control and Prevention. 2010. *2010 Report on Tobacco Control in China: Gender and Tobacco—Reducing Tobacco Marketing to Women.* Retrieved from http://www.360doc.com/content/10/0613/17/656136_32913862.shtml (February 19, 2011).

Tobacco Marketing Lures Chinese Women. 2010. *China Daily.* Retrieved from http://www.chinadaily.com.cn/china/2010-05/31/content_9912847.htm (May 31, 2010).

Tong, E., M. Tao, Q. Xue, T. Hu. 2008. China's tobacco industry and the World Trade Organization. In *Series on Contemporary China*: Vol. 12. *Tobacco Control Policy Analysis in China: Economics and Health* (211–244). Singapore: World Scientific.

Turner, L. 2003. "Zones of consensus and zones of conflict: Questioning the "common morality" presumption in bioethics." *Kennedy Institute of Ethics Journal*, 13, 193–218.

Veatch, R. M. 2003. "Is there a common morality?" *Kennedy Institute of Ethics Journal*, 13, 189–192.

Wang, J. 2003. "Framing Chinese advertising: Some industry perspectives on the production of culture." *Continuum: Journal of Media & Cultural Studies*, 17, 247–260.

Wanli, Y. 2010. Beijing really is the big smoke. *China Daily.* Retrieved from http://www.chinadaily.com.cn/cndy/2010-06/03/content_9926212.htm (June 3, 2010).

Wei, S. 1999. *Whether corruption affects FDI* (working paper). Sydney: National Center for Economic Research.

Whitcomb, L. L., C. B., Erdener, C. Li. 1998. "Business ethical values in China and the U.S." *Journal of Business Ethics*, 17, 839–852.

Woodruff, D. M. 2004. "Property rights in context: Privatization's legacy for corporate legality in Poland and Russia." *Studies in Comparative International Development*, 38, 82–108.

The World Bank. 1996. *World development report 1996: From plan to market.* New York: Oxford University Press.

The World Bank. 1999. *Curbing the Epidemic: Governments and the Economics of Tobacco Control.* Washington, DC: Author.

World Health Organization. 2005. *World Health Organization Framework Convention on Tobacco Control.* Geneva.

World Health Organization. 2009. *WHO Report on the Global Tobacco Epidemic: Implementing Smoke-Free Environments.* Geneva.

Wright, A. A., I. Y. Katz. 2007. "Tobacco tightrope—balancing disease prevention and economic development in China." *The New England Journal of Medicine*, 356, 1493–1496.

Wu, X. 1999. "Business ethical perceptions of business people in East China: An empirical study." *Business Ethics Quarterly*, 9, 541–559.

Yang, G. 2008. Prevalence of smoking in China. In *Series on Contemporary China*, edited by T. Hu, Vol. 12. *Tobacco control policy analysis in China: Economics and health* (pp. 13–31). Singapore: World Scientific.

Yang, G., J. Ma, A. Chen, Y. Zhang, J. M. Samet, C. E. Taylor, K. Becker. 2001. "Smoking cessation in China: Findings from the 1996 National Prevalence Survey." *Tobacco Control*, 10, 170–174.

Zhang, H., B. Cai. 2003. "The impact of tobacco on lung health in China." *Respirology*, 8, 17–21.

Zhong, W. 2006. China: A smoker's paradise. *Asia Times.* Retrieved from http://www.atimes.com/atimes/China_Business/HG11Cb01.html (July 11, 2006).

Zhu, Y. 2009. "Confucian ethics exhibited in the discourse of Chinese business and marketing communication." *Journal of Business Ethics*, 88, 517–528.

Zhu, T., B. Feng, S. Wong, W. Choi, S.-H., Zhu. 2004. "A comparison of smoking behaviors among medical and other college students in China." *Health Promotion International*, 19, 189–196.

ADDITIONAL READING

Benedict, C. 2011. *Golden-Silk Smoke: A History of Tobacco in China, 1550–2010.* Berkeley, CA: University of California Press.

Chan, S. S. C., L. Sarna, D. C. N. Wong, T.-H. Lam. 2007. "Nurses' tobacco-related knowledge, attitudes, and practice in four major cities in China." *Journal of Nursing Scholarship*, 39, 46–53.

Gao, J.-N., P.-P. Zheng, J.-L. Gao, S. Chapman, H. Fu, 2011. "Workplace smoking policies and their association with male employees' smoking behaviors: A cross-sectional survey in one company in China." *Tobacco Control*, 20, 131–136.

Gonzalez, M., L. W. Green, S. A. Glantz. 2011. "Through tobacco industry eyes: Civil society and the FCTC process from Philip Morris and British American Tobacco's perspectives." *Tobacco Control*, 20. doi:10.1136/tc.2010.041657.

Li, L., G. Feng, Y. Jiang, H.-H. Yong, R. Borland, G. T. Fong. 2011. "Prospective predictors of quitting behaviors among adult smokers in six cities in China: Findings from the International Tobacco Control (ITC) China Survey." *Addiction*, 106, 1335–1345.

Liu, Y., L. Chen. 2011. "New medical data and leadership on tobacco control in China." *The Lancet*, 377, 1218–1220.

Stanton, C. R., A. Chu, J. Collin, S. A. Glantz. 2011. "Promoting tobacco through the international language of dance music: British American Tobacco and the Ministry of Sound." *European Journal of Public Health*, 21, 21–28.

Yang, Y., D. Hammond, P. Driezen, R. J. O'Connor, Q. Li, H.-H. Yong, G. T. Fong, Y. Jiang. 2011. "The use of cessation assistance among smokers from China: Findings from the ITC China Survey." *BMC Public Health*, 11, 75–82.

2

STAKEHOLDER LEADERSHIP IN PUBLIC RELATIONS

7 CHAPTER

THE STAKEHOLDER CONCEPT
Empowering Public Relations

Clarke L. Caywood, Ph.D.
Professor and Past Chairman, Department of Integrated Marketing Communications
Medill School of Journalism, Media, Integrated Communications
Northwestern University

The challenge facing the men and women who will lead or consult with our human institutions in the early decades of the twenty-first century will be to use all of the knowledge available to them to manage their organizations' responses to their stakeholders. Stakeholders are the organizations and the individuals that have an interest in the success and failure of a company, a nongovernmental organization (NGO), a government or other organization.

Single stakeholders, like customers, have become a nearly fanatic focus for marketing, and particularly integrated marketing communications, in the past two decades. Now, the entire host of stakeholders will be a critical focus for organizations. We can assume that, moving forward, organizations will be restructured nearly continuously at different levels on the basis of the demands of stakeholders, market and society. The dated traditions in our graduate schools of business, producing approximately 156,250 master of business administration degrees annually in the United States[1] and emulated all over the world, have emphasized a narrow focus on the customer or investor for too long. This emphasis will give way to what some might consider a more European social democracy of business and organizations or even a more governmental definition of capitalism in China.

The failure of business education and training has been the single stakeholder focus. The marketing focus on the customer may have given the field a competitive advantage 30 years ago. The focus of finance on the shareholder may have given that specialty access to the CEO and board. However, as former U.S. President Bill Clinton stated to the New York University graduating class of 2011,

> I was probably [in] the last generation of Americans until the present day who could have gotten an MBA, if I went to business school instead of law school, with the prevailing theory being that American corporations had obligations primarily to their stakeholders. Ever since then we've been teaching our young people that your primarily obligation is only to the shareholder. The problem is that if you do that you ignore the other stakeholders.[2]

This breakdown is due, in part, to the failure of accredited business education programs to teach communications as a strategic advantage in business and other complex organizations. Without communications as a management strategy and tactic, the idea of building relationships with hundreds of stakeholders is nearly impossible. The traditional tools of management, including finance, accounting, marketing and human resources, are simply too limited to incorporate the wide range of stakeholders. The "stake" of other companies, organizations or individuals in a company or NGO can only be fully managed with a rich communications program.

In my opinion, the day has already come when corporations, NGOs, not-for-profit organizations and government have become high visibility public organizations. From a communications perspective, there are no truly private companies, organizations or members of government, as several government officials have recently found out. If the web and its messaging systems like Facebook, Twitter and WikiLeaks (wikileaks.org) did not explode the myth of privacy and anonymity for you, then I hope this book's broadening of the field of public relations and the recognition of the importance of a stakeholder point of view will.

Companies and individuals might continue to fight for their former privacy. However, the pressure of dozens of stakeholders insisting on more information, greater transparency and a forum for their points of view puts companies, NGOs and all institutions in the limelight. This more open system has an unsettling effect on the prevailing forms of capitalism and democracy. In a stakeholder world, the local environmental group may bring its light to bear on a global corporation. A single blogger may focus the attention of the world media, which may have missed the actions of an organization. Although it now seems obvious that long-standing national dictatorships can fall from microblog messages and blog posts, the same lessons must be learned by corporations, governmental bureaus and universities.

At the time of this writing, the Middle East is in an even greater uproar with Egypt as one center of disruption. The resignation of Egyptian president Hosni Mubarak in 2011 was credited in part to the work of citizens on social media bringing a constant and unwavering flood of attention to Egypt. CNET noted, "We shouldn't go so far as to call this a social media revolution, but it nevertheless is arguably the first time in history that we've seen Facebook and Twitter, a crucial part of the way we now communicate, speedily and successfully conveying the ideas and beliefs that do lead to a revolution." CNET not only differentiated the efforts of people who went to the Tahrir square in Cairo as a key force but also acknowledged "the fusion of millions of observers, pundits and supporters around the world into a sort of leaderless digital watchdog, an unwavering force that ensured the international eye would not stray from Egypt." Confirming the notion of the new power of social media, CNET sermonized, "It's the latter where we can credit social media."[3]

The barriers of entry for using social media, and increasingly accessing traditional media, are at an all time low, if they exist at all. The empowerment of stakeholders, with extraordinary powers of communication for little or no investment except time, energy, mind and heart, has redefined the relationship between institutions and stakeholders.

Although Europe moves from a more government-controlled stakeholder environment and the United States finds greater pressures from government and stakeholders abrogating some of the traditions of economic freedom, new enterprises and institutions rush to fill the gap of power, expertise and influence. Governments shift their stakeholder focus because of the power of stakeholders and their own internal power shifts to rebalance business and other institutions. The U.S. model of economic and social independence becomes more of a mix involving an increasing number of stakeholders, which means it will become more like the European governance model.

For example, Kevin Hassett, an economist at the American Enterprise Institute, a conservative Washington, D.C., think tank, notes that European governments are becoming more like the United States by not controlling their business-directed economies as much. He states, "They've moved much more towards having an economy that looks like an American, or a traditionally American economy." At the same time, he sees a contradiction of the United States' mimicking the traditional European model: "I'm not saying that that's what I would do if I were dictator, but I think that it's clear that's the path that seems to be emerging," he says.[4]

Ken Rogoff, now a Harvard professor and a former chief economist at the International Monetary Fund, says there will be changes in the United States as well. He notes, "I think the United States is clearly going through a sea change to become more like Europe." According to National Public Radio, Rogoff warns "that Americans need to understand there will be consequences. He says a move toward European-style capitalism, with its more generous social safety net and tighter regulation, will mean higher taxes—and not just for the wealthy."[5]

Stakeholders will gain new powers to redefine organizational boundaries and make them more transparent. Stakeholders will also possess more and more communication tools as well as the ability to speak freely and directly to other stakeholders. In the past, government and business used their nearly endless resources to manage and control privacy and message delivery. If business and organizational life are to be planned, operated and evaluated in a more transparent world, then the lessons and predictions of this book could be the operating manual for the next decades.

Returning to Former President Bill Clinton's graduation commencement address to New York University held in Yankee Stadium on May 11, 2011, I share his view of stakeholder education. Former President Clinton's work as a globally minded president, and his work with fundraising for his and other foundations since his presidency, is a specific endorsement of the stakeholder concept. He and I are both critical of American business education and hopeful that the stakeholder concept will take precedence in the thinking of future leaders. After noting that a shareholder focus means you ignore the other stakeholders, he went on to say the following:

> That could be why wages have been virtually stagnant for the past 30 years, because the workers are stakeholders. It could be why communities have been unable to undertake economic transformations in many places, because communities are stakeholders. It could be why customers don't care so much what the sources of their purchases are; they're stakeholders. Ever since then we've been teaching our young people that your primary obligation is only to the shareholder. The problem is that if you do that you ignore the other stakeholders.[6]

Perhaps the greatest lift to the concept of a stakeholder society was the election of Barack Obama in 2008. It seems logical to note that the association of stakeholder with his name, more than any other U.S. politician in history, proves a very public point. Slicing the Google search tool several ways, it seems that the President is associated with the word stakeholders over a million times in a very short time. Not quite as impressively but still notably, former President George W. Bush was linked to stakeholders prior to 2009 more than 400,000 times. Allowing for a lot of wow and flutter in this simple counting metric, the term has become presidential, global, prevalent and powerful.

Enough credit has not been given to Giuseppe Bassini, who came to my attention when, in 1986, he was named Vice President of NCR, the former National Cash Register Company, which was later bought by AT&T. Normally, the appointment would be one of hundreds of anonymous corporate jobs, but in his case, his title became "VP of Stakeholder Relations." It may have been his European heritage, the nature of the company broadening to new technological horizons or just his Renaissance approach that matched the new corporate title to a new view of public relations.

After I participated in a seminar for academics and others interested in the stakeholder work at NCR in Dayton, Ohio, my teaching and thinking became more precisely defined by these terms. It had already been influenced by E. Freeman, a Harvard professor, and later a professor at the University of Virginia. In 1984, Freeman had written a small book called *Strategic Management: A Stakeholder Approach*.[7] He has written with others several books using the stakeholder perspective.[8-10] If I had not been nearly finished with my dissertation on a developing theory of the First Amendment and threats to political advertising, I might have followed the clarion call of the stakeholder model, so aptly and richly described by Freeman.

NEGATIVE, NEUTRAL AND POSITIVE USES OF THE STAKEHOLDER LANGUAGE

NEGATIVE

Naturally, not everyone, and I mean anyone in the social media sphere, might object to the word *stakeholder*. For example, in the following irascible blog, *stakeholder* seems to irritate the writer as further "corporatism,"

> I decide who's a "stakeholder" around here, buddy! President Obama held a big immigration meeting this afternoon with "senior administration figures and stakeholders" to plot how to revive the drive for amnesty. This was not a big tent meeting. I guess low-wage American workers (who have to

compete with unskilled immigrants) aren't "stakeholders." Or maybe they were represented by Michael Bloomberg . . . . P.S.: If you were going to compile a lexicon of corporatism, "stakeholders" would be a key entry.[11]

NEUTRAL

In some cases, the use of the term is more neutral and becomes part of the lexicon of policy and public debate. Here the government posts schedules of stakeholder meetings on health reform. The word is merely part of the description of who is expected to attend the meetings held around the nation following a speech by President Obama in March of 2009.

White House Forums

Stakeholder Discussions. "The Obama Administration has invited small business owners, rural Americans, physicians and other key stakeholders to the White House for a series of roundtable discussions on health reform. The Health Care Stakeholder Discussions bring together Administration officials and Americans from around the country to discuss their experiences with the health care system and the urgent need for health reform this year."

Features and Events. "The Obama Administration has released a series of online reports, held town halls and forums and participated in stakeholder meetings to discuss the urgent need for Health Reform this year."[12]

POSITIVE

Some users of the word are strong advocates. The opportunity to create a new book in the field of public relations brought me back to the stakeholder model, which I have taught through the years using E. Freeman's articles. The first edition of this book was centered on two theoretical principles: the integration of communication at various levels of management and society and the importance of communications in developing relationships with stakeholders.

The new edition has expanded more on the stakeholder model, on the basis of years of experience and work with business professionals. Every time I conduct a training program in China, Nigeria, Europe, Venezuela, Canada, the Philippines, Great Britain, Australia, Chile, Japan, Korea and the United States or elsewhere, I find that the stakeholder exercise reveals more about its power. Over the years, managers and students have been able to conceive hundreds, if not thousands, of very specific stakeholders. It might be the name of a politician, a great customer (or a not so great one), a specific supplier, an attorney, a tough regulator, a former employee or any number of individuals or organizations that might have a stake in the success or failure of their specific company or organization. A local politician in my hometown of Madison, Wisconsin, once proclaimed, after we shared a stakeholder process with her, that she had no idea she was responsible to so many different individuals and organizations. Frankly, it was surprising to hear her utter the general statement because my background in politics had always made me constantly and increasingly aware of the number of publics, audiences, voters and detractors—stakeholders—who might be involved in a policy, a strategy or even a simple tactical action. Still, her exclamation made me even more appreciative of the term *stakeholder* and the more interactive nature of the concept over the more traditional and aggregating term *public*.

I find global business and NGO audiences resonate increasingly to the stakeholder concept. However, there have been some notable translation difficulties with the word *stakeholder* in the Mandarin and Cantonese languages. The term does not always translate easily around the globe. Deputy Secretary of State Robert Zoellick's September 2005 speech to the National Committee on United States–China Relations is a case in point. "We need to urge China to become a responsible stakeholder," said Zoellick. According to professional translator Song White and *The Wall Street Journal* story cited by White, the problem arose because there is not an official Chinese translation for the word *stakeholder*.

The Song White translation in Chinese includes "相关成员" (xiang guan cheng yuan) ("related member"), "相关团体" (xiang guan tuan ti) ("related group"), or "相关团体成员" (xiang guan tuan ti cheng yuan) ("related group member"). For reference, it should be noted that the U.S. State Department's translation is "利益相关的参与者" ("participants with related interests"), whereas Chinese scholars have offered "利害攸关的参与者" ("participants with related benefits and drawbacks"), "共同经营者" ("joint operators"), "参股人" ("shareholder"), and "合伙人" ("partner").[13]

These subtle distinctions are, in my experience, most often overcome by example. The meaning can also be defined through the creation of a stakeholder map and follow-up discussion. However, the fact that such a potent word has many meanings in another language gives pause to the assumption that many of our words in business and organizational management may not translate as fluidly as we wish or assume. Using the term *stakeholders* assumes some degree of ambiguity, but terms like *public* carry some burden of uncertainty too.

STAKEHOLDER MAPS

Stakeholder is not only a newly applied word, but it also can be very visual and interactive. Creating stakeholder maps is an exercise that provides a visual insight to the multiplicity of organizations and individuals that have a stake in a particular company or organization. I have used this exercise in educating and training sessions for managers in China and other parts of the globe on the topic of crisis management. In such a vivid and high-risk management situation as a crisis, the listing of stakeholders usually flows quickly. As managers immerse themselves in the exercise, they realize that their company and management position may depend on the support or nonsupport of groups and individuals they may take for granted under less stressful management circumstances. However, I have completed equally productive stakeholder maps for noncrisis issues including mergers, takeovers, acquisitions, new relationships with not-for-profit programs and new market launches and would argue that nearly any management activity, large or small, would benefit from a stakeholder mapping.

Figure 7.1 shows an example of the introductory theoretical model stakeholder map. Also illustrated is a more custom model of stakeholder maps. The theoretical model simply illustrates the most common stakeholder groups with equal stature. The list of employees, suppliers, government offices, customers, investors, analysts, universities and labor unions are each pointed out as examples of stakeholders that businesses and NGOs can consider in their first round of identifying stakeholders.

FIGURE   7.1

General Stakeholder Map

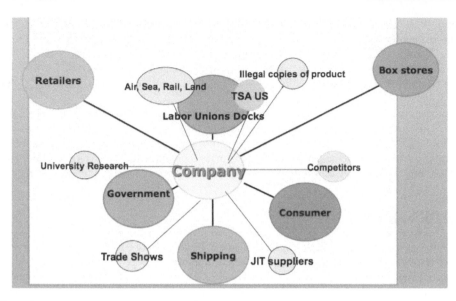

FIGURE 7.2

Stakeholder Map for Chinese Company

The map has circles (bubbles), lines, boundaries and a center to illustrate the relationships between the stakeholders. The image is one of two-dimensional bubbles around a center bubble representing the company, the CEO, a department or a project. The center of the map will be the first decision for the map. The center of the globes suggests that the unit or individual will be the focus of the relationships with the many stakeholders. The company, NGO or government unit is most often used, but each case must be considered uniquely.

Initially, the other bubbles are labeled as key stakeholders without a level of detail. That is, initially, the stakeholder bubbles may simply represent the customer, the institutional investors or even the employees. The work beyond the theoretical model gets more exciting and also debatable as specific customers are ranked by profitability, or employees are divided into circles of management, staff, labor or government into local, state, regional, national or even global segments. All key stakeholders are listed without the dynamics that are later offered to differentiate the stakeholders by influence, economic power, or other dimensions. Again, a simple theoretical model may represent only some degree of reality for the organization. The first map is intended to merely illustrate the process.

The applied model has a range of dynamics that gives the image more power and more of an opportunity for discussion and debate. It is possible that each of the common stakeholder groups can be divided and subdivided into many stakeholders. For example, local government might be represented by several circles of zoning departments: safety departments, such as of fire and police; infrastructure departments, such as streets and sanitation; local government offices, such as the city council and office of the mayor and council president (Figure 7.2).

Each circle will bear a name and be linked to specific contact information and other dynamics discussed in the next paragraph. If you multiply a theoretical list of 12 stakeholders times 6 to 12 sub-stakeholders, the number of globes can quickly morph into hundreds and become overwhelming. There are logical limits to the detail on the central stakeholder map that might be considered for ease of understanding and reading. Each sub-stakeholder will be "assigned" to a management team, or individual manager, staff member or consultant. Once the circles and subcircles have been created, a highly dynamic set of dimensions can be added both visually and in the notes. The dynamics (or size), the power of the company, the partnerships and the contacts that can be built into the model include many relationships with the center circles of the company or NGO. The relationships are listed in some detail as follows:

Stakeholder Dynamics—Map Code 1–10

1. Estimated degree of economic impact on the center globe (size of circle representing sales, investment and budget)

2. Past, current, future influence timing (dated start and stop points)

3. Linkages between stakeholders (alliances shown by lines)

4. Conflicts between stakeholders (battles shown by jagged lines or notes)

5. Boundaries of openness to a relationship or not (thickness of globe line)

6. Frequency of contact with center (proximity to core circle from near to far)

7. Number of contacts between stakeholders and with center stakeholder (thickness of line to circles)

8. Public and media perceptions of tone of positive or negative relationship (number of + or – symbols)

9. History of dynamics tracked and monitored (dated and saved) on several maps or a rapidly changing map

10. Other dynamics relevant to an industry, for example, degree of government regulation, bankruptcies, new technology interruptions and so forth

The process is quite simple but requires dedicated time, the benefit of a team and reference to the theoretical model to remind the map maker of the general categories that must be made more specific. The maps, at their highest level of development, can be considered proprietary because they may reveal a great deal about the relationships, contracts and contacts.

Stakeholder Map Construction—With Interactive Steps

The steps of the process include a combination of individual and group work:

1. A brief presentation of the theoretical model and definition of a stakeholder

2. A group facilitator definition of the assignment

3. The clarification of what organization or individual is in the center of the map, whether it is the CEO, the company, a division, the customer or another

4. Opportunity for the participants to take time (10–20 minutes) to list in columns as many relevant stakeholders as possible

5. Roundtable listing of stakeholders by participants through listing on a white board

6. The addition, through brainstorming, of more names

7. The balancing of the list where there are holes or fewer names

8. The clarification of the lists by stakeholder category, including adding more detail, including names. Clarification is not a debating period of whether someone or an organization belongs on the list, but only clarification on the stakeholder

9. The individual evaluation of the dynamics of each stakeholder by ranking and scoring

10. The compilation of the dynamic scores and drawing of the map

With the completion of a more comprehensive customer stakeholder map, the management process may continue with further discussion, checking the facts of the stakeholders' current relationship with the company. Finally, as discussed further in Chapters 21 and 26, there may be management assignments to each of the stakeholders or stakeholder groups to monitor, to track and to build relationships.

I have found, however, that the idea of a community of stakeholders is easily understood and accepted by the more than 3,000 Chinese business leaders I have spoken to. The concept of the worker, although perhaps not as refined in benefits as in the West, is still heartily accepted. Certainly, the role of government is strongly understood in China. The press still operates with less freedom than in parts of the West, but the demand for traditional and social media is still very strong. That role will be empowered, as the need for information from more than just a governmental source is needed. Probably the least understood stakeholder is the NGO. It has been described in China as a government-operated NGO or GONGO. Currently, the former governor of Wisconsin, Scott McCallum, one of the authors of Chapter 18 on NGOs, and I are working toward introducing Aidmatrix.org as a viable NGO in China.

The most frequent erroneous experience I have had with the term is the simple misunderstanding when people think the word is shareholders, not stakeholders. Given the proclivity of business leaders to be concerned with the shareholder, the similarity of the words, and the fact that the term is still not a common subject taught in graduate schools of business, it might be an understandable error. However, the term has grown into acceptance, so that this mistake is now not made as often. At the beginning of working with the idea of stakeholders, I used notations of "sh" for shareholders and "SH" for stakeholders to show the umbrella value of the stakeholder term. I still use the annotation, when it is helpful.

The section of stakeholder chapters has been expanded substantially since the first edition. Although some have advised me that second editions sometimes become overwritten, we have invited a whole new group of authors to contribute to this section. This section will be very important to your knowledge of public relations.

DISCUSSION QUESTIONS

1. Define stakeholder. How is it different from the public?
2. What are the common audiences in the language and learning of business education? How does stakeholder theory and practice overcome this focus?
3. Create a list of 10 key stakeholders for a business meeting that is concerned with the manufacturing of toys with lead paint on the surface of the toy. What advice would you give the board members of the American licensed company who say they were not able to do anything about the error of manufacturing?
4. How would you organize a company's communications function to be prepared to address the concerns of key stakeholders?

NOTES

1. *NumberOf.net.* http://www.numberof.net/number%C2%A0of%C2%A0mba%C2%A0graduates%C2%A0in-the-us-per%C2%A0year (accessed May 5, 2011).
2. Aimee Groth, "Bill Clinton Tells NYU Grads Why Business Schools Are Fundamentally Flawed," *Business Insider* (2011), http://www.businessinsider.com/bill-clinton-nyu-business-schools-2011-5 (accessed May 29, 2011).
3. http://news.cnet.com/8301-13577_3-20031600-36.html#ixzz1Q1XkSDMV
4. http://www.npr.org/templates/story/story.php?storyId=111420898 (accessed August 3, 2009).
5. Ibid.
6. Aimee Groth, "Bill Clinton Tells NYU Grads Why Business Schools Are Fundamentally Flawed," *Business Insider* (2011), http://www.businessinsider.com/bill-clinton-nyu-business-schools-2011-5 (accessed May 29, 2011).
7. R. Edward Freeman, *Strategic Management: A Stakeholder Approach* (1984). Boston, MA: Pitman.
8. R. Edward Freeman, Jeffrey S. Harrison, and Andrew C. Wicks, *Managing for Stakeholders Survival, Reputation, and Success* (2007). New Haven, CT: Yale University Press.
9. Zakhem, Abe J., Daniel E. Palmer, and Mary Lyn Stoll. *Stakeholder Theory: Essential Readings in Ethical Leadership and Management.* Amherst, NY: Prometheus, 2008. Print.
10. Phillips, Robert. *Stakeholder Theory and Organizational Ethics.* San Francisco, CA: Berrett-Koehler, 2003. Print.

11. Mickey Kaus. *Kaus Files*. http://dailycaller.com/2011/04/19/dont-call-me-stakeholder/#ixzz1NmTV2M8h (accessed May 15, 2011).

12. Mickey Kaus. *Kaus Files*. http://www.healthreform.gov/forums/index.html (accessed May 15, 2011).

13. Song White, "Untranslatable WordsThree Chinese Puzzles," *NCTA's Translorial Online Edition*. http://translorial.com/2006/02/01/untranslatable-wordsthree-chinese-puzzles (accessed June 21, 2011).

ADDITIONAL READING

Freeman, R. Edward. 2010. *Stakeholder Theory: The State of the Art*. Cambridge, UK: Cambridge University Press.

Freeman, R. Edward. 1984. *Strategic Management a Stakeholder Approach*. Boston, MA: Pitman.

Freeman, R. Edward, Jeffrey S. Harrison, and Andrew C. Wicks. 2007. *Managing for Stakeholders: Survival, Reputation, and Success*. New Haven, CT: Yale University Press.

Friedman, Andrew L., and Samantha Miles. 2006. *Stakeholders Theory and Practice*. Oxford, UK: Oxford University Press.

Zakhem, Abe J., Daniel E. Palmer, and Mary Lyn Stoll. 2008. *Stakeholder Theory: Essential Readings in Ethical Leadership and Management*. Amherst, NY: Prometheus.

8
CHAPTER

THE KEY STAKEHOLDERS
Your Employees

Keith Burton
President
Insidedge

Pottinger's Entry is an arched passageway that knifes into Belfast, Ireland's onetime waterfront streets that snake between warehouse blocks, and proceed down to the quayside that was destroyed by a German aerial assault in World War II. It remains the gateway through which multiple generations have connected to the world of commerce, social trends, lifestyle interests and sources of knowledge that fueled their lives. Pottinger's Entry was named for a prominent local family, one of whose number was Sir Henry Pottinger, the first Governor of Hong Kong and the man who, coincidentally, forced the Chinese Imperial government to give up the island (Figure 8.1).

Walking through Pottinger's Entry on a visit to Northern Ireland, it didn't escape me that this historic portal, one of a series of seven narrow alleyways dating back to the 1600s, is a powerful allegory for employee communication today: If we find the right point of entry, the right passage to the hearts and minds of the men and women who populate the leading companies of our world, we can access higher performance, transform cultures, and achieve greatness together.

When the original *Handbook of Strategic Public Relations & Integrated Communications* was first published in the 1990s, employee communication was a nascent discipline. And that's being kind. For decades, it had been relegated to a back room, where its practitioners toiled with old-school newsletters, overhead foils, speeches, video and benefits communication. It wasn't strategic. It wasn't valued. Nobody cared. And the band played on.

Fast forward. Corporate re-engineering took center stage in 1991 and the game changed forever.

In 1992, I teamed up with Dr. Clarke Caywood, editor of the *Handbook* and a true thought leader in integrated marketing communication, and Dr. Robert Berrier, one of the world's foremost employee research specialists, to innovate the first integrated employee communication model for IBM Corp. For the first time, we used research as a "listening" tool to mine for knowledge and to plumb the perception gaps that exist between executive leaders and frontline employees. We created a new model that eclipsed the classic top-down communication by placing frontline managers and supervisors into the role of privileged carriers of information. And we created a new anthem—"One Voice, One Look"—to signify the critical importance of aligning the internal brand with the external voice of the organization.

From business process re-engineering to cultural transformation, to the dot-com boom and bust, to the mergers and acquisitions explosion, to internal branding and now to the Employee Value Proposition—we've seen it all during two decades of internal communication consulting. And in my experience, great organizations like

FIGURE 8.1

IBM, FedEx, Genentech, American Airlines, Boeing, the Federal Aviation Administration, Dow Chemical, NASA, Toyota, Molson Coors and Covidien all have contributed to the progress we've made globally with this discipline.

What have we learned? As we conduct ongoing soundings and best practices reviews among our clients and other leading companies, we've learned that employee communication has evolved from a perfunctory component of corporate communication and HR functions to one that is firmly tied to corporate strategies and business objectives. Companies are putting more money and effort into their employee communication programs, and employee communicators are being more aggressive in pushing their leadership teams to see them as strategic consultants.

As a result, employee communication has evolved from a state of "sharing information" to one of driving employee behavior by helping people understand how their work influences the success of the company.

CEOs and other top corporate executives who've ascended during this evolutionary period now better understand and value effective employee communication, and they're more supportive of those who lead it. Many companies place their top employee communicators at the director level and above, and within one or two reports of the CEO or president (that is, if you can find and hire them, as experienced employee communicators are becoming one of the hottest commodities in our profession). We've found that on average, about a third of today's corporate communication budgets are spent on employee communication staffing and programming—and that number is growing with the adoption of new digital channels and mobile applications required to reach a distributed workforce.

About two-thirds of the companies we've surveyed have told us they measure their internal communications programs in some way—be it qualitative or quantitative. The most common measures include cultural or employee engagement surveys (often in association with human resources), internal communication audits (to measure the effectiveness and credibility of communications vehicles and channels) and surveys around specific programs (e.g., the quality of communication around a one-time event, such as an employee town hall). Beyond the employee climate studies, we've also witnessed an increase in the use of field "pulsing" and targeted internal focus groups to test ideas and validate the efficacy of messages, messengers and programs. Insidedge also has pioneered a model known as the "Challenge Team," comprised of a cross-functional group of men and women who come together to review and critique internal communication strategies and tactics before a launch. Challenge Teams help us ground our ideas in the realities of how employees will receive and act on the information we communicate.

It seems strange to say today, in 2011, that blogs are becoming somewhat passé. It was not long ago that we innovated two of the earliest CEO blogs for Andrew Liveris of Dow Chemical and John Swainson of CA, Inc. Today, wikis, portals, apps, webcasts, social media and an explosion of digital solutions are providing internal communicators with a new arsenal of tools with which to do their work. Even the vanguard among us, however, would caution that companies should not concentrate on electronic communication at the expense of print or face-to-face communication. Each has a role, and each should be used in a way that reflects the wants and needs of the employees at a company. As Al Golin, the founder of GolinHarris, has said: "Don't let high-tech replace high-touch!"

What will the future hold for employee communication? Here are the collective predictions of our Insidedge team:

- *Authenticity is the new green.* Sustainability and green-friendly practices are still in, but they are no longer it. Today's employees are looking for total values alignment with their employer, and environmental stewardship alone is no longer sufficient. Authenticity—which calls for demonstrating integrity, telling employees the truth even if the news is bad, being consistent in what is said and done internally and externally and acting in an honest, trustworthy way—is the new standard.

- *The wisdom of virtual teams.* Technologies that captivate us are enabling greater agility and collaboration. Or so we hope and pray. In truth, we know that nothing is more complex than welding together global virtual teams because of geographic, cultural, linguistic, emotional and procedural distance. Terence Brake, author of *Where in the World is My Team? Making a Success of Your Global Virtual Workforce*, tells us that if virtual teams are to be effective, they require more attention, discipline, and effort than colocated teams. The key to success, Brake says, is providing guidance on "how to think coherently and holistically" when setting up or running a virtual team. That's where employee communicators come in: Our job is to create a communication "road map" that will help employees fully understand what we expect of them, how they can contribute and collaborate, how their differences will bring strength to the enterprise and ultimately, to demonstrate that our plans will support their growth.

- *Return on investment = standard operating procedure.* The time has come for communicators to deliver more than just messages. Although communicators live in a world of words and images, the people who lead organizations live in a world of processes and numbers, and they expect us to relate to the way they keep score. Measurement is a business imperative, not just something to justify budgets. Go beyond *acknowledging* the need to measure: define, deliver, and demonstrate the value of employee communication to the business with tangible outcomes that show success or the need for adjustment. Use the many tools available to justify a program's impact on the bottom line.

- *Corporate speak is dead (or it should be).* The Internet and social media have changed the way we write, speak and receive information. A long, stuffy memo from the CEO will be forgotten or ignored. These days, employees expect fast, direct and informal communication—24/7/365. The workplace is shifting from experienced, reliable baby boomers to savvy, demanding Gen X, Gen Y and Millennial employees. To keep their attention, we must communicate in a way that's relevant to them. Whether you're blogging or not, communicate like a blogger: tell it like it is with personality and purpose.

- *Don't control conversations. Join them.* In this era of Facebook, Twitter and the surge of digital channels, what was once a whisper in the break room is now heard around the world. I'm reminded of the medical technology company that had planned for every possible contingency in announcing a wave of layoffs. To everyone's surprise, word of the downsizing quickly leaked out on Facebook among 25 affected employees connected as "friends," and then it spread like wildfire to the larger workforce, the media and other stakeholders before the company could release an official statement. As much as you might want to, you can't govern the kinds of viral conversations that take place on the Web. Learn to love this loss of control and embrace it to your advantage. Our job must be to persuade CEOs and executive leaders to blog directly with employees. Develop grassroots networks and eschew one-way, top-down communication.

- *Listen up.* Before you e-mail, blog, script or print, ask yourself, "Is this something that matters to employees?" In a refinery location of a client organization, we found that managers were receiving a mountain of e-mails, multiple voice messages and myriad meeting requests that paralyzed their ability to do actual work and act as communicators with their frontline reports. As an IBM manager once said in the heat of change, the clotted communication in his company left employees "gagging on data and starving for information." Information overload and desensitization creates less-engaged employees. There's no magic formula to determine what kind of information employees want or how they want to get it. Take the time to listen and understand your unique workplace culture, the issues employees are concerned about and the channels through which they prefer to receive information. Then communicate about the things that matter to them in the way they want to hear it. And remember—a good rule is "Less is *more.*"

- *Corporate cultures are woven with stories. Share them.* Since the dawn of time, people have used stories to make information memorable. Why, then, has the corporate world seemingly become an ever-escalating competition over who can prepare the most elaborate presentations? If you want to capture employees' hearts and minds, go back to the basics and tell a good story. Facts are merely information, but storytelling brings information to life. Storytelling is the anti-PowerPoint. Employees want to feel like they're part of something, and a good story forges that essential emotional connection. Microsoft, Pepsi, Dow Chemical and Molson Coors all have used storytelling to teach managers and frontline employees how to communicate less formally, more personally and more effectively (see Chapter 52 on storytelling).

- *It's time for emerging professionals to teach their leaders.* Gone are the days when the senior executive mentored the fresh-faced associate just starting out in his or her career. Now, the young are removing the mystery of technology and social networking for their bosses and their bosses' bosses—teaching them how to set up Facebook pages, send tweets and use wikis. Workforce dynamics have changed and communication has a role to play in easing the transition and removing the awkwardness of reverse networking.

- *The world is your backyard.* All companies are global. For those who don't think they're a global firm, just take a look at the Google Analytics for your company's website—you'll be stunned to see where you have followers. Employers must look at every issue from a global perspective, not just from the viewpoint of the home office. Language, cultural differences and geography should all play a role in your communication planning.

- *Managers are corporate communicators' best friends.* Employees trust their immediate supervisors more than anyone else to deliver important information. Developing the communication skills of managers is critical. But don't just train your managers; give them tools they can use. We know that approximately two-thirds of all employees work in a factory, manufacturing, telemarketing or support environment where time and technology for communicating may be very limited or not available. So a PowerPoint presentation or Web video is of little use to a manager in these settings. Something like a simple set of pocket-sized note cards with important information, or a "toolkit" for use in a "tailgate session" (literally setting up shop on a truck's tailgate for a conversation with telephone linemen, as it happened with one client), have far more value.

- *Get outside by going inside.* Companies can invest time, talent and resources into nurturing their reputation, but a brand is only as good as the people who deliver it. Although external image is important, what's inside is *vital.* If companies don't enlist their employees as brand advocates, arming them with the information they need to live the brand and spread the good word, consider your marketing budget wasted. Engaged employees are at the core of every extraordinary brand. Engaged employees comprise the new face of the Employee Value Proposition that is now taking center stage in our world.

- *When worlds collide.* I've long said that one of the most critical aspects of our work is to understand the importance of cultural compatibility. A celebrated example of this is the failed merger of Pharmacia and Upjohn in the 1990s, when The *Wall Street Journal* reported that the consolidation would cost hundreds of millions of dollars more than was originally planned because of the difficulty in unifying the American and European cultures in four geographies and poor communication efforts. Sadly, this pattern has been repeated countless times through the years with other leading brands—and at a very high cost of human capital, productivity and squandered market opportunities. I believe we'll see a resurgence of M&A activity in the coming years, and we should not be surprised that many of the "acquiring" brands will be companies from India and China like Lenovo, Tata Group or Reliance Industries, to name a few. How will European and North American workers respond when they're expected to embrace Eastern values and management philosophies that don't synch with their expectations and experiences? We've already seen the affects of such mergers in the technology field, and it has not been pretty. Stay tuned. It will be a big part of our work as employee communicators.

I spent a weekend once in Seattle with Jeff Bezos and his team at Amazon.com. The executives were working through a very difficult decision, at that time, about shuttering new distribution centers to reduce costs in a drive for pro forma profitability. It was a tough call. Tax abatements and covenants had been struck with the economic development authorities and governors of certain states where the distribution centers would operate. Jobs that had been planned would be in doubt.

In the heat of the discussion, questions flew throughout the conference room. "What do we say?" "How do we honor the commitments we've made?" "What will our people think?" "Will this hurt our reputation?"

I remember watching Bezos as he sized up his team and reflected privately on their questions. Silence fell in the room. Then he spoke, and his words pierced the cloud of uncertainty: "We have to remember that our reputation is what people say about us when we're not in the same room. We have to do what is right for us and for those communities that have honored us with their commitment." And that's exactly what happened in the difficult days ahead. The company honored all of its commitments. And it communicated—honestly, openly, transparently—with its people. As promised.

I've long been a fan of alternative rock music. My Chemical Romance is an alt-rock group whose music I've enjoyed. As I think about the days ahead, I'm drawn to lyrics of their hit, "Sing"

> *Sing it out,*
> *Boy you've got to see what tomorrow brings*
> *Sing it out,*
> *Girl you've got to be what tomorrow needs*
> *For every time that they want to count you out*
> *Use your voice every single time you open up your*
> *mouth*

INSIDEDGE

Insidedge, a specialty brand of The Interpublic Group of Companies, is recognized as the world's leading employee communication consultancy. Its team of specialists weds the rigor of management consulting, the science of research and the art of marketing and communication into a strategic package that fosters employee commitment and motivates their performance.

Insidedge works with an array of global clients to help "translate" and explain business plans, organizational change, and corporate strategies in language employees can understand, and—more importantly—act upon. Insidedge team members have broad experience supporting client programs related to the following:

- Change management
- Employee engagement and employee value proposition
- Labor relations
- Crisis management
- Communication organization reviews
- Communication skills training
- Human resources and benefits communication
- Internal communication research
- Leadership communications/ mission, vision and values development

Insidedge serves global clients from its offices in Chicago, New York and London. Its Website is www.insidedge.net.

Through these words, the artists encourage a new generation to speak up and become the leaders of tomorrow, to look ahead and to learn what our world will need. I feel that way about our role as employee communication strategists—we've got to be what tomorrow needs. I'm confident that the men and women learning on college campuses today, as well as those entering our field, have what it takes and will rise to the occasion. We need them even now. Life moves quickly, and we have much to do as employee communicators.

Pottinger's Entry has stood the test in Belfast. The world has changed, but the truth we find once we pass through the portal will never change. Our job is to remember that our reputation is what people say about us when we are not with them. Employee communication must be that touchstone, that authentic voice that will carry us forward to a new place.

Sing it out.

STORYTELLING CASE STUDY: THE DOW CHEMICAL COMPANY

In 2006, The Dow Chemical Company announced aggressive 2015 Sustainability Goals, including a commitment to achieving breakthroughs in the areas of sustainable water supplies, adequate food supplies, decent housing and personal health and safety by 2015. The goals are the foundation for Dow's "Human Element" advertising and public relations campaign, a key aspect of the company's overall efforts to enhance its reputation. The campaign is centered on the concept that the missing element in the periodic table is the human element, which when applied to chemistry, can help solve the world's most pressing problems. The company understood that the credibility and success of the entire reputation program would depend in large part on active engagement from its employees around the world.

However, soon after the launch of the overall Human Element campaign in June 2006, a global internal pulse survey examined employee reactions to the campaign and found the following:

- Only 55 percent of employees had seen images from the Human Element campaign at their site.

- Only 59 percent of employees felt informed about the Human Element campaign.

These results indicated an opportunity to develop a sustained internal component to the Human Element campaign to recognize Dow employees and increase awareness of Dow's sustainability goals, as well as to foster support for the overall Human Element reputation program and the important role reputation plays in achieving the company's goals.

OBJECTIVES

Dow had several objectives that it wanted to accomplish through this global effort, all of which tied naturally to developing a storytelling campaign. These included:

- Building business literacy among employees for the Human Element campaign and Dow's 2015 Sustainability Goals, as well as ensuring that a majority of employees understand the importance of reputation to Dow's achieving its vision of being the largest, most profitable and most respected chemical company in the world.

- Motivating employees to be brand ambassadors for Dow by gaining the support of a majority of employees for the Human Element campaign.

- Fostering employee understanding of the types of work being done by Dow employees across the world to further progress toward the achievement of its 2015 Sustainability Goals.

- Bolstering pride in Dow among its employees and employee commitment to the company.

- Recognizing and celebrating Dow employees for the work they do that embodies the spirit of the Human Element and helps Dow to achieve its goals.

STRATEGY AND TACTICS

Insidedge set out to engage all 46,000 Dow employees who work in a variety of positions from scientists to manufacturing, to research and development, to administrative roles in nearly 40 countries around the world.

Our overall strategy involved the "I am the Human Element" peer-driven internal storytelling campaign, whereby employees nominate colleagues to be featured in the series as living examples of how Dow can achieve its 2015 Sustainability Goals through employees who embody the spirit of the Human Element. To ensure the campaign would be global in scope, and would recognize employees from all geographies, levels and job functions, we launched an easy-to-use online nomination form translated into the six languages of Dow's key regions: English, Spanish, French, Italian, Portuguese and Dutch. In 2007, the program received more than 150 nominations, representative of all the regions of the Dow world.

From these nominations, Insidedge interviewed the employees and developed articles and internal ads intended to share each employee's story and how he or she helps the company achieve its goals. The ads— close-up photographs of the employees' faces—are treated with the Human Element graphic and are accompanied by a brief overview of their story. The ads are published with an internal news story and are also printed as oversized posters displayed at Dow sites around the world and on *DowTV*, Dow's own internal television broadcast channel. New stories and posters are published every three weeks on the *Dow Today* global Intranet home page.

RESULTS

- A September 2007 employee survey indicated that an overwhelming 90 percent of employees strongly agree or agree that Dow's efforts to build its reputation are beneficial to achieving company goals and 61 percent of employees are very favorable or favorable to the Human Element campaign.

- The survey showed that 79 percent of Dow employees were aware of the "I am the Human Element" program and 82 percent reported having seen posters from the campaign, up from 55 percent after the campaign's initial launch. Sixty-nine percent of Dow employees felt "very informed" or "informed" about the Human Element campaign, up from 59 percent at the launch of the campaign in June 2006.

- Employees from around the world have been recognized and celebrated for their work to achieve the 2015 Sustainability Goals. Since the program's inception, 25 employees have been featured at a global level, representing all five geographies where Dow operates: Europe; Asia-Pacific; Latin America; India, the Middle East, Africa; and North America. Many more have been featured at a regional and site level (Figure 8.2)

CASE STUDY: MOLSON COORS

Category	13—Internal Communications
	A Business (Fewer than 10,000 Employees)—Products
Title of Entry	Rallying Employees Behind "Our Brew" at Molson Coors
Agency	Insidedge
Client Name	Molson Coors Brewing Company

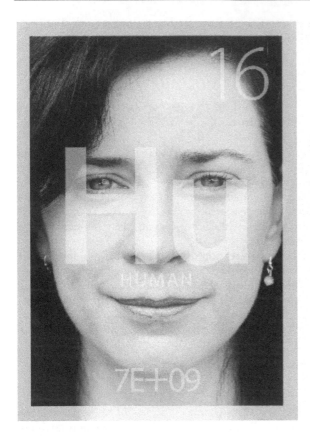

F I G U R E   8.2

OVERVIEW

In a shrinking global economy, differentiating your business among many is a problem not unique to beer, and not unique to Molson Coors. But before you can build your brands and identity externally, you must build an internal culture that understands—and is engaged in—your path forward.

At Molson Coors, one of the core beliefs is that the only two sources of sustainable competitive advantage come from the quality of your brands and the quality of your people. We work to build extraordinary, iconic, inspiring brands that are based on enduring truth and principles, and a relevant, consistent experience. In turn, we need people who are passionate about delivering exceptional results and holding themselves accountable for achieving our ambitions and challenging the expected to deliver these extraordinary brands.

Obviously, we knew this mission was not a simple one, but we also knew that it was not mission impossible. We knew it would take the insight, input and commitment of our entire organization to develop, implement and sustain our winning recipe. Enter "Our Brew."

RESEARCH

1. *Clue-finding mission.* Our Brew was not born from leaders brainstorming about our vision. It was a nine-month journey with input from more than 300 employees. Employees participated in "clue-finding exercises" to discuss likes, dislikes and beliefs about Molson Coors. This resulted in 3,000 "clues" that would serve as the foundation for Our Brew.

2. *Communications audit.* We also conducted a global communication audit to measure the effectiveness of existing internal communications, as well as affinity for the enterprise strategy and change readiness.

3. *Annual People Survey.* Molson Coors also gathered input from our annual global "People Survey." The survey measures seven areas of engagement: (1) engagement, (2) growth and development, (3) involvement and empowerment, (4) decision making and future vision, (5) supervision, (6) goals and objective, and (7) work culture.

4. This research provided insight into preferred and trusted communication methods, communications and work needed to change employee mindsets. For example, employees were eager for a more visible leadership team and to better understand where we were heading.

The findings indicated three focus areas: decision making and future vision, goals and objectives and growth and development. Our Brew was developed to address these areas of engagement.

PLANNING

Budget: $500,000 including collateral production and printing costs and consulting fees.

Audience: Our Brew needed to connect with a diverse global population of approximately 6,000 full-time employees, including salaried G&A and hourly production employees in the United States, Canada, United Kingdom, China, Japan, and other small sales/marketing locations.

Objectives:

1. Increase employee engagement scores 4 percent in four years (2008 score of 80% to 84% by 2012) as measured by our annual People Survey.

2. Improve employees' trust in leadership and leadership decision-making as measured by our annual People Survey.

3. Clearly define and increase employee awareness and understanding of the company's ambition, strategic goals and values.

4. Rollout Our Brew to all salaried employees by March 2009; rollout to hourly production employees by end of October 2009.

5. Unite disparate business units under one company name, brand and strategy.

6. Translate all major communication vehicles into "pub talk–approved" look, feel and language.

Strategy: Our multipronged strategy focused on the following:

1. *Print.* The physical manifestation of Our Brew is a book distributed to all employees.

2. *Leadership visibility.* In addition to being involved in Our Brew development, consistent messaging presented by visible leadership was key to ensuring employees saw Our Brew as more than just words on a page.

3. *Pub-talk approved.* We left corporate speak in the boardroom and talked to people like people. Pub-talk became the "stamp of approval" for all employee communications going forward.

4. *Interactive, two-way dialogue and storytelling.* This took a personal and virtual approach. Leaders had frequent meetings with employees outside their function to talk about Our Brew and share stories. These conversations continued through a new intranet site, "Our Brew Board." This featured a weekly blog and a storyboard where employees could post, read and comment on stories. We also started a social networking site, Yammer, a Twitter-like environment.

5. *Ongoing visibility*. As mentioned previously, the look, feel and sound of Our Brew is not just used when talking about Our Brew. The communications approach and design permeate all aspects of our employee communications campaigns to keep Our Brew "top of mind."

EXECUTION

- *January*: Our Brew rolled out to global leadership team during a three-day January leadership conference. Our Brew was the focus of the entire conference, preparing leaders to leave the conference as certified Our Brew ambassadors.

- *February–March:* The global leadership team conducted town halls to introduce Our Brew to salaried employees. This included a standard presentation format including messaging and video. Employees also were provided with the Our Brew Book. Materials were translated into French, Japanese and Chinese to accommodate geographies.

- *April–May:* After the rollout, global leadership conducted staff sessions to talk more directly with their teams to see if Our Brew messages were resonating and what questions or communication opportunities we had. The communications department also began applying the Our Brew look, feel and pub-talk language to existing and new communication mediums and launched the Our Brew Board site.

- *June–July:* In preparation for the hourly rollout, all managers of hourly employees attended an Our Brew Communication workshop to be reimbursed in Our Brew and their role as communicators.

- *August–November:* Hourly rollout, following a similar format to salaried rollout, with storytelling sessions added at the end of town hall to gather stories of Our Brew in action. "Sip Survey" conducted of 1,000 salaried employees to measure awareness and effectiveness of Our Brew rollout at midyear (see results under Measurement and Evaluation).

MEASUREMENT AND EVALUATION

1. *Objective:* Increase employee engagement scores 4 percentage points in four years (2008 score of 80% to 84% by 2012) as measured by our annual People Survey.

Result: Employee engagement results jumped from 80 percent in 2008 to 86 percent in 2009, representing an unprecedented six-point increase in one year, clearly exceeding the goal of a four-point increase in four years. Our survey vendor, Towers Perrin-ISR, said these engagement results were unprecedented within the history of their client base.

2. *Objective*: Improve trust in leadership and leadership decision making as measured by our annual People Survey.

Results: Trust in leadership and confidence in leadership decision making were among the most improved individual question scores within the annual People Survey. Specifically:

- I trust the senior leaders of my division—score increased 14 points to 80 percent agree or strongly agree.

- I have confidence in the decisions made by the senior management team of Molson Coors—score increased 15 points to 80 percent agree or strongly agree.

3. *Objective:* Clearly define and increase employee awareness and understanding of the company's ambition, strategic goals and values.

Results: A November 2009 Sip Survey of 1,000 salaried employees showed an overwhelmingly positive reaction to Our Brew. More importantly, it showed that people were connecting the dots between Our Brew and the company's strategy. Some results included (% agree or strongly agree):

- I believe senior executives at Molson Coors are committed to Our Brew (90)

- Our Brew helps me understand what the company is trying to achieve (82)

- I understand the Big, Hairy, Audacious Goals defined in Our Brew (82)

- I understand what is expected of me to help us become a Top 4 global brewer (79%)

- I feel comfortable challenging the expected at work (81)

- I know how I help deliver extraordinary brands that delight beer drinkers (83)

4. *Objective*: Rollout Our Brew to all salaried employees by March 2009; rollout to hourly production employees by end of October 2009.

Results: Rollout completed to entire employee population within pre-established timeline.

5. *Objective*: Unite disparate business units under one company name, brand and strategy.

Results: In addition to a common alignment around Our Brew key messages and corresponding goals, the leadership, HR and communication teams took a series of "iconic actions" such as the business unit name changes, HR process changes and launch of one global employee intranet.

6. *Objective*: Translate all major communication vehicles into "pub-talk approved" look, feel and language.

Results: All major communications vehicles revised to be pub talk–approved, including Our Brew Board, Yammer social media community, printed collateral and global portal.

- Average 1,500 to 3,000 unique users to Pub Talk portal per day (Monday highest average; Friday lowest).

- Average 1,750 distinct Our Brew Board users per month; 175 average users per day.

- Yammer enrollment more than 1,600 in first six months.

DISCUSSION QUESTIONS

1. How has employee communication evolved as a communication discipline, and why?
2. How have major business cycles affected employee communication?
3. What are the key elements of effective employee communication cited by the author?
4. How can employee communication be measured to demonstrate its effectiveness, reach and return?
5. What trends will influence the evolution of employee communication?
6. What did the author mean when he cited the following quote: "Don't let high-tech replace high-touch?"
7. What does the concept of "One Voice, One Look" represent?
8. What role does storytelling play in companies today?
9. How is globalization influencing the role of employee communication?
10. How important will digital communication and new technologies be to the internal communication efforts of organizations in the coming years?

ADDITIONAL READING

BOOKS

Belasco, James and Ralph Staver. *Flight of the Buffalo: Soaring to Excellence, Learning to Let Employees Lead.* New York, NY: Grand Central Publishing, 1994.

Berry, John and Ed Keller. *The Influentials: One American in Ten Tells the Other Nine How to Vote, Where to Eat, and What to Buy.* New York, NY: Free Press, 2008.

Bethune, Gordon. *From Worst to First: Behind the Scenes of Continental's Remarkable Comeback.* Hoboken, NJ: Wiley, 1999.

Bossidy, Larry and Ram Charan. *Execution: The Discipline of Getting Things Done.* New York, NY: Crown Business, 2002.

Buchholz, Todd. *New Ideas from Dead CEOs: Lasting Lessons from the Corner Office.* New York, NY: HarperBusiness, 2007.

George, Bill. *True North: Discover Your Authentic Leadership.* San Francisco, CA: Jossey-Bass, 2007.

Golin, Al. *Trust or Consequences.* New York, NY: Amacom, 2006.

Keen, Andrew. *The Cult of the Amateur.* New York, NY: Crown Business, 2008.

Larkin, T.J. and Sandar. *Communicating Change: Winning Employee Support for New Business Goals.* New York, NY: McGraw-Hill, 1994.

Smith, J. Walker and Ann Clurman. *Rocking the Ages: The Yankelovich Report on Generational Marketing.* New York, NY: Harper Paperbacks, 1998.

WEBSITES

www.insidedge.net
technorati.com
www.eiu.com/public
www.apple.com
plankcenter.ua.edu
www.instituteforpr.org
www.iabc.com
www.prsa.org
www.prweek.com
www.awpagesociety.com

BLOGS

intake.insidedge.net
intranetblog.blogware.com
atomicbomb.typepad.com
www.edelman.com/speak_up/blog
byrnebabybyrne.com

NEWSPAPERS AND PERIODICALS

The Wall Street Journal (iPad)
The New York Times (iPad)
The Economist
Talent Management
MacLife
Outside
The Strategist (PRSA)
Harvard Business Review

9

C H A P T E R

CONSUMER INSIGHT IN A DIGITAL AGE

Geraldine Henderson, Ph.D.
Associate Professor, School of Business
Rutgers University

Consumers are just one set of the many different stakeholders that an organization has. However, it is easy to argue that consumers are the most important stakeholder group because they bring in the revenue (funds) for most organizations and because there are so many of them. For instance, there are many more consumers (in sheer number) than other stakeholders such as board members or suppliers. An organization may have a product or service, a method of distribution and an internal support structure but if it does not have a consumer, it cannot exist or sustain itself. In the corporate world, consumers buy products or services, generating the cash flow that allows an organization to grow and expand, to invest in improving itself and to make a profit. In the not-for-profit world, consumers are the end users of an organization's services, creating for that organization a sense of purpose and focus. The opportunity that consumers represent is the reason we organize in the first place. Consumers are an organization's greatest assets and ones to be carefully managed.

To influence consumers, we need to understand them; thus this chapter on consumer insight. We want to be able to have some type of interaction with them. Hopefully, they will do something that will be in the organization's best interest. We need to understand them and to make ourselves available to them as much as possible. Influencing, persuading and motivating this critical stakeholder group is a fundamental activity of any organization. Marketers and communications professionals are particularly dedicated to this task and always have been. Public relations professionals, as one type of communications expert, are also highly involved in this influence function, but their role has evolved over time.

DEFINING CONSUMERS

Consumer is a word used quite broadly, but it generally refers to the "end user" of an organization's product or service, that is, the person who pays for and "consumes" that product or service. In a not-for-profit context, a consumer may be a client of a public organization, benefiting from the services that organization has been created and funded to offer. In a political context, a consumer may be a voter. Because the corporation or organization provides a product, service, issue or candidate to someone to be used or affiliated with, the corporation or organization has a consumer. Equally, a consumer can be defined as the person on whom the organization depends for the money, effort, time or votes that sustain it. The relationship between an organization and its consumers is indeed an interdependent one, which should work to the benefit of both parties.

There is a difference between customers and consumers. For purposes of this chapter, we broaden the definition of consumer to include a type of person often called a customer. Customers are in fact consumers, but in a business-to-business context. For example, a food manufacturer's first consumer is the grocery store buyer. A clothing manufacturer's first consumer is a department store buyer. A mutual fund organization's first consumer may be the stockbroker whose own consumer is the investor. Because these people are essential elements of the distribution system of most corporations, they should be considered part of the broader consumer audience.

The diversity of the consumer audience is also a unique characteristic of this stakeholder group. They are heterogeneous. They are all over the place. They are from every demographic, psychographic, geographic, need-based and behavioral segment. We group consumers together into one audience simply because they share a common behavior; that is, they have purchased or used a product or service. However, the needs that prompted their desire for that product or service may differ widely as may the benefits they derive from it. Both the size and the diversity of our consumer audiences present exciting challenges to public relations and communications professionals.

Consumers are heterogeneous, and thus one size does not fit all—so we can't assume that what we do for one set of consumers is going to work for another. Thus, we need to constantly update what we know about consumers because what we know about a particular consumer segment most likely is not going to apply to all people, places and occasions. However, an important issue shared by all communications practitioners is the need to understand consumer motivations fully and richly enough to be able to design programs that persuasively and effectively connect with those consumers. As any communications professional knows, the programs she creates are far more likely to be effective at influencing, persuading and motivating a consumer audience if they are constructed from the beginning with the wants, needs and motivations of that audience in mind. To that end, this chapter will focus on ways in which communications professionals and their organizations can learn more about consumers as a foundation for effectively influencing and persuading them.

Once we identify desirable consumer segments, we must profile them. Profiling segments includes asking how big a segment is, how fast it is growing, who is in each segment, what are their demographic characteristics, how do they spend their free time, what do they care about, where do they shop, where do they collect product information, how do they buy, who makes or influences the purchase decision, how often do they buy, how much do they buy, how do they use the product and what benefits are they seeking. Segment factors to consider include size, growth rate, competitive intensity, fit with our organization skills and resources, profitability and whether the segment warrants targeting. To be useful, market segments must be measurable, substantial, accessible, differentiable and actionable.

DEFINING CONSUMER INSIGHT

Often, the question gets asked about what consumer insight is. Succinctly put, it is a cross between consumer behavior and marketing research (Figure 9.1).[1]

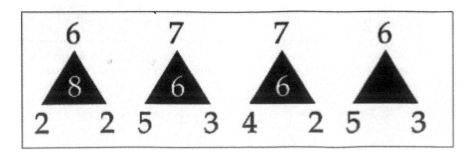

F I G U R E   9.1

Pattern Recognition

What number comes next? Consumer insight is all about pattern recognition and making sense out of chaos. The idea is to convert data into nuggets of knowledge about consumers. Hulu has great insight into consumers.[2] They observed the data of consumers increasingly using services such as TiVo and other DVRs, NetFlix and SlingBox to control their own television and film programming. Hulu provides a similar type of service except that the consumer does not have to remember to set a device to record or pay per view of each movie or show. Instead, they may go to hulu.com and watch current season programming for free or join Hulu Plus for added benefits. Some have argued that the Hulu business model will not be able to sustain itself, but it is actually a perfect win–win for advertisers, content providers and consumers because Hulu allows consumers to tailor their programming and marketers to tailor their advertising to the particular target. Levi's has also been able to see the pattern in the data. For years, their research suggested that the process of buying jeans was a frustrating one for women, with each woman trying on an average of 10 pairs of jeans before finding a pair that suited her. Of particular frustration were the standard leg and waist measurements that failed to capture the differences in shape of each woman's body. Thus, this consumer insight led to the development of the CurveID that not only selects jeans based on leg or waist measurements but also according to whether they have a slight curve, a demi curve, a bold curve or a supreme curve (Figure 9.2).[3]

One of the reasons that Levi's was able to be so effective is that they were able to gather data from their existing base of consumers and use that for both the retention of existing consumers and the recruitment of new consumers. An organization's consumer marketing is only as good as the data on which it is based. As with any persuasive activity, a marketer or communicator's programs are only as effective as the insights into consumers and customers who inform them. Indeed, we will always find that an organization that is effective

FIGURE 9.2

Levi's Curve ID Campaign

with its consumer audience is one that is highly skilled at gathering and interpreting useful information about those consumers. It is an organization dedicated to distilling key insights into its most important stakeholder and aligning its programs with those insights. Therefore, perhaps the most critical foundation stones for organizational success are the development of a base of knowledge about the consumer, the ability to carefully listen to and interpret that knowledge and the ability to disseminate consumer and customer insights throughout the organization.

ANALYZING

Gathering and analyzing the data needed for consumer insight are the fundamental purposes for consumer research. The role that consumer research has played in organizations has varied over time. In many organizations, consumer and market research have long been important tools in planning marketing and communications strategies and tactics. The research techniques vary widely, but they are well established and range from small-scale qualitative research (often called *soft soundings* in a public relations context) to large-scale and projectable quantitative research, including surveys. There are many ways of gathering these data. It is difficult to say which of the many available techniques is most appropriate in a particular circumstance, but many excellent marketing research organizations exist in virtually every country, which can help formulate a program of marketing research relevant to a particular consumer target. It depends on your objectives and your disciplinary perspective.

There are different perspectives to keep in mind when gathering this information such as psychological, sociological, and/or economic. There are so many different researchers from diverse backgrounds interested in consumer insight that it begs the question as to which is the proper or correct discipline to look into these issues. Depending on what your goal is, you are going to look at it through different lenses. Michael Solomon equates this type of interpretation with the age-old concept of three blind men in a room with an elephant; all will give different interpretations of what it is.

You might remember a children's story about the blind men and the elephant. The gist of the story is that each man touched a different part of the animal and as a result the descriptions each gave for the elephant were quite different. This analogy applies to consumer research as well. A given consumer phenomenon can be studied in different ways and at different levels depending on the training and the interests of the researchers studying it.[4]

As you formulate a program of marketing research or consider the base of information your organization has already collected, it is important to remember that there are many ways of knowing and understanding consumers and customers. Although there are a great number of techniques available to help us learn about consumers "in general" or "on the average," and they are critical to intelligent decision making, other techniques help us to get closer to the consumer, closing the inevitable distance between ourselves as marketers, communicators and public relations professionals and the consumer. With the advent of the social Web, many of these techniques may be conducted online, and thus we spend the bulk of this chapter focusing on these newer, online data gathering techniques.

ANALYZING ONLINE CONSUMER DATA

The Internet is full of nuggets of data for organizations to grab up. Thus, in addition to commissioning research and eliciting data from consumers, it is of tremendous value to listen in on the organic conversations that consumers are having because that's not something that is primed by a researcher's inquiry. Online consumers may disclose real-life situations and frustrations that they may be too embarrassed or modest to disclose in face-to-face settings. In addition, the online community affords them the ability to identify other like-minded and like-conditioned individuals beyond the confines of geographic limitations and to form cliques (groups and subgroups) with them. Netnography techniques (also known as online listening) represent a growing market research industry from which organizations may gain tremendous insight into the minds of consumers.[5] Netnography is "a specialized form of ethnography adapted to the unique computer-mediated contingencies of today's social worlds."[6] Both archived and elicited data may be gathered online. Data archival is a less obtrusive means of data collection.[7]

Companies that specialize in this type of research are Communispace,[8] Radian6[9] and Zuberance,[10] among others. Radian6 is the modern-day equivalent to a news clipping service on steroids. Their platform trolls the Internet looking for mentions of your organization. Anytime they come across a mention, they capture it and tell you whether it was positive or negative. They give you some indication of the context. It's like a content analysis of your organization, and they tell you whether the overall sentiment is good or bad. Radian6 gives its customers a "complete platform to listen, measure, and engage with [their] customers" via the social web.

Although the Radian6 platform is proprietary, what they deliver to their clients is similar to a content analysis of sentiment expressed about brands and organizations via the social web. However, data collected online may be analyzed in many other ways including discourse analysis. Discourse analysis includes a recurrent process of data abstraction, grouping and coding either manually or automatically by using software such as Nvivo[11] or Atlas.ti.[12] To develop theoretical grounding, codes are developed on the basis of the informant or archived data as well as the extant literature.[13] Definitions for codes and subcodes are created using informant key words and phrases as well as definitions from the literature. Data should be coded by more than one consumer researcher. That way, any discrepancies between coders may be identified, discussed and resolved. Codes are then aggregated to develop the themes used to understand your findings. Data are thus analyzed using a hermeneutic approach.[14,15] You know you have consumer insight when you achieve triangulation or convergence. That is, you reach a point that any new data points found only confirm what you have already found across people, places, occasions and time. According to Blake Cahill, former Senior Vice President of Marketing at Visible Technologies, firms like to provide social listening platforms such as Radian6 and Visible Technologies. These platforms also assist organizations in differentiating between signal and noise with respect to consumer insights derived from data.[16,17]

Some organizations understand the concept of online consumer insight more than others. For instance, organizations that were primarily direct marketers before the advent of the social web have adapted to it very well. After all, they had a more distributed approach to marketing communications, so it was an easy slip into social media. The door-to-door Avon sales representative has now taken her business to the social web and has been able to renew herself.[18] Her customers are now able to self-select in and out of purchasing products, and the representative may have both an online and an offline interaction with customers.

LISTENING

Because consumers are out on the social web communicating with one another about brands and organizations, organizations may listen in on those conversations. Traditionally, if two individuals were having a conversation about the Red Cross during the aftermath of a natural disaster, that conversation might be held in private and thus the Red Cross would not be aware of it. However, with the advent of the social web, the conversation may now happen on Twitter or some other medium. If so, this conversation becomes public and the consumers don't seem to care about having this conversation in public; everyone can see it. They may even use the hashtag #redcross so that others may find and join in on that conversation, including the Red Cross. Because the Red Cross uses Radian6, they are able to listen to what their consumers are saying about them online, to measure consumer sentiment and then to engage their consumers.[19,20] Thus, if a tweet or a series of tweets were found that was inconsistent with the Red Cross brand image, the Red Cross could engage their (potential) consumers by posting a reply to that individual (@individual) or post generally (and include #redcross). The result is more effective public relations efforts and an increase in giving associated with those efforts.

The social web is replete with consumers crying out for attention from companies. They want a conversation either with the company directly or with other consumers who may help them work through their frustrations (e.g., lack of wireless network coverage) or help them celebrate their victories (e.g., the newest iPhone). They want to know if anyone is listening to them. If an organization is not willing to listen to them, their competitors may be.

This is an opportunity for organizations to get involved with these conversations because, in this instance, the consumer is not writing a private letter to the organization and saying you messed up. No, the conversation they are having is a public one—so the onus is on the organization to correct, not only in the mind of that particular consumer but also in the public face. Otherwise, there is unanswered negativity out there that the organization has chosen not to address.

Consider a Coach Leatherware or a Tumi Luggage brand enthusiast. They love these brands. They may have purchased their first purse or piece of luggage decades ago and have been with them ever since. Unlike their counterparts, who have had several different brands and styles over the years, some of these committed consumers may have some of the same pieces for the duration of their long relationship with these brands. Whereas others may seek variety, these individuals enjoy the durability and reliability of these brands. These pieces may be items that travel with them everywhere they go like a constant companion and thus have a lot of wear and tear.

However, these brand enthusiasts know that if they should ever have a problem with their Coach purse or Tumi luggage, they can take them back to the store, have them send it back to the factory to be fixed and mailed back to the consumer. After all, these are probably individuals who over the years defended Coach and/or Tumi time and time again when asked why they would pay so much for a purse or a piece of luggage. As long as this relationship proceeds as expected, these individuals are ripe for brand advocacy.

However, there is a potential for a love–hate relationship with Coach or Tumi should they ever change the nature of the relationship. Recently, many Coach or Tumi enthusiasts have taken to the social web to express their dismay at being refused repair by the respective firms.[21] Many of them have expressed that they felt as though they were in a relationship with them for quite some time and they hurt their feelings. According to them, Coach or Tumi violated one of the fundamental bases of their relationship with them. Through their brand loyalty, these brand enthusiasts told Coach or Tumi that they loved them but with this new policy they heard Coach or Tumi say that they didn't love them back.[22] In recognition of these types of problems, some advertising agencies actually bring in psychologists to review a client's relationship with its consumers. They would say things like "you have violated trust; you've broken a promise, and now they don't want to deal with you anymore. You can't just say 'hey, I've got this new thing, why don't you come back?' It's really going to take some time and some healing." Without such healing, brand advocates may become brand badvocates and voice their displeasure via twitter, Facebook and other social media platforms.

In steps a firm called Zuberance led by Rob Fuggetta. Zuberance matches up organizations with their brand advocates, and they also identify brand badvocates. This notion is that there are people out there who will promote or demote your brand in the public mind. One of the things Zuberance does is help you find these people. These brand (b)advocates provide invaluable market research.

CASE STUDY

CDW is a leading supplier of computer hardware, software and technology supplies with IT professionals as its major consumers (customers). Lauren McCadney, Senior Segment Marketing Manager of CDW, cites Forrester Research, which states that although 3 of 4 consumers mistrust traditional media, 9 of 10 consumers do trust other consumers. In fact, CDW's own research indicates that after personal experience, advice from a colleague is the second most influential way to learn about IT providers like CDW. A manager in possession of this insight may engineer a social marketing campaign that takes advantage of the Internet's ability to reach massive audiences to help identify and target brand advocates (those consumers who indicate a willingness to recommend your brand).

Lauren led her CDW team in constructing a three-part strategy to locate and activate advocates: identification, acknowledgment and multiplication. In particular, CDW sought to learn effective advocate outreach tactics, the willingness of advocates to act in a way that benefits the company and the monetizing of opportunities. For example, reviews written by advocates offer an opportunity to help educate other customers and prospects by explaining, in terms relevant to the target, the benefits associated with doing business with CDW. The captured reviews were used in several ways including sharing on the website, as a copy in catalogs and a call to action in direct mail. CDW also discovered that one of five nearly advocates writing a review also elected to share via social sharing (i.e., mail, Facebook or Twitter). The short-term goal of leveraging the reviews was increased brand consideration through peer-to-peer message reinforcement. CDW took advantage of their already established goodwill with a segment of their customer population to help drive more consideration and ultimately revenue.

Their success story is not about the single (albeit awesome) accomplishment of securing their advocates but about their process. CDW, while working with knowledgeable partners such as Zuberance, simply endeavored to acknowledge the existence of their most satisfied tribe members and centered their activities on the customer and community. They didn't follow the crowd, but they did do what made sense for their brand.

In this case, a company ought to determine whether an individual who discusses company products is a valuable marketing resource (advocate) or a threat to the brand (badvocate). A manager should consider the value of advocates in the pursuit of marketing success and should reflect on the methods of sustaining advocates.

Everyone knows that positive feedback for an organization is good news. However, negative feedback is great news. If an organization delivers a less than satisfying customer experience, all is not lost. In fact, if the organization has a service failure and has a service recovery to the satisfaction of the consumer, the consumer is likely to be more satisfied than they would have been if the service failure never happened.[23] This is not to suggest that organizations should go around creating service failures. However, to the extent that an organization is able to discover a service failure, then it is in their best interest to attempt to recover from that failure. Not all people complain. The more people are invested in the relationship they have with an organization, the more likely they are to voice their (dis)pleasure.[24] In fact, we know that people have several different ways in which they might respond to less than satisfying customer experiences: exit, voice and loyalty.[25,26] Exit is when they get so fed up with the experience that they walk away from it and the associated organization. There are several forms of voice, which include internal voice and external voice.

Internal voice is to the organization itself via direct face-to-face communication, telephone, e-mail or regular mail. These internal communications may be anywhere up the food chain from frontline service personnel or entry-level customer service representatives all the way up to the C-suite or the board of directors. External communications include word of mouth (online and offline), media reports, legal and other regulatory notifications and other interested parties such as the Better Business Bureau. Social media, in particular, and the Internet, in general, blur internal and external voice and thus are the perfect locale for consumer insight data collection.[27]

Consider the Tempur-Pedic example. In 2010, Tempur-Pedic ran a commercial in which they challenged consumers to not just take their word for it but to ask anyone that they know that has a Tempur-Pedic mattress what they think about that Tempur-Pedic relative to any other mattress they have ever owned. They said that they would let existing consumers convince the potential consumers. After all, they tout themselves as being "the most highly recommended bed in America." An organization that is going to open itself up to word of mouth like that has to be so confident about its product offering that they are willing to have someone else whom they don't know be that mediator of the relationship between the organization and the potential consumer. In addition, they are especially susceptible to competitive postings about their products (remember the Whole Foods CEO John Mackey who got in trouble for posting negative things about his competitors).[28]

Thus, Tempur-Pedic launched the Connect & Share portal on their website in which people who don't already know a Tempur-Pedic consumer may ask and hear what others have to tell about their experiences.[29] Of course, an organization is not going to throw something like that out there unless they are able to engage (listen in and respond to) conversations (such as the one being held on the Tempur-Pedic page of pissedconsumer.com). One of the reasons that the Internet is such a fertile ground for data collection is that if two consumers talk to one another in a private conversation (e.g., in restaurant over lunch), there is virtually no way for the organization to ever find out the exact details of that conversation. Online, an organization may watch that conversation unfold before its very eyes. There is tremendous value in information online, and organizations may find this treasure using consumer monitoring and engagement.

ENGAGING

As markets in more industries and in more countries mature, and as supply exceeds demand in many of those markets, it will become increasingly clear to organizations that the ability to maintain a long-term relationship with consumers should be the organization's most important goal.[30] Organizations that embrace consumers as true stakeholders in their success will benefit from the long-term asset value those consumers represent.[31] Organizations that find unique and effective ways to engage the consumer to reach into the organization will be ones with the greatest chance of building those relationships. Apple is one such organization. The Apple Store

Genius Bar is sheer genius.[32] When you are there to get your computer fixed, they tell you to wait anywhere in the store. They have computers and gadgets set up everywhere along with chairs so that you may sit and play with them. They want you to get attached to them, buy one and take one home. In this instance, Apple provides an in-store environment that is conducive to future sales. In contrast, many other organizations that have the same opportunity choose to keep their gadgets behind counters, where the only way that a consumer can get access to it is to have a sales person mediate that interaction.

ENGAGING CONSUMERS

There are a variety of ways to engage the consumer, all within the capabilities of every public relations practitioner, marketer and communicator. These days, the simplest is to spend time online with consumers, observing the way they shop for, purchase and use your products or services. For instance, after years of selling hardback and paperback books to consumers, Amazon.com realized that their e-book business was increasingly robust. Thus, they launched the Kindle business to allow e-book consumers to take their books with them. The way that Kindle works is that a consumer goes online to amazon.com or to the WhisperNet on their Kindle and orders a book, a magazine or a newspaper. After the transaction is complete, the item is downloaded to their Kindle. A record of all transactions is stored on Amazon's server and associated with an individual user's account.

Amazon even has a way to deal with a stolen Kindle. If someone calls Amazon and tells them that their Kindle has been stolen, they immediately disable the device so that it is no longer able to download any new content or access content already resident. If the person in possession of the stolen Kindle calls Amazon for technical assistance to get access to the content, Amazon does not reveal that they know the device has been stolen. Instead, they encourage the individual in possession of the Kindle to send it back to Amazon so that they may "fix" the problem. However, what Amazon really does is provide the stolen device back to the owner of record on the account. The Kindle owner is not only not held responsible for any charges after the device was reported stolen, but as soon as the consumer gets the stolen device or a replacement device, they are able to retrieve all of the content that they had previously purchased.

More importantly, Amazon demonstrated great consumer insight through its release of the free Kindle application for iPhone, iPad, Droid, Mac, PC and other platforms.[33] When the iPhone was introduced, people had a choice between using the iBook application or the Kindle application. Amazon could have attempted to force consumers to purchase the Amazon Kindle to get the functionality that the application provides. However, their knowledge of consumers led them to understand that many consumers are more interested in converting to a digital library than being tethered to a particular platform. Similarly, Amazon realized that the true revenue derives from the content downloads and not the device, and thus they are also not tethered to it. It is like the old Gillette razor handle versus razor cartridge example in which the handle is basically given away because the real revenue comes from the repeat purchase of the cartridges. Likewise, Amazon makes its money from the sales of Kindle books just as Apple makes money from its sales of music via iTunes.

JetBlue uses multiple approaches in social media to get in contact with its customers and to build its brand through its website, blog, YouTube channel, Twitter feed, Facebook and so forth. Paul Levy, the President and CEO of Beth Israel Deaconess Medical Center in Boston, Massachusetts, had a long-standing blog entitled "Running a Hospital." This was a great way for him to establish and maintain contact with Beth Israel's consumers. Of course, there is an inherent challenge for the organization of having the CEO brand be too tightly connected to or confused with the organization's brand. For example, when Paul Levy left Beth Israel, he took his blog with him and renamed it "Not Running a Hospital."[34]

The higher up in the organization you are, the less likely you are to know about your consumers. You are more distant from them. This is one of the reasons that social media is so important. It removes the distance between the CEO and the consumer. The information is out there, but it is not gated. Many CEOs have their own blogs now. It is a way to allow people to have access to CEOs when they ordinarily would not. Many facets of organizational life conspire to keep an organization's members at all levels away from direct contact with their consumers, but it is a tendency that must be fought. The more often organizational managers, and particularly communications professionals, decide how to best influence consumers on the basis of executive summaries of distantly collected data, the greater the likelihood that those decision makers will miss important nuances and details of the consumer's experience. In addition, it is often the nuances of the consumer's experience that lead to greater and deeper insights into their motivations and better ideas about how to use communications tools to persuade them.

The most important activity a forward-thinking manager can do to help encourage this way of thinking is to set a good example. If the highest levels of an organization dedicate themselves to some form of regular and direct contact with consumers, other levels of the organization will follow. Indeed, if the management of an organization goes further to reward the contributions of all employees or members who get closer to the customer, the organization will much more easily orient itself in that direction. A manager can never allow disassociation from the consumer or customer to become a corollary of increasing authority in the organization.

Our marketing efforts and communications programs can often be vastly improved when we use these techniques to help us understand the employees who directly serve consumers. Certainly frontline employees are important "communications tools" themselves, leaving indelible impressions on the consumer about how much the organization cares about them and is interested in delighting them. It clearly behooves us to keep our fingers directly on the pulse of employee sentiment as much as it does on that of the consumer. Imagine if each nail technician at the local nail salon felt this aligned incentive to be a consumer champion. Each time a new customer would arrive at the salon, they would be greeted immediately and made to feel welcome. The consumer would be asked what services he or she wanted and how long the wait would be for such a service. There would be interaction with the consumer before, during and after the service that would make him or her feel like the object of attention (as opposed to a distraction for the nail tech). After all, tips and perhaps commissions would be paid according to the level of consumer service provided and perceived. An organization such as GameStop has great consumer insight. One of the things that makes them successful is that the people that they have working in their stores are gamers, so who could be better to interface with the consumers?[35]

ENGAGING CONSUMER COMMUNITIES

There are ways in which organizations can provide more formal opportunities for consumers and customers to enter into its decision-making processes. Today, many organizations have created online consumption communities that may be consulted at a variety of points in the processes of devising business, marketing and communications strategies and tactics.[36,37] The organization has ready access to people who can serve as representatives of the larger consumer audience and as a reality check for decisions and programs under consideration.

Beyond traditional market research panels, organizations often form communities of consumer experts and opinion leaders to help them stay on top of trends that can affect their marketing and communications programs. This kind of advisory community is particularly useful in a fast-moving industry such as the computer industry or in industries subject to quickly shifting trends such as the toy and fashion industries. Here, an organization might identify early adopters of new technologies or innovations or people who have amassed an influential expertise in a particular area. An organization can monitor the information-gathering, shopping and purchase behavior of these consumers in a detached and unidentified way, or it can directly interact with them and question them in a roundtable discussion format. Of course, there is always the fear that such direct interaction will taint the validity of the information and insights these consumers have to offer. On the other hand, if the members of the organization learn to interact with these consumers in a way that emphasizes their ability to listen and observe, then this risk can be minimized, and these consumers can serve as extremely valuable advisers to the organization.

Beta testing products is one particular function that these consumer advisors may play. For instance, in 2010, Chevrolet provided 15 consumers with its Chevy Volt automobiles for a 90-day period and had them not only incorporate them into their everyday lives but also blog about it.[38] Thus, Chevy had constant (albeit public) feedback regarding these early user experiences. Close contact with a set of early consumers of one brand helps the organization anticipate when and why a consumer eventually moves on to another brand. Armed with that information, particular communications programs can often be designed and used, which helps to keep the brand fresh and relevant to current drinkers over time and to generations of new consumers as they emerge.

It can be very valuable for an organization to establish a long-term, ongoing relationship with a set of everyday consumers who can be consulted for their opinions on both broad and specific questions. It may be that consumers are selected as consultants or advisers for only a year's time, but during that year, they can be available to the organization for visits online, via Skype (or similar technology), over the phone, or even in person. Having these kinds of consumers readily available encourages organization members to contact them spontaneously and also encourages the consumer to contact the organization with thoughts or ideas. In addition, having contact with the same consumers over an extended period helps to make the consumer's point of view better understood by the entire organization. It is easy to see how this kind of contact can help draw the consumer and the organization closer together by making the consumer a real person rather than a set of summary statistics. In fact, visits with consumers and customers should be a part of the routine activities of people in all functional areas of an organization. If an individual's work touches the consumer in any way, there is always the opportunity to improve that work on the basis of a greater insight into the consumer.

To make these types of long-term connections with consumers easier, Communispace, led by Diane Hessan, designs online communities for companies for just this purpose. They have created private communities for companies such as Blue Cross Blue Shield, Home Depot, and Harrah's. Kraft Foods, which has a long history of creating face-to-face communities, says,

> . . . we immediately saw the benefit of having consumers talking with us and with each other around the clock. It enabled us to stay in almost constant touch with our consumers. Although Kraft certainly benefits from getting their reactions to new product ideas and the like, the true benefit is developing deeper relationships and the dialogs that result. Our consumers were no longer demographic statistics—they became real people with strong opinions, deep feelings and daily challenges that they were willing to share with us. Knowing our consumers at this level is invaluable in helping us deliver the best possible products and programs to meet their needs (Gretchen Waitley, Consumer Insight Manager with Kraft).[39]

Organizations who seek to have their products purchased by specific age groups, such as financial services, may find these types of communities of particular use. It is often the case that consumers don't even consider their financial future during their young adult years, but then as they age, they realize that they need to start investing and saving. Charles Schwab used Communispace to help them indentify GenX'ers before they would normally seek out investment help. Identifying and engaging them early, and thus having them engage each other in conversations about their financial future, has turned out to be a winning strategy for Charles Schwab.[40]

LIBERATING CONSUMERS

Too often today, we think of consumers as the quasi-military objective of our marketing and communications efforts. We speak of "capturing" the consumer, "locking up" their purchase patterns, using "guerrilla" tactics or "flanking" maneuvers to "destroy" the competition and establishing a "beachhead" with a consumer market. This way of conceptualizing our efforts and of describing them to one another is antithetical to the view described earlier and the feeling we must have toward consumers to ensure our organization's future survival.[41]

Rather than a military metaphor, we might be better served with an agricultural one, conceiving of our consumers the way a farmer might of his land. Our consumers are people we cultivate and care for. If they are stewarded carefully, they ensure our survival.[42] Like the farmer, we can never afford to forget the consumer. All of the resources of our organizations must be expended in ensuring the complete satisfaction, if not delight, of the consumer. If successful, consumers will reward us with their continuing goodwill and loyalty and will work with us through any crisis or difficulty that we may encounter.

JetBlue had people sitting on the Tarmac for hours. They had to do something to get people back in line. There must have been people on their phones on the tarmac complaining. JetBlue CEO gave a talk at Northwestern. He talked about what JetBlue learned from that situation and how to regroup from it.[43] What is really important to recognize now is that because of the lack of control over brand and identity, you have no control over it; either you get with the program or you get lost because otherwise people will take you over. If one bad thing happens, you can never get rid of it. Once it is on the web, it is there for life; you can't get rid of it.

American Airlines does some things well. JetBlue decided to equip their planes with luxurious seats and DirectTV. American Airlines does not have leather seats but they have retrofitted all of their planes with power ports available to most seats on the plane. Thus, consumers may bring their own personal entertainment and have a power port. In addition to that, many flights have Internet, so if consumers want to watch TV, they may watch Hulu or they can catch up on their work or personal e-mail. Not everyone wants to watch TV on the plane. American Airline's investment in technology was much smarter than JetBlue's DirectTV investment.[44] People can also talk about how they are e-mailing someone while flying on American Airlines. It is a better use of technology because it allows the consumer more versatility. Other airlines spent an enormous amount of money to retrofit their planes.

However, American Airlines mistakenly believed that they could charge a premium for those seats and thus pulled themselves off orbitz.com.[45] Loyalty is bittersweet. On one hand, the organization has the benefit of the buyers' repeat patronage and even repeat purchase; however, on the other hand, repeat purchase does not equal loyalty, and as soon as a better alternative presents itself, the consumer may disappear.[46] In the case of American Airlines, powerports and Internet availability give consumers a reason to fly American Airlines relative to its competition, but that preference does not necessarily quite reflect an ability to charge a premium price for that opportunity.

In 2011, it is amazing that service providers such as cable, phone and home delivery services still insist on arriving during the hours when most people who can afford to engage them are at work earning a salary to pay them (e.g., a 4-hour window between 8 A.M. to noon). When individuals ask for either later hours, or at least a narrower window of time, they say no. Even when the organizations employ independent contractors, the organization still keeps and makes the master schedule that is not flexible. Hospitals are quick to blame the ranks of the uninsured for overwhelming their emergency room departments. However, a closer look at the data often reveals that many of the nonemergency cases presenting to the emergency room are individuals who are insured and have access to regular physicians and specialists. Insight into their behavior might lead hospital executives to understand that emergency rooms provide instantaneous service at more convenient hours to many patients. Perhaps if primary care physicians offered a wider array of office hours, they might find a tremendous boost in their patient visitations. Organizations need to have more accommodating hours.

Convenient hours aren't the only accommodation that organizations can make for consumers. Best Buy realized that one of the reasons their sales had leveled off over the years (and why companies like Circuit City collapsed altogether) was that consumers weren't trading up. Thus, Best Buy started a buyback program, which is a recognition that people are reluctant to upgrade to the latest and greatest when they already possess an older generation device that still works perfectly fine, albeit more slowly and without as much whizbang.[47] By all accounts, the buyback program isn't a great deal for consumers (as compared with selling the old technology on places like ebay.com); however, Best Buy realizes that by giving their consumers this option, they are giving them permission to trade up to the latest and greatest.

Likewise, Costco discovered through its consumer research that consumers really disliked the traditional process for purchasing a vehicle in which the price they paid was a function of their negotiation skills and the integrity of the car dealership. Thus, the experience of buying cars from Costco is changing the perspective of how people acquire cars. It's a win–win for the consumer and the manufacturer. Effectively, with this program, consumers are able to purchase virtually any make and model of automobile in the same way that they would order a refrigerator or other durable goods from Costco.[48]

Progressive, E-surance, and Geico have changed the way that people purchase auto insurance. You don't have to go to your neighborhood insurance broker to buy insurance. You may go online, compare rates based on the type of coverage that you would like and order automobile insurance the same way that you order books from Amazon. The Progressive spokesperson "Flo" is portrayed to be like a cashier or frontline service provider in a retail setting. E-surance allows you to purchase insurance online when you want it and to use people when you don't. This is a true recognition that consumers are not one-size-fits-all and that they have many different ways in which they want to interface with the marketplace.[49]

It is often valuable for an organization to maintain particularly close ongoing ties with its outside distribution system. Whenever an organization relies on dealers, distributors, trade partners or another form of nonproprietary sales force to interact with the ultimate consumer, the organization must stay on top of their attitudes and ideas, which certainly affects the consumer. For instance, some of the earliest online communities were in the high-tech sector and were called *user groups*. These user groups were populated by IT managers and technicians, along with other "heavy users" of information technology within a variety of firms. Because they could not reach enough critical mass within their own organizations (either because their organization was not large enough or because their particular function was highly specialized and no organization, no matter how large, would need more than one of them), they found each other at a user group meeting and on the Internet via forums and chat rooms. However, with the advent of the social web, firms like Spiceworks have really changed the user group phenomenon into living online communities for various hardware, software and solutions platforms.[50] Spiceworks boasts having active participation from a wide range of sectors such as education, entertainment, finance, government, health care, travel, legal, nonprofit, retail and transportation. As of 2011, the Spiceworks community was home to more than 1.4 million IT professionals in small to medium businesses who join to research products they need, to get answers to questions they post, to connect with other IT professionals and to share what they know.

Naturally with any of these techniques, there is always the fear that, with the limited time available to any member of an organization, particularly a key decision maker, the interactions she can have with consumers are likely to be very idiosyncratic and unrepresentative, and therefore the conclusions this decision maker might draw could be suspect. This, of course, is possible. However, if we agree that the most fundamental purpose of our organizations is to gather and share information and that all employees should be committed to this purpose, then there is little to fear. All of the information, gathered in any way by any person, becomes a part of the organization's collective knowledge base, and the effect of any single piece of information is tempered by the rest of what the organization knows.

DISCUSSION QUESTIONS

1. Distinguish between a consumer and a customer. Can a company have both customers and consumers? What communications differences are there in strategies to reach consumers versus customers?
2. Profiling seems to have some risk associated with it in public discussions. In marketing, however, how is the term used? What are the segments of profiling in marketing? What are the traits of segments that allow marketers and PR professionals to use targeting? Give an example of how a consumer goods company might use the segments to increase the likelihood of making a sale?
3. Discuss the importance of feedback in PR and marketing communications. When is negative feedback more useful than positive feedback? Write a 200-word memo to a manager explaining why it is a good idea to encourage negative feedback about your product or service. Provide some ideas on how you can open channels of communications to get that feedback.
4. Are consumers and customers really targets? Write a brief story of 200 words of how you were treated as a new consumer of a company or organization. Was it a relationship or an effort by them to just "grab your money"? How would you improve the contact between you and the company?

NOTES

1. Lisa Fortini-Campbell, *Hitting the Sweet Spot: How Consumer Insights Can Inspire Better Marketing and Advertising* (Chicago, IL: The Copy Workshop, 1992).
2. J. Bennett, N. Strange, and L. Spigel, *Television as Digital Media* (Durham, NC: Duke University Press Books, 2011).
3. Jess Greenwood, "Levi's Case Study," *Contagious* (2011), Issue 24, 50–61.
4. Michael R. Solomon, Russell-Bennett Previte, Rebekah Solomon, Jo Russell-Bennett, and Josephine Previte, *Consumer Behaviour: Buying, Having, Selling* (Australia: Pearson Education, 2009).
5. Gerald Zaltman, *How Customers Think: Essential Insights into the Mind of the Market* (Boston, MA: Harvard Business School Press, 2003).

6. Robert V. Kozinets, *Netnography: Doing Ethnographic Research Online* (London, UK: Sage Publications, 2010).

7. Gregor Jawecki and Johann Fuller, "How to Use the Innovative Potential of Online Communities? Netnography—An Unobtrusive Research Method to Absorb the Knowledge and Creativity of Online Communities," *International Journal of Business Process Integration and Management* 3.4 (2008): 248–255 (May 6, 2009).

8. Communispace (2011), http://www.communispace.com/home.aspx (accessed May 24, 2011).

9. Radian6 (2011), http://www.radian6.com (accessed May 23, 2011).

10. Zuberance (2011), http://www.zuberance.com (accessed May 25, 2011).

11. QSR International, *Nvivo* (Computer software, 2011).

12. Scientific Software Development, *Atlas.Ti* (Computer software).

13. Glaser, Barney G., and Anselm L. Strauss. *The Discovery of Grounded Theory; Strategies for Qualitative Research*. Chicago: Aldine Pub., 1967. Print.

14. Craig J. Thompson, Howard R. Pollio, and William B. Locander. "The Spoken and the Unspoken: A Hermeneutic Approach to Understanding the Cultural Viewpoints That Underlie Consumers' Expressed Meanings." *Journal of Consumer Research* 21.3 (1994): 432.

15. Craig J. Thompson, "Interpreting Consumers: A Hermeneutical Framework for Deriving Marketing Insights from the Texts of Consumers' Consumption Stories," *Journal of Marketing Research* XXXIV (1997): 438–455 (Nov 1997).

16. Cahill, Blake (2010) "Leveraging Social Insights." Consumer Behavior Class. University of Texas, Austin, TX.

17. Visible Technologies (2011), http://www.visibletechnologies.com (accessed May 26, 2011).

18. Willie Pietersen, *Reinventing Strategy: Using Strategic Learning to Create and Sustain Breakthrough Performance*. (Hoboken, NJ: John Wiley and Sons, 2002).

19. Radian6, *American Red Cross: Small Changes Making Big Differences* (2010), http://www.radian6.com/resources/library/american-red-cross/ (accessed May 15, 2011).

20. Ted Hart, et al. *Internet Management for Nonprofits: Strategies, Tools and Trade Secrets*. (Hoboken, NJ: John Wiley and Sons, 2010).

21. Anonymous, *Tumi Luggage Does Not Honor Warranty* (2008).

22. Kevin Roberts, *Lovemarks: The Future Beyond Brands* (New York: Powerhouse Books, 2004).

23. Valarie A. Zeithaml and Mary Jo Bitner, *Services Marketing: Integrating Customer Focus across the Firm*, 3rd ed (New York: McGraw-Hill Higher Education, 2003).

24. Colin Shaw, *The DNA of Customer Experience: How Emotions Drive Value*. (London, UK: Palgrave Macmillan, 2007).

25. A. O. Hirschman, *Exit, Voice, and Loyalty: Responses to Decline in Firms, Organizations, and States* (Cambridge, MA: Harvard University Press, 1970).

26. Anne-Marie G. Harris, Geraldine R. Henderson, and Jerome D. Williams, "Courting Customers: Assessing Consumer Racial Profiling and Other Marketplace Discrimination," *Journal of Public Policy & Marketing* 24.1 (2005): 163–171.

27. Robert V. Kozinets, Kristine De Valck, Andrea C. Wojnicki, Sarah J. S. Wilner. "Networked Narratives: Understanding Word-of-Mouth Marketing in Online Communities," *Journal of Marketing* 74.2 (2010): 71–89 (March 2010).

28. David Reich, *Whole Foods CEO: Busted!* (MarketingProfs Daily Fix Blog, July 17, 2007), http://www.mpdailyfix.com/whole-foods-ceo-busted/.

29. Tempur-Pedic (2011), http://connect.tempurpedic.com/connect (accessed May 18 2011).

30. Roland T. Rust, Katherine N. Lemon, and Das Narayandas, *Customer Equity Management* (Upper Saddle River, NJ: Pearson Prentice Hall, 2005).

31. Robert C. Blattberg, Gary Getz, and Jacquelyn S. Thomas, *Customer Equity: Building and Managing Relationships as Valuable Assets* (Boston, MA: Harvard Business School Press, 2001).

32. Mike Lewis, "Great Customer Experience at the Apple Store," *Social Episodes* (2009).

33. Stephen D. Rappaport, *Listen First!: Turning Social Media Conversations into Business Advantage* (Hoboken, NJ: John Wiley & Sons, 2011).

34. Paul Levy, "Transitions," *(Not) Running a Hospital* (2011).
35. Market Force, *Gamestop Partners with Market Force for Customer Case Study: Intelligence* (Marketforce Information, 2011).
36. Bernard Cova, Robert V. Kozinets, and Avi Shankar, *Consumer Tribes* (Oxford, UK: Butterworth-Heinemann, 2007).
37. Charlene Li and Josh Bernoff, *Marketing in the Groundswell* (Boston, MA: Harvard Business Press, 2009).
38. Sebastian Blanco, *GM Announces Customer Advisory Board for Chevy Volt* (2010 of Autoblog Green).
39. Communispace (2011), http://www.communispace.com/clients/Testimonials.aspx.
40. Communispace, *Communispace and Charles Schwab Win Social Technologies Award for Generation X Online Customer Community* (2007).
41. Colin Shaw, Qaalfa Dibeehi, and Steven Walden, *Customer Experience: Future Trends & Insights. Beyond Philosophy* (London, UK: Palgrave Macmillan, 2010).
42. Jeff Howe, *Crowdsourcing: Why the Power of the Crowd Is Driving the Future of Business* (New York: Crown Publishing Group, 2009).
43. Adrienne Murrill, *When Bad Times Turn out Good Strategy* (Evanston, IL: Northwestern University, 2007).
44. Donna M. Airoldi, *In-Flight Internet News: Free Facebook, Gogo Grabs $35 Million in Funding* (Uptake, 2011).
45. Doug Cameron, "American Airlines Wants Expedia, Orbitz to Come Around," *Wall Street Journal* (January 5, 2011).
46. Paco Underhill, *Why We Buy: The Science of Shopping* (New York: Simon & Schuster, 1999).
47. Flexo, "Best Buy's Buy Back Program," *Consumerism Commentary* (2011).
48. Larry Gerston, *The Costco Experience*, revised and updated ed. (E-reads/E-rights, 2010).
49. Aryya, Gangopadhyay. *Managing Business with Electronic Commerce: Issues and Trends.* Hershey, PA: Idea Group Pub., 2002. Print.
50. Paul Gillin and Eric Schwartzman, *Social Marketing to the Business Customer: Listen to Your B2B Market, Generate Major Account Leads, and Build Client Relationships* (New York: John Wiley & Sons, 2011).

ADDITIONAL READING

Cova, Bernard, Robert V. Kozinets, and Avi Shankar. 2007. *Consumer Tribes.* Oxford: Butterworth-Heinemann.

Fortini-Campbell, Lisa. 1992. *Hitting the Sweet Spot: How Consumer Insights Can Inspire Better Marketing and Advertising.* Chicago, IL: Copy Workshop.

Gillin, Paul, and Eric Schwartzman. 2011. *Social Marketing to the Business Customer: Listen to Your B2b Market, Generate Major Account Leads, and Build Client Relationships.* New York: John Wiley & Sons.

Harris, Anne-Marie G., Geraldine R. Henderson, and Jerome D. Williams. "Courting Customers: Assessing Consumer Racial Profiling and Other Marketplace Discrimination." *Journal of Public Policy & Marketing* 24.1 (2005): 163–171.

Hart, Ted. 2010. *Internet Management for Nonprofits: Strategies, Tools & Trade Secrets.* Hoboken, NJ: John Wiley & Sons.

Hirschman, Albert O. 1970. *Exit, Voice, and Loyalty; Responses to Decline in Firms, Organizations, and States.* Cambridge, MA: Harvard University Press.

Howe, Jeff. 2009. *Crowdsourcing: Why the Power of the Crowd Is Driving the Future of Business.* New York: Crown Publishing Group.

Kozinets, Robert V. 2010. *Netnography: Doing Ethnographic Research Online.* Los Angeles, CA: SAGE.

Li, Charlene, and Josh Bernoff. 2009. *Marketing in the Groundswell.* Boston, MA: Harvard Business Press.

Market Force. 2011. *Gamestop Partners with Market Force for Customer Case Study: Intelligence.* Marketforce Information.

Rappaport, Stephen D. 2011. *Listen First!: Turning Social Media Conversations into Business Advantage.* Hoboken, NJ: John Wiley & Sons.

Shaw, Colin. 2007. *The DNA of Customer Experience: How Emotions Drive Value.* Basingstoke, UK: Palgrave Macmillan.

Shaw, Colin, Qaalfa Dibeehi, and Steven Walden. 2010. *Customer Experience: Future Trends & Insights. Beyond Philosophy.* London, UK: Palgrave Macmillan.

Underhill, Paco. 1999. *Why We Buy: The Science of Shopping.* New York: Simon & Schuster.

10

C H A P T E R

MARKETING PUBLIC RELATIONS
Cementing the Brand

Patricia T. Whalen, Ph.D., APR
President, Whalen Communications Group

WHAT IS MARKETING PUBLIC RELATIONS?

In our book *A Marketer's Guide to Public Relations in the Twenty-First Century*, Thomas L. Harris and I defined marketing public relations (MPR) as "the use of public relations strategies and tactics to achieve marketing objectives. The purpose of MPR is to gain awareness, stimulate sales, facilitate communication and build relationships between consumers, companies, and brands."[1]

Perhaps more important than knowing a simple definition is understanding that MPR is one of the cheapest forms of branding known to man. Al and Laura Ries expressed this sentiment a decade ago in their book *The Fall of Advertising and Rise of PR*,[2] and it is still being echoed today by such public relations (PR) agency executives as 4WPR CEO, Ronn Torossian, in his New York agency blog on the value of PR, when he says, "It's one of the most affordable forms of marketing—for under $100,000 you can have an effective campaign (and for less than seven figures you can't do advertising properly)."[3]

However, the effectiveness of public relations in a marketing campaign goes well beyond its low cost. Its chief strength, garnering third-party endorsements—from opinion leaders, the news media and other key influencers—can lend a brand credibility and authenticity that advertising and direct marketing cannot. In addition, MPR strategies and tactics can bring a brand to life by building brand loyalty and generating word-of-mouth buzz, often by integrating an event, a mascot, providing useful or interesting information or incorporating a nonpaid promotional activity into an existing marketing campaign.

Examples of these types of MPR activities have ranged from the silly to the very serious, including Aflac Insurance giving its signature toy duck to celebrity Ben Afleck during a TV show appearance; Legacy.com, an online obituary service, undertaking and releasing the results of a survey in an election year comparing the type of music Republicans and Democrats prefer for their funeral services; Taco Bell posting to its own website a very funny YouTube video by two bloggers doing a live drive-through serenade; Home Depot posting heartfelt interviews from its female customers about why learning how to do their own home repair was so important to them; and, General Motors staffing a round-the-clock social media "war room" after its financial restructuring announcement to be able to respond immediately to online comments and answer questions from bloggers and, most importantly, its customers.

These wide-ranging activities are collectively known as MPR, and they differ from more traditional public relations activities in that their primary goal is to support an organization's sales and marketing efforts rather than supporting broad corporate reputation goals. But they also differ from traditional marketing efforts, which typically pitch the product or service with a goal of achieving an immediate sale, and instead, focus on building trust and developing relationships with the marketing targets.

SOME HISTORY ABOUT MPR

The concept of MPR has been around since some of the earliest days of business. Scott Cutlip, in his PR history book, *The Unseen Power*,[4] suggested that it was an MPR approach that the National Biscuit Company and its agency N.W. Ayer & Co. took in 1899 when they decided to position their product against the cracker barrel of old by putting their Uneeda Biscuits in an airtight package. They promoted sanitation first and the product second, and the concept connected well with both the media and customers.

Other historically significant marketing campaigns that have successfully used MPR tactics to cement the brand have included Ivory Soap, which got its message out about it being "so pure that it floats" by hosting soap carving contests in the 1920s; Pillsbury, with its 100-year-old bake-off contest, which of course requires the use of Pillsbury products in the recipes that are widely distributed through the product packaging and reported in the news media; and McDonald's, which has amazingly been able to use the Ronald McDonald clown as a very serious and well-respected symbol of the company's commitment to sick children and their families through Ronald McDonald Houses around the world.

DOVE—A "REAL BEAUTY" OF AN MPR CAMPAIGN

A more recent campaign that integrated traditional marketing efforts with more relationship-building MPR efforts was Unilever's very successful Dove campaign, which helped to rejuvenate the brand and make it relevant to a whole new and younger target audience. It was Ogilvy & Mather's very creative "Real Beauty" advertising campaign that started it all, but it was Edelman's MPR campaign, in strategic alliance with the overarching advertising theme, that created a global conversation about standards of beauty that deeply resonated with customers and the news media. That campaign, which launched in 2004, was truly an integrated marketing communication effort and continues to keep the brand alive today half a decade later. Certainly, the center of the campaign was an extensive series of print and television ads featuring "average size" women in their underwear, but why did they strike such a chord with customers and why did the "real beauty" message get carried so far beyond the paid advertisements?

It was MPR that generated the unprecedented news coverage of the campaign using tactics such as the well-publicized model search and subsequent media tours by the models, who became spokespersons for the brand. It was also public relations that developed a website to promote women's self-esteem and to report on company research about how women perceive themselves differently worldwide. The public relations elements of the campaign have continued to generate buzz and attract new and younger followers in subsequent years by adding sponsorship activities related to improving young girls' self-esteem and providing workshops, a book and training materials on the Dove website.

A part of that effort was the creation of a "morphing" video of what an already reasonably attractive woman has to go through to fit the definition of beauty for a magazine cover. It was reportedly the most watched video on YouTube in 2006. Another video, called "Onslaught," which shows how young girls are being constantly bombarded with sexualized images and unrealistic standards of beauty, continues to be viewed regularly today, several years after the campaign's launch.

The question for public relations professionals and marketers alike should not be, which agency or which part of the integrated marketing communication equation was responsible for the increased sales and brand awareness? Instead, they should be asking, why was this campaign such a grand success? And can we imitate that success in *our* next marketing campaign?

THE IMPORTANCE OF MESSAGE CONSISTENCY FOR EFFECTIVE MPR

Interestingly, another question that should be asked, "Can the campaign be sustained over time?" is one that Unilever itself will have to grapple with since the campaign has been criticized in the years after the launch because the parent company seems to be giving conflicting messages about real beauty as it markets a skin-lightening product to dark-skinned women in several countries, and owns and markets its Lynx beauty line using more stereotypical young and thin models. However, the biggest criticism toward Unilever comes from those who view the ads for its AXE brand of deodorants as particularly hypocritical because they use overtly sexual messages aimed at young men and objectify the women featured in the ads.

In some ways, Unilever was a victim of its own success. The Dove Real Beauty campaign struck such a positive chord with certain female target groups that accolades went out to Dove's parent company as well. Unfortunately, Unilever was letting each of its brands set its own positioning strategies, which led to obvious inconsistencies in tone and message. It would be like Nabisco, after its 1899 success with its sanitary packaging campaign for Uneeda Crackers, acquiring a cracker barrel company and promoting the low cost of bulk crackers. Inconsistency can kill the goodwill established by an MPR campaign, and it is something that needs to be considered early on when brand positioning strategies are set. Positioning is not just a clever slogan for how you want your customers to think about your brand. It is a promise to your customers of how your brand will behave.

This chapter provides a number of examples of standout MPR campaigns and addresses the trust factors that will help sustain a brand message over time. The chapter also provides a specific set of steps for planning and implementing an effective MPR campaign, but before doing so, let us first look at some barriers to integrating public relations into the marketing communication efforts and discussing ways to overcome these barriers.

BARRIERS TO CONVERGING PR AND MARKETING

A recent PRNewswire white paper, "The New Face of Public Relations: Navigating the Convergence of PR and Marketing,"[5] lauded the ever-growing list of brands that have begun to incorporate MPR strategies into their marketing activities. The paper, however, begins by reminding us that public relations and marketing were "once rigidly separate (and often competitive) disciplines" (p. 1). The paper suggests that the convergence of these disciplines is nothing short of "a paradigm shift in communications; a shift that is blurring the line between PR, marketing, and even advertising" (p. 1).

As an example of this convergence, the paper cites IKEA's award-winning 2008 webisode campaign "Mark Lives in IKEA," where comedian Mark Malkoff lived in a New Jersey IKEA store for a week and reported on his activities via online video and a blog. He also interacted with customers live at the store, did media interviews and spoke with employees. He ultimately posted 25 short videos that featured furniture and other products including the in-store restaurant. The result was a lot of free media coverage for the store and the brand, a more engaged workforce and customer base and, yes, a 5.5 percent increase in sales at the New Jersey store and a 6.8 percent increase in web traffic over the previous year.[5]

However, despite successful examples like this, the concept of having public relations support the sales effort is still a controversial topic among academics and public relations "purists." Why the controversy? There seem to be two main reasons for resisting the use of public relations in the marketing mix.

A FAILURE TO COMMUNICATE

The first barrier to truly integrating PR into the marketing mix is an organizational issue, in which the two functions still often work in independent silos, neither truly understands the language of the other, and both are concerned about becoming subordinate to the other. Bill Wagner, in a 2010 *PR Tactics* column on careers, suggested that "the relationship between marketing and public relations can be tenuous, with parties on both sides thinking that the other doesn't get it."[6] This communication barrier tends to keep the public relations and marketing folks at arms length and suspicious of each other. The best way to get past this is to create joint planning meetings to ensure that all communication tools are strategically integrated into a marketing campaign.

This means sharing research findings, setting common business objectives, jointly deciding on which targets should be approached and agreeing on measurement standards.

Another way to break this barrier is to have one group report to the other, and Wagner tells us that when this happens, it is usually PR that is absorbed into the marketing function. If an organization is large enough to support both a corporate PR and a MPR function, then having the MPR function report to marketing can be a reasonable solution. However, if the organization can only support one PR function, I, personally, do not believe that it should report to marketing. This is because there are so many other targets and corporate communication goals beyond those of marketing, and the PR function needs to be free to pursue those without being hindered by only sales and marketing goals.

However, if the organization is decentralized along lines of business, then a very workable solution is to have the head of communication at the headquarters office oversee all corporate public relations efforts including internal communication, government affairs, investor relations, media relations and community relations, and have a marketing public relations specialist reporting to the marketing director of each major line of business. This MPR person would have a dotted-line reporting relationship with the head of corporate communication and would keep him or her apprised of any marketing activities that could have media implications for the corporation as a whole. In my 17 years as a corporate executive, I always operated under this type of structure: at various times as the head of corporate communication, as the MPR specialist within the line of business and as the head of marketing for a line of business. It worked well in all these scenarios when all parties recognized that they had interrelated goals and agreed to work as a team to accomplish them.

COMPETING TARGETS AND GOALS

The second barrier to an effective and truly integrated MPR effort is in how public relations professionals and marketers differ in their views of the targets and goals of a campaign. This is an area in which marketers can become very shortsighted, focusing exclusively on sales goals and customers and potential customers. Marketers are often saying things like, "Everyone in the company is in sales," or "Without customers, we are out of business."

Although this may be true over the long term, there are many times when non-customer targets are very important to achieving a critical short-term goal, and measuring an improved relationship with those targets may be more critical to the organization's survival than meeting a particular sales or profit goal. For example, a cable TV company may have many potential customers who would like to buy their services, but if the local public utilities commission or other government regulators block the firm's ability to serve the community, then the critical focus may need to shift away from customers and move toward improving relations with the local public utilities commission. Other targets that could be critical to a firm's success, but that are typically ignored by marketers, are employees who need to gain a better understanding of how the product works to be able to meet customers' needs, bankers and other investors who are needed to fund a plant expansion, community or environmental groups who may want to block a retailer or manufacturer from building there, and suppliers who may be asked to provide resources on faith or with extended credit terms until sales hit a critical mass.

When not overtaken by pure marketing activities, public relations professionals would typically consider all of these targets under a broad "stakeholder" model and seek to develop a two-way dialogue with them. Many public relations practitioners and academics are concerned that these targets will be ignored in the future as more public relations departments lose their autonomy and are required to report within the marketing department. San Diego State Professor Martha Lauzen labeled this as a concern about "marketing imperialism" nearly two decades ago, and it is still a legitimate threat in those organizations that do not have a public relations professional reporting to the chief executive to provide public relations guidance and counsel about audiences outside the marketing realm.

MEGAMARKETING—GETTING PAST THE GATEKEEPERS

At least one marketing guru, Northwestern University's Phillip Kotler, has recognized the importance of these other non-customer targets and has acknowledged the value of reaching out to them through MPR strategies. Kotler used the term *megamarketing* to describe these activities in a 1986 *Harvard Business Review* article. He defined the term as,

The strategically coordinated application of economic, psychological, political, and public relations skills to gain the cooperation of a number of parties in order to enter and/or operate in a given market.[7]

Of course, public relations professionals might still object to Kotler's focus on these audiences solely for the purpose of gaining their cooperation to "enter and/or operate in a given market." Kotler does not address the value of creating a two-way dialogue with them, nor does he address the issue of changing corporate behavior to improve reputation or the value of developing deep, lasting relationships with key audiences. But he does, at least, acknowledge the importance of targets beyond the customers, and lends credibility to the use of public relations to reach them.

Thomas L. Harris describes this as a "pass" strategy for getting around gatekeepers who are blocking access to a market. Some examples of MPR pass strategies could be anything from partnering with advocacy groups, signing on to fair trade and fair wage agreements and lending support to lobbying efforts that are important to your target audience. Harris suggests that these strategies work best when the targets know and trust the company and, as Harris says, "Trust is earned by providing quality products at a good value. It is also earned by sponsoring activities and identifying with causes that demonstrate the company's appreciation of the consumers' patronage."[8]

BUILDING RELATIONSHIPS—IT'S A MATTER OF TRUST

And therein lies the real value of MPR—its ability to help build trust by using more authentic means of communication than a screaming advertisement that says, "Buy Me!" One of the most authentic messages for a member of a target audience to receive is not from the company at all, but from a neutral third party. The message delivery system could be anything from a news story to word-of-mouth buzz or e-mail comments by friends and family. The important thing is that it come from someone other than the firm.

Edelman's 2010 Trust Barameter found that more than twice as many people trust what they read or hear about a company or a product in a news story than they do seeing an advertisement for that company or product.[9] Conversations with "friends and peers" received an even higher trust score. Why? Because those third-party comments are assumed to be more honest since there is no perceived benefit to the individuals making the comment.

With that in mind, a good marketing public relations campaign typically focuses on building trust, creating dialogue with its key target audiences and creating a conduit for getting useful information into the hands of key influencers such as traditional news media, bloggers, industry analysts and other opinion leaders. However, good MPR isn't all one-way communication. To be truly authentic requires that MPR professionals understand what is important to the target audiences, and this often requires a two-way communication mechanism that bypasses the traditional media gatekeepers and allows a direct interaction with key audience members. The rapid growth of social media in the last few years has greatly aided in this endeavor.

MPR done well matches what BET Network's chief marketing officer, Janet Rollie, outlined in a recent *Ad Age*[10] article as her five "guiding brand pillars" that have accounted for her network's rating renaissance. Paraphrasing, these brand pillars are:

1. Understand your target audience and assign them attributes that inform your messages.

2. Be authentic and practice what your messages promise.

3. Listen by creating feedback mechanisms.

4. Follow the conversation (especially on social media sites).

5. Give the audience a voice and let them do the talking for you as often as possible.

THE GROWTH OF SOCIAL NETWORKING TO EXTEND THE DIALOGUE

In 1994, Cutlip and colleagues[11] summarized the public relations role as "the management function that establishes and maintains mutually beneficial relationships between an organization and the public on whom its success or failure depends" (p. 2).

The interactive nature of social media is the perfect mechanism for establishing what those mutually beneficial relationships should be. High-tech firms, such as Dell and Apple, were among the first to explore these relationships, allowing customers to get faster and more complete customer service information online, but also getting the benefit of its customers acting as free support staff to answer other customers' questions and post helpful information on customer forums. These highly engaged customers act as an early warning system when product or service problems arise and they serve as brand ambassadors when things are going well.

Another popular MPR use of social networking involves integrating some type of interactive or viral activity with existing marketing campaigns to fully engage customers. An example of one of the most successful campaigns was the OfficeMax "Elf Yourself" holiday campaign that let people affix pictures of themselves and their friends to the bodies of the dancing elves used in their holiday commercials and then forward them via e-mail. A second was Procter & Gamble's three-day live Twitter campaign with the new and very popular Old Spice Guy, Isaiah Mustafa, which generated more than 140 million YouTube views of his famous "I'm on a horse" ad along with some 200 other customized videos. A final well-remembered campaign was Kotex brand's "Break the Cycle" campaign that broke from the normally hushed tones of feminine care products by creating several online viral videos of segments of their current ad campaign, including one of men's reactions when they were approached on the street and asked to buy tampons, one of women's reactions when a man in a supermarket asks women for help selecting a feminine care product for his girlfriend and one video on how to use a tampon. These are just a few of the social networking tactics that savvy public relations professionals have used in support of existing advertising campaigns.

In addition, smart public relations professionals are also finding ways to target influential bloggers and use online tools to get key information into the hands of targets not easily reached through traditional media. David Meerman Scott, in his book *The New Rules of Marketing and PR* (2009),[12] explained the importance of bypassing traditional gatekeepers to reach more important influencers in today's digital world. He said,

> Instead of spending tens of thousands of dollars per month on a media relations program that tries to convince a handful of reporters at select magazines, newspapers and TV stations to cover us, we should be targeting the plugged-in bloggers, online news sites, micropublications, public speakers, analysts and consultants that reach our targeted audiences that are looking for what we have to offer. Better yet, we no longer even need to wait for someone with a media voice to write about us at all. With blogs, we communicate directly with our audience.[12]

THE IMPACT OF ETHICS IN SOCIAL MEDIA ON REPUTATION

This is good advice, but one should keep in mind that all the social media efforts in the world can be for naught if the social media strategy is created without regard to sound ethical practices. Any perceived lapse in ethics, once it becomes public, can cause permanent damage to an organization's reputation.

This warning is particularly important given the results of a 2009 *PRWeek* survey of marketers who had used social media in their campaigns, with more than a few admitting to some lapses in ethical judgment. Twenty-one percent had positioned company-generated content as if it were consumer-generated content, 13 percent had edited the content about the brands on sites like Wikipedia, 11 percent had removed negative comments or content from a customer forum, 7 percent had offered gifts to bloggers for positive reviews and 4 percent had offered outright payment for positive online reviews (Maul 2009).[13] All of these ethical lapses could have gone viral in a matter of a few days or event minutes, causing incalculable damage to their firms' reputations and to established relationships with key audiences.

PLANNING TO SUCCEED

To avoid these types of potential disasters and to ensure the best outcome for an MPR campaign, it is always wise to be strategic and develop a plan that relies on consumer insights to avoid the use of messages or tactics that would be offensive to the key targets. I rough out a strategic plan for every marketing activity that I undertake—from the smallest tactical idea to a long-term, complex year-long plan. The following is a brief outline of the seven planning steps that I follow for my MPR activities. They are described in greater detail in Chapter 7 of the Harris/Whalen book, *A Marketer's Guide to the Twenty-First Century*.[14]

ELEMENTS OF THE MPR PLAN

In the Whalen Seven-Step Strategic Planning Process, the seven steps are often written in a circular pattern to show that the MPR plan does not have an absolute beginning or end. Rather, it is a continuous process that recognizes a current situation, undertakes activities to change that situation, gauges the results of those activities and then addresses the new situation that has developed.

The seven steps are situation analysis, objectives, targets, strategies, messages, tactics and evaluation. Let's look at each step in more detail.

1. *Situation analysis.* This first step in a strategic plan includes a discussion of up-front research undertaken to identify internal strengths and weaknesses and external threats and opportunities. Often, this can be accomplished with a review of internal business plans and existing marketing research, but should also include a summary of media articles about the organization and its competitors to identify how the outside world views the brand. It is also useful to interview some key internal and external experts to get their take on the most important problems and issues that need to be addressed. It is important to note that that the situation analysis does not attempt to solve the problems—it simply identifies them. Please save any creative ideas for the body of the plan.

2. *Setting objectives.* This step is one of the most crucial to the plan because it identifies what you need to accomplish with your MPR activities and how your success should be measured. The objectives should always be specific, measurable and set within a timeline. They include short-term communication objectives, sometimes referred to as outputs; intermediate-term objectives that address changes in attitude or awareness, sometimes referred to as outtakes; and long-term business objectives, which are typically behavioral or financial in nature, such as changes in purchasing behavior and revenue generation, sometimes referred to as outcomes.

    Typically, the entire marketing effort is aimed at achieving the intermediate and long-term objectives, thus the main focus of the MPR plan is to achieve the communication objectives, which are often described in such terms as generating a certain amount of media and online coverage, dissemination of key messages to particular audiences, generating attendance at events, driving hits to a website and generating requests for more information. Despite the main MPR objectives being centered on these types of communication goals, a good MPR plan will not shy away from identifying attitudinal, behavioral and financial changes that can result from the MPR efforts.

3. *Identifying the targets.* As crucial to MPR as to any other marketing campaign is the ability to gather demographic and psychographic information about the key targets. Things you should gather and report include: who they are, how many there are, where they are and what they do. It is important to gain as much insight about them as possible, especially what motivates them and who influences them. Often, the MPR professional will have access to the same consumer research that is available to the advertising experts, and can incorporate this information into the MPR strategic plan. If this is not the case, small MPR budgets often do not allow for extensive consumer research, but there is often a wealth of secondary literature on key consumer groups that can provide useful insight into them. It is also possible to gain great depth of information with just a few interviews, focus groups or online monitoring of customer forums.

4. *Strategy.* Once you know who the targets are and what is important to them, the next step is defining a strategic direction or "big idea" that will resonate well with them and sustain the campaign over a long period. This is often an area of weakness for public relations campaigns, which too

often incorporate a jumble of tactics—an event here, a cause-related tie-in there and a series of news releases on a wide array of unrelated topics. A strong MPR campaign will be based on an overarching theme that gives purpose and direction for all of the tactics used to reach a particular target group. For example, a recent Carnival Cruise Line marketing campaign used the overarching theme, "Fun For All, and All For Fun" to illustrate the cruise line's point of differentiation from its more conservative competitors who target older customers looking for a quieter, more sophisticated cruise experience. Carnival used the tag line in its print and TV ads to promote its focus on younger passengers and families, and its MPR efforts included staging two extreme media events around the "fun" theme. One was to drop the world's largest beach ball off a 10-storey building and the other was to build the world's largest piñata and give the candy to area children.

5. *Messages*. Once the strategic direction of the campaign has been decided on, the next step is to create specific messages to address each target's needs and interests. The theme, "Fun For All, and All For Fun" might resonate well with all of Carnival's targets, but the definition of "fun" will be very different for a middle-aged empty nester couple, than for a group of single women in their twenties, and something different again for a thirty-something couple with three young children. A strategic MPR campaign will target the media that these different consumer groups use and will develop information materials and generate articles that will show how Carnival can deliver on their idea of fun. Note that the MPR messages cannot reply on the catchy slogan, as the advertising campaign can; but they can reflect the idea behind the slogan.

Also, note that any MPR message directed at the news media has to have a news value. That is, if you want a journalist to run a story about your product or organization, it has to be newsworthy. Otherwise, you will need to take out a paid advertising space to get your message across. The same is true for viral campaigns. If you expect people to pass information along to friends and family, it has to be "buzz worthy." Some of the things that will make your messages newsworthy or buzz worthy are being high in human interest, especially if it is very funny or very sweet; high in significance, with key information about how it will affect a large number of people or is important to one's health and happiness; uniqueness, with its being very unusual in terms of size, the first of its kind, or something that rarely happens; timeliness, tied to current events, holidays or trends; proximity, tied to local events or facts; prominence, including involvement by an expert or a celebrity; and conflict, or showing a struggle or something to be overcome.

6. *Tactics*. The tactical section of an MPR campaign is nothing more than identifying the tools you will use to disseminate the messages and to generate the news and the buzz, and developing timelines and budgets for creating these tools. Of course, this is where the bulk of the time and budget is spent during the actual execution of the campaign, so it is often the case that MPR novices find themselves starting with the tactics. This can happen when overzealous project managers or marketing directors incorporate MPR tactics into their own strategic plans and simply direct the MPR professional to execute a series of tasks such as writing up some brochures and press releases, putting on an event, developing a website, creating a blog, staging a press conference, etc. It is unlikely that this approach will ensure that the tactics will come together in a cohesive manner to support one another or sustain a key brand position. Savvy marketers will share their strategic marketing plans with their MPR expert, but will let them tailor that plan into a strategic MPR plan that puts tactics at the end where they belong.

7. *Evaluation*. The last step in the plan is to evaluate its effectiveness. This step is inseparably linked to Step 2 (*Setting objectives*). As a rule of thumb, an MPR plan should never include an objective in Step 2 that does not have a way to measure it in Step 7. It could be written as simply as repeating the objective, but adding "as measured by . . ." after it. This measure should specify the time period to be evaluated and the method that will be used to see if the objective was met.

In the past, public relations results were typically measured in terms of the number of news stories generated, and gross media impressions were measured in terms of the total audience potentially exposed to the media coverage. Unfortunately, these measures have little to do with marketing or business objectives. The good news is that PR measurement has started to become much more sophisticated, and many online tools now exist for measuring how well MPR efforts did in terms of tone, message pick-up, share of voice and other far more nuanced measures than simply counting clips. Intermediate, outtake measurements of MPR campaigns have included asking if people comprehended the message and retained it over time. Did they change their opinions or beliefs based on the content? And, did they take any actions as a result of that publicity?

However, the most important evaluation is probably the long-term outcome of the MPR campaign. It is now possible to track media coverage, both traditional and online, to such a degree that it can be correlated with changes in sales revenue, market share and sales volume. Bank of America has used media measurement software to combine media relations information into an analytical measurement with customer data to show how MPR can drive new customers to the bank and drive the bottom line. Miller Brewing Company has used media metrics to measure the quality of the news and the circulation of its traditional media and then determined which brand or brand programs were effectively being portrayed, which spokespeople were being quoted and which journalists were covering Miller, compared with its competitors.

THE FUTURE OF MPR

This level of sophistication will only get stronger as media measurement tools improve and become more widespread and user-friendly. This bodes well for MPR moving up the ladder within the marketing discipline and perhaps, someday in the not too distant future, getting an equal billing with advertising and direct marketing in terms of its contribution to the bottom-line.

For this to happen, however, those who practice MPR will need to become marketing experts, not just PR experts. They must understand the language of marketing and such concepts as return on investment, positioning, product life cycle, market share, lifetime customer value, etc. They can no longer just focus on earned media. They need to be able to address consumers directly using the wide array of interactive tools available to them through social media, including photo- and video-sharing sites, social-bookmarking, webinars, microblogging and the dozens of new social networks that appear on a weekly basis.

This, I believe, is truly the future of MPR, and as Bill Wagner pointed out in his *PR Tactics* column, "PR should own social media."[6] This, he says, is because PR professionals have an inherent advantage over other business functions in that "PR's background in working with objective editorial influencers makes the PR professional well-suited for driving corporate social media strategy."[6] Wagner went on to suggest that despite marketing professionals not seeming to understand "social media's adversity to commercialization," if PR "doesn't step up to own social media, then marketing will."[6]

I agree with him, but I believe that those practicing MPR are in the best position to lay claim to social media, given their proximity to the marketing function. Their biggest threat is in losing their PR perspective, which takes a long-term, relationship-oriented, stakeholder view, in favor of a marketing perspective that can be focused just on the bottom-line and customers only.

MPR has the ability to merge cost-effective PR tools with strategic marketing concepts to reap greater benefits than either discipline can achieve on its own. As PR Newswire's white paper on PR and marketing convergence suggests, "Rather than marketing's eclipsing public relations, it's elevating the practice to new heights and making the need for each discipline more relevant. Forward-thinking practitioners are preparing for the changes—and the opportunities—of the months and years ahead."[15]

DISCUSSION QUESTIONS

1. How does MPR differ from public relations in general?
2. Where should MPR report within the organization?

3. If your client was a large national pet supply retail chain, use each of the news values listed in the chapter to create an MPR tactic for each.
4. Should the media be treated as a target in an MPR plan?
5. Should an MPR plan include non-PR strategies and tactics such as sales promotion and adverting ideas?

ACTIVITIES

1. Go to the Internet and find a current consumer goods advertising campaign that is not using any PR activities. Identify two or three MPR strategies or tactics that could enhance this campaign to add value to the marketing efforts.
2. Look up a current PRSA Silver Anvil winner two-page description at www.prsa.org/Awards/SilverAnvil/SilverAnvil_Results, and rewrite the plan following the seven-step planning process. Then assess it. Were all parts of the plan there? Where was this plan strongest? Where was it weakest?
3. Find any advertisement that describes a product or service. Then, using each of the news values listed under strategic planning Step 5 (*Messages*), identify an MPR tactic for each news value that would compliment the ad campaign.

NOTES

1. Thomas. L. Harris and Patricia. T. Whalen, *A Marketer's Guide to Public Relations in the Twenty-First Century* (Thomson/Southwestern, 2006), 7.
2. Al Ries and Laura Ries, *The Fall of Advertising and Rise of PR* (New York: HarperCollins, 2002).
3. Ronn Torossian, "Value of Public Relations," March 10, 2011, ronntorossian.com/value-of-public-relations.
4. Scott Cutlip, *The Unseen Power* (Hillside, NJ: Lawrence Erlbaum, 1994), 7.
5. PRNewswire, "The New Face of Public Relations: Navigating the Convergence of PR and Marketing" (2010), 1.
6. Bill Wagner, "What Marketing Expects from Public Relations," *Public Relations Tactics* (October 2010), 7.
7. Phil Kotler, "Mega-Marketing." *The Harvard Business Review* (March 1, 1986).
8. Thomas. L. Harris and Patricia. T. Whalen, *A Marketer's Guide to Public Relations in the Twenty-First Century* (Thomson/Southwestern, 2006), 42.
9. "Opinion Leaders Doubt Credibility of Advertising." WARC. Data sourced from Edelman; additional content by Warc staff, January 28, 2010–March 4, 2011, www.warc.com/LatestNews/News/ArchiveNews.news?ID=26244.
10. Andrew Hampp, "BET Finds New Life in its Guiding 'Brand Pillars,'" *Ad Age* (October 25, 2010), 16.
11. S. M. Cutlip, A. H. Center, and G. M. Broom, *Effective Public Relations* (Engelwood Cliffs, NJ: Prentice-Hall, 1994).
12. David M. Scott, *The New Rules of Marketing and PR* (New York, Wiley, 2009).
13. K. Maul, "Reality check." *PRWeek* (U.S.), 12 (22), 34–41. (2009).
14. Thomas L. Harris, and Patricia T. Whalen, *A Marketer's Guide to Public Relations in the Twenty-First Century* (Thomson/Southwestern, 2006), 57–72.
15. "The New Face of Public Relations: Navigating the Convergence of PR and Marketing," (2010), 6, PRNewswire.com.

ADDITIONAL READING

A Marketer's Guide to Public Relations in the Twenty-First Century, by Thomas L. Harris and Patricia T. Whalen (Thomson/Southwestern, 2006).
The Fall of Advertising and Rise of PR, by Al and Laura Ries (New York, HarperCollins, 2002).

"Mega-Marketing," by Phil Kotler, *Harvard Business Review* (March 1, 1986).

The New Rules of Marketing and PR, by David Meerman Scott (New York, Wiley, 2009).

"The New Face of Public Relations: Navigating the Convergence of PR and Marketing," (2010), PRNewswire.com.

Outcome-Based Marketing New Rules for Marketing on the Web, by John D. Leavy (Entrepreneur Press, 2011).

11

C H A P T E R

INVESTOR RELATIONS FOR SHAREHOLDER VALUE
Communicating with the Market

Nancy A. Hobor, Ph.D.
Retired Senior Vice President, Communications and Investor Relations
Grainger
Senior Lecturer
Northwestern University

A STRATEGIC APPROACH

Imagine John (or Johan, Jean, Joanna), a portfolio manager for a large investment firm. He or she has to make a decision about whether to buy (or sell) your company's stock or bond. Paul (or Paula), an individual shareholder, does the same. Both individuals will make a decision based on information (with some emotion as well). The goal for both is the same: to make money. The trading of shares takes place on an exchange, independent of the company, and the company does not get any money from the transaction (unless, of course, the company is an exchange). So, why does a company have a function called investor relations?

Investors need information to make the right decision on which stock or bond to buy. Most investors research the company before investing, and, as long as they remain shareholders, they require ongoing news and information.

That's where the investor relations function comes in. A working definition of the investor relations professional is one who brokers information between the investing community (audience) and publicly traded corporations. For most of the chapter, the examples relate to trading stocks, not bonds.

Many companies hire an individual investor relations professional or officer, although some might split the duties among the financial, legal and communication departments. According to a 1998 study carried out for the Ernst & Young Center for Business Innovation by Sarah Mavrinac and Tony Siesfeld, an investor relations program can add between 0.3 and 0.9 to the price–earnings ratio of a company. Much less scientifically, others have estimated that a robust investor relations program can add as much as 10 percent to the price of a stock. Why? Because sharing credible, accurate and timely information with investors and potential investors gives them confidence in what's going on.

Another way to think about it is to consider that a small cap stock (i.e., the stock price multiplied by the number of shares outstanding is less than roughly $1 billion) might be trading at $50 per share and have 20 million shares outstanding. The investor relations professional would potentially add $100 million to the value that the company's shareholders receive. Considering that the average salary of an investor relations practitioner in the United States ranges from approximately $100,000 (with a 10 percent bonus potential) for managers to up to $450,000 (with 50 percent bonus opportunity and long-term incentives between $200,000 to $400,000) for a senior professional, investors should consider that a good return indeed.

What does the investor relations professional do to earn that salary? Reflecting work done by Thomson Reuters in 2009, job of investor relations includes the following:

1. Communicating a clear, consistent, credible story

2. Communicating within the legal and disclosure requirements

3. Communicating regularly with security (sell-side) analysts so they are able to share information with their clients

4. Communicating with the right investors for a company's profile

5. Communicating with the company's senior executives and its board of directors to ensure shareholder value is considered in decisions

The stakes are huge. Today's investors are more actively involved with the companies they own than they were even 10 years ago. Making sure the investors are informed of where the company is headed and what and when the payoff for their investment will be is not just a nice-to-do activity. It is vital to the long-term health and survival of a company in the competitive marketplace for invested capital. Examples of those companies that don't do this job well are found daily in stories in the financial papers. For those companies, it sometimes was as much a failure of communication as operational or financial missteps. For companies that get investor relations right, a strong investor relations program can also reduce the volatility of the stock.

Communication is never one way. Strong companies take advantage of the dialogue with investors and consider the perspectives they bring. To start, a company needs an understanding of who and where investors are. An investor is someone who is a long-term owner as opposed to a renter, or an individual or institutional shareholder who trades in and out of the stocks hoping for quick, short-term gains.

THE AUDIENCES OF INVESTOR RELATIONS

To practice investor relations, a communicator needs to know the key players worldwide, including the important intermediaries between individuals or portfolio managers (the actual owners) and the 63,000 publicly traded companies around the world. These intermediaries are sell- and buy-side financial analysts, portfolio managers, stockbrokers or registered representatives and reporters and editors from influential financial publications. Let's start with a few definitions:

- A sell-side analyst is someone who works for an investment bank and researches an industry and selected companies within that industry to be able to analyze them. The information he collects is communicated to the bank's clients through written reports and conversations with the bank's sales force as well as the clients.

- A buy-side analyst or portfolio manager is someone who works for a money management firm such as a bank, mutual fund, foundation or endowment, pension fund, insurance company or hedge fund. She uses the sell-side information (along with research carried out by the buy-side analyst) to determine whether the company analyzed fits with what the firm is looking for in a holding. These firms are ones that actively manage money (as opposed to following an index). Passively managed money (an index fund) is not interested in the company or its story, just how significant a weight is assigned to the stock.

- Stockbrokers or registered representatives are people who work for institutions to help individuals make investments. They may help clients find opportunities or just execute the trades based on what the clients order.

- Reporters and editors today include people who work for traditional print media, television and cable companies (with an emphasis on financial stories) and electronic media, including blogs. These people provide news and entertainment about stocks and what's happening in the economy.

To communicate to these audiences, an investor relations professional creates targeted messages to inform and to persuade the audiences to buy or hold the stock. For the company, those messages are anchored in its strategic direction. What is said is a topic of importance to the chief executive officer and his or her key management team.

When investor relations professionals are actively involved in discussions relating to where the company is heading and how it plans to get there, they can provide the key management team with a perspective on how investors would perceive those decisions. Involvement also allows the investor relations person to answer investors' questions accurately and, more importantly, to develop communications plans to address the reasons why investors would want to own the stock or bonds of the company.

Many publicly traded companies in the developed world have investor relations activities that go well beyond the required filings and meetings prescribed by law. However, other parts of the world are just beginning to develop investor relations functions. In Brazil, for example, the Brazilian Investor Relations Institute offers its almost 500 members courses, events and webinars to learn about the latest trends in the profession.

Most investor relations professionals also play a key role in the integrated communications of the firm because the audiences for investor relations' messages are not just investors.

Audiences include the following:

- Employees, even if they don't own stock in the company they work for, are aware of the financial community's opinions about their company. One important employee group, senior management, frequently has a financial interest if the compensation program includes stock options or other long-term incentive programs such as performance shares. Executives follow the price of the company's stock with intense interest, and it's not unusual for the investor relations professional to get a call from a leader wanting to know what's going on with the stock price.

- Customers, too, are influenced by what the financial community is saying about the company from whom they are buying. The products might be great, the service outstanding and the price right, but if the financial media have picked up stories of investment firms attacking the company (think how activist firms might describe the company's leadership), the resulting press can raise concerns about what the future may hold. Customers may pause and want more guarantees. They, too, are influenced by the company's reputation as defined by the investment community.

- Similarly, suppliers watch and read about the companies they sell to, as do the community leaders in the areas where a business operates. In fact, mayors of small towns are among a company's supporters if activists attack because they worry about repercussions to their citizens.

So, the economic health of companies as defined and discussed by the financial community has repercussions well beyond the shareholders themselves. This is why investor relations professionals must become critical partners with communication teams in all publicly traded companies. What a company says reverberates beyond the individuals or group with whom it communicates. All company spokespersons should be telling the same story.

COMMUNICATING A CLEAR, CONSISTENT AND CREDIBLE STORY

What investors want is a reason to buy (or hold) a stock. In the white paper written by Sarah Mavrinac and Tony Siesfeld in 1998 for the Ernst & Young Center for Business Innovation titled "Measuring Intangible Investment," they assessed what mattered to portfolio managers when deciding whether to buy (or sell) a position. Although financial results (e.g., earnings, cash flow and capital expenditures) mattered, also important to the investors were the intangible factors, such as quality of management, new product development, market share, R&D productivity, innovativeness and customer satisfaction. They found that 35 percent of the reason why a sophisticated portfolio manager reported she bought a stock related to the intangible factors, although which specific factors were most important varied by industry. This study repeated and confirmed an earlier study performed by Professor Mavrinac. The idea that intangible factors are reasons for buying and holding the stock in a company reinforces why investor relations is so important and why the role of an investor relations professional is so critical in the strategic management of a company. Smart CEOs recognize this and involve investor relations professionals whenever the company makes a major strategic shift. Understanding and positioning that shift to investors matter.

How can investors make an evaluation without understanding the business strategy and model? A large part of the time that an investor relations professional spends with investors deals with the industry the company operates in and the competitors, customers and suppliers within the industry. Investors are trying to determine the following:

- What makes the company's business model successful and allows it to grow

- Why the company expects to gain market share in the future

- Who the critical leaders within the organization are (their backgrounds and what they bring to the company)

- How the company intends to leverage its financial and human assets to win in the marketplace

- When the investor should get into the stock

To attract and maintain the interest of investors requires taking a great deal of information and developing a persuasive story. Investor relations professionals can't just list the attributes that make their company great. They must illustrate those attributes through concrete examples that bring the company to life and make it memorable for the investors. Research has shown that what people remember is stories, not statistics. That doesn't mean that investor relations professionals shouldn't know and understand the financial numbers that go into the investors' models, but they won't get the chance to prove that the story is working, financially speaking, if the investors don't already find the story clear and compelling or believable.

Investor relations professionals are expected to be positive about the company they work for. That does not mean naively optimistic. If there are problems, shareholders want and deserve to hear about them early and completely. Some investors are worried about the cockroach theory—the idea that there isn't just one small problem, just as there isn't just one cockroach. Being transparent and honest is critical to building and retaining the credibility needed to see a company through a rough patch. This was the great lesson of the early twenty-first century. Some companies (Enron, WorldCom and others) obfuscated or downright lied. The result was additional regulations (see next section).

Trying to hide or twist information ruins the credibility of the investor relations professional and his or her company. If the investor can't trust the company, the risk of owning its stock goes up. If the investor believes there are really more problems than the company admits to having, the investor could instead short the stock. That means he sells the stock (by borrowing stock from someone else) and plans to buy it back later for a lower price. Hedge funds use this strategy frequently.

COMMUNICATING WITHIN THE LEGAL AND REGULATORY REQUIREMENTS

One of the greatest changes to the investor relations profession over the past decade has been the plethora of new regulatory requirements from the agencies that watch over the investment environment. All communication between companies and investors takes place in a well-regulated world. In the United States, the Securities Acts of 1933 and 1934 created the basic framework for the interchange between companies and investment community. The Securities and Exchange Commission (SEC) is the watchdog. All legally required documents (such as 10-Ks, 10-Qs, 8-Ks and proxy statements) are filed with the SEC in a prescribed manner.

In addition, the courts have and are interpreting the provisions of the acts to ensure there is no selective disclosure of material information. When companies disseminate information that could move the stock price, such as earnings, everyone should have equal access to that information, not just a few.

Some of the most recent, important legislative and regulatory actions are as follows:

- Regulation Fair Disclosure (Reg FD), which went into effect in August 2000, mandates full and fair disclosure of material information, meaning that companies cannot provide information that could move the stock price up or down to one person or a small group of people without informing everyone.

- The Sarbannes–Oxley Act of 2002 requires chief executive officers and chief financial officers to certify the company's financial results and internal control methods.

- The Frank–Dodd Act of 2010 (among many other provisions) requires a shareholder vote on executive compensation at least every 3 years and more disclosure between how executive pay and company performance are linked.

Not only does the SEC regulate companies in the United States—so too do the exchanges on which stocks are traded and the Financial Accounting Standards Board, which dictates the way financial information is reported. This is true for companies outside the United States as well. One of the upcoming changes to the way companies report is the movement to get companies to standardize accounting treatment across more countries.

To ensure that a company remains within the law and rules, the investor relations professional must understand the requirements of the appropriate governmental bodies, the exchanges and the accounting standards board. To do that, he or she collaborates constantly with lawyers and accountants when communicating with the firm's shareholders or bondholders. In a practical sense, this happens more with formal, written communication, such as the annual 10-K filing or quarterly press release. Investor relations professionals, however, should always rely on help and input, even when speaking informally to investors, especially when they are uncomfortable with the topic. It pays to know when to solicit guidance and when it's unnecessary. It also pays to develop good working relationships with the key members of these organizations.

The company whose investor relations professional masters the communications challenges within the legal and accounting framework (in other words, the company in which lawyers and accountants don't stifle communication with investors) should see the benefit in its shareholder value. Investor relations consultants argue that an effective program reduces the risk of owning a stock and that is therefore reflected positively in the price of the stock.

COMMUNICATING WITH SELL-SIDE ANALYSTS

One way companies get their messages out to the financial community is through the sell-side community of financial analysts, both equity and fixed. Although the roles and responsibilities of the sell-side analysts have been altered because of recent regulatory changes and judicial settlements, there are myriad ways that information is now disseminated electronically and the sell-side analyst remains an important player.

Historically, the analyst worked for an investment bank and did original research on the companies. She provided invaluable insight on the companies to the bank's clients, the investors who bought the research (hence the name buy-side). The analyst also provided support to investment bankers within the firm as they provided companies with help accessing the capital markets (such as private placements, secondary offerings or floating bonds).

The first challenge to the sell-side analyst came when commissions—that is, what the investor paid to buy the stock through the bank—were deregulated in 1975. Investors now traded on the basis of how much it cost, and a new group of discount brokerage firms helped make the transactions highly competitive. Thus, the investment banks turned to other ways of making money, including helping companies go public or raising additional capital through secondary offerings and debt placement. Brokerage houses asked their sell-side analysts to begin following some of the new companies, dramatically increasing their workload. At the same time, bankers hoped that the analysts' recommendations to clients would help the newly public companies' stock price increase. This benefited those clients who bought the stock when it first went public and helped the bankers win new business if the companies needed to raise more money.

Then, in 2003, New York regulators stepped in and stopped the more egregious actions. One outcome was the complete separation of research and investment banking. This caused many of the largest banks to reexamine how much research they could afford. With fewer analysts covering more and more companies, they lost the ability to do in-depth, original research.

Combining heavy workloads with the buy-side's desire for more information faster has meant that the quality of research has declined, despite the increase in the quantity of information. Some sell-side analysts felt they had become reporters instead of analysts. Analytical work on the models became the responsibility of research assistants, who may not have much experience or understanding of the companies they were analyzing.

Today, sell-side analysts may rely on investor relations professionals even more to gain access to information and to provide their clients with access to the senior leadership in the companies. Can the sell-side analyst reach the company ahead of competitors and get information on earnings or other events? Can they take management teams around to visit clients in the major money markets? Can the sell-side analyst provide the firm's major clients, the ones who pay the most in commissions, with specialized insight? These are just a few of the new challenges facing sell-side analysts and investor relations professionals.

For companies, the sell-side analyst is not as important an audience as it once was. As discussed in the next section, companies today are going directly to the buy-side analyst and portfolio manager and telling their story without the filter of the sell-side analyst. Investor relations professionals have reallocated their commitment of time to the buy-side from the sell-side analyst. Yet, the investor relations professional must still maintain good relationships with the sell-side firm, even while limiting the amount of time spent responding to them. It's important to make sure that sell-side analysts have the right information so time isn't spent trying to counter misinformation. Preventing miscommunication from leaking into the market is critical; it's a delicate balancing act.

COMMUNICATING WITH THE RIGHT INVESTORS

The best investor relations professionals work at finding and attracting investors who are right for the company. It's not easy. There are approximately 7,700 mutual funds in the United States, 12,200 hedge funds, and a very large number of other investment firms including pension funds, university and charitable endowments and insurance companies. Finding the ones interested in investing in the company and staying with that position for more than a short period requires knowing the investment firms' investing parameters and meshing those with the company's attributes.

One easy example: an investment firm with a small-cap approach is not going to buy into a company with a market cap over the limit set by how that investor defines small cap. The same is true for an investment firm that only buys growth companies. If a company does not meet the earnings per share (EPS) growth requirement, the firm is not likely to devote time to talking to an investor relations professional.

Consequently, the first task the investor relations professional has is to assess the company's attractiveness *from an investor's perspective*. With a variety of investment styles including special situations, there is a group of investment firms for every kind of stock. Targeting starts with finding the fit given each investment fund's parameters. There are many analytical tools to match company and fund, which can speed up the process.

Investor relations professionals can develop their own targeting list. Sell-side analysts can be helpful in identifying the firms which have expressed an interest in a particular company. Many funds identify their set of parameters on their websites (this is particularly true for mutual funds–seeking investors). Other investor relations professionals can suggest investment firms on the basis of their experience with the firms. However, the easiest way is to buy a targeting service from one of several consultants in the field.

Once the target has been identified, the sell-side analyst can be helpful in finding the right contact within the investment firm (this is something that consultants provide in their targeting software as well). Getting in touch with that person depends on many factors. Again, the task is not easy: 40 percent of the buy-side analysts' time at many large investment firms is spent on the firm's top two holdings. Another 50 percent of their time is spent on two to four "interesting" ideas. Special situations take up 7 percent of their time (companies involved in mergers or emerging from bankruptcy would be examples). That leaves just 3 percent of the analysts' time for companies of no interest. It sounds challenging, and it is. However, investors are always interested in a good story. The investor relations professional needs to know how to become part of the evoked set. Even if analysts call just to add information about the industry or trends, the investor relations professional can help make his or her company's role or position important.

When trying to get the interest of already busy analysts, the investor relations professional needs to be able to give those people something that warrants their time, and information about the industry is one way of hopefully attracting the beginning of interest in the investor relations professional's company. Sharing information is, in fact, important not only externally but also internally.

COMMUNICATING WITH SENIOR MANAGEMENT AND THE BOARD

Although the investor relations professional often works alone or with peers in finance and communications, there are two groups within the corporation who are (or should be) very interested in what the investor is thinking. The first is the senior executive team. These men and women often have some or all of their financial future tied up in the success of the company's stock price. In addition, they are the people most able to affect the company in ways that benefit the shareholder. Yet, like many, their focus is on their specific area: customers (for sales and marketing leaders), employees (for human resources leaders), production (for manufacturing leaders) and so forth. That's how they are measured and rewarded in the short term.

The goal of the investor relations professional is to make the information gathered from investors relevant and important to the senior team through an appeal to their long-term interest in the stock price. However, the information gleaned is also valuable as competitive intelligence. Because analysts are often talking to competitors about their challenges and what will be done to overcome them, sharing that information can be helpful when a marketing leader plans how to approach a customer group, especially if that group has been loyal.

Similarly, investor relations professionals can help the senior leadership think differently about an issue by having the leader present to a gathering of investors, either in a small group or at a conference. The questions posed to the leader may help him think and problem solve differently. CEOs and chief financial officers are the leaders most commonly exposed to investors. These are the individuals who are responsible for the issues of greatest importance to the investor: where is the company going and what are the financial implications of those actions? Giving other leaders in the company a venue that provides familiarity and an understanding of investors can strengthen the management team as a whole.

Communicating about what's going on with shareholders and investors to the board of directors is common in most companies. It's customary for chief financial officers or investor relations professionals to share analyst reports, EPS expectations, and stock price analysis. Yet, this doesn't actually help board members know what shareholders are thinking. They need to know.

Boards make decisions that influence the value of shareholders' holdings when the members vote on share repurchases, the annual and strategic plan or an acquisition or divestiture. An investor relations professional who has relationships with the decision makers (portfolio managers) and the buy-side analysts can provide insight that helps shape the decisions of the top actively managed shareholders.

These five responsibilities—telling the company's story, telling it within the legal framework, working with sell-side analysts, targeting the right shareholders and sharing information with senior leadership and the board of directors—mean the investor relations professional is a busy person. He is always juggling time and money. Making the best use of both is what the next section is about.

PLANNING AND BUDGETING FOR INVESTOR RELATIONS

An investor relations function needs its own strategic plan to move ahead. In addition, just as a corporation's strategic plan has measurable goals, so too should the investor relations function.

What those goals are depends on the company. For example, some companies are heavily institutionally held, while at others, it is individuals who own a sizable percentage of the shares. To shift that mix might be an appropriate investor relations goal. Similarly, an investor relations goal could involve the geographic distribution of the stock, with a desire to move more shares into North or South American, European, Asian or Middle Eastern accounts.

To accomplish the goal will require a clear understanding of where and why the shares are currently held. To find out where, there are several services that monitor stock activity and report results on a regular basis, as discussed in the following paragraphs. As to why a shareholder bought or sold, research firms using techniques similar to those of marketing research firms can help companies better understand investor motivations.

Attracting more individual shareholders may be an appropriate goal for companies with a strong consumer brand and a desire to encourage customer loyalty among its shareholders. Achieving the goal, however, requires more resources. Connecting to and communicating with individual shareholders typically demands a significant amount of money. Consider the task of reaching the millions of Americans (or Brazilians, Europeans or Japanese) who own stock. Motivating them to buy a particular stock requires the same tools and techniques used to get the public to buy a consumer product.

In the United States, many active individual shareholders belong to investment clubs, so reaching them through the National Association of Investment Clubs is an avenue some companies have embraced. National or regional investment club conventions with booths manned by investor relations professionals allow companies with active individual shareholder programs to distribute their messages to potential shareholders.

Some companies are using social media techniques to reach and attract individual investors. Understanding and connecting with individual investors is not much different than understanding and connecting with consumers, something that successful companies have honed. Working with marketing or communications professionals in companies with a business-to-consumer approach is one important strategy.

Because of the expense of reaching individual investors, many companies—particularly those without any consumer presence to help with recognition—concentrate on institutional shareholders, who typically require less expensive communications efforts. However, institutional shareholders require more executive time. Because institutional investors in the United States are located in major money centers—New York, Boston, Chicago, Los Angeles, San Francisco, Denver, Houston, Dallas, Newark, Kansas City, Detroit, Philadelphia, Baltimore, Pittsburgh and Minneapolis—efforts to reach these investors can be more targeted. However, meetings with senior portfolio managers typically require the attendance of senior executives such as the CEO, chief financial officer or chief operating officer.

Shifting the geographic distribution of shares to Europe or Asia also requires a commitment of executive time to meet with investors in the major European money centers, including London, Paris, Zurich, Geneva, Frankfurt and Edinburgh, and in Asia, including Tokyo, Hong Kong, Sydney and Singapore. Increasingly, Latin America offers new opportunities as well. European and Asian investors, by virtue of their distance, often place more importance on meetings with senior management, especially the CEO. They also require regular visits, not just visits when results are good. The commitment is to establish a relationship that can create the trust required for these long-term shareholders.

If you consider the long-term capital flows, you realize that it's a mistake not to participate globally. Companies that recognize the trend will take advantage of the future opportunity and begin to establish the relationships now. Having a global investor relations program will become the norm, and companies not making the effort jeopardize the longer-term stock price.

Whatever the investor relations goal, the tools and techniques to reach that goal will require resources. One traditional expense has been the annual report, but that's changing as companies move more and more of their communication to websites. Instead of spending the time and money on printed annual reports, companies are using their 10-K, the year-end equivalent to a 10-Q, or quarterly report. 10-Ks and 10-Qs are documents required by the SEC for any U.S.-listed company and are typically done by a team of financial reporting, securities lawyers and investor relations staff. For the 10-K, the investor relations professional, perhaps in conjunction with a financial communications professional, adds a letter from the chairman and/or the CEO. With that, companies have the functional equivalent of an annual report. With the SEC's "notice and access" regulations allowing companies to provide information on their websites, hard copy printing of the "10-K plus shareholder letter" annual report is on the decline.

Taking the place of the time and expense an annual report requires is the effort that goes into the company's investor relations website. The goal is to make this communication vehicle more relevant and timely for investors. There are consultants who can help companies with their webites, but they can be costly. Whether the consultant helps make the website easier to use or faster to post, the responsibility of the investor relations professional is to include content on the site that investors find valuable. That content contains information traditionally found in an annual report or in other printed documents. Consultants may help investor relations package the material, but gathering the information that's needed remains the duty of the investor relations professional.

One source of information may come from the materials put together to host analyst meetings or to make visits to larger shareholders in money centers around the globe. Posting the presentations on the website is a good way of making sure information is broadly disclosed.

Analyst meetings, conferences, and visits are keys to success in targeting the right shareholder, but they are also factors to consider in developing a budget. How many trips can an investor relations professional reasonably make in a year? Will the chief executive officer or chief financial officer devote the time? What about others in operations such as the chief operations officer or the head of important divisions? In addition to considering the time and travel costs, would the investor relations professional need to rent a room and equipment for presentations? If it's a sell-side analyst conference, is there a fee to webcast the company's presentation and Q&A session, and if not, can it be arranged for Reg FD compliance purposes? These are the key questions that will determine your spending on investor meetings and conferences.

Increasingly, investor relations professionals rely on databases to find appropriate prospective investors. Similarly, some way of monitoring the shareholder base is important, particularly if the goal is to switch that base to a more stable one. Firms now specialize in following the buying and selling of stock, so investor relations professionals have a pretty good idea in real time which institutions have liquidated their positions or which are adding, becoming major shareholders. Knowing the trends is important in targeting investor visits as well as in determining the success of the overall investor relations program. If an investor relations professional is bringing along her chief executive officer or chief financial officer, it's imperative the visits are to the most important investors or potential investors. Consultants, again, can provide information, but that may be too costly for some companies. One alternative is using sell-side analysts who are eager to help set up meetings, but investor relations professionals need to make sure the analysts' top choices are the right investor, not just the investor who is the sell-side firm's best client—often a hedge fund.

In addition, there's a need to keep track of what is being said, not just in analyst reports, but also in blogs and other social media vehicles—which can be done through clipping services and other, more sophisticated monitoring services. When inaccurate or misleading information is public, correcting that misimpression becomes more difficult and time consuming the longer it goes unchallenged. Several firms will provide that service, again for a price, and today it is usually offered in an electronic format. Teaming up with the communication or marketing department can help defray some of the costs.

Increasingly, consultants are also encouraging companies to use social media tools to reach investors. Clearly, companies need to know what's going on in social media, but institutional investors are not likely to be big users of these vehicles because they want to protect the decisions they have made or are planning to make. However, social media tools are potentially attractive for individual investors. Companies with an important individual shareholder base or those wanting to shift more shares into important individual shareholders should consider the various ways people are communicating today and determine how to reach these shareholders within the legal guidelines (see Communicating within the Legal and Regulatory Requirements).

The size of the investor relations budget, therefore, depends on the goals set in the investor relations plan and the strategies that will allow the investor relations professional to achieve the goals. Once the investor relations professional has developed an approved plan with specific goals, he creates the strategies and tactics, which include annual reports, presentations before financial audiences, fact books or fact sheets, press releases, letters or bulletins and a variety of telecommunication devices from the Internet to the telephone.

The investor relations professional is a conduit of information about what is happening within the company. By marshalling resources, he or she can increase the probability that a buy- or sell-side analyst will follow a particular company, understand the growth and profitability dynamics of that company and encourage the buying or holding of its stock. Each of the tactics needs to help accomplish that goal. In addition to the ones discussed earlier, consider the following.

PRESENTATIONS

Presentations involve preparing material and PowerPoint or slides to highlight information. Every project starts with determining the target audience and the message. The goal of the presentation is to persuade investors to buy or hold the company's stock. All presentations should be scripted, if for no other reason than to be able to post the script on the web. PowerPoint or slides should be used only as memory enhancers, not to supplement the message or detract from the presenter. Those that are too busy or include confusing graphs or charts dilute the effort. If there are specific graphs or charts that bolster an argument, the investor relations professional should use them in handouts rather than cluttering the presentation with too much detail.

FACT BOOK OR FACT SHEETS

The fact book or fact sheets augment the annual report and other financial documents. The fact book contains information that the stockbroker, financial analyst or portfolio manager typically wants. For many industries, statistical data over time are crucial; for other industries, descriptions of complex businesses help the analyst dissect and understand the company.

The information in the fact book or fact sheets can usually be found in other documents produced by the company. By gathering these facts and grouping them together in a simple format, the investor relations professional makes it easier for the financial community to follow the company. Fact sheets also can help supplement and reinforce the messages.

PRESS RELEASES

Press releases are used to disseminate time-critical, material information widely and simultaneously, such as quarterly earnings and dividend declarations. Typically, the company sends via modem a copy of the press release to one of the services (such as PR Newswire and Business Wire), which then makes the release broadly available to newspapers and wire services. Whether any newspaper or wire service picks up the release, however, is up to the various editors.

One way to enhance the possibility of coverage is to ensure the news is easily understood. Although that thought is not very profound, accomplishing it is extremely difficult. Talk to any business editor, and she will have many examples of poorly written or bland headlines.

It's imperative that the news jump out of the headline and first paragraph and not be buried in later paragraphs. However, if the news isn't positive, it is human nature to want to bury that news. Don't let the lawyers and accountants add jargon or obfuscate what really happened. In addition, don't use too many numbers in the text; include the numbers in appropriate tables at the end of the text. Finally, treat each important news release as an opportunity to explain how the information accomplishes the corporation's goals or strategies. For a description of best practices, Dix and Eaton's website has an informative piece titled "Times Are Tough."

In addition to using press releases for material information, investor relations professionals can use press releases to emphasize a message. For example, new contracts, new products or even the chief executive officer's speech to a group of analysts can be transformed into a press release. Although the speech may not merit the attention of the media, it represents another opportunity to reach the financial community by posting on the website and microblogging to key analysts and shareholders. Just be careful to include information in the press release (and the speech) that has some value for the audience, such as the potential size of the market for the new product or what the contract can do for future sales. A worthless press release wastes everybody's time and will cause the recipients of future press releases to ignore them.

LETTERS AND OTHER WRITTEN MATERIALS

At times, companies should write directly to their shareholders. Events that happen between quarterly earnings or receive a great deal of media attention may warrant a letter to shareholders. When companies change strategies and/or CEOs, the CEO can write to shareholders to explain what was happening and to assure them of his or her attention to their concerns.

Similarly, information may need to go to financial analysts to put events into perspective. Many years ago, Morton International had a problem: too much demand for road salt. Investors immediately wanted to know what the impact on the quarterly financials would be. The company had no news, so a press release was inappropriate and unnecessary. However, a brief white paper that described the situation and tempered expectations allowed Morton to explain how the demand was affecting the company. This paper was then widely disseminated.

TELECOMMUNICATIONS

Even with ever more sophisticated electronic devices, most investor relations professionals spend much of their time on the telephone, answering the myriad questions asked by financial analysts and individual shareholders. One way some companies have answered these questions successfully is with a formal conference call. After major news announcements such as quarterly earnings, analysts are invited to call a number and hear what happened from the company's executives. Usually, the analysts can ask questions or probe further if the information is unclear.

Conference calls help the investor relations professional be efficient and effective because repetition of the same information to each of the analysts is frustrating and time consuming. The message is also kept more consistent because many analysts can hear the same news simultaneously. However, conference calls don't necessarily reduce the number of calls, and getting back quickly to the financial community remains an ongoing challenge. Also, the call is dominated by sell-side analysts. Buy-side analysts won't usually ask questions as they don't want to tip their hands as to how they are thinking. To find out what's on their minds, the investor relations professional has to reach out and have a dialogue with the buy-side analyst. Finally, conference calls should be webcast to ensure public access to the information, in line with Reg FD.

ADDING VALUE: INVESTOR RELATIONS HELPS ACHIEVE CORPORATE OBJECTIVES

A well-planned and executed investor relations program facilitates the achievement of corporate objectives. That's a bold statement. Here's how the function can do that.

On one side of the communication is the investing community wanting accurate, timely information to make the best decisions. On the other side is the company with facts and figures marshaled logically and persuasively to convince investors that the company's future is sound. Although stock price appreciation does not directly affect corporate results (as indicated earlier, it may do so indirectly by influencing customers, suppliers, etc.), savvy corporations pay more attention to what investors know and expect, recognizing that these external stakeholders help company leaders think about the industry, competitors, strategies, appropriate capital allocation and even achievable goals.

However, the benefit is equally strong internally. In addition to helping ensure senior executives and the board of directors consider what shareholders need and want, investor relations programs can distill for all employees an idea of what direction the company is going and how it plans to get there. Among the most avid readers of the communications produced by the investor relations professional are the company's employees.

Fundamentally, what the investor (and the employee) want is an understanding of the strategic direction of the firm. What competitive advantages will allow it to improve returns for the shareholder?

DO NOT FORGET TO CONSIDER THESE ITEMS WHEN PUTTING TOGETHER A PLAN AND BUDGET

Salary and fringe benefits of investor relations professionals

Administrative support for investor relations

Telephone, fax, computer, modem and access to various services

Annual report (perhaps including design, printing and photography)

Website hosting, maintenance and content development

Fact books, fact sheets and other hand-out materials

Annual meeting space, refreshments, giveaways

PowerPoint slides, videos and other audio visual materials

Analyst meeting(s) and visits

Conferences

Letters or dividend stuffers to shareholders

Travel

Consultants, including those able to help in targeting, stock watch and social media monitoring

Unfortunately, because of a natural, human unwillingness to be measured for performance, not many companies are willing to lay out the firm's goals and strategies with milestones to allow shareholders to gauge results as the company grows. So, investors are left to guess at them and develop their own measurements.

> Fundamentally, what the investor wants is an understanding of the strategic direction of the firm and the competitive advantages that will allow it to improve returns for the shareholder.

When investors' expectations get ahead of reality, the result is disappointment and a declining stock price. Low stock prices can hurt if a company needs to raise additional capital. Even if the company does not contemplate a secondary offering of stock, a low stock price makes a company vulnerable—to another company or to activist shareholders willing to push for outcomes that may not be in the best interests of either the long-term shareholders or the management team.

THE FUTURE OF INVESTOR RELATIONS

This chapter has worked to persuade the reader that the investor relations function is a critical part of an integrated strategic communications program. In most companies, the role reports to the chief financial officer. In a few companies, it reports directly to the CEO, who then gets an unfiltered read on what'a going on. The person in the role must have strong financial as well as communication skills to be successful. When investor relations professionals and communication teams join together, the company and its stakeholders benefit.

The investor relations professional of the future will take advantage of how information flows. The role needs to engage the audience and communicate in an open, honest way. What makes a successful program is credible, clear, accurate and timely information. It's about transparency.

The profession recognizes that the transparency created by the new electronic world knits together all stakeholders, including investors. The web is more important than traditional printed pieces. Social media vehicles are the way people are communicating. Companies no longer control the message (if they ever did). Investor relations professionals must understand the rules that govern disclosure requirements and behave accordingly. If information is material, let everyone know at once, not just a few. That's being transparent.

Sophisticated investors know that beta (or how a stock price changes in relation to the stock market as a whole) accounts for approximately 80 percent of the value of a stock. The investor relations professional must work hard to find those investors who are seeking information about the remaining 20 percent. Where? They can be found all over the world.

The future of investor relations comes back to answering the question posed at the beginning of the chapter: why should a firm invest in an investor relations function? Because the men and women on Wall Street looking to make money want quality information—with context—as to why to invest in a particular company. The savvy company will ensure it has a solid investor relations function with professionals who, through the effective use of both old and new techniques, can answer their questions and tell the company's story credibly and accurately.

CASE STUDY

Your company is within weeks of finishing the quarter. Unfortunately, the expected last-minute realization of revenue has not yet materialized. It could be due to weather, the lack of an anticipated flu season or to another exogenous event. It could also be due to some event within the company's control. Whatever the cause, the result is a shortfall in sales but, more importantly, in earnings per share. This is likely to cause a surprise when earnings are reported. What should you do?

Let's start with what you can't do: you can't tell any single analyst or small group of analysts without telling everyone. No smiles, no winks. Nothing.

You can preannounce earnings when you are sufficiently sure of the outcome and are prepared to answer the questions that will come. The result will be a decline in the stock price, but that's going to happen once you report earnings on your regularly scheduled day. The benefit is that you may gain some credibility for telling Wall Street early. The problem is that analysts will want more information to fine-tune their models. However, chances are that not all the numbers are finalized (including EPS), so you may actually lose credibility for not sharing more. Also, research has shown that stock prices take a double dip: once when you release that you will fall short of expectations and again when you release the actual results.

You can remain silent and release when you normally do, but that's often a long month or a month and a half without saying anything. Analysts will surely call during this time. What do you say if one of them questions you on exactly the topic you know accounts for the problem? The questioning could be along the lines of typical inquiries you get (such as what will the impact on sales be if the weather remains hot, or cold or wet). If you respond accurately, you will be giving that analyst information that is material. If you try to duck the question, this may generate additional speculation and potentially more calls.

There are things you could have done: you could have provided, in advance, what the major drivers are on your business. Some companies let analysts know that for each degree of cold or number of persons experiencing flu, what the percentage impact is on sales. This works when companies are less complicated and good financial records allow for quantification. Alternatively, you could have scheduled an opportunity for the CEO to speak to a trade association or other group (you would not have scheduled anything with investors being so close to the end of the quarter). In his or her remarks, you can work in the fact that the exogenous event is causing concern for revenue growth comparisons. Before the speech, the company sends out a press release alerting the Street to lower sales. Analysts will call, but you are not under any obligation (nor should they ask) to describe what the impact might be on earnings. Analysts should adjust their numbers downward and put out notes letting investors know the reasons for the revision.

However, without being lucky or prepared, the prudent investor relations professional usually opts for a prerelease of earnings. This protects the company from inadvertent release of material information and gives the financial community confidence that even bad news will be released promptly. Long-term shareholders may find a buying opportunity if they believe the story is intact.

DISCUSSION QUESTIONS

1. What choices does an investor relations professional have if the company is expected to fall significantly short of the consensus earnings estimates?
2. How can a company avoid an inadvertent Reg FD violation and have to rush out an earnings release if a preliminary internal estimate shows that EPS is coming out significantly below consensus earnings estimates?
3. Can the investor relations professional improve the way investors think about the company even if there is a shortfall in earnings?

ADDITIONAL READING

Blumenthal, Karen. 2007. *Grande Expectations: a Year in the Life of Starbucks' Stock.* New York: Crown Business.

Bragg, Steven. 2010. *Running an Effective IR Department: A Comprehensive Guide.* New York: Wiley.

Charan, Ram. 2001. *What the CEO Wants You to Know: How Your Company Really Works.* New York: Crown Business.

12

C H A P T E R

MERGERS AND ACQUISITIONS
Communications Between the Lines

Joele Frank
Founder and Managing Partner
Joele Frank, Wilkinson Brimmer Katcher

AN INTRODUCTION TO THE WORLD OF MERGERS AND ACQUISITIONS

As an executive of a public company, you are entitled to legal, investment banking and public and investor relations counsel, but everything you've said can and will be used against you in the court of public opinion. There are no "gimmes" when it comes to deal making—but there are some lessons to heed when it comes to communicating about deals.

Although mergers and acquisitions (M&A) are often driven by the level of confidence in the economy, sometimes the exact opposite is true. Companies often seek M&A opportunities to compensate for a lack of confidence in a business unit or in its ability to further drive organic growth. In either case, our job as communicators is to clearly articulate why a transaction better positions a company to drive growth for its shareholders, customers, employees and other key stakeholders.

Once upon a time, management teams and boards of directors could do no wrong. They set the corporate strategy—including M&A—and shareholders accepted it. During the mid-2000s, strong economic growth and easy access to credit propelled a boom in corporate finance and private sector deal making. Companies were confident about the future, and sought new, riskier growth opportunities. Management teams and boards of directors were aggressive and forward-thinking, rather than defensive and risk-averse.

No matter what the motivation, the right acquisition can help a business leapfrog its competitors and define its competitive position for years to come. When companies maintain strong balance sheets, interest rates are low and access to capital is easy, the number of deals soars. This helps explain why the level of M&A activity is taken as a lagging indicator of the overall health of the economy.

There's no better example of this than the recent financial crisis. The housing bust that originated in the U.S. spread across the globe, affecting nearly every industry in the process. Revenues dropped. Business and consumer confidence plummeted. And, most importantly, banks severely limited access to financing. Instead of aggressive growth strategies, companies took defensive positions. For most, it was a time to stockpile cash in case things got worse, and M&A activity suffered.

In 2010, as we began to emerge from one of the greatest global economic downturns in history, boards began to feel more empowered to pull the trigger on strategic actions that in previous years or even months might have been shelved. By the end of 2010, global M&A activity had improved 23 percent from 2009 to $2.4 trillion (KPMG 2011, par. 1). The surge was characterized in the media as a "sure sign that the nascent economy recovery is well on its way," by Boon Sim, head of global M&A at Credit Suisse Group (Chon and Das 2011, par. 10). Many companies that survived the downturn—ones that previously took a more conservative approach to managing their balance sheets—now had a lot of cash and were looking for ways to spend it and improve their returns via targeted acquisitions.

One complicating factor for many companies, however, was the advent of a more empowered shareholder base. Although the pendulum once rested with management teams and boards, shareholders now reigned supreme. The corporate raiders of the 1980s were back, and they were not afraid to let people know. And more importantly, as the real owners of a company, they held considerable power in the M&A process.

No matter where this pendulum rests, though, it doesn't change the importance of a transaction for a company. A major acquisition can single-handedly define a company's future—both positively and negatively—for years to come and is often the seminal event for the leaders of a company. Given this magnitude, when it comes to communicating the rationale for a deal, you must get it right the first time.

Although the specific situations will ultimately vary, there will always be two types of transactions: friendly and unsolicited. Communications in a friendly transaction can sometimes be more difficult—communications have to be coordinated among two executive teams, each with a slightly different message to sell to their constituencies, but with the same goal of consummating the transaction. In hostile M&A, communications is different whether you are the acquirer or target, but the same basic principles apply.

THE BEST DEFENSE IS A STRONG OFFENSE—THE BATTLE OVER POTASH

In 2010, we saw a handful of unsolicited takeover attempts that underscored one of the most important aspects about communications in M&A: the best defense is a strong offense.

A great example of this played out in the world's fertilizer industry, which was affected significantly by the recession. Prices for the three primary crop nutrients—potash, phosphate and nitrogen—plummeted after a commodity boom peaked in 2008, sending market capitalizations for fertilizer companies down.

The stock price for the world's largest fertilizer company by capacity, Potash Corporation of Saskatchewan, Inc. (Potash Corporation), dropped from a peak of $241 in 2008 to $67 by the end of the year. This made it an attractive (and potentially inexpensive) acquisition target. However, it also meant PotashCorp had to sell at perhaps its lowest valuation. So, when BHP Billiton (BHP), a global mining company with headquarters in Australia, lobbed in an unsolicited bid to acquire PotashCorp, it was no surprise that PotashCorp wanted to fight back.

Rather than wait for BHP to announce that it had made a proposal to acquire PotashCorp, PotashCorp did something unconventional that in the end paid huge dividends. PotashCorp pre-empted a public announcement from BHP and publicized BHP's $39 billion unsolicited proposal, which essentially put PotashCorp into play. Some speculators wondered why PotashCorp wanted to take that risk. Others knew that, given where they were in the industry cycle, BHP's bid would put a spotlight on the business and help reshape public opinion regarding valuation. And that's exactly what happened.

PotashCorp's investors responded swiftly to the announcement that the board of directors had unanimously rejected BHP's proposal as grossly inadequate, among other things. PotashCorp's stock price soared a record 28 percent that day and eventually settled 13 percent higher than the $130 per share proposal at $147. Analysts speculated the bid might have to near $160 to $180 a share for it to work. "A fair deal is not at $130 a share," one shareholder said (Onstad and Rocha 2010, par. 6).

One point was clear—BHP wanted a way to grow and PotashCorp was at the absolute low point in the cycle. Like most unsolicited offers—BHP tried to take advantage of opportunistic timing in the market. This was PotashCorp's opportunity to demonstrate to the world that it was poised to deliver far more value to shareholders and other stakeholders than BHP was offering. And that's exactly what the company did.

Although BHP sought to exploit PotashCorp's low valuation, the fundamentals of PotashCorp's business were still strong, and PotashCorp's board remained confident in its future growth prospects. The nearly universal conclusion that potash demand is expected to grow steadily as incomes and populations increase in emerging markets helped the board's analysis. PotashCorp's board also implemented a shareholder rights plan, which is a tactic used by corporations to prevent coercive takeover attempts.

The battle for PotashCorp played out on the world stage and attracted widespread media interest as the largest transaction of the year. The location of the companies (BHP was based in Australia whereas PotashCorp had headquarters in Canada with major shareholders in the U.S.) only added to the drama. To make matters more interesting, PotashCorp sued BHP to block the tender offer because it felt BHP had made "false statements, half-truths, and contradictions" (PotashCorp).

Government officials in Canada voiced their opinions throughout the process because they have to review all takeover offers by foreign companies to ensure that there would be a net benefit to Canada as a result of the transaction. In the end, as one of Canada's largest companies and an owner of an important natural resource, PotashCorp inspired nationalistic pride. After lobbying from both sides, the Canadian government voted to block BHP's bid because it did not believe that the deal was in the country's best interest.

BHP's failed takeover attempt illustrates the crucial role that communications and public relations play in articulating the benefits (or drawbacks) of a potential transaction to all key stakeholder groups and, most importantly, to shareholders. Communications only work well in M&A if it's done in concert with the investor relations efforts at a company. Simply put—public relations in M&A should not be done for the sake of publicity, but rather to best support a company's growth strategy.

In most special situations, there can be as many as 40 to 50 influential opinion makers, and every constituency counts. In fact, success hinges on the ability to target these key influencers and communicate a clear and consistent message to them with enough frequency so it resonates. You know you've done a good job when you hear those messages coming back to you.

In the case of PotashCorp, consistent, effective communications with shareholders, government officials, employees, the media and others dictated the outcome. Stakeholders were convinced of the future value inherent in PotashCorp on a stand-alone basis and continued investing in the company at prices well above BHP's proposal. Employees executed well and contributed to strong earnings results, which further supported the company's story. Government officials also demonstrated their confidence in the value of the company remaining a national treasure.

DRIVING FORCES FOR M&A

To communicate the rationale for a strategic transaction effectively, it is critical to understand why a company is pursuing a merger or acquisition. Companies often look to external acquisitions as a way to grow their business and deliver greater shareholder value. For some, it might be part of a deliberate diversification strategy. Others might look to acquire a competitor to gain economies of scale. Sometimes, companies seek acquisitions because they believe their target is significantly undervalued and thus a bargain.

Even though specific situations vary, the answer almost always has to do with growth. Although one company might face financial pressure to divest a business, the acquiring company might see it as an opportunity to expand into a new market and gain new talent. One company might feel pressure from shareholders to pursue a new strategy and explore a sales process, but the acquirer might see it as a way to gain new products and technologies or simply to run business better. There are always at least two sides to every deal, and each has its own story to tell.

This is important to remember because acquiring companies almost always pay a premium—sometimes a substantial one—to the stock market value of the company they buy. Shareholders accept it because of the promise of synergies. Companies believe that by combining two organizations, they can eliminate duplicate roles or functions, exploit economies of scale, share technologies and, generally speaking, work more efficiently. This results in both cost savings and additional revenue, although on announcement Wall Street will only give companies credit for cost savings.

When a company announces a transaction or offer, the expected synergy total is closely watched by investors and analysts as a sign for what the new company expects it can deliver after integration. The best way to justify a high premium is to demonstrate the value the transaction will deliver. This means not only clearly and effectively communicating the total amount of the synergies, but also exactly how the company will deliver those results.

There have been many high-profile situations in which a company grossly underdelivered on the promises of its deal. AOL and Timer Warner are infamously linked for a failed merger that never delivered its potential. Upon the announcement of a transaction, analysts and investors will closely scrutinize what a company says it can do. It falls on the communicators to work closely with investor relations to articulate how a company will realize the benefits. The higher the premium paid, the harder it is for a company to justify the acquisition. Anyone can promise a big number. Not everyone can effectively communicate the rationale.

TYPES OF M&A COMMUNICATIONS

The communications strategy for a transaction depends entirely on the type of deal: friendly or unsolicited. A friendly deal is when the target's board of directors and management team are receptive to the offer, negotiate, and recommend the company's shareholders vote in favor of the transaction. Communicating the announcement to shareholders, the media, employees, customers and other key stakeholders can and should be carefully planned and executed.

Not all companies are open to acquisition offers. A hostile takeover occurs when the initial, unsolicited approach is resisted by the target's board, and the acquiring company still pursues the transaction. The acquiring company may revise the terms of its offer, circumvent management by offering to buy the shares directly from shareholders (a hostile tender offer, or exchange offer if part of the consideration is being offered in stock) or even seek to install new directors to the target's board. It's important to note that whereas a deal may begin on a hostile basis, if a deal is ultimately struck, it has to be done on a friendly basis.

In any scenario, communications is often the last thing an executive wants to think about, but the first thing the market, vendors, regulators and all stakeholders see. A company has only one chance to launch a deal, and the risk of a mistake is huge.

FRIENDLY

In developing a communications strategy for a transaction, it's important to have a seat at the table when strategy is actually discussed. And the only way to get one is by advancing those discussions. In a friendly transaction, communications must address transaction-related market developments that are unknown and can change at any time. Although some planning is possible, the precise tactics used and timing will ultimately depend on how events unfold. In all instances, though, messages should be clear and consistent.

In advance of an actual announcement, the companies should be prepared for and continue to manage any speculation surrounding a possible deal. This will include preparing executives ahead of public appearances and having stand-by statements ready.

As communicators, it is our job to pressure-test executives about the rationale for the merger. We must understand how and why the deal supports the company's go-forward strategy. We do not want any surprises on announcement day; we want all audiences to understand how the transaction will benefit them. Equally important, both companies' executives and boards should be aligned on key themes, including how the transaction came together and who approached whom. We want everyone to sing from the same song sheet.

The goal of a successful Launch Day strategy is to maintain control of the message. This can be achieved by managing all aspects of the launch, including the timing of the announcement, coordinating timely communication with key audiences and determining which outlets and reporters get time with management.

When it comes to the actual announcement, who issues the release isn't as important as the content and overarching strategy. The press release is usually the "core document" because it's the first thing all audiences see and the primary marketing piece. The release will also contain the main messages that will be used to develop other communications materials.

Specifically, the release needs to accurately and effectively communicate a company's rationale for its decisions to all the stakeholder groups. A poor announcement can be disastrous. The stock price might plummet.

Shareholders might come out against the proposed transaction. Hundreds of millions or billions of dollars are often at stake, and a deal can be ruined.

After announcement and until close, both companies must develop and execute communications strategies targeted at the constituencies that are critical to the success of the proposed transaction: shareholders, elected officials, employees, customers, analysts and media. The primary role of communications in the M&A process is to articulate the benefits of the potential transaction to these key constituencies, minimize the effect of any opposition and demonstrate that the transaction can and will get done. As such, as part of the communications strategy, it's imperative to prepare comprehensive, thoughtful and realistic answers in advance to certain questions. For the target company executives, shareholders and other stakeholders tend to ask:

1. Why are you selling now?

2. What is the strategic rationale?

3. Did you run an auction? Perform a market test?

4. How does this benefit me?

5. What would you do if a third party made a bid for the company?

6. Did you explore other alternatives to maximize value for the company?

For the acquiring company executives, shareholders and other stakeholders tend to ask:

1. What is the strategic rationale?

2. Why is this deal in my best interests?

3. Why this combination? Were there other candidates that you considered?

4. When will you realize the synergies?

5. Are there any antitrust concerns to consummating the transaction?

6. Are you concerned about a possible interloper breaking up the transaction?

In addition to defining answers to the previous questions, it's important to clearly articulate the "path to completion." The financial community pays close attention to the approval process, including any requisite regulatory approvals. If a shareholder vote is required, or if the transaction is structured as a tender offer, the shareholder meeting or tender deadline serves as an "election day" that necessitates a campaign to secure the support necessary to complete the transaction. The campaign period typically entails one-on-one in-person or telephonic meetings with the target's top shareholders and numerous press releases or letters to shareholders urging them to vote or tender.

On and immediately after Launch Day, the target's shareholder base is likely to turn over as traditional holders take profits and arbitrage investors build positions. Understanding what the arbitrage shareholders, who often provide valuable intelligence on market sentiment as a transaction proceeds toward completion, think can be useful. In addition, financial analysts, and potentially investors, will make their opinions and concerns known publicly. Therefore, the perception of a challenging completion process in the financial markets can resonate through the media, affect the target company's stock price and create new challenges for the acquiring company.

Different constituencies, such as employees, media, customers and shareholders communicate with each other—not only with the companies involved—and therefore it is critical that communications be consistent, coordinated and focused. A combination is received best by a company's key constituencies when they learn about it from the company itself. Because companies only get one chance to roll out a major announcement, careful planning is key. It will be necessary to communicate with a number of audiences simultaneously, including:

- *Shareholders.* There are likely to be concerns and questions about deal value versus the upside potential of the stock and the path to close.

- *Analysts.* Analysts are significant influencers in any merger of publicly traded companies and their opinions are quoted in the media.

- *Employees.* All employees need immediate communication on what the transaction means for them and what they should be communicating to customers. Generally, the areas of concern for employees include how the transaction will affect jobs and benefits.

- *Customers and Vendors.* Customers and vendors are a priority and the ways in which they will benefit—or see no effect—as a result of the transaction should be clearly articulated.

- *Elected Officials.* Communicating to government and community leaders on Launch Day is very important and can be done via press release, letter, phone calls and face-to-face meetings.

When it comes to dealing with the media, companies must maintain a disciplined approach. The number of spokespeople should be limited to ensure consistency. In preparing for a friendly deal announcement, companies can identify the key outlets and reporters at national publications, newswires, local publications and trade media in advance. The goal would be to reach as many key outlets as possible while making maximum use of management's time.

Many journalists covering the transaction may have very little experience in M&A. In those instances, it may make sense to arrange for one of the financial and/or legal advisers working on the transaction to speak to reporters on background (not for attribution) to provide further context for an announcement. This helps educate the reporter and provides greater perspective than can be accomplished in an on-the-record conversation. Keep in mind that the actual coverage of an announcement will vary depending on the size of the transaction and the current volume of announcements in the market. To enhance a story, it may also be appropriate to proactively provide to a reporter select analyst reports and/or direct a reporter to specific third parties for comment, including supportive shareholders, industry experts and analysts.

Friendly transactions are announced every day, but not all garner significant media attention like Merck and Schering-Plough's $41 billion friendly transaction did in March 2009. Merck's successful rollout of the friendly transaction was the result of a well-planned and coordinated effort, achieved through constant communication between the communications and investor relations at both Merck and Schering-Plough.

Merck realized that, in a transaction of such large scale, many eyes would be watching. Therefore, the company used all opportunities for strategic communication, focusing the announcement on the companies' complementary pipelines and portfolios, research and development capabilities, expanded global presence and combined upside potential. The companies emphasized their shared vision of creating a strong, global health care company aimed at meeting the unmet medical needs of patients around the world.

Launching a transaction of this magnitude, especially during the financial crisis, was a complicated task, in particular given the nation's focus on jobs. Merck was attuned to this issue and made sure to always be forthright and transparent with its employees and the communities in which Merck operates. Furthermore, Merck communicated with employees through every step of the integration process to ensure a smooth and seamless integration.

Another important consideration to the communications planning was the awareness of consolidation in the pharmaceutical industry. For example, only six weeks before Merck and Schering-Plough announced the transaction, Pfizer and Wyeth announced their intent to combine. From a communications perspective, it was important for Merck's constituencies to understand that the Merck and Schering-Plough transaction was not a knee-jerk reaction to industry consolidation, but rather an extremely well-thought, strategically and financially sound opportunity that would redefine the companies and set a bright path for the future.

It is often noted that coordination between two parties to a friendly transaction can be challenging. There are often cultural issues that prevent harmonious integration and threaten the overall objective of the transaction. None of this happened with Merck and Schering-Plough. Rather, the merger proved to be a textbook case of bringing two strong and complementary companies together after a well-thought and well-executed integration. Ultimately, the Merck and Schering-Plough transaction announcement was well received by the financial community and by the employees and customers of both companies. And most importantly, several years later, the transaction was considered a great success for both companies.

HOSTILE DEFENSE

Communications in a hostile are fluid, and it is critical as communicators to remain flexible so that we can address unexpected and unpredictable transaction-related market developments. Although some planning is possible, especially on defense, the precise tactics and timing used will depend on how and when events unfold. In all instances, however, messages will need to be clear, consistent, coordinated and supportive of the company's overall strategy. In preparing for any hostile defense, it's important that the target company's board and management team consider the following:

- *Currency fights take time.* Although value is an important element in any contested transaction, in a stock-for-stock contest, there is greater opportunity for other factors to influence the outcome. For example, by emphasizing the benefits of the target's stand-alone plan and future valuation potential and by demonstrating the weaknesses of the acquirer's plans and currency, the target can discourage support for the acquirer's proposal and sometimes cause the acquirer to drop its bid. The longer the process, the more opportunity the target has to influence both companies' shareholders, as well as the acquirer's board.

- *The target company—and its board—go under a microscope.* Media interest in hostile situations is likely to dramatically increase coverage and scrutiny of the companies. Consequently, it's important to understand that both the acquirer and the target—including the management teams and the boards—will be critically examined and/or challenged. Moreover, should the hostile evolve into a proxy fight, it's not uncommon for board members to be personally targeted. Although at times uncomfortable, occasional aggressive tactics are part of the overall process and will likely be used by both sides.

- *Opposition.* In unsolicited transactions, particularly when the proposal is stock-for-stock, it is a battle of stamina—it's a marathon, not a sprint. Unlike most other corporate situations, in a hostile defense, there's opposition, and the aggressor will test the endurance of the target's management and board. Although there may be good days and bad days, the best counsel is for the board and management to develop a thick skin.

- *Similar to a political campaign.* Much like a political campaign, the rhetoric can be heated at times and it's important to set expectations and understand that everything can and will be responded to. However, what matters is getting the votes for the deal. A successful defense is dependent on anticipating the offense to the extent possible, controlling the agenda and not letting others define the target company or its position.

As is the case in a friendly transaction, it's critical to maintain a disciplined approach to the media. The themes used to defend against a hostile bid will be based on the target board's response to the acquirer and will become the basis for subsequent communications. These themes will be repeated throughout the contest and the messages will become the target company's mantra. The possible approaches could include attacking the following:

- Economics of the proposal

- Poor stock performance

- Acquirer's ability to manage the target business

- Acquirer's conflicting organizational/management structure

- Considerable transaction costs

- Transaction approval process

On the other side of the coin, the target will advocate the following:

- Currency: stock price today versus future potential

- Stock performance during the last 5 and 10 years

- Long-term growth potential

- Stand-alone growth plan

- Fiduciary responsibility

- Management and track record

The communications "weapons" used in a hostile include press releases, stockholder letters, investor presentations, Securities and Exchange Commission (SEC) filings, employee letters (which can often be filed with the SEC as well) and advertisements (however, advertisements are less likely to be used). All of these documents should be as comprehensive as possible, and ancillary documents will echo the strategic rationale in these documents.

Announcements will likely include:

- *Response to acquirer unsolicited offer.* An announcement such as this affords the target company the opportunity to publicly describe the board's consideration of the offer and detail why it believes that an offer is or is not in the best interests of the target's shareholders.

- *Responses to the acquirer's announcements.* Defending against a hostile bid is a fluid process, driven by unknown market developments, and the target company must be ready to take a responsive position on all announcements from the aggressor. Typically, the aggressor has a wide window to create an event (most likely every three to four weeks), and its actions and announcements could include, among others:

  - Launching an exchange/tender offer

  - Writing letters to shareholders

  - Commencing litigation

  - Naming a slate of directors for nomination at the target company's annual meeting

  - Providing updates on the progress of its exchange offer

Though on the defensive, the target company has the opportunity to respond to these announcements and reinforce its position. Although ideally, the target would respond within the same news cycle, there may be times or circumstances in which it makes more sense to delay and ensure a more measured response.

Although the target's board recommendations will have an immediate effect on the company's shareholders, the company should also consider outreach to important constituents such as key customers, partners, elected officials and so forth. By outlining the rationale behind the board's recommendations and explaining potential future events and their effect on them, communications to these parties can help garner support in the weeks and months to come. Third parties, including institutional investors, sell-side analysts, business partners, industry analysts and so forth, are also sought to validate or refute a company's messages. For unsolicited transactions, third parties can also be used strategically to help build support for the target company's position and/or mitigate criticism.

In October 2008, NRG Energy became the target of a hostile takeover attempt from Exelon Corporation and, subsequently, a proxy fight for board seats. After numerous, unsuccessful efforts to reach an agreement with NRG, Exelon took its offer directly to shareholders via an exchange offer. NRG believed that the unsolicited offer was opportunistic, inadequate and reflected a depressed valuation given the overall market decline. Given time to execute on its strategic initiatives and for the market to recover, NRG was confident that greater value could be realized as a stand-alone company.

During an intense, 10-month defense campaign, NRG developed messages and arguments to serve as the company's defense platform. These included advocacy points regarding the company's track record of value creation, the opportunities for additional growth, the credibility of the management team and attacks on the aggressor's ability to actually finance its offer. NRG repeatedly argued the inadequacy of Exelon's offer, the inadequacy of the currency it was using (i.e., stock rather than cash) and its inability to obtain the required regulatory approvals. These messages became NRG's mantra and were used in all materials.

NRG also worked to develop relationships with the core set of reporters covering the company to disseminate the relevant messages. In a fight, M&A and finance reporters often take over for the beat reporters, with whom a company traditionally works. NRG made a point to capitalize on every opportunity to communicate its central message that the value that NRG would contribute to the potential combined company was not reflected in the acquirer's valuation.

The highly regulated nature of the industry also aided NRG's efforts. Public affairs matters quickly became a hurdle for the potential acquirer. In the event of an acquisition, the possibility of a drawn-out regulatory approval process was inevitable. This became an important point of defense for NRG, which raised this point in all of its communications, stating that a deal between the two companies could not be consummated quickly, if at all.

NRG reinforced these points in presentations to analysts, interviews and background conversations with the media and communications to the company's shareholders and employees. In addition to stand-alone press releases and media interviews announcing the company's position, NRG also leveraged regular corporate events like earnings calls as forums to communicate these thoughts.

NRG carefully anticipated several possible scenarios based on the landscape and drafted necessary materials for each scenario, which usually included a press release or public statement, a list of potential questions from various stakeholders, talking points and letters to employees and shareholders. These contingency plans ensured that the company was prepared to fire a rapid response when necessary—a key element in a successful communications defense strategy.

NRG also communicated often and effectively to all its constituents. Under the circumstances, SEC law required that both parties publicly file all communications that pertained to the situation. Turning this legal obligation to its advantage, NRG sent communications to various constituencies frequently, knowing that its position would inevitably reach a wider audience.

The company sent weekly communications to its employees and posted these letters on its intranet site. It dedicated a section of the site to the hostile offer and posted a FAQ and a glossary of terms to help employees better understand the situation. The company also sent shareholders an update on business strategy and recent achievements to defend against attacks from Exelon. These fight letters aimed to convince shareholders of the inadequacy of the offer and the fact that shareholders would not receive a fair share of the combined company given the stock component of the offer.

As part of NRG's strategic initiatives program, in early 2009, the company announced the acquisition of a business that would serve to strengthen NRG's position in an important and highly competitive market in the industry. The combination created an ideal business model that would deliver greater value to customers, employees and shareholders. In the press release, NRG detailed the strategic and financial benefits of the combination, including credit synergies, significant collateral reduction and the company's expectations that the transaction would be immediately accretive to earnings before interest, taxes, depreciation and amortization (EBITDA) and free cash flows.

The acquisition was well received by NRG's shareholders and revered by Wall Street. The positive effect of NRG's announcement with its investor base, combined with its exceptional first quarter earnings results, further damaged the potential acquirer's efforts to discredit NRG's stand-alone strategy. In the end, NRG successfully convinced investors and all four leading proxy advisory firms that the hostile offer undervalued the company and its future prospects, and Exelon ultimately withdrew its offer.

HOSTILE OFFENSE

Although still very much like a political campaign, a company's role and approach to communications changes dramatically as the aggressor in a hostile. When on offense, a company has to not only communicate to its own investors, but also has to convince the shareholders of the target company that an acquisition is in their best interests, too. Ultimately, the goal is to have the target's shareholders exert so much pressure on the target's board that the board is forced to negotiate with the acquirer.

Communications need to be assertive, but appropriate, and always reiterate the rationale for the transaction. Although a target's best defense is a strong offense, an acquirer's best approach is a "pillow" offense. There is no added value to inflaming the target even more—the goal is to win the hearts and minds of the shareholders. Communications should convince them that the value offered exceeds what they stand to make by sticking with the target. And if it's an all-cash offer, shareholders get that value immediately.

How does an acquirer generally approach communications? Among other things, an acquirer will attack the following:

- The target's track record and strategy

- How the target is denying shareholders near-term value and upside potential

- A breach of fiduciary duty by target's directors (i.e., failure to give appropriate consideration to the proposal)

At the same time, an acquirer will advocate the following:

- The acquirer's compelling offer

- The strategic rationale for merger

- That financing is not an obstacle

- The ability to close transaction in timely manner

- The synergies and accretion

The communications used in a hostile offense often include press releases, shareholder letters, launching an exchange/tender offer, litigation, naming a slate of directors for nomination at the target company's annual meeting, investor presentations, SEC filings, employee letters (which are usually filed with the SEC as well) and potential advertisements. All of these documents should be as comprehensive as possible.

Not all hostile attempts are successful, but one such example is O'Reilly Automotive, one of the largest specialty retailers of automotive aftermarket parts, tools, supplies, equipment and accessories in the United States. O'Reilly went public with an $845 million, $8 per share tender offer to acquire CSK Auto Corporation in 2007 after nearly a year of denied approaches—a deal coincidentally launched on the exact same day Microsoft made its unsolicited $44.6 billion proposal to acquire Yahoo!

O'Reilly felt it had been "forced to take (its) proposal directly to CSK's shareholders," the company stated in a press release announcing its tender offer (O'Reilly Automotive 2008, par. 2). In addition to justifying the move to its own investors, O'Reilly's real audience was CSK's shareholders, whom it hoped to convince to tender its shares and sell the company.

In its initial release, O'Reilly included a letter it sent to CSK's CEO outlining the strategic rationale and benefits of a merger. In the letter, O'Reilly's CEO, Greg Henslee, wrote that repeated efforts to engage CSK in negotiations had failed, even after signing a confidentiality agreement. The letter and release also repeatedly highlighted O'Reilly's desire to work together. "We would unquestionably prefer to work cooperatively with you to complete a negotiated transaction that would produce substantial benefits for our respective stockholders," Henslee wrote (O'Reilly Automotive 2008, par. 11).

The "pillow" approach is important because negotiations can change rather quickly. Although CSK responded rapidly to the hostile offer by instituting a shareholder rights plan that would dilute any shareholder who acquired a stake (of more than 10 percent) in the company, the company's position eventually softened, and CSK agreed to negotiate on friendly terms. CSK eventually opened its books for O'Reilly, and the sides settled at a purchase price of $12.00 per share several months later, a 50 percent premium to O'Reilly's initial hostile offer. In this case, a hostile deal ended on friendly terms.

ACTIVISM IN M&A

When all is said and done, the real owners of a company are its shareholders and when they want to speak up, they can cause real trouble. Understanding the composition of a company's shareholder base on a regular basis is an important component of any investor relations program. Activism is a common way for an investor to exert rights as a shareholder to influence a company's behavior. Oftentimes, an activist feels that management is doing a bad job and that either a change to the board or company strategy will result in improved results for shareholders. More importantly, in M&A, shareholder activism can play a crucial role.

Activists normally try to meet directly with management and suggest business operation improvements, changes to corporate governance, a spin-off, or even a sale or acquisition. When management is unreceptive to these ideas or even refuses to meet with an investor, an activist may force the issue by trying to replace directors or even trying to take over the company themselves. In a transaction, a dissident shareholder will often try to seek more value by pressuring for better deal terms or for management to even consider a different bid or a sale process.

To do this, a dissident shareholder will attack a company's track record and strategy for value creation by arguing that it can be done better. They'll claim that the board and management's interests aren't aligned with the interests of shareholders or that they're not independent. The most powerful tool activists have is their alignment with other shareholders. When a company underperforms relative to its peers, shareholders are much more receptive to activism because the shareholder is seen as right no matter what the company says.

COMMUNICATION DOESN'T END WHEN A DEAL CLOSES

It's important to remember that our role as communicators doesn't end when a deal publicly closes. In fact, many successful transactions fail because of postclosing integration mistakes: top employees leave, customers go to competitors, and unexpected costs eat into profits. A well-planned postmerger communications plan can address many of these issues and position the company for future success.

For example, the closing of the transaction provides a natural time to proactively reach out to all important stakeholders, including key shareholders, employees, vendors, business partners and local government officials. Communications should be carefully constructed depending on the specific constituent. For friendly transactions, companies can work together to ensure that messages are consistent and delivered to the appropriate groups.

Employees are of particular concern. Any merger or transaction creates some uncertainty and speculation about how the deal will affect the day-to-day lives of employees. They will be concerned about everything from benefits to reporting relationships to the organizational structure. Companies can take advantage of their traditional internal communications vehicles (e.g., company newsletters, intranet sites, video messages, town hall meetings) to communicate key messages about the transaction and to set expectations about the integration plan and timetable. Communications need to reassure employees that the company is focused on growing with all of its employees and that any effect from the transaction will be minimal on day-to-day business. These communications can also highlight successes during the process and reinforce the potential of the new company.

In the end, companies and executives are often defined by deals—both good and bad. Although we as communicators can't control the outcome of the transaction and most certainly the timing, we can make sure that there aren't mistakes when it comes to communicating. It's our job to make sure that the public, shareholders, employees and all other stakeholders understand why a deal is right for the company. Every transaction offers its own challenges and unique opportunities, but what's consistent about every deal is that a company only has one chance to launch and it can't afford to make a mistake.

DISCUSSION QUESTIONS

1. Why do companies pursue acquisitions?
2. Who are the audiences that a company should communicate with when announcing a transaction?
3. Why was PotashCorp successful in defending a hostile bid from BHP?
4. How will the aggressor in a hostile transaction typically attack a target company?
5. What tactic did O'Reilly Automotive use in announcing its hostile bid for CSK?
6. How did NRG approach employee communications during its hostile defense?
7. What role do activists play in M&A?

REFERENCES

Chon, Gina, and Anupreeta Das. 2011. "Big deals are back as US firms seek growth." *The Wall Street Journal.* online.wsj.com/article/SB10001424052748704810504576305363524537424.html (May 6, 2011).

Onstad, Eric, and Euan Rocha. 2010. "BHP goes hostile on $39 billion Potash Corp." *Reuters*. www.reuters.com/article/2010/08/18/us-potashcorp-idUSTRE67G1R620100818 (May 3, 2011).

O'Reilly Automotive. 2008. *O'Reilly Automotive Proposes to Acquire CSK Auto for $8.00 per Share in Cash*. Springfield, MO.

KPMG. 2011. "M&A Practitioners Express Optimism for the Year Ahead." 2011, www.kpmg.com/US/en/IssuesAndInsights/ArticlesPublications/Documents/ma-spotlight-ma-practitioners-express-optimism-for-the-year-march-2011.pdf (May 5, 2011).

Potash Corporation of Saskatchewan, Inc. v. BHP Billiton Ltd. No. 10-cv-06024. U.S. District Court for the Northern District of Illinois Eastern Division. October 28, 2010.

ADDITIONAL READING

Bruce Wasserstein. *Big Deal: 2000 and Beyond*. New York: Warner, 2000.

Bryan Burrough and John Helyar. *Barbarians at the Gate: The Fall of RJR Nabisco*. New York, NY: Collins Business, 2008.

Julie MacIntosh. *Dethroning the King: the Hostile Takeover of Anheuser-Busch, an American Icon*. Hoboken, NJ: Wiley, 2011.

James B. Stewart. *Den of Thieves*. New York: Simon & Schuster, 1992.

Connie Bruck. *The Predators' Ball: The Inside Story of Drexel Burnham and the Rise of the Junk Bond Raiders*. New York, NY: Penguin, 1989.

Steven M. Davidoff. *Gods at War: Shotgun Takeovers, Government by Deal, and the Private Equity Implosion*. Hoboken, NJ: John Wiley & Sons, 2009.

Andrew Ross Sorkin. *Too Big to Fail*. New York: Penguin (Non-Classics); Mti Upd Edition, 2011.

13
CHAPTER

CHARITIES AND CORPORATE PHILANTHROPY
Giving Back

John A. Koten
Founding Director
Arthur W. Page Society
Former Vice President, Corporate Communications
Ameritech

CASE STUDY

It's budget time at the Magenta Butterfly Corporation, a maker of sports apparel for women headquartered in Edina, Minnesota, with annual sales of approximately $285 million. After an all-vegan lunch at a nearby restaurant, the company's senior executive team is scheduled to hear the final four presentations in a series of budget meetings with company department heads. The 16-meeting agenda already has left the team feeling a bit uneasy as they munch away on kalamata and roasted red pepper tapenade. Although Magenta's sales have been growing at a 10 percent annual rate, cost pressures have held profits flat during the past year. The day before, Magenta's CEO kicked off the budget meetings saying that the time has come to clamp down on expenses. So far, however, each department's presentation has made a compelling case for more rather than less funding.

The afternoon will bring more of the same. First up: Magenta's chief legal officer will ask for a 10 percent increase to cover higher litigation expenses associated with defending the company's Butterfly trademark. Next, the IT department will request a 25 percent spending increase to purchase more servers for the company's expanding website and replace outmoded equipment (a year ago, the company elected to save money by waiting four years instead of three to replace computers). Now some machines are literally falling apart). Up third is the human resources (HR) department. HR doesn't plan to ask for anything, but instead will take the budget committee through a PowerPoint presentation showing why Magenta is facing an imminent 14.9 percent increase in its annual health care insurance premiums.

Finally, Karen Jennings, Magenta's newly hired chief corporate affairs officer, will get her turn. Karen plans to offer to keep her department's spending flat in the coming year—with one exception: she wants the company to raise its annual pledge to a charity that funds shelters for runaway teenage girls. Her presentation will ask for an increase of $160,000, or 10 percent more than the $1.6 million the company is giving to the charity in the current fiscal year. She plans to conclude her presentation, which she has rehearsed over and over again the past week, with what she hopes will be a dramatic flourish. "Because it's the right thing to do," she'll declare.

Pause. So what do *you* think Karen's chances are of getting her full $1.76 million? Note that she's up against requests that seem either essential to Magenta's DNA or fundamental to keeping its operations functioning. Recall the CEO's admonition about cutting expenses and keep in mind the company's fiscal situation; Magenta simply doesn't have enough money to fully fund every request. On the face of it, it's hard to see how Karen's well-intentioned pitch has much chance of success. It's unfortunate, perhaps, but it's the way things often are in business. In a pinch, generosity gets jettisoned.

However, before you give your final answer, let's add a few more details to the picture. Suppose we mentioned that Magenta's CEO was recently elected to serve on the board of the charity Karen singled out. Would that change your call? Or, suppose the charity had been founded by employees and had become a crucial part of the company's culture. What if the largest retailer carrying Magenta's clothing lines also is a huge supporter of the charity? Or suppose that, integral to its marketing and advertising campaigns, Magenta has, for years, pledged to contribute a fixed percentage of its sales to this charity every year. Perhaps it has even become the single most mentioned thing about Magenta by the users of Facebook and Twitter, along with testimonial videos on YouTube?

This example of a budget meeting at the fictitious Magenta Butterfly company isn't meant to be a pop quiz. Rather, it aims to illustrate some of the real-world factors that come into play in the realm of corporate philanthropy. As a business discipline, corporate philanthropy has evolved greatly over the years—arguably at an even faster rate than the fields of advertising, marketing, finance or operations. Yet, although now practiced with considerable sophistication at some corporations, charitable giving still remains a blurry or underexploited discipline in many enterprises.

Indeed, for some time now, corporate charitable giving has been the fastest growing segment of philanthropy in the United States. It reached an annual rate of approximately $14.9 billion in 2010. That's still a fairly small amount compared with the $225 billion given yearly by individuals the United States. It is also less than 30 percent of what companies could donate if all of them gave the full limit allowed by the Internal Revenue Service. Over the last 25 years (1985–2010), in good years and bad, inflation-adjusted increases in total corporate giving have averaged more than 7 percent.

Today, the main recipients of corporate donations fall into the following categories: education, health and human services, arts and culture, the environment, science and technology, social sciences and international affairs. The two largest beneficiaries are education and health and human services. International giving by corporations has grown steadily over the past decade, during which nearly 15,000 organizations in more than 200 countries received grants totaling over $7 billion. Charities in Switzerland, England and Kenya were the largest major recipients.

As recently as 2008, a study of philanthropic practices conducted by the McKinsey & Co.[1] consulting firm found that the "personal interests" of the CEO or board of directors continues to be a top-three factor in determining the focus of giving at more than 45 percent of the 721 companies McKinsey surveyed. It's possible to believe that many of these directors and CEOs operate with the best intentions and keep the interests of the company well in mind. Still, leaving such decisions exclusively to the boardroom can be an invitation to the inappropriate pursuit of purely personal agendas or other unethical behavior. At the very least, it's questionable for a company to treat its philanthropic activities as a kind of executive perk.

It is also far from current best practice. Today's most advanced practitioners carefully weave their company's philanthropic efforts with the strategic goals of the business. They thoroughly research philanthropic options, seek to achieve measurable results on dollars they spend and try to demonstrate a long-term return on investment.

The potential for the misuse or even abuse of corporate resources is one reason some serious corporate thought leaders still oppose the notion that businesses should engage in philanthropy at all. They argue that companies should either reinvest profits to do what they presumably know how to do best—providing a specific good or service to their customers at a profitable price—or return any spare assets not used for this purpose to shareholders to do with the funds as they please (including giving to charitable causes). Shareholders, this argument continues, simply do not retain senior managers to be philanthropic agents. It just isn't part of the job description.

Although opposition to charitable activity was actually the prevailing view within business a century ago, it is a far less common way of thinking today.

This increase in corporate charitable activity reflects changing social and customer expectations. As recently as 20 years ago, few consumers paid any attention to the philanthropic activities of businesses and had few expectations of them in this regard. Businesses were considered accountable for their legal contractual obligations, not for their impact on issues as far-flung as childhood obesity and foreign sweat shops. Yet, as consumers have become more and more aware of their own social, moral and environmental impact, they have increasingly sought out businesses identified with causes they relate to and shunned companies whose activities violate their values.

Consumers obviously also now have more access to this sort of information than ever before. The Internet has become a powerful and ubiquitous research tool, and companies are expected to talk about and disclose their philanthropic activities prominently in public view. The rise of online social networking has made it possible for individuals and groups to champion causes they support and also call out questionable activities or even engage in online protests against corporations whose practices they disagree with.

Institutional investing also has accelerated the pressure on companies to meet their social obligations. As they put their own reputations at stake and advocate on behalf of the investors they represent, pension funds and other investment organizations have made the examination of a corporation's values and practices an integral part of their due diligence.

Companies also may be giving more in hopes of combating the overall public erosion of trust in business institutions. In 1968, when the pollster Daniel Yankelovich asked Americans whether business behaves responsibly, 70 percent said yes. By 1985, only 30 percent and by 2010, just 20 percent answered the question in the affirmative.

The decline in public trust clearly has to do with many events and factors outside the realm of corporate charitable giving. But it also has given companies greater incentive to do more philanthropically and be much smarter and more sophisticated in how they go about it (something we will explore in more detail later in this chapter).

At its best, corporate charitable giving can support every aspect of a company's activities. It can create goodwill among consumers, regulators, investors, employees and other business partners. It can help clarify and distinguish a company's mission and culture. It can provide leadership training for executives. And, by taking a business outside of its normal sphere of operations, philanthropy can introduce it to new ideas, new partners, and innovations that might not otherwise come its way.

One often cited example of a company that appears to have benefited in all these areas is General Mills, a member of a group of businesses in the Minneapolis–St. Paul area that has committed to spending 5 percent of each company's annual pre-tax net income on charitable activities. The yardstick puts General Mills at the $100 million level annually, an amount that not only allows the company to make significant ongoing commitments but also to respond in a powerful way during a crisis such as the 2010 earthquake in Haiti. When General Mills became concerned about multicultural affairs, it increased giving by 40 percent to such groups as the National Urban League, National Council of La Raza, the Congressional Black Caucus and the Congressional Hispanic Caucus.

Yet, consistent with its corporate mission, food and hunger remain its primary focus. In 2009, for example, General Mills donated more than $18 million in food products to Feeding America, the nation's largest hunger relief organization. It also gave Feeding America 49 million bowls of whole grain cereal worth $10 million. To encourage youth fitness and nutrition programs, the General Mills Foundation partnered in 2002 with the American Dietetic Association Foundation and the President's Council on Fitness, Sports and Nutrition. Its "Champions for Healthy Kids" program has reached more than 5 million children since its inception.

General Mills encourages all employees to take part in its charitable activities—and an astonishing 82 percent of its U.S. employees do. It would be hard to find a more ringing endorsement of corporate philanthropy than that.

James Burke, former chairman of Johnson & Johnson, linked a corporation's level of charitable giving not only to what he considered to be the essential components of business success but also to its self-preservation. He once remarked, "I have long harbored the belief that the most successful corporations in this country ... the ones that have delivered outstanding results over long periods of time ... were driven by a simple moral imperative—serving the public in the broadest possible sense—better than their competition. We as businessmen and women have extraordinary leverage on our most important asset ... goodwill. The goodwill of the public ...

(I)f we make sure our enterprises are managed in terms of their obligations to society ... that is also the best way to defend this democratic, capitalistic system that means so much to all of us."[2]

Another example of corporate giving that benefits companies and society alike is the case of the Aidmatrix Foundation. This nonprofit organization uses supply chain technology to meet disaster need and to supply food banks and free clinics. Companies can donate overruns or unneeded goods through an online system, which benefits them as well as those in need. In addition, transportation companies can donate empty backhauls to get goods to where they are needed. (See Chapter 18 on Nongovernmental Organizations.)

BRIEF HISTORY OF CORPORATE CONTRIBUTIONS

In 1981, the Business Roundtable, an association of CEOs of leading U.S. companies, proclaimed that "all business entities should recognize philanthropy as good business, and an obligation if they are to be considered responsible corporate citizens of the national and local communities in which they operate." Importantly, the Roundtable statement stopped short of saying that any profitable business was morally obligated to contribute to charity. Instead, it made charitable activity the price companies should pay if they want to enjoy a reputation as a responsible corporate citizen.

Even with that caveat, the thinking behind the Roundtable's pronouncement took many decades to evolve. Although philanthropy has been an integral part of American tradition since the country's founding, charitable activity by business has developed much more slowly over a longer period of time. It may never, in fact, have evolved if early corporations hadn't been so closely tied as private enterprises to a single or small group of owners who could legally comingle their personal charitable impulses with those of the companies they owned.

Americans may be among the most generous givers in the world, but we are also among the most conflicted when it comes to charity. On the one hand, we celebrate charity and associate it with altruism and selflessness. On the other, we are acutely aware of the benefits that can accrue from charitable acts and can be quick to view them with a jaundiced eye. Introducing business into the mix tends to make us even more suspicious of supposed eleemosynary behavior. A corporation, almost by its very definition, is organized self-interest. So why would anyone expect it to behave charitably?

In practical terms, this means companies often find themselves walking a fine line in their philanthropic pursuits and laying themselves open to criticism on all fronts. A shareholder group might complain that a gift will dilute the company's efforts to expand and grow; employees might complain it did little more than allow the CEO a moment of glory as he or she presented an oversized check to the gleeful charity; a customer might say the money should have been used to lower prices; a regulator might call out questions about a potential quid pro quo.

Philanthropy in the United States was initially fostered by the religious community; later, wealthy families and individuals joined in accepting the responsibility of helping others by making financial contributions. Echoing the philosophy of stewardship (a then popular belief that all property ultimately belongs to a higher authority than its current possessor), Standard Oil founder John D. Rockefeller told others he had been singled out by God to receive a great fortune precisely because of his willingness to pass it on to charitable causes. "It has seemed as if I was favored and got great increase because the Lord knew that I was going to turn right round and give it back," he once said. Given the enormous contributions made by some of these wealthy families, it probably shouldn't be surprising that names like Rockefeller, Carnegie and Mellon now have far more favorable reputations as civic-minded philanthropists than as the hard-driving, monopolistic businessmen they were in their lifetimes.

The first companies to gain wide notice for combining charity with business strategy were the railroads in the late 1800s. Recognizing that many of their passengers and employees needed clean, comfortable, inexpensive places to stay overnight as they made cross-country journeys, the railroads gave money to Young Men's Christian Association (YMCA) facilities. Typically, the railroads provided 60 percent of the YMCA's operating budget; rentals from passengers and employees were expected to cover the rest. These contributions (for what were known as "supervised economical accommodations") not only furthered the railroad's goal of helping passengers travel safely, but also had a huge effect on the growth of the YMCA in the United States. By 1890, it had built nearly 200 facilities using railroad funds. What's more, as the railroads continued to prosper during those days of extensive train travel, another group of beneficiaries emerged: railroad investors.

Even so, the concept of the corporation as anything other than a vehicle for generating shareholder profit would remain an elusive one for many decades. In a telling ruling in 1915, the Michigan Supreme Court found that Ford Motor Co. had violated the interests of its shareholders (who included the Dodge brothers) when it suspended a special dividend to pay for the increased production of a cheaper car. The court cited Ford's publicly expressed desire to "employ still more men, to spread the benefits of this industrial system to the greatest possible number, to help them build up their lives and their homes" as a secondary goal at best. The court concluded, "A business corporation is organized and carried on primarily for the profit of stockholder."

During World War I, the American Red Cross broke down many barriers to giving by companies. Benefiting from its designation as the nation's official relief agency and auxiliary of the military, the organization counted more than 1,200 corporations among its donors by 1918. Among the largest were General Electric (GE), Anaconda Copper and Ford, which contributed 5,000 Model Ts. To address the concerns of companies hesitant to pledge shareholder funds, the Red Cross came up with an alternative. It gave them a form to send out with dividend checks that would make it easy for the stockowner to sign the proceeds over to the charity.

In 1936, in hopes of stimulating greater charitable activity at the height of the Great Depression, President Franklin Roosevelt agreed not to veto a bill that for the first time allowed companies to deduct up to 5 percent of their pretax net income from their federal income taxes for any contributions they made to charities (the charitable deductions for individuals had already been established in 1911). At first, Roosevelt opposed the measure. Reflecting sentiments that were shared by many at the time, he said he thought that the tax exemption "would mean the sanctioning of two unsound practices. First, the purchase of goodwill by companies, and second, the authority of corporate officials to exercise a right in bestowing gifts that belong properly to the individual stockholders in the corporation." Columnist Walter Lippmann wrote at the time that the president appeared to have branded corporate giving as "immoral."

However, the national organization of Community Chests—many of which were struggling mightily to raise funds—fought back with a national campaign in support of the deduction. A fusillade of support for the bill poured into Congress, and Roosevelt dropped his veto threat. However, the bill he signed into law nevertheless contained the provision that all corporate donations be tied to a clear benefit to the company. Just what that meant would be a source of dispute for many years to come.

The issue was finally clarified in a landmark case in 1953, when the New Jersey Supreme Court ruled against a shareholder suit arguing that a $1,000 gift to Princeton University from the A.P. Smith Manufacturing Company had violated the company's fiduciary responsibilities. In its decision, the court eliminated the "direct benefit" provision of the federal law and said a company also had a social responsibility to the entire community. It specifically cited education as an important social benefit and thus helped usher in an entirely new era of corporate giving to higher education.

In 1955, the Ford Motor Car Company announced plans to spin off $641 million of stock to the outside charitable foundation it had first established in 1936. The gift would coincide with a public offering to shareholders that would end Ford's status as a privately owned company. A year later, the Ford Foundation made grants totaling $260 million to more than 600 private four-year colleges and universities to help increase faculty salaries. Although the foundation no longer had a connection with the company following the public offering and owed all of its generosity to the largesse of the Ford family (whose stockholdings provided the endowment), the action was widely noticed throughout corporate America and helped generate new interest in the goodwill and public attention that could be stimulated through philanthropic activity.

Also in 1955, GE launched its landmark matching gift program. GE's innovative approach let employees have a say about where corporate money was donated. Originally conceived as a fringe benefit to attract and retain talent, the program produced unexpected benefits as an effective device for directing corporate contributions.

It wasn't long before matching gift programs were adopted by a wide variety of cultural, social and health-related organizations. Andrew Heiskill, former CEO of Time, Inc. said, "Matching gifts are one of the best ways of boosting employee morale and building a good feeling about working for an organization that supports the causes chosen by its employees." Heiskill went on to assert that, "Fifty percent of a company's giving should be 'employee driven.'"[3]

In its first year, GE matched approximately $200,000 in employee contributions to colleges. Twenty-five years later, more than 900 companies were participating in the educational "match"—providing approximately $40 million for higher education. By 2010, the total match by companies to educational, cultural, health-related and other nonprofits exceeded $100 million annually.

In the late 1950s, Sanford Cousins, a vice president at AT&T, wrote an article in the company magazine proposing that the company and its employees "begin helping the communities we serve." He argued that, given the nature of its business, the telephone company would benefit because as communities grew and prospered, it would, too. Employees also would be helping neighbors in their communities with the company's support. Shortly thereafter, Illinois Bell (an AT&T subsidiary) made "help the communities we serve" its fourth "guiding principle" after (1) serve the public, (2) benefit investors, and (3) deal squarely with employees. Years later, AT&T executives would cite Cousins's inspiration as one of the factors that contributed to the company's success and its reputation as the most admired corporation in America.

The technological revolution that gained steam throughout the latter half of the twentieth century also influenced corporate philanthropic giving. Companies began to fund research and develop closer relationships with educational institutions in hopes of gaining insights or access to innovation that might provide a competitive edge in the marketplace. In the mid-1970s, seeking to improve its management recruiting efforts on college campuses, General Motors decided to concentrate its educational giving on the 13 business schools and 14 engineering schools it deemed crucial to its own future.

The more companies widened the scope of their giving, however, the more they created a new problem for themselves. By raising public expectations, they had opened the floodgates to requests for gifts. In 1980, Kenneth L. Albrecht, a vice president at Equitable Life Assurance Company, was moved to point out that, "There is really no point in any corporation wasting its time (or contributions) on matters in which it has no interest and with which it is not equipped to deal. For example, Equitable, a life, health and pension company—will almost always have a segment of its program devoted to health. If we made musical instruments, our interest in the performing arts would likely be great."[4]

McDonald's Corporation was one of the first large companies to successfully tie its philanthropic efforts to brand building. When it opened its first Ronald McDonald House in 1974, it integrated a fictitious advertising mascot with a charity dedicated to establishing facilities that could be used by the family members of critically ill children during overnight hospital stays. Ronald McDonald became an icon for children everywhere as a symbol of care and concern.

In fact, McDonald's was so successful in establishing the concept through its Ronald McDonald House Foundation that it has been able to get other companies (including many of its suppliers) to contribute to its foundation. A recent page on the charity's website, for instance, featured the donation of more than 2,000 pieces of furniture to the charity by La-Z-Boy. Officials at McDonald's today say that the company's entire product line benefits from its association with the more than 300 Ronald McDonald Houses built around the world, where employees serve as volunteers.

Over time, as corporate philanthropy has grown and become more visible, so too has corporate vulnerability to criticism over giving policies. In 2003, Berkshire Hathaway discontinued a philanthropic program that allowed holders of its Class A stocks to each choose up to three charities the company would donate to from profits set aside for the purpose. Although the program contributed approximately $17 million annually to more than 3,500 charities, it stirred a protest and boycott because some of the designated funds went to controversial groups like Planned Parenthood. At the time, CEO and Chairman Warren Buffett complained that he couldn't persuade the public that the program was legitimately spending investor rather than company money.

CORPORATE PHILANTHROPY TODAY

Under current tax law, the IRS permits a company to give in cash or property up to 10 percent of its profits for a given tax year to qualified charitable (nonprofit) organizations. Qualifying entities are known as 501(c)(3) organizations after the section of IRS code where they are described. As of 2010, there were more than 1.2 million organizations in the United States with this designation.[5] Few companies give the maximum amount;

most give in the range of 1 to 2 percent of their pretax net income. Charities may not provide goods and direct services back to individuals or companies in return for charitable deductions.

Contributions to political parties and candidates also are not tax deductible. Nevertheless, some contributions may be made to the educational arm of a political organization if they are qualified under IRS code section 501(c)(3) or (4). This loophole is not without controversy and, as of this writing, remains a subject of debate in Congress.

The Council of Better Business Bureaus counsels companies to avoid misunderstanding the difference between organizations that are "tax deductible" and ones that are "tax exempt." The IRS defines more than 20 different categories of tax-exempt organizations (those that do not have to pay federal income taxes). Of these, contributions to only a few categories are tax deductible. The status of any organization may be determined by asking the local IRS office or by asking the prospective recipient for a copy of its "Letter of Determination" from the IRS.

As more companies formalize their institutional giving, more have formed their own foundations to handle the task. Some do so simply to insulate the CEO and other executives from the minefield of fielding requests for bequests so they can focus exclusively on the task of operating the company. When someone does ask for money, either through formal business channels or in an ambush setting like an awards banquet, the CEO can refer the person to the foundation. CEOs are often especially happy to exercise this option when approached by an important business partner, a personal friend or valued subordinate. These people are often due serious consideration and a thoughtful response, something the CEO can't quickly or easily provide. Even denying a charitable request can sometimes take a company into treacherous territory.

Establishing a foundation also can send a positive signal to a company's various stakeholders that its charitable activities are accounted for and measured, that the company has at least some way of ensuring that it makes careful and serious choices about its giving and that it has made a serious commitment to philanthropy that it intends to stick to. This is true whether the company establishes the foundation as a pass-through vehicle or with an endowment, which can help companies with inconsistent earnings make longer-term commitments.

By far, direct giving programs still account for the largest amount of money contributed to charities by corporations. That's partly because employee matching gift programs, in-kind giving, and pro bono services fall into this category. However, the total assets of corporate foundations (of which there are approximately 3,000 in the United States) surpassed $20 billion in 2010 and showed every sign that they would continue to increase, with annual receipts from their affiliated companies running at approximately $5 billion. Many companies have both a foundation and a large internal direct giving program.

Foundations that operate like endowments rarely spend all of the money they receive, but instead try to build their overall corpus and give a percentage of their revenue away. Though there are many variations of the formula, one commonly used rule of thumb is to set annual spending at 5 percent of the average total assets for three years. In 2010, there were approximately 500 U.S. company foundations that gave at least $1 million annually to charity. The five largest were Sanofi-Aventis ($321 million), Walmart ($216 million), Bank of America ($186 million), GE ($97 million) and Wachovia Wells Fargo ($93 million). The top donors of cash *and* products were Pfizer ($2.3 billion), Oracle ($2.1 billion), and Merck ($923 million).

All company foundations, whether structured as endowments or not, have a board of directors composed of officers of the company and, often, directors from the outside world. A good outside director can bring significant value to a foundation's giving efforts by exposing the company to charitable avenues and opportunities that it might not encounter in the usual course of business. In the best of circumstances, all directors are tasked with ensuring that the foundation's giving remains in proper alignment with the goals and strategy of the company.

Trouble can result when the mission of a foundation drifts too far from its corporate parent. Throughout the 1970s and 1980s, the Exxon Education Foundation was regarded throughout the philanthropic world as a leading model of enlightened corporate giving. Although funded by Exxon, the foundation paid little attention to the business of the company and gave instead to causes it felt were the most needy. The idea behind this separation of church and state was, at least at the time, partly noble: the foundation's motives could genuinely be seen as more altruistic if they didn't involve the interests of the company.

There was little serious argument with this thinking until the company was confronted with the disastrous Exxon Valdez oil spill in Prudhoe Bay in 1989. With the benefit of hindsight, it was painfully clear that Exxon could have come through the crisis much better if it had cultivated at least some allies and partnerships among environmental groups. Instead, because its foundation had focused almost entirely education, it was left without a single friend or resource in the crisis. The resulting blow to the company's reputation and finances in the end not only crippled the company but hurt the foundation as well.

Geography has almost always had a major influence in contribution decisions, with the bulk of the money going to headquarters or plant or office locations. This is because most companies—regardless of size—can see the clear benefit in helping the communities in which most of their employees live. Improving the quality of life locally not only generates employee loyalty but helps attract prospective employees.

An increasing concern of many communities has been the rise in corporate mergers, which has reduced the number of givers (particularly in the banking area) and centralized giving policies in companies with many branches (drug stores, restaurants, hardware stores, etc.). Some describe this as "the Walmart Effect."

Walmart Stores itself has sought to counteract such criticism by focusing its efforts on community giving. The Walmart Foundation is now the largest cash contribution program in the United States. It operates on three levels: national, state and local (zip codes). The local program is run by store managers and deals with community issues. Each state has a state council that deals with unmet needs, including complaints from groups who believe they have been neglected or not listened to on a local level. The national program deals with major issues affecting society (hunger, education, etc.), recently granting $2 billion over five years to help reduce hunger worldwide. Margaret McKenna, a former college president and the current chair of the Walmart Foundation, says the three-tier system has allowed the company to be both fair and comprehensive in giving back to the communities that are home to its stores.

Seeking to maximize the return on investment from their philanthropic activities, more and more companies have also sought to more carefully target their giving. Rather than simply contributing to a charity's general operating funds, they've increasingly asked partners to create custom programs that relate to a specific aspect of their business. This might mean something as simple as asking a local art museum to help create a special evening for a company's customers or something as complicated as a multiyear program that takes both the company and the charity in new philanthropic directions.

The previously mentioned 2008 McKinsey study found that of 721 responding executives, 70 percent said the number one motivation behind their company's charitable activities was to "enhance the corporate reputation and/or brand." The seven other motivations they cited (they were allowed to pick more than one) ranked as follows:

- "Build employee and/or leadership capabilities and skills" (44%)

- "Improve employee retention or recruitment" (42%)

- "Differentiate itself from competitors" (38%)

- "Manage current or future risk" (19%)

- "Build knowledge about potential new markets or products" (15%)

- "Meet industry norms" (12%)

Only 12 percent of the respondents to the McKinsey survey said their companies do not try to achieve any business goals with their philanthropy programs.[6]

At the same time, the survey respondents expressed less than utter satisfaction with their company's programs. When asked how successful they had been at achieving their companies' goals, only 14 percent described their philanthropic programs as "extremely or very successful." Nearly 30 percent, in contrast, called their companies' efforts "a little or not at all successful." The rest of the respondents checked "somewhat successful."

Corporate philanthropy will never be an exact science, and there will always be room for improvement. But when assessing a company's charitable activities, it is important not to expect short-term results: saving the world takes time. It is also good to keep in mind that to engage in new philanthropic activities a company must, to at least some degree, venture outside its area of historical expertise (which it may already have spent decades or more to perfect). Learning curves come with new territory.

DEVELOPING EFFECTIVE CONTRIBUTION PROGRAMS

The role of chief philanthropy officer (when it exists at all) can be one of the easiest or one of the most difficult at a corporation. A company that regularly limits its giving to one or two charities and an employee match program probably doesn't require even one full-time employee to orchestrate its philanthropic efforts (it is also likely foregoing significant opportunities in the process). A company with a large budget and the desire to generate as much long-range return on investment from its charitable spending as it receives from other activities may need a large staff of highly imaginative and energetic people to make the best philanthropic choices.

The task also can be more or less demanding depending on the activities the business itself is engaged in. A company that provides ambulance services might need look no further than local hospitals for strategic allies in its philanthropic efforts; a company engaged in multinational strip mining may find it hard to find any allies at all. Or sometimes the nature of the business, no matter how harmless, simply doesn't suggest an obvious charitable complement. Quick: name the perfect charity to match up with a large accounting firm. As John E. Corbally, former president of the $3 billion MacArthur Foundation, once remarked, "Giving money away intelligently is the hardest job there is."

To effectively "broker" the interests of society with the interests of a particular business, a contributions executive must be able to understand both extremely well—melding a healthy marketing sense with a sensitivity for community and social needs. At the same time, the executive also should have enough practical business experience to determine the likelihood that any plan or proposal will actually deliver the results that are promised—a far from certain outcome in many instances.

Proactive strategies—actively researching and seeking potential partners—require more effort but usually yield better results than purely reactive strategies. Proactive companies often issue a request for proposals, inviting organizations to send proposals that meet specific criteria.

The job definitely isn't suited for someone who finds it hard to say no. In all but the least visible and smallest of businesses, the person in the position will be besieged with requests, many of which (perhaps even all) will seem worthwhile. Giving to too many causes virtually assures a less-than-optimum return for charitable giving. By diluting the company's efforts, complicating administration and pulling all results (when they are even measured) toward the mean.

That's the position in which Southwest Airlines found itself in the late 1990s. Although the company had a solid record of philanthropy, its efforts were often decentralized and based on employee initiative. "We've had a long tradition of being involved in the community, but it wasn't well understood because we didn't talk about it," Debra Benton, Southwest's director of community relations and charitable giving, told the *Chronicle of Philanthropy*.

In 2010, the company selected five types of charities that its customers and employees identified as important: groups that focus on children, disasters, the environment, health and members of the military and their families. It uses its blog, *Nuts About Southwest*, to report on its charitable enterprises (a recent article discussed a playhouse it built for children shaped like a jet airplane) and bundles separate reports about its environmental practices and its corporate social responsibility into its annual financial report.

There are at least four other advantages of a narrower, more clearly defined focus: (1) it improves the opportunity to create complementary and even synergistic programs; (2) it provides a better opportunity for learning and measuring progress over time; (3) it provides an effective rationale for rejecting charitable causes that don't fall within the company's framework; and (4) it improves the odds that the company will develop a clear reputation for its charitable efforts.

Matching gift programs, by their nature, disperse giving widely. They allow employees (and retirees) to make gifts to any qualified charities that interest them. The loss of strategic focus, companies believe, is offset by the gains in generating employee goodwill. At last count, matching gifts accounted for approximately 15 percent of all corporate giving. Some companies match their gifts on a one-to-one basis, others on a two-to-one basis. Usually, there is an annual upper limit to the total match per employee.

Other currently popular employee programs include providing paid time off. The charity receives knowledgeable and competent help, the employee can plan his or her home and work schedule accordingly and the company can adjust its workload and receive a tax benefit. In some cases, teams of employees are assigned to help a specific organization such as Habitat for Humanity, the housing builder. Such employee programs have been shown to improve employee morale—not only from the satisfaction they get from helping their neighbors, but from feeling they work for a company that has positive values that they can take pride in. Improved morale, in turn, typically translates into lower employee retention costs and higher productivity. Cisco Systems has actually gone so far as to place laid off workers with charities at reduced salaries, often hiring the employees back when business conditions improve.

"Making a difference is one of my values, and it is one of the key reasons I like working at General Mills," explains Anita Hall, senior system engineer. "The company has supported my desire to teach children throughout my 30-year career. They helped me find volunteer positions; connected me to others who share my passion; and they have supported a flexible work schedule so I can do the two things I love—engineering and teaching."

Many companies now use their websites to recognize providing exceptional community service. Websites not only honor the employees who participate, but encourage others to do likewise. It also frequently lists other opportunities to undertake volunteer services.

Companies have also learned how to leverage another corporate asset for charitable purposes: stuff that they once tossed in the trash. In 2009, for instance, Southwest Airlines donated more than $10 million in free tickets and cargo space to charity; IBM gave $145 million in computers and software, and Comcast gave $367 million in free air time, cable services and Internet access.

The pharmaceutical industry is probably the standout example of in-kind giving today, donating enormous amounts of both new and surplus medicine to needy patients who have a limited ability to pay for them, through pass-through foundations set up for this purpose (see the Chapter 18 case on free clinics). In 2008 alone, Sanofi-Aventis distributed more than $206 million in medicine through its Patient Assistance Foundation.

J.P. Garnier, former Chief Executive Officer of GlaxoSmithKline, said, "I have witnessed first-hand the difference our community programs are making. Our partnerships offer more than just a helping hand; they transform the lives and prospects of people all over the world. Employees don't come to work each day motivated by the next quarter's financial results: they are driven by making a difference for others." In 2010, GlaxoSmithKline gave approximately $600 million in cash and in-kind contributions.

The first step in designing a corporate philanthropy program is the same as it is in any other task where the outcome matters: decide on an objective. In all cases of corporate philanthropy, the goal should be driven by the same mission as the company. It helps to remember at all times that the spending is coming from funds that belong in every sense to the company stockholders. How would they view a charitable proposal if they knew all the details? Indeed, every time a CEO or board of directors approves a spending measure, they risk violating their fiduciary responsibility to investors. Philanthropic donations are no exception.

For similar reasons, no giving program should be undertaken without some idea how progress toward the goal will be assessed over time. There's no question that some programs will be easier to measure than others and that not all will achieve the expected results. There's still room for creative, seat-of-the-pants judgment in most situations. However, the difficulty of measuring results doesn't exempt corporate philanthropy from efforts to do so. Risks should be assessed just as they are in any other business activity. As with any corporate initiative, the plug should be pulled and resources redeployed when things don't go as planned. Chief giving officers should not hesitate to share this fact of business life, as well as their expectations for any program, with their philanthropic partners.

It often (usually, in fact) isn't possible to clearly link the measurement of charitable performance to bottom line results. However, companies can and should use such tools as reputation surveys, awareness studies and direct customer feedback to assess progress. In the past, corporate philanthropy officers often could get away with pointing to the success of the charity that received the money. In today's climate of more rigid accountability, she will invariably be told, "All right, but what, exactly, did it do for us?"

Often, companies that fail to see benefits from their charitable efforts simply aren't thinking broadly or imaginatively enough. Some of the less frequently imagined routes for corporate philanthropy include:

- Positioning senior executives by creating visibility for them as board members or participants in important community projects such as a hospital addition

- Establishing a political presence by hosting opinion makers at schools or cultural events

- Building relationships to improve access to research and innovation

- Contributing to nonprofit competitors—a strategy often referred to as "opening a dialogue"

- Funding a cause favored by elected officials (must be careful not to be construed as "buying" the official)

- Investing in media strategies conducted by nonprofits (to help build a consensus in favor of the company's viewpoint)

Budgeting for philanthropy can be both controversial and ticklish. An increasingly common way that companies avoid this yearly issue is to fix their gifting at a specific percentage of profits. Many who do cite the ongoing success of Patagonia, which for two decades has promised consumers that it would donate 10 percent of its pretax profits or 1 percent of its sales to environmental causes. The program makes obvious strategic sense for the outdoor clothing maker, in part, because it is so closely allied with the specific interests of its customers. It also has benefited from being bold and ambitious enough to break through the clutter and cement Patagonia's reputation as a leading corporate citizen.

Gaining recognition for charitable acts, particularly attracting national media attention, has become more difficult. Public skepticism accounts for some of this, but it's also true that the outsized activities of some philanthropists, most notably the Bill and Melinda Gates Foundation, have significantly raised the bar for what constitutes news in the realm of charitable giving.

However, the rise of online and social media has provided companies with an alternative strategy for telling their story. Where once corporations needed to promote a brief message to millions in hopes of reaching thousands, the rise of accessible information resources like Wikipedia and networking sites like Facebook and Twitter has given companies the opportunity to tell a more detailed story in hopes of connecting with thousands to reach millions.

The explosion of new media makes employee information programs all the more important. Employees are by far a company's best ambassadors, and their support is essential for any company reputation–enhancing efforts. Contributions programs help build a bridge between employees and the company. Company giving programs can help build employee self-esteem and combat negative publicity by their ability to tell others about the good things the company does. They need to know the facts and rationale about any company program well ahead of the public. In the case of corporate contributions, it is likely some employees will disagree with certain causes, and the contributions staff needs to be sensitive to that fact, but employees need to know why the company believes in the cause or the organization it is supporting.

Looking at corporate philanthropy from the recipient's viewpoint at the outset can help build a better relationship between the company and donor and will likely lead to further ventures if the activities are beneficial to both. Nonprofits fear the "overcommercialization" of their activities, the risk that their mission could be undermined by association with an organization motivated by different forces. They also need to cover their ongoing expenses and don't always have the resources to undertake the level of customization a corporate partner might demand. A flashy corporate partner might also create problems among the charity's other benefactors, who might ask, "What are you doing to get me recognition for my gifts?"

The support of company decision makers (including the board of directors) is extremely important. Many companies address this by creating a senior level management contributions committee. Doing so usually gives key decision makers a better understanding of how contributions resources help the corporation prosper over the long run. An executive's interest is often stimulated when he or she joins nonprofit boards that share their passion or require their specific talent. Over time, this will also raise awareness about community needs and opportunities.

Larger companies often also create an external affairs committee at the board of directors level. This raises decision making to a level only one step from shareowners, who have the most direct claim on corporate assets.

Ultimately, it is important that the person in charge of the charitable giving program be recognized as its leader throughout the company and become the primary source of making recommendations about the giving program (although all employees should be encouraged to offer suggestions about how the program can further the company's interests). The chief contributions person should be consulted on all company sponsorships and cause-related marketing ventures to make sure they are consistent with corporate goals and contributions programs and that they are unlikely to damage the company's reputation.

The public relations person as the external "eyes and ears" of the company is often the best position to assess shifts in societal trends and economic conditions. It is already part of their job to assure that the way the company chooses to identify itself will truly help to perpetuate it and not diminish it by reflecting negatively.

Salespeople often ask for the responsibility of making corporate donations. Although many of them undoubtedly have the best of intentions, they may easily find themselves grappling with the temptation to make a donation for the wrong reasons: to boost short-term sales. IRS regulations specifically prohibit donations tied to a direct return benefit to the company.

Staffing requirements vary because charitable giving operations are not profit centers, per se, but are sometimes delegated to lower levels in the organization. Thus, opportunities to fully benefit from the reputation-enhancing activity philanthropy provides aren't fully realized. One study showed that corporations had one person for every $2.3 million in grants, whereas foundations averaged one person for every $1.2 million. The total dollar amount isn't as critical a measure as the number of requests received, actual grants made, and whether the company is proactive or reactive. An accurate assessment of the amount of staffing needed should relate to the volume of work required.

LOOKING TO THE FUTURE

With most major companies having restructured during the past decade, it is no surprise that corporate philanthropic programs are also undergoing change. By 2010, after years of acquisitions and rapid growth, J.P. Morgan Chase found itself partnered with charitable organizations in 500 communities in 33 nations and providing a range of financial support, technical expertise, volunteerism and banking products and services. To both rationalize and maximize all of this activity, it required a more orchestrated effort. It called the resulting program Live, Learn and Thrive. "Live" focuses on basic needs, such as housing, job training and financial literacy. "Learn" focuses on helping young people succeed in the educational process, from birth through higher education, especially in impoverished areas. "Thrive" supports vital environmental, artistic and cultural initiatives. The three-pronged efforts gives the company a way to guide and administer its $100 million in annual spending that is consistent with community economic development and therefore its own long-term interests as a banking institution.

The competitive marketplace will continue to push companies to look for ways to differentiate themselves (usually in a positive way) from their rivals. That's generally good news for corporate philanthropy which, along with the rapidly growing areas of sponsorship and event marketing, clearly can help in this process. Similarly, winners in the competitive arena should always wind up with more money for philanthropic purposes than losers, so unless business activity itself diminishes or somehow becomes less lucrative, the overall philanthropic pie should increase. Charities should want businesses to succeed.

In 2004, Suzanne DuBose, president of the Verizon Foundation, complained to *Business Ethics* that most large corporate givers behave like "ATM machines"—just waiting reactively for prospective recipients to come to them. Verizon took the opposite approach, moving toward proactive giving. At the time, it was the fourth-largest company foundation in the United States. Now, Verizon seeks out potential recipients rather than waiting for charities to approach them. Since taking that approach, the foundation has succeeded in raising its percentage of proactive donations to 60 percent of its annual total giving.

DuBose explained that Verizon's corporate mission includes helping to close the digital divide between rich and poor. One example of meeting the corporation's and foundation's mission involved helping Boys and Girls Clubs located on Native American reservations to create computer centers with Internet access. In that context, the decision to help wire the reservations made perfect sense.

The trend toward proactive giving should continue. As corporate missions become more specialized and complex, it may be less and less fair to expect outsiders to provide ideal or highly customized solutions. Of course, companies can make it easier for their outside partners to devise solutions by clearly defining and explaining just what their corporate objectives actually are.

Global expansion is also requiring that companies become more sophisticated in their giving, as charitable customs (and laws) may vary widely from one country or region to the next. Often, a decentralized approach involving local employees makes the most sense. That is what motivated IBM to institute a model hiring program for the handicapped in Japan. As a result of this and other employee-driven activities, it has won favor with government, business and its customers. In fact, a recent survey in Japan ranked IBM second only to Sony in social responsibility.

Improvements in communications technology, including the phenomenal growth of social media, have made it increasingly possible to bring the benefits of charitable activities back home and vice versa as cross-border exchanges of students, cultures and business practices enable both ideas and trade to move globally with greater ease. Given the rapid pace of technological change, it's likely that by the time this chapter appears in print, many companies will have developed new Social Media 2.0 strategies to compliment their global philanthropic efforts by engaging in a deeper dialogue with customers, employees, investors and other interested parties.

Interestingly, foreign companies are taking a cue from their American counterparts and aggressively introducing philanthropy into their marketing mix. Companies like Siemens, Hitachi and Sony have found that a sure way to win acceptance in the American marketplace is to become identified as sharing some of their good fortune with American nonprofit organizations. As of this writing, more than 200 Japanese companies were operating formal giving programs in the United States.

Surveys in cities elsewhere in the world show that people's expectations for corporate social responsibility are just as high there as they are in the United States. Yum! Brands, the parent of such well-known fast food chains as KFC, Taco Bell, Pizza Hut, and others, feeds six billion customers a year and desires to be known as the "company with a huge heart." It seeks to become the "Defining Global Company that Feeds the World" (see Chapter 39 by Jonathan Blum of Yum! Brands). The Yum! Brands Foundation supports charities in the areas of hunger relief, youth, and the arts through annual unrestricted and restricted grants. It encourages its "associates" to provide financial support and to be active on nonprofit boards that are working to end hunger in their communities. Their Harvest Program is the largest prepared-food donation program in the world in terms of pounds donated.

Yum! Restaurants International has major efforts in such countries as the United Kingdom, Australia, South Africa, Thailand, South Korea, and others. Its largest effort is in China. Through its First Light Foundation, it provides scholarships to Chinese students in need. In its first 10 years, more than 10,000 students benefited from this program. Similarly, the Yum! China World Hunger Relief Program began in 2008. In its first three years, more than 3 million Chinese participated, causing it to be named, by the Chinese Enterprise News, the most successful social responsibility cause carried out by a multinational company in China.

CONCLUSION

The economist John Kenneth Galbraith inadvertently may have made one of the strongest arguments ever for corporate philanthropy when he declared that companies should be banned from corporate giving. His argument was that allowing business to do so unduly extended its influence in social and economic matters in the pursuit of corporate interests.

Businesses themselves seem far less persuaded. Few spend anywhere near the tax-deductible maximum allowed by the IRS and the average, as previously mentioned, is less than 30 percent. If more companies truly believed that they could improve their business objectives through philanthropy, it's likely the percentage would be much higher. Some of the companies that do contribute more than 5 percent of their pretax profits are Pfizer (24%), Oracle (9.3%), Abbott Laboratories (9.3%), Wells Fargo (6.2%) and Target (5.2%).

The chief contributions officer will continue to devise improved practices for charitable giving. These are likely to include:

- Further narrowing the areas funded by corporations to assure they are consistent with corporate goals and community needs.

- Using new technologies to develop more information quickly to aid decision making.

- Forming more partnerships with both governmental and nongovernmental organizations who can bring expertise to solve specific problems.

- Developing more sophisticated methods to determine the success (or lack thereof) of programs.

- Discouraging unsolicited proposals. More and more companies will send out requests for proposals outlining activities they are willing to support, and will decline all others.

- Awarding more multiyear grants because of new Financial Accounting Standards Board rules.

- Outsourcing of routine tasks, such as the matching gift program or the sending of acknowledgment of gifts to meet the tax code requirements.

Corporate philanthropy can be an important aid to advancing a company's positive reputation. Handled wisely, it can benefit the company's financial health, employee morale and its reputation as a good trusted citizen. The contributions manager, however, must be attentive to what is being said internally and externally about the company's contributions program regardless of the media being used to transmit information. Although the state of the economy will play a major role in the corporate giving programs, the likely outcome is that corporate philanthropy will continue to increase steadily and help make the world a better place.

So, there is a lot that goes into the budget decision back at Magenta Butterfly. The senior executive team has finally made its budget decisions. It has decided to reject the bullying of the IT department, instruct the HR department to renegotiate the company's health care contract (holding out additional years of commitment as an incentive to the provider) and award both legal and corporate giving their full budget requests. In granting Karen's request, the committee takes the time to note that it was impressed with the way her presentation tied the company's charitable activity to a rigorous annual brand awareness survey that not only showed growth over the past year, but demonstrated that over half the company's new customers had first heard of the Butterfly brand in conjunction with its centers for runaway teenage girls. "Because it's the right thing to do," the CEO said with a chuckle.

DISCUSSION QUESTIONS

1. What is the "right reason to give" from a corporation or corporate foundation? Discuss.
2. Which stakeholders are most directly affected by a corporation's philanthropic decisions? Why? If the corporation is global will the list change? Why?
3. Write a memo to your CEO outlining the possible strategic models on which a corporation or a new foundation could base a giving model?
4. What is your opinion of the public value of profitable companies donating used office equipment, over stock in the warehouse or even free, excess airline tickets (for an airline) or used computers (computer company)?
5. Discuss the opinion of John Kenneth Galbraith and other economists and critics on why corporations should not be able to make contributions to society? State your opinion.

NOTES

1. www.mckinseyquarterly.com/The_state_of_corporate_philanthropy_A_McKinsey_Global_Survey_2106.
2. Andrew W. Singer, "Ethical conduct pays off for corporations—probably," *Christian Science Monitor*, November 10, 1991.
3. Brian O'Connell, "Unique dimensions in philanthropy," *Philanthropy in Action, The Foundation Center*, 220.
4. Mary Tuthill, "The growing impact of corporate giving," *Nation's Business*, October 1980, 68.
5. Williams, Grant. "Number of Charities and Foundations Passes 1.2 Million," *The Chronicle of Philanthropy*, March 15, 2010. http://philanthropy.com/blogs/government-and-politics/number-of-charitiesfoundations-passes-12-million/21832.
6. www.mckinseyquarterly.com/The_state_of_corporate_philanthropy_A_McKinsey_Global_Survey_2106.

ADDITIONAL READING

Benioff, Marc R., and Carlye Adler. *The Business of Changing the World: Twenty Great Leaders on Strategic Corporate Philanthropy.* New York: McGraw-Hill, 2007.

Brest, Paul, and Hal Harvey. *Money Well Spent: A Strategic Plan for Smart Philanthropy.* New York: Bloomberg, 2008.

Burlingame, Dwight, and Dennis R. Young. *Corporate Philanthropy at the Crossroads.* Bloomington: Indiana UP, 1996.

Crutchfield, Leslie R., John V. Kania, and Mark R. Kramer. *Do More than Give: The Six Practices of Donors Who Change the World.* San Francisco: Jossey-Bass, 2011.

Harvard Business Review on Corporate Responsibility. Boston: Harvard Business School Pub., 2003.

Kotler, Philip, and Nancy Lee. *Corporate Social Responsibility: Doing the Most Good for Your Company and Your Cause.* Hoboken, NJ: Wiley, 2005.

Levy, Reynold. *Give and Take: A Candid Account of Corporate Philanthropy.* Boston, MA: Harvard Business School, 1999.

Saul, Jason. *Social Innovation, Inc., 5 Strategies for Driving Business Growth Through Social Change.* New York: John Wiley & Sons, Inc., 2010.

Weeden, Curt. *Smart Giving Is Good Business: How Corporate Philanthropy Can Benefit Your Company and Society.* San Francisco: Jossey-Bass, 2011.

14 CHAPTER

GOVERNMENT PUBLIC INFORMATION
Portal to the Public

Brent Baker
Rear Admiral (Ret) and Former Chief of Information
U.S. Navy
Dean Emeritus, College of Communication
Boston University

While the United States is one of the leaders in the practice of governmental public relations, it has never had a government Ministry of Information or government-run domestic national newspaper, radio or television station. However, U.S. government leaders, beginning with President Andrew Jackson in the 1830s, began to hire ex–newspaper journalists as press assistants to help get their messages out to the American people. So, the American model of government public relations practice has always involved a democratic government informing the public via a free, independent and privately owned news media establishment. A study of U.S. government public relations is the baseline for this chapter and the term *public affairs* is the government term for public relations (PR).

Beginning in the 1900s, officials in the U.S. Department of Agriculture (USDA) began to institutionalize the governmental public relations or public affairs function. The USDA operated a press bureau in the Division of Forestry, which upset some pro–timber company congressmen. The other federal government "early adopters" of public relations (then called *publicity*) included the Commerce and Interior Departments. The U.S. Congress (legislative branch) has always been skeptical about the executive branch's use of public relations or publicity people to inform the public. In 1913, Congress passed the Deficiency Appropriations Act, which stated, "No money appropriated by any act shall be used for compensation of any publicity expert unless specifically appropriated for that purpose." The Congress traditionally fears that the president will use the government's public relations machine for political propaganda. In the U.S. government, the president sets the leadership example as the Public Relations Commander in Chief. The major U.S. steps in the evolution of governmental public relations or public affairs came during World War I and World War II. (See Chapter 5 on the history of public relations.)

In summary, the government integration of the public relations or public affairs function began in earnest in the 1920s and expanded greatly with the wartime work of the Committee on Public Information and the Office of War Information. Today, the U.S. government is engaged in a global war on terrorism, and is one of the world's largest government employers of public information or public affairs personnel with over 12,000 practitioners. State and local governments have also had to build large public relations or public affairs organizations.

Today's 24/7 news flow and dynamic mix of mainstream media and Internet digital–social media have added to the government's communication challenge. How government leaders and public affairs officials react to that challenge is explained in the following pages.

In planning an overall communications strategy, a public affairs officer in the White House or at any level of government must understand the cultural and communications environment. There are a number of important differences between the practice of public relations in government and in the private sector.[1] The stakeholders in government public relations are a vast and diverse group of internal and external publics and audiences with different agendas. These groups include leaders and employees in the executive, legislative or judicial branches of government and government agencies; public interest groups; political party leaders; political action committees; state and local officials; private businesspeople; professional interest groups; news media; social media; and the domestic and international publics. Some of these vested-interest groups closely monitor the government's public relations programs, and the legislative branch has budgetary power, not to mention the power of public opinion, to influence the government's actions.

In all governments the goals and functions of public relations activities are linked closely to the personal leadership style of those in charge, as well as to unique cultural factors and the formal or informal structures of the political system. Even in democratic countries, where citizens freely elect their leaders, the nature and practice of government public relations can vary widely. For example, in the United Kingdom there is an Official Secrets Act that restricts the free flow of certain types of information to the citizens. In the United States, the Freedom of Information Act (FOIA) is designed to give citizens relatively open access to most kinds of government information and records. In contrast, in nations with difficult domestic or national security concerns, such as China, Russia, Iraq or Israel, the government may exercise very tight information controls in selected circumstances.

Political scientists also note the importance of the personal communication style of senior government leaders. A change in leadership can significantly influence how the government communicates with its publics.[2]

American journalists and advocates of openness or transparency in government believe President George W. Bush's administration (2001–2009) was one of the most restrictive administrations regarding freedom of government information. To be fair, it is clear that the terrorist attack on the New York World Trade Center on September 11, 2001, forced President Bush into a global "war on terrorism." This in turn, increased the tension between open government and wartime and homeland security challenges.

During the 2008 Presidential election campaign Senator Barack Obama stressed his pledge to lead a more "open and responsive government."

On his first day in office, President Obama signed a January 21, 2009, Memorandum on Transparency and Open Government. He wrote,

> My Administration is committed to creating an unprecedented level of openness in Government. We will work together to ensure the public trust and establish a system of transparency, public participation and collaboration. Openness will strengthen our democracy and promote efficiency and effectiveness in Government.

But, even after making such policy statements, President Obama's administration has been under attack by journalists for not following through on open government. A cultural factor among American journalists, as political scientist Thomas E. Patterson points out, is that the media generally share a negative view of politics and government.[3] Furthermore, the formal structure of government in the United States requires that political executive leaders must share the public stage and power with congressional leaders. In contrast, European prime ministers mostly operate with a ready-made legislative majority.

In America there is a constant tension between the president and Congress, and between the major political parties. There is no clear locus of control, but a so-called balance of power. The danger in America is "partisanship," which can lead to frustration and political gridlock. For example, in December 2010, Senate Minority Leader Mitch McConnell (R-KY) threatened to blockade all Obama administration–sponsored legislation in a "lame duck session" unless a deal was made to extend the Bush-era tax cuts. McConnell said, "For the past two years, Democrat leaders in Washington have spent virtually all their time ticking off items on the liberal wish list. . . . Here we are just a few weeks left in the session, and they're still at it." In response, Senator Clare McCaskill (D-MO) stated, "If anybody's been paying attention, they would understand that our friends across the aisle have been blocking everything, including motherhood and apple pie for the last year."[4]

These statements were made just after the 2010 midterm elections, when frustrated citizens voted for Republicans, who gained control of the House of Representatives after four years in the minority. The Senate remained in Democrat control but with less of a majority. At the end of 2010, President Obama and the Republicans reached a compromise on tax cuts. Congress also overturned the Pentagon's "don't ask, don't tell" policy regarding gays in the military, and the Senate ratified the new START Treaty with Russia. But that was only a temporary cease-fire, and partisan tensions rose again as the new divided Congress convened in January 2011.

This division of power between branches of government causes another important difference between private business and government public relations. Business organizations generally have the legal right to advertise or seek publicity in almost any manner they choose. In contrast, those conducting public relations in government have unique legal, political and cultural restrictions placed on them.

For example, in November 1995, U.S. Energy Secretary Hazel O'Leary was rebuked by the White House and Congressional critics because her public affairs office had spent $46,500 to hire a commercial media tracking company to do a content analysis of media stories on the Energy Department's activities. The tracking company's reports "ranked" the news reporters in relation to whether their stories were favorable or unfavorable to the Energy Department. O'Leary attempted to defend her department's action saying she stood for increased government openness with the public. Nevertheless the energy secretary came under bipartisan congressional political fire and news media criticism. She was ordered by the White House to repay the $46,500 to the treasury from her personal office account. The *New York Times* lashed out at the Energy Department's attempt to evaluate the content of the news media saying,

> It was a flagrant misuse of taxpayer money by a department with plenty of its own propaganda specialists. The compiling of a [media ranking] list smacks of a readiness to manipulate the press by rewarding friends and punishing enemies.[5]

Actually the government payment for an evaluation of the media content was not illegal. In fact in business public relations practice it would have been considered normal, but in government practice it was just "politically incorrect."

Congress often uses its power over the budget to restrict the size and scope of this public affairs area of the executive branch. The late Senator J. William Fulbright was an especially vocal critic of government public relations. He wrote, "What is one to think when the apparatus is used, as we all know it sometimes is, to guide public opinion toward controversial objectives? What of the use of the government's information resources to promote intensely controversial political or foreign policy objectives?"[6]

In 2009 Congress asked the Government Accountability Office (GAO) to investigate whether the Department of Defense (DOD) violated the Fiscal Year 2010 Defense Appropriations Act (which prohibited spending for publicity or propaganda activities unless specifically approved by Congress) by offering special access to retired military officers (RMOs) acting as media analysts. The GAO reported, "Clearly, DOD attempted to favorably influence public opinion with respect to the Administration's war policies in Iraq and Afghanistan through the RMOs. However, we conclude that DOD's public affairs outreach program to RMOs did not violate the prohibition."[7]

In summary, government public affairs specialists communicate with a vast and very diverse group of both internal and external publics. In reaching these constituents, the goals, nature and functions of public affairs are carried out by political appointees, civil service personnel or uniformed personnel. They are influenced by three major factors. These are (1) the personal communication styles of the leaders they serve, (2) shared understandings and cultural norms prevailing in the media and nation, and (3) both the formal and informal nature of the political process in their particular governments.

JUSTIFICATIONS FOR GOVERNMENT PUBLIC RELATIONS

In broad perspective, the practice of government public relations within a democratic society is justified by three major propositions:

1. A democratic government is best served by a free two-way flow of ideas and accurate information so citizens and their government can make informed choices.

2. A democratic government must be transparent and accountable to the citizens it serves.

3. Citizens, as taxpayers, have a right to government information—but with some exceptions.

Exceptions to a completely open flow of information are based on such factors as national security or homeland security concerns, sensitive business proprietary issues and, of course, citizens' rights to privacy and to a fair trial. For example, in the United States, a legal tug-of-war sometimes occurs between the Privacy Act and the FOIA when the government's release of information is at issue. Career public affairs officers frequently find themselves involved with both government and private lawyers, discussing the "balance" between the public's right to certain information versus the legal protection of that information due to one of the above exceptions. The government leader's decision on whether to release information leads to a judgment on the balance between public interest and individual citizens' rights.

BASIC STRATEGIC GOALS

While each country's government may have a different type of public relations or information context, there are four rather basic *strategic* approaches to all government public relations practice. In these four approaches, the existence of a two-way communications process is assumed; that is, a free flow of information back and forth between the government and the citizens it serves. These approaches are focused on the goals of providing political communication, information services, positive institutional images and on generating public feedback.

POLITICAL COMMUNICATION

The goal in political communication is to persuade and win domestic or international acceptance of a government's existing, new or proposed budget, policy, law or regulation. In pursuing this goal, political leaders actively "sell" their policies and positions to various constituencies. Simply put, this is a battle to win public opinion and gain public support. An example is President Obama's visit to a Chrysler Auto Plant in Kokomo, Indiana, amid a 2009 economic recession, to tell auto workers that his administration "acted aggressively" to boost the American automobile industry and "We are coming back . . . We are on the move."

After the Republicans took control of the House in the November 2010 midterm election, President Obama was asked what happened. He responded that his administration, "probably spent much more time trying to get the policy right than trying to get the politics right." He then stated, "Anybody who's occupied this office has to remember that success is determined by an intersection in policy and politics and that you can't be neglecting marketing and PR."

The president's weekly national radio and Internet address (and the other political party's response) is another example of political communication. In 2011 to 2012, the House of Representatives was controlled by a Republican majority. White House Communications Director Dan Pfeiffer stated, "In a world of divided government, getting things done requires a mix of compromise and confrontation. What are the things you can do without Congress? In some cases, that involves executive orders. But it also involves using the bully pulpit of the presidency to make a political argument about the direction of the country."[8]

The public expects elected political leaders to advocate for their programs. But the public also expects open and fair debate. This political communication strategy often sets the public agenda and drives the most time- and content-sensitive inquiries from citizens and the news media. Government public affairs officers must deal with "political coordination and direction," sometimes at the highest levels of government. Moreover, ethical concerns often come into play when there is a conflict between political loyalty and what the career government public affairs officer believes is the right thing to do in accordance with government laws, rules or ethical standards of conduct.

INFORMATION SERVICES

The least controversial goal is delivery of government information services. This involves informing various publics about the types of government information and services available so citizens can access them. This is the day-to-day government's customer service role—disseminating information or answering questions from citizens or the media concerning such areas as education, citizen entitlements, public health, public safety, public transportation, commerce, agriculture and government reports. But even this goal comes under fire by critics.

In 2005 the Bush Administration came under news media attack for doing what businesses do all the time, that is, for releasing "video news reports" about their products. On March 13, 2005, the *New York Times* headline was "Under Bush, A New Age of Prepackaged TV News." The report stated, "At least 20 federal agencies, including the Defense Department and the Census Bureau, have made and distributed hundreds of television news segments in the past four years, records and interviews show. Many were subsequently broadcast on local stations across the country without any acknowledgement of the government's role in their production."

The newspaper slammed the government's effort to generate positive TV news coverage and at the same time slammed the TV stations, which aired the segments for ethical violations by not disclosing the segments were government produced. The government-produced TV reports covered areas such as regime change in Iraq and Medicare reform. The *Times* reported that TV segments "focused on less prominent matters, such as the administration's efforts to offer free after-school tutoring, its campaign to curb childhood obesity, its initiatives to preserve forests and wetlands, its plans to fight computer viruses, even its attempts to fight holiday drunken driving. They often feature 'interviews' with senior administration officials in which questions are scripted and answers rehearsed. Critics, though, are excluded, as are any hints of mismanagement, waste or controversy."

The electronic communication channels came under fire as the newspaper concluded, "It is a world where government-produced reports disappear into a maze of satellite transmissions, web portals, syndicated news programs and network feeds, only to emerge cleansed on the other side as 'independent' journalism."[9]

One of the best government public health information services was the public health case of the 2009 to 2010 concerns about influenza and the outbreak of H1N1. The Centers for Disease Control (CDC) became the government's spokesperson. The CDC even launched a new website (flu.gov) where anyone could get all they need to know about the flu, including where to get flu shots. The web-distributed information included news releases and video news conferences with Dr. Anne Schuchat, assistant surgeon general.

DEVELOPING AND PROTECTING POSITIVE INSTITUTIONAL IMAGES

The goal in developing and protecting positive institutional images is to build a trusting relationship between government and its publics. Having a positive image influences short- or long-term public support for a government branch, department, agency or unit. This goal often is pursued within a complex matrix of contention, criticism and crises. Uneasy feelings and controversies can be expected when government officials try to openly "sell" a positive image. Unique problems often arise when internal government critics (in Congress) or external antagonists (special interests or news media) claim that government PR activity is a form of self-serving propaganda and a waste of taxpayers' money. Defensively, the government spokesperson usually replies that the public has a right to know what the unit is doing, and its public affairs efforts are designed to inform the public about its mission, operations and people.

What happens when the government fails in its mission, and then the government tries to recover its positive image? On August 29, 2005, Hurricane Katrina hit the Gulf Coast. President Bush described the Katrina disaster as being three disasters—a storm that wiped away miles of the Gulf Coast, a flood caused by breaches in the New Orleans levees, and an outbreak of violence and lawlessness in the city. The television news carried dramatic videos of people in New Orleans trapped in the Superdome, or on the top of their waterlogged houses. There were positive TV images of Coast Guard helicopters rescuing victims from the rooftops. Videos also showed the lawlessness in New Orleans and the slow and inadequate response at all levels of government, local, state and federal. At all levels, the government image was one of incompetence.

One Katrina news image was of President Bush on Air Force One, looking out the plane's window flying high over the Gulf Coast a day after the storm hit. The image conveyed to Americans that of a leader who was detached from the victims of Katrina. In his memoir, President Bush wrote that this decision not to land at New Orleans was correct because it would have disrupted the first responders from their work. But he said he should have had his plane land at Baton Rouge. He wrote, "Landing at Baton Rouge would not have saved any lives. Its benefit would have been good public relations. But public relations matter when you are president, particularly when people are hurting."[10]

Another Bush Katrina video image was of the President on day five of the disaster relief, when he flew to Mobile, Alabama, to talk to Governors Bob Riley and Haley Barbour about disaster relief efforts. At the meeting was Mike Brown, Director of the Federal Emergency Management Agency (FEMA), which was in charge of Katrina federal relief operations. They all had a press availability, in which Bush turned to Brown and said on camera, "Brownie, you're doing a heck of a job!" Critics of the slow and inadequate federal government response showed that video over and over (in Bush's words) "as a club to bludgeon me." Bush was forced to fire Brown and replace him with Coast Guard Vice Admiral Thad Allen, who had been in charge of the Coast Guard's first responders, who had been seen on the news doing an excellent job saving Katrina victims.

Bush admitted that the Katrina federal response was "flawed and unacceptable," but he defended himself in his memoir writing, "The problem was not that I made the wrong decisions. It was that I took too long to decide. I made an additional mistake by failing to adequately communicate my concern for the victims of Katrina. This was a problem of perception. Not reality."[11] Unfortunately, in public relations, the public perception, whether true or not, becomes the reality. Also, after a negative image is established in the public mind, it is difficult to reestablish credibility. The only path to rebuilding credibility is for the agency to show again and again that it is doing a good job.

In December 2010, the U.S. House of Representatives, the Commonwealth of Massachusetts and the Boston City Council all had scandals and a credibility or image problem. Again, when discussing image or credibility, we are talking about public trust.

In Boston, one of the city council members, Chuck Turner, was convicted in a federal court of taking a $1,000 bribe from a Federal Bureau of Investigation undercover agent. Turner refused to resign from the City Council, and was vocally supported by his constituents. He was popular and had been a black community organizer for 30 years. He had been on the City Council since 1999. The other members of the Council begged Turner to resign, but he still refused. Then the council members decided they had no choice but to remove Turner from his seat. The City Council president, Michael P. Ross, said, "We are not above the law. If we act as if we are, this body loses its credibility, its integrity, and the trust of the people we serve."[12] On December 2, 2010, the *Boston Globe* reported, "The Boston City Council voted overwhelmingly yesterday to throw Chuck Turner out of office because of his bribery conviction. An unprecedented rebuke after a racially charged hearing that elicited tears from elected officials and angry taunts from Turner's supporters."[13]

In Washington, DC, on December 2, 2010, 80-year-old Representative Charles E. Rangel (D-NY) stood before his House peers and was censured for bringing discredit upon the House. He had failed to pay federal taxes and misused his office to solicit college fund-raising donations. He was the first House member to be so censured in the previous 30 years. After the censure vote, Representative Zoe Lofgren (D-CA), chairwoman of the House Ethics Committee, said, "We need to hold ourselves to a higher standard. Mr. Rangel himself has acknowledged that."[14]

The bottom line in each of these image cases is that the government institutions must maintain a positive reputation to maintain the moral authority in a democratic society. *Image* is a synonym for public *trust* in government. Trust must be earned over time. This includes government's admitting mistakes and taking responsibility for all actions.

PUBLIC FEEDBACK

Part of a public affairs officer's job is to ensure a two-way flow of information from the public to government leaders, who must make informed choices in the government's policy decision-making process. This is the most misunderstood task of government public affairs staff. In a large government bureaucracy, leaders can become isolated from those people who may be most affected by their policy decisions. In contrast, government public affairs officers have daily contact with a wide range of people (e.g., other government employees, news and social media, community and civic leaders, special interest groups and the general public). The public affairs staff must have a unique insight into how these segments of the society feel or might react to a particular government policy or decision. Often the public affairs officer must deliver "bad news" that a proposed policy would not be accepted by the affected audience.

Leaders must have enough trust and confidence in their public affairs adviser to ensure that such information is listened to within the executive's decision-making process. The public affairs advisor provides a public "reality check" at all stages of discussions, not just after the decisions already have been made. Senior

BOX 14.1 TRANSPORTATION SECURITY ADMINISTRATION AND INCREASED AIRPORT SECURITY MEASURES—THANKSGIVING 2010

All of the above strategic communication goals, including the government institution's credibility and mission, came under congressional, media and public attack in the case of the Transportation Security Administration's (TSA) increased airport security screening in the busy air travel days of the Thanksgiving 2010 holidays. At U.S. airports, this was a rare case in which millions of citizens were personally affected by the increased security screening policies of a government agency. Many citizen travelers going through airport screening had to submit to either a full-body scanner or a more rigorous "pat-down" procedure.

Headlines in the November 23 to 26, 2010, mainstream and social media highlighted critics, who maintained that the scanners and pat-downs were ineffective to stop terrorists, unsafe because of radiation from scanners, or an invasion of personal privacy because of scanners' ability to see through clothes. Some critics claimed the pat-downs for those who refused the scanners were "sexual assaults or rapes." Social media was a major player in this case. Travelers themselves took video pictures of people going through the security checks with their mobile phones and the viral video was quickly posted on the Internet. In some cases that viral video was picked up and broadcast by the mainstream television media. Of course there were the late night and comedy television shows like *Saturday Night Live* skits that mocked TSA officers.

In the digital world, Brian Sodergren, a pharmaceutical executive in Virginia, started an online campaign to ignite a "National Opt-Out Day" on the Wednesday before Thanksgiving. He suggested that, as a protest, travelers "opt-out" of scanners and submit to the pat-down, which would slow down the security process. On Twitter, there were many messages saying people would not fly until the security procedures were changed. There was even a website called, "We Won't Fly." The mainstream media jumped on the "National Opt-Out Day" campaign bandwagon. All major news media gave the critics' messages headline coverage. This forced the government leaders and spokespersons to react in real time.

Adding to the public and media controversy was the American Pilot's Union, which complained that their members were subjected to far too much radiation from full-body scanners because they were forced to pass through them many times a day going to their assigned flights. They ordered their pilot members to not submit to scanners. This led to a fast TSA change in procedures, so that the uniformed pilots (and later the uniformed flight attendants) were allowed to bypass the scanners. The pilot's union had protested to the TSA about the scanners long before the Thanksgiving holiday, but the publicity storm caused TSA to reach a change in policy.

The political messages were flying. To add to the controversy, the Associated Press reported that Government Cabinet Secretaries and Congressional leaders, including Homeland Security Secretary Janet Napolitano and House Speaker-elect John Boehner (R-OH) did not have to go through the airport security screening.[16] The November 24, 2010, the *New York Times* included an editorial, "Politicizing Airport Security," which indicated conservative Republicans, such as former Arkansas governor Mike Huckabee, Governor Chris Christie of New Jersey and Governor Rick Perry of Texas had attacked the Obama administration for the use of full-body scanners and "intrusive" pat-downs. The *Times*' editorial said that Americans should realize that these attacks were purely partisan and ideological.[17] The *Times* also carried a political commentary by Matt Bai, under the headline, "Mistrust of Government Crystallized." Bai stated that the airport security crisis reinforced the central theme of the Obama administration, that is "America's faltering confidence in the ability of government to make things work." He opined that, "The administration and its Congressional allies have sometimes furthered the image of government as less than ruthlessly efficient."[18]

As the mainstream and social media increased the pressure on the government and TSA, it forced Janet Napolitano, the Homeland Security secretary; John Pistole, administrator of the TSA; and Robert Gibbs, the White House press secretary, to hold news conferences to defend the increased airport screening process as necessary to keep travelers safe. Pistole said, "As we said in the beginning, we are seeking to strike the right balance between privacy and security."[19] Media interviews with airport travelers indicated a majority of travelers would comply with the increased security procedures, but a vocal minority spoke out against the full-body scanner and pat-downs. On November 23, 2010, a *Washington Post*–ABC poll indicated that two-thirds of Americans in their survey supported the full-body scanners, but half the people surveyed were against the pat-down procedure.[20]

(continued)

BOX 14.1 Continued

The day before Thanksgiving, the TSA used its own online blog to report airport-by-airport how few travelers had opted out of the scanners. TSA public affairs people were stationed at all major airports armed with their Blackberries. The media interviewed TSA screeners. They said they did not like the pat-downs anymore than travelers did, and defended the screening procedures. The *New York Times* reported that the TSA administrator, John Pistole, went to Reagan National Airport on November 24, "to Buck Up Troops and Defend Tactics."[21] With the news media watching, he even went through the full-body scanner and a pat-down.

It was clear at the end of the Thanksgiving holiday that the TSA security screening had gone amazingly well. The TSA had added security-screening officers at all airports and mobilized its public affairs team effectively. The TSA had used the mainstream and social media. TSA spokespersons were on duty at almost every major airport ready to supply information to the local and national media. The TSA administrator was highly visible and available for media interviews. For his part, John Pistole said he was "happy to take the heat if it meant keeping travelers safe."

On the other hand, critics also skillfully used the social and mainstream media. On November 25, 2010, the *New York Times* reported, "Even if protests did not materialize in any significant numbers, the fact that people were discussing the issue at all meant that the [critics'] campaign had succeeded, said Brian Sodergren, who originated the idea of the National Opt-Out Day." The *Times* quoted Sodergren saying, "For me, the outcome has probably been achieved. There has been more attention given to this than I could ever imagine."[22]

---

government public affairs officers often tell their leaders, "I want to be in on the takeoff (of a policy) and not be called in only after it has crash landed and we are in a crisis."

Feedback from the public can take the form of scientific public opinion polls. But the U.S. Congress is very restrictive when it comes to the executive branch funding domestic opinion polls, owing to its concern that such information would be used to pressure the Congress on pending legislation or on foreign policy. Thus, U.S. government–sponsored polls usually focus only on international public opinion. That does not keep the government from using the data from outside commercial or political party–sponsored public opinion polls.

Social media is an excellent way for government leaders to connect with the public and receive direct feedback. This does not mean that the busy executive personally has to monitor social media channels; that is done by the public affairs staff. One of the busiest executives in the Pentagon is the chairman of the Joint Chiefs of Staff, Admiral Mike Mullen, USN. He also realized that he could become isolated from the public he serves. So he has a Facebook account, a Twitter account, videos on YouTube and a website called "Travels with Mullen: Conversation with the Country." The Pentagon spokesman Geoff Morrell said that Chairman Mullen has "a compulsion to communicate."[15]

ORGANIZATIONAL RESPONSIBILITIES AND FUNCTIONS

The U.S. government has one of the world's largest public relations operations, with about 12,000 civilian and military public affairs people spending over $1 billion annually on various information programs.[23] For purposes of this discussion, assume that the public relations function is located in a major executive branch department such as State, Defense, Energy, Homeland Security, Treasury or Transportation and that the senior civilian public relations officer works directly for the civilian department secretary. Normally, the senior civilian public affairs officer has the title of Assistant Secretary for Public Affairs or Director of Public Affairs. If the head public affairs officer is a civilian political appointee and holds the title of Assistant Secretary, the Senate usually must confirm him or her. This person is normally given overall formal responsibility for several functions, including public relations planning and policy and media relations (includes social media). The duties also include coordinating with other government departments or agencies, and with higher authorities, such as the White House on public affairs matters.

LEGISLATIVE AND PUBLIC RELATIONS FUNCTIONS

It is important to note that the department secretary has overall responsibilities for both public affairs and for congressional affairs. In some government offices, these two functions will be combined in one central Office of Legislative and Public Affairs, which make sense with constrained administrative resources but also presents practical problems. For example, such a single office may get the same type of inquiry from a congressional office, a news organization or a special interest group. Assuming the answer to the three inquiries is the same, it seems logical for one office to coordinate the answer within the bureaucracy and respond uniformly to the customers. However, the main administrative problem is one of timing and priority. Bear in mind that thousands of information inquiries move through government public affairs and legislative offices every day. All information customers want their answers *now*! These inquiries come from all kinds of sources and there is always the question of which should get priority. Does the government employee provide answers in the order in which the inquiries were received, or in some other way?

The solution to the inquiry priority problem is shaped in part by politics. The secretary of a department is very aware that he or she must gain the support of Congress during the annual "battle of the budget." The secretary or some "higher authority" is always trying to curry favor with Congress, and his or her success or failure is measured partly by the ability to get the department's budget or program requests approved. This simple political fact of life means that legislative inquiries usually get top priority. Indeed, most governments use special color-coded folders to distinguish top priority legislative inquiries from public or media inquiries. Congressional members or staff who oversee the department's budget usually receive top priority. For example, if a request for information from the State Department is from a member or staff of the Foreign Relations Committee, which has budget authority over that agency, that request will be given top priority. As a general rule, congressional inquiries will be answered first, followed by those from the news media, and finally public inquiries.

Because both public affairs and legislative affairs are full-time jobs, most large government departments separate these functions to achieve better customer satisfaction. Within this structure, the heads of both offices carry the title of Assistant Secretary (or Director) for Legislative Affairs or Public Affairs.

To assist in legislative and public affairs coordination and to give firsthand feedback to the secretary, a daily morning "lineup" meeting is usually held between the secretary, legislative advisor, public affairs advisor and the secretary's other top personal advisors. At this meeting there is normally an informal review of the events of the previous 24 hours and a forecast of expected actions in the next 24 hours, from both the legislative and public affairs points of view.

INTERGOVERNMENTAL AFFAIRS

In U.S. government departments that interface routinely with other levels of state, local and international government, there are separate offices headed by a person with a title such as director or assistant secretary for intergovernmental affairs. For example, within the Department of Commerce there is the assistant secretary for legislative and intergovernmental affairs. Other major departments with similar posts are Transportation (assistant secretary for intergovernmental affairs) and Homeland Security (office of intergovernmental affairs).

The federal government itself is a large bureaucracy, and it is hard for employees and government contractors to communicate informally and exchange ideas in a timely manner. In 2010, the General Services Administration (GSA) created a new Facebook-style social networking website for federal employees. The site, called FedSpace, is a secure intranet (open only to federal employees and contractors) and provides federal employees with more opportunities to communicate, collaborate and share information. Bev Godwin, director of GSA's Center for New Media and Citizen Engagement, coordinated the FedSpace effort, and worked on other government initiatives to make it easier for agencies to point to websites using Twitter and other social media.

PUBLIC RELATIONS DIRECTOR OR ASSISTANT SECRETARY

Again, for purposes of further discussion, it is assumed that the head civilian public affairs officer reports directly to the department secretary. The title of this person is either Director of Public Affairs or Assistant

Secretary for Public Affairs. This person is either a political appointee or a civil service career public affairs officer. The normal responsibilities of such a person include the following:

1. Acting as the senior department public affairs advisor. This means the public affairs advisor sees the secretary daily and attends most senior staff meetings, where policy and actions are decided.

2. Serving as the senior public spokesperson for the department. This means he or she usually does the major department news media briefings. The routine daily "care and feeding" of the media is usually done by a media relations division or directorate.

3. Coordinating communication strategy policy and programs within the department.

4. Functioning as the senior public affairs adviser for crisis management. This crisis role may involve public affairs coordination with other government departments or agencies, as directed by the secretary or higher authority.

5. Coordinating public affairs actions, as deemed appropriate, with the office of legislative affairs.

6. Releasing information of special interest concerning the department in coordination with the secretary or designated higher authority. (This may or may not include coordination of requests for information under specific laws, such as the Freedom of Information Act or Privacy Act. All government public affairs personnel must be familiar with the provisions of all laws and regulations pertaining to the release of information that may affect their unit.)

7. Supervising the coordination of community relations, internal information and audiovisual programs within the department.

8. Coordinating department policy and security review of speeches, articles or books by department officials.

FUNCTIONAL ORGANIZATION WITHIN A GOVERNMENT PUBLIC RELATIONS OFFICE

To fulfill these public relations responsibilities, the typical department public affairs office has divisions or directorates focused on the following major work areas:

Administration. This office keeps the paperwork flowing and usually handles such things as security and policy review and FOIA coordination. Sometimes the FOIA coordination is handled by the legal counsel's office.

Media relations. This office includes processing and coordinating department information for release to the public and/or the mainstream news media. The media relation's function is fast paced, and often requires senior-executive-level coordination or approval of news releases.

Public inquiry or civic relations. This office is in direct contact with the public. It handles all public inquiries. In these programs there is an attempt to gain local public support and to establish a positive image within the community through such routine activities as arranging public speaker appearances, conducting open houses and tours for local government facilities and arranging cooperative community service projects and local people-to-people cooperative programs. An especially sensitive political aspect of community relations is that related to environmental law compliance and public safety.

Internal relations. This office is the link between government management and employees, specifically the government's employees, their families and in some cases retired employees and their families. Internal information refers not only to the communication themes and messages, but to the means by which such messages are communicated; including, for example, employee newsletters or websites covering such topics as the department's vision and plans, personnel policies, promotion opportunities, professional education or training and retirement. In the case of the Defense Department, they have a Defense Media Activity (DMA). DMA provides news and information to U.S. Armed Forces worldwide. The agency presents news, information and entertainment on a variety of media platforms, including radio, television, Internet, print media and emerging media technologies. DMA informs millions of active, Guard and Reserve service members, civilian employees, contractors, military retirees and their families in the United States and abroad.

Communication strategy, plans and policy. This office is focused on the longer-range public affairs strategy and plans. The office coordinates planning to ensure the most effective and efficient use of all public affairs resources. Some offices also do a follow-up evaluation process after a plan is executed. But, in most cases, the government (due to a shortage of resources) merely does a short "lessons learned" evaluation after a plan is executed.

Emerging media. Since social media is a relatively new area of communication, there are different ways to handle this area, which will be explained later. For example, in the State Department there is an Office of Innovative Engagement working for the Under Secretary for Public Affairs and Public Diplomacy, and in the Defense Department there is a Senior Strategist for New–Emerging Media within the Office of the Assistant Secretary of Defense (Public Affairs).

In summary, government public relations or public diplomacy organizational structures are based on what publics or audiences they serve on a daily basis. The policy and priorities of leaders and their missions define and limit what is communicated, in what manner, to whom, over what medium and for what purpose.

PLANNING APPROACHES TO GOVERNMENT COMMUNICATION

The first research step in communicating a government policy or program is that of central issue identification and focus. In a complex democratic governmental process with many political players (some outside the government leader's control), it is difficult to tackle too many issues at once. The best communications strategy is to pick an issue and concentrate all communication assets on that topic before moving to the next. Many veteran observers refer to seats of government as "one-issue towns," with the implication that the public can handle only one issue at a time. Also, some experts believe that if a government leader attempts to present more than one major topic in the news cycle, the public attention is lost. This one-issue-at-a-time approach is not an easy one in practice because there are always many important issues in government. There are other powerful political players in Congress, for example, who may want to focus on tax reduction, while someone else wants to focus on job creation or health care. However, it is clear from a public affairs viewpoint that "mixed messages" should be avoided. In his first two years in office, President Obama faced a major economic recession, but his critics say he spent too much time on health care reform and lost his focus on getting unemployed Americans back to work. This loss of White House one-issue-at-a-time focus is not new.

BOX 14.2 FOCUS—KEEP IT SIMPLE

George Stephanopoulos, President Bill Clinton's first press secretary wrote, "Obsessed by the idea that we had to keep all our promises at once, we were trying to do too much too fast." He listed the events of a single day in the White House on April 14, 1993. The issues included the deficit, abortion rights, gays in the military, jobs, stimulus strategy, health care reform, environmental policy and Bosnia.

Mike Deaver, President Reagan's counselor said, "The largest hurdle that President Clinton's going to have is to keep himself focused. There is so much coming in and there are so many people that want him to do things; there are so many requests to divert his attention from this economic goal, he is going to have to be single-minded about what he does with his time and who he speaks to and where he speaks; because, otherwise, with all the information that's coming at us, this message is going to get very diluted."

Karen Hughes, President George W. Bush's communications director wrote, "One of the keys to delivering an effective message is consistency and repetition; whenever we had too many things jumbled on the president's calendar, I used to joke that we had message ADD."[24]

The second planning step is formulation of a coordinated communications plan, customized to the issue. All the major government players should agree on and be familiar with the plan. The advantage of such a coordinated plan is that the entire administration can "sing from the same sheet of music." This communications plan outlines the specific messages or themes and tactics to be followed and avoids the complaint that the administration is not speaking with one voice. Such a plan would contain a general strategic goal or objective, major themes and tactical steps. Usually the plan will contain "talking points" and an action listing of all multimedia targets and/or other public relations events used to communicate to the various target publics. For example, a member of the administration may be scheduled to appear on a television program such as NBC's *Meet the Press*, or on a web blog. A leader who is scheduled to make a public speech would be able to review the plan's talking points to ensure agreement with the chief executive's position. It must also be stated that while a politician can get away with only a general theme such as "It's the economy stupid" or "change you can count on" in an election campaign, when one is governing the themes must be focused with more specific and detailed programs and talking points.

The third step is to execute the communications plan. While the top leaders will be involved in the execution, many players within and outside of government (such as political party organizations) will also be involved. The more officials that actively communicate the same message over many multimedia channels, the better the chances are of reaching target audiences. The people in the field, who are and will be most involved with an issue or policy, are the most credible spokespersons.

The fourth step of evaluation is usually poorly done in government. This is due to the more restricted political and bureaucratic context. In addition, short-fused requests for public affairs plans and budget limitations have a negative effect on practicing the evaluation step. If there is a crisis in the public affairs office, the first place people are pulled from to reinforce the news desk or on-scene crisis team, is the "plans and analysis shop." Evaluation (the question of how successful public affairs efforts were from the target audiences response) is usually answered by who won or lost the policy vote, either on the floor of the legislature or in the court of public opinion—or both. However, new digital tools such as social media allow public affairs officers to gain direct public feedback to evaluate how well a message has or has not been received by the target audience. Social media also allows early warning of public affairs problems.

STRATEGY AND TACTICS IN GOVERNMENT MEDIA RELATIONS

The use of all media (mainstream and social media) is vital to all government public affairs plans, strategies and tactics. Each communication party needs the other if citizens are to be fully served by a free two-way flow of information. Sometimes those in high office "just don't get it" when it comes to this basic truth. For example, President Clinton was talking to a friend and he mused, "I did not realize the importance of communications and the overriding importance of what is on the evening news. If I am not on, or they're with a message, someone else is, with their message."[25]

One of the most significant features of the relationship between government public relations officials and the media is the deep cynicism and negative attitude most journalists have toward government and government spokespersons. Marlin Fitzwater was a civil service public affairs officer for 17 years before spending 10 years as President Reagan's and President George H. W. Bush's press secretary. As press secretary he noted, "Any show of patriotism or sympathy for the government was condemned as 'soft' by the press corps."[26] Career public affairs officers learn to live with this tense media relationship and build their own personal relationship with members of the media.

One of the best-documented facts about the government–mainstream media relationship is that *government sources dominate traditional media coverage of government*. As writer Walter Karp reported, "The overwhelming majority of stories are based on official sources—on information provided by members of Congress, presidential aides and politicians."[27] Therefore, the cards are not so stacked against government officials in terms of getting out their messages as some stressed-out spokesperson might think.

But in today's online social media environment, it is the outsiders and government critics that too often dominate the public dialogue. These same social media sources have become prime sources for the mainstream media reporters who grew up in the online world. Government must integrate all media (including social media) into its communication plans and policy. This holistic media approach takes a lot of daily and even hourly public affairs monitoring attention and can never be taken for granted.

GENERAL OUTREACH STRATEGY

The first step in designing a multimedia outreach is to decide on a general communication strategy. Essentially, there are four options available in designing such a strategy. One is to be *reactive* to the media, which is the norm during unexpected "breaking news." A second is to be *active* and create multimedia opportunities on a regular basis. A third is to use a *combination* of the first two. Finally, one can have no systematic media strategy and just "wing it."

There is little to recommend the last option and it should be avoided. Using a combination of active and reactive multimedia strategies is usually the best bet because it allows a leader to customize the media outreach to the issue, the situation, and his or her personal style. It also allows some flexibility. At the same time, most successful government public affairs practitioners believe that their experience indicates a good, proactive strategy that keeps the media busy and focused on the government leader's agenda. Another reason to be active is that when a crisis arises, the official already is a known quality to the media and the public. Above all, closing the door and hanging out the "no comment" sign sends the media to your critics, who are always willing to talk.

TACTICS FOR DEALING WITH LEAKS

Government leaks have always involved classified national security information or sensitive political material. During World War II, posters in places where cargo was loaded on vessels bound for the war zone cautioned, "Loose lips can sink ships." This referred to wartime leaks of classified ship movements. Today, with social media such as Twitter, the Navy has a digital version of the old World War II poster that says, "Loose Tweets Sink Fleets." (Tweets are short messages sent on Twitter.)

Leaks got so bad in President George W. Bush's administration that Karen Hughes, his communications director, wrote that it changed the nature of her daily White House message meetings. She recalled that the daily message meetings were used to discuss policy and to "brainstorm ideas," but changed to mere "venues to distribute marching orders" because of the fear of leaks, "We instituted a new meeting in which the real decisions about schedule and message could be made in a smaller leakproof group."[28]

One of the most famous [leaks] of government-classified information was the "Pentagon Papers" case in June 1971, during President Richard Nixon's administration. The papers were a 7,000-page classified history of American involvement in Southeast Asia from World War II through 1968. The leaker was Daniel Ellsberg, who had worked at both the National Security Council and at the Pentagon. The Nixon administration went to the federal court to restrain the *New York Times* from publication of the papers citing the Espionage Act. However, the government lost its case against the *Times* because as federal Judge Murray Gurfein wrote, the government "did not convince the court that the publication of these historical documents would seriously breach the National security."[29]

In July 2010, a new Internet chapter in the government leak history exploded in the media headlines as an online organization called WikiLeaks made public thousands of pages of classified documents from the Afghanistan and Iraq Wars on the web. Then, in late November and December 2010, WikiLeaks was involved in the largest ever leak of some of 250,000 classified State Department cables. (A cable is like e-mail.) Scott Shane reported in the *New York Times*, "Traditional watchdog journalism, which has long accepted leaked information in dribs and drabs, has been joined by a new counterculture of information vigilantism that now promises disclosures by the terabyte."[30]

In November 2010, The White House issued a statement concerning the State Department cable leaks saying, "We condemn in the strongest terms the unauthorized disclosure of classified documents and sensitive national security information."[31]

WikiLeaks posted its mission on its website in December 2010. According to WikiLeaks,

> We provide an innovative, secure and anonymous way for sources to leak information to our journalists (our electronic drop box). One of our most important activities is to publish original source material alongside our news stories so readers and historians alike can see evidence of the truth. We are a young organization that has grown very quickly, relying on a network of dedicated volunteers around the globe. Since 2007, when the organization was officially launched, WikiLeaks has worked to report on and publish important information.[32]

On its website, WikiLeaks called itself a "new model of journalism" and stated that, "Publishing improves transparency, and this transparency creates a better society for all people." The website then stated, "In its landmark ruling on the Pentagon Papers, the U.S. Supreme Court ruled that 'only a free and unrestrained press can effectively expose deception in government.' We agree."

In reviewing the WikiLeaks 2010 release of classified State Department cables, three things standout. First, the unintended consequence of the public disclosure of classified cables was that it was not so damaging as government spokespersons claimed it would be. David E. Sanger wrote in the *New York Times*, "While WikiLeaks intended to expose duplicity, what struck many outside readers was that American diplomacy looked rather impressive. The day-to-day record showed diplomats trying their hardest behind closed doors to defuse some of the world's thorniest conflicts. . . ."[33] Second, WikiLeaks was more responsible than generally believed. WikiLeaks coordinated its release of classified documents with traditional media, such as the *New York Times* and four European newspapers. Also, WikiLeaks did not post all 251,287 classified cables on the web. As of mid-December 2010, it only released about 1 percent of the cables, and often redacted (censored) names of people in the cables who might be endangered by public release of their identities.[34] Third, for the most part, United States diplomatic relations were not seriously affected by the WikiLeaks disclosures.

Today, leaks can affect government policy and planning. Because such leaks of classified or sensitive information are a serious problem, government leaders and spokespersons must understand how and why they occur. Moreover, in the words of former American cabinet secretary Harold Brown, officials must "view with some equanimity the inevitability of such leaks." In fact, most seats of government are the "leak capitals" of the nation. Passing on confidential information to unauthorized persons is part of the regular balance of power discourse in government. Leaks are inevitable, and a number of observations help place them in perspective:

1. Leaks, in this discussion, are defined as involving both classified and unclassified but sensitive government information. The information is provided in an unauthorized manner to people without current government security authorization for access to the information.

2. It takes at least two people to spring a leak—an inside government source and an outside receiver, usually a journalist or government critic.

3. Leaks require an outside transmitter, usually a news media or social media outlet, to publicize the information.

4. Leaks of classified or politically sensitive information are widespread throughout government.

5. Leaks usually feed controversy. Therefore, they benefit the vested interests of the source and sometimes the economic or prestige interests of the news media or other transmitter.

6. Leaks generally occur around key decision milestones, and are timed by sources to influence government decision making.

7. Leaks from inside a bureaucracy may reflect an internal power struggle that the source has an interest in airing publicly.

8. Leaks may have a multiplier effect, with one leak stimulating another countermeasure leak championing the opposite position.

9. Leaks by their nature highlight the more dramatic aspects of an issue and seldom present a balanced view of a complex issue.

10. Once leaked, information is in the public domain. The future course of the issue is not controlled by anyone. In other words, the person who leaks, or who publicizes the leaks, cannot forecast the final effect of such action. This is often called the "myth" of the controlled leak or plant. The effects of neither leaked (unauthorized) nor planted (authorized) information can be orchestrated once in the public domain.

11. The sources of leaks are almost impossible to track down, and while it may be necessary to seek them, investigations aimed at finding such sources seldom succeed and can actually be counterproductive since the inside government sources are sometimes congressional officials.

12. The government leak investigation will add to media coverage of an issue and keep that issue alive, which may not be desirable. [35]

There are a number of specific tactics that can be used in trying to control damage that results from leaks. The challenge is to reply to a leak on the public record, without causing further classified security problems—or in the case of sensitive information, without further fanning the flames of controversy. These tactics assume that government spokespersons are on the defensive or reactive in the case of leaks. If that is indeed the case, the following defensive public affairs options are possible:

Refuse to confirm or deny. This is not considered a "no comment." The "refuse to confirm or deny" tactic is used when the information is classified or sensitive. Some spokespersons view this as a neutral response. However, the net effect from the media and public's point of view is, "There must be some truth to it or they would give a better answer."

Demand a retraction, or write a letter to the editor or enter social media discussion. It is almost impossible to get a mainstream media retraction. However, any "official" discussion keeps the story alive even though it may not get any action from the media outlet, and even if "official comments" are run, they may not be presented in the context of the original story. Also, the timing or placement of the rebuttal will not be under the government's control. Overall, however, it beats doing nothing.

Issue a public statement or news release. Usually, this is fighting to catch up after the damage is done. Nonetheless, if aggressively pursued, the effort may change the momentum of the story. But it does keep the story going.

Hold a news conference or social media conversation. This involves the same problems as the previous option. However, if one wants to take a strong public rebuttal stand, there is nothing like a leader taking charge, who can change the dynamic from reactive to a more active driving of the story. If truth is on your side, this is the best option, with the government spokesperson face-to-face with journalists or critics.

Give a background interview or provide a counter-leak (plant). Most reporters want official on-the-record responses, not more anonymous leaks. However, if the topic is hot and reporters feel they will get new angles, or they are worried that the competition is moving in, they will attend a backgrounder and dutifully report a new angle to the story.

Prepare an "answer for query only." This old passive tactic is useless if the right question is not asked. Of course, the spokesperson can tell a reporter, "Why don't you ask me this question?"

Prepare a side-by-side or "questions and answers." This is a process in which each leaked allegation is taken on, issue-by-issue, with points that are (or are likely to be) raised by reporters and the official comments on each. It can be actively marketed or passively held for answer to query.

Use a third-party surrogate expert. This tactic uses an expert from outside the government or a retired government official who attacks the credibility of the leaked information and/or source. Some believe this is the best option because it can cause reporters and/or editors to worry about the credibility of the information used in a news story and, consequently, about their personal and professional reputations among peers. Again, the social media are a good place to have a surrogate defend the government action.

Preemptive leaking or public release. This tactic best meets the needs of reporters, and it takes preventative maintenance measures against being blind-sided by unauthorized leaks. For example, reporter Stephen Rosenfeld, writing in the *Washington Post*, suggested:

> The best way to balk "damaging leaks" of special interest material, however, is to make a broad range of material available routinely in a context devised not by special interest but by the government itself. Call it preemptive leaking or public information.[36]

DECISIONS AT THE SPEED OF DIGITAL MEDIA

Today the speed at which rumors and stories spread via digital global communication systems (cable TV, Internet and social media) means the response time for government leaders and their public relations officers has become more critical. There is little time to think about, not to mention effectively plan, a response strategy when there is a social media or cable TV deadline every minute, 24 hours a day, seven days a week.

People forget that it was the Internet blogger Matt Drudge who first alerted the mainstream media to the gossip about President Clinton's affair with a White House intern. That blogger's chatter led to the impeachment of a president.

Government public relations personnel have learned to deal with decision-time compression driven by the Internet. The social media are important as an early crisis warning net and rumor control system. A CNN executive admitted on the air that CNN first learned about the January 2010 Haiti earthquake by reading status updates on Facebook.

Today, from the White House to the State Department to the Pentagon and to every other government public affairs office, cable news networks and the Internet news and social media are closely monitored. The federal government's operational and intelligence worldwide reporting systems often cannot keep up with digital multimedia chatter. Electronic speed of news or rumors not only drives the timing of decisions and responses by government but also it may get "inside the government's decision cycle." In today's world, leaders learn of the event on satellite cable TV or on the Internet and they must react via the same media within minutes.[37]

Secretary of State Hillary Clinton addressed the issue of decision-time compression.

> But the kind of slow, patient diplomacy that is necessary for the vast majority of problems that have been faced in diplomacy, going back in history, is so much more difficult today. I mean, think about some of those critical moments that we look back at with admiration when breakthroughs occurred. How hard is it now to imagine doing that with Twitter, with blogs, with 24/7 media coverage so that the necessary ingredients of building some level of trust, to understand opposing points of view, to have the luxury of time, even if it's just days and weeks, to think through approaches, that has all been telescoped. . . . It's just a constantly accelerating mechanism that requires people to act often more quickly than the problem deserves. Yet that is the world in which we find ourselves. And so therefore, we have to adapt to it and we have to understand what it will take to meet the requirements of the times in which we find ourselves.[38]

Arthur Molella, director of the Smithsonian Lemelson Center for the Study of Invention and Innovation in Washington, DC, points out how the Internet has changed our lives, and how governments have to run to catch up. He said, "Governments usually have to catch up if they want to stop something proliferating on the Internet. I think it's this instant communication and talking back to authority, as it were, that is changing the political scene."[39]

Increasing demands for speed put most democracies at a disadvantage in the war of words and images. Our democratic process is one of bureaucratic coordination aimed at getting consensus on a response. Add the international element of United Nations, North Atlantic Treaty Organization or European Community coordination, and democratic government officials have a response-time disadvantage when dealing with groups such as terrorists or dictatorship-style governments. Those who have worked in government crisis management also know that the first media reports suffer the problem of all initial reports: they are single-view snapshots. At best, they are usually incomplete and at worst, wrong.

STRATEGIC COMMUNICATIONS PRACTICE

So what do government public affairs people do today to keep up with global digital media? They change the way they plan and communicate. They adapt their messages to emerging communication technology as they have always done. They engage in strategic communication to connect and have conversations with people!

The U.S. State Department (www.state.gov) and the Defense Department (www.defense.gov) are the best U.S. government examples of adjusting to the changing global information environment. Both State and

Defense leaders and their information–public affairs staff have learned the hard way—from the unique global communication demands in public diplomacy and public affairs; fighting two wars (Iraq and Afghanistan); and at the same time being involved in many humanitarian actions such as Hurricane Katrina at home and Haiti relief operations abroad. The secretary of state and defense secretary have streamlined and integrated all public diplomacy, military public affairs and strategic communication resources.

STATE DEPARTMENT

The State Department follows President Obama's Open Government Plan and focuses on three imperatives:

- *Transparency.* Providing information to enable the American people to view the department's activities and products, and ensure accountability for results.

- *Participation.* Enabling the public to engage on issues of importance and make their voices heard.

- *Collaboration.* Sharing information and ideas, and working cooperatively with partners around the world to promote the foreign policy interests of the United States.

The State Department's Foreign Affairs Manual discusses the use of Internet and social media. It cites the following opportunities enabled by social media:

- Conduct activities with non–U.S. government organizations (such as the International Red Cross during Haiti Relief).

- Use for official consular, public affairs and public diplomacy activities on websites that are available to the general public.

- Use for engaging in activities that are of official concern to the department.

The Foreign Service Institute (www.state.gov/m/fsi) is the training and professional development school for the State Department in Washington, DC. It offers short courses for State personnel on how to integrate the Internet and social media into foreign diplomacy operations. There is PY 360, Introduction to Social Media, and PY 363, Social Media for Practitioners.

State's Office of Innovative Engagement also takes these courses and other "disruptive technologies" training workshops on the road regionally and locally. There is a teaching challenge when teaching government employees about social media. Even if government employees have "personal experience" with social media, it is very different to be in the social media as an official. For example, as a government official, the types of things in your "profile" and what you share may be more restrained. You have to tell your family and friends (real and virtual) that you work for the government. State does not prevent employees from having personal social media accounts, but they are educated about privacy and safety protections. State requires if an account is used for public engagement (official business) that your profile clearly state your government position and that you are using the social medium in your professional capacity.

Another key point is that public diplomacy is decentralized in execution. Local embassy people are focused on what media mix is right for the country and culture they are in. While Facebook is the largest global social network, it may not be the one used in a particular international culture. There may already be a local social network that is used in a particular situation. The messages or conversation is always customized to the local language and culture.

The State Under Secretary for Public Diplomacy and Public Affairs has one public affairs bureau and two public diplomacy bureaus.

- *The Public Affairs Bureau* is focused on communicating to American domestic publics what the Secretary of State and the department is doing.

- *The Education and Cultural Affairs Bureau* does all sorts of cultural affairs programs such as music, arts, sports and Fulbright and other exchange programs.

- *The International Information Programs Bureau* explains to international publics what U.S. government policy is and how it affects them on a local level.

The State Department is restricted from disseminating public diplomacy information directly to the American domestic publics. The U.S. Information and Education Act of 1948 (PL 80-402), referred to as the Smith-Mundt Act, contains a prohibition on domestic dissemination of materials intended for foreign audiences by the State Department. The original intent of the law was that Congress did not want executive branch propaganda to affect the American public. Congress felt that the free American news media would be the only appropriate information channels to inform U.S. citizens about what the State Department said overseas. However, in a practical sense, the Internet and social media networks are open public global networks, so there is no way to restrict U.S. citizens from having direct access to the open information or conversations. For example, because of Smith-Mundt, State has a separate www.America.gov website aimed at the international publics, which they cannot mention in domestic public affairs outreach, but any American citizen has access.

Since 2001, State officials have talked about digital diplomacy and State uses a wide range of Internet media, such as the State blog called DipNote, Facebook, Twitter, Flickr and YouTube. The State website called Connect (connect.state.gov) is an online international community managed by State's Bureau of Education and Cultural Affairs. Many ambassadors have their own blogs, which deal with local issues and the dialogue is in the local county's language.

Since 2002, the State Department has been focused on emerging media first using locally produced video products and then online chat in 2005. One site that initially attracted State's attention in 2005 was the virtual world called Second Life launched in 2003 (www.secondlife.com). It is a virtual community where users can connect. Users are called "residents" and avatars represent residents. The reason this social media site was attractive to State was that at that time 70 percent of the users (average age 35) were non-American and at any given time about 3 million users are engaged on the site.

State also uses more familiar social media such as Facebook and Twitter. In October to November 2008, one of the most successful state-sponsored Twitter feeds focused on the U.S. presidential election. Over 75 percent of the 580 million Facebook users in January 2011 were from outside the United States. Indonesia is the largest Muslim nation in the world with 240 million people. Just before President Obama's November 2010 visit to Jakarta, the U.S. Embassy's Facebook page became very active with public comments. In one case, within 15 minutes of a new posting, there were over 200 public comments. It is not how many "fans" a government Facebook Page has that is important, it is how many people are engaged with comments and active conversations.

In Turkey, also a Muslim country, a Facebook group called "Young Civilians" is composed of individuals who advocate "peace, tolerance and democracy." In December 2008, Facebook, AT&T, MTV, Google and an online video company called Howcast, brought representatives from 17 Facebook overseas activist groups (including "Young Civilians") to Columbia University in New York City. The idea was to let these groups share ideas and return to their home countries refreshed by the exchange. The Under Secretary of State for Public Diplomacy, James Glassman, addressed this gathering. He saluted them for taking the personal risk to express their views publicly on Facebook. He then said, "This is public diplomacy 2.0. The new technologies give us a significant competitive advantage over terrorists. Some time ago I said that Al Qaeda was 'eating our lunch on the Internet.' That is no longer the case. Al Qaeda is stuck in web 1.0. The Internet is now about interactivity and conversation. Now, the Net itself is becoming a locus of civil society 2.0. Meanwhile, Al Qaeda keeps its death cult ideology sealed off from discussion and criticism."

Within State's Bureau of International Information Programs there is the Office of Innovative Engagement created in June 2009 to manage emerging public diplomacy media policy and advocate emerging media initiatives. The Office's mission includes the following objectives:

- To support and educate embassies and public diplomacy professionals on their use of Internet-based, mobile and computer technologies with an emphasis on social media to enhance their outreach strategies and ability to build local communities

- To support major international events, including presidential and secretarial trips, by increasing engagement and fusing traditional and nontraditional media

- To serve as a think tank to extend the reach of public diplomacy engagement by experimenting with cutting-edge technologies that can be used for public diplomacy and evaluating their potential to deliver effective programming

The Director of the Office of Innovative Engagement is William E. "Bill" May. His office is recognized as a government center of excellence in the use of social media. He explained that his office is all about "engaging the people and responding to the people." He gave the example of President Obama's visit to Ghana in 2009. He said, "We used a combination of old and new media. We were able to ask and hear back from the populations of Africa using text messaging. We asked in four different languages what questions and comments did they have for the president? We were able to actively listen to 15,000 comments and have the President respond back via a podcast and the traditional media." In simple terms the office is trying to find innovative ways to reach non-American publics that have not been reached in the past or who have been difficult to reach.

May stated, "We need to know who we're trying to reach, know where they live and then go there and engage. Not just talk but engage them in active listening." He also says an official must have an objective in mind, and the hard part is measuring the results.

May pointed out that engaging international people is not all about Facebook. The majority of social media users in some countries such as Brazil, China, Japan and Russia do not use Facebook, preferring other regional and local social media. Again, the government must use the local and regional social media to engage the public where they are living.

Lovisa A. Williams is the deputy director of the Office of Innovative Engagement. She has a blog (lovisawilliams.wordpress.com) where she discusses such things as "The Power of One" (the individual) and the global citizen rights and responsibilities.

She believes the hardest part of using social media or "disruptive technology" as she calls it, is the fact that this is a huge cultural shift and how one thinks about the work he or she does (public diplomacy), and the processes used to do that work. She believes the shift requires people to change how they think too. She cites three key things that public affairs officers should think about regarding emerging media.

1. This is disruptive technology. It is social media today, but will be called something else tomorrow. There is always going to be technology change, which will have an impact on culture and how you communicate. So do not focus so much on the specific tools, but recognize more the concept of reaching out to people and creating communities of people.

2. Your (government's) reputation is the biggest risk in this type of open communication. You have got to be transparent about who you are, and what your intentions are. You have to be open and honest in dealing with people. If you or your organization makes a mistake, better to admit it and move forward. You cannot "spin" anything. The way the Internet works, "spin" is not possible anymore.

3. This is about building communities as opposed to the traditional broadcasting. You know that it is a successful community when you are no longer leading the conversation. You want other people to join the conversation and bring up their ideas and opinions.

From a crisis prevention perspective, social media can give early warning before something leads to a crisis. For example, a rumor on Twitter claimed that an unpopular ex-president of a troubled country was seeking protection in the local U.S. Embassy. It was not true, and U.S. officials were able to engage in the Twitter conversation and explain that the rumor was not true in real time.

Again, at State, the social media management is decentralized in each country, using the specially trained local U.S. Embassy staff. The communications strategy is to customize conversations to the local language and culture. One of the tools the Innovative Engagement staff teaches is to design a "Listening Dashboard" of tools to determine what social media are used in that country and culture, and how the media are used. Tools such as Twitter, Google Alerts and Google Reader are used. The local social media manager wants to know what topics are being discussed and when they are talking about the United States. The thing to remember is that with social media, everybody gets to be an affairs officer in direct communication with the public.

THE FUTURE IS EASY ACCESS TO EVERYTHING—RIGHT NOW

What will be the nature of government public affairs relationship with the public in the future? This is an especially important question considering the changes that have already come about in the twenty-first century digital information age. In 1995, Bill Gates forecast this change while he was still chairman and CEO of Microsoft Corporation. He defined the information age as a time when, "People should have easy access to information of any type, for use in business, information, entertainment or education. Anywhere they go, they should find that easy to do."[40]

Fast forward to today. In discussing the new 4G high-speed smart phone networks, the *Boston Globe's* technology writer, Hiawatha Bray wrote, "You're in your living room, watching a high-definition movie with the kids. Time to go to the airport; but the movie follows you to the car, playing on a screen behind your seat so the kids can watch. Your car (technology) tells you the best way to avoid a traffic jam, then warns you that your flight has been delayed. You detour to a restaurant, and the movie follows you on your smart-phone as you wait for a table."[41] One can substitute "news" for "movie" in that scenario.

The public affairs lesson is that the information consumer goes from digital device to digital device always connected to the content that he or she wants. It is not the medium or device that is important, it is the message. The trick is for your message to be in sync with local culture, be in a personal voice and be fun. The fun part is difficult for government agencies. But it is hard to be on the consumer's digital channel of choice anytime everywhere.

GOVERNMENT PR PRACTICE IN THE DIGITAL ECOSYSTEM

The government public affairs officer's job in the digital age is the same as in the past—to communicate with the many publics, in the most efficient and effective way possible. The question is not, "Will we use the Internet and new digital social media?" It is, which media channel combination (old and new) will we use to most effectively reach our target audiences? It is true that audiences have become more fragmented in the huge Internet universe. Streaming video services such as YouTube, Hulu and NetFlix offer a wide and increasing variety of content online, a possible reason that cable TV providers are losing TV subscribers, but gaining broadband subscribers. Younger busy Americans are getting most of their news online.

GOVERNMENT 1.0 WEB COMMUNICATION

As mentioned before, the American government launched their initial websites in the mid-1990s. The U.S. Congress and executive branch have used government websites, such as the U.S. Congressional Library's "Thomas," thomas.loc.gov/, or the White House site, www.whitehouse.gov, as routine public affairs tools. Through the Internet, citizens are able to access more and more government information, including news releases in a timely manner. For example, the Massachusetts Internet "Access to Government Network" website is www.magnet.state.ma.us and the City of Boston's website is www.ci.boston.ma.us/.

GOVERNMENT 2.0 SOCIAL MEDIA COMMUNICATION

Since 2004, Internet social media sites became major communication hubs, and government public affairs must integrate the communication power of sites such as Facebook (launched in February 2004), YouTube (February 2005) and Twitter (July 2006). For government public affairs, the social media use is a "work in progress." Social media has the potential to add fresh knowledge for public affairs strategic planning and evaluation. A lot of public affairs time is now spent monitoring and interacting with people in social media, including blogs. This is part of the feedback function.

STATE GOVERNMENT ONLINE ENGAGEMENT EXAMPLE

Governor Chris Christie (R-NJ) took office in January 2010. He was the first Republican to be elected to New Jersey statewide office in the past 12 years. He and his public affairs staff are plugged into the digital world. The New Jersey Governor's website is his communications hub (www.nj.gov/governor). On his home page you can click on the newsroom button or the blog button or scroll down to the Twitter section and click with a link to www.Twitter.com to register and then connect with the governor's Twitter account. The governor's wife also has her own web page, www.nj.gov/firstlady.

If that was not enough digital communication, Gov. Christie's public affairs staff has also posted videos on YouTube. Gov. Christie is shown in town hall meetings exercising hard-hitting humor and an aggressive style of leadership. According to the *New York Times*, Christie's YouTube videos have been edited to help his tough-guy image and in one case show him in a "testy exchange" with a teacher. That particular "testy" YouTube video had 766,000 views. In 2010, Christie's staff posted 163 videos on YouTube, which helped make Christie a YouTube sensation. "A lot of the political stuff online is really dry, but with Christie, there's an entertainment factor," said Nicco Mele, who teaches a class on the Internet and politics at the Kennedy School of Government at Harvard. He said, "These videos don't seem professionally produced, even though they are."[42]

CITY GOVERNMENT ONLINE ENGAGEMENT EXAMPLE

Mayor Cory A. Booker and the City of Newark, New Jersey (www.ci.newark.nj.us), are also a great example of using the digital tools to communicate. The mayor does his own "tweets" on Twitter, which alerts him to citizen's complaints and he responds with the action taken.

TRANSPARENCY AND PUBLIC ENGAGEMENT IN PLANNING

Today, the public affairs planning process must involve transparency and public input. For example, the issue of *open citizen access* to government information means involving citizens in how information is delivered. The U.S. government web content guide (www.usa.gov/webcontent) states:

> All citizens are entitled to access government information and services, including those who don't use advanced technologies. While more and more visitors have access to higher-end technologies, research shows that a significant percentage of the public still uses relatively low connection speeds, lower screen resolutions, and prefers a variety of different Internet browsers.

Therefore, the government web planners recommend that:

> Designing, developing and testing your website for a broad range of visitors—including those with lower-end hardware and software capabilities—is one of the best practices for managing your agency's external website. You should routinely evaluate your website to be sure you are giving your visitors an equal chance to get the information and services you offer.

In planning for ways to integrate emerging digital media, the relationships summarized in Table 14.1 provide a point of departure. In developing plans for new strategies based on the future interactive multimedia marketplace, keep in mind four prime providers whose roles must be considered: the providers of *content*, *hardware*, *software* and *network services*. Today's citizens are online content providers using blogs and social media.

T A B L E   14.1

Strategic Communication Planning for Government Public Affairs

Area	Old Way	Digital Way
Strategy creation	Senior officials	Team effort with citizen input
Key players	Senior officials	Officials and public customers
Audience size	Local or state or national	Global—but, localized
Audience makeup	Mass—undifferentiated	Internet—niche communities
Transmitting media	Mass (one-way)	Digital multimedia (two-way interactive)
Public access to government information	Limited, with gatekeepers	Open and interactive

DEALING WITH SOCIAL MEDIA

In March 2009, Nielsen Company reported that for the first time in history the time people spent on social media exceeded the amount of time they spent on sending e-mail. According to the U.S. government web content guide (www.usa.gov/webcontent):

> Social Media integrates technology, social interaction and content creation, using the "wisdom of crowds" to collaboratively connect online information. Through social media, people or groups can create, organize, edit, comment on, combine and share content.

The U.S. government web content guide gives government public affairs people all they need to know to engage with social media. Also, the Navy has created a "Navy Social Media Handbook" designed to help Navy people create and use social media (www.slideshare.net/USNavySocialMedia/navy-command-social-media-handbook-web).

Some points to think about include the following:

- Have a plan for how you will integrate social media into your overall communications strategy.

- With social media you are in the niche audience two-way conversation, not just in the one-way mass transmission business.

- Target your content (messages) to those niche audiences.

- Know your time limits with social media. (Do you have the daily time needed to interact on Facebook or Twitter?)

- Online audience measurement (metrics) needs close attention.

- Keep content simple and interesting.

- Lighten up on social media. (Use humor.)

- The moment of interaction or message is the important thing, not what device people are using in the digital conversation.

Government agencies now work the social media networks daily. Social networks are a way to connect with fragmented audiences. The online audience will "self-select" to join or follow a government-sponsored social media presence, such as on Facebook or Twitter. A guiding interactive principle is that the government must reorganize its public affairs team to actively maintain the ongoing public conversations.

SOCIAL MEDIA INTEGRATION AND PUBLIC AFFAIRS EXAMPLE: FACEBOOK

Facebook is a privately owned social network service and website launched in February 2004. In January 2011, Facebook had more than 580 million active users, with 50 percent of those logging onto Facebook daily. The average user had 130 friends and users spent over 700 billion minutes per month on the site.[43] Users create a personal profile, add other users as friends and exchange messages, including automatic notifications of friends when there is new action on their pages. Additionally, users may use the search engine for common-interest user groups, organized by workplace, school, subject or other characteristics. Mark Zuckerberg, Facebook's founder and *Time* magazine's Man of the Year in 2010 said,

> There is a big misconception around what social networks are. People think they are communities or sites where people are going to meet new people or make new connections or consume a lot of media. But what they really are is a completely different paradigm for people sharing information. The traditional media models are all centralized. What we're enabling here is decentralized individual communication. When that happens with a certain level of efficiency, it starts to become easier for people to communicate and get a lot of their information through this network rather than through a lot of centralized approaches they used before.

TABLE 14.2

U.S. Navy Facebook Guidelines

Think before jumping into creating a Facebook page, there are three key questions you should consider to determine if Facebook is right for your command:

1. How will engaging with the public in an open forum help you better achieve your mission?
2. Have you identified someone who can spend at least 1 hour a day to monitor, post and respond to comments to build an active and engaged community online?
3. What is your **goal** in establishing a Facebook page? What are the **measurable objectives** associated with that goal? Note: Getting 10,000 friends is NOT a goal—it's one metric, but your goal should be tied to your communications strategy.

If you are able to realistically answer these questions you are ready to establish a Facebook fan page and are on the path to setting your command up for success in using this tool.

Establishing Policy and Roles & Responsibilities:

Prior to creating your command's fan page, you should establish some **standard operating procedures** that will determine who will manage the Facebook community (including what material to post, when to respond, how to engage, what to do when a crisis occurs, etc.). The standard operating procedures should also include your command's policy on comments and commenting.

TABLE 14.3

U.S. Navy Facebook Content Guidance

Disclaimer for use on Official Sites:

(To be added to the "info" tab of your fan page)

Welcome to the Facebook Fan page sponsored by (unit name). This page is intended to provide updated information and discussion on (. . . .). Please visit our official homepage at (. . . .).

While this is an open forum, it's also a family friendly one, so please keep your comments and wall posts clean. In addition to keeping it family friendly, we ask that you follow our posting guidelines here. Comments and posts that do not follow these guidelines will be removed:

–We do not allow graphic, obscene, explicit or racial comments or submissions nor do we allow comments that are abusive, hateful or intended to defame anyone or any organization.

–We do not allow solicitations or advertisements. This includes promotion or endorsement of any financial, commercial or non-governmental agency. Similarly, we do not allow attempts to defame or defraud any financial, commercial or non-governmental agency.

–We do not allow comments that suggest or encourage illegal activity.

–Apparent spam will be removed and may cause the author(s) to be blocked from page without notice.

–You participate at your own risk, taking personal responsibility for your comments, your username and any information provided.

–For Official Use Only (FOUO), classified, pre-decisional, proprietary or business-sensitive information should never be discussed here. Don't post personnel lists, rosters, organization charts or directories. This is a violation of privacy.

The appearance of external links on this site does not constitute official endorsement on behalf of the U.S. Navy or Department of Defense.

You are encouraged to quote, republish or share any content on this page on your own blog, website, or other communication or publication. If you do so, please credit the command or the person who authored the content as a courtesy (photo or article byline can be U.S. Navy or MC2 Joe Smith, for example).

Thank you for your interest in and support of the men and women of the U.S. Navy. For further information visit the Department of Defense user agreement at www.ourmilitary.mil/user_agreement.shtml

Zuckerberg also spoke of how social media will effect governments. He said, "It's really changing the way that governments work. A more transparent world creates a better governed world and a fairer world."[44]

The federal, state and local governments are large bureaucratic organizations. Therefore, each component office must look at its public affairs goals and decide what guidelines or rules to follow in using social media. Within the Defense Department, the Navy guidelines were created, and on December 1, 2009, the first Navy Facebook guidance was issued as outlined in Tables 14.2 and 14.3.

The official government social media accounts must adhere to a higher standard of content control than would be necessary for a private individual or business account. This is usually called "terms of use" guidance. The navy's social media account content user guidance is in Table 14.3.

SUMMARY—PUBLIC TRUST IS KEY

In summary, digital technology and the Internet is transforming the government's relationship with its citizens. But one thing has not changed. The government public affairs mission is still about connecting government with people.

Government public affairs must reach people who are in a digital *self-serve* multimedia ecosystem. The mainstream media are still important because of the mass distribution. But emerging social media allow a message to be aimed at a small target community of individuals. In the end, it is important to just strip away all the technology and when you look at it, it is just about people talking, building relationships and forming a sense of community with other people around issues of mutual interest and value.

The mainstream and social media are an open public system. Public affairs leaders must assume that everybody (friend and foe) gets to see their messages. This is where truth and trust comes in. If what you say is not true on TV or Twitter, you break the bonds of trust with your audience. Truth and trust is still the glue that brings credibility to government and its public affairs efforts.

DISCUSSION QUESTIONS

1. Discuss the barriers to the President's being able to honor his "transparency policy." On his first day in office, President Obama signed a January 21, 2009, Memorandum on Transparency and Open Government. He wrote, "My Administration is committed to creating an unprecedented level of openness in Government. We will work together to ensure the public trust and establish a system of transparency, public participation and collaboration. Openness will strengthen our democracy and promote efficiency and effectiveness in Government."

2. Do you agree or disagree with former President George W. Bush (and why)? One Katrina news image was of President Bush on Air Force One, looking out the plane's window flying high over the Gulf Coast a day after the storm hit. The image conveyed to Americans that of a leader who was detached from the victims of Katrina. In his memoir, President Bush wrote that this decision not to land at New Orleans was correct because it would have disrupted the first responders from their work. But he said he should have had his plane land at Baton Rouge. He wrote, "Landing at Baton Rouge would not have saved any lives. Its benefit would have been good public relations. But public relations matter when you are president, particularly when people are hurting."

3. In the digital world, Brian Sodergren, a pharmaceutical executive in Virginia, started an online campaign to ignite a "National Opt-Out Day" on the Wednesday before Thanksgiving. He suggested that, as a protest, travelers "opt out" of scanners and submit to the "pat-down," which would slow down the security process as a protest. As chief of communications for the Transportation Security Administration what would your communication recommendations be about this potential protest?

4. Admiral Baker gives advice on the possible use of Facebook in government and military communications: "Think before jumping into creating a Facebook page, there are three key questions you should consider to determine if Facebook is right for your command." Using his three questions (and another you might ask) locate a government Facebook page and comment on its effective use of the Baker questions and the additional question you might ask.

NOTES

1. In government offices, the terms *public relations* or *public affairs* describe the same function. The term *public diplomacy* describes the overseas public relations efforts of the State Department. In the U.S. military, the term *strategic communication* covers the management task of integrating the planning, coordination and execution of public affairs and overseas information operations. It also includes the coordination with the State Department on public diplomacy aboard. The military term *information operations* is the new term for *overseas military psychological war operations*. The military's rethinking of strategic communication was the result of experience in the wars in Afghanistan and Iraq, and at the same time dealing with the war on terrorism at home.

2. Stephen Hess, *The Government/Press Connection* (Washington, DC: Brookings Institution, 1985), p. xiii.

3. Thomas E. Patterson, "Legitimate Beef—The Presidency and a Carnivorous Press," *Media Studies Journal*, 8, no. 2, Spring 1994, p. 23.

4. Ibid, pp. 25–26.

5. Herszenhorn, David M., "Republicans Threaten to Bring Senate to Halt Over Tax Dispute, New York Times, December 2, 2010, p. A20.

6. Matthew L. Wald, "Energy Chief Expresses Chagrin Over Monitoring Reporters, and editorial, "Energy's Friends and Enemies List," *The New York Times*, Nov 11, 1995, pp. 9 and 22.

7. James William Fulbright, *The Pentagon Propaganda Machine* (New York: Liveright, 1970), pp. 21–22.

8. GAO Report B-316443, "DOD—Retired Military Officers as Media Analysts," July 21, 2009, and See 38, Part I, U.S. Stat. 212.

9. Ibid, p. 310.

10. George Bush, *Decision Points* (Crown Publishers, New York, 2010), p. 318.

11. Ibid, p. 310.

12. Andrew Ryan, "Votes Mount for Ouster of Turner," *The Boston Globe*, November 39, 2010, pp. A1, A10.

13. Ryan Andrew and Travis Andersen, "Amid Outcry, Council Expels Turner," *The Boston Globe*, December 2, 2010 pp. A1, A14.

14. David Kocieniewski, "Rangel Censured Over Ethics Rules," *The New York Times*, December 3, 2010, pp. A1, A23.

15. Bob Woodward, *Obama's Wars* (New York: Simon & Schuster, 2010), p. 173.

16. Eileen Sullivan, "Officials Sidestep Airport Security," AP, *The Boston Globe*, November 24, 2010, p. A13.

17. Matt Bai, "Politicizing Airport Security," *The New York Times*, November 24, 2010, p. A22.

18. Matt Bai, "Mistrust of Government, Crystallized," *The New York Times*, November 24, 2010, p. A17.

19. Erin Aillworth and Katie Johnson Chase, "Turbulence over airport security," *The Boston Globe*, November 23, 2010, pp. A1, A13. Dan Berry, "At Checkpoints, Looking for Threats and, Now, at Testy Travelers," *The New York Times*, November 23, 2010, pp. A1, A18.

20. Ibid, pp. A1, A13.

21. Ashley Parker, "T.S.A. Chief Visits Airport to Buck Up Employees and Defend Tactics," *The New York Times*, November 25, 2010, pp. A22, A26.

22. Campbell Robertson, "Passengers Unmoved By Protests Against Scan," *The New York Times*, November 25, 2010, p. A22.

23. It is very difficult to obtain an exact number of public affairs people working in the federal government because of the use of so many occupation categories (civilian and military) that do not specifically say public affairs. For example, the author has used his 30 years of federal government service to make a judgment, including the occupational categories of public affairs, visual information, and writers and editors. The latest U.S. Office of Personnel Management, "Occupations of Federal White-Collar Workers Statistics as of September 30, 2010," indicated 5,543 public affairs specialists, 1,794 visual information specialists, 1,368 writers and editors for a total of 8,705. (See www.fedscope.opm.gov and click on employment cube, and then click on Sept. 2010.) In addition, the Defense Department's military departments (Army, Navy, Air Force, Marine Corps) have about 3,500 uniformed public affairs specialists. Under the Homeland Security Department, the Coast Guard has an additional 100 uniformed enlisted public affairs specialists. So, not

counting other administrative support staff, the uniformed public affairs staff totals 3,600. Totals are 8,705 civilians and 3,600 uniformed for a federal government reported total public affairs staff of 12,305. The amount of federal funds spent on the public affairs function is almost impossible to find, since many costs are buried in administrative costs. The $1 billion figure is the author's best estimate after talking to officials in the Office of Management and Budget.

24. George Stephanopoulos, *All Too Human* (New York: Little, Brown and Company, 1990), pp. 140–141; and ABC News, "Nightline," February 15, 1993; and Karen Hughes, *Ten Minutes From Norma* (New York: Viking, 2004), p. 219.
25. Bob Woodward, *The Agenda: Inside the Clinton White House* (New York: Simon & Schuster, 1994), p. 254.
26. Melvin Mencher, *News Reporting and Writing* (Madison: Brown and Benchmark, 1994), p. 486; and Fitzwater, Marlin, *Call the Briefing* (New York: Times Books, 1995), p. 8.
27. Walter Karp, "All the Congressmen's Men: How Capital Hill Controls the Press," *State of the Art: Issues in Contemporary Mass Communication* (New York: St. Martins Press, 1992), p. 109.
28. Karen Hughes, *Ten Minutes from Normal* (New York: Viking, 2004), p. 222.
29. Floyd Abrams, *Speaking Freely: Trials of the First Amendment* (New York: Viking: The Penguin Group, 2005) pp. 1–31.
30. Scott Shane, "Keeping Secrets WikiSafe," *The New York Times*, December 12, 2010, Week in Review Section, p. 1.
31. Ginger Thompson, "Official Assail WikiLeaks and Try to Curb Damage," *The New York Times*, p. A16.
32. See www.wikileaks.org.
33. Sanger, David E., "Engage, But Move To Plan E," New York Times, December 5, 2010, Week in Review Section, pp. 1, 5.
34. Shane, p. 5.
35. Brent Baker, "Leakology: The War of Words," U.S. Naval Institute Proceedings, Vol. 103/7/893, July 1977, pp. 43–49.
36. Ibid, p. 49.
37. Brent Baker, "Decisions at the Speed of TV Satellites," *Vital Speeches of the Day*, Vol. 58, no. 19, July 15, 1992, pp. 581–583.
38. Hillary Clinton, Secretary of State, remarks on "The Obama Administration National Security Strategy," to Brookings Institute, Washington, DC, May 27, 2010.
39. Arthur Molella comments, "Instant Communication Changes Customs, Politics in Developing World," at Voice of America News website (www.voanews.com/english/news/9-13-2008-07-18).
40. Bill Gates, *The Road Ahead* (New York: Viking, 1995), pp. 20–21.
41. Hiawatha Bray, "What 4G Cellular Networks Mean to You," *The Boston Globe*, December 3, 2010, p. B5.
42. See website, nytimes.com/2010/12//01/nyregion/01/youtibe.html. No longer online.
43. www.wikipedia.org/wiki/Social_network_service.
44. Arthur Molella comments, "Instant Communication Changes Customs, Politics in Developing World," at Voice of America News website (www.voanews.com/english/news/9-13-2008-07-18).

ADDITIONAL READING

Abrams, Floyd. 2005. *Speaking Freely Trials of the First Amendment*. Prince Frederick, MD: RB Large Print. Print.
Baker, Brent. 1992. "Decisions at the Speed of TV Satellites," *Vital Speeches of the Day*, Vol. 58, no. 19, July 15. Print.
Baker, Brent. 1977. "Leakology: The War of Words," *U.S. Naval Institute Proceedings*, Vol. 103/7/893, July. Print.
Reedy, George E. 1987. *The Twilight of the Presidency: From Johnson to Reagan*. New York: New American Library. Print.
Stephanopoulos, George. 1999. *All Too Human: A Political Education*. Boston: Little, Brown and Co. Print.

Woodward, Bob. 2010. *Obama's Wars*. New York: Simon & Schuster. Print.

The First Presidential Communications Agency: FDR's Office of Government Reports (SUNY Series on the Presidency: Contemporary Issues). 2006. New York: Mordecai Lee State of New York University Press. Print.

The News and Public Opinion Media Effects on Civic Life. 2011. Boston, MA: Polity Pr. Print.

Wring, Dominic, Roger Mortimore, and Simon Atkinson (Editors). 2011. *Political Communication in Britain: TV Debates, the Media and the Election (Political Communications)*. Basingstoke, Hants, U.K.: Palgrave McMillan. Print.

15

C H A P T E R

BROADCAST MEDIA AS BROADCAST PUBLIC RELATIONS

Tim Larson, Ph.D.
Associate Professor, Department of Communication
University of Utah

Craig Wirth, MA
Adjunct Assistant Professor, Department of Communication
University of Utah

Broadcasting and public relations are often treated as unique in the media tactical mix, seemingly with little in common, each making its separate contribution in the marketing and management process. In this chapter, we update the broadcasting and public relations digital link, show what the two can synergistically accomplish integrated with other marketing components, engage a video news release (VNR) case study to test our thinking and suggest a hybrid marketing promotion tactic labeled *broadcast/public relations (PR)* that often finds its product showcased in VNRs. *Product* refers to a service, an idea, a destination, an institution, an organization, an individual (such as a politician running for office) or anything else that can, broadly speaking, be marketed.

We look at broadcast/PR as a synergistic tactic in the integrated marketing communication (IMC) process where the result of the two combined working for a client in the *customer buying* process is greater than the sum of their individual effects or capabilities. Broadly, public relations includes ongoing activities to ensure that an organization, its reputation and its products have a strong public image. Often this involves promotional activities conducted through the mass media. Broadcasting involves the production and transmission of television and radio programs and other content using airwaves, wired and wireless technology or the Internet.

The roles of broadcasting and public relations are changing because of the shift from traditional to online media. Over-the-air broadcasting has been reinvented by incorporating Internet broadcasts into its repertoire. PR has changed from an esoteric, standalone discipline and practice to one necessitating integration in the marketing communication process with other media, including broadcast media. In this chapter, we have morphed broadcasting and public relations into a hybrid tactic we call broadcast/PR. We focus on the customer buying process and the tactical integration of broadcast/PR in the IMC model. This is in contrast to the combined pejorative or depreciative application of PR in the Nixon Watergate scandal, or BP's use of PR to target members of Congress in the wake of the Deepwater Horizon disaster or the prospective presidential candidates' use when testing the political waters with exploratory committees. Instead, the focus is on the consumer and the equivalent in not-for-profit organizations of patients, donors and others.

We first offer some definitions and explain our understanding of the IMC process before embarking on the broadcast/PR synergistic tactical relationship.

THE IMC PROCESS AS WE SEE IT

A distinction between *integrated marketing communication* and *integrated marketing communications* is warranted. A good way to distinguish communication with and without an "s," is to examine other concepts with and without "s's." Some examples include the following:

- Medicine versus medicines

- Philosophy versus philosophies

- Language versus languages

- Communication versus communications

All the "s-challenged" words above describe a broad field of study or a profession, while the "s-gifted" words describe the tools and tactics employed within a field of study or profession. For example, if you are in the profession of medicine, you are a doctor or other health care provider. If you are in the field of medicines, you likely deal with the "stuff" of medicine—drugs or remedies for treating illness. Similarly, philosophy is the branch of knowledge devoted to the systematic examination of basic concepts such as truth, existence, reality and freedom. Philosophies, on the other hand, are the "stuff"—the precepts, beliefs, principles and practice—of philosophy. Try your hand at language versus languages.

Likewise, *communication* involves the face-to-face or mediated exchange of information or meaning among individuals; for example, by means of speaking, writing or using a common system of signs or behavior. *Communications* involves the tools, tactics, technologies and systems used for sending and receiving messages and meaning; for example, postal and telecommunications networks and mass media.

Integrated marketing communications and integrated marketing communication are similarly distinguished:

- *Integrated marketing communications.* Strategic communication with customers using any and all available marketing promotion methods in combination, including, among others, mass media advertising, public relations and publicity, broadcast/PR, sales promotion, personal selling, Internet, events, packaging, point-of-purchase, word-of-mouth and social media.

- *Integrated marketing communication.* The strategic *communication* process involving the integration, sharing or exchange of information among all people, departments and functions in an organization, including and involving, among other elements, *integrated marketing communications tools* and *integrated marketing communications tactics* to find, satisfy and retain customers and make a profit.

We put these definitions into an understandable framework in Figure 15.1. It shows a model of the *integrated marketing communication* (**IMC**) process and the place of *integrated marketing communications tools* and *tactics* in that process.

The interactive steps in the IMC process are shown in the context of an organizational structure, in which the marketing manager coordinates the marketing *communications tools and tactics*, making sure corporate, marketing and marketing communication strategies and objectives are integrated. The model lists the several functions an organization engages, not necessarily dictating that each requires an individual person to manage it. Certainly, in smaller organizations, an individual may wear several hats managing a stable of these departments or functions under different names.

You will note in Figure 15.1 that broadcast/PR, public relations and social media are integrated marketing communications tactics, not part of the five major IMC tools (5Ps). That is not to say they are not important in the strategic mix, but they are only three of several available integrated marketing promotion tactics, not esoteric functions, separate from the other measurable IMC tactics.

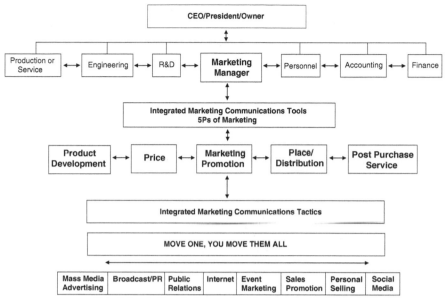

F I G U R E   15.1

Integrated Marketing Communication Model

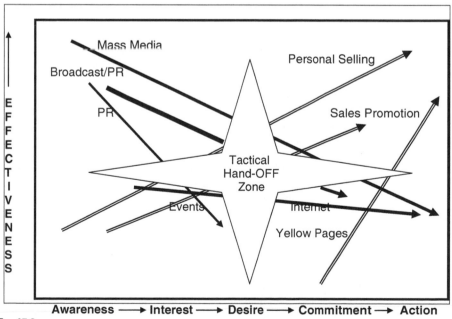

F I G U R E   15.2

A.I.D.C.A—A Hierarchy-of-Effects Theoretical Model and Applicable Marketing Communications Tactics. Adapted from Manning, G.L., and Reece, Barry L. (1987), *Selling Today: A Personal Approach*, Dubuque, IA: Wm. C. Brown, (201).

We maintain a marketer without great knowledge of the IMC process and the strengths and weaknesses of the competing media tools and tactics is an anachronism in today's customer-focused marketplace. From our perspective, although a marketer may work in a particular medium or specialize in a marketing promotion tactic, he must have the knowledge and ability to integrate all the competing media and the integrated marketing communications tools and tactics, to find, satisfy and retain customers while making a profit for the client and his organization.

Generally, as depicted in Figure 15.2, broadcast/PR and other mass media tactics, with their higher reach, are best at creating awareness and less effective in creating action (purchase), where more personal tactics are needed. Note that personal selling, with its fewer contacts, is of less value in creating awareness but more valuable in creating action. The Internet, depending on what uses it is put to, can serve both ends of the continuum, providing information as well as facilitating purchase.

An important point to be gleaned from Figure 15.2 is that there is a *tactical hand-off zone* in the awareness, interest, desire, commitment, action (AIDCA) model. Because no marketing communications (marcom) tactic is totally effective at every AIDCA step, an integrated mix of tactics must be employed. As such, a marketer might use a mass media tactic such as broadcast/PR to create *awareness* at the beginning of a campaign and later hand-off the responsibility to create *action* to a more personal tactic, such as personal selling. The marketer's knowledge of the strengths and weaknesses of each marketing communications tool and tactic and their strategic mix is put to a test in the *tactical hand-off zone*.

CHANGES IN THE PAST DECADE

There was a time when broadcast media relations was relatively simple to do. You had three major television broadcast networks in the United States: ABC, CBS and NBC; each had an affiliate station with regularly scheduled newscasts in every market. And, to target radio audiences, sellers looked to the powerful 50,000-watt clear-channel AM stations in large markets. However, those days are now long gone. This thought conjured in 1997 by John Bace of J.A. Bace, Inc., is now reality.[1]

On June 12, 2009, all full-power U.S. television stations gave up their analog channels and renewed using digital technology. Profound changes were brought about in the way television was delivered. The changes are having profound effects on the use of what we had comfortably thought was broadcast television. Digital television threatened the very existence of over-the-air television broadcasting, with regulators and public interest groups suggesting cutbacks in television station spectrum space and allocating it to wireless broadband. U.S. FM radio stations also went digital, allowing for multiple formats airing in spectrum space where only one was possible.

The old model of delivery for radio and television began to change collaterally for public relations, even before the digital transition. Radio was transformed as a result of station ownership deregulation promulgated with the passage of the Communications Act of 1996. Some form of broadcast media ownership rules before 1996 had been in place for decades at both the national and local levels, evolving from the "Rule of 7s," which limited broadcast station ownership to seven AM, seven FM and seven TV stations nationwide. After 1996, for the first time, ownership of multiple radio and television stations as well as some market cross-media ownership of radio and TV stations, cable systems, telephone services and newspapers in many local markets was allowed.

The Federal Communications Commission (FCC) maintained ownership restrictions, which, from its perspective, propped up the doctrine-of-wagging-tongues, proffered First Amendment ideals, and promoted competition to ensure the efficient use of scarce spectrum resources. The result of broadcast ownership deregulation, however, was fewer owners, less localism, decreased diversity and options and a concentration of spectrum allocations in the hands of a few. In radio, for instance, six large corporations and equity groups bought and merged the 80-plus individual radio ownership units, resulting in a company such as Clear Channel Communications owning over 1,200 radio stations nationwide—as many as eight in a single market—with multiple radio and television stations, newspaper, outdoor and other cross-media holdings allowed in the larger U.S. markets. The FCC, while exercising oversight, now evaluates radio and television station ownership and proposed cross-media ownership combinations nationally and locally on a case-by-case basis using established market criteria to determine whether it would be in the public interest, specifically, whether it would promote competition, localism and diversity.[2]

Before the digital television transition, the remote control allowed couch potatoes to channel-surf television programs without getting up. Using VCRs, viewers time-shifted recorded programs for later playback, and cable and satellite delivery exponentially increased program options beyond the three television network choices. But after the digital transition, Internet Protocol television (IPTV) evolved along with the advent of the digital video recorder (DVR). Thus began the reinvention of television from a one-way, time-based, linear program delivery model controlled by large corporations to a nonlinear delivery model controlled by individual television viewers—often content providers in their own right. The DVR employs a computer hard drive that records programming for playback at the viewer's discretion, resulting in skipped commercials and other messages, dramatically forcing advertisers and public relations practitioners to rethink their marketing strategies and tactics.

Changes were accelerated when the Internet, with its personal digital mobile devices—PDAs, cell phones, iPods and other MP3 players—allowed listeners and viewers from anywhere in the world to *place-shift* and receive only the radio and television programs, advertising and public relations messages they selected or were addressed to them via nearly ubiquitous Wi-Fi and wired broadband connections worldwide. With this, the Internet, audio and video are no longer controlled by professional programmers. Viewing and listening are now in the purview of consumers who control content and media use on their video and audio digital devices, requiring a shift from a *push* to a *pull* marketing promotion strategy.

Radio and television stations, however, have benefited from ownership deregulation and by going digital, even though the Internet has siphoned audiences. For instance, using automation, radio stations can be programmed using the hard drive of a computer, and fewer people are required for an owner to operate multiple radio and television stations located in the same market. Economies of scale are gained for both radio and television.

BROADCAST/PR

David Meerman Scott, an online thought leadership strategist, posits the Internet dramatically changed the broadcasting and public relations synergy. According to Scott, public relations old-school rules were nearly synonymous with mass media advertising, and PR practitioners were dependent on broadcasting and other mass media for distribution of their press releases and VNRs—specifically, on journalists who decided what was "newsworthy." In addition, marketers under the old rules did not strategically employ integrated media, but, instead, practiced parochial marketing promotion strategies, objectives and tactics. New marketing and public relations rules introduced by the Internet promoted PR beyond its perception as a twin to advertising and allowed broadcasters and PR practitioners to join the buyer in two-way conversations, shifting thinking from mainstream mass media marketing and toward underserved buyers via the web.

Under old-school rules, broadcasting, public relations, print and other mass media functioned separately under a model in which a *seller* went indirectly in search of a *buyer*, often with strategically "dis-integrated" marketing promotion methods. Going digital turned this around. Broadcast/PR functions under a model akin to the traditional and online Yellow Pages or Switchboard, in which a buyer goes directly in search of a seller for products in which he has interest.

As such, the transition to digital, broadcast deregulation and the Internet fostered broadcast/PR tactics and promoted the use of a variety of web-based services to reach buyers directly. Included was broadcast/PR content delivery using podcasts, online forums, wikis and list servers, blogs to cultivate viral marketing, e-mail, geo-location services, sites for posting video, social media and, of course, over-the-air broadcasting.

BROADCAST/PR MEDIA RELATIONS

To explicate broadcast/PR media relations, we searched in Google, Bing, Yahoo! and other prominent search engines using a stable of key words and phrases, primarily the term *broadcast/PR*. The following self-described broadcast/PR firms were chosen as examples of those providing the broad range of broadcast/PR services.

- DWJ Television (www.dwjtv.com/broadcastpr) DWJTV produces video press kits, satellite media tours, radio news releases and radio media tours for its clients.

- A-1 Broadcast (www.a-1broadcast.com) A-1 Broadcast is a full-service broadcast public relations company specializing in Satellite and Radio Media Tours.

- zcomm (www.zpr.com) zcomm integrates strategic, traditional, and broadcast public relations and online media services with tactics such as podcasts, webcasts, corporate video and out-of-home media.

- PRNewswire (www2.prnewswire.com/services/resources/vnrs.shtml) PRNewswire, a commercial news distribution company, places video, audio and satellite news releases, B-roll and other content on the Pathfire Digital Media Gateway, the same system most broadcast affiliates use to get their network news and program feeds. It leverages multimedia content to engage clients in digital, social media and multichannel marketing.

- MediaForce (www.mediaforcepr.com/whymfpr.html) MediaForce PR focuses on nonprofit and government clients. It developed branding for the U.S. Customs and Border Protection Agency's Global Entry pilot program.

    Although most broadcast/PR firms differentiate themselves from competition by specializing in some unique services, the following are standard broadcast/PR client services typically offered by most.

- Video, audio, satellite, multimedia, social media news releases (VNR, ANR, SNR, MNR, SMNR)

    These releases are client-sponsored reports produced by broadcast/PR agencies and released to radio, TV and online media. There has been some controversy of late over VNRs and the practice by television stations not to identify VNRs as sponsored when included in a newscast and made to look like a real news report. The VNR controversy is discussed in more detail below and is engaged in a case study.

- Radio, television, satellite, and Internet media tours

    These tours involve a series of interviews booked on nationally syndicated and local talk and news shows enabling a client's spokesperson to deliver key messages to listeners. These interviews can originate from almost any place on earth to reach TV and online audiences with technology, health, green and entertainment news, among other topics.

- Podcasts, online audio and video webcasts and e-mail broadcasts

    These audio and video productions are uploaded on such aggregators as iTunes, Yahoo! Video, GoogleVideo, YouTube, Odeo, Vimeo and other customized sites. The audience for these services is especially valuable because its members are already interested in the product and seek it out online.

- Public service announcements (PSAs)

    This service includes audio and video PSAs to a national audience or to targeted regional and local audiences.

- In-store, airport and health club broadcasts

    These broadcasts reach a captive audience with information and news that is location related and topical.

- Media presentation training
    This service involves training for media presentations, public speaking, interviews and executive coaching.

- Social media

    Social media can stand alone, but most often should be integrated with other marketing promotion tactics and with communication components of a client's marketing promotion campaign. Social media sites are developed for clients and usually employ search engine optimization strategies to drive people to a client's website. A discussion of social media is engaged in the "Futures" section below.

As ubiquitous as Otis elevators, the mainstay of nearly every broadcast/PR firm is the VNR. Its fortified place in the broadcast/PR repertoire, however, has weakened in recent years. Possibly sensing pending FCC intervention as a result of a study conducted by the Center for Media and Democracy (CMD) putting VNR distributors and stations in a negative light, a group of 15 PR firms formed the National Association of Broadcast Communicators (NABC) in the summer of 2006. (See the discussion of the CMD study and subsequent FCC rulemaking in the case study below.)

As of 2008, the NABC is a consortium of broadcast public relations firms that produces VNRs. Its stated purpose is "to establish standards and guidelines for its member companies" and to "represent the broadcast PR profession before the broadcast industry, regulatory community and PR industry."[3] However, its focus clearly was on VNRs and sponsorship identification.

NABC Membership Code

- Affirming that "the appropriate use of VNRs is an important and integral part of the dissemination of information to the public"

- Respecting "the First Amendment rights of their customers to use VNRs, as well as the First Amendment rights of individual broadcasters to exercise appropriate editorial control and discretion concerning their use of VNRs"

- "Assisting all broadcasters in fully complying with the FCC's news and program sponsorship requirements by including attribution and source identification information as required by FCC rules and policies"

- Condemning "the payment of money or other valuable consideration to broadcasters in return for the broadcasting of VNRs, without disclosure as required by FCC regulations"

- "Educating the public regarding the appropriate use of VNRs, consistent with FCC requirements and the First Amendment rights of broadcasters and NABC members' customers"[4]

VNRs became widely popular in the 1980s and lasted into the new century as an important marketing tool. The largest VNR producer was Medialink Worldwide, a sophisticated marketing, production and analytical data company with offices in New York, Los Angeles and London. Medialink, MultiVu, KEF, Media Associates, DS Simon Productions (all original NABC members), as well as smaller organizations, produced videos in the form of news packages that ideally conformed to what a particular TV station or network expected. A producer supervised a script that usually included short interview answers from an expert or a customer and featured shots of the product or service. A "reporter" in the employ of a VNR company would read a script just as an actual news reporter would do. VNR companies also provided a script in hopes a station reporter, a known commodity in the market, would read the script instead of its in-house "reporter."

The report was distributed by mail, overnight delivery, via satellite or as a news feed to local stations. News feeds are closed circuit feeds between stations, and commonly between networks and stations. VNR bookers tirelessly called newsrooms, hoping to gain interest for the VNR. They often purchased lists of station employees who might be interested in a certain product, service or topic, such as medical reporters for drug or supplement stories. Their appeals, however, were not only to reporters specifically selected for their likes or interests, but were customized for specific reporters with whom the VNR producer had developed a relationship and knew how he or she wished to receive a story. For instance, a Los Angeles company that specialized in celebrity VNRs would offer up an "A list" of stars that could appear live on a station's morning news. Local entertainment reporters would not pass up the opportunity to speak with a star hawking his or her latest movie. In a true IMC sense, the VNR booker researched the market to know which particular reporter was most influential in targeting the message to the desired demographic.

A sophisticated recording service monitored the VNR showings. The twentieth and twenty-second lines of a TV scan of 525 lines of the old NTSC TV system (standard definition) was encoded with a measuring tool called SIGMA—provided by the Nielsen Media Research company—which gave the VNR company a report of when a piece aired and the demographics reached.

There was a constant effort made to combat the perception that VNRs were not legitimate journalism—rather than a commercial disguised as a news story. VNR distribution focused on doing about anything to blend in with traditional journalism in style. The biggest boost to legitimizing VNRs came when networks and wire services carried VNRs for hire on their news feeds that went to local stations, using such services as Pathfire mentioned above. While networks supplied these feeds with the understanding that they were "pay-to-play" stories on the feed mixed in with their other reports, the fact that they came from the trusted network source gave VNRs credibility. The stories were packaged as network-produced stories and often were sandwiched between network news stories.

In its time the VNR was a terrific broadcast/PR tactic. In reality, VNRs were far more economical than commercials; featured credible spokespersons—often the friendly anchor or credible local reporter who had years of trusted association with the audience; were considered legitimate news stories by many viewers; and were targeted and placed in segments to reach the demographic the VNR producer and client desired, usually for free.

The success stories abounded throughout the industry. For instance, coauthor Craig Wirth once produced a VNR in which celebrities, including Paris Hilton and Nichole Richie, appeared for free to sample a dairy product at a film festival. Footage from that VNR appeared for several years in TV news programs showing the stars drinking out of a cup with the client's logo. Audience measurements equaled many millions. In another case, the medical reporter for a New York TV station, a doctor, read word for word in his featured segment one of Wirth's VNR scripts for a supplement. His primary audience was caregivers, mostly women, who watched his segment and with whom the reporter had built a near fiduciary relationship.

Because of contractual agreements of nondisclosure, proprietary restrictions and ethics, we cannot identify VNR clients in this chapter, but all of coauthor Wirth's VNRs, although promoting a client's product and subject to client approval, were truthful. In fact, the four VNR companies and numerous PR firms for whom Wirth produced insisted he use truthful information. Video content was never staged, nor were actors used instead of a client's employees or users of a product. Of course, the people used in VNRs reflected the sponsor's message.

Stations and networks often tell the public that they never use VNRs, or that they decry their use. However, that simply is not the case among some specialists such as medical reporters who otherwise do not have access to video of technical operations or research. Also, entertainment reporters use promotional film, satellite tours and star celebrities to discuss upcoming releases. Additionally, VNR producers never request or ask broadcasters to not disclose that a client paid for the report. In all of Wirth's VNRs, the client was identified in the paperwork that went with the release and on a slate at the beginning of the on-air report.

However, transparency is not necessarily practiced by all the stations who aired VNRs. *PRWatch* reported the VNR business took a series of major hits with the nonprofit watchdog group CMD, which conducted an extensive study of television news and VNRs. The landmark study followed 77 television stations and reported that in virtually all cases, these TV stations aired VNRs without disclosing that they came from a source other than the TV station's own reporters.[5]

The federal government, most notably the FCC, took on the issue. In November 2006, FCC Commissioner Jonathan Adelstein released a statement commending the CMD study and issued a stern warning:

Many broadcasts are apparently ignoring the FCC and their own ethics guidelines in running VNRs without disclosure. All the warnings in the world don't help if nobody's listening. When the flock ignores the shepherd, it's time to build a fence. Since the industry is patently incapable of self-regulation it's up to the FCC to enforce our disclosure rules. Some stations have developed such an ingrained pattern of running VNRs that even a direct investigation by the FCC isn't enough to snap them out of it. Maybe some have run so many red lights it seems like the normal way to drive. It's time to start handing out citations. This is not a First Amendment issue. Newsrooms are not allowed under the law to run commercials disguised as news without an honest and adequate disclosure. Clearly, the embarrassment of informing viewers they are merely transmitting corporate propaganda in lieu of real news is leading many to actually eliminate disclosure supplied by the VNR producer. The issue is not free speech—it is identifying who is actually speaking.[6]

The FCC saw a need to protect consumers from what was termed "propaganda." The irony is that the federal government was one of the major users of VNRs at the time. The agency assigned to protect consumers, the Consumer Protection Agency, was in fact one of the most visible VNR users. The agency frequently generated alerts and offered guidelines to its staff members on how to produce VNRs. Of course, the FCC wasn't directing comments to VNR producers, but to stations, networks and news services that aired VNRs without disclosure. Producers and their clients didn't abuse VNRs. They were doing nothing more than promoting products to consumers and giving stations the option to air those marketing efforts.

We honestly don't think any legitimate VNR producer hid the facts in the VNR paperwork. However, they all did their best to see that reports didn't look like VNRs. All put sponsor IDs on the VNR paperwork, leaving it up to the station to identify the video as a VNR. Of course, it was a homerun for the client and producer when the station didn't identify that the VNR was a sponsored piece. Lazy reporters or insufficient news budgets may also have contributed VNR nondisclosure.

However, the arena was already messy when the FCC's Adelstein issued his 2006 warning that evolved into an FCC investigation. A year earlier, two federal agencies, the Department of Health and Human Services and the Department of Education, issued VNRs that promoted concepts being promoted by the George W. Bush administration. Most notably, they were VNRs about a new Medicare plan and a push for No-Child-Left-Behind. The General Accounting Office determined the two agencies violated the law in pushing what were political initiatives. Democrats introduced legislation to stop what they described as government propaganda, but the Republican Congress never acted.

The result was a decrease in VNR production but not a total elimination of this broadcast/PR tactic. Cable and satellite presentations and distribution through blogs and YouTube and other Internet offerings kept VNRs alive, albeit at a decreased level. The strong accusations that regulation was needed naturally affected much more than a careful analysis of the beneficial use of VNRs might have revealed.

The FCC took enforcement actions against stations on the CMD list after sending FCC letters to those stations. In March 2011, the FCC Enforcement Bureau issued notices of "apparent liability" against a Fox TV station in Minneapolis and a New Jersey station. The Fox station aired 12 shots of General Motors (GM) cars in a story about convertibles. GM provided video of the cars, which was aired without a disclaimer. The issue is murky. When a story about convertibles that used GM video is aired, is this propaganda? Does a Fox TV reporter assigned to promote the network's own *American Idol* television program violate VNR guidelines?

In trying to make sense of what was legal and not, the Radio Television Digital News Association (RTDNA) wondered, for instance, if the Insurance Institute releases about car safety crash results, or expensive movie clips provided by Hollywood studios require VNR source identification. Sports video also frequently was used that came from organizations such as Major League Baseball through its internal television network. Virtually all sports stories at local stations come from marketing departments associated with teams or leagues, or at least are done in cooperation with those marketers. Tickets to games are provided to those who cover sports. New product videos, such as those for computers or telephone devices, come from manufacturers. The viewing public likely knows the station or network didn't shoot the video that was aired. But the question remains: Do American viewers care what the regulators were trying to protect them against?

Marketing also exists behind the scenes in television news. Many story ideas come from PR agencies that have strategic relationships with reporters. Press conferences, new product announcements and the like do not just happen. A marketing/PR agency generally contacts a reporter and/or a station to pitch the event. The station seldom identifies that it is covering an item simply because a PR practitioner, for instance, informed the station about the event. The optimum end result is having the actual consumers then create the product buzz. A staggering 900,000 people have offered information about Apple computers on YouTube. Are these VNR violations?

Previously as a reporter in New York and Los Angeles TV, Wirth never had a person tip him to a story who didn't have a vested interest in getting the story on the news. They usually represented a cause or client that had hired them to pitch a story. The good ones, according to Wirth, presented an argument about how "his reporter consumers" would benefit by a story about some concept or product they were pushing. The good ones were simply good marketers with a transparent agenda also common in traditional news.

Commissioner Adelstein concluded his release of November 14, 2006:

No wonder the public is having a hard time distinguishing between news and propaganda. Americans have a legal right to know that what appear to be independent news reports are actually bought and paid for by a private corporation. Broadcasters need to provide disclosures so viewers can make up their own minds about the story. Stations that fail to disclose who is behind these stories show a lack of respect for their viewers, as well as the FCC and the broadcast industry's ethics guidelines.[7]

It appears that VNRs are alive and well, as long as one does not call them a VNR.

CASE STUDY

This case study is presented with permission from the Radio Television Digital News Association (RTDNA) and from author Kathleen Kirby, partner in the Wiley Rein law firm.[8]

VNR "SPONSORSHIP" IDENTIFICATION

"FCC Issues Fines for Airing Video News Releases Without Sponsorship Identification." By Kathleen Kirby, Partner, & Ari Meltzer, Wiley Rein

On March 24, 2011, the Federal Communications Commission's (FCC or Commission) Enforcement Bureau issued Notices of Apparent Liability for Forfeiture (NAL) against two television broadcast licensees for airing material from VNRs in violation of the Commission's sponsorship identification rule. The licensees, Fox Television Stations, Inc. and Access.1 New Jersey License Company, LLC, each face forfeitures of $4,000. The fines stem from complaints filed with the FCC against numerous television stations by Free Press and the Center for Media and Democracy in 2006. At that time, RTDNA met with FCC Commissioners and filed pleadings raising the significant First Amendment concerns associated with these investigations.

Under Section 317 of the Communications Act, broadcasters are required to disclose to their listeners or viewers if they have aired matter in exchange for money, services or other valuable consideration. Notably, the Act exempts from the disclosure requirements material "furnished without charge or at a nominal charge." This safe harbor seemingly would cover situations in which a broadcaster receives no payment and makes its own independent judgment about what to air, such as when a broadcaster derives story material from a VNR.

In the Fox case, however, station KMSP-TV aired material in one of its newscasts from a VNR that the station obtained from the Fox News Edge service. The segment, which addressed consumer demand for convertibles during the summer, featured 12 different shots of three General Motors cars, each of which was named in the segment. Even though Fox stated that neither the station nor its employees received any consideration in exchange for broadcasting the VNR, and that no third party had reported to the station a consideration exchange, the Bureau concluded that the VNR material itself constituted "valuable consideration."

Analogizing to an example the Commission first offered in 1963, where a bus company furnishes a travel film free to broadcast stations and the bus is "shown to an extent disproportionate to the subject matter of the film," the Bureau concluded that, because the KMSP-TV's story focused on the GM convertibles in both the script and video footage, rather than "merely quoting editorial comment from a press release," sponsorship identification was required. By its use of the VNR, the Bureau reasoned, the station had "impliedly agreed to broadcast an identification beyond that reasonably related to the subject matter of the film."

Similarly, in the Access.1 case, station WMGM-TV included material from a Matrixx Initiatives Zicam VNR during a sponsored "Lifeline" health segment. The broadcast included four different shots of Zicam and the cover of the Zicam Travel Well Survey as well as a sound bite with a medical doctor recommending Zicam by name. Here, the station included a sponsorship announcement—not for Zicam, but for the hospital that paid for the segment. Nevertheless, the Bureau determined that because the VNR focused "almost exclusively" on Matrixx's Zicam product, the station was required to identify Matrixx as the sponsor of the VNR material.

Notably, the Bureau expressly rejected Fox's arguments that the investigation unconstitutionally intruded into the station's journalistic and editorial discretion in the presentation of news and public information, and would ultimately result in broadcasters self-censoring and eschewing legitimate speech under the threat of government sanction. In dismissing these assertions, the Bureau stated that (1) Section 403 of the Communications Act gives the Commission broad authority to investigate any matter relating to enforcement of the Act; (2) the Bureau's decision leaves broadcasters free to exercise newsgathering and editorial functions; and (3) the Commission's rules are simply disclosure requirements, not direct speech restrictions.

The Notices mark the second and third enforcement actions since the FCC sent letters of inquiry to 77 stations in 2006 seeking information about the airing of VNR material. In order to enforce a civil forfeiture, the Commission must bring a lawsuit within five years of the date when the claim "accrued"—generally the date of the incident. With this deadline approaching, it would not be surprising for the Commission to address many of these dormant inquiries in the coming months.[9]

RTDNA said it would keep members apprised about developments concerning FCC enforcement with respect to sponsorship ID. It told stations in the interim that it may be advisable to review sponsorship identification and payola policies as well as newsroom practices with respect to disclosures.

CASE STUDY QUESTIONS

1. Is the FCC sponsorship ID ruling fair?
2. Is it anachronistic? Is it relevant to apply in today's television news marketplace?
3. Is the $4,000 fine appropriate? Is it large enough to send a message or just a slap on the wrist to stations?
4. Are VNRs inherently dishonest, unethical or unprofessional when included in a newscast?
5. If the VNR itself is a "valuable consideration" under the Communications Act, wouldn't every VNR require "sponsorship" identification? Wouldn't NASA-provided video inside the space shuttle, for example, be considered a valuable consideration? Doesn't that video have more value than video of convertible cars?
6. If the FCC limits "sponsorship" identification requirements to VNRs that identify brands "disproportionate to the subject matter," wouldn't Insurance Institute for Highway Safety (IIHS)-provided video of their vehicle crashworthiness tests require a disclaimer? Do IIHS VNRs go beyond disproportionate identification into the realm of praising certain brands and condemning others?
7. How about the segments on the newest medical devices and procedures, almost all of which are VNRs obtained from medical providers and device manufacturers? Do those segments brazenly promote specific procedures and devices, almost never provide any balance, independent investigation or dissenting voices, and are they more deceptive to viewers than video of convertible cars with visible nameplates?
8. How about clips of Hollywood films in the ubiquitous "in theaters now" and "weekend box office numbers" segments, all movie studio provided?
9. Do VNRs about high-tech product releases, which most often focus exclusively on a particular brand, require "sponsorship" identification?
10. Is it self-evident that VNR material originates outside the newsroom? Is the answer now to headline brands contained in VNRs, rather than to simply allow oblique glimpses of logos?

(Adapted from Bob King's online response on March 25, 2011, to the RTDNA article. www.rtdna.org/pages/posts/fcc-issues-fines-for-airing-video-news-releases-without-sponsorship-identification1305.php)

WHAT DOES THE FUTURE HOLD FOR BROADCAST/PR?

We tapped some broadcast/PR experts on their predictions for the future of broadcast/PR. The Internet, press releases and social media significantly come into play. Here is what the experts predict:

Doug Simon, President and CEO of DS Simon Television[10]

- Two services that will grow in popularity in the broadcast/PR industry are Internet Media Tours as well as Internet Interview Tours.

- Corporate communicators are going to be looking to hire people for project assignments and those assignments increasingly are going to be about creating content and also distributing them via social media.

- Satellite media tours have been transformed to include radio, web media, in-market tours and, in some cases, brand integration. New services include helping clients organize, share and control the video on their own sites so customers are not clicking through on YouTube to competitors' content.

- Broadcast/PR is driving relevant, strategic placements on television, radio and the Internet.

- Press releases are becoming VNRs and corporate events are broadcast over the Internet.

- The rise of multimedia PR gives public relations professionals new ways to reach target audiences in nontraditional settings.

- Social media is changing the face of PR and affecting the future of the press release.[11]

- We have witnessed a shift toward what some are calling the "social media release." Services like PitchEngine, PressLift, PRX Builder and MindTouch are bringing the press release into the new millennium with embedded multimedia and easy distribution through various channels, including social media and e-mail.

Amanda Miller Littlejohn, Founder of Mopwater Social Public Relations[12]

- The press release has been transformed, to become this living, breathing thing. If a release doesn't have a social element—that is, a way for viewers to comment or share to their social networks—it doesn't have legs.

Lindsay Groepper, Vice President of BLASTmedia[13]

- What we see now is new methods of distributing the info, driven by social media. Rather than e-mailing a press release, PR people are sending journalists to custom landing pages created just for that specific announcement, contacting them via Twitter with a BUDurl link to the release, or even directing them to a YouTube video with a message from the CEO making the announcement.

Jeff Esposito, Vistaprint's Public Relations Manager[14]

- Press releases will continue to evolve into multiple iterations for various audiences, channels and situations.

David McCulloch, Director of Public Relations at Cisco Systems[15]

- The press release's future may simply depend on media consumption trends. We have seen a marked shift in [the press release's] format to reflect the accelerating societal shift from mass consumption of media ("push" media) to personalized consumption or "pull" media.

Kelly McAlearney, Account Supervisor at Edelman Digital[16]

- Based on natural progression, the press release will continue to get shorter, for concision's sake. And interactions have naturally become more concise as many brands are in constant, direct contact with consumer audiences and media via online channels.

Lou Hoffman, CEO of The Hoffman Agency[17]

- Backlinks—incoming links to a website or a web page—generated by press releases are reason enough to continue syndicating them. Even if the syndication of this content has little impact on the target stakeholders, they will still be generating backlinks, which by themselves deliver a decent return on investment.

Dragon Blogger Technology and Entertainment[18]

- Advertising will continue to be the primary driver of content.

- User-inspired or partially created content will become more likely as entire TV shows or episodes could be developed based on users' feedback or participation in helping shape the direction of a show.

Proactive[19]

- Social Media is no longer a fad, or something to try out. It will become an integral part of PR programs. And PR people have to master social media and use it strategically to be effective.

Communiqué pr[20]

- As services such as Hulu continue to influence the broadcast media landscape and provide viewers more control over what they watch and when they watch it, the company has the potential to change how PR and broadcast media interact. For example, we anticipate it will become more challenging to place stories as network coverage may become more limited. As networks strive to keep their shows on top, producers will be looking for stories that resonate with a local or niche audience and also provide information that is truly valuable to their viewers.

No matter what other prognosticators predict for its future, Doug Simon argues that the broadcast/PR industry controls its own destiny.

"What our industry has missed is a coherent plan to communicate the value of our new products as we did in the VNR days. We have a strong case to present—especially about earning media on the web. Clients are able to measure value in improved search rankings and increased traffic to their websites. The critical challenge now is, Can we get beyond the hypercompetition to move the broadcast/PR industry forward into the new era?"[21]

NOTES

1. Adapted from John A. Bace, "Broadcast Media Relations" in Caywood, Clarke L. *The Handbook of Strategic Public Relations and Integrated Communications.* New York: McGraw-Hill, 1997, pp. 77–89. Print.
2. www.fcc.gov.
3. www.sourcewatch.org/index.php?title=National_Association_of_Broadcast_Communicators.
4. Ibid.
5. www.prwatch.org/fakenews/execsummary.
6. FCC News Release November 14, 2006.
7. transition.fcc.gov/headlines2006.html.
8. www.rtdna.org/pages/posts/fcc-issues-fines-for-airing-video-news-releases-without-sponsorship-identification 1305.php.
9. www.rtdna.org/pages/posts/fcc-issues-fines-for-airing-video-news-releases-without-sponsorship-identification 1305.php.
10. www.vlogviews.com/categories/broadcast-pr.
11. mashable.com/2010/08/16/pr-social-media-future.
12. www.millerlittlejohnmedia.com.
13. www.blastmedia.com.
14. www.vistaprint.com.
15. www.cisco.com.
16. edelmandigitial.com.
17. www.hoffman.com.
18. www.dragonblogger.com/future-broadcast-media.
19. www.proactivereport.com/c/pr/pr-trends-in-2010-the-future-of-pr.
20. www.communiquepr.com/blog/?p=403.
21. Douglas Simon, "The Future of Broadcast PR: Acquisitions, Bankruptcies and Web Video Point to New Era of Opportunity," *Bulldog Reporter's Daily 'Dog* (May 30, 2011).

ADDITIONAL READING

Bace, John. 1997. "Broadcast Media Relations." In: Caywood, Clarke L., ed. *The Handbook of Strategic Public Relations and Integrated Communications*. New York: McGraw-Hill. (pp. 77–89.) Print.

Dominick, Joseph, Barry Sherman, and Fritz Messere. 2007. *Broadcasting Cable the Internet and Beyond: An Introduction to Modern Electronic Media*. McGraw-Hill 7 edition 2011. Hoboken, NJ: John Wiley & Sons. Print.

FakeNews, www.prwatch.org/fakenews/execsummary.

Hendershot, Heather. 2011. *What's Fair on the Air?: Cold War Right-wing Broadcasting and the Public Interest*. Chicago: University of Chicago. Print.

Hutton, James G., and Francis J. Mulhern. 2002. *Marketing Communications: Integrated Theory, Strategy & Tactics*. Hackensack, NJ: Pentagram Pub. Print.

National Association of Broadcast Communicators www.sourcewatch.org/index.php?title=National_Association_of_Broadcast_Communicators.

Manning, Gerald L., and Barry L. Reece. 1990. *Selling Today: A Personal Approach*. Boston: Allyn and Bacon. Print.

Rudin, Richard. 2011. *Broadcasting in the 21st Century*. Basingstoke Hampshire, UK: Palgrave Macmillan. Print.

Scott, David Meerman. 2008. *The New Rules of Marketing and PR: How to Use News Releases, Blogs, Podcasting, Viral Marketing, & Online Media to Reach Buyers Directly*. Creative Commons. E-book.

Wertime, Kent, and Ian Fenwick. 2008. *DigiMarketing: The Essential Guide to New Media & Digital Marketing*. Singapore: John Wiley & Sons (Asia). Print.

LINKS

A-1 Broadcast. A-1 Broadcast is a full-service broadcast public relations company specializing in Satellite and Radio Media Tours. www.a-1broadcast.com

DWJ Television. DWJTV produces video press kits, satellite media tours, radio news releases and radio media tours for its clients. www.dwjtv.com/broadcastpr

zcomm. zcomm integrates strategic, traditional and broadcast public relations and online media services with tactics such as podcasts, webcasts, corporate video and out-of-home media. zpr.com

PRNewswire. A commercial news distribution company, places video, audio and satellite news releases, B-roll and other content on the Pathfire Digital Media Gateway, the same system most broadcast affiliates use to get their network news and program feeds. It leverages multimedia content to engage clients in digital, social media and multichannel marketing. www2.prnewswire.com/services/resources/vnrs.shtml

Media Force. MediaForce PR focuses on nonprofit and government clients. It developed branding for the U.S. Customs and Border Protection Agency's Global Entry pilot program. www.mediaforcepr.com/whymfpr.html

National Association of Broadcast Communicators. www.sourcewatch.org/index.php?title=

Fake News. www.prwatch.org/fakenews/execsummary

16 CHAPTER

DIGITAL COMMUNITIES
Social Media in Action

Richard Edelman
President and Chief Executive Officer
Edelman

Robert Holdheim
Managing Director, Edelman India
Edelman

Mark Hass
President, Edelman China
Edelman

Phil Gomes
Senior Vice President, Digital Integration
Edelman Digital

Steve Rubel
Executive Vice President, Global Strategy and Insights
Edelman

Derek Creevey
Contributor, Executive Vice President, Corporate Communications
Edelman

PR AND THE MEDIA CLOVERLEAF: THE ROAD TO PUBLIC ENGAGEMENT

BY RICHARD EDELMAN

Over the past two decades, the media has undergone a profound metamorphosis. After World War II, consumers relied on a select number of national broadcasters and newspapers, underpinned by local newspaper, radio and television news outlets. The early 1990s saw the advent of cable television dispersing the audience among specialist brands from the Weather Channel to MTV to CNN. And over the last 10 years, there has been an acceleration of the dispersion of both audience and authority to Internet-based channels, premised on proliferation of broadband and near-universal access to mobile devices. Audiences have even become co-creators of news and information by posting comments, stories and videos as part of a continuing conversation.

The average informed person now has eight daily sources of information, according to a recent Pew Foundation report, a complete change from the morning newspaper and evening television news of prior generations. The reader spends 90 seconds on each medium, instead of the 35 minutes devoted to the print version of the newspaper. In a given year, 40 percent of readers will contribute a comment; the Huffington Post has one million comments a week. News is accessed throughout the day, with the expectation of immediate updates as stories unfold. Instead of going directly to media brands for news, search engines are the new door to the house, with 90 percent of readers inquiring on subjects then clicking through to highest ranked articles. Increasingly, peer recommendations on social networks such as Facebook and Twitter are as relevant as media's concierge: one-third of Huffington Post readers come this way.

THE FOURTH ESTATE IS DEMOCRATIZED

Today's media ecosystem is akin to a cloverleaf (Figure 16.1). The first leaf, mainstream media's traditional delivery modes of newspaper, television, radio and magazine are still the largest drivers of established media

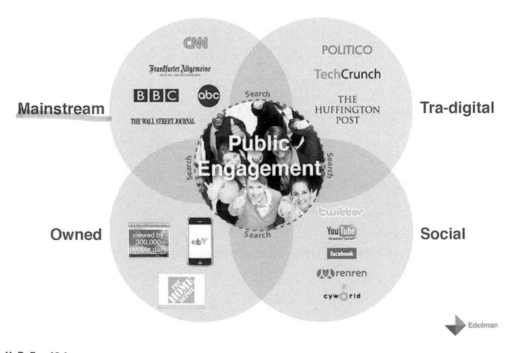

FIGURE 16.1

Media Cloverleaf

business in terms of their revenue. For instance, the print edition of the *New York Times* still accounts for 85 percent of the revenue and a higher percentage of profit.

The second leaf is Tra-digital, the morphing of the new and traditional media on the web. All mainstream brands now provide their content across digital platforms, increasingly behind some form of pay wall, allowing limited free sampling. There are stand-alone web products that are subject-specific such as Mashable, TechCrunch and Gawker.

The third leaf is social media—the communities that have been built by companies including Facebook, Twitter, Renren, Cyworld, Friendster and Foursquare. Organizations/brands encourage individuals to converse with them directly on these sites.

The fourth leaf is "owned" media, a company's website or content posted on its YouTube channel. BP's livestream of the gushing well during the Gulf of Mexico spill provided a 24/7 channel of information, helping BP provide details of the recovery effort directly to the general public.

HOW PR FUNCTIONS ACROSS THE MEDIA CLOVERLEAF

According to Edelman's annual Trust Barometer, which tracks the attitudes of more than 5,000 influencers across 23 countries, people need to hear or see or read news about a company three to five times before believing it (even more often in the United States and United Kingdom), and from multiple channels and sources.

For example, in the Tra-digital section of the cloverleaf, Edelman worked with nonmedia influencers and select bloggers well in advance of the launch of Microsoft's Kinect for Xbox 360, to critique the beta version and drive conversations about the product and its potential. Kinect for Xbox 360 subsequently became the most successful consumer technology product introduction in history, surpassing the iPhone in sales in the first 60 days.

In the social part of the cloverleaf, Edelman Digital created an augmented reality application for Ben & Jerry's to enable a smartphone user to learn where the ingredients were sourced as well as sustainable and "fair-priced" sourcing facts. For Edge Shaving Cream, Edelman used the common shaving problem of skin irritation to encourage consumers to say what was irritating in general about life. Via Twitter Edge asked, What Irritates You? Edge Shave Gel Wants To Know! This got people tweeting about anything from the lack of time to get things done to the slow driver in front of us, to the person who cuts across two lanes that makes us slam on our brakes. Edge would then respond to people's everyday problems.

In the owned part of the cloverleaf, companies have the opportunity to use new technologies to illustrate key messages in creative ways. During a campaign to end the Prohibition era ban on New York State supermarkets offering wine, opponents held a press conference claiming that supermarkets would only sell low-end wines from massive, out-of-state distributors rather than promote and sell local New York brands. Rather than respond with a press conference of our own, we produced a video that featured one of our campaign members calling liquor stores statewide and asking if they carried New York wines. Almost all of the stores said they did not stock local wines, and some boasted of their selection of foreign wines. The video became an online hit promoted by bloggers, then the basis of a dozen editorials moved legislators to reconsider the old ban.

PR is most effective when it engages audiences through each of the four parts of the media ecosystem. When GE announced the Ecomagination Challenge—a commitment to invest $200 million to fund clean technology ideas—in the summer of 2010, they organized a traditional press briefing in San Francisco, with CEO Jeff Immelt, venture capitalist Ray Lane of Kleiner Perkins Caufield & Byers, and a room full of entrepreneurs who could benefit from GE's investment. The tried and true outreach was made to mainstream media, resulting in articles in the *Wall Street Journal,* the *New York Times* and *Financial Times,* as well as coverage on CNBC. Influential bloggers such as Treehugger.com were brought in, and the team garnered blog posts on Huffington Post and GigaOm after the event and an online broadcast interview with TechCrunch TV. GE's Facebook and Twitter pages were turned into eco-innovation embassies, funneling potential entrants to register and others to comment on the Challenge website. The GE home page had a special button for the Challenge, while GE Reports and GE's YouTube channel offered video views from the company on the initiative. The overlapping of the four leaves is evident from the links by bloggers to the GE Reports and YouTube videos and the use of the Challenge community site as source of story angles for mainstream media. In the first month, GE had created a community of 70,000 entrepreneurs from around the world, received 4,000 entrants and provided this community with direct access to the firm's top technical experts and research.

THE PATH TO PUBLIC ENGAGEMENT

The new media ecosystem profoundly changes public relations. PR has been dismissed by some as trivial flackery or a well-controlled manipulation of facts under the cloak of a "spin room." Today, at its best PR is deeply involved in the formation of policy and strategy as well as transparent communication. PR provides all stakeholders with a continuous two-way flow of information, as part of a genuine conversation with the organization about its services and products.

PR is now charged with the creative leadership by brands and with pushing the evolution of corporate reputation. PR is best able to inspire a passionate conversation among stakeholders who feel that a brand is listening rather than selling, engaging instead of dictating. PR thrives on the complexity of the time by encouraging transparency, which is essential to credibility.

At Edelman, we characterize our approach as "public engagement," meaningful participation in the networked world, and it is premised on a number of key tenets, including the following:

> *Think and act like a media company:* Today, any company—not just a media company—can drive the conversation in subject areas where it had comparative advantage. For example, eBay hired a former editor of *Lucky* magazine to troll through the entire eBay-created *Inside Source*—an online weekly magazine in which industry influencers for fashion and other key verticals contribute content on latest trends, styles and innovations in the space.

> *Actively listen:* PR engages stakeholders to inform a firm's strategy, and by engaging consumers, organizations can cocreate their brands. For instance, the website mystarbucksidea.force.com solicits new product ideas from the crowd, reinforcing the company's relationship with its customers.

> ***Content creators:*** PR is now the creator of compelling, entertaining and relevant content. We generate video programming and employ our own bloggers. PR empowers subject matter experts to provide credible well-researched data on its own website, and correct ongoing conversations, whether on discussion forums or in the press. Spirits giant Diageo created a series of video and audio recordings of "walks with giants," including Richard Branson, adventurer Ranulph Fiennes and Formula One

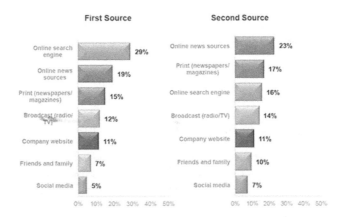

Source: 2011 Edelman Trust Barometer
Question: There are a number of sources one could use to find general news or information about a company. When looking for general news or information about a company, which one type of information source would you generally consult first? I140. And after [INSERT I139 RESPONSE], which one type of information source would you generally consult second when looking for general news or information about a company? I141. Now, thinking about a business crisis, are [INSERT I139 AND I140 RESPONSE] the same types of sources you consult first for information about a business crisis? Informed Publics ages 25-64 in 23 countries

FIGURE   16.2

Where 'Informed Publics' Go For Company News and Information

driver Lewis Hamilton, to evoke the Johnnie Walker striding character on the brand's label, on the brand's website and on promotional materials across social media. Diageo regards the program as a gold standard because it provided content that truly resonated with its consumers.

Continuous engagement, not sporadic campaigns: PR involves audiences consistently across all mediums, adapting the discussion and style to the specific medium, collaborating on Facebook, entertaining on YouTube and providing customer tips on Twitter. For instance, Butterball Turkey Talk-line now offers mobile texting tips, hosted web chats, a partnership with Bravo's *Top Chef* show, and a Cellufun mobile game.

Activating influentials—idea starters, amplifiers and viewers: Good PR practitioners have always engaged credible experts to provide independent insights for mainstream media. Today, online search engines are the first source people to turn to for news about a company (Figure 16.2). Recognizing that popularity does not equal influence; PR needs to uniquely engage with different types of influentials, depending on their characteristics. PR uncovers passionately interested people in a given area—we call them *idea starters*—and provides them with early access so they can publicly discuss product or corporate initiatives. We also identify people and/or organizations who act as "amplifiers" because of their significant number of relevant followers and readers. Credential media are often key amplifiers because 8 of 10 Google search links are to newspapers. Hewlett-Packard (HP), the world's largest technology company, adopted an influencer marketing model to build their imaging and printing business across Europe, the Middle East and Africa. To increase awareness of their premium printers, HP engaged niche influencers from fashion, music and lifestyle, inviting dozens of bloggers to a Summit in December 2010. The event resulted in the lifestyle bloggers producing videos, photos and blogs that brought HP's product experiences to life, and ultimately helped drive conversation, endorsement and action among consumers.

PR is becoming the discipline that melds strategy and communications, constituting the bridge between corporations and their stakeholders. The PR practitioner's position in the modern corporation is much enhanced. Leslie Dach at Wal-Mart, Gary Sheffer of GE, Jon Iwata of IBM and Kelly Semrau of SC Johnson sit at the right hand of the chief executive officer. At these corporations, PR informs the business strategy and policy formulation, in addition to being responsible for communicating the decisions externally. PR is responsible for marketing and communications, public policy and charitable activities. PR is entrusted with policy creation and implementation; it engages nongovernmental organizations (NGOs), regulators, elected officials, academics and media. PR has moved from pitching to informing, engaging new influencers through continuous conversation and appropriate behavior across the media cloverleaf.

DISCUSSION QUESTIONS

1. Can you think of PR programs that engage audiences through each one of the four elements of today's media cloverleaf?
2. Can you think of PR programs that engage audiences across all parts of the media cloverleaf?

PR AND SOCIAL MEDIA IN INDIA: THE GULF BETWEEN THE OLD AND THE NEW

BY ROBERT HOLDHEIM

Public relations in India is caught between the traditional and the modern, the tactical and the strategic, the "back channel" and the transparent. Practice—and quality of service—tends to be bunched at the two ends of the spectrum, with little in between. The fact that this division mirrors India itself should be no surprise; PR is, ultimately, a demand-led sector.

PR in India is, by and large, still synonymous with media relations. In a market where "we have plenty of five-year plans but no decent roads,"[1] the focus is on execution over strategy. This effectively commoditizes the offering, with price as the major variable (at the expense of efficacy or value). Clips are the primary deliverable, with little attention paid to content. As a pure cost center delivering little strategic value, PR becomes a game of the lowest bidder. PR firms take on vendor status. Cost management via constant pressure and frequent staging of competitive reviews becomes the core competency of the corporate communications department.

Indeed, Indian marketing in general has traditionally relied on two relatively blunt levers: celebrity endorsement and price promotion. In a market in which demand has historically exceeded supply and consumer choice has been highly restricted, building brand equity seemed superfluous.

Add to that, digital communications—while broadly recognized as the "next big thing"—is primarily related to online advertising. This effectively limits the ultimate two-way medium to a one-way use, and fixes it firmly in the domain of advertising agencies. Within this context, the potential of social media as an interactive communications platform is both feared and underestimated, and often as misunderstood by those selling it as those buying.

INDIA RISING: THE RAPIDLY CHANGING CONTEXT

Consider the pace of change in India today, however. GDP growth is back up to 9 percent, and flirting with double digits. Over one-half of the total population of 1.2 billion is under the age of 25; two-thirds are under 35. While poverty is still rampant, the rapidly growing middle class now numbers over 300 million. The economy has doubled over the past decade; by many estimates, it will rival that of the United States in size by 2050.

This potential makes it difficult for global companies from any industry to ignore the Indian market, despite the continued difficulty of doing business here. The potential for consumer products is obvious, as well as the potential for energy, education, health care, infrastructure, defense, technology, telecommunications—all sectors that address tremendous societal needs and, therefore, speak to the priorities of the Indian government. International companies are coming, or expanding, in droves. Indian companies are tapping international markets and bringing back significant know-how. Consider the following changes:

- Dramatically more products are available to a much larger (and fast growing) consumer base. At one time there were only three brands of cars available to the Indian consumer, today there are multiple super-luxury brands available (Audi, Mercedes, BMW) among many, many others.

- Consumers are substantially more sophisticated and well traveled, with a much broader geographic spread—well beyond the major urban centers of Delhi, Mumbai and Bangalore.

- Despite facing continued infrastructure challenges, comparatively low landline and broadband penetration, India boasts a huge mobile phone penetration upward of 600 million units.

Addressing a larger consumer base of higher sophistication faced with exponentially greater product choice will force marketers to raise their game.

MORE CONTINENT THAN COUNTRY: MARKET COMPLEXITY FAVORS COMMUNICATIONS

This greater geographic spread will present yet another distinct challenge: how to reach a population spread across 28 states (plus seven union territories) with 23 official languages and 1,600 dialects, multiple religions and highly distinct cultures. Once again, consider the following:

- Of the 10 Indian daily newspapers with the highest circulation, only one—the *Times of India* at number 7—is a national paper.

- TV is fragmented, focused on local channels and content and languages, with penetration still low outside of the major urban areas.

- Limited broadband penetration is also highly concentrated in the urban centers.

- Mobile penetration is the greatest unifier, cutting across demographic and geographic sectors.

This highly diverse, fragmented and complex environment presents a nightmare for advertisers. Add to this the huge infrastructure challenges India faces, the lack of centralized systems and institutions, the relationship imperative as a strong element of Indian culture, and the need to build these relationships locally. All of this favors communications as the "medium of choice" in addressing the opportunities arising from a rapidly changing Indian market.

A BRIGHT FUTURE FOR PR AND SOCIAL MEDIA IN INDIA

Favorable demographics and growing purchasing power, the flood of new products into the market and the ensuing pressure to increase marketing sophistication, the complexity of the market and hefty infrastructure challenges—all of these things create a "perfect storm" that will cause a dramatic change in Indian PR. India has the ability and the proclivity to "leapfrog" stages of development that other markets have gone through in the past. As one visiting CEO stated, "Everything in India is on a J-curve."[2]

Given the youthful population and the prevalence of mobile communications, social media is likely to be the trigger for this leapfrogging, and to lead the way as the communications channel of choice. For example, consider the following:

- With over 12 million users, India is the second fastest growing market for Facebook, following Indonesia.[3]

- Professional networking platform LinkedIn doubled its Indian user base from 3 to 6 million within 6 months of opening an office in India.[4]

- Twitter is gaining massive traction in the market, becoming the de facto newswire. In just the past 12 months:

  o A government minister lost his job over Twitter posts.

  o The high-profile head of a sports association had to flee the country due, in part, to his posts.

  o LinkedIn, a highly credible platform in and of itself, has used Twitter as a medium to engage with users to teach them how to better leverage the site.

Consider, finally, the case of General Motors (GM) in India.[5] While other automobile brands use social media purely for advertising, the GM brand Chevrolet "went social" with online customer relationship management. As an after-sales service, the company initiated an online "listening" program that monitored service-related complaints. These were directed to owned media properties such as a Facebook page, where they were addressed promptly, adding to the online buzz. Proactive competitions were held, encouraging customers to share content on the important role their car plays in their lives. Finally, GM India CEO Karl Slym went online to respond directly to customers' questions in live chat sessions.

The reach this program was able to achieve, the level of consumer engagement and ability to leverage user-generated content, the willingness to communicate directly—right up to the CEO level—on topics positive or critical of the company: all these are relatively new to India. And all are hallmarks of the type of program that can leverage the unique opportunities, and address the tremendous challenges of the Indian market.

THE GULF REMAINS

Despite all of this change and opportunity, the divide between old-style and modern PR in India remains. Nowhere is this more evident than in the public affairs space, where the concepts of "fixing" and "file pushing" are alive and well, as demonstrated by a series of recent public sector scandals.[6]

In public affairs, and Indian public relations generally, the sector is splitting into two distinct models. These models will continue to coexist at opposite ends of the spectrum for as long as there continues to be demand for both. The true opportunity, however, lies in modern strategic (though locally relevant) communications with digital and social media as a, if not the, primary channel.

DISCUSSION QUESTIONS

1. What characteristics make up the traditional practice of public relations in India?
2. What factors are driving the change in how PR is practiced?
3. What role will digital and social media play in modernizing Indian communications?
4. Why will this be such an effective tool?

SOCIAL MEDIA AND PUBLIC RELATIONS IN CHINA

BY MARK HASS

When Li Guoqing, CEO of the Chinese B2C site Dangdang, involved himself in an obscenity-laced flame war attacking the bank Morgan Stanley on a microblogging service in China, he unexpectedly confronted the new reality of public relations in China. Perfect fast start with unexpected word choice! Grabber.

Just 18 months before, in July 2009, the powerful Chinese Ministry of Industry and Information Technology learned a similar lesson when it proposed, in its "Green Dam" initiative, to require that every computer sold in China have filtering software preinstalled to make the task of government censorship easier.

In both cases, the growing ranks of Chinese "netizens" erupted in what researchers have begun to call "spontaneous Internet protests." In the first example with Morgan Stanley, Mr. Li became the object of ridicule across various social media platforms, with users raising serious questions about his ability to lead a prospering online business. In the second example, the Chinese government ran into a hailstorm of protest about its censorship proposal and, in an unprecedented reversal, quietly let Green Dam die in a very unusual change of policy.

AN INTRODUCTION TO CHINESE SOCIAL MEDIA

Nothing has had a more profound effect on communications and public relations in China than the emergence of the world's largest online community, with more people using social media on the Chinese mainland than there are people in the United States. By 2013, researchers expect more than 800 million people will be using social media in China. This community would be vaguely familiar to social media users in the West, but the platforms themselves would be as foreign as a stroll through a Beijing neighborhood or *hutong*.

Twitter, Facebook and YouTube, the big three social media brands that dominate in the West, are largely nonexistent in China. Aside from a group of expats and affluent Chinese living in the country's tier 1 cities on the east coast, and using virtual private networks to gain unrestricted Internet access, the vast majority of Chinese engage with social media in their own, unique national context.

Many with limited Internet access still rely on older bulletin board systems (BBSs), which are important and vast platforms. Web 2.0 platforms with names such as Sina Weibo (China's Twitter), RenRen (China's Facebook) and YouKu (a version of YouTube) have also organized vast online communities and host what academics and others in China refer to as social media "with Chinese characteristics."

These platforms have in many ways outperformed their cousins in the West, through aggressive innovation and feature enhancement. Sina Weibo, unlike Twitter, is friendly to multimedia content, and RenRen's use of geo-location and video is more advanced than Facebook's, even though the Chinese platforms are younger.

These social media outlets, while closely monitored and sometimes censored by the government, provide a relatively open media forum for the first time in China's modern history. Since coming into existence in 2005 and becoming a key communications vehicle in 2008, they have become an outlet for expression of grassroots sentiment, with important implications for corporate reputation, government relations and brand awareness in China, and also for the Chinese government itself, as the "Green Dam" incident illustrates.

They have also created a vibrant platform, while still young and undeveloped, for brand marketers eager to engage this audience through mobile outreach, e-commerce and influencer campaigns.

PLANNING AND IMPLEMENTING SOCIAL MEDIA CAMPAIGNS

China's social media community tends to be young, and those living in the largest cities tend to be well educated. The four largest social networks are Renren, Kaixin001, Qzone and Pengyou, and their users are typically younger than 30, with the majority of Qzone users, the nation's largest network, between 10 and 20 years old. Older users tend to be from China's tier 1 and 2 cities, while rural areas have the youngest users.

Data from the Edelman Trust Barometer research show that urban, informed, affluent people in China have a greater level of trust in mainstream media than their peers almost anywhere else in the world. Findings from 2011 show that 74 percent in China trust television news, 54 percent trust print media and 42 percent trust radio. Those are among the study's highest levels in 23 countries.

However, a pattern has emerged in recent years indicating a growing dependence, if not trust, in online sources of news and information. While broadcast news (34 percent) is the first place that informed people in China turn for news about companies, the second choice is online search engines and news sources (30 percent), making it clear that opinions are being heavily influenced by this two-part media environment. The level of dependence on online news has also been growing steadily in recent years, even though trust in traditional media remains high.

But the key challenge in planning social media campaigns in China is the fragmentation of those media. Each of the core platforms (news, community, microblogs and video sharing) has multiple big players offering marketers innovative and unique features. Platforms also tend to reach different demographic groups.

The accessibility of social media and online news outlets, and the way both aggregate other news sources, has made social news a critical component of Chinese information habits. That is something Chinese social media have in common with their Western counterparts. But the differences outweigh the similarities, with at least three key differentiating factors that must be considered when planning and executing social media campaigns in China:

First, *Behavior is affected by censorship*. China's social media users are all too familiar with the ever-present "Golden Shield," a term used to describe the Internet filters used by the government to block certain terms from search engines or remove social media posts that contain those terms. With all Internet traffic entering China through just four global Internet nodes, it is relatively easy for the government to block or filter incoming and outgoing traffic.

It has proven more complex to do so within China's social media, largely because of the resourcefulness of the social media community. For example, when news broke in April 2011 that artist and activist Ai Weiwei had been detained in Beijing, government censors removed references to Mr. Ai from popular microblog platforms. But an alternative phrase, *ai weilai*, meaning "love the future," quickly emerged to substitute for Ai's name. So the conversation went on.

Second, *Issues go viral quickly, and often become large, spontaneous protests*. The so-called herd effect in social media is more pronounced in China than anywhere in the world, which is one of the reasons issues go viral so quickly. In the case of Dandang, regarded as the Chinese Amazon.com, its CEO Mr. Li used his Sina Weibo account to attack Morgan Stanley and Credit Suisse for what he claimed was a poorly executed initial public offering that undervalued his firm. The first post from Mr. Li, which he described as lyrics for a rock song: "You f**kers knew first day of launch that valuation would be 2 billion, but you still priced USD 16 per share, which comes to 1.1 billion. My CFO was in panic mode, I held back a breath and silently cursed you motherf**kers."

The tirade continued in a series of over 50 weibos (Chinese tweets) and incurred the wrath of the online community, which furiously attacked Li, his family and his wife, and caused the story to spill over into traditional business and consumer media.

A few days later, Dangdang tried to call a truce and limit the damage the brand was incurring among online consumers, its primary customers. Mr. Li issued a terse, seven-point statement, trying to explain his behavior. The statement may have been too late, however, because it came after social media users turned *dangdang* into a verb meaning unacceptable, self-centered online behavior.

Third, *There is a lack of transparency*. Unlike the West, where social media behavior by organizations is guided by principles of openness developed by the Word of Mouth Marketing Association, a lack of engagement rules and a history of media opaqueness have made "real" opinions less common in Chinese social media. Speculation in the West is strong that the Chinese government uses the Wumao Dang, a "50-cent" army of paid social media commentators who receive a 50 Mao note, or half a Yuan, for each social media post that spreads government opinions. Many local public relations firms have adopted the same tactic, and have deployed their own armies of paid commentators on behalf of both major Chinese and Western brands. Most social media outlets are also willing to sell companies a presence on their sites that guarantees a certain audience size, although the level of engagement by these artificial audiences tends to be very low.

This is an eloquent example of the risks of private and owned content in the market versus news.

This has created an atmosphere in which some marketers expect, and even demand, that nontransparent techniques be used to manage social media opinion about their brands and products. This is true even though Chinese social media communities are becoming adept at spotting bogus posts, and marketers face reputation risks if they use nontransparent techniques.

The Mengniu Dairy PR debacle of 2011 provides an informative case study about how PR and social media were employed to spread misinformation. Mengniu hired firms to create fraudulent blog posts and fake consumer comments about a competitor, inciting fears that tainted milk products caused premature sexual development among children. There was a time when these no-holds-barred techniques were considered a legitimate approach to pursue business goals in China. This campaign, however, backfired after online communities unmasked the bogus posters, leading the government to arrest staff from Mengniu and its PR agency for spreading lies about the competition.

Events such as this have created a growing willingness among marketers, especially those that have been successful elsewhere in the world using social media as an engagement tool, to build their brands in a more believable and sustainable way online.

Starbucks, generally regarded as a best-practice social media user, offers numerous examples of how social media are being woven into China public relations campaigns in a transparent and impactful way. One was its 2010 "Black Is Chill This Summer" campaign, in which it used social and traditional media to connect to China's "golden generation," the men and women who have benefited tremendously from the nation's economic growth.

A holistic campaign, relying heavily on buzz within social media and BBS sites, used a local designer to create a unique Starbucks Black fashion show that tied to the brand's special summer food and drink offerings, while also establishing a virtual platform for aspiring local designers to interact and grow professionally.

Within two months of launching, the program garnered widespread lifestyle media coverage and connected on social media with more than 400,000 highly engaged members of the target audience by relying not on paid posts, but rather on stakeholder outreach and compelling content.

THE FUTURE

As China's social media continue their dramatic growth in coming years, three trends are likely to emerge:

1. It is inevitable that companies and brands will be offered more ways to buy their way to big followings online. Marketers who choose this route will need to weigh the worth of a guaranteed, but unengaged, audience versus one that is more valuable because it is built through transparent engagement and content creation.

2. The Chinese government will continue to struggle to control grassroots social media efforts and content. Social media communities will become increasingly vigilant watchdogs over regional and local government activities, and there is great potential for a government confrontation with the online community. The technology tools the government currently uses to block certain content will not scale to manage a community of 800 million users or more. If seriously challenged online, the only option will be to pull the plug on certain popular social media sites entirely. This is why social media strategies are now an important element of many government affairs campaigns being developed by Western multinational corporations.

3. Chinese social media, now largely confined to users on mainland China, will spread and become a more global phenomenon, especially among people elsewhere who prefer to communicate with Chinese characters as opposed to Western alphabets. An estimated 40 million ethnic Chinese live outside China, with large communities across southeast Asia, as well as in North America. As this occurs, savvy global marketers will begin to look at social media in China as more than a one-market play.

DISCUSSION QUESTIONS

1. In creating social media programs in China, how should PR professionals balance their desire to act transparently with the realities of pay-for-play and other nontransparent techniques sometimes used in the Chinese market?
2. Is it all right for companies and organizations to use "50 Mao Armies" to spread a message on Chinese social media, given that it is a common practice?
3. How would you suggest that a corporate CEO in China use social media as a personal communications platform? How should these strategies be different than his or her counterpart in the West, given the unique nature of Chinese social media?
4. Why do issues go viral, the so-called herd effect, more quickly in China than in the West?
5. Assuming social media continues to grow in China as forecast, how will the sheer size of the social communities affect Western competitors, such as Twitter, Facebook and YouTube?
6. Will social media programs by brands and organizations need to be replicated in multiple communities?
7. How is it possible to preserve messaging or brand values in these two widely different social media environments?

EARS TO THE THIRD RAIL: A PERSONAL HISTORY OF PR IN SOCIAL MEDIA

BY PHIL GOMES

In spring 2005, I was moderating a BusinessWire-sponsored panel in Silicon Valley about the emerging intersection between PR and social media. By this point, I had been blogging on my site and writing in the trade media about this still-nascent phenomenon for about four years.

When the conversation tilted toward the topic of *listening* to online conversations as a corporate communication imperative, I mentioned the old cliché of "keeping your ear to the rail." In an age of social media, I argued it was more akin to "keeping your ear to the *third* rail", referring to the high-voltage track used in public transit systems, often indicated by severe-looking warning signs.

After a beat, journalism visionary Dan Gillmor asked, "But, wait . . . Isn't that third rail *the one that kills you?*"

"Sure," Mike Masnick of Techdirt playfully added. "But it's also where all the power is."

Years later, this dilemma has not changed all that much. Some companies have connected to this "third rail" of online community engagement and tapped powerful energies that helped move their brands and reputation forward. Others were not so careful, mishandling those currents and walking away charred, dazed and smoldering for weeks, the event recorded on Google for posterity. Sometimes, a company had to be publicly zapped in the latter case to achieve enviable status within the former. Precious few got it right the first time.

My point is not to praise or decry the social media activities of companies and organizations. All told, even though some people are better (and often *much* better!) at online community engagement than others, everyone is in the learning game. Anyone playing the "so-and-so doesn't 'get it'" card—as many in the PR 2.0 space are unfortunately wont to do in a counterintuitive attempt to demonstrate their online community knowledge—is only leaning on the last desperate crutch of the intellectually lazy and politically correct. In any event, as one client recently said with regard to the use of case studies, "Just because someone did something that *worked* doesn't necessarily mean that it was *good*, broadly applicable, or worth repeating."

Rather, I hope to deliver some kind of context for readers who might view a pre-social-media era for PR much like I might view that relatively recent time—stone knives and bearskins for certain—when people blast-faxed press releases and fully 15 percent of an agency's hourly fees went to compiling clip reports. Since my PR career precisely straddles that border, I hope to deliver a perspective that's helpful and not merely of the uphill-both-ways-in-the-snow-and-we-were-*thankful*-back-in-my-day variety.

With scarce attention testing the limits of the art of compression, I'll try to boil my 15 years in this space into three simple lessons.

PR EVOLUTION IS LIKE GEOLOGY

The story begins straight out of undergrad. I started in technology PR (as opposed to, say, consumer or health care) because I thought that the technology industry might drive PR professionals to be every bit as innovative as the people and advancements that they were tasked to promote.

This turned out to be disastrously naive. It was as if, decades earlier, legendary technology marketer Regis McKenna wrote and saved a program onto the great mainframe that formed the collective brain of the Silicon Valley PR community. Then, laughing maniacally, Mr. McKenna sheared off all the knobs, thus irreversibly turning it into a read-only device, and walked away.

```
> LIST TECH_PR.BAS
10 brief industry analysts under NDA
20 brief long-lead publications under NDA
30 brief short-lead publications under NDA
40 brief dailies and wires under NDA
50 transmit news announcement or just do something really, really cool
60 Goto 10
> RUN
```

The crushing monotony of this method—with *innovation* generally defined as adaptations *atop*, never *within*, this framework—would really chafe at you if, well, it didn't work really, really well at the time.

In any event, to say nothing of what has happened in the years since the BusinessWire panel, the experience of PR folks who saw the potential of social media early on (and up to that point) was a bumpy one.

Thanks to what was then an emerging blogosphere of PR professionals, I found that I was not alone. One of the earliest PR-blogging entrants was Tom Murphy, then of Cape Clear Software in Dublin, Ireland. While the focus of PR on media relations (at the expense of exploring new media) was frustrating, he says "What did surprise us, at the time, was the bleed into traditional mainstream media. And that transition drove a lot of traffic." In one particular instance, Cape Clear had a service called "Google Mail" that allowed you to e-mail search queries to the company and have the results from Google e-mailed to you. "Given there was zero marketing budget—and revenue—for the application we thought it would be a great opportunity to see if we could promote it via bloggers." It was so popular that it earned the company significant mainstream coverage . . . and a cease-and-desist letter.

From my own experience:

- At my first job, while working with an enterprise software company, I noticed that Usenet postings by the company's customers served as a strong indicator of what stories we would be able to tell on behalf of the client. The effort was derided as "Gomes in his chat rooms again."

- At my second job, the fact that I was writing about social media in the trades was brought up in my 2002 performance review—slotted into the negative column.

- A year after that, I was castigated for forwarding a blog post of interest (written by a decades-long technology veteran, no less) to a client. If an activity did not involve pitching *FORTUNE*, it did not have value.

- One client even told me, "Don't blog. No one really wants to hear from a PR person who *thinks!*" (Eight years later, I was retained to write that company's social media strategy framework.)

I started in PR in 1996. I am writing this in 2011. These stories span 15 years and, again thanks to the art of compression, you'll have to wait for the DVD release to get the rest of them. Many people today marvel at the volume and velocity of social media. From my perspective, we are seeing a sustained eruption of violent activity, caused by the release of gentle pressures acting over a long time.

Like geology.

USING SOCIAL MEDIA TO SOLVE IMPORTANT COMMUNICATIONS PROBLEMS, NOT JUST INTERESTING ONES

I had the great fortune of working with the historic nonprofit research institute SRI International for about five years. Their CEO, Dr. Curtis Carlson, used to encourage the researchers in his charge to focus on solving important problems, not just interesting ones.

Deserved or otherwise, I have received a lot of attention as PR's first blogger. Fact is, though, online community engagement was not the primary or even a *major* reason why I pursued this medium. In fact, I wish I *could* say that I was exploring the interesting problem of social media engagement. As it turned out, though, I needed blogging to help solve what was, for me, an important problem. Fortunately, though by accident, my focus was in the right place.

My important problem was this: Back in 2000 or so, anybody who could fog a mirror was in public relations. Journalists, quite rightly, complained that the people who were pitching them appeared to know little about their beats or the outlets they wrote for.

"Fine," this cocky then-27-year-old countered. "I'll top *that*. Plus, I'll even supply public proof-positive that I not only *read* your work, but have a reaction to it!" After an abortive attempt or two, my first blog was born.

My point certainly is not to encourage readers to adopt an antagonistic stance with people they are tasked with influencing. Rather, I hope I am encouraging readers to keep the communications objectives in mind first and determining how the vast array of new tools and communications philosophies can be adapted to serve those ends. In my case, I had to find out a way to distinguish myself as a media relations professional in order to break through the clutter.

Today, it's easy to be distracted by the latest social media platform, technology or destination in much the same way that the dogs in the movie *Up* were easily pulled off-task upon spotting a squirrel. When you get down to it, though, they are all tools that can help strong, strategic communicators do their jobs by helping companies participate credibly in places where their audiences are. Granted, these tools carry with them heavy expectations in terms of their use—knowledge of good online citizenship and digital mores chief among them—though the best PR professionals know how to help clients find their voices online and work toward the mutual, objective benefit of all parties.

This transcends the gosh-and-wow that the breathless social media pundits have used to muddy the marketplace of ideas, contributing little else but what I like to call "tactical glossolalia." ("gloss-oh-LAY-lee-uh" [noun]: "an incomprehensible speech in an imaginary language, sometimes occurring in a trance state, an episode of religious ecstasy, or schizophrenia." Source: Dictionary.com.) Plenty of interesting problems. Precious few can identify the important ones and determine whether (or if!) social media helps achieve that objective.

Which brings me to my third point.

MOVING FROM THE BOARDROOM TO THE LIVING ROOM

Young PR professionals who pride themselves on their writing skill all quickly find themselves asking the same question once they have written about a dozen press releases or so:

"Dear Lord, does anyone *really* talk like this?!"

As mentioned earlier, I was almost exclusively working in the technology industry for the first decade of my career. (Even today, I can tell you all about polycrystalline silicon, tantalum pentoxide and other high-k dielectrics, and so on.) Press releases in this industry were once described by Dan Gillmor as sounding like a conversation between a Turing machine (an idealized artificial intelligence system) and a lawyer, and for good reason: due to a perfect storm of executive ego, excessive regulatory compliance and the political clout of most marketing departments over their public relations colleagues, most press releases are truly awful.

What I offer here as parody is, unfortunately, not too far from a representative sample of the genre:

- "Acme Roadrunner Solutions, the leading provider of feature-rich, end-to-end, robust solutions for seamless integration, today announced the appointment of Jason Smith as the Assistant Vice President of Avian Eradication . . ."

- "'We are pleased to have entered into this end-to-end strategic partnership with Acme Roadrunner Solutions,' said Jeff Jones, CMO of Spacely Sprockets."

When I was 24 and already fully up to *here* with the jargon, I asked one client if we could convince others at his company to substitute the feature-rich-seamlessly-integrated stuff, as well as the laundry list of standard features, with the simple phrase "fully buzzword compliant."

"Think about it!" I enthused. "PR pros hate writing this stuff. Everyone else hates *reading* it. If we want to make friends with journalists and analysts, this is most certainly one way to do it!"

Our shared crusade lasted about 14 hours, half of which I spent dreaming about a world when crusty, inherited PR conventions deliquesced and evaporated, leaving a world where people used and consumed truly meaningful terminology and language.

Gamely serving their purpose, press releases and their turgid wording live on, though something truly important happened in the meantime. Thanks to social media, communicators are forced to relearn the language of the living room in addition to their mastery of the language of the boardroom.

Think about the consequences of confusing the two:

- If you use the language of the boardroom in the living room, you might find your invites coming to an abrupt halt.

- If you use the language of the living room in the boardroom, you might find your *employment* coming to a halt. (Or maybe that is just the language of *my* living room, but you get the point.)

When someone opens up their lives to Twitter, Facebook, their blog or any online social platform, they bring their living rooms online: the discussions, the news, the memories, the heartaches, the joys, the hobbies, the job stress, the hopes and the dreams. Many—solo or in aggregate, intentionally or deliberately—have become media, influencers, pundits, or any number of descriptors that are so often applied to the parties with whom PR professionals are tasked with building and maintaining relationships.

We now live in a world where personality can be just as important as positioning in terms of winning sustained attention or credibility. To those communicators who have long struggled under the yoke of boardroom language, now is your chance. Your boardroom skills are highly valuable, but stakeholders also want to hear from *you*, not just the organization you represent. To those who are just now exploring a public relations career, I cannot think of a better time.

The third rail is yours.

DISCUSSION QUESTIONS

1. Who is credited with being a pioneer in Silicon Valley marketing?
2. What is the difference between an important problem and an interesting one? Why does this matter?
3. Why do you think that PR practitioners experienced resistance by their peers and clients in the early days of social media?
4. Phil's onetime client said, "Don't blog. No one really wants to hear from a PR person who thinks!" To what degree should a PR person be an industry participant and to what degree is there riskin "becoming part of the story?"
5. There's a distinction made between the language of the boardroom and that of the living room. What is meant by this and why is it important for a communicator to know the difference?

THE FUTURE OF PUBLIC RELATIONS

BY STEVE RUBEL

Future casting is a notoriously tricky practice. It is easy to be consistently wrong.

Five years ago, for example, Twitter, Facebook and YouTube were tiny or nonexistent. Today, all three are giants. They command significant chunks of our attention and therefore, understandably, ad dollars.

What's more, five years ago many of us, including this writer, were questioning what the rise of social technologies would mean for the media's long-term viability. It turned out that journalists' embrace of these channels actually made them stronger.

Consider ABCNews.com, for example. Today the majority of the site's video views come either from social networking sources or search engines.[7] This means that for communicators, there is now another layer: new social filters sit on top of the traditional filters.

The upshot here is that in the near-term future, communicators will need to study the dynamic between these layers, harness them and build appropriate plans. The pace of change won't slow anytime soon. The noise in the media and technology sectors, with its daily twists and turns, makes it harder than ever to spot meaningful trends. There is still too much focus on what Twitter and Facebook are doing versus how news circulates and how consumers digest, interact and collaborate around it.

With this as the backdrop, we outline three key global medium-term trends that are fairly bankable, independent of the specific channels that may prevail. Specifically, we will look at how technology will do the following:

- Scale content, yet leave attention relatively finite

- Shift trust toward validated authority figures

- Adjust how stories are told and retold

ATTENTIONOMICS

Without question, in the future we will be consuming more information in digital form than analog.

Already, Amazon sells more Kindle eBooks than it does paperbacks. Video viewership on mobile devices is increasing dramatically. And large newspapers are beginning the painful transition to a completely digital future.

According to Google Executive Chairman Eric Schmidt, the amount of information generated every two days[8] is equal to what had existed in entirety before 2003. Much of this comes from new sources—our tweets, videos, status updates and more.

All of this information, however, comes at a premium. The digital space is infinite. It will scale to accommodate whatever we want. Our time and attention, however, are limited resources. They remain finite.

The Internet is rewiring our brains. The data is already beginning to show just how this will influence how we consume and vet news and information.

According to the 2011 Edelman Trust Barometer[9], informed publics need to hear things three to five times before they trust it. In addition, the same study found that we turn first to search engines over online news sources.

Studies by the Nielsen Norman group found that people, in general, read just 20 percent of any given web page and spend just seconds on it before deciding to move on.

This means that planning and measuring campaigns purely on reach—which is how we have operated for years—can no longer be the norm. Communicators will understand that attention is the first step toward economic value. And they will adjust their thinking.

For example, many emerging pure-play digital outlets such as Mashable and Sports Blog Nation have lower circulations than traditional outlets, yet have far higher rates of attention in terms of time spent, amplification on Twitter and their ability to influence search results. These will start to be front-loaded in programs.

In addition, communicators will begin to show rather than tell and make greater use of images and videos.

DIGITAL THOUGHT LEADERSHIP

Authority is shifting yet again. There are signs that we are beginning the *next* great digital era. In this age it will be critical for companies to propagate new ideas.

During the first era, Commercialization (1994–2002), only well-capitalized media companies and brands could command authority. During this time, the mainstream media incumbents and a few first movers, such as Yahoo!, were the sole voices of authority.

The dot-com crash deflated cost of bandwidth and storage and made publishing technologies easier to use and open to all. This, coupled with the rising sophistication of mobile devices, gave rise to the age of Democratization (2002–2010).

During this time anyone could use social technologies to become influential. This was evident in the 2006 Edelman Trust Barometer when peers became the most trusted sources of authority.

Now, a new day is dawning. Too much of anything is never a good thing. And that's exactly what we're seeing with social media. There is too much content and not enough time. There has been a glut of "friending," and many are unsure of whom to trust.

The 2011 Edelman Trust Barometer, much like the 2006 study, brings this to light. It revealed that informed publics are increasingly looking at accredited and technical experts as the most credible sources of authority. We are now entering the age of Validation.

For communicators to succeed in this epoch, they will need to increasingly work within their companies or clients to identify individuals who can become thought leaders. Social media will be one way to do this, and in the future it will not be just 100 percent of 1 person's job, but 1 percent of 100 people's role.

TRANSMEDIA STORYTELLING

If there is one constant in a world of change, it's that we love stories. Storytelling is an art. It remains essential for helping companies connect.

However, technology is changing our expectations for what a story should look like. Witness, for example, the way that *Toy Story* and *Avatar* altered film. The end result is that today, a narrative is no longer sequential—a beginning, middle and an end. Rather it unfolds in different places at different times, leaving it to the stakeholder to decide how to connect the pieces.

What this means is that communication professionals will need to learn how to hand craft their content for each part of the cloverleaf Richard Edelman speaks to, and also harmonize them. The stories we tell (and others tell) in each section of the cloverleaf needs to lead our stakeholders to pursue the rest of the story across the others.

Content is key to this. Public relations professionals will need to learn how to help their clients and employees become their own media companies so that the stories we tell in other clovers encourage stakeholders to seek our own content for greater depth and meaning.

DISCUSSION QUESTIONS

1. How do you and your peers filter information? Are there leanings here that can inform your view of how news and information spreads across channels?
2. What is an example of a strong PR campaign that leveraged lots of different spokespeople across the media cloverleaf and elevated the company as a thought leader?
3. How has the use of mobile devices changed how we consume and create news? How will it continue to do so going forward and what does this mean for attention?
4. Will Facebook and other social networks as well as Google become our primary filter for news? If so, how do we need to prepare?

NOTES

1. Indian government official in a private conversation.
2. Terry McGraw, CEO of McGraw-Hill Companies.
3. June 2010 figures released by Facebook.
4. LinkedIn blog, July 7, 2010. Note: Edelman client.
5. Note: Edelman client.
6. Both practices relate to influencing corrupt government officials to make decisions favorable to certain individuals or companies. The recent 2G telecom scandal, where licenses were sold at well below market value, is one recent example of this.
7. "ABCNews.com Gets Seventy Percent of Video Views via Links and Search, Says Digital Chief," *Beet TV*, April 8, 2011.
8. Eric Schmidt, "Every Two Days We Create As Much Information As We Did Up to 2003," *TechCrunch*, August 4, 2010.
9. www.edelman.com/trust/2011.

ADDITIONAL READING

www.edelman.com/speak_up/blog. Edelman.
www.edelmanfellows.com/pages/home.aspx. Edelman.
blog.philgomes.com. Phil Gomes.
www.awpagesociety.com. Arthur W. Page Society.
www.prsa.org. Public Relations Society of America.
www.steverubel.me. Steve Rubel.

17

C H A P T E R

GLOBAL MEDIA RELATIONS
Traditional through 2.0

Matthew P. Gonring
Vice President, Corporate Communications
Jackson National Life Insurance Company

STRATEGY: MEDIA RELATIONS DEFINED

Balance.

This one word best summarizes the challenge for this particular area of public relations management and communications. From delivering your message to key audiences to meeting the requirements of journalists, media relations is an exercise in tightrope walking. In an era of global and networked communications, the difficulty lies in practicing a worldwide strategy while keeping local interests in mind.

Media relations—communicating with the news media verbally or through assorted media channels—must also balance public opinion and transparency with business strategy. It does so by monitoring social trends and political landscapes, counseling management and cultivating relationships both internally and externally. For today's global companies, media relations must also manage to successfully straddle the convergence between digital dialogue, emerging trends and the worldwide public's thirst for news and information. This broad perspective differentiates media relations from publicity. Media relations professionals around the world use press releases and a broad array of tactics to manage information flows and, ultimately, media exposure. In effect, they strategize on multidimensional levels to manage press coverage in shaping the opinions of important constituents.

Who these constituents are varies by organizational objectives. In a networked world it becomes increasingly challenging to target specific audiences via the media because virtually everything is in the public domain. Twitter feeds that expose the misdoings of various celebrities, political and Hollywood. Journalists and the general public alike use search engine technology to find and research qualified (and occasionally, unqualified) information on any subject matter.

The following factors shape the role of the media relations function:

Type of organization
Public/private nature of the enterprise
Relationship between visibility-reputation and revenue-profitability
Media interest in the products, services or other organizational activities
Expectations of the organization
The importance of and extent to which its stakeholders are networked.

Depending on media relations' role within the organization, its activities can assume one or more of these three approaches: reactive, proactive or interactive, as seen in the media relations continuum in Figure 17.1.

Reactive media relations fields and responds to inquiries. Professionals should follow these general guidelines when the media call:

Always avoid immediate comment and off-the-cuff remarks.
Keep an up-to-date file of issues likely to attract media attention.
Understand and acknowledge deadlines.
Always be available and respond to inquiries promptly.
Be curious and ask questions.
Place yourself in the journalist's "shoes."
Provide a balanced perspective or know which company expert will be able to provide it.
Identify helpful background information.
Set internal expectations appropriately.
Keep records: whom you talked to and what you said.
Never lie.

Proactive media relations builds on these 11 reactive steps, going further to promote and publicize the organization. A proactive role is equivalent to thought leadership positioning—essentially about generating business. It is an organized approach to capture share of mind and voice in the media about a specific subject or subjects. Virtually all proactive media relations begin by answering these 12 questions:

Do you know the messages you want to deliver and the desired outcome?
What is the most effective way to communicate your message?
What is the "right" medium for your message?
Are your messages clear, concise and straightforward?
Which media do you want to reach in order of priority?
Which reporter and/or editor should you target?
What are the newsworthy elements to your message and how do they relate to trends in the news?
How should you package or sell your item?
What else is in the public domain?
Who are the key third parties, and what will they say? Journalists often seek out other qualified sources.
When contacting reporters/bloggers, have you listened for signs that they are busy or uninterested?
Do reporters understand you will go elsewhere if they are uninterested?

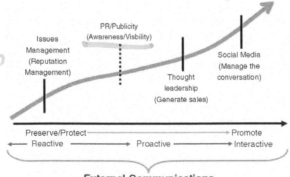

FIGURE 17.1

Media Relations Continuum

Professionals who major in interactive media relations go even deeper to develop a "give and take" rapport with the press. Their reasoning: media interest and subsequent coverage evolve from positive, regular ongoing interactions. In working with bloggers, for instance, media relations experts look to understand their specific communities of interest; that understanding leads to providing them targeted information about products, services or specific issues that interests their followers. Here are a dozen ways to reach this level:

Discuss issues other than your news that may be of interest, including topics they have covered.
Be a source; make yourself available for comment as an expert in your industry or category.
Always think in terms of their needs and deadlines; a few minutes of advance notice may make you a hero.
Exclusivity should depend on the subject, organizational objectives, fair disclosure laws and other ramifications.
Be able to converse in depth on timely news topics and industry trends.
With blogs, periodically participate in the conversation as well as regularly track the content of popular bloggers.
Talk about other publications and reporters and how they approach different issues.
Be complimentary, not thankful, about articles they have written. Reporters are taught to be unbiased and do not want to be considered simply a mouthpiece.
Call to talk about relevant news and to keep in touch.
Look for legitimate non-news reasons to interact with the news media.
Avoid asking favors; only make suggestions.
Adjust your message and conversation according to the reporter's time constraints and level of interest.

Taking an interactive approach to media relations is more easily said than done. Professionals who seek to develop their position within an organization can do so by developing a framework for success based on the following:

Knowledge of the business
Knowledge of the subject matter
Understanding of what is news (news must be timely, relevant and compelling to the audience)
Extensive internal network that will provide information and knowledge
Knowledge of external third-party experts for referral
Familiarity and comfort with conversations on world events and business news
An approach that is consistent with internal management expectations
Practical, hands-on experience in dealing with news media
Knowledge of each reporter's reputation and track record
Understanding of how particular news media outlets have covered news
Interpersonal skills
Relationships built over a professional lifetime

Since the media are a conduit that reaches thousands, millions, even billions of your audiences, these efforts can pay substantial dividends. Depending on the medium, they also have the advantage of being perceived as independent, lending your message third-party credibility.

Effective media relations begins with understanding the inherent differences in the media's needs and approaches. Those differences are determined by readers, viewers and listeners, since each medium must address its own users and their perception of the content's value. Although unique characteristics differentiate the world's media, many "basics" apply across the globe. Here are descriptions for the general media:

Daily newspapers structure their newsrooms around beats, assignment desks and sections. They cover breaking and local news and features and need access to quotable sources, background information and visuals. Usually on tight deadlines, editors of daily newspapers must weed through hundreds of press releases, looking for the few that break through the clutter. Increasingly, daily newspapers are placing greater emphasis on their online versions. Daily newspapers have undergone considerable restructuring as advertising revenue has shifted more to online; the cost of newsprint and physical distribution has increased;

MEDIA INFLUENCE

The media's influence with the general public is particularly strong since most people rely heavily on the media for their information. However, there are no guarantees. The media retain their influence because they shape and control what information is disseminated, when and in what form. Thus, media relations becomes a management practice with influence but without control.

and new generations of consumers are more accustomed to getting their regular dose of daily news online.

Weekly newspapers operate with limited editorial staff. They generally take a feature or local focus. Many weekly newspapers demand a local focus and will not use information without it. Suburban weekly papers frequently rely on freelancers and local sources of information.

Regional and national magazines have varied resources, depending on their subject matters, circulations and advertising revenues. Their editorial staff are frequently dedicated to a specific subject or regional coverage. They want high-level access, often exclusivity, for visuals and quotes.

Trade magazines usually operate with skeleton editorial staff and limited resources. They take a subject focus and rely heavily on freelancers and outside sources. Industry professionals often write articles and provide case studies.

Special-interest publications target niche audiences, such as ethnic groups, sports enthusiasts, collectors and other groups with distinct lifestyles or interests. These media seek information that can benefit their specific audiences, presenting this information in the language or jargon of their audience.

Newsletters usually specialize in one subject area and tend to take a more detailed, in-depth approach. They generally assume readers have previous knowledge of the subject.

Regional and national television stations have a breaking news and entertainment orientation and will sometimes present features. They need access for visuals and are always on tight deadlines.

Cable television has given rise to a host of special-interest channels and communities. They generally take a feature orientation and serve a specific purpose.

Regional and national radio stations have limited staff support and focus on breaking news with occasional features. They need audio for on-air broadcast. (Radio news releases include localized interviews and are a good way to obtain a great deal of coverage in a short period.)

Wire services—such as financial/investor research wires—track breaking or market-moving news with spot assignments. News wire services, including the Associated Press, cover the day's breaking news with occasional features. Wire services need accurate facts and data *fast*.

Internet or online services are becoming the preferred choice for Gen X, Gen Y, the Millennials and Baby Boomers alike. Because online has low distribution costs and an ability to build communities of interest, advertisers increasingly favor these media. Online offers companies a means of communicating instantaneously and interactively with customers, investors and employees globally. The company can gather database information and provide up-to-the-minute news, product information and financial data.

Social Media

Blogging. Blogging allows almost anyone to become a published journalist. Think of it as an online editorial, attracting readers through the value and popularity of content. Plus, readers can weigh in via a comment stream that allows multiple parties to contribute their perspectives on particular areas of interest or strains of dialogue.

Vlogging. Video blogging continues to grow in popularity driven by sites such as YouTube, where anyone can post Flash and video information on the web. The proliferation of relatively low-cost, high-quality HD video equipment like the Flip camera, not to mention the traditional media's promotion of clips on air, has converted many to videography. While not a traditional medium, the influence and viewership of YouTube and other video sites is an important part of the arsenal of a media relations professional. Whether simply monitoring or actively "pushing" video to the web, professionals need to consider YouTube one of the critical media of choice to get broad viewership. It is, however, highly dependent on the content, which, in turn, relies on viewer interest.

TRENDS AND DEVELOPMENTS

The business community's perception of the media (and vice versa) has been called everything from starry eyed to mutual contempt. The latter opinion was fueled by the global financial crises of September 11, the dot-com bubble and meltdown of global financial markets in 2008 to 2010. In the 1950s, public relations professionals viewed the media as targets for positive publicity. Reporters believed they were contributing to the economic system by reporting positive product and company news. That is not to say media attacks on business are a new phenomenon; they have been affecting American industry since the early 1900s. It is difficult, however, to pinpoint the moment when reporters began to envision themselves as the drivers of business reform. Specific industries, companies, products and business practices came under siege by critical reporters who initiated a wave of investigative reporting.[1]

While this skepticism continues today, a greater degree of personal respect is building between journalists and public relations practitioners. Both are beginning to realize that their relationship depends on mutual influence and dependence. For example, it is estimated that 25 to 95 percent of the editorial material contained in published or broadcast media either originates with, or involves, a public relations professional. Similarly, business relies on the media to tell its story and to help identify the potential impact of major decisions. At most of the prestigious journalism schools, aspiring journalists are counseled about their responsibility to be unbiased, accurate, fair and balanced.

To develop relationships with the media, communications professionals should provide access and information designed and packaged to meet the needs of journalists. This is even more critical today, as media staff have been pared to the bone. More than ever, many reporters need and rely on outside help. At the same time, cutbacks in media staff, contracting newspapers and less editorial space make it more difficult to get coverage. This requires you to "sell your story" by personalizing it to meet the journalist's needs, ultimately reflecting the expectations of their consumers.

As the journalists' reliable source, you can help them do their jobs and avoid their two greatest fears: missing the story and having their integrity challenged. Supply journalists with enough information to uncover all the angles and insights, but never allow them to become your mouthpiece. Instead, learn what approach the journalist is taking and offer the relevant information. Start with these descriptions of common media approaches to news reporting:

Hard or breaking news—reports facts and balances them

Forward spin—looks ahead or analyzes future impact; used in features

Point of view—draws a conclusion based on research, sometimes biased

Consumer interest—carries particular interest to buyers of products and services; uses surveys and research to provide information that the average shopper can use

Opinion—represents reporter's or publication's view on a subject, supported by rationale and studies

Entertainment—has novel or even sensational appeal and is favored by TV and tabloid media

Profiles—takes an in-depth look at interesting personalities

Introspective analysis—examines a subject through the eyes of an individual

Historical—describes what has occurred before and its influence on today's events

Tension—uses controversy or opposing viewpoints, often played up by reporters

The media's mission to report the news is being made more difficult by the industry's fragmentation, forcing media to fight for market share and cut operating costs. The number of media options—online and cable programming, in particular—continues to proliferate. Technology and the Internet are creating these new outlets, while both simultaneously change the way the media cover the news. Technology in all its forms has quickened the pace of reporting, while the Internet enables anyone with computer access to download information in the seconds it takes for Google (and other search engines) to complete the query.

Reporters from all media outlets have quickly adapted to the instant information age as local outlets compete with online media and use news gathering and interconnections to be complete, timely and interesting for their own consumers. Media relations professionals must tailor their approach to meet the information needs of this new breed of reporters while understanding how they service the needs of their subscribers.

Fortunately, new software products and services provided by a variety of vendors are enabling media relations professionals to easily store, organize, transmit and use large amounts of media-related information. Some are hosted by the vendor in an on-demand manner and others are available with software that can be regularly updated.

EMERGENCE OF THE BLOGOSPHERE

As a consequence of the Internet revolution, aspiring journalists and amateur writers have jumped on the opportunity to produce information or "blogs" that could be viewed, accessed and commented on by others. Bloggers have grown in popularity, building communities of interest and garnering the support of advertisers and organizations seeking publicity. Search engines direct traffic to these bloggers, and sophisticated digital marketing firms track, direct and analyze content and drive traffic.

This increasing media sophistication extends to local markets throughout the world. Media fragmentation can also be seen in the growing number of publications targeted toward specific communities of interest. Nonetheless, traditional media relations activities still predominate. Developing economies and varying economic systems compound the challenge of delivering effective media relations. New opportunities abound in developing economies across the globe, where living standards are rising and countries are adopting more flexible trading policies. Thus, understanding the varying nuances between these countries is vital. The Japanese, for instance, have a sophisticated press club system in place and rarely accept a news release at face value. In Hong Kong, however, a press release written in Cantonese will often be printed almost as is.[2] According to a 2004 report by Weber Shandwick, in recent years the Chinese media has had more flexibility and editorial control, but the regulation of media outlets by the Propaganda Department of the Central Committee of the Communist Party of China can still be a challenge. It is important to keep in mind that the Chinese government tightly controls all media outlets, and media are required to cover important government events.

As a result, media relations campaigns need to time news releases to ensure announcements do not clash with major national events. Issues labeled sensitive by the government also need to be handled carefully. It's also good practice for companies operating in local jurisdictions to underscore their commitment to contributing to the local economy and community, and acknowledging local partners. However, this could come into conflict with the Foreign Corruption Practices Act of the United States; corporate legal counsel will be invaluable here.

In developing economies, it is not unusual for news media to expect reimbursement for expenses and to be compensated for press exposure. The form varies from country to country, outlet to outlet. Controls on the media in developing economies are also a frequent reality, with officials censoring foreign newspapers, controlling web access and banning direct satellite dishes. The same challenges of government-controlled media exist in Latin America, although Puerto Rico and Mexico are two Spanish-speaking markets where public relations has developed rapidly.[3]

Consumerism is spreading worldwide, fueling business growth and a demand for business communications. The next section explores business' immediate need for media relations.

CONTRIBUTION TO OVERALL CORPORATE GOALS

In an era of increased accountability, "contributing to corporate goals" often means demonstrating your impact on the bottom line. Showing the "link" between business outcomes and the goals of media relations is an ever-present challenge. More business executives are beginning to understand the interconnections between responsible media relations, corporate image, brand building, reputation and sales. In other words, media relations' credibility-building attributes help companies secure investors and lenders, attract and retain talent and strengthen supplier-customer relationships—all of which contribute to bottom-line success. These considerations are of particular importance for truly global companies. By being seen as a credible, contributing member of the local community, a U.S.-based company can link its corporate name to its products and services—without taking on the guise of a foreign invader.

Unifying the communications of local operations with those of the corporate office requires open, collaborative and candid channels of information. Communication to the media must also embody those characteristics.

Top executives must therefore participate and be accessible, even in the midst of "bad news." Despite companies' conditioned fear of in-depth reporting, candid communication pays off in more objective coverage. The same theory applies to risk communication, or reporting on the hazards of everyday life. Bringing your management into the communication loop enables you to train them to proactively address potentially controversial issues. Media relations professionals must also work to make risk communications part of a larger risk management program.

> Media relations' credibility-building attributes help companies secure investors and lenders, attract and retain talent and strengthen supplier–customer relationships—all of which contribute to bottom-line success.

Media and public relations should also be incorporated into the larger business strategy, with every communication considering and cognizant of its impact on specific stakeholders. It almost goes without saying that professionals must clearly understand the company's goals and how it plans to achieve them. For a corporation's international companies or divisions, individual business-communication plans will be based on local markets, issues, culture and products. The news media approach, then, will vary from country to country, all integrated by a global communications strategy.

At the same time, local-market media communications must support the organization's mission, including its sales and marketing objectives, if media relations is to increase its stature inside the organization.

It starts, in part, by collaboration between media relations and marketing, working together to build credibility that protects and increases sales of company products and services. Media training can sometimes be used to gain better preparedness and understanding on behalf of non-PR professionals to more effectively execute campaigns.

When both functions are learning new ways of operating overseas, each benefit from the other in terms of experiences. By reviewing marketing plans, strategies, white papers and research, media relations professionals quickly get up to speed on the vagaries of local markets. Similarly, media relations helps marketing identify broader issues that might affect sales. By keeping a pulse on the marketplace, media relations will counsel against marketing ideas that just won't fly in a local market or that might have unintended consequences to other important stakeholders. Marketing executives also turn to media relations for creative ideas that act as viable and less-expensive advertising substitutes to reach audiences efficiently.

The advice to "think globally, act locally" has become cliché. Media relations professionals have learned that their approach must depend on the local market's culture, media sophistication, and the economic and political situation. However, one need not separate national from international news. With fewer companies limiting business activities to domestic only and the global nature of web-based communications, many issues now matter to Asians as well as Europeans and Latin Americans. Moreover, editors often want to hear from public relations professionals inside corporate headquarters. They are also eager for contact with top executives since most reporters often deal only with corporations' overseas representatives.

Local considerations still come into play, however. People and companies with high profiles in one country may not be as well known in other parts of the world. Relevance, timing and wording are key requirements when operating across time zones. *International Public Relations in Practice* suggests that companies answer the following questions before carrying out public relations efforts in local overseas markets:

Does the local press accept news releases? Or do they expect payment?
What types of promotions work?
Do the local media accept tie-in promotions?
Does the government have a strong "corrupt practices" branch? (If so, it can be very restricting.)
What is the local attitude toward sponsorships?
Are charity donations accepted or construed as bribes?
Is there a local trade or technical press? (This is a good beginning for media relations campaigns.)
Has public relations drawn up an attitude survey, which differs from marketing research?
How will the organization's local standing affect its credit rating and hiring ability?

BUDGETING AND MEASUREMENT CONSIDERATIONS

Cost management challenges all multinational companies. And the fact that media relations is relationship based and must be executed locally creates extra program costs. Careful budgeting takes goals and objectives into consideration, as well as a thorough understanding of the effectiveness and capabilities of the many media channels. Careful planning becomes crucial, not only as a way to determine the cost of a media campaign but also for management evaluation. Dispelling the myth of "free" publicity enables media relations professionals to prove their worth. This requires educating management about the differences between disseminating press releases and building credibility for a company's products and services. The former, unfortunately, is the popular definition of publicity; the latter is what responsible media relations accomplish. But neither effort is "free" or easy or without potential risk.

To play the budgeting game effectively, media relations professionals must remain flexible and creative and know how to do more with less. Creating skeleton budgets of all relevant expenses helps document media relations' efforts while providing valuable insight into an array of considerations. With news conferences and special events, in particular, always expect the unexpected. Budgeting is made easier by consulting such resources as *The Professional's Guide to Public Relations Services* (H&M Publishers, Rhinebeck, NY). The services listed can be contacted and then compared based on current prices and written estimates.

TACTICS: EXECUTING A MEDIA RELATIONS STRATEGY

Tactics set media relations objectives in motion and thus play an important role in media relations strategy and planning. A company trying to build sales in a specific industry, for example, could use media relations to provide trade media helpful information on the company's products and services. The tactics to achieve the strategy can include engaging industry journalists, sending press kits to industry trade media, and connecting with relevant bloggers and thought leadership forums at industry trade shows. See the following example of a media relations plan for a manufacturing automation supplier (Figure 17.2).

Example of Media Relations Plan for Manufacturing Automation Supplier

Objective:	Increase awareness of the application of products and systems in manufacturing technology by 25 percent.
Strategy:	Engage journalists important to the industry by inviting them to a daylong demonstration in advance of the company's annual trade show.
Possible tactics:	• Share case examples showing successful product applications with quantified productivity improvements.
	• Give them access to customers and members of senior management to discuss successes
	• Provide supporting visuals, data and background information to enable them to understand and ultimately tell the story.
	• Address the macro-economic trends affecting the business environment; provide participation in actual working session applications.
	• Have a noteworthy, keynote speaker address timely and topical issues in manufacturing.
	• Provide an economic outlook for the year ahead with a leading economist.

FIGURE 17.2

Sample Media Relations Plan

For instance, Rockwell Automation, a Fortune 250 systems, technology and components automation supplier, decided it wanted to create a thought leadership platform for its capabilities and accomplishments in helping manufacturing companies automate. To help implement the marketing of this strategy, the media relations department invited journalists to a thought leadership day to meet with executives and to hear and see case examples of how the products and systems improved manufacturing productivity, effectiveness and output.

Tactical examples include setting up a proprietary website to access information including videos, product demonstrations, testimonials and image libraries; distributing timely, useful information to industry trade publications; and personally calling editors and syndicated writers. The choice of tactics depends on your media relations objectives. Here is a list of just a few tactical options:

Audio releases or podcasts (for radio)

Backgrounders (as a supplement for news)

B-roll (unedited video) or background footage gives video outlets the opportunity to pick and choose elements for development of a story

Bylined articles (authored by "experts")

Community calendar listings (similar to public service announcements)

CD or DVD disks (can include product demonstrations and other detailed graphics)

Fact sheets (as a supplement to news releases)

Faxes (while outdated, is still an alternative means to gain attention)

Features (publication articles or broadcast programs)

Fillers (supply sidebars, illustrations, lists and other "quick reads")

Letters to the editor (one of the most underused media relations tools)

Mat releases (camera-ready copy and photos)

Media advisory (for press invitations and very timely items)

Media roundtables featuring subject matter experts

Media kits (range from simple folders filled with information to elaborate packages of giveaways and samples)

Op-ed pieces (take a point of view on an issue)

Phone calls (preferred by some editors, especially when breaking news)

Photos (avoid clichés and make them eye-catching; may help get your story published or used alone as filler or, when offered exclusively, go over wire services networks)

Pitch letters (personalize them)

Press conferences (make sure your reason is *very* newsworthy)

Press releases (target recipients carefully to avoid wasteful mailing)

PAs or PSAs (public service announcements)

Q&A's (most relevant questions and answers)

Quote sheets (gives media qualified quotes they can use)

Search engine optimization (gets your product, company or service at the top of the list when users are searching information)

Talk and interview shows (more risk involved, but can be worth it)

Trade shows (multitude of opportunities from exhibiting products to hosting elaborate press and customer receptions)

Tweets (links to press releases, announcements, advisories, etc.)

Video (be careful not to skimp on quality)

Video news releases (video feed to TV stations; aim for broadcast quality and make your news integral to the story)

When selecting appropriate tactics, know what your target media prefers. With financial news, certain disclosure requirements *must* be followed. News that could have a bearing on your company's stock price should be disclosed simultaneously by the quickest means possible. This requires sending it through a qualified newswire service. Choose these services carefully and ask lots of questions, particularly about distribution.

Overseas, these tactics can vary—and widely. For instance, the press in other countries often meets with companies at the close of the business day, not at the time-honored U.S. lunch meeting. And news conferences in some countries begin promptly at the appointed hour, while others make it customary to wait 30 minutes. Also, the list of attendees for news conferences can include everyone from government officials, local bankers and dignitaries to the company's customers and sales representatives.

The language issue can be resolved by having translators or technology-enabled translations and by composing press kits in English as well as the host country's official language. Company spokespersons should also be trained to avoid American slang and business jargon. Also, any giveaways must consider local taboos. Ways to learn about local customs and make media contacts include in-depth briefings from local public relations agencies, the expat U.S. community, local press clubs, and your own marketing people.

INTERNAL MEDIA RELATIONS

Before approaching the media, sell your story internally. By earning the trust of senior management, you can teach them the benefits of open communication and prepare your organization for possible media confrontations. Achieving this level of respect within the organization better enables you, as media relations professional, to turn potentially negative situations to your company's advantage.

Here and abroad, relationships depend not only on cultural understanding but also on professional conduct. For instance, media relations professionals must understand journalism and be knowledgeable about their subject matter. Knowing how to "sell" one's story using strong written and verbal communications skills is also crucial.

MEASURING THE SUCCESS OF TACTICS

Demonstrable results build credibility and strengthen the media relations function. Accurate program measurement is difficult enough here at home and multiplies significantly as media relations takes on a global reach. Given the challenge of pan-European comparisons, for instance, media relations must depend on country-by-country evaluation. Media delivery measurements vary between countries, creating inconsistent data. Increasingly sophisticated databases and instant access to all web-based information is simplifying measurement, but understanding the actual *effects* of media coverage will continue to elude many.

Monitoring and distribution services currently provide audience profiles and can detect whether the message was mostly positive or negative and can search for the inclusion of key words or phrases. On the other hand, technology lacks the human ability to analyze. As a result, media relations professionals must rely on limited sentiment tracking technologies while combining them with their own interpretation. Measurements currently available are as follows:

Clipping services. Same-day services are an alternative to databases; pertinent clips are gathered on the date of publication. Some vendors even "analyze" clips and assign ratings on the basis of the clippings' position in the publication.

Transcript services. Clients can access transcripts or electronic clips from news summaries of network, cable and local news.

Content analysis services. Using sophisticated computer analysis, these services go beyond readership and audience figures, tracking media comprehensively. Data tracking will prove helpful in articulating progress to management as well as identifying opportunities or shortcomings of media relations programming.

Surveying. Periodic surveying of journalists to ask if they are getting what they need and what they find helpful is a good way to ascertain to what extent you are meeting their needs.

Sentiment analysis. This derivative of content analysis uses sophisticated modeling to identify positive or negative human "feelings" associated with media coverage of organizations. Several firms have taken content analysis further by tracking and analyzing sentiment, or the degree to which media relations efforts have affected attitudes, opinions and sentiment. While not officially a science, many organizations have used this methodology to articulate progress of media relations efforts.

CASE STUDY: PACTIV GETS PUT IN PLAY—2010

It all began with a call from the *Wall Street Journal* on a Friday afternoon at 3 PM, when a journalist called with a rumor that private equity investors were considering making an offer to acquire Pactiv Corporation. The first order of the day is to understand exactly what the journalist had in terms of qualified information and what his intentions were in writing something. The second order of the day was to make certain that I understood what was actually going on so that I could advise senior leadership on the proper course for handling this inquiry and, of course, the countless number of additional queries that would follow any media coverage on the topic. The journalist began by testing his information with me. He seemed to be giving Pactiv a chance to respond. He also seemed to be trying to ascertain if he was the "first" to break the story.

On the website of Pactiv on June 14, 2011, it states:

> Pactiv Corporation is a leader in the consumer and foodservice–food packaging markets it serves. With 2009 sales of $3.4 billion, Pactiv derives more than 80% of its sales from market sectors in which it holds the No. 1 or No. 2 market-share position. Pactiv's Hefty brand products include waste bags, slider storage bags, disposable tableware and disposable cookware. Pactiv's foodservice–food packaging offering is one of the broadest in the industry, including both custom and stock products in a variety of materials. Pactiv Corporation was acquired by Reynolds Group Holdings Limited on November 16, 2010. As a result of the acquisition, Pactiv is now privately held and its stock is no longer traded on the New York Stock Exchange (www.pactiv.com/).

On June 14, 2011, it was reported that Rank Group, owned by New Zealand's richest man Graeme Hart, was the mystery bidder behind a US$1.64 billion (NZD$2.01 billion) bid for Graham Packaging Co, said a source familiar with the situation, trumping an earlier bid from Silgan Holdings. Privately held Rank, led by Hart, a former tow-truck driver now estimated by Forbes to have a net worth of US$5.5 billion, has a track record of big acquisitions. In 2008, Rank bought Alcoa Packaging & Consumer Group for US$2.7 billion, a business it later renamed Reynolds Packaging Group. Last year, Reynolds acquired Pactiv, the maker of Hefty garbage bags, for $US4.6 billion, plus debt, in one of the largest packaging industry deals in years (www.stuff.co.nz/business/world/5140181/Harts-Rank-Group-behind-mystery-bid).

He appeared to hold off for the weekend apparently seeking to further qualify his sources. He called on Sunday evening to advise me that it would be in Monday's edition of the *Wall Street Journal (WSJ)*. Of course we had no choice other than to go with "no comment." We had spent the weekend advising the Board of Directors of the potential *WSJ* story and organized a meeting of senior leadership for first thing Monday morning. The goal of the weekend planning was to make sure the work force understood that financial offers and rumors about them happen in business and might happen again. We would advise them of any pertinent actions, but we asked that they stay focused on their jobs.

Subsequent media inquiries were handled mostly on a reactive basis, always trying to learn more about the source and nature of the rumors and advising journalists of their responsibility to make certain that rumors were from credible, qualified and multiple sources. Media management was a daily exercise in responding, keeping records, monitoring and keeping senior leadership advised in real time. Maintaining a rapport with journalists, keeping tabs on what they were pursuing and trying to help them avoid "looking foolish" without publicly commenting were among the challenges. Ultimately, we announced that the Board of Directors had agreed to a deal of $33.25 per share from private equity player Rank Group Limited of New Zealand. Once the news media learned of the deal, press coverage quickly advanced to the next stage focusing on Rank's efforts to raise capital and close the deal. Media interest quickly waned once the deal mania was sorted out. The media were not as interested in a story about Pactiv's moving into private equity ownership.

1. How can a company effectively manage press exposure when its official stance is "no comment"?

2. How can company spokespeople maintain contact with the media without commenting on the record?

3. What is the best method to ensure that journalists carefully sort out the qualified nature of their sources?

4. How is it possible to encourage a journalist to avoid going with information that is inaccurate?

5. Is it clear why "no comment" is the only safe comment in the face of rumors?

THE FUTURE

FUTURE TRENDS WILL CHANGE MEDIA RELATIONS

New forms of media monitoring and information dissemination will build on the progress described previously. The proliferation of online sources and the replacement of print are changing the manner in which news is absorbed and viewed. Online is traditionally shorter in length of copy, but greater space is allocated for specialty communities of interest. New, imaginative forms of information distribution will continue to emerge, requiring media relations professionals to continue if not anticipate the trends. It will become increasingly difficult to control the speed of two-way, interactive communication, while the visual influence of these communications will have impact on the corporate image more than ever before.

THE FUTURE BELONGS TO FORWARD-THINKING MANAGERS

This new high-impact media will have a profound influence on public opinion around the globe. As a result, media relations must become more of a knowledge-based profession. The competition to reach these key constituencies will become even more intense.

Just as the speed and quantity of information will increase, so too must its quality. This means honing information and personalizing it for increasingly diverse audiences. Technology will continue to drive this segmentation, introducing new ways to reach defined targets. More media relations professionals will use these new e-communications to distribute information to targeted communities of interest and local media. Already online global media services are localizing versions as they identify users and adjust content according to a specific profile. At the same time, messages must remain consistent if they are to unite the corporation's local and global interests. This integration requires media relations to join forces with issues management, law, human resources, finance and marketing. Together, the various corporate functions can ensure clear and consistent emphasis on key messages. A constant state of readiness enables global companies to manage and influence events *before* they occur.

EDUCATION AND TRAINING RESPOND TO FUTURE NEEDS

Media relations must be part of this integrated marketing communications mix if it is to provide consistent messages and achieve measurable results. The first requirement—an understanding of how other disciplines operate—is achieved through training in government relations, employee communications, advertising, marketing, social media and other related functions.

Add to this a business and management background and media relations gains an even broader framework on which to build itself into a knowledge-based profession. Public relations education must prepare graduates for positions that combine a strategic management focus with strong written, verbal and interpersonal communication skills. At the same time, public relations and business must join forces. Business schools must overcome their traditional prejudice caused by a lack of understanding of the public relations practice. Public relations professionals also need to embrace business planning and accountability and be able to speak the language of business.

By strengthening its position *within* the organization, media relations will be better equipped to respond to external constituents. This balance between business strategy and public opinion is achieved by keeping an eye out for emerging social and political trends. Public relations are uniquely positioned in that it is virtually the only functional accountability with a multistakeholder view. This perspective enables news media relations professionals to see the effects of programming across publics. It also means offering guidance about how management should respond. This is what true media relations is all about. For today's global companies, the added challenge is to stay alert for emerging trends in the United States and overseas. Such a broad perspective takes media relations beyond mere press coverage to become an influencer of public perception and behavior toward the organization.

DISCUSSION QUESTIONS

1. What should be considered in developing a media campaign for a product or service?
2. When managing a tough issue with the press, how can you make sure you are most effectively prepared to be successful?
3. How do you go about developing good-standing relationships with the news media?
4. How can you most effectively understand the cultural differences in how media operates in different parts of the world?
5. Is it possible to talk "off the record" with the press, and what are the risks in trying to do so?
6. In working for an organization, how can you create a broad understanding of the strategic role that media relations plays in driving corporate strategy?
7. How does digital media differ from traditional media? And, how does this affect media planning and programming?

NOTES

1. David Finn, "The Media as Monitor of Corporate Behavior," *Business and the Media*, Craig E. Aronoff, ed. (Santa Monica, CA: Goodyear Publishing Company, Inc., 1979), p. 119.
2. Alan Macdonald, "Financial Public Relations in a Global Context," *International Public Relations in Practice*, Margaret Nally, ed. (London: Kogan Page Limited, 1991), p. 58.
3. Fraser P. Seitel, *The Practice of Public Relations* (New York: MacMillan Publishing, 1989), p. 516.

ADDITIONAL READING

Jones, Alex S. 2009. *Losing the News: The Future of the News That Feeds Democracy*. Oxford: Oxford UP. Print.

McChesney, Robert Waterman, and John Nichols. 2010. *The Death and Life of American Journalism: The Media Revolution That Will Begin the World Again*. Philadelphia, PA: Nation. Print.

Mersey, Rachel Davis. 2010. *Can Journalism Be Saved?: Rediscovering America's Appetite for News*. Santa Barbara, CA: Praeger. Print.

Tuchman, Gaye. 1978. *Making News: A Study in the Construction of Reality*. New York: Free. Print.

18

C H A P T E R

NONGOVERNMENTAL ORGANIZATIONS
Solving Society's Problems

Ray Boyer
Communication Consultant and Owner
Boyer Media

Governor Scott McCallum
Chief Executive Officer
Aidmatrix Foundation

A STRATEGIC APPROACH

PUBLIC RELATIONS AND COMMUNICATIONS IN THE NONPROFIT SECTOR

Every organization, whether it realizes it or not, is actively engaged in communications and public relations activities each and every day. From the simplest phone call to the most complex presentation, each contact conveys a message about the organization and its work. Regardless of their position, staff members answering simple questions over the phone or by e-mail are delivering a message about the organization just as surely as the executive director in a formal speech. And there are many more phone calls and e-mails than speeches.

It would be fairly straightforward to discuss the function of a communications office within a nonprofit organization, but it would be less than useful for two reasons. First, it is perfectly likely that a typical community-based nonprofit group will not have a communications staff. Second, even for those that do, it is important that communications and public relations be considered from an integrated and organization-wide perspective, not as a function that can be neatly sliced off from others.

It is through the process of communications and public relations that an organization systematically identifies the audiences for its various messages and ensures those messages are conveyed and reinforced in an effective way. Communications is integral to an organization's strategic plan and deserves special focus. Every person who represents the organization is part of the communications effort.

For nonprofit groups, there are very useful and inexpensive approaches to this work that can, if designed and implemented wisely, tend to communications issues at every level.

THE NONPROFIT SECTOR

There are more than 1.5 million nonprofit organizations registered in the United States, employing approximately 12.5 million people or about 10 percent of the workforce. Statistics published by Independent Sector, the organization representing the entire cross section of philanthropic and nonprofit organizations in the United States, indicate that such groups make up approximately 10 percent of the nation's workforce, a number equal to those employed by the finance, insurance and real estate industries combined. The nonprofit sector generates more than 5 percent of the nation's gross domestic product[1], about $750 billion in 2011 dollars.

Included under the nonprofit umbrella are many organizations that look and act very much like for-profit businesses. A hospital or a private college can look very much like a for-profit business. However, the difference is significant. In very general terms, the main difference in qualifying for nonprofit status, and the tax exemption that goes with it, is that the money raised must be used to advance the mission of the organization, not to enrich its owners. And they must serve a qualifying public service.

While organizations that look and act like traditional for-profit firms, complete with healthy balance sheets from businesslike operations, may find useful guidance in this chapter, they are more likely to find their best guide to public relations and communications strategies in other chapters of this book. Under discussion here will be strategies for nonprofit organizations that are (1) heavily dependent on fund-raising activities for support and (2) typically local or regional in the scope of their work. Annual operating budgets for such groups tend to be from a few hundred thousand dollars to the low millions per year. Salaries are modest and money is always tight.

Even in this smaller arena, according to Independent Sector,[2] there are approximately 700,000 organizations in the United States. Missions vary widely. There are groups, for example, that provide direct services, while others focus on issues with an emphasis on finding solutions to social problems. Many are advocates for action around various issues. It is such a complex web of activity that Independent Sector, working with a national sampling of tax returns from nonprofit organizations, developed a classification system that is broken down into 10 major categories and 26 major groups. It is a very busy corner of the economy. Between 1998 and 2008, the number of registered nonprofit organizations grew by more than 60 percent.

KEY AUDIENCES OF NONPROFIT ORGANIZATIONS

The discussion of communications and public relations for nonprofit organizations can, in general, be considered in terms of two primary sets of audiences.

The first is composed of those on the receiving end of the nonprofit's work. If it is a service provider, it is those who would receive the service; if an advocacy group, those the organization is attempting to influence.

The second is communications geared toward the people and institutions providing the money and other forms of support a nonprofit organization needs to do its work. There is a very straight line between the amount of money an organization has and the scope of its work. Assuming wise management, more money translates directly into more good work being done. Properly carried out, effective communications strategies can translate into greater financial support just as surely as product advertising translates into increased sales.

Determining the audiences linked to the work of a nonprofit organization is a key component of a communications planning exercise that will be discussed in detail in the "Tactics" section of this chapter. The first step of that exercise is a listing of audiences, followed by a determination of messages appropriate for each and the techniques that might be employed to reach and engage them. While the communications task of a nonprofit organization can be roughly broken down into the two large sets of audiences, there will be considerable overlap between them.

TRENDS AND DEVELOPMENTS THAT HAVE SHAPED THE NONPROFIT SECTOR IN THE UNITED STATES AND INTERNATIONALLY

The nature of nonprofit organizations varies considerably from nation to nation and culture to culture. From the very earliest days of the United States there has been a tradition of voluntarism that evolved into the nonprofit sector of today. Lester Salamon, of the Johns Hopkins University Institute for Policy Studies, has traced the history of nonprofit groups.[3] He notes that in the early days of the nation, despite a great spirit of self-reliance, the colonists formed voluntary associations to provide services that the government could not. As the nation grew, the number and importance of the nonprofit groups grew as well. For a variety of reasons, following the Civil War and continuing through the Depression, the link between nonprofits and the government grew considerably, despite efforts to downplay this relationship for political reasons. During the Great Society era of the 1960s and 1970s, however, this partnership between government and the nonprofit sector grew massively, as the federal government entered the human service field in a major way with resources designed to address people's needs while relying on the nonprofit sector to do much of the work. Salamon writes that by the late 1970s, "nonprofit organizations were delivering a larger share of government-financed human services than all levels of government combined . . ."

In other nations, the development of the nonprofit sector has followed many different paths. Salamon and his colleagues have found that nonprofit, nongovernmental organizations (NGOs) are present in virtually every country, and their presence has expanded significantly. Research by Salamon and colleagues revealed that if the international nonprofit sector were a nation, it would have the world's seventh largest economy with a GDP of $1.3 trillion.[4] The workforce of those in this sector, about 39.5 million full-time and 190 million volunteers would be more than the entire population of Russia. Worldwide, as the in the United States, the nonprofit sector is a significant presence.

KEY INFLUENCES ON THE PRACTICE OF COMMUNICATIONS AND PUBLIC RELATIONS IN THE NONPROFIT SECTOR

Because the nonprofit sector is defined by legislation, there are many rules and regulations governing the work of these organizations. There are clear limits, for example, on the extent to which nonprofits that receive federal funding can engage in lobbying activities. Philanthropic foundations are forbidden to engage in lobbying activities unless it is directly related to the rules governing their operations. In 2004 the Pew Charitable Trusts changed its structure so it could be more vigorous in advocacy. The Supreme Court in a 2010 decision opened the door for corporations to spend freely on political campaigns.[5] The ruling did not, however, change the rules with respect to foundations.

There is, however, one unchanging fact of life confronting virtually all nonprofit organizations, especially in the wake of the Great Recession: there is never enough money. Reading the annual budget of most nonprofits is a visit to the world of tradeoffs. Choosing one course of action invariably comes at the expense of other work the group would like to do. It is the rare nonprofit manager who can sit back at the end of the day and reflect on how the financial statements never looked better. It is small wonder then that such organizations have traditionally put concern about communications and public relations well down on the list of priorities. With so much that needs to be done, the argument goes, how can one possibly spend scarce resources on self-promotion?

The answer lies in one's perspective. If viewed as the need to hire a new staff member, retain public relations counsel or engage in a stream of attention-grabbing special events to hype the organization, building such capacity could easily (and rightly) be seen as a frill. By adopting the perspective that communications and public relations are critical to carrying out the mission of a nonprofit organization and a powerful tool in fundraising, it becomes too important to ignore.

THE RELATIONSHIP OF PUBLIC RELATIONS AND COMMUNICATIONS TO THE ORGANIZATIONAL MISSION AND GOALS OF A NONPROFIT GROUP

When nonprofit organizations approach foundations for financial support, it is unusual to see a request for communications support included. There is frequently a perception both on the part of the groups doing the asking and the groups doing the giving that communications is an add-on, something that can be done when the time is right—if there is something to communicate. The director of a nonprofit group in Chicago described it as "feeling like there are only so many things you can ask of the tooth fairy. You don't want to spend your wish on public relations when there are so many other needs."

The good news in this scenario is that funders are increasingly recognizing the importance of communications in the efforts of those they support. In earlier years, it was only the very largest foundations that had communications specialists as staff members. At the urging of veterans in the field such as the late Frank Karel, who was head of public affairs for the Rockefeller Foundation and later vice president for communications of the Robert Wood Johnson Foundation, the Council on Foundations established an affinity group today called the Communications Network, which currently has almost 300 members. The view of communications in the nonprofit sector is captured on the organization's website:

> . . . .Growing numbers of foundations have recognized the value of using strategic communications as a tool for advancing their missions and extending the impact of their grantmaking. Several forces drive the resulting investment in more robust communications: a desire by foundations to demonstrate the results of their philanthropic efforts; a desire to be more transparent; and a need to respond to increasing scrutiny from policy makers and the media seeking proof that foundations deliver value to American society.[6]

THE LINK WITH MARKETING

Nonprofit organizations tend not to use the term *marketing* in discussing their work, but it does not take much of a conceptual shift to think of the two main areas in which communications and public relations is key—fund raising and service delivery—as marketing efforts. For nonprofit groups, in the absence of significant advertising budgets, communications and public relations strategies that can be carried out at low or no cost take on special significance. Social media and other online activity have dramatically shifted the landscape, giving nonprofits global access to highly targeted audiences.

The link between money and message is a blunt one, but happily less blunt than as recently as a decade ago, thanks to communications technology. The fact remains, though, that with lots of money, it is possible to buy a great deal of awareness of an issue by the public. Consider, for example, the Disney film *Mars Needs Moms*. The *New York Post* noted that the film was launched with approximately $60 million worth of advertising, publicity and product tie-ins.[7] Twenty-five of the top 100 foundations had total annual grantmaking budgets that were less. It is tempting to think about the impact $60 million advertising budgets could have on attitudes about issues such as war, peace, racism and poverty. However, that is not the way society has arranged itself, so the nonprofit sector uses strategies that make the greatest possible use of online approaches and free media.

INTERNATIONAL CONSIDERATIONS

For U.S.-based organizations doing communications and public relations work in other cultures, it is very important to exercise caution. The worldwide reach of media organizations such as CNN may lead one to think that communications strategies are cross-cultural. They are not. A safe rule of thumb is to simply assume that each time borders are crossed, the rules of the game change. The ways in which public relations people work with newspaper reporters in Mexico, for example, is significantly different from the customary techniques in the United States. Asian media climates are vastly different from those of the United States, and in the former Soviet Union many of the rules are written as one goes along.

Along with the importance of understanding and being sensitive to different cultures, it is important, in many nations of the world, to consider security issues as well. If there is even the slightest question about whether calling public attention to a person or organization can lead to physical danger, it is obviously best to err on the side of caution. Communications tools as basic as press releases should not be used unless there is complete confidence that the information contained in the release is safe for all concerned.

Nonetheless, it is still perfectly possible to do effective communications and public relations work in other nations. A useful step for first timers is to seek guidance from colleagues or people in organizations already engaged in communications activities within that culture. A great deal of useful information about customary practices and fees can be quickly gathered from a trusted person with firsthand experience. In seeking such advice or in moving to the stage of implementing a communications strategy, it is important to keep values in mind. There may be significant differences in the way this work is done from country to country, but if the approach that is recommended does not feel comfortable, it is probably best to avoid it.

The landscape is shifting rapidly, courtesy of the Internet, which has brought vast and instant global connection. But it would be a mistake to confuse ease of access with more effective international communications programs. The cost is less but the cautions remain.

Many organizations have defined themselves in global terms and move smoothly in that arena. An organization named Environmental Law Alliance Worldwide, for example, with headquarters in Eugene, Oregon, connects environmental lawyers throughout the world who work through their nations' legal systems to protect and improve the environment. Legal information and documents are instantly available.[8] There are memorable stories about Twitter, YouTube and mobile phones as catalysts to the events of the Arab Spring in 2011. The days of communications blackouts are all but over.

Chicago-based consultant Emily Culbertson,[9] the former web managing director of the Robert Wood Johnson Foundation, notes that international organizations that seek to use technology to improve communications have their roots in volunteer efforts. Initially launched as a real-time repository of reports of violence after elections in Kenya in 2008, Ushahidi provides tools to people to collect and share information about breaking news events through the web or through mobile phones. CrisisCommons organizes volunteer web developers to work together on technology and telecommunications needs after natural disasters. (See sidebar, "Integrating Social Media into Nonprofit Communications," by Culbertson.)

Nonprofit organizations throughout the world have found they can seek out people and organizations doing similar work and engage in electronic conversations in ways that were simply not possible only a decade ago.

RULES OF THUMB FOR BUDGETING

As with so many aspects of nonprofit management, it is safe to assume that work in communications or public relations will be done with an eye on keeping costs as low as possible. This generally means aggressive use of Internet-based communications, minimal advertising budgets, less than glossy publications—if publications are put on paper at all, the least expensive ways to use the mail and so on right down the line. Given these constraints, it might be useful to review several considerations that can have an impact on the cost of communications efforts.

Websites and Social Media. Every organization has its website. Many organizations use e-mail to tell stories about their organizations' activities, keep them informed, and drive actions and fundraising. Everyone is aware of the potential for social media to connect and engage directly with key audiences. The most important thing to understand about use of electronic communications is that it allows a nonprofit organization to be proactive in reaching out to its audiences through social media. It allows nonprofits to participate in conversations about their field in ways that were simply not available in the past. A website remains the centerpiece of an organization's electronic communications effort. Used together, e-mail and social media will bring people to that website, help connect like-minded people together, and reach people interested in these issues at the websites where they are already talking about ideas and issues. For many nonprofits, online advertising can be an inexpensive way to reach people as well.

Get competitive bids when redesigning or redeveloping a website and, whenever possible, look for technology that the nonprofit can own or modify (ideally, open source content management systems such as WordPress or Drupal).

While the technology that drives websites can be complex, and no simple rule of thumb exists for pricing websites, a good webmaster or web consultant should be able to explain clearly the choices and tradeoffs for certain features or needs in a way that communications staff can understand.

For further resources in this area, check the Nonprofit Technology Network.

Beyond electronic communications, it is important to keep more traditional communications tools and techniques in mind.

Design and printing costs. Printing is a highly competitive industry that has been dramatically altered by computerized design and layout technology. There can be enormous variations in the costs of these services. The importance of competitive bids cannot be overstated.

INTEGRATING SOCIAL MEDIA INTO NONPROFIT COMMUNICATIONS

Emily Culbertson

Social media has transformed the way many people stay informed and connected about news, how people decide to donate to organizations, and how people share stories, good and bad, about the experiences they have. Now more than ever, it is important for nonprofit communicators to stay abreast of developments in web and social media. Why?

People are already talking about either your organization or issue online. No two audiences congregate in exactly the same place or at the same intensity. Yet it is important to find those talking about your issues already and learn what they are saying. If they are unhappy with your organization, you can listen to them and learn from them, even if you cannot change their minds. If they are happy with your organization, they are now evangelists for your work.

Social media speeds up the pace of conversations, but provides more opportunities for your organization to participate in them. In a social media environment, you have the challenge, but also the opportunity, to position your organization's point of view into the context of real-time conversation about news and events.

Social media allows you to tap into the wisdom of crowds and to learn from people you may not even know. To improve both the communications and the performance of nonprofit organizations, organizations can turn to social media for feedback in real time. Whether it is responses to online surveys or collaborative edits to a strategic white paper, soliciting feedback online can help your organization gain insight it might not have gotten otherwise and help create evangelists for your work.

The tools needed to create and share stories, video or photos about an issue keep getting cheaper and better. Thanks to mobile phones and wireless networks, videos, photos and news updates can be shared moments after they are created. Your organization no longer needs a large budget to shoot video or compile a photo essay about your work. What it needs, apart from skill and practice using the tools, is a compelling story, which is no different from what traditional communications plans need.

To succeed in social media, you will want to take a few first steps.

Make sure your organization's messages are short, conversational and easy for others to share, even if you do not yet use social media. Social tools such as Facebook and Twitter rewards short and clear messages and a conversational tone. Likewise, create content people will want to share on social media: focused, conversational content on web pages (not PDFs) with charts, short video or photos.

Conduct a few pilot projects before committing to a particular social media effort in the long term. Begin a few social media efforts that can be ended if need be and can reach your influencers. Take time to consider what works and what does not.

Create policies, guidance and coaching resources for people using social media. Social media policies and guides should not be just a list of prohibitions. They also should include guidance on ways to engage with people online, which may vary from field to field. All policies should include a reminder that staff, volunteers and board members should disclose their identities if they talk about the organization or issues related to it. Once developed, organizations should discuss policies with staff and modify them as needed.

Do not hand responsibility for social media to the intern, but do not do it all yourself. Online interactions should represent your organization's values, as they may be the first, or only, contact people have with your organization. It can best do so when a broad range of people share their knowledge, activities and insights online and use social media to build relationships. Effective policies and good coaching can help ease an organization's jitters about broader use.

Consider how social media contributes to larger goals. While it is possible to measure the number of people who follow or engage with your organization, the contribution of social media to organization goals may be more difficult to gauge. It is important to meet regularly to review progress and missteps so the organization can learn from them.

An overview of ways to use social media to create social change is *The Networked Nonprofit: Connecting with Social Media to Drive Change*, by Beth Kanter and Allison H. Fine (Jossey-Bass 2010).

Emily Culbertson is a Chicago-based web and social media consultant for foundations and nonprofit organizations and is the former web managing director of the Robert Wood Johnson Foundation.

Consultants. A great deal of valuable information and guidance can be provided by consultants. It is important to have a clear agreement with them about the budget and who covers expenses. It is equally important to have a clear understanding of the task the consultant is asked to do. It should be the organization that drives the consultant, not the other way around.

Freelance writers. Most freelancers charge by the hour. It is virtually impossible, however, to arrive at a precise number of hours and unwise to simply leave the meter running. It is best to arrive at an overall estimate for a job based on a reasonable estimate of the time involved. Partial payments at the beginning, middle and end of a project are a good practice, as is agreement on procedures for cancelling a project. Be sure to secure rights that allow publishing of writing in print and online, and when making assignments, brainstorm with the writer about the various ways the copy can be used or adapted to serve multiple needs.

Public relations firms. Such firms can be invaluable in carrying out a communications or public relations strategy. They can also be expensive. It is possible, however, to find high-quality counsel for affordable prices. As with consultants, it is important to have a clear vision of what is to be accomplished. It can be expensive, and frequently unsatisfying, to depend on a firm to provide vision as well as follow-through. Again, advice from experienced colleagues can be invaluable. In some cities there are nonprofit organizations such as Chicago's Community Media Workshop that provides low-cost high-quality communications services and training.[10]

Volunteers. Excellent counsel can be provided by volunteers serving on boards and committees. Remember that while such advice might be free, the cost of those recommendations may have a very real price tag.

A FEW SUGGESTIONS FOR THE PURCHASE OF PRODUCTS OR SERVICES

It is difficult to state in general what communications services should cost, but it would be quite easy to establish what the nonprofit sector is paying in any one city or region. There will generally be a local group of nonprofit organizations, and those doing the most effective work in communications and public relations can usually be easily identified. People working in the nonprofit sector are, in general, more than willing to share information about resources and expenses. Remember, it is possible to spend a great deal of money and get terrible results. It is equally possible to develop creative, low-cost strategies that will have a substantial impact. Pay attention to social media strategies. The entry barrier is low; the potential impact is high. The greatest cost is time spent learning and trying new tactics and persistently using the tools of social media.

TACTICS

THE COMMUNICATIONS PLAN

There is a tendency to think of communications as an episodic activity. In the simplest and most traditional terms, this means calling a press conference to make an announcement, harvesting a few inches of newspaper space or a moment on the nightly news and feeling like the work has been done. Using a press release service can produce eye-popping lists of websites that scoop up everything offered for free and offer it on a dizzying array of seldom, if ever, used websites. In this scenario, a public relations firm might be hired to work on the project and there will be a lot of activity for a short period of time. The project will end and a quiet status quo returns. It probably cost a lot of money, and that might prompt a diligent board member to wonder out loud if the short burst of media exposure was worth the time and expense. It probably was not.

The key to gaining acceptance of a communications strategy, both within an organization and by external funders, is to be clear on the ways in which the work will be done and the ways in which communications supports other priorities of the organization.

Such a plan should map out:

- Each of the audiences for information about the organization and its work

- What the organization wants each of those audiences to understand—its messages

- The people, publications, websites and other resources that members of each audience view as trusted sources of information

- Strategies for delivering those messages

This communications planning model can be applied to the communications objectives of an entire organization or implemented when a very specific project is under discussion. It provides an excellent framework for thinking about multiple audiences, the ways in which they overlap, and the ways in which specific messages can reach them from multiple sources.

THE COMMUNICATIONS GRID

A useful and practical approach to developing a communications plan is to set up a communications grid composed of audiences, messages tailored for each audience, and strategies for delivering the messages. The exercise of building the grid lends itself well to a moderated group discussion. The leader need not be a communications professional, just the person within the organization whose job most logically includes concern for such matters. For tens of thousands of small nonprofit organizations, this usually means the executive director.

AUDIENCES

Those who develop an organization's communications grid should first identify each of the main audiences important to the group. For a nonprofit organization, this list would typically include two large subcategories: (1) those critical to fund-raising efforts such as foundations, individual donors and governmental agencies and (2) those who are the object of the main work of the organization such as those who might receive the group's services, local and state politicians, policymakers and the general public.

Typical audiences for the work of nonprofit organizations might include the following:

- The staff of the organization

- The organization board

- The people and groups served by the organization

- The people or groups whose attitudes or behavior the group would like to influence

- Other organizations doing similar work

- State and local politicians

- The general public

- The media

MESSAGES

When Sharon McGowan, a Chicago journalist who turned her considerable energy to public relations, was developing her approach to spokesperson training, she focused on the importance of the carefully developed message.[11] She emphasizes that the message is not a recitation of an organization's mission statement but a plain language, conversational sentence that describes the nature of a group's work. There is often lively debate in her classes as trainees struggle to agree on how to say what it is that they do.

The same lively debate will usually occur during development of the messages that must lie within the communications grid.

McGowan led a spokesperson training session for the senior management of the social science research organization National Opinion Research Center (NORC) at the University of Chicago, leading them to the following message statement:

Successful efforts to understand and improve society begin with objective, high-quality social science research and data. NORC at the University of Chicago is an independent research organization that collaborates with government agencies, foundations, educational institutions, nonprofit organizations and businesses to develop enduring knowledge that supports evidence-based decisions.

The message statement clearly answers the question, "What is NORC at the University of Chicago and what does it do?" Imagine the number of times and the different settings in which a person is asked about their work and the importance of a well-planned answer is clear. Further spokes training sessions added layers to the message about the role of each individual in the organization.

Short and simple messages become especially important when you want to share them by mobile phone or text message. A word of caution: keep the messages consistent. Touting world-class facilities to potential users while describing the deplorable state of facilities to potential funders, for example, can be a sure-fire source of embarrassment.

VEHICLES

Having agreed on audiences and messages, the planning process moves to the question of delivery. Just as messages overlap, the same will be true of vehicles. Some, such as media placement, have the potential to reach every audience. Others can be highly targeted. In thinking about the audiences and the methods for communicating with them, useful considerations to keep in mind would include knowing the attitudes of the audience at the start of the project; their stage of understanding; the appropriate ways of reaching them, including consideration of their culture; and other matters that are competing for their attention.

The process of thinking through communications vehicles is an opportunity to tap into the planning group's ingenuity. It would be a pretty dull plan if, after working through audiences and messages, the vehicles were limited to a website, brochures and press releases. The world of communications and public relations does, after all, include both craft and creativity; it is a world made much larger through the tools of electronic communications.

MEDIA RELATIONS AND MEDIA PLACEMENT

While the essence of a sound communications plan is deliberate thought about how to reach all appropriate audiences, it is still important to pay special attention to good old-fashioned media placement work. There is ample research showing that for all the glamour of the Internet, most content about social and political issues still appear first in traditional media. It is an understanding of the agenda-setting role of the mainstream media that lies behind the well-known presidential "bully pulpit," in which the president is able to influence the content of the news by simply choosing what to say on any particular day. Savvy communications specialists at the local, national or international level can accomplish the same by carrying out effective media strategies.

The right kind of media attention at the right time can play an important reinforcing role in a communications effort. If, for example, a story appears that profiles the work of a nonprofit group at the same time a fundraising appeal arrives on an executive's desk, the impact can be considerable. Thus, an important consideration in planning a media relations effort is the way in which more targeted communications focused on selected audiences can be carried out simultaneously.

Groups attempting to call attention to an issue will have an easier time if their work is reinforced by a media that has created a general bed of awareness about it. This holds true regardless of where the story appears. Whether a story shows up in the newspaper or online makes much less difference than in the past. The story can be retransmitted in so many different ways; the most important first step has become getting it published in the first place. Do not ignore, however, the impact of appearing in a place like the *New York Times* or being picked up by the Associated Press.

If circumstances allow, it can often be easier to time an organization's communications efforts to a moment when an issue of interest to the organization is in the news, as opposed to doing the hard work of getting an item on the agenda from scratch. When Wisconsin Governor Scott Walker launched an effort to greatly reduce the power of public employee unions in his state, it became a moment for the union movement to convey a lot of information about unions in American society. The story was in the news, so it became an opportunity for coverage from many angles. It is, of course, important to try to bring new issues to the nation's attention, and many nonprofit groups are in business for the purpose of encouraging society to consider one issue or another. However, there is no person more grateful than a journalist offered a solid source or idea about a story already under way.

The *Bulletin of the Atomic Scientists* has long included media relations in its work to focus attention on the challenges to humanity posed by nuclear weapons, climate change and emerging technologies in the life sciences. Its staff is savvy in recognizing that when issues on those three topics are in the news, it can deepen the conversation by offering experts to comment on the issues and by holding special events to discuss them. Shortly after the 2011 earthquake and tsunami in Japan triggered the nuclear tragedy at the Fukushima nuclear power plant, the *Bulletin* hosted a conference at the University of Chicago, home of the first controlled nuclear reaction, on "The Lessons of Fukushima."[12]

There are few days quite so pleasant for a communications specialist as the day a favorable story about his organization is in the paper, on the air or online.

A good media specialist can be hard to find, but is worth the search. As with so much of the communications field, effective media placement blends craft with art, and there can be many approaches that work. Some prefer simply picking up the phone and pitching an idea, others feel strongly about leading with an e-mail message. Good media specialists tailor their tactics to the preferences of the reporters and bloggers they seek to reach. It is results that count.

In considering whether to work with a particular media relations person, all the usual rules apply about checking references and track record. This is important in establishing a person's capacity for attention to detail and reputation for follow-through, but these steps only provide clues to a person's ability to place a story. One of the best tests of this skill takes place when the candidate is asked how a story that appears fairly dull on the surface might be handled. If creative ideas start to flow about things that might be tried or angles that might work, it is a very good sign. Also, pay attention to how well a person sells her own qualifications for the job. If placing a story is at its heart a sales job, a person who does such work should be able to sell himself or herself as well. Finally, checking a person's reputation with reporters who have worked with the candidate can be very useful.

THE COMMUNICATIONS STAFF

One of the most frequently asked questions about communications in nonprofit organizations is whether to have a staff communications director. The answer depends in part on the nature or size of the organization. The first issue to address, though, is the perception of communications within an organization.

As hard as it may be to imagine, there was a time, during the height of the post–World War II Baby Boom, that colleges and universities did not have sizeable marketing departments. There were plenty of customers.

College or university news bureaus were largely responsible for hometown press releases and announcements for the local papers about college events. How times have changed. When the Baby Boom generation moved through college, schools that once had more applicants than they could handle suddenly faced a dramatic marketing challenge as competition for applications heated up. The cost of maintaining a first-class educational facility shot up, so the need to reach out to alumni and other donors in new ways became pressing. Higher education in this nation did a remarkable job of meeting the challenge. Colleges and universities recognized that developing increased interest among prospective students and stimulating more financial support was in large measure a communications task. Today it is the rare college or university that does not have a seasoned communications specialist holding a senior position in the administration.

What college and university administrators recognized was that communications is not a function that can be neatly relegated to a tidy corner. It is a function that permeates an organization; each person who works there is, in some way, engaged in the communications process.

For some organizations it is perfectly appropriate to have communications as a staff function; for others it may not be feasible. The challenge for the nonprofit organization is to recognize the importance of the work and properly tend to it. For groups that have sufficient resources, having a communications specialist on staff as a member of the senior management team can generate results that justify the investment many times over. This can be particularly true when the communications strategy is linked to fund-raising efforts and the link between a successful message and money in the bank is a direct one.

OUTSIDE CONSULTANTS

According to Paul Argenti, professor of corporate communication at Dartmouth College's Tuck School of Business, communications and public relations are never something that can be simply farmed out. While there are many excellent firms and individual contractors who do fine work, Argenti's view is that at least one person within the organization must understand its communications needs, have an appreciation of their importance and be responsible for tending to them.

Argenti feels that there is no substitute for working within an organization to understand both the big picture and the fine points of what needs to be done. It may well be, says Argenti, that such a person would retain communications counsel on a long-term basis, a project basis, or both. But he stresses the importance of someone in-house defining communications needs, being the driver in developing a communications plan, and overseeing its implementation.

SHOESTRING STRATEGIES

Some of the most cost-effective communications and public relations strategies that can be adopted by a non-profit organization are advocated by Thom Clark, the founder and president of Chicago's Community Media Workshop.

Established in 1989, the workshop is a nonprofit organization that provides communications training for Chicago's nonprofit community. According to Clark, it is a mistake for cash-strapped organizations to spend scarce resources on special events or other activities that are primarily designed to attract attention.

Using Clark's approach, a nonprofit manager should take a close look at the organization's strategy, with an eye toward the opportunities it offers to advance communications efforts without adding significant new costs. Examples might include the following:

Building visits with journalists into travel schedules. A group doing interesting work on an issue in one city may find that the news media in other cities are interested in learning about it. A low-cost but potentially high-impact media relations project can consist of simply arranging media sessions for traveling staff members.

Taking advantage of conferences or other gatherings of people with whom a group wants to communicate. Somebody is responsible for putting together the agendas for such meetings. An offer to do a workshop may well be eagerly accepted. It is only a short step beyond that to arranging meetings with the trade press covering a conference.

Writing for the trade press or guest blogging for a prominent blogger in your issue or industry. There are literally thousands of special-interest publications with print and online editions serving nonprofit organizations or the people who use their services. Contacting the editor of such publications with an offer to write a column or an article may well be accepted, especially if the offer is based on some prior research about the editorial needs of the publication. Online opportunities to comment on a story are abundant and an effective way to get a point of view into circulation, something that is especially important given the long life cycle of online information. Contributing to other blogs allows you to get used to the back-and-forth of engaging with readers while relying on the support of the blog's primary author.

Staying in touch with key audiences. Thanks to the Internet, the cost of producing an attractive, informative newsletter has plummeted. Such a strategy can be used to stay in touch with key audiences on a regular basis. Allowing people to subscribe to an organization's e-newsletter gives a sense of the breadth of interest in the organization's issues. Commercial e-mail services allow nonprofit to manage their subscriber lists simply and inexpensively and to stay in compliance with federal anti-spam laws. A few sentences and a link can accomplish as much as a fully written story did in the past—perhaps more because of the virtue of its brevity.

One-to-one communication. Some audiences, especially those most important to an organization, deserve more than a newsletter. For such people, a highly personalized e-mail message, or even an old-fashioned letter can be extremely effective. A personal salutation can go a long way toward causing a person to cut through the clutter of their e-mail traffic and respond to a group's communication. Anything with the look and feel of a personal message will be treated as such. Make sure the information provided lives up to the high touch of a personal message.

PRO BONO SUPPORT

The notion of pro bono support has a great deal of appeal because of the implication that it is free. Indeed a great deal of excellent communications and public relations advice can be provided by volunteer board members or through other arrangements with communications firms or corporate communications officers. The way such arrangements come about depends largely on the ingenuity of the nonprofit manager. Whatever the case, it is virtually always a good idea for a nonprofit group to include a communications specialist on its board. It signals recognition of the importance of communications to a nonprofit organization and ensures a communications perspective will reach the top level of management.

An interesting and useful approach to pro bono services has been developed by a national organization, the Taproot Foundation, which has offices in Chicago, Los Angeles, New York City, San Francisco and Washington, D.C. It offers three core programs that provide the equivalent of millions of dollars worth of support to organizations working local social issues. Between its inception in 2001 and 2011, Taproot volunteers provided more than 780,000 hours of pro bono service on over 1,300 projects.[13]

It should also be understood that pro bono support has its limits—usually the point at which the support goes beyond advice and involves direct expenses, which typically are paid by the organization receiving the free service.

ELECTRONIC COMMUNICATIONS

Revolutionary changes in the technology of communications have brought about vast new opportunities for nonprofits to communicate and tell their stories. The centerpiece, of course, is the Internet, an incredibly rich source of information and connection that simply did not exist two decades ago.

MEASUREMENT

Evaluating the success of a communications or public relations strategy should take place at two different levels. First is the strategic level, in which communications is seen as integral to the goals and objectives of the organization. It can be difficult teasing out of a larger strategy the precise impact of the communications efforts. If, however, there is a communications plan that identifies audience, messages and vehicles for conveying those messages, and if there is some baseline information about the level of awareness before the communications strategy is launched, follow-up survey work can determine if the effort was successful and suggest areas that need more attention.

The tools of electronic communications can provide incredibly precise information about who is seeking information about an organization. The free service provided, for example, by Google Analytics, takes much of the guesswork out of the analysis of Internet-based efforts.

The narrower the communications task, the more straightforward the process of measuring results. It is also important to keep fairness in mind. A media relations effort, for example, should be launched with the intention of achieving a certain level of coverage in print, broadcast and online outlets. Measurement of results should be how well it accomplished those objectives, not on a vague larger objective such as the impact of coverage on helping improve public education or reduce poverty. There may be a very direct link to such matters, but there will always be other factors involved as well. It is important to measure results, but also important that the criteria used for such measurement be appropriate.

FUTURE TRENDS

If there is a lesson from the past that is certain to continue into the future, it is to stay alert and responsive to the relationship between government and the nonprofit sector. The Great Recession triggered financial issues that severely constrained the budgets of nonprofit organizations of all sizes at the very moment their services were needed the most. If sentiment about cutting the size of government that ebbs and flows in American society takes root, the role of the nonprofit sector will be forced to adjust accordingly, with sources of support always central to its direction.

Social media will continue to grow as a tool used by nonprofit organizations to listen to the sentiments of key audiences online, even if the organizations themselves do not make strong use of social media. Finally the continued fragmentation of news coverage means that individual organizations will have to do more and more of the storytelling work themselves, even if just to catch the attention and interest of journalists.

THE CHALLENGE FOR MANAGERS

Despite the sense of change, the two major sets of audiences—those who provide support and those who are the focus of the organization's work—will remain the same. Nonprofit organizations will need innovative communications strategies designed to reach both.

One of the most significant opportunities, of course, is the greatly expanded marketplace for information. There may be more people and organizations competing for public attention than ever before, but the opening up of societies throughout the world coupled with new techniques for gaining access to them is unprecedented as well.

Nonprofit groups have been among the leaders in recognizing the value of electronic communications as a very cost-effective way to reach targeted groups worldwide. But the value of electronic communications in advancing the work of nonprofit goes far beyond efficiency. It has brought ways of reaching far more people in more highly targeted ways than has ever been available in history, and the pattern of growth and change is certain to continue. Where once there was concern that the cost of new technology would be a barrier, access to technology has proven remarkably universal.

The challenge for communications people is to learn the basics of sound communications strategy and apply those basics to the new generation of communications tools that are so rapidly developing, and offer such opportunity in meeting the communications objectives of nonprofit organizations.

A great deal has been written about how successful business organizations in the new century will be able to adapt quickly to changing competitive environments. By the same token, nonprofit organizations must adapt to changing economic and social environments. Effective communications and public relations strategies will be central to their success.

The preceding discussion of public relations in nongovernmental associations was written by Ray Boyer, former assistant dean for external relations at Northwestern University's Kellogg School of Management and head of public affairs for the John D. and Catherine T. MacArthur Foundation.

The following case study, by Governor Scott McCallum, former governor of Wisconsin and now CEO of the Aidmatrix Foundation, shows the effects of the proper use of these public relations strategies to meet the goals of a non-governmental organization with worldwide objectives.

CASE STUDY: FREE CLINICS

Free clinics today are defined by the U.S. National Association of Free Clinics[14] as "private, nonprofit, community-based organizations that provide medical, dental, pharmaceutical and/or mental health services at little or no cost to low-income, uninsured and underinsured people. They accomplish this through the use of volunteer health professionals and community volunteers, along with partnerships with other health providers." Some free clinics rival local government health departments in size and scope of service with multimillion dollar budgets, specialized clinics and numerous locations.

There has been a major difference between traditional health care in the United States and free clinic care. The cost of identical medical products has often been many times more expensive to most free clinics than it has to the large medical facility around the corner. This has occurred due to a lack of information and the lack of a better communication system. Through the use of technology this imbalance is being addressed.

The Aidmatrix Foundation is a global nonprofit organization that utilizes information solutions—technology—to help meet disaster needs as well as to supply food banks and free clinics. Those in this field need to have a mission passion beyond that of a job. When that passion is combined with communication and marketing skills, the impact is enormous.

In this case, Aidmatrix technology was used to link medical donors to the end users—the free clinics. This program started utilizing a model similar to that of U.S. Charitable Food, in which most donated food is transacted from food companies through Aidmatrix solutions to U.S. Food Banks affiliated with America's Second Harvest. The food program is run under the auspices of Feeding America. The medical program was administered by the National Association of Free Clinics (NAFC).

The success in the medical program was realized as the over 300 free clinics throughout the United States not only received donated product but were also able to become a market for the sale of this product. By leveraging the collaborative aspect of technology, the free clinics were able, in the period of 18 months, to expand from just receiving donated product, to combining to drive down the price of other needed materials. From the perspective of the medical manufacturers, there was a scale reached for a new market. This technology program eventually reached having over 1,500 products marketed on the system before it was spun into a completely market place solution. In terms of savings, the cost of diabetic kits, as an example, went from $45 or $55 per kit for individual free clinics, to a clinic cost of $9.50. There were savings of millions of dollars for organizations serving people in need. Manufacturers gained as well through access to a previously diverse market.

The case study reports the following:

- Over 200 free clinics in 35 states were providing their patients with higher quality care through FreeClinicLink.

- In 2008, Mission Arlington saved more than $3 million on medical supplies to treat their 5,500 patients.

- Free clinics were able to purchase a box of 50 diabetic test strips for as little as $9.95, saving over 75 percent off the normal price of $40 a box, with the added bonus of receiving free glucometers, filling yet another need.

TECHNOLOGY CREATING BETTER COMMUNICATION

FreeClinicLink is a web-based solution that allows members of the NAFC to purchase medical supplies in bulk. Bulk purchasing is an incentive to the medical suppliers to give the NAFC a much greater discount on their products. Donor companies can also provide a larger array of products that previously would have been destroyed due to short shelf-life dates. Now, these products can be successfully donated by using this system.

RETURN ON INVESTMENT

Using FreeClinicLink provides free clinics access to many more donated and discounted medical products than was previously possible. Free clinics are able to save 75 percent on some diabetes supplies. They also have access to new donations from donors across the country. With these new medical supplies, free clinics are able to treat more patients and provide better care. All these benefits enable free clinics to lower operating costs and, as a result, improve the lives of those in need. In 2008, more than 200 NAFC free clinics saved more than $17 million on both donated and discounted products. According to Nicole Lamoureux, the NAFC executive director, free clinics have seen up to an 80 percent increase in volume through FreeClinicLink.

CONTINUOUS CARE

A 62-year-old woman was recently laid off after working the past 30 years in customer service, the last 9 years of which had been at the same IT center. With her husband already on Medicare, she needed a way to receive medication to manage her diabetes. Her first thought was applying for private, temporary insurance, but those were all too expensive considering her recent job loss. Undeterred, but cautious, she went to her local free clinic for treatment. To her surprise, the care that they provided her was equivalent to the care she had received from her previous doctors. Suzie Foley of the Greenville Free Medical Clinic in South Carolina reported the woman's gratitude: "I was thrilled with the continuous care I received at a time when I didn't know where I would be receiving care the next week. I never thought I would be the one asking for help, but I am really glad that I did." Fortunately, her local Free Clinic was a member of the NAFC and the medical supplies on hand were received through FreeClinicLink.

FIGURE 18.1

NGO Case Studies: Aidmatrix.org

CASE STUDY: HAITI EARTHQUAKE

CRITICAL HUMANITARIAN CHALLENGE

A magnitude 7.0 earthquake struck 10 miles west of Port-Au-Prince on the afternoon of January 12, 2010, causing massive damage to the small country of Haiti. The Haitian government estimated that 3 million people were affected by the earthquake and the 52 aftershocks measuring a magnitude 4.5 or greater. During disasters, it is a challenge for relief agencies to manage all of the unexpected goods and volunteers that arrive. This challenge is especially prevalent during international disasters, when the transporting of donations and volunteers becomes the biggest challenge. The airport and the seaport were damaged during the earthquake, so airplanes and boats attempting to bring relief workers, donations and equipment to and from Haiti were being delayed or cancelled altogether.

Disaster response communications is critical for many organizations. The public messaging, donor messaging and solicitation and internal information sharing reinforce each other. The operations need to be coordinated and this must be done rapidly with the overall plan of action.

The size of the organization affects what type of communications it is able to engage in during a crisis. Smaller nonprofits are fully aware of the crowded public media market. They may devote more attention to market segments, notably their own donor base.

Haiti meant special problems generally not seen before. For example, it became important for efficient response to be coordinating with other bodies. Usually a national government takes the lead in disaster response but, in this case, the Haitian government was overwhelmed by the earthquake. International organizations such as the United Nations have disaster response agencies that were attempting to coordinate. The U.S. government took a special role with the State Department and U.S. Agency for International Development (USAID) within the country, and for transportation and other logistics the U.S. Defense Department under Southcom was able to coordinate, especially with shipping, and to access the major airport in Port-au-Prince.

Any organization wanting to respond would be at an advantage if they were able to communicate with umbrella organizations. Not doing so would make their job extremely difficult. There were further advantages to this coordination, not only to the organization but also in overall response efficiency.

Not all of this responsibility would necessarily fall in the jurisdiction of a communications or media operations director. But clearly, all activity includes a communications plan and understanding.

Program Benefits from Better Communication (through Aidmatrix)

- Provided increased amount of goods, money and volunteer donations

- Gave relief to victims of disaster more quickly

- Reduced time and effort organizing and distributing donations and volunteers

- Improved the efficiency for rebuilding efforts

- *Bottom Line: More people receive the right aid more quickly*

THE CASE OF BUSINESS

The USAID, in partnership with more than 100 NGOs, unveiled an online donations management website to facilitate the public's assistance in the relief efforts for the Haiti earthquake. Aidmatrix worked with USAID to provide technology that helped coordinate the U.S. in-kind donations and volunteer response to the January earthquake in Haiti. Cooperative for Assistance and Relief Everywhere, the International Society of Transport Aircraft Trading's (ISTAT) Airlink program, American Logistics Aid Network (ALAN), MedShare, Adventist Community Services, Mission Outreach, Powered by ACTION, the State of Florida, the Government of Puerto Rico's Departamento de la Familia and other agencies activated their portals or joined other installations on the Aidmatrix Network to post needs, accept donation offers and match them to help those in the region affected by this devastating earthquake.

Behind the scenes, these NGOs use a web-based warehouse management module, provided as part of the Aidmatrix Network, to provide real-time visibility into available quantities and to share the inventories in their disaster warehouses with local relief teams. Each NGO has the ability to share views into their inventory with other NGOs as well. The situation is highly fluid as pallets of products are arriving, checked in, broken down into smaller units, repackaged and then transported out on demand as the heroes on the scene order directly what is needed for their area. In addition, many of these NGOs and governments set up temporary emergency warehouses to stage the incoming in-kind donations and supplies as the items were transported closer to Haiti from around the world.

More than 200 NGOs were able to easily and efficiently communicate needs to prospective donors. Individuals and companies could use this intuitive system to offer donations and match the needs of the organizations in Haiti. More than $51 million in donations were offered and accepted by individuals and companies to the organizations responding in Haiti, including offers of transportation. Once the donations were matched, the technology could connect NGOs with potential transportation donors to facilitate the movement of product. The transportation of donations and volunteers was provided by such groups as UPS, ISTAT and ALAN.

"We are focused on the multiplier effect of connecting our program with the Aidmatrix Network of NGOs who are seeking transportation services—especially on the Haitian Earthquake Relief efforts," stated Robert Brown, project manager of ISTAT's AirLink program. "We are already tracking our transportation donations in the system and getting them visible to this large, centralized, online audience of NGOs while coordinating flight plans for the immediate future as the Port-Au-Prince airport opens up to more relief flights this week."

Individuals interested in volunteering in the disaster relief were able to enter their volunteer details into the system, inputting their training certifications and skills, languages spoken and the duration of service. Those wanting to support the recovery through financial donations were able to be directly funneled to the Clinton Bush Haiti Relief Fund through the Aidmatrix technology on the USAID Haiti relief website.

The AT&T Foundation provided funding to help Aidmatrix launch the Warehouse Management Modules to responding NGOs in the region. Warehouses were successfully set up to manage the inventory and distribution of goods to those affected by the earthquake in Haiti. The AT&T funding also helped provide Aidmatrix with the bandwidth to deploy personnel into Haiti in the days and weeks following the disaster.

Throughout the relief efforts, 40 separate NGOs posted needs on the Aidmatrix network, while 48 NGOs accepted donations through the system. There were a total of 33 different products that were donated in response to an organization's needs, valued at more than $2.2 million. A total of 103 donation offers were accepted.

Crisis communications in a natural disaster were required of many organizations following the devastating earthquake of January 2010.

Government organizations were expected to respond with support. The United States in particular was looked to as the major developed country in the region. Government is made of many entities, all with their own communication needs. The U.S. Defense Department was charged with response both in terms of fleet movement and transportation. The U.S. State Department was in charge of foreign policy, and within the department was the U.S. Agency for International Development, most specifically the Office of Foreign Disaster Assistance. The Federal Emergency Management Agency (FEMA), while charged with domestic response, was asked to take on a significant role. The White House took the overall leadership role.

All of the organizations had responsibilities. In some cases these responsibilities were more clearly defined for an agency. In a number of cases the responsibility was either defined during the crisis, was overlapping, or was of a competing nature.

The competition came from the fundraising efforts of most of the nonprofit organizations operating in Haiti. According to the Institute of Peace, "At least 3,000 NGOs are operating in Haiti. Struggling with insufficient capacity in the face of overwhelming poverty and environmental disasters, the government has been unable to coordinate or capitalize on what some in Haiti refer to as a 'Republic of NGOs.'"

The lifeblood of many U.S.-based NGOs is through donations. Those that get the message out to supporters and the public are winners in the financial race.

The American Red Cross unveiled the first widespread effective use of mobile phone giving. They were joined by several other organizations that took their message to the public through television advertising. Press conferences, releases, staged events, mailings and phone banks, from dozens of the nonprofits went into high gear to capture dollars from a supportive public.

Communications were important from several perspectives. First, there needed to be information sharing to the general public on what the organization was doing to help Haitians. Mainstream media outlets had the earthquake as the lead story in the aftermath.

The other target audience—in many cases the prime target audience—was to organization members, supporters and donors. Speed in getting the message out is important. The media attention span is short. The competition for public donations is fierce. The desire to be "first in" is heavy for many of the organizations in the field.

Not to be forgotten is communication needed internally to get the mission accomplished. Volunteers may be needed. Field staff needs to be heard from and directed. Administrators need information for coordinating relief activities. All occurs simultaneously with limited resources. In the case of the earthquake in Haiti, as in other disasters, the need for medical supplies, food, clothing and shelter can be addressed by many NGOs in many different ways. But the importance of communication, coordination and logistics management cannot be overestimated.

CASE STUDY: CRITICAL HUMANITARIAN CHALLENGE—NORTH DAKOTA

With snowfall levels exceeding more than 500 percent above normal in parts of North Dakota, the state braced for an active flooding season in the spring of 2009. That flooding began in earnest the week of March 20 when floodwaters destroyed a portion of the small town of Linton. The flooding continued when an ice jam caused major flooding in the capital city of Bismarck beginning March 23 and rivers throughout the state began to exceed their flood stages. While fighting floods in other parts of the state, emergency management officials cast a wary eye toward the state's largest city of Fargo, where the Red River began a rapid rise that would eventually result in a record crest. The rising Red River set the stage for a possible evacuation of more than 90,000 people from the Fargo area. While record crests were achieved throughout the state, preplanning helped avoid major evacuations. By the end of the flood event, more than two months later, all but 5 of North Dakota's 53 counties had received a presidential major disaster declaration.

Program Benefits

- Increased donations meeting the needs of the community

- Provided relief to victims in an efficient manner

- Decreased time spent organizing and distributing donations and volunteers

- Received 211 donations into the system within the first three days that the system was operational

- Received several hundred thousand dollars worth of donations through the National Donations Management Network (NDMN) system during the flood event

- *Bottom Line: More people receive the right aid more quickly*

THE CASE OF BUSINESS

In March of 2009, several factors collided creating the worst springtime flooding in the history of the state of North Dakota.

As the nation's eyes focused on the efforts to battle the flooding there, offers of donations began to pour into the state.

State officials recognized the potential problems associated with a disorganized donations management system and signed a Memorandum of Understanding (MOU) with the Aidmatrix Foundation on March 25, 2009.

DISASTER RELIEF IN ACTION

With the MOU in place, the state put together a donations coordination team (DCT) with members from the state, Voluntary Organizations Active in Disaster (VOAD), North Dakota Citizen Corps and the North Dakota League of Cities.

FEMA was able to provide invitational travel to bring in a representative from Aidmatrix and an Adventist Community Services representative who helped to implement use of the NDMN during the California wildfires to complete the DCT. The team was tasked with implementing the NDMN in the State of North Dakota.

The DCT's first task was to obtain buy-in from the North Dakota VOAD organizations that would be using the NDMN.

This task was achieved through conference calls with VOAD membership and trainings on the use of the NDMN. North Dakota VOAD members in good standing became the first vetted organizations that were assigned usernames and passwords for the NDMN.

NORTH DAKOTA BRINGS FAST DISASTER RELIEF DURING SPRING FLOODS

Aidmatrix and the NDMN have helped us reduce paperwork and focus on relief efforts so communities and individuals with unmet needs can be helped more quickly. After buy-in and training of VOAD members was achieved, the next step for the DCT was to create awareness of the NDMN among the general public. This was achieved by placing a link to North Dakota's NDMN portal on the North Dakota Department of Emergency Services website and distributing a news release through the governor's office. Through North Dakota's use of the NDMN, the state was able to avoid opening a multiagency warehouse by heading off unsolicited donations until they were needed. "Aidmatrix and the NDMN have helped us reduce paperwork and focus on relief efforts so communities and individuals with unmet needs can be helped more quickly," stated Sarah Werner, Citizen Corps coordinator for the North Dakota League of Cities and VOAD officer.

There were 211 donations entered into the system within the first three days that the system was operational. North Dakota accepted several hundred thousand dollars worth of donations through the NDMN system during the flood event. North Dakota VOAD members also posted several needs on the NDMN portal for potential donors to fulfill. The system helped VOAD member agencies to work better together and with the state to get the items they needed.

FEMA's ability to bring in NDMN experts to help the state implement the use of the NDMN system was also very helpful in getting North Dakota's portal up and running in a short amount of time.

LESSONS LEARNED

In the midst of a humanitarian crisis and ensuing media spotlight, North Dakota courageously undertook implementing a system for disaster relief that they had never used before. Their commitment to seeing it through in the midst of the chaos helped minimize wasted donations. The NDMN system, along with seasoned veterans who had used the system in countless other disasters, helped them quickly coordinate the donations process and route necessary relief items to the responding relief agencies on the ground. North Dakota now stands well prepared for future disasters.

CASE STUDY: CRITICAL HUMANITARIAN CHALLENGE—CHILDREN INTERNATIONAL

Household incomes for the poor in developing countries typically amount to less than $150 per month. For many impoverished children, surviving into adulthood is considered a success. Children International is a nonprofit humanitarian organization that serves over 330,000 children through 84 community centers in 11 countries. Aidmatrix partnered with Children International in 2009 to help them manage their global in-kind donations through humanitarian relief supply-chain management tools.

Program Benefits

- Improved inventory management
- Increased visibility and reporting of in-kind donations
- Enhanced tracking on shipments en route to their destination
- Ability to aggregate needs from all international programs
- Increase Children International's donor network
- *Bottom Line: Enterprise visibility of products and needs, available 24/7*

Children International, through its local community centers, offers care to children ages 2–19 years, providing them with basic health and dental care, nutritional aid, educational support and other programs to help children grow to become self-reliant adults. They are headquartered in Kansas City, Missouri, but they rely on their field offices and partner agencies to carry out their mission around the globe. Children International partners with Blusource, a warehousing and logistics provider, to manage the delivery of urgently needed items. To manage these processes, the team had been using a 1998 Microsoft Access database software system. Children International approached Aidmatrix about updating their technology with a new, more robust tool to help them more efficiently deliver aid.

A CASE OF BUSINESS

Children International manages a product donations program in which they ship approximately $52 million worth of products to their field offices and partner agencies. Forty-foot container shipments are loaded with supplies mostly comprised of textbooks from American schools. These books are replaced by newer textbooks in the schools and then shipped to Children International.

Managing a humanitarian relief supply chain of this magnitude requires an incredible amount of coordination as the products flow through different logistics channels. The products are first shipped from the donor's warehouse or school, and then they are processed and stored in the Blusource warehouse, eventually selected and shipped internationally to the sponsorship operative agency, and then finally distributed to schools and relief workers in the field. The Children International product donations manager and the Blusource warehouse manager must maintain close communications to coordinate the process and document the shipped products.

Children International and Blusource saw many limitations in their current system that inspired them to look for upgraded software that best fit their program requirements and the advancing technology of the time.

- This database required the maintenance of an old hosting server because the new operating systems would not support the program.

- The old server was deteriorating and slow, requiring costly maintenance and worrying Children International staff of potential failure.

- The database was rigid and inflexible, not able to be adapted as the program progressed.

- The database was only accessible through a special virtual private network from the Children International headquarters.

SPEEDING DELIVERY OF GLOBAL CARE TO CHILDREN IN NEED

Field offices could not connect to the system, and all communications were done outside of the system through e-mail.

There was not a functionality to collect donation needs and perform forecasting, which was seen as a new requirement to improve Children International program efficiencies.

In the fall of 2008, Children International began the search to find a new platform to manage the inventory and logistics of their Product Donations Program, replacing their Access Database system. As they searched the Internet for a new solution, they found Aidmatrix and began the conversation that resulted in their adoption of the Aidmatrix In-Kind Donations Management module.

IMPLEMENTATION PROCESS

Phase I of the implementation involved Children International, Blusource and Aidmatrix working together to map the entire donations process. Children International has an interesting process in that Blusource receives and catalogs the in-kind donations. Donations range from small to very large, at times consisting of multiple container loads.

Phase II of the program was a pilot that involved training headquarters administrators, identifying regional participants, training them, identifying additional requirements and building key reports. In phase III, updates were incorporated and Children International began using their Aidmatrix technology to support the day-to-day donations management process. In phase IV, Children International disabled their Access database and moved 100 percent of their operations on the Aidmatrix platform. In addition, in this phase, Children International was able to do something they had never done before. Their international partners, from Guatemala to Zambia, from India to the Philippines, were able to enter their 2011 needs in the Aidmatrix network.

James Cook, president and CEO of Children International, stated,

At Children International, we always look for ways to make our programs run as efficiently and effectively as possible. The key to a successful donations program is moving items to where they are most needed as quickly as possible—to get them in the hands of a poor child. It's about getting the right pair of shoes, or the right book, to the right child at the right time. Aidmatrix is helping us do that, and we are very excited about the partnership.

GLOBAL IMPACT

Using the Aidmatrix system, Children International has shipped out more than $45 million worth of textbooks, school supplies, clothing, shoes, hygiene items and medical supplies to their partner agencies around the world. Children International has collected over 1,100 product needs from their international offices to provide accurate information for their donation solicitation and procurement efforts, saving at least 25 percent of their time and money. This technology partnership has improved the gift-in-kind program's international logistics, data reporting, and communications with their donor and partner communities. Children International has increased its prospect donor base by 80 percent. Additionally, the network membership is expected to grow at a rate of 40 percent per year providing Children International a growing procurement channel. Children International has communicated that this partnership will enable them to realize a savings of approximately $3 million in budget costs associated with procurement from using Aidmatrix solutions.

ABOUT CHILDREN INTERNATIONAL

Children International, a nonprofit, humanitarian organization, was founded in 1936. Its mission is to bring real and lasting change to children living in poverty, made possible through its Child Sponsorship programs. Individual sponsors are united with a single child in need to give them an opportunity to succeed, primarily through educational and medical care. Children International augments this assistance with gift-in-kind donations. During the last year alone, Children International delivered more than $52 million.

Whether it is responding to disaster needs, supplying free clinics or food banks, Aidmatrix is an NGO that utilizes supply chain technology combined with many public relations strategies and tactics to bring needed aid to the right people at the right time. Through the use of social and other attention, Aidmatrix has saved and improved lives and is an NGO to emulate.

DISCUSSION QUESTIONS

1. The authors note "With so much that needs to be done, the argument goes, how can one possibly spend scarce resources on self-promotion?" What is your response to this fundamental question about the marketing and public relations support for a not-for-profit or NGO?
2. If not-for-profit organizations were not allowed (were outlawed), what would be the economic and social impact on society?
3. What advantage gives such a small organization with fewer than 40 employees the power to raise $2 billion in aid each year? What are the differences between Aidmatrix and other charities?
4. What can be done about the millions of dollars in value of heartfelt donations of clothing, food and other supplies sent to disaster sites only to be put in landfills? Discuss the major reasons for destroying the goods.
5. Searching online, find a relatively unknown not-for-profit and read about it on their website. Describe the organization, its goals and its accomplishments. From what you learned in this chapter suggest at least three ways the organization could improve its work and public relations.

NOTES

1. Global Philanthropic. Web. June 21, 2011. www.globalphilanthropic.com/subpage.php?p=66.
2. Independent Sector. Web. June 21, 2011. www.independentsector.org.
3. Lester M. Salamon. Web. June 21, 2011. ips.jhu.edu/pub/Lester-M-Salamon-Ph-D.
4. Lester M. Salamon, S. Wojciech Sokolowski, and Regina List. "Global Civil Society: An Overview." The Johns Hopkins University Comparative Nonprofit Sector Project, 2003.
5. Supreme Court Decision: Citizens United V. The Federal Elections Commission. 558 U.S. 08-205, 2010.
6. The Communications Network. Web. June 21, 2011. comnetwork.org.
7. "Box Office: *Mars Needs Moms*–A Megaton Bomb." *The New York Post.* March 13, 2011.

8. Environmental Law Alliance Worldwide (ELAW). Web. June 21, 2011. www.elaw.org.
9. Emily G. Culbertson. Web. June 21, 2011. www.egculbertson.com.
10. Community Media Workshop. Web. June 21, 2011. www.communitymediaworkshop.org.
11. centerforhighperformance.com/about/global-team/sharon-sutker-mcgowan.
12. "Lessons from Fukushima." UChicago News. Web. June 21, 2011. news.uchicago.edu/multimedia/lessons-fukushima.
13. Taproot Foundation—Make It Matter. Web. June 21, 2011. www.taprootfoundation.org.
14. www.freclinics.us/AboutUs/WhatIsaFreeClinic/tabid/63/Default.aspx.

ADDITIONAL READING

Blecken, Alexander. 2010. *Humanitarian Logistics Modelling Supply Chain Processes of Humanitarian Organisations*. Berne: Haupt. Print.

Christopher, Martin and Peter Tatham. 2011. *Humanitarian Logistics: Meeting the Challenge of Preparing for and Responding to Disasters*. London, England and Philadelphia, PA: Kogan Page. Print.

Ross, Molly, Katrin Verclas and Alison Levine. 2009. *Managing Technology to Meet Your Mission: A Strategic Guide for Nonprofit Leaders*. New York: Jossey-Bass. Print.

19

C H A P T E R

ASSOCIATIONS
A Strong Voice

Richard L. Hanneman
Former President
Salt Institute

Changing public attitudes and opinions and motivating others to act can be honored as the essence of human progress and happiness or condemned as deceitful manipulation. This credo stems from one of my early and formative public affairs positions, as assistant to Wisconsin Governor Warren P. Knowles, who lived as he taught: "Good government is good politics." In public relations and communications, our tools can be misused; but, employed in a good cause, they can help us achieve greater human understanding, productivity and happiness.

Our standard of living and quality of life reflect both the productivity of the private sector of our economy and the decisions of governments. The United States allocates about 40 percent of the gross domestic product directly to sustain our standard of living and regulations impose additional costs. The Obama administration's massive "stimulus" spending, "bailouts" of firms deemed "too big to fail," and resurgent regulatory activism make government an important audience for corporate communications. In the private sector, marketplace consumer choices govern the flow of goods and services, which are heavily influenced by organizational communications as well. Inadequate or inappropriate public communications can doom virtually any enterprise or cause.

WHY ASSOCIATIONS?

Associations exist for just these reasons. Associations are voluntary, not-for-profit organizations formed in recognition of the greater, even synergistic, potential of uniting in common purpose. In some ways, associations act as any business in defining their core purpose or niche, developing and marketing their goods and services. They provide employment, produce goods and services and pay taxes. However, the bottom line is not only the reserve fund balance of their financial statements but also the success of their mission. Most associations achieve this goal along the path traveled, not at their financial destination.

America has long recognized this voluntary segment of society, and the U.S. tax code makes specific provision for code section 501(c), organizations spanning the breadth of religious, educational, charitable, scientific, social, recreational and fraternal activity as well as those organized for primarily economic interests (e.g., labor unions and business leagues). Most of these fall into one of two groups: 501(c)(3) public interest groups and

501(c)(6) trade associations. The differences between the two, in terms of public policy objectives, strategies and tactics is, in practice, often indistinguishable.

Associations are almost as varied as people. Each is unique. They come in all sizes and shapes, from the local Parent Teacher Association to the International Red Cross, from labor unions and business leagues to professional associations for narrow professional specialists. Associations represent all types of charitable purposes, providing private sector responses to societal concerns that would otherwise grow into a demand for government action.

Once associations were essentially local. They dealt with city governments or addressed community problems. But the spurt of central government dominance beginning with the New Deal in the 1930s has led to stronger national associations. The 1980s decentralization of governmental activism from Washington to state capitals reinvigorated state-level associations dealing with governmental issues. Multinational corporations are commonplace, but more and more trade associations and professional organizations also bridge national boundaries when their charters identify broader concerns.

Many associations provide valuable education and training, supplementing public schools. They foster professional in-service, lifetime-learning educational experiences and inter- and intra-industry exchanges of expertise to improve productivity, worker safety, environmental protection and a host of other socially sanctioned services.

ASSOCIATIONS AS IDEA MERCHANTS

Apart from feeding the hungry, promoting the arts or teaching businesspeople how to cope with changing work and marketplaces, associations also exist to present ideas, to advance ideological causes and to promote efficient industrial production or product acceptance through generic marketing of ideas and philosophies. These are the "special interests" so commonly debated in newspapers or at cocktail parties. Yet these interests reflect the individual opinions of citizens in their multitude of ethical, political, philanthropic and economic diversity.

Our political and social structure rewards effective group action; naturally, then, advocacy groups are formed in response. So, whether the view is that more money needs to be spent for AIDS research, that government is "too intrusive" or "not doing enough," that zoning should protect the integrity of neighborhoods, that bald eagles need protected nesting areas or that dairy farmers need price supports, citizens vote not just with their ballots on election day but with their memberships in associations created to advance their interests. The scope of government today includes which medical research should be funded, how the marketplace is to be policed and which technologies should be promoted (and which deep-sixed). Lawmakers and regulators would be lost and rendered ineffective without the specialized expertise of the "special interests" represented by voluntary associations.

Associations are governed by charters and bylaws that define their general purposes and objectives. Achievement of these objectives—well recognized by sophisticated association management professionals— requires consideration of the role of communications in both strategic planning and tactical implementation. Thus, "Save the Whales" and eating "Five a Day" servings of fruits and vegetables elucidate organizational strategies. The core strength of any association is the power of their espousal of ideas motivating action by either its members or some targeted individual or group. If the motivating idea is the source of power, the communications strategy is the essence of an association's mission.

The mission of an association is different from that of its members. Members of the Salt Institute, for example, have been tutored to distinguish their business—to make and sell salt—from the business of their trade association—to develop and sell ideas on their behalf. This maxim replicates the mission of many associations providing a targeted communications function on behalf of their members, whether advocating humanitarian aid to the least developed nations or to central cities or expanded consumer acceptance of a product or service.

Government regulations influence communications strategies adopted by associations. Take meetings, for example. While associations have long held meetings as a primary means of communicating with members and conducting organizational governance, phone and fax technology, Skype, video teleconferencing, webcasts and e-mail have negated the need for many face-to-face meetings. Removing the tax deduction for spousal travel has also undermined in-person association meetings. Classifying association expenditures for lobbying as nondeductible has retarded associations' ability to represent members' views.

Associations are walking a fine line. They have invited governmental scrutiny not only by emerging as effective agents in promoting their members' causes, but, in some cases, by stretching the boundaries of their income-tax-exempt status. Some association activities are performed by for-profit subsidiaries (such as magazine publication and insurance company ownership) and associations are becoming increasingly reliant on non-dues income. Sales to members and nonmembers alike of various materials, charges for special services, rental of mailing lists—these, and many more creative money-raising initiatives—often blur the line between associations and for-profit ventures. In many associations, the greatest growth in communications is to support marketing of the expanding array of non-dues revenue programs.

ASSOCIATIONS SHARE CHARACTERISTICS WITH FOR-PROFIT COMPANIES

In many ways, public relations and communications in associations mirror the strategic and tactical decision-making processes of for-profit enterprises. Sellers of toothpaste, municipal bonds or pork belly futures share common principles with those funding kidney research, upgrading worker safety procedures in salt mines and expanding markets for California raisins, industrial machinery or computers. Many of the challenges of communications within the for-profit sector are also shared by nonprofit associations.

The biggest difference is not that nonprofit associations do not make money, produce consumer goods and services or pay taxes; they do. The difference is implicit in the membership concept: many individuals or businesses voluntarily unite to support the association. In this complex setting, strategic and even tactical decisions in association public relations and communications must be devised and implemented against the backdrop of internal political decisions that usually are more significant to organizational survival and explicit than those in business and industry.

Associations are characterized by the same sort of merger and spin-off machinations as the for-profit corporate sector. The most specialized of business or ideological interest can be found represented with its own association. Associations represent interests A to Z, from those advocating making the aardvark the United States' national symbol, to zoo keepers pursuing best professional practices. There is even an association for association executives. Based in Washington, DC, that association absorbed its local counterpart several years ago. New industries or emerging growth segments of an association's membership often choose to establish new organizations to promote their specialized interest not addressed by the original association. Countering that are mergers driven by cost-conscious boards who consider a specialized organization an unaffordable luxury. Evolving missions imbue the association's internal communications program and its strategic external communications efforts with a critical role.

ASSOCIATIONS HAVE VITAL DIFFERENCES FROM FOR-PROFIT COMPANIES

Association governance is a key variable distinguishing association public relations and communications in the for-profit sector. Boards of directors, often augmented by standing public relations committees of member volunteers, bring to the table a diverse set of interests and concerns. In some association cultures, the members predominate. Small associations, of course, often lack paid staff and the function is entirely volunteer. But growing associations with fewer than 10 staff members, and often larger ones as well, frequently remain member driven, with members moving far beyond setting policy into an active hands-on management role. Such instances invite substituting the members' individual, sometimes private, interests and views for those of the association in general. The opposite model is the staff-driven organization in which association management professionals are given broad latitude to manage the program. Unfortunately, as in any group of people, there are managers who mismanage their duties or abuse their trusts. The association management profession, obviously, favors a hybrid of the member-driven and staff-driven extremes.

Whether an association's objectives are to prepare its members for effective industry participation, establish best practices or product standards for the marketplace, market non-dues revenue programs to its members or advocate for its members to legislators, regulators, judges or consumers, its mission relies heavily on effective communications.

PRINCIPLES OF STRATEGIC COMMUNICATIONS IN ASSOCIATIONS

The principles of successful public relations and communications by associations are the same as for other entities. Essentially, success depends on aligning the group's interests with those of the public. Skilled association communicators define the issues. The association either must convince a significant segment, if not a majority, of the public that its perspective is worthy of support or abandon its programs and advocacy objectives. For some associations, addressing gun control is a question of the public's insisting on removing criminals' access to weapons, while for other associations, the issue represents an individual's constitutional rights and ability to protect self and family. The salt industry's interest in selling deicing salt becomes transformed into a salt-for-sand substitution strategy in communities with elevated wintertime airborne particulate levels that seek to satisfy the requirements of the Clean Air Act. The public has little sympathy for gun merchants or shooting clubs and cares little whether the salt industry sells more salt, but it certainly endorses preserving public safety, protecting constitutional rights and supporting the ability of people to protect themselves and their families while breathing clean, healthful air.

Effective association communications consists of developing a coherent strategy to conflate the association members' interests with the interests of the entire polity. Strategic communications encompass developing a winning message and selecting both relevant audiences and communication tools. A few examples will illustrate these principles in action.

When the Ontario Solid Wastes Management Association catalogued problems of Toronto-area trash truck operators, it identified a specific policy of the regional government that increased operators' costs. After 3 PM private waste haulers were denied access to public transfer stations convenient to their customers. "Too bad, but what can we do about it?" was the waste haulers' lament. Staff knowledgeable about the policymaking process suggested a simple, direct meeting with the agency to outline the problem. The meeting was held, and the hours adjusted. Never before had the operators cooperated. Never had it occurred to them that they could appeal even a manifestly unfair governmental policy. A simple problem with a simple solution.

MOVING FROM DEFENSE TO PROACTIVE ADVOCACY

Most challenges are more complicated. Let's consider the issues management strategy for highway deicing salt.

Since the 1960s, a major barrier to widespread use of wintertime deicing salt has been the documented adverse impacts on vehicle corrosion, water quality and vegetation. In 1972, the Salt Institute won a Silver Anvil strategic campaign award from the Public Relations Society of America for its Sensible Salting Program. The program included a series of free, staff-provided training seminars for equipment operators employed by state and local highway agencies and toll road authorities teaching them to use only the minimum amounts required to reach service objectives. Responsibly, salt-using agencies have experimented with alternative products; governments have studied environmental impacts. Salt remains the "deicer of choice." In fact, after relatively flat sales from the late 1970s until the early 1990s, varying only due to winter severity, road salt usage has increased by about 60 percent. Why?

In the early 1990s, the Salt Institute shifted its communications strategy for road salt. The primary audience had been customers and the message had been: use only as much as you need. The Institute switched from this essentially defensive stance to a proactive explanation to the general public, to highway users (shippers, bus companies, etc.) and to road safety advocates. The Institute pointed out that provision of winter roadway maintenance is the key to unlocking the values of safety and mobility for winter roads. The Institute sponsored university engineering studies of traffic crashes and road conditions and commissioned econometric analyses of the costs of paralyzing blizzards. The messaging focus shifted from minimizing costs to achieving benefits. When the public and concerned interest groups realized that deicing roads was both possible and valuable to them, they demanded improved winter roadway maintenance. A rising tide lifts all ships, so salt sales increased. The strategic communications shift anticipated an era of budgetary pressures on roadway maintenance agencies and equipped them with credible information to secure the budgets needed to deliver the demanded service levels.

The Salt Institute today focuses on mobilizing highway users and traffic safety advocates and officials to support performance metrics for highway operations leading to public support for high levels of winter maintenance service. Longtime allies such as the American Public Works Association (APWA) have been enlisted not only to promote environmentally safe salt management practices by their member agencies but also to work building public support for the service they provide. APWA, with Salt Institute encouragement, created a booklet entitled "Fight Winter and Win" designed for use by public works managers to educate their locally elected officials and concerned citizens.

The success of the program is measured in terms of acceptance of the Institute's advocacy positions by the targeted groups, fewer attempts to ban the use of salt, improved access and credibility accorded to the Institute's staff by various target groups, and formal endorsements of the Institute's advocacy of support for high quality winter maintenance by these groups. It exemplifies how the enduring strategic objective of facilitating the use of road salt for winter safety and mobility can be furthered by changing tactics of promoting the benefits of high service levels as opposed to emphasizing techniques to reduce environmental insult.

Some issues management strategies can be developed and implemented proactively; others are reactionary responses to challenges in the marketplace or from government, either legislative or regulatory. The proceeding case examines a 15-year issues management effort by the Salt Institute.

CASE: CANADA'S PRIORITY SUBSTANCES LISTING OF "ROAD SALTS"

In December 2001, Environment Canada (EC) recommended that road salts should be listed as "toxic" on Schedule 1. Up until then, every substance recommended to be listed as "toxic" was added to Schedule 1 and regulated by the federal government. But road salts were never listed, and therein lie the lessons.

That road salts are environmentally problematic was hardly news. Well before "Earth Day" was first celebrated on April 22, 1970, the public in North America and Europe, at least, knew of the environmental threat and both the salt industry and its municipal and state or provincial government customers had initiated efforts to reduce the adverse environmental impacts of salt or replace salt altogether.

In 1991, the Transportation Research Board (TRB), an arm of the National Academy of Sciences, completed a comprehensive investigation of the environmental consequences of using sodium chloride on U.S. highways. After calculating the damage inflicted by road salt and comparing it with damage caused by calcium magnesium acetate, a popular alternative, the report concluded that salt would remain the deicer of choice for the foreseeable future.

Unforeseen by either TRB or the Salt Institute at the time of the TRB report, just a few years later, in 1995, Canada ordered an environmental assessment of all chloride salts used for wintertime deicing and summertime dust suppression, adding "road salts" to its Priority Substances List (PSL) under the Canadian Environmental Protection Act (CEPA). This required EC and/or Health Canada to assess road salts to determine whether they are "toxic" as CEPA defined that word and, if so, to add them to Schedule 1 to be regulated. Substances not listed on Schedule 1 would be regulated at the provincial level; those listed as "toxic" would be regulated by EC risk managers.

That road salts were never listed owed much to a campaign of strategic communication. The CEPA statute required the bureaucrats' "toxic" recommendation to be endorsed by the Canadian Cabinet, a political decision, and political support for a "toxic" listing proved inversely related to successes in upgrading salt management practices.

While the assessment was still ongoing, the Salt Institute took an initiating role within the Transportation Association of Canada (TAC) to revisit the effectiveness of TAC members' salt management techniques. TAC represents public agencies (directly supervised by elected officials) and large-scale road maintenance contractors. TAC codified best practices and produced a Salt Management Guide in 1999, two years before the assessment report was released. The product, in effect, updated the Salt Institute's Sensible Salting guidelines and the entire project was designed, consciously, to serve as the blueprint for EC's anticipated salt management risk managers. Since it was developed by the very transportation agencies that were using salt, it was practical; since those agencies themselves were led by elected politicians, it set demanding standards for best management practices to protect the environment.

Thus, as the unsympathetic EC salt assessor team was wrapping up its report, and the risk management team was organizing to take its hand-off, significant groundwork had already been laid organizing road salt users and suppliers and launching a proactive campaign to upgrade salt management practices. The sanguinary struggle over the toxic listing that filled the news waves and front-page headlines concealed the broad consensus of salt producers and salt-using roadway agencies that careful management was the key ingredient in environmental stewardship.

To its great credit, EC took seriously its policy to consult affected stakeholders. It created a Road Salt Working Group and included all the parties from farmers and environmentalists to salt companies, the Salt Institute and road salt customers, including TAC. Not only did EC host frequent stakeholder meetings; it also employed a professional facilitator to develop consensus.

Consensus was reached relatively quickly. Early in the process, the stakeholders coalesced behind a strategy of emphasizing operator training as the top priority. Other major elements included creating "salt management plans," promoting ground control automatic spreaders, covering storage piles and filing annual public progress reports. The evident commitment of salt producers and users legitimized a voluntary approach and EC embraced a collaborative rather than combative risk management strategy.

Using the stakeholders group, EC produced a Road Salt Code of Practice and an implementation plan. Again, just like the TAC Guide, the end product looked a lot like the Salt Institute's Sensible Salting guidelines.

Taking advantage of the media visibility and the concern by provincial and local public officials that they would be put in the untenable position of using local tax revenues to put "toxic" materials into the environment, the Salt Institute recognized the opportunity to promote more vigorously its decades-old Sensible Salting message. Rather than becoming defensive, the Salt Institute became a cheerleader for the new EC Code of Practice. The Salt Institute funded projects by such salt customer groups as the Ontario Good Roads Association, to develop model salt management plans for their members and to conduct training workshops to implement improved salt management practices.

The positive momentum was sustained by two important facts. First, most previous PSL substances bore disturbing multisyllabic chemical names and were used by chemical companies out of sight "behind the fence"; road salt was inherently harmless (it is, after all, an approved food) and well known by the public. Second, the agencies "discharging" road salts into the environment were headed by elected officials committed to protecting public safety and jobs. The issue advocacy featured both themes.

Opposition to a "toxic" listing and support for a program of voluntary compliance with state-of-the-art salt management practices united the Canada Safety Council, shippers and other groups concerned that restrictions on road salt use would jeopardize the safety and assured availability of Canadian roads. It pitted "white hat" causes against each other and asked: "why can't we have both?" Rather than allowing salt users to be demonized as environmentally insensitive, the message was one of reaching the achievable balance of protecting the environment, ensuring safety for roadway users and keeping Canadian businesses open year-round. Had the campaign to defend best practices in road salt management not been based on a bedrock public purpose (in this case, at least two), it could not have withstood the attack of extremists who sought to ban salt use altogether. Likewise, those who would employ public safety and economic competitiveness arguments to excuse sloppy salt usage were frozen out of the stakeholders group and gained no public credibility.

As a result, EC completed a five-year assessment of its progress in implementing the Code of Practice at the end of 2010 and gathered data demonstrating that the voluntary program had produced significant results. Again, the Salt Institute and its road salt customers welcomed the notion of a science-based review and, in fact, the Salt Institute cofunded with Environment Ontario the most significant scientific assessment—chloride penetration into groundwater. The results, released at two international symposia at the University of Waterloo, indicate that best practices reduce chloride loadings and will gradually repair the damage of poor salt management practices in past decades.

DIFFERENT STROKES FOR DIFFERENT FOLKS

Sometimes strategic communications involve protracted and sustained advocacy of simple solutions, often using multiple communications channels. Other times, novel solutions can be quickly implemented when creative minds discover win-win opportunities. Consider enactment of the Post-Closure Liability Fund, a brainchild of the National Solid Wastes Management Association (NSWMA; now part of the Environmental Industries Association).

With the enactment of the landmark federal solid waste statute—the Resource Conservation and Recovery Act of 1976 (RCRA)—Congress created a federal regulatory program to ensure that hazardous chemical wastes were properly treated and disposed of by closing improper sites. Waste technology was evolving, but few state-of-the-art facilities existed. Some advanced facilities operated by NSWMA members had difficulty attracting sufficient volumes of waste to be commercially viable because less-costly but less-protective options were still legal. At the same time that the public interest lay in directing wastes to state-of-the-art facilities as quickly as possible, NSWMA members' interests lay in opening as many of these modern-technology facilities as necessary to receive these wastes.

The issue landscape was in chaos. Industries generating chemical wastes were often unfamiliar with proper waste management procedures and uncertain how to cover these new operating costs, or minimize them to meet international marketplace competition. Some environmentalists opposed any generation of hazardous wastes in the first place, hoping to "constipate the system" by denying approval of any legal disposal facilities and force the offending industry out of business or compel it to use a nonpolluting alternative technology (which often did not exist). Other environmentalists were intent on retribution for environmental sinners, punishing anyone responsible for environmental discharges.

The NSWMA developed the idea of the Post-Closure Liability Fund. The concept was that modern treatment and disposal facilities using state-of-the-art technologies would eventually receive Environmental Protection Agency (EPA) permits, and that those permits and the regulatory system overseeing their enforcement could be used to manage industry liabilities. A significant concern in bringing these expensive facilities into being was the potentially huge liability for unknowable future failures and the resultant environmental contamination. If some insurance mechanism could be provided, the insurance cost could be incorporated into the disposal fees charged up front, at the time of disposal. The proposed Post-Closure Liability Fund would bear the entire cleanup costs for properly licensed and properly closed facilities. It would be funded by a special disposal fee levied at the time of disposal and retained in a separate account for the generations to come.

The fund was a creative response to the public desire to manage the wastes properly since it provided a significant incentive to facility operators to qualify for the fund by properly managing and closing their facilities. It provided otherwise-unavailable insurance for the operators to encourage investment in facilities that would qualify for RCRA permits.

The NSWMA issues management program targeted Congress. The concept was new, different, narrowly focused and likely to be opposed by significant political forces. Broad consensus would be impossible, and implementing RCRA, a priority. Environmentalists would likely oppose the fund measure as encouraging additional disposal capacity and shielding operators from long-term liabilities associated with their activities. Industrial producers of waste materials could be counted on to oppose the new fees that they would be paying.

The NSWMA adopted a two-part strategy. First, the concept was broadly legitimized through discussion in public forums, articles published in environmental and trade journals and one-on-one meetings with EPA staff and a number of key congressional staff. Then, highly credible congressional staff who were sold on its merits promoted it within the staff drafting committee of the Senate Environment and Public Works Committee to be included as a minor provision of the massive Superfund (Comprehensive Environmental Response, Compensation and Liability Act). The waste service industry registered its support for the final Superfund bill containing this provision. When other lobbyists discovered the Post-Closure Liability Fund was part of the final version of the act, it was already a "done deal." Environmentalists and industrialists all conceded they were familiar with the idea; they just had no idea it was going to be in the final bill enacted in 1980.

Different issues demand different strategies. In the Canadian campaign, vocal public support by a strong and politically potent coalition was crucial for success. In the Post-Closure Liability Fund, quiet negotiations brought success.

One technique used with increased frequency and great success has been the creation of ad hoc alliances and coalitions, some with their own staff apparatus, many without. If the rationale for associations is that there is strength in numbers, association activists recognize that joint action of many associations raises the truism exponentially. Just as "politics makes strange bedfellows," ad hoc coalitions exist issue by issue; today's antagonist is tomorrow's valued ally.

The basic functions remain critical to successful strategic communications: define the vision and desired outcome; position the message to align with the public interest; and develop sustainable support within the association and among potential allies.

ASSOCIATIONS MASTER USE OF NEW COMMUNICATIONS TECHNOLOGIES

The basics are not enough today, however. Strategic communications for associations also requires integrating those messages and policy objectives with fast-developing new technologies and public communications expectations. Communications is a competitive enterprise. Counter messages seek outcomes detrimental to the association communicator. More subtly, the vastly expanding universe of information being communicated challenges the talents of association communicators to differentiate their message and master the media.

Sound strategy remains absolutely necessary, but it is insufficient. Tactics separate the sheep from the goats. Even if the fireman has the ladder leaning against the right house, if he can't climb, aim a hose or wield an ax, fire will destroy the house. Knowing who needs to be convinced and what they need to be convinced to do—but not knowing how to convince them—is a recipe for communications impotence. Effective strategic communicators need to understand the big picture, but also master the tactical tools of the trade.

Over the past decade, association use of strategic communications has been evolutionary rather than revolutionary, spurring effective association issues managers to evolve with them. Ten years ago, seven-pound laptop computers were considered mobile devices. Today, we have lightweight netbooks, but even they are being supplanted by tablets like the iPad and all manner of smartphones. The capacity of these devices to connect to the Internet virtually anywhere and to process, quickly, all manner of content, including graphics and live video, has launched a new chapter in association communications. Social media is only the tip of the iceberg as this new mobility has created expectations of immediate access to information and interactive opportunities. Turn-around communication responses that were once aspirational are now insufficiently responsive. Time is compressing.

Ten years ago, blogs were just drawing attention as communication vehicles and RSS feeds were pie-in-the-sky. Communication theorists predicted online, virtual communities, but technology was still too clunky to realize that vision. No longer. Facebook is faster than the phone. Think viral.

Technologies also have enabled such basic services as cloud computing, online backups and storage and, most of all, online collaboration. It is hard to realize that Wikipedia was only launched in January 2001, one decade ago. Today, Wikipedia is often the first-named search result for online searches. While webmasters from the mid-1990s understood the importance of optimizing their sites for search engines, the term *search engine optimization* (SEO) was only beginning to take hold as a website essential 10 to 12 years ago and the advancing sophistication of SEO and search engine algorithms has become valued intellectual property defining the communications playing field.

Never before have the tools available to issues managers and strategic communicators been so powerful, affordable and broadly available. Likewise, never before has the targeted "public" had higher expectations about the speed, quality and responsiveness of the information they seek. While information overload is hardly a new phenomenon, it is clearly more important with each passing year that both information management technology and consumer communications expectations are driving imperative advances in practitioner skills. Associations recognize the truth spoken by the Red Queen to Alice in Wonderland: "Now, here, you see, it takes all the running you can do to keep in the same place. If you want to get somewhere else, you must run at least twice as fast as that!"

Indeed, some associations are running faster than ever before. Myriad examples fill the pages of *Associations Now!*, the magazine of the American Society of Association Executives, and the related literature. Four examples illustrate. The Ecological Society of America produces a series of podcasts created by recording Skype interviews with explanatory voiceovers and music. The International Game Developers Association uses blogs and wikis to stimulate member collaboration in a series of special interest groups that publish their own news and develop industry standards and white papers. The National School Boards Association has a long-standing blog, *Board Buzz*, which it employs to respond to media stories and legislative or regulatory issues. The Salt Institute posts a series of vodcasts by "The Salt Guru" to the web, opining and informing on common questions about salt and offering perspective on public policy issues. Other examples abound.

KNOW YOUR TARGET AUDIENCE

Tools vary according to the audience and objective. Associations have internal and external audiences.

A key strategic need of associations is in the area of internal marketing. This includes not only getting members to renew their dues but also to buy association-produced books and videos, register for association meetings, raise assessments for special projects, buy insurance from the association's captive company, use the association-sponsored credit card and place ads in the association's magazine. In short, plans include the use of any number of special services from which the association derives non-dues income. Associations use brochures and fact sheets, internal newsletters, telemarketing, direct mail, broadcast fax, computer bulletin boards and membership meetings.

The second major communications area for most associations is to communicate and "sell" ideas to external audiences. While the communications objectives are external, they often involve both member education and grassroots mobilization. The tools include the full range of member communications listed above. In addition, the tools are used to mobilize potential allies in a temporary alliance or coalition. Examples of these tools include direct mail to concerned publics; paid advertising in the consumer or trade media, formal legislative and/or regulatory testimony; personal visits with legislators and regulators; third-party endorsements, particularly of especially credible individuals or groups or by celebrities; and political action contributions with elected officials.

SYSTEMATIC ISSUES MANAGEMENT PLANNING

A systematic top-down process is most effective. It derives strategies and tactics from the association's mission. They reflect the organizing principles of the group.

For example, the mission of the Salt Institute is to ensure that the public is able to enjoy the many benefits of using salt. Although each association is unique, the principles of issues management at the Salt Institute, including the tactical tools and planning process, reflect the process in all associations. Consider the process exemplary.

People have discovered more than 14,000 ways to use sodium chloride, the principal ones being the raw material for the entire chlor-alkali industry, highway deicing, water softening, use in food processing and preparation and in feeds for poultry and livestock. The Salt Institute issues management program has established objectives in each of these areas and in the area of production and distribution issues related to enhancing the productivity of salt production and shipment to customers, reducing their costs.

Until recent years, association policy makers met twice a year and worked their way through a detailed book of the association's strategies and tactics. Today, that same group meets monthly via teleconference. A members-only website captures the key data and strategy decisions and the discussion is more lively and timely. Instead of a thick book, policy issue summaries are now available online with supporting documents distributed via e-mail or posted to the members-only website.

The tactical discipline remains unchanged. For each issue, staff prepares for a discussion statement of the goal, a listing of the priority target audiences, a series of short summaries of the strategy for each target audience, a listing of the projects that are being used to implement the several target audience strategies, a listing of the measures of results and evaluation by which the issues management strategy performance will be evaluated, a listing of the priority networking contacts with a subsidiary listing of other networking contacts worth mentioning, a similar listing of priority media outlets including both institute publications or audio-visual materials and outside publications and electronic media and finally, a list of the priority communications vehicles being employed in each strategy.

CULTURE AND COMMUNITY—USING SOCIAL MEDIA

Nonprofit associations have much in common with for-profit companies, but vive la différence! The two can learn much from each other. Successful for-profit firms offer clear lessons to the nonprofit sector in evaluation and accountability. Successful nonprofit associations have mastered issues of culture and community. Both community and culture, and evaluation and accountability deserve attention.

Today, community means connecting and belonging, and technology again has revolutionized possibilities and expectations. And, since mobilizing for action these communities of shared interest-holders is at the core of the nonprofit association mission, associations have embraced the social media.

A generation ago, associations created communities largely by newsletters and meetings. Most associations launched websites in the mid- to late-1990s. A decade ago, a membership community featured listservs and intranets. Then came blogs. Today, "community" includes Facebook, LinkedIn, Twitter, YouTube and others like them. The principles are the same, but communication flows more quickly and in all directions.

The lawyers cringe! No longer can association communications be prescreened for potential antitrust sensitivity. Associations, and particularly trade associations composed of marketplace competitors, invest heavily in robust antitrust compliance programs to educate their members about sharing inappropriate competitive information such as plans for pricing, marketing and production. No system is perfect, but newsletter copy and website postings can be prescreened and meeting-goers warned of the antitrust ground rules. Listservs and intranets can be monitored in the same manner the Federal Communications Commission polices the airwaves for profanity. But real-time "posts" from all comers from all directions all the time? Impossible. Risky. Irrepressible.

ENDURING PRINCIPLES OF STRATEGIC COMMUNICATION

The point is, everything has changed and nothing has changed. The principles of integrity, credibility and transparency are inviolate.

Social media are more immediate than previous technologies. They can be more personal and represent a powerful tool in the communications toolbox. But credibility and quality information remain central to strategic communications, whether the author uses a quill pen or an iPad. And while the superficial metric changes from number of phone calls received to the number of website "hits" to the number of Facebook friends, the real measure of success is in achieving policy objectives. Technologies come and go. Social media will give way to something else. What endures is the value of the information transmitted, the integrity of the communicator and the willingness and ability to deliver the message conveniently to the target audience.

Mastery of the communications process and technology options confers power on the expert communicator. With that power—the ability to move an issue, to direct a policy outcome—comes a responsibility beyond that owed to a cause or an employer. We lament incivility in our public discourse. Rightly so. But as we master the tricks of the trade and amass the power to move public opinion or influence any of the various publics whose actions influence our goals, we are admonished by such varying authorities as the Bible (Luke 12:48), President Theodore Roosevelt and Stan Lee's *Spiderman*, that with power comes responsibility.

For-profit public companies are regularly chastised for failing to look beyond their next quarterly "numbers." Likewise, strategic communications is a long-term endeavor depending on the communicator's reputation; abuse that trust and forfeit any future influence.

Insecure advocates cherry-pick the evidence. They fail to prepare those they hope to influence with the basic education on an issue; they fail to disclose the arguments that will be raised counter to their case. Transparency works. For example, all news releases and public statements issued by the Salt Institute since 1996 (when the institute launched its first website) are available on the website today. Few would care to mine this historical mother lode, but all can appreciate what this transparency says about the Salt Institute's openness and willingness to accept responsibility for its advocacy representations. Information changes over time and, with it, advocacy positions. But an organization that embraces truth and data quality strengthens its reputation and, ultimately, this translates into effective strategic communications.

DID WE WIN? EVALUATION AND ACCOUNTABILITY

All of this leads naturally to the question of evaluation and accountability. How do we know if we have won? How do we know if we have been effective strategic communicators?

Association public relations and communications staffers often learn a harsh lesson at the hands of their boards, particularly if those boards are composed, as they often are, of hard-nosed, successful business executives. And the lesson is equally applicable if the organization is charitable, education oriented, devoted to some ideological cause or pursuing the economic interests of its corporate members.

Measure outcomes, not outputs. Sure, the board wants an accounting of the resources they provide, the inputs. They are interested in outputs such as newspaper and magazine clippings and calculations of the number of column inches or the potential combined readership of the distribution or the number of viewers or listeners. But quantifying outputs is a trap, whether it be column inches of yesteryear, the number of business cards collected in a fishbowl at trade shows, the number of people in the audience for key presentations or, in the past decade, the number of website "hits," Facebook "friends," or "likes" for their Facebook posts. Outcomes are what matters, not outputs.

Strategic communicators cannot settle for bean counting. Issues management deals with outcomes. And this issue demands hard thinking on the front end: what will represent "success"? Is it passage or defeat of a specific legislative bill or regulatory proposal, some nuanced policy outcome, association visibility, increased membership or some improvement in the industry's economic position? Strategic thinking in public relations and communications demands that publicity be only a side indicator; an interim measure at best. The objective is some behavior change on the part of the target audience. That is true whether the audience is a congressional conference committee or 310 million Americans. The board of directors wants to know whether the publicity produced additional membership and dues revenues, whether it resulted in an expanded market for the association members' products or services, whether additional and effective research areas were opened or whether hungry people were fed or homeless were housed. They want the bottom line. It is never easy and it is sometimes impossible to document all the answers to the right questions. But it is always appropriate to address the right questions. Professionals do just that. They show that they know what is really important, and what is not.

By measuring and delivering outcomes, communicators earn a place at the table when strategic planning decisions are discussed. No effective association can operate without input and guidance from a board sensitive to strategic public relations and communications. In associations with paid staff, the public relations or communications director should be at the table and on the inside. But the status must be earned, not offered because it was recommended in a handbook of proper practice.

FACING THE FUTURE

A few historical statistics will help us crystal-ball the years ahead. A century ago, governments at all levels spent about 8 percent of the U.S. Gross Domestic Product and it was not until the Great Depression that total government spending exceeded 10 percent. Today, governments spend 40 cents of each dollar produced by American workers and federal regulations alone are estimated to add an additional 18 cents per dollar. Clearly, governments are directing more and more economic decisions.

Look at a second set of historical statistics; these on technological change. Change is always destabilizing. A millennium ago, the Chinese invented paper currency and movable type. A century ago, Thomas Edison demonstrated the first talking motion picture. A decade ago, Apple introduced the iPod. Just last year, surgeons began using plasma scalpels. The point is, technology is accelerating. The world is both smaller and more complicated. Governments are desperately struggling to control these destabilizing changes. Sure, it is possible we could retreat to another Dark Ages by virtue of global terrorism or World War III. More likely, we'll face a future where many decisions touching our lives have been socialized; associations will be needed to ensure those decisions reflect real-world understanding of the issues involved to avoid unintended consequences. Likewise, our children face the challenge of a world where absorbing the exploding quantity of technical knowledge is essential to ensure economic competitiveness and the quality of life it enables.

Associations are an indispensable aid to the process of keeping government on track and preparing the next generation of doctors, engineers and the rest of our workforce with the skills they need to maintain our momentum forward toward more healthy and abundant lives. Associations will play a vital role in framing issues for public discussion. They will aid citizens' petitions to government. They will help define the basic educational curriculum both to prepare professional specialists and provide in-service training for those who need access to an accelerating knowledge base.

The "special interests" who are castigated as "lobbyists" are, rather, educators. What legislator, in a state capital or on Capitol Hill, could possibly have enough specialized knowledge in our complex, interrelated economy to make informed policy judgments? Even seasoned regulatory specialists often misunderstand how "the rubber meets the road." The term *unintended consequences* is becoming a common explanation (i.e., excuse) of why well-intended interventions didn't quite work out as planned.

This is neither new nor particularly American. Witness the decades-long failure of successive waves of Soviet "five-year plans" or the twenty-first century absurdity of congressional bills thousands of pages long. Pick any professional specialty and you'll quickly find additions to the body of knowledge emerging so fast that even specialists cannot keep pace. If peer reviews and guidance were unavailable, technology transfer would grind to a halt. Associations face a bright future as tour guides through the information jungle.

Communications, likewise, will remain the central mission of associations as long as there are associations. The tools will change. Association intranets, websites, listservs, blogs, e-mail, webcasts, social media and other new technologies will characterize the operations of even small association staffs. Gathering information is an even greater challenge. The Internet and the panoply of available commercial databases and information services threaten to overload our circuits, but they offer needed information at the same time.

Members of associations and members of the various publics with which they interact are all facing the prospect of information overload. Communications professionals understand the challenge, and they recognize the opportunity for those who can meet the challenge. The postindustrial society is information based. Those who have it, those who manage it and the associations who employ them have an edge on the future.

DISCUSSION QUESTIONS

1. How are associations different from for-profit companies?
2. What technologies and techniques have associations employed for strategic communication over the past 50 years? The past decade? Today?
3. Does the planning and execution of strategic management in associations vary between local, state, national or global organizations?
4. What is the single most important consideration in ensuring successful strategic communications?
5. What steps should be included in an organization's strategic communications plan?
6. Why was the case example a success story?

ADDITIONAL READING

American Society of Association Executives, "Associations FAQ," www.asaecenter.org/Advocacy/content ASAEOnly.cfm?ItemNumber=16341, accessed May 18, 2011.

Chase, W. Howard. 1985. "Issue Management: Origins of the Future." *Issue Action Publications*, September. ISBN 0913869015; ISBN 978-0913869017.

Dalton, James G. 2006. "Strategy Management for Associations: From Issues to Action." *Journal of Association Leadership* (Fall 2006). www.asaecenter.org/Resources/JALArticleDetail.cfm?ItemNumber=19978.

Heath, Robert L. and Michael J. Palenchar. 2009. *Strategic Issues Management—Organizations and Public Policy Challenges*, 2nd ed. www.sagepub.com/books/Book230592.

Jaques, Tony. 2000. "Don't Just Stand There—The Do-It-Plan for Effective Issue Management." www.issue actionpublications.com/documents/literature/lit.dont.just.stand.html.

McGrath, George B. 1998. *Issues Management: Anticipation and Influence*. International Association of Business Communicators, ISBN-10 1888015128; ISBN-13: 978-1888015126.

Schattschneider, Elmer Eric. 1960. *The Semisovereign People: A Realist's View of Democracy in America*. ISBN-10: 0030133661; ISBN-13: 978-0030133664.

Scheel, Randall L. 1991. "Maxims for the Issues Manager." *Issue Action Publications*. ISBN-10: 0913869023; ISBN-13: 978-0913869024.

20 CHAPTER

AGENCIES
Managing a Global Communications Firm

Ray Kotcher
Senior Partner and Chief Executive Officer
Ketchum

We are living in revolutionary times. Literally.

We see entrenched leaders overthrown and societal structures profoundly, sometimes radically, transformed. These tectonic shifts have many underlying sociopolitical causes, with nuances as varied as the history and culture of whichever group we are examining. However, as communicators, we cannot help but see a strikingly common thread in each transformational moment—the power of ideas, the ability to share them in real time and the opportunity to engage with people and mobilize them. This power is literally at our fingertips, just a click away, and it brings consequences that only recently were beyond our imagination.

While a global communications firm, to my knowledge, has never been tasked with navigating a revolution on the streets, we are indeed charting a course through our own revolution: the convergence of globalization, digital empowerment and near-total transparency. How then, does a twenty-first century global communications company harness these extraordinary forces to deliver what clients need, namely, gold standard reputations and brands that stand out from the crowd to earn consumer loyalty? To help translate this to perhaps a more typical assignment, picture this:

> An established consumer brand has been working to make its products more appealing to young adults. Now, it needs to raise awareness among those young adults in important markets around the world. Shortly before it announces the product changes, however, a key competitor launches a campaign aimed at the same consumers. That will make getting attention for the brand's messages an even tougher challenge. Young adults already are bombarded by marketing messages every day, making it difficult to get their attention. The brand's competitor is better known, with more resources. And the brand knows that what works in one part of the world may not work in others.

The company calls on brand marketing consultants in, let's say, its agency's New York office. New York taps San Francisco, then London, Sao Paulo, Hong Kong and Munich. Within a few short days, each office offers strategic and tactical ideas to help the brand cut through the clutter. So what's the issue? The ideas aren't connected, they aren't talking the same language and they haven't sufficiently engaged the clients.

Simply tapping offices around the world will not solve a client's challenge. For a global communications firm to provide superior client service, it needs more than just offices around the world. It needs to have a unified vision of how to service and engage those clients. Here's a different scenario:

Same brand. Same challenges. This time, though, the client is provided with an integrated experience in every aspect of its engagement. From one city to another, across continents, across areas of expertise, the client is actively engaged throughout the collaboration. The agency is a near expert in the business of the client. There is an open dialogue about the work. Tools are used to communicate efficiently with the client and to determine the metrics of success and measure them in real time. There is a global commitment to constantly driving innovation and ideas that break through for clients' businesses.

But wait. There's more. Even as the communications firm's professional consultants work together across geographies, ideas also pour into the agency from students at Bournemouth University in the United Kingdom; the Chinese University of Hong Kong; the Mudra Institute of Communications in Ahmadabed, India; Georgetown University in Washington, DC; and from other schools around the world. The agency pairs its ideas with the students' to give its client the combined benefit of the thinking of seasoned communications professionals and virtual real-time crowdsourcing.

This is not a focus group or a one-off classroom experiment. Called Mindfire and used through a close partnership with clients, it is one of an agency's many approaches to using social technology to bring our clients fresh thinking from diverse minds—wherever they might be around the world.

But ideas are only one part of the equation. Meeting clients' needs and providing truly differentiated service is what will empower the agency and its clients to achieve business goals. That brings us to the subject of the rest of this chapter—what it means to run a globally successful public relations firm today.

NO BOUNDARIES

Managing a global communications firm requires a no-boundaries approach. But communications without boundaries presents both perils and promise. And today's communications firm must be prepared for both.

Today's media is always on, and it's everywhere—from the constant streaming of social media where bloggers can post anything from anywhere, to consumer product reviews available to anyone with a smartphone. We're living in a world with no communications boundaries, so to be successful, a global communications firm must commit to the same thinking. Stories that could harm companies or their brands and products can come from anywhere at any time. But today's always-on media offers an unprecedented opportunity to engage in authentic conversations that are already taking place online. That can yield great benefit to companies and brands that participate.

A successful global agency must be willing to go beyond conventional thinking—and in some cases its own walls—to solve client challenges. We call this our "no-boundaries approach" to client service.

Managing a global communications firm with a no-boundaries approach demands four key components:

1. A clear understanding of how recent and ongoing changes in communications tools and technology continue to change how we use communications to meet client needs

2. The ability to integrate global resources to benefit clients, which may include working with agencies from across the marketing disciplines

3. A structure that enables a multinational firm to maintain a common cultural glue

4. A willingness to embrace and anticipate an ever-changing communications environment

Throughout this chapter, I will discuss each of these in relation to our agency's approach. Let's start by looking at some of the changes that led to a world without boundaries.

UNDERSTANDING WHAT HAS CHANGED

To fully grasp how changes in the media landscape influence the way global communications firms must operate, it is essential to understand what those changes are. Three stand out: the Internet revolutionized the media infrastructure; it became critical for organizations to boost employee engagement and synchronize internal communications; and measurement of public relations became focused on what the discipline brings rather than trying to simply mirror existing advertising measurement models.

CHANGES IN THE MEDIA INFRASTRUCTURE

Before 1996, most major news organizations did not have an online presence. Even after some of the world's largest newspapers and broadcast networks launched news websites, the media continued to operate the same way it always had. News editors and producers served as gatekeepers, deciding what constituted news and how it was reported. Most local and regional news stayed local. And public relations professionals cultivated relationships with seasoned journalists who typically covered a particular beat in a particular market.

However, by 2000, independent news aggregators already were posting news stories online for anyone with an internet connection to see. Bloggers were providing their own analyses of news stories. Initial concerns about the credibility of unedited reporting soon gave way to the reality that consumers were deciding for themselves whom to trust—and often choosing the first mover reporting on the ground as events unfolded. Before long, major news organizations were racing to keep pace with upstarts.

Today, news is nonstop. Everyday consumers, the so-called citizen journalists, are supplanting professional news editors and reporters—sharing and even reporting stories about brands, companies and countries and often doing so in 140-character messages from hand-held, mobile devices. Consumers are commandeering official brand communications, too. Their ability to engage in uncensored conversations about what they like and don't like arguably has shifted control of a brand's image to the public just as much as to the companies that market them.

Whether it's coming from consumers, corporations or institutions, people have expressed preference for a continuous flow of information, and they seem to expect more of it. To match the demand for news, established media outlets now must meet multiple deadlines and file in multiple formats throughout the day. And they must be ready for anything.

Just as the Internet and related media tools have raised the bar for news organizations, they also have raised the bar for communications firms. Companies can now take their side of a story directly to consumers, rather than relying solely on media outlets for accurate interpretation. Communications firms must have full access to and command of the latest communication tools, along with skilled PR professionals, to help their clients do this in a way that's both credible and effective.

Also as with news organizations, global communications firms must be prepared to respond to breaking issues around the world, as clients are now doing business on a multinational basis. Whether that means they make or sell products in many countries, provide services to businesses in multiple countries, or have international investors, it most certainly means that they have greater exposure to public scrutiny than ever before and greater opportunities to positively position their companies and brands.

To support clients within a global media framework, a communications firm must operate on a global platform. In the past, managers of a public relations agency could choose whether their firm would be global or local and still operate as a full-service agency serving a range of clients. Today, a mid-sized firm focused on only one market is considered a specialty shop. To serve global clients, a firm must be strong on the ground in the markets where its clients do business. It must be able to act quickly and creatively to boost its clients' profiles. And it must be able to respond rapidly to protect its clients' reputations.

CHANGES IN INTERNAL COMMUNICATIONS

Internal communications has always been important to keep employees abreast of news and changes at a company; however, it has not always been a part of the work a firm does for its clients. For the most part, corporations traditionally relied on their agencies for external communications support while handling internal communications, well, internally. Indeed, a firm's primary relationship within a client company might well have been with an individual who had little to no direct involvement in communicating to employees. (See Chapter 8 for more on employee communications.)

Things have changed. The communications function for organizations is no longer about external communications alone. C-suite-level executives understand that what's said inside an organization is just as important as what's said outside, and corporate communicators view employees as key stakeholders. To go further, what companies preach outside the company must line up with management practices and how they behave inside the company. When they don't, a company's own employees often will be the first to let the public know. Likewise, when internal communications is done well, employees can have a significant positive impact.

Legendary public relations practitioner Arthur W. Page recognized this decades ago. In 1927, Page became the first person in a public relations position to serve as an officer and member of the board of directors for a public company. One of the seven principles he practiced in managing public relations for the American Telephone and Telegraph Company sums up employees' impact on a company's reputation this way: "Realize a company's true character is expressed by its people."

Employees represent a company's brand, and in some cases, are perceived to *be* the brand. If you are at all uncertain about whether this is so, think back to the last time you walked into a store and ordered coffee and someone greeted you with a smile, listened carefully to your order and got it exactly right. Now, think back to a time you walked into a store and the salespeople were too busy to notice you.

In the case of the latter, didn't it at least make you want to tell a friend, post it to Facebook or consider whether you would ever go back?

Employees can be a company's best advocates or its worst detractors. Communications firms have significant opportunities today to help their clients align messaging from multiple employee-facing functions and engage employees around the world as brand and reputational ambassadors. To do so, a firm must have a deep knowledge of a client's company or brand, industry and markets in which they operate. More importantly, it also must counsel the client to make sure the messages it is asking employees to carry line up with reality.

One other interesting and very recent development relating to communicating with employees is that today many clients are building open employee communities using social media channels such as Facebook as a means to share information and connect. Further, no-boundaries communications also means that social networks and online media have given employees a voice they never had before.

FedEx, which provides customers and businesses worldwide with a broad portfolio of transportation, e-commerce and business services, provides a great example. FedEx learned through integrated research that its nearly 300,000 team members around the world wanted not only an opportunity to engage and learn from one another—everyone from managers to front-line drivers—but they also wanted a chance to tell their story. What was so compelling was the pervasive theme of sharing their passions as employees, and their responsibilities to customers and the communities where they work and live. Ketchum worked with FedEx to create "I am FedEx," a digital, social and communications platform that houses a variety of content including videos, audio clips, photos and the like. Less than one year after its launch, I am FedEx is one of the most embraced, utilized and valued platforms for dialogue and storytelling by the FedEx team member communities.

While all of these platforms offer tremendous opportunity for dialogue and participation, they also fuel the need for policies on engagement. Therefore, global firms also must develop or acquire the expertise to counsel organizations on developing social media policies and guidelines to help shape the way employees around the world talk about their companies online. Guidelines can serve two purposes: they can help govern the use of corporate identity and what can or cannot be shared, and they can support employee ambassadors who want to use social media to build a stronger reputation for the company online.

An in-depth proprietary study conducted of corporate communications leaders at 60 well-known companies by Ketchum and its client FedEx suggests a few areas in which communications firms might offer needed help in developing social media policies from start to finish. First, the study found that most effective communications policies are natural extensions of existing codes of conduct related to confidentiality, privacy and disclosure. Next, policies were often developed or strengthened by benchmarking what other companies are doing and then facilitating cross-functional collaboration among corporate communications, human resources, marketing, legal and other departments to tailor according to the specific company. Finally, employee acceptance and adoption of such policies is driven by clear internal communication and relevant learning opportunities. In all instances, global agencies are in a strong position to support these efforts.

CHANGES IN PR MEASUREMENT

The measurement of success tied to actual business results has long been one of the most critical factors in how business leaders judge the relevance of—and allocate resources for—their various marketing activities and corporate communications. Yet, for far too long, the public relations industry had no standard guidelines for measuring PR. In the absence of a PR-focused approach, clients typically used advertising metrics (namely, advertising value equivalencies) to measure public relations results.

However, from agency to agency and client to client, what counted as acceptable measurement had been inconsistent, making it difficult for the industry as a whole to pinpoint the value of communication programs. Thanks to an ambitious and essential effort by multiple public relations organizations around the world, things are changing.

In 2010, a group led by the International Association for Measurement and Evaluation of Communication gathered together in Barcelona, Spain, to agree on a set of standards and principles for measuring public relations. Among other things, the Barcelona Principles of Measurement articulated the importance of quantitative goal setting and measurement. (See Chapters 2 and 3 on research.)

David Rockland, managing director of Ketchum Research and an agency partner, was a key contributor to that effort. He summed up the need for measurement this way: "The value of PR lies in how earned media drives changes in audience awareness, comprehension, attitude, behavior and, ultimately, business results such as sales. As an industry, we need to be very clear about how you get to these (PR) results."

The insightful nineteenth century marketing pioneer John Wanamaker articulated the measurement challenge in a different way, many decades ago. "Half the money I spend on advertising is wasted," he said. "The trouble is I don't know which half."

Today, clients just do not accept that. They want to understand the value of every marketing and communications dollar they spend. We need to be very clear about the fact that PR *can*, in fact, deliver results, and that we are better at planning and modeling than ever before as clients are demanding that certainty. A dollar spent will generate more than a dollar in business returns. The focus on standard measurement principles is a game changer for the PR industry as a whole, as well as for any global PR client in need of consistent measurement across its markets.

In that regard, a recent development that must be highlighted is the application of sophisticated analytics to public relations research and measurement. One example is that we are now able to incorporate PR metrics into marketing mix modeling (MMM). MMM uses historical data to determine the sales impact of different marketing activities. Traditionally it has been used to determine the impact of advertising, even down to the level of a specific ad. As we begin to apply it to public relations, agency and client alike can plan even more effectively and optimize budgets by allocating them properly to the most effective elements of a campaign. This presents one of the areas of greatest promise and opportunity for public relations, particularly as it relates to marketing communications and linking what we do to business results.

In addition to the potential of MMM, the focus of PR research and measurement also has turned to applying analytics to social and digital media. We now are able to determine the arc of a social media conversation and the impact of our efforts on that conversation.

The focus on standard measurement principles and the application of analytics are game changers for the PR industry as a whole, as well as for any global PR client in need of consistent measurement across its markets.

WHAT HAS NOT CHANGED

With all the ways communications has changed and continues to change, it seems worthwhile to point out the one thing that has remained constant: the power of an idea. Creativity is essential. A creative idea grounded in business strategy and executed properly can be powerful enough to break through any or all media channels and yield returns for the client no matter where they happen to be in the world. (See Chapter 49 on creativity.)

PUTTING GLOBAL STRENGTH TO USE FOR CLIENTS

Working with a large, global communications firm offers many benefits for clients, including the following:

1. A wide breadth and depth of communications services and specialized offerings—ranging from branding to media relations, from corporate reputation management to sports marketing, and from issues and crisis management to public affairs

2. Service in countries where clients are doing business—providing an understanding of local communications culture and expectations while at the same time linking clients to a broader communications network and infrastructure

3. A range of talent and experience across functions

4. A business operations infrastructure spanning information technology, budget management and reporting

As important as each of these things is, they are not enough to effectively serve clients in a world of 24/7, global communications. If a firm has a large number of employees but those employees are not collaborating and working together effectively, success is far less likely. Integration is essential.

A strong global communications agency must be integrated across geographies, areas of expertise and in its approach to client challenges. This includes the obvious, such as being able to communicate across language and cultural barriers and being accessible, at times on demand. But it also means understanding the strengths that lie across the firm and being able to tap into those strengths to improve on the level of work being delivered and to produce measurable results. Furthermore, it requires trust. Integration will only be successful if employees are willing to trust each other and share the responsibility with other colleagues—even those halfway around the world. Together they can then collaborate back and forth and produce the best results for clients.

CASE STUDY

Work for the Häagen-Dazs brand provides an example of integrating areas of expertise. In 2007, Häagen-Dazs asked Ketchum to help reinvigorate public perception of the brand and increase sales. The agency responded with an integrated campaign that resulted in the brand's introducing a new flavor of ice cream to help raise attention for what was then a little-known epidemic that was killing off honeybee populations in North America and parts of Europe—colony collapse disorder (CCD).

Agency social media strategists identified CCD as a potentially hot topic after observing online conversations among consumers. Soon after, the client's account team learned that more than 40 percent of the all-natural ingredients used in Häagen-Dazs products are reliant on honeybee pollination and thus threatened by CCD. The brand committed to donating funds for honeybee research whenever consumers bought certain products.

Teams across the agency contributed to the program. Members of Ketchum's brand marketing team designed the "Häagen-Dazs Loves Honey Bees" campaign based on the social media team's discovery about CCD. Members of the public affairs team helped raise legislative awareness of the issue on Capitol Hill in Washington, DC. Media specialists helped secure more than 1,000 news placements. And the agency's research team provided further insights on which to base the work, as well as measurement of the campaign.

These integrated efforts earned the client praise and recognition for supporting an important environmental cause and for its commitment to using all-natural ingredients in its products. Most significantly, the award-winning campaign also helped drive Häagen-Dazs' largest single-volume sales increase in more than a year. To top off that treat, the second year of the program won one of the first-ever Lions awards for public relations work from the Cannes Lions International Advertising Festival, one of the most important professional gatherings in the global communications industry.

Anecdotal and quantitative evidence suggests that today clients are not only seeking integration, they are demanding it. *Marketing in the Brave New Digital World*, a 2010 report from The Boston Consulting Group (BCG), makes the following observation about the need for better integration of marketing efforts:

> Once they decide where to invest, companies need to integrate their chosen marketing vehicles, creating campaigns where the channels complement—and boost—each other. "Siloed" activities might net positive results, but not the big payback that justifies big investments. That only comes when the parts are carefully, and intelligently, linked. Unfortunately, few companies—and few agencies—are presently able to create integrated campaigns across all media.

That's not just public relations agencies. In fact, BCG's research looked across the full spectrum of marketing and advertising, asking survey participants, "How effective is your company's planning and budgeting process for each of the following marketing/advertising vehicles you use?" The list included point-of-sale marketing, direct marketing, mobile marketing and advertising through television, radio, magazines and bill-boards, alongside public relations and other marketing efforts.

The list itself underscores another important point about integration: not only must communications firms be able to integrate within their own companies, but they also must be able to work with clients' agencies from other disciplines to conduct integrated programs. While the BCG report laments the lack of this kind of integration, clients are asking for it more and more. As companies continue to rely on multiple firms representing a range of disciplines, calls for integration among agencies will only grow louder. That will make it inevitable.

CASE STUDY: ACTIVATING AGENCY MULTICENTER ENGAGEMENT FOR CLIENTS

A prime case in point for the way the agency works to provide a seamless, outstanding experience in every facet of a client engagement is the Ketchum multicenter engagement program. We work for many of our clients in a variety of locations, and may offer different services as needed in different locations. It is essential that every client have the same high-quality experience in every location, and that we leverage the value of our entire global network to give clients a maximum "return on their spend." In many cases, clients look to us to break down silos between regions. Launched in 2009, multicenter engagement codifies and formalizes Ketchum's approach to globally integrated and superior client service through a detailed methodology and account director training program.

From one continent to another, across multiple practices and specialties, from strategic thinking to the management of the business relationship, multicenter engagement delivers a coherent, efficient Ketchum experience. The end goal is simple: provide consistently high global service, via engaged agency employees who deliver an outstanding client experience, and make doing business with Ketchum as easy as possible.

Currently, multicenter engagements constitute some of the most robust and expansive work in Ketchum's portfolio. One of our largest multicenter engagement programs is in support of Eastman Kodak. A client since 2002, this iconic brand and global company of nearly 20,000 employees faced a twofold challenge in the 2000s: transforming itself from a film to an imaging technology company amidst the digital media revolution, and developing a social media marketing strategy for the consumer technology space. To meet this challenge, it was essential for Kodak to have globally differentiated yet consistent strategy and execution, and Kodak and Ketchum joined forces in a multicenter engagement effort.

Today our work with Kodak spans 11 markets on five continents. It operates under a global client service director who has primary responsibility for the engagement and is supported by a global account team with clearly defined roles. Further, Kodak and Ketchum developed mutually agreed-upon standards to evaluate the success of each activity along with the overall program, and they are reviewed during regular monthly, quarterly and yearly check-in periods.

Today, multicenter engagement has been established as the foundation for Ketchum's service promise and serves as the agency's "true north."

MAINTAINING A "CULTURAL GLUE" IN A NO-BOUNDARIES ENVIRONMENT

Seamless integration, even within a single organization, does not happen automatically. In a world where individuals must work together across multiple geographies, as well as levels of professional experience and areas of expertise to deliver a consistent client experience, purposeful effort is needed to bind them together.

As of 2011, Ketchum's global network included more than 2,300 people in more than 120 operations in 70 countries. Essential elements to enabling collaboration and cooperation throughout the network are a dedication to talent management with a strong training and professional development curriculum and a commitment to ethics and transparency. These are two of the critical components of our firm's "cultural glue."

KETCHUM UNIVERSITY, PROFESSIONAL DEVELOPMENT AND TALENT MANAGEMENT

Ketchum University is a comprehensive training program that offers employees opportunities for both personal growth and professional development. The program has a curriculum that is developed globally and implemented at both the global and local levels. Agency leaders and outside consultants alike provide training to help employees improve critical skills, keep current on the firm's capabilities and stay abreast of new and emerging industry tools and practices among many, many others. The program offers courses both in person and online via aided tools and live webinars. With nearly 1,500 hours of courses available in 2010, more than 80 percent of employees took advantage of course offerings, representing a total of more than 18,000 hours of employee training. In fact, Ketchum's training program was cited as a contributing factor in the agency's recognition as the 2010 Large Agency of the Year by industry publications the *Holmes Report* and *PR News*.

In addition to employees' personal development, ongoing training also helps ensure that clients receive a consistently high level of performance no matter where they engage us throughout our global network. To that end, key programs included "Delivering an Outstanding End-to-End Client Experience," taught by Ketchum's senior partner and chief client officer; a series of team-building programs taught by an external expert; and the Ketchum Leadership Institute, led by key partners and agency president and focusing on cross-boundary leadership.

We have learned that on-the-job training, or coaching, can be a powerful tool, as well. Our people have been "coached on coaching" and apply it every day on client engagements and for continuous development of our people. As part of this coaching effort, we have added a twist with something that we call "reverse mentoring." This is a program through which senior staffers have the opportunity to build their own social media skills by working on a regular basis with junior staffers who have grown up with and are well versed in social media technologies.

Training is an important part of an effective overall talent management program—but it is just one part. To attract and retain great talent, a firm needs a comprehensive human resources strategy that is linked to— and supports—the firm's global business strategy. The human resources strategy must be driven by a group of experienced, world-class human resources professionals and, as with training, must be implemented locally as well as at the global level. The primary mission of the human resources team is the effective management of the agency's talent pipeline with programs that support the key phases of the employee lifecycle from recruitment to hiring to orientation to promotion up and through the organization and to departure—if or when that occurs. One example of a human resources program that enables employees to engage in their own career development is the Career Development Toolkit. It provides a collection of resources to assist employees at all levels to proactively mine and map their strengths, clearly and accurately identify areas for development, and chart their own career paths. In addition, a large, global communications firm needs to put in place formal succession planning to allow the agency to plot deployment of talent and identify a strong lineup of talent to fit and fill current and anticipated client and agency needs.

ETHICS, TRANSPARENCY AND SOCIAL RESPONSIBILITY

Part of being the very best is having the highest professional standards. There are no shortcuts to this. Routinely, we counsel clients that transparency and a commitment to ethical business practices are essential in a media environment where consumers are demanding to know more and more about how companies do business. As a global organization, we recognize that the new rules of communication apply equally to us and to our clients. And we take our own counsel seriously.

In addition to signing a code of conduct at the beginning of employment, employees must complete an online quiz to receive ethics certification. Because this quiz is updated each year to reflect changes in the communications landscape, the certification must be renewed annually. Our ethics guidelines govern the way we do business as a firm and on behalf of our clients. The annual, agency-wide certification is consistent across national borders, and it ensures that the standards are understood by every employee, everywhere.

The idea that corporations have a responsibility to the world beyond producing products, providing services and minding profits has been around for decades. As more companies became multinational in the 1960s and 1970s, this idea started to be known as corporate social responsibility (CSR), and it meant that companies took an active part in improving environmental and social conditions, either through financial contributions, employee volunteerism or changes in the way they did business. In the past decade, consumers have asked for more. Rather than waiting for companies to announce their CSR efforts, consumers who bought their products and services (not just their stock shares) began demanding that businesses take a more active role in addressing societal challenges. They wanted to know exactly what companies were doing and what difference those efforts made.

CSR has become a critical component of marketing and corporate public relations. As a global agency, we advise our clients not only on developing CSR programs and initiatives but also on meeting stakeholders' expectations for accountability and disclosure. And we practice what we preach.

In 2010, Ketchum published its first annual report on the agency's global commitment to corporate social responsibility. The agency's signature program is a pro bono partnership with Room to Read, an international literacy and education advocacy organization. The agency donates staff time (professional hours) through a vice-president-level employee who devotes 50 percent of her time to the organization. In addition, our world-wide offices provide communications support and conduct fundraising campaigns. As of the end of 2010, the agency had contributed nearly $900,000 and more than 3,600 hours to Room to Read.

Our first Ketchum Social Responsibility report also detailed our pro bono work with the World Economic Forum (WEF), to which we provide strategic counsel and a full-time employee who works from WEF's head-quarters in Geneva, Switzerland. Along with other efforts aimed at preserving the environment and supporting causes in local communities, Ketchum donated the equivalent of more than $3.3 million in time to pro bono efforts in 2010.

For global communications firms, like any other organization, demonstrating a commitment to the communities where you do business is essential. It is also fundamental to attracting and maintaining talent, and it is the right thing to do.

EMBRACING AN EVER-CHANGING COMMUNICATIONS ENVIRONMENT

In 1964, Canadian educator and media theorist Marshall McLuhan coined the phrase "the medium is the message" in his book *Understanding Media: The Extensions of Man*. Around the same time, he also introduced the notion of a "global village," predicting that people around the world would eventually share a collective identity brought on by electronic media.

Nearly five decades later, the broad and immediate reach of the Internet and social media has indeed made the world a global village—with common experiences shared online. Social media have enabled each of us to live in our own little villages, too. Every day, small groups of people from places throughout the world gather online around specific interests. A single medium is facilitating everything from a collective identity to smaller communities to countless individual identities.

This represents extraordinary potential for global communications firms. To fully realize that potential, PR practitioners and other professional communicators will have to continue to study and understand the power of today's media and its ability to drive what may, at times, be distinctly different behaviors. Indeed, at Ketchum that is a key initiative for a team of more than 250 individuals from around the world who collaborate as part of our Global Media Network. However, we must be mindful that our learning will never be complete because the media and methods of human communication are continuously evolving and changing dramatically.

While McLuhan's predictions about the future of media turned out to be uncannily accurate, it is nearly impossible to know where the next evolution will lead. But we can make some assumptions about how on-going changes in media will influence public relations and then apply our learnings to suggest how global firms must operate. On the basis of the frequency with which new media tools are being introduced and how quickly consumers are adopting them, there are four upcoming realities for which communications firms must be prepared:

1. *Social media will continue to drive change.* Over a relatively short period, social media has advanced from simply facilitating communication with networks of family and friends online to enabling businesses to make strong, personal connections with consumers based on anything from their interests to their physical location. Social media has been a dynamic source of change, and there is still more to come. Existing social media tools will continue to become more sophisticated and create infinite opportunities for new tools as entrepreneurs can use open protocols to tap into the social graph being created all around us. They will bring with them social business opportunities for brand communications, cause marketing, reputation management, financial communications and more.

PR professionals have already learned that they must engage consumers where they are already having conversations and showing interest. Communications firms must build on that knowledge and make sure they have the best talent to help clients keep pace with the most effective ways of communicating with various stakeholders, particularly the ever-changing online world. Continual training will play an important role in keeping talent current as will real-world experience. Global agencies also will need to be tuned into differences in how consumers access and embrace new media tools in different parts of the world. Socioeconomic conditions in some countries will mean that traditional media formats, such as newspapers, radio and TV, are the best ways to reach people. Some countries may skip the desktop generation of access to the Internet entirely, and only access the Internet via mobile devices.

2. *Communications firms will work better together.* As clients continue to work with multiple firms with different and the same expertise concurrently, it will be critical for those firms to work together seamlessly. In fact, questions about a firm's experience integrating with other agencies are becoming routine during the process of being considered for new client assignments. Agencies will become better at working together as one team because it will be a requirement for doing business.

3. *Communications firms will work "smarter" to compete.* At the end of 2010, the Council of Public Relations Firms, an association of the leading firms in the United States, surveyed its members about the top trends they expected to see in new business in the year ahead. "More competitive pitches" was the second most common answer, ranking behind only "more requests for social/digital media." One reason pitches have become more competitive is that social media has changed the game. Full-service PR firms often must compete with digital shops, boutique agencies and advertising agencies for new business. To emerge successful, all firms will have to compete in a smarter way. This could take many forms—from continuously driving creativity and innovation that anticipates clients' needs to underscoring the point of difference PR firms bring to the table—earned engagement—to more carefully choosing which pitches to invest in on the basis of the firm's capabilities and available resources.

4. *Investment in public relations will grow.* In its 2009 Communications Industry Forecast, investment firm Veronis Suhler Stevenson estimated that spending on public relations will increase about 17 percent by 2016, over what it was in 2008. That is also in comparison to a 6 percent growth in advertising spending over the same period. Various surveys of marketing professionals also project increased investment in public relations and PR activities. For instance, 42 percent of respondents to Boston Consulting Group's 2010 Future of Marketing and Advertising Study said they expect their companies to increase PR spending over a three-year period. In what is perhaps a more important finding in the same survey, 94 percent said they expect to increase spending on social media. That, too, underscores the bright future for the public relations industry and represents tremendous opportunity for PR. Social media and other changes in communication have blurred many of the lines that once separated marketing disciplines. Today, anyone can play in anyone else's space as long as they can prove they can do the work. PR can.

Communications is one of the most profoundly powerful forces in the world today, and that power most likely will continue to grow. Global communications firms must manage their investments in talent, tools, time and other resources to be prepared to grow along with it . . . and perhaps even to lead the way. There are no boundaries. The potential for what we can do for our clients and as an industry is unlimited.

DISCUSSION QUESTIONS

1. What are the four imperatives of managing a global communications firm?
2. What are some of the most significant changes in public relations and how have these changes influenced the industry?
3. What role do a company's employees play in communications today?

4. Describe the multicenter engagement approach to client service and how it benefits clients. What are some of the challenges with this approach?
5. What future "realities" does the author hypothesize the industry will see?

ADDITIONAL READING

BOOKS

Friedman, Thomas L. 2009. *Hot, Flat, and Crowded 2.0: Why We Need a Green Revolution: and How It Can Renew America.* Hampshire, UK: Picador. Print.
Zakaria, Fareed. 2011. *The Post-American World: Release 2.0.* New York: W.W. Norton & Co. Print.
Zakaria, Fareed. 2008. *The Future of Freedom Illiberal Democracy at Home and Abroad.* Harlow, Essex, England: Penguin UK. Print.

WEBSITES AND BLOGS

www.awpagesociety.com. Arthur W. Page Society.
www.fareedzakaria. Fareed Zakaria.
www.thomaslfriedman.com. Thomas L. Friedman.
www.prfirms.org. Council or PR Firms.

MAGAZINES

The Economist. The Economist Group. Hayward Health, U.K., St. Louis, MO.
PR Week. PR Week. New York.

21

C H A P T E R

ISSUES MANAGEMENT METHODS FOR REPUTATIONAL MANAGEMENT

James E. Arnold, APR, Fellow PRSA
Chief Executive Officer, Arnold Consulting Group
Former President Chester Burger & Company
Former Chief Executive Officer, Legis 50: The Center for Legislative Improvement

Raymond P. Ewing
Industry Leader in Issues Management (Ret)
Professor, Department of Integrated Marketing Communications
Medill School of Journalism, Media, Integrated Communications, Northwestern University

> *"The Public Be Damned"*
>
> —Commodore William H. Vanderbilt, 1882

> *"All business in a Democratic society begins with public permission and exists by public approval."*
>
> —Arthur W. Page, 1947

The environment in which all organizations exist, especially corporations, has changed dramatically since Mr. Vanderbilt, the founder of New York Central Railroad, offered his oft-quoted opinion about public opinion. Today most CEOs and leaders have learned to speak like Mr. Page, the first vice president of public relations at AT&T—but many CEOs secretly agree with the commodore. What changed in the intervening years between Vanderbilt and Page? Public opinion became a force to be reckoned with in American society.

Ida Tarbell's *Rise of the Standard Oil Company* (1904) depicted the rise of John D. Rockefeller's integrated oil producing, transporting, refining and marketing juggernaut. Standard Oil became the world's largest refiner, operated as a major company trust, and was one of the first multinational corporations until it was broken up by the Supreme Court in 1911. Rockefeller, the richest man in modern history, defended his company's business strategies, practices and tactics as "lawful" but he forced many smaller businesses out and became very unpopular with the public—thanks in large part to Tarbell's book, its serialization in McClure's magazine and the heyday of muckracking "yellow journalism" fostering a rising resentment against robber-baron capitalism.

Even this early in the twentieth century with the rise of national newspaper chains, it was not unusual for companies to employ "press agents" to tell their side of a story and rebut criticism. In 1906 Ivy Lee, a former journalist, represented the coal mining bosses, who were facing a big strike and enjoyed little support in the press because the unions had built good relations with reporters in a previous strike. Lee saw the emerging mass media as a conduit for his client's point of view as well as that of critics. Unlike other press agents, he wanted to organize ongoing campaigns of information on behalf of his clients, not just engage in tactical skirmishes. He sent a steady stream of statements to newspapers, laying out the mining bosses' case and responding to criticisms and allegations—earning his clients a fairer hearing going forward.

Lee's "Declaration of Principles" looked forward to the ideas Arthur Page would use to counsel his colleagues at AT&T: "This is not an advertising agency . . . Our plan is frankly, and openly, on behalf of business concerns and public institutions, to supply the press and public of the United States prompt and accurate information concerning subjects which it is of value and interest to the public to know about."[1]

When Page offered his "public permission, public approval" guidance in 1947, he did so with the full understanding of the importance of public opinion to the success of AT&T's enterprise. Since AT&T chose to be regulated as "a natural monopoly," Page wisely understood the downside of being "king of the mountain" and advised in favor of a business model called "universal service" (emphasis on service), which would put a telephone in virtually every home, making it a utility, and keeping the residential charge low with social-based pricing and raising the charge on business accounts as a cross subsidy. In this way Page made the largest possible number of people part of, and proud of, the Bell Network—the world's finest telephone system.

From Page's day until the present, the matter of dealing with public opinion has grown increasingly difficult and complex for all corporations, organizations, institutions and even the government. Our society is more multicultural, our interests more narrowly drawn and often advanced at the expense of competing interests; we seem sometimes to lack a central narrative that would help us find the grace to "disagree without being disagreeable." You hear more win–lose than win–win as outcomes of conflicts. There was a point when public relations would be thought of simply as "telling the story of your organization in terms of the larger public interest, thereby establishing its credibility and legitimacy." But today, defining *public interest* is no easy matter. One person's sacred cow is another's Big Mac.

For example, is it more in the public interest to protect inefficient producers in the United States with government tariffs and trade quotas, thereby saving jobs and businesses at home but penalizing consumers who have to buy more expensive goods (perhaps of lesser quality) than would be necessary without protection of these markets? Or is it in the public interest to allow the free flow of goods and services into reciprocating economies even though it means losing jobs and businesses at home and creating ill will with some unions but benefiting consumers who will have a greater range of choices and prices? Clearly, making public policy choices in a pluralistic society requires the wisdom of Solomon and the karma of a schizophrenic Zen master: "I am at two with the world."

From within this attitude-intensive environment, hotly wired, rich with proliferating media, driven by technology slicing-and-dicing audiences into ever smaller segments, searching for common ground while spinning outward like a centrifuge on the globe of earth—here we begin to explore *issues management* and how it has changed since Ray Ewing wrote his chapter "Managing Trends through the Issues Life Cycle" in the 1997 original *Handbook of Strategic Public Relations & Integrated Communications*.

Ray was intimately involved in the early beginnings of issues management, working closely with Howard Chase and the Public Affairs Council (PAC). He was the first senior officer to have issues management in his corporate title, and at Allstate Insurance Companies he worked closely with the CEO Archie Boe, who was to be an early adopter of issues management, especially as it could be partnered with *strategic planning*. Ray offered this quote from his boss: "Issues management and strategic planning are both born of the dynamic tradition in American business management that rejects the passive approach of hoping to know the future and merely adjusting to it, for an affirmative posture of *creating* the future and *fitting* the corporate enterprise into it."[2]

From the very beginning, those who pioneered the development and definition of issues management considered it to be a management process concerned with *public policy* foresight and planning for an organization in the *private* sector. It is not the management of issues through the public policy process in our democracy or the management of the public policy process itself. Instead, it is the management of an institution's resources and efforts to participate in the successful resolution of issues in the public policy process that will affect the future viability and well being of the organization and its stakeholders.

The term *issues management* was formally and publicly coined by W. Howard Chase on April 15, 1976. That is the date of volume 1, number 1, of his newsletter, *Corporate Public Issues and Their Management.*

The newsletter, now usually called *CPI*, stated that its objectives were "To introduce and validate a break through in corporate management design and practice in order to manage corporate public issues at least as well or better than the traditional management of profit-center operations."

Chase went on to say, "The thesis and impact of *CPI* inevitably led to fundamental revisions of costly and divisive practices of traditional line-staff management. There can be today only one management with one objective: survival and return on capital sufficient to maintain productivity, whatever the economic and political climate."

Chase was 66 years old when this newsletter came out in 1976, having retired the previous year as public affairs vice president of American Can Company. In 1977, he and his associates, Barry Jones and Teresa Yancey Crane (now the publisher of *CPI*), created the first issues management process model, which involves five steps:

1. Issue identification

2. Issue analysis

3. Issue change strategy options

4. Issue action programming

5. Evaluation of results

Early full-time practitioners of issues management have always called Chase the "father" of issues management. He has more than earned that title for coining the term, publishing the first newsletter on the subject and creating the first issues management process model.

- Issues management as a new process management concept evolved from the public relations and public affairs (PR/PA) professions after Chase coined the phrase in 1976.

- Chase did not "invent" issues management (although he created the name) because, from Ivy Lee's time to 1976, counselors of senior management had been "doing" issues management—but on an ad hoc, hit-or-miss basis under various names. Chase moved the field to a foresight and planning basis from the ad hoc practice.

- Chase's basic concept of issues management (for senior management's use in integrating the management of public policy and profit matters) moved public relations/public affairs professionals who could practice issues management to the center of corporate or organizational management.

So long as PR was confined to media relations, practitioners were operating at the outer edge of the organization. In the 1960s, when PR and government relations were combined to create a public affairs function, they moved closer to the center of operations because senior management became more involved in decision making. With the evolution of issues management (public policy planning) as a companion to strategic planning (profit planning), again they moved to the heart of the company where senior management focuses"(see Figure 21.1).

According to the Institute for the Study of Issues Management at the University of Houston, over 240 scholarly and professional articles, scholarly books and PR textbooks dealing with issues management have been published. This is proof to Professor Robert Heath, director of the institute, that issues management is a new discipline that has emerged, not to replace public relations but to strengthen it. Most professional

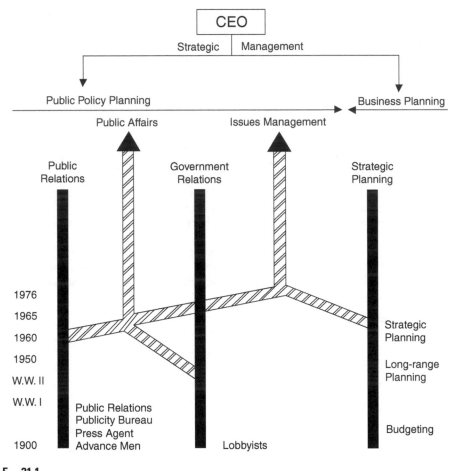

Timeline of Evolution of Issues Management

practitioners agree, and formal courses in issues management have appeared at universities teaching public relations as well as at some business schools.

Many CEOs have seen the advantage of an issues management system since Chase first gave it a name. By one count, over 200 issues-related titles could be identified in as many companies, and more than 60 public relations and management consulting firms were offering issues management services.

The earliest companies adopting the technique were mainly the regulated industries: chemicals, petroleum, banking, insurance and so forth. That is, the earliest practitioners were found in companies like Allstate, Bank of America, Chase, Dow Chemical, PPG, AT&T, Rexnord, Sears, Monsanto, Union Carbide and various electrical utility companies. However, over time, this management system spread to companies in all sectors.

Although Howard Chase argues that issues management is a new profession that transcends the PR/PA profession, we consider issues management to be one of the major functions that the PR professional can perform today. It is of equal or more importance than our other major functions: media relations, marketing public relations, investor relations, public affairs, employee communications, community relations and corporate philanthropy. The addition of strategic planning and issues management to our duties in the past decades completed our maturing into a modern profession.

THE RELATIONSHIP OF ISSUES MANAGEMENT TO BUSINESS SCHOOL STRATEGIC PLANNING

Issues management and strategic planning together form the planning platform on which CEOs and their senior management team can stand to strategically manage their organizations.

While issues management focuses on *public policy* research, foresight and planning for the organization, strategic planning is concerned with *business* research, foresight and planning for the organization. The first is concerned with policy planning; the second is concerned with profit planning. This chart illustrates what each system is concerned with or can affect.

Issues Management	Strategic Planning
Outside-in planning	Inside-out planning
Issues 1–5 years in future	Issues 1–5+ years in future
Operational (annual) plans	Organizational plans
Defense/opportunity	Opportunity/defense
Best of a contentious bargain	Best of self-created bargain

Under this construct, issues management is concerned with plans that groups outside the corporation are making in the sociopolitical and economic environment (the public policy process) that would influence the corporation's future and viability. It is also concerned with the outside plans it must make to counteract or support the plans of others as the corporation seeks to participate in the public policy process where the issues will be resolved.

Strategic planning is primarily concerned with the corporation's internal planning for its own business future, as it seeks to meet and beat its competitors in the economic arena.

On the time frame, issues management is primarily concerned with issues that will be resolved 12 months to 5 years in the future. (Of course, it monitors issues that will not be resolved for many years into the future—and brings those into the system as they move toward the five-year time frame.)

Because of the shorter time frame and the need to react quickly to public issues, issues management is more concerned with adjusting current operations and operational plans to best benefit its stakeholders.

Issues management's first responsibility is to make sure the corporation is well defended against whatever tactic or move the many organized actors in the public policy process choose to execute. This is designed to meet the first planning and management goal of every CEO: "No surprises!"

Issues management's next goal is to search out inherent opportunities in issues others generate or the company decides to generate in the public policy forums.

The primary duty of strategic planning, on the other hand, is to seek economic opportunities and to find ways to exploit them with internally created business plans.

Thus, issues management is concerned with achieving the best resolution for its company's stakeholders in a contentious arena where bargains are struck. Strategic planning is concerned with harvesting the benefits of marketing that its plans have created.

Both issues management and strategic planning are guided by the corporation's mission statement, which attempts to tell who the corporation is and what it hopes to become, and makes commitments to its primary stakeholders—customers, employees, the general public and shareholders. For issues managers, the company's mission statement frames the issues they must seek.

Issues managers scan for, monitor and seek resolution only of those issues that might have significant impacts on their company's stakeholders, and hence the company's future.

The practice of issues management has always required an understanding of how the laws and regulations get made at the local, state and federal level in the United States, and by extension the processes in place in other countries around the world to accomplish the same purposes.

The public policy process in a free society is the meeting ground of the public sector (federal, state and local governmental units) and the private sector (citizens, corporations, organizations, etc.). It is the process, facilitated by the media, where the public's aspirations and dissatisfactions work their way up through public issues debates into law and regulation, if they are not voluntarily resolved in the private sector.

The social control of business is affected through this mechanism. It has only been in the past three decades that business has come to realize that it is not only controlled by the economic environment, but is in fact effectively controlled through the broader social and political environments. This realization forced the development of issues management to give corporations a rational way to manage their participation in the process.

The public policy process can best be understood through a simplified graphic model (Figure 21.2), developed by Ray Ewing from an earlier Yankelovich, Skelly and White description of the process.

The base of the pyramid is where public dissatisfactions with the present emerge, prompted by perceived injustices and exclusions, new aspirations, new concerns about the environment, new ideas relating to "rights" and "entitlements" or other issues. But at this level, nothing happens until it gets a name and visibility, when the media can take it up and talk about it, broadcasting the issue of concern beyond those affected.

The media do not create issues unless there is an underlying reality, but they are essential in issue development and its life cycle. However, nothing really happens to the issue until an organized group takes it up and adds it to its action agenda.

Once an organized group decides to add it to its agenda, the pressure group—a public interest group, Chamber of Commerce, trade association, religious institution, political party or other group—seeks to mobilize social and political forces beyond its own membership. Because the media become critical at this point, the pressure group holds demonstrations and public meetings, making headline-grabbing charges. When this happens, the pressure group becomes the issue champion and, in effect, co-opts the issue, defining it as it wishes.

Frequently, the pressure group approaches a leading company as representative of a targeted industry, or some service organization, demanding a meeting to negotiate the issue, complete with notices to the media. If the

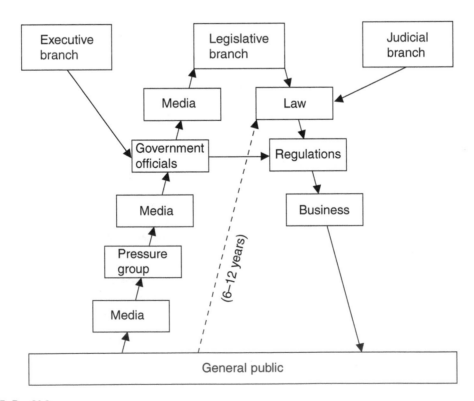

FIGURE 21.2

Public Policy Process Model (Social Control of Business)

company or other organization in the private sector does not respond, the pressure group moves on to the appropriate regulatory agency, demanding public hearings. Again, this is accompanied by notices to the media.

The regulatory agency, because of the publicity and accompanying demands of the pressure group, will take notice of the issue and consider holding public hearings to investigate the charges. These actions generate more media attention. If the agency decides that new laws and regulations are needed, it moves the issue to the elected legislative bodies—the U.S. Congress or state legislatures.

Finally, the Congress or the state legislature, standing at the top of the public policy process, considers the conflicting demands and the interests of key publics. The legislative body will pass a new law if it thinks a law will resolve the problem the issue represents, and if it thinks there is sufficient public consensus for a legislative solution. If the legislators do not think the issue can be resolved or that there is not sufficient public consensus for any one solution, they will not act. In effect, they kick the issue back down into the public arena, hoping the issue will be privately resolved through voluntary actions in the private sector.

If the Congress or state legislature decides a law is needed, it passes one. This law and any accompanying regulations come down like a straitjacket on the business community.

As many commentators have pointed out, the business community gets involved in the life cycle of an issue far too late—at the regulatory or legislative phase when business is considered the problem, not the solution. That is why business is famous for killing legislation, not advancing broad solutions. This was true before the issues management system was developed.

Researchers have found that, at the federal level, it takes from 6 to 12 years for an issue to emerge at the general public level before legislation is passed. (At the state level, legislation can be passed in 1 to 2 years under certain conditions.)

Issues management is designed to take advantage of the time lag so that senior management can develop policy positions and supporting action programs. It sets up systems to monitor all stages of the public policy process stream to identify emerging and developing issues.

ISSUE MANAGEMENT TACTICS: 2011

Without question, the most fundamental aspect of issues management is summed up in the first sentence of the book *How to Grow Asparagus*: "Dig a trench—three years ago." Or as they say in politics, "Don't wait until you need a friend to make a friend." Or as the lobbyists are famous for saying: "You can't just show up at the office of a government official, lawyers and experts in tow, and expect to get a fair hearing on the 'merits' from your self-serving point of view. First, you have to lay a little pipe into that office."

The practice of issues management is usually described as a process over time that begins with discovery and ends with a resolution at the most advantageous or possible level in the issue cycle. Here is how Teresa Yancey Crane, a founder of the Issue Management Council (IMC) and a team member with Howard Chase who developed the first issue management process model, describes the process in January 2011 (issuemanagement. org/learnmore/origins-of-issue-management):

> We have always emphasized that this model is not conclusive. It will vary according to the specific needs of any user. The primary purpose in our exercise is to demonstrate that a systems approach could apply to the strategic management of issues. At the heart of each step in the model is the interaction among citizens, business and government, the push and pull relationship that governs the core of our society, and serves as the birth place . . . of all issues.

- *Issue identification* consists of three primary steps:

  1. Consideration of trends in the social, political and economic realms; now we would add other trend areas, such as technological

  2. Comparison of those trends to your basic organizational goals, in other words, your business plan

  3. Identification of primary issues

- The major focus of the *issue analysis* step is to draw on past experience with the issue, as reflected in quantitative and qualitative research on how people feel about the issue, what actions have been taken, how the company is geared for dealing with it and, in general, how the issue can impact the organization.

- Now, as for the circle with the odd name *issue change strategy options*. What does that mean? Basically, each issue requires a carefully determined stance. It may be desirable to let others take the lead, remaining in a reactive mode. Perhaps it is best to "go with the flow" and adapt where necessary. Or, a dynamic posture may be taken. This whole step is designed to incorporate an element of strategy into plans and actions.

- *Issue action* is the fourth step. The components of action include setting a goal, objectives, strategies and tactics. Then one has to organize all resources at hand to achieve targets that are set. We wanted to emphasize that all parts of the organization should be tapped and synchronized. This was a radical approach in 1977.

- Finally, there is the emphasis on the *evaluation of results*. At times, we said, the issue management cycle begins again, with new players, new results, new attitudes and so on.

Issues are resolved, not ever really solved and will often spring back to life, sometimes without even a decent mourning period. This is the nature of a pluralistic society where the legislative and/or regulatory processes force compromise to settle legitimate but competing interests.

There are many models for the issues management process, each containing a number of steps from 5 to 10, usually falling into three major categories:

1. Issue identification and analysis

2. Strategic decision making and action

3. Evaluation

Emphasis by practitioners and academic researchers has usually been on the first two categories with little done on evaluation. I especially like Heath's argument that issues management is the proactive application of four strategic options:

1. Strategic business planning

2. Getting the house in order—corporate responsibility

3. Scouting the terrain—scanning, identification, monitoring, analysis and priority setting

4. Strong defense and smart offense—issues communication

Evaluation, a management function that looks at results in the outside environment and makes a subjective cost/benefit analysis, is dependent on setting measurable objectives and measurable results indicators at the outset for each issue as it enters the issues process. What can be measured generally is the response capability of the company or organization, outlined in Figure 21.3 on the next page: (1) issues correctly anticipated and issues avoided, (2) timeliness of response and (3) appropriateness of response. These three dimensions of capability can be quantified, and those measurements then form the basis of the qualitative evaluation of the effectiveness of the response capability by the owners of the issues and the clients of the issues management process inside the company.

Since publication of Ewing's chapter in 1997, the Issues Management Council has identified nine best practice indicators. The IMC Best Practices Project was led by Tony Jacques and presented in full on the Council's website. They are organized in three categories: structure, implementation and integration. Here is a summary:

Structure

1. There is an established mechanism to identify current and future issues through environmental scanning/issue analysis.

In this environment, strategy formulation is matched or exceeded by strategy execution when it comes to defining a winning strategy. In this time of increasing transparency, strategies are easily discovered or divined by competitors and duplicated or foiled. Execution, then, requires nimbleness and a coevolution of strategy execution against a competitive business set, some of whom come from around the world. "The best companies are emulated by those in the middle of the pack, and the worst exit or undergo significant reform. As each player responds to and learns from the actions of others, best practice becomes commonplace rather than a market-beating strategy."

Silos are out, or should be. Centers of excellence are coming in. There are indications that management wants more alignment among and accountability from such practices as corporate marketing, public relations, public affairs, issues management, government relations, CSR, reputational management, enterprise risk management (ERM) and related stakeholder activities. Looking back to the beginnings of issue management, there was a difference of opinion about whether issues management was to be a separate and new management discipline, standing apart from public relations and operating on a parallel track to strategic planning. According to the PAC, the trend now is to have issues management done as part of public relations or public affairs in the majority of companies. In some instances, it has been subsumed into the strategic planning process itself.

A more important trend (the evolution of risk management from a compliance- and/or financial-based function to ERM including risk to such intangibles as reputation) may eventually bring together all the various external audience-facing public relations and communications functions. An *Economist* study of reputation risk found that it is the number 1 concern of companies worldwide. However, those questioned were evenly divided as to whether reputation risk was a factor unto itself or a derivative of other risks. And the respondents believed that reputation should be managed as a differentiator of value since it is a valuable asset. It is likely that a trend now under way will accelerate to organize, integrate or in some way align many of the functions that have dealt with reputation in the past into a more cohesive, focused business unit. This suggests to me a consolidation of public relations, public affairs, issues management/stakeholder relations, corporate marketing, investor relations, government relations and likely new media (social media). Some have correctly observed that risk is proportional to reward, and not something to be automatically mitigated or avoided—perhaps public relations leaders are not the appropriate mind set to lead such a cross-disciplined team. That remains to be seen, but the internal organization of these different and distinct areas would seem to be on a course for a new organizational structure.

AN ISSUES MANAGEMENT CASE STUDY

In 2006 the Issus Management Council presented its W. Howard Chase Award to Swiss Re for the best Issues Management Case of the Year. Here is a summary of the winning case.

WHY IS THE ISSUE IMPORTANT TO SWISS RE?

Understanding and anticipating the developments that shape the risk landscape are essential elements of Swiss Re's business. As a leading global reinsurer, Swiss Re's success is based on high-quality risk assessment and industry recognition of its broad knowledge of risk transfer and financing. Swiss Re established an issues management process called Top Topics in 2001 to help identify and tackle fundamental trends affecting the insurance industry, and to ultimately shape the group's business environment. In 2005, Swiss Re advanced its issue management practices with the creation of the group issue management (GIM) process and through the work of the Issue Steering Committee (ISC), aggregating further intelligence on the changing expectations of stakeholders on the risk landscape and enhancing the group's communications agility. ISC members are senior professionals representing the broad range of stakeholders' views on topics. Long-term objectives of the ISC include the following:

1. Ensuring that topics are positioned vis-à-vis stakeholders in a consistent manner and that communications activities are aligned with the group's interests

2. Foster stakeholder dialogue

3. Support knowledge transfer into real business opportunities

4. Promote best practices in dealing with issues and topic management

The topics identified represent both opportunities and changing risks affecting various Swiss Re's units or functions, and therefore requiring coordination at the group level: these topics involve either significant market and economic trends, regulatory changes or key scientific and social developments that have or could have an impact on the group's current and future book of business. Currently 20 topics are monitored and analyzed and a large range of research and external communications activities are conducted on these.

AT WHAT LEVELS DO MEMBERS OF THE ORGANIZATION PARTICIPATE IN ADDRESSING THE ISSUE?

The GIM discipline is a global function at the corporate center benefiting from all levels of seniority. Overall responsibility for decision making related to the issues lies with the ISC. The chief risk officer and the head of communications and human resources are sponsors of GIM and members of ISC. All stakeholder views are represented in the ISC. Swiss Re's Centre for Global Dialogue in Switzerland is the central platform to foster stakeholder dialogue. The ISC provides regular updates on the Topics portfolio and makes recommendations on Top Topics. The ISC meetings and GIM process are managed by a senior manager in the group communications function. The head of issue management (senior position) ensures ongoing monitoring and scanning of a broad range of potentially new topics. Experts for individual topics are embedded in functional units such as risk management, product development and so forth. Topic managers are supported by communications managers.

WHICH CONSTITUENT GROUPS ARE AFFECTED?

Existing and potential clients
Investors and financial analysts (including rating agencies)
Regulators and/or legislators
Employees
Industry associations
Media
Academic institutions
General public

HOW ARE CONSTITUENT CONCERNS CONSIDERED AND ACTED ON?

Feedback from the various constituent groups is fed into the regular evaluation process of individual topics at the ISC level and the GIM process. The executive committee of ISC is consulted twice a year to collect feedback and guidance on actions conducted and/or planned. Concerns raised by various external constituencies are usually discussed with specific business partners within the organization. For example, clients will typically consult with their client manager and regulators discuss issues with Swiss Re regulatory affairs. All stakeholders are represented in the ISC and their feedback on Swiss Re positions is shared on a regular basis. The group conducts regular surveys with stakeholder groups, and regular media benchmarking of communication in the insurance industry reveals that Swiss Re's voice is being heard and compares well in comparison to industry peers.

WHAT IS THE KEY OBJECTIVE OF THE ISSUE MANAGEMENT PROGRAM?

The key objective of GIM is to enable Swiss Re to identify economic, regulatory and risk-relevant trends, and monitor their impact on the group's strategy and/or earnings so that Swiss Re can actively shape its business environment. In addition, the research and communications activities generated on Topic as a result of GIM underpin Swiss Re's reputation as a leading knowledge company in the field of capital and risk management. Finally, as a global organization of some 8,800 employees in more than 70 offices in over 30 countries, the GIM supports Swiss Re's objective to deliver consistent messages globally. The GIM's mission statement: "position Swiss Re as a knowledge company and industry leader on topics of strategic relevance, representing market opportunities or potentially impacting Swiss Re's balance sheet and entrepreneurial freedom."

DOES ISSUE MANAGEMENT MAKE A DIRECT CONTRIBUTION TO SWISS RE'S PROFITABILITY? IF SO, HOW?

Yes, GIM contributes both to business growth as well as protecting the group's balance sheet. Identifying new business opportunities at an early stage allows Swiss Re to become market leaders in its chosen fields (e.g., insurance-linked securities as innovative risk transfer solutions, Solvency II in terms of adequate capital and disclosure requirements). On the other hand, detecting potential new risks before they develop into serious issues enables the group to set up appropriate mitigation procedures including underwriting guidelines, pricing recommendations and capital allocation (e.g., nanotechnology- or obesity-related claims).

WHAT ARE THE RESULTS?

GIM is acknowledged as a contributor to Swiss Re's strategic decision-making process as well as an important factor in the group's external positioning and communications. Greater coordination has resulted when launching major communications initiatives. Increased transparency in Swiss Re's key messages and dissemination of these messages internally and externally has been achieved. Business benefits are felt in many Top Topics where additional communications resources have been allocated, particularly for climate change, insurance-linked securities and Solvency II.

THE FUTURE OF ISSUES MANAGEMENT

Given the three trends mentioned above, the importance of effective company responses to emerging trends before they become well advanced in the issues process will be greatly enhanced in the foreseeable future. Ideally, issues management strategists will find more effective ways to create communities of interest among all a company's stakeholders. Technology will play a larger role in segmenting stakeholder groups and establishing personal relationships with the key actors. As Peter Drucker noted, IT thus far has fulfilled the promise only of the *technology* and not delivered on the *information*. As we become more proficient at collecting data and interpreting it, databases can be mined to learn more about not only the demographics of stakeholders but also values and psychographics.

This will make possible more effective use of messages and symbols because we can create appeal for our point of view with more insight into the attitudes of those to be persuaded. Being able to target our audiences by familiarity levels such as aware, informed, leaning toward or against, committed for or against, ready to act for or against, advocates for or against will help choose the right channel of communication and kind of conversation to have.

With the new social media we should be able to create platforms and viral trails for all our advocates and other influencers as well as being able to track what others say about us and our positions. In this new environment, getting the engagement of shareholders, customers or clients, and especially employees will be critical to the success of a company's response to gaps between stakeholder expectations and actual performance. Not delivering on the brand promise or living up to the reputation multiplied over hundreds of individual experiences can be a daunting challenge to the issues management strategist. But be of good cheer: as Aristotle said, "rhetoric is the ability to find, in any given situation, all available means of persuasion."

Besides being the sentry, issues management must be a part of the response. There is an advantage to putting issues on the team with public relations (*public affairs* is using public relations strategies and tactics to influence the actions of government). In most companies, the best media expertise and creative messaging comes from the public relations unit. And public relations is usually in charge of leading the effort to optimize a company's reputation as well as defending and/or mitigating risks. With stakeholders creating context for actions (use reputation), improving understanding (use reputation), shaping the opinion environment (use reputation)—all fit like a glove with the mission of public relations.

At the intersection of shareholder and stakeholder relations sits the growing practice of CSR—the second act of something once known as *corporate citizenship*. The original foundation of CSR was based on companies voluntarily doing good in order to do well. The European Commission defines it as "a concept whereby companies decide voluntarily to contribute to a better society and a cleaner environment." It is related to sensitive issues—environmental protection, human resources management, health and safety at work, relations with local communities, relations with suppliers and consumers and so forth.

The shareholder view would be that corporate managers should serve the interests of shareholders, using resources to increase the profits and wealth of the company. The stakeholder view would posit that in addition to shareholders, other groups and constituencies may be affected by the company's actions or policies and those interests must be considered by corporate managers as well. In the past five years, CSR has increasingly become an important strategy for issues managers to solidify relations with stakeholders and make alliances with related organizations who may not be central to the company's economic story but can have a direct impact on creating value and wealth inside the company. It seems a logical evolution that, as a company decides to dedicate some resources to causes outside the mainstream business purposes, those resources would necessarily be linked to influencing opinions of stakeholders identified as key to achieving business goals.

In a wonderful essay, "The Next Information Revolution" (ASAP, versaggi.net/ecommerce/articles/drucker inforevolt.html), Peter Drucker bemoans the failure of computers to revolutionize the work of top management. It has paid off for operations, he says, all internal, but nothing for "creation of value and wealth. This requires risk-taking decisions: on the theory of the business, on business strategy, on abandoning the old and innovating the new, on the balance between the short term and the long term, on the balance between immediate profitability and market share. These decisions are the true top management tasks."

Drucker once told me (Arnold) over lunch that the failure of public relations to live up to the promise of Arthur W. Page was its reluctance to bring the outside environment into the organization, to overcome executive isolation, while concentrating on "getting the message out" through publicity because it was "what management expected." Drucker says managements, especially in large corporations "focus inward on costs and efforts, rather than *outward* on opportunities, changes and threats. This tendency is becoming increasingly dangerous considering the globalization of economies and industries, the rapid changes in markets and in consumer behavior, the crisscrossing of technologies across traditional industry lines, and the increasing instability of currencies. The more inside information top management gets, the more it will need to balance it with outside information—and that does not exist yet."

Drucker would support the efforts of issues managers to bring to management's attention both the threats and the opportunities that can be discerned from survey research, trend analysis and careful listening—something to be done more easily and quickly now with new digital media in hand. In the *Effective Executive*, Drucker observed poignantly:

> The truly important events on the outside are not the trends. They are the changes in the trends. These determine ultimately success or failure of an organization and its efforts. Such changes, however, have to be perceived; they cannot be counted, defined or classified. The classifications still produce the expected figures—as they did for the Edsel. But the figures no longer correspond to actual behaviore . . . The important events on the outside cannot be reported in the kind of form a computer (or any other logic system) could possibly handle. Man, however, while not particularly logical, is perceptive—and that is his strength.[5]

It is now in vogue to treat a company's reputation with much greater respect than the mere lip service of saying "it's very important to us and it's one of the building blocks of our strategy formulation process." Most top management who talk this way have no idea what the most important attributes of their reputation are; is the quality of management ranked high by those who know the company? In the wake of the trust crisis created post-Enron and now the financial crisis that has called into question the ethics and competence of the leaders of many major financial institutions, "aren't these the guys who set up world class risk management practices, approved by the Audit Committee of the BOD, blah, blah, blah"?

Interestingly enough, a McKinsey Quarterly classic, "Running with Risk," recently reissued in the wake of the global conversation now about risk management, cites financial institutions as a model for emulation when it comes to being out-front about risks.[6] In 2009 we find out what good models they were: turns out the risks were all about threats to profits or cash flow only, they were siloed, and the risk tolerance for compliance matters was zero percent while tolerance for risky schemes to make money was quite high because it could always be hedged against investments handled for clients. All the risk managers met once a week for happy hour at a bar called "See No Evil, Hear No Evil, Say No Evil."

One nice piece of man-bites-dog news did appear at the end of 2009 when Goldman Sachs Group, America's favorite "hate" company from the financial crisis, filed its Form 10-K providing fascinating insights into management's assessment of risks the business faces going forward: "Item 1A: Risk Factors: We face a variety of risks that are substantial and inherent in our businesses, including market liquidity, credit, operational, legal, regulatory and reputational risks. The following are some of the more important factors that could affect our businesses:

- We may incur losses as a result of ineffective risk management processes and strategies.

- Our businesses may be adversely affected if we are unable to hire and retain qualified employees.

- Our businesses and those of our clients are subject to extensive and pervasive regulation around the world.

- We may be adversely affected by increased governmental and regulatory scrutiny or negative publicity.

- Conflicts of interest are increasing and a failure to appropriately identify and deal with conflicts of interest could adversely affect our businesses.

- Substantial legal liability or significant regulatory action against us could have material adverse financial effects or cause us significant reputational harm, which in turn could seriously harm our business prospects."

Imagine: negative publicity is a risk for Goldman Sachs. Here is an example of a company needing a massive dose of visionary issues management.

Now there is a clamor to make reputational risk an important part of the ERM. A Conference Board report, "Managing Reputation Risk and Reward" (2009), found high percentages of public affairs and corporate communications executives listed as primarily responsible for reputation risk management, but the authors believe it is because reputation risk management was heavily siloed into communications and/or public affairs and not integrated into enterprise-wide risk management processes.

In 2010 the PAC study "Public Affairs and Enterprise Risk Management" showed survey results surprisingly different: "Nearly 80 percent of companies participating in a PAC survey had an enterprise risk management program. Of those, close to 80 percent involved public affairs staff in ERM." Of course, those who responded self-selected and that would probably affect the results somewhat.

As to the future of issues management in this period of soul searching, transition and realignment of corporate functions, it is safe to say issues management's relevance and value to top management and line operators alike is hardly going to decline. And the tools to do an even better job of finding common ground with and persuading conflicted stakeholders and stakeseekers alike are improving. The PAC is now offering a seminar on reputation management to go along with its traditional issues management program.

The Committee for Economic Development study *Restoring Trust in Corporate Governance* finds there has been a negative impact on the reputation of all businesses because of the behavior of a significant number of institutions during the financial crisis: "And other corporations in both the financial and industrial sectors, even those which are well-run, are not immune from general reputational harm to business caused by almost two years of headlines about corporate problems, excesses and failures."[7]

Peter Drucker's *The Practice of Management* (1954), the book that defined management as a discipline and made it important to companies, concludes by mentioning the political satirist and pamphleteer de Mandeville whose **"Fable of the Bees" (subtitled "Private Vices, Public Benefits")** espoused the theory **"selfishness unwittingly turns into common good."**

Drucker counters in the final sentence: "But today it has become possible if not commonplace in this country to assert the opposite principle: the business enterprise must be so managed as to make the public good become the private good of the enterprise."

DISCUSSION QUESTIONS

1. Define issues management. Give an example of two issues facing an organization that you choose (e.g., automobile, computer, charitable aid, consulting).

2. What is the difference between issues management and futurism? Please provide two specific organizational examples with an issue and a futurist topic for each.
3. Outline the issues management process. Describe very briefly how you would organize the steps in an organization.
4. Issues management is one of the highest paying specializations in public relations management. Discuss why that seems to be a reasonable expectation to pay higher fees and salaries for issues managers and consultants.
5. Give three examples and discuss research methods that are used in issues management. What is different about research methods for issues management?

NOTES

1. Archie R. Bol, "Fitting the Corporation to the Future," *Public Relations Quarterly* (Winter 1979), p. 5.
2. I have always detested that limp rag of a word "proactive," which some PR people stole from educational psychology. Proactivity, however, has muscle and direction. It reminds me of Mark Twain's observation: "The difference between the right word and the almost-right word is the difference between lightning and the lightning bug." (Ray Ewing)
3. Committee for Economic Development, "Restoring Trust in Corporate Governance: The Six Essential Tasks of Boards of Directors and Business Leaders" (2010).
4. *The New York Times*, March 2011.
5. Peter Drucker, *The Effective Executive*.
6. "Running with Risk," McKinsey Quarterly (November 2003). www.mckinseyquarterly.com.
7. Committee for Economic Development study "Restoring Trust in Corporate Governance," January, 2010. p. 2.

ADDITIONAL READING

Ashley, William C., and James L. Morrison. 1995. *Anticipatory Management: 10 Power Tools for Achieving Excellence into the 21st Century*. Leesburg, VA: IAP. Print.

Brown, J.K. 1979. *This Business of Issues: Coping with the Company's Environment*. New York, NY: The Conference Board. Print.

Chase, W. Howard. 1982. "Issues Management." In: Nagelschmidt, Joseph S, ed. *The Public Affairs Handbook*. New York, NY: AMACOM. Print.

Chase, W. Howard. 1984. *Issue Management: Origins of the Future*. Stamford, CT: Issue Action Publications. Print.

Coates, Joseph F. 1986. *Issues Management: How You Can Plan, Organize, and Manage for the Future*. Mt. Airy, MD: Lomond. Print.

Elkins, Arthur, and Dennis W. Callaghan. 1975. *A Managerial Odyssey: Problems in Business and Its Environment*. Reading, MA: Addison-Wesley Pub. Print.

Ewing, Raymond P. 1980. "Sociopolitical Forecasting: Managing the Black Hole of the Future." In: Feather, Frank, ed. *Through the '80s, Thinking Globally, Acting Locally*. Washington, DC: World Future Society. Print.

Ewing, Raymond P. 1987. *Managing the New Bottom Line: Issues Management for Senior Executives*. Homewood, IL: Dow Jones-Irwin. Print.

Heath, Robert L., and Michael J. Palenchar. 2009. *Strategic Issues Management: Organizations and Public Policy Challenges*. Los Angeles, CA: Sage Publications. Print.

Nowlan, Stephen E., and Diana R. Shayon. 1984. *Leveraging the Impact of Public Affairs: A Guidebook Based on Practical Experience for Corporate Public Affairs Executives*. Philadelphia, PA: HRN. Print.

Renfro, William L. 1993. *Issues Management in Strategic Planning*. Westport, CT: Quorum. Print.

Stanley, Guy D.D. 1985. *Managing External Issues: Theory and Practice*. Greenwich, CT: JAI. Print.

22
C H A P T E R

STATE AND LOCAL GOVERNMENT RELATIONS
Guiding Principles

L. James Nelson
Public Affairs Consultant

When covering government, the media in the United States, and generally the world for that matter, invariably tends to focus its attention on Washington, DC. While no one would deny the importance to the direction of the country of the federal government—the administration, Congress, courts, the hundreds of regulatory bodies and everything else that lies within the infamous "Beltway" between Virginia and Maryland—increasingly it is at the state and local levels of government where "the rubber meets the road."

Over the past 30 years, American business and organizations of all types have found that many of their challenges and opportunities with government rest in the legislative bodies of cities, counties and states. The ideal—a single standard to comply with or measure up to—is more often than not more of a patchwork of laws and regulations that varies widely from jurisdiction to jurisdiction.

Good examples are the issues of product liability and medical malpractice, where what might be relatively innocuous for a manufacturer or physician in one state presents a major challenge in another. At the same time, the cultural, political, media bias and other intangible, vaguely measurable but very real aspects that go into decision making in a jurisdiction weigh heavily as well.

When a company or any organization with nationwide locations or customers must deal with government, it can be and often is a multilevel, multilayered proposition. To effectively deal with it requires, among other things, superior data gathering, financial resources and exceptionally effective troops on the ground, not unlike war. The twists and turns public policy development takes at the state and local levels are limitless and can be profoundly unpredictable.

Someone who knew something about both war and legislative battles, former U.S. President Dwight D. Eisenhower, once said something apt regarding the challenges faced by any company or organization including state and local levels of government:

"PLANS ARE NOTHING; PLANNING IS EVERYTHING"

And so it goes for any business or organization that needs to approach and effectively deal with state and local governments as those bodies do the bidding of voters and other stakeholders in what can loosely be called a *process*. Both preparedness and the ability to measure ever-changing situations and to quickly and adroitly change direction and tactics, while preserving strategy and objectives, are the keys to effectiveness.

Many corporate chieftains often echo the sentiment, "half our advertising budget is wasted, but we're never sure which half." This statement also sums up well the challenge of the work and the allocation of resources for the state and local government relations function. There are, in life and in business, more than enough banana peels to go around. Avoiding hazards is a central part of anyone's job. Mostly we learn what to avoid by trial and error. Perhaps, through others' experiences, we can both shorten the learning process and keep from making critical errors with dire consequences.

Here are two *don'ts* to consider and then hold near and dear, as you begin your trek to excellence in dealing with state and local government.

DO NOT ASSUME ANYTHING, EVER.

The Washington representative for a multinational manufacturing conglomerate was infamous for distributing small marble paperweights inscribed with the simple admonition "Assume Nothing" to members of his staff, who from time to time might have transgressed this, his cardinal rule. Perhaps it was a touch heavy handed, yet his minions usually got the message. Few ever got a second paperweight.

Arnold Dornfeld, former editor at the City News Bureau of Chicago was equally as direct when he would offer this counsel to his reporters: "If your mother says she loves you, check it out."

The message is this: advocacy at any level of government requires constant care and healthy skepticism, but first and foremost the necessity to always check and recheck whatever information you are basing your plans and work on. If your sources are wrong, you are wrong. It is as simple as that.

DO NOT PUT ANYTHING IN WRITING YOU DO NOT WANT TO SEE ON FACEBOOK OR THE FRONT PAGE OF ANY NEWSPAPER OR A BILLBOARD.

The situation today is complicated for those representing their organization or company to government, especially state and local. The advent of the Internet, prevalence of e-mail and wide variety of social media only underscore the necessity of keeping in mind the old English adage that "A lie will go round the world while truth is pulling its boots on."

Electronic and social media, and particularly e-mail, make it all an even more slippery slope nowadays. Consider these true confession horror stories:

> A "helpful" human resources person in my company sent an employee phone extension list to everyone at our company. But the spreadsheet had hidden columns that were easily unhidden to reveal everyone's pay, bonuses and stock options—including senior managements'. She wasn't with our company much longer.

or,

> I received an e-mail from an assistant at a competing consulting firm, cc'd to the entire firm's entire e-mail address book. What a piece of luck! Now I know who all their employees, associates and many of their clients are. Attached was the proposal to one of their clients, so much the better. Now I know how much they charge. Several hours later, I received another e-mail from this assistant, again cc'd to everyone, with a revised proposal. The next day I received a third e-mail from the assistant "Please ignore the previous e-mails."

You get the message.

A good rule of thumb is that if you think something you intend to put in writing might become publicly misinterpreted and likely misused, chances are it will be. Write everything with this public possibility in mind and with all communications practice the old carpenter's rule, "Measure twice—cut once." And, of course, think twice before sending once. In other words, compose and then set it aside and let your angst or whatever emotion you are feeling cool before you send *any* message.

And here are 16 *do's* for anyone seeking proficiency in dealing with government, at any level.

DO BECOME, TO THE GREATEST EXTENT POSSIBLE, THE EMBODIMENT OF WHO OR WHAT YOU REPRESENT TO ANY LEVEL OF GOVERNMENT.

You are the message. You are your organization. The legendary Bryce Harlow once said, when asked who he reported to when he ran Procter & Gamble's Washington, DC, office, "To the chairman and the chairwoman." Harlow's point was that when meeting with anyone on the Hill or anywhere in Washington, he was at that moment "the company." What he was relating to any public official he spoke with unequivocally represented both the internal consensus and public policy needs of Procter & Gamble.

Make sure you are able to speak similarly on behalf of your organization when representing it to government and those in government who will play a role in its destiny. You may not get a second chance. You *are* the company. You *are* your organization.

DO RESPECT GEOGRAPHY.

Keep in mind that the disastrous results of The Charge of the Light Brigade were the result of the charge having been ordered by someone more than a thousand miles from the event. If you are *not* "on the ground" in the city hall or state capitol where the destiny of your organization is being determined by well-meaning but possibly misinformed elected officials and regulators, then things will *not* likely go your way. Simply put—effective representation or advocacy is not something easily sustained through e-mail or by picking up the phone. Better to get on a plane and go where you can see, smell and hear about the situation and best represent yourself and your interests.

Written reports and memoranda cannot do the job that the on-the-ground inspection can do. The chief operating officer of a large environmental service company tells stories of operating managers who spent company resources on giant models of Santa Claus riding spaceships on the front lawns of regional offices, boxes of pet snakes under the desk of one regional manager and bizarre, inappropriate art work hanging in field corporate offices, inflicted on employees and visiting customers alike. He summed it up with "You never see the boxes of snakes if you don't get out there and visit your offices."

DO GET THE VERY BEST CONTRACT REPRESENTATIVES AND ADVOCATES FOR WHEN YOU CAN'T BE THERE YOURSELF. THIS CAN BEST BE DONE BY FOLLOWING THE LEADERS.

It is likely that at some point, you in combination with your local or regional managers and your industry's trade group and any other internal resources relevant to your cause will simply not be enough. At that point it will become apparent to all the overworked folks on your team that an outside contract lobbyist needs to be brought on board to provide political savvy and "boots on the ground" in the fight ahead.

This can seem like a daunting task, but it needn't be so. Identifying and hiring a contract lobbyist is not unlike doing so with any sort of vendor. Researching, completing staff work and making sure everyone in the organization is on board with the options and eventual choice are all important and can be time consuming as they are with any executive search.

To speed the process along somewhat, learn and review which firms and particular lobbyists the leading companies (*not* those in your industry) operating in a state capitol or city hall are engaged with. The very best lobbyists are likely already working for others, so check who the leading brewer, car manufacturer, pharmaceutical house, giant retailer, etc., is engaged with in terms of lobbying talent. Chances are that when the top two to three are using one specific lobbyist, then the majority of the sifting work has been done for you.

Approach and dialogue with that contract lobbyist can be undertaken more quickly and probably more easily than approaching your choices with original research and a shot in the dark.

DO RESPECT THE INEVITABLE DISTINCT DIFFERENCES BETWEEN JURISDICTIONS YOU ARE DEALING WITH.

Every state capital, county building and city hall is different from every other one. Never forget that. The biggest mistake you can make is the same one made by a very long-term top aide and later cabinet member to Ronald Reagan. He made the mistake of thinking Washington, DC was just a big Sacramento, which of course could not be further from the truth. Equally bad is to think for an instant that any state capital is like a small Washington, DC. Springfield or Columbus or Indianapolis or Olympia or Pierre are *not* small Washingtons. Each is a three-ring circus unto themselves. Never forget this.

And while any and every seat of government may resemble a three-ring circus, they should not be treated the same, by anyone, ever. Economic realities, public policy priorities, regional preferences and biases on hundreds of social and cultural issues, quirks of local media and the inevitable unique political differences from city to city and state to state will all have an impact on your organization's legislative and regulatory agendas. No two localities, or government structures, are the same, ever. Treat all governmental bodies in the same way at your own peril.

DO STUDY, UNDERSTAND AND BECOME AN EXPERT IN THE USE OF SOCIAL MEDIA.

For better or worse, the Internet and social media no longer just fill in the cracks in and around traditional print and electronic media. Social media has now become the preferred bearer of news, gossip and substantive information on public policy of all sorts. And by its very nature, change comes to social media in quantum leaps. Changes emerge and evolve, and new sites, apps and systems are born every day. Social media's importance to how everyone, particularly those in business and government, communicates with one another become more important with every passing news cycle.

Do what you must to stay current. Such personal strategies as taking college courses, attending internal corporate seminars, following worthwhile blogs and subscribing to publications online just to observe information flow and management will work to your benefit and serve to your mastery of social media. The Public Affairs Council (www.pac.org) of Washington, DC, regularly holds training sessions of all sorts designed to spread understanding of practical elements on any number of topics and has recently done so extensively with Internet and web-based communication.

A word of warning (and perhaps a glimpse of the blindingly obvious!)—the Internet is perhaps one of the greatest time sinks ever created. Central to your ongoing success as an advocate will be being able to separate the wheat from the chaff and develop an expertise over time to differentiate, instinctively and intuitively, between the *useful* and the *useless* on the Internet.

DO MEET PEOPLE AND THEN ASSIDUOUSLY KEEP TRACK OF EVERYONE, BY BOTH NAME AND LOCALITY, THAT YOU HAVE MET SOCIALLY AND PROFESSIONALLY.

We only get things done through other people. Generally speaking, the more people you know, the more you will get done.

For anyone working in public affairs or government relations, so geographically tuned, it is particularly important that each contact be listed in two data systems, once alphabetically and once geographically, whether you use a sophisticated electronic data system or an old-fashioned rolodex.

That way, when you are considering who can help or serve as a potential strategic partner on a given challenge in a given location, you will have that list of everyone in Lansing, Michigan, or Sacramento, California, or wherever your next campaign takes you.

David Rockefeller, former chairman of Chase Manhattan and a globetrotting titan of public affairs, was always able to take with him in person a small loose-leaf book of everyone he had ever met in this or that city and be able to automatically remember, and contact them again when working any given business or governmental wiring diagram.

Such a two-tiered system can and will be, invaluable.

DO UNDERSTAND THAT, AS JESSE UNRUH, FAMED CALIFORNIA POLITICO, ONCE SAID, "MONEY IS THE MOTHER'S MILK OF POLITICS" ULTIMATELY, TO BE EFFECTIVE, YOU WILL NEED TO COPE WITH A PATCHWORK OF CAMPAIGN FINANCE LAWS FROM LOCALITY TO LOCALITY AND ENGAGE IN THE BASIC NEED OF POLITICIANS OF ALL STRIPES FOR MONETARY HELP WITH THEIR CAMPAIGNS.

Those who are able to run effective political action programs for their organizations get more done than those who do not. It is as simple as that. Learn how leaders in your field do it, work hand in hand with knowledgeable corporate legal counsel and establish your own program. It can be time consuming and difficult in terms of accounting and human resources, but for better or worse, it goes with the territory.

Even then, political action will, at best, gain you access to politicians' time and attention. Making your case will depend on a host of factors.

DO LEARN TO CREATE AND MAINTAIN HELPFUL AND GOOD WORKING RELATIONSHIPS WITH YOUR ORGANIZATION'S LEGAL COUNSEL, WHETHER THEY BE INTERNAL OR WITH A LAW FIRM FROM "OUTSIDE."

There is a nexus where public policy and politics meet the law. The effects of how that happens and shapes your organization is the responsibility and absolute purview of your lawyers. Keeping "legal" informed and part of the process could not be more important to eventual outcomes. While most lawyers believe they understand the political and public policy processes, few actually do. Never assume "legal" understands completely what you are working on. Take the additional time to completely and transparently describe and explain what your organization is facing in governmental venues and bring legal counsel along and make them part of the process.

DO LEARN TO WRITE A ONE-PAGE, CLEAR, CRISP OPTIONS MEMORANDUM ON ISSUES AND RECOMMENDATIONS FOR NEXT STEPS.

To be able to do so for stakeholders, your management, public policy makers and potential coalition members in your effort on issues at hand adds immense value to your organization.

Your options memo should be able to stand on its own with background provided if asked for. Critical components of *your* one-page options memo should include:

- A concise statement of the issue

- Brief background on the problem

- Relevant analytical and factual data

- Policy alternatives for decision makers

- Advantages and disadvantages of each alternative

- A recommendation, either yours or a consensus recommendation of those working the issue

Can it be done on one page? The legal marriage vow has two words. The *Gettysburg Address* has 271 words. The *Ten Commandments* have 297 words. The *Lord's Prayer* has 71 words. The president of the United States receives an endless stream of one-page option memoranda on the wide variety of issues daily. Those you communicate with deserve the same thought, editing and complete staff work as does the president.

DO LEARN TO DISCERN INSTINCTIVELY AND INTUITIVELY WHAT INFORMATION IS SUBSTANTIVE, RELEVANT AND SUSTAINABLE, AND THE TRUE SPEED AT WHICH SOMETHING IS MOVING THROUGH THE PROCESS AS OPPOSED TO INFORMATION AND "FACTS" THAT ARE READILY APPARENT OR IMMEDIATE.

Understand that virtually all information you receive, particularly that having to do with public policy development, on any given day is invariably simply the tip of the iceberg. The other 95 percent of any situation is out of sight and below water. With icebergs it is always the case that that which is at the surface can be merely something you power through, while that which is below the surface is, more likely, something that can, and will, sink your ship if not treated with the respect it deserves. Former U.S. Secretary of Defense Donald Rumsfeld termed such information as "known unknowns." In other words, there will always be a lot of things we know we do not know, but which we can find out.

It is your job, as an effective advocate, to find out whether the legislative bill introduced or regulation proposed has the legs to make it through the process and become a fact of life for your organization, company or whatever you represent. Local and state governmental bodies can and often do act with lightening speed. A legislative bill can pass one house one day, glide through the other house the next day and be signed by the governor by the end of the week.

Other measures are put forward for political or other purposes without really having any chance of passage or enactment but serve their sponsors as stalking horses and trial balloons for other, down-the-road legislation they are thinking of introducing.

Timely information management, and knowing which information is accurate and important *and which is not*, is your responsibility.

DO BECOME EXPERT ABOUT PUBLIC OFFICIALS' SPHERES AND ORGANIZATIONS OF INFLUENCE AND LEARN TO WORK WITHIN THOSE ORGANIZATIONS.

All professions, whether dentistry, accounting, the clergy, academia or whatever, network among themselves, work toward common goals, create "best practices" and do many like things together.

In industry this networking and cross-pollinating is done in and through trade associations (see Chapter 19 on associations). Similarly, elected and nonelected government officials at all levels exchange gossip and ideas and work toward common objectives through myriad especially created groups. These include prominent ones such as the Council of State Governments, National League of Cities, National Conference of State Legislatures, National Association of Attorneys General as well as some less-well-known ones such as the National Association of State Budget Officers, National Association of State Boating Law Administrators and many others. Also, there are ideological groups, such as the American Legislative Exchange Council, which works for a 50-state standardization of rules and regulation with its guiding principle being smaller, more efficient government.

You need to recognize any and all "wholesale" groups for what they are, what they can and cannot do as components for the accomplishment of your strategic objectives. All such organizations invariably welcome private sector input and participation, but to different degrees. Getting involved and active can pay dividends and enhance your network of contacts and resources. Working with and through these groups, when possible, on behalf of what you advocate can provide you with both an excellent periscope and added effectiveness when moving your own organization's agenda forward.

When the pharmaceutical giant, G.D. Searle, encountered almost 50 different state codes regulating artificial sweeteners, the company helped found the American Legislative Exchange Council (ALEC), where state legislators of all stripes could come together and determine a single standard. ALEC worked at it and succeeded greatly on this particular issue, and is still working at similar challenges imposed by the fact that there are, in the final analysis, 50 states all concerned about and constantly working on societal problems, but many times coming up with and pushing different solutions to those societal problems.

Washington, DC, is the center for the lion's share of this sort of professional and coalition activity and can be a great resource to your building of contacts and effectiveness. The State Governmental Affairs Council is the hub of much of this. Start learning through the State Governmental Affairs Council's website, which spells out who generally belongs to which organizations and what those organizations are doing. Try to attend and observe annual and semiannual meetings of these organizations. Getting to know public officials "off campus" when they are more relaxed and out of the glare of the media is easier than trying to do so in the state capital while they are on a working schedule.

DO CREATE STRATEGIC ALLIANCES WITH MODERATE ELEMENTS OF THE ENVIRONMENTAL MOVEMENT WHENEVER AND WHEREVER POSSIBLE.

Every business and organization these days is, or has some element of, an environmental challenge to society. The days of confrontation, argument and denial over the various elements of the environmental movement, including service, intellectual and manufacturing, throughout the past 40+ years (roughly since the first Earth Day in 1970), have come together and worked together on issues facing the environment.

For instance, after many years of ducking the debate over whether huge amounts of waste are created by millions of to-go meals sold every day around the world, McDonald's has gone to work hand in hand with the Natural Resources Defense Council and Waste Management Inc. on an ongoing basis on packaging challenges, bringing a solid "reduce-reuse-recycle" ethic and process into McDonald's day-to-day operations at over 30,000 outlets worldwide.

Hundreds of companies have similar success stories to tell. Florida Power Corporation, Dow Corning, Consolidated Coal, Chevron and Borden's all have assessed their solid waste, carbon emissions, water pollution and other challenges; chosen strategic partners in the environmental community; and gone to work to successfully reduce their contributions to a fouled atmosphere and environment. Sustainable corporate environmental responsibility is the word of the day. They know they are not going to clean up the world by themselves, but they do understand that the devil is in the details and every bit counts.

DO LEARN TO TELL THE TRUTH ABOUT ANY GIVEN EXTERNAL EVENT(S) TO THE ISSUE YOU ARE DEALING WITH EARLY, QUICKLY AND AS COMPLETELY AS POSSIBLE TO ALL STAKEHOLDERS.

Bryce Harlow always told those he took under his wing that "Trust is the coin of the realm," and the only way you get and maintain trust from others is through being straightforward and complete in your communications. The entire story will come out one way or another, and it might as well come from you. This is particularly true when and where state and local government officials are concerned. They will appreciate your candor and completeness and will be all the more willing to trust you in negotiations in the future. Whether it is an environmental crisis, or human resources event such as a layoff. Whatever it is, get it out there for the public and media and those governmental officials you are working with.

Treat every adverse situation as if it were a matter of life or death. Remember what Apollo 13 astronauts advised mission control at NASA, "Houston, we have a problem," the minute their craft was in trouble. Treat your challenge in the same way and answers will become apparent and solutions will happen that much more quickly.

DO UNDERSTAND THE CENTRAL MOTIVATION OF ELECTED OFFICIALS. GOOD GOVERNMENT IS ADMIRABLE, BUT ALWAYS REMEMBER, AT ANY LEVEL OF GOVERNMENT, AN ELECTED OFFICIAL'S PRINCIPAL JOB IS TO GET REELECTED—NOT TO CREATE "GOOD GOVERNMENT."

The basic assumption and formula is this—no elected official can ever expect *all* of his or her constituents to agree on an issue. His or her job is to represent the majority of those constituents on any given issue. Sometimes, probably too often, it comes down to 50 percent plus 1 of the constituents being pleased with a decision and those 50 percent plus 1 going to the polls and reelecting the official at the next election. It can be a messy process, but in the end that is how it generally works.

If you keep this in mind as you advocate, negotiate and advise public officials, you will much sooner reach a meeting of the minds. Knowing what they need to do to get reelected serves as a reliable compass for your own work.

23 CHAPTER

CORPORATE GOVERNANCE
Operating as an Open Book

Ted McDougal
Founder and Principal, McDougal + Associates
Principal, Jacobs + McDougal
Former Director of Ketchum's Midwest Corporate/Healthcare Practice

Kurt P. Stocker
Director, New York Stock Exchange Regulation Inc.
Member, Board of Governors of Financial Industry Regulatory Authority, Inc.
Former Chief Communications Officer of Continental Bank Corporation

> *Corporate Governance is concerned with holding the balance between economic and social goals and between individual and communal goals. The corporate governance framework is there to encourage the efficient use of resources and equally to require accountability for the stewardship of those resources. The aim is to align as nearly as possible the interests of individuals, corporations and society.*[1]
>
> —Sir Adrian Cadbury

*G*overnance describes the mechanisms an organization uses to ensure that its constituents follow its established processes and policies. Corporate governance prescribes the rights and duties of a corporation's shareholders, board of directors and management. The term also encompasses the efficiency and transparency of a company's financial and information structure, defines expectations, grants powers and verifies performance.

A company's stockholders elect members of the board of directors who represent the interests of the stockholders and make long-term decisions that shape the future of the corporation. For example, the chief executive officer (CEO) reports to the board of directors on matters ranging from long-term corporate strategy to financial transactions and overall productivity. Board members in turn are directly accountable to stockholders and must abide by the company's code of ethics when discharging their responsibilities. As such, the board of directors forms the foundation for the structure of corporate governance.

Barron's defines governance as "the system of checks and balances designed to ensure that corporate managers are just as vigilant on behalf of long-term shareholder value as they would be if it was their own money at risk. It is also the process whereby shareholders—the actual owners of any publicly traded firm—assert their ownership rights."[2]

A CENTURY OF SELF-DEALING

The practice of federal corporate governance dates to the early twentieth century (see box on Corporate Governance Chronology) with the 1912 Pujo Committee congressional hearings into the concentration of power and influence in the national banking system, which was orchestrated primarily through interlocking directorships. Following the 1929 stock market crash amidst the Great Depression, Congress enacted the Securities Act of 1933. Part of the New Deal under President Franklin D. Roosevelt, the law was the first major federal legislation regulating the sale of securities. Previously, securities regulation was governed by the states.

Often referred to as the "truth in securities" law, the Securities Act of 1933 had two basic objectives: to require that investors receive financial and other significant information concerning securities being offered for public sale and to prohibit deceit, misrepresentations and other fraud in the sale of securities.[3]

The following year, the Securities Exchange Act of 1934 created the Securities and Exchange Commission (SEC) and gave the new agency broad authority over all aspects of the securities industry. This included the power to register, regulate and oversee brokerage firms, transfer agents and clearing agencies as well as the nation's securities self-regulatory organizations (SROs).

The various stock exchanges, such as the New York Stock Exchange (NYSE) and American Stock Exchange, are SROs. The National Association of Securities Dealers, which operates the Nasdaq system, also is an SRO. The law also prohibited certain types of misconduct in the markets and provided the SEC with disciplinary powers over regulated entities and persons associated with them.[4]

The aftermath of World War II saw the rise of multinational corporations. The regulatory system as we know it today took shape gradually over the ensuing 30 to 40 years, struggling to keep up with the rapid post-war global expansion. Business experts observe that "many large corporations [had] dominant control over business affairs without sufficient accountability or monitoring by their boards of directors." The pace of regulatory transformation accelerated dramatically as the twentieth century came to a close.[5]

The progressive effort by shareholders to hold boards accountable in their oversight role over management and to represent the interests of investors has evolved over at least three decades. Through the 1970s, individual investors held the dominant number of shares in public companies of all sizes. The 1980s and 1990s were a time of corporate excess, closed boardrooms and sweetheart deals. Correspondingly, the era of shareholder activism began to change when a few prominent public pension funds began challenging boards and CEOs over corporate social policies.

The first decade of the twenty-first century saw more changes in the governance landscape than at any time since the Great Depression because of high-profile scandals involving abuse of corporate power and, in some cases, criminal activity by corporate officers. A series of financial reporting and corporate governance scandals shook the U.S. securities markets (see MCI WorldCom case study) and led to the Sarbanes-Oxley Act, which was signed into law by President George W. Bush on July 30, 2002. Sarbanes-Oxley mandated a number of reforms to restore investor confidence by enhancing corporate responsibility, improving financial disclosures and combating corporate and accounting fraud. The NYSE and Nasdaq followed suit by updating their own corporate governance rules.

In March 2008, a seminal event turned the tables on boards of directors: the collapse of Bear Stearns under the weight of bad investments in various collateralized securities backed by subprime mortgages. Shortly thereafter, Lehman Brothers became another victim for many of the same reasons, including a marginalized board and too much leverage.

The Lehman Brothers bankruptcy filing triggered the largest federal bailout of the financial services industry in U.S. history. While there were numerous fallouts from the financial crisis, one was the focus on boards' responsibility for risk assessment. In the aftermath, boards of directors were criticized for failing to understand the inherent risks behind their firms' investments.[6]

FINANCIAL SYSTEM BREAKDOWN

The federal bailout, called the Troubled Asset Relief Program (TARP), was created by the U.S. Treasury in 2008 to help stabilize the U.S. financial system. The Treasury invested approximately $250 billion in more than 200 banks to acquire bad mortgages, mortgage-related instruments and other debt-related products in exchange for preferred stock and warrants from those institutions.

These developments led to a concerted push to improve governance and disclosure practices through legislation, regulation, stock exchange rules and private sector efforts. Serving as an applied case study to dramatize the need for more stringent governance guidelines, financial services concerns that either voluntarily granted shareholders a vote on how the companies should compensate their top executives (say-on-pay), or were mandated through TARP to do so, received overwhelming shareholder approval.

The worst market freefall since the Great Depression spawned the Dodd-Frank Wall Street Reform and Consumer Protection Act, which was passed by Congress and signed into law by President Barack Obama on July 21, 2010. In his remarks before signing the Act, President Obama outlined the regulatory changes that would be required to implement the new law, which in turn promises to have a profound effect on the practice of public relations and its role in furthering economic reform:

> [The new Act] demands accountability and responsibility from everyone. It provides certainty to everybody, from bankers to farmers to business owners to consumers. And unless your business model depends on cutting corners or bilking your customers, you've got nothing to fear from reform.
>
> Reform will also rein in the abuse and excess that nearly brought down our financial system. It will finally bring transparency to the kinds of complex and risky transactions that helped trigger the financial crisis. Shareholders will also have a greater say on the pay of CEOs and other executives, so they can reward success instead of failure.[7]

Dodd-Frank contains numerous provisions that affect the governance and communications practices of issuers. For example, the new law requires advisory votes of shareholders about executive compensation and golden parachutes; it mandates disclosure about the role of compensation consultants and it requires clear disclosure about certain specific compensation considerations, including pay-for-performance and the ratio between the CEO's total compensation and the median total compensation for all other company employees.

CORPORATE GOVERNANCE CHRONOLOGY

1912—Congress begins Pujo hearings into concentration of power among U.S. banks through interlocking board directorships and financial transactions.

1933—Securities Act of 1933 requires that investors receive key information about securities being offered for sale; prohibits misrepresentations and imposes penalties on directors.

1934—Securities Exchange Act of 1934 creates the SEC, with authority over all aspects of the securities industry; requires periodic reporting of information by companies.

1940—Investment Advisers Act of 1940 requires that professionals advising others about securities investments must register with the SEC.

1955—*Fortune* magazine introduces the Fortune 500 ranking, bestowing status on directors of the nation's largest corporations.

1974—SEC requires disclosure in proxy statements about whether corporations have independent audit committees.

1985—Institutional Shareholder Services debuts as a consultant to institutional investors on corporate governance.

1993—Chief executives ousted at such major underperforming companies as General Motors, IBM, American Express, Eastman Kodak and Westinghouse.

2000—SEC Regulation FD (fair disclosure) sets out new, more restrictive guidelines on how companies can communicate to the market.

2002—Enron implodes from mismanagement and accounting scandal, heightening public awareness about the importance of transparent financial dealings; President Bush signs the Sarbanes-Oxley Act, tightening accountability standards for officers, directors and auditors.

A NEW CORPORATE DEMOCRACY

2003—SEC approves NYSE, Nasdaq rules to strengthen corporate governance standards; audit, compensation and nominating committees must have only independent directors.

2004—Executive pay indignation swells as NYSE CEO Richard Grasso's compensation tops $180 million, surprising some board members who approved pay package.

2005—WorldCom CEO Bernard Ebbers convicted of participating in the largest accounting fraud in U.S. history; sentenced to 25 years in prison.

2006—SEC approves sweeping overhaul of compensation reporting to take into account fuller disclosure of perquisites, retirement benefits and total compensation.

2007—Merrill Lynch reduces value of securities linked to risky subprime mortgages; Citigroup reports net income plunge, citing weakening consumer credit environment.

2008—JPMorgan Chase pays $2 a share to acquire Bear Stearns after firm was driven to brink of bankruptcy; Lehman Brothers enters largest bankruptcy filing in U.S. history; TARP established for U.S. Treasury to purchase assets and equity from financial institutions; TARP expanded to support U.S. auto industry.

2009—Judge refuses to approve Bank of America settlement of SEC lawsuit in connection with Merrill Lynch acquisition, accusing both parties of blindsiding shareholders and taxpayers.

2010—President Obama signs Dodd-Frank Wall Street Reform and Consumer Protection Act, a sweeping overhaul of the U.S. financial regulatory system.[8]

The question under the new regulatory paradigm becomes who is running the nation's publicly traded companies and whom do they represent? The answer reflects a shift toward corporate democracy as shareholders demand greater involvement in the process and significant events shape the new view of corporate governance as defined by regulators, SROs and beneficial owners or retail investors who actually own the publicly traded shares of these same companies.

Historically, boards of directors comprised primarily company management, key vendors, clients and associates of the CEO. These imperial boards were treated like members of exclusive clubs: lots of perks, little homework and minimal accountability. As long as the economy was expanding, corporate share prices were climbing and financial performance was strong, few complained.

That all changed after highly publicized lapses by so many corporate boards. Financial results were not as they seemed, especially from the perspective of the corporations' owners. In the case of high-profile failures such as Enron, MCI WorldCom, Tyco, Bear Stearns and Lehman Brothers, management was less than truthful about how and what their companies were doing, while the boards of directors were either in the dark or complicit. Investors lost money, management was fired, lawsuits were filed and boards were replaced. In these cases, there was no direct communication from boards of directors to the shareholders they represented. Investors in turn had no access to the boards.

Despite declining operating results, these same directors authorized handsome compensation for the corporate leaders they were supposed to be supervising, even when share prices were declining. In many cases, stock options were rewritten so that incentive compensation could be paid to executives who had not achieved their performance objectives. At the same time, plurality voting for directors was dominated by brokers claiming to represent beneficial owners, but who voted almost exclusively with management for board retention.

Making matters worse, many securities analysts were accessories in the process by providing "buy" recommendations for failing companies right up to the bankruptcy announcements. Securities analysts provide research on companies and make recommendations on their stocks. When analysts are employed by brokerage firms and provide information for the firms' retail and institutional clients, they are called *sell-side analysts*.

For example, on November 29, 2001, of a reported 13 sell-side research analysts covering Enron, one issued a "strong sell," six had "strong buys," and six advised investors to "hold." Incredibly, Enron CEO

Kenneth Lay filed one of the largest bankruptcies in U.S. history on December 2.

Under Sarbanes-Oxley, and subsequently reinforced by Dodd-Frank, the NYSE and other SROs now impose stricter listing standards for companies whose stock is traded on those public exchanges. For example, the NYSE mandates that boards of directors for its listed corporations be made up of a majority of independent directors, meaning not members of internal senior management or anyone associated in any way with leadership of the companies they serve.

> *We are in constant contact with shareholders. We listen very carefully to what they think and what they think good corporate governance should be. The creation of trust depends on good corporate governance. Employees want to work for a company that has integrity. Shareholders want to invest in a company that has good corporate governance. Consumers want to know how a company is being run, if it is honest and if it is controlled.*[9] —Peter Brabeck-Lemathe

POWER SHIFTS TO INDIVIDUAL INVESTORS

A year before the passage of Dodd-Frank, another significant regulatory change affecting investor relations involved amending NYSE Rule 452. As previously written, the rule permitted brokers to cast votes for customers who chose not to respond to requests for voting instructions in proxy solicitations. Investors can hold shares in their own name (shares of record) or in the name of a broker (street name). For shares held in street name, which account for approximately 85 percent of exchange-listed shares, investors are called beneficial owners.

On July 1, 2009, the SEC approved an amendment to Rule 452, which eliminated the ability of brokers to vote in their discretion with respect to elections of directors. The amendment promises to have broad consequences for annual shareholder meetings because broker votes in director elections typically represent a significant percentage of the total vote.

Companies, especially corporations that have large retail shareholder bases, will need to educate their shareholders about the rule change. It is important for shareholders to understand that failure to instruct their brokers to vote in elections of directors for companies with a majority voting standard will be equivalent to voting against those directors.

Consequently, corporations need to more clearly communicate with shareholders about the increased

OPPORTUNITY FOR PUBLIC RELATIONS

Retail investors regaining their collective voice and investor dialogue expanding to include boards of directors potentially opens enormous opportunities for the public relations industry to take the lead in an evolving dialogue, which formerly was the exclusive province of financial and legal staffs.

Public relations professionals historically deferred investor-related issues to the chief financial officer and investor relations team, who generally were responsible for managing relationships with a company's largest institutional investors, as well as securities analysts who file research reports recommending investment in its stock.

However, with the balance of power shifting to individual investors and beneficial owners, companies must actively manage those relationships, or risk losing control of matters such as director elections, board composition and executive compensation.

In many corporations, the PR function frequently was asked to implement strategic decisions, without having been involved when decisions were being made. The threat posed by new and pending corporate governance regulation presents an issues-and-crisis-management challenge similar to those encountered by specialized public relations professionals on a regular basis. These include creating clear and persuasive messaging strategies to simplify complex positions and a proven ability to shape opinions and influence behavior by communicating to diverse audiences through mass media.

With regulatory upheaval, boardrooms and corporate staffs were buffeted by activist demands, investor expectations, employee concerns and shareholder confusion as never before. They needed to prepare themselves by focusing strategic considerations on investors with the boards of directors.

Public relations professionals need to be aware of what impact these momentous changes will have on virtually all public companies and what communicators can do to improve the outcomes. The corporate governance reforms sweeping through Wall Street and Washington go way beyond what conventional investor relations functions had been expected to execute in the past.

BUILDING TOWARD UNDERSTANDING

Governance is all about communications. Regulators and exchanges talk about disclosure and transparency, but the ultimate goal is to keep investors—all investors, regardless of size or sophistication—informed about what their companies are doing. What regulators are now demanding is that investors must *understand* the disclosures, no matter how transparent they may be.

It is the act of dissemination that is mandated, which does not necessarily achieve the more important objective of comprehension. Contractual language and regulatory compliance are nothing new to public relations professionals, who pride themselves on translating and interpreting complicated concepts to foster better communication and understanding.

One goal of recent governance regulatory reform is to help boards of directors perform their primary function, which is to assess organizational risk. From a public relations perspective, the purpose of a strategic governance communications program is to manage reputational risk in such a way that highly publicized abuses such as those that occurred around the turn of the twenty-first century can be avoided.

The consequences of failing to develop a governance vision and communication strategy are many. Certain directors or an entire board committee could be voted down by stockholders. An activist investor could be elected to the board and become a disruptive influence. Owners could object to the compensation being paid a corporation's top management team. Special-interest groups could advance their agendas within a company's proxy.

It is incumbent on the corporate communications team to put its company's story in context. In other words, communications must match actions so that financial and business disclosures support shareholders' reasons for investing in the stock. A well-executed governance program can serve to *activate* investors by giving them reasons to support a company's business strategy for building long-term sustainable growth.

Nestlé Chairman Peter Brabeck-Letmathe may have put it best when he accepted an award for that company's approach to corporate governance from *World Finance Magazine*. Brabeck-Letmathe emphasized that good corporate governance depends on regular and open communications.

importance of voting at annual meetings. This shareholder education may take the form of simpler language in annual reports and proxy statements, or companies may choose to prepare separate documents to be filed as additional soliciting materials.

Communication with all of a company's—or issuer's—shareholders is complicated by the fact that brokers, rather than issuers, maintain the lists of street-name holders. Companies are only able to communicate directly with beneficial owners of their stock who have not objected to such contact (nonobjecting beneficial owners). Therefore, in planning any shareholder education or solicitation campaign with respect to director elections, companies will need to rely on the brokerage community to reach objecting beneficial owners.[10]

Public relations professionals therefore need to think of a company's shareholders in a new light. Since the 1980s, when the balance of power shifted from individual shareholders to huge pension funds and other institutional investors holding massive numbers of shares, individual shareholders had little power in proxy voting. With the changes to proxy voting rules, brokers and institutions no longer can impose broad non-company-specific standards on proxy votes.

What's more, Dodd-Frank gives the SEC explicit authority to set new rules for proxy access. These rules would allow shareholders meeting certain ownership requirements to place their board nominees on the company's proxy materials. At the time of this writing, the rules are still being finalized, but it's clear the SEC will move quickly to implement the final regulations and that activist investors, including unions and public pension funds, are gearing up for action once the rules are in place.

Taken together, the Dodd-Frank Act and other regulatory measures have important implications for companies. The combination of proxy access, majority voting and the elimination of broker voting means there may be an increase in contested elections and that "vote-against" campaigns will be much more challenging, particularly if the SEC makes it easier for investors to work together. As a result, companies may find themselves having to campaign for their own directors.

ADVOCATING CORPORATE POSITIONS

Companies will need to make a stronger and more public case for their positions on such matters as executive compensation, director qualifications, the composition and diversity of their boards and corporate sustainability efforts. Successful companies will do more than adapt. They will turn these changes into opportunities to strengthen relationships with shareholders and other important constituencies.

Many governance issues must be proactively managed like other aspects of reputation. In fact, year-round communications and education obligations created by Dodd-Frank will require full-time staff attention and tight coordination across functions, particularly the office of the chief financial officer, investor relations, legal affairs, communications and human resources. Corporate communicators can help create and implement strategies to make sure the right information reaches the right audiences in the right way.[11]

When directors must be elected by a majority of a company's shareholders, and not just a plurality, there will be greater scrutiny on director performance, qualifications and independence. In plurality voting, the winner is the candidate with the most votes. There is no requirement that a director receive votes representing a majority of all the issuer's shareholders. Typical corporate investor relations staffs have neither the expertise nor the resources to run internal and external canvasses. Companies, and by extension their communications teams, will have to familiarize shareholders with director candidates and make the case for their governance.

Essentially, companies will need to run their directors for election, manage more information on risks defined by nongovernmental organizations (NGOs), defend the board's governance and make sense of its decisions on executive compensation. A well-conceived public relations program will be required to help corporations gain acceptance for how they create value, as well as to explain the board's advocacy for shareholders.

Key audiences range from institutional investors, many of whom don't vote their proxies, and individual investors—retail, 401(k), mutual funds and retirement funds—to proxy advisors, regulators, activists and employees, who often comprise one of an issuer's largest shareholder blocks.

GOVERNANCE STRATEGIES

1. BLOW UP SILOS

Outdated organizations that isolate the investor relations function from the public relations group are destined to lose ground in today's climate. Both the knowledge and contacts of investor relations and the media savvy of PR are necessary to manage this increasingly important component of corporate governance. Corporate America is just entering the early stages of a more open and intrusive system of regulatory oversight and consumer advocacy.

2. CONFRONT IMPERATIVES

Issues such as majority voting for directors and unrestrained board access promise to define an emerging interactive relationship between corporations and their owners and can no longer be ignored. Conversations in nominating committees likely will be transformed. The first step is to review the current board and make sure each director brings a skill set and unique perspective to the mix. Careful preparation and critical, objective analysis reduce the possibility that an incumbent director is voted off the board or replaced by an independently nominated candidate in an open election.

3. CONDUCT SELF-ASSESSMENT

The 2010 Spencer Stuart Board Index confirmed an encouraging trend toward governance practices favored by shareholders, even though those changes were not required by regulators at the time the survey was conducted. For example, 72 percent of boards now elect directors to one-year terms, up from 40 percent a decade ago. Majority voting is also becoming the norm: 71 percent of boards—up from 65 percent in 2009—require directors who fail to secure a majority vote to offer their resignation. In addition, boards are paying more attention to their own performance. Nearly all (96 percent) conduct annual performance evaluations for the board as a whole and more than a quarter evaluate individual directors as well.[12]

4. DEPLOY THE EXPERTS

Public relations core competencies can help boards vet directors by conducting vulnerability assessments of all publicly available information on each board member. Launching campaigns in advance of director elections is another area of expertise within the profession. The new governance order demands more than just a list of names in a legal document. Definition and insight into individual backgrounds, qualifications and independence will be necessary to activate shareholders and turn out the vote. Companies now must communicate beyond the proxy and consider using more accessible channels, such as electronic shareholder forums, issuer websites, social media and even direct mail to reach, educate and motivate retail investors.

5. WALK THE TALK

Communication strategies must be rooted in boards making enlightened, clearly visible and understandable decisions, particularly at the committee level. Public relations counsel can provide insight to nominating committees about how individual candidates are portrayed in public sources. From a messaging standpoint, compensation committees could benefit by formulating the rationale behind executive compensation plans in simple language.

6. PROVIDE CONTEXT, PERSPECTIVE

Boardrooms will be turned inside out as complex decisions that heretofore were made behind closed doors now must not only be disclosed, but also understood. Again, a function that previously did not exist appears ideally suited for the public relations team. Whether it's say-on-pay, separation of chairman and chief executive officer titles or the highly sensitive issue of management succession planning, the SEC is demanding greater visibility and explanation of board decisions for the benefit of all investors. The complexity and sensitivity of these issues demands a carefully coordinated cross-disciplinary approach involving communications, finance, law and human resources.

7. ENGAGE INVESTORS

Currently most proxies are, at best, uninspiring because votes to confirm public accountants and elect a group of unfamiliar directors are only marginally relevant to the average retail investor. With the shareholder powers granted by Dodd-Frank, annual meetings will no longer be rubber stamp affairs. The bar has been raised beyond declaration and transparency, to engagement and activation of those holding a majority of an issuer's shares.

8. MANAGE REPUTATION

Companies that recognize governance is more than just compliance, but an essential component of reputation management, will separate themselves from the pack. This is another responsibility for public relations. Being stewards of effective corporate governance is yet another important new application of the business of conveying benefits to stakeholders and influencing their behavior.

9. INNOVATE CHANNELS

One significant departure, particularly in the previously archaic realm of financial disclosure, is the channels available to post material information. For example, most company-sponsored investor websites have the potential for much more effective interactive communication to both persuade and motivate. The SEC is exploring how to improve the use of the Internet for distribution of proxy materials to stimulate greater participation among beneficial owners.

CASE STUDY: WORLD CLASS FRAUD

In 1997, WorldCom was one of the world's largest telecommunications companies, with 20 million retail customers, thousands of corporate clients and 80,000 employees. Headquartered in Jackson, Mississippi, WorldCom that year reported annual revenues of $7.35 billion. In 1998, WorldCom merged with MCI Communications Corporation, then the fifth largest telecom provider in the world, creating MCI WorldCom, which had total revenues of more than $30 billion. By 1999 the combined company reported annual revenues of $33.9 billion, a trajectory that could not be sustained and in fact proved to be illusory.

At its apex, the company's operations included the second largest long-distance company in North America, which provided local phone service, data, Internet and other communications services. Other units of MCI WorldCom provided local access to the Internet throughout the United States, Canada, Europe and Asia-Pacific, as well as corporate facilities support across Europe, Scandinavia, Australia, Latin America and the Pacific Rim.

Under Chief Executive Officer Bernard Ebbers, who became CEO in 1995, WorldCom had grown quickly through almost continuous mergers and acquisitions, culminating with MCI and two other mergers in 1998, all of which burdened the company with huge debt.

In October 1999, MCI WorldCom announced its intent to acquire Sprint Corp., which would have combined the nation's second and third largest long-distance suppliers. However, U.S. and European regulators blocked the proposed merger, voicing antitrust concerns about its anticompetitive effects.

FABRICATED INCOME STATEMENTS

With revenue growth flattening and the acquisition route thwarted, management began to fabricate income statements to provide a favorable financial picture that would allow MCI WorldCom to meet Wall Street's earnings targets. In the years following the aborted Sprint deal, the company reported earnings that met those targets, but only through various accounting schemes. Later it was discovered that actual operating earnings not only did not meet the Street's expectations, but in fact the company should have reported net operating losses in many of those reporting periods.

> To sustain a share price, based on high rates of corporate revenue growth, with acquisition forestalled, WorldCom resorted to shifting of reserves into revenues, generating false reports of revenues, and as a last resort converting substantial portions of its line cost expenses into capital items. Its peak share price was sustained by false information just when WorldCom executives were cashing in.[13]

It all came to an end less than three years after the disallowed Sprint acquisition, when an internal auditor blew the whistle on the improprieties. The SEC arrived, executives were fired, a criminal investigation was initiated, and, in July 2002, WorldCom filed for Chapter 11 bankruptcy, the largest bankruptcy in corporate history.

The conditions that enabled a $34 billion telecommunications giant with stock that once traded at $64 per share to declare bankruptcy just three years later are difficult to pinpoint, but pervasive corruption was the order of the day. A bad tone was being set at the top of many large companies in response to corporate governance practices that emphasized stock and options as the preferred form of incentive for management performance.

> Option-based compensation, for executives of firms with $5 billion of revenues, rose from tens to hundreds of millions of dollars per year . . . Management in numerous cases undertook to maintain the share price, against the interests of the shareholders in the corporation. When their misleading activities were revealed, investors led a collapse in share price that in turn triggered debtor demands for payment with adverse effects on corporate liquidity. The resulting collapse, in at least a dozen of the largest corporations, raised the question as to whether there was a failure of corporate governance. Management self-dealing had involved misinforming shareholders as to the true condition of the corporation, causing share prices to be too high.[14]

Subsequent legal action placed much of the blame for management self-dealing on the boards of directors, especially the audit and compensation committees. These committees, before Sarbanes-Oxley and Dodd-Frank, typically were led by internal directors.

FAILURE OF CORPORATE GOVERNANCE

Where did the board members fail and why? They did not ask tough questions, did not conduct rigorous due diligence and essentially accepted what turned out to be illegal accounting statements. The MCI WorldCom board approved multibillion-dollar deals with insufficient information or discussion—sometimes in brief phone calls, with little or no documentation of the transactions. This was characterized by the WorldCom Bankruptcy Court Examiner as a "culture of accommodation."

The gatekeepers—the audit and finance committees—overlooked fabricated reports and the outside accountants, Arthur Andersen, blinked because management hid its scheme from directors and their advisors. Should the board have seen through the falsified revenues? Presumably they noticed that operating growth was leveling off and reserves were diminishing. Governance experts Paul MacAvoy and Ira Millstein attribute the WorldCom bankruptcy and other corporate breakdowns to recklessly executed strategies, compounded by dysfunctional corporate governance systems that enabled the breakdowns to occur:

> We do not with 20/20 hindsight choose to indict boards of directors although we note that many of them appear to have operated with a significant degree of passivity and/or deference to management. Rather, we are searching for the cause of this too-common passivity and deference. We (and others) believe there is a governance mechanism in the engine of the corporation that is broken and has allowed an excessive number of company collapses.[15]

In today's world, outside accountants are hired by audit committees, which comprise independent directors who are qualified financial experts. Would the current regulations have helped? Would these changes have mitigated the problems?

Possibly, but a director's job still is to ask probing questions, be skeptical, act like an investor and look for clues in the tone of the organization. In the case of MCI WorldCom, Bernard Ebbers and Chief Financial Officer Scott Sullivan eventually were found guilty of conspiracy, fraud and making false statements about WorldCom's financial health to regulators. Nevertheless, the board's compensation committee had extended them personal loans with shaky underpinnings, while the investment banks that had led the company's forays into ill-advised public offerings gave the former officers preferential terms that made them small fortunes.[16]

A board with an independent majority and mandated meetings without management might have helped. Greater transparency and disclosures would certainly have been beneficial. New regulations that require attorneys to report material violations of securities laws or breach of duty could have provided early warning signals. Requirements regarding the rotation of outside accounting staff likely would have changed the course of this case.

A FUTURE OF INFORMED INVESTMENT DECISIONS

The future of governance practices at public companies is in the hands of the beneficial owners. While they do not make the laws or enforce regulations, they have been empowered by those who do. Until very recently, retail shareholders have been apathetic toward proxy statements, as the documents were primarily concerned with tedious matters such as electing full slates of unfamiliar director candidates and confirming independent accounting firms.

That has now changed, and retail shareholders can influence the election of individual board members, target specific committees, challenge executive compensation and affect a host of new proposals from a variety of sources.

Where does regulatory reform go from here? Data tagging—interactive statistics labeled by analytical software—is on the menu. Investor-to-investor communications would enable shareholders to interact with investors and other interested parties through electronic forums on proxy issues. While many proposals have been put forth to make it easier for individual shareholders to vote their stock, participation remains disturbingly low. New measures must be found to engage and motivate previously passive investors.

The Wall Street Journal noted that entrepreneurs and activists are trying to urge individual investors to use their newfound power. Websites and social networking tools that compile information and offer voting recommendations already exist. The SEC is interested in modifying techniques to attract more investor votes, but lack of a uniform system for online proxy voting remains an obstacle. Companies also are increasing efforts to engage individual investors online. eBay uses Twitter to send updates on financial disclosures; Amgen has used its proxy to survey shareholders on pay practices; and Intel experimented with an interactive online annual meeting.[17]

Institutional shareholders increasingly are shown how to vote a particular stock by advisory organizations. Many believe that the same companies that independently rank stocks, yet also derive revenue for advisory services in connection with proxy voting, should be regulated. There are others who feel such service providers have grown so large and possess such influence that the proxy voting system is becoming distorted. Whether they eventually fall under the purview of the SEC remains to be seen.

With board access regulation, we will see campaigns for board members. We will see more shareholder education campaigns. We will see more movement by companies to communicate directly with their retail investors, but enabling access to objecting beneficial owners other than through their brokers still needs to be addressed.

Executive search firm CTPartners recently identified key changes that are likely to motivate directors to embrace the new regulatory environment, as well as emerging media. They suggested that boards should engage new technologies or risk becoming their victims. Likewise, boards are advised to take the lead on contentious issues such as compensation and board governance, or shareholders likely will. Finally, directors need to act on internal barriers to change because corporate culture can sink or save a company.[18]

We will definitely see more communication from and to boards of directors, especially about board leadership and director qualifications. These are the right conversations, but to ensure that they are going in the right direction, public relations professionals need to align and lead an integrated approach to the proxy process.

DISCUSSION QUESTIONS

1. What public relations competencies can be brought to bear to support boards' efforts to improve shareholder understanding about board composition, executive pay decisions and companies' enterprise risk management practices?
2. What are the primary objectives of a strategic governance communications program? Who are the key audiences the program is designed to reach and what are the most effective communication channels to reach them?
3. What are the obstacles to activating beneficial owners to vote in support of their company's board of directors, its business strategy for long-term sustainable growth and the compensation and benefits paid its top executives?
4. What new tools can activists and NGOs employ to advance their agendas in corporate shareholder meetings and proxy statements? How can communication teams best offset or neutralize adversarial corporate challenges?
5. Which corporate staff functions are the most essential to coordinate with public relations to articulate the company's position and activate its shareholders?
6. What is your opinion of whether the governance changes offered in this chapter are sufficient to prevent another WorldCom? What corporate communications actions could have been taken to have lessened or prevented the final outcome?
7. Should the SEC consider whether to permit or require proxy statement and voting information to be provided in interactive data format?

NOTES

1. Sir Adrian Cadbury, *Global Corporate Governance Forum* (Washington, DC: World Bank, 2000).
2. Barron's Accounting Dictionary. *Dictionary of Accounting Terms.* Copyright © 2005 by Barron's Educational Series Inc. All rights reserved.

  3. U.S. Securities and Exchange Commission; www.sec.gov (April 26, 2011).
  4. U.S. Securities and Exchange Commission; www.sec.gov (April 26, 2011).
  5. J.W. Lorsch and Elizabeth MacIver, *Pawns or Potentates: The Reality of America's Corporate Boards* (Boston, MA: Harvard Business Press, 1989).
  6. Louis Thompson, "The New Board Role in Investor Relations," *The Corporate Board* (November/December 2010).
  7. Barack Obama, "Remarks by the President at Signing of Dodd-Frank Wall Street Reform and Consumer Protection Act," The White House (2010).
  8. James Kristie, "The Evolution of Corporate Governance, Continued . . ." Directors & Boards (2006).
  9. Nestlé Chairman Peter Brabeck-Letmathe, "2011 Corporate Governance Awards," *World Finance Magazine* (2011). World News Media.
 10. Amendment of NYSE Rule 452: Elimination of Broker Discretionary Voting in Director Elections. © 2011. The Mayer Brown Practices. All rights reserved.
 11. John Weckenmann, "Dodd-Frank's Impact on IR and Beyond," IR Alert (2010). © 2010 Infocom Group. All rights reserved.
 12. 2010 Spencer Stuart Board Index. © 2011 Spencer Stuart.
 13. Paul MacAvoy and Ira M. Millstein, *The Recurrent Crisis in Corporate Governance* (New York: Palgrave MacMillan, 2003) pp. 80–81.
 14. Paul MacAvoy and Ira M. Millstein, *The Recurrent Crisis in Corporate Governance* (New York: Palgrave MacMillan, 2003) pp. 76–77.
 15. Paul MacAvoy and Ira M. Millstein, *The Recurrent Crisis in Corporate Governance* (New York: Palgrave MacMillan, 2003) p. 7.
 16. Copyright 2011 Fox News Network, L.L.C. All rights reserved.
 17. Cari Tuna, "Proxy-Voting Advocates Pool Resources on the Web," wsj.com (2009).
 18. CTPartners' Second Annual Board of Directors Human Capital Institute. TradersHuddle.com (April 26, 2011).

ADDITIONAL READING

Lorsch, J.W., and Elizabeth MacIver. 1989. *Pawns or Potentates: The Reality of America's Corporate Boards.* Boston: MA: Harvard Business Press.

MacAvoy, Paul, and Ira M. Millstein. 2003. *The Recurrent Crisis in Corporate Governance.* New York: Palgrave MacMillan.

2010 Spencer Stuart Board Index. © 2011 Spencer Stuart.

24

C H A P T E R

CAREER PATHS IN PUBLIC RELATIONS

Jean Cardwell
President
Cardwell Enterprises Inc.

Dana Rubin
Rubin Creative

Welcome to the brave new world of careers in public relations.

New dynamics and developments have demolished the last vestiges of the old order, but what will emerge as its replacement is not yet clear. Globalization, the demands of the hyperconnected world, the rise of social media, the recession and slow economic growth—all these have undermined the traditional job ladder, eroded organizational loyalties and transformed expectations for success within the industry.

Competition is tougher than ever, and the marketplace for communications professionals has become a Darwinian struggle. New skills, new specialties and new strategies are crucial both for those who are just starting out, and for those who want to give their careers a boost.

Yet before you discard the old thinking altogether, I believe some perspective is called for. Because in certain fundamental ways, the basic requirements for success in this profession have not changed. For PR practitioners, there is a set of competencies that remains the bedrock.

Make no mistake, knowledge of the current state of public relations is still essential. Mastering the latest technical skills is also crucial. But at heart, PR is about connecting people with information. Learn how to work effectively and powerfully with both and you will have a solid foundation for success, one that is as relevant today as it was a century ago, in the earliest days of public relations.

THE RISE OF MODERN PUBLIC RELATIONS

Public relations as a profession in its own right emerged in the first half of the twentieth century. Individuals such as Ivy Lee and Edward Bernays are considered the industry's founding fathers. Both men understood a basic truth about the art of influential communications—that people are open to persuasion and willing to have their opinions shaped, but they have to trust the source. They must have confidence in the information they are receiving. No one wants to be misled or manipulated.

Lee, Bernays and other pioneers of the field were masters at establishing that basis of trust and building on it. Their work was rooted in an understanding of human nature.

FROM PROPAGANDA TO PUBLIC RELATIONS

Like many PR practitioners before and after him, Ivy Lee came from the world of journalism. He began his career as a newspaper reporter in New York City, then founded a public relations firm. During World War I, he directed PR for the American Red Cross, then returned to New York. In his book *Declaration of Principles*, published in 1906, he was the first to articulate the idea that PR practitioners have a public responsibility that extends beyond their obligations to their client.

Later that same year, his ideas were put to the test when a train derailed in New Jersey, fell into a river and 53 people drowned. Lee persuaded his client, The Pennsylvania Railroad, to disclose information about the horrific accident to journalists before they could hear it elsewhere. He issued what is considered the very first press release, which was published in the *New York Times*. Lee demonstrated how to establish credibility, convey authority and take control of a story—what is known today as "getting out in front of the story." That is why many call him the founder of modern crisis communications.

Lee's principal competitor in the new public relations arena was Edward Bernays, who combined recent theories on the psychology of crowds with the insights of his uncle and teacher, Sigmund Freud.

Bernays grew up in New York City but his family roots were in Vienna, and he was keenly aware of the role propaganda and manipulation had played in European history. He famously said "If you could use propaganda for war, you could certainly use it for peace." Instead of propaganda, he called it public relations.

Like Lee, Bernays chose journalism as his first career. He was also a Broadway press agent, then worked for the Committee on Public Information, an independent agency of the U.S. government that sought to influence public opinion in favor of American involvement in World War I.

In 1919, he set up shop in New York City as a "public relations counselor" and four years later published a groundbreaking book, *Crystallizing Public Opinion*.

Both Lee and Bernays were farsighted pioneers who grasped that psychology was at the heart of the profession, and the principles they applied remain as relevant today as ever. A savvy PR practitioner understands the public mood, is adept at using words and images for persuasive ends and knows how to build effective relationships—because PR is at heart a people business.

A JOURNALIST'S SKILL SET

Following in the tradition of Lee and Bernays, the predominant feeder field for public relations for many decades was journalism. For someone with a journalist's skill set, the transition to PR could be relatively seamless. Newsmen (and the occasional newswoman) already had knowledge of current events, an understanding of social and cultural trends and strong communications skills including the ability to write quickly and tell powerful stories.

Particularly in the area of media relations, former journalists brought an advantage in that they understood what reporters were looking for. They knew instinctively what made a good story. They came to the job prepared to pitch story ideas to media outlets and get their clients mentioned in the newspapers.

In mid-twentieth century America, much of PR involved media relations, employee communications (including newsletters and other internal print vehicles) and what was then known as product publicity—in other words, generating positive public opinion about a company's product or services.

PUBLIC RELATIONS FACES NEW CHALLENGES

A watershed moment in PR came in 1965 with the publication of Ralph Nader's book, *Unsafe at Any Speed*, which argued that many American automobile makers were focusing on styling, speed and power at the expense of public safety. The first chapter focused on the Corvair—"the One-Car Accident"—manufactured by General Motors, one of America's largest and most powerful corporations.

In its wake, the deluge of media attention, lawsuits and the emergence of what became known as the consumer movement led many corporations to create consumer affairs departments, among the first specialized areas within public relations. Consumer affairs departments were staffed by professionals who could respond with speed and sensitivity to the concerns of the public and public interest groups about product viability. As before, many were former journalists or others with social awareness and strong communications skills.

As American corporations grew and consolidated, and as consumer culture expanded in the prosperous years following World War II, so did the need for effective public relations to support the corporate sector. Part of the need was for a corps of communications professions who understood "inside the Beltway" practices and thinking and could help their clients win favorable treatment from politicians in Washington, DC.

Another emerging area was public policy PR, both in the United States and abroad. Domestically, those who excelled were skilled at managing issues on Capitol Hill and improving their client or industry's image.

In subsequent years, public policy PR has grown into a powerful specialty whose practitioners play an important role influencing policy in areas such as trade, global warming, water rights and intellectual property rights. These areas could only be addressed through global coordination, so practitioners today need an international mindset and an in-depth understanding of diverse stakeholders around the world.

THE RISE OF FINANCIAL PR AND INVESTOR RELATIONS

Also in the post-war years, the rise of mergers and acquisitions activity and initial public offerings led to the emergence of financial PR as another specialized area of focus. In 1970, Gershon Kekst founded one of the most successful financial PR firms, Kekst and Company, headquartered in New York City. The firm specialized in corporate and financial communications, with a focus on external communications within the financial and business press.

Kekst and other large financial PR organizations, such as the financial division of Hill & Knowlton, served a large clientele among publicly traded companies that were required by the Securities and Exchange Commission to issue documents such as annual reports and quarterly earnings releases on a regular basis.

Investor relations, or IR, also emerged as a niche area within financial PR that focused on helping a company's securities achieve fair valuation in the public financial markets. In addition to keeping close tabs on current and upcoming issues that could influence the functioning of a publicly traded organization, IR specialists had to ensure their clients were fulfilling their fiduciary duties to their shareholders.

PR professionals seeking a career in financial PR and investor relations must have solid communications skills as well as a strong grounding in the financial and capital markets. IR as a function within a large corporation typically reports to the chief financial officer or treasurer, rather than the communications department.

In general, whenever there is volatility and upheaval in the business and finance world that leads to a diminishment of public trust, the need for public relations intensifies. This is exactly what took place after the dot-com bubble from 1995 to 2000, and again during and after the wave of accounting scandals from 2000 to 2002 involving global companies such as Enron, WorldCom and Tyco International.

Senior officers were increasingly recognizing the importance of corporate reputation to their bottom line and were dedicating more resources to PR. This trend gave rise to the specialty now known as reputation management, which emerged with the growing awareness that a company's reputation and brand are fragile assets, and that enhancing and maintaining them requires an orchestrated effort and considerable investment.

A related trend was the expanded duties of the chief marketing officer (CMO), the executive who oversees a range of sales and marketing activities. "CMOs used to stick to the pay side of things," notes David Chamberlin, a senior vice president and director of issues and reputation management in North America for MSL Group. "They never had to understand the reputation side of communications." But as reputational issues came to the forefront, that changed. CMOs began to take responsibility for areas in which marketing intersects with reputation, such as government, community and media relations.[1]

Increasingly, PR began to be seen as the guardian of public trust and a reflection of the values of a changing society. And American society was changing—dramatically.

CSR OR CORPORATE DO-GOODERS?

On June 22, 1969, the Cuyahoga River in Ohio erupted in flames. *Time* magazine put the disaster on the cover and described the Cuyahoga as one of the most polluted rivers in the United States—the river that "oozes rather than flows." It was just one of a series of environmental disasters in the late 1960s that helped spur the environmental movement.

As consumers began demanding corporate behavior and products that did not harm the environment, companies responded with a concerted effort to clean up the way they did business, and make sure the public knew about it. They wanted public relations programs that would not be defensive, and that would proactively establish a favorable public association with a company's brand.

Along with the environmental movement came the emergence of corporate community relations and volunteerism. One visionary was Walter Wriston, the CEO of Citibank, who realized that for a corporation, communities could be about something other than the bottom line. He actively promoted the notion that companies should be engaged productively with their communities, which he called *community relations*. Not surprisingly, some skeptics were quick to dismiss it as corporate "do-goodism." Nevertheless, a corps of communications professionals emerged who specialized in the growing field of community relations.

In the 1980s, this movement would evolve into *corporate social responsibility*, or CSR—a new awareness and form of corporate self-regulation that generated its own public relations speciality. A number of major PR firms established specialist CSR practice groups within their organizations.

Effective CSR programs establish a powerful link between a company and its various constituencies, so that, for example, communities become not just a corporation's labor pool but a positive asset. CSR-minded companies do not just make philanthropic donations to their communities—they partner with them to create healthy neighborhoods and a high quality of life. Their CSR activities are described in annual sustainability reports and "triple bottom line" reports—specialized PR vehicles that let the public know how they are doing and are designed to foster favorable public opinion.

GLOBALIZATION AND BRANDING

Another recent movement with a tremendous impact on the PR profession has been the rise of corporate brands for organizations, products and services. The idea of a corporate brand as a powerful marketing element is by no means a new one—just think back to 1891 when Ivory soap's first slogan—"It floats!"—was introduced. But the institutionalization of branding and the rise of specific PR branding agencies and consultancies emerged in the late 1980s and 1990s. PR practitioners in this area function as part of a comprehensive focus on strengthening and promoting a distinct corporate brand through the use of a logo, slogans, stories and other identity elements so that consumers instantly recognize the brand and feel good about it. Today the practice incorporates areas such as product design, retail design and point-of-purchase marketing. In addition to strong overall communication skills, a foundation in marketing and marketing communications is essential for those pursuing a career in this area, as well as an understanding of how communications supports advertising and marketing programs.

At the same time, as corporations have become more global and their clients have encountered reputation problems that extend across national borders, they have increasingly required PR strategies that encompass the same global breadth. Firms like Hill & Knowlton, Edelman and Burson-Marsteller have extended their range around the world and brought on board talent with the ability to be internationally competitive. This expanding global marketplace calls for a new range of skills, and candidates who can demonstrate broad internationalist thinking, cultural fluency, a cross-national mindset and language skills have a distinct competitive advantage.

Beginning in the 1970s and 1980s, the consolidation of media ownership put intense pressure on news organizations—print, television and radio—to generate higher profits. As a result, news operations across the country have been folding, consolidating and downsizing.

Fewer news outlets and a shrinking news hole have made it significantly harder for PR professionals to get their stories placed. At the same time, a flood of journalists newly out of work set their sights on transitioning into public relations. But with so many angling to get in, the competition has stiffened and the barriers to entry have risen.

MORE DIVERSITY, BUT STILL NOT ENOUGH

In the 1980s and 1990s, social barriers began rapidly breaking down in American society, and the workplace was becoming more diverse. For the first time, women, Hispanics, African Americans and representatives of other ethnic groups began entering the corporate world in significant numbers.

Diversity had long been a concern for the PR industry. Consider the role of women: historically they have had an outsized role in the public relations world, but very few were in top leadership positions. There have been very few female creative directors, even fewer managers and almost no owners of PR firms. Margery Kraus is a notable exception—in 1984 she founded APCO Worldwide, based in Washington, DC, and built a strong clientele in public affairs, communication and business consulting.

While the situation has changed over time, it is still true today that the only women-owned firms are those that the women themselves have launched—in other words, they did not rise to positions of power from within their organizations.

Why not, after all these years? Among the many reasons, surely one must be the persistent lack of an effective mentoring system for women. How can a young female communicator learn about strategic thinking and positioning unless she attaches herself to a senior professional, male or female, who is willing to guide, lead and teach? It is not as if there is a significant old girls' network, although a few organizations for women in communications do exist. Unfortunately they do not compare to their powerhouse male counterparts, which have been working at full speed for generations, grooming candidates for coveted leadership spots in the elite corridors of power.

With regard to minority groups, there has been a longstanding perception that the public relations industry has not actively promoted minorities or recruited ethnically diverse students. Although measurement is difficult, polls show that change has indeed been slow in coming. According to the 2009 PRWeek/Hill & Knowlton Diversity Survey, 42 percent of respondents believe the PR industry has become more diverse than when they entered the industry, 9 percent say it is less diverse, and 49 percent say it is about the same.[2]

In recent years, more agencies have established diversity committees and have focused not just on recruitment, but retention. Though strides have definitely been made, the PR industry still faces the challenge of recruiting and retaining a diverse workforce.

TECHNOLOGICAL UPHEAVAL

The rise of the Internet from the 1990s onward has had a profound and transformative impact on public relations. As readers and viewers turned to the Internet for news, even more media outlets lost advertising revenue and went out of business, or became Internet-only publications.

As digital media and social networking have come into ascendancy and the number of media channels has continued to multiply, companies are struggling to keep up by hiring new individuals with specialist skills to manage these channels. Many if not most companies have developed a distinctive presence on social networking sites such as Facebook and Twitter, overseen and managed by specialized public relations professionals. Those individuals who can design, write for and maintain websites are finding their skills are in demand.

According to *Advertising Age*, in the years to come there will be even more nontraditional hires within the PR industry. Probably more than any other marketing sector, PR is drawing talent from different areas into the fold, such as social media analysts and bloggers in specialized areas such as health or wellness, to direct targeted PR programs for their clients.[3]

PR firms are also helping their clients start blogs and create web-only magazines. And they are beginning to encroach on what used to be the territory of advertising by designing and orchestrating live events, telecasts and web launches.[4]

Increasingly, PR firms are being called on to gauge the impact of their efforts by using the measuring tools of the Internet such as visitor traffic or numbers of Facebook fans. This marks a big contrast to the old days, when it was much harder to measure the number of people who actually laid eyes on conventional advertising, such as a TV ad or an element of outdoor advertising such as a billboard or placards on the side of a bus.

It has now become apparent that the digital network revolution did not merely introduce technological change, but has fundamentally altered ways of doing business and created a new economic and social environment. As James Gleick writes in his 2000 book, *Faster: The Acceleration of Just About Everything*, communications have been speeded up to the point that society is now in "the epoch of the nanosecond." With corporate reputations made or destroyed in a day, or even an hour, public relations practitioners are required to work 24/7 with the speed and responsiveness of day traders.

With the flood of information has come greater demand for organizational transparency. As the tools of reputation and influence have become available to all, companies are finding they have far less control over their identities and reputations. Anyone can make an accusation online, post a bad review or complaint on a blog or shoot an unflattering video and post it to YouTube and instantly undermine decades of carefully nurtured goodwill. In a 2007 report, the Arthur W. Page Society noted that businesses, communities, nations and individuals find themselves in "an acute and high-stakes battle for their identities and global reputations."[5]

THE ROAD AHEAD

As public relations has become more fragmented and specialized, the threshold for entrants has risen. Those who are just starting out can enhance their career opportunities by combining a degree in public relations, journalism or another communications-related field with an internship or other practical work experience, whether paid or unpaid. When it comes to landing that first position, any real-world experience will be a big help.

To meet the growing demand for PR practitioners, the higher education world has exploded with new PR programs at both the undergraduate and graduate levels. Master's degree programs in public relations have become popular not just for young aspirants but also for older practitioners hoping that a graduate degree will give their careers a boost.

And with good reason. PR practitioners are expected to be both more broadly educated and have more specialized knowledge than ever before. According to the *New York Times*, "To avoid being limited to pitching stories about clients or writing the company newsletter, a public relations employee needs to understand business, finance, marketing, strategic planning and research—the language of corporate America and the company boardroom."[6]

PUBLIC RELATIONS IN THE RECESSION

The global recession that began in 2008 and ushered in the most challenging economic climate in recent memory has left its mark on the public relations industry. Like other marketing sectors, the PR industry took a beating. The million-dollar-plus retainers from global corporations that PR firms used to count on have largely disappeared, replaced by project work—assignments with definite beginnings and endings.

Many PR professionals who left large corporations or agencies in the upheaval have chosen the path of independent consultancies and specialty agencies, or mini-boutiques. Some have carved out thriving specialties in strategic communications, thought leadership communications or corporate speechwriting.

Despite the industry contraction, some analysts say the recession has actually intensified competition and increased corporate demand for PR. "We used to be the tail on the dog," says Richard Edelman, president and CEO of Edelman, the world's largest independent PR firm. "Now, public relations has become 'the organizing principle' behind many business decisions."[7]

One open question is, What will be the long-term impact of social media on the field? As Melanie Wilt of Ohio-based Wilt PR notes, now that any individual has the tools and means to become his or her own publisher and publicist, why would anyone need to hire a professional?[8] And yet for the time being, companies and organizations are continuing to hire.

Now that most any information can be accessed on the go from a smartphone or a tablet device, there is an even greater emphasis on knowing how to create pitches and campaigns that grab the attention of a wary, distracted and saturated public. E-mail inboxes, websites, blogs, forums and social media platforms are over-flowing. The new challenge for the PR practitioner is ensuring their client's story will be heard above the noise and chatter.

"We're talking more than ever, but in a totally disconnected way," notes Beth Comstock, chief marketing officer and senior VP at GE. "Never has meaningful connection been in such short supply. We use these great new tools to shout at each other. We emphasize telling over listening. We celebrate page views over human connections."[9]

And yet, it bears noting that while social media is about networking and building relationships through online platforms, the basic principles of PR remain the same: understanding client needs, communicating with authenticity and connecting with people.

Even as new technologies have exploded with sophistication and versatility, there has never been a greater need to transcend the limitations of technology. "As humans and as a planet, we have never been more connected—economically, socially, culturally, technically," says Jon Iwata, VP of marketing and communications at IBM. "But . . . We are realizing that being connected is not enough."[10]

A CRYSTAL BALL FOR THE INDUSTRY?

So what do all of these unsettling trends—demographic changes, the digital revolution, information overload and economic upheaval—mean for the aspiring and ambitious public relations professional?

It hardly requires a futurist to see that the primary challenge facing workers in this environment is the ongoing, relentless, exhilarating and yet often destabilizing process of change. In this environment, PR professionals have to be more broadly educated and yet more technically savvy, more focused and yet more flexible, more strategic in the way they shape their careers and also more open to reinvention.

At the same time, it is true that the foundations of effective public relations have not changed much since the days of Ivy Lee and Edward Bernays. As always, PR professionals still need a good grasp of current events and social trends. They need to think analytically and be able to apply lessons and strategies from one industry to another. And they need a core set of strong communication and interpersonal skills—because despite all the technological advances, public relations remains a people-to-people business.

As communications consultant Roger D'Aprix has put it, "Technology, as wondrous as it is, tends to be distancing, even alienating in those situations where we truly need human presence and reassurance."[11]

So even as you brush up your technical skills, make it your practice to carve out time away from the tools of technology. Polish up your people skills. Join a professional organization and serve on a committee. Network broadly and nourish longstanding relationships. Find a mentor. Become a mentor. Be a lifelong student of human nature.

In short, the Brave New World of career paths in public relations is one that you create for yourself. So go out there, create it, and enjoy!

A CASE STUDY: "BUCKETS OF SKILLS"

Over the course of a long career, every public relations practitioner faces many junctures when a decision must be made about the next step—which direction to follow, which area to focus on, which job to pursue. Often it is not easy to know which way to go.

John Onoda, a senior consultant at Fleishman-Hillard in San Francisco, has reached the point where he is reflecting on the crucial steps he took in a 30-year career as a PR professional.

Like many in public relations, Onoda began as a daily newspaper reporter—first in Omaha, then Houston. The work came fairly easily. He had strong writing skills, the ability to assimilate new information quickly, the discipline to meet deadlines and the willingness to be edited. But after a few years he and his wife wanted to start a family. Seeking higher earning potential, he shifted into PR.

When he became a Communications Associate at Mitchell Energy & Development, an independent oil and gas company, his salary increased by 50 percent. At first it seemed as if he was doing almost the same job as before. But he quickly found himself on the verge of being fired. "I was acting like a reporter, but it was a PR job," he recalls.

TOP 10 TIPS FOR GETTING AHEAD IN PR

1. Become a good writer. The foundation of this profession will always be persuasive and powerful prose. Develop the ability to write clearly and concisely. Your language must engage the reader and create a sense of urgency.

2. Be a member of the team. Learn to work with others, whether within your discipline or in other fields. The ability to subsume your ego to the greater cause is essential. So is the ability to adapt to various corporate styles and cultures.

3. Make a commitment to lifelong learning, whether formal or informal. Workers will always be rewarded for their specialized knowledge and skills. Make sure yours are up to date.

4. Broaden thyself. The most successful PR practitioners understand something about finance, law, operations, human resources, technology and more. The "key to the public relations kingdom," says Gary D. McCormick, chairman and CEO of the Public Relations Society of America, is the ability to "think holistically."[12]

5. Become a master storyteller. As movie executive Peter Gruber notes in *Tell to Win: Connect, Persuade, and Triumph with the Hidden Power of Story*, getting ahead means harnessing the hidden power of stories. ". . . Reams of data rarely engage people or move them to action," he says. "Stories, on the other hand, are state-of-the-heart technology— they connect us to others."[13]

6. Listen to your clients. Those who succeed in public relations have an exceptional ability to listen intuitively and understand their client's needs, whether it is within a PR agency or senior management.

7. Accept that job security is a thing of the past. The recession has forced companies to focus

In public relations jobs, the primary objective is advocacy—advancing the agenda of the organization. In the for-profit sector, where the vast majority of the jobs are, that means helping the company become more profitable. Many journalists are not comfortable or do not understand this, and cannot make the transition.

Onoda realized he needed to change his mindset. "It seemed to me that in PR, there were buckets of expertise, and that each bucket contained certain skills." He saw that the people at the top had mastered all the buckets. To advance, he adopted a strategic approach to the long-term shaping of his career that would give him the buckets and the breadth he needed to get where he wanted to go.

At Mitchell, he started out doing internal communications, including an employee newsletter, as well as media relations, a natural fit for someone straight out of journalism. He was also given a project management assignment—he served as part of a team that ran a series of conferences on sustainability. That gave him early exposure to an area later known as corporate social responsibility, which would become tremendously important in public relations.

It was a good beginning. At each of Onoda's following three career moves, compensation was not the determining factor. Nor was getting a bigger title, a fancy office or more job perks. Most important was the portfolio of new skills he would learn on the job.

From Mitchell he went to the Holiday Corporation as Director of External Communications in Memphis, Tennessee, where he learned to manage a global brand. He also picked up his first managerial assignment, which opened the door to a multitude of other opportunities down the road. At Holiday he was also exposed to financial communications, including annual reports, quarterly statements and shareholder meetings.

His next move was to the Chicago area, where he joined McDonald's as Director of Global Media Relations. For the first time, Onoda found himself dealing with brand management issues for a global consumer brand. At McDonald's, he was exposed to all the issues involved with the protection and enhancement of the brand, including crisis management.

As part of that job, he also learned to oversee a complex assortment of public relations agencies. McDonald's had a key, long-term relationship with the Golin Harris agency as well as smaller engagements with dozens of other firms around the world. "It was like being the conductor of an orchestra with different musicians that had to be coordinated," he says. Agency management became a key part of his portfolio.

His next stop was Levi Strauss & Co., in San Francisco, where Onoda became Vice President of Corporate Communications. For the first time, he was given the opportunity to head up an entire department, with responsibility for integrating various functions. That was also the first assignment in which he reported directly to the chairman and CEO. Learning to engage effectively with C-suite leaders was a key skill—actually a set of many skills—that proved to be crucial to his future advancement.

At Levi Straus, leadership was heavily emphasized. Top management was influenced by the ideas of Thomas Peters and Bob Waterman, expressed in *In Search of Excellence: Lessons from America's Best-Run Companies*. The company held regular conferences where management received "360 degree feedback." Onoda recalls it as a tough learning process. "Sometimes you felt like you'd been kicked in the teeth," he says. "You might think you're doing great, but there are always some people who think otherwise. You have to be vulnerable so you can learn."

Perhaps the most important skill he learned at Levi Strauss was the difference between leadership and management. Management is the ability to steer projects forward, oversee effective processes and manage budgets. Leadership is about having a vision of where the organization should go.

In some respects, Onoda sees his job at Levi Strauss as a transition to a new phase of his career. Until then, he had been tapping into new buckets, picking up skills as he went along. But after Levi Strauss, he was not seeking buckets anymore. He was looking for opportunities to grow as a leader.

Onoda's next move was to General Motors, in Detroit. His decision to take the position as Vice President of Corporate Communications was driven by the desire to operate on a larger scale—he went from a $7 billion company to a $178 billion company. But he found himself struggling to adapt to the GM corporate environment.

relentlessly on costs, and job cuts will continue. As former Labor Secretary Robert Reich put it: "People are going to have to get used to the idea of involuntary separations—sometimes four, five or six times during a career."[14]

8. Be responsible for your own career. Think of yourself as a business. Invest in your own growth and development, just like a company invests in R&D. Make sure your resume works as a marketing piece that promotes you and your accomplishments.

9. Build relationships. Develop your networking skills, and build career-long relationships. Look for a mentor, and be one in return. As Rosanna Fiske put it: "People build relationships with other people; people make decisions on brands based on other people; people purchase products from people."[15]

10. Know your profession. Do you know what is going on across the PR world? What are the latest trends? What is considered "best of breed?" Could you just possibly be becoming obsolete? If you see the warning signs, it is time to upgrade your skills.

He took over a function that had been using communications primarily to inform and educate customers about vehicles and cars. His intention was to shift resources to strengthen the company's corporate reputation and improve relations with employees, especially unionized workers. It was not an easy process. "I was a fish out of water," he says. He had a great boss, but when that boss fell ill and left the company, Onoda decided to move on.

As Executive Vice President at Visa USA in San Francisco, Onoda continued to strengthen his managerial and leadership skills: his business acumen, his judgment and his effectiveness as a counselor to top management. In that capacity, he was called to advise on urgent PR challenges. "Very often in those types of situations there's no road map or clear precedent," Onoda says. "There's no right or wrong, and your recommendations might be opposed by one or more departments. You have to make a judgment call and be persuasive."

In his next position, as Chief Communications Officer at Charles Schwab & Co., in San Francisco, Onoda's career was up-ended by events beyond of his control. The attack on 9/11 occurred not long into his tenure there and changed everything. Suddenly people stopped trading. Instead of helping to strengthen a world-class brand, as he had hoped, Onoda had to downsize. He ended up leaving.

Now he was ready for a different kind of career move. He had been working nonstop for 20 years, he says, and "it seemed like a good time to take a break." Onoda joined Fleishman-Hillard as a part-time, in-house consultant.

Onoda finds his depth of experience in different sectors and at different organizational levels is valued at the global PR firm. So is his client-side perspective. "Agency people see things very differently from the way their clients do," he says. He finds his views are particularly helpful when the agency is trying to win new business and a team is preparing for a major pitch.

Onoda advises aspiring PR practitioners—as well as those who are mid-career but reconsidering their future—to take a strategic approach to achieving their long-term goals. The majority of PR professionals focus on their job and not on their career. "When you're changing jobs, what primarily should be driving you is the ability to accumulate skills that will carry you forward," he says. PR professionals should continuously update their product, which is themselves. They should invest in themselves—their skills, their image, their brand.

"I never wanted to be seen as a car guy or a jeans guy, an internal or an external communications guy," Onoda says. While it may not matter at the start of a career, having a broad portfolio pays off down the road, where there are fewer jobs at the top and fewer opportunities to get ahead.

As you move up, relationships are also crucial. "It's important to learn to network beyond your job—outside your industry, outside your geographic area, even outside your profession," Onoda says. Having a strong network becomes key to advancement when you are higher up the ladder.

Although he never actually lived and worked in a different country (he did a great deal of international business travel), Onoda advises those who are starting their careers today to get foreign experience, and do it in their early years before it becomes difficult to move your family. An international perspective is crucial to success in this age of global communications and PR.

The best counsel Onoda offers to those starting out is to do an honest self-assessment and consider what buckets of skills they need in order to get where they want to go—and then go get them.

Also critically important: understanding the mega-trends that are reshaping our society and the business world, such as globalization, demographic changes, the rise of social media, the growing importance of Asia—and in particular China. "All these will have a major impact on business," Onoda says, "and ultimately the course of your career."

DISCUSSION QUESTIONS

1. Write your own 5 year career plan citing suggestions from the chapter for support.
2. List the 10 ways to "get ahead" in PR. Be prepared to discuss them in a group of professionals or students.
3. Why is journalism still an integral part of the career path in PR? Do you think it will continue?
4. What makes PR a profession?

NOTES

1. David Chamberlin. Personal interview. March 23, 2011.
2. Kimberly Maul. "Diversity Survey 2009: Progress at Work." prweekus.com. *PRWeek*, December 1, 2009. Web. February 23, 2011.
3. Rosanna Fiske. "The Year Ahead: 2011 Predictions for Agencies." PRSA.org. PRSA, January 17, 2011. Web. February 22, 2011.
4. "Good News: Other Firms' Suffering Has Bolstered the Public-Relations Business." *The Economist*, January 14, 2010. Web. March 10, 2011.
5. "The Authentic Enterprise: An Arthur W. Page Society Report." awpagesociety.com. Arthur W. Page Society, 2007. Web. February 22, 2011.
6. Cecilia Capuzzi Simon. "A Career Detour." *The New York Times*, January 7, 2011. Web. February 22, 2011.
7. *The Economist*, op. cit.
8. Melanie Wilt. "PR Here to Stay in 2011." WiltPR.com. Wilt PR, December 23, 2010. Web. March 1, 2011.

9. Beth Comstock. "2010 Hall of Fame Acceptance Speech." awpagesociety.com. Arthur W. Page Society, September 26, 2010. Web. March 1, 2011.

10. Jon Iwata. "2009 Hall of Fame Acceptance Speech." awpagesociety.com. Arthur Page Society, September 14, 2009. Web. March 1, 2011.

11. Roger D'Aprix, press release. "Despite Social Media Tools, Face-to-Face Interaction in Organizations Has Remained the Same: IABC Survey." iabc.com. IABC, August 3, 2009. Web. February 22, 2011.

12. Simon, Cecilia Capuzzi. "A Career Detour." *The New York Times*, 7 Jan. 2011. Web. 22 Feb. 2011.

13. Gruber, Peter. *Tell To Win: Connect, Persuade and Triumph with the Hidden Power of Story*. New York: Crown Business, 2011. Print.

14. Reich-Topolnickui, Denise. "Down and Out?" *Chicago Tribune*. May 1994: pp. 1ff.

15. Fiske, Rosanna. "Memo to Corporate America: Five Questions Every CEO Must Ask About PR in the WikiLeaks Era." *www.commpro.biz/blog*. Commpro.biz, 1 Apr. 2011. Web. 11 Apr. 2011.

ADDITIONAL READING

Beinhart, Larry. 1993. *American Hero*. Pantheon, New York City.

Bernays, Edward. 1928. *Propaganda*. Liveright, New York City.

Buckley, Christopher. 1994. *Thank You for Smoking*. Random House, New York City.

Burson, Harold. 2004. *E Pluribus Unum: The Making of Burson-Marsteller*. New York: Burson-Marsteller, New York City.

Edelman, Richard. 2011. Convocation Speech at S.I. Newhouse School of Public Communications, Syracuse University. May 14, 2011.

Gruber, Peter. 2011. *Tell to Win: Connect, Persuade and Triumph with the Hidden Power of Story*. Crown Business, New York City.

Lawrence, Mary Wells. 2003. *A Big Life in Advertising*. Simon & Schuster, New York City.

Maister, David H., Charles H. Green, and Robert M. Galford. 2000. *The Trusted Advisor*. Free Press, New York City.

Matalin, Mary, and James Carville. 1991. *All's Fair*. Random House, New York City.

Ogilvy, David, and Sir Alan Parker. 2004. *Confessions of an Advertising Man*. Southbank Publishing, London, UK.

Sandberg, Sheryl. 2011. "The Women of My Generation Blew It, So Equality Is Up to You, Graduates." Commencement address, Barnard College, May 17, 2011.

Tye, Larry. 2002. *The Father of Spin: Edward Bernays and the Birth of Public Relations*. Picador, New York City.

White, Ronald C., Jr. 2005. *The Eloquent President*. Random House, New York City.

25

CHAPTER

THE CHIEF EXECUTIVE OFFICER
The Key Spokesperson

John D. Graham
Chairman
Fleishman-Hillard International Communications

Public relations has reached a significant turning point in its evolution as a profession. In today's highly competitive, global business environment, with more public attention focused on business actions and their consequences, public relations has the opportunity to become one of the key management disciplines of the future. But our success in meeting this challenge will depend heavily on how well we, as communications counselors, can perform one crucial function. I am talking about our ability to advise the senior executive team on how best to protect, manage and market an organization's single most important asset—its reputation.

Data shows that business leaders are increasingly focused on corporate reputation. A 2009 Conference Board survey found that 81 percent of executives polled said they had increased their attention to reputation risk in the last three years, and 63 percent believed that reputation risk spending would increase over the next three.[1] The importance placed on corporate reputation echoes an earlier Opinion Research Corporation survey, which showed that 90 percent of the business executives polled (two-fifths of whom were senior executives) agreed strongly that a company's reputation is a vital corporate asset that must be maintained as carefully as any other asset.[2]

As more and more corporations around the world rely on public relations professionals to guide them through the complex communications issues they face in an increasingly global marketplace, those professionals must have expertise in strategic and analytical skills as well as tactical tools.

For example, they must be "futurists" in their thinking—able to anticipate with reasonable accuracy the potential impact of trends and issues on corporate growth and profitability. They must also have a broad perspective on their entire industry (and related industries), rather than a narrow focus on a few companies. They must be mindful of the consumer's growing influence over corporate behavior—an influence greatly strengthened by the use of social media—and be able to interpret how that influence will affect specific products and services. They must know how to fully align communications plans with the organization's current and future business objectives, and be willing and able to change accordingly. At the same time, public relations executives must have the ability to respond rapidly in handling an unforeseen crisis or in supporting a new marketing effort.

These are all skills that the communications executive must have to provide the level of strategic counsel that senior management requires. And, to my mind, there are three other attributes that complete the package—good judgment, unflinching integrity and the courage to "speak truth to power" when there are tough issues to be dealt with.

Key Issues Affecting Public Relations

- Global competition
- Rapidly evolving media environment
- Revolution in digital technology
- Corporate governance, composition of corporate boards, shareholder activism
- Sustainability/corporate social responsibility issues
- Business ethics
- Product liability
- Workforce education and training, professional development
- Workforce satisfaction
- Labor-management relations
- Management team diversity
- Hiring and promotion, equal opportunity, managing diversity
- Mergers and acquisitions
- CEO compensation
- Regulatory issues
- Healthcare management and costs
- Retirement benefit costs

F I G U R E   25.1

Key Issues Affecting Public Relations

Communications executives who confidently and persuasively bring these qualities to the table are creating the conditions for their own success, empowering themselves to do the following:

- Have access to the highest levels of management, thus enhancing their effectiveness in managing the organization's reputation

- Persuade senior management that strategic communications is a key management discipline—one that cuts across all management functions to address a wide range of issues that bear on reputation

- Help the PR function earn and keep the respect and credibility of the other management functions within the corporation

Increasingly, public relations will be called on to interpret external developments and formulate plans to address a broad range of issues. As a result, public relations executives must understand the major issues and trends confronting business and society, and be able to effectively communicate their long-term implications to management.

Key issues of concern today include such things as global competition, the ongoing revolution in digital technology, privacy, security (both in the personal and the geopolitical sense), health care, sustainability and a range of regulatory developments at the local, national and international levels. These issues and others (Figure 25.1) will persist and will continue to command high visibility in communications plans.

A STRATEGIC APPROACH TO COUNSELING SENIOR MANAGEMENT

The challenge confronting the public relations profession is partly a function of technology and rapidly changing times. Media coverage of business has increased exponentially, putting companies under a level of scrutiny that would have been unthinkable two decades ago. There was a time when business news primarily focused on relatively routine areas such as the rise and fall of stock prices, new products and services, largely uneventful stockholder meetings and the occasional labor dispute. Today, the situation is far different. Comprehensive business news is available online around the clock from a mind-boggling range of media outlets around the planet. Not only is electronic coverage of business news more extensive and wide-ranging than ever before, people increasingly have access to that news wherever they are on a growing array of devices—from laptops to mobile phones to tablet computers.

The attention focused on today's business enterprises obviously can have profound effects on a company's reputation. Some chief executive officers (CEOs)—for example, Bill Gates of Microsoft, Mark Zuckerberg of Facebook, Steve Jobs of Apple and Richard Branson of Virgin Group—have attained a degree of celebrity status rivaling that of movie stars or professional athletes. Other business figures, such as Bernard Madoff, Kenneth Lay and Jeffrey Skilling have achieved notoriety in the much more literal sense.

At the same time, consumer activist movements have continued to successfully bring pressure to bear on a wide variety of companies and industries in areas such as product liability, social responsibility, corporate governance, labor relations, nutrition and health. Whatever the specific issue, activist pressures have afforded public relations professionals an uncommon opportunity to develop ways to more closely and responsibly align the goals of the businesses they represent with the goals of society.

But it is also important to note that the concerns of activists have a way of going mainstream over time. One area where we have seen that happen over the past decade or so is in the area of sustainability. And I am using the word here both in its connotation of environmental responsibility and stewardship, as well as in the broader sense of a company's focus on social, economic and environmental concerns—commonly referred to as the "triple bottom line."

Consider a few statistics:

- In 2010, 75 percent of consumers wanted to buy products from socially responsible companies—that is up from 45 percent the year before.[3]

- Socially responsible investors, who factor corporate responsibility and societal concerns into their investment, are no longer on the fringes. In fact, socially responsible investment (SRI) encompasses more than $3 trillion—representing a little over 12 percent in the U.S. investment marketplace today. Nearly 1 out of every 8 dollars under professional management in the United States today is considered an SRI—and that is growing at a rate of more than 13 percent.[4]

- The investment community is not alone in wanting to understand more about companies' commitments to environmental sustainability. Customers, employees, governments, nongovernmental organizations and the media all want more information. They want data. They want compelling stories. They want transparency and disclosure. As stakeholder groups demand this information, companies are increasingly providing it. Eighty percent of the top 250 Global Fortune 500 companies issued CSR reports in 2010—a 700 percent increase from 2009 to 2010.[5]

- Even if companies don't willingly and proactively report this information, there are organizations that compile it and will share it, with or without a company's knowledge or permission. For example, the UK-based Carbon Disclosure Project (CDP) takes material sustainability information, such as a company's greenhouse gas emissions or water use, and makes it available to investors. In 2010, 150 percent more institutional investors used CDP data to evaluate companies' water management practices than in 2009.[6] And the availability of CDP data on 350,000 Bloomberg terminals worldwide is pushing sustainability reporting from transparency to accountability.

This expanding interest on the part of a range of stakeholders has fed, and been fed by, a corresponding growth of media interest in sustainability issues. As just one indicator, in 2010 the *New York Times* published 196 articles on the topic of "sustainable business." In 2005, the *Times* published only 63 articles—an increase of more than 300 percent over five years.[7]

I expect this trend to continue, and I believe that we will see in the future that a company's record for sustainability will be taken more and more as an indicator that it is a well-managed company, period. Going forward, I think helping communicate a strong sustainability story that is fully aligned with business strategy and objectives is one of the greatest opportunities the PR executive has to build a company's reputation.

Of course, effectively communicating a company's sustainability efforts—or its successes and accomplishments in any arena—means tackling a much more pervasive trend. And that's the emergence of social media.

There is no doubt that this is one of the greatest challenges that communicators have faced in recent memory. Even the Internet itself wasn't as disruptive for marketers as the open, connected, consumer-controlled conversations of the social web. It's a challenge that most companies will consider and reconsider for the fore-seeable future.

Unlike traditional channels, these channels are designed for two-way, interactive communication. Unlike a press release or TV or print ad, the content in these channels is intended to be consumed, shared, taken apart, put back together and offered back up for a response from any and all comers.

Going forward, communicators who want to add maximum value to their companies' reputations need to have more than just a working knowledge of these channels. They need to go on from there—integrating fully with the marketing and internal communications functions—to put the resources in place to cultivate and manage these one-to-one, two-way conversations that, for all intents and purposes, play out in full view of everyone.

So, the people who just saw an ad from your company's new print campaign are now telling you what they think on the spot, not through the billboard, but through social media. You've missed an opportunity if you're not able to respond. Or a customer who just spent two hours on the phone with your company's call center, but still can't resolve her problem, is Tweeting at you—and your company's lack of a response is apparent to all of the others who are watching the discussion play out. Or, your company has run afoul of an activist group that is inspiring throngs of people, including many of your customers, to line up on Facebook to express their indignation.

These are all real issues. And each of them requires coordination across different parts of the business. This presents one more major opportunity for the communications executive and his or her team to make a major contribution to protecting the company's reputation. It's the opportunity to help all their colleagues across the organization understand the uncontrolled, real-time nature of social media, as well as to understand the roles that they play in helping the company address and meet the expectations of a connected world with all its connected members and connected issues.

Within that world lives a general public that is better informed than ever about business organizations, business issues and how corporations are managed. And surveys of public opinion lend credence to the fact that public approval increasingly is necessary if sales are to be maintained, if plants are to be sited for construction or relocated, if crucial legislation is to be passed or defeated or if people feel comfortable holding a company's stock or choosing its products.

AN ORGANIZATIONAL STRUCTURE FOR REPUTATION MANAGEMENT

In that environment, executives have become increasingly aware of the importance of corporate reputation as a bottom-line asset—an asset that must be managed carefully and given as much professional attention as other corporate assets. And corporations that acknowledge this fact must be willing to let their organizational structures evolve in ways that may depart from traditional models, in order to more effectively manage their reputations.

The most useful organizational model suggests a CEO at the top of the organization, and an office of the chief executive consisting of several individuals who work collaboratively with the CEO. These executives should include the chief financial officer, the chief legal officer, the chief operations officer and the chief communications officer (CCO). The first three individuals are, for the most part, already in today's corporate boardrooms helping make decisions. But in too many cases, that fourth player is not. That's a situation that needs to change if a company is serious about the importance of its reputation.

Every time a significant corporate decision must be made, these four people should sit down with the CEO and review its ramifications. And I'm talking about decisions that address more than just marketing issues or obvious external forces. I mean decisions about such actions as changing a company's capital structure, opening or closing a plant, laying off employees, choosing new outside directors, introducing new products or changing a major supplier. The legal officer discusses the legal implications of the action, the operations officer details the operational implications, the financial officer deals with the financial implications and the CCO discusses the implications for the company's reputation among a wide range of audiences. This suggests a primary responsibility to *protect* the company's reputation. More important, the CCO has the unique ability to serve as a catalyst for positive change as a result of the additional responsibility to *enhance* a company's reputation among a wide range of audiences.

Now, clearly, the purpose of this structure is not merely to confer status on the position of the CCO. On the contrary, this approach is all about ensuring that major corporate actions, including, when the need arises, crisis management, are communicated properly. Unless management gives corporate reputation the sort of consideration it gives to many other issues of equal importance, the potential for reputational damage is greater than it has ever been in today's media environment. Moreover, unless companies recognize the value of the corporate communications function, consumers and the general public will become increasingly skeptical of business and its ability to act responsibly.

This structure is only one organizational possibility. Many companies continue to debate who should fill the role of the CCO. Some believe that the CEO should fill that role. This is a difficult task, however, given all the other responsibilities that compete for his or her attention.

In a general sense, however, the CEO must be considered the de facto CCO of a corporation. The CEO is viewed not only as the individual who makes the final decisions regarding a company's operations—everything from what and where it manufactures, to the services it provides, to marketing, advertising, acquisitions, divestitures and so forth—but also as the individual who sets the tone for the corporation. A CEO cannot avoid this role. As a result, the job of a public relations executive is influenced by at least two factors: (1) the unique communications needs of the individual organization and (2) the degree to which a CEO wishes to emphasize his or her role as the CCO.

THE ROLE OF THE CCO

Given the inherent importance of the CEO as the chief communicator of a corporation, the appropriate role for the CCO is twofold. First, he or she is the person who brings news to top management or to the boardroom of what interested third parties are saying about the company. In this sense, the CCO provides intelligence and counseling based on the perceptions of others that will help the CEO make the right decisions. Second, the CCO's role is to communicate to internal audiences a central message: that everyone in the organization—from the top down, throughout the company—shares responsibility for protecting and enhancing the company's reputation, just as they have a responsibility for helping the company meet its operational and financial goals. This is the direction in which public relations is headed and must continue to move.

In this regard, it is useful to contrast the public relations function with the marketing function. Clearly, marketing is much different in scope than public relations, except when it is in the form of an integrated marketing communications program designed to reach multifaceted, multitiered audiences. Marketing typically focuses on one audience, the B2C or B2B customer, and on only one transaction or a single stage of the commercial process in which goods change hands from the company to the customer. Public relations, however, involves a diverse range of audiences: employees, stockholders, local communities, governments, consumers and the general public (whether or not they buy the company's products or services). Public relations has the flexibility to focus on those audiences that are appropriate to a company's priorities and objectives.

Marketing professionals often argue that the customer must always be the most important audience because if customers do not buy the company's products or services, then the company will cease to exist. This is a superficially attractive argument, but it focuses on only one corner of the picture. For example, if employees are on strike, then the company's ability to serve customers will be at risk. If your products are being boycotted, then the existence of your company is in jeopardy. If shareholders and lenders lose confidence in the company, its ability to raise debt and equity may be significantly impaired. If federal, state or local governments restrain you from operating a plant or selling your products or services, then you may not have a company for long.

Businesses must transcend the exclusively customer-oriented focus of marketing. The marketing perspective is too narrow to serve the scope of the company's key interests. Corporations must realize that the job of reputation management involves a wide range of significant perspectives, and the concerns of marketing are only one slice, though an important slice, of the issues public relations professionals must deal with.

This viewpoint is supported by the 2009 Conference Board survey I noted above. It found that two-thirds of the executives polled believe that reputation risk management is the responsibility of multiple departments. These include communications (74 percent), enterprise risk management (42 percent), legal (38 percent), marketing (31 percent), finance (27 percent), business unit management (23 percent), human resources (18 percent), COO function (10 percent) and reputation management group (8 percent).[8]

TACTICAL MODELS OF REPUTATION MANAGEMENT

So, we have just discussed the importance of the CEO as the chief communicator of a corporation. That model structure is described in Figure 25.2.

In this prototype, the communications strategy of a company involves spotlighting the CEO as the visionary leader who embodies the direction and culture of the organization.

This approach has several clear advantages, not the least of which is simplicity: it involves a single individual and one straightforward approach. It also appeals to the media's tendency to focus on personalities, as well as the general preference of investor audiences to see and hear from a company's CEO. An additional strength of this approach is the fact that a strong individual personality helps create a distinctive personality for the entire organization, with the further benefit that employees will react strongly and positively to a charismatic leader whom they want to follow. This personality can serve as a further point of differentiation from competitors.

Disadvantages of this model are its frequent use as a strategy when little else sets the company apart, and when a company's products are fundamentally not unique. Moreover, if anything happens to the CEO, it is difficult to provide a transition for internal or external audiences.

The CEO as a Visible Symbol

Strategy: Spotlight the CEO as an exemplar, leader, visionary and embodiment of the organization.

Tactics: Focus the majority of communications to all audiences on the CEO as the spokesperson and/or symbol for the organization.

Advantages:

- The CEO provides ease of control in communications.
- The media gravitate toward personalities.
- Investor audiences like to see and get a personal sense of the CEO.
- A strong individual personality can create a strong personality for the organization.
- Employee audiences react positively to an individual they want to follow.
- A distinctive personality can be an inherent differentiator from other organizations.

Disadvantages:

- This structure most often used as a strategy when little else is possible and/or when a commodity product or institution is involved; the structure itself may convey an impression.
- Media can turn on a person quickly and, by extension, on the organization.
- Investor audiences want a sense of depth beyond the individual at the top.
- If anything happens to the CEO, transitions are difficult—internally and externally.

F I G U R E   25.2

The CEO as a Visible Symbol

The Executive Team Model

Strategy: Spotlight the senior executive team for its unified vision and its depth and breadth of expertise and experience.

Tactics: For major media and internal audiences, focus on the whole team; use individual members to deal with appropriate individual audiences (the CFO with the financial community, the chief scientific officer with technical audiences, etc.).

Advantages:
o   Time and energy commitment are spread over a group of people.
o   The team approach makes use of both individual and collective strengths.
o   The team still involves the CEO as a leader and visionary.
o   The team provides an external image of institutionalized excellence.

Disadvantages:
o   A team can be faceless at a time when a human face is what's needed most.
o   Getting time and energy commitment from a group of people can be difficult.
o   Team-developed strategy can be conducive to counter-productive internal political jockeying.
o   The company may be difficult to differentiate from other organizations if its industry includes similar organizations with similar management teams.
o   A team approach requires open discussion of business strategy (which may not be welcomed) and proof of problem-solving successes (which may not be available).
o   The team model works best when the financial community provides external endorsement of management's capabilities.

FIGURE 25.3

The Executive Team Model

A number of other models are worth examining for their differing methods of positioning a company's top management and promoting corporate reputation. These approaches may not necessarily be employed in a pure form, but may be mixed and blended to one extent or another.

The Executive Team model (Figure 25.3) spotlights the executive team as a whole, both for its unified vision for a company and for its depth and breadth of experience and management expertise. Tactically, this approach focuses on all top executives as a team, and uses individual members to deal with appropriate individual audiences. This model not only offers built-in efficiency—spreading commitments over a number of people—but it also makes use of individual and collective strengths, provides an external image of institutionalized excellence and still involves the CEO as a leader and visionary.

The Products and Services Model

Strategy: Emphasize *what* the organization is doing, rather than *who* does it.

Tactics: Focus on customer successes with existing products and services and on new products and services.

Advantages:
o   Products and services are tangible and, potentially, tell a compelling story.
o   Focus on products and services provides a clear sense of the present and an expectation of the future.
o   The model allows for third-party verification of credibility through case studies and endorsements.

Disadvantages:
o   Investor audiences need individuals as well as products and accomplishments.
o   The media are attracted to real people who can embody a company's accomplishments.
o   R&D people are not always the most effective spokespeople.
o   Heavy reliance on customers for credibility can be risky and is often cumbersome.
o   A product emphasis requires publicizing innovations at the time of a patent filing or at commercialization, which can limit news value.

FIGURE 25.4

The Products and Services Model

The History as a Guide to the Future Model
Strategy: Use the (successful) history of an organization as an implicit predictor of its future.
Tactics: Focus on past successes and on the responsible individuals who are still with the organization and who are creating the success of the future.
Advantages:
o   Past successes provide third-party credibility.
o   Success sustains, or builds, a strong internal sense of self.
o   History can be orchestrated to indicate future directions, implicitly or explicitly.

Disadvantages:
o   Heavy reliance on "Trust us, we've done it before" is risky in anything but the short term.
o   Essentially a backward-looking strategy.
o   The company needs an established, celebrated past with few, if any, difficulties.
o   The approach requires that an organization have a view of the future that it wants to talk about, in order to provide context for expectations of future achievements.
o   The model may not allow adequate differentiation from other successful organizations in an industry characterized by a rapid pace of innovation.

FIGURE 25.5

The History as a Guide to the Future Model

Disadvantages of the Executive Team model are that it is faceless (especially at those times when a familiar, human face is what is needed most), it can prove difficult in getting time and energy commitments from a group of people, it can be conducive to internal political jockeying, and it may not be sufficiently differentiated from other companies with similar management teams. Perhaps more important, the approach can involve discussion of business strategy that some companies may not want to engage in, and proof of problem-solving successes that may or may not be available. The Executive Team model generally works best when management's capabilities enjoy the strong external endorsement of the financial community.

An approach that avoids the issues of personality altogether is the Products and Services model (Figure 25.4), which emphasizes *what* a company does rather than *who* does it. The approach focuses on customer successes with existing products and services, as well as on new products and services.

The positive aspects of this model are that products and services are tangible in the sense that they are used by or affect customers, and those products and services potentially can be used to tell compelling stories. It also provides a clear sense of the present and future via the company's goods and services, and allows for third-party credibility through case studies, endorsements and similar testimonials. The drawbacks include the fact that this approach could become faceless among general or investor audiences, that research and development people who may be called on to discuss products often are not good at PR and that a heavy reliance on customers for credibility can be risky and cumbersome. The approach can also be time sensitive since it may require publicizing innovations at the time of patent filing or commercialization, when they may yield less news value than they might at other times.

The History as a Guide to the Future model (Figure 25.5) makes use of the successful history of a company as an implicit predictor of future performance. The approach focuses on past successes and the individuals still with the corporation who are creating future successes. Past successes tend to provide a sense of third-party credibility, and help sustain a strong internal sense of self for the organization. Among its other advantages, the approach also can be orchestrated to at least imply the company's future direction. On the other hand, heavy reliance on this historical approach is risky in anything but the short term, since trust based on past performance has inherent limits. It is also a strategy that essentially looks backward and requires an established, celebrated past with few, if any, difficulties. At least implicitly, this model also requires that an organization have a view of the future that it wants to talk about, so as to provide a context for expectations of future achievements. It also may not afford a company adequate differentiation from successful peer companies, especially in industries characterized by a rapid pace of innovation.

The Financial Performance Model
Strategy: Concentrate on financial performance of the organization and of its financial supporters.
Tactics: Include financial messages in all communications, even those which are not obviously about financial performance matters.
Advantages:
o   Investor audiences may say they prefer this approach.
o   Unlike other approaches, this one is essentially quantitative.
o   External validation and positive comparisons with peer organizations are easier than with qualitative approaches.
Disadvantages:
o   The company must have smooth, predictable financial trend lines, or retribution will be swift.
o   This is a more quantitative variant of the History as a Guide model.
o   This approach does not work as an internal communications device, and can be counterproductive.
o   It ignores a basic fact. Financial performance is not what a company does, it's a *result* of what it does.

F I G U R E   25.6

The Financial Performance Model

Another approach that avoids any focus on personalities and individuals is the Financial Performance model (Figure 25.6), which includes financial messages in all communications, even those that are not obviously about financial performance issues. This method, essentially a quantitative variant of the History as a Guide model, is best suited to organizations that must concentrate on investor audiences, who are likely to prefer this approach. It is worth noting that external validation and positive comparisons with peer companies are easier to obtain with this approach than with more qualitative approaches. However, a drawback is that a company must have smooth, predictable financial trend lines to make this approach successful, or retribution by critics will be swift. This method also has little attraction as an internal communications device, and can, in fact, be

The Defining/Redefining an Industry Model
Strategy: Spotlight the business strategy and vision of the organization as a proxy for the industry as a whole.
Tactics: Focus on the larger environmental context for strategic decisions; offer predictions for future directions of aspects of the business.
Advantages:
o   The approach conveys vision and leadership.
o   Media like to look ahead and project future trends.
o   There's safety in the fact that predictions can be wrong, as long as they're thoughtfully communicated.
o   It allows a company to speak beyond itself, which is especially useful when news is neutral or bad.
o   It give employees a sense of pride in being part of a company that sets the pace for an entire industry category.
o   It gives employees a sense of pride in being part of a company that sets the pace for an entire industry category.
Disadvantages:
o   The method needs legitimate content to work.
o   It requires confidence in the strategy and a vision of the future.
o   It requires underpinnings of actual company business success to be credible.
o   The effect can be shortlived, and can make a company an easy target in an environment of continuous change (e.g., "So what will they do for an encore?").

F I G U R E   25.7

The Defining/Redefining an Industry Model

counterproductive among employees. Moreover, it may not focus enough on what a company does—a questionable approach, given the fact that financial performance is essentially a result of what the company does and how it is managed.

A final method takes a broad, panoramic approach to managing a company's reputation by spotlighting the business strategy and vision of the company as a proxy for the industry as a whole. The Defining/Redefining an Industry model (Figure 25.7) focuses on the larger environmental context for strategic decisions, and operates within it to offer predictions for future directions of aspects of the business. The approach has the advantage of conveying vision and leadership and appeals to the media's interest in looking ahead and making projections about the future. This method also allows a company to speak beyond itself—a useful device when news is either neutral or bad—and gives employees a sense of pride in being part of a company that sets the pace for an entire industry.

Cautions involved in this approach include the fact that to be credible, it requires the right combination of legitimate content, complete confidence in the company's strategy and vision and a strong underpinning of actual business success. It also can be relatively shortlived in its effectiveness, since a company that sets itself up as a proxy for an industry can be an easy target for criticism in an environment of continuous change or negative results.

In the real world, any company consciously—or, more often, unconsciously—uses a mix of strategies to communicate about itself, with one model being dominant and another, or others, being subordinate themes.

For many companies, the most effective strategy would seem to be a slight modification of the Defining/Redefining an Industry model. It allows—actually, demands—the use of the whole executive team, with the CEO as an important voice and the key player. However, it also allows each member of that team to be visible for his or her important audiences. In addition, this approach allows each individual to stress what is important in his or her own area—financial performance, new research breakthroughs, new customer products and services and so forth.

What must be made clear in this approach, particularly internally, is that the group is, in fact, a team, not a huddle of people jockeying for power. Another implicit factor is the role of the CEO as team captain, team manager and overall strategic visionary. The key to making this modified approach work is the corporate communications function. With the concurrence and active support of the CEO, corporate communications collects information internally about the content and substance of the company's story, and collects information externally about how to make that story most compelling across the range of audiences the company wants to reach. Then, the corporate communications function determines (or, at least, strongly recommends) who should take which opportunity to convey the company's story. It is the only way to avoid a confusing jumble of voices and messages.

MINI-CASE: ENTERPRISE HOLDINGS

With annual revenues of $14.1 billion and more than 68,000 employees, Enterprise Holdings is the largest car rental company in the world measured by revenue, employees and fleet. In 2007, the Taylor family—which owns Enterprise Rent-A-Car—purchased National Car Rental and Alamo Rent-A-Car. Overnight, what was already the world's largest vehicle fleet surpassed 1 million cars. And the company hit that milestone at a time when Corporate America's record for environmental responsibility and sustainability was coming under increasingly close scrutiny.

The situation presented Enterprise with a choice: it could prepare to defend itself against criticism from NGOs, government agencies and others over the environmental impact of its fleet. Or, it could take the initiative on environmental sustainability issues as one more way to strengthen the company's industry leadership and expand on its tradition of sustainable management.

Chairman and CEO Andrew C. Taylor quietly took stock of the situation and clearly saw the opportunity within the challenge. Under his guidance, Enterprise Holdings chose leadership, and went on to build the industry's most comprehensive environmental sustainability platform. The underlying principle that drove the effort was not presuming to save the world, but responsibly addressing the parts of the world the company touches with its business. Taylor also recognized Enterprise's opportunity to play a constructive role as a catalyst—bringing together the public, private and nonprofit sectors to address issues of common concern.

This catalyst role was certainly front and center when the company launched its 50 Million Tree Pledge—a private/public/nonprofit partnership with the Arbor Day Foundation and the U.S. Forest Service. This is a commitment to plant 50 million trees over 50 years in national forests in countries where Enterprise operates—funded by a $50 million gift from the company's charitable foundation.

The other major planks in Enterprise Holdings' environmental platform include the following:

- Offering consumers the world's largest fleet of fuel-efficient vehicles

- Embracing new, clean fuels and engine technologies, such as electric vehicles and hybrids, and working with the manufacturers to help build consumer acceptance of these technologies

- Offering customers the opportunity to offset the emissions associated with the average vehicle rental—with a dollar-for-dollar match of up to $1 million to fund additional projects

- Helping remove vehicles from the road to reduce emissions and traffic through WeCar car sharing and Rideshare vanpool services

- Committing to what Enterprise calls its 20/20 Vision—a plan to achieve a 20 percent reduction in both energy use and energy costs across the company's operations by the end of 2015

- Investing more than $150 million through 2016 in sustainable construction of company facilities

- Funding renewable fuels research through a $25 million gift that created the Enterprise Institute for Renewable Fuels at the Donald Danforth Plant Science Center in St. Louis, the company's headquarters city

Enterprise has told the story of its sustainability efforts across its key audiences, including consumers, business partners, government and community leaders and—importantly—employees and job prospects, who view Enterprise's active and visible commitment as one more good reason to build a career there.

The company has used a wide variety of online and offline channels, including media relations, blogger outreach, social media programs, speaking opportunities and company websites. (That includes www.driving-futures.com—a website that serves as a communications hub for Enterprise's sustainable approach to doing business.)

Enterprise's sustainability commitment is more than a communications program. With the appointment of a head of corporate sustainability and the establishment of a cross-functional Chairman's Task Force on Sustainability, the company is working to incorporate more and more business practices that make sense for the environment and for the long-term success of the company. One of the first things to emerge from this Task Force was the 20/20 Vision initiative noted above.

As a result of these and other ongoing efforts, Enterprise Holdings has emerged as the clear sustainability leader in its industry. *Fortune* writer and sustainability expert Marc Gunther summed it up nicely with the comment: "More than the logo at Enterprise is green."

THE FUTURE: CEOs WILL HELP SET COMMUNICATIONS AGENDAS

A company's reputation, and sometimes its very survival, depends on how well it communicates with key audiences, including stockholders, the financial community, governments, business groups and partners, suppliers, the media, consumers, the general public and others. This is especially true at a time when corporations are under unprecedented, round-the-clock public scrutiny from one end of the globe to the other. Strange as it may sound, it is no longer good enough for a company to be ethical and forthright in its dealings; it must be perceived as such. That's why many companies continue to invest in communications efforts aimed at ensuring that their good deeds are communicated to the right audiences.

In the future, corporations will face increased challenges in maintaining a positive corporate image, but the benefits of having such an image will also increase. Those companies with a strongly favorable image are likely to have an advantage over those that do not. Communicating quickly and efficiently with a diverse range of audiences will be more important—and more challenging to manage—than ever before.

But I think corporate management increasingly realizes it is a challenge well worth meeting. And I think they realize as well that important audiences cannot be treated merely as communications targets; they must be treated as partners in the communications process. This positive change in objectives has significant consequences for the public relations executive who must analyze, understand and approach key audiences with arguments that are compelling, authentic and easy to understand.

CEOs in the future are likely to play a more active role in setting communications goals for their firms, as well as insisting on measurable programs to achieve those goals. Attaining the best reputation for the organization will be an asset prized by management, and more chief executives, assuming the responsibility of communicating clear visions and strong values, will set aggressive benchmarks on which to build their corporate reputation goals.

Going forward, the communications executive has the potential to be much more than just one more senior partner in that process. He can serve as the integrator who helps ensure that all the major functions are pulling in the same direction when it comes to promoting and protecting the company's reputation, and who brings an integrity and consistency to the company's story across all its key stakeholders.

DISCUSSION QUESTIONS

1. In your mind, what is the single most important skill or quality involved in being an effective communications executive?
2. In your opinion, what companies are doing an especially good job of managing and protecting their reputations? What sets them apart?
3. A core premise of this chapter is that "the CEO must be considered the de facto CCO of a corporation . . . viewed not only as the individual who makes the final decisions regarding a company's operations . . . but also as the individual who sets the tone for the corporation. A CEO cannot avoid this role." Do you accept that premise? Why or why not?
4. This chapter asserts that "we will see in the future that a company's record for sustainability will be taken more and more as an indicator that it is a well-managed company, period." Do you believe that is true?
5. The exploding use of social media has presented a whole new array of challenges and opportunities for those charged with managing their companies' reputations. In your opinion, what companies are particularly effective in using these interactive, real-time channels to their best advantage?
6. Of the tactical models outlined in this chapter, which one strikes you as the most effective overall approach to managing a company's reputation? The least effective?

NOTES

1. The Conference Board, Research Working Group, *Managing Reputation Risk and Reward* (April 2009).
2. Opinion Research Corporation, Corporate Reputation Center, *Management Profile: The Corporate Reputation* II (June 1994).
3. Penn Schoen Berland, *Green Brands Survey* (October 2010).
4. Social Investment Forum Foundation, *2010 Report on Socially Responsible Investing Trends in the United States* (November 2010).
5. The Economist Intelligence Unit/SAP, *Global Trends in Sustainability Performance Management* (March 2010).
6. Carbon Disclosure Project, *2010 CDP 2010 Water Disclosure Global Report* (November 2010).
7. Fleishman-Hillard internal content analysis of *The New York Times* (March 2011).
8. The Conference Board, Research Working Group, *Managing Reputation Risk and Reward* (April 2009).

ADDITIONAL READING

Friedman, Thomas L. 2008. *Hot, Flat and Crowded: Why We Need a Green Revolution—And How It Can Renew America* (New York: Farrar, Straus and Giroux).

Harris, Thomas L., and Patricia T. Whalen. 2006. *The Marketer's Guide to Public Relations in the 21st Century* (Mason, OH: Thomson/Southwestern).

Hayes, Tom. 2008. *Jump Point: How Network Culture Is Revolutionizing Business* (New York: McGraw-Hill).

Henderson, David. 2006. *Making News: A Straight-Shooting Guide to Media Relations* (Lincoln, NE: iUniverse Star).

26

C H A P T E R

CRISIS COMMUNICATIONS
Brand New Channels, Same Old Static

Hud Englehart
Managing Partner
Beacon Advisors, Inc.
Adjunct Professor, Integrated Marketing Communications
Northwestern University

Crisis is any threat that, when reported to one or more key constituents, disrupts company operations or causes a set of negative outcomes for a company or brand. Such peril from a public relations perspective goes beyond disruption, however, because unlike any other business situation, crisis puts a company's reputation on the line in full view of its stakeholders. It tests principles, positions and values. It magnifies every misstep, compounds every error, fuels every emotion and heightens every agenda while everyone watches—and judges—from a front row seat.

The definition has not really changed over the decades; nor have the tenets for managing serious, media-fueled business interruptions. Warren Buffett described the stakes: "It takes 20 years to build a reputation and five minutes to ruin it. If you think about that, you'll do things differently." And effective crisis managers tend to do just that. They respond in ways that, under normal business circumstances, might seem unusual, even risky because they (1) let their actions lead their words and (2) adhere to the tried and true dictum for crisis communicators: maximum disclosure–minimum delay (or as one professional crisis counselor puts it: "Tell it all and tell it fast").

The other thing that has not really changed, unfortunately, is the nature of the mistakes that companies are prone to make when crisis strikes. The ones that stumble do so because they are guilty of (1) missing, ignoring or covering up warning signs and thus lack a plan for response, (2) thinking that legal liabilities are the same as the "cost" of the crisis and (3) choosing to protect self-interests rather than brand interests.

Tactically, it is a far different story. In fact, by virtue of a rapidly fragmenting media industry, the execution of crisis communication strategies has changed dramatically since Y2K. Back then, Northwestern University's *Journal of Integrated Communication* dubbed 2000–2001 the Year of Crises for American business. Arthur Andersen, Enron, WorldCom, the Catholic Church, Major League Baseball, Martha Stewart and Jack Welch, among others, found themselves in crisis mode, grappling with public revelations of misconduct and the explosive headlines they created.

Managing communication for these organizations and individuals was complicated, for sure. Institutions faltered. Near-sacred trusts with stakeholders had been broken. Careers were pillaged. Employees lost jobs along with their retirement savings and investments. Government intervened. CEOs and CFOs were seen on network news literally being bound over for trial. It was nothing if not chaotic.

Yet for all of the game-changing events that occupied the headlines during this period of U.S. business history, crisis communication managers could rely on the constancy of the media's content delivery model. Reporters were assigned to stories and stuck with them. TV relied on newspapers for breaking news. Stories had hard deadlines tied to printing schedules and airtimes. The key media universe comprised the home-town metro daily, the *Wall Street Journal,* the *New York Times, Business Week, Fortune, Forbes, Time, Newsweek, USN&WR, USA Today*, network morning and evening TV news and a smattering of cable TV programs.

Sure, "celebrities" moved some news from the business page to the cover of *People Magazine*, which could not resist Martha Stewart's insider trading story, R. Kelly's sex tapes or a GE CEO's involvement with the editor of the *Harvard Business Review*. Yet when pressed into duty, crisis PR staffs generally knew how, when and where to engage with the media. And the media generally performed its role of delivering the news to key audiences.

THIS IS NOT YOUR FATHER'S NEWS MEDIA!

Contrast that scenario with the one that confronted companies and individuals in another Year of Crises: 2009–2010. The period saw behemoth Wall Street brands like Bear Stearns and Lehman Bros. vanish from the investment bank universe. Toyota had its value proposition come unhinged in a typhoon of product recalls. BP's green image turned black with a sea-floor oil gusher that brought 4.9 million barrels of crude to the surface of the Gulf of Mexico. And Tiger Woods, the most recognized athlete in the world and a near-iconic family man considered by many to be on track to become the greatest golfer ever, finally met a foe he could not beat: himself.

Like the spate of disasters that captured headlines earlier in the decade, many of these incidents violated the public trust and, in so doing, sounded public alarms, shook foundations, challenged conventional wisdom and brought on unprecedented levels of government action and reaction.

But it was different in 2009–2010—a lot different—because the traditional news media world had trans-formed itself from its organized journalism base to an entirely new platform of social media that empowered public involvement with instant messages, life followers, self-publishing and word-of-mouth marketing. The key words in this seismic media shift were not even in dictionaries until after 2004, the year that marked the start of a revolutionary advance in global connectivity and grass roots communication.

The upheaval began when a young Harvard entrepreneur launched Facebook, the social network-ing website that today boasts 600 million members and grows by 10 million members a month. That same year, 2004, while Mark Zuckerberg's invention was gathering its first followers, three other Internet entrepreneurs—leaders from companies named BzzAgent, Intelliseek and BuzzMetrics—formed WOMMA, the Word of Mouth Marketing Association, to provide an ethical foundation for a growing new marketing and research discipline focused on harnessing and deploying the power of digital conversation. The as-sociation's rapid rise acknowledged that the Internet had lifted dialogue and conversation from the dinner table to the airwaves.

In February of 2005, the next digital shock arrived. YouTube gave motion to messages by letting its users upload visual content to the web for anyone to see . . . anytime. So "hot" was YouTube's consumer appeal that just a year after its launch, *Google paid $1.65 billion to acquire it.*

Then, in July of 2006, Jack Dorsey launched Twitter, the social networking and microblogging service that lets its 200 million users send messages called Tweets to followers down the hall, around the corner and across the world.

In the preface to *Twitterville*,[1] Shel Israel's 2009 examination of history's most rapidly adopted commu-nications tool, Altimeter Group founder Charlene Li gives context to the social media phenomenon. "Twitter was made for my Mom," she wrote. "That's because she's always infinitely interested in what I am doing and thinking, no matter how mundane—or inane."

Li's description puts forward the immense communications potential of social connections—and the almost equally immense skepticism with which social networking is often greeted by businesses. After all, not everyone wants to know as much about you as Mom does.

Having said that, however, these new digital communication forms elevate conversation and dialogue among stakeholders to levels that companies simply cannot ignore. To drive home the point, a Keller Fay Group FastTrack[2] study conducted in 2009 revealed that consumers have 112 marketing-relevant conversations a week; and 56 times a week those conversations include brand mentions. Imagine how the results of a similar survey would look if a well-known brand—say Tiger Woods—saturates nearly all the lead acreage in both the traditional and digital media space.

Skeptic or not, it is hard to deny that the social media model makes possible rocket-like branding—and wildfire-like crises. That is because channels like Twitter and Facebook, each barely a half-decade old and each approaching generational ubiquity, have not only hastened message delivery, but they have also personalized and dimensionalized it. In effect, they are the technological equivalent of the fall harvest, bringing together communities of friends—globally—for collaboration, commerce and conversation.

Put in a public relations context, the once popular counseling parlance rooted in "news cycles" and "mass media coverage" has evolved—some might say devolved—to a new vocabulary of instant message delivery and social media. Digital communication makes every user of computers and mobile phones a potential media channel. Where crisis managers once worried about news radio as the ignition of public exposure, in the digital age they now have to consider more viral and potentially damaging delivery channels that exist on desktops, laptops, tablets and PDAs.

What can make this channel proliferation so confounding for a company in crisis is the premise on which the delivery mechanisms thrive, namely the credibility of word-of-mouth communication. Nearly 70 percent of those interviewed for Edelman's annual Trust Barometer (see Chapter 16), for example, say that they most trust people "like themselves" when it comes to information. Amplifying the point in the affirmative, a 2009 study on word-of-mouth communication by Millward Brown, the Madison Avenue marketing research company, revealed that more than 85 percent of consumers rely either solely (19 percent) or in part on recommendations when choosing brands.[3]

Switching to the negative, auto sales people were once famous for saying that only 1 satisfied customer in 10 would tell others about their new car; while dissatisfied buyers grumpily spread the news at a rate of 6 in 10. Though the order of magnitude may be subject to some distortion, the old axiom about bad news traveling farther and faster has survived into the digital age, and it holds prescient significance for companies in crisis, which by definition is "bad news."

The point is that, in examining any set of today's legitimate (or illegitimate) business news sources, it is hard to escape a sense of inevitability when it comes to crisis. Business has become more complex and far reaching. Customers and employees have become more sophisticated. Business itself has become an arena where ethics and values, alliances and disputes, culture and diversity, finance, fairness and equal opportunity are arbitrated. Acknowledging all this, can anyone really argue that the unexpected seems much more likely to occur?

WHAT TO CONCLUDE FROM A HALF DECADE OF MOVING AT THE SPEED OF DIGITAL

So, in an era when advocates as well as adversaries have globally capable instant message delivery devices at their fingertips 24/7, two crisis management conclusions ought to be evident.

The first is that *planning for the unplanned* has never been more important. It is the only way to have an effective defense against the onset of crisis. It ensures the capacity to launch an aggressive offense to lessen the damages. With speed at a premium, preplans help avert the kind of decision gridlock that makes the clock an enemy and eats away at both the pocketbook and the brand equity bank. Finally, preplanning necessitates a discovery process that allows companies to prioritize influential audiences and identify the message channels to reach them.

The legendary John Hill[4] theorized that companies operate with the permission and under the watchful eye of their publics or stakeholders, i.e., share owners, customers, suppliers, employees, legislators, regulators and the press who empowered their points of view by acting as their eyes and voices. The Hill & Knowlton founder, who was the firm's CEO until 1962, could never have imagined how diffuse the "press" would become. In his day, the "public eye" was represented by large metropolitan daily newspapers whose editors and reporters had desks down the hall from the printing presses.

Today, of course, the print editions of daily newspapers are being supplanted by online publications that boast no deadline but the time it takes to write and post stories, by a blogosphere of unaffiliated "journalists" who produce endless streams of news and commentary and by a community of consumers who incessantly communicate brand encounters—good and bad—to their friends and followers. As a result, even absent the paralysis that often infects decision making during a crisis, the tasks of aligning audiences with delivery channels and finding the "reporters" who supply channel content is exponentially more difficult in this social media age.

All of this does not mean we should ignore the mainstream media. They remain the single most credible sources for news despite the advent of digital spontaneity and connectivity. As such they offer crisis communicators a critical leverage point. Consistent and repeated airings of facts in or on traditional—and trusted—media still trump the rumor mill. Moreover, as these more familiar media forms adapt to the social networking revolution, they are likely to recapture some of their lost news leader status.

Above all else, then, while companies are doing their best, they need to plan in advance for coping with their worst.

The second conclusion from this media centric introduction has to do with *cost* and *survivability*. The last decade has delivered plenty of crisis-related fatalities, the ultimate cost. Multinational enterprises like Arthur Andersen, Enron and Lehman Bros. collapsed under the pressure of public exposure causing billions in lost partner and shareholder equity. Major League Baseball (steroids) and the Catholic Church (pedophilia) have survived under relentless lenses, but one has to wonder if these entities might have eased their pain by looking beyond the hard dollars and trying to inform their crisis decisions with realistic calculations of the near and longer term monetary impacts on their brands.

More recently, once highly regarded brands like Toyota and Tiger Woods have paid extraordinarily high near-term prices as they faced off against enterprise-threatening accidents and scandals. But each might have averted their own forms of water boarding by asking their communication staffs to add calculated brand values into the decision mix. Both brands might have behaved differently confronted with the true magnitude of the problem.

Here is an example of how a calculation of "loss magnitude" can effect decisions and outcomes. The owner of a quick service restaurant, embroiled in a payments dispute with an ethnic franchisee, threatens to disenfranchise his operations if he doesn't pay $5 million in delinquent franchise and marketing fees. The franchisee responds to the threat by claiming that the owner's stance is racially motivated and that he is working with activist groups to support his call for a boycott of the owner's urban stores.

Using a worst-case approach, the owner calculated that a boycott, fueled by attending negative publicity and potential service disruption and employee backlash, might result in $15 to $20 million in lost revenue—and even more if boycotting customers switched their loyalty to a competing chain.

Within the parameters of this cost calculation, the fee delinquency issue took a different turn. The owner felt that any settlement that cost less than $15 million was a "victory" for his company. So his crisis strategy took shape. In the court of public opinion, he would defend his brand and its integrity by delivering the facts and letting his customers decide. At the same time, he would try to negotiate a quiet and quick settlement to rid his balance sheet of the debt, even if it meant swallowing it; to disenfranchise the unruly franchisee; and to avert the downside effects inherent in a protracted boycott.

Jumping back to reality, had Toyota "run numbers" on the loss magnitude of its troubles with accelerator defects—an issue that dated back to 2002 but came to light in 2009—it might have opted for a Tylenol approach much earlier in its year-long recall crisis, i.e., announcing that affected vehicles were *not* going to be sold to any customer anywhere until the defects were corrected.

The lesson for companies in crisis is to weigh *all* the costs, not just those that influence short-term results.

IT IS WHAT YOU DO THAT COUNTS, NOT WHAT YOU SAY

For all of this, one suspects that there is not much different about crisis itself. Bad things happen to good companies. Media of almost any sort and origin decry mistakes, missteps or misdeeds. Stakeholders fear for the performance of their investments. Customers question their loyalty. Government panders. The public demands reform.

But in the end, crisis outcomes are determined by how companies *behave*—by what they do, how they do it and when they do it. When behavior doesn't line up with the story (message), companies have to be prepared to suffer the consequences. It seems human nature supports this notion. For the public-at-large, the cliché "seeing is believing" is just another way of saying that credible company behaviors hold more sway than noncredible (or incredible) statements.

That behavior is the critical element in crisis response was the true learning from the now iconic response of Johnson & Johnson to the Tylenol tampering incident way back in 1986. J&J's entire story was footed in one straightforward, easy-to-comprehend decision: remove the product from the shelves. The action said it all, and said it better than any set of words: J&J cared first and foremost about its customers and they refused to put any of them at risk, no matter what the financial and marketing consequences.

In more recent times, there have been plenty of cases to test the theory. In the 1990s, Monsanto was busy pursuing a life sciences mission that it boldly touted in a logo that connected the company's products with "Food. Health. Hope." But when the British discovered that health and hope revolved around genetically modified food—"playing God" with the food supply was the way Prince Charles put it—it seemed to them to be the antithesis of life and science. The messages did not line up and, in the ensuing media storm, biotechnology suffered a significant global setback.

Heading to their vacation homes on a Friday night, Long Island residents tuned into their car radios to hear news that a Boston Chicken employee had turned gravely ill at work, was transported to a local hospital and diagnosed with acute hepatitis B, a disease that sounds scary but adults usually have for a short time, experiencing flulike symptoms before it just goes away. Nonetheless, the news reader teased the story that evening with words that went something like, "It's dangerous, it's contagious, and it's on Long Island. More after this word from our sponsor." The news obviously put a scare into Boston Chicken customers, so much so that sales plummeted as much as 80 percent over the weekend in question.

The crisis evoked a completely aligned response from the company. The CEO set an unequivocal strategy in place by instructing his crisis team to ". . . Do whatever it takes to convince me that it is safe to bring my nine-year-old son back to Boston Chicken for dinner." And that's what they did. With no evidence to suggest that anyone on Long Island had contracted the disease other than its own employee, the company immediately took the steps to persuade its customers and protect its brand. It shut down the store in question and sterilized it. It contacted and worked with concerned authorities in the community to make sure the company understood the public health implications. It offered to help pay for an emergency education program to help residents recognize and understand hepatitis strains, symptoms and treatments. And it made its local management team completely accessible to the press.

When the media, and through them the community, took note of what Boston Chicken was doing, the crisis vaporized like steam from a hot turkey sandwich and within a few weeks the company's business was back to normal. The latter was helped along by editorials in the local press praising the company's aggressive response on behalf of its customers and the public at large.

Another case when actions spoke louder than words involved a situation in which HIV-positive organs had been transplanted in patients at three major medical centers in the Chicago area. At one of the hospitals involved, the University of Chicago Medical Center (UCMC), then VP of Communications Kelly Sullivan was made aware of the problem through the center's legal department. Lawyers for the affected patients, she was told, were readying a press conference to announce a lawsuit against UCMC and several other area hospitals seeking damages.

Sullivan, a seasoned communication executive who built her reputation by using her PR post to advocate for patients, had heard the ensuing arguments many times before. On the one side, faced with the prospect of a front-page story on the lawsuit, the hospital attorneys, concerned about litigation issues and patient privacy, urged UCMC not to comment. On the other side was Sullivan who argued, successfully as it turned out, that UCMC should get ahead of the story by making a full and proactive disclosure of the circumstances. In other words, she lobbied to have UCMC and the other hospitals break the negative news themselves. She prevailed by arguing convincingly that it was the only way to marginalize allegations from the plaintiffs, avert a confidence crisis among UCMC's current and prospective patients, inform and calm the physician referral network and blunt a series of sensational headlines that might cause patients to withdraw from transplant wait lists around the country.

Following Sullivan's lead, UCMC agreed to give an exclusive on the story to the science writer at the *Chicago Tribune* who learned every substantial detail (except patient names) from UCMC medical experts involved, with backup and support from the Centers for Disease Control (CDC) in Atlanta. The story that subsequently appeared on the front page was a balanced, completely accurate report of the complex circumstances that included the plaintiff's point of view. In the days that followed, when calls from journalists poured in from around the country, Sullivan simply pointed them to the Tribune account and declined any further comment.

The medical and legal staffs were somewhat amazed but thoroughly impressed by the outcome. The CDC, an experienced media and public relations–literate government enterprise, got the balanced result they expected from a reporter whose view of the story was shaped by who released what and when. The act of having the hospital expose the problem clearly led to a much less sensational account than the one that might have appeared if the plaintiffs had first say. Why? Because the hospitals' proactive and transparent revelations put them on the side of the patients.

PLAN FOR THE UNEXPECTED

On the surface, planning for the unexpected may seem to be an exercise at odds with itself. But the fact is that most organizations have a somewhat advanced sense of their vulnerabilities. And it is from there—from attempts to address weaknesses long before they build into an unanticipated threats—that a well-conceived crisis response plan will inevitably spring. Perhaps the most compelling argument for doing a plan in advance is that once a crisis event occurs, there is no time for a considered, thoughtful approach. Another way of looking at it is to note that the absence of an advance plan vastly improves the chances of failure. Finally, there are no rush orders in crisis. Companies cannot lift their readiness quotient by opening up the company checkbook or putting more bodies against the task. Bluntly put, there simply is no substitute for a top management–sponsored crisis plan.

WHERE TO BEGIN, WHAT TO PROTECT?

Start by deciding what could go wrong and figuring out what needs to be done to deal with the breakage. Good plans do more than establish tactical responses. They actually set out goals and objectives and concisely articulate an approach to crises so that every decision has a context and a path. In effect, the company has to decide, as a matter of corporate conscience, what it wants to protect when something hits the proverbial fan. Is it the brand, the public, the shareholders, directors, managers, employees, customers?

To bring costs to bear on the discovery process, do some simple arithmetic. Calculate the financial effect of a crisis on shareowners and managers. Use a 1 percent fall in stock price as a baseline. Then up the ante to 5 percent, 25 percent and 50 percent to arrive at what some crises generate in near-term stock losses. The math exercise is purposeful because it establishes the "value" of the planning exercise and, for those with company shares, it engages them personally and financially in the effort.

Once the key vulnerabilities are identified, it is time to envision and address the details and twists and turns that might arise. Figure out who will speak for the company, who to communicate with, what channels to use, what media to contact/follow, what influencers need to be in the loop and what contingencies need to be in place. During the process, make sure to designate a communications chain of command. There is nothing more frustrating or debilitating than having a great plan and no clear sense of who has authority to make decisions. The truth is that companies that have meetings at the onset of a crisis to figure authority issues usually take their first crisis step on the wrong foot and it can take weeks to get the operation back on pace.

A GOOD REPUTATION: THE BEST TACTIC OF ALL

Having a good reputation is like having a rainy day fund to tap into when things are going wrong. In hard dollars it ranks among the lower cost assets in a time of crisis. In soft dollars its value is nearly incalculable as it is a resource that companies usually will need plenty of: the benefit of the doubt. During a crisis, organizations with a solid standing among stakeholders invariably fare better in the court of public opinion.

BUILD A CRISIS TEAM AND GIVE IT A LEADER

The crisis team's membership needs to reflect the company's inner workings as well as its outside influences. The most effective planning teams are those that develop decisions using perspectives from operations, finance, sales, marketing, research, human resources, investor relations, government affairs and communications.

    The team has to have a decisive leader, preferably someone from top management who has won the trust of the Board, who possesses an unflappable temperament and in whom top management colleagues have unshakeable faith to do the right thing. That kind of leader generally inspires respect from the crisis team. Each discipline represented on the team needs a leader, too, the most critical of whom will oversee crisis communication.

SET UP A CRISIS COMMAND CENTER

When the waves of crisis begin breaking, companies need to have a command center at their disposal, a place where they can go to focus solely on the task at hand and where they have unfettered access to critical resources. The center can be a conference room on site or a room at a neutral site—it does not really matter as long the team has access to the appropriate communications resources such as satellite television and wire services, Internet-enabled PCs, video conferencing and audio/video recording applications.

SET UP THE COMPANY'S OWN SOCIAL NETWORK

A well-prepared crisis unit will have developed resources that they can tap on a moment's notice to help manage events, gauge reactions and mitigate damages. The resources might include the following:

- A *list of allies* in industry, on Wall Street and Main Street, in academia, NGOs, think tanks, policy institutes and the like that would agree to support or affirm the company's points of view on crisis response with opinion editorials, blogs, broadcast news appearances, webcasts, white papers, congressional testimony and so forth. Creating the list is the first step. Nurturing the ally group into a community is next. Use Facebook, Twitter and LinkedIn to glue everyone together through information sharing and periodic dialogues.
- A *list of freelance news producers* who can be called on to write, shoot and edit videos for distribution to the news media and for posting at YouTube.
- A *public opinion polling resource* like Pulse Opinion Research, a Rasmussen Reports polling affiliate, to develop and conduct statistically reliable overnight public opinion surveys. The value of knowing what people think and how they are responding to events and messages cannot be quantified. Every communicator will argue that having timely data affirming either the direction or intensity of crisis response is a critical element of effective crisis communications management. Pulse, and other robo-polls, offer key advantages in this time-compressed era: (1) they can field surveys within hours; (2) they can conduct surveys within targeted geographies; and (3) they can analyze and cross tab results by key demographics: income, employment, ethnic origin, education, etc.
- *Excess server capacity* so that the company's web presence can be expanded rapidly to accommodate additional traffic, video streaming and other new web functionalities, perhaps including chat and survey and feedback loops.
- *Ready-to-go mobile app(s)* that stakeholders can add to their Internet-enabled phones to follow progress, receive outbound messages and deliver critical on-the-ground feedback.

- *E-mail and/or text addresses* of every potential ally and stakeholder to facilitate direct, integrated communication with key audiences.
- *Adaptive new technologies* like the new Microsoft Tag reader application or QR code readers for internet enabled camera phones. These apps bring information to the "point of impulse" and can be attached to print articles, embedded in videos, posted on billboards or kiosks, printed on packages, etc. With a simple scan, users are taken to a web server that features company sponsored information.
- *Employee engagement plans*—perhaps the most underutilized, and underappreciated, resource during crisis is the work force. The shame is that in most companies, employees represent a pool of support. They are usually willing community ambassadors with personal credibility that goes well beyond the company's. So activate them. Short of activation, make sure there is a way to keep them in the loop. Their loyalty to the brand is key.

BUILD AN INTERNAL NETWORK

Today's corporate communications departments are plagued in some instances by the old PR adage: "last to know, first to go." The way to attack the syndrome is to forge links to key managers for the express purpose of being in the loop on problem identification. Top corporate communications practitioners form exchange alliances with department and division heads so communications is informed and can prepare for potential problems. The legal department is where most of them start because the chief counsel and the legal staff tend to be the repository for all the serious complaints against the company. What makes the network successful is the initiative of the communicators who understand that lawyers do not volunteer information. They need it pried out of them.

BE CONTENT READY, FORMAT FLEXIBLE

Once a company has taken the time and expended the effort to identify and prepare for its nightmare crisis scenario, it should not be too difficult to anticipate the content needs of the company's most important delivery channels. TV, print and online outlets may need different formats, but the content—the message—is not likely to vary. The question to pose is, "What do I need to respond to immediately?" The answer will depend on the crisis, of course, but a few ideas come to mind. You should have the following ready:

- A press statement that can be e-mailed, faxed, posted, Tweeted, taped or verbalized that (1) reserves specific comments until the company has more or all the details, (2) states the company's overriding concern, (3) reveals the company's approach ("We're going to get to the bottom of this!") and (4) pledges to inform in a timely way.
- A starter set of "best answers" for product failures, contaminations, crashes, leaks, discrimination suits, work stoppages, etc.
- Files of generic company and product or service information that can be distributed to help give context to a story and deliver positive messages about the company's performance, safety record, etc.
- Charts, graphs, diagrams and illustrations to provide visual context. A water company might have media-ready diagrams of its pipelines accompanied by inspection data and safety records.
- Crisis-specific Twitter and Facebook accounts that can be activated at the onset along with a set of early posts to drive Internet traffic to credible news outlets.

SOME GUIDING PRINCIPLES FOR CRISIS RESPONSE

Companies in crisis need to pay attention to their behavior, certainly. But the images and words are important, too. Just ask BP CEO Tony Hayward. In the midst of an otherwise splendid operations and communications response to the massive release of oil into the Gulf of Mexico in 2010, he called the worst oil spill in U.S. history "relatively tiny," was seen hobnobbing on his yacht and then compounded these visual and verbal insensitivities with a statement that was way too self-involved: "I'm sorry," he said. "We're sorry for the massive disruption it's caused their lives. There's no one who wants this over more than I do. I'd like my life back."[5]

Hayward personally paid for this "string of out-of-touch statements"[3] with his job. The company, though, paid a far greater price in lost goodwill when the public tuned in to the gaffes and tuned out on the truly responsive work that company was doing in the region.

So how can companies say the right thing when crisis strikes? Most experts agree that the best guide for delivering messages is contained in the rules of complaint handling, and specifically the "4Rs" whereby companies should express:

Regret. Say that you are sorry it (the crisis) happened. Not that you are guilty, or even responsible; just that you regret the circumstances. Lawyers will lobby hard against the idea that saying the words will come back to bite you in court. The problem with this lawyerly counsel is that it assumes the real costs of crisis are exacted in court, when they are actually paid in far greater magnitude in the market. What's more, if the company does not express regret, nobody will listen to anything else the company has to say.

Resolution. Say, if you can, what the company will do to resolve the issue. Put safety caps on the medicine, buy double-hull ships, test the chips before you ship, stop buying from the offending supplier or nothing if the company is not at fault.

Reform. Tell stakeholders that the company will do everything it can to ensure that the accident or incident or malfeasance will not happen again.

Restitution. Finally, see to it that everybody gets something, not in legal judgments, but in coupons, temporarily reduced rates or free gifts with future purchases.

So, now that the company spokesperson is saying the right things, how does the company make sure that the media accurately and fairly reports the facts? There are several techniques to consider.

One is to become a self-publisher, a tactic that is made possible by the shift to digital communication. Post blogs, publish op-eds, e-mail newsletters and news releases, webcast events, upload videos, publish books and white papers, and then drive audiences to the content using a combination of traditional and social, paid and earned media techniques. Remember, companies have a right to a point of view and a right to have it disseminated in clear air, so to speak, thus giving readers and viewers a chance to decide on their own.

Another is to hold the media accountable. Form a "Truth Squad" to monitor and correct any and all media errors or omissions. Understand that every error discovered probably won't result in a published correction. But the technique puts the media on notice that someone is watching and fully intends to hold them accountable. The other objective here is to make sure that the search engines—Google, Yahoo!, Bing, Ask Me—are revealing the most accurate accounts possible to people who search for information on the crisis.

Companies can also test messages to gauge understanding and impact. The focus group technique often used in advertising, for example, can be incredibly helpful in detecting the nuances of the public's reaction to company output.

Speaking of ad models, don't discount paid advertising. It can be an effective delivery channel for company messages, especially in a protracted crisis situation. BP may have set the standard on this score in 2010. Faced with 90 straight days of actual and inferred negative press that focused on the off-shore effort to plug the Deepwater Horizon oil spill, the company's on-shore response fell out of public view. With a truly inspired message adaptation, BP launched a paid advertising program using its Gulf Coast employees to tell a compelling—and quite believable—cleanup story.

Next, companies can use experts they identify as allies to convey third party support for the company positions on the circumstances surrounding the crisis. The PR staff should keep a log of press reports and opinion pieces from credible sources and use it to brief reporters new to the story.

Finally, depending on the nature of the crisis, companies can provide a location for the press to meet and communicate, and to receive periodic briefings from company spokespersons and experts.

WHAT NOT TO DO WHEN THE BALLOON GOES UP

In his wonderful book *When the Balloon Goes Up: The Communicator's Guide to Crisis Response*, expert crisis manager in the oil and chemical fields and former Northwestern University Adjunct Professor Bob Roemer[6] succinctly mapped the road to disaster when it comes to handling crisis. He cited seven serial failings that ring as true today as they did 40 years ago when the principals to the Watergate scandal first brought them to the attention of this generation of top corporate communicators. Here they are.

No plan. Perhaps the most critical mistake made by executives is the sin of pride. Not planning is the ultimate hubris because it assumes the company and its people will know what to do when the worst happens. Of course, the opposite is much closer to the truth.

Circle the wagons. Going on the defensive cedes control of the crisis communications agenda. Getting it back before the damage is done is almost impossible to pull off.

Ignore and Deny. Almost every crisis has warning signs. Some are subtle and others are as plain as the logo on corporate stationery. But somewhere along the way, the company decides that "this won't get any worse" and even if it does, "we can control the information." Big, big mistake.

Creative writing. Many a failed crisis management program can trace their downfall to the belief that companies can talk their way out of a problem. The evidence, of course, substantiates a far different reality: talk is cheap and actions speak louder than words.

Defend and/or protect the wrong thing. The best example of this failing occurred during Tiger Woods' marital crisis. He desperately tried to protect his privacy but in deciding to do so he ignited an avalanche of speculation and relentless attention.

Conflict with stakeholders and the media. When Toyota decided to defend a faulty accelerator system, it was in direct conflict with the interests of its customers. It is a losing position.

Damage to reputation. The inevitable conclusion reached by stakeholders is summed up in a question: "Do I really want to do business with a company this callous and this inept?"

CASE: TIGER'S WOODSHED

Situation: Tiger Woods burst on to the American cultural and sports scene as a two-year-old, appearing with driver in hand on Mike Douglas' daily syndicated TV show to hit golf balls while Douglas, guests Bob Hope and Jimmy Stewart and a national TV audience looked on. On that day, Woods delivered the first of his signature thrills—a mind-blowing strike of the ball, launched high and true against odds-defying pressure.

From the Douglas appearance the legend grew as Tiger reeled off one golf marvel after another. He shot a 48 at the Cypress Navy course at age three. He won his first tournament—an under 10-year-old event—at age seven. He broke 80 for the first time at age eight. He won six Junior World Championships, four of them in a row between 1988 when he was 13 and 1991. He became the youngest ever U.S. Junior champion at age 15; is the only golfer ever to win three U.S. Amateur titles; and in 1997, at age 21, became the youngest Masters Champion and the tournament's first African American winner with a record 12-shot margin of victory.

A dozen years later, in the fall of 2009, Woods seemed destined to break every record in professional golf and break through every financial barrier previously known to athletes (he was the nation's first billion-dollar athlete). Adding perfection to destiny, Woods was believed to be the quintessential family man. Devoted husband, loving father and attentive and dedicated son. In almost every way, he was bigger than life.

Crisis: So when word spread across the Internet that Tiger crashed his Escalade into a tree outside his Orlando home and that the accident followed a tumultuous night during which wife Elin Nordegren first learned of serial infidelities, the shattering of his image was literally heard round the world. In a flood of news reports—starting with celebrity gossip's TMZ, amplified by a torrent of Tweets and texts and ultimately legitimized by coverage at every media outlet in the country—Woods' carefully constructed public image actually drowned to death.

The proof was in the numbers. A Rasmussen poll conducted a week after the car accident showed that just 38 percent of Americans had a favorable opinion of the golf superstar. That was down from 83 percent from two years before. Corporate sponsors, one of the mainstays of Tiger's income, reacted, too, and quickly terminated endorsement contracts worth more than $50 million a year.

Response: Meanwhile, Woods and his advisors circled the wagons to defend against intrusions by law enforcement agencies, curious onlookers and the media. It was a fatal mistake for it meant that Woods, one of the most recognized celebrities in the world, had decided that his privacy was more important than his brand. It also meant that Woods intended to violate the "maximum disclosure, minimum delay" principle of crisis communication.

The combination of errors was as ironic as it was lethal. The more Tiger tried to keep the media out, the harder they tried to get in. The less he decided to tell, the more he ceded his own story agenda. The longer he delayed making some sort of full disclosure, the more speculation raged. And the fewer tournaments he entered, the less chance there was that he could win his way out of the tabloids and back onto the sports pages.

History is left to wonder what might have happened if Tiger had told it all and told it fast. For sure, the prolonged agony of six months of media scrutiny, virtually all of it bad, could have been averted. The "crimes" may have outweighed any PR attempt to win back sponsors in the near term.

Outcome: In the meantime, his brand was left with a two-iron shot into the wind to an island green. That's golf talk for a really tough spot.

His Nike equipment and apparel lines suffered declining sales, and the declining promotional presence of Woods himself. The Tiger Woods Foundation faced previously unimagined fundraising challenges. Tiger's course design and endorsement businesses shriveled to half their former selves.

In 2008, Woods topped Forbes list of Top-Earning Athletes, banking $127 million in Tour winnings and endorsements. The crisis cut that amount by 40 percent by 2010. A March 2011 Rasmussen poll showed only 31 percent of American adults shared a favorable opinion of Woods. None of his previous sponsors—Accenture, AT&T, American Express, Tag Heuer—had resigned him by 2011.

Woods holds the record for the most consecutive weeks at number one in the World Golf Rankings (281, from June 12, 2005, to October 24, 2010), as well as the most total weeks in the position at 623. In early November 2011, he ranked fifty-eighth.

WHAT IS AHEAD?

There are certainties about the future. There will be businesses in crisis as long as people run them and, human nature being what it is, history will not be as great a teacher as textbook writers might hope. Crisis management asks company managers to get outside the lines and consider strategies that may seem antithetical to the normal conduct of business communications: reveal the negatives, decide what to do before deciding what to say, cooperate with the press and, often hardest of all, put brand ahead of self.

Given the evolving nature of personal (i.e., digital) communication, it also seems quite likely that crises in the future will be much more complicated to manage. Social networking services have the potential to elevate casual conversation to the level of national and international news. Companies will have to hone their own networking to ensure that they have Toyota-like net-positive balances in their goodwill accounts if crisis strikes.

The new media environment will continue to redefine the idea of transparency. The world is such that everyone is reading everyone else's mail. In addition, virtually every stakeholder carries a potential mass communications device that puts companies just 140 characters away from their next public relations disaster. Companies simply cannot delude themselves into thinking that no one is watching, no one will notice or that facts won't eventually find their way into the public domain.

"Comebacks" may be harder in the future, too. The public tends to be a forgiving bunch. They give their brands the benefit of the doubt, particularly when traditional media, whom they generally hold in fairly low regard, is the prime message carrier. As social media constructs embed themselves, however, the bigger concern will be what friends are telling friends. In that delivery system, the trusted friend gets the benefit of the doubt, not the brand. This is yet another reason for companies to use digital techniques to engage their customers and constituents.

How quickly companies recover from crisis is a function of how big their goodwill bank was before the crisis and how well they behaved during and after. Companies that do it right will inevitably find that customers reward behaviors perceived to be in their best interest. So post-crisis brand loyalty could actually improve despite the threats to reputation posed by unexpected events.

Crisis will go global more quickly and more intensely. Global brands, therefore, will have to understand and learn to cope with a social networking community that runs well beyond national borders and deep, deep into international cultures. The wildfire—some would say viral—nature of crisis in the years ahead will have insurers insisting on plans to deal with them. The question is whether the plans will address communication as completely as it addresses operating responses.

That said, the hardest thing to gauge about the future of crisis is whether companies actually will be more inclined to plan for it. Given the loss magnitudes that the market witnessed in the first decade of the twenty-first century, it is hard to imagine why more planning wouldn't take place.

But then again, human nature often leads executives to think that the longer crisis is averted, the less likely it is to occur. Crisis teaches a different lesson, however, one that generations of baseball fans may recall from listening to legendary Pittsburgh Pirate broadcaster Bob Prince. One of his favorite sayings was: "The longer you win, the closer you get to losing." Those are words a crisis manager can live by.

DISCUSSION QUESTIONS

1. Describe your first actions as the crisis manager immediately upon learning that a crisis has occurred in your company.
2. What are the "costs" of a crisis to an organization?
3. Write a memo to the CEO explaining why a crisis plan is necessary.
4. What discussions should you have with your corporate or organizational attorney as part of the crisis plan?
5. Is crisis management the same for a personality as it is for a corporation? Why?

NOTES

1. Shel Israel, *Twitterville: How Businesses Can Thrive in the New Global Neighborhoods* (New York, NY: Portfolio, 2009). Print.
2. www.kellerfay.com.
3. www.millwardbrown.com.
4. John Hill founded Hill & Knowlton. He managed the company from before the Great Depression (1927) to 1962 and was active until shortly before his death in 1977.
5. Huffington Post, June 1, 2010.
6. Bob Roemer, *When the Balloon Goes Up: the Communicator's Guide to Crisis Response* (Victoria, BC: Trafford, 2007). Print.

ADDITIONAL READING

Augustine, Norman, et al. 2000. *Harvard Business Review on Crisis Management*, Harvard Business School Press.

Caywood, Clarke L., and Hud Englehart. 2002–2003. "Crisis Management: The Model Unchanged But the Costs Are Skyrocketing," *Journal of Integrated Communications*, Medill School, Northwestern University, pp. 46–50.

Coombs, W. Timothy, and Sherry J. Holladay. 2010. *PR Strategy and Application: Managing Influence*. Wiley Blackwell.

Roemer, Bob. 2007. *When the Balloon Goes Up*. Bloomington, IN: Trafford Publishing.

Stocker, Kurt. 1997. "A Strategic Approach to Crisis Management," Chapter 12, In: *The Handbook of Strategic Public Relations and Integrated Communication*. New York, NY: McGraw-Hill, Clarke L. Caywood, editor.

Weick, Karl E., and Kathleen M. Sutcliffe. 2007. *Managing the Unexpected: Resilient Performance in an Uncertain Age*, Second Edition. New York, NY: Wiley & Sons Inc., Jossey-Bass.

CURRENT AND CONTINUING ISSUES IN PUBLIC RELATIONS

At first glance, some readers might be surprised at the collection of topics in these chapters. Public relations is concerned with key business and social issues: positive, neutral and negative. Positive issues that PR might communicate about include new miracle drugs, safety features in automobiles and new Wi-Fi technologies. Negative issues might include oil spills, food poisoning, air crashes and product failures. There are also more neutral issues including the hiring of employees, changes in leadership and mergers and acquisitions.

This section is a strong combination of important selected issues. Each issue has been in the news and increasingly in the academic literature. These issues are likely to be found on the agenda of the board of directors and the short list of concerns for CEOs and other C-suite officers. Each issue also represents the movement away from the American business model or the European government model, to an institutional approach that can problem-solve the complex issues facing society. The solutions are found with the full engagement of strategic communication and represent an opportunity for stakeholder-oriented communicators to lead their organizations.

The lessons from these chapters are perfect illustrations of communications professionals taking the lead with sustainable policies in organizations (Lake and Calandro, Chapter 27) or with smart and continuing environmental programs beyond mere advertising claims of being "green" (Kelly, Chapter 28).

Opportunities also abound. The nearly infinite potential of the digital revolution has granted communicators new tools and entirely new ways of explaining their worlds and organizational goals to stakeholders (Clark, Chapter 29). In the same way, the concept of *reputation* exceeds the simpler notion of mere product or even corporate branding (Carroll, Greyser and Schreiber, Chapter 30). Branding beyond the historical meaning of marking cattle for ownership is elevated by a redefinition of how organizations can better perform with transparent, authentic definitions of their reason for existing, as their reputations precede them.

Other substantial issues included in the Industries and Organization section might have just as easily found a place in this section of the book. For example, food safety will continue to challenge citizens but the topic is nicely managed by Blum in Chapter 39, and Copel and Nelson in Chapter 44. The issue of loss of confidence in the world financial system, led by American failures and distorted leadership, are addressed by McDougal and Stocker in Chapter 23, and Anonymous in Chapter 43. The author of the chapter on the financial services industry has chosen to remain anonymous, because of the continued controversy surrounding the financial crisis and the resulting regulations and changes imposed on the industry.

The profusion of issues that public relations professionals can solve is virtually unlimited. Each subsequent edition of the book will add or, in some cases, subtract from the list as was done in this revision. What's important is that the issues presented here inspire overarching strategic communications thinking that transcend time and place.

27

C H A P T E R

SUSTAINABILITY FOR BUSINESS
A New Global Challenge

Charlene Lake
Senior Vice President Public Affairs and Chief Sustainability Officer
AT&T

Tony Calandro
Senior Vice President and Partner
VOX Global

AT&T CASE STUDY: A WORK IN PROGRESS—INTEGRATING BUSINESS NEEDS WITH THOSE OF SOCIETY

OVERVIEW

AT&T's legacy spans more than a century, but in many respects, the AT&T of today is a new burgeoning company. The "new" AT&T—a Fortune 12 company with more than 255,000 employees and well over $100 billion in annual revenue—emerged in 2007 after a series of mergers. The largest of the merged companies were SBC, AT&T, BellSouth and Cingular, but the mergers also included several smaller companies that were also folded into the new AT&T. Each of the legacy companies had its own culture, operations and policies, and the workforce was geographically diverse. After AT&T completed the major steps involved in integrating these companies, it recognized the need to reevaluate and realign its strategy around social and environmental sustainability and ensure alignment between that strategy and the business strategies throughout the company.

THE BUSINESS CASE FOR ACTING

There were many reasons for the company to strengthen its commitment to citizenship and sustainability. Initial discussions centered on potential reputational issues, customer pressure and on AT&T's existing environmental profile. At the time, some in the business community tended to believe that keeping a low profile would pose much less risk than voluntarily raising the stakes—particularly in an area considered by many inside the company to be uncharted territory. To counter that challenge, early advocates within the company focused on an idea that would resonate with people inside the company: AT&T needed to define its own image in this space, rather than allow others to do so.

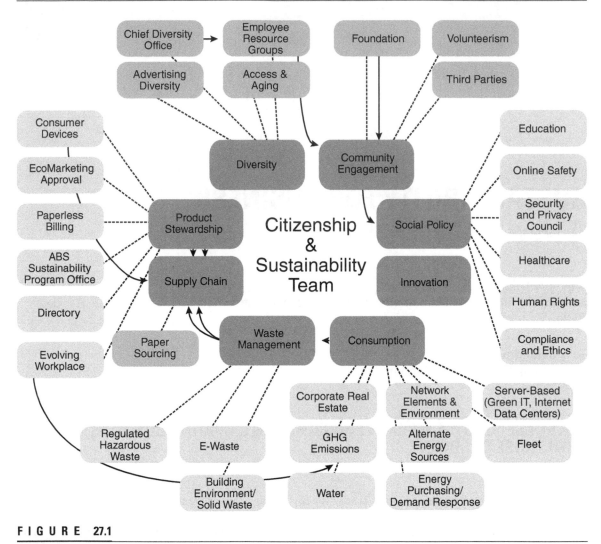

FIGURE 27.1

Citizenship & Sustainability Team

A host of additional reasons provided support for that central idea.

- Policy makers were increasingly inclined to take action, particularly in energy and environmental areas where the company was potentially exposed to legislative and regulatory impact simply due to the sheer size of the new company.

- The investment community and shareholders were increasingly focused on the subject. The company was beginning to see an increase in investor surveys and RFP's asking the company to report on its social and environmental impacts. Additionally, the first shareholder meeting of the new company saw a shareholder resolution asking the company to be transparent in its sustainability commitments.

- Customers increasingly expected corporations to be sensitive to social needs. The United States had seen a string of company executives abusing the public trust, and customers were looking for proof that companies were ethical, community focused and responsible.

- Social concerns captured the interest of employees. Employees wanted to work for a company that was a good corporate citizen.

- Environmental stewardship supported new market opportunities. There was a realization that the company's products and services could help customers minimize their environmental impact. At the same time, there was a recognition that the company would need to "walk the talk"—i.e., if the company were to credibly promote the environmental benefits to their customers, AT&T would need to demonstrate that it was helping its employees do the same.

- The explosion of bloggers and "citizen journalists" was creating an era of greater transparency and disclosure with companies. A company's impact on its communities was now becoming a matter of public record and a topic for open discussion.

Since those early days, sustainability has started to evolve into an explicit and defined aspect of AT&T culture and business operations. AT&T has achieved significant milestones—including the announcement of a commitment to spend up to $565 million to deploy approximately 15,000 more fuel-efficient vehicles in its corporate fleet through 2018—but these achievements were not without hurdles. AT&T knows its efforts are a work in progress, with ongoing challenges and setbacks that are economic, operational and institutional. While change sometimes comes slowly in such a large organization, AT&T leadership is committed to fully integrating sustainability and sustainable business practices throughout the company.

Maintaining this commitment requires many different strategies and approaches—and one fundamental condition: corporate recognition that sustainability brings value back to the business. Defining sustainability as a key business approach ensures that it is assigned appropriate significance at all levels of the company. Such high-level commitment also promotes sustainability as a more efficient way to meet bottom line goals and to drive shareholder value.

AT&T's sustainability journey has led to six key lessons that may be helpful to any business or organization looking to integrate sustainability into its business operations.

DEFINING SUSTAINABILITY: BEYOND BEING GREEN

Sustainability has no uniform, consistent definition, and it encompasses more than just environmental issues. For AT&T, it came down to recognizing the natural link between its business and society—understanding that the long-term financial health of the company is inextricably linked to the health of its communities. Therefore, AT&T used phrases such as *citizenship and sustainability* and *social and environmental sustainability* and focused its efforts on those issues that are found at the intersection of society and AT&T.

A good example is the issue of world hunger. While it is a serious global issue, it does not as naturally overlap with the company's core business or expertise as some other potential areas of focus. Instead, the company concentrated its efforts in areas where it could provide valuable business and expert input such as energy management, maintaining a diverse and highly trained workforce and deploying more fuel-efficient vehicles in its fleet.

This approach to sustainability also included a major education initiative, AT&T Aspire, which is championed by AT&T's CEO, Randall Stephenson. Aspire was launched in 2007 as a four-year, $100 million initiative created to address a true national crisis—the growing epidemic of high school dropouts. About 25 percent of U.S. high school students drop out before they earn their diploma, and the number is about 40 percent for African American, Hispanic and Native American students. The Aspire program is dedicated to addressing this crisis by improving high school retention rates and workforce readiness. The company believes that people, not capital, are the critical business resource of the future. Concentrating resources on developing a high-quality labor pool addresses a serious problem in which the needs of the business community intersect with the needs of society.

While the company had a long history of social commitment dating back to Alexander Graham Bell, this focused approach placed a business value on addressing specific societal issues and infused the philosophy throughout the company's operations.

OPERATIONAL ALIGNMENT: A METHOD TO THE MADNESS

Key to AT&T's effort to implement sustainable business practices across the company was the ability to gain understanding of and build relationships with a variety of stakeholders. With that concept as a foundation, AT&T based its sustainability leadership in the Public Affairs business unit— a core function of which is to build relationships with key stakeholders in society through understanding their issues and finding commonality in purpose. The same relationship-building and listening skills employed with key public affairs stakeholders were applied internally to help AT&T drive sustainability further into the company. These skills helped AT&T better understand its employees' motivations, to identify the communications that would most resonate with them and, ultimately, to better work with them to find long-term business success.

Regardless of where this function resides inside a company, success requires some type of internal structure that seamlessly integrates sustainability into an organization's business operations. This helps ensure that sustainability is not seen internally as an "add on" that is confined to a particular function of one business unit.

For AT&T, the first step of operational alignment was taken by AT&T's Public Policy Committee of the Board of Directors, which, led by the Chairman and CEO, changed its charter in the first quarter of 2008 to include oversight of citizenship and sustainability initiatives. Followed by this action, the company created a Citizenship and Sustainability Steering Committee. The committee is made up of senior executives and officers from across the company who meet quarterly to determine company priorities, align resources and help further integrate these issues into its core business operations.

As part of the structure, the company now has more than 25 active "expert teams" aligned around specific citizenship and sustainability issues. Each team has cross-functional business representation, serves to assess company operations through the specific lens of sustainability initiatives and drives projects and initiatives around sustainable business practices. The strategy, execution and public messaging of these expert teams and initiatives are coordinated by members of the company's corporate citizenship and sustainability core team, which helps the "expert teams" determine key performance indicators and goals, undertake new initiatives and strengthen existing ones.

While AT&T's approach produces consensus and ownership within the various business units, it is not an effortless operating system. For instance, the goal of an initiative and the time it takes to be achieved are open discussion points between the company's corporate sustainability team and the affected business units. Shared understanding and consensus on a path forward must be resolved. The goal and pace of this process may not be as significant or fast as preferred, but the final outcome is stronger because the decisions receive buy-in from the business unit, and decisions are made with full understanding of business impacts.

Given the uncommon nature of the system, and the reliance upon consensus vs. command and control, there was an initial lack of role clarity for the Steering Committee, causing some inertia early in the system development. Today, however, committee members have taken ownership of their roles; they more readily embrace driving change, and they are setting the agenda and pace for the company's sustainability efforts. The company further strengthened its sustainability operating structure by appointing its first chief sustainability officer.

ISSUE ALIGNMENT: MORE THAN STARS NEED TO BE ALIGNED

With a more explicit definition of sustainability in place and a strengthened internal alignment, AT&T turned its attention to identifying priorities for the company to pursue.

AT&T started by conducting a series of in-depth interviews with employees, focused on senior executives, officers and mid-level managers inside business units. The interviews gave greater insight into the challenges and opportunities sustainability presented for each sector of the business. AT&T balanced these internal conversations with a variety of key external stakeholders' views on what they felt were the key issues to AT&T.

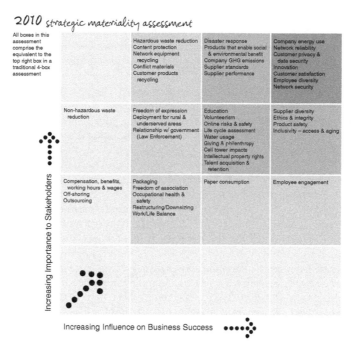

FIGURE 27.2

2010 Strategic Materiality Assessment

AT&T then undertook a "materiality assessment" designed to achieve three primary goals:

1. Identify and align the company's greatest risks and opportunities with key stakeholder expectations

2. Prioritize the risks and opportunities based on importance to stakeholders and relevance to business operations

3. Help inform subsequent decisions regarding which issues to pursue and the level of activity

The full results of the materiality assessment are available online at http://att.centralcast.net/CSRBrochure09/Default.aspx. The analysis presented a clear picture of the areas of confluence between business success and stakeholder priorities, and clarified the connection between sustainability and the bottom line. Simply put, the process provided AT&T with a road map to identify the issues that mattered most and allowed the company to restructure its efforts into several focus areas that would guide the company's sustainability efforts.

UNDERSTAND THE CULTURE AND BLEND

The culture that develops around a business is a reflection of both the individuals involved and the group dynamic. As such, being mindful of a company's culture is critical to success in any corporate endeavor, including sustainability. AT&T's challenge was particularly unique as it was integrating several separate corporate cultures into one cohesive company.

Nothing better illustrates the need to be mindful of a company's culture than the effort that was undertaken at AT&T to produce and publish the company's first carbon footprint. Simply suggesting that developing and publishing a carbon footprint would be the right thing to do would not be sufficient. It had to make sense to the company from a business perspective, too. To garner support, efforts were made to link the need to produce the carbon footprint with the company's efforts to better understand its energy use and control its energy-related costs. AT&T had continually assessed its energy consumption; conducting a carbon footprint analysis was presented as another way to examine energy output and provide additional data points to identify the key drivers of AT&T's energy consumption.

Disclosing AT&T's footprint was another matter altogether. This ran counter to a culture disinclined to publish otherwise closely held numbers absent a compelling reason. Again, understanding this aspect of the internal culture helped guide the rationale on why to publish this information. AT&T is in a very competitive market, and it was this competitive element that presented the best opportunity to build a business case supporting the disclosure of this information.

AT&T examined Fortune 10 companies, as well as peers in the telecommunications industry, and discovered that many of the other companies already had published their carbon footprints. AT&T also watched and reported on the generally favorable public response to corporate disclosure of this information. AT&T went on to track the increasing number of customer, investor, media and analyst requests asking for information about its carbon footprint. Finally, the sustainability team sought the opinions of credible third-party organizations in the environmental space. The team shared the potential risks and opportunities that could be lost over the coming months and years if the company did not disclose its carbon footprint.

The findings compiled from internal research dovetailed with evidence of the increasing external pressure of government regulation, as well as a growing interest from key nongovernmental organizations and socially responsible investors to disclose this information. Collectively, these elements built a compelling and ultimately successful case for disclosure and allowed frank conversations about the reputation risks associated with failing to do so. Ultimately, AT&T disclosed its U.S. footprint in December 2009.

While this was a significant achievement, the sustainability team recognized it was one step in the journey. The next step is how to address the issue of potential carbon emission reduction goals. There are strong cultural currents that must be considered in connection with this decision, including both the competitive nature of the company and the corporate culture that demands accurate and detailed information and comprehensive plans before committing to any goal. Plans to move forward are under robust discussion and development.

TAKE BABY STEPS: LEARN BEFORE YOU LEAP

AT&T is a large company, and each decision has the potential to affect shareholder value, company profits and employee morale, among myriad other effects. As with any initiative, small steps that enable the company to assess impact are often favored over sweeping actions. AT&T's corporate fleet effort provides the best illustration of this approach.

After the mergers, AT&T found itself with one of the largest commercial fleets in the country. With the unpredictability and spikes in fuel prices, the company realized it would need to reduce its fuel consumption—particularly when an increase of just a few pennies at the pump could cost the company millions of dollars each year. In 2007, AT&T put more than 100 alternative fuel vehicles, including compressed natural gas trucks and hybrid electric passenger cars, through an initial trial. AT&T deployed the vehicles in different geographies and weather patterns to better assess their performance. AT&T had been concerned that people would say the effort was miniscule given the size of its fleet—a proverbial "drop in the bucket." But it made business sense to first conduct a trial before committing to a larger fleet. Although anticipating negative feedback, AT&T was pleasantly surprised by the positive response the initiative received both in the media and from environmental groups.

The effort was almost universally reported as a smart approach to a complex issue—experimenting with different technologies to see which worked best before making significant investments. The trial was successful, and although there remains no single alternative fuel technology that can answer all the company's needs, AT&T learned which type of alternative fuel vehicles performed best in specific geographies across the company's broad geographic footprint. AT&T was also able to calculate the long-term fuel savings the company could potentially achieve if a significant investment were to be made in these vehicles.

After the successful trial, in 2009 AT&T announced its intention to deploy approximately 15,000 alternative fuel vehicles through 2018. The fuel cost savings certainly helped the bottom line, and the announcement also signaled a demand for more fuel-efficient vehicles. AT&T is applying the same "learn before you leap" approach to all-electric vehicles. By early 2011 AT&T had deployed more than 3,500 alternative fuel vehicles, including more than 2,500 compressed natural gas vehicles. AT&T is testing several all-electric vehicle models, along with heavy-duty trucks, to assess performance before determining whether to make significant investments. Beyond the bottom line and environmental benefits, this effort has produced an unforeseen internal benefit: the initiative has become a source of employee pride throughout the company.

A WORK IN PROGRESS: SISYPHUS WOULD BE PROUD

Driving sustainability throughout the company remains a work in progress. At times, it can feel much like Sisyphus did in the ancient Greek myth—always pushing a boulder up a hill. Never quite able to get the boulder to the top, it would fall back down. Sisyphus would forever keep trying. But, AT&T also understands that meaningful change does not happen overnight, and it is important to adjust expectations accordingly. Three years into this journey, the pace of integration is steady, but at times it is a slower pace than some would like. AT&T has numerous business units across the company. Many of these business units understand the relationship between sustainability and its core business function; others are less mature in their development.

Beyond the pace of progress, AT&T communicates its sustainability efforts in ways that, at times, have run counter to a traditional approach. The tendency for most companies is to discuss its efforts in very bold terms. This approach, however, is not always appreciated or viewed as the most credible by those in the sustainability space, many of whom expect companies to express their commitments and achievements with humility and candor. While this effort remains a work in progress, AT&T tries to follow four criteria when communicating about sustainability:

1. Communicate in a humble tone, and discuss efforts in terms of aspiration.

2. Be transparent with information and progress.

3. Let others speak out on its progress.

4. Discuss results in tangible and understandable terms.

Additionally, when the company releases its annual Sustainability report, it attempts to discuss in specific and quantifiable terms its impact on the communities in which it operates. For example, it will discuss the total number of hours employees and retirees volunteered in their communities, the total amount of philanthropic contributions and employee giving and the specific reductions in energy and fuel consumption.

Despite the challenges the company faces when publishing goals, over the past two years AT&T has made significant progress in both the development and disclosure of goals and metrics to measure the company's success in nearly all of its initiatives. The goals that AT&T develops are based on consensus. Some goals may not go far enough for some, but they are established in ways that work within AT&T's culture. AT&T will continue to strive for transparency in its goals and key performance indicators. AT&T's 2011 goals can be found online at www.att.com/Common/about_us/citizenship/Our_Goals.pdf.

Finally, economic realities and factors beyond anyone's control, like the price and availability of alternative energy, can sometimes limit the ability to make wholesale changes in operations as quickly as desired. These issues will not reverse AT&T's long-term path, but as with other companies, they do sometimes present challenges to developing aggressive short-term goals.

AT&T's sustainability efforts remain a work in progress. Success comes in many forms, whether it be a company-wide change in policy or an incremental step forward within one business unit.

THE FUTURE

MOVING FORWARD: WHAT IS NEXT

When AT&T started this effort, the decision was made to operate with a well-thought-out approach—one that had a formal governance structure with committees in charge of driving sustainability into the business operations. Since that time the company has come to realize that each employee can be a source of new, innovative ideas that drive sustained change and better position AT&T for long-term success. Over the past year AT&T has begun to take steps that would empower and engage its total employee base in a voluntary initiative called "Do One Thing," or "DOT."

A simple concept, the effort is an invitation for employees to voluntarily adopt a practice—"do one thing"—that positively influences them personally, their community or the company. In 2010, the company launched a series of four pilot programs for DOT. The information and key findings are helping inform and guide the employee roll-out this year.

AT&T is also taking additional steps to further drive sustainability into the culture of its company. One example in particular bears mentioning. In 2010 the company initiated an energy scorecard of its top 500 energy-consuming buildings, while providing incentives for corporate real estate managers to meet or exceed specific energy reduction targets. This brought about more than 4,200 energy projects being implemented in one year that saved the company a total of $44 million in annualized revenue.

Finally, for AT&T to credibly promote its products' effectiveness in minimizing its customers' environmental impact, it needs to ensure that efforts to minimize its own environmental impact are in sync. Employee telecommuting is such an example of "walking the talk," and is an issue that presented some challenges. Similar to internal concerns about publishing AT&T's carbon footprint, some viewed the benefits as counterintuitive, being concerned about sacrificing productivity and effectiveness of their work groups. It also was a source of culture clash, as the premerged companies had vastly different telecommuting policies.

These challenges have diminished as AT&T has communicated the areas of shared values: senior management understands that, when properly implemented and managed, there are many sound business reasons for the company to expand the number of employees who telecommute, all while supporting an action that helps society. Over the past two years, the company has made substantial progress in this effort and has realized significant real estate cost reductions. The company also has noted an increase in employee productivity and job satisfaction among the employees who are telecommuters.

AT&T has enabled virtual working for nearly half of its total workforce with mobile and remote access technologies. The company recently surveyed the telecommuter population to determine the environmental impact of the program, as well as to measure its effectiveness and ancillary benefits. The survey asked a series of questions related to transportation method, commute distance, number of telecommuting days or weeks, vehicle type and year and number of errand miles.

Coupling that data with the Fuel Economy Guide from the Department of Energy and the Environmental Protection Agency, the company found that by reducing its employees' commute, AT&T's telecommuters avoided 175 million total commute miles, saved approximately 8.7 million gallons of gasoline and avoided total greenhouse gas emissions of 76,000 metric tons—the equivalent of removing 14,788 passenger vehicles from the road for a year.

In turn, this saved on average 54 minutes of commute time per employee. Approximately 85 percent of survey respondents agreed that increases in productivity and work-life balance were the top reasons they telecommute. More than 95 percent of telecommuters surveyed agreed or strongly agreed that they are more productive when working from home, and an equal number similarly agreed that telecommuting is important to their job satisfaction.

While AT&T has been getting its own house in order by allowing a greater number of employees to telecommute, the company has also been aggressive in communicating the economic and environmental benefits of its products and services to customers, helping it to capture market share in the emerging low carbon market. To help identify and communicate these benefits more effectively, the company created a sustainability council, comprising leading environmental nongovernmental organizations, academics, customers and suppliers.

THE JOURNEY CONTINUES: THE ONLY CONSTANT IS CHANGE

Sustainability is not a static endeavor. To be successful in the long term, a company must continually evolve to meet the changing needs of society. In the beginning of this chapter, we discussed the main reasons that drove

AT&T's renewed desire to strengthen its commitment to integrate sustainability into its business operations. Those issues still exist today.

Over time, however, issues ebb and flow. A company needs to continually assess trends and determine their impact on its business operations. To answer this need, AT&T conducted a second materiality assessment three years after its initial assessment. This new assessment enabled the company to identify new trends and their impact on the business success of the company. It also enabled AT&T to evaluate progress that had been made, and changes still needed on the path of progress. For AT&T, the most significant issues identified in this recent assessment included:

- Energy consumption

- Network security and reliability

- Supply chain standards

- Innovation

- Education

Over the next two to three years, the above issues will be key priorities for AT&T. And while the company's approach to sustainability will remain focused on identifying those societal issues that directly intersect with its business strategy, the ways in which the company expresses this relationship will change, too.

The public at times shows cynicism for company actions that aren't completely altruistic. But growing demands by consumers for transparency are beginning to reveal the public's acceptance, and in fact respect, for companies that point out the business value of their actions. There is growing recognition of "shared value," and growing understanding that, without business value, a company's action cannot be sustainable. Shared value is not "social responsibility"; rather, it is a recognition that social good and economic success can and should co-exist. It is not on the margin of what companies do, but at the center. AT&T and others believe that this approach is beginning to transform business thinking.

CONCLUSION

AT&T's definition of sustainability is simple: it is a way of doing business that benefits both society and the company in specific and tangible ways. The fact that AT&T has been in existence for more than 130 years is proof that sustainable business practices have been part of its operating system. What has changed, however, is the realization that businesses need to take additional steps to bring more focus, discipline and value to these efforts. It is not a passing fad at the company, and AT&T strongly believes sustainability is increasingly important to customers, investors and to its bottom line.

This belief is the main motivation for AT&T to detail publicly its approach to addressing these issues. It did so with the hope that other companies might be able to learn from AT&T's experience, and perhaps find useful insights that could help their own journeys. AT&T's intent is for this report to have made the business case for operating a company in a way that recognizes the positive value found at the intersection of society and business—a value that translates into long-term health of the company and the communities where it does business.

DISCUSSION QUESTIONS

1. How would a company define sustainability that is relevant to its business?
2. What would some of the criteria be to make the business case for integrating sustainability into its long-term business strategy?
3. For a company coming out of a series of mergers, how should this new company approach developing its sustainability strategy?

4. Is it more effective to adapt the culture of a company to its sustainability strategy or try to integrate sustainability into the company's culture?

5. If sustainability is not personally championed and driven by a company's CEO, what recommendations would you provide to integrate sustainability into its business operations?

6. What are some of the methods a sustainability officer can use to further integrate sustainability into the company's business operations when the officer has no ability to mandate that it be done?

7. What are the steps a large, multinational company should take to identify the most relevant sustainability issues important to its business success?

8. What are some of the communications challenges a company might face while promoting green initiatives?

ADDITIONAL READING

AT&T Sustainability media kit: http://www.att.com/gen/press-room?pid=2644.
AT&T Sustainability news room: http://www.att.com/gen/press-room?pid=2644.
2010 AT&T Sustainability report: http://www.att.com/csr.

28

C H A P T E R

ENVIRONMENTAL COMMUNICATION
A Matter of Relationships, Trust and Planning

Susan Croce Kelly, APR
President, Kirkpatrick International, Inc.

> *Think like a wise man, but communicate in the language of the people.*
>
> —William Butler Yeats

These days, in our world of instant communication and instant access to information, there is no wiggle room between talking the talk and walking the walk. There are too many people watching.

A company that wants to be seen as a good environmental citizen or wants to effect a positive outcome on an environmental issue/initiative has to *be* a good environmental citizen or be taking significant steps in that direction. The public demands action, wants answers and will tell the rest of the world if those things are not forthcoming.

There is real value for companies to be seen as "green." Green products, manufacturing processes and an environmental philosophy all can contribute to an organization's bottom line and public acceptance. But woe to the organization that promotes greenness without being able to back it up. This is called "greenwashing," and it carries such a stigma that some companies are afraid to speak up even about positive developments for fear they may be misconstrued. Likewise, any industrial or real estate project that requires public approval had better meet the green smell test as well. Today, there is a whole blogosphere and activist industry of its own just waiting to match up corporate talk and actions—and point out the discrepancies.

At the same time, more companies are adopting an environmental ethic, looking for alternative energy sources and changing to environmentally friendly manufacturing processes and other earth-friendly ways of operating. Many developers place environmental concerns front and center before launching building projects. The food industry recognizes that consumers want to purchase products that come from nearby and (if they do not cost too much more) are grown organically.

All in all, this is a great time to be practicing environmental communication. This chapter suggests ways that a communicator can support a company's or client's environmental efforts by helping prepare for, think through and launch an environmental initiative, whether it be *positive*, as in gaining public acceptance for a new real estate development, *defensive*, as in holding the line to save an existing product/practice from being eliminated or *reactive*, as in responding to an environmental crisis.

CHANGES IN THE PAST DECADE AND HISTORY

Back in 1990, Deloitte Touche and the Stanford Graduate School of Business conducted a survey of industrial businesses. Among those surveyed, 45 percent of the executives believed that environmental issues are critical to a company's well-being. A larger group, 68 percent, rightly said that environmental issues would increase in importance.[1]

Since then, the American public has embraced environmentalism. Even in an economically difficult year like 2010, fully 61 percent said they were either active or sympathetic to the environmental movement.[2] A significant number of us recycle and are willing to purchase products that advertise themselves as green.[3] Laws and regulations favor waste minimization, green practices and alternative energy.

The green ethic in this country has come in waves, ebbing during tougher economic times, only to reappear later with new strength.

The first great American environmental movement began in the late 1800s and was championed by people like John Muir, who sought preservation of the country's unspoiled wilderness. Although President Theodore Roosevelt disagreed with Muir in that he saw value in putting forestland to "wise use," he pushed for creation of our wonderful National Park system. The Sierra Club was founded in 1892 with Muir as its first president.

At roughly the same time, the industrial revolution was ushering in concerns about working conditions and issues with pollution. In the 1920s, dirty air from coal-powered factories was so invasive that in St. Louis, the now world-famous Missouri Botanical Garden purchased property 35 miles out of town and prepared to move its most delicate plants. Fortunately, industry found ways to remove enough soot from the air that the Garden—and American cities—survived.

Later, in the prosperous aftermath of World War II, the public again became concerned about what was happening to the nation's air and water. Smog issues in Los Angeles were in the national news almost daily. In the 1950s, a generation of children probably had their first view of environmental responsibility by taking part in the national "Don't be a Litterbug" campaign to clean up America's highways.

Then in 1962, a slim book riveted the nation's attention on an increasingly polluted United States. *Silent Spring*, by naturalist Rachael Carson, pointed to the problems of pesticides in the environment, ultimately resulting in the banning of the pesticide DDT. The book was a success because the problems were real, and they were obvious. One of the most dramatic occurred in 1969, when Cleveland's polluted Cuyahoga River spontaneously caught fire.

The next decade was a time of wake up and awareness. These years saw the formation of the Environmental Protection Agency (EPA) and the Occupational Safety and Health Administration (OSHA) and the passage of the Clean Air and Clean Water Acts. Because of these laws, this was also a decade when companies were brought to task for past actions involving the environment. Public concerns about old chemical dumps, asbestos contamination and links between chemicals and cancer all forced corporations into actions to clean up, stop producing and look for new ways to deal with the environment.

Water quality improved rapidly. Air pollution was cut back dramatically partly as a result of installing catalytic converters on cars. Nuclear safety increased after an accident at the Three Mile Island nuclear reactor.

It was during this period that companies began to employ public relations professionals specifically to help tell their side of the environmental story. Although early environmental public relations involved assisting companies that found themselves in crisis, the profession also had a hand in helping companies find their way in the new world of environmental awareness and corporate responsibility. Monsanto Company in St. Louis was a leader among technology companies during this era, initiating the Chemical Facts of Life program in the late 1970s—with the tagline "No chemical is safe all the time everywhere, but without chemicals, life itself would be impossible"—as a proactive communication initiative for the company's business. Monsanto issued the first report on Corporate Social Responsibility in the early 1980s.

The ante was upped when one of the words most often associated with *environment* was *disaster*. These were years in which a pesticide plant in Bhopal, India, blew up poisoning thousands of people, a nuclear disaster occurred in the Ukraine, and the Exxon Valdez spilled hundreds of thousands of gallons of oil in Alaska's coastal waters.

Congress passed toxic waste legislation, and established a Superfund for orphan site cleanup. And corporations began to talk seriously not just about cleanup but also responsibility.

By the 1990s, public attention was shifting from pollution and toxics-related issues to global concerns about such things as food safety, climate change, biodiversity and alternative energy. The environmental movement became an industry of its own as these concerns only grew after the turn of the century. More than ever, corporations learned to embrace a green ethic and, with it, saw the need for a cadre of environmental professionals to help focus their efforts and communication professionals to tell their side of the story. In more than one case, environmental groups and industry found common ground for successful collaborations.

At the same time, a relatively static communications world of television, newspapers, meetings and mailings was beginning to see the first inklings of competition from the Internet.

The result is that what began as a defensive public relations specialty is now three:

- *Environmental communications.* Today, there is still a need for sophisticated communication professionals to guide management in its relationships with a variety of publics when the subject is the environment.

- *Green PR and marketing.* A growing specialty that encompasses all kinds of businesses and products. Because an environmentally minded public prefers to know that the products and services they consume have been provided in ways that do not harm the environment, green PR has become a prominent part of corporate publicity and marketing, just as green products are a plus for a company's bottom line.

- *Sustainability communication.* Likewise, companies want consumers and the public to know that they operate with an eye to their place in the world. Sustainability, defined as meeting the needs of the present without compromising the ability of future generations to meet the needs of the future, is a goal that a vast number of today's businesses strive for—to the point that sustainability communications is big business. (See Chapter 27 for further discussion.)

PLANNING, IMPLEMENTATION AND EVALUATION: BEGIN WITH A HEALTHY CORE

It is greed to do all the talking but not want to listen at all.

—Democatus

At its core, the practice of environmental public relations is not much changed from what it was a decade ago, nor is it different from other aspects of modern communication. It is about carefully assessing a situation, building relationships and finding ways to gain people's emotional support for what the company is doing. It is also about listening.

The world, however, has changed a great deal in the past decade. The immediacy of our electronic world, especially the social media, can preclude the luxury of taking weeks to plan and obtain approvals. This is why up-front preparation is so vitally important.

Today, any organization or company should have a core communication program in place that acknowledges its many stakeholders and their need to know the company's history, philosophy and present activities.

This should include at least a website, corporate blog, traditional news release and video news release program, You Tube, Facebook and Twitter accounts. If you do not have an electronic employee newsletter, start one. Speakers bureaus, open houses, mailings—traditional means of communication are still necessary, but they cannot substitute for an active Internet presence.

A website, of course, is the face of your or your client's organization and should provide the basic information not only about who you are and what you do, but your philosophy toward the environment. Many company and organization websites present the sustainability of operations as well as explain day to day operations.

At Monsanto Company, an international producer of seed and agricultural chemicals, the Monsanto Pledge, which began as a way for executives and public relations staff to talk to the rest of the world, has truly become institutionalized as the way the company conducts business.[4] The Monsanto Pledge is posted on the homepage of the company website:

The Monsanto Pledge is our commitment to how we do business. It is a declaration that compels us to listen more, to consider our actions and their impact broadly, and to lead responsibly. It helps us to convert our values into actions, and to make clear who we are and what we champion. (Monsanto.com)

Beyond a website, start a regular blog about day-to-day business, products, events of interest, news that affects the company and the like. And have a Twitter account. Twitter will serve two purposes: it will allow you to keep your stakeholders aware of what you are up to and be the most immediate way to get in touch should a crisis occur. You will also be in touch with some of your most vocal detractors. This is valuable for two reasons: you will know what they are saying, and you can initiate contact to correct mistakes or get your message out before someone else speaks for you.

Glynn Young, director of Social Media for Monsanto, notes that since much of what is on the web is out of date, it is not uncommon for particularly juicy nuggets to find their way back into the Internet conversations years after they were put to rest. Young recalled correcting the date on a bit of tweeted "information"—it was 10 years out of date—with a timely tweet of his own, which kept the misinformation from going viral. Had Monsanto not been engaged in social media, the old information could have caused a real headache for the company.

Be familiar with media and blogs that regularly cover your client/company, and know the political leaders in your industry and home community. This way, when the time comes to initiate or defend the company's environmental activities, gain acceptance for an environmental project, launch a green product or manage an environmental crisis, the basic tools and communications networks will already be up and running.

Despite the ubiquitous presence of the electronic media, do not overlook traditional communication channels, especially in places where your company, organization or client has a physical presence or large group of customers. Build a line of communication with the people and members of the media who will most likely be out in front should an environmental disaster occur or if a back-burner environmental issue comes to the forefront. Despite concerns about the disappearance of traditional news sources, they serve as a resource for the social media. Media lunches, executive briefings, miniseminars on environmental issues, editorial board meetings and tours of building sites, research, manufacturing, or waste disposal facilities all help educate the media and public and build relationships that are so important when something goes awry.

LAUNCHING AND MANAGING AN ENVIRONMENTAL INITIATIVE

To be prepared is half the victory.

—Miguel de Cervantes

Any successful environmental communications initiative, whether mounted by an old line corporation, a non-government organization (NGO), a marketing team, or some other organization, will include four steps: goal, planning, implementation and evaluation.

STATE YOUR GOAL

State the desired outcome. This sounds simple but may be the most difficult part of the whole exercise. What exactly does your company, client or organization want to accomplish? Your statement should be as specific as possible (e.g., change the zoning laws to allow our construction project). Manage the successful introduction of a new green product as measured by dollars in sales. Convince the public that your client, company or association is working in good faith to rectify the results of an oil spill and regain their trust so we can continue to work in this environment. Manage the food recall in such a way that our company/product is not ruined, etc.

Make sure that there is agreement among those involved—management, legal, marketing, government affairs, manufacturing and so forth—that this is in fact what you want to accomplish. It will guide you in the development of your plan and also be the basis for your after-the-fact evaluation.

PLANNING

First, Assess the Situation

Every company or organization should have, or have access to, an ongoing issue-scanning program to stay abreast of environmental initiatives, new legislation and public concerns. It should also conduct an assessment when launching a new initiative or when faced with a crisis (the latter will clearly need to be done very quickly).

This information is vital to accurately understand the strengths and weaknesses of the initiative or project, and what key stakeholders are thinking and also what they feel. Although there are a number of commercial groups that monitor issues for businesses, there are also plenty of low-cost approaches, beginning with Google alerts. And do not forget to ask employees, customers and supplier groups!

Regardless of how it is accomplished, every organization should make a point of knowing what is being said about it and by whom.

Even if you conduct regular assessments, it's a good idea to conduct a specific assessment before you launch a new initiative so you know in economic, environmental, political and human terms where your strengths lie, your vulnerabilities, the opportunities that exist and potential threats to your success.

Sometimes you will not have the luxury of time, as spinach growers found in 2008 when salmonella in fresh spinach packages caused several deaths and a nationwide recall.

Especially in a crisis situation, though, it is valuable to understand public emotions at that particular point in time and know where you can marshal support. How much better it is to be able to quickly update existing information and relationships than to have to react totally in the dark.

Next, Conduct an Analysis

Basically, the analysis should look at how well you are equipped to achieve your goal. What are the strengths of your company, product or situation? What are the weaknesses? Opportunities? Threats? How does this translate economically? To the environmental situation? In human terms?

Put together a cross-functional group to conduct your analysis. Such a group should include, as appropriate, operations, legal, human resources, manufacturing and communications. This will help assure the comprehensiveness of the resulting plan, its ultimate acceptance and your ability to put it into play.

If, for example, an agricultural chemical company is seeking to launch a new biological pesticide, the analysis might consider the following:

Strengths

- The company may market only pesticide products with extremely good environmental profiles.

- The CEO is considered an industry leader and is a good spokesperson.

- Other manufacturing strengths might be a state-of-the-art manufacturing plant, an occupational safety and health program that shows a history of healthy workers and a healthy workplace or an energy co-generation process that minimizes the use of fossil fuels.

- The new product probably has its own list of strengths: high efficacy, totally natural—found in nature in small amounts produced biologically.

- The company has an ongoing communication program in place and an interactive relationship with employees, customers, government officials, plant communities, regulators and activist groups that follow food and agriculture issues.

- The CEO and other officers regularly give speeches, which are shared throughout the industry and shared with customers.

Weaknesses

- The company's products are sold only in throwaway plastic jugs, a disposal problem nationwide.

- There is an old hazardous waste site on land once used for chemical loading operations where the new plant will be constructed. (However, if the loading site cleanup is dealt with effectively, it also may be a potential opportunity to talk with the media and position the company as a leader in taking responsibility for the environment.)

Opportunities

- Communication opportunities may exist in the product itself, which is naturally derived rather than a synthetic chemical, and is not genetically engineered.

- The CEO is known in the industry and is willing to be an active participant in the initiative.

- The company is developing some new kind of packaging for the product, thus upping the environmental profile and giving it an advantage over competitors.

Threats

- The EPA has pending regulations that limit bulk transportation of certain kinds of chemical pest control products. This might pose issues for the company's manufacturing operation and other products while the new product is being introduced, thereby causing confusion among the stakeholders.

- There also may exist a crossover threat from the general public's concerns about chemical pesticide residues in food.

- Some activist groups seek to eliminate all pesticides from the environment.

- Potential confusion exists about the new biological pesticide—that because it is biological it is a genetically modified product. This may result in legislative concerns about food safety.

From this list, and yours will probably be much longer, a picture will emerge of how your goal fits into the company's world. Look at potential political and economic cost and benefits. Consider which items are most significant and prioritize them according to what must immediately be dealt with and what needs to be prepared for.

Your company or client will have scientists, lawyers and other professionals to handle the facts of the situation. Facts are important, but all too often, facts are not enough. The communicator's unique challenge is to take on the emotional component—the relationships. How do customers, neighbors and/or others feel about your issue, product or goal? What do they fear? How will you address that?

CONSIDER YOUR STAKEHOLDERS

Life is partly what we make it, and partly what it is made by the friends we choose.
— Tennessee Williams

Where the environment is concerned, people at all levels are more inclined to believe people they know than those they do not. And although they tend to have a great deal of trust in scientists for information on science-related issues, they next look to friends and family, NGOs and citizen groups. Next on the list are journalists. Companies and elected officials are at the bottom.[5]

An environmental communicator should waste no time in developing networks of stakeholder groups, both the traditional way and online. Ideally, you should know your stakeholders—those on your side, and those who oppose what you are trying to accomplish—before this project even comes up, and be in touch via social media.

What groups are important to the company in this situation and how do they feel about it?

- *Employees.* Employees should always be kept inside the information loop. This is an obvious statement, but rarely as easy as it should be.

- *Governments.* Develop a working relationship with government officials at all levels, from local mayors and state legislators to members of Congress and appropriate regulatory officials. Should trouble hit, an existing relationship pays big dividends.

- *Neighbors.* Work with community relations professionals to be sure that plant city neighbors in particular are kept apprised of company activities.

- *Interest groups*. Who might care about what you are doing? Develop a working contact list for everyone from local Rotary (in plant cities and small communities) to environmental groups and other NGOs that care about what you are doing. Thanks to the Internet, others who care about what you are doing will make themselves known as well.

- *Shareholders, customers, suppliers, trade associations.* These are all potential allies. Keep them informed.

- *Media*. While traditional media is dwindling, they serve as a source to the blogosphere. Find out who covers your company, issue or products—get in touch and go visit them if you can.

Today, it is impossible to overemphasize the need to create and maintain networks of friends—and also people who would be most likely to question your actions.

Once issues, audiences and potential sources of expert support are identified and your analysis completed, draft your communications plan.

STRATEGY AND TACTICS

STRATEGY

What is your overall communication strategy to achieve your goal? Do you want to be transparent and available? Limit communication? Speak only on specific occasions or through experts? Work through industry associations or other groups?

Ideally, you should be able to state your strategy in a sentence or two. Where you can, opt for transparency, get out in front with your messages and plan to be available.

List the tactics that will achieve your strategy. As you develop your tactics, consider the following: How can you engage with your target audiences in such a way that they not only hear what you have to say, but move to your side? How will you introduce your project or initiative to your stakeholders? What support material or activities need to be created? What activities need to take place? What are the political aspects of the project? How will you inform politicians or government organizations and/or regulators? What kind of information or reassurance do they need in order to proceed as you would like? What are the economic considerations? What if the project is delayed? Can you marshal experts to your goal? What are the groups and organizations that support your cause? What is in it for them?

Somewhere between setting a strategy, creating a hierarchy of tactics and beginning implementation, prepare a budget. This will dictate the scope of the final communication initiative. You may not be able to do all the things you believe are needed, but if you set a budget and prioritize activities by their importance, you will be able to remain focused and stay on track.

The following are some of the tactics to consider.

TACTIC 1: MAKE IT INTERACTIVE AND EMPATHETIC

Since so many environmental issues turn on questions of public risk, a communication strategy that does not consider the emotional side of the issue probably will not succeed. Companies that once said, "Trust us," have learned that what the public wants to hear first is an acknowledgement of and a respect for their concern. People often are actually less concerned about the risk to themselves than they are outraged over their lack of control and the sense of fairness of a situation. This is why smoking and driving, both high-risk but voluntary activities, are accepted in a much different way than airline accidents or the threat of contamination in food, which are low risk but not controllable by the individual. The rise of social media has made this all the more obvious.

Acknowledge that people have a right to be concerned and that technology is often scary. A key to successful risk communication is ultimately based on honest, open, two-way communications that offer the audience opportunities to express fears and concerns and allow companies to address those particular fears.

Understanding the trigger points on both sides of an issue can greatly increase the opportunity for real dialogue to take place. Otherwise, if the public is concerned about one thing and you are busy telling them about something else (as is often the case), nothing is resolved and the problem is magnified. And do not forget that people may know exactly what you are saying and still may not agree with you.

TACTIC 2: EMBRACE THE MEDIA

Be first with information about your company/project to both traditional media and social media. This is the best way to ensure that people will hear what you say.

Tap social media to communicate with key audiences at a moment's notice. Or they will communicate with you. Or communicate with the rest of the world about you.

This speaks to the importance of quickly establishing an ongoing social media presence—Facebook, You-Tube, RSS feeds, Twitter accounts and so forth—something BP discovered to their sorrow in the aftermath of the Gulf Coast disaster when a rogue "tweeter" sending messages as @BPGlobalPR temporarily took control of BPs hapless communications.

Can the message be personified? Use your CEO if you can. This is the person in charge, and his or her word carries a lot of weight.

For years, business has believed, and members of the media agree, that news gatherers generally pay more attention to statements of environmental activists than businesspeople.[6] Part of the reason for this bias is that activists are traditionally more accessible and willing to talk to the press. They are also broadly active on the Internet. Businesspeople often feel that when they do talk to the media, they are misquoted and misrepresented and so are not eager for more encounters. Even if that is the case, business really has no choice but to try again. Similarly, many companies are far more comfortable sending out well-digested news releases or formal statements than engaging in conversations.

However, as was shown so graphically as far back as the 1992 presidential campaign when candidate Bill Clinton captured the nation's attention by appearing on MTV, engaging in face-to-face communication can have a huge impact on targeted audiences. That long-ago campaign was a precursor to the person-to-person engagement that exists today with social media.

TACTIC 3: BUILD RELATIONSHIPS WITH PERTINENT ENVIRONMENTAL GROUPS

Look for environmental or other groups who may share a common interest. True partnerships are not possible between all businesses and all environmental groups but they are valuable in situations where business and environmental groups share common goals.

Back in 1990, in one of the first major corporation–environmental collaborations, the Environmental Defense Fund (EDF) teamed up with McDonald's Corporation to phase out polystyrene burger containers. Since 2007, EDF has had an office in Bentonville, Arkansas, for the purpose of helping Walmart, the world's largest retailer, improve energy efficiency and reduce waste. A current project for EDF is creating a sustainability index for Walmart to use to assess the environmental performance of its 100,000 suppliers.

However, although industrial–environmental group collaborations can be beneficial to both sides, situations sometimes change. BP, for example, engaged in a number of projects with environmental groups, only to have those collaborations called into question when the April 2010 explosion and oil spill in the Gulf of Mexico led to a closer look at BP's existing shortcomings in areas of employee safety and environmental protection.

The Nature Conservancy, for example, has taken more than $10 million in cash and land contributions over the years from BP and has, in return, given BP a seat on its International Leadership Council. After the BP explosion, donors and the press questioned Nature Conservancy's actions. And although it might not have satisfied a lot of people, Nature Conservancy CEO Mark Tercek posted a statement that "Anyone serious about doing conservation in this region must engage these companies, so they are not just part of the problem but so they can be part of the effort to restore this incredible ecosystem."[7]

Other kinds of partnerships between business and environmental groups include unrestricted grants, cooperation on technical projects, political coalitions and workplace fundraising. If handled correctly, these partnerships can result in positive publicity, access by the corporation to group members, credibility for the corporation and even access to the group's political clout.

TACTIC 4: PLAN FOR A CRISIS

Even with a carefully thought-through strategy, it is a good idea to also have a crisis plan should an environmental issue erupt in an unforeseen manner. The crisis plan will vary somewhat depending on the industry and the potential for disaster, but all should share the same core segments and all should be updated on a regular basis. Although it might not be considered "environmental" communication per se, one wonders how much the marketing team knew about the content of the "fake blueberries" that were loaded into cereal and other foods sold by such giants as Betty Crocker, General Mills and Kellogg's before that story broke in January 2011.[8] Did they have a group of food experts on hand to diffuse the situation?

Confrontational media training for company executives and a blueprint for contacting key publics at a moment's notice, plus an internal emergency network that is tested periodically, are always a good idea, as is a list of well-informed outside experts who can speak on behalf of the company, or at least offer an informed perspective on what happened. Moreover, an active crisis plan keeps executives attuned to the need to stay on top of key issues, and that in itself is worth the time and effort. Creating and maintaining top-of-mind awareness among company management can go a long way toward preventing a crisis.

TACTIC 5: INCREASE VISIBILITY IN WASHINGTON AND STATE CAPITOLS

If an environmental issue can be associated with public laws or regulations, then it is a certainty that disgruntled or worried voters will be contacting their appropriate city council person, state legislator or member of Congress about it. Yet Congressional staff members who handle environmental issues are quick to point out that while activists are on the Hill year-round talking about their issues, industry or business people rarely show up until they have a concern. In dealing with Washington, as in dealing with any other relationship, an ongoing association is bound to be more successful than an intermittent, adversarial approach. One well-known lobbying firm in Washington always registers "FOR—with amendments" regarding bills they are working on because they believe that anything can be modified effectively, and a positive approach is always in their, and their client's, best interest.

TACTIC 6: DO THE LITTLE THINGS RIGHT

Before you decide to project your company or client as green, make sure that they are. Small things such as using recycled paper, recycling and other conservation measures can make a difference. What kind of environmental footprint do you have? Remember when the auto company leaders took their corporate jets to Washington, D.C., to ask for bailouts?

Although such gestures may not make a difference individually, taken together they send a message to employees and other stakeholders about an organization's commitment to bigger issues.

The Yellow Pages Group in Canada, for example, has taken a look at their practices and made paper conservation and recycling both a big part of what they do commercially and an everyday way of doing business. The phonebooks, of course, are totally recyclable and the company has mounted programs to help consumers do just that. In addition, one Yellow Pages company's Enviro-Action team looked at the company's internal needs and launched a duplex printing initiative to reduce the amount of paper used, plus an internal recycling program that goes beyond traditional collections of paper, plastic and glass to include recycling printer cartridges, batteries and even cellular phones.[9]

IMPLEMENTATION

Once you have established your plan and budget, create a timeline or a matrix showing known events such as hearings, meetings, plant open houses and planned communications. A public hearing might require a brochure to hand out, letter to the editor, video news release, issue-related blog and following the key testimony or countering factual errors on Twitter. Do this for each event and the result will be a work plan, budget and a blueprint for success.

This document will change as time passes and events occur, but it will serve as a starting place, a rallying point and a road map for the project.

If the organization has done its homework, a carefully prepared and executed communications plan should pave the way for a project's success.

EVALUATION

Every planning process should also include preparation for evaluating what you have accomplished. You might even want to conduct evaluations several times if the project is a long one so that changes can be made to correspond to changing aspects of the project.

Is there a readily quantifiable way to assess your outcome? Did you achieve a zoning change? Secure a permit? Launch a project? Perhaps your goal is to increase awareness. If that is the case, you might look at changes in hits, retweets and/or blog mentions. Measure changes in attitudes through questionnaires, increased activity of some anticipated type or decreases in negative activities, that is, picketing stopped, anti-organization blogging and Tweets diminished by x amount.

Did your program come in as budgeted?

However you decide, it is important to include an evaluation in your environmental communication planning.

CASE STUDIES

Here are examples of two environmental communications initiatives. Both are long term and involve the relationship between heavy industry and the rest of the world. The first is from the perspective of an industrial trade association: the communications aspect of a decision to phase out mercury in the chlorine manufacturing process in Europe. The other is an initiative undertaken by a citizen's group in Florida to fight encroachment by an industrial phosphate mining company.

MERCURY PHASE-OUT IN EUROPE

By Peter Whippy, former Communications Manager at Euro Chlor, the European association of chlorine producers. Whippy spent several years deeply involved in a pan-European communication initiative to phase out a key use of mercury in chlorine production.

Mercury is a toxic metal that is being progressively phased out of industrial applications worldwide because of concerns about its persistence in the environment and impact on human health.

The largest emitters of mercury to the environment are coal-fired power stations and waste incinerators. Cremation is also a significant source due to the volatilization of dental amalgam. The largest users, but not direct emitters, are chlor-alkali producers, which use mercury as a catalyst. However, environmental NGOs have attacked many applications of chlorine, particularly its major use in the manufacture of PVC plastics.

Greenpeace was the first to put the sector under the spotlight when it launched a worldwide anti-chlorine campaign in the late 1980s–early 1990s. Europe was particularly vulnerable because the majority of chlorine production was then based on the mercury electrolysis process.

European producers concluded early on that for broader health and environmental reasons, mercury production and use was vulnerable and could be eventually banned. The primary objective of producers, therefore, was to win enough time for the progressive, but costly, switch to an alternative non-mercury process. A key goal was to win breathing space to amortize existing plants (they have 30- to 40-year economic life spans) and reinvest billions of dollars in primarily the lower-energy membrane process.

The European Union (EU) strategy for mercury is to ban exports from 2011 onward, then require chlorine producers to safely store thousands of tons from decommissioned mercury-based plants deep underground as the remaining chlorine capacity is voluntarily phased out by 2020.

Euro Chlor, a Belgium-based business association of European chlorine manufacturers, spearheaded the sector's regulatory and communications strategies. Since the early 1990s, the association's role has been to help manage public expectations and neutralize efforts by industry opponents to accelerate the sunset of mercury cells.

The European public relations strategy was to adopt a policy of openness and transparency, particularly on scientific and technical issues. Euro Chlor was one of the first industry associations to implement a long-term industry sustainability program. It also launched several voluntary agreements as a way to influence legislation.

Communications tactics included a steady stream of data and information about chlorine production and use, along with scientific and regulatory developments. Besides keeping many key publics such as regulators and scientists informed, this information stream enhanced the association's reputation as a reliable and credible source of accurate information and prevented the formation of a vacuum that could be filled by opponents.

Some specific tactics include:

- A major international conference in 1994, titled "Chlorine and the Environment," targeted European and national regulators, scientists and media and was a platform for launching an industry sustainability program.

- Media visits to chlorine and PVC plants in Norway and rock salt mines in the United Kingdom were organized to show the inexhaustible nature of chlorine's main raw material, and how chlorine is made and used.

- Regular symposiums in Europe every three to four years on technical and safety matters. (See banner on home page at www.eurochlor.org.) Trade media is invited, but this is an internal industry event to share experience and encourage best practice in operating chlor-alkali plants.

- A steady stream of print material and website updates, including annual report showing progress on sustainability program; detailed information on location of all plants within the EU, process used, capacity, data on applications, etc., available on the website; monthly news releases (NRs) detailing EU chlorine and caustic soda production changes; and NRs on various topics of interest related to HSE (www.eurochlor.org, newsroom archives). Note: In recent years, there has been an increased reliance on the Internet as a communications tool, but because of the many languages spoken in the EU, there will always be more of a role for traditional media than would happen in the United States.

- Brochures, including a major cooperation with the United Nations Environmental Program to publish recommendations on municipal water treatment plants in a wide range of languages, along with a video on chlorine production and use.

- First-ever industry association poster campaign on chlorine applications in metro stations surrounding EU institution offices in Brussels.

- Humanitarian water relief program through World Chlorine Council, offering water purification chemicals in the aftermath of the December 2004 tsunami.

- First-ever industry association advertising campaign on Google.

- In 2010, a 20-year timeline brochure captured the communications strategy with its title: "About Transparency, credibility, having a good story and getting it accepted."

To date, the campaign has gone on for more than a decade, although the trade association has been scaling down communications activities for several years, and most country chlorine working groups have substantially reduced or ceased communications activities. This is because attacks on chlorine applications have substantially declined and most NGOs recognize the industry's 2010 voluntary commitment to cease using mercury cells.

For Euro Chlor, the challenge of promoting the sector and defending against opponents is not yet over, but much reduced. Undoubtedly, the decision, taken almost 20 years ago, to base the industry's defense strategy on openness and transparency has been successful. (See eurochlor.org.)

RESIDENTS RULE: THE FIGHT TO STOP PHOSPHATE STRIP MINING IN FLORIDA

By Honey Rand, Ph.D., APR. Rand is president of The Environmental PR Group, Tampa, FL. As she notes below, this case study involves only one skirmish in a long-running situation.

Environmental issues, like all issues, are complicated—at least for those of us who know too much. For those who don't not know "too much," the issues are much simpler and, many times, more emotional. Of course, this is true of all issues. Generally, the more we know, the more complicated the issues; the less we know, the easier it is to tease through them.

Dealing with environmental issues is more than "educating" or "engaging." Everyone who is married knows that the hardest thing in the world is to change an adult human's mind. Just because someone understands doesn't mean that person is going to agree.

Even more challenging, in environment-centered situations, is the fact that in too many instances the difference between "environmentalist" and "anti-growth" factions has blurred. They are not the same, although they can be on the same side. In many cases, no-growthers have hijacked environmental issues. All of this is to say that although there are some stable consistencies from issue to issue, there is also great variability. And, anywhere in the issue, politics can shift, changing everything.

In short, this work is not for the squeamish or for those who resist change. That applies to the "activists" as well as the agency.

In Florida, as in most states, there are specific rules, regulations and processes that provide the parameters of resource management, protection and allocation. These rules are developed through a public process in which all sectors have a say in their development. For business, the rules dictate what is required. For environmentalists and other watchdogs, the rules provide a benchmark to hold a certain standard.

Charlotte, Sarasota and Lee Counties, along with environmental and economic development groups, had been fighting the spread of phosphate strip mining into the Peace River basin. Strip mining and the failure or reclamation had already had a negative impact on river flow in communities upstream. Reduced water flows, opponents believed, would diminish the necessary inflow to Charlotte Harbor, a nationally designated estuary, and the heart of economic vitality for an entire region (Figure 28.1).

In one skirmish, the Florida Department of Environmental Protection (FDEP) offered the phosphate company a water quality variance. A variance typically allows an applicant some latitude in meeting rules. In this case, the variance was an allowance to have water with reduced oxygen discharged downstream to the river.

However, the variance had no restrictions so it really amounted to a waiver of water quality standards, and the FDEP did not have the authority to do that. Water quality is a federal issue.

Charlotte County filed suit to stop the variance.

People love their nearby waters and the residents living along the Peace River are no different.

Working with Charlotte County's attorneys, we developed a "shell" petition that made it much easier for residents to object. Assured that they were within their rights, many were still afraid. Lawyers offered to support the residents in the process at no cost, although they were threatened with time-consuming depositions by the phosphate company. Some were even told that if they refused to be deposed, liens would be placed against their homes.

Even in the face of phosphate company employees' threats of liens against their homes, the residents held firm.

Nearly 110 individuals joined the suit, which resulted in the attention of the media and the EPA. While 110 petitions may not sound like a lot, the media coverage underscored the bullying tactics of the phosphate company.

The FDEP had never had so many individuals intercede in a legal process. With their poor decision making highlighted to the media and EPA, the FDEP dropped the variance in a few short weeks.

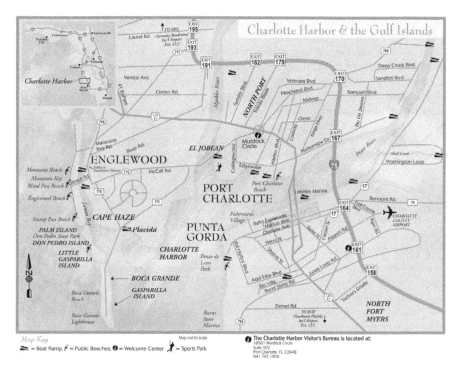

FIGURE 28.1

Charlotte Harbor, Port Charlotte, Florida

It was one skirmish victory in a battle that continues—ongoing for at least nine years. Extending the fight to wear out the combatants is a baseline tactic in many issues.

SOME FINAL CONSIDERATIONS

...Remember...on both sides that civility is not a sign of weakness and sincerity is always subject to proof...

—President John F. Kennedy
Inaugural address 1/20/61

Unfortunately, it is all too common for businesspeople—and communicators—to forget that there is a ceiling on successful communication efforts. That ceiling is the truth. If a company is not actually committed to operating in an environmentally sound way, or if the product is not really green, no environmental communication campaign can succeed for long. BP for example, shed their British Petroleum name a number of years ago for a slick marketing campaign that positioned BP as a company "Beyond Petroleum"—one that was actively working toward alternative fuel sources and systems. That message carried them through a deadly explosion at their refinery in Pasadena, Texas, but was shown for what it was when the Deepwater Horizon drilling ship in the Gulf of Mexico exploded, killing a number of people and spilling millions of gallons of oil in the Gulf. Today, as one Florida resident recently related, many people have trouble even turning into a BP station.

The need to walk the walk is so important in regard to the environment that fear of being accused of greenwashing has actually kept many companies, especially many industrial companies that are making incredibly positive changes, from talking about their actions.

So here the message is two-sided. Beware of greenwashing. The public will find you out and broadcast your sins across the Internet.

On the other hand, if you have your ducks in a row and a positive story to tell, don't hide your light under a bushel. Stakeholders need to hear that you have improved minimized waste, retrofitted a plant, changed a product line or introduced a new environmentally friendly product or process.

Part of a communicator's job is to convince clients and management of the value of knowing what's happening around them, looking forward and finding ways to move their operations in that direction. Even in down economic times, a majority of the public consider themselves to have an environmental ethic, and there is a growth market in environmental activist groups dedicated to changing the world.

As environmental communicator and writer Shel Horowitz commented, many of the technologies today that we consider new, different and creative will be common in five years. "Green is a process. There's always more to be done."[10]

Likewise, environmental communication is an important and growing field. There will always be more to do.

DISCUSSION QUESTIONS

1. Why is it particularly important to build long-term relationships with stakeholder groups when you are dealing with an environmental issue?
2. How has the history of environmental awareness in the United States contributed to present attitudes?
3. What are the four things to consider when conducting an analysis?
4. How big a role should social media play in environmental communications?
5. Since most people today get their news from the Internet, what is the value of traditional media in environmental communications?
6. Is the practice of environmental communications always confrontational? Should it be?
7. What role does emotion play?
8. Environmental communications situations or initiatives are often drawn out over many years. Why is this? Should they be?

NOTES

1. James T. Harris, "Working with Environmental Groups," *PR Journal* (May 1992), 24.
2. Gallup's 2010 Environmental Poll. Gallup.com
3. "Environmental Advocacy Grows Stronger for LGBT Americans," Harrisinteractive.com 12/15/10. http://harrisinteractive.com/NewsRoom/PressReleases/tabid/446/mid/1506/articleId/656/ctl/ReadCustom%20Default/Default.aspxhttp://harrisinteractive.com/NewsRoom/PressReleases/tabid/446/mid/1506/articleId/656/ctl/ReadCustom%20Default/Default.aspx.
4. Glynn Young, Director of Social Media, Monsanto Company. Interview, January 5, 2011.
5. The Editors, "In Science we Trust: Poll Results on How You Feel about Science," *Scientific American*, The Editors. October 2010.
6. Knapp, Inc., "Journalists Admit Environmentalists Get More Attention than Business." PR Newswire (January 13, 1992). This is a report on a survey of 100 media and 100 business people in 43 states.
7. "BP and Environmental Nonprofits: Conflicts and Complaints," OMB Watch. June 15, 2010, http://ombwatch.org/node/11068.
8. Shari Roan, "Fake Blueberries Abound in Food Products," *Los Angeles Times*, January 20, 2011. http://articles.latimes.com/2011/jan/20/news/la-heb-fake-blueberries-20110120.
9. "Yellow is Green," Think Green column, Yellow Pages Association, http://www.ypassociation.org/AM/Template.cfm?Section=Homes&TEMPLATE=/CM/HTMLDisplay.cfm&CONTENTID=5035.
10. Shel Horowitz, "Greenwashing Alert: Green Expert Shel Horowitz on BP, Green News & Tips," Commpro.biz Interview. 14 January 2011. http://www.commpro.biz/#slide+interviews&id=13.

ADDITIONAL READING

Cox, J. Robert. *Environmental Communication and the Public Sphere*. Sage Publications, Thousand Oaks, CA, 2010.

Dryzek, John S., and David Schlosberg. *Debating the Earth: The Environmental Politics Reader*, Second Edition. USA: Oxford University Press, 2005.

Layzer, Judith A. *The Environmental Case: Translating Values into Policy*, 2nd Edition. Washington, D.C.: CQ Press, 2006.

Levinson, Jay Conrad, and Shel Horowitz. *Guerilla Marketing Goes Green: Winning Strategies to Improve Your Profits and Your Planet*. Hoboken, NJ: John Wiley & Sons, 2010.

Rand, Honey. *Water Wars: A Story of People, Politics & Power*. Xlibris, 2001.

Shroder, Tom, and Kenneth Conrad. *Fire on the Horizon: The Untold Story of the Gulf Oil Disaster*. New York, NY: HarperCollins Publications, 2011.

29
CHAPTER

RELATIONSHIP TRANSFORMATION
Shifting Media Boundaries

Kevin Clark
President and Founder
Content Evolution LLC
Director, Emeritus, Brand and Values Experience
IBM Corporation

Markets Are Conversations

—Searles and Weinberger, *The Cluetrain Manifesto*[1]

A STRATEGIC APPROACH TO RELATIONSHIPS AND MEDIA EMERGENCE

Creating and maintaining relationships is at the core of communications and marketing practice. Media as an institution is moving off center stage and being joined and diffused by the constituencies that use and increasingly create content.

Even as media's boundaries shift, the fundamental role of media as extensions of human perception remains unchanged.[2] Media collapse time, overcome distances, extend the range of the human senses and increasingly connect and create conversations.

Push strategies in marketing and communications are being replaced by conversations, by interaction, by participation and co-creation of meaning.

The primary change agent for marketing and communications is the potential for global relationships and global culture. The primary driver for media transformation is digital technology. Digital media move with ease from one form to another, and blur the boundaries between organizations and individuals.

DIGITAL INTERACTORS

"Technology helps customers to adopt digital lifestyles," says Erich Joachimsthaler, president of Vivaldi Partners, a strategy consultancy based in Manhattan.

> Businesses drive toward digital processes. This development is based on two trends that make the world a smaller and more connected place: broadband networks being everywhere and the presence of ever more

powerful devices. Today, customers pull information whenever they need it, wherever they need it. Gone is the traditional thinking in channels or media options or alternatives. As a result, the media landscape is changing.[3]

New forms of media are being created at an astounding rate. They have made it possible for the nature of vocation and play—life and avocation—to merge. The publics we relate to are increasingly self-made categories that are constantly remixing, not a set of monolithic attitudes and attributes.

Increasingly, we're inheriting a generation of *interactors*—a term borrowed from biology to describe the real-life interactions with the environment. With a mobile phone in hand or networked game at hand, people growing up digital are wired to interact and make demands on the world around them.[4]

As player experience and interaction expert Nicole Lazzaro says,

Games connect goals with actions, motivations and emotions to create engagement and create value for all parties. Media from newspapers to email will become more gamelike to increase engagement. Traditional broadcast media shouts at the target market several million at a time. The web creates two-way conversations. Game-inspired media creates experiences that invite potential companies to come over to play.[5]

CONVERSATIONS AND COMMUNITIES

As the distinction between going to work and being engaged in social settings diffuses, the challenge will be choosing forms of interaction that help co-create meaningful and economically beneficial relationships. "Delivering messages" and "moving products" is giving way to conversations in an exponentially increasing marketplace of ideas.

New forms of digital media also change what constitutes a customer or public and where they exist. We live in a sea of virtual communities. Geographic boundaries are becoming less relevant as new virtual communities of interest spring up and gain strength. Where digital media is in wide use, people derive their identities from self-selected communities of interest rather than just national, professional or company affiliations.

These multiple roles place a new demand for client counsel based on improved access to and synthesis of relevant information and conversation streams from around the world.

David Martin, president of Interbrand, the world's largest brand consulting entity, says,

Our work reveals a dramatic shift in the relationship between companies and the people they serve, brought on in large measure by the rise of new forms of media. The emerging wide array of new interactive tools and social media has given people the ability to build a dialogue with the brands they bring into their lives. Through these tools, people can interact with brands similarly to the way they interact with humans in their lives. Increasingly people expect, even demand that their brands "relate" with them—to behave as if they are in a true partnership. This is giving rise to a whole new set of customer demands on the brands that want to play an important role in their lives.[6]

SOCIALLY NETWORKED ICONS AND BURSTS

One implication of digital communications and media convergence is a global population that is becoming increasingly iconic, gaining information from short bursts of written words and visual communications. This trend has profound implications for education, commerce and governance.

In an interactive world more suited to the "constituencies" and "publics" referred to in public relations practice for decades, the profession is deeply rooted in the written word. Today's practitioners need to continue developing keen ears—along with eyes and the rest of the human sensory system to be ready for a short-burst communications and icon-driven world.

In fact, gesture recognition is likely a new form of device interaction right around the corner. The Microsoft Kinect for the Xbox platform starts as game interaction, yet likely migrates quickly from gaming to other useful device interactions in everyday life. Notice how the touch-screen revolution has quickly created a generation of youth that expect screens to respond to touch. It is now common to hear parents report toddlers crawling up to traditional video screens or televisions and touching them, expecting something to happen, with disappointment or frustration.

We're now raising a generation expecting an interactive and socially networked world.

"By enabling interactions across organization boundaries not before possible, social media has altered how organizations attract and retain employees, increase the strength of their brands, and expand the outreach of their communications," says Andrea Goldberg, founder of Digital Culture Consulting.

> This more open and collaborative environment has resulted in organizations rethinking some of their basic tenets of membership, structure, and control and it has changed expectations of employee roles, engagement and leadership. In the near term, social media platforms will not only continue to grow as selection and retention tools, but they will become a vital part of how employees perform their jobs, how organizational knowledge is disseminated, how innovation is harnessed, now organization members select and engage with their leaders—and perhaps most important, the relationship employees are able to forge with internal and external stakeholders.[7]

Andy Hines, Lecturer and Executive in Residence at the University of Houston Futures Studies Program and founder of Hinesight, says, "social media are enabling not just two-way, but 'multi-way' conversations. The 'markets are conversations' insight described a decade ago is in full flower. Traditional communications models seeking to speak to an average or representative customer or segment are increasingly ineffective. The one-size-fits-all approach in effect fits none."

THE RISE OF COLLABORATIVE PERFORMANCE

Control systems are weakening; collaboration systems are strengthening and growing.

"We know more about people, companies, and things than ever before—and the implications for companies spread like the conversation threads themselves," says Ed Zuber, president and founder of Human Brandsources.

> The content and frequency of things that people say, or don't say, about their companies speak volumes. The companies that will thrive, I suspect, will be the ones that do first, and communicate those stories second. They will give employees and constituency's reasons to believe along with factual stories to inspire them. They will also unify the company brand characteristics and reputation throughout public relations, marketing, human resources and recruiting. That is, the successful won't be telling scattered schizophrenic stories; they'll be telling the same stories that are uniquely theirs, based on shared values, mission and vision, and those stories will have elements that speak to everyone.[8]

VALUE, VALUES AND VALUATION

The words value, values and valuation are used every day in organizations. They form a constellation of interlocking concepts that help inform business decisions and allocate scarce resources.

Value is understood as a fair exchange of money, or barter, for commodities, goods, services, experiences or transformations.

Values represent common ground for drawing economic actors and interactors together while creating trust for each other and the customers they serve.

Valuation is a translation of current and predicted ongoing economic worth, with intangible valuation being a repository of future sales—the estimate of customers' future desire to do business with a company. Intangible valuation is also a bank of goodwill that allows businesses to keep operating through periods of economic distress. Economic valuation is what attracts and retains investors.

An earlier version of these "3 V's" was first penned for Don Sexton's thoughtful book, *Value Above Cost*. [9]

Taken together, *values* inform why economic actors and interactors are drawn together to deliver *value* to a particular set of customers, resulting in *valuation* that attracts and retains investors. This, in turn, reinforces the *core value systems* that create and deliver customer value, forming a virtuous cycle of *value creation*.

In reverse order, valuation gets most of the attention from investors and Wall Street. What is it worth? You choose the "it"—product, service, experience or enterprise. Valuation is an expression of worth, good as far as it goes, yet limited in its numeric vocabulary.

Values tell you more. What a company has believed in the past and believes today will be more predictive in how it will behave and increase its valuation in the future. Values are more fundamental and express the long-term view of a sustainable enterprise.

In my book *Brandscendence*,[10] from the chapter "In Crisis, Culture is Destiny," I argue that values also inform members of the enterprise when to use their own judgment in the context of the company culture, and also predict how the enterprise will behave in crisis.

When you blend the core values of an organization and the valuation of what people are willing to pay for what they make or do, value is right in the middle of both concepts. Value encompasses both the tangible and intangible benefits that represent the total worth and frequency of transactions.

The dance of value, values and valuation represent both the art and science of brand management and customer experience strategy. Companies will pay close attention to all three when they embrace long-term customer relationships that are the foundation for sustained revenue and profit.

Elsie Maio, founder of Maio&Co, even sees the fabric of corporate social responsibility (CSR) dissolving into the way business is done. No longer a separate activity performed by a specialized staff, "doing well and doing good" become one continuum of seamless performance. Doing good is not the residue of having done well in the past for a limited set of constituents, and doing well is turbocharged and creates resilience when informed by a broad view of mission and service. The tectonic plates of commerce and governance are shifting in directions that point to an integrated view of all operating environments.

"Emerging values shifts are suggesting that people are making less of a distinction between their personal and their work life," says Andy Hines.

> They don't want to be one person at work and another at home, but seek to be their authentic self in all they do—and emerging communication media are making this increasingly possible. Prospective customers and employees can investigate organizations and see if their values are in alignment. They are bringing their values to their work, to organizations they believe in, in order to influence the organization to behave in a way that aligns with their values.

RELATIONSHIP BRANDS

"You can't make a bad company a good brand," says David Martin, president of Interbrand. He goes on to say,

> People are besieged with options as never before. Lives are more complex, time passes more quickly and choices are more numerous. Something's got to give for living to be more manageable. People cope by being far more selective regarding the brands they bring into their lives. They make quick decisions. Brands that don't make the cut are relegated to a locked mental box labeled "not for me." Once in that box, it's virtually impossible for a brand to escape.

> Those brands that make the cut are quickly sorted into two distinct groups—acquaintance brands and relationship brands. Acquaintance brands are like human acquaintances. They're in people's lives primarily for functional reasons; they are given little thought and can be out of people's lives as fast as they come in. On the other hand, relationship brands are central to people's lives. As with human relationships, these brands forge important multifaceted bonds that grow deeper over time. Without them, people feel a void. The best relationship brands become indispensable over time.

Like their human counterparts relationship brands earn people's relationship first and foremost by playing a unique and meaningful role in their lives. Something important and special happens as a result between people and their relationship brands. Life is enhanced through what happens in that relationship. Relationship brands play a meaningful, sustained role. Relationship brands secure long-term revenue flows by delivering value that is core to the lives of those they serve. This gives rise to a whole new set of customer demands on the brands that want to play an important role in people's lives. Success in the long run is predicated on understanding and fulfilling a unique role in the lives of those people companies want to serve. New media gives companies the tools they need to interact with those they serve in the fashion they wish to be related to—and unless companies carve out a distinct role, it will be easy for those they wish to serve to edit companies out of their lives.[11]

Jerry Michalski, founder of Sociate and REX (the Relationship Economy eXpedition), refers to an emerging "relationship economy" that thrives on trust and delivers abundance. His working thesis is that most economies function on the basis of allocating and distributing scarce resources, while the tools of the new economy taking hold make sharing more valuable than protectionist strategies, and the cost of replicating and distributing knowledge and capabilities starts to widely approach a zero marginal cost. The wiki phenomenon is a good example of this open contribution and availability model; most notably the creation of Wikipedia and the demise of the printed encyclopedia. These trends potentially usher in a whole new age in which our motivations and approaches to problem solving are completely rewired, and the role of communications and marketing is recast in new and more meaningful roles.

INTRINSIC MOTIVATION

Motivation is also a new battleground with the traditional forces of extrinsic rewards and punishments giving way to intrinsic motivations of individuals and organizations. Extrinsic is a vestige of command and control hierarchies, intrinsic is the world of opt-in, collaborative communication and innovation.

Both Daniel Pink in *Drive* and Clay Shirkey in *Cognitive Surplus* explore the concept of intrinsic motivation and its power to truly change hearts, minds, and get things done.

Pink shares examples in which "we leave lucrative jobs to take low-paying ones that provide a clearer sense of purpose." He talks about the behavioral scientists categories of algorithmic work where there is an "established set of instructions down a single pathway to one conclusion," and heuristic tasks that are the opposite where "you have to experiment with possibilities and devise a novel solution."[12]

In the heuristic world you have to come up with something new.

Pink cites work from McKinsey that estimates "In the United States only 30 percent of job growth now comes from algorithmic work, while 70 percent comes from heuristic work."[13] A key reason: "routine work can be outsourced or automaticed; artistic, empathetic, non-routine work generally cannot."[14]

Clay Shirkey says, reinforcing the Michalski premise, "Information can now be made globally available, in an unlimited number of perfect copies, at zero marginal cost. As a result, every mode of communication that once had to rely on market pricing can now have an alternative that relies on open sharing."[15] Shirkey cites the explosion of Wikipedia that essentially put *Microsoft Encarta*, *Encyclopedia Britannica*, *World Book*, and every other non-web encyclopedia reference out on the stoop. It's about intrinsic motivation and nontraditional economics and sharing. Note: I would not go so far as to say Wikipedia is "authoritative" yet; that is to say I don't believe it has fully found all the processes to ensure accuracy of what is contained in it. That said, it is a wonderfully collaborative phenomenon.

"Alexis de Tocqueville, the eighteenth-century historian, would have understood the advantages of cognitive surplus," continues Shirkey. "In this book *Public Associations in Civil Life*, he wrote: 'In democratic countries, knowledge of how to combine is the mother of all other forms of knowledge; on its progress depends that of all others.' Social production increasingly relies on de Tocqueville's 'knowledge of how to combine.'"[16]

People and organizations increasingly want to combine to create mutual benefit.

People are less interested in being customers than they are being members.

People want to be members of something where they have a voice. As American Express has been saying for decades, "membership has its privileges."

They do not want marketing; they want to be part of a movement, and they want to be heard.

RELATIONSHIPS IN CONTEXT

One way to listen with precision is social network analysis. Myra Norton, president of Community Analytics, is an expert in this emerging field. "Social network analysis allows organizations to uncover the relationships of trust and advice seeking among its key constituents," says Norton. She continues,

> These relationships drive the perceptions, decisions and behaviors of those constituents in ways that often wreak havoc for organizations. Boundary spanners typically spend a lot of time seeking to understand *what* is important to key constituents. Social network analysis, when executed properly, empowers them to understand *who* is important to them. In many ways understanding *who* allows marketing and communications professionals to actually change the *what*. When marketing and communications professionals learn to leverage the trusted networks that are already in place among the audiences they seek to impact, they find that changing perceptions, decisions and behaviors is no longer an uphill battle.

The other side of this dynamic is that identifying and then *listening* to the trusted voices among constituents empowers marketing and communications professionals to be ahead of the game in terms of what will and will not resonate with the constituent base at large. This creates the space for real-time strategy adjustment and co-creation. It also saves immeasurable time and energy spent trying to force messages, initiatives and behaviors on a network of individuals who are simply not going to adopt them. The leading marketing and communications professionals of this decade will be those who have developed a solid understanding of network dynamics and have applied that understanding in their organizations.

Who knows who and where the sources are changing the nature of disclosure for investor relations. Who knows what in web-driven information ecologies is radically different. What will constitute simultaneous disclosure on market-making news will push the professional communicator to scrupulously orchestrate the release of information.

Indeed, speed itself is a new competitive advantage, overtaking traditional forms of intellectual property ownership and value extraction. Getting offerings and ideas to market quickly and sharing is now often more important than restrictive ownership plays.

IMPLICATIONS FOR PUBLIC RELATIONS

Speed is and has long been a key advantage of public relations. Professionals practicing public relations are well equipped to deal with breaking events and to think in terms of stakeholders and constituencies, not just customers and shareholders. With greater percentages of knowledge and information moving at the speed of light thanks to digital technology, public relations should continue to benefit from the quick response capability it brings to the table.

As information moves faster and faster, more and more of the problems organizations face will be defined as public relations problems. They will be problems rooted in an imbalance of information—either incorrect, misinterpreted, incomplete or in disinformation.

The role of the public relations practitioner could become so pervasive that it is no longer a specialty staff function. Many skills will be transferred to the management team itself, since public relations is simply part of the fabric of many organizations. Practitioners must redefine themselves to be highly relevant within these trends and become the coaches, teachers and inventive consultants who create and deploy new ways of practicing public relations, not just perform the tactics themselves.

The greatest advantage beyond speed, then, may be in the practitioner's ability to define new ways of using the new media being developed. The practitioner must fully understand all forms of media and the roles they play between organizations and individuals.

In this role, the public relations professional must continue to find ways to understand and create credibility. This is the role of advocacy communication. As new media emerge, the credibility of the source will become a much larger issue than it is even today.

For instance, what is source credibility in the age of the Internet? Is information received online sitting at a workstation hooked up to a network the same as getting information from the Associated Press (AP)? For some, the distinction will be lost that the AP is a news-gathering organization that puts information into some kind of edited order and context for viewers, while the Internet, at the time of this writing, continues to be a form of organized chaos. The underlying value system of the Internet is freedom of expression and expanding frontiers—popular themes for democracy. Witness Facebook, Twitter, Wikileaks and many other forms of electronic discourse. Are they source-credible?

They are caveat emptor—buyers beware.

DIGITAL DEMOCRACY

New forms of digital media make it possible for democracy to flourish. Digital information is democratic information; it likes to spread and does not respect the boundaries of authoritarian ownership, of objectivity or accuracy.

The implication for public relations is that source credibility will continue to blur during the ongoing digital communications revolution, and people will get burned.

Just as in a new democracy, having information freedom does not mean having access to useful information, such as information that will sustain a strong economy. It does not guarantee jobs. Freedom does not mean that if the right information is available it can be found or put to any useful purpose.

This is why source credibility will invoke itself. Information franchises such as the Associated Press, Dow Jones, Nikkei and Reuters will find renewed following around the world as people seek accuracy, order and priorities out of information chaos.

The introduction of new media forms has inevitably reflected the needs of the culture introducing and using them.

In the case of North America, the first use of digital media was to send money electronically. This export caught on rapidly around the world, and the digital dollar is now the common denominator for the world economy. Since accounting is a command-and-control language that expresses value by what gets funded and what doesn't, the first phase of the digital media deployment taught the world to trust numbers more than words. A decided preference exists now for automated teller machines (ATMs)—the first public-access terminals. It's now considered a hassle to stand in line and wait for a person.

DIGITAL CULTURE FLOWS

North America has traditionally been a net exporter of culture, information, consulting, processes and education around the world. Existing media fuel the dissemination of popular culture in the form of film, video, recordings and software to even the most remote locations. New forms of media will speed this trend with the addition of instantaneous networked delivery of content worldwide. When global broadband interactive media, such as telepresence and virtual worlds technologies move vast quantities of information to people around the world, we will search the globe for ideas to create local solutions. The reversal will be the ubiquitous availability of wireless communications, with most people in the world having some connection to a network of data, voice and, increasingly, multimedia communications.

The European continent will continue to find pressure to unite, trading sovereignty for economic power. Media patterns will follow this trend. The practice of public relations will become less of a local phenomenon and more of a continental one. Finding and creating durable relationships across borders will become a staple of the public relations business during this consolidation period.

Asia will likely reverse the trend of being net global importers of information and increasingly be exporters as well. Information acquisition, which will then be adapted to their needs, will have a strong role in these societies. As a result, Asia likely will be among the greatest information aggregators in the world. These cultures may more rapidly develop the ability to synthesize new knowledge from that which exists. In this environment, public relations will provide a strong role to help organizations adapt to a rapidly changing world. Many leading-edge counseling practice methodologies will be developed for clients in Asia and then be disseminated as new public relations methodologies.

In the same way that a garage became the birthplace of the personal computer decades ago—and small workshops gave us the telegraph, telephone and the technology of flight—so will some remote parts of the world find their way racing into the age of knowledge.

What seem to be insurmountable barriers to the deployment and use of new communications and information technologies are melting in the face of equally new communications practices and techniques.

The least-wired half of the world, the Southern hemisphere, is quickly finding it has the leverage to compete in the communications revolution as wireless communications make the need for copper strands and extruded glass unnecessary over broad expanses of unwired oceans and continents.

The *Wall Street Journal* reported in 1994 that, "The rebellion that erupted in Mexico January 1 began on the edge of a rain forest in the poorest part of the country. Yet within days, the insurgents or their supporters had signed on to the Internet and used its collection of electronic bulletin boards to broadcast the rebel manifesto around the world."[17] We now witness similar trends at the time of writing emerging in the Middle East that is likely to spread around the world. Saul Alinsky would have been proud and might have added a chapter about the Internet, if it had been around at the time, to his 1971 book *Rules for Radicals*,[18] essentially proactive public relations in the cause of reform.

MEDIA TRANSFORMATION

We now turn to an in-depth conversation with Chris Beaumont, founder of Beaumont and Partners, and vice chairman, emeritus, McCann-Erickson Asia and Grey Group Japan. His insights in this interview point to a media landscape that is being rapidly transformed by technologies and techniques only now being fully grasped, and is a good preface to our case about Google.

Kevin Clark (KC): Chris, thank you for sharing your thoughts with us about the future of media transformation and customer relationships. What do you believe is underway?

Chris Beaumont (CB): The media landscape is changing fundamentally; not simply the often called digital *new media* becoming mainstream, as an adjunct to *traditional media*, but with the explosion of smartphones and tablets providing people with ubiquitous access. Some time ago I created the term *vireal* because technology is increasingly woven (in the background) into the everyday. The virtual world is becoming more realistic and with the Asian lead in mobile marketing the Internet has become ubiquitous, and usage of web-enabled phones far exceeds that of the West. For example, Japan is the global leader in mobile in its broadest sense and with Near Field Communication (NFC) technology becoming more pervasive we are likely to see some fundamental changes in what we need to carry around with us. For example, more than 20 million Japanese regularly use their Suica, a near field communication card to buy train tickets and other items while on the move; they can now use their NFC-enabled mobile phones of which there are already some 50 million in Japan. The phone can be your wallet, your ticket or your home key, and thus save significant time.

KC: What about the intersection of GPS technology and wireless mobile devices? What does this hold for the future?

CB: The ability to access and analyze vast amounts of data with a spatial (GPS) overlay enables people to interact on many more dimensions. Indeed, one might hypothesize that the provision of navigation mapping on handheld devices is the next "killer app" in this space. With such shifts brand owners can now move online across the complete continuum of marketing activities from awareness building to sales and loyalty. This is the natural evolution of digital marketing that builds on fundamental changes in behavior of the people across Asia who naturally now go on-line to get information.

KC: What about social media and social networks?

CB: A major structural discontinuity can be witnessed by the development of social networks and their associated market valuations! In this new era, technologies are also empowering people to influence brands and not vice versa, lending new meaning to the phrase "a brand is not about what you think it is but what consumers think it is." The real power is with the people as brand attitudes—enabled by CGM such as SNS and blogs—are being shaped more through the shared experience of the "many small," rather than by messages from "a few large."

Despite earlier fears that standardization and globalization would massify the human race, we are witnessing still further evidence that people are moving in a different direction. The individual is triumphing and becoming more significant!

KC: What are the implications for communications and marketing professionals?

CB: Marketers need to recognize the fact that increasingly they have less control. There will be even more user-generated content. Product and service reviews by users will impact all marketing; for example user-generated content influencing natural search. People are proactively sharing their experiences with one another and brands are being shaped through such natural conversations as a result.

Moreover, it will become more important to recognize that such people are a disproportionate part of the brand franchise as potential brand advocates. Marketers express fear about losing control of consumers in the digital space, but what they really need to worry about is losing touch with customers. Marketers must empower people to actively participate in brands so that they have delightful involvement with a brand, and share it with their peers as "*my* delightful experience," "*my* story," "*my* brand"—and it's passed on. In this sense, the true impact of Web 2.0 is the nature of the interaction and the fact that brand owners can focus on longer-term relationships rather than transactional moments.

WEB 2.0 TO PEOPLE 3.0

KC: So we now have the ability to better understand, over time, the people visiting. We can develop a relationship with the people we're doing business with again as we did in local businesses?

CB: Yes, but with the natural evolution from Web 2.0 it is the primacy of People 3.0, who are becoming more sophisticated and empowered that will prevail. Thus marketers will truly see the need to personalize and enhance relationships within their brand franchises. Brands are being nurtured through chain reactions of delightful involvement by people who are empowered by technologies. But let's remember that technologies have changed the way people get connected, but not the people themselves. Marketers need to see the channel as a two-way interaction opportunity: Think domestic rather than digital!

KC: You're pointing away from the technology to people. Say more.

CB: Indeed. The Information Age with its technologically empowering solutions is giving way to the Imagination Age where ideas are the predominant capital. People delight in surprises that help them discover more themselves and more about themselves. Making things and managing people are becoming less important in the post-industrial economy, and increasingly, wealth is created through the creation and nurturing of value-adding ideas. This plays a significant role in the shift away from social hierarchy-based notions of branding to an equally inspirational, emotionally driven, experiential definition of brands.

For people, I use the term *People 3.0* because people set trends. Therefore, brand owners need to think people first. By calling them people, this is not a simple kind of symbolic repositioning. It should be central to how marketers think: inside out or outside in.

People are seeking more quality time to refresh and escape—"me time" if you will, but not in a selfish way. The ultimate goal: to be time rich, since cash rich, in many cases, is not achievable. Consistently we see people trying, in their daily lives, to manage an inherent imbalance that drives this stress. Life is not work; work is not life. Thus, people want to find more time in their schedules and marketers need to think about how to help people find it, especially since quality is only relative.

ECOSYSTEMS OF LISTENING AND ACTING

KC: What about ecosystems of people listening to each other? Is there a hierarchy or aristocracy of idea people we need to pay attention to?

CB: Key influencers are part of a bigger movement, which is change. Even more interesting are the people who are the embodiment of change itself. In our industry's obsession with the stereotype, and sometimes the archetype we often fail in looking to the future or even the emerging present to identify these manifestations of change. These are not change agents—those are the cultural creatives. These are the living breathing embodiments of change.

It might seem strange that participation has not been adopted before. But we have come from an authoritarian age of the parent/child into the age of the sibling. And this has led how brand managers think about their consumers. Previously, they thought all they needed to do was tell consumers. Now we need to participate with them. Yet participation is already happening. But often we are still thinking about participation within a single touch point, namely the Internet. And most marketers' thinking has not matured about how we can apply this as a strategy across multiple touch points. We need to move Marketing 1.0 to Marketing 3.0 and become more strategic!

The idea that a brand owner can own a single touch point is misguided. It comes from the share of voice thinking. What we have found is that participation works best when we engage consumers across multiple touch points. In other words, the brand has become part of people's lives. This is not shouting the brand. What we do is to find reasons for the consumer to interact with the brand across multiple touch points. The brand at one touch point leads the consumer to another touch point, so that they are truly participating.

KC: Can you measure what we're talking about?

CB: Conventionally lifetime value gets measured as the sum of transactions that a customer can have over their potential lifetime of category consumption. What if, instead. lifetime value were measured in the amount of participation that a person had with a brand? And what if value were measured by what was given as well as what was received. Dynamic, interactive strategies that span touch points require a new type of agency. Integration is not a catchword to sell marketers and agencies services, but the very way that creative business intelligence needs to be practiced.

By creating brand participation, what will be achieved is a more intelligent interaction between brands and their consumers. Participation means never being stuck in the past and moving with the People 3.0!

A GREAT TIME TO PRACTICE

KC: What do you think about this as an era for communications and marketing practice? Are the professions diminishing or growing relative to the opportunities we're discussing?

CB: In the same vein, for the CMO, I do not think there has ever been a better time. If you are willing to lead, doing things right is not the same as doing the right thing. With our accelerating age, fragmenting media, creating more consumer choices, enabling new competitors, burgeoning numbers of touch points, as well as materially empowering customers, no other senior executive position will be subject to as much change over the next few years. But, to date, in general the CMO has not walked the talk, and led. Too many chief marketers still have narrowly defined roles that emphasize advertising, brand management and market research. They will have to spread their wings. It is all about marketing from the inside out, and making marketing part of the organization. Marketing should not just be the icing on the cake, but part of the cake itself. Indeed, one might anticipate in many countries the role of the corporate brand becoming more important. This will not be because many more see social responsibility as a genuine action, rather the wider acceptance that brands mean business.

As such, it is key to recognize that what have been recipes in the past will not be successful in the future. Marketers are limiting themselves to retaining a focus on the classic "4 P's" of marketing (price, promotion, position and placement). They should think only of 1P: People 3.0, who are with greater social networking, the real brand custodians. This should be coupled with a passionate attitude about the central power and role of a brand(s) in driving sustainable business success. It is far better to own the customer franchise, which are hearts and minds, than it is a factory. Such a centricity implicitly recognizes that the biggest shift in today's marketing world is not the much-discussed declining effectiveness of television advertising but the changes in how consumers research and buy products.

It is the Internet and dynamic, distribution models, which are structurally changing the way consumers research and buy products and services. Moreover, third parties such as bloggers and their consumer-generated content are having a greater influence on corporate reputations. Collectively, these disruptions are necessitating that companies transform not just the marketing function but also everything from corporate affairs and product development to distribution and manufacturing models to be more engaged with customers. As the scope of marketing broadens, the central role of the CMO will be singular as the "voice of the customer" recognizing/embracing, as Kumar advocates, the "3 V's" (valued customer, value proposition and value network).

In the present economic situation, firms are understandably obsessed with measuring marketing performance. They should rightly demand marketing and the CMO to be more accountable! There is nowhere to hide. One of the consequences of our digital era and analytic modeling technologies is access to a breadth of timely information. Unfortunately this ability does not seem to sit well with many marketers; this is quite simply because the numbers would be bad! Poor because of the tactical and executional mentality that has become pervasive in many marketing functions at the expense of a more strategic and discriminatory focus.

The need for return on marketing investment (ROMI) metrics has never been greater and there are no longer technological barriers. Creating metrics and committing to being objective will not be sufficient because strategies themselves are often flawed and thus investment is inefficient. Measuring marketing ROMI will not improve performance. Fixing broken strategy and optimizing the marketing investment will!

KC: When you talk about the CMO, I know this is a surrogate for all communications and marketing practitioners in the enterprise. What about new roles for practitioners in the wake of new media forms?

CB: Today's competitive environment is made for marketers and it is important that CMOs stand up and broadcast their strategic roles for growing brands, rather than sit back and narrowcast a role that is merely communications orientated and therefore tactical. In this way the lifespan of CMOs will average longer than that of a rat.

THE BRANDS LIVE ON

KC: I remember your saying people move on and business changes, yet well-managed brands remain—what I refer to as enduring brands.

CB: Indeed, over time, buildings age and become dilapidated. Machines wear out. People die. But what lives on are the brands. Brands will need to evolve and remain contemporary, fulfilling evolving people's values; the issue will largely be one of brand maintenance, rather than brand building, but that does not require any less innovation! When one is speaking of change it seems all too easy to only talk about growth. For every innovation, there has to be at least one competitor who will need to fight harder to retain its revenue and share. Brand consistency over time can be a critical weapon in defense as well as attack! Going forward there needs to be a more balanced view, with consideration by many, on how one nurtures their current marketing assets. This should not focus on cost cutting and restructuring but marketing innovation and less reliance on product innovation.

Brands are becoming more integral to our lifestyle experiences. But it is unlikely brand loyalty will increase, as people in category after category wish to have different experiences and engage in "repertoire" buying. That said, the message must be that if your brand is not number one or number two you may be kicked out of the market! The competitive necessity will be to have vision/foresight and commitment to win opportunity share, not simply market share since that is looking at our futures through today's spectacles. In other words to be a market driver not market driven!

This brand new world demands we will change. Marketing programs will need to be designed, developed and implemented consistent with targeting and specialized brand messages, ensuring the content reflects the context of the connection. This brand new world, which everybody seems to think is about information and knowledge, is really about imagination. It is the idea that matters! Therefore we need to leverage emotions to build a greater intimacy with consumers, recognizing their increasing desire to stimulate their imagination and enhance their personal creativity. It's the fine art of being close to consumers... without getting in their faces; in essence, listening, understanding and then acting. As brand custodians we need to understand human vulnerability, emotions and optimism to really connect. There is a famous quote from Calne which says "Emotion leads to action, while reason leads to conclusion."

The bottom line is to ensure that brands empower! And we need to be respectful—create a dialogue rather than a monologue, recognizing they have choice and wish to be more in control. With multiple communication channels we must focus our communication connections—narrowcast the message. We must also think of our BrandWidth—the multiple interactive, multichannel, nature of today's brand connections—with a seamless, and yet, original brand voice:

- Always talk to the target community from the perspective of their personal concerns.

- Always feed their desire to be empowered.

- Always talk to them in a tone, manner and environment that demonstrates accessibility, involvement and personal dialogue.

- Always project consumer advocacy when conveying the message of personal drive, recognizing that brand management is more than product management, it is the holistic approach that will make the difference.

EXPERIENCE RULES

KC: We don't always have all the resources you're talking about at our disposal.

CB: At a time when much is said of austerity marketing, experience is more important than ever. When people look for a certain experience, not a specific product, your competition may be anyone fighting for your customers' money. More significantly it means experience expectations are being set in other categories than your own. For example, Starbucks redefined retail experience beyond coffee, while Apple is setting the standards for e-commerce experience through iTunes store.

This has important implications for brand strategy. No longer can we think of brand positioning; "Brand Position" is too static a concept to embrace the dynamism of today's competitive marketplace.

For the retailer, the importance of shopper marketing will increase as more choice is made in store (the so-called First Moment of Truth) whether off- or on-line (as e-commerce continues to provide more convenience). People are increasingly better informed and connected with like-minded communities telling them "how it is" (Second Moment of Truth). The choice of new products and services is multiplying, yet at the same time, consumers have become more skeptical about product claims. As shoppers gain unprecedented strength, customization, differentiation and consistency are business and brand imperatives.

Thus the market place has a new freedom which needs a new people, shopper–consumer model, with the recognition that behavior will never be easily nor completely predictable. In the era of choice, there is a paradox of choice, where consumers can make apparently the wrong choice. There is a surplus of almost everything in most categories; success will come only to companies that change directions fast and add value through quality, service, innovation and relationships with customers. These virtues are achievable by companies who are energetic, spirited and obsessive—the small company soul inside the big company body.

The overriding reality of today's life is not so much that change is increasingly embraced by peoples, and how much change there is but, the overwhelming pace and the nature of change itself; life accelerating for us all. Indeed, on the business side, the speed at which business is being conducted is moving faster than most companies acknowledge. Those that do not start accelerating will be left behind; business cycles are absolutely collapsing. Paradoxically, there is often a tendency to overestimate how much things will change in the next two years, but also, a tendency to underestimate how much things will change in 7 or 8 years. We need to understand "what is," but have a passion and enquiring mind for "what can be."

The media today frees us to focus on our strategic marketing imagination.

KC: Thanks, Chris.

GOOGLE: THE NOUN AND THE VERB

Google is a brand phenomenon.

Studying the rapid rise of its brand value and global awareness is the personification of the saying "the medium is the message" in the seminal book *Understanding Media* by mass media prophet Marshall McLuhan.[19]

Google is both a medium and a message. Google is a medium of access, delivery, and connections—and a message about how to find things and get things done.

Google is both a noun and a verb. It is a company, and when we "google something" or "google someone," we acknowledge this as a key way to find out something quickly on the web.

It is relevant. Millions of people use the Google search engine to find information every day. Gone are the days of questions going unanswered when you have access to Internet search engines, including the most used search engine in use today—Google.

It is mutually beneficial. Every query with a resulting set of findings and user selections strengthens Google PageRank link analysis and search algorithms and the ability to serve the next set of information seekers. It is a virtuous cycle of co-creation by question and answer. Socrates would applaud.

Google breaks the rules of brand building, since it does little advertising or promotion beyond just being itself. It has its own inherent awareness-building and promotion capacities.

It is also a story and emerging myth about the unrestrained ambition to organize and make available all human knowledge.

Interbrand currently values Google at US$43.5 billion, up 36 percent year over year in 2010. It is ranked at the number four position worldwide out of the top ten, as shown in the Interbrand Best Global Brands 2010 study:

- Coca-Cola: US$70.4 billion +2 percent

- IBM: US$64.7 billion +7 percent

- Microsoft: US$60.8 billion +7 percent

- Google: US$43.5 billion +36 percent

- GE: US$42.8 billion −10 percent

- McDonald's US$33.5 billion +4 percent

- Intel: US$32.0 billion +4 percent

- Nokia: US$29.4 billion –15 percent

- Disney: US$28.7 billion +1 percent

- HP: US$26.8 billion +12 percent

As Google continues its upward path, it increasingly finds it difficult to reconcile its brand promise, "Don't be evil," with the realities of a powerful global brand. Although it continues to leverage this messaging through investments in Google.org (its not-for-profit philanthropic arm) and a number of other initiatives, its access to user information and what it is doing with it is increasingly being scrutinized. Recently, it compromised a key value—trust—when it violated 176 million users' privacy with Google Buzz. And though its effort to pull out of China, which was censoring the search engine, and realign with its message demonstrated its commitment to its promise, only a few months later, Google was quietly persuaded to work with China again. Still, Google's reach and record for innovation is undisputed. Expect the brand to continue to diversify and expand, even as it experiences increasing backlash. (Interbrand Best Global Brands 2010, pg. 18)

With the EnduringBrands™ stage maturity model first described in my book *Brandscendence*™—three elements are used to understand the strength and resilience of great brands and the organizations behind them:

- Relevance: Why is the brand here?

- Context: Where and when does the brand show up (economic and cultural)?

- Mutual Benefit: Who is served and how—what is in it for both of us?

The EnduringBrands™ model can diagnose how mature a brand is today and paths to growth.

At stage one, brands act *dependently*—where they form an early personality, reflect, remember and mimic the environment, and act conditionally in working with others (brand as child).

At stage two, brands act *independently*—where they start to have character, are adaptive to the world around them, and act in mindful and with reciprocity to create goodwill (brand as adolescent).

At stage three, brands act *interdependently*—where the brand knows its purpose in life, projects a context that others feel compelled to follow and adapt to, and creates integral mutual benefits where the collaboration together is greater than the two economic actors acting on their own (brand as lifelong learning adult).

Google has been acting at stage three almost since its inception. To remain at the top of its game, it needs to be able to have a values system that transcends its founders. This is the story of the other top brands today— Coca-Cola, IBM, Microsoft, GE and McDonald's.

Rough patches? Yes.

Reinvention and resilience? You bet.

As a comparison benchmark, Interbrand talks about the 10 principles of brand strength:

1. Commitment: A measure of an organization's internal commitment to or belief in its brand. Commitment is the extent to which the brand receives support in terms of time, influence and investment.

2. Protection: This component examines how secure a brand is across a number of dimensions—from legal protection and proprietary ingredients to design, scale or geographic spread.

3. Clarity: The brand's values, positioning and proposition must be clearly articulated and shared across the organization, along with a clear view of its target audiences, customer insights and drivers. It is vital that those within the organization know and understand all of these elements because everything that follows hinges on them.

4. Responsiveness: This component looks at a brand's ability to adapt to market changes, challenges and opportunities. The brand should have a desire and ability to constantly evolve and renew itself.

5. Authenticity: This component is about how soundly a brand is based on an internal capability. Authenticity asks if a brand has a defined heritage and a well-grounded value set, as well as if it can deliver against customers' expectations.

6. Relevance: This component estimates how well a brand fits with the customer needs, desires and decision criteria across all appropriate demographics and geographies.

7. Understanding: Not only must customers recognize the brand, but there must also be an in-depth understanding of its distinctive qualities and characteristics, as well as those of the brand owner.

8. Consistency: This measures the degree to which a brand is experienced without fail across all touch-points and formats.

9. Presence: This measures the degree to which a brand feels omnipresent and how positively consumers, customers and opinion leaders discuss it in both traditional and social media.

10. Differentiation: This is the degree to which customers perceive the brand to have a positioning that is distinct from the competition.

In an earlier era, there was a business with similar ambition: IBM. The ability of IBM to reinvent itself is one of the great stories of business. Weight scales and time clocks gave way to mechanical tabulating machines, and eventually a pioneering move into electronic computers. Little of IBM's revenue today comes from the sales of physical devices; it has reinvented itself to be mostly a software, services and consulting business today. One hundred years young, IBM today is the most valuable business-to-business (B2B) brand in the world, with only Coca-Cola ahead of it in the Interbrand rankings.

In all three cases—Coke, IBM and Google—these brands have global reach and impact. Coke is a physical world distribution master, Google is an Internet and virtual realm genius and IBM possesses world-class complex problem-solving skills. The harder the problem, the more IBM likes it.

Both Google and IBM share a proclivity for hiring smart people. Google has more Ph.D.s per capita than most university communities. IBM has one of the last freestanding pure research organizations in the world (T.J. Watson Laboratories) and functions collegially much like a university.

Having spent 30 years at IBM (measured by career) and my entire life (measured by a father who worked for IBM and learning about the company by osmosis), the sheer scale and ambition of both companies signals to me that Google has the staying power and values maturity guidance system to have its own 100th anniversary celebration with pride just less than 90 years from now.

DISCUSSION QUESTIONS

1. Why is the concept of relationship at the core of communications and marketing practice today?
2. What are the implications of increasing connectivity and wireless capabilities for integrated communications and marketing practitioners?
3. What is the difference between an enterprise that has values and an organization that lives its values?
4. IBM is an example of a values-driven company; IBM employees embrace:

   • "Dedication to every client's success

   • "Innovation that matters—for our company and for the world, and

   • "Trust and personal responsibility in all relationships"

   What can these foundational values do to guide individual professional and overall IBM company behavior?
5. Google's goal to organize all human knowledge is clearly ambitious. Compare and contrast the access needs required to make this possible, and the information and knowledge rights of copyright and patent owners.
6. What is the role of collaboration vs. competition in the emerging relationship economy?

NOTES

1. Doc Searles and David Weinberger, *The Cluetrain Manifesto* (New York: Perseus Books, 1999), 75.
2. Marshall McLuhan, *Understanding Media, the Extension of Man* (New York: Mentor, 1964), 8.
3. Erich Joachimsthaler, interview with author, www.vivaldipartners.com.
4. Interactor, http://en.wikipedia.org/wiki/Interactor.
5. Nicole Lazzaro, interview with author, www.xeodesign.com.
6. David Martin, interview with author, www.interbrand.com.
7. Andrea Goldberg, interview with author, www.dccinsights.com.
8. Ed Zuber, interview with author, www.humanbrandsources.com.
9 Don Sexton, *Value Above Cost: Driving Superior Financial Performance with CVA, the Most Important Metric You've Never Used* (New York: Pearson Prentice Hall, 2009).
10. Kevin Clark, *Brandscendence: Three Essential Elements of Enduring Brands* (New York: Kaplan Business, 2004).
11. David Martin (ibid).
12. Daniel Pink, *Drive* (New York: Riverhead Books; Penguin Group, 2009), 29–30.
13. Daniel Pink (ibid); B. Johnson, J. M. Maynika, and I. A. Yee, "The Next Revolution in Interaction," *McKinsey Quarterly* 4 (2005): 25–26.
14. Daniel Pink, *A Whole New Mind* (New York: Riverhead Books, 2006).
15. Clay Shirkey, *Cognitive Surplus* (New York: Penguin Group), 110.
16. Clay Shirkey (ibid), 111.
17. Paul Carroll, "Foreign Competition Spurs Mexico to Move into High-Tech World," *Wall Street Journal* (July 5, 1994), 1.
18. Saul Alinsky, *Rules for Radicals* (New York: Random House, 1971).
19. McLuhan, 8

ADDITIONAL READING

Alinsky, Saul David. *Rules for Radicals—a Practical Primer for Realistic Radicals*. New York, NY: Random House, 1971. Print.

Clark, Kevin A. *Brandscendence: Three Essential Elements of Enduring Brands*. Chicago, IL: Dearborn Trade Pub., 2004. Print.

Levine, Rick, Christopher Locke, and David Searls. *The Cluetrain Manifesto the End of Business as Usual*. Cambridge, MA: Perseus Publishing, 2000. Print.

McCracken, Grant David. *Chief Culture Officer: How to Create a Living, Breathing Corporation*. New York, NY: Basic, 2009. Print.

McLuhan, Marshall. *Understanding Media: The Extension of Man*. London: New American Library, 1964. Print.

Pink, Daniel H. *Drive: The Surprising Truth about What Motivates Us*. New York, NY: Riverhead, 2009. Print.

Sexton, Donald E. *Value above Cost: Driving Superior Financial Performance with CVA, the Most Important Metric You've Never Used*. Upper Saddle River, NJ: FT, 2009. Print.

Shirky, Clay. *Cognitive Surplus: Creativity and Generosity in a Connected Age*. New York, NY: Penguin, 2010. Print.

Woodhouse, Barbara Bennett. *Hidden in Plain Sight: The Tragedy of Children's Rights from Ben Franklin to Lionel Tate*. Princeton: Princeton UP, 2008. Print.

Zaltman, Gerald. *How Customers Think: Essential Insights into the Mind of the Market*. Boston, MA: Harvard Business School, 2003. Print.

30
C H A P T E R

REPUTATION MANAGEMENT
Building and Maintaining Reputation through Communications

Craig E. Carroll, Ph.D.
Associate Professor and Department Chair of Communication and Journalism,
Lipscomb University

Stephen A. Greyser, D.B.A.
Richard P. Chapman Professor of Business Administration (Marketing/Communications)
Emeritus
Harvard Business School

Elliot S. Schreiber, Ph.D.
Clinical Professor of Marketing and Executive Director of the Center for
Corporate Reputation Management
Bennett S. LeBow College of Business
Drexel University

BUILDING AND MAINTAINING REPUTATION THROUGH COMMUNICATIONS

The purpose of this chapter is to examine the role of communications in corporate reputation brand-building.

We first provide background on reputation and the role that communications can play on its behalf. Our primary focus is on managing stakeholder expectations. Our principal perspective is that of the chief communications officer (CCO). We then address the context for corporate communications and reputation management, with particular emphasis on external and internal challenges to effective communications. Under this setting, we look at three underexamined phenomena: the willingness to disclose and to be open to feedback (i.e., managing reputational intelligence); the awareness that companies have multiple reputations; and the desirability of managing organizational-constituent expectations about the congruence among the multiple reputations.

We close with our perspective on the roles of substance (actual corporate behavior) and communications in building and maintaining reputation. Finally, we offer some questions management should ask in the course of considering and undertaking reputation-directed communications.

BACKGROUND

Although there is a vast amount of literature on corporate reputation, there is relatively little systematic development from the perspective of corporate communications. The term *corporate communications* appears to be widely used now, with some companies creating positions of CCO, responsible for a range of communications to numerous stakeholder groups. Corporate communications is not limited just to corporations. It can be applied to any organization. By corporate, we mean organization-level communications on behalf of companies, government entities, and nonprofit organizations. Corporate communications is a broadly used term of organization-level communications that encompasses public relations, public affairs, employee communications and other functional activities, to name just a few.

We also recognize that corporate communications is not the sole company actor affecting reputation management. Reputation is built and maintained by the actions and communications of an organization at all "touch points" with the many stakeholders of the company. As such, corporate communications plays a major—but not an exclusive—role in the reputation of the company. In fact, no single function in the corporation can manage reputation, which is a derivative of so many behaviors and communications of the enterprise. We think that all functions in the organization, through their actions and communications, share the responsibilities of supporting and protecting its reputation.

Corporate reputation is a topic of conversation among boards and in the C-suite in every major corporation. However, there has not been a consistent perspective on how to manage reputation. We believe that there are two different perspectives on reputation: (1) a marketing and communications perspective and (2) a management perspective. We favor the latter since it is holistic and strategic. Too many companies believe that they can communicate themselves into a reputation, while ignoring the structural and organizational issues that must be addressed to allow them to behave the way they want stakeholders to perceive them.

There also have been countless definitions of reputation. If one cannot define a term, it is difficult to propose a process to measure and manage it. So, although CEOs generally agree that reputation is one of the most important assets they manage, often they are also confused about how to define and manage it.

OUR PERSPECTIVES

We propose that *reputation* is what stakeholders say about the expectation of an organization's value vis-à-vis an organization's peers and competitors (Korshun, Schreiber & Andras, 2010). There are several operative terms in this definition. *First*, reputation is based upon expectations of value that stakeholders believe they have a right to expect from the organization. For example, employees expect that they will receive appropriate pay and an acceptable work environment. To the extent that an organization exceeds these expectations, it becomes known as a good place to work, whereas those that barely meet or fall below these expectations gain a reputation for having a poor workplace environment.

Second, reputation is not monolithic, but rather is stakeholder-group specific. There are often vast differences in the expectations of value by employees versus those of investors or customers or other stakeholders. *Third*, reputation is competitive. In any industry sector, particularly in the more mature sectors, there is a relatively consistent level of value in terms of both talent and capital. Reputation allows an organization not only to build value, but also to take value from others in the industry, allowing it to attract and retain talent more easily, lower its cost of capital, reduce its credit costs and raise its market value relative to its competitors, among other benefits.

We believe that communicators should focus primarily on expectations, for the following reasons: (1) Expectations are established and maintained by communications in support of the actions of the organization. (2) If an organization can meet or exceed the expectations of stakeholders versus competitors, it will increase its reputation and attraction to them. (3) When experience falls below expectations, the organization is facing a reputation risk with the stakeholder, a risk that often calls for communications.

As one might suspect, the expectations of stakeholders are in a continual state of flux due to competitive offerings or socioeconomic–political–technological changes. The corporate communications department plays a major role in helping the organization stay abreast of these changes and assuring that it remains current and relevant to stakeholders.

Although corporate communications does not have an exclusive role in reputation management, we believe it has or should have a lead role. We find, furthermore, little to guide practitioners who are often charged with corporate reputation management. Among the few are white papers from the Arthur W. Page Society, but these are not exclusively focused on corporate reputation. What we are trying to do here is to offer a more straightforward guide for those who must conduct and manage the planning and execution of their organizations' desired reputations.

Corporate communications, then, has a primary role in building, enhancing and maintaining corporate reputation, both inside and outside of the organization, but it must do so in conjunction with other functions in the company, including marketing, human resources, government affairs, finance and sales, among others. How this can effectively be done will be suggested later in this chapter.

CONTEXT FOR CORPORATE COMMUNICATIONS AND REPUTATION MANAGEMENT

There are a number of factors that create the context for corporate communications in reputation management. There has been a movement to a "knowledge economy" (Drucker, 1993), where the intangible value of what employees can do with their brain has, in many industries, supplanted what they can do with their "muscle."

The market value of corporations today is composed primarily of intangible assets. The more effectively an organization utilizes its intangible assets, the more it builds its reputation (Low and Kalafut, 2002). We can classify intangible assets in three general categories: human capital, structural capital and relationship capital. Corporate communications has a major role to play in identifying the intangible assets in the company and finding ways to connect these intangibles to the needs and interests of stakeholders.

A key role for communicators is to assure that the organization is both transparent and authentic in its communications, and does not attempt simply to "hype" its intangible values. When organizational "outsiders" can know more about inside operations than many "insiders," when definitions of insiders and outsiders are constantly changing (Carroll, 1995; Cheney & Christensen, 2000) and when organizational constituents may share multiple roles (e.g., being both an employee and a customer), there will be growing organizational tensions. We believe that such tensions are best articulated through conversations about expectations.

Moreover, there is a mismatch between the way organizations are structured and the expectations of the organization's significant others. As Zaltman (1995) describes, customers seldom distinguish one function (accounting, management information systems human resources, marketing) from another when attempting to evaluate and understand an organization's offerings. Instead, they judge the organization as a whole. Furthermore, Zaltman points out that companies are discovering that their self-perceptions do not correspond with those of their customers. These mismatches and discrepancies are best framed in terms of identity and reputation: who we are, who they think we are or even who they want us to be.

PARTICULAR CHALLENGES FACING CORPORATE COMMUNICATIONS IN REPUTATION MANAGEMENT

In attempting to harness its communications to build and support corporate reputation, organizations confront a variety of issues and situations that affect the environment for both their transmission and the target audiences' reception of the messages. Here are some that we consider to be significant challenges and impediments.

- *Information overload.* Publics that organizations want to reach already are flooded with messages in the communications world where the sheer necessity for companies to establish, communicate and position its version of "who we are" contributes to the very predicament that prompted our need to establish, communicate and position "who we are" (Cheney & Christensen, 2000).

- *Lack of differentiation.* There is a growing tendency for stakeholders to have difficulties distinguishing organizational offerings in terms of their product capabilities, quality, price and traditional measures of differentiation. Communication scholars call this *semantic similarity.* Organizations within an industry sector seem to "morph together" to many but the most informed of stakeholders. Still, one company within an industry sector typically finds a way to distinguish itself and to build a reputation separate from that of the others in the industry. For example, Johnson & Johnson has held that position within the pharmaceutical industry and DuPont has distinguished itself within the chemical industry. Although the industry sector certainly filters perceptions and expectations, it is possible to distinguish oneself from others in the same industry, even one that has a negative overall reputation. BP was such a company within the oil industry. It had staked out an aggressive position of being "beyond petroleum," and had redesigned its logo and corporate colors to signal its greater commitment to the environment. However, after the massive Gulf of Mexico oil spill, BP's reputation was quickly tarnished when stakeholders realized that the reputation built by BP was not real. It had not taken steps to assure that its organization could live up to the standards it communicated it believed in. Balmer, Powell and Greyser (2011) provide a recent analysis of BP in the context of ethical corporate marketing.

- *Maintaining organizational integrity.* Organizations striving to maintain a special identity (or for that matter, an identity distinguishable from others) must consider the challenge that arises from working with others in the course of doing business, "being in the world, but not of the world" and maintaining their sense of self and their core values. This is true of customers and stakeholders demanding the organization maintain particular social values as well as efficiency, quality and customer orientation (Cheney, 1995). Cheney (1997) describes organizational integrity as the extent to which an explicitly value-based organization can maintain its basic values and character over time. The central question is can an organization be true to itself over time, adhering to its own professed standards for decision making and behavior? This is especially challenging in global organizations.

- *Understanding real values.* It is useful, we believe, to differentiate between real and manufactured values. Real values are those that the company truly holds, are embedded in the culture and to which everyone in the organization is held accountable. Manufactured values are those that an organization claims with the goal to make itself appear more favorable to its various stakeholders. (See Urde 2009 for an empirically-based, culture-rooted treatment of "building real values and avoiding hollow values.") As we noted in the BP example above, manufactured values can achieve desired results for a short time, but they are not sustainable. Corporate communicators have a major role to play in being a catalyst within the organization for developing and adhering to real values.

  In the past several decades, it has become fashionable for companies to develop "vision and values." These have been an attempt to shape the corporate persona. If done well, these are very effective tools. If done poorly, these become "wallpaper" that few people think about or follow. Those organizations that do these well involve employees in their development, challenging them to think about what the values are and should be and engaging them to shape the desired persona. Those who do this poorly develop the vision and values with a small group and then announce them to employees. The persona of a company lives with its employees. If they do not understand the persona and know how to live it, it will fail.

  We have all known people who claim to be one thing but act a different way. Companies are no different. Our persona—who and what we are—is the critical element to our reputation. We cannot sell our reputation to others to believe if we cannot live it and act accordingly.

- *Competing targets of identification.* Competing with organizational identities are personal, professional and work group identities (Scott, 1997), among almost limitless others. Companies must determine whether they want to focus on a single enterprise-wide identity or base their reputation on the products and services they offer. Here we should also mention the competing demands between the broader organization with the local community culture, national culture or political socioeconomic systems (Cheney, 1991).

- *Successful socialization*. It may actually be the case that organizational members can identify so closely with organizational values and premises that they take them to extremes. Members may identify more with value premises of the organization than with the organization's current reality (Bullis, 1991). An example would be the unwillingness of the Catholic Church in the United States to recognize publicly the early problems of its priest sex abuse events. Thus, when there is conflict (or perhaps a need for a change), there exists a loss of control as the organization's already-successful identity lies in the heart(s) of the individual(s). Because a lot of both who we are and the actions we take come from our justifications and premises as reference points, we can become trapped into preferred ways of thinking (Christensen, 1997), both for the individual and the organization. This means that there is a danger to organizations when they begin to believe the best about themselves while denying that their critics have any justified perspective. To manage expectations, we must respect and appreciate them, regardless of how difficult it may seem.

- *Disenfranchisement (unsuccessful socialization)*. Just as oversocialization can occur, so can undersocialization. It may be the case that there are individuals who are never socialized into the organization's culture constituting the largely "hidden" or forgotten segments of an organization's workplace; a primary example would be the support staff (Deal & Jenkins, 1994), many of whom have a difficult time relating what they do to the central mission of the organization—be that making "widgets," checking in customers at hotels or educating students—except through conversations about efficiency. Although we can all think of voices that have been marginalized, staff people usually constitute an under-recognized group.

MANAGING REPUTATIONAL INTELLIGENCE

One role of corporate communications is managing the organization's reputational intelligence. A useful framework for understanding reputational intelligence comes from the Johari window. Imagine a window that contains everything that could be known about your company's reputation. (See Figure 30.1.)

Like everyone else, the company is not aware of everything about the company's reputation, only certain components. To represent the idea that there is only so much that the company knows about its reputation, the Johari window can be cut in half, representing the components that members of the company know about its reputation knowledge that (any) organizational members do not have about the company's reputation (Figure 30.2). The reputational knowledge can be of any type: information known to any member of the organization or information known to a specific group such as corporate communications.

The original Johari window can be divided in another way. In this division, one box represents what others know about your company's reputation, and the other is what others do not know about your reputation (Figure 30.3). "Others" can be any group: a group of employees, consumers, investors, or even the general public.

Everything Knowable about a Company's Reputation

F I G U R E   30.1

Everything Knowable about a Company's Reputation

F I G U R E 30.2

Everything Known and Not Known about a Company's Reputation

When the two divisions are laid on top of one another, four quadrants are created. When compared with the original box, one can see that everything about the company's reputation can be divided into one of these four quadrants. These quadrants together are modified, based on the Johari window, from interpersonal communications research and theory (Figure 30.4).

The lower left represents information that is unknown to both the company and some other public. In its purest sense, this cell represents information that cannot be known, or at least is impossible to verify with this specified public. After all, if neither the company nor others know what it contains, how can one be sure it exists? Its existence is deduced because organizations are constantly learning new things about themselves through research, accidents or discoveries.

The lower right represents the company's hidden reputation: information the company knows about its performance, but is not willing to reveal to the other specified public. Information in this hidden area becomes public primarily through the company's self-disclosure.

The upper left represents the blind area: this is where information resides of which the company is unaware, but the other-specified public knows. The company learns about this reputational information in the blind area primarily through feedback or research. The upper right represents reputational information of which both the company and the specified public are both aware. This part is referred to as the company's "open" or public reputation.

The relative size of each area in an organization's reputational intelligence changes from time to time, according to the situation. Despite the varying contexts, most organizations' overall style of disclosure could be represented by a single Johari window, depending on the climate or culture of the organization or the company's overall disposition toward the general public or any one of its publics. The goal for corporate communications is to reduce the size of the unknown, hidden and blind boxes. Briefly, we will describe these four reputational intelligence scenarios.

F I G U R E 30.3

Everything Known and Not Known to Others about a Company's Reputation

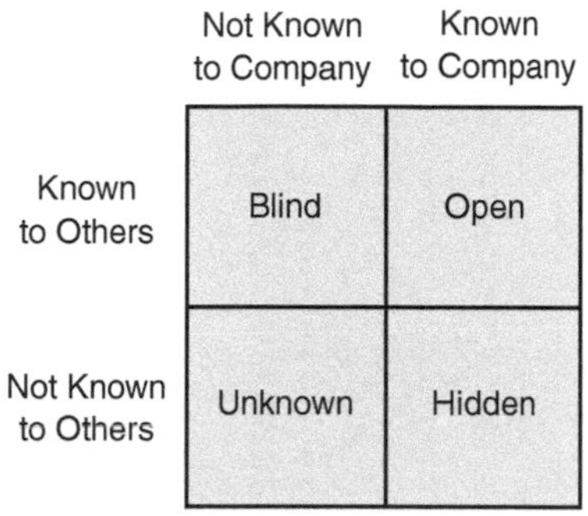

Not Known   Known
to Company   to Company

Known
to Others   Blind   Open

Not Known
to Others   Unknown   Hidden

FIGURE 30.4

A Johari Window for Corporate Reputational Intelligence Scenarios

Reputational intelligence scenario #1 depicts an organization that is neither receptive to feedback about its reputation nor is willing to self-disclose about its performance (Figure 30.5). The organization takes few risks and may appear aloof and uncommunicative. The largest quadrant is the unknown area. Such organizations have a lot to learn about their reputations, as do others.

Reputational intelligence scenario #2 depicts an organization with a large hidden reputation area: the company is open to feedback from others about its reputation but does not voluntarily self-disclose about its performance (Figure 30.6). This company may fear exposure, possibly because of not trusting others. Companies fitting this pattern may appear highly supportive at first. They may want to hear a customer's story and appear willing to deny themselves by remaining quiet. Then this first impression fades, and eventually the public sees them as distrustful and detached.

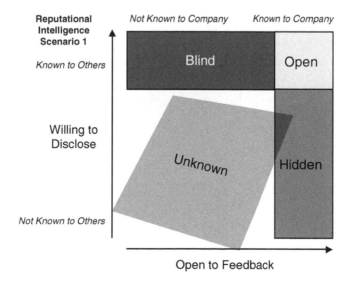

FIGURE 30.5

Corporate Reputational Intelligence Scenario 1: The Unknown Reputation

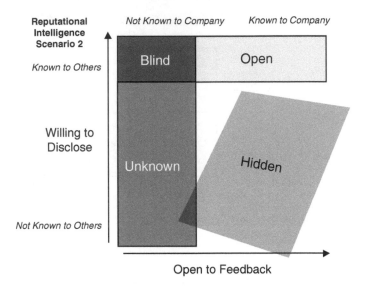

F I G U R E   30.6

Corporate Reputational Intelligence Scenario 2: The Hidden Reputation

Reputational intelligence scenario #3 has the blind cell as the largest (Figure 30.7). It describes companies who discourage feedback from others, but who disclose freely. Like the companies depicted in scenario #2, they may distrust others' opinions. They certainly seem self-centered. They do not encourage feedback, and so fail to learn much about how others view their reputations.

Reputational intelligence scenario #4 depicts companies that are both willing to disclose information about their performance and are open to others' opinions and ideas about their reputations (Figure 30.8). They

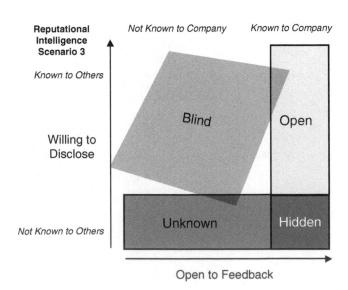

F I G U R E   30.7

Corporate Reputational Intelligence Scenario 3: The Blind Reputation

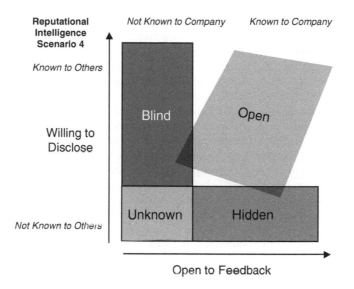

FIGURE 30.8

Corporate Reputational Intelligence Scenario 4: The Open Reputation

trust enough to seek the opinions of others and disclose their own. In extreme, this scenario of reputation can be intimidating and overwhelming because it violates the usual expectations of how organizations and publics with whom they do not have strong relationships ought to behave. In moderation, however, an open style provides the best way to build strong organization–public relationships.

CORPORATE PERSONIFICATION AND MULTIPLE REPUTATIONS

An organization personifies itself through its brand activities. It is through branding, as well as through communications, that a company sets the expectations that are to become the foundation of its reputation.

A brand is composed of three components: symbols, attributes and associations. Although a great deal of money and time are often devoted to developing a logo, the more important work in branding is often given less time and attention: how the organization wants to be known and thought of in the marketplace and the associations that it will or will not accept that illustrate or highlight its desired attributes.

A useful exercise often used by brand professionals is to ask a company to think of itself as a person. What would it look like to its stakeholders? What kind of car would it drive? Where would it live (urban, rural, suburban, etc.)? In conducting such an exercise, we in the company are learning about what we believe our stakeholders think of when they think of us. We personify ourselves. This is helpful, because that is exactly what stakeholders are doing all of the time. When they hear about our company, they think of certain things. We may not like what they think about, but this is where we need to start.

There is a saying that positioning is what a company does, whereas position is what the stakeholder does. That is, we attempt to influence the personification of our organization, but in the end, the stakeholder positions us vis-à-vis others on a mental or perceptual map. Until we take stock of this and understand where we are in the minds of our various stakeholders, we cannot impact the personification of the organization. If we deny the view of stakeholders or write them off as being inconsequential or old or based on too small a data set, we are setting ourselves up for problems. We must be willing and able to look in the mirror and see ourselves as others see us.

Companies can take many forms in the way they present themselves. In brand management terms, companies have different brand architectures that determine how they are seen in the market. For example, Procter

& Gamble or Unilever go to market with a brand architecture called *house of brands*. As consumers, we know these companies through the product brands that they sell rather than as a company. Although there is advertising and public relations support for the various brands from these companies, the support is about the product brand, not about the corporate brand, Procter & Gamble.

On the other hand, for such stakeholders as investors and retailers, the P&G or Unilever corporate brand has far more value. We invest in P&G, not in Tide or Pampers. A buyer at Walmart buys a large number of goods from P&G. The P&G persona means more to these stakeholders than the individual product brands do.

This duality of personality, so to speak, can cause some problems for such companies. Unilever makes both Dove products and Axe products. On the one hand, Dove has had a campaign to sell young girls on "inner beauty" and not allowing themselves to be defined by the standards of the beauty and fashion industry. At the same time, Axe is sold to young men using advertising that suggests that using Axe can help attract a young woman, many of whom appear scantily clad in Axe commercials. The conflict between these two brands brought Unilever undesired controversy in the blogosphere as some customers suggested that Unilever had to choose between its two competing personas. The company deflected the criticism, noting that each brand manager in the company is focused on meeting the brand persona that appeals most to his or her target market.

In stark contrast to the house of brands are companies such as IBM, HP or Nivea, to name but a few, that are *branded houses*, which are often called *umbrella brands* or *master brands*. All of the focus is on the corporate brand, and all products and services are sold under the corporate umbrella. In between these two extremes are other ways to personify the company, including *sub-branding* and *ingredient branding* that take on different personifications for the company. In sub-branding, the company allows a separate brand to exist to appeal to a certain segment of the market, but is tied back to the corporate brand to enhance the equity. An example would be Fairfield Inn by Marriott. The companies that go to market as ingredient brands offer themselves as enhancements that help the brand carrier to its persona. For example, Intel or DuPont Stainmaster are both ingredient brands that enhance the perceived value of computers or carpets, respectively.

Which brand architecture or "persona" to select depends on a number of factors. Schreiber (2002) noted that there are two variables that need to be considered in determining the right brand architecture; the amount of fear, uncertainty and doubt (FUD) perceived by the purchaser when making the decision, and the complexity of the buying decision. As the amount of FUD and complexity increase, we tend to move toward master brands because we want the customer to feel more comfortable knowing the company behind the product or service. In a house of brands, we accept the fact that most people likely think Tide is made by the Tide Company rather than by P&G. The efficacy of the product is contained in the product. This is possible because FUD and complexity are relatively low for most consumer products. The communications challenge in supporting different persona also depends on the brand architecture.

For companies such as P&G, the focus is on marketing communications to support the product brands, while the corporate communications group focuses on stakeholders for whom the corporate persona matters, including investors, the community and employees. In addition, P&G corporate communications would be involved in helping to ensure that the various brands live within the parameters of an established family persona. P&G does this through committees. Johnson & Johnson, a highly decentralized company with a J&J line of products but also a large number of companies operating without the J&J brand, manages its persona by its legendary credo. The J&J Credo is a document written in the late 1940s that focuses on the various responsibilities that the company has to its key stakeholders. Everyone working in a J&J company is expected to understand the Credo and what it means to defining the company. The Credo lists its key stakeholders as being consumers, employees, communities and investors, in that order. The Credo was the document used in 1982 during the Tylenol crisis that led the management team at the time to decide that it had to withdraw Tylenol from all shelves rather than just from the shelves of stores in Chicago where people died by cyanide poisoning. It is a set of values that shapes the J&J persona.

Research by the Reputation Institute has found that in the past few years, the public's view of companies has shifted from products and services to the overall value of the companies. The Reputation Institute suggests that we have entered a "reputation economy," in which consumers are concerned with the "company behind the brand." At one time, there was a belief that individual product names versus a corporate brand (a so-called house of brands architecture) protected the corporation and the other products should a problem occur with one product. This possibility, if it ever really existed, certainly no longer exists in our web-based world, in which information is transparent.

There appears to be a change in brand architecture, even for companies such as P&G and Unilever. We note that P&G began its first corporate advertising campaign during the Vancouver Winter Olympics of 2010, and Unilever has begun putting its corporate logo on the commercials of its various products.

"STRESS TESTING" CORPORATE VALUES

Balmer, Stuart and Greyser (2009) articulated the AC³ID Test (originated by Balmer) to identify six *identities* that are present in any company. These can be modified to examine the multiple *reputations* that organizations can also have. They are the actual reputation, communicated reputation, conceived reputation, covenanted reputation, ideal reputation and desired reputation. We add to this list the construed reputation, making it the AC⁴ID Reputation Framework. (The descriptions below are adapted and augmented from those in the 2009 article.)

1. The *actual reputation* ("what we really are") consists of the current attributes of the company, privately held by individuals. These may be tacit and unexplored, based on the impressions, perceptions and experiences of individuals and is shaped by a number of factors, including corporate ownership, the leadership or management styles, organizational structure, business activities, the range and quality of products and services and the firm's overall business performance.

2. The *communicated reputation* ("what we say we are") consists of attributes that occur through communications, whether controllable (advertising, marketing, public relations or sponsorships) or uncontrollable through word of mouth, media criticism or commentary or social media.

3. The *conceived reputation* ("what we are seen to be")—or to break away from the acronym, the *perceived* reputation—is how the company is seen by various audiences. The difference between the actual and the conceived (perceived) is that the actual is and the conceived is learned from research on stakeholder views.

4. The *construed reputation* ("what we think others see") is top management's view of a(nother) stakeholder's (e.g., consumers or customers) views of the organization's reputation.

5. The *covenanted reputation* ("what the brand stands for") refers to what the brand promises and the stakeholders expect.

6. The *ideal reputation* ("what we ought to be") consists of the optimum positioning of the organization in its market within a given time frame. This is based on current and forecasted information from strategic planners and others about the organization's capabilities and prospects in the context of the general competitive environment. It is often based on research and accumulated data about an organization's prospects.

7. The *desired reputation* ("what we wish to be") is analogous to the ideal reputation, but it resides in the hearts and minds of organizational leaders rather than empirical data, and is based on a guiding image or vision of what the organization should be, not limited to what it can be based on forecasts and estimates.

The AC⁴ID Reputation Framework is grounded on the premise that organizations have multiple reputations. A lack of alignment between any two can create dissonance or a situation in which two reputations are juxtaposed against one another, highlighting their differences, in turn creating a potential moment of crisis, if the dissonance is not addressed or resolved. Imagine situations where corporate rhetoric (communicated reputation) is meaningfully ahead of or behind reality (actual reputation), where vision (desired reputation) is at odds with strategy (ideal reputation) or where corporate performance and behavior (actual reputation) falls short of expectations held by key public stakeholder groups (conceived reputation).

It is the task of corporate communications to learn about these reputations and make relevant executives in the organizations aware of them. Consequently, the executives are always cognizant of the alternate realities the organization faces with its markets, audiences and publics. Table 30.1, adapted from Balmer and Greyser (2002), lists the key stakeholder groups involved with each type of reputation.

T A B L E   30.1

Key Stakeholder Groups Involved with Each Reputation Type

Type of Reputation	Key Stakeholder Groups Involved
Actual	Internal (those who "comprise" the company)
	Individual tacit impressions, perceptions and experiences held privately by stakeholders, shared informally
Communicated	Internal (marketing, communications)
	Marketing partners (e.g., advertising, marketing, public relations firms)
	Media (interpreting the company)
Conceived	All external publics (e.g., financial community, government or regulatory sector, headquarters or local facility communities, customers or consumers)
Construed	Internal (usually top management)
Covenanted	All internal and external publics
Ideal	Internal (e.g., strategic planning)
	External (e.g., financial analysts, consultants, regulatory or legislative entities)
Desired	Internal (CEO/Board)

Adapted from Balmer and Greyser (2002). Managing the multiple identities of the corporation. *California Management Review* (Spring 2002) 44, 3, 72–86.

CO-ORIENTATION THEORY AND EXPECTATION MANAGEMENT

Reputation management is based on an alignment of multiple reputations. Co-orientation theory gives some insights into expectation management. Co-orientation involves the alignment of expectations stemming from the agreement of expectations, perceived agreement of expectations and the accuracy of the two expectations. (Figure 30.9.)

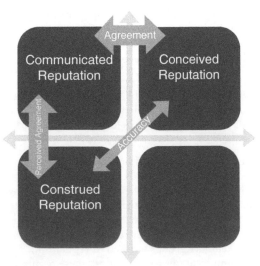

F I G U R E   30.9

Co-Orientation of Reputation and Expectations

An organization is in perfect alignment when the expectations of those in each quadrant match those of the corresponding quadrants. However, such balance is rare and expectations need to be either modified or an organization needs to attempt to persuade others to adjust their expectations.

Identifying expectations is straightforward. It is simply a matter of finding alignment between the communicated reputation and the conceived reputation, which requires finding what the relevant public's expectations are via their conceived reputation. If a set of expectations can be materialized on paper, then it is possible to ask both groups—through personal interviews or through surveys—what their expectations are, and what they perceive the expectations of the other party to be. Construed reputation and conceived reputation are important to assess for their perceived agreement or congruence with the other's expectations and their perceived level of agreement. Organizational leaders and stakeholders make these comparisons implicitly, but the corporate communications professional helps make them explicit through research.

Organizations should never assume that they know their relevant publics' conceived reputations of the companies, but should conduct research to confirm assumptions. Many organizations have been surprised to learn that they either misconstrued the expectations of others or that expectations had changed, either due to social–political–economic–technical changes in the environment or because a stakeholder (i.e., competitor, media, NGO) had changed expectations for the industry.

In this research scenario, both groups are asked the same questions. It is usually best to gather this information by using approaches: first through personal interviews, with the answers computed into survey questions that can be converted to 5- or 7-point scales for assessing the levels of agreement. When the time comes to conduct the surveys with each stakeholder group, start off by asking the top management team about their expectations regarding the communicated reputation. Then ask the top management team to articulate what they consider the other (stakeholder) group's expectations to be. This, as noted above, is called the *construed reputation*. These two sets of expectations can be compared for their degree of agreement.

Then, using the same surveying techniques, the corporate communications professional asks the other stakeholder group to articulate what *their* expectations are. Using the same set of questions, ask the stakeholder group to identify what they think the top management team thinks; this produces the construed reputation. The produced set of expectations—stakeholders' expectations (conceived reputation) and the construed reputation—can be compared for their level of perceived agreement.

Congruence of expectations and perceived expectations leads to a consensus; incongruence of expectations and perceived expectations leads to conflict. It is the corporate communications professional who is responsible for assessing the degree of consensus and conflict in expectations between the two groups—one group being the top management team, the other being the "other" stakeholder group.

Four different views emerge from whether there is conflict or consensus in the expectations between the communicated reputation and the conceived reputation of any particular group of stakeholders, and whether the accuracy between the groups exists. These four views are *true consensus*, *true conflict*, *false consensus* and *false conflict*. The accuracy of expectations is important to identify because it affects the degree of resources that organizations expend, and corporate communications professionals, in particular, allocate to the management of expectations.

TRUE REPUTATION CONSENSUS

True consensus exists when the expectations are mutual between the top management team and the group of stakeholders, that is, the communicated reputation and the stakeholders' conceived reputation are in agreement, and the groups perceive that they are in agreement. True consensus can be identified by comparing the expectations of (1) the top management team with those of (2) the stakeholders, as well as (3) the construed reputation (Figure 30.10).

The role of the corporate communications professional here is to make true consensus known. True reputation consensus (Figure 30.10) exists when there is agreement between the top management team's reputation expectations and stakeholder's reputation expectations; in addition, there is perceived agreement between the top management team's reputational expectations and the construed stakeholders' expectations (what the top management team thinks the specified stakeholder expects).

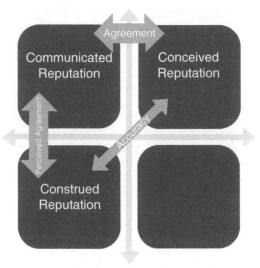

F I G U R E   30.10

True Reputation Consensus

TRUE REPUTATION CONFLICT

True conflict exists when the expectations of both parties diverge, that is, the top management team's communicated reputation and the group of stakeholders' conceived reputation are in disagreement, and the groups recognize they are in disagreement. Although the groups may perceive there is disagreement, the parties do not know for sure the degree of disagreement until it is brought to their attention. Here, the role of the corporate communications professional is to try to manage the conflict between the two sets of expectations (Figure 30.11).

   True reputation conflict exists when there is disagreement between the top management team's communicated reputation and the specified stakeholder group's conceived reputation, and both groups perceive the disagreement.

   Of course, two other scenarios exist: *false consensus* and *false conflict*. These particular scenarios are important because they lead to mismatched resources in the management of corporate reputation (Dukerich & Carter, 2000).

FALSE REPUTATION CONSENSUS

False consensus exists when there are divergent expectations between the dominant coalition's communicated reputation and the group of stakeholders' conceived reputation, yet one or both groups perceive that their expectations are shared. The false consensus between expectations and the perceived expectations of others is troublesome because it involves the identification of conflict where neither party sees it at first (Figure 30.12). A false reputation consensus occurs when there is disagreement between the expectations of the dominant coalition and the specified stakeholder, yet the top management team perceives agreement between the two parties.

FALSE REPUTATION CONFLICT

False conflict occurs when the expectations between the top management team's communicated reputation and any group of stakeholders' conceived reputation are mutual, but the groups perceive the expectations as

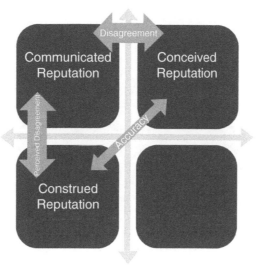

F I G U R E   30.11

True Reputation Conflict

divergent. This type of conflict is the easiest for the corporate communications professional to address and try to correct because the expectations between the two groups are, in fact, in alignment (see Figure 30.13). False reputational conflicts are when there is disagreement between the top management team's expectations about the reputation and the specific stakeholder's expectations, yet the top management team thinks there is agreement.

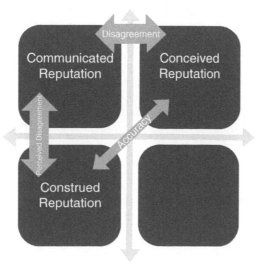

F I G U R E   30.12

False Reputation Consensus

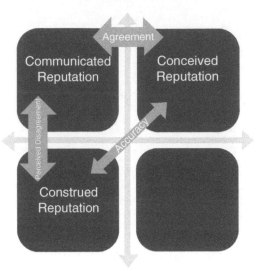

FIGURE 30.13

False Reputation Conflict

The value of gathering information on the alignments and misalignments linked to stakeholder group expectations is that it provides guidance to CCOs—specifically, in both understanding and prospectively addressing desirable adjustments in the conceived (perceived) perspectives held by stakeholders. In addition, significantly, it can aid them in resolving incongruences on the part of management.

WHEN SUBSTANCE TRUMPS COMMUNICATIONS

Reputation typically takes a long time to build, but can be fragile under the pressure of perceived serious misbehavior or performance/activity that falls short of stakeholder expectations. This is particularly true if the issue involved is central to what one of us has called "the essence of the brand," described as "the distinctive attribute/characteristic most closely identified with the brand's meaning and success" (Greyser, 2009). Widely recognized examples are Toyota (product quality), Arthur Andersen (integrity), the U.S. Catholic Church (faith and trust), and Intel's Pentium chip (accuracy); in all of these cases, situations arose that challenged the positive reputation built over many years by company and product performance, achievements and positive impacts for customers and other stakeholders.

We believe, as noted above, that a company's actual behavior and performance are at the core of its reputation. Furthermore, "substance is the foundation of effective communications, supported by authenticity" (Greyser, 2011). Another way of expressing this is to "live your brand and grow your reputation" (Schreiber, 2011). Stakeholder-perceived authenticity about an organization helps validate its communications. Greyser cites four contexts for authenticity: *talking authentic* (communications per se); *being authentic* (based on a company's core values and track record); *staying authentic* (organizational stewardship of values and behavior); and *defending authenticity* in troubled times (most effectively done when able to draw on a company's "reputational reservoir" of trust built over time).

Good communications cannot overcome bad substance. Furthermore, we think that companies should be far less concerned with trying to kill bad news and more often ask whether its action or inaction would be harmful if news of it appeared in blogs, tweets, in the newspaper or on TV.

The role of communications is obviously important, including the daily work "in the trenches" of corporate activity. However, beyond traditional support for R&D achievements, financial performance and so forth, maintaining and enhancing reputation is often done via communications that supports unusual initiatives. Such initiatives in recent times have included those in the corporate social responsibility area, such as "green" programs, partnerships with nonprofits and employee engagement in their communities. Although not normally material for headlines or major stories for TV, such communications is the ongoing work that supports corporate reputation.

To achieve effective communications, CCOs and their colleagues need to build and maintain the strength of their internal network so that they can know the facts of any given situation—especially difficult in a large and/or global organization or in a multidivisional one with units in very different industries. This kind of network management constitutes a set of "collegial conduits." The effort can also encompass the use of a reputation council or stakeholder relations council (Schreiber, 2011), which may include outside experts, to help monitor external conditions and stakeholder inputs that can affect a firm's reputation and help guide the firm's reputation-directed communications and initiatives. The councils should be composed of all of those who have responsibility for stakeholders and the various touch-points at which reputations can be built or damaged. Jon Iwata, head of marketing and communications at IBM, says that the role of communications should be as a "chief collaboration officer" for such councils.

The organization also needs to be able to harness a range of traditional and nontraditional communications expertise (including outside communications counselors) for its work. The consequent programs now frequently encompass integrated marketing communications (IMC), including traditional public relations, paid advertising, use of the company's website and social media. Social media require conversations *with* stakeholders rather than communicating *at* stakeholders.

Some companies may question whether they should have a social media strategy. The answer is that they should have a *reputation* strategy that includes the full utilization of the capabilities of social media. Such programs, particularly in the sensitive area of reputation, need to be consistently monitored to ensure that the central messages stay on target. Many CCOs look to the Arthur Page Principles, developed decades ago by the "old" AT&T's legendary longtime communications head, as guidelines for both communications and corporate behavior.

QUESTIONS FOR MANAGEMENT

What should top management be asking itself (and others) with regard to building and maintaining reputation through communications?

To us, the most important question is, *does the company understand the expectations of its various stakeholders?* This question must be addressed before one can know what the organization's reputation is. This leads to related questions: What is the value that stakeholders *expect* from the organization versus that of its competitors? How do relevant stakeholder groups see the organization, its strengths and weaknesses, and the elements that are at the heart ("the essence") of the corporate brand, and that may distinguish the firm from its competition as well as from other organizations with which it may be compared for certain purposes? The latter might include such areas as the financial marketplace, partner companies for coventuring and executive recruiting. This will help enable a company to define its reputational goals.

Obviously, the matter of what an entity's reputation is has multiple facets, as discussed in earlier sections.

Another key question is, *does the company understand itself?* Its core values are key internally, but not always visible externally. More broadly, the aims are to understand how various significant constituencies see the company, and to do the same internally. If top management can explain the multiple reputations at least to itself, then the CCO and senior executives have the basis for both meaningfully managing the company's organizational-constituent expectations for the firm (and its reputations), and for undertaking and, where necessary, modifying the communications programs.

A third major question is, *does the company have the skills and the will to be effective guardians of its reputation?* Furthermore, the company must have enough relevant information to make intelligent decisions on reputation issues. As stated earlier, this encompasses willingness to disclose, to be open to feedback and the ability to monitor many stakeholder groups on many dimensions—and for some companies, in many places.

A fourth question is particularly appropriate in the wake of 2010—the "year of reputational travail," as one of us characterized it: *What could cause your brand to undergo a reputational crisis?* In most cases, organizations had "cracks" that should have been noticeable at some level. Crises begin with a triggering event. Companies need to understand whether their cracks are normal or abnormal and require further investigation. In many crises, someone says, "we should have known" from some indicator. Companies that maintain strong reputations keep a focus on those indicators and do not rationalize them away.

The most notable reputation crises include the following:

- The Toyota problems, during which corporate behavior presumably bred from its corporate culture, as interpreted in its own company report, caused the company's reputation for product quality to erode rapidly.

- Johnson & Johnson's renewed problems, not only with Tylenol in the McNeil division, but elsewhere in the firm. The company's once-vaunted Credo seems now to be questioned in terms of its "leading star" role for J&J's reputation.

- BP's reputation-wounding actions and non-actions in the Gulf of Mexico oil explosion, clean-up and so forth, constitute for many a veritable manual of how not to address protection and rescue for reputation. As noted earlier and by one of us elsewhere, BP in some ways prepared its own problems by considerably overstating its "green credentials" and some years ago repositioning the corporate brand (including a new logo) to be more environmentally friendly in an inherently difficult industry for such a position.

- Tiger Woods' brand reputational swoon through widely perceived personal misbehavior and its consequences (e.g., efforts to stonewall and dribbled-out information). Tiger's brand and brand value virtually collapsed quickly, as almost all firms employing him as an endorser or marketing partner dropped him or let a veil of communications silence fall over its programs with him.

These illustrations point to the importance not only of understanding one's reputation (as noted above), but also to considering the kinds of events or phenomena that could adversely affect the brand reputation. For example, for a research-based university, such an event could be a renowned professor being found to have contrived or deliberately falsified data in an important article (e.g., a scientist whose work affects public policy).

The complement to considering what could cause a reputational crisis is, how would the company—and the CCO's group—try to help the firm address it? Again, we come back to such guidelines, which we think must be embedded in the organization, such as being willing to find the facts, tell the truth about them and address the problems (even if costly) via acts, not ads.

There are obviously many operational questions that derive from these macroquestions, or for which the answers will support the company's capacity to address them.

In closing, we want to remind readers that *the corporate brand is as wide as the organization*, so the CCO can serve only as a guide and an advocate (especially internally) for the company's reputation, cognizant that *the CEO is the ultimate guardian* of that reputation.

COMCAST CASE

The competitive landscape of pay television service in the United States has changed significantly over the past few years with the entry of new providers, including telephone companies like Verizon. For cable operators, like Comcast, this has presented some challenges and opportunities.

Around 2008, Verizon introduced a new offering called FiOs that it claimed could provide better quality TV signals through fiber optics. Verizon already provided telephone, wireless and Internet services, and Comcast had broadened its offerings to include digital telephone and high-speed Internet services.

It first appeared this was a "fight" between two competing technologies: cable versus fiber optics. However, it soon became clear that customer service was also a key differentiating factor for consumers. And Comcast, the leading U.S. cable company, had experienced some well-publicized customer-service incidents in recent years, whereas Verizon had fared better in external customer satisfaction surveys such as JD Power & Associates.

In late 2007, several senior leaders in Comcast's Customer Service organization put together a "listening tour" for executives. They visited a number of cities to listen to customers in open focus groups and also to meet with employees to help Comcast executives understand the expectations of its customers and to assure that its employees had the tools and resources to meet those expectations. The feedback from customers was, in the company's words, "humbling" as customers were very vocal in their descriptions of unsatisfactory experiences with Comcast.

Recognizing that it needed to make some serious changes to how it operated, Comcast launched a companywide initiative to evaluate its service network—from its people and processes to systems, technology and materials—to identify issues and resolve them. After making several significant operational changes, the company introduced a Customer Guarantee in 2009, which it describes on its website as "our promise to you."

During the process of working to improve its customer service and reputation, Comcast chose not to do any major advertising or public relations programs touting its refocused attention to customer service, concerned that customers would see it as "hype." However, in 2010, the company began running commercials featuring its employees talking about the Customer Guarantee.

In 2011, Comcast is continuing to focus on improving the customer experience, and research, including external surveys that measure customer satisfaction, has found that it has come a long way from 2008. Customer retention is on the rise and Verizon has found it more expensive to attempt to acquire Comcast customers than it had expected when they started their competitive push in 2008.

CASE QUESTIONS

1. What does the Comcast case demonstrate in terms of how reputation is built and maintained?
2. If reputation is based on stakeholder expectations of value vis-à-vis competition, what do you think Comcast found were differences of expectations among its various stakeholders?
3. If you were an employee of Comcast, how would you feel about the company's renewed interest in customer service in 2007? Would you be proud of the company or disappointed that it took competition to help bring awareness to the issue?
4. What other companies can you think of that are similar to Comcast in focusing reputation-building activities on specific segments of their business?
5. If you were in the communications organization at Comcast, how would you feel about not promoting the new customer service focus? Do you believe Comcast was right in initially holding back on communications?

DISCUSSION QUESTIONS

1. How does the approach to reputation in this chapter fit with the perspective you have had regarding the role of communications in building and maintaining reputation?
2. The authors suggest that "substance trumps communications." How do you feel about this statement? Can communications overcome bad substance in some situations?
3. Is the role of branding and brand management connected to reputation, or are these truly separate activities in the corporation?
4. If you were charged with putting together a reputation council for your university, whom would you put on the council and what would be your agenda?
5. What companies do you believe are true to their values? Are these companies the best in terms of reputation? What is the connection between values and reputation?
6. Many studies of reputation focus on overall "esteem" of a company. What do you think of the authors' focus on reputation as being related to expectations of value?
7. Related to Question #6, many studies of reputation tend to aggregate perceptions to produce a single overall reputation score for the company. Do you agree that reputation is stakeholder specific and based on competitive analysis?

8. If reputation can build competitive advantage, how might you use reputation to build the value of your university versus others that attract similar students or faculty?

9. Do you think that an organization can have a great reputation that it finds meaningful, even though members of the general public have never heard of it?

REFERENCES AND ADDITIONAL READING

Balmer, J., and S. A. Greyser. "Managing the Multiple Identities of the Corporation." *California Management Review* 44, 3 (2002): 72–86.

Balmer, J., S. Powell, and S. A. Greyser, S. A. "Explicating Ethical Corporate Marketing. Insights from the BP Deepwater Horizon Catastrophe: The Ethical Brand that Exploded and Then Imploded." *Journal of Business Ethics* 102, 1 (August I) (2011): 1–14.

Balmer, J. M. T., H. Stuart, and S. Greyser. "Aligning Identity and Strategy: Corporate Branding at British Airways in the Late 20th Century." *California Management Review* 51, 3 (2009): 6–23.

Bullis, C. A. "Communication Practices as Unobtrusive Control: An Observational Study." *Communication Studies* 42, 3 (1991): 254–271.

Carroll, C. E. "Rearticulating Organizational Identity: Exploring Corporate Images and Employee Identification." *Management Learning* 26, 4 (1995): 463–482.

Cheney, G. *Rhetoric in an Organizational Society: Managing Multiple Identities*. Columbia: University of South Carolina Press, 1991.

Cheney, G. "Democracy in the Workplace: Theory and Practice from the Perspective of Communication." *Journal of Applied Communication Research* 23 (1995): 167–200.

Cheney, G., and L. T. Christensen. "Organizational Identity: Linkages between Internal and External Communication." In *New Handbook Of Organizational Communication*, ed. F. Jablin and L. Putnam, 231–269. Newbury Park, CA: Sage Publications, 2000.

Christensen, L. T. "Marketing as Auto-communication." *Consumption, Markets and Culture* 1, 2 (1997): 197–227.

Deal, T. E., and W. A. Jenkins. *Managing the Hidden Organization*. New York, NY: Warner Books, 1994.

Drucker, P. *Post Capitalist Society*. New York, NY: Harper Business, 1993.

Dukerich, J. M., and S. M. Carter. "Distorted images and reputation repair." In *The Expressive Organization*, ed. M. Schultz, M. J. Hatch, and M. H. Larsen (97–112). Oxford, UK: Oxford University Press, 2000.

Greyser, S. A. "Authenticity and Reputation." A paper presented at Lipscomb University's Media Masters Award Ceremony, Lipscomb University, Nashville, TN, 2011.

Greyser, S. A. Corporate brand reputation and brand crisis management. *Management Decision* 47, 4 (2009): 590–602.

Korshun, D., E. Schreiber, and T. Andras. "Stakeholder Capitalism: It's How We Meet or Exceed the Expectations of Stakeholders that Determines a Company's Reputation." Working paper, 2010.

Low, J., and P. C. Kalafut. *Invisible Advantage: How Intangibles Are Driving Business Performance*. Cambridge, MA: Perseus Publishing, 2002.

Schreiber, E. "A Process for Enhancing Brand and Reputation While Mitigating Risk." A presentation to the Public Relations Executive Leadership Forum, New York, 2011.

Schreiber, E. "Brand Strategy Frameworks for Diversified Companies and Partnerships." *Journal of Brand Management* 10, 2 (2002): 122–138.

Scott, C. R. "Identification with Multiple Targets in a Geographically Dispersed Organization." *Management Communication Quarterly* 10, 4 (1997): 491–522.

Urde, M. "Uncovering the Corporate Brand's Core Values." *Management Decision* 47, 4 (2009): 616–638.

Zaltman, G. "Amidword: Anthropology, Metaphors and Cognitive Peripheral Vision." In *Contemporary Marketing and Consumer Behaviour: An Anthropological Sourcebook*, ed. J. F. Sherry Jr. (282–304). Thousand Oaks, CA: Sage Publications, 1995.

4
P A R T

INDUSTRIES AND ORGANIZATIONS

There are at least three loyalties in organizational life for a true communications professional: to the multiple stakeholders, to the organization and to the profession and its standards. In a perfect world, these standards would align with both the needs of the stakeholders and those of the organization.

In the stakeholder section of this book, you will discover how intense and important the relationship between communicators and stakeholders can be. You will also read, see and sense the pride that the authors have in developing educated loyalties to their organizations and professions, institutions which they help define as ethical, transparent and responsive to stakeholders. I have chosen a representative list of industries, but this is by no means a full list of all influential industries. Do not feel bad if your industry is not included in this section as this list is meant to be merely a sampling of industries in the field. Each industry or organizational area has its own unique requirements for communications and management leadership. Each author takes pride in his or her business or nongovernment organization (NGO).

The selection of the industries and institutions depended on several criteria, including:

- Each author's ability to fairly and responsibly report on the communication challenges of his or her industry

- The matching of institutions to demonstrate the importance of the full stakeholder focus, so that no chapter is narrowly defined by only one stakeholder

- The selection of a wide range of service and manufacturing industries to include profit and nonprofit organizations

- A representation of a mix of vertical industries, described in Chapter 1, chosen as examples of strong pillars of developed economies, such as manufacturing, hospitality, entertainment, food, energy, health, NGOs (logistics), government, information, telecommunications, banking and automotive

- An effort to include a mix of business to business (B2B) and business to consumer (B2C) organizations

The idea of a mix of businesses and organizations that direct their communications primarily to other businesses that sell or serve consumers, or to organizations that directly sell or serve the end user, is reflected in these chapters. For example, B2C is represented by the automotive, airline, insurance, hospitality, sports, computer, entertainment, health care, restaurant, retail and mobile telecommunications industries. The B2B side is represented by the pharmaceutical research, consulting, financial products, food and beverage, oil and law industries. Naturally, each industry could partially serve consumers or other businesses. One way of addressing these somewhat artificial categories is to remind businesses that primarily sell to resellers (other businesses, or B2B) that they should always be concerned with the consumer and stakeholders of their end customers. We suggest that the term *consumer* be used for end users (B2C) and the term *customer* for resellers (B2B.)

One additional criterion for selecting these firms (other than the authors' obvious willingness to participate) is what I have called "high risk" or "high visibility" organizations. It is logical to rank organizations by the stakeholders they serve or with whom they communicate. Some stakeholders, as consumers or relationships, are in a number of ways higher profile than others. Any misstep or miscommunication can lead to a crisis, or at least the attention of society, that would challenge the management team, specifically the communications professionals. In the same way, certain products are related to this high-profile and high-risk perspective. Some products and services (food, beverage, restaurants, finance, sports, personal care goods from retailers, entertainment, autos, energy, air travel and, logically, insurance) require greater care than thousands of "unseen" products (the keys on your keyboard, the veneer wood on your desk, the mouse pad and other more incidental products and services of life and business.) Of course, every product has some risk, or there would not be product and service insurance. I have argued that every industry or product represented in the chapters in this book has some degree of risk, a higher degree of visibility and perhaps an even greater responsibility to protect stakeholders. A PR professional has the responsibilities of a risk manager. The beauty of this field is that we are educated and sometimes born to warn our clients about risk. Nevertheless, "read the headlines" is still a famous warning to CEOs and managers, so that they avoid negative press coverage by their actions. Today, a better warning might be "read the Tweets." And who knows what it will be tomorrow.

31

C H A P T E R

THE AUTOMOTIVE INDUSTRY
A Race to the Future

Ray Day
Vice President, Communications
Ford Motor Company

Steven J. Harris
Vice President, Global Communications (Retired)
General Motors Corporation
Senior Counselor
McGinn and Company

AUTOMOTIVE COMMUNICATIONS: AT THE BEGINNINGS OF PR AND LEADING THE WAY INTO THE FUTURE

The practice of modern corporate public relations or communications is generally believed to have begun with the naming of Arthur W. Page as the first vice president of public relations for AT&T in 1927. And few, if any, could argue with the trailblazing achievements and legacy of Page.

About that same time, the U.S. auto industry was also recognizing the value and necessity of effective communications with customers and a wide variety of constituencies. So, in 1931 General Motors (GM) named Paul Garrett as its head of communications. During his 25 years at GM, he emphasized quality performance, public interest and honesty as corporate public relations principles. His effectiveness inspired other corporations to establish public relations departments. The Ford Motor Company was not far behind, hiring its first PR agency in 1927 and establishing the Ford News Bureau in 1942 with dedicated leadership of corporate PR, publications, photographic and government information.

Mary Henige, GM's director of social media and digital communications, did her masteral thesis on Paul Garrett and GM Communications, and her research uncovered that Garrett, like Page, had a set of clear and concise objectives:

- "The art of public relations is in the art of multiplication—that is, the art of multiplying endlessly the good impressions of a company."

- Industry must also learn to be "for" rather than "against" so many things.

- Doing the job well is the first dimension; the doing is more important than the telling. But the doing alone is not enough; the public must be told. The third dimension is explaining "how" and "why" behind what a company is doing. "The knowing why is what makes an idea stick."

"Hardest problem a practitioner of public relations in any company has is to impress upon the company's executives is that the job is *theirs*—not that of any public opinion department," Garrett said.

And Garrett had a number of themes he impressed upon his communications team as well as the senior management of GM. Among these themes were:

- Decentralize operations down to the point of contact with the customer. "Putting the entire organization to work on PR." PR is everyone's job.

- Master that sense of timing.

- Develop new ideas.

- Ensure that the industry must interpret itself.

- Understand the public.

- Unify the corporate stance/institution is greater than the product.

- Give importance to the role of the press.

- Understand the importance of the customer and research.

- Remember GM as a good neighbor/social responsibility.

- Keep in mind that good PR is saying and doing.

- Integrate PR as a management function.

- Adopt an inside/out philosophy: good employee relations.

- Maintain PR as an operating philosophy/consider the PR aspects.

Most, if not all, of these could have been written today. Many of the foundational elements of effective and leading-edge communications used today are included here.

THE AUTO INDUSTRY IN AMERICA

Few industries have had the impact—both good and bad, depending on your point of view—that the U.S. auto industry has had on so many facets of American culture, economics and lifestyle.

Cars and trucks produced by GM, Ford and Chrysler—and hundreds of other American car companies that did not survive to today—gave Americans unprecedented mobility and freedom. This led to the growth of our cities and the creation of suburban communities across the United States.

The industry provided well-paying jobs to hundreds of thousands of workers, many of them minorities. It provided health care and pensions, and many people credit the industry with a major role in the creation of the middle class in America.

At one point, it was estimated that one in seven jobs were connected with the auto industry when you include the manufacturers themselves, dealers, suppliers and those who finance the purchase of automobiles.

The industry, especially through its independent dealers, has played a significant charitable and support role in thousands of communities across the country. Through innovation and technologies initially developed for the auto industry and then applied to other industries and applications, the R&D efforts of the auto companies have touched and improved the lives of everyone in America.

While the past two decades have seen a great deal of consolidation and shrinkage in the domestic U.S. auto industry, it remains a powerhouse of technology and environmental innovation and has the potential to create thousands of well-paying jobs as projected economic growth resumes.

What is automotive PR?

A better question might be, "What isn't automotive PR?" Because, with the scale, complexity, diversity and global footprints of modern auto companies, you can expect to be asked to handle just about any type of communications issue or challenge you can imagine.

On a global basis, auto company communications staffs may number into the hundreds, and individuals are assigned to cover just about every facet of these mega companies. An easy way to think about it is to visualize a full-service PR agency residing within the corporation. Of course, auto companies have always had numerous PR agency partners in addition to their own staffs to help when specialized communications skills are needed or to provide additional resources during periods of heavy workloads.

An incredible diversity of activity is handled by the auto companies' communications staffs. Let's look at some of the responsibilities and challenges that these communicators take on.

Regardless of what kind of communications work you want to do, it's happening at the auto companies.

PRODUCT PR

Although everything that corporate communications staffs do should be in support of their company's business objectives, in the auto industry none is closer to those core objectives than product public relations. From the basics of providing performance data and specifications and photography to elaborate media launches at global auto shows, the majority of auto communications spending and personnel are assigned to product PR. Special programming is designed to introduce a wide range of media—magazines, social media, newspaper, radio, TV and so on—to new models and provide an opportunity to test drive new models and talk to designers, engineers, marketing people and senior executives. Vehicles are later provided to media representatives for longer test drive evaluations. Company blogs and websites supply incredible amounts of product information to anyone interested.

If your imagination can create an opportunity for media—and often specific consumer groups—to be exposed to a vehicle, it can be done and probably has been done by one of the car companies in the past.

Chris Hosford, vice president for Communications at Hyundai, which has had a string of successful product launches, lists the following steps for a successful automotive product launch:

1. Understand and be consistent with product and marketing messages and goals.

2. Clearly define your media objectives.

3. Define the competitive set.

4. Differentiate your product.

5. Create momentum.

6. Create a product experience.

7. Strategically time media coverage (when possible).

8. Evaluate and evolve.

DESIGN COMMUNICATIONS

The auto industry is one of the most covered industries globally. As a result, virtually every aspect of the design, engineering, manufacturing and sales efforts for cars and trucks is of interest to an ever-growing group of traditional and social media.

Design communications is the "fashion" element of automotive PR. It is closely followed by not only automotive publications but art and architecture media as well. Concept cars, usually revealed at auto shows, are the stars of the design world, but the media and the general public have long been fascinated with car design. It is an interest in an art form that people develop very early in life. Cars are often called "rolling sculptures."

ENGINEERING COMMUNICATIONS

At the core of product communications is engineering. It often is the story of fuel economy, weight reduction, packaging, suspensions and steering, technology and environmental innovations. There is a nontraditional audience of suppliers, equipment manufacturers and government officials who are keenly interested in automobiles, and a great deal of "vertical" or specialty media services their need for information.

Other auto communications functions sometimes included under this category are *technology*, *environmental*, *safety* and *vehicle recall* communications.

MANUFACTURING COMMUNICATIONS

This activity centers on the plants that produce parts and whole vehicles. There is a significant audience that is specifically interested in manufacturing techniques and equipment, but these communicators also work with media located near the manufacturing facilities and provide information on employment, updates and expansions to the plant, production schedules and many other issues of interest to the local community.

MARKETING AND SALES COMMUNICATIONS

A significant number of marketing and sales specialty publications, as well as general auto and business media, follow these issues. Subsets of this activity are *advertising* and *fleet sales* communications.

People who follow these areas are interested in month-to-month and year-to-year sales totals, the levels of incentive spending, sales to fleet operators such as rental car companies versus retail sales to individual customers, advertising campaigns, new taglines and advertising agency issues, positioning of a vehicle versus the competition and much more.

EMPLOYEE AND OTHER CONSTITUENCIES' COMMUNICATIONS

Once considered the responsibility of the human resources or personnel departments, employee communications has become a critically important task within auto companies.

As the business itself has become more complex, so has communicating with employees. Instead of just bombarding employees with what management wants them to know, it has become a dialogue and a two-way conversation. Information on industry conditions, competition, quality, costs, globalization and many other subjects are communicated to salaried employees, giving them the opportunity to make up their own minds on what is happening in the industry that will affect their company and their jobs.

In addition to communications to *salaried* and *hourly* employees, the companies also make a significant effort to communicate with *retirees*, *dealers*, *suppliers* and others.

Gary Grates, president and global managing director, Edelman Change and Employee Engagement, and the former global head of internal communications at GM, indicates that the following trends are at play in organizational communications:

1. Employees are your next new product.

2. Managers are no longer the center of an employee's universe.

3. Leadership rhetoric challenges versus cheerleads.

4. Conversations inform decision making not vice versa.

5. Socializing strategy throughout the enterprise correlates with success.

6. Story sharing defines brands from the inside out.

7. Engagement equals experience.

8. Credibility is constantly shifting.

9. Adding visual dimension to one's work leads to greater comprehension.

10. Situational awareness trumps all.

11. Self-identity is found through a career path versus a company destination.

FINANCIAL AND SHAREHOLDER COMMUNICATIONS

This critical area includes reporting of quarterly and annual financial results and timely and broad-based communication of material information relative to the company's financial performance, product issues, production schedule changes, ratings and so forth.

Financial communications also works closely with the *investor relations* staff within the company to coordinate release of information to financial analysts and the media.

MEDIA RELATIONS/NEWS DESK

Inside most companies' communications department is a newsroom, where a wide variety of media inquiries are handled. Questions about lawsuits, international operations, corporate policy and anything else not covered by one of the other assigned communications teams comes in here. Team members need a very broad knowledge of the company, great resources within the company and the abilities to be quick and responsive to questions and good at building strong relationships with the media to be successful and effective.

EXECUTIVE COMMUNICATIONS

Many communications teams also include a group that works directly with the most senior management to assist in all their communications needs. The assignment can include speechwriting, letter writing, talking points for interviews or employee discussions and scheduling interviews, speeches and internal appearances.

Tony Cervone, who held senior communications leadership positions at Chrysler, GM and United Airlines, and who recently joined Volkswagen in the United States as CCO, gives this advice for dealing with the CEO:

Do

1. Use the CEO as the "communicator in chief."

2. Know who the CEO is and capitalize on his or her natural communications abilities.

3. Be respectful of, and responsible with, the CEO's time.

4. Understand that, as the CEO's reputation goes, so does the company's.

Do not

1. Try to make the CEO something he or she is not.

2. Crumble under the pressure of dealing with the CEO.

3. Be irresponsible with your access.

RESEARCH, ISSUES MANAGEMENT AND TREND ANALYSIS

This category is an important piece of the communications equation that is often not given the budget or human resources it deserves.

Research into the image and reputation of the company, message effectiveness or movement of opinion on various issues and events, can prove invaluable in developing a communications strategy and tactical plan.

CHARITABLE COMMUNICATIONS, COMMUNITY RELATIONS AND CORPORATE SOCIAL RESPONSIBILITY

Community participation is an increasingly important activity. Recent difficulties experienced by the U.S. auto industry reduced contributions to charitable and community organizations but the industry will return to this role over time.

Communications in connection with these financial contributions and involvement at the community level are very important in building a strong image and reputation, especially in those communities where the companies have a significant manufacturing presence.

SOCIAL MEDIA

By any measure, the impact of social media in all its forms has been the communications game changer over the past decade. It has given everyone a voice, including the auto companies. The rules of the road may be different and the speed and potential for good and bad are enormous, but no one can afford not to be aggressive in this space.

A more complete discussion of the use of social media in the auto industry will appear later in this chapter.

CRISIS COMMUNICATIONS

The U.S. auto industry has certainly had its share of crises throughout it 100-plus-year history, but never more so than in 2008–2010. Although you can never accurately predict the exact type or fact basis a crisis will take, you can practice how you and your communications team will react in a crisis situation. Practice will build confidence in your response system and test your organization to make sure you have the right people and right resources to respond to a crisis quickly and effectively.

Dan McGinn, one of the leading crisis counselors in the United States, suggests keeping the following things in mind when dealing with a communications crisis:

1. Unusual events tend to cluster.

2. Be quick but do not hurry.

3. You have to process information quickly.

4. You have to know the most about the facts.

5. Crisis is a bad time to make new friends.

6. Know your advisors before a crisis happens.

7. Use opinion research.

8. Understand who will tell you the truth.

9. Crisis is a spend, spend, spend situation—emotion, money and mind share.

PLANNING, IMPLEMENTATION AND EVALUATION

Automotive communications represents an intense segment within the overall public relations industry, in part because of the many different audiences it engages and the significant interest in the automotive sector among the news media.

In an industry that directly employs more than 1.7 million people across design, engineering, manufacturing and supplying, with another 8 million jobs in indirect industries (suppliers, dealers, etc.),[1] speaking to a variety of audiences is essential. At the same time, with more than 245 million passenger vehicles on the road today, the industry must be able to both support an auto enthusiast's desire to hear the latest and greatest technical specifications of a new model and convey easy-to-understand messages about the same vehicle to parents who may only seek out automobile information when shopping for a new car.

Rarely was the importance of speaking directly to a variety of audiences tested more than in 2008 at the start of the global economic recession. The economic crisis had pushed the auto industry to the brink, including two companies that ultimately filed for bankruptcy, leaving the public skeptical—if not antagonistic—regarding the future of the industry. Automakers not only needed to rebuild their reputations, they also needed to rethink how they reached consumers and conducted their business, including an opportunity to change the way they communicated with their audiences, such as consumers, reporters, lawmakers and dealers.

To succeed, the auto companies needed to speak clearly and with one voice to diverse audiences. This effort required planning, implementation and evaluation to be essential pieces of their plans. Each company would need a clear idea of how it would move forward as well as the ability to make that vision a reality and a way to ensure the plan was working.

In this section, using recent events as examples, we will explore how planning, implementation and evaluation are critical to executing successful campaigns in the auto industry, with an in-depth look at how the industry is leveraging social media tools and working to be more transparent and responsive to consumers.

PLANNING AND IMPLEMENTATION

Of course, every media effort is different, but there are some key elements and standard considerations that should be part of every effort. The five steps covered in this section form a checklist that will help develop a successful campaign, from launching a new vehicle model to rebuilding a company's image following a crisis.

CHOOSE THE MESSAGE AND IDENTIFY THE GOAL

In such a large industry, with so many audiences and competing interests, creating a clear vision and simple message from the outset is essential. Maintaining message discipline and clearly identifying goals from the outset will help ensure that the message cuts through the clutter and reaches the intended audience. Establish a vision that can be shared

---

PR CAMPAIGN CHECKLIST

What is the message or goal?
What is the event or announcement?

- Auto shows
- Ride and drives
- Local dealer events
- Consumer Electronics Show
- Local, state and federal government demonstrations

Who is the audience?

- Employees
- Labor groups
- Policymakers
- Suppliers
- Stakeholders
- Media

What tools or resources will be used?

- Videos, B-roll
- Animation
- Press release

What mediums will be used to drive messages?

- Print
- Radio
- Broadcast
- Social media

MAXIMIZE IMPACT ONLINE

Reach more audiences

- Car enthusiasts
- Parents
- Green
- Technology
- Bloggers

Opportunities

- Online car reveals
- Behind the scenes content
- Live chats with executives
- Celebrity spokesperson live chats or exclusive content

with stakeholders and a message that everyone on the team can deliver so an audience hears the same message through multiple media.

For example, when Ford Motor Company implemented its "One Ford" campaign in 2006, it provided its employees with a wallet-sized laminated card with four goals printed on one side and a revised definition of the company printed on the other. These goals and messages are reflected in every aspect of Ford's business and are incorporated in all communications and/or PR campaigns. Regardless of the event or type of news item, every message and plan must point back to the idea of "One Ford."

IDENTIFY TYPE OF EVENT OR ANNOUNCEMENT

The auto industry is fortunate in that it has a variety of events and announcements to help creatively convey messages and provide information to audiences, from auto shows or "ride and drives" to less obvious opportunities, such as technology trade shows and demonstrations with lawmakers at the local, state or federal level.

Different formats cater to different audiences, so team members should identify at the outset which kind of event or announcement makes the most sense for your goal and audience. For example, ride and drives are great opportunities to showcase new auto features to auto enthusiasts that want in-depth information and have the time to spend absorbing it. Hands-on demonstrations are perfect for broadcast media because of the visuals they provide to viewers, and bloggers may prefer behind-the-scenes informational visits that provide special information for their readers.

IDENTIFY THE AUDIENCE

Years ago, the auto industry largely focused its communications efforts on reaching automotive reporters. Today, successful auto companies know that this alone is not enough. From car bloggers to environmental reporters and from parents to technology media, the opportunities to use these audiences to amplify messages are vast—and essential.

In planning an event, think about the audience and what messages resonate with different groups. Target audiences will vary depending on the kind of announcement. Release of financial information will target financial reporters, stockholders, analysts and others, whereas a new product announcement will be geared more toward consumers.

Even when sharing one announcement to multiple audiences, it is important to identify what matters most to each audience within that announcement and tailor it to appeal to that group. Learn what reporters or bloggers are interested in and, from there, provide information that is useful or unique. Strategically identify and engage the most influential and relevant audiences and forge new relationships to deliver messages and information.

IDENTIFY TOOLS AND RESOURCES

When beginning outreach to key audiences, keep in mind that the universe of reporters is stretched thinner and thinner as traditional news outlets cut staff or ask more contributions from reporters in order to be more competitive. Outreach must be tailored and comprehensive, giving them all the "extras" they may have created by themselves before.

During the planning stage, determine which tools and resources will help tell the story to target audiences. Resources include:

- B-roll footage (used for TV reporting)
- Animation showing a new feature "in action"
- Demonstrations
- Press releases
- Fact sheets
- Samples of new materials (leather, high-strength steel, etc.)
- Sound files to demonstrate quiet engines and so forth

IDENTIFY MEDIA TO DRIVE MESSAGES

Today, there are many ways for PR professionals to deliver messages to various audiences. This may be achieved through traditional forms such as broadcast interviews on local morning shows or outreach to automotive columnists or through new means, such as leveraging social media networks. Once again, utilizing a combination of media will reach more audience members and will further support efforts to drive home messages and information. Think strategically about how to implement each, and how one medium can encourage coverage among others.

For example, the 2011 Super Bowl provided the auto industry with the opportunity to marry a traditional media strategy, advertising, with nontraditional outlets, social networks, to reach varied audiences: football fans, auto enthusiasts, reporters and consumers. Auto companies not only bought ad time, but also leveraged social networks to get the most bang for their buck and keep momentum and buzz going around new product launches and overall campaigns.

MAXIMIZE IMPACT—TRADITIONAL MEDIA + NONTRADITIONAL MEDIA

In 2010, Ford Motor Company Reinvents the Reveal

- Launches the new Explorer first on Facebook.
- Team conducts extensive research; analyzes success and failure of other launches on Facebook; determines content; and supports social media reveal activities with traditional ad buy and media campaign.
- Traffic to FordVehicles.com nearly crashed servers; top U.S. search trend on Google; 99 million social media impressions in three days.

Chrysler and VW Maximize Super Bowl Ad Buy

- Chrysler's "Imported from Detroit" ad viewed more than 6 million times on YouTube.
- Chrysler's Facebook page "liked" by more than 92,000 people.
- VW's ad "The Force" hit more than 1 million views in less than 24 hours following its broadcast during the Super Bowl.

VW posted "behind the scenes" footage on its Facebook page a week after the Super Bowl—thereby giving more "legs" to the ad.

GAME CHANGER: SOCIAL MEDIA

Across all generations, more car buyers than ever are utilizing social networks to connect with other enthusiasts, learn information about product launches and stay connected to their favorite brands. To reach those consumers, four out of five auto companies use social media tools today, with that number only expected to grow. By 2012, 88 percent of all automotive marketers will use social media to reach their audiences. As more and more consumers turn to online media for their news, it is critical that every communications effort include a plan for social media outreach today.

CASE STUDY: A MORE SOCIAL FORD MOTOR COMPANY

In November 2008, the domestic automotive industry was on the brink of disaster, facing increased competition, declining sales, a global economic meltdown and a series of contentious congressional hearings. Ford Motor Company emerged as the only domestic automaker to reject a government bailout and was confident in its product lineup—with all vehicles best-in-class or among best-in-class in fuel efficiency, quality, safety and technology. However, Ford had to find a way to communicate this to consumers. Its traditional, automotive industry–focused communications model was broken and no longer served Ford's needs.

Social media would play a pivotal role in this new communications plan. By strategically identifying and engaging with the most influential and relevant online voices, Ford could give them a Ford Story they could share with the world.

OBJECTIVES

Ford needed to differentiate itself from other Detroit manufacturers, convince consumers, opinion leaders and the general public that "Ford is Different" and has a plan and quality vehicles to succeed.

Ford looked to social media to:

Look beyond auto bloggers to identify new categories on the web that could care about Ford with the right opportunity
Develop breakthrough social media programs that got online influencers talking
Improve perception of the Ford brand among consumers online

STRATEGIES

Ford would show online influencers (and ultimately their audience) the human side of Ford. They would introduce these influencers to the real faces and stories of the Ford brand and its products.

Influencers would need different information tailored to their audiences and first-hand experiences.

These endorsements could be used to strengthen Ford's image and amplify other efforts to send a powerful message to consumers.

TACTICS

Enterprise Transformation

To truly capitalize on the power of social media, Ford would need to look at how it approached social media internally and externally, regionally and globally and outside of the Communications team across the entire enterprise. Social media could not be the job of one; it needed to be integrated into the planning and tactics across the organization.

To start, Ford launched official corporate presences on top social networks, including Facebook, Twitter, YouTube and Flickr, and vehicle-specific presences where appropriate on these same sites.

Ford drafted guidelines showing its internal and external approach to social media and posted them on Scribd, the social media sharing site. In addition, Ford convened its own global Center of Excellence to bring its social media team members together around the world on a regular basis for sharing best practices, guidelines, campaigns and opportunities for collaboration. Ford launched a Sharepoint site to act as an online hub for these activities. Finally, Ford began the development of standardized playbooks for team members in Communications and Marketing to have one set of rules and standardized procedures for handling various platforms and types of campaigns.

Market-Facing Programs

With so many new audiences to reach, Ford developed innovative new market-facing programs for vehicle reveals and influencer engagement. For the launch of the Taurus, Ford rolled out a 100-city tour with targeted social media outreach in 10 cities known for having larger social media communities. There, local influencers were able to test drive the vehicle and talk to executives including CEO Alan Mulally, and Ford was able to film test drive testimonials and share photographs across its social platforms.

To better reach female buyers, Ford hosted 60 bloggers at the Chicago Assembly Plant the day before the 2009 BlogHer Conference for the *What Women Want* Quality and Technology Forum. The women in attendance met the Ford team responsible for putting sustainable materials in seats and tried the latest in-vehicle technology. In addition, they got a tour of the Chicago Assembly Plant and saw the Taurus being rolled off the line—an experience most highlighted as being once in a lifetime.

Digital Media Relations

With the constant goal of bringing all communications efforts and experiences to digital influencers, Ford maintains strong relationships with the online influencers they hear from and meet at events. These influencers are lent vehicles through the Blogger Drive program and often share their stories on their own blogs as well as the Ford Story, providing Ford with new and authentic vehicle experiences to share on its own network.

Event Activations

To generate real-world awareness and increase content creation and coverage, Ford builds social media into its events on the ground. At the 2010 North American International Auto Show, Ford had its top executives participate in a full day of social media activities with blogger interviews, Q&As on Twitter and Facebook, and photo and videos live from the show floor. For the 2011 North American International Auto Show, Ford took its established commitment to social media even further and invited 100 bloggers from around the world to a Green and Technology event. Bloggers spent one day at the show blogging live from the show floor and the next day saw the best of Ford's green and technology innovations, including touring the local Dearborn truck plant and seeing firsthand how Ford takes sustainability into account in the manufacturing process. Along the way, these bloggers created three straight day's worth of content, sharing all of this information across the social Web.

RESULTS

Ford achieved impressive results with its bloggers. Before launching its social media initiatives, an average of 29 percent of bloggers would have considered purchasing Ford vehicles. Afterward, 89 percent of them said they would, based on a company survey. The bloggers' coverage resulted in more than 200 million social media impressions. The industry recognized these achievements as well, awarding Ford the Cannes Lions Silver Lion for Social Media in 2010 and *PRWeek*'s Best Use of Social Media Award in 2009. Mashable named the Ford Explorer reveal one of the five "game-changing" social media campaigns of 2010, and Ford was named the top automotive brand in social (and #11 overall) by Vitrue in 2010.

TRANSPARENCY AND ACCOUNTABILITY

Recent product recalls and congressional hearings, combined with the increased popularity of social media, have put a premium on transparency and accountability in all communications efforts. Auto companies have had to recognize that problems existed, whether financial or product oriented, and determine a way to address those problems and identify solutions. By and large, this meant being more transparent with consumers, policy makers and the press.

Audiences today want to be able to speak directly with people involved with a company or someone who represents that company. They want to ensure they have

TRANSPARENCY AND "GOING GREEN"

"Greenwashing" is a relatively new term coined to describe deceptive use of "green PR" to mislead consumers into thinking a company's products or policies are more environmentally friendly than they are.

The auto industry is careful to avoid such charges as it works to put new types of vehicles to market, as evidenced through recent confusion over what constitutes an electric vehicle and how many miles per gallon a vehicle truly achieves.

Transparency is key to avoiding this situation. Providing more information to support a company's claim will go a long way toward building credibility and trust.

If You Want to . . .	Try Measuring with . . .
Reach influencers	A survey to capture specific thoughts among a small, specific group
Determine image changes	Looking at changes in tone of voice in articles
Determine reputation changes	Word clouds
Increase awareness	Tracking number of clips
Increase social media presence	Track Twitter followers or Facebook fans

been heard and want to ensure they are being treated fairly. Social media gives auto companies an additional resource to provide audiences with straight, honest answers.

In 2009, Toyota came under scrutiny following reports that it delayed providing information to the U.S. government about mechanical issues with some of its vehicle models. For months, the company mishandled how it relayed information about the mechanical failures. While both NASA and the National Highway Traffic Safety Administration ultimately found no electronics-based reason for the mechanical problem, Toyota was forced to pay millions in fines and came under heavy fire from the press, consumers and lawmakers, in large part because of a perception that Toyota hid information from consumers.

EVALUATION

Judging the success or failure of any campaign can be tricky and often subjective; one person's definition of success may not be another's. Just as every campaign is different, measuring its success also will be, which is why evaluation should be included at the start of every plan to ensure an accurate assessment of an event or announcement.

Success for a campaign can range from traditional media hits to increased traffic on a website to how many people "like" something on Facebook or share a video posted to YouTube. In order to determine if objectives and goals have been met, metrics should be put in place during the planning stage in order to manage expectations and identify a method that best reflects the stated objective.

HOW FAR CAN YOU SEE AROUND THE CURVE?

Much of what this chapter covered occurred in roughly the first 100 hundred years of the U.S. auto industry. But what do the next five years and beyond hold for those practicing communications in the auto industry or in just communications in general?

A few things are obvious:

1. The world continues to shrink. The globalization of the auto industry and business in general is accelerating. Barriers and borders are being eliminated.

2. The global auto industry has consolidated, and many believe this trend will continue for many years to come. So you will have fewer companies with those surviving selling in markets around the world and representing a number of brands.

3. The speed at which information and news—and rumors and untruths—will move around the world will continue to accelerate. You will need a response mechanism and process in place that can respond in minutes, not hours.

4. The blurring and real integration of communications and marketing will continue. Few, if any, organizations have achieved true integration but its logic is so compelling that it is only a matter of

time. The question remains as to whether communications will have an equal voice in the ultimate integration.

5. What we consider a crisis today will become much more of the norm. Many will come and go quickly, but an organization's ability to deal with them efficiently and with transparency will be critical.

6. Engagement will become a key activity of all business organizations, and communications will play a vital role in engagements with a wide variety of audiences. Only those companies that can truly find a way to engage with customers will succeed in the long term.

7. Social media will continue to evolve and play an even more dominant role than it does today. But will the auto companies and all users be overaggressive and too heavy handed and ultimately turn off the audience and users of social media? This is a real risk, and so the challenge will be to anticipate and leapfrog to where those audiences will move next to engage, get information and have conversations.

8. Content versus context. Warren Buffett has said, "The value of information has gone to zero. But the value of expertise and ability to interpret information will someday go to infinity." In an age when anyone, anywhere can get equal access to information, those organizations that can provide context and credibility will be the most successful in changing minds.

9. A number of very bright communications people have begun writing about the "wisdom of crowds" (James Surowiecki) and "crowd surfing," but the bottom line is that groups—often consumers—are smarter than individuals. Listening has always been an underutilized skill but those who can apply deep listening will profit greatly. The answers are found in our customers, employees, suppliers, dealers, etc. The power shifts that we have already witnessed and will witness in the years ahead are permanent.

10. Winning and losing will be magnified and accelerated. We are given examples almost daily that the riskiest position to be in today is biggest, best, first or most.

11. And finally, the public expects, and is entitled to, more than scientific data and legal fine print.

What they really want to know is, are you a predator or a partner?

DISCUSSION QUESTIONS

1. What was there about the major auto companies that caused them to set up internal PR departments earlier than most corporations or industries? Are the car companies leaders in communications today in your opinion? If not, what companies or industries do you think are doing the best job of communicating today?

2. Communications within the auto companies is very diversified, lots of very different types of communications expertise are called for. Can this be effectively done internally? What role can and should external resources (PR agencies, freelancers, etc.) play in the development and execution of modern corporate communications?

3. How important is research in contemporary communications? If you feel it is important, why do you think so little is being spent on it today? Why can't communicators agree on how to measure what they do?

4. What are core elements of effective PR planning and implementation? Would you add any to the list outlined in the automotive chapter?

5. The U.S. auto companies were very earlier adopters of social media trends and tools. How familiar are you with what they have done? How effective do you think they have been? If you were advising the car companies on social media, what suggestions would you give them?

6. Do you agree with the future of communications outlined at the end of the chapter under "How Far Can You See around the Curve?" Are there any that you disagree with? Are they any observations of your own that you would add?

NOTE

1. Report: Center for Automotive Research. "Contribution of the Automotive Industry to the Economies of All Fifty States and the United States." Ann Arbor, Michigan, 2010.

ADDITIONAL READING

Ingrassia, Paul. *Crash Course: The American Auto Industry's Road to Glory to Disaster*, 1st ed. New York, NY: Random House, 2011. Print.

Lutz, Robert A. *Car Guys vs. Bean Counters: The Battle for the Soul of American Business*. New York, NY: Portfolio/Penguin, 2011. Print.

Taylor, Alex, III. *Sixty to Zero: An Intimate inside Look at the People and Cars That Led to GM's Collapse*. New Haven, CT: Yale Univ. Press, 2010. Print.

Vlasic, Bill. *Once upon a Car: The Fall and Resurrection of America's Big Three Auto Makers—GM, Ford, and Chrysler*. New York, NY: William Morrow, 2011. Print.

32 CHAPTER

THE AVIATION INDUSTRY AND CIVIL AVIATION
Flying High for Business

Robert P. Mark
Chief Executive Officer
CommAvia

Good public relations for the aviation industry is a simple concept really . . . at least theoretically.

Engage people with a cleverly written story that convinces them to think differently about a product, service, organization or idea, a new belief you know is critically important to their life. Then, persuade them that it is a piece of information they cannot possibly live without for another day. Naturally, the message they hear, the message that changes their view of the aviation world, is one that comes from you, a message that just a few days, sometimes only just a few hours prior, was no more than an idea in your head or words on the screen of a laptop or smart phone. The key is to also be a strategic communicator, since any PR practitioner can react to a crisis.

The public relations function within the aviation realm is more dynamic than in most other industries, often requiring reactionary PR, as in the case of an accident or significant incident. The chaos of September 11 not only forced PR professionals to solve problems they never learned about in school, but forced them to develop strategies on the fly. The aviation industry, however, was never the same, despite the incredible communications efforts of both airline and public safety officials in New York and Pennsylvania. The events of September 11 also reinforced the idea that the most significant public relations draw in aviation is safety. Like automotive, health care or energy, if the case can be made that public safety is somehow at risk, a story is sure to follow like dawn follows night.

Throughout this chapter, our goal is not simply to highlight examples of good or bad public relations in the aviation industry, but to call attention to the issues and methods used that clearly outline elements of PR that are more common to this industry than to others. This chapter sifts through the facts, the stories and the people to find those learning experiences that will most easily allow new PR practitioners to more easily make that leap from the industry uninitiated to communicators with enough knowledge that their first day on a new job in aviation will be much less anxiety producing for themselves and their new employers. This chapter also highlights significant elements of the aviation industry often left unmentioned, such as business aviation and general aviation, in addition to the more well-known airline sector.

AVIATION 101: A QUICK LOOK AT THE INDUSTRY

Some PR practitioners believe a public relations career in aviation means working for an airline. Setting your sights on an airline PR career might well mean missing out on some other fascinating aspects of the aviation industry.

Here is a bit of what might slip under your nose:

In addition to working for the major airlines, PR people might find industry employment in business aviation, those private jets owned and used by large corporations to fly executives and middle managers all over the world. Fleets of these aircraft are often owned by high-net-worth individuals and celebrities, or charter companies, which means the need for PR folks to help guide the media through the mayhem that often occurs when a Michael Jordan or Shania Twain arrive for an event. The reason these very busy, rich and guarded people almost never travel on the airlines is simple. The newest business aircraft such as the Dassault Falcon 7X can fly 8 to 10 passengers in lavish comfort from any point in the United States to almost anywhere in Western Europe nonstop without the need for passengers to wait in line or share luggage space.

General aviation—often including small single-engine aircraft—also demands a considerable PR force, especially at airframe manufacturers such as Cessna, Hawker Beechcraft, Cirrus, Piper, Gulfstream, Dassault Falcon and Bombardier. Electronic equipment manufacturers such as Honeywell or Rockwell Collins also maintain a considerable PR force, as do builders of aircraft engines, landing gear, tires and hydraulic systems. Large aircraft manufacturers such as Boeing, Airbus, Bombardier and Embraer are also worthy employment targets. The defense aerospace industry, giants such as Northrup Grumman, Lockheed, General Dynamics and Raytheon, also demand considerable numbers of PR people.

Although an engineering degree in addition to a communications degree is not necessary to qualify, nor is a pilot's license for that matter, the best aviation PR people are passionate about the industry. Why? Because most of the people they will encounter on a regular basis from media covering the industry to customers and even company employees tend to be very dedicated to and excited about the products they build and the services they deliver.

Good aviation industry practitioners acknowledge the dynamics of aviation itself, which is considerably different from the situations a person encounters working for Palmolive or Citigroup. Sloppy work or a poor attitude can cost an airline, charter or aircraft management company customers at best, lives at worst.

Certainly after an aircraft accident, the immediate crisis often focuses on the degree of control PR practitioners can maintain, which is very little actually. A solid response means following the crisis communications plan almost all aviation companies have at the ready—or should.

It is critical to have level-headed, compassionate spokespersons who are media ready. Because an aviation accident is so spectacular—often with a loss of life or serious injuries—choosing the right spokesperson can be one of the most critical decisions any corporate communicator might make. A person too focused on the company and not enough on the passengers and crew can make for disastrous and far-reaching PR results. The questions every reporter or relative wants to know are usually the ones any PR practitioner is least likely to have answers to, such as, "How could this happen?" and "Are the passengers safe?" Any answer short of, "We are doing all we can to learn the state of the aircraft, the passengers and the crew" or "As soon as we have any update on the people involved, we will update you," and finally, "It is far too early to speculate on the cause" (see Case study #1) is probably the wrong answer. Aviation communicators do not simply sit around waiting for the next accident or incident to occur, however. Sometimes, just a phone call, e-mail or Tweet from a customer service representative trying to soothe an angry or frightened passenger can draw them into a conversation, something that seldom occurs in the packaged goods or publishing industries. In aviation, the learning never stops.

An example of this scenario occurred on my recent trip aboard a regional airliner—50 seats—a wholly owned subsidiary of a major carrier. The aircraft was taxiing out from Chicago O'Hare International Airport for a two-hour flight west toward Denver. As most pilots will do after the flight is airborne, this one offered passengers an idea of the trip ahead, telling us it would take longer than normal because the aircraft would be flying more slowly than normal. "The reason is that the aircraft is missing a metal panel." You could have heard a pin drop, even inside the noisy jet, as many passengers wondered just how an airplane could possibly be flying with some sort of metal panel missing. Indeed, many commented, "Why is this airplane flying with a panel missing? It can't possibly be safe, can it?" There were no additional comments from the cockpit until we landed.

After all passengers had left the airplane, the PR guy and pilot in me simply had to find out what the captain had been talking about. I approached the cockpit door, which by now was open and asked. "Oh that?"

he said. "We're missing a fueling panel door on the fuselage. No big deal at all. The aircraft manufacturer recommends we fly slower when the piece is missing though. It's all perfectly legal." I took a minute and explained that some passengers were just short of terrified at the idea of flying an airplane with missing parts.

The pilot was seriously shocked that his statement, intended simply to inform, had actually frightened anyone. He promised not to be quite so blunt the next time. This incident reinforces a major issue aviation PR folks must deal with. Pilots who operate the aircraft are often "left-brained people," meaning, of course, that they understand how things work, or do not. Unfortunately, if you are a right-brained communicator trying to communicate with a left-brained aviator, the conversation can be enlightening, as we saw here. But it happens all the time when employees get caught up trying to help. As the PR person, you will put out a lot of fires—figuratively, of course. The key is to not confuse passion with a high communications emotional quotient (EQ) score.

Aviation public relations can be—at the same time—fascinating, exciting and terribly challenging for a number of reasons. One, aviation is highly regulated, which means that practitioners must clearly understand not only their own jobs and the products or services the company delivers, but also appreciate the vast group of government regulators that oversee every aspect of the industry. Practitioners must become familiar with the Federal Aviation Administration (FAA), the major regulating body for the industry. They also should understand the position—operationally and politically—of the Department of Transportation (DOT), the cabinet-level organization that oversees the FAA. There are also a number of significant associations related to the industry that carry immense weight on Capitol Hill.

Aviation communicators must learn about the National Transportation Safety Board (NTSB), a powerful, independent federal watchdog organization responsible for investigating all aircraft accidents and incidents, as well as for developing regular safety recommendations to the FAA. The public relations aspects of an NTSB recommendation on an airline, a charter company or the flying industry in general can be enormous, as they can on the FAA itself. This is especially true when the agency decides *not* to implement an NTSB recommendation, which are, by the way, nonbinding on the FAA. This option alone often creates a hostile dynamic of one regulator versus the other. It also creates confusion in the public's mind about whether the industry is as safe as it should be.

At present, there are a half-dozen outstanding NTSB recommendations—the board calls them their "most wanted"—sitting without action on a desk at the FAA. Some of the recommendations are more serious than others. At present, they range from the NTSB's suggestion that the FAA improve the quality of pilot proficiency training, to improving the safety of emergency medical services helicopter operations, to reducing the dangers of flying aircraft in icing conditions, to an extremely controversial recommendation to add digital video recorders in the cockpits of airliners. Video recorders would not only record the audio of cockpit conversations, but show pictures of what transpires during the flight. Snoozing, for instance, would be tough to hide, an issue that brought the house down on the FAA when some of their air traffic controllers tried it at work.

The idea about video recorders leads to yet another organization, the Air Line Pilots Association (ALPA) and a cornucopia of operational matters and issues PR practitioners must deal with, one of which is labor and professional unions. Aviation's labor force is actually one of the most highly organized of all U.S. industries, and one that new communicators seldom have experience with. Although union influence on the American workplace has declined significantly over the past few decades, it is alive and well in aviation and government. Everyone from pilots to flight attendants, mechanics, ground workers, even aircraft manufacturing labor all belong to unions. Public relations efforts with a unionized workforce are so unique that it has grown into a discipline of its own: labor relations.

New practitioners must, for instance, learn to stand strong against a first "gut" reaction to a union-induced incident such as a strike or work slowdown. Harsh or reactionary statements to the media during an already highly charged job action can itself inflame the situation. So, it is not at all unusual in a unionized organization to have the company PR people saying one thing, whereas the union's PR spokesperson seems to be taking a completely opposite position. What makes the practitioner's job more difficult when working from either side of the unionized workforce is that volunteer union members will often work side by side with full-time PR practitioners because they *want to help*.

As a quick example, let's look again at the ALPA. These are highly respected, well-educated professionals capable of "leaping tall buildings in a single bound." Oh wait, that's Superman, isn't it? But pilots think they are pretty darned close, which is why the motivated union volunteers (I was one) believe communicating with the public is a piece of cake. Few pilots have any formal communications training (I was an exception). Think back to my earlier comments about pilots being good at commanding electronics and airplanes, but not as strong on people skills. This applies to the union leadership as well as the individual volunteers. They believe in the cause, but are often not able to segment stakeholders and messages. The downfall for some of these volunteers is that their egos tend to be large, which makes them seldom ask for help and often not appreciate it when offered. This, of course, does not mean that a professional communicator should not keep trying, however.

As an example of labor communications, let's delve a bit deeper into the case of video recorders in the cockpit, a subject most outsiders would say sounds like a marvelous safety improvement. Yet, this improvement suggestion has gone nowhere because of the pilots union's refusal to allow them. Imagine the implications for the transfer of safety data to the ground that might prevent an accident, as in the case of Air France 447, an Airbus A330 lost over the South Atlantic in 2009 with the loss of all 228 aboard. The reason there are no video recorders aboard airliners anywhere in the world is that the pilots unions, regulators and company management have failed to agree on terms that would ensure those recordings would not be used in disciplinary actions against union (pilot) members. However, both sides acknowledge the value of digital video technology.

PRACTITIONER INSIGHTS: ROB DOUGHTY, OWNER, DOUGHTY COMMUNICATIONS, MIAMI, FLORIDA

Before opening his consulting business, Rob Doughty served as vice president of communications for Burger King Corporation and vice president of public relations for Pizza Hut, Inc., before that. He has also served in various communications positions for United Airlines. While at United, Doughty was responsible for overhauling and then implementing the crisis communications plan used following two fatal aircraft accidents just five months apart. He received numerous awards for his work and is a frequent speaker and author of articles in professional journals about his experiences managing crisis communications. We spoke about his experience as a PR practitioner in the airline industry.

FIGURE 32.1

Rob Doughty

Q: What makes working as an airline industry communicator somewhat unique from other industries?

A: My experience was with a major international carrier (we were the largest airline in the world at that time). Smaller carriers I'm sure are different. I found the sheer volume of information we handled in my department to be unique. We were the mirror image of the City Desk of a major metropolitan newspaper. Our offices even looked like it with papers stacked everywhere.

Also, we dealt with real-time, very short deadlines. You have to work fast in the airline business. Almost always, we were dealing with news that was breaking that day or within a few days (such as a fare announcement or a new route). Generally, other industries have more time to plan than airlines.

Aviation is very competitive and highly visible. Airlines are seen as critical to commerce. . . the business traveler was our target passenger. When the airline was running on time, it was great. When there was bad weather or other disruptions occurred, it was a very trying time for both passengers and staff. Having a major airline serve a market is a big deal to the local economy, something we take for granted now. However, when we made changes, such as pulling out of several smaller markets in the Midwest in the late eighties and replacing our jet service with United Express and their very small prop planes, these communities felt slighted, wounded and deeply betrayed. These moves made it more difficult for them to attract business. It certainly gave us a black eye with those cities.

Secondly, we were big supporters of tourism as an industry. We had the largest market share of the air-service market to Hawaii, for example, which was both good and bad. When we had a pilot strike in 1986 we brought Hawaii, a state that depends almost exclusively on tourism, to its knees. When we sought to bring needed changes to the Mileage Plus program in the late 1980s, the state of Hawaii was very upset since the new rules were perceived as not fair to Hawaii residents. The Hawaiian state legislature planned to censure us. We stopped the changes. I had to go there in person when we announced the revised changes to make sure our story was told accurately and to show that we had taken Hawaii residents into consideration to be treated fairly.

Q: What are the personal qualities a good public relations practitioner needs in order to be successful in his or her first year at an airline?

A: In the first year, you have to be like a sponge and maintain a strong sense of intellectual curiosity. Ask "What" and "How?" Also ask "Why?" Sometimes "Why?" is the most important question, and its answer is the one most likely to lead to clarity because airlines are very complex. There is a lot to learn in a very short period of time. You also have to work very fast and expect to put in long hours and work at odd times, like late at night and on weekends and holidays. This doesn't change much in subsequent years as there will still be a lot to learn and long and irregular hours will continue. By then, though, you will have a better understanding of the industry, which will make things fall into a clearer context.

Q: Have new forms of social media communications changed what a person needs to know in order to be a successful communicator in the airline industry?

A: No, not really. You must still be a good writer. Even with the truncated language of social media, you will need communications skills such as establishing a clear objective, strategies and messages that explain what you're trying to accomplish. And you will need to do it fast.

Q: Some people remember the 1989 United flight 232 crash in Sioux City [Iowa], certainly a case of extreme airline crisis communications. Are there less dramatic stories you can share?

A: Actually, I'm not sure everyone thinks about UA 232. I meet a lot of people who do not remember it or who were too young or not alive when it went down. There are still lessons to learn from that and other accidents however.

But outside of handling accidents, an airline PR person needs to think like a reporter. . . absorb every fact and distill what is important to get to the real issue or opportunity. This process happens very fast in aviation, much faster than in any other industry I've worked in. As the world's largest airline, we also had to think *big*. Our news needed to be truly newsworthy in an innovative way. We also had to think through all the implications of what we did (i.e., pulling out of or entering a market).

Q: What events stick out in your mind most as a communicator at an airline?

A: Two stick out the most (and there was a lot of stuff), like the launch of United's Pacific service when we acquired Pan Am's Pacific Division, for starters. Literally on a single day, we entered the entire trans Pacific market to Asia, Southeast Asia and the South Pacific. Most airlines entered one or two markets at a time. We launched service to 13 new international destinations on a single day. We also took over Pan Am's operations, crews and aircraft, which were very different from ours. The first year, we operated in the most service-sensitive air market in the world, while also transitioning the operations, aircraft and culture at the same time. It was a huge communications challenge and not without constant issues, such as delayed or cancelled flights that irritated high-paying customers.

    The other events were two accidents—UA 811 and UA 232—just five months apart. I had just finished overhauling the crisis plan in December 1988. UA 811 happened in Feb 1989 and UA 232 in July. They both involved intense work on our part with long days. Often we got no sleep, yet had to be at the top of our game since we were in the public eye. These were both major international news stories and they commanded the media's attention for a good 10 days each.

Q: Is there a strategic value to the new social media tools communicators have at their disposal today?

A: Social media, of course, did not exist then. Now, I would make sure we had communications staff dedicated to monitoring and participating in the social media space to make sure the conversations taking place were accurate and timely, just as we sought to do with traditional media.

(Rob Doughty is also the author of Chapter 37 of this book, which focuses on the Entertainment Industry, based on his work with the Walt Disney Company.)

CASE STUDY #1

As this book goes to press, an incident occurred in March 2011 that tested the reputation of the third largest U.S. air carrier, Southwest Airlines. A Boeing 737, cruising at 34,000 feet en route to Sacramento from Phoenix experienced a cabin decompression when the outer aluminum skin of the 15-year-old aircraft split open, setting off a series of alarms in the cockpit. The alarms also set off a monumental PR disaster for the airline on the ground. At that altitude, the time of useful consciousness for passengers without adequate oxygen is about 45 seconds. After that, people would begin passing out in their seats, unable to grasp the yellow oxygen cups dangling above their heads.

    With knowledge in the cockpit that passengers could quickly perish, flight crews are trained to quickly descend to an altitude of 10,000 feet, where the oxygen levels will allow normal breathing. This means the airplane must lose 26,000 feet as quickly as possible. The math translates into the pilots pulling the engine throttles back to idle and literally shoving the nose of the aircraft down to begin a steep dive. Inside the cabin, it would have felt as if the airplane were pointed almost straight down. Although it really was not, the sensation no doubt added to the panic. Despite crew instructions, the sense inside the cabin would be almost surreal. A once-calm cabin would be suddenly disturbed by an explosion with an accompanying roar of air rushing out of the cabin while oxygen masks would dangle in front of passengers' faces. The pilots would have no time to talk as they wrestled the airplane to a safer altitude and depended on three flight attendants to manage the cabin.

    The aircraft finally did reach a safe altitude with only a few passengers needing assistance. When the media caught wind of the incident, of course, TV and radio, not to mention the Internet, lit up with details of the story. Media such as CNN, Fox News and MSNBC rushed to interview passengers and industry experts, this writer included. Not surprisingly, airline employees refused any and all interviews as strict company policies normally spell out. Pilots also refused to comment for concern that anything they say in an emotional moment might later be used against them in a court of law.

What makes the Southwest Airlines cabin decompression incident a valuable learning tool for public relations practitioners is that, as an airline, they were already experienced with this issue because Southwest had experienced a similar decompression just a year before. No one was injured in that incident either. Southwest is no stranger to difficult PR situations. In 2007, it paid a $7.5 million fine to the FAA for repeated maintenance violations, involving inspections of the aircraft's outer skin.

Although many people still enjoy flying, just as many others view commercial airline flying as about as enjoyable and common as riding a Greyhound bus. When an issue significant enough to warrant media attention like this one pops up, everyone who flies quickly sits up and takes notice. Public relations focused on customers put in life-threatening situations is about as tough as it gets. And yet, just days after the March 2011 incident, TV cameras were anxiously searching for someone who would say something newsworthy about their fears of ever again flying aboard Southwest Airlines. None could be found. Southwest Airlines had avoided a public scandal . . . once again. The question was how.

A few weeks after this event, the story was still playing out in the press, keeping Southwest's PR people on their toes, despite the fact that no specific cause for the malfunction had yet been identified. This did not stop people from making several predictions—anxiety-producing enough for any CEO.

In a *New York Times* story on April 18, 2011, John Goglia, a former member of the NTSB, referred to both the 2011 Southwest incident and an earlier 2009 event in which an 18-inch hole opened up on top of the cabin of another Southwest 737. "Here's a case where we have a small hole [in this incident], a big hole [in the first incident] and if we're not going to do something serious about the entire airplane, we're going to end up with a smoking hole. FAA and other industry officials say they are reviewing their policies on aging planes. But they note that fatigue problems have not caused any deaths on jetliners since the Aloha accident, even with millions of flights a year in the United States."[1]

In an April 24, 2011, statement, the NTSB announced the possibility that Southwest Airlines maintenance —or the lack of it—was not responsible for the decompression incident. Initial reports showed that some of the rivets that hold the skin together were misaligned on the aircraft, suggesting an emerging PR problem at Boeing, where the aircraft was built.

Or, was it simply the short-term memory of a seasoned crowd of Southwest Airlines Rapid rewards members that seemed to get the airline off the hook in this instance? Perhaps it was a snappy spin the airline's PR people put on the incident. After all, Southwest's PR department was one of the first to use social media effectively by anyone's measure.

Here are some questions to consider before you read on:

1. What do you think allowed Southwest's image to remain intact?

2. What would you expect to be your first reaction when CNN calls your cell phone to announce the incident before you have even heard anything from the company?

As it turns out, the most pragmatic reason Southwest Airlines recovered and continues to thrive in situations like this when other airlines have not, really points to the culture of the company itself, a personality trait buried deep within every Southwest employee.

From its humble three-aircraft beginning in 1967 as an intrastate Texas carrier offering service between Dallas, Houston and San Antonio, Air Southwest, as the company was originally called, was viewed as an underdog in a competitive industry. Yet, this scrappy little company was not adverse to communications tactics its legacy airline industry competitors, such as United, American or Delta, would never consider, much less attempt. Despite the seriousness of operating 3,400 daily flights all over the lower 48 states, Southwest Airlines empowers employees with the knowledge and the tools they need to cope—and communicate—during these kinds of problems. Southwest learned early on that keeping everyone in the loop, including customers, encourages those valuable passengers to keep coming back.

Most large airlines cautiously guard all business information. Corporate communications decides who hears what and when. However, Southwest views the company's priorities somewhat differently, which also explains quite a bit about the company culture. At United, for example, shareholders and profit maximization are the airline's top priority, with the debate on whether employees come next and then customers, or customers second and United employees winning a third place slot in overall importance. At Southwest, founder Herb Kelleher, a chain-smoking, Wild Turkey–drinking lawyer-turned-airline CEO saw the world a little differently. He believed employees should be the company's number one priority, with customers second and shareholders, well. . . . Kelleher believes shareholder issues and profit maximization all work out if the first two priorities are firmly established. The company acts this way with information dissemination from corporate communications too. (See Chapter 8 on Employee Communications.)

From a public relations standpoint, Southwest Airlines' culture translates into a fairly open-door opportunity for the media to meet and get to know the communications practitioners the airline brings on board. Kelleher was always known as a guy any reporter could stop in the halls of the airline's Dallas Love Field HQ with a question. The PR staff at Southwest—with their use of social media tools such as the "Nuts About Southwest" blog,[2] as well as company-managed Twitter feeds and podcasts—encouraged relationship building early on with bloggers in addition to the usual cadre of TV, radio and print reporters. Beginning with the airline's "annual media days" in 2008, bloggers from every aspect of the aviation industry found themselves eating a scrumptious meal right alongside travel writer Peter Greenberg or Andy Pastor from the *Wall Street Journal*.

Southwest's PR department offered these introductions to the airline itself and to other reporters that fundamentally paved the way for additional relationship building, which was good for the reporters and bloggers and, of course, very good for Southwest Airlines. The PR department at Southwest also made a point of regularly reading and commenting on other aviation and travel blogs, encouraging even more participation by social media geeks with the airline, as the carrier continued building a critical mass of solid public opinion, better known as social capital, building goodwill for the day when it's needed.

For the PR department at Southwest, this meant that when a crisis hit the fan, the blogosphere could be counted on to light up with opinions, usually positive. People wanted to like the people at Southwest Airlines because the airline's communicators had spent years building valuable relationships with reporters of all shapes and sizes, from all points on the globe.

Not long after the skin peeled back from the Southwest airplane, communicator resource, Ragan.com, ran a story about another incident at the airline and how valuable social media had been to connecting with stakeholders.

In this event, a Southwest aircraft slid off a wet runway while landing at Chicago Midway Airport. The statement about the incident went out almost immediately through traditional channels, but was also posted to the airline's Facebook page where it quickly drew 170 comments and 128 "likes." Almost at the same time, Southwest sent a Tweet to its 1.1 million followers.

CASE QUESTIONS

1. Does building this sort of goodwill mean reporters and other media professionals are being bribed in advance to positively slant the stories they write about the airline?

2. If this sort of tactic is so successful, why don't other airlines consider using it?

3. What drawbacks do you see with the kind of chummy relationship the Southwest Airlines PR people have with the media and other stakeholders?

Through its organized communications plan to build social capital, Southwest Airlines has broken down, and continues to crush, some significant barriers to effective communication about the company's core operations. When there is a crisis, the airline PR office can certainly never guarantee current CEO Gary Kelly that they will emerge from a skirmish unscathed. But when a crisis does occur, Southwest's PR people can be guaranteed that they will be explaining the situation to a group of media professionals they have come to trust, sympathetic ears if you will. These are people who are not so focused on a sound bite that they are willing to indict the

FIGURE 32.2

Media Example after Southwest's Skidding Incident

company to produce it. This is because the airline's PR team has worked hard to be people reporters, who can be trusted to easily share as much information as possible.

PRACTITIONER INSIGHTS: DAN HUBBARD, VICE PRESIDENT OF COMMUNICATIONS, NATIONAL BUSINESS AVIATION ASSOCIATION, WASHINGTON, D.C.

Although an understanding of good public relations skills combined with solid industry knowledge is important to climbing the ladder of any organization, practitioners must never lose sight of the idea that PR is about people communicating with people and not people communicating with things or about things as can happen in a complex, technical industry.

Dan Hubbard is the vice president of communications at the National Business Aviation Association (NBAA)—the trade group for owners and operators of business aircraft in the United States. Prior to this position, Hubbard worked at one of the largest global communications companies in Washington and also on Capitol Hill during a number of political campaigns. "Working at NBAA seemed like it would present quite a challenge because business aviation is always so misunderstood," he said when asked why he took the job. "But I also saw it as a chance to tell a really good story about an industry that is important to businesses and job creation, and where the U.S. still leads the world in manufacturing and business aircraft flying. You just don't come across that kind of opportunity every day in communications. So while I thought it would definitely be challenging, I thought it would be an exciting challenge."

FIGURE 32.3

Dan Hubbard

Q: What do you do?

A: If a communications job realizes its full potential in any organization, it fulfills the role of bringing a singular voice to an organization. At NBAA, communications is primarily responsible for insuring the consistency of association messaging to key audiences that include the media, association members and people in the Washington policymaking community.

Q: Who decides what that voice is?

A: The voice should come from the leader of the company or organization. The final decision here rests with Ed Bolen, our CEO. Other organizations seem to do well, though, working that out in a collaborative fashion. I think it's based on the style of the leadership. And honestly, I don't know if there is one single answer to that question. Our CEO is good at gathering opinions and building a message from that.

Q: What are important communications challenges today?

A: The trial for many communicators these days is that they are often in touch with lots of people in an organization as they gather intelligence. And, for whatever reason, they are still routinely brought in late to the discussion of the organization's key communications. When I interviewed for this job, I told them I wanted a seat at the table before key communications decisions are made, not after the strategy was already developed when I would then be expected to implement it. I've worked at some organizations where this is a chronic disability. I said I wanted to know the plan, the goal, because adding a communications component to that strategy mix will greatly strengthen the outcome. I established and maintained that perspective here from the beginning. Part of doing this job right is finding that balance between being too forceful and too passive.

Q: How important are writing skills?

A: This is the area where I get pretty sour grapes [on hiring people]. The importance of good writing cannot be overemphasized. If you don't like writing or don't write well, you really need to think about whether a communications job is for you. I'm not a Hemingway myself, but I can assemble a sentence correctly. I am simply stunned at how many communicators I meet these days cannot do that. Writing samples are nice, but I don't hire anyone for day-to-day communications positions without giving them a writing test right here in front of me. And they can't use the Internet. I often give applicants a bunch of facts and ask them to write a news story or a press release to see how they handle it. People return writing tests that include sections that are not even complete sentences, or show absolutely no creativity or innovation. I had a candidate at another firm who gave me great writing samples and did well on the interviews. Then, the candidate took the writing test and never came back. What he handed in was not even close to what he had been showing us. Make of that what you will. (See also Chapter 51 on writing for more ideas.)

Q: What do you look for in a communicator?

A: Our entry-level job is probably a communications manager whether they work in government affairs, membership marketing or operations. I look for a person who understands the fundamentals of effective communications. I've often heard people say we should hire a communicator who flies. There are some great pilots who don't want to write press releases. But I also think there are some great communicators who can understand the fundamentals of this industry and figure out how to communicate its value. We need a person who understands how to explain information in a very basic way. When writing a speech, or choosing content for a monthly print publication, they must learn how the audience sees the world. Prioritization and time management are very important. In a communications organization it is easy to get pulled in many different directions making you believe that everything coming to you is of equal weight. Good communicators need to learn how to navigate some of that. Those skills are key—know the audience, how to manage priorities and how to ferret out information by building relationships in the organization. Communicators should be curious about the organization and all the issues that the organization is involved with. Be enthusiastic about coming to work and seeking out new opportunities to develop effective communications. They certainly need to be professional with other people. That's the market basket of things that you're always going back to as a communicator.

Q: Can you give us an example of your work?

A: Sure. Remember when the pilot flew the small airplane into the IRS building in Austin in 2009? This was not a traditional business airplane and the guy flying it wasn't using it for business. But to the broader public, the media and legislators, anything that's not an airliner is one of those little private planes. They make no distinction. We needed to educate the media and legislators about what flying little airplanes really do and what security measures are in place. We also needed to explain that the "that's not an airliner" might look like a threat. They ask what the government is already doing to prevent these kinds of situations. We had to work hard on a local level because people in Austin were trying to figure out what to do next. Responsiveness can quickly turn into an action with unintended consequences. We gave people all the relevant information so they could make informed decisions. That's our job.

Q: Where does technology fit in aviation-industry communications today?

A: Technology is a tactical tool, not a strategy. People get lost sometimes trying to bump it up to the strategic level. They need to understand how to use it, certainly, but we develop the message first and then try to figure out which tool to use. There are some messages, for instance, that simply work better as an audio production than as written text.

I think communicators owe it to themselves and their organization to do the best job they can. PR can be a very challenging line of work... very tough actually. No two days are the same. But as a communicator, you can be a storyteller and have a real influence on how decisions are presented. You also have a chance to experiment and innovate. I think the communications challenges are equaled by the opportunities. Communications is not always steady and predicable, but it is rich with potential opportunities.

CASE STUDY #2

In late 2008, the U.S. economy began to sink into the gloom of one of the worst recessions since World War II. Many large, well-known financial institutions failed, such notables as Fannie Mae and Freddie Mac, Lehman Brothers, AIG, Wachovia, Bear Sterns and National City. Corporate giants such as General Motors, Ford and Chrysler teetered on the brink of bankruptcy with Chrysler and GM finally taking the plunge.

It was not easy for titans of industry—like the CEOs of the Big 3—to arrive hat-in-hand on November 18, 2008, asking Congressional legislators for a bailout. But the public relations fiasco that unfolded that day caused far more anxiety and embarrassment than their need for money ever could.

This event focused not on the commercial airlines, but on business aviation: private owner/operators of jet aircraft that often cost $15–20 million—with some costing as much as $60 million.

Although the price of private flying is actually as irrelevant to people who fly aboard business airplanes as it is to business passengers aboard an airliner; as in all things public relations, how things appear is just as important as how things actually are.

On this chilly November morning, still early in the great American recession, some members of Congress had already grown tired of listening to senior business leaders plead for federal funds to repair what had begun to look very much like sloppy management. "There is a delicious irony in seeing private luxury jets flying into Washington, DC, and people coming off of them with tin cups in their hand, saying that they're going to be trimming down and streamlining their businesses," Rep. Gary Ackerman, D-New York, told the chief executive officers of Ford, Chrysler and General Motors at a hearing of the House Financial Services Committee. "It's almost like seeing a guy show up at the soup kitchen in high hat and tuxedo. It kind of makes you a little bit suspicious." On camera, the three CEOs were silent in response to the congressman's apparent accusations and looked, in fact, much like three little boys who had just been caught with their hands in the cookie jar. None of them seemed able to articulate a sentence about why they used their private airplanes to attend the hearings.

Each of the three automakers had for decades actually owned and operated relatively large fleets of business airplanes to shuttle senior executives and middle managers between the Motor City and plants scattered around the United States, as well as to manufacturing and parts suppliers all over the globe. So much, in fact, did auto manufacturers for decades depend on their business airplanes for transportation, that within business-aviation circles, it was common knowledge that General Motors operated almost no plants anywhere that could be easily reached by *anything other* than a business airplane landing at an airport locale. The only airline options were often valuable time-consuming trips combined with long drives in an automobile. Business airplanes had for decades allowed executives to travel to more places in a single day than could ever be possible on an airliner while discussing proprietary business with the utmost in corporate security.

Upon hearing the CEOs' response, or rather the lack thereof, Congressman Brad Sherman, D-California, reacted with shock. "Let the record show that none of the executives who came here today [to beg for a federal bailout] used the airlines..." but instead arrived on their lavish private airborne yachts... or so it appeared. Communicators for all aspects of manufacturing held their breath to see what would happen next. How would the CEOs eventually defend their use of private airplanes they had been effectively using for years to conduct business faster and more efficiently than it could possibly be handled aboard an airliner?

Auto-industry communicators could not have been more disappointed at this point in the hearings, as the CEOs remained effectively silent to questions about their aircraft. At the news conference following the testimony, TV and radio reporters descended upon the auto executives and peppered them with questions about their apparently lavish transportation methods, a style they seemed not to want to discuss. The three were singularly unable to defend the use of their airplanes, which of course made them appear even guiltier, as if they were trying to hide something from prying eyes. Later that day and for weeks to come, the news was filled with stories about auto executives running for cover trying to pretend they knew nothing about the ownership or use of their big birds.

Media relations experts employed by the auto companies attempted to minimize the damage to the automakers—not to mention save the testimony about bail-out funds that had been detoured, but the damage was done at a time when tens of thousands of Americans were losing their jobs. Within days of the public relations fiasco, all three auto makers seemed ready to throw in the towel—any towel—to grab their piece of federal bailout money. All announced they would sell their entire fleets of aircraft and completely disband their flight departments, as if to precisely confirm the deeds for which the congressman had accused them.

Damage to the business aviation fleets of the auto makers was only the tip of the iceberg as suddenly, company executives all over the United States began disavowing ownership and use of their business airplanes to deflect the heat they thought they'd receive from the public. Within weeks, most of the major aircraft builders found their sales lines going almost quiet as they experienced a rash of order cancellations. At first, it was just a few dozen jets, but eventually it became hundreds with all manufacturers feeling the heat. The media had a field day with story after story implying that most highly paid executives traveled on private jets not simply for the luxury, but also to avoid the security scrutiny traditional airline passengers faced. Media attention was vicious as company after company caved in to the pressure rather than admit the aircraft had any legitimate business purpose, which of course they did. Even Barack Obama jumped on the bandwagon at one point denouncing the use of "those fancy private jets." Every dark cloud in the economic world seemed to have found its way to Wichita, Kansas, the city nicknamed "the aviation capitol of the world."

Wichita is home to some of the largest aircraft manufacturers in the world, such as Cessna Aircraft Company, Hawker Beechcraft and Bombardier's Learjet division, as well as a host of parts manufacturers that produced elements necessary to keep the lines flowing. Cessna alone employed some 15,000 people in Wichita and surrounding towns building aircraft that translated into hundreds of millions of dollars of exports of the outwardly expensive machines around the world. Someone needed to do something fast to save an industry that was worth billions, yet had prided itself on staying below the radar of shareholders for decades.

The media machine of the NBAA, as well as the General Aviation Manufacturer's Association, swung into action with an extensive, action-packed media relations campaign including letters to the editors of the *Wall Street Journal,* the *New York Times*, the *Washington Post* and dozens more publications. NBAA president and CEO Ed Bolen took to the road of major TV outlets with a message attempting to counter the bad publicity created by the Big Three. On one occasion, he hit CNN with Cessna CEO Jack Pelton, where both explained to listeners precisely what a business aircraft was and how effectively such aircraft were used by companies all across the globe. They explained details that until that moment, only people inside the industry understood; such as that most of the Fortune 100 companies operate business aircraft. Pelton and Bolen also pointed out that companies that use business aircraft effectively are by and large measurably more profitable than companies that rely on traditional transportation like the airlines.

But while the pro–business aviation media campaign roared on, new aircraft order cancellations continued. Even companies operating older aircraft began selling them rather than facing potentially critical scrutiny. The aircraft manufacturing industry, already stumbling through the initial months of the recession, tripped and fell even further. Wichita production lines idled more workers. More than 15,000 workers were laid off from Cessna Aircraft, Hawker Beechcraft and Learjet from 2008 to 2010. Save for the media relations efforts of the NBAA, the business aviation industry would have been in a freefall.

However, one company, Cessna Aircraft Company, a subsidiary of giant Textron Corporation, decided to fight back and threw the first communications punch in February 2009 with a marketing department–conceived outreach campaign called RISE. This campaign was designed to counter the misinformation about the value and use of business aircraft. According to CEO Jack Pelton,

We think it's time the other side of the story be told and that support be given to those businesses with the good judgment and the courage to use business aviation to not only help their businesses survive the current financial crisis, but more quickly forge a path toward an economic upturn. Today, we are demanding business leaders and managers work at their absolute peak to turn their companies, and our economy, around.

Business aviation provides the means to do just that. A business aircraft is a tool of industry, and one that should see its highest and best use during times of fiscal crisis. Anyone who has ever seen managers board a business aircraft at dawn and return well after dark, having visited multiple cities and attended countless meetings in one day can attest to the fact that business aviation allows companies to get the most out of every minute of every day—exactly what is needed to work our way toward economic recovery.

Pelton said the reality of business aviation is that some 85 percent of business aircraft are used by small or medium-sized companies, and that the large majority of the passengers are middle managers and technicians. The aircraft, for the most part, are single- and twin-engine propeller and turboprop aircraft or small or medium-sized jets, not simply large aircraft. "Business aviation is a far cry from the misconception of CEOs flying in

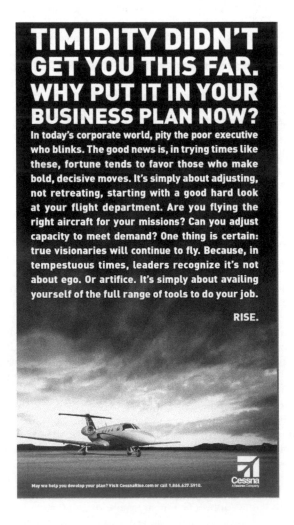

FIGURE   32.4

Timidity didn't get you this far. (Cessna)

large luxurious airplanes," Pelton said. "Most of these aircraft are fairly spartan, designed for business, with a cabin about the size of a minivan or SUV interior."

Cessna's integrated RISE campaign spent millions on traditional media and public relations, as well as direct marketing, video production and conventional full-page advertising in many of the same newspapers and publications where the company's letters to the editor had appeared. But although all aircraft manufacturers were affected by the economic chaos—a place in time one Cessna executive aptly called a battlefield—as well as the public relations nightmare created by the Big Three, Cessna stood alone in the fight. Despite the turmoil and need to fight for their economic futures, other aircraft manufacturers felt the risk of further negative publicity from media outlets far outweighed any benefits to be gained from joining with Cessna. One company, Hawker Beechcraft, actually took a moment during the RISE campaign to poke its competitor in the eye with a sales campaign that blatantly attempted to convince buyers that their aircraft were a better option than Cessna's, while Cessna fought the good fight for the entire industry.

Cessna's PR department recorded—on average—50 e-mails a day, most in support of the campaign promoting a better understanding of business aviation. In the 18 months the RISE campaign ran, Cessna held strong, despite the other manufacturers' refusal to publicly support the concept. Cessna executives later acknowledged that the RISE campaign held a very significant internal communications role for the giant manufacturer as well. In an internal company newsletter, Pelton said, "We want you [Cessna employees] to know we are aggressively pursuing measures designed to ensure the health of our company and our industry. By all accounts, this [RISE campaign] is a bold move that is causing business owners to rethink hasty decisions while giving them support as they defend the use of the business jet." The campaign ended in late 2010 when Cessna decided the message had run its course and that it was time to return to some semblance of business as usual.

DISCUSSION QUESTION

If you worked at a Cessna competitor, would you have tried to convince your boss to join Cessna's campaign? Why or why not? After the Big Three CEOs created their own PR quagmire, how would you have suggested any or all of them fix the problem?

A FINAL THOUGHT

Despite the chaos of 9/11 as well as the turmoil caused by a host of external affairs and internal economic failures, most communicators who enter the industry never leave. They do, of course, network continuously with their counterparts at other companies, which, of course, is how they land some of the most interesting and lucrative communicator jobs on the planet.

NOTES

1. "Scrutiny Lags as Jetliners Show the Effects of Age," *New York Times*, April 18, 2011.
2. http://www.blogsouthwest.com.

ADDITIONAL READING

BOOKS

Bell, Dana. *Smithsonian Atlas of World Aviation: Charting the History of Flight from the First Balloons to Today's Most Advanced Aircraft*. New York: HarperCollins, 2008. Print.
Kasarda, John B. *Aerotropolis*. New York: Farrar, Straus and Giroux, 2011. Print.

MAGAZINES

Air & Space magazine. Washington, D.C.: The Smithsonian Institution.
Flying magazine. Winter Park, FL: Bonnier Corporation.

BLOGS AND PODCASTS

The Airplane Geeks podcast. Web. www.airplanegeeks.com.
CommAvia.com – Leading Edge Media for the Aviation Industry.
"Cranky Flier," the inside scoop on what makes the airline industry work. Weblog. www.crankyflier.com.
Jetwhine.com, the blog of aviation buzz and bold opinion. Weblog.

33

C H A P T E R

THE INSURANCE INDUSTRY
Reputation Management in Good Hands

Robert P. Gorman, Jr.
Principal
Robert E. Gorman Communication
Former Sr Communication Consultant,
Allstate Insurance Company

James M. Dudas
Communications Consultant and Former Senior Director
Allstate Insurance Company

> *Insurance is the "oxygen" of free enterprise . . . it acts as the engine of growth in the United States and around the world.*
>
> —Edward Liddy
> Former Chairman, President and CEO, The Allstate Corporation,
> to the Detroit Economic Club, May 3, 2004

You can't drive without it. You can't own a home or business without it. You can't operate a school, hospital, nursing home or day care center without it. Yet insurance is easy to take for granted.

Insurance is vital in other ways. It employs about 2.2 million people. It pays about $300 billion in claims to help restore customers' cars, homes and businesses. Insurance carriers and related activities account for $464 billion, or 3.2 percent of the gross domestic product.

Insurance also pays more than $11 billion in taxes and invests about a trillion dollars in corporate and municipal bonds that help build roads, parks and public improvements across the country.

Reputation is especially important to insurance companies because theirs is a business built entirely on trust. What consumers hear, read, watch and experience influences the level of trust they feel about a particular company, or even about an entire industry.

FIFTEEN YEARS AGO VERSUS TODAY

Today's marketplace for home and auto insurance has both similarities and differences to that of 1995, when the authors first examined it.

On the similarities' side, it is still a marketplace driven by low price and heavily influenced by marketing, media, word of mouth and advertising. It also is influenced by the "good news" and "bad news" following catastrophes such as Hurricane Andrew, which hit southwestern Florida in 1992 and, up to that point, was the most damaging natural disaster ever.

Allstate was and is a major player in the insurance industry. Its role in Andrew and post-Andrew is emblematic of the industry during this period.

ADVERTISING WARS

Fifteen years ago, Allstate was the industry's spending advertising leader. Since then, ad spending by the top insurance companies has surged and leadership has changed. According to Kantor Media, in 2009, GEICO spent more than $600 million on advertising. State Farm, Progressive and Allstate spent $385 million, $323 million and $272 million, respectively. The ad message has been almost exclusively about which company has the lowest auto insurance price.

Another difference between today's and yesterday's market: the advent and wide acceptance of measures such as *FORTUNE* magazine's "Most Admired" rankings, the *Global Reputation Pulse Study* published annually in *Forbes* and the Edelman Trust Barometer. Essentially, the business community took to heart the adage that "good news is good for business."

In this spirit, the ideals of corporate social responsibility and of operating ethically took on added importance as more companies made the strategic and tactical connection between good reputation and positive financial results. "Doing well by doing good" became the mantra of many corporations.

Another difference now versus then: the broad use and speed of social networking adds further challenges to managing reputations.

Finally and very importantly, since Andrew, two related events have influenced the marketplace.

First, in 2004, four large-scale hurricanes hit Florida within six weeks. Damage to homes and business totaled more than $22 billion.

Second, in 2005, Hurricane Katrina engulfed and devastated New Orleans and neighboring areas of Texas, Mississippi, Alabama, Arkansas, Georgia and Florida. This wind-driven devastation was exacerbated by the failure of a levee that drove floodwaters far and wide.

These large-scale disasters not only cost insurance companies billions of dollars in losses; they presented huge challenges in settling thousands of claims concurrently. This required managing these claims competently, empathically and fairly—with the interests of both customers and the company (staying solvent and financially stable) in mind. Finally, these disasters presented opportunities to protect and polish reputations, as well as to tarnish them.

HOW INSURANCE WORKS

The insurance industry suffers from what the Reputation Institute[1] calls a "negative halo effect." Among other things, this means that customers are paying for something they hope they will never have to use. They pay premiums in case they do have an auto accident or the wind blows off shingles or an entire roof. But they may pay for months or years without any need to file a claim. So there is a perception of paying a lot out and getting very little back.

When there is a loss, claim adjustors are starting off on negative footing. At best, the settlement will "make the customers whole" or bring the car, home or business back to the way it was. At worst, the customer experience is reminiscent to some of a root canal—painful both financially and viscerally.

Customers experiencing a claim need to worry about how policy language will be interpreted. Was the basement flooded because of storm damage? Or was it because the sump pump failed? Or both?

Adding to the problem is that sometimes customers thought their policies included certain coverages, when, in fact, they did not. Even if an agent reviews the policy with a customer at the point of sale, it could be years before the policy language is tested by an accident or other insured loss. And in today's marketplace, unlike 20 years ago, many customers choose to buy via telephone or through the Internet, bypassing agents altogether.

BAD NEWS IS BAD FOR BUSINESS

Similar to other industries, unhappy insurance customers generate negative "word-of-mouth" comments to friends, family, neighbors, investors, the media, legislators and regulators.

Negative reputational buzz is especially bad news for insurance companies. A policy is simply the legal statement of a promise to take care of the policyholder. Less legal in form, promises also are made by agents, sales literature and advertising. For insurance to work, customers need to trust the company standing behind the promise.

For example, Allstate, which owns one of the most recognized brands in the industry, built its entire consumer franchise on the promise that "You're in Good Hands with Allstate." Given the challenging environments of customer claims as a result of a hurricane such as Andrew, this is a promise easier to make than to keep.

That promise extends, at least in theory, to investors. They have a right to expect that Allstate will not write too much business in areas prone to natural disasters, and if they have taken on too much risk in these areas, that they will take appropriate action. Investors also expect the company to charge rates that will generate competitive returns. One former Allstate CEO noted that it was the company's responsibility to pay claimants what the policy guarantees—but not one penny more or less.

Still, as Gordon Stewart[1] has noted, reputational risks abound in the property/casualty insurance business when disasters strike. These include, but are not limited to the following:

- How responsive insurers appear in adjusting and settling claims.

- How insurers manage or exaggerate expectations. "Advertising that portrays accurately company personnel extending themselves far beyond their normal duties to assist customers with serious personal needs may create inflated expectations at a moment when even the most basic claims functions are difficult to perform."[2]

- How fair the claims process appears to be.

- How litigators portray insurer practices.

Conversely, notes Stewart, "successful performance, well communicated, has more upside for the reputation of insurance than any single factor."[3]

GOOD NEWS IS GOOD FOR BUSINESS

The flip side, of course, is that customers who are happy about the way a claim was handled, whether it was a "fender bender" or a home totally rebuilt from the foundation up, can generate positive buzz. This can burnish both a company's, and to some extent, an industry's reputation.

IT STARTED WITH ANDREW

On August 24, 1992, Hurricane Andrew roared over 1,100 square miles with wind gusts reaching 175 mph.

Andrew spawned and nurtured more than 200 tornado-like vortexes that ripped a 20-mile swath through Dade County and 50 miles into the Florida peninsula.

At an estimated $41.5 billion[4] in USD 2011, Andrew is the second most costly hurricane ever, surpassed only by Katrina. In Dade County alone, 117,000 homes were destroyed or damaged. Additionally, there was incalculable damage to the tourist and the agricultural industries. When property insurance is difficult to buy because of companies' reluctance to take on more risk and possibly threaten their financial stability, banks become reluctant to write mortgages. And this has a significantly negative effect on the real estate market.

Insurance companies were scrambling to bring the financial capital and physical resources they needed to manage the claims while remaining solvent.

ANDREW'S IMPACT ON ALLSTATE AND THE INDUSTRY

By summer 1993, Andrew's effects had come full circle. Most claims had been paid. People were rebuilding their lives, homes and businesses. Insurance companies were doing what they could to take care of customers and bring them back as close as possible to their life before Andrew made its devastating landfall.

Now it was time for Allstate and other insurers to take a look back at what had occurred and ask: What can we do to make things better if another Andrew, or worse, hit southwestern Florida, if not the city of Miami?

Indeed, computer models had shown that a storm of Andrew's force was possible. What was unknown was the unprecedented level of destruction Andrew caused. It seemed unfathomable that one storm could wipe out 53 years of Allstate's earnings in Florida in just 30 hours. But that's what happened.

Allstate paid out nearly $3 billion in claims, nearly half of its capital. That was more than the company's combined payout for the previous 17 years.

Allstate and other insurers faced a new reality. Another Andrew could jeopardize the company's ability to protect policyholders not only in Florida, but also across the nation.

Insurers had several options to begin to change the very challenging circumstances they faced in the future:

1. Establish a state catastrophe fund that would transfer some of the total hurricane risk from insurance companies to a public funding vehicle. Sharing the risk with the state would help insurers to provide property with coverage against future severe hurricanes.

2. Fight for stricter enforcement of building codes and structural changes to existing homes and businesses so that they would be less susceptible to hurricane damage.

3. When companies determined that they were "overexposed" to hurricane risk in certain areas, consider, as a last resort, canceling these policies. As distasteful as this option was to companies, customers and regulators alike, these property owners could potentially receive coverage from the newly formed state catastrophe fund.

ANDREW'S AFTERMATH: OPTIONS EXERCISED

Option 1. Establish a State Catastrophe Fund

Allstate supported the creation of a risk-sharing fund that would be managed by the state of Florida. It would be paid for by the insurance companies according to their levels of exposure to hurricanes and other natural disasters.

Establishing the fund would require an increase in consumer costs for property insurance. But in return, consumers would have the security of having insurance protection equivalent with private insurance coverage.

Although establishing a fund such as this would help make property insurance more available in areas with high exposure to hurricane losses, insurance companies would still be required to *nonrenew* (another expression for canceling) some current policies so that they would no longer be overexposed to losses like those caused by Andrew.

The challenge: balance the financial risk of insolvency with the reputational risk t of dropping even a small number of their customers.

Option 2. Enact and Enforce Stricter Building Codes

In the wake of Andrew's winds, the need for stricter building codes became clear. The irony is that many of the homes destroyed avoided the worst of the winds. One insurance executive told the *Miami Herald* that many of the losses of $100,000 to $150,000 should have been $25,000 to $50,000 if building codes had been stricter.

The South Florida Building Code, once hailed as the strongest hurricane code in the country, had eroded steadily since its original enactment in 1957. Founded on the principle that "people's safety is the highest law," South Florida counties nonetheless chipped away at the codes in response to the demand for lower costs and more rapid construction. For example, in the 1980s, staples and particleboard replaced sturdy nail and plywood roofs.

A loophole in the code let builders, architects and engineers gain exemptions from attaching tie beams with steel rods. Another culprit was the vagueness of the code with respect to horizontal reinforcement of roof trusses.

Many of the losses could have been reduced if homeowners had invested in materials to strengthen their homes. After Andrew, construction quality and design won renewed respect. But complacency taught a very costly lesson.

Option 3. Reduce the Number of Insureds in High-Risk Areas

In explaining how it planned to continue to provide coverage for more than 2 million Florida customers despite losses caused by Andrew, the company said that it would have to find alternatives for about 300,000 customers who resided in high-risk hurricane areas. Allstate said that future losses the size of Andrew were simply beyond the scope of private insurers to cover. The company was hopeful that a public–private partnership could be fashioned with the state of Florida that would provide additional financial resources to bear in a post-Andrew loss environment. Such a partnership offered the prospect that insurers could minimize the number of nonrenewals and make insurance more available to Florida customers.

PAYING A PRICE FOR SUNSHINE AND LOW COSTS

It was Florida's sunshine that first attracted people to the state. It was the low cost of living that kept them there. Housing was affordable if not downright cheap compared with other areas of the country. Taxes were low and opportunity abounded. During a critical growth period from 1960 through 1992, fewer intense hurricanes made Florida landfall than in any 30-year period since 1871. The cost of insuring property reflected those trends. They were among the lowest in the United States.

For much of the 1960s and 1970s, property and casualty insurance companies raced to write new business and keep up with burgeoning real estate sales of single-family homes and condominiums.

The circumstances—rapid growth and low hurricane activity—contributed to loose enforcement of building codes. This left homes and business more vulnerable.

Consequently, "economic impact" took on a new meaning in the aftermath of Andrew. The Category Five storm was the first of its force to hit a prime Florida growth area and to leave a gaping trail of destruction in its wake.

Through the rapid growth years, insurance companies became disproportionately exposed to hurricane losses because of the high volume of policies they wrote in hurricane-prone areas of the state.

Andrew forced these companies to reevaluate their exposure to hurricane risk so that they could remain financially capable of continuing to provide property coverage to their millions of customers across the country. But this meant telling some customers that they could not renew their current policies.

No company wants to turn away business. But their past propensity to write in the wrong areas left these companies few options. In Allstate's case, this meant working with about 300,000 Florida customers to find alternative coverage.

STAKEHOLDER RESEARCH INFORMED STRATEGY DEVELOPMENT

Allstate needed to mobilize action internally and externally. But as part of the planning process, the company wanted to know how employees, customers and the public across the country were reacting to its announcement that it was planning to nonrenew about 300,000 customers.

The surveys it conducted showed that employees were aware of the company's decision. Although most understood the rationale for the decision and thought it was the right thing to do from a business standpoint, some felt less favorable about Allstate as a place to work.

According to data generated by Allstate's Research Center, only about 30 percent of consumers and customers outside of Florida were aware of the decision. But customers who were aware of the decision were less likely to recommend Allstate to friends and family. Agreement that "Allstate has a good reputation" was significantly lower among those customers who were aware of Allstate's nonrenewal plan.

These results were cause for concern on both employee and customer fronts. Among employees, it was clear that company communications had been successful in capturing their "heads." They understood that the risk reduction, nonrenewal action was necessary. But the company also wanted to capture their "hearts." It needed their help in building grassroots support for a catastrophe bill that was being drafted to help stabilize the property insurance market.

With customers across the country, Allstate worried that the decision could devalue company core strengths: the Allstate brand name and the company's reputation. Would customers' decisions to do business with Allstate be negatively influenced by the nonrenewal announcement? The company needed to act quickly and decisively to mitigate any loss of trust.

The strategy that developed was to work from the inside out—starting with Allstate employees and sales agents, and through them, reaching out to customers, legislators and business owners who would stand to benefit from a stable insurance market.

The plan had four components: employee and agent communication, political action, media contacts and coalition building.

COMMUNICATING WITH EMPLOYEES AND AGENTS

The message to employees and agents was that this issue affected much more than insurance companies. A stable property insurance market affected every Florida resident and was critical to the state's economic well-being. Communications explained that an industry-sponsored bill would stabilize the market by establishing a risk-sharing fund with both public (the state of Florida) and private (insurance companies) components.

Allstate sent a communication package to all employees. It included highlights of the Florida research so that they could understand how the nonrenewal decision was being received by customers and the public. The package included "talking points" that employees could use to inform themselves and to answer questions they could get from friends, family members, neighbors and other employees. The communicators assembling the package also wrote questions and answers, a chronology of key events and a sample letter to customers that addressed issues and concerns. Also included were the accolades Allstate was getting from customers and the media for its exemplary claim service despite the very challenging circumstances.

Another employee communication package was distributed a month later. This presented a more detailed historical summary that led up to the legislative challenge ahead and detailed how employees could help support the proposed bill.

POLITICAL ACTION INITIATIVES

Political action efforts capitalized on an active group of Florida employees. Their strategy was to sponsor roundtable discussions and educational forums that would mix employees with legislators. These meetings focused attention on the advantages of an industry-sponsored catastrophe fund that was then under review by a special session of the state legislature.

About 100 employees participated in open houses in company offices throughout the state. They also contacted their state representatives and encouraged other employees to do the same.

MEDIA STRATEGY

The media strategy involved partnering with other insurance companies, industry groups and other businesses with a stake in a successful outcome for the catastrophe fund bill (bankers, realtors, builders, etc.). This cross-functional group made editorial board with state and national newspapers and magazines, as well as with radio and television stations.

COALITION BUILDING

Allstate and other companies worked closely with the Florida Insurance News Service, an industry information and advocacy group. Also working the coalition-building front was the Hurricane Insurance Information Center, which was sponsored by the Insurance Information Institute, a national trade organization.

INITIAL CAMPAIGN RESULTS

The Florida Hurricane Catastrophe Fund Bill was passed by the legislature on November 9, 1993. This was an important day for Allstate and the rest of the industry because it established a risk-sharing mechanism—a public–private vehicle that meant Allstate could reduce the number of proposed nonrenewals from the original 300,000 to only 30,000. This mechanism eventually morphed into Citizens Insurance, managed and underwritten through the Florida Department of Insurers. Citizens Insurance is now Florida's largest residential home insurer, with about 1.2 million policies.

BUILDING CODES STRENGTHENED

Although there were plenty of lessons learned as a result of Andrew, none had as much impact as the realization that many buildings were poorly constructed and certainly no match for hurricane force winds.

As the trade publication *Insurance Journal* noted:

> The storm exposed inadequate code standards that were based on old data or flagrant violations that slipped inspection.
>
> In some cases, there were not enough nails affixing plywood sheets to roof trusses, or the nails used weren't strong enough. In others, unprotected windows and doors were too weak to withstand flying debris. Many of the damaged or destroyed roofs were not braced or strapped down properly, and roof shingles and tiles were not properly installed."[5]

The new building codes resulted not only in sturdier structures, which suffered far less damage from hurricanes Charley, Ivan, Frances and Jeanne, all of which came ashore in Florida in 2004.

The codes and their enforcement has helped to encourage Florida insurers to get back into the business, albeit more carefully, of homeowners insurance. In some cases, insurers offered discounts to customers who had their homes retrofitted to the new and stricter building codes.

KEY LESSONS FROM HURRICANE ANDREW

Growing out of some painful lessons learned in Florida during 1992 and 1993, Allstate began taking several steps to improve its image.

These steps were based on a better understanding of the severe catastrophe risk the company faced and actions it could take to mitigate that risk. They also were based on a better understanding of reputational risk—the possibility to erode stakeholder trust in the company and the opportunities to preserve and deepen that trust.

In addition to the company's ongoing efforts to reduce exposure to natural disasters in states such as Florida, Texas, California and New York, Allstate formed a senior-level Image Team that reviewed pending business decisions and considered how they might affect Allstate's image.

This heightened sensitivity to and appreciation of its image will likely serve Allstate well. As its employees seek to deliver on the "Good Hands" promise Allstate makes to its 17.5 million customers every day.

FAST FORWARD TO 2005: KATRINA ENGULFS NEW ORLEANS

When Hurricane Katrina made landfall in southern Plaquemines Parish, Louisiana, on August 29, 2005, it quickly established itself as the most destructive storm ever, more than doubling Andrew's economic losses. It caused devastation along the Gulf coast from central Florida to Texas. Eventually, 80 percent of the city and large tracts of neighboring parishes became flooded. Floodwaters lingered for weeks.

Having survived Andrew, insurance companies such as Allstate once again had the challenge of balancing financial risk and reputational risk. Although passage of the Florida Hurricane Catastrophe Fund had helped to stabilize the property marketplace since Andrew, Allstate and other property insurers remained overexposed to potential hurricane losses. Part of the solution was to raise rates to reflect the true risk hurricanes posed. But that was not enough by itself. Once again, companies had to consider nonrenewing some customers in Katrina's highest risk areas.

The combination of rate increases and nonrenewals brought bad news to bear not only on customers, but the state regulators who have jurisdiction over insurance companies and with whom these companies must negotiate proposed rate and coverage changes. Increasing rates and reducing policies-in-force were on the table not only for Florida, but other large exposure states such as Texas and New York.

REPUTATION MEASUREMENT AND MANAGEMENT

"The reputation measurement we were doing after Katrina indicated that we had some challenges with regulators in certain states," said David Woolwine, Allstate's director of reputation management (like all insurers Allstate is regulated in each state in which it does business). "Our measurements at the time were helpful in guiding our strategy development," he said. "But we were looking for something more rigorous and national in scope.

Woolwine interviewed several reputation measurement firms and decided that the Reputation Institute best fit Allstate's needs. The Institute has a presence in 25 countries and since 1997, it has been dedicated to advancing knowledge about how reputation works, how companies can build better relationships with stakeholders and how companies can improve business results. The Institute's *Global Reputation Pulse Study* is published annually in *Forbes* magazine.

In early 2008, Allstate formed the Reputation Leadership Council. It is composed of the chairman and other members of the senior management team. The council's purpose is to use reputation to drive business results and to gain competitive advantage.

Slugging it out with key competitors GEICO, Progressive and State Farm in a market driven largely on low price, Allstate hoped to use what it learned about stakeholder expectations to attract more consumers into the purchase consideration set. For example, someone shopping for auto insurance considers one or more companies. A positive reputation could be thought of as a "gateway" into a consumer's consideration set. According to Allstate's Woolwine, once someone considers purchasing insurance from one or more companies, other factors, such as low price, come into play.

A positive reputation, according to the *Reputation Institute*, also would increase recommendations, referrals and stronger relationships with key constituents such as employees, agents, opinion leaders, policy makers and investors.

Reputation is defined by the Institute as: "An emotional bond. The level of trust, admiration, good feeling and overall esteem a stakeholder has for a company."

Charles J. Fombrun, founder of the Reputation Institute and author of *Reputation, Realizing Value from the Corporate Image*, says, "A corporate reputation embodies the general estimation in which a company is held by employees, customers, suppliers, distributors, competitors and the public. The key point is that reputation consists of *perceptions*, how others see you."

In differentiating reputation from image, Fombrun goes on to say, "Marketers, advertisers, and public relations specialists help create attractive images of a company. . . . But unless those images are anchored in core characteristics of the company and its products and services, they will decay. . . . Many companies today are beginning to recognize the difference between image and reputation. They go beyond mass marketing and traditional image management by try to build strong relationships with customers."

Fombrun adds that to build an enduring and resilient reputation, however, a company must go beyond customers to establish strong relationships with other key constituents.

Given that the market for auto insurance today is driven by low price, Allstate is using the survey data from the Reputation Institute to anticipate and ideally mitigate the "bad news" that rate increases and exposure management (or nonrenewals) could generate in a given market.

For example, if it knows that nonrenewals are coming in an area such as Long Island, the company can plan and execute remedial actions that might be called corporate social responsibility (CSR) initiatives.

Working with the Reputation Institute for the past two years, Allstate has learned that customers, employees and other stakeholders form their perceptions of a company in three ways:

1. *Product experience.* They purchase a product or service or they have a claim or customer service interaction.

2. *Heard/seen.* They hear and/or see communications that includes marketing, advertising, and public relations and website information.

3. *Third party sources.* They receive messages through traditional media such as television, radio and publications, as well as social media such as Facebook and Twitter. People also may receive "word-of-mouth" messages from friends, family, neighbors and other members of their social network.

According to the Institute, what we now know about reputation management can be summarized in four lessons:

- Reputation is the trust, admiration, good feeling and overall esteem people have for an organization.

- Reputation is formed by the perceptions people have.

- Strong reputations lead to supporting behavior such as purchase and recommendation.

- Supportive behavior leads to improved organizational performance.

The Institute goes on to say that the key to create stronger reputations centers on answering four related questions:

- What are the actions that stakeholders expect from companies?

- How can a company partner with external stakeholders to co-create a better future?

- What are the most effective ways to influence employees to support other stakeholders?

- What are the best ways to manage the risks and leverage the opportunities more systematically?

The Institute measures reputation with seven stakeholder groups: sales agents, consumers, investors, customers, policy makers, employees and opinion leaders. A company like Allstate could enjoy an excellent reputation with customers, for example, and a weak reputation with another group, such as agents. These diverse reputational positions require distinct strategies.

For example, in its most recent surveys, Allstate's reputation was strongest with consumers who have had "personal experiences" with the company, its products or its services. By definition, consumers are not customers. They do not currently do business with Allstate. Since it's not legal to provide free insurance to anyone, the opportunity Allstate saw was to create another type of experience that consumers could have.

THE "GOOD HANDS" ROADSIDE ASSISTANCE PROGRAM

This background led to the creation of a new Allstate roadside assistance program. It allows any driver—not just Allstate customers—to call the company for help when becoming stranded on the side of the road.

The program, launched November 2010, will not require an annual fee. Drivers need not sign up in advance. Allstate hopes that those who call for help will think of the company when their policy comes up for renewal.

Stranded motorists will play a flat fee of $75 for a tow, or $50 if they lock their keys in the car. The company says that the average driver calls on his or her motor club once every three years. So they could save money by using Allstate's service instead of paying annual membership dues. They also have the peace of mind that answering 3 million calls for roadside help should be able to take care of them in a moment of real need.

The company's primary targets are the 35 million U.S. households who do not belong to a motor club. Research indicates that these tend to be younger drivers who tend to own their vehicles longer and are more likely to experience a breakdown. "It's a great way to get more people associated with Allstate," said Mark LaNeve, Allstate's chief marketing officer.

It is too early to know how well Roadside Assistance is winning new customers. But the company continues to roll out the program from its initial local testing.

Although Allstate continues to be successful bringing in new customers, it has been challenged to keep the customers it already has. As of the third quarter of 2010, the company had a 2.5 percent increase in new auto insurance customers, which works out to about 13,000 policies-in-force.[6] New business has been up in double digits in some quarters in traditionally difficult states such as Florida and California. But the company was challenged to retain its current customers, and overall, it saw a decline in policies.

With car insurance, ". . . We see price playing a very strong role (in customer decisions) compared to other industries,"[7] says David VanAmburg, managing director at American Customer Satisfaction Index LLC, a consumer survey firm.

The pressure to cut prices is certainly present as low-cost competitors GEICO and Progressive gain customers and increase premium revenues. But the company thus far has resisted taking rate cuts choosing to increase customer satisfaction in order to boost retention and preserve Allstate's industry-leading margins.

The effort to increase customer loyalty in states in which Allstate recently raised rates, has not yet stopped customers from defecting.

With these defections in mind, last year, Allstate initiated a new advertising campaign called "Mayhem," in which it attempts to convince customers that it is worth it to pay more for car insurance, because, unlike "cut rate insurers," Allstate will take care of customers when something bad happens. The intent is to influence potential defectors to stay.

"The intense focus on price played well during the recession," said Mark LaNeve. "But we are sensing a return to value along the lines of 'The company you do business with matters; you get what you pay for.'"[8]

"For many people, value isn't just based on price," said Brad Casper, president and chief executive officer of Henkel Consumer Goods whose products include home care and personal care. "Low price isn't necessarily a good value if quality and performance are not where their expectations are."[9]

The "Mayhem" campaign is part of the company's effort to reposition the company from just selling insurance, which tends to be considered a commodity, to proving valuable protection. This is emphasized by what spokesman Dennis Haysbert says at the end of "Mayhem" spots: "Dollar for dollar, nobody protects you like Allstate."[10]

The "Mayhem" advertising is supplemented internally by a program called Ambassadors (the company describes it as a grassroots employee movement). Data from the reputation research signaled an opportunity to create internal advocates who would volunteer to act as ambassadors of the company.

The goal is to engage 70,000 employees, agents and agency staff in improving customer satisfaction and loyalty, while decreasing negative perceptions about the company and increasing positive perceptions.

Anticipated outcomes for this totally voluntary program are as follows:

- Improve products and services.

- Tell the Allstate story whenever and wherever possible.

- Provide employees, agents and their staffs with the tools to make decisions that enhance reputation.

- Increase the ability to make referrals and answer customer, consumer and other employee questions.

- Further the elimination of enterprise silos through collaboration and celebrating successes.

- Look for ways to improve Allstate's reputation in their everyday jobs.

- Encourage and champion new ideas.

Beginning in March 2009, the Allstate Ambassadors network now has grown to 4,400. In one measure of the group's work, 40 percent of ideas offered in Company Ideation meetings (brainstorming sessions) came from Ambassadors who comprised only 10 percent of the sessions' attendees.[11]

Whether the "Mayhem" advertising and the Ambassador's effort help Allstate retain more customers remains to be seen. But the reputation scores indicate improvements across all stakeholder groups, and that is a good trend for the "Good Hands" people.

CEOS MUST TAKE THE LEAD

One leading business school educator advocates that reputation management is too important to delegate to lawyers or PR experts. "The responsibility for reputation management lies with CEO. . . ,"[12] says David Diermeier, IBM professor of regulation and competitive practice at the Kellogg School of Management and director of the Ford Motor Company Center for Global Citizenship. He goes to say,

> Most reputational challenges arise out of a specific business context and thus require management and execution as an integral part of business decisions," Diermeier says. He further states: "The key is for a CEO to have the ability to maintain an external perspective throughout the decision-making process. Companies must develop a proper governance structure that mirrors their organizational structure. Companies must have an intelligence capacity. Reputational challenges can emerge from anywhere in a company's operations or external business environment. Lack of intelligence capabilities jeopardizes a company's ability to manage such issues proactively.

Finally, Diermeier says that CEOs must understand that even the most advanced reputation management system is implemented by people.

> They need to assess the situation, evaluate its risk, and take the appropriate action. Getting this right requires not only a strategic mindset, but also values and culture to provide guidance to individuals. We can't expect every employee to correctly assess the reputational risk of an issue, but we can expect them to raise a red flag when something does not look right. It is here that the CEO's leadership matters most.

With the tools that are available to help companies measure and manage their reputations, Allstate and other industry players now have the data available to use this process to gain or maintain competitive advantage.

After Andrew, conversations started among Allstate's senior management about the importance of reputation. Fifteen years later, business decisions are being informed by stakeholder perceptions and guided by considerations of potential reputational risk. Allstate is likely to continue benefitting from these considerations.

THE ART, SCIENCE AND REALITY OF REPUTATION MANAGEMENT

To be sure, Gordon Stewart notes,

> One term of art in recent ascendance must be regarded with special wariness and that is "reputation management." Like most appealing movements it grows from a useful idea—in this case that serious concern for one's reputation is really important. The fact that this has been a central concern of sentient human beings since at least the time of Homer's heroes makes it no less timely today. But quick sand surrounds the vague allure of the word "management." For the majority of leaders, firms, and industries that succumb to the lures of reputation manipulation (sorry, "management"), the usual outcome is less likely to be prison garb than a public parading in that traditional line of ceremonial clothing long favored by naked emperors.[13]

Stewart fears that reputation management runs the risk of devolving into old-fashioned propaganda or new fashioned spinning. He asks: "Why does behaving reputably require management in the first place?"[14]

Finally, Stewart notes: "Where and when insurance does its job very well, listens to its customers, corrects its own shortcomings (we all have them), and communicates honestly and well, its reputation is generally good."[15]

THE HURRICANE THAT REDEFINED THE BUSINESS OF INSURANCE COMPANY COMMUNICATORS AND POSSIBLY OTHERS

Corporate speechwriters and PR professionals have gotten so used to using the phrase "sea change" to describe even piddling challenges to markets and industries that it now carries about the same cachet as describing an idea as having "gone viral" or someone experiencing an "aha moment" or some minor event being touted as having "epic proportions."

Notwithstanding its misuse and overuse, a "sea change" did, indeed, manifest itself within the Property and Casualty Industry in dealing with the after-effects of Hurricane Andrew (and what could be a more appropriate phrase, found first in William Shakespeare's *The Tempest*, to describe an unprecedented natural disaster?).

Nothing so affected the way homeowner's insurance was priced, marketed, sold, bought and thought of than the destruction brought on by a Category 5 hurricane making landfall in one of the nation's most populated peninsulas.

Equally impacted was the small army of corporate and insurance trade communicators who found their companies pilloried and their reputations tattered. Already smarting from public perception of its poor response to the 1991 Oakland wildfires, and the Golden State's attempt to literally take over auto insurance underwriting within the same time frame, Hurricane Andrew added another blow to the industry's image.

"We had never suffered anything like the Oakland fires. Industry critics organized claimants. While individual companies responded to policyholder concerns, there was no collective communications response and we got hammered for it," says Cary Schneider, executive vice president of the Insurance Information Institute (III),[16] an association of insurance companies that describes itself as having a mission "to improve public understanding of insurance—what it does and how it works."

From a communications standpoint, Andrew set in motion a new, more aggressive and more transparent approach to communicating industry messages, but not before sharp distinctions were drawn between "image" and "reputation." Up until then, the former too often was thought to drive the latter, particularly among individual companies who relied on community events (e.g., fingerprinting for child safety, safe bike-riding events) and foundation grants for playgrounds, after school programs and socially responsible organizations. If you were in the business of printing giant checks in those times, you did very well, indeed, with insurance companies as your clients. Agents were encouraged and enlisted to sponsor little league teams and participate in company-sponsored community center groundbreakings (while making sure to hand out their business cards). Local insurance company media relations teams spent freely on lunches and other social or business outings with reporters. Little wonder that regional and home office executives displayed paroxysms of anger, angst and misunderstanding when negative stories over customers whose complaints of unfair claims settlements made the news. They were blissfully ignorant of the reality that few mitigation bank accounts can withstand a run on their deposits when insurance companies are perceived to have failed in any of their primary reasons for collecting premiums.

To be fair, many corporate communicators and Insurance Information Institute professionals knew in their guts that the axiom "actions speak louder than words" would only break positive if the actions were the right actions; the expected actions and not simply the actions of intention, of advertising, of grants or lobbying.

The Insurance Information Institute helped lead this effort, convincing insurance executives that although it is the job of the insurance company to clearly communicate to its policyholders what its promises mean and how they will be kept, a collective response by the industry as a whole is needed to explain in broader terms the essential role the industry plays in rebuilding devastated communities by responding promptly, efficiently and compassionately.

Although sometimes glacial in its progress, that message eventually got out. But nowhere was it more or better manifested than in the aftermath of 9/11/2001, when terrorists destroyed the World Trade Center.

It was maybe the industry's finest moment, according to Julie Rochman, president and CEO of the Institute for Business and Home Safety (IBHS),[17] an insurance industry group whose mission, according to its website, is "to reduce the social and economic effects of natural disasters and other property losses by conducting research and advocating improved construction, maintenance and preparation practices." Her credentials include positions as senior vice president of public affairs for the American Insurance Association and the Insurance Institute for Highway Safety.

Rochman notes that once President Bush and other government leaders rhetorically labeled the World Trade Centers as "a war," insurers could have tried exercising a war exclusion that long existed in various policies. Rochman notes that,

The term "war" has a contractual meaning. If the 9/11 attacks were part of a war, the industry would not have had to pay. But the industry did not hesitate, did not litigate. Instead, the companies stepped up quickly and paid some $32 billion of losses. It was a defining moment for the industry. The PC (property and casualty) industry did an amazing job. The companies did the right thing, stayed strong, and never bragged about it.

And although the industry never got much credit for its actions, neither did it have to dig itself out from the mountains of negative opinion it would have gotten for denying claims based on legal policy language. It was not about image, it was about reputation.

That the industry was sharpening and broadening an enlightened view that image does not a reputation make was clearly in evidence when The Geneva Association, an international think tank for the study of insurance economics, sponsored a "Reputation and Reputational Risk Management" conference in Zurich, Switzerland in 2006.[18]

In an editorial introducing the publication of the papers presented at the conference, Kai-Uwe Schanz, chief communication and corporate development officer, Converium, LTD, Zurich posed this question: "Why does reputation increasingly matter to insurers?" He went to say,

> The answer is the increasing relevance of reputation as one of the insurance industry's key assets, offering attractive returns when properly cultivated but also threatening considerable damage if eroded or lost. In the case of the former, the potential return from reputation can materialize as increased sales, as the ability to command a premium on market prices, as access to talent, or as stock market valuation in excess of book value.

Among the most provocative of the papers is one entitled: "Can Reputations be 'Managed'?" by Gordon Stewart, who was president of the III and is now retired.

"Fortunately," wrote Stewart, "the latest thinking in business includes the rise of 'reputational risk' to the forefront of institutional threats. It has even replaced 'image,' and this represents progress."

> The two are similar and related, but not identical or interchangeable. Fundamentally, reputation results from actions taken over time. Thus, reputation arises from, carries the force of, and embodies a thing itself. Image implies a disembodied, external projection, detached from the thing itself, in this case, actions over time. Both are real phenomena, but the excessive, even obsessive, focus on one's "image" tends to divert attention and resources away from a company's or an industry's own actions, which are the foundation of any reputation, and onto "others," such as critics, business adversaries, predatory lawyers and the dreaded media—all of which exist and present threats but do not, in the end, create or destroy reputations.

Since 1968, the Insurance Information Institute has been conducting a blind poll of Americans' opinions of the banking, auto and home insurance, mutual funds and electric utility companies. In 2000 it added health insurance, in 2002 financial services companies, in 2008 the banking, pharmaceutical and oil and gas industries, and in 2009 it split auto insurance and homeowners insurance into separate entities. The auto and homeowners industry reached its nadir in public opinion in 1991 with 33 percent of those polled feeling very/mostly favorable (it had been as high as 61 percent). Largely due to enhanced and aggressive communication that was transparent and tutorial in its approach post 1992's Hurricane Andrew, the industry experienced a steady improvement in its opinion ratings. It climbed steadily, even after Katrina.

This, according to Jeanne Salvatore, senior vice president of the Insurance Information Institute, had much to do with the way companies and the industry approached communication. "Andrew was the turning point," she says. The media was also changing. Major newspapers could no longer afford to have reporters dedicated to insurance. Even fewer papers had business reporters who understood how insurance works. So the Institute worked hard to be a credible and honest wellspring of information. They also worked hard to be responsive, particularly with the advent of social media and the 24 hour news cycle, and to let responsible action speak louder than words.

Is that what kept Hurricane Katrina from turning into a public relations and reputational disaster for insurance companies and the industry? Rochman of the IBHS, says that was certainly a part of it.

"Companies were on site, sometimes with three claims adjusters per claim. Looking at the evidence, determining whether the damage was from flooding, wind or wind driven rain, all criteria that determined if and the amount of a claim a company would cover," says Rochman. And communication was constant.

In his article, Stewart noted other things at work. The Insurance Information Institute's survey showed that, post Katrina, the auto and home insurance industry favorability ratings dropped a mere one point to 56 percent from 57 percent. "Why did our rating not decline more precipitously given the slow and difficult claims handling process and the well publicized disputes over flood and wind damage?" Stewart said the Institute's research showed that most people believed that government at all levels failed. "Very few people (only 4 percent) thought that insurance companies were the entity principally responsible for dealing with Katrina. State and local government (33 percent) and FEMA (26 percent) were viewed by the public as most responsible."

Still, the industry remained favorably viewed at 56 percent in November 2010, up 11 points from 45 percent in November 2009.

Clarity around policy language and promises kept are two of those drivers. The constant drum beat of communication is another.

"Today," says Salvatore, "a lot of reporters are not on staff. They are freelancers. They often get it (insurance issues) wrong and it is not in our favor. So we have to be more aggressive in getting information out directly to consumers."

The social network has enabled that. "We don't have to go through filters (agents, mainstream media) the way we once did," says Salvatore. Companies and the industry groups representing them can get right to customers with accurate, credible information. "Today," Salvatore says, "I think a website is more credible than a news release."

None of this is to suggest that companies should stop being socially responsible or sponsoring community events or funding worthwhile causes. To be sure, auto companies today have teen safe driving programs that push for and fund initiatives around graduated licensing and electronic monitoring of vehicles when teens are behind the wheel. But individual companies understand that those efforts must work hand in glove with fair and personal interaction with policyholders.

As Stewart noted: "Successful performance, well communicated, has more upside for the reputation of insurance than any single factor."

It appears the message has been received, and is being acted upon, by the messengers.

Editor's note: After the catastrophic results of Hurricane Andrew, Katrina and others, a group of insurers, led by Allstate, formed an organization called ProtectAmerica.org whose goal was to provide federal backup funds to cover damages from natural disasters beyond a certain ceiling. It proposed a House Bill (HR 2555) to establish this fund. The bill has not yet passed. Its opponents, and they include a number of insurance companies and insurance trade organizations, oppose it for a number of reasons, not the least being that it encourages building in areas where natural catastrophes are likely, since insurers would not be on the hook for the entire loss exceeding a certain limit: the taxpayers would be.

Groups that oppose the concept and legislation, most notably, smartersafer.org, cite its likely cost [the Congressional Budget Office estimates that H.R. 2555, the Homeowners' Defense Act, will cost the federal government $1.7 billion over five years (2011–2015)], and call it a "federal bailout program principally designed to benefit hurricane-threatened Florida at the expense of taxpayers in all 50 states."

The debate continues.

ACKNOWLEDGMENTS

The authors wish to express a deep debt of gratitude to Jeanne Salvatore and Cary Schneider of the Insurance Information Institute; Julie Rochman at the Institute for Business and Home Safety and, especially, Gordon Stewart, retired president of III whose provocative, revealing and erudite paper: "Can Reputations be Managed," is part of the Geneva Papers (2006) published by The International Association for the Study of Insurance Economics. The questions Mr. Stewart raised and the wisdom he revealed warrants close inspection by public affairs and public relations practitioners in and beyond the insurance industry.

DISCUSSION QUESTIONS

1. In today's insurance marketplace, is reputational risk the equivalent of financial risk?
2. How does reputation factor in decisions to buy or renew policies?
3. Does reputation need to be managed, or is it really about managing the business itself well and taking care of customers? Who defines whether the customer is well cared for and how is it measured?
4. How is the balance in consumer decision-making between low price and value being played out in other industries?
5. What are the elements of reputation recovery in the insurance industry? In what order should they be implemented? What needs to be done immediately?
6. Who is ultimately responsible for an insurance company's reputation?
7. In a commodity business, as the insurance industry is quickly evolving into, where does reputation fit?

NOTES

1. Gordon Stewart, "Can Reputations be 'Managed,'" Insurance Information Institute, The Geneva papers, 2006, The International Associations for the study of Insurance Economics.
2. Gordon Stewart, ibid.
3. Ibid.
4. National Hurricane Center, National Oceanic and Atmospheric Administration, http://www.nhc.noaa.gov/pdf/NWS-5-TPC-5pdf.
5. Allstate presentation, January 4, 2011.
6. *Crain's Chicago Business*, November 8, 2010.
7. Op cit.
8. Stuart Elliott, "Allstate 'Mayhem' Character is Aimed at Spicing Up Ads."*The New York Times*, June 21, 2010.
9. Stuart Elliott, "Allstate Adds Villain, With Car Insurance as the Hero." *The New York Times*, June 21, 2010.
10. Stuart Elliott, "Allstate Adds Villain, With Car Insurance as the Hero." *The Wall Street Journal*, June 21, 2010.
11. Allstate interview, January 20, 2011.
12. Daniel Diermeier, "CEOs must lead the way in reputation management." *PR Week US*, January 11, 2011.
13. Ibid.
14. Ibid.
15. Ibid.
16. http://www.iii.org/index.html.
17. http://www.disastersafety.org/about.
18. Papers from this conference, as well as others, can be accessed via http://www.genevaassociation.org/Home.aspx and using the key word *reputation* in the search key.

ADDITIONAL READING

Bernstein, Peter L. *Against the Gods: The Remarkable Story of Risk*. New York, NY: John Wiley & Sons, 1996.

Fombrun, Charles J. *Reputation, Realizing Value from the Corporate Image*. Cambridge. MA: Harvard Business School Press, 1996.

Gregory, James R., and Jack G. Wiechmann. *Marketing Corporate Image, The Company as your Number One Product*. Cambridge, MA: Harvard Business Press, 1996.

Reichheld, Frederick F., and Thomas Teal. *The Loyalty Effect: The Hidden Force Behind Growth, Profits and Lasting Value*. Cambridge, MA: Harvard Business School Press 2001.

34

C H A P T E R

THE HOSPITALITY INDUSTRY
Communicating with Our Guests

John Wallis
Global Head, Marketing and Brand Strategy
Hyatt Hotels & Resorts

People who work in marketing and public relations always have their eyes on the future, in large part because our field relies on media and technologies that are constantly evolving. Hospitality, by contrast, is an ancient word. It has been passed down to us with three distinct, interrelated meanings: being a guest, being received and entertained in a friendly manner and being treated with generosity. For this reason, every person in the hospitality business is in "marketing" as hospitality has always been about genuine public relations, the kind that requires one-to-one, caring interactions.

Personally, I cannot imagine working in a better industry than hospitality. We have the opportunity to play a part in some of the happiest moments in people's lives. Every day, our hotels host honeymoons, vacations, business meetings that make careers and reunions that forge lasting memories. If we do our jobs right, we have the opportunity to turn a guest's pleasant trip into an unforgettable experience.

I'm also fortunate to work for a great company, the Hyatt Hotels Corporation, which began as a family business. Jay Pritzker founded Hyatt in 1957 when he purchased the Hyatt House motel adjacent to the Los Angeles International Airport. Over the following decade, Jay Pritzker and his brother Donald Pritzker grew Hyatt into North American and international hotel management and ownership companies that were consolidated in 2004 under a single entity, now named Hyatt Hotels Corporation, which debuted on the New York Stock Exchange in November 2009.

To be in the hospitality industry, whether you run a bed and breakfast or help manage a global hotel, resort and convention business, is to care deeply about your guests and your reputation. Therefore, even though my career in the hospitality industry began with the job of working in a bar, I feel I have always worked in marketing and public relations. In some very important ways, the basics of that business and our relationship with guests are the same today as it was when I began. Our focus is still on creating and maintaining safe, clean and comfortable resting places for travelers of all types. It is also about showing gratitude for everyone who chooses to spend time in our properties—and who take away enough positive memories from those experiences to return again, sometimes to the same properties, but also to those hotels that share the same brand.

As global head of marketing and brand strategy for Hyatt, I spend a great deal of time focused on that word, *brand*. At Hyatt, we think of our brand from within the context of our mission, which is to provide authentic hospitality by making a difference in the lives of the people we touch every day. Simple to understand, although not always so simple to execute. In our industry, not only is it accurate to say that our bell persons are part of our brand marketing and public relations strategy, it is also impossible to talk about the brand without discussing how every customer contact integrates with marketing. In the hospitality business, it is our associates who deliver our brand every single day. Think of all the people you come into contact with when staying in a hotel: bell person, front desk clerk, housekeeper, waiter/waitress in the restaurant and fitness club manager. Did you ever have the occasion to ask any of these people a simple question to which they did not know the answer? Or on a more positive note, have you ever been pleasantly surprised when someone at a hotel steps out of his or her prescribed role and does something for you that make your stay more pleasant? The image a guest carries away after staying at a hotel is based on the collective impressions formed during that stay. Each one of these impressions is a contact that ultimately impacts a customer's feeling about the brand.

If one believes that a customer's perception of a brand can easily change with each interaction, then the bell person is more important than the glossy image advertisement in *Conde Nast Traveler*. Finding ways to communicate to employees the importance of their roles in a manner that is simple for everyone to understand is a key part of our internal communications. Even the employee responsible for washing the pots in the kitchen must become aware that his or her role supporting a restaurant enables the cook to prepare the meal more quickly and the waiter to serve a hot meal to the customer more efficiently.

In essence, marketing is all about strengthening, promoting and protecting the brand. The Hyatt brand takes a worldwide portfolio of more than 450 properties and combines them under a single identity. But at the same time, each of these properties and every other engagement with the Hyatt brand—from a conversation with our customer service staff over the phone to a review posted on a website like TripAdvisor—affects our brand reputation.

More than in most industries, managing a brand in the hospitality industry requires an integrated form of marketing and communications, one that affects the way we communicate to customers and other stakeholders—who could be a reporter, but could also be the woman writing a review of one of our hotels on a smartphone, just moments after checking out.

In this chapter, I will highlight the rapid changes in hotel industry marketing and public relations and discuss some of the rising challenges we face as the traditional experts and gatekeepers in the hospitality industry are replaced with anonymous customers communicating in real time. I will review how technology is being deployed as a communications tactic, but I will also discuss how the revolutionary changes in the way people share information around the globe demand new communications strategies.

Had this chapter been written in the spring of 2008, it would have described a seemingly more predictable industry than the one that exists in more turbulent economic times. Looking back at that time, it appears that our industry was running on autopilot. We based our forecasts on our business history, assumed our customers would continue to behave in the future as they had in the past and expected history to repeat itself. Our confidence in our ability to predict the future was shattered by an event no computer program could foresee: the global financial crisis. The collapse of investment banking giant Bear Stearns, followed by the fall of Lehman Brothers, touched off chaos throughout the economy. Financial service companies held 119,000 room nights at Hyatt properties, and these events were followed quickly by rampant reservation cancellations across the globe.

Every industry, in nearly every country, was affected deeply by the financial crisis. But there were moments in early 2009 when it seemed like our industry might also be teetering. Conventions were cancelled and vacations put on hold. At a time when many Americans were worried about being able to pay their mortgage, checking into a hotel seemed like a luxury. Shortly after the financial crisis hit, PKF Hospitality Research was predicting a modest 1.1 percent decrease in lodging demand for 2009. Yet by January, hotel demand was contracting at an alarming velocity. According to the PWC Lodging Industry Outlook in 2009, U.S. hotel room demand was contracting at twice the pace of the overall GDP.

By November 2008, we discovered that the only reliable customers we had left were those staying in our hotels at that moment. That was our first lesson in back-to-basics customer marketing. If, in the heat of the financial crisis, a guest was staying at a Hyatt hotel, odds were pretty good that this customer still had a job, still needed to travel or otherwise felt comfortable enough about the future to keep visiting our properties. Before 2008, all of this information made us confident about our future business; however, this data had become so unreliable that we had to toss it out and start over.

How do you talk to future customers when you no longer know who they are? Knowing that the methods we had used to fill hotel rooms over the previous few years would no longer work, Hyatt shifted its focus toward the customers who remained most loyal to us. If we could give these customers incentives to keep choosing Hyatt in the midst of a brutal price war, and perhaps even convince them to stay in our hotels more often than usual, we could survive the downturn, and perhaps reemerge in a stronger position.

It was also a perfect opportunity for us to form stronger relationships with the customers who meant the most to us. We decided that an enhanced loyalty program would not only help us keep rooms filled, it would also strengthen these customers' emotional engagement with the brand. In an increasingly inhospitable world, we wanted our hotels to seem like a safe haven—a place where loyal customers will be met not with less service, fewer extras, stingy access and unattainable status—but with genuine welcome and gratitude.

CASE STUDY: MANAGING CHAOS WITH GRATITUDE

"Gratitude is not only the greatest of virtues, but the parent of all the others," said Marcus Tullius Cicero, the great Roman statesman and philosopher. Hyatt reached out to its loyal customers with this philosophy in mind, and by involving operations, we realigned the company around our relationships with our most loyal, frequent guests. Today, our loyalty program, Hyatt Gold Passport, is at the heart of everything we do.

We relaunched Hyatt Gold Passport as a best-in-class loyalty program. Our goals were to increase both the number of stays and nights among members by shifting market share and to enhance customer engagement with our program and brand. We anchored our redesigned program with one key idea: BIG generosity when the world needs it most.

This is the way we would distinguish Hyatt in a marketplace dominated by larger companies that manage substantially more properties—companies like Starwood, Hilton and Marriott—who will always be able to dominate a marketplace built solely around loyalty points.

The 2009 film, *Up In the Air*, accurately dramatized the hospitality industry reward system as dominated by the biggest players. It is a world that encourages robotic behavior, gaming the system and accumulating markers of status rather than encouraging customers to actually enjoy every visit. At one point in the film, the protagonist, played by George Clooney, orders three dinners, not because he is especially hungry, but because it fits within his company meal allowance and he intends to maximize his loyalty points. He then explains to his young colleague that the purpose of accumulating the points is not to bank the points for a memorable vacation, but simply to accumulate the points.

Traditional loyalty programs are often far removed from the true meaning of the word, becoming a means to an end for frequent travelers. Increasingly these days, customers are going on to sites like Points.com and exchanging points in one program for points in another. In rethinking Hyatt's loyalty system, we focused on creating a system that was not about the points—or even a system—but pure generosity. We wanted to show the importance of being there for our members in tough times and to engage them in a meaningful relationship.

If Hyatt wanted to demonstrate genuine gratitude, we could not do it by playing the traditional loyalty points game. We had to make our program enhance each moment and build an emotional attachment with our best customers. Our goal was to use Hyatt Gold Passport to demonstrate a genuine difference. We would express our best qualities through this program: gratitude, generosity and authentic hospitality. The initiative had three core elements.

First, we made the system simple. This meant dumping the complicated program rules that only corporate insiders understood and nobody liked—getting rid of capacity controls and blackout dates for standard room redemption. In addition, we decided to stop nickel-and-dime practices. We were the first major full-service U.S. hotel chain to provide complimentary Internet access to elite members. We launched expedited check-in at a dedicated area for our elite members. And for the most loyal customers, those who obtained Diamond status, we added suite upgrades four times annually on paid nights to our best rooms available and free breakfast at every hotel.

Second, we decided that a true loyalty program should offer something more than rewards based on points; it should demonstrate our gratitude in ways both big and small, every day. To do this effectively, we had to get every employee involved. So we launched a program called "Random Acts Of Generosity" that empowered our employees to demonstrate authentic hospitality by providing complimentary Hyatt services. There were no strings attached and these acts were truly random; Hyatt Gold Passport membership was not a requirement. Employees were free to decide when and where to surprise and delight their guests with services like complimentary laundry service, picking up the tab at dinner or even providing a weary traveler a free massage in one of our spas. It was a random and unexpected gesture of goodwill, and it spread the Hyatt spirit of generosity to both employees and guests. A total of $1 million in services was dispersed by Hyatt in 2009 alone.

Third, if we were going to relaunch Hyatt Gold Passport, we needed to reach out and encourage more travelers to participate in the program. Thus, we launched a global attention-grabbing campaign, which was a grand gesture of generosity and authentic hospitality. The Big Welcome campaign encouraged travelers to dream again by asking how they would use 365 nights at Hyatt. Three lucky winners would receive 365 complimentary nights and receive a million air miles to realize their dream. Thirty thousand other winners would get a free night at any Hyatt hotel. This campaign had a budget of $8 million and took full advantage of our integrated marketing–communications approach, using a broad range of media, including print and digital advertising, direct mail and e-mail, as well as public relations.

It worked. The campaign generated a massive amount of attention for our company, in total, 976 million media impressions. This included more than 700,000 hits on the program's YouTube home page and more than 300 placements in unpaid media via our public relations outreach. We also received more than 1 million visitors to "The Big Welcome" website and received 280,000 entries to our contest. The submissions included 30,000 pictures, 400 videos and 100 audio files.

Bear in mind that all of this was happening during the worst year for the hospitality industry anyone can remember, and in a global economy worse than any time since the Great Depression. And the results speak for themselves. Among our Diamond Members in 2009, as compared to 2008, stays increased by an astonishing 40.9 percent and room nights increased by 51.5 percent. Overall, total stays increased by a strong 3.4 percent, with their total room nights increasing by 3.1 percent. For members who redeemed awards through "The Big Welcome" contest, stays increased 125 percent per member, with revenue increasing by 92 percent.

Increasing Hyatt Gold Passport overall satisfaction was even more important than putting customers into rooms. Program members aware of the new benefit enhancements reported higher preference and satisfaction with Hyatt Gold Passport and Hyatt overall. "Top Box Satisfaction" with Hyatt Gold Passport increased among Gold members from 24 percent to 35 percent. This means the number of Gold tier members surveyed who rated their satisfaction with the program as a 5 on a 5-point scale increased by 11 percent. Among Platinum members, satisfaction rose from 32 percent to 52 percent. And among our Diamond members, Hyatt's most loyal, frequent guests, satisfaction soared from 46 percent to 63 percent.

The campaign turned out to be highly influential. Those who were most aware of The Big Welcome were those most favorable toward the Hyatt brand. Respondents aware of the campaign registered a 34 percent increase in brand awareness, a 50 percent increase in willingness to recommend and a 117 percent increase in brand preference. The success could also be marked by a significantly higher brand preference for Hyatt among our Hyatt Gold Passport members. Gold members increased their preference from 61 percent to 90 percent, Platinum from 78 percent to 84 percent and Diamond from 88 percent to 89 percent.

What this shows is that across the board, regardless of status, our Hyatt Gold Passport members overwhelmingly prefer our brand to that of our competitors.

The Big Welcome campaign helped Hyatt thrive in a difficult environment, but it also taught us several invaluable lessons. It demonstrated the power of being bold and generous when everyone else was focused on cutting costs and becoming stingier with service. Traveling customers quickly discovered in 2009 that hotels that focused purely on cost to ride out the recession often skimped on maintenance, added new "resort fees" and severely cut back on staff.

Another key lesson we learned is the importance of employees. Great strategies and tactics are wonderful, but they are meaningless in our industry unless they are delivered passionately and in a manner that enhances our brand and program. By inspiring Hyatt employees to make the most of customer engagements, we brought the program to life.

Since 2009, we have continued to refine Hyatt Gold Passport based on the lessons we learned. Because our data showed that the greatest loyalty gains were among those who redeemed awards points, we made a special effort to simplify and streamline our awards redemption process. Our goal is to turn the typical experience of redeeming rewards on its head—taking a process that is often complex and cumbersome and turning it into something simple, something that is encouraged, and another opportunity for us to express our gratitude for continued loyalty.

As a result of these efforts, in 2010 Hyatt won the "Innovation in Travel/Hospitality Loyalty Award" from the Colloquoy Loyalty Awards, the only peer-based award in the loyalty arena and the only loyalty awards that span all major industries, including retail, travel and financial services.

AFTER THE STORM: CHANGE CONTINUES

Thriving amid the tumult of 2008 and 2009 required just the right combination of innovation and discipline. But as the clouds have lifted, the hospitality industry that has emerged in the new economy is not the same one we left behind three years ago. In fact, change in the industry seems to be evolving even more rapidly. Before I explain the new age of the hospitality industry's integrated marketing efforts, I need to say a few words about how our industry itself once operated.

Forty years ago, the public relations manager's role in a hotel was to entertain important guests, handle customer complaints, and go shopping with the wives of important customers. The public relations manager was, in fact, a glorified VIP guest relations officer. In those days, a heavy emphasis was placed on the hotel sales department. The "sales call" was believed to be the single most effective means of filling a hotel. It was easy and fast and it achieved results.

In the 1970s and 1980s, the hotel's director of sales was responsible for working with the press because the public relations executive employed in the department typically had no formal training in communications. Any interaction with the press was promotional or advertising in nature and driven by the press, not by the hotel. Although hotels would participate in such promotions, the newspaper or television station would derive the most direct benefit.

By the 1990s, hotels had established marketing departments and professionally trained public relations specialists. Even as the role of the hotel public relations manager began to be better understood, public relations management was still more reactive rather than proactive. The hotel public relations manager answered calls from the press, wrote and distributed press releases based on the news the hotel wanted to tell, and sat back and waited for the telephone to ring.

Even at the corporate level, marketing and public relations were conducted in a far simpler manner than it is today. In the first edition of this book, published in 1997, I wrote about how we were just starting to get a handle on tailoring press releases and media outreach based on reporters' interests.

I wrote that each year, Hyatt would attend a number of industry trade shows. Inevitably, we would carry with us 5-pound press kits complete with every possible story our company had to tell. And we could never understand when a journalist was not eager to walk away from our booth with the information we deemed so valuable. At the time, I also wrote about transforming this process by distributing press materials to those with a receptive ear, to those on our target database, or to journalists we had identified as being willing to accept the information and interested in doing something proactive with it. In these "good old days," our public relations challenge consisted largely of personally knowing the world's top 10 travel journalists, letting them know when new resorts were opening and making sure they got there. This was an effective way for hotel operators to influence guests and potential guests because those top 10 journalists had enormous power and influence. They were the information gatekeepers and the tastemakers who could make or break a hotel's reputation with a single review.

Today, by contrast, we operate in an environment that is constantly in flux. With the dramatic rise of social media and mobile technology, the power in the communications pendulum has shifted from the brand managers and hotel operators to the customers themselves. We are managing an industry that is transforming, changing so fast that the process of change itself is almost imperceptible. I like to say it is like being in a hot air balloon: you do not feel the wind, you are a part of the wind. Everyone in our industry is struggling to figure out how to use social media most effectively and most strategically. We are in an era of total transparency, where anonymous reviewers on sites like TripAdvisor.com are even more influential than those top 10 journalists of old. In addition, the brand is subject to constant reevaluation and redefinition, and a company's behavior and environmental footprint can have a major global influence and impact as strong as its marketing communications efforts.

THE GROWTH OF SOCIAL MEDIA

I want to start this examination of the current, rapidly changing environment with some words about social media. Today, there probably is not a company in the world, regardless of its size, that is not thinking about ways to use online tools such as Facebook, Twitter, YouTube, blogs and check-in sites such as Foursquare to increase their customer base and drive loyalty. Recently, I saw a trash truck drive by on a Chicago street with a small sign affixed to the side urging people to seek out their Facebook page. For what purpose, I have no idea.

That waste management company is not alone. Every company today feels the need to be on Facebook and Twitter, but not necessarily to drive a strategic purpose. When you consider that at the time of this writing, Internet websites have been around for roughly 17 years and many companies in many industries have yet to figure out how to best leverage these always-on, instantaneous publishing tools for a strategic business purpose. With this, you can better appreciate why social media has yet to fully revolutionize how the hospitality industry operates.

Yet, in many industries, there is a genuine fear that a competitor will soon find Excalibur and start wielding the power of social media to change the business model of that industry at any moment. So if you are not experimenting with an effort to do that yourself, you stand at risk of being left behind when and if the instantaneous change hits. The hospitality industry is not immune to that concern.

At Hyatt, we think of social media such as Twitter feeds and our Facebook pages the same way we do our loyalty program—as opportunities to reengage our customers. For example, we have found Twitter to be a remarkably fast and efficient concierge service for our hotel guests. Guests who Tweet to @HyattConcierge can make dinner reservations or spa appointments rapidly, which is especially useful when away from the hotel, because you do not need to recall a telephone number.

THE ERA OF TRANSPARENCY

A more immediate trend that is rapidly changing the face of our industry is transparency. I believe that we are entering an era of complete transparency, one where the power has been taken away from brands and placed in the hands of consumers.

Our customers are talking to each other, moment to moment, without our even knowing about it. In a way, companies now manage the brand on behalf of the consumer. In today's world, people want to be part of a community. They have probably always trusted their friends' opinions most of all, but now they have new ways of communicating those opinions rapidly and in a systematic manner. From a brand perspective, we used to rely on advertising to convey our message; now, we rely on every interaction between users and buyers. In many respects, we are just sitting on the sidelines watching our brand interact with the world.

The exclusive role once reserved for major travel magazines and columns in influential newspapers has been taken up by websites such as Hotelshark.com, IgoUgo.com, NileGuide.com and, especially, the wildly popular Expedia.com subsidiary, TripAdvisor.com. Individual reviews written by largely anonymous travelers are having an enormous impact.

There are three ways to approach this new era of open criticism: you can ignore it, fight it or embrace it. Ignoring the power of customer critiques is the most perilous route. It essentially surrenders your brand to the wild, allowing customers to pick apart your image and reputation one property at a time. Fighting it, by disputing the statements made on these sites, attempting to scrub the sites of negative comments or creating fictitious favorable reviews to outweigh the negative is also a short-sighted strategy, one that will almost inevitably lead to a backlash as your company gains a reputation for hostility and deception.

Hyatt has determined that the best way to engage hotel review sites is to enter into the communities and to engage customers who post reviews. On TripAdvisor.com, we read every comment made each day about Hyatt properties and our direct competitors. The good news is that six out of seven customer comments within this group of hotel brands are positive. We believe consumers want to write about their good experiences because it reaffirms the decision they made to stay in a particular hotel in the first place and allows them to show how smart they were for making such a great choice for their vacation. But review sites like these are forcing us to learn a new art—how to manage the negative. We use negative customer experiences as an opportunity to explain what went wrong, how we fixed the problem and how we will learn from it to try to prevent it from happening again. Interestingly enough, we are also learning to manage the negative by adjusting to relying on brand advocates and the self-policing or self-correcting dynamic that seems to be occurring naturally in so many online communities. In those rare instances when an unhappy guest takes to cyberspace to vent or to exploit the power of the community to advance his own agenda, we consistently see other guests pipe up in our defense, providing a more balanced perspective and a tempering tone. As review sites proliferate and gain influence, there will be a larger number of people who seek to game the system. When that happens, if we have done a good job engaging the community, they will help support our brand.

What we have discovered is that customers do not want complicated rationales and extravagant promises; they want simple explanations. I believe that the brands that can be the most transparent are the ones that will end up winning. Every brand has its weaknesses. But if those deficiencies are effectively managed, the brand may become loved, and loyalty will soon follow. Operating in this newly transparent environment is uncomfortable for most of us who have spent our careers seeking to control every mention and representation of our brands. But those who learn to perform their brand promise in the social universe as well as they do in the physical world are the ones who will succeed in using the new technologies to drive preference for their brands.

THE EFFECT OF GREEN POLICIES

Brands are also being redefined by the way we behave in the world. In the wake of the financial crisis, corporate responsibility has become a larger issue than ever before. With growing concerns about climate change and periodic energy price spikes, brand reputations are being redefined by the way companies handle environmental challenges, and the influence of "green" behavior on the brand will only grow in the years ahead.

Hyatt Hotels Corporation has a deeply rooted environmental program that is driven by our hotels in the field. From Santiago, Chile; to San Diego, California; to Sydney, Australia; each Hyatt hotel has its own green team, working proactively to reach aggressive corporate goals regarding our carbon footprint and energy consumption. In fact, the corporation was ahead of the field in understanding the importance of greater environmental responsibility.

By 2015, Hyatt's goal is to decrease its 2006 level of energy consumption per square meter and greenhouse gas emissions per square meter by 25 percent. Also by 2015, we are working to reduce water consumption per guest-night by 20 percent (from the 2006 levels) and reduce waste sent to landfills per guest-night by 25 percent.

Our commitment to protect our planet is backed by the strength of more than 85,000 associates and dedicated Green Teams. Together, we strive to take care of our environment with the same commitment with which we care for our guests.

We are making significant progress toward our goals, and we were recently one of three companies (along with Nike and Toyota) to be invited by the Department of Defense to talk about the ways we have implemented green policies across the company, and how our practices could help the U.S. military become more energy efficient and reduce its carbon footprint.

OUR EYE ON THE FUTURE

Given the current dynamics in our industry, it would seem to be a perilous, even foolhardy, venture to speculate on what the future might bring. But given the risks of inaction, and the possibility, as mentioned in the social media section, that someone else will find a way to harness these emerging technologies and revolutionize the industry overnight, it would be even more foolish to take a wait-and-see approach. Hotels are physical, not virtual, properties and will not just disappear. But as real estate was dramatically revalued in waves of foreclosures, the ability of companies to manage room rates can be dramatically affected by technologies that pick apart property reputations and steer customers in large numbers.

That's the negative way of looking at the future. The positive is that, as we have learned when we re-launched Hyatt Gold Passport, philosophy has a funny way of triumphing over simple prognostications and rote mechanics. We learned quite a bit about how to use customer data in the wake of the financial crisis and the new models that will replace those deemed outdated by the crash. This is a high priority program within Hyatt that is central to our future marketing efforts. The ability to gain a variety of snapshots about our customer base and to parse that data to predict future behavior will be an important part of our company's future.

Even more important than this data, however, are the lessons we learned in our industry's darkest hours in 2008 and 2009. By returning to our core values—mutual respect, intellectual honesty and integrity, humility, fun, creativity and innovation—we did not just entice our guests to dig into their wallets; we formed a new emotional bond. This emotional bond engendered loyalty, driving future sales. Our challenge now is to apply this philosophy to the chaotic world we live and work in.

CREATING COMMUNITY

It all starts with publishing. Today, every brand is a publisher. Hyatt Hotels Corporation is not just a series of hotels and corporate offices; it is also a website, a Facebook page and a Twitter feed. Millions of stray comments about us appear on websites around the world. To thrive in this environment, we need to also thrive as a publisher. For people who work in communications, our roles are moving beyond simply pushing out definitions of the brand. Our roles increasingly revolve around our reactions to the individual and property-by-property brand redefinitions driven by our guests.

So, how will we use social media? Our industry needs to find a way to communicate with customers the moment they walk in the door and up to the moment they check in again. As consumers become increasingly comfortable "checking in" on their mobile devices in exchange for small rewards, these media give us an opportunity to form those bonds. But how do we create relevancy? And how do we get into the space where people have conversations about lifestyle, where they start to dream about those big, memorable moments in their future, and also get them to consider our brand.

If we ultimately believe that Facebook or some other form of an online community is here to stay and will take on an increasingly central role in publishing our personal and corporate brands, then we are facing the first major paradigm of the new century and no brand has figured out the way to best interact with it. While it is true that brands are entering the space and in some cases creating impressions, few are actually fostering genuine, lasting interactions. Just as Facebook could be a game changer, it could also be a colossal time waster and cash furnace.

In the meantime, as everyone tries to figure this out, Hyatt is engaging with smaller, invitation-only online communities in an attempt to further refine our brand and extend our loyalty efforts. Hyatt is making great use of the online community of loyal customers it has established into a perpetual virtual focus group. The community is hosted by Communispace.

This community of loyal customers allows us to develop a high level of customer engagement while also receiving valuable feedback from them about ways that we can make our properties more appealing. One use of the community, for example, was to find out what bathroom amenities our customers would like to enjoy. We sent samples of shampoo to everyone in the community, gathered their feedback and used the results to make a decision. And in the process, our customers had a chance to try out some products free of charge.

We have also made an effort to reach out to specialized communities. A good example is flyertalk.com, which bills itself as the world's largest frequent flyer community. Although we may not want to build our travel loyalty program for characters like the one George Clooney played in *Up in the Air*, we do have great affection for the world's travel warriors and we are always looking for ways to make our loyalty efforts more appealing to them. If you want to find the modern equivalent of those 10 most influential travel journalists in today's publishing world, you should probably check out the FlyerTalk hotel forums.

Will it be possible to move the people who frequent these kinds of forums to pages and sites hosted by our brand? Probably not. But that does not mean that we cannot create opportunities for these influencers to touch our brand.

MANAGING BRAND REPUTATION

The second great challenge of the social media era will be reputation management. Any time you perform a Google search of your name to check what is freely available about you on the Internet, you are engaged in a form of reputation management. For a company like ours, reputation management is as critical to the strength of our brand as our advertising campaigns.

I have already discussed the ways that Hyatt interacts with sites like TripAdvisor. But learning how to manage opinions posted on sites like these is an evolving art and, as the nature of reputation management changes both on the consumer and corporate sides, how to manage it will continue to evolve. Making the most of these interactions will require not only figuring how to respond, but also whether to respond at all.

One factor in the future of reputation management, for example, is the proliferation of Facebook Connect. A growing number of websites, including TripAdvisor, allow customers to log onto their site via their Facebook accounts. Because Facebook requires its users to publish under their own name, the growth of Facebook Connect could change the nature of interactions on websites. Numerous studies have shown that people are far less likely to post heavily negative information if they have to take personal responsibility for the comment.

Another consideration is the question of authority on review sites. Today, review sites are dominated by the masses; reputation is measured by an average rating and by the most recently posted reviews. But it is very easy to envision a future in which reviewers start to build their own platforms, and websites provide an opportunity for their readers to "review the reviewers," as is done on Amazon.com. This could create greater authority for some voices, which adds a new layer of stakeholders for reputation managers to take into account. Perhaps someday, we will be back to a list of 10 authorities whom public relations managers will have to manage first—the only difference being that these reviewers could be critiquing for free.

Yet another layer of complexity is added by the fact that the websites themselves are starting to offer reputation management training courses back to the industry. TripAdvisor, for example, offers free courses to help property owners and marketers enhance their listings, increase traffic, maintain a positive reputation and respond to guest reviews posted on their site. Numerous marketing companies are offering similar services, for a fee. Some have suggested that online reputation management will soon replace search engine optimization as the number one service offering from Web 2.0 consulting firms.

CONCLUSION

No matter how closely we monitor trends—or how effective we become at analyzing data—we will never be able to accurately predict the future of marketing and public relations in the hospitality industry, or any industry for that matter. But what we can anticipate is how human beings might respond when they are treated with special care.

When you think about it, the entire nature of the Web 2.0 social media economy revolves around generosity and the maintenance of a good reputation. When people post reviews, they are not doing so to gain fame and fortune. Sometimes they go online to vent, but mostly they offer honest advice to help fellow travelers find a decent place to stay. When people follow the rules buying and selling products on eBay or Craigslist, they are building and maintaining reputations. Someone who creates a video and posts it on YouTube is sharing a small piece of art with the world, setting it free to achieve "viral" status.

For a company to thrive in this environment, we need to keep learning to match these small selfless acts with rewards of our own. For this reason, the hospitality industry is the perfect place to experiment with the future of marketing communications. Our business has always been about delighting customers—making wonderful moments just a bit more memorable. For Hyatt, a company built around generosity, gratitude and genuine hospitality, these are exciting times.

We look to the future, eagerly embracing the chaos.

In a "social" spirit and in the interest of transparency, I invite you to let me know if you have questions or if you would like to have a dialogue on these topics. Please do not hesitate to email me at john.wallis@hyatt.com.

DISCUSSION QUESTIONS

1. What skills might someone seeking employment in a marketing–communications function within the hospitality industry need today, that were unnecessary 10 years ago?
2. Why is hotel guest data, including phone numbers and e-mail addresses, so important to the hospitality industry?
3. Given the importance of building and attracting loyal customers for the hospitality industry, why are websites like Hotels.com and Expedia.com seen as a challenge?
4. Who are the most important "journalists" in the hospitality industry today?
5. Why is online reputation important for both the writers of reviews and the subject of the reviews?
6. What are the potential downsides to a hospitality industry company investing heavily in an online community such as Facebook?
7. What use has Hyatt made of Twitter? What other potential uses can you envision?
8. How could a company's "green" policies affect their reputation management and community-building strategies, both positively and negatively?

ADDITIONAL READING

http://www.hyatt.com. Hyatt Hotels.
http://www.hotelblogs.org. Hotel Blogs.
http://pritzkerprize.com. Pritzker Architecture Prize.

35

CHAPTER

SPORTS MARKETING
Champion Communicators

Amy D. Littleton
Vice President
KemperLesnik

Steven H. Lesnik
Founder
KemperLesnik

A STRATEGIC APPROACH TO SPORTS PUBLIC RELATIONS

Sports public relations is one of the fastest-growing segments of the PR industry. This arena is defined by the use of public relations tactics to achieve the communications objectives of a team, venue or property and/or to support and enhance the sports marketing activities of a company or brand.

Over the past two decades, spending in sports sponsorship has continued to increase. Throughout the 2008–2010 economic recession, sponsorship was one of the few forms of marketing in which spending remained in positive territory. With sports sponsorship engagement comes activation of sports-related activities. Public relations is a significant sponsorship "activation activity" and has benefited a great deal from the boom in sports.

The 26th annual year-end industry review and forecast from the IEG Sponsorship Report shows that sponsorship expenditures by North American companies grew 3.9 percent in 2010 to $17.2 billion. Spending globally grew 5.2 percent to $46.3 billion. (IEG Sponsorship Report, 01/04/11).

Furthermore, the number of people watching general television programming has steadily declined while the number watching sports events has increased. According to a report published by Horizon Media, 85 percent of the television programs that drew more than 30 million viewers over the past year (2009–2010) were sports related. That percentage was 47 percent in 2004–2005.[1]

Super Bowl 2010 (New Orleans Saints vs. Indianapolis Colts)	Most watched television show in U.S. history, 106.5 million viewers, an eight percent increase over the 2009 Super Bowl
Kentucky Derby 2010	Most watched horse race since 1989
Stanley Cup 2010	Strongest performance in 13 years

Game six of the Stanley Cup playoffs 2010 (Chicago Blackhawks vs. Philadelphia Flyers)	Most widely watched NHL game in 36 years
NCAA men's basketball tournament championship 2010 (Duke vs. Butler)	23.9 million television viewers, the highest since 1999, 36 percent higher than in 2009
BCS championship game 2010 (Alabama vs. Texas)	Reached 30 million viewers for the second time in the event's 12-year history
NBA Finals 2010	Most watched since 2001
World Series 2010	Most watched since 2004

"Why Sports Ratings Are Surging on TV," *Time*, August 14, 2010.

SPORTS IN AMERICA

The impact of sports on American culture has been well documented. Popular language and business language are filled with sports clichés and analogies. Many people can remember the starting lineup of their favorite team more easily than the names of their local government officials.

The sports phenomenon is easily understood. The same principles and values upheld on the playing field—loyalty, competition and teamwork—mirror those that drive America's competitiveness in international affairs and business as well as in the individual need many Americans have to succeed.

Although more Americans are playing sports, many more are watching sports on television, over the Internet and via mobile technology. The biggest contributors to the popularity of sports on television are as follows:

- *High-definition television (HDTV)*. In 2010, 63 percent of U.S. homes owned at least one HDTV set, an increase of 13 percent over 2009.[2] Sports ratings are 21 percent higher on HDTVs.[3]

- *Digital video recorder (DVR)*. Consumers can record and watch whenever they like and cut out commentary and commercials to condense viewing time.

- *Internet*. Many games are streamed live over the Internet. This makes it easy for fans anywhere to bypass local television programming and watch their favorite teams in real time. For example, international football fans in Iowa can watch Union of European Football Associations (UEFA) matches taking place in the United Kingdom in real time.

- *Social media*. Sporting games are now shared experiences. Microblogging and social networking sites make it easy for fans to banter online with friends and followers about their teams, players, coaches and plays. The amount of Twitter traffic related to the 2011 Super Bowl was so great that it virtually shut down the system. People tracking the #superbowl11 hash tag had a difficult, if not impossible, time keeping up as the traffic jammed up many computers and mobile devices.

WHAT IS SPORTS MARKETING?

Marketers may be wise to take advantage of sports trends to reach key audiences, but just how do they do it? What is this widespread and ambiguous industry of sports marketing?

Any program that uses sports to realize one or more corporate, sales, marketing or communications objectives falls within the parameters of sports marketing.

It could include inviting a client to a professional or college ball game, buying an ad in a team's program book, hanging an authorized sign with a corporate logo at a sporting event, purchasing commercials during a sports telecast, inviting an athlete to deliver a motivational speech to employees or even sponsoring a local or employee-involved Little League team. Any of these tactics are the basis of local to global sports marketing campaigns.

The best sports marketing campaigns will vertically integrate program components that together achieve many objectives. Integrated public relations is a critical piece of sports marketing campaign activation with advertising, sales, promotions and other communications.

By engaging in any sports marketing activity, a marketer hopes to tap the emotional investment that bonds most sports fans: loyalty to a favorite sport or event or a favorite team or player. Because consumer brand loyalty is perhaps the most important attitude a marketer must influence, marketers align their companies with entities and personalities to whom their target consumer is loyal. In theory, over time the consumer will become a loyal follower of the company as well. Figure 35.1 shows the most active non-media sponsor categories.

Marketers use sports to reach specific target audiences with sales and brand messages. Research has shown there is a distinction between fans of different sports; for example, a typical National Basketball Association (NBA) fan differs from a typical PGA Tour fan. As a result, specific sports are used by marketers as a reliable way to reach targeted audiences. Marketers also use sports to conduct research—deeply delving into the consumer's thoughts and behaviors. In addition, sports provides the means for marketers to try targeted or niche marketing strategies aimed at ethnic, regional, age, income and other segment-based audiences.

The following section summarizes the major areas of sports marketing. The integration of public relations with marketing and corporate goals is critical to the successful implementation of many, but not all, of these strategies.

WHY COMPANIES SPONSOR

- Increase brand loyalty
- Create awareness and visibility
- Change or reinforce image
- Drive retail traffic/sales
- Differentiate brand from that of competitors
- Demonstrate commitment to niche market
- Sample/display brand attributes
- Create business-to-business marketing/hospitality[4]

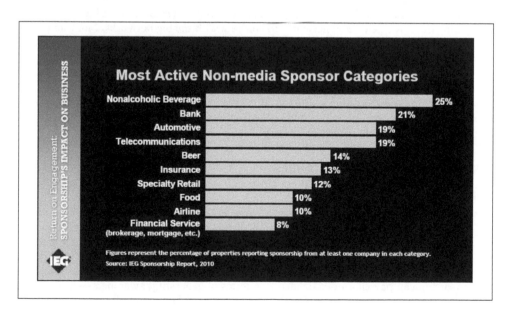

FIGURE 35.1

Most Active Non-media Sponsor Categories

SPORTS MARKETING

The pervasive presence of sports in our culture is one of the major reasons for the growth of sports sponsorship. In fact, according to the *2010 IEG Sponsorship Report*, sports sponsorship spending in North America was $11.66 billion, eclipsing all other forms of sponsorship.

North American Sponsorship Spending by Property Type

2009 Spending	2010 Spending	Increase from 2009	2011 Spending (Projected)	Increase from 2010 (Projected)	
Sports	$11.28 billion	$11.6 billion	3.4%	$12.38 billion	6.1%
Entertainment tours and attractions	$1.64 billion	$1.75 billion	6.3%	$1.85 billion	5.9%
Causes	$1.51 billion	$1.62 billion	6.7%	$1.7 billion	5%
Arts	$820 million	$842 million	2.7%	$885 million	5.1%
Festivals, fairs and annual events	$756 million	$782 million	3.4%	$820 million	4.9%
Associations and membership Organizations	$496 million	514 million	3.6%	$543 million	5.6%

Sports is big business and getting bigger. More children are participating in sports now than ever before, and many colleges and universities now offer undergraduate and graduate degree programs in sports management. From high school events, such as the McDonald's All American High School Basketball Games, to major college sports, such as basketball and football, to every professional sports league in the nation, sports permeates the airwaves, radio waves and Internet.

Where the major networks (ABC, NBC, CBS) and ESPN once owned the market for distribution of sporting events, college conferences, such as the Big Ten, and professional leagues, including the National Hockey League, are creating their own television networks to compete with the big networks. Nontraditional networks such as TBS and TNT are airing sporting events, including Major League Baseball (MLB) games, NBA games and, as of 2011, portions of the NCAA Tournament (basketball) in a share with CBS. In addition, independent sports networks like Versus (subsequently purchased by NBC) and Comcast SportsNet have emerged to compete in recent years for sports viewers.

Each of these new channels delivers content on television and has a robust presence over the web. The emergence of mobile smartphone technology and convenient electronic pad technology (e.g., iPad) even further enables competition in the area of content distribution.

SPONSORSHIP FOR BUSINESS AND CAUSES

Event Sponsorship

College's Tostitos Fiesta Bowl, the PGA of America's Senior PGA Championship presented by KitchenAid and NASCAR's Quaker State 400 auto race are all examples of title sponsorships. The legal definition of corporate sponsorship is: a form of advertising in which companies pay to be associated with certain events. When the sponsorship of a nonprofit or charitable event is involved, the sponsorship activity is often referred to as event marketing or cause marketing.

Title sponsorship can pay enormous dividends in terms of generating awareness—through advance promotion, television coverage and direct contact with event attendees. Many if not all times an event is mentioned —during its television broadcast, by fans around the office water cooler, on that evening's sportscast, via social media channels or in the local newspaper—the sponsor receives mention and expands its reach.

Generally, title sponsors negotiate benefits from event owners and organizers. These include placement of the sponsor's logo on-site and within television camera view (often on the actual playing field), the inclusion of one or more commercial spots during the event's telecast, the opportunity to distribute product or coupons at the event, other consumer promotions, a supply of tickets, attendance at one or more VIP parties tied to the event and corporate hospitality venues. Benefits may also include mobile content, live web streaming and other technology-enabled communications or promotions.

The price tag for such packages can be quite steep. Title sponsors of nationally televised events frequently pay more than $5 million for their sponsorships.

Most event organizers will sell less expensive sponsorships to marketers that for one reason or another do not wish to purchase the title sponsorship. The benefits included in these lesser sponsorship packages can include many, but not all, of the same benefits received by the title sponsor.

Property Sponsorship

For marketers looking for a sports link in their advertising or perhaps in retail, property sponsorship makes sense. Sponsorship of a property means that a marketer has purchased the right to use the logo, name or likenesses of the players of a team, franchise, league or organization in promotional efforts.

Most sports properties, such as the Olympics, UEFA and the National Football League, sell similar sponsorship packages to many different marketers by offering one exclusive package to just one marketer in many different business categories. For example, McDonald's (restaurant), Coca-Cola (soft drink), Omega (watch), Visa (credit card) and seven other companies constitute the group of worldwide Olympics sponsors.

Venue Sponsorship

Purchasing the rights to the name of a stadium or arena presents another area of sports sponsorship.

Here are some examples: Staples—Staples Center, Los Angeles; Phillips Electronics—Phillips Arena, Atlanta; and United Airlines—United Center, Chicago.

In 2010, JPMorgan Chase agreed to a massive sponsorship deal with Madison Square Garden worth at least $30 million a year. At the time, this deal stood as the most lucrative annual venue sponsorship agreement to date. Although it did not include naming rights, this comprehensive media buy included all teams and events in the building as well as all content on Madison Square Garden Network.

A professional sports and entertainment venue sponsorship investment can pay big dividends in terms of number of impressions made each time members of the community and the media mention the building. In a way, the venue sponsor is inherently linked to every event that takes place at the facility.

ATHLETE SPOKESPERSON

Professional athletes are frequently associated with skill, dedication and performance. Many marketers strive to derive value from professional athletes by associating those athletes with particular companies and brands. The income of many professional athletes is elevated solely because of sponsorship or spokesperson contracts for brand or product endorsements and appearances.

For top athletes, such as Tiger Woods and Lance Armstrong, sponsorship can translate to as much as 10 times their sports earned salary. While watching TV on any given night, you might see Peyton Manning promoting Gatorade or Shaun White endorsing Red Bull.

The rewards of associating a product with an athlete in terms of image enhancement are great, but it is important to remember that athletes, like the rest of us, are only human, and athlete endorsements do come with risk. Take the Thanksgiving holiday episode in 2009 when Tiger Woods wrecked his car and subsequently his image as the incident exposed him as a prolific adulterer. This embarrassing situation led many sponsors to pull their endorsements and others to deeply question their relationship with the star golfer.

Bloomberg Businessweek regularly ranks the 100 most powerful athletes that dominate in the world of sports and business. The 2011 ranking (top 10) follows:

Bloomberg Businessweek (Top 10) Power 100 List—2011

Rank	Name	Sport	Sponsors	Earnings
1	Peyton Manning	NFL/Indianapolis Colts quarter back	MasterCard, Reebok, Gatorade, Oreo	$30 million
2	Shaun White	Snowboarding, skateboarding	Red Bull, Target, Burton, Oakley	$8.8 million
3	Tiger Woods	PGA golf	Nike, EA SPORTS, Rolex	$71.3 million
4	Phil Mickelson	PGA golf	Barclays, Callaway, KPMG, ExxonMobil, Rolex	$53.8 million
5	Tom Brady	NFL/New England Patriots quarter back	Under Armour, UGG, Glaceau, Movado, Audi	$30 million
6	Shaquille O'Neal	NBA/Boston Celtics center	Li-Ning, Oreo, Comcast	$15.3 million
7	Drew Brees	NFL/New Orleans Saints quarter back	Nike, Visa	$17 million
8	Lance Armstrong	Cycling	Trek, Nike, Oakley	$15.3 million
9	Albert Pujols	MLB/St. Louis Cardinals first baseman	Nike	$23.5 million
10	Apolo Anton Ohno	Speed skating	Coca-Cola, AT&T, Alaska Airlines	$1.7 million

Bloomberg Businessweek, January, 26, 2011.

SIGNAGE AND LOGO PLACEMENT

Perhaps the simplest form of using sports to generate consumer impressions is a marketer's purchase of the right to feature content and images, particularly company logos, in sight of event goers, television audiences and fans.

The next time you are at an MLB game, count how many commercial signs you see: on the scoreboard, by the outfield wall, behind home plate and so forth. Rotating boards that provide signage space to more than one company during a game are also prevalent at MLB games and courtside at NBA arenas. The goal of well-positioned signage is to generate awareness for marketers both in the ballpark or arena and in the thousands of homes where people are watching sporting events on television. The better the position of the signage, the more times it will appear during the event's broadcast.

Logos appear on more than just signs. In many sports, athletes themselves are walking billboards. From golfers to tennis players to racecar drivers, athletes are often seen with sponsor logos on caps, helmets, shirt pockets, uniforms, equipment and even socks.

Take for example, the deal signed in June 2009 between Aon Corporation and the Premier League European football team, Manchester United. The four-year deal, the most lucrative in soccer at the time, cost approximately $32 million per year and included most prominently the Aon logo front and center on Manchester United jerseys.

On the front page of the company's website (www.aon.com), visitors may click to read Aon's statement about the sponsorship:

Partnering in tradition, integrity and success.

One unique opportunity to partner the preeminent global professional services firm with the world's most powerful sporting property. A shared desire for excellence and winning, based on tradition, integrity, teamwork and success. Unparalleled global reach. Unprecedented partnership.

It is a rather unique opportunity in the business world when two leaders in their respective fields can come together in a global partnership such as the one we have announced with our friends at Manchester United, the world's #1 sports brand.

Through its partnership with Manchester United, Aon, a leading global provider of risk management services, insurance and reinsurance brokerage and human resource consulting and outsourcing, is:

- Exposed to more than 300 million Manchester United fans worldwide

- Associated with the #1 sport in the world and the most widely followed team

- Enabled to reach 1.15 billion households in 227 countries with 88 million fans watching weekly

As a further example of the global nature of the Aon–Manchester United partnership, the company advertised a marketing position with specific duties related to Manchester United in Hong Kong. It said:

Manchester United Shirt Sponsorship responsibilities:

To support implementation of global Manchester United sponsorship initiatives in Asia

To act as coordinator and communicator between global marketing and local countries to ensure success implementation in each country in Asia

To follow up and keep track of results of each initiative in every country

To support Asia-initiated Manchester United sponsorship initiatives including PR events, advertising activities, internal communication and inter-country communications

To support Asian countries in their local client campaigns leveraging the sponsorship platform on marketing material, communication to media, coordinating with external agencies, etc.

PRODUCT PLACEMENT

Although marketers pay a hefty price for athletes to wear their companies' logos on apparel during competition, sporting goods companies battle, and pay handsomely, to have athletes use their equipment in play.

Nike, Reebok, Adidas and many other athletic apparel manufacturers, for example, pay colleges millions of dollars to outfit their teams during the season. Louisville Slugger provides thousands of free bats to professional baseball players every season.

CORPORATE HOSPITALITY

Tickets to many professional and college sporting events are often difficult to obtain. Providing a number of seats to key clients or employees generates goodwill among important audiences and fosters relationship building. Many marketers, especially those who sell to businesses rather than consumers, use their sponsorships to provide unique hospitality experiences to customers and prospects.

SPORTS PUBLIC RELATIONS

Many public relations practitioners in corporate communications departments or at public relations agencies face the challenge of supporting sports marketing ventures.

Each sponsorship or sports celebrity endorsement is different, and each requires a unique public relations program. Typically, public relations programs in these areas have two important components:

- Traditional media relations
- Social media

TRADITIONAL MEDIA RELATIONS

From sporting events to properties, venues and athletes, the news media plays an important role in building awareness, driving ticket sales/attendance and shaping brands. Many events and properties are covered by a group of reporters whose primary job is to report on certain sports. For example, golf writers cover only golf, and basketball writers cover only basketball. Each of these specialized groups focuses on being experts in their sports, and many belong to organizations such as the Golf Writers Association of America and the U.S. Basketball Writers Association of America. Public relations professionals concentrating on these sports focus on building relationships with the writers that most cover the sport.

In addition, there are many broadcast reporters who cover sports in general—from national ESPN reporters to sports anchors at local network affiliates. These reporters, while familiar with many sports, typically don't have the deep knowledge and long history with any one sport in particular. In addition, their coverage parameters are much more constricted. For example, they may briefly cover game highlights but are not able to publish in-depth analysis of an event or a feature story about a sponsor's activation activities.

Some media relations techniques focusing on supporting sports sponsorship include:

- Media credentialing for on-site event coverage

- Media room set up and management

- Player and coach interviews

- Press conferences (pre- and post-event)

- Proactive story angle development and pitching

SOCIAL MEDIA

Today's most important emerging public relations skill is the effective use of the social web. The *social web* is a term used to describe how people socialize or interact with each other throughout the Internet, including on social networks and content sharing sites made possible through Web 2.0 technology. *Web 2.0* refers to Internet technology applications that facilitate participatory information sharing, interoperability, user-centered design and collaboration.

Social media has become so relevant in the public relations industry that many public relations agencies have sprung up to focus solely on social media. All public relations firms today offer social media services in one form or another. Corporate public relations departments have also created social media functions, whether outsourced to an agency or insourced through additional staff and resources.

The realm of social media, as with any emerging technology, is ever-changing. It is likely that some tools used prominently today, such as Facebook, Twitter and Foursquare, will be less relevant or even nonexistent in a few years. Twitter, for example, while being the fastest-growing microblogging engine around, has not yet figured out how to monetize its business model. It will only be able to operate on venture funding and private equity money for so long until investors begin to demand return.

Nevertheless, the action of people connecting with people over the web using Web 2.0 technologies is not likely to diminish. In fact, as more and more people across the globe gain access to computers and the Internet, social media activity will only increase.

There are many ways for public relations practitioners to utilize the social web to benefit their companies, properties, venues and events. These tactics go beyond simply conversing over the web, although that is a key component. Many times, social media tactics also include:

- Event promotions

- Sales promotions

- Sweepstakes and giveaways

- Contests

- Games

Most often, it is the conversation and discussion surrounding the above tactics that drive interest and participation. These conversations take place over social networking sites as well as in online reviews, forums, discussion boards and blogs. Much of the creative conversation associated with these tactics can be found on sharing sites, such as Flickr. Hulu and YouTube.

The key to relevant social media engagement centers on being authentic. People do not want to interact with brands that are always trying to sell them something. They want to engage with brands that mean something—whether cause or affinity related. Luckily, most sports fans have affinity for just about everything in sports. That's why many athletes have thousands of friends and followers on Facebook and Twitter, why thousands of people choose to "like" their favorite sports teams and why fans follow the happenings at sports events and venues through conversations taking place in real time over social media. Fans also like to share their personal experiences with athletes, teams, and events by posting content, images and videos on social media channels.

Social media is an increasingly important tool in the public relations professional's toolbox.

EVENT SUPPORT

As the title sponsor of an event, a company expects, above all else, recognition of the sponsorship by all target audiences, including consumers, the media, employees and other key influencers. It is the responsibility of public relations to help generate that recognition by undertaking all communications-related activities for the marketer, including creating, developing, producing and disseminating media materials.

Managing all proactive media relations and social media efforts, including regularly distributing information and discussion on a variety of sponsorship-related stories, responding to media inquiries and serving as the marketer's liaison with employees regarding sponsorship support activities, are all important public relations functions that support event communications.

PROPERTY SUPPORT

Sponsorship of a major sports property costs millions of dollars. Supporting this heavy marketing investment requires an integrated activation program that includes advertising, internet marketing and public relations. Oftentimes, the public relations component includes media relations, social media and grassroots or community relations.

Many organizations use their property sponsorships as platforms to progress their corporate social responsibility agendas. For example, GE gives a legacy gift to each market in which the Olympics is held. In Toronto, it rehabilitated a rundown inner-city hockey rink and left the new facility to the community. In London, it created mobile medical facilities for use in low-income neighborhoods where healthcare options are few. In China, it donated two advanced water treatment systems to provide clean drinking water to residents in Dongguang City.

VENUE SUPPORT

Sponsorship of a stadium or arena is big news to local media and citizens. If the site is used by a professional team, it may be of national interest as well. Although the media opportunity for venues is less than that of teams and events, a carefully designed media relations and social media plan can ensure that the venue's profile is high. This is particularly important for sponsors who have purchased venue naming rights, for example, Staples—the Staples Center in Los Angeles; United Airlines—the United Center in Chicago; and Miller Coors—Miller Park in Milwaukee, Wisconsin.

ATHLETE SPOKESPERSON SUPPORT

Public relations can strengthen the relationship between a marketer and a spokesperson in a variety of ways, depending on the specifics of the endorsement contract.

The announcement of an endorsement provides a first opportunity for publicity. Many spokesperson announcements

The following examples show how companies can take advantage of athlete spokesperson appearances:

- Secure media interviews during which the athlete can deliver predetermined messages about the marketer and/or wear apparel featuring the company's logo.
- Arrange for the athlete to visit with employees at the marketer's headquarters for an afternoon or perhaps deliver a speech at the company's national sales meeting.
- Schedule the athlete to appear at the company's booth at an industry trade show to help build traffic.
- Distribute information to media about a new advertising campaign or promotional effort that will feature the athlete.
- Produce candid videos for distribution and discussion over social media.
- Host community clinics and other grassroots activities to generate awareness and media attention.

are made during press conferences showcasing the athlete and his/her relationship to the brand. Thereafter, the spokesperson typically agrees to appear in marketing collaterals (advertising, direct mail, internet, etc.) and contributes some amount of time to public relations activities, including public and media appearances, charities or cause marketing, social media engagement activities and community relations events. Athlete spokespeople are also often used for business relations purposes, including making appearances at company functions and interacting with important company clients and prospects.

CASE STUDY, MEDIA RELATIONS: CHAMPIONS CHANGING LIVES—THE LAUNCH OF HARBOR SHORES

OVERVIEW

In the economically struggling southwest Michigan city of Benton Harbor, golf is being used as a catalyst to economically, environmentally and socially revitalize the community. The grand opening of Harbor Shores, a beach and golf resort community that features an 18-hole Jack Nicklaus Signature Golf Course, in one day became a local and national sensation. With four golf legends, Jack Nicklaus, Arnold Palmer, Tom Watson and Johnny Miller, an entire region of support, a national golf audience and a miraculous 100-foot putt, the Champions for Change grand opening event did much more than simply put Harbor Shores on the map.

BACKGROUND

In the mid-1980s, Benton Harbor, a once thriving manufacturing community, was devastated by the closing of several factories. More than 5,000 jobs were lost over an 18-month period. With the vision to revitalize Benton Harbor, Whirlpool Foundation and other nonprofit groups created a plan to clean up contaminated land left over from old factories and develop a lakefront resort to drive tourism and create jobs.

The signature component of this effort is Harbor Shores, a 530-acre beach and golf resort community featuring an 18-hole Jack Nicklaus Signature Golf Course.

RESEARCH

In 2003, following civil unrest in Benton Harbor, then governor of Michigan Jennifer Granholm formed a task force to determine how to bridge social and racial gaps and provide opportunities for sustainable economic growth and employment in Benton Harbor. Countless focus groups and community meetings yielded an over 100-page report that included the recommendation to "develop an entertainment venue." It was determined that opportunities could be created by utilizing the area's abundant natural assets, including Lake Michigan, and, as a result, Harbor Shores was conceived. The research identified the program need and outlined the measure for success: build Harbor Shores into a premier Midwest destination and stimulate the local economy.

With research in hand and deep community support, Champions for Change—a one-day public golf exhibition featuring four of the most famous golfers of all time and benefiting nonprofits in the Benton Harbor community—was created. Target audiences were (1) Benton Harbor and surrounding Southwest Michigan communities, (2) primary and second home buyers throughout the Midwest, with a concentration in Chicago, and (3) golf enthusiasts across the nation.

PLANNING

Champions for Change objectives were to (1) build awareness of Harbor Shores and its community building mission locally, regionally and nationally; (2) drive residential real estate sales; and (3) stimulate golf rounds and revenue at The Golf Club at Harbor Shores.

Champions for Change was a concept to galvanize the community around the common goal of creating important social and economic changes to benefit all citizens.

Champions for Change was a series of three events in one day (August 10, 2010). The day started with a golf clinic during which the players engaged in lively banter and gave lessons for success on and off the golf course. This was followed by an 18-hole skins match. The players competed for a $1 million purse, which was provided by Whirlpool Corporation. This purse, in the end, was donated in the names of the four players to the Boys and Girls Club of Benton Harbor and The First Tee of Benton Harbor.

The golfers also participated in An Evening for Champions, an intimate fireside chat, which attracted thousands to the Benton Harbor Civic Center, was moderated by CBS Sports anchor Bill Macatee, and featured a lively, insightful and candid conversation among the four former competitors and long-time friends. CBS Sports captured the day's activities.

EXECUTION

Using Champions for Change to achieve the three primary objectives (listed above), the public relations team implemented a three-phased approach, which included a detailed pre-, during- and post event media relations campaign. The goals of each phase were to (1) garner top-tier media coverage in advance of Champions for Change, (2) secure more than 100 media to cover the event and (3) extend the life of the event through the year.

Phase One: Pre-Event

The team pursued the goal of national recognition and awareness by starting the Harbor Shores conversation at the highest level in two national media placements.

A *USA Today* Money Section exclusive cover titled "Building Hope on Golf's Allure" appeared the day Champions for Change was announced and served as the first national introduction of the event and real estate project. The article focused on how Benton Harbor was using golf as a catalyst for social and economic change. The *Wall Street Journal* article, "Can a Golf Course Save a City?," told the history of Benton Harbor and Harbor Shores. It appeared two weeks prior to Champions for Change and set Harbor Shores on the national stage.

One week before the event, the PR team held a media teleconference featuring all four golfers. More than 30 reporters from local, regional and national media outlets participated in the call generating 15 pre-event news stories.

Phase Two: During-Event

The day of Champions for Change, the PR team managed credentials for close to 130 media—from CBS Sports to the *Herald Palladium*—exceeding the goal by 30.

The team twice distributed B-roll footage online (at 1 PM and 7 PM) to meet various broadcast deadlines and generate early and end of day sports report stories. Video footage was available for media to download online and was also distributed via satellite. This effort garnered 33 news placements totaling more than 3 million impressions. On the 10th hole, Jack Nicklaus sunk an incredible 100-foot putt. The PR team quickly trumpeted this news, which was captured both professionally and by numerous fans on the course. In addition to securing coverage on countless sports broadcasts across the nation, the team landed the Nicklaus' putt on ESPN SportsCenter numerous times as a "Play of the Day" and "Play of the Week." Amateur videos of the putt made it to YouTube, and have generated more than 1 million views.

After play, Jack Nicklaus, Arnold Palmer, Tom Watson and Johnny Miller recapped their experience and spread the good word of Harbor Shores to a packed house during the post-event press conference.

Phase Three: Post-Event

In addition to concentrated post-event efforts to close many of the pending news stories from the event, the PR team engaged CBS Sports to concept and produce a 30-minute feature program about Champions for Change and Harbor Shores. This program aired on Saturday, April 9, 2011, just before the third round of play during one of golf's greatest annual tournaments, the Masters.

EVALUATION

1. Build awareness of Harbor Shores and its community building mission locally, regionally and nationally.

   - All three Champions for Change activities (the golf clinic, match play exhibition round and An Evening for Champions fireside chat) were sold out weeks in advance.

   - The public relations effort garnered more than 832 million media impressions and achieved a total advertising value of close to $7 million (a client-directed measure).

   - The team secured ranking of The Golf Club at Harbor Shores as one of the "Best New Courses" by *Golfweek*, *LINKS Magazine* and *GOLF Magazine*.

   - *Golf Digest* named The Golf Club at Harbor Shores "Lightning Rod of the Year."

   - CBS Sports aired the Champions for Change television special on Saturday, April 9, 2011, during The Masters Tournament.

   - A total of 100 local, 20 regional and 10 national media attended the events.

2. Drive residential real estate sales.

   - Prior to Champions for Change, 11 home sites at Harbor Shores had been sold.

   - During the event month (August 2010), 17 home sites were sold.

   - Almost everyone who purchased a home site in August contributed his or her awareness of and affinity for Harbor Shores to Champions for Change.

   - By September 2010, 50 percent of the residential real estate inventory was sold.

3. Stimulate golf rounds and revenue at The Golf Club of Harbor Shores.

   - Golf rounds spiked 20 percent immediately following Champions for Change.

   - Golf rounds are up more than 500 percent today.

To further underscore the impact of this one-of-a-kind event, following Champions for Change, the PGA of America selected The Golf Club at Harbor Shores to host the Senior PGA Championship tournament in 2012 and 2014.

CASE STUDY, SOCIAL MEDIA: THE EA SPORTS MAUI INVITATIONAL

ACTIVITY

In 2010, the EA SPORTS Maui Invitational experienced unprecedented reach through social media. The social media team communicated with millions of online users gathering information minute by minute by employing an on-site staff completely dedicated to social media.

In addition, the social media team sat courtside during all 12 games and listened to the ESPN audio feed, providing accurate, engaging and interesting information to social media users in real time and immediately responding to conversations as they happened.

Among other vehicles, the social media team posted links to Twitter, Facebook, Flickr and YouTube on the official Tournament's homepage, mauiinvitational.com. It also tweeted up-to-the-minute, behind-the-scenes notes from the Lahaina Civic Center, provided Facebook updates at halftime and at the end of each game and updated Flickr with game photos consistently throughout the event.

RESULT

In 2010, the social media team more than tripled the Tournament's online presence, with 7.4 billion online impressions. This increase was in large part due to the increased use of social media on site.

Twitter: @EASPORTSMauiInv, 2,770 followers (46 percent increase from 2009), 1,979 Tweets sent (136 percent increase from 2009)

Facebook: EA SPORTS Maui Invitational Fanpage, 699 fans (235 percent increase from 2009)

Flickr: EA SPORTS Maui Invitational Photostream, 200 Tournament photos (66 percent increase from 2009)

CASE STUDY, SOCIAL MEDIA: KITCHENAID AT THE PGA MERCHANDISE SHOW

ACTIVITY

KitchenAid made a splash at the 2011 PGA Merchandise Show on January 26–29 in Orlando. At Demo Day, the KitchenAid brand was exposed to 6,754 people. While at the show, KitchenAid reached 6,564 PGA professionals and more than 50,000 show attendees.

Brand manager Deb O'Connor met with 30 reporters from *Sports Illustrated* to the *Wall Street Journal*. During this time, the group revealed the new Senior PGA Championship presented by KitchenAid logo and disclosed KitchenAid's exciting sponsorship activation plans.

With the goals of establishing an online presence for KitchenAid in golf; providing daily updates to fans about happenings at the PGA Merchandise Show; engaging in relevant conversations with fans, media and show attendees; and populating channels on YouTube and Flickr, the PR team supported KitchenAid's presence at the 2011 PGA Merchandise Show with a robust social media program.

The team focused its energy on Twitter, YouTube and Flickr, and worked with the KitchenAidUSA social media team to extend the reach of golf-specific content to all brand audiences. The PR team created the @KitchenAid_Golf Twitter handle and used show hashtags #PGAMR11, #PGAShow. It also created and populated YouTube and Flickr content.

RESULT

- Achieved close to 400 followers in one week

- Tweeted 68 times during the course of the Show

- Used appropriate hashtags in 40 tweets

- Tweeted 15 times during Demo Day

- Tweeted 19 images

- Tweeted 6 times during the press conference

- KitchenAid was mentioned in 62 conversations

- Replied to 22 tweets from other users (@replies)

DISCUSSION QUESTIONS

1. Which companies do you think do the best job using sports marketing and public relations? Why?
2. How has technology changed the role of the sports public relations professional?

3. How do you see sports changing over the next 10 years? How will this impact sports marketing and public relations?
4. Is sports marketing and public relations local, global or both? Why?
5. How important are athlete spokespeople to a company/brand? Why?
6. What are the biggest risks associated with sports marketing and public relations?
7. Have you ever considered purchasing a product or service because the company was associated with a sport? If so, give an example. If not, why not?
8. How important is it to you that companies, sports teams and/or athletes are engaged in charitable, cause-related activities? Does this involvement motivate you to change your attitude, perception or behavior? If so, how?

NOTES

1. Sean Gregory, "Why Sports Ratings Are Surging on TV," *Time*, August 14, 2010.
2. Consumer Electronics Association.
3. Neilson.
4. Jim Andrews and William Chipps, "Fundamentals of Sponsorship," March 13, 2011.

ADDITIONAL READING

Helitzer, Melvin. *The Dream Job, Sports Publicity, Promotion and Marketing.* 2004.
Hopwood, Maria, James Skinner, and Paul Kitchin. *Sport Public Relations and Communications*, 2010.
Pitts, Brenda G., and David K. Stotlar. *Fundamentals of Sport Marketing*, third edition, 2007.
Rein, Irving, Philip Kotler, and Ben Shields. *The Elusive Fan, Reinventing Sports in a Crowded Marketplace.* New York, NY: McGraw-Hill, 2006.
Stotlar, David K. *Developing Successful Sport Sponsorship Plans*, second edition. 2004.

36

CHAPTER

EFFECTIVE TECHNOLOGY COMMUNICATIONS
Innovation that Matters

Edward Barbini
Vice President of External Relations
IBM

Rob Flaherty
Senior Partner and President
Ketchum

For decades, technology public relations was primarily communications for high-technology companies and their highly technical products. A case in point: in the last edition of this book, this chapter was titled "Public Relations for High-Technology Industries." Today, because of the pervasiveness of technology in our lives, "tech PR" can be communications about the technology of a transportation, energy or healthcare company. It can be about consumer electronics products, like smartphones and GPS devices. It can also be about the services of a technology company, not just its products. As has been noted elsewhere in the book, communications is also now an integrated exercise that may incorporate everything from internal communications and social media to influencer outreach and live events—frequently on a global scale. Consequently, the opportunities for a skilled technology PR practitioner are limitless and this is a great time to build those skills.

This brings us to the thesis of this chapter: to be an effective practitioner in technology public relations today, you have to be adept at identifying and working at the *intersection* of technology and society's broader needs. Successful technology communications calls on your ability to elevate your product or service to a higher level, to place it within the context of larger business or societal issues and broaden its relevance to those issues. Some call this being a "T-shaped" professional, deep in technical knowledge—the vertical trunk of the letter "T"—and also broad in your perspective about business and society—the horizontal top of the T. (It can also mean that you are not only deeply skilled as a communicator, but are also broad in your ability to manage or lead a team.)

However, it may be more accurate to think of this combination of skills as an "X" or a cross because it symbolizes an intersection. For years, innovation was thought of as a brilliant invention emerging from a laboratory to be marketed to manufacturers and end users. Now, there is a better formula:

Insight + Invention = Innovation

The plus sign in the formula is that critical intersection. Real innovation today starts with insight into what is needed in society and business, spurring an invention that leads to innovation. At IBM, it is called "Innovation That Matters." Effective communicators must learn to live at this intersection.

For example, as a technology PR practitioner, you may be asked to introduce into the marketplace a new medical diagnostic technology for the detection of skin cancer. In order to do that well, you not only need to have a level of knowledge about the technology of medical diagnostics, but you will also need to know about the key players in the skin cancer diagnosis and treatment ecosystem, from primary-care physicians and dermatologists to oncologists and hospital information technology buyers. You will also need insight into the patient's mindset: What is their level of knowledge of the different forms of skin cancer? Why do they avoid treatment? You will also need to prepare to engage buyers, physicians, patients and influencers through multiple channels.

As you can see, doing well on this assignment calls on more than your aptitude and ability to understand and communicate about sophisticated technologies. It also requires that you learn a considerable amount about the healthcare marketplace and what influences purchase decisions.

AN EXAMPLE OF THE INTERSECTION: IBM'S VISION FOR A SMARTER PLANET

Today, IBM expresses the role that its technology products and services can play entirely through the lens of what is needed in society and business (Figure 36.1). Beginning in 2009, IBM shared a vision for a smarter planet—an opportunity to infuse intelligence into every system through which the world works. The vision was based on the insight that smarter systems can help with most of the world's tough problems, from disconnected healthcare systems and energy-guzzling transportation systems to questionably safe food systems and less-than-transparent financial systems. The vision started with the external insight, not the invention in a laboratory. This is because a smarter planet, while global by definition, happens on the industry level. Capturing the story meant understanding three broad trends that made the opportunities possible: (1) everything is becoming instrumented with sensors and computational power; (2) the world is becoming interconnected via vast networks; and (3) many things are becoming intelligent by applying analytics to the mountains of data they can collect.

Since then, IBM communicators have been telling the story of the remarkable progress that has taken place to make the complex systems that people rely on smarter, including cities, energy grids, food distribution chains, healthcare networks and banking systems. One key to explaining what can be complex systems is to show how people's lives will change in the short-term future because of these advances. For example, smart retail systems will soon allow you to fill up your shopping cart at a supermarket and proceed to the parking lot without stopping because everything in the cart is automatically charged to your credit card—and registered as removed from the store's inventory.

FIGURE 36.1

An Example of the Intersection: IBM's Vision for a Smarter Planet

This progress underscores an important point: critical to the success of these stories has been to bring it to the level of individuals. To do this, IBM communicators have been showing how, as the global network of people becomes instrumented, interconnected and intelligent, dramatic shifts are taking place. The ways individuals interact, relationships form, decisions are made, work is accomplished and goods are purchased are fundamentally changing. Consumers now wield unprecedented power over how brands are perceived. Crowd sourcing is changing industry landscapes by leveling the intelligence playing field at an extraordinary rate. Instrumentation, in the form of smartphones, has put unprecedented power literally in people's hands, anywhere they go. The meteoric rise of social networking, which now accounts for 22 percent of people's time spent online, has connected nearly every individual on earth. And the emergence of social analytics means that not only are individual people intelligent, but networks of people have become intelligent as well and are able to learn from interactions and associations to deliver recommendations and take action. As you can see, this is as much a story about the impact on people's lives as it is about the technology.

THE IMPORTANCE OF GREAT STORYTELLING

As noted, the technology public relations field has expanded and changed over the past decade. Five of the most significant ways it has changed are discussed below. Before examining those changes, it is important to note that an essential aspect of effective technology communications has not changed.

As discussed in the Smarter Planet example, great storytelling is still central to success in technology communications. Compelling storytellers remain rare and in demand even though stories are told across more varied forms of media than ever. Strong writing is clear thinking on a screen. This talent will always be valued. Hallmarks of great storytelling include the ability to find the human interest in the story and take the reader across the arch of the story from beginning to middle to end in a way that achieves relevance and allows the reader or viewer to see themselves in the story.

Social media has only heightened the value of good stories as brands increasingly recognize the importance of their customer telling their story for them. Indeed, it is increasingly vital to identify the "shareable story," the story others will tell about your product or service, rather than the one you will tell about it yourself. There is more on how to shape great stories about technology later in this chapter.

UNDERSTANDING WHAT HAS CHANGED

Here are five ways technology communications has changed:

1. Moving from "what" to "how and why"

2. Responding to polarization in the media

3. Evolving from media relations to integrated communications

4. Seizing the opportunity for reinvention

5. Embracing the era of "social business"

1. MOVING FROM "WHAT" TO "HOW AND WHY"

Some of the changes in technology communications are driven by changes in journalism. As newsrooms have downsized due largely to the decline in mass media advertising, there are fewer reporters covering more stories. To gain their attention and break through is increasingly difficult. Reporters and bloggers are less interested than ever in serving as the marketing arm of a company by running their news releases. Smart communicators are delivering more compelling stories by focusing less on "what" is being announced, a new product with faster speed than the old one, for example, and more on "how" the technology makes a difference and "why" it matters to the viewer or reader. How will it make life better? How will it make a company smarter or more effective? How will it make society better?

2. RESPONDING TO POLARIZATION IN THE MEDIA

Another by-product of the scaling back of newsrooms and the fragmentation of journalism online is a polarization in media coverage. We discuss above the more sophisticated coverage—larger feature stories in major media that tell a sweeping story of transformation. But it would be misleading to suggest that this is the only or even the most plentiful form of storytelling about technology today. Experienced journalists will tell you that there has been a polarization of coverage. There are some great features on the high end, but also hundreds of smaller, more transactional stories on the lower end that fall into two categories: stories that have the potential to move the stock markets (acquisitions, new products, venture funding) and "gadget" stories that are simply announcing a new device and are not destined to be seen as transformative at all. Doing well initially in technology communications probably requires doing your fair share of the transactional stories, but hopefully always with an eye toward the larger potential in each.

3. EVOLVING FROM MEDIA RELATIONS TO INTEGRATED COMMUNICATIONS

This book has already prepared you for a much more integrated communications world. Working with the media will remain central to effective technology communications, but to this is added reaching out to influencers, engaging with bloggers, developing a presence through social media, harnessing the power of your own employees and many other aspects. People look to many sources for information and advice. Effective communications enables your story to be told through all of those channels and eventually for your "shareable story" to be told by others.

Indeed, the communications function is undergoing its own transformation, just as other functions within corporations have over the years. The accounting department is now the office of the chief financial officer. The personnel department is now human resources or the chief talent officer. The advertising department is now under the leadership of the chief marketing officer. As the PR department becomes the purview of the chief communications officer, there is an evolution in roles and sophistication as shown below:

Role	Then	Now
Mainstream and trade media relations	Placing stories	Setting an industry agenda, cultivating a network of advocates
Social media relations	Establishing an online presence (website, Facebook page)	Earning engagement, enabling two-way conversation, building communities
Internal communications	Informing employees	Shaping the culture and workplace of tomorrow
Executive communications	Conveying direction	Articulating vision and strategy
Analyst relations	Briefing analysts	Building deeper understanding, cultivating advocates

Elevating your role and the communications function's contribution requires all of the skill mentioned before about seeing the larger picture and context. It also calls on the communications leader to work across the company, collaborate with other functions and help to drive alignment, from the close proximity functions such as marketing and advertising to the other cross-enterprise functions of human resources, investor relations, sales and distribution and others.

SEIZING THE OPPORTUNITY FOR REINVENTION

One of the most exciting aspects of all of the change happening right now is that everyone entering the field has the opportunity to reinvent the definition of communicator or public relations practitioner. It is an era of experimentation and evolution. What are some ways in which communicators can reinvent the field?

As one example, take a look at how some previously mainstream journalists have reinvented themselves. Many have moved from being exclusively print reporters at a major magazine to now being a prominent blogger, a book author, a sought-after speaker and panelist. They may have thousands following them on Twitter and a series of videos on YouTube. What they have done is transition from being a conveyor of someone else's news to being a content provider, offering a point of view of their own.

The same opportunity exists for public relations practitioners, especially in the technology arena. It is increasingly likely that you will see in-house and agency communications pros establishing their own identity and brand as providers of commentary and content, functioning as somewhat-independent observers and analysts of their industry or of new technologies. This reinvented PR practitioner may have multiple channels offering his own point of view and content, from a blog and video channel to speeches, by-lined articles and a Twitter feed. Obviously, you have to have an employer that accepts this new interpretation of the role. Full disclosure of any company or client ties would be an essential part of this new model (in a section later in this chapter, we discuss ethical considerations), but it offers the advantage of becoming a visible, credible voice in the market, not just an invisible intermediary for a company's products and services.

Not only are communicators becoming content sources, many employees in every part of a company are becoming content providers and participating in the dialogue about technology today. This is one reason why IBM and Ketchum were both early to encourage blogging and other forms of responsible dialogue and collaboration with people outside the company. Both organizations issued blog policies or social computing guidelines in 2005 so that their greatest asset—the expertise of their employees—could be shared with clients, shareholders, and the communities in which it operates.

EMBRACING THE ERA OF SOCIAL BUSINESS

Over the past 10 years the web has come to the workplace and has become a serious business tool for organizations and industries of every kind, from e-commerce to the emergence of web-based solutions for financial, accounting and supply chain systems. And the evolution continues.

Now, social networking services are on track to replace e-mail as the primary communications method for many business users in the next few years. It is a concept IBM has advocated for several years. But this new paradigm impacts more than your e-mail inbox. As each company looks to incorporate social networking technologies, it is, in fact, becoming what IBM calls a Social Business.

This approach shifts the communications focus from static content to collaboration and the source of the energy, creativity and decision making that moves the business forward: people. As a result, people not only find what they need, but also discover valuable expertise and information they were not even looking for that might solve a problem in a new way. What does it mean to be a social business? It means that a company is (1) *engaged*—a social business connects people to expertise; (2) *transparent*—a social business strives to remove unnecessary boundaries between experts inside the company and experts in the marketplace; and (3) *nimble*—a social business leverages social networks to speed up business, gaining real-time insight to make quicker and better decisions.

As companies become social businesses, there are profound implications for communicators. Centralized control of communications is a thing of the past. We move from the era of mass communications to the era of masses of communicators. But it is also an era that is rich with opportunities to engage employees, business partners, students (prospective employees), retirees and many others in the dialogue about your company, its products and services. This next section can help you prepare to do just that.

PLANNING, IMPLEMENTATION AND EVALUATION

Elsewhere in the book, there are sections on research, planning and evaluation. In this chapter, we will focus on the steps that are most helpful in technology communications and particularly those that support the points made about storytelling at the intersection of society, business and technology, as well as the multichannel communication that is most effective today.

As a starting point, here are the steps most frequently used at Ketchum in the development of campaigns for the firm's clients.

KETCHUM PROGRAMMING PROCESS

1. *Discover*. Answer fundamental questions, including the business goals you must drive, to the behaviors and beliefs you must change.

2. *Set goals*. Articulate what you aim to deliver—in terms of media outputs, target audience outcomes and business results.

3. *Strategize*. From key insights, construct a strategic framework that includes messaging and media channels.

4. *Create*. Engage right-brain thinking to produce original tactics—through the left-brain lens of your clear strategy.

5. *Evaluate and evolve*. Select an evaluation methodology and commit to tracking success during the entire campaign.

You can see that the "Discover" phase is very focused on aligning the campaign with real business results, which may be as tangible as computer software or hardware, or it might be a longer range goal such as establishing thought leadership for your company in a category.

The "Set Goals" section challenges you to set objectives that not only include media outputs such as stories placed, but also business results and target audience outcomes, such as measurable changes in attitudes or behavior.

It is in the "Strategize" phase that you will begin to shape your story, from determining the messages you want to communicate to developing visual and digital content.

Figure 36.2 shows one of the tools used by Ketchum to arrive at the most compelling message. It prompts you to think about what makes your product or service *competitively unique*? What makes it *current* and relevant to individuals, businesses or society? What is *compelling* about it and, in this era of complete transparency, what can you say about it that is more *credible* then your competitors?

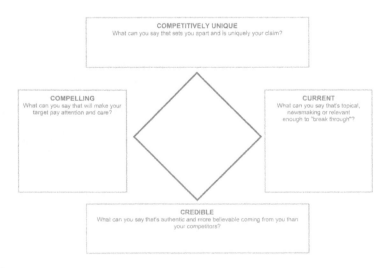

FIGURE 36.2

Message Map

MESSAGE MAP

Of course, arriving at messages does not complete the task of effectively framing a compelling story in all of its dimensions. To do this, communicators should think about how their product or service can be transformative; how it can transform its entire category. They should ask how the story can be a larger feature story about the future of a category, not just a one-day, smaller hard news story. The point is that most new technologies can either be thought of as just another brick in a wall, or they can be seen as the start of a new cathedral, the start of a larger transformation (see box).

Seeing the Big Picture: The Three Stonecutters

One day a traveler came across three stonecutters working in a quarry. Each was busy cutting a block of stone. Interested to find out what they were working on, he asked the first stonecutter what he was doing. "I am cutting a stone!" Still no wiser, the traveler turned to the second stonecutter and asked him what he was doing. "I am cutting this block of stone to make sure that it's square so that it will fit exactly in its place in a wall." A bit closer to finding out what the stonecutters were working on but still unclear, the traveler turned to the third stonecutter. He seemed to be the happiest of the three and when asked what he was doing replied: "I am building a cathedral."

—Various sources

The lesson for technology communicators is to look at the intersection of the technology with society's needs to find the larger issues or "cathedral" in the story.

Your challenge is to see the larger role your technology can play and tell that story. If you identify the transformative nature of a technology and the service it provides, this will give you permission to tell a bigger story; permission to tell a more relevant story. Your company can then be seen not as just a technology vendor but as a leader.

THE FIVE M'S

A story is more than the literal content and words; it is also the person telling the story, the pictures and video that accompanies it and the ways that people can link to the story. These days, a story without links is irrelevant. One helpful way Ketchum uses to think about shaping and conveying a story is to brainstorm ideas in each of these five M's: Message, Messenger, Media, Moment and Measurement. To do this, you need to answer these questions:

- What's the story you are trying to tell (Message)?
- Who is best suited to tell it (Messenger)?
- Through what channels: mobile, online, video (Media)?
- At what time and place (Moment)?
- How will you know you were successful in its delivery (Measurement)?

When debating the messenger, try to think unconventionally about your potential spokesperson and remember that today the most credible source for most people is not an authority but rather "someone like me." For example, in the hypothetical example of launching a new skin cancer diagnostic technology, a company executive or a doctor might be the obvious messenger. Less obvious, but potentially more compelling, might be a skin cancer survivor who benefitted from the technology or a famous surfer whose deep tanning for years produced skin cancer that he or she now wants to help others avoid.

As you will see in this case study about an IBM computer named Watson, storytelling that is relevant to specific industries and to people in their daily lives was central to the success of the initiative.

A COMPUTER NAMED WATSON

The story of a computer named Watson is a story about talent, skill, fortitude and calculated risk taking. It demonstrates all of the points made in this chapter: the importance of good storytelling, the need to tell a story through multiple channels and the power of turning that story into a two-way conversation between people, not just an exercise in broadcasting your version of events.

Fittingly, the larger Watson story begins with a short story. Watson, named after IBM founder Thomas J. Watson, was built by a team of IBM scientists who set out to accomplish a grand challenge—build a computing system that rivals a human's ability to answer questions posed in natural language with speed, accuracy and confidence. They were pursuing breakthrough achievement in the scientific field of question answering, also known as Deep QA.

While working long hours to scale the computing system's literal learning curve, IBM scientists and communicators were also thinking about how they could capture the public's imagination and bring the potential technological achievement to life. IBM has a rich tradition of doing this, showcasing its Deep Blue supercomputer in 1997 with a victory over reigning world chess champion Garry Kasparov and more recently demonstrating the power of its Blue Gene supercomputer in everything from protein folding to predicting climate change and global financial risk.

While contemplating the possibilities in 2004, Charles Lickel, one of the scientists on the Deep QA project was dining at a restaurant in Fishkill, New York. Suddenly, the restaurant emptied into the bar to watch something happening on television. Ken Jennings was making his record-breaking 75th appearance on the game show *Jeopardy!* The attention and enthusiasm of the crowd that night prompted Lickel to suggest that Watson could challenge *Jeopardy!* champions on television to showcase the power of IBM's latest achievement. While a game show may seem like a simple venue to showcase a major achievement, answering the complex, nuanced questions on *Jeopardy!* could provide the ultimate comparison of computer to human answering capability.

Fast-forward to 2011. For three consecutive evenings in mid-February, millions of TV viewers tuned in to *Jeopardy!* to watch history in the making—a man-versus-machine faceoff that pitted two of the quiz show's grand champions against the computing system named Watson. Watson won by a decisive margin. Its winnings totaled $77,147, more than triple Ken Jennings's $24,000 and the $21,600 earned by Brad Rutter (Figure 36.3).

Watson represents a breakthrough achievement in the scientific field of question answering. But its public debut posed a different kind of communications challenge. How could IBM make Watson relevant and interesting to business leaders and the general public, not just fellow scientists?

It would have been easy to focus on telling the "speeds and feeds" story of Watson. Both the media and the general public wanted to know the answers to questions such as whether Watson was connected to the

FIGURE   36.3

Jeopardy!'s two most successful and celebrated contestants–Ken Jennings and Brad Rutter–challenge Watson in the first-ever man vs. machine Jeopardy! competition

Internet (it was not), or if it had an unfair advantage in hitting the buzzer faster. (No. In fact, as part of its ability to process language and estimate accuracy, the system took longer to buzz when it was less confident in its answer.) The final configuration that went into preparing Watson for *Jeopardy!* represents an impressive array of hardware and software. If Watson had been built to operate on a single computer processing unit (CPU), it could have taken as long as two hours to answer a single question. A typical *Jeopardy!* contestant can accomplish this feat in less than three seconds. Thus, to rival the speed of human competitors in delivering a single, precise answer to a question, Watson needed custom algorithms, terabytes of storage (able to hold the equivalent of about one million books) and thousands of POWER7 computing cores working in a massive parallel system.

But Watson was not designed simply to win a quiz show. While the grand challenge driving the project was to win on *Jeopardy!*, the broader objective was to create a new generation of technology that can find answers in unstructured data more effectively than standard search technology. The real test will be to apply Watson's underlying systems, data management and analytics technology across different industries.

GOALS

Watson's creation led to the following communications goals:

- Engage the scientific community and validate Watson's achievement in the field of QA.

- Demonstrate the potential impact this kind of technology can have on business and society, particularly in areas such as health care, government, financial services and consumer products.

- Capture the imagination of a broader audience and communicate the "wow factor" of computer intelligence, with a special emphasis on reaching college students.

STRATEGY AND TACTICS

The communications strategy was to place Watson at the intersection of technology and society's broader news by discussing the ways it could be applied to solving societal and business problems, long after its fame as a quiz show winner had died down. The three-night run on *Jeopardy!* was not viewed as the end point of the campaign, but rather as a pop culture moment in time that was supported by an integrated "before, during and after" communications strategy aimed at the media, clients, prospective clients, shareholders, employees and university students.

Initiating the external part of the campaign was an exercise in calculated risk taking. In early 2009, Watson was making steady progress in the percentage of questions answered and answered correctly, but it was nowhere near the batting average of Ken Jennings and other top champions. However, the lead time for a major "curtain raiser" story is several months, especially if you want to give a reporter inside access to the process. So, without knowing if Watson would ever be able to ultimately beat a top *Jeopardy!* champ, IBM communicators took the calculated risk of approaching John Markoff, one of the leading technology reporters for the *New York Times*.

Consistent with IBM's corporate culture, the story was told through relevant IBM employees who work day to day in roles that involve some aspect of research and development related to Watson or work on one of the industry teams where Watson-like technology could be used. This contrasts with a common corporate practice of featuring the company's top executives for all major press announcements.

With these spokespeople well prepared, the campaign got off the ground more than six months before the *Jeopardy!* match with the cover article on Watson in a June issue of the *New York Times Magazine*. IBM launched an introductory video on Watson, the first in a series, to coincide with the article and ensure that the desired messaging and positioning were conveyed. A bylined article was placed in *AI Magazine* (Artificial Intelligence), helping to engage the scientific community and validate the technology. After that, a steady drumbeat of announcements related to the *Jeopardy!* match were made, leading up to a special called "The Smartest Machine on Earth" that aired on PBS' Nova just prior to the match.

During the *Jeopardy!* game, one of the many communications activities taking place was to invite reporters to one of more than 200 client and university viewing parties across the United States, where many conducted on-site interviews with IBM researchers and industry executives. After Watson's dramatic performance on *Jeopardy!*, IBM focused on communicating Watson as an innovation that matters, announcing a research collaboration with several top university medical centers to apply Watson technology to health care. Industry-specific stories and bylined articles were placed in trade and major media to offer thought leadership on how the technology underlying Watson can transform government, health care, water, banking, electronics, transportation, insurance, oil and gas, retail and personal investing. Throughout all of these phases, social media was used extensively to create two-way conversations, using vehicles that included blogs, Facebook, Twitter, YouTube and Reddit.

RESULTS

In the two months that followed the *Jeopardy!* match, 6,000 articles appeared in the United States alone, generating coverage in media outlets that include the *New York Times*, *USA Today*, the *Wall Street Journal*, *Time*, *Forbes* and the wire services. Segments on Watson also appeared in all national network and cable broadcast news shows, many of them carrying the messaging about the technology's ability to solve business and societal issues like improved health care.

Injecting Watson into pop culture via a national quiz show was also a success. References to Watson in editorial cartoons, David Letterman's Top 10 list, *The Daily Show* with Jon Stewart and daytime talk shows such as *The View* and *The Ellen DeGeneres Show* illustrated the success of linking technology to a well-known pop culture icon and telling its story in ways that are entertaining and relevant.

The social media tactics showed similar momentum. In the two months following the *Jeopardy!* match, eight of the world's highest ranked blogs (as ranked by Technorati) posted entries about Watson. Twitter impressions reached 213 million, with "Jeopardy" hitting the #1 tweet topic in the United States and "Watson" #2 on the first day of the *Jeopardy!* contest. Facebook garnered 6 million impressions and over 20,000 fans. In addition, IBM and Ketchum teamed to make members of the Watson Research team available for a Q&A session on Reddit, which proved to be immensely engaging. One of the most powerful, opinionated and influential communities on the Web, Reddit is a news aggregator site on which Web users submit links and vote on other users' submissions. Within 1 hour, the post shot to the #1 position on the whole site, generating more than 16 million unique media impressions. It was the first branded link to ever reach the #1 position, and was followed by more than 1,270 comments about Watson, which generated thousands of up-votes within the comments thread alone. The Communications team worked with Watson project leader Dr. David Ferrucci to answer the top 15 reader questions, which then also rose to the #1 position on Reddit. IBM capped the victorious week with full-page ads in major newspapers and proclaiming "Humans Win!" underscoring the long-term benefits of Watson rather than the short-term victory on *Jeopardy!*

The overall results of the communications efforts around Watson are continuing to develop and be assessed. What is clear after only two months, however, is that this approach to technology communications represents a new and high-impact way to talking about bits of silicon and zeroes and ones. The Watson communications strategy underscores the importance of good storytelling, the effectiveness of telling a story through multiple channels and the power of making the story a two-way conversation between a wide range of audiences.

TECHNOLOGY INFLUENCER ENGAGEMENT

As noted in the Watson case, the work is not done. Some of the most important extensions of the Watson project are the effective application of Deep QA technology in specific industries. One of the most effective strategies to engage with decision makers in key industries is to systematically identify and reach out to influencers in those industries. This can be applied in a consumer product campaign, in which the influencers might be prominent bloggers, best-selling authors and consumers who love the product or brand (brand evangelists). It can also be

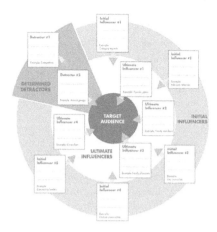

FIGURE 36.4

Influencer Identification Map

applied in a business-to-business technology campaign in which the influencers might be analysts, consultants, academics and business leaders.

The key steps in planning to engage influencers are segmentation (prominent bloggers, analysts, authors, etc.), identification of specific influencers (name, organization, contact information), assessment (current relationship and attitudes), engagement (meetings, briefings, invitations to events), activation (tapping them as a speaker or source) and evaluation (tracking of relationship and attitudes). Figure 36.4 shows a visual tool, from the Ketchum Programming Process, that can help to develop an initial set of influencers.

TRANSPARENCY AND ETHICS

In this chapter, we discussed a number of factors that raise new ethical issues today. Among them:

- Communicators and companies becoming content providers

- The blurring of lines between a commercial source of information versus an independent source

- The radical transparency enabled by social computing

One of the most important tenets to remember is to always disclose who you represent, whether you are issuing a formal communication such as a news release or posting a comment on a blog. If it is about your product, your industry or your company, you must disclose your affiliation. Here is how that point is made in IBM's Social Computing Guidelines.

BE WHO YOU ARE

We believe in transparency and honesty; anonymity is not an option. When discussing topics relevant to IBM, you must use your real name, be clear about who you are, and identify that you work for IBM. If you have a vested interest in something you are discussing, be the first to point it out. But also be smart about protecting yourself and your privacy. What you publish will be around for a long time, so consider the content carefully and also be judicious in disclosing personal details.

BE THOUGHTFUL ABOUT HOW YOU PRESENT YOURSELF IN ONLINE SOCIAL NETWORKS

The lines between public and private, personal and professional are blurred in online social networks. By virtue of identifying yourself as an IBMer within a social network, you are now connected to your colleagues, managers and even IBM's clients. You should ensure that the content associated with you is consistent with your work at IBM. If you have joined IBM recently, be sure to update your social profiles to reflect IBM's guidelines.

VALUES AND THE FUTURE

Beyond ethical considerations, there are other significant issues associated with the democratization of communications channels. Because of social media and other computing technologies, there are now billions of "publishers" in the world. Today, every employee, every retiree, every customer, every business partner, every investor and every neighbor associated with every company can share an opinion about that company with everyone in the world, based on their firsthand experience. The only way a company can be comfortable in that world is if every employee of the company is truly grounded in what their company values and stands for. Although this book is largely about communications, today a brand is what a brand does—actions are even more important than words.

Recognizing this, IBM has created a new discipline within its organization that puts together brand management and workforce enablement, or what the company used to call internal communications. This may sound to some like external and internal messaging coming together and enlisting the employee as a brand ambassador. Sure, that is an aspect of it. But the centerpiece is something quite different. It is called the IBM Brand System. This system is not about creating conformity or standardization; indeed, diversity of thought and background is an essential part of IBM's identity. It is about being clear and consistent about what IBM stands for and what its talented employees should aspire to represent in the marketplace (Figure 36.5).

Simple enough. The same framework could be applied to any other company. But of course it would—and should—take much longer to fill in the details. Every word, every phrase and description in that framework should be painstakingly chosen, because this is a corporation's genome. It describes what makes a company unique. Developing the framework is hard work, but it is only the foundation. Because, like a genome, the real work—and value—are in bringing it to life.

For example, after defining what it means to "look like IBM" (and that's not a reference to IBM people; they all look different!), the company has to ask the tough questions: Does IBM look like that in all of its advertising, websites, sales collateral? In all of its client briefing centers, all of its laboratories, offices and buildings in every part of the world? Where are the gaps? How does the company know? How will the company go about systematically closing the gaps—to become truer to its brand and its values?

Similarly, having defined what it means to sound like IBM, think like IBM and perform like IBM, it is important the following questions: Where are the gaps? How does the company know? How will it go about systematically closing the gaps—to become truer to the company's brand and values?

A couple of things become obvious as one moves to the right in this framework. To really activate the System, you go from managing expressions and manifestations of the company—visual identity, naming conventions, messaging, design and the like—to the behavior and performance of people. This Brand System is necessarily inclusive of corporate culture. And that means that the System cannot be activated without close collaboration with other parts of the company—from sales and service delivery, to product engineering and

| To Look Like IBM | To Sound Like IBM | To Think Like IBM | To Perform Like IBM | To Be Like IBM |

F I G U R E   36.5

The IBM Brand System

human resources. For example, IBM marketing and communications is collaborating with colleagues in human resources to redesign IBM's leadership competencies.

For smart companies, for great companies, values are not the work of positioning, messaging or storytelling alone. For great companies, what they value defines who they are along with who they hire, what they make and the broader constituency of aspiration they seek to define. And they methodically and intentionally align their operations and cultures to authentically be that. This emphasis on behavior combined with integrated communications keeps all of us grounded in the values and priorities of our business and keeps us faithful to the true identity of our clients. It is not just about "random acts of placement," but a concerted effort to live up to a corporate culture, or to help change that culture.

The opportunities for communications professionals who can be stewards of corporate character and can work at the intersection of technology and society—and of actions and words—are limitless.

DISCUSSION QUESTIONS

1. What do you think are some of the implications of a "reinvented PR practitioner who is a multichannel content source" as described here?
2. How can communicators develop the broad perspective needed to "work at the intersection of technology and society's broader needs"?
3. What do you think were the potential risks to IBM's reputation associated with the Watson project?
4. The IBM Social Computing Guidelines assert that "the lines between public and private, personal and professional" are increasingly blurred. When it comes to social networking and online communications, when is a person a professional and when are they a private citizen?
5. The Five M's model that Ketchum uses places equal emphasis on the Message, Messenger, Media, Moment and Measurement. Which one or two are most important in your view?
6. What insights, skills and experience will communicators need to have if they are to play a major role in shaping the actions, policies and character of a corporation?

ADDITIONAL READING

Arthur W. Page Society. *The Authentic Enterprise*. The Arthur W. Page Society: New York, NY, 2007. Available online at http://www.awpagesociety.com/images/uploads/2007AuthenticEnterprise.pdf.

Maney, Kevin, Steve Hamm, and Jeffrey M. O'Brien. *Making the World Work Better: The Ideas That Shaped a Century and a Company*. Upper Saddle River, NJ: IBM, 2011. Print.

Thompson, Clive. "What Is I.B.M.'s Watson?" *New York Times Sunday Magazine*, June 20, 2010, p. MM30. Available online at http://www.nytimes.com/2010/06/20/magazine/20Computer-t.html.

37

C H A P T E R

THE ENTERTAINMENT BUSINESS
Lights, Cameras, Promotions

Rob Doughty
President
Rob Doughty Communications

The entertainment industry is a diverse and wide-ranging offering of leisure time activities. Since its launch in the early twentieth century, it has grown rapidly both in terms of the numbers of customers and in the breadth of entertainment types available. For the first part of the twentieth century, the industry was primarily defined as major movies, most often produced in Hollywood, California. Technological innovations throughout the century quickly evolved entertainment to a wide range of activities that appeal to a diverse population and are now available both at special venues as well as in private homes. In the second decade of the twenty-first century, the proliferation of new technology, especially digital technology, is accelerating the release of new entertainment options at a dizzying rate. This innovation will certainly continue, making for an exciting industry for the aspiring public relations practitioner.

The entertainment industry, once considered the domain of the United States, is now truly global. For the most part, the industry was launched and is still centered on the motion picture industry, based in Hollywood. Today, however, major films are produced throughout the world, including the now famous Bollywood of India. Movies have also spawned related activities, including theme parks and music. Many computer games and children's toys also have themes carried over from the movies. American-style theme parks operate in Europe as well as in Asia. In some cases, the flow has gone in the opposite direction, and movies have been made from ideas that started in another form of entertainment. Popular books that are turned into movies are an obvious example. *The Pirates of the Caribbean* movie franchise actually grew out of the popular attraction created by Walt Disney for his Disneyland theme park in the 1960s.

One of the biggest growth segments has been entertainment available in homes via television, computers and other media designed for in-home use. More recently, entertainment has moved into the "on-the-go" category as new technology allows us to carry our music, our games and even movies wherever we go. The dawn of the century saw a number of Latin musicians cross over into the mainstream.

This multibillion-dollar industry includes such diverse activities as:

- Major films and movies
- Television programming

- Award shows (e.g., Oscars, Emmys and Tonys)
- Theme parks
- Amusement parks
- Cruise ships
- Hotels and resorts
- Casinos
- Theatrical plays
- Recorded music
- Concerts
- Road tours for musical groups and theatrical productions
- Themed restaurants
- Gaming
- Books
- DVDs
- Professional sports
- Recreational sports
- Celebrity management

Many more innovative entertainment options are sure to come.

HISTORICAL PERSPECTIVE

The twentieth century arguably saw the greatest rise in entertainment options in the history of the world. Technology, combined with shorter workweeks and greater disposable income, introduced Americans and others in the developed world to a relatively new phenomenon: leisure time. The post–World War II economic boom in the United States with high rates of employment and the rise in popularity of the family automobile and homes in suburbia fueled demand for something to do during nonwork hours.

Much of the growth in entertainment can be traced back to Hollywood-produced movies. In 1891, the Edison Company introduced the Kinetoscope, which allowed one person at a time to view moving images. In 1895, Frenchman Louis Lumiere invented a portable camera called the Cinematographe. That same year, he and his brother were the first to present moving images to a paying audience of more than one person and the entertainment industry was born.

D.W. Griffith made the first film made in what we now call Hollywood in 1909, a 17-minute short film titled, *Old California*. At about the same time, East Coast producers started moving to Hollywood to escape the restrictive licensing fees and less-than-perfect weather back east. By 1920, Hollywood was the film capital of the world. By mid-century, television and music recording studios followed suit and Hollywood evolved to become the "Entertainment Capital of the World."

In 1955, Walt Disney, a Hollywood producer known for his series of family films and maker of the first full-length animated feature (*Snow White and the Seven Dwarfs*, 1937), introduced the world to a new form of entertainment when he opened Disneyland, a family-friendly theme park in Anaheim, California. Disney's inspiration came from his own leisure time with his two daughters and his frustration that the entertainment options available at the time were not suited for younger family members. Walt wanted to be entertained while he was simultaneously entertaining his young daughters; he wanted a place where he could take his daughters and "have a little fun" himself. Amusement parks of the time were viewed as rather seedy and not especially family friendly.

Disney had a vision for a new place and took his skills as a storyteller to immerse his "guests," as he called them, in three-dimensional stories. The attractions that created Disneyland in the mid-1950s came from stories Disney had already told on film: *Snow White and the Seven Dwarfs* (1937), *Alice in Wonderland* (1951), *Peter Pan* (1953), *Sleeping Beauty* (1959) as well as adventures from his fledging television productions. "Westerns" that captured the days of America's notorious Wild Wild West were especially popular in the 1950s. When Walt Disney chose to tell the story of American hero Davie Crocket, he also offered coonskin caps for sale in Disneyland. Those caps became a runaway success and nearly every boy in America had to have one. One website reports that over $100 million was spent on them in the first year alone.[1] Today, Disney parks are located in Florida, France, Japan, Hong Kong and a soon-to-be-built park in Shanghai. Universal Studios has also capitalized on the segment with parks featuring its films in Los Angeles and Orlando.

The mid-century uprising of television brought entertainment into the home and people no longer had to leave the comfort of their own homes to be entertained. Even with the opening of Disneyland, Mr. Disney understood that not everyone would be able to visit his dream place so he launched a television program, "Disneyland," that made the magic available to everyone with a television set. That move also acted as a strategic public relations and marketing tool that encouraged customers to visit the theme park and to purchase the themed toys, apparel, games and other merchandise sold in the park. Decades later, it is still viewed as one of the best PR moves ever.

Walt Disney also helped redefine television when color televisions became available in the early sixties. The Sunday evening program "Disney's Wonderful World of Color," brought family-friendly entertainment in color right into the home at a time when most other programs were still broadcast in black and white. Many Americans purchased their first color televisions just to watch this popular weekly program.

Over time, the entertainment industry has become ingrained in American culture. The industry helps to capture and record the evolution of our culture. It also provokes and challenges us on difficult questions and issues. Just as with fine art that is meant to make us think, movies and recording artists often stretch our views of the world by telling stories that shed light on new ways of viewing the world or exposing larger audiences to the blight of smaller segments of the population. Many movies in the 1990s, *Philadelphia* (1993), for example, helped to show that the HIV/AIDS epidemic was a disease that impacted real people. Movies in the sixties, such as *Guess Who's Coming to Dinner* (1967), in which a white woman brings her African-American boyfriend home to meet her family, challenged prevailing views of race relations in America at the time. Similarly, television shows often explore controversial and taboo topics, such as abortion, domestic violence and sexual abuse. These types of programs can cause challenges for the entertainment public relations practitioner as special interest groups seek to censure and boycott television stations and their advertisers. It is in controversial entertainment that public relations practitioners most often meet the First Amendment of the Constitution, which protects the freedom of speech and the freedom of expression.

The entertainment industry has had a major impact on how companies promote and sell their products. Television, most notably has brought an ever-evolving stream of advertisements that are produced with Hollywood quality into our homes. Big advertisers today will often hire Hollywood-caliber directors and producers to film their commercials. There is a world of difference in the quality of advertisements produced in the 1950s and the high production values we see today. In fact, the phenomenon continues in the digital world as advertising agencies seek ways to leverage the new media channels in this space.

The public relations profession within the entertainment industry also has a structure unlike any other. In the early days of Hollywood, the movie studios viewed publicity as the force that drew audiences into theaters. Studio publicity departments focused only on driving news coverage for the stable of stars under contract with each studio as well as the release of each movie. They did not have the broader view of today's more evolved public relations, including issues and crisis management. So ingrained were the publicity departments that the name survives in most parts of the industry today.

In fact, many larger entertainment companies, such as Disney, have split the communications function into two departments. The publicity departments typically reside within the marketing function and continue to focus only on driving media for movies and celebrities. Public relations, or public affairs, has been added as a separate function reporting to senior executives, such as the chief executive officer, and carries a broader communication mission than just publicity. This function will support such activities as corporate positioning, issues and crisis management, internal communications, executive communications, government relations and corporate communications that communicate the broader business story in support of investor relations for companies that are publicly traded.

PUBLIC RELATIONS IN TODAY'S ENTERTAINMENT INDUSTRY, A CASE STUDY 50 YEARS IN THE MAKING: DISNEYLAND'S GOLDEN ANNIVERSARY

July 17, 2005, marked the 50th anniversary from the day that Walt Disney opened Disneyland in Anaheim, California, and introduced the world to a new form of entertainment in which guests would be immersed into a story, surrounded by the sights, sounds and emotions of well-known and well-loved tales. While many companies struggle to leverage an anniversary effectively, Disney believed that its core of loyal guests, as well as the millions of others who had visited Disneyland and its sister theme park, Walt Disney World in Orlando, Florida, would enjoy celebrating the occasion.

Starting two years in advance, the Disney team began strategizing how to best promote the anniversary. Ultimately, they saw it as a chance to present their guests with a new reason to return to the parks, which by now had grown to include Disneyland Tokyo and Disneyland Paris. Also in the works was the opening of the newest Disneyland theme park in Hong Kong. The strategy was to leverage the 50th anniversary of the iconic American theme park to encourage guests to come to any of the parks to celebrate by reliving their memories and creating new ones for younger members of the family.

The effort became a multidiscipline approach that ultimately would involve all aspects of the company: marketing, public affairs, operations, human resources, even legal and finance. As you will see, the story captures all the aspects of public relations in the entertainment industry, including celebrities and a red carpet that, in this case, magically turned gold to fit the theme.

Matt Ouimet, president of the Disneyland Resort, set the tone and direction for the celebration. He realized that it could be much more than just another marketing campaign. Matt saw that it could also be a chance to revitalize the Disneyland Park, which was beginning to show its age. Built in just one year during 1954 and 1955, Walt Disney used the building techniques he knew best, building facades for a studio back lot. Since the park had never closed, major maintenance had not been an easy chore. The declining condition of the park even became a focal point of the now-famous boardroom battle during which Roy Disney, Walt's nephew, complained that Disneyland was falling into disrepair and that there were burned-out lights on Main Street, something his uncle would never have tolerated.

Matt decided that Disneyland had to look its absolute best on July 17, 2005, and set out to paint, replace and overhaul every inch of the park. The project included closing popular attractions for months on end, including shrouding the famous Sleeping Beauty castle that sits as the anchor to the entire Disneyland experience. When the shrouds were lifted, the castle had a new coat of paint and many new features that would make it even more dazzling. One of the most difficult decisions was the closing of Space Mountain for an overhaul that would take the popular attraction out of service for two years.

Matt also saw that the anniversary could be used to drive Disneyland's legendary guest service, already at very high standards, to a new, even higher, level. The 50th anniversary would be a complete renovation, including the service its "cast members," as Disney calls its employees, offer to their guests.

Matt also realized that the Disneyland anniversary had to blend the past, present and future of the park. Focusing too much attention on the Disneyland of the parents and grandparents of the 1950s or 1960s would have been irrelevant to the nine-year-olds of 2005, and risked turning Disneyland into a museum. In addition to sprucing up the place, the anniversary would also be a great chance to introduce new elements to keep the park relevant and to keep giving guests reasons to return.

Marketing set out to develop the look, tone and feel of the 18-month celebration, which they themed "The Happiest Homecoming on Earth" as a play on the famous quote from Walt Disney's inaugural speech on opening day in which he called Disneyland, the "Happiest Place on Earth." The marketing theme also encouraged guests to revisit the park to relive memories. The public relations department, housed within the marketing department, also set a plan to drive media attention. At the same time, the public affairs department, which reported directly to the president, set out to leverage the anniversary to position the resort in a new way. Public affairs owned different audiences such as cast members, community and government leaders.

While the public relations department sought media coverage of the actual elements of the celebration, including several new attractions that would be launched or reopened, the media relations function within public affairs focused on telling the business story of the Disneyland Resort. The overlapping functions can be confusing and required extremely close coordination between the two functions that handled media relations. Careful attention to help the media understand the difference between the two media-facing departments prevented confusion and mistakes.

Since the celebration would last 18 months, it was up to PR to kick-start the conversations at the time of the anniversary. Marketing would support the effort with a series of advertisements that would keep the promotion in front of the public via purchased space and time on radio, television, newspaper, magazine and billboard advertising. PR's job would be to earn space and time in the media by supplying them with compelling and newsworthy stories. PR is often referred to as *earned media* for this reason.

The "curtain raiser" for the Disneyland anniversary came on New Year's day (January 1, 2005), when Mickey Mouse rode up Pasadena, California's famed Colorado Boulevard as the Grand Marshal of the Rose Bowl Parade. Behind him, a completely flora version of Disneyland's iconic Sleeping Beauty castle with Sleeping Beauty and Prince Charming holding court. Disney's other princesses and princes as well as numerous Disney characters danced and sang as the float moved along the parade route. Clearly, the excitement was building.

To earn maximum media attention, the public relations department set up a plan that invited valued media from around the world to the Park for three days in May 2005. They chose May to give the media time to write stories that would encourage their audiences to arrange their vacation time to visit Disneyland over the next year and a half. Since most families have to arrange vacations well in advance, the May launch of the anniversary provided that time. The PR team chose May 5, 2005, or 05-05-05, as the launch date. Invitations to the launch were an elaborate box that opened to an image of a castle that including parts of all five of the Disney castles from around the world. As you moved the image in your hands, fireworks sparkled overhead. The box also contained the agenda for the event. In addition to encouraging reporters to attend, it would also become a keepsake.

The event kicked off on May 4 in the Hyperion Theater located in Disney's California Adventure, a new theme park carved out of the former Disneyland Parking Lot in February 2001. Hosted by television actor Kelsey Grammer, the evening outlined for the media the events they would see over the next two days. Each day would see multiple new attractions, including a new parade, the official unveiling of the Sleeping Beauty Castle and a collection of golden ride vehicles that would be placed in each of the original attractions that greeted guests on July 17, 1955.

On May 5, Disneyland Park was closed to the public for the first time in its history. Only those with the special invitations, primarily media from around the world, were allowed in. The anniversary launched in front of the Sleeping Beauty Castle with an entertainment program that only Disney could pull off. Hosted by Mickey Mouse, the program included remarks from several Disney executives and luminaries. Art Linkletter, who served as the MC on opening day 50 years earlier, gave a moving speech about the vision his friend, Walt, had despite many naysayers who thought the park would be a flop. Diane Disney Miller, Walt's daughter gave a rare public appearance and spoke of her father's desire to create a place where fathers could "have a little fun too."

Christina Aguilera sang the iconic Disney song, "When You Wish Upon a Star" and LeAnn Rimes sang "Remember When," the Disneyland 50th anniversary theme song composed by famous composer Richard Marx. Actress Julie Andrews, who played in numerous Disney movies and who was named the official 50th anniversary ambassador, dedicated a golden horse on the carousel located in Fantasyland, just beyond the castle gates. Several of the original Mouseketeers from the original "Mickey Mouse Club" television show from the 1950s also sang and danced. Daytime fireworks, another Disney icon, completed the opening program. The 50th anniversary of Disneyland Park was officially underway in true Disney fashion.

The entire park was transformed with sparkling, renovated attractions. The park had never looked better. To accommodate the media, tents had been set up throughout the park for broadcasting with iconic views such as the Sleeping Beauty Castle, Space Mountain and Main Street as backdrops. The media were invited to ride all the attractions and plenty of Disney Imagineers, the creative geniuses who create the magic, were on hand for interviews. Even one of the morning talk shows from Australia broadcast live every day that week.

The evening of May 5, 2005, turned Disneyland into the place to be. A gold carpet had been rolled down the length of Main Street to receive the many Hollywood celebrities who had been invited to a special event in the New Orleans Square portion of the park. The media had been lined along one side of Main Street behind a velvet rope. A select group of cast members and guests had earned the right to stand on the opposite side of the Main Street forming a backdrop for the media.

As celebrities arrived, they first passed in front of a "step and repeat wallpaper" often used to ensure that photos captured by the media included the name and logo of the sponsor or sponsors. In this case, the wallpaper repeated the special logo that marketing had created for the 50th anniversary. The logo was the Disneyland castle wrapped with a royal blue banner declaring "50" and "Disneyland." The tagline "Happiest Homecoming on Earth" appeared below the banner. Mickey Mouse and Minnie Mouse led off the parade of celebrities and showed off their new costumes that had been designed especially for the 50th anniversary.

Hollywood stars followed down the golden carpet posing for the media from around the world and answering interview requests along the way. Publicists accompanied most celebrities down the long carpet. The publicists worked the media and made sure that each star spoke with the media most important to them and their positioning. The celebrities then entered New Orleans Square for a private party away from the prying eyes of the media to celebrate the milestone for the most famous theme park in the world.

Meanwhile, news coverage of the Disneyland 50th anniversary was buzzing around the world. The investment the company made in closing the park and focusing on providing the media with a high-quality visit that would capture the essence of the guest experiences to come certainly paid off.

The public affairs department leveraged the anniversary as well. One area of great impact was with internal communications, which is called Cast Communications in Disney parlance. More than a year prior to the event, the Cast Communications team worked with operations to ensure that cast members were well prepared. One of the tenets of good customer service the Disney Operations holds dear is having knowledgeable cast members. Cast Communications decided to own this tenet.

Starting in July 2004, a year before the actual anniversary, Cast Communications set an objective that would align cast members with the expectations that marketing was creating with guests. Marketing in the western United States focused on a homecoming theme that encouraged guests to return to Disneyland to relive their memories and create new ones. Even though Disneyland is blessed with an above-average number of longtime cast members, many were younger and would not fully understand or relate to a guest who last visited the park in the 1950s or 1960s.

Each week the team focused all of the various Cast Communications channels, which included a weekly magazine and closed-circuit television station called "Cast TV," on one of the last 50 years. The articles and news pieces talked about the attractions that opened during that specific year, interviewed a cast member who started that year, and recounted other significant news items from the year. One such event was Elizabeth Taylor's 60th birthday party hosted by Michael Jackson on February 27, 1992. The plan gave cast members a better guest perspective, which in turn allowed them to engage in conversations with guests as they have been trained to do from their first day on the job. Guests loved the tidbits of history they picked up from the cast and left the park feeling like they had been given an insider's view of their favorite park. It cost Disneyland very little, but the perceived value to guests was huge. Operations gave Cast Communications due recognition for their role in actually increasing guest satisfaction scores from an already high level to an even higher level.

Public affairs launched its part of the 50th anniversary on March 4, 2005, with the release of an economic impact report it commissioned CB Richard Ellis Consulting and Allan D. Kotin & Associates to conduct. The report confirmed that Disneyland was the number one theme park in the Western United States (Walt Disney World in Orlando holds the distinction of being the number one theme park in the world). It also declared that Disneyland was a "critical driver of tourism in Southern California." Tourism is a multibillion dollar industry in Southern California. The report also stated:

- The Disneyland Resort generates $3.6 billion in third-party annual economic impact to non-Disney businesses throughout Southern California.

- The Disneyland Resort supports 65,700 jobs in Southern California.

- The Disneyland Resort is the most popular theme park destination in the Western U.S.

- Disneyland Resort and its visitors, who stay in the Anaheim Resort area and surrounding locations, generate $225 million in taxes to various Southern California cities and counties.

- The impact of spending by Disneyland Resort patrons outside of the resort totals $1.9 billion annually.

The report, which was released at a special breakfast event at the Hyperion Theater before civic, business and government leaders in Southern California, drew significant media coverage throughout the five counties of Southern California. The leading paper in all five counties covered the report as the lead item in their business section. The media relations department localized the story for each by giving them economic impact data for just their county and even identified vendors such as florists, balloon makers, taxi and bus companies, among others who benefit from the tourist traffic generated by Disneyland. Although the media knew that the city of Anaheim and Orange County benefitted from Disneyland, the real news and surprise was the geographic extent of the economic impact. Even Disneyland cast members drive to work from each of the five counties.

The Economic Impact Report successfully told a fresh story of Disneyland and showed that it was more than just a place to go to "have a little fun." Disneyland is a major economic contributor. By narrowing the news down to a few choice facts, Public Affairs made the story memorable. Years after its release, civic and government officials were still able to recite the three major facts: $3.6 billion, 65,000 jobs and $225 million in taxes.[2] Elected officials often used the information in their speeches. While the Economic Impact Report was prepared for the 50th anniversary, it would become particularly helpful a few years later when Disney became embroiled in a land use dispute with the city of Anaheim that resulted in the first lawsuit Disney had ever filed against its host city. In that dispute, a zealous housing developer coveted land that had been included in the zone known as the Anaheim Resort area. The zone had been set aside for development only for resort use and specifically prohibited residential development. The housing boom caused land zoned for residential development adjacent to the resort to skyrocket in cost. By constantly repeating the economic value, including the jobs it created, Disney and other hotels, restaurants and other resort-related businesses were able to gain public support to keep the resort area zoned exclusively for its further expansion. Ultimately, the rapid decline in housing values in southern California caused the residential developer to lose interest, and the whole issue faded away.

Public affairs, which includes community relations, saw an opportunity to show the residents of Anaheim and Orange County how much Disney appreciated them as neighbors. For this reason, public affairs arranged for Disneyland to give back to the community in big ways. On the eve of the May 5, 2005, celebration, Disneyland announced a $1 million donation to the Boy & Girls Club of Anaheim. Mickey Mouse and his friends drove the short distance from Disneyland to the Boys & Girls Club in downtown Anaheim arriving in the famed Main Street fire truck to deliver the check. Similar presentations were made to the Boy & Girls Club of Central Florida from the Walt Disney World Resort at the same time.

When Disneyland drew its 50th anniversary celebration to a close on July 17, 2006, the day that also marked its 51st birthday, Matt Ouimet also presented a check for $1 million to the Children's Hospital of Orange County (CHOC). Disney has enjoyed a long-standing relationship with CHOC ever since Walt Disney himself served on the board of directors and helped create the teddy bear the hospital still uses as its mascot. Mickey and Minnie make regular calls to the hospital to brighten the day of the children there. The presentation took place in front of the mayors of all 34 cities that make up Orange County. It was a fitting end to a hugely successful promotion that far exceeded expectations in increasing guest visits to Disneyland, even setting a number of records in terms of guest visits and guest satisfaction.

PUBLIC RELATIONS IN TODAY'S ENTERTAINMENT INDUSTRY, CASE HISTORY: VIRAL MARKETING GETS A SPOOKY START—THE MARKETING OF *THE BLAIR WITCH PROJECT*

While "viral marketing" is almost a household word today, it may surprise you that it was a low-budget film produced on a shoestring budget from a group of film students that first used the Internet to drive consumer interest in a product. It was a brilliant move, and our world has not been the same since.

Filmed by Haxan Films, interest in the movie started well before its July 1999 release with a campaign on the Internet telling the story of three film students who set out to film the notorious Blair Witch, a local legend in the Black Hills around Burkittsville, Maryland. Gradually, reports began to circulate on various Internet chat rooms that the three film students entered the Black Hills with their camera and were never seen again. Their camera, sound equipment and the footage they shot during their last few hours was all that was left of the project. The so-called recovered film footage is then presented as the film known as "The Blair Witch Project." It was a compelling and intriguing storyline that drew the viewer into the story well before they arrived at the theater. Most viewers were obsessed with the question of "What happened to these poor students?" The buzz and legend of *The Blair Witch Project* and its lost film students drew so much attention on the Internet that public anticipation for the movie grew rapidly.

Trailers and snippets of the movie released ahead of the theatrical premiere added to the drama and intrigue. Shot as a real-life documentary, later it would be called a "mocumentary" for obvious reasons: the film captures the journey in a less-than-polished manner. Often shot with night vision equipment, the students appeared frightened. They frequently turned the camera on themselves to reveal their true internal fear, often in tears. The fuzzy, green hue of the night vision lens extended the fear to the viewer. Increasingly, the buzz grew louder, "What happened to these poor students?"

During the film, one by one, the students disappeared. However, they were reunited at the very end in the basement of an old house where they were last seen with one man facing a wall and an ear-splitting scream. The camera fell to the floor and the footage ended. Quick, tell me. What did happen to these poor students?

Shown at the Sundance Film Festival in 1999, the low budget film went on to gross more than $248 million in worldwide syndication, making it one of the most successful and profitable independent films of all time. Not bad for a film that reportedly cost between $20,000 and $25,000 to produce. It is useful to remember that the production budget of a movie is often used to earn news. Blockbuster movies like *Avatar* (2009) and *Titanic* (1997) were promoted for their record level production costs to draw early, prerelease interest in the movie. *The Blair Witch Project* eventually received great news value for its position at the other end of the scale with a very low production cost.

Originally, the producers planned to release the film on cable television only, and had not anticipated a wide release. Artisan acquired the film for $1.1 million and spent approximately $25 million to market it. It is believed to be the first widely released film ever marketed primarily through the Internet. Books, comic books and computer games followed the movie. A sequel never took off, perhaps because the ruse had been exposed, making it hard to duplicate.

Studios spend heavily on marketing their movies. As a comparison, MGM spent $30 million to market *Hot Tub Time Machine* (2010), which cost $35 million to produce. Disney spent a reported $75 million to market the *Prince of Prussia: Sands of Time* (2010) that cost $200 million to produce and only grossed $63 million. However, they spent about the same amount making and marketing Tim Burton's *Alice in Wonderland* (2010), which grossed $334 million worldwide.

Despite the normal, expensive, traditional media practices in the entertainment industry, *The Blair Witch Project* received wide acclaim as one of the best horror films of all time. For public relations and marketing students and professionals, the film opened a new door we now call viral marketing. As social media sites such as Facebook and Twitter (remember, this movie predated these social media outlets) grow, public relations practitioners now have many more avenues available.

Since *The Blair Witch Project*, viral marketing has become widely used, especially in the entertainment industry. PR practitioners and marketers continually seek ways to build buzz for their movies, albums and computer games well in advance of their release. This anticipatory strategy is especially critical in the film world where a movie is made or broken on the sales it generates in just its first box office weekend. Conventional wisdom in Hollywood is that a movie has to earn the spot as the best box office during its first weekend to ensure its success. The number two spot at the box office for a film's opening weekend is considered a failure. Who said there's no business like show business?

Publicity departments play a huge role in building this anticipation. They book the film's stars on talk shows before the release. In addition to talking about their personal lives, the star's main objective on *The Tonight Show* or *Late Night with David Letterman* is to promote the film, which is most likely to be released the next weekend. They will introduce a short clip of the film, which their publicist has selected and arranged for the talk show to broadcast. It's all about free (earned) publicity to drive audiences to the opening weekend premiere.

Oh, yes. And, what did happen to those students? Well, luckily, this was a film and a story they made up. University of Central Florida students Heather Donahue, Joshua Leonard and Michael C. Williams went on with their lives. They signed an agreement to receive a portion of the profits from the release of the film. Indeed, they did not vanish.

THE FUTURE OF ENTERTAINMENT

There is little question that the entertainment industry will do anything but grow and evolve, most likely at an increasingly faster pace. This growth will provide even more opportunities for communications practitioners to support and help this exciting industry. Many of the coming opportunities are not even visible to us today. The growth will also bring more challenges, many of which we cannot begin to predict at this time. This uncertainty, however, is what makes this industry one for careful consideration as you think about your own career path in public relations.

TRENDS

Given the rapid advances that technology is creating within the entertainment industry, we are almost reluctant to forecast its future. While we do not have the crystal ball that will allow us to predict specific new entertainment options, we do see a number of broad trends at the start of the second decade of the twenty-first century. Each of these trends opens job opportunities for future communications practitioners. It will be an exciting industry.

ENTERTAINMENT WILL BE MORE GLOBAL

Already, Hollywood, California, can no longer contain the entirety of the entertainment industry. Once a clearly defined geographic domain, Hollywood today is more aptly defined as a state of mind, an image of the power and potential that entertainment has had and will continue to have on our lives. Hollywood today is a concept, a short-handed symbol for entertainment in general. This evolution is already underway as film centers have cropped up all over the world. Most notably, Bollywood in India has become the entertainment capital of one of the most populous nations in the world. Other entertainment centers have cropped up in the United Kingdom, China and other countries in Central and South America. As people realize the economic and influential power of entertainment and the costs of producing high-quality entertainment falls, we are likely to see more and more "Hollywood"-type entertainment centers develop throughout the world.

American entertainment companies are already working to ride the wave around the world. Disney, for example, has opened theme parks in Paris, Tokyo, Honk Kong and, most recently, Shanghai. The launch into China has been particularly challenging and provides a model for how entertainment companies will have to embrace local cultures and mores to be successful. Chinese audiences, for example, did not grow up with images of Mickey Mouse and all his friends. Similarly, stories of Sleeping Beauty and Cinderella, whose castles are so central to the Disney theme parks, are foreign tales to the Chinese. As Disney opens these new parks, it is also being sensitive to telling the stories already embedded in those cultures.

In addition, Disney is using other media, such as television and movies, to introduce their stable of characters and their stories to these new audiences. These introductions will theoretically entice Chinese audiences into the theme parks as guests to experiences the stories in the Disney story immersion model. This approach is still in its early days and it will take time to see if it will pay off. Along the way, Disney will monitor the acceptance of its stories, and the various modes in which it tells those stories, and may very well need to make some adjustments along the way to ensure their success. The global expansion of Disney will be an important one to watch as a barometer to the global future of the entertainment industry.

In the music segment, we will continue to see the crossover of Latin musicians into the larger and more lucrative mainstream market. The growth will be driven by a combination of the growth of the Hispanic population, music lovers developing a wider range of musical interest and musical artists who develop musical arrangements that appeal to the broader mainstream market.

ENTERTAINMENT WILL BE MORE ACCESSIBLE TO MORE PEOPLE MAKING TARGETING AUDIENCES EVEN MORE STRATEGIC

More people will have access to more entertainment both from the global expansion of the industry, and also from the technological advances and the ever-decreasing costs of access that is rapidly removing the economic barriers to the newest and more sophisticated forms of entertainment.

This trend of increasing accessibility will provide public relations practitioners in this industry even more tools to reach audiences that were not reachable in the past. It will also allow for even greater targeting of specific audiences. Reaching only people who have an interest in tennis, or nutrition or fashion has become so much easier than it was a few decades ago.

ENTERTAINMENT WILL BE MORE HOME-BASED

Once the domain of movie theaters, theme parks, resorts and other venues that we had to travel to, entertainment is now available from the convenience of our own homes. Starting with radio in the 1930s, home entertainment evolved greatly with the advent of television in the 1950s. The launch of cable television service in the 1970s grew the offerings from only three national network channels to hundreds of channels ranging from 24-hour news to special interests such as food, travel as well as a multitude of sports channels. "Channel surfing" has entered the popular lexicon as we sit home in our easy chairs pushing a button that spins us through all the offerings.

Beyond channel surfing, we have also taken control of our televisions in other ways. Gaming systems such as Wii and X-Box have altered our televisions from a once passive medium to a now interactive one. It is possible to use your television as an alternative to the gym, jogging track, tennis court, golf course or bowling alley. The gaming industry has become a rapidly growing segment of the entertainment industry with companies such as Sony, Lucas Entertainment and many start-ups actively developing innovative interactive uses for your television.

ENTERTAINMENT WILL GO MOBILE

Although it may seem strange today, cellular phones actually started as a device to hold a conversation without being connected to a wire. Today, iPhone, Android and other new cellular and wireless platforms have moved this portable device deeper into our lives and have unbound us from the confines of our homes or the length of a wire. One of the fastest-growing industries now is the development of applications, or apps, that we can download onto our phones that allow us to do multiple tasks including surfing the Web, watching our favorite movies and television shows, listening to our favorite music and playing games either on our own or with people far away, just to name a few. We are sure to see ever more innovative applications every day, and many are available for free.

ENTERTAINMENT WILL BE MORE DIVERSE

As you can see from this chapter, the evolution of the entertainment business has touched many new people and continues to be shaped by new technology and other innovations. This evolution will only continue and with it will open entertainment to new audiences. Already, for example, innovators are able to use new technology to send electrical impulses through a person's tongue to allow blind people to see. The evolution of medicine into genetics is opening new therapies, thinking and treatment for people with numerous chronic diseases and genetic deficiencies.

MANY COMPANIES ARE MOVING INTO THE ENTERTAINMENT SPACE

Many companies are realizing that they, too, are in the lucrative entertainment industry. Companies that once focused on telephone service (such as AT&T) have realized that they, too, are now in the entertainment business. As discussed above, our phones have become as much, if not more, about entertainment than communications. Communicators of the future will enjoy the opportunity of exploring the entertainment options their employers or clients may offer. Some of these companies may not even realize their entertainment options at this point.

CONCLUSION

The entertainment industry is one of the most exciting industries for an aspiring public relations practitioner. Steeped in tradition and history, Hollywood publicists are here to stay. They are considered vital to the success of a movie, a recording artist, even the opening of a new attraction at a theme park or the launch of a new cruise ship. The buzz they create well in advance of a movie's release helps drive that all-important opening weekend box office ranking that can make or break a movie. With millions of dollars at stake, creatively telling the "making of" story is as important as the movie itself; just remember the enormous success of *The Blair Witch Project*.

If publicity is not your thing, the entertainment industry offers public relations and public affairs functions that cover a wider gamut of audiences including employees, communities and investors. The success of the Disneyland 50th anniversary had as much to do with involving these audiences as it did attracting guests to pass through the turnstiles. Disneyland cast members knew they had a role to play in the "Happiest Homecoming on Earth" and the information they gained from the internal communications team at Disneyland helped them make a significant difference in guest experience and satisfaction at the Happiest Place on Earth.

DISCUSSION QUESTIONS

1. What business value does public relations add to the entertainment industry?
2. What challenges can public relations help the entertainment industry overcome now and in the future?
3. What role can internal communications play in helping an organization reach its goals?
4. How did the internal communications function at Disneyland support the success of the 50th anniversary of Disneyland?
5. Can you think of new ways to conduct a viral campaign using the tools now available to a public relations practitioner? Use your wildest imagination.
6. Can you define new communications channels that PR professionals in the entertainment industry will be using in the next few years to build awareness of their movies, songs, theme parks, resorts and so forth?
7. Imagine you are the publicist for *The Blair Witch Project* and that it is being released this year. What would you do differently using tools and channels available now that might not have been available in 1999?
8. How is public relations in the entertainment industry different from public relations in other industries you've read about in this book? How is it the same, or similar?
9. What role did the Economic Impact Report play in the 50th anniversary of Disneyland? Were you surprised to read about this report as part of the celebration? Why or why not?
10. What role did community relations play in the Disneyland anniversary?

NOTES

1. http://www.fiftiesweb.com/fashion/coonskin-caps.htm.
2. http://corporate.disney.go.com/corporate/board_news/2004/2005_0305_dlrstudy.html.

ADDITIONAL READING

Balio, Tino. *Grand Design: Hollywood as a Modern Business Enterprise, 1930–1939. History of the American Cinema*. Berkeley, CA: University of California Press, 1996.

Birchard, Robert S. *Cecil B. DeMille's Hollywood*. Lexington, KY: University of Kentucky Press, 2004.

Brown, Gene. *Movie Time: A Chronology of Hollywood and the Movie Industry*. Hoboken, NJ: Wiley, 1995.

Bruck, Connie. *When Hollywood Had a King: The Reign of Lew Wasserman, Who Leveraged Talent Into Power and Influence*. New York, NY: Random House Trade Paperbacks, 2004.

Carr, Steve A. *Hollywood and Anti-Semitism: A Cultural History up to World War II (Cambridge Studies in the History of Mass Communication)*. Cambridge: Cambridge University Press, 2001.

Carter, Graydon. *Vanity Fair's Tales of Hollywood: Rebels, Reds, and Graduates and the Wild Stories Behind the Making of 13 Iconic Films*. City of Westminster, London, England: Penguin, 2008.

Daniel Alef, *Jack L. Warner: Last of the Hollywood Empire Builders (Titans of Fortune)*. Ebook: Fortune Publishing, 2010.

Davis, Ronald L. *The Glamour Factory: Inside Hollywood's Big Studio System*. Dallas, TX: Southern Methodist University Press, 1993.

Epstein, Edward Jay. *The Hollywood Economist: The Hidden Financial Reality Behind the Movies*. Brooklyn, NY: Melville House, 2010.

Frost, Jennifer. *Hedda Hopper's Hollywood: Celebrity Gossip and American Conservatism*. New York, NY: NYU Press, 2011.

Gabler, Neal. *Walt Disney: The Triumph of the American Imagination*. New York, NY: Knopf, 2006. Print.

Hirschhorn, Clive. *The Warner Bros. Story: The Complete History of Hollywood's Greatest Studio. Every Warner Bros. Feature Film Described and Illustrated*. New York, NY: Crown Publishers, 1987.

Keith, Gaelyn Whitley. *The Father of Hollywood*. Amazon Digital Services, 2010.

Levy, Frederick. *Hollywood 101: the Film Industry*. Los Angeles: Renaissance, 2000. Print.

McDonald, Paul. *The Contemporary Hollywood Film Industry*. Hoboken, NJ: Wiley-Blackwell, 2008.

Polard, Tom. *The Hollywood War Machine: U.S. Militarism and Popular Culture*. Boulder, CO: Paradigm Publishers, 2006.

Richard, Alfred Charles. *Contemporary Hollywood's Negative Hispanic Image: An Interpretive Filmography, 1956–1993*. Santa Barbara, CA: Greenwood Press, 1994.

Robb, David L. *Operation Hollywood: How the Pentagon Shapes and Censors the Movies*. Amherst, NY: Prometheus Books, 2004.

Rose, Frank. *The Agency: William Morris and the Hidden History of Show Business*. New York, NY: Harperbusiness, 1996.

Segrave, Kerry. *Product Placement in Hollywood Films a History*. Jefferson (NC): McFarland, 2004. Print.

Smith, Dave, and Steven Clark. *Disney, the First 100 Years*. New York, NY: Hyperion, 2002. Print.

Stewart, James B. *Disney War*. New York, NY: Simon & Schuster Paperbacks, 2006. Print.

Thomas, Bob. *Walt Disney: An American Original*. New York, NY: Hyperion, 1994. Print.

Williams, Gregory Paul. *The Story of Hollywood: An Illustrated History*. Los Angeles: BL Press, 2006.

Yule, Andrew. *Fast Fade: David Putnam, Columbia Pictures, and the Battle for Hollywood*. Los Alamitos, CA: Delta, 1989.

38

C H A P T E R

HEALTH CARE
Harmonizing the Healthcare Message

Richard T. Cole, Ph.D.
Professor, Department of Advertising, Public Relations and Retailing
Michigan State University, East Lansing

> *Public relations practitioners today experience a multifaceted profession, which comprises communication and relationship building with internal as well as external publics, and they face new challenges driven by development in communication technology and continuously changing organizations.*
>
> —Catrin Johansson

Despite its growing complexity, and the orientation of modern public relations as relationship management, the CEO of an American healthcare enterprise would likely see issue management, specifically *influencing government healthcare policy*, as public relations's most important function. After all, politicians make policy, and public opinion drives politicians. The publicity that shapes opinion is the work—sometimes described as the principal work product—of PR. CEOs would likely understand that PR frames the debates that shape U.S. healthcare policy, building arguments and selling them to the public. The high stakes of healthcare reform create the need for more and better publicists, which in turn contributes to growing healthcare costs, which increases frustration and expands controversy about America's inability to provide universal health care—and the dance goes on. And with it goes a greater and greater need for communicators.

The 1990s witnessed huge amounts of PR activity focused on derailing proposals that could have reshaped hospitals, insurance companies and the role of the American physician. In the early days of the Clinton administration, one of the most intense lobbying efforts to ever hit Washington, DC, hit it full force. "Hillarycare," President Bill Clinton's attempt to restructure American health care, was pummeled into a nearly two-decade retreat. This victory for the status quo elevated the standing of, if not the respect for, PR. It also signaled a shift in how large-scale policy campaigns are designed and executed, demonstrating, perhaps as never before, the efficacy of grassroots pressure on the Congress.

Sixteen years later, healthcare reform returned to Washington, DC, this time as the principal initiative of another new U.S. president, Barack Obama. Obama had been swept into office in November 2008 on a wave of a different kind of grassroots pressure stimulated by the best-orchestrated social media campaign in the young history of the Internet. With Obama's victory came a strengthened, and largely supportive, majority in the U.S. House of Representatives (21 new Democrats) and nine new Senate Democrats, giving Obama increased leverage to move his agenda forward. President Obama used this leverage to orchestrate a full-court press to pass comprehensive healthcare reform.

In retrospect, this most comprehensive reform of American health care seemed to have occurred at break-neck speed. And as it is said that for every action there is a reaction, before the ink had dried on Obama's healthcare reform package, dubbed the Affordable Care Act of 2009, armies of PR practitioners had begun to assemble. Battle plans were drawn for removing a sufficient number of Democrats from Congress in the next round of elections (2010) to shift the balance of control from Obama to a new Republican majority. Their driving force was to reform the reform. First mission accomplished—a sufficient number of Republicans having been elected in the U.S. House of Representatives to shift the balance of power—the first official action of the new majority was to announce an all-out assault on "Obama Care." Their objective: to pass legislation they artfully framed "Repealing the Job-Killing Health Care Law Act."

So, for much of the last two decades, and with no end in sight as of this writing, the most visible role of public relations in U.S. health care has been the role of the publicist and lobbyist in denying, then providing, then attempting again to deny national health care reform. Yet, while the spotlight continues to shine on the healthcare wars in Washington, the much larger role of PR in health care seems to have been lost in the shuffle. This irony should not be missed. Many of the most effective tactics used to derail U.S. healthcare reform reflect PR skills learned by healthcare communicators engaged in efforts to improve America's health.

As far back as the early 1900s, public relations pioneer Edward Bernays, the "Father of Public Relations," was using integrated communications to address significant healthcare issues. Fresh out of college, and working as an editor of a small New York–based medical publication, Bernays recognized that America's social taboo against public discussion of the epidemic of sexually transmitted disease was making it impossible to educate the populous about prevention and cures. He decided that a well-orchestrated campaign centering on the production of an off-Broadway play, *Damaged Goods*, about the tragedy of syphilis, if properly promoted, could break through this taboo, and could be the beginning of lifesaving public education effort on the issue.

Integrated communication campaigns remain in use, today, to promote cigarettes, alcohol and the consumption of high-calorie foods. Other campaigns, however, are helping reduce smoking, control family size, prevent and treat sexually transmitted disease and prevent infant deaths. Integrated communication management has demonstrated its power to increase seatbelt use, reduce drunk driving, promote the donation of human organs and prevent child abuse. And though results of these campaigns are often less than hoped for, Americans are, nonetheless, better off today due, in part, to the work of healthcare public relations.[1]

Public relations textbooks focus mostly on commercial or political applications. But much of the best evidence of the power of PR is in the work product of the health communicator. Quality communication is central to the success of many healthcare products and services. Healthcare communicators are issue managers, marketing partners, behavior shapers and crisis "firefighters."

JOBS IN HEALTHCARE PUBLIC RELATIONS

Many public relations skill sets are demonstrated through a marketing-support role of PR in disease-prevention and treatment strategies aimed at individuals and groups. For example, the pharmaceutical communicator assures that both the diabetic and the doctor are aware of his company's new treatment. PR practitioners dramatize, and sometimes popularize, heretofore-unnamed health conditions, priming the public for cures that their clients or employers have developed for sale. However, the most important and lasting work of healthcare PR practitioners may be demonstrated by the social marketing role PR plays saving and improving lives. And the new applications of healthcare PR strategy and tactics seem to grow daily.

Data provided by the Public Relations Society of America (PRSA), the largest PR membership organization in the United States, support similar findings from the U.S. Bureau of Labor Statistics that identify continued employment opportunities for healthcare communicators (see http://www.prsa.org/Jobcenter). Healthcare communication job opportunities are expanding at a rate even faster than are PR job opportunities in general.

Healthcare public relations practitioners work under a variety of titles including many that disguise the PR nature of the position, and they work in an even wider variety of organizations ranging from health insurance, hospitals, nursing homes, physician groups, temporary nursing agencies, laboratories, fitness clubs and trade and professional associations representing virtually every health-related occupational group. Local, state and federal agencies, foundations and large corporations hire increasing numbers of communicators to work in social marketing campaigns that address environmental concerns, child and worker safety and vaccination rates, or that encourage employees to adopt healthier lifestyles. The U.S. Department of Health and Human Services (HHS), for example, employs large numbers of communicators within their cadre of nearly 65,000 employees in departments and agencies as far reaching as the National Institutes of Health (NIH), the Food and Drug Administration (FDA), the Centers for Disease Control and Prevention (CDC) and the Indian Health Service.

Health insurance companies provide an expanding number of PR-related opportunities. Competition between insurance carriers and healthcare organizations (HMOs), for example, shows no signs of slowing down, especially if the federal requirement stays in effect that every American, not covered in an employer-based insurance program, must buy his or her own coverage.

Each of the larger health insurance carriers and managed care organizations—and there are hundreds that fall into this category—employ many employees for whom healthcare communication occupies an increasing amount of their workday. The number of PR-related jobs in these companies expands even further if one counts employees engaged as lobbyists, or in online and in-person customer relationship management, public opinion or marketing research or the operation of corporate foundations that support research and charities.

Despite the dwindling number of traditional reporters covering U.S. health care, an otherwise reduced need for traditional "media relations" staff members appears capable of being offset by the growing need for social media–savvy employees who develop and nurture relationships with a rapidly expanding number of blog and healthcare website managers.

Provider relationships remain the bread and butter of health carriers and HMOs. Provider-relations jobs provide a strong employment category for PR practitioners who meet face to face, develop stock letters and brochures and, increasingly, run the websites used to manage day-to-day relationships with doctors, hospitals, equipment suppliers and others in the healthcare food chain.

Insurers employ armies of PR practitioners working in marketing or sales communications developing relationships with agents, trade associations and other intermediaries essential to business survival. These employees work with company community affairs departments making sure that customer pet projects are acknowledged with donations, or that clients are provided tickets to athletic events. These employees participate in charity golf outings, dinners or other client or civic events. PR employees also staff carriers' special events departments planning and staging activities to bring attention to their employer's "corporate social responsibility" mission.

Entry-level PR work occurs in 6,000 U.S. hospitals. Heavy demand for communicators in hospital work, combined with the spending constraints of insurance carriers and governments, makes U.S. hospitals fertile fields for students and graduates, seeking internships and entry-level positions.

Across every aspect of PR, writing is an unmet aspect of the success of entry-level practitioners. A recent survey of 800 U.S. PR practitioners found that, despite the obvious importance of good writing, supervisors express great disappointment over the quality of the writing skills of entry-level employees.[2]

Western Michigan University, Kalamazoo, graduate William Fitzgerald appreciates the value of good writing. He was hired into the public affairs office at the world-renowned University of Texas MD Anderson Cancer Center, Houston, the nation's largest cancer hospital directly from an internship with Detroit's Weber Shandwick.

"Starting out in such a large institution involves a significant learning curve," Fitzgerald says, "however I found that relevant coursework and solid internships helped ease this transition for me." Fitzgerald went on to say,

What I quickly appreciated is how important communications is to MD Anderson's mission of eliminating cancer. Communications is a main vehicle positioning the institution as a leader in the field. Solid two-way communications result in patient referrals and increased cancer awareness. The more large organizations engage their constituents, customers and patients in dialogue, the more credible institutions become in the eyes of those they serve. There is probably no field in which this honest communication is more important than in healthcare, as most people gravitate toward institutions they trust and understand.

Fitzgerald, who gained much of his social media experience as an intern, believes that experience was a big factor in his transition to practice. "The social media revolution is making it easier and faster to make the connections that gain the trust of various constituencies we depend upon. Facebook, Twitter and other interactive platforms are redefining communication. For example, physicians use social media to help them find candidates for life-saving clinical trials."

Cancerwise.org (http://www2.mdanderson.org/cancerwise) has become an important voice of MD Anderson. "Some of my time each week is spent identifying influential bloggers who can disseminate cancer knowledge and create a larger conversation about important cancer issues."

Fitzgerald says his best advice to entry-level PR practitioners and interns is to ask questions. "No one knows everything, but the healthcare industry requires an uncommon level of expertise. Asking questions is a valuable way to learn and to ultimately help management make quality communication decisions."

The increasing number of independent health-related websites also provides a significant source of employment in PR. These websites span a range of government, nonprofit and for-profit ventures.

Since 1997, Boston-based Web Marketing Association (http://www.webmarketingassociation.org) has selected the best healthcare website. A review of recent award winners demonstrates a diverse range of robust health-related websites ranging from pharmaceutical companies (2010, Prilosec: http://www.prilose cotc.com/en_US/consumer/Pages/Home.aspx) to private advertising-based health information networks (2009, Healthline: http://www.healthline.com/) to a pro-social site for gay men about street drugs, alcohol and sex (2008, Terrence Higgins Trust: http://www.tht.org.uk).

A brief examination of the official HHS website (http://www.healthcare.gov) overviews work being done by federal communicators. For example, one section of the website details provisions of the new "Affordable Care Act," whereas another provides options for finding private insurance and qualifying for government-sponsored programs. A third section provides detailed information on wellness.

Another significant force in U.S. healthcare is the pioneering advertising-based website WebMD. Headquartered in New York City, WebMD (http://www.webmd.com/) employed 1,400 employees in 2009. Recent estimates place the number of viable health and medical U.S.-based websites as exceeding 4,000.

Healthcare communication, with its often pro-social mission, wide range of job responsibilities and entry-level opportunities, is a proven discipline for entry-level practitioners to develop rewarding commercial careers, as well as to work in the service of mankind.

COMMUNICATION FOR BEHAVIOR CHANGE

Not to be confused with social media, healthcare communication campaigns are described as social marketing—"a framework in which marketing concepts are integrated with social-influence theories to develop programs better able to accomplish behavioral-change goals."[3]

As previously noted, integrated communication techniques were applied to health care long before the phrases *social marketing* or *healthcare communication* or *integrated marketing communication* (IMC) were used. And two essential IMC characteristics—its consumer orientation and its dependence on relationship building—are mainstays of effective PR.

In 1985, Silicon Valley marketer Regis McKenna recognized the importance of relationship building in his vision of "new marketing" for technology industries. "While information is fleeting, relationships have a permanence that is very powerful in a fast-changing world. By forming the right relationship, a company can gain credibility and recognition that it would never gain through advertising."[4]

To create an authentic earth-friendly image, for example, a chemical company must develop an obsessive aversion to pollution. Once company behavior is consistent with a planned message, PR can integrate communications to make the organization's behavior more obvious to the target audience. This approach—called the adjustment and high-pointing functions—strengthens the organizational–public relationship in much the same way as "changing our ways" can strengthen personal relationships. PR, since its earliest days, has been described as supporting relationship building by adjusting organizational behavior to the values of the audience upon which the organization depends, and then high-pointing the adjustment through publicity or other means.

For more than 20 years, Larissa and James Grunig (and colleagues) have been stressing relationship building as a central activity in excellent public relations.[5] This notion of using communications for relationship building seems especially relevant to health care.

Despite health care's life and death consequences, for many consumers, healthcare services are commodities. Health care is complicated, mysterious, technical and intimidating to many consumers. A health care organization's position in the marketplace, therefore, is influenced significantly by how well it expresses its commitment to the patient relationship.

Position is that magical quality that separates one organization from the rest in the mind of the consumer. It is difficult to imagine any better way for a health care entity to position itself than as one that is totally dedicated to its patients. So as the recognition takes hold that the central function of public relations is organizational-relationship management, healthcare organizations increasingly turn to PR practitioners for consulting, and sometimes, management of basic customer relationship activities such as their "1-800" call centers.

CUSTOMER SERVICE AS PR JOB NUMBER ONE

In 2004, KALPA systems, a Michigan-based consulting firm, was hired by a major healthcare system to review and improve its centralized call center operation. The firm's goal was to identify options for better call-center effectiveness defined as "improving the customer experience." The CEO of the healthcare system believed that his "garden-variety" patient-contact interface could do far more than generate revenue. He wanted an improved call center that could build strong relationships between callers and system's personnel and demonstrate that his system is passionate about patient care.

At that time, system hospitals had nearly as many independent call center teams as it had hospitals. These nurse-staffed phone operations were scheduling appointments and procedures, handling prescription refills, fielding insurance questions and providing care advice. KALPA's controversial plan required consolidation of the various independent hospital call centers into a single "super contact center." New technology and centralized processes would facilitate workforce planning, coaching and quality monitoring. On the surface, the new and improved call center plan might appear as nothing more than a basic operational improvement. The broader picture that emerged, however, was its demonstration as a public relations centerpiece for building relationships between callers and system personnel. "The transformation to a customer-centric call center was a signal to callers and to system employees of a new service standard," said KALPA president Joe O'Connor.

Joanne Crispignani, founder of Allegra Direct Communications, a Troy, Michigan–based contract call center, believes competent telephone-based patient contact demonstrates many of the key components of excellent public relations:

> When it comes to healthcare, it's not enough for an agent simply to answer a caller's question. The caller often calls with emotions running hot. One simple answer often is not enough to provide our desired level of satisfaction. We make sure our whole process gives the caller a sense of the client's competence and commitment, and provides the caller with a sense of ownership of the outcome. Our goal is to give that caller, from the beginning to the end of the dialogue, a sense of being in control of the situation.

Integrated communication proponents believe brand strength stems from such "control mutuality," and with it produces consumer confidence in the organization. Since, to the average consumer, one healthcare product or service may be "virtually the same as your competitor's product, you cannot depend upon the product alone to build confidence. It's the rapport, the empathy, the dialogue, the relationship, and the communication you establish with this prospect that makes the difference. These separate you from the pack."[6]

As hospital–patient relationship becomes paramount, so too does the significance of *dialogue*. Even a social media–facilitated dialogue can create the trust and commitment that help form and enhance, or if handled improperly can destroy, a relationship. Adopting a relationship-based integrated communications strategy forces a healthcare enterprise to examine every aspect of its organizational behavior to understand what it is communicating to the patient in every situation. And since an organization's actions are its most powerful form of communicating, nearly all aspects of organizational performance are within the jurisdiction of the

PR practitioner. Effective healthcare PR begins by identifying, understanding, inventorying and monitoring all patient–organization exchanges, and *owning* them.

HARMONIZING THE HEALTHCARE MESSAGE

Adopting a strategic public relations approach in health care requires an organization's willingness to act in a manner consistent with its messages. What you do speaks in a voice louder than what you say.

Integrating communication demands that messages be evaluated from the perspective of the message receiver. The appropriate perspective is from outside the organization in, not inside out. Communicators must assume a broad sense of responsibility for all actions of the organization because ultimately relationships are built on actions not words.

All successful PR is built upon clear strategy. Strategy, the *clever plan* that drives the messaging, must be consistent with and derive from organizational goals and must reflect the vision of the organization. At the same time, strategy should remain flexible enough to adapt to changing circumstances.

Being able to articulate a clear public relations strategy is an early step in the creation of any successful integrated communications plan. Strategy that is understood by everyone in the organization is most likely to be executed. Using effective employee communication, another important PR function, to create a "line-of-sight" between every employee's job and the organization's vision statement is a critical component of successful strategic execution.

Each audience member forms different impressions of an organization depending on what it sees and hears and feels about the organization. No organization fully controls how every member of their target audience receives the messages *they think they are sending.*

The essence of integrated communications reveals itself through the process of discovering and understanding the impressions target audience members are getting from the actions and messages of the client organization. The effect of integrated communications involves redirecting these actions and messages in the direction of the explicit strategy. Not all actions and messages are under direct organizational control. In fact, communications researchers contend that many fewer audience impressions are truly "controlled" than may have been previously assumed. So-called *controlled communications* such as advertising, special events, community activities, employee publications and marketing communications depend on the context within which they are delivered and received, and thus are subject to great variation in interpretation. Therefore, successful integrated communications must attempt to influence messages being sent to stakeholders from sources beyond the client organization's direct control. Media coverage, competitive information, customer, supplier and employee word of mouth and the expanding world of social media work together to shape organizational image.

Developing an integrated communication strategy is like creating a score for an orchestra. Unfortunately, integrated communication is often characterized not as much as a symphonic score as it is simply providing all the musical instruments on concert night. The fact, however, is that integrating communication requires more than just making every communication instrument available to the client on concert night. True integration requires *harmonics*—bringing together the otherwise disparate sounds audiences might receive from segregated units of the organization. Different instruments play different notes at different times and in different intensities. To produce an appealing symphony, a score is written for each section of the orchestra. That score, when properly played, produces the harmonics necessary to deliver a cogent and appealing sound for the concert audience. This is the essence of effective strategic public relations and integrated communications.

Besides harmonizing messages for a specific audience at the appropriate time, effective public relations integration also harmonizes the various communication tactics employed throughout the client organization. Organizations have many audiences. Audiences, themselves, are dynamic; people are in more than one audience at the same time, and they move from one audience to another. The skills of the healthcare PR team are most challenged when attempting to harmonize the various corporate communication tactics that may include those designed to increase market share; develop new markets; erode competitor viability; educate audiences about new products or services; enhance employee, customer and supplier loyalty; increase product use; reduce product use (as with healthcare utilization); reduce unhealthy behavior (as with wellness programs); avoid or manage crises; and inoculate audiences against upcoming negative news.

The importance of harmonizing the message can be illustrated with a number of examples. One department of an HMO may employ one tactic to *increase* the use of its preventive health services while another department uses a separate tactic to *reduce* emergency room use. Unless these tactics are harmonized, the HMO may, at once, look both stingy and generous—a recipe to produce the appearance of confusion, if not hypocrisy. Every effective organization must have a variety of overlapping tactics to achieve the complex mission of healthcare delivery. But no organization can afford to send messages that confuse its multiple audiences.

SOCIAL MARKETING: A PARADIGM FOR CHANGING PEOPLE

Think of social marketing as a framework for integrating marketing techniques with social-influence theories to get people to change the way they behave. Traditional media combine with social media as instruments of IMC and social-marketing campaigns, but social marketing is a distinct PR discipline. Social marketing borrows planning variables from marketing—the product, price, promotion and place—and reinterprets them, often in a health-related context. The approach mixes these marketing–planning variables with knowledge of modern social psychology.[7]

Jeffrey Barach outlined differences between social marketing programs and traditional sales-related marketing.[8] Social marketing practitioners see themselves as "educating" the target group. Attitude change is often seen, sometimes incorrectly, as a necessary precursor to a desired behavioral outcome. For example, in commercial marketing the goal is to move consumers toward a purchase. Positive attitudes often result from good product experiences. Commercial marketing campaigns are often aimed first at getting trials to occur—getting prospects to use a product. Favorable experience with the product promotes positive attitude change. Advertising reinforces the new positive attitude and reduces post-adoption anxiety. It capitalizes on a person's tendency to want to justify an action he has already taken. To create behavioral change first, with the knowledge that attitudes will eventually follow, is a principle of great interest to the healthcare communicator.

Social marketing can reduce the psychological distance between an individual consumer and the desired behavior. Marketing techniques are used to identify markets and individual consumers, and to develop a behavior-change message that they will buy. Behavior change provides evidence that the message has been bought.

Social networks and organizational relationships accelerate the delivery of messages to the target audiences. In a celebrated case, Kellogg Company teamed with the National Cancer Institute (NCI) to stimulate public understanding of the relationship between eating habits and cancer.[10] NCI publicized the association of increased cancer risks with eating habits and suggested grain cereals as an alternative food. A massive Kellogg advertising campaign reinforced this message, resulting in a higher awareness of the NCI message and an increased consumption of Kellogg high-grain cereals. According to Wallack, "social marketing attempts to make it easy and attractive for the consumer to act in compliance with the message by creating the ideal marketing mix of right product, price, promotion and place."[11]

In some cases, the product in the social marketing mix involves encouraging the use of a specific item such as a condom to prevent an unwanted pregnancy or disease. In other cases, the product is a more subtle behavioral change such as turning to low-fat foods as a risk-reducing alternative. In social marketing theory, the price variable is described as the effort "paid" to make the behavioral change. Promotion translates into how the social marketing message is delivered and what it means to the consumer. Place refers to the availability of the product.

Atkin and Freimuth found that social marketing campaigns aimed at health-behavior change often fall short of their promise because too many organizations have begun massive behavioral change campaigns without engaging in necessary formative research.[12]

Formative research helps develop campaign messages from the framework of tested impact on consumer behavior before the campaign begins. It helps develop the campaigns for which it is used by testing campaign tactics, themes and messages to determine if they are likely to have the desired effect on target audiences.[13]

Formative research (in contrast to evaluative research, which is used to determine campaign effect) adapts PR efforts to specific audiences. Focus groups representing segments of the target audience might be convened to solicit ideas about program strategy and to test reactions to specific messages. The actual campaign messages may emerge from these sessions. At least, modifications to strategy and message can be made on the basis of focus groups. Formative research also includes audience analysis of media habits and assessment of attitudes in the target population. Simply said, formative research reduces uncertainty.

Formative research is essential to integrating communication for many reasons, not the least of which is its ability to keep campaign focus on the individual customer. The basis of all marketing is that people are willing to exchange their commitment in time, effort, attention and sometimes money, in return for a result they see as being of greater or equal value. By teasing out the motives of prospects, formative research demonstrates its power to increase the likelihood of a positive outcome.

Social marketing principles have been used, with varying success, to encourage consumers to change behavior and to increase the likelihood of healthier, longer (and medically cheaper) lives. For any marketing program to be effective, it must be built on a clear strategy. Effective strategy is revealed through solid research and is evolved from the core values of the client organization.

ORGANIZING THE CAMPAIGN

Integrated communication can be sequenced in a variety of ways. Schultz and his colleagues suggest that the IMC process should begin with a determination that the client-organization has an opportunity to connect with the target audience. Without such opportunity, further efforts are pointless. "We are simply saying that the conditions under which the communication will be delivered are as, or more, critical than determining message content of the communication."[14]

Most communications campaigns begin with some sense of a desired outcome. Nonetheless, focusing at the earliest possible moment on existing vehicles for creating dialogue (rather than focusing on persuasive message options) forces the communication manager to address interactions already occurring between the organization and the target audience. Doing so may unveil numerous opportunities for bolstering dialogue through existing communication channels, or by developing entirely new channels.

The second step in campaign development requires answering the question: "What do we want consumers to do?" Defining the outcome as "doing" reminds communicators that the object of every campaign should not be what you want your target audience to see or to hear or even to say. The key question is what do you want audience members to do?

Sinai-Grace Hospital was formed with the merging of three separate hospitals by Detroit Medical Center (DMC) in the early 1990s. Each hospital had a distinct culture, and uniting them into a single culture was a difficult process with near-catastrophic results. The hospital consolidation had cost the new Sinai-Grace physicians, community support and market share. By 2005, Sinai-Grace was beginning to turn the corner with new leadership, new physicians and new services and investments in buildings and equipment. But it was, nonetheless, teetering on the brink of bankruptcy. Far too many of its patients, especially those with health insurance coverage, were taking their business to upscale suburban hospitals. Sinai-Grace needed to establish itself as the new Sinai-Grace Hospital, and its communication team realized this could not be done with slick advertising and press releases. It needed to find a way to get people to visit.

The next step in the strategic PR and integrated communications process requires stating clear campaign objectives in measurable terms that will allow the client organization to know if the campaign is working.

In order to regain community trust and, ultimately, market share, the Sinai-Grace team needed to improve perceptions of the quality of its facility, and to introduce the community to its new medical teams. The only evidence that would satisfy the hospital president became the campaign's top objective—increasing the number of insured patients using Sinai-Grace services.

Strategy is that clever scheme capable of guiding action. A simple, memorable strategy statement helps the team select the tools and tactics for the campaign.

The challenge was to connect the newly formed hospital with insured members of surrounding communities through a convincing demonstration of competence. The idea of using a "strategy of engagement" emerged and resonated well with the hospital team. Nearly every aspect of the hospital's communication, from revamped customer service to advertising, would be aimed at establishing and reinforcing community engagement with the hospital and its physicians, nurses and staff members.

A "strategy of engagement" borrows from the PR discipline of "development"—fundraising and enlisting volunteers. By its very nature, development is based on behavioral outcomes—getting people to provide the funds and manpower needed to meet organizational needs.

The job of the communications team at Sinai-Grace Hospital was to get local residents to recognize their local hospital as a new community asset, and to get them to invest their trust and loyalty in it. The team had to find a vehicle to involve as many community leaders and residents in visiting the new hospital. This vehicle was "People's Medical College."

A principal function of a clear and unambiguous strategy statement is the influence it has upon the actions of the team. Think of the strategy statement as a template upon which the team can check its tactics.

The next step in developing fully integrated communications involves picking the tools and tactics that best fit the strategy, and then testing them out and tuning them up. A strategy of engagement assumes that the primary focus of involvement is behavior change. In fact, the concept of engagement—as defined by the involvement of target publics with the client organization—is action oriented. It ignores or minimizes the presumption that attitude change is somehow a necessary precursor to behavioral change.

Development officers use a pneumonic device— "the four I's of fundraising"—to explain the process they use to secure donations. The first "I" in the sequence is *identification*. The target market must be identified. In most development cases, the target is an individual. Agreeing on a target can be a daunting task. But just as in the act of firing an arrow, the target must be recognized, correct and in clear focus. The second "I" in the fundraising sequence is *information*. Persuasion, it is thought, must come before the involvement that results in the *investment*. However, public relations has evolved to recognize that, rather than persuasion, as it was once thought, PR's critical skillset is increasingly understood to be developing and maintaining relationships.

So an alternative sequencing emerges, one that better fits a strategy of engagement. This new sequence may require involving the target audience at the earliest possible stage in the process—even before any attempt at persuasive attitude change has occurred. This new sequence requires initiating involvement through methods that do not require the target for investment to change her attitudes first. Using this approach of *involvement before information* requires accepting that a faster route to attitude change may stem from creating conditions that appeal to a target's felt needs, regardless of how inconsistent this involvement may be with existing attitudes.

The communications management team, which included a top administrator from Sinai-Grace's parent system, recognized that they needed to "connect" the community with the "new" hospital. People's Medical College, a concept that had been earlier tested by the parent hospital system, might provide the bait the team at Sinai-Grace needed to entice community members with insurance to visit the new facility.

There are a variety of ways to motivate audience involvement before attempting to deliver persuasive messaging. Persuasive information, albeit normally thought of as a necessary precursor for involvement, too often falls on deaf ears. In commercial marketing, strategies designed to engage the prospect first, and let the product do the persuading, are called *trials*. Once the prospect has a rewarding experience with a product or service, resistance to information, even that which may be in conflict with preconceived notions, begins to wane. Because *involvement* has already occurred, the *information*, which now becomes the third "I" in the sequence, is relevant. Because the information is now relevant, it is seen as authentic, rather than if it had been presented as an attempt to alter attitude.

People's Medical College was announced to the public with fanfare that included features in newspapers, announcements on the corporate website, and television and radio advertising, and was accompanied by a promotional partnership with a "news and talk" radio station. The system had earlier introduced the concept of People's Medical College in an upscale, suburban community center. The first class had focused on "heart health" (where one of the system's well-meaning cardiologists had to be talked out of using an audience conspirator from faking a heart attack as a stunt to demonstrate the importance of portable defibrillators). The public's reception to the idea of a hospital system sharing lifesaving information in a community classroom verified the efficacy of proceeding with a series of future classes. In the future, however, and consistent with Sinai-Grace's "strategy of engagement," the People's Medical College was to be held in system hospitals, beginning in the newly rehabilitated Sinai-Grace Hospital.

Many of public relations history's great campaigns have been built around special events. "Spectacular events" designed to make large public points can generate significant publicity. They become the subject of social media that produce great word of mouth, sometimes going viral on the Internet. Events inspire employees and introduce products or services to customers and prospects. If the event is held at a corporate site, the effect can be similar to how inviting the boss home to dinner helps ensure that the home looks especially tidy. After all, "important company is coming."

Making Sinai-Grace the inaugural DMC hospital home of People's Medical College involved a complex set of activities from selecting "class topics" aligned with area residents' healthcare concerns to choosing the physicians and nurses to serve as "class professors." The hospital CEO used People's Medical College to welcome the community to "their new hospital," giving him a chance to rave about its physicians and staff, buoying employee attitudes and selling hospital pride. Physicians, who had been splitting their time at various competitive hospitals, began to request an opportunity to be featured "professors" at Peoples' Medical College sessions at Sinai-Grace. This gave the CEO new leverage to create physician–hospital loyalty.

Over the years that People's Medical College has been running at several DMC facilities (see http://www.dmc.org/pmc), doctors, nurses and other staff members of Detroit's Sinai-Grace Hospital have come to understand this strategy of engagement not only for how it began—a plan to bring the community into a local hospital—but also for how it has become the relationship-building mechanism that demonstrates the best of strategic PR. It is said that while the manager's product is efficiency, the leader's product is culture. For the community as well as the employees of Sinai-Grace, the People's Medical College has been an ongoing spectacular event that demonstrates the role communicators play in building—more than a strategy—a culture of engagement. *Investment*, the fourth "I" in the sequence, be it a charitable contribution or a willingness to recognize the competence, in this case, of a neighborhood hospital, flowed more quickly from a sequence of activities built on the earliest possible involvement of target audience members.

"COMMUNICATIONS" AS THE HEALTHCARE MARKETING POSITION

The healthcare communicator's toolbox can include advertising, public and community relations, employee communications, media relations, customer and provider communications, special events and, where appropriate, development.

In their seminal work, *Integrated Marketing Communications*, Schultz, Tannenbaum and Lauterborn stressed that effective communications can help offset commoditization in the marketplace.[15] In many cases, effective communications may be the only thing consumers use to differentiate one healthcare organization from another.

For healthcare organizations to achieve a strategic command of the marketplace, and a clear position in the minds of targeted consumers, communications activities must be fully integrated with research and marketing. The power of strategic public relations and integrated communications derives from its central focus on behavior. To be successful, the healthcare communicator must find ways to engage target audience members with the organization's products and services. Through engagement, the consumer is better able to view persuasive information as authentic.

Strategic public relations and integrated communications depend on solid research to identify audiences and their needs, and to modify behavior and messages accordingly. Relationships flourish once parties understand that adjustments are made to accommodate one another's needs. Encouraging organizational adjustments, and then once made, underscoring the adjustments to make them obvious to target audiences, is the work of strategic PR. Integrated communications are driven by an obsession with ensuring that both the organization's behavior and its messages achieve the harmonics of a well-scored symphony.

CASE STUDY: SHARE AND SHARE A BIKE: HUMANA BRINGS BIKE SHARING TO THE MASSES

Humana Inc. markets and administers health insurance nationwide. With a customer base of more than 11.5 million, and more than $25 billion in annual revenue, Humana employees number more than 26,000.

In 2007, in what became a test for a larger program, Humana had launched an innovative and "green" employee relations initiative called *Freewheelin*, a bike-sharing campaign offering free bikes for employees to use for short daily trips, running errands, getting to and from public transportation or taking a leisurely spin during the day. The program's success with employees gave Humana's public relations team an idea for how they could garner positive public attention while addressing America's obesity epidemic with a strong pro-environment statement.

Humana teamed up with the national nonprofit "Bikes Belong" of Boulder, Colorado, to take its Freewheelin program public at the Democratic and Republican 2008 presidential nominating conventions. The idea was to provide 1,000 bikes for free use by conventioneers in the convention cities of Denver and Minneapolis–St. Paul.

Humana's agency, New Jersey–based Coyne PR, conducted a media, industry, health and environmental audit to determine Freewheelin's newsworthiness. In 2008, U.S. private bike sales were on the rise. At the same time, several U.S. cities were considering bike-sharing programs. Humana calculated that the 1,000 bikes in use during both conventions could reduce the nation's carbon footprint by 12 tons and participants would burn over 1,000,000 calories. Introducing Freewheelin at America's two highly visible conventions could provide great material for national news and local stories in delegate hometowns across America.

PLANNING

Advance publicity supported the program's objective of challenging conventioneers and host-city residents to pedal their way to health while demonstrating the environmental benefits of community bike-sharing. For Humana, the program could provide an authentic demonstration of its position as an innovative, socially responsible company. The integrated communications effort capitalized on this opportunity by targeting, principally, four key audiences:

- Nearly 5,000 Republican and Democratic delegates at each convention—community opinion leaders who could flow the word back to their hometowns

- Federal and state legislators, critical to Humana's business interests, Humana customers and prospects who would experience the health and environmental benefits of *Freewheelin* first hand

- More than 15,000 representatives of traditional news outlets and the social media that would spread word of Freewheelin virally

STRATEGIC OBJECTIVES

The Freewheelin strategy would team public relations pros and volunteers with each host city's convention committees to establish a bike-sharing presence in all convention-related communications. Humana's partnership with Bikes Belong would provide instant credibility in the bicycling world. Team strategists decided to "let the Freewheelin program be the star" and allow the attributes of the program to tell the story. No celebrities need apply. The team saw the program as an unusual opportunity for authentic and direct media involvement, more than as commentators, as bicyclists. Government affairs professionals would get legislators and congressional leaders to advocate for the program among their colleagues and, through the media, to their constituents. Multiple media "flashpoints" would generate ongoing bursts of news coverage emphasizing both personal and environmental health in all aspects of the program. A robust social media effort could create "buzz."

EXECUTION

To avoid becoming a "one-day story," the Freewheelin team introduced and executed their integrated communication program with a series of activities including:

- *The Congressional Challenge.* Four Congressmen (Democrats and Republicans) issued a national "bike-partisan" challenge in July to all convention-goers: "Use Freewheelin to ride 25,000 miles and burn 1,000,000 calories."

- *The Convention Countdown.* Coyne PR arranged "Santa's Workshop" media previews in convention city warehouses where the 1,000 Freewheelin convention bikes were being assembled.

- *Inaugural Rides.* Host-city mayors took 150+ bicyclists on a 3-mile ride through their cities.

- *Legislator Rides.* Rides were "pitched back" to media in legislators' districts, providing progress reports on the Congressional Challenge. (With the arrival of Hurricane Gustav, Humana added a charity twist by establishing a "$10-per-mile" hurricane relief drive.)

- *Keeping it Green.* "Social media press kits" were delivered via e-mail, and on-site materials were provided on flash drives rather than on paper, consistent with the environment-friendly theme of Freewheelin.

- *Virtual Freewheelin.* Bike sharing was tailor made for a social media campaign, given the strong interest in green initiatives and the role of new media at the conventions. To maximize Freewheelin's impact, the team developed a social media press release, Facebook and Flickr groups, and a YouTube channel for program and user-generated content. Humana set up webcams at Freewheelin bike stations so people could watch the action live.

- *Post Convention.* To keep Freewheelin at top-of-mind for local residents, Humana donated 70 bikes to each host city.

EVALUATION SUMMARY

Participants. Freewheelers exceeded all expectations for biking 41,724 miles, burning 1.3 million calories and reducing their carbon footprint by 14.6 metric tons. Additionally, Humana's Hurricane Gustav challenge raised $150,000 for relief efforts.

Key stakeholders. Humana held eight legislative bike rides, during which national and local representatives led constituents on Freewheelin bikes through Denver and Minneapolis–St. Paul. Photos of the rides were pitched to the Congress members' hometowns. Nearly 300 convention delegates participated.

Nationwide media coverage. Freewheelin garnered 2,342 stories across print, broadcast and on-line media, totaling 185.7 million impressions. Media highlights included five AP stories, two *New York Times* articles, two *USA Today* articles, two *Washington Post* stories, stories in *The Wall Street Journal* and *Newsweek*, and across the county. More than 250 journalists rode including Tom Brokaw, David Gregory and *The Daily Show* staff.

Peer recognition. 2009 National PRSA Silver Anvil Award. Category: 4B. Events 7+ Days—Business Service Title of Entry: "Share and Share-a-Bike: Humana Brings Bike-Sharing to the Masses." Humana Corporate Communications and Coyne Public Relations. Client: Humana, Inc.

DISCUSSION QUESTIONS

1. A wide-variety of PR-related units and functions within the company were required to be involved in the planning and execution of Humana's "Share and Share a Bike" events. Identify eight discrete functions of PR and speculate on their involvement in the event, and identify how the outcome of their involvement might have been measured and evaluated.

2. Identify the various kinds of formative research that was used and may have been used by the company and its PR agency to formulate the "Share and Share a Bike" event.

3. Identify two ways in which this national event was localized and identify one way that was not reported that Humana might have used the event on a localized basis.

4. The Humana legal department could have come up with a number of "reservations" about the event. Name three legal issues that could have caused the event to be scuttled. Develop arguments to counter these legal reservations.

5. Humana and its agency developed a number of ways to prevent their bike-sharing event from becoming "one-day stories" at the two conventions. Identify five things that could have gone wrong and that would have turned the story into a public relations nightmare for Humana.

6. PR practitioners are well advised not to forget to "kick the extra point" after a successful event. Come up with three "extra points" that the PR agency could have recommended for Humana.

NOTES

(Introductory statement) C. Johansson, "On Goffman—Researching Relations with Erving Goffman as Pathfinder," in *Public Relations and Social Theory, Key Figures and Concepts*, ed. O. Ihlen, B. van Ruler, and M. Fredriksson (New York: Routledge, 2009), 126.

1. C. Atkin and L. Wallack, Eds., *Mass Communication and Public Health* (Newbury Park, CA: Sage, 1990).
2. R. Cole, L Hembroff, A. Corner, and Andrew D, "National Assessment of the Perceived Writing Skills of Entry-Level PR Practitioners," *Journalism and Mass Communication Educator* (Spring, 2009): 10–26.
3. L. Wallack, "Improving Health Promotion: Media Advocacy and Social Marketing Approaches," in *Mass Communication and Public Health*, ed. C. Atkin and L. Wallack (Newbury Park, CA: Sage, 1990), 155.
4. R. McKenna, *The Regis Touch* (Reading, MA: Addison-Wesley, 1985), 8.
5. L. A. Grunig, J. E. Grunig, and W.P. Ehling, "What Is An Effective Organization?," in *Excellence in Public Relations and Communication Management*, ed. J. E. Grunig (Hillsdale, NJ: Lawrence Erlbaum Associates, 1992), 66–89.
6. D. Schultz, S. Tannenbaum, and R. Lauterborn, *Integrated Marketing Communications* (Lincolnwood, IL: NTC Publishing Group, 1993), 84–85.
7. Wallack, *Mass Communication and Public Health,* 155.
8. J. Barach, "Applying Marketing Principles to Social Causes," *Business Horizons* (July 1984): 65–69.
9. Wallack, 155.
10. Atkin and Wallack, 11.
11. Wallack, 156–157.
12. C. Atkin and V. Freimuth, "Formative Evaluation Research in Campaign Design," in *Public Communication Campaigns*, ed. R. Rice and C. Atkin (Newbury Park, CA: Sage, 1989), 131–150.
13. Schultz et al., *Integrated Marketing Communications,* 57–75.
14. Schultz et al., 44–45.
15. Schultz et al.

ADDITIONAL READING

Argenti, Paul A., and Janis Forman. The Power of Corporate Communications. Boston, MA: McGraw-Hill, 2002.

Atkin, C., and V. Freimuth. "Formative Evaluation Research in Campaign Design." Public Communication Campaigns, ed. R. Rice and C. Atkin. Newbury Park, CA: Sage, 1989.

Atkin, C., and L. Wallack, Eds. Mass Communication and Public Health. Newbury Park, CA: Sage, 1990.

Barach, J. "Applying Marketing Principles to Social Causes." Business Horizons (July 1984): 65–69.

Cho, Sooyoung. "The Power of Public Relations in Media Relations: A National Survey of Health PR Practitioners." Journalism and Mass Communication Quarterly, 83, 3 (2006): 563–580.

Cole, R., L. Hembroff, and A. Corner. "National Assessment of the Perceived Writing Skills of Entry-Level PR Practitioners." Journalism and Mass Communication Educator (Spring 2009): 10–26.

Dozier, D. M., L. Grunig, and J. E. Grunig. Manager's Guide to Excellence in Public Relations and Communications Management. Mahwah, NJ: Lawrence Erlbaum Associates, 1995.

Grunig, L. A., J. E. Grunig, and W. P. Ehling. "What Is An Effective Organization?" Excellence in Public Relations and Communication Management Hillsdale, ed. J. E. Grunig. Hillsdale, NJ: Lawrence Erlbaum Associates, 1992.

Johansson, C. "On Goffman—Researching Relations with Erving Goffman as Pathfinder." Public Relations and Social Theory, Key Figures and Concepts, ed. O. Ihlen, B. van Ruler, and M. Fredriksson. New York, NY: Routledge, 2009.

Levenshus, Abbey. "Online Relationship Management in a Presidential Campaign: A Case Study of the Obama Campaign's Management of Its Internet-Integrated Grassroots Effort." Journal of Public Relations Research 22, 3, (2010): 313–335.

McKenna, R. The Regis Touch. Reading, MA: Addison-Wesley, 1985.

Schultz, D., S. Tannenbaum, and R. Lauterborn. Integrated Marketing Communications. Lincolnwood, IL: NTC Publishing Group, 1993.

Scott, D. M. The New Rules of Marketing and PR. Hoboken, NJ: John Wiley & Sons, 2009.

Thomas, Gregory D., Stephen Smith, and Joseph Turcotte. "Using Public Relations Strategies to Prompt Populations at Risk to Seek Health Information: The Hanford Community Health Project." Health Promotion Practice 10, 1, (2009): 92–101.

Wallack, L. "Improving Health Promotion: Media Advocacy and Social Marketing Approaches." Mass Communication and Public Health, ed. C. Atkin and L. Wallack. Newbury Park, CA: Sage, 1990. For Chapter 38 by Richard Cole—Healthcare

Waters, Richard D., Natalie J. Tindall, and Timothy S. Morton. "Media Catching and the Journalist—Public Relations Practitioner Relationship: How Social Media Are Changing the Practice of Media Relations." Journal of Public Relations Research 22, 3 (2010): 241–264.

39 CHAPTER

THE GLOBAL RESTAURANT INDUSTRY
Communications Strategies

Jonathan Blum
Senior Vice President and Chief Public Affairs Officer
Yum! Brands

The global restaurant business revolves around satisfying customers better than anyone else, providing employees around the world with the opportunity to have a career of a lifetime and making a huge difference in the world by giving back.

It is a fiercely competitive category with a daily battle for "share of stomach" as the stakes get higher all the time due to changing consumer needs, shifting demographics and the economy.

Yum! Brands, Inc., based in Louisville, Kentucky, is the world's largest restaurant company and the parent company of KFC, Pizza Hut and Taco Bell, the leaders of the chicken, pizza and Mexican-style food categories, respectively. We have 1.4 million associates around the world in more than 117 countries and territories. We open approximately four new restaurants each day of the year, making Yum! a leader in international retail development.

The passion we have for our people, our customers, our franchisees and communities around the world has generated consistent recognition over the years—from our unique reward and recognition culture to our diversity leadership, community giving and consistent shareholder returns.

Over the past 14 years, we have been able to transform our company into a global powerhouse, generating approximately 65 percent of our operating profit from outside the United States, an increase from approximately 20 percent in 1998 following our spin-off from PepsiCo in 1997. In 2015, we expect our global operating profit to increase to 75 percent. Undoubtedly for Yum! Brands, the future is focused on global growth. We believe we are on the ground floor of this opportunity.

YUM! BRANDS' FUTURE BACK VISION

Yum!'s "Future Back Vision" is to be the "Defining Global Company that Feeds the World" and we do that in three important ways:

1. We continue to build a famous recognition culture in which everyone counts by attracting and retaining the best people and inspiring greatness. We love celebrating the achievements of our employees as part of our corporate culture.

2. We make our brands dynamic and vibrant everywhere, with operational excellence as our foundation. We are committed to providing customers with delicious and relevant food choices. This includes our commitment to offer balanced options and to continuously improve the nutrition of our products.

   At the same time, we are educating our customers online and in our restaurants so they can make informed purchase decisions about the food choices they are making. We are also committed to sustainability by working to make our restaurants more energy efficient, our packaging more environmentally friendly and to reduce our overall carbon footprint.

3. We demonstrate that we are a "Company with a Huge Heart." Yum! is a company that truly cares for its employees by training them, developing them and providing them with the skills to grow in their careers. We also demonstrate that we are a company with a huge heart by giving back to the community and working to make the world a better place.

   We give back in many ways through each of our brands by supporting education, the arts, teen mentoring, literacy and many social services around the globe. We are also giving back across Yum! with our long-term commitment to the United Nations World Food Programme (WFP) and other hunger relief agencies that are dedicated to alleviating world hunger.

COMMUNICATING FUTURE BACK VISION

External and internal communications play a vital role in achieving organizational success. Our team is responsible for making that vision come to life in a dynamic and engaging way globally. Yum! Brands' global presence from the United Kingdom to South Africa to India to China, creates the need to have a powerful communications strategy. With a diverse portfolio of brands and an immense geographical spread, communications is a valuable component to the overall success of the business.

Our public affairs vision is to deliver world-class communications. We do that by creating very strategic breakthrough, proactive external and internal plans and continually raising the bar on our performance.

We view our employees as our most important asset as well as our secret weapon. Effective communications educates, motivates and inspires employees to achieve great heights.

Our chairman and CEO, David Novak, uses a personal touch that makes a big company feel small by sending out handwritten notes and blogging internally on a regular basis to provide updates about our people and our business developments around the world. He connects a vast organization in a highly engaging manner. Every quarter, Novak and his leadership team host an engaged dialogue with employees wishing to participate in "Talk to David" conference calls. During these calls, David and his team listen to employees and answer any questions they may have about our business. The "Talk to David" calls are an effective part of our internal communications process and reinforce the notion at Yum! to "Believe in All People."

In addition to our employees, we have a wide range of stakeholders, from customers that enjoy our products to shareholders that invest in our company, plus analysts and the media. We use communications to engage, excite and inform. We provide important information about our growth strategies as well as transparency to external audiences. In an age when the rise of social media has changed consumer and stakeholder expectations, we are focused on engaging our different audiences through various integrated communications platforms.

We are an organization of avid learners and constantly seek best practices inside and outside the company to ensure that we are on the vanguard of the latest corporate communication trends. We conduct full reviews after the introduction of every initiative to see what worked, what did not and what elements require fine-tuning in order to achieve success.

Yum! conducts annual global summits for the entire public affairs function spanning external and internal communications, corporate social responsibility (CSR), community and government relations and diversity. Employees from around the world share know-how and best practices that they can apply in their work.

IMPORTANCE OF BRAND BUILDING

Brand equity is paramount to all companies. Everything you do has to go through the filter of how it impacts the brand and perceptions from consumers and other relevant stakeholders. You need to determine if what you want to do strategically builds a positive perception or connection with your brand in an engaging manner.

How to do that is what makes the communications field so exciting and challenging. The reality today is that it has become even more challenging to cut through the clutter. The best ideas are rooted in consumer insights.

At Yum!, we are focused on solving for the "unmet" needs of our customers. We frequently ask, "What habit, belief or perception do you need to change, build or reinforce to grow the business?" This question leads you to insights rooted in consumers' needs. It applies to all functions from communications to marketing to operations.

EVOLVING COMMUNICATIONS

As consumer habits change, we adjust how we communicate with our customers. The media landscape continues to evolve as more and more people turn to social media and use the Internet to get their news and information. Social media is one of the biggest and most important ways a brand can engage customers. It is important to know what people are saying about your brand from a positive and negative perspective. Negative commentary can be magnified and have a longer online life span and a local rumor can become global in seconds. Communications professionals must be sensitive to this new reality.

There are hundreds of social networks and platforms such as Facebook for social networking, Twitter for microblogging, YouTube for video and Foursquare for location-based interaction. The emergence of these networks has created an increased desire from consumers to engage with their favorite brands. Therefore, communications must meet such desires wherever they appear in a transparent and conversational manner. In terms of communicating our initiatives around the world, we maintain a sense of openness and honesty around all of our brands. Only through this approach can brands remain relevant in the eyes of consumers.

Word of mouth is very powerful. Whoever creates a blog, tweets or posts something on Facebook has the power in today's world. Given this development, it is important to know what is being said about your brand or company. This means "listening" vs. "monitoring" and nurturing conversations. Conversations about your brand are happening everywhere online. Find out where the discussions are happening, who is saying what and become part of the conversation. Build relationships along the way to cultivate key influencers and brand ambassadors. A two-way, honest dialogue is key. Do you know what is being said about your brand? Are you engaged in conversations with your consumers? If you replied no to either of these questions, it's time to reconsider your communication practices.

Smart companies, for instance, tap into empowered consumers and bloggers by inviting them to participate in new product ideation by soliciting feedback and input. If you are not engaging the relevant stakeholders to be a part of the conversation, you run the risk of being left behind.

PLANNING, IMPLEMENTATION AND EVALUATION

From a planning perspective, adopt a 360-degree approach. Identify all the ways your consumers get news and information and where they share this information. Include traditional and social media as part of your overall strategy for internal and external audiences. Social media should be part of corporate communications, individual brand marketing plans and customer service.

Information can span news about CSR, expansion plans, new products, the latest promotions and special offers. When planning, determine from the onset what success will look like. Who is your audience, what is your brand essence, and how can you tell your story in an engaging way? Think about all the aspects that are involved from staffing to budget to measurement. Determine how much budget can be set aside for each including search engine optimization and online advertisements? There is not a single approach that works universally to staff and organize around communications and social media. Rather, each company finds a different way of doing so. Some have dedicated individuals or teams, whereas others utilize resources in public relations, marketing or human resources.

Just as there are numerous ways to organize communications and social media teams, there are many ways to measure the effectiveness of your outreach. Each company and brand has a unique model. In some cases, you may just want to drive awareness or engagement; in other instances, driving sales is key, as is the case with brands with very high levels of recognition. Some companies prefer to measure conversation volume or buzz, website traffic or customer satisfaction and approval ratings. Decide what is important to your company or brand and build a measurement plan with those elements in mind.

Finally, it's important to be compelling as you compete against all the chatter from competitors and others seeking to gain share of voice. Rich content with visuals that reflect the brand personality is vital. Handheld cameras can be used to capture the authenticity of a brand for a more grassroots, social media component to your communications and marketing campaigns. Consumers today are looking less and less for overproduced video content, as it is perceived as not having a genuinely social feel. This development calls to mind another shift in consumer behavior: consumers are now more likely to trust a product recommendation from a friend or peer rather than from a traditional advertisement. It is important for companies to realize this shift as they develop communications strategies aimed at reaching key influencers.

CRISIS COMMUNICATIONS

In corporate communications, a company must be prepared for the worst. Crises do happen, and it is important to have a plan in place to deal with potential emerging issues. An excellent example is Taco Bell's communications plan and crisis response efforts behind a lawsuit brought against its beef. In January 2011, a lawsuit was filed against Taco Bell claiming that its beef did not meet the U.S. Department of Agriculture (USDA) standards. The lawsuit generated thousands of news stories and a high volume of online buzz. The lawsuit's claim served as a direct threat to brand equity and product quality.

Taco Bell had a tremendous weapon on its side—the truth. Taco Bell's beef is high-quality 100 percent premium beef inspected by the USDA. The law firm that initiated the lawsuit unfortunately decided to sue first and ask questions later. The incident required a bold response from Taco Bell via mainstream outlets and social media channels. Armed with the facts, Taco Bell implemented a massive campaign that was clear-cut, transparent and bold in communicating the truth about the brand's beef to consumers. This was one of those moments in a brand's history in which corporate communications played a vital role.

The campaign included interviews with the CEO of Taco Bell by mainstream media outlets such as *Good Morning America* and CNBC following Taco Bell's full-page ads in *USA Today,* the *Wall Street Journal* and the *New York Times* facing the lawsuit head-on by saying "Thank you for suing us" (Figure 39.1). A video statement on YouTube was also posted that enabled consumers and brand advocates on various social media platforms and blogs to share the brand's key messages around its beef quality.

Brand advocates throughout the crisis came to Taco Bell's defense. Taco Bell's Facebook page received an overwhelming amount of support from the community. Taco Bell rewarded Facebook fans with a free taco as a thank you and to generate further positive online buzz. The increased traffic on Taco Bell's Facebook page gave the brand an opportunity to drive consumers to a page where Taco Bell could further communicate to set the record straight.

Next, the brand sought to communicate the facts to consumers with a transparent and aggressive value offer of one of its signature products: the Crunchwrap Supreme, for just 88 cents. Supported by national television ads, the offer included real Taco Bell employees discussing the quality of Taco Bell's seasoned beef.

The next phase of the strategy focused on the conclusion of the crisis. The law firm that initiated the scandal withdrew the lawsuit. Taco Bell prevailed by aggressively defending the brand and communicating the truth. The brand made no changes to its products or advertising campaigns as a result of the baseless claims set forth in the lawsuit. Taco Bell quickly spread the news across traditional and social media outlets,

Thank you for suing us.

Here's the truth about our seasoned beef.

The claims made against Taco Bell and our seasoned beef are absolutely false.
Our beef is 100% USDA inspected, just like the quality beef you buy in a supermarket and prepare in your home. It is then slow-cooked and simmered in our unique recipe of seasonings, spices, water, and other ingredients to provide Taco Bell's signature taste and texture.

Plain ground beef tastes boring.
The only reason we add anything to our beef is to give the meat flavor and quality. Otherwise we'd end up with nothing more than the bland flavor of ground beef, and that doesn't make for great-tasting tacos.

So here are the REAL percentages.
88% Beef and 12% Secret Recipe.

In case you're curious, here's our not-so-secret recipe.
We start with USDA-inspected quality beef (88%). Then add water to keep it juicy and moist (3%). Mix in Mexican spices and flavors, including salt, chili pepper, onion powder, tomato powder, sugar, garlic powder, and cocoa powder (4%). Combine a little oats, caramelized sugar, yeast, citric acid, and other ingredients that contribute to the flavor, moisture, consistency, and quality of our seasoned beef (5%).

We stand behind the quality of our seasoned beef 100% and we are proud to serve it in all our restaurants. We take any claims to the contrary very seriously and plan to take legal action against those who have made false claims against our seasoned beef.

Greg Creed

Greg Creed
President, Taco Bell

TacoBell.com
Facebook.com/TacoBell

TACO BELL

FIGURE 39.1

Taco Bell's Full-Page Ad Explaining Use of High Quality Beef

including full-page ads in national newspapers asking the law firm, "Would it kill you to say you're sorry?" (see Figure 39.2).

The communications strategy behind the campaign in both mainstream and social media received numerous kudos from PR experts and consumers for being highly responsive, creative and transparent. It successfully integrated traditional news, social media and marketing and demonstrated the tremendous relevance communications has for companies.

Would it kill you to say you're sorry?

The law firm that brought false claims about our product quality and advertising integrity has voluntarily withdrawn their class action suit against Taco Bell.

- **No changes to our products or ingredients.**
- **No changes to our advertising.**
- **No money exchanged.**
- **No settlement agreement.**

Because we've ALWAYS used 100% USDA-inspected premium beef.

Sure, they could have just asked us if our recipe uses real beef. Even easier, they could have gone to our Web site where the ingredients in every one of our products are listed for everyone to see. But that's not what they chose to do.

Like we've been saying all along, we stand behind the quality of every single one of our ingredients, including our seasoned beef. We didn't change our marketing or product disclosures because we've always been completely transparent. Their lawyers may claim otherwise, but make no mistake, that's just them trying to save a little face.

We were surprised by these allegations, as were our 35 million customers who come into our restaurants every week. We hope the voluntary withdrawal of this lawsuit receives as much public attention as when it was filed.

As for the lawyers who brought this suit: You got it wrong, and you're probably feeling pretty bad right about now. But you know what always helps? Saying to everyone, "I'm sorry."

C'mon, you can do it!

©2011 TACO BELL CORP.   TacoBell.com • Facebook.com/TacoBell

F I G U R E   39.2

Taco Bell's Ad After Lawsuit is Withdrawn

USE OF SOCIAL MEDIA

The Taco Bell beef crisis clearly illustrated the power of social media and the importance of integrating this new medium in a company's communications strategy. In fact, all brands at Yum! are fully engaged in social media.

In the United States, KFC continues to grow its base of social neighbors to create brand advocates. They leverage Colonel Sanders' authentic brand personality and connect with fans in a genuine, sincere way. KFC engages regularly and responds quickly to inquiries or questions.

KFC created one of the most innovative social media efforts when it announced it would give away a $20,000 college scholarship through its Colonel's Scholars program based entirely on a 140-character Twitter "application."

The offer generated tremendous online and traditional media coverage, driving positive awareness for KFC and its Colonel's Scholars program. The number of followers on Twitter jumped by 25 percent in just one month. The winning tweet was: "#KFCScholar Hey Colonel! Your scholarship's the secret ingredient missing from my recipe for success! Got the grades, drive, just need cash!"

More than 60 million media impressions were generated including coverage by the Associated Press, CNN and *USA Today*. The KFC Twitter scholarship example also shows how you can create breakthrough news and buzz based on a clever idea.

Taco Bell has also achieved tremendous social media results and is one of the top brands on Facebook. The brand's Facebook following increased from roughly 600,000 to 5 million Facebook fans in just one year. One of the most innovative social media initiatives uses Twitter for the Taco Bell food truck. On Twitter, the Taco Bell Truck is a fun way for fans to find the truck and enjoy delicious food. It became #5 on Maxim's Top 100 Twitter Accounts Every Guy Should Follow.

Pizza Hut also leverages social media extensively. The brand effectively combined traditional and social media with the introduction of phase one of the $10 Any Pizza campaign around the 2011 Super Bowl. Pizza Hut kicked off the product offer via traditional, mainstream media outlets including Jimmy Kimmel Live, to generate buzz during the first phase of the campaign. To change the perception held by some consumers that Pizza Hut is unaffordable, the company announced the deal that any Pizza Hut pizza was just $10.

The second phase of the launch included a voting campaign that encouraged consumers to vote to extend the $10 offer via Facebook. Pizza Hut's "Tweetologist" campaigned across America and tracked her progress on Twitter and Foursquare, giving fans exclusive news and access to photos and updates from the campaign trail. Pizza Hut drove widespread online engagement and received positive feedback from fans across the nation.

ENVIRONMENTAL IMPACT

Successfully demonstrating a company's ethics can have a great effect on connecting consumers to brands on an emotional level. For Yum!, communicating CSR is essential in showing the world that we are a "Company with a Huge Heart," with leaders and employees that truly care about making the world a better place.

Corporate social responsibility is an important and integral part of every company. Consumers, shareholders and employees expect companies to acknowledge their responsibility to do the right thing from environmental and philanthropic work to employment. Consumers want a brand's ethics to reflect their own. It is the responsibility of companies and brands to provide answers to consumers' questions, to address concerns and, above all, be transparent about information provided. Successful brands understand this and put it into practice across the organization from marketing to consumer insights to communications.

As the chief public affairs officer at Yum! Brands, I believe it is important to communicate our goals, strategies and progress with transparency. We publish this information in our CSR Report. Yum! takes its responsibility to environmental sustainability very seriously, and we have reduced our carbon footprint around the globe. We have decreased energy usage and taken the equivalent of 11,000 cars off the road. We have also introduced environmentally preferable packaging with napkins and cup carriers made from 100 percent recycled content along with reusable food containers and pizza boxes made with recycled material. We are making great strides and continue to work toward more CSR initiatives.

The work we do in this area continues to be exciting. We are raising awareness, volunteerism and funds for our World Hunger Relief effort through our partnership with the United Nations World Food Programme (WFP). We are truly saving lives by moving millions of people from hunger to hope and this has become a hallmark of our company's "huge heart."

As a leading global company, we believe it is our privilege and responsibility to give back. Coinciding with our 10-year anniversary in 2007, the public affairs team was challenged by the chairman and CEO to find a way to make a difference on a global scale, leave the world a better place and demonstrate our higher purpose.

For the first 10 years of the company's existence, we had a track record of feeding the hungry in the United States through the Yum! Harvest Program (formerly Yum! Meals). We recognized that hunger is a worldwide problem and that we had the reach and capability to tackle the issue on a global scale. Our global footprint is unique: with approximately 38,000 restaurants in more than 117 countries, we have tremendous reach to engage our consumers and more than 1 million employees to help make a difference.

We saw that hunger was at the worst point in history with nearly 1 billion people going to bed hungry every day, many of them children. In short, it was the "perfect storm"—a convergence of higher commodity and global food prices, increased competition for products that produce energy, severe droughts and floods due to climate change and increasing demand from growing economies. All these things came together at the same time to make the problem worse than ever.

We were determined to find out how Yum! could become part of the solution and formed a cross-functional team that looked at all the top food relief agencies. We zeroed in on WFP because of their capability, track record of success and global span. Numerous Yum! leaders and top franchisees visited such places as Sudan, Kenya, Nicaragua, Guatemala, El Salvador, Honduras and Haiti to see WFP's work firsthand. WFP does not just offer a handout but rather a hand up, helping to build sustainable communities.

Yum! started with the company's global leadership and cascaded the systemwide rollout of World Hunger Relief to our restaurants and frontline employees. In just one year, our World Hunger Relief effort became the world's largest private sector hunger relief effort in support of WFP and other hunger relief agencies.

The initiative started by setting aside a week in our restaurants around the world to raise awareness, volunteerism and funds. Each brand and each market makes the program come alive in a way that is relevant to them. Each employee takes ownership by choosing his or her own personal form of volunteerism.

World Hunger Relief quickly took hold of people's hearts around the world and is now a campaign defined by months rather than weeks, as well as ongoing efforts throughout the year. The positive feedback we hear from our customers and employees reinforces how vital it is to give back. Employees were both proud and heartened by the efforts of their brands and coworkers. Customers also became more engaged with brands they viewed as vibrant, caring and responsible.

In 2009, multi-Grammy award-winning artist Christina Aguilera became World Hunger Relief's spokesperson. Her incredible star power has helped to greatly increase awareness of the issue. She has made field visits with WFP in Haiti and Guatemala to see firsthand the impact of the earthquake in the region.

As of 2010, World Hunger Relief has raised nearly $85 million for WFP and other hunger relief agencies and is helping to provide approximately 350 million meals, saving the lives of millions of people in remote corners of the world. Our employees and franchisees have volunteered 21 million hours from a number of initiatives.

Employees and franchisees around the world are volunteering and reaching out to consumers to truly make a difference and communicate that Yum! is a company with a huge heart. In 2010, Yum! China engaged employees and consumers to donate, generating a 152 percent increase in donations from the previous year's campaign. KFC South Africa's "Add Hope" national campaign included a number of activities and competitions to encourage consumer participation and raise funds. KFC U.K. employees organized 145 events for World Hunger Relief, including hiking over 32,000 miles for hunger awareness. In Dubai, teams launched a "Battle of the Bands" as well as a cycling event from Dubai to Oman to raise money and awareness. In Singapore, team members organized a "Carnival for Hope" event. In Malaysia, KFC and Pizza Hut employees organized a "Be the Movement" charity walk with more than 5,000 people in attendance.

We have everything it takes to make this goal a reality over time. Although we recognize that we have much more to do, we are energized about how much more we can contribute to serving the world.

Yum! is also addressing hunger across the United States through our Yum! Harvest program. Since its launch over two decades ago, Harvest has become the largest prepared-food donation program in the world. Through Harvest, Yum! has donated over 125 million pounds of wholesome food, with a value of over $500 million, to needy families and children. We have also been the primary sponsor of the Dare to Care Food Bank in Louisville, the home of our global headquarters and have donated nearly $9 million to this local agency over the last nine years.

In addition to hunger relief, our brands and franchisees are supporting countless nonprofit organizations in thousands of communities across the world, focusing on education, literacy, social services, the arts, teen mentoring and much more. We believe our community support, with hunger relief as our primary cause, is a hallmark of Yum! Brands.

Equally important is our commitment to health and nutrition. Across Yum! we are actively focused on making balanced options available to our customers, while continuously improving the nutrition of our menu and serving delicious food. We also help promote physical activity because we know the key to a balanced life-style is all about energy in and energy out.

We fully understand and are actively participating in the global debate on health and nutrition, and the role restaurants should play. We are committed to helping identify solutions and have taken many actions, including the following:

- Kentucky Grilled Chicken at KFC; the Fresco Menu at Taco Bell, offering nine items with fewer than 9 grams of fat; grilled chicken options such as KFC's Brazer sandwich in a number of international markets; and an entire line of delicious, healthy roasted foods in China.

- Offering choice and variety of products, including items that are lower in fat, calories and sodium

- Converting cooking oils to 0 grams trans fat per serving in most countries

- Making continuous and meaningful reductions in the level of sodium in our food

- Reducing the use of high fructose corn syrup and other added sugars

- Introducing whole grains and other wholesome ingredients

- Dialoguing with regulators, special interest groups and health officials, along with our suppliers, to ensure open communication and understanding

- Educating consumers through in-store materials, websites, brochures, trayliners, packaging, posters and advertising

- Offering training to our associates so they can develop their own personal action plan and meet with experts on nutrition and exercise to help them put their plan into action

It is our firm belief that we have an obligation to serve the world and make it a better place. This is fully integrated into our corporate culture and factors into our communications strategy. The scope and depth of our CSR efforts is a source of pride for our employees and enables them to feel good when they interact with customers. We want to be engaged with our consumers and stakeholders and we want them to know that we are a company with brands they can believe in. By showing consumers our beliefs and demonstrating them with CSR efforts around the world, we have a much greater chance of engaging them and building the trust required to strengthen brand equity.

FUTURE OF COMMUNICATIONS

Yum! is a company with two wildly popular global brands, KFC and Pizza Hut, and over the past two years we have started to make Taco Bell our third global brand. As previously mentioned, we are a company that is experiencing dramatic increases in our international development. How does a company with a global presence implement a communications strategy? Should communications be filtered to adapt to local perceptions and sensitivities? A localized filter should be in place, but that should not deter a company from creating one global vision and organizing communications around that vision.

For Yum!, our strong global corporate culture helps facilitate a vision that all employees share, whether in China, France or Australia. Our culture emphasizes a belief in all people and their capabilities. Our employees around the world know that they are valued, and this helps create more than 1 million ambassadors for Yum! Brands. The positive work culture and strongly communicated company principles allow Yum! to create a global communications strategy while also adhering to varying contexts within international markets.

At no time has this global approach been more important for Yum! as a leading international retail developer and the world's largest restaurant company. With the rise of the middle class internationally, our growth is coming from emerging markets and requires us to meet consumer expectations not just within the United States, but also in countries such as China, India, Russia and Vietnam. As companies become more global, it is essential to strike the balance between global and local in order to produce a solid communications strategy.

Ironically, global communications and localization will continue to converge. Consumers around the world expect a localized dialogue, but they also expect a company to be accountable regardless of where they are in the world. The Internet and social media have blurred the lines between countries and cultures. A public relations statement or commercial is not contained within a country, but publicized globally on YouTube, blogs and so on for the entire world to see. PR professionals and communication specialists, for example, will need to take into account how their message to a French audience will be perceived by audiences across the globe. This will be an increasingly important component to consider and an even finer line to walk in the future. To meet these demands as effective communicators, communications professionals must be prepared for public relations to become even more public.

DISCUSSION QUESTIONS

1. What perceptions is your company trying to build, change or reinforce to grow the business?
2. Do you have a well-rounded communications plan and calendar around various news categories within your organization (CSR, HR, Finance, etc.)?
3. Are you going for breakthrough with your plan? Does your plan drive the business?
4. How can you leverage social media to amplify communication efforts?
5. How can you best engage customers and employees?
6. Are you aligned globally with your communications strategy? Have you gained the participation of all relevant parties within the company?

ADDITIONAL READING

Fombrun, Charles J. *Essentials of Corporate Communication: Implementing Practices for Effective Reputation Management*. London, UK: Routledge, 2007. Print.

Ihlen, Oyvind, Jennifer Bartlett, and Steve May. *The Handbook of Communication and Corporate Social Responsibility*. New York, NY: Wiley-Blackwell, 2011. Print.

Keller, Kevin Lane. *Strategic Brand Management: Building, Measuring, and Managing Brand Equity*. Upper Saddle River, NJ: Pearson/Prentice Hall, 2008. Print.

40

C H A P T E R

THE RETAIL INDUSTRY
Not Your Father's Drugstore

Michael Polzin
Divisional Vice President, Corporate Communications
Walgreen Co.

Retailers are defined by the products they sell and the services they provide. Consumers head to the electronics store for a computer or Blu-ray DVD player. They do their weekly food shopping at a grocery store or mass merchandiser. For clothing, it's typically the department store or specialty apparel store.

If a store's focus is not clear, customers will not know why to shop there. To earn and keep customers' loyalty, a store has to meet their expectations—and, more specifically, the customer's needs for that particular shopping trip. Changing the mix of products or services carries the risk of confusing or alienating shoppers if they perceive the change as out of character for the particular retailer.

At the same time, retailers must change and adapt to economic and social forces to remain competitive and profitable. Fashions change. LP records are replaced by CDs, which are replaced by digital downloads. Working parents look for easy-to-make, fresh-food dinners instead of frozen meals.

Finding the balance between meeting existing customer expectations and offering something new or different can be challenging. The retailer can seriously harm its business if its customers don't understand why changes to products or services are being made and how they will benefit from them.

In 2009, Walgreens embarked on a significant addition to its product offering. The nationwide drugstore chain decided to begin offering beer and wine at most of its 7,500 stores. Simultaneously, the company was repositioning itself from "The Pharmacy America Trusts" to "America's First Choice for Health and Daily Living Needs." So, how does selling beer and wine make sense for a provider of pharmacy, health and wellness solutions? In this chapter, we will look at how Walgreens went about adding this product category, positioning the category as a logical extension of its offering, and successfully garnered support from customers and other stakeholders for the change.

As part of the process, the company needed to identify key stakeholders, determine its key messages for the issue and figure out the best way to deliver those messages to the various stakeholders. Without a successful communications program, the new beer and wine products could not have achieved the level of success that they did in their first 12 months and enhanced the company's sales results.

HISTORY

THE 1990s—FOCUS ON CONVENIENCE

The decision to reenter the beer-and-wine category, a category that Walgreens had largely deserted in the late 1990s, came as the company underwent significant changes to its merchandising approach, operating structure and even its overall strategic positioning in the marketplace. Like most retailers, and most companies in general, Walgreens has had to regularly reinvent itself to remain viable, relevant and growing. Its drugstores today bear little resemblance to the one founded in 1901 by Charles R. Walgreen Sr. on Chicago's South Side. The clerk-assisted stores of the first half of the twentieth century eventually gave way to larger, self-service stores in the 1950s as customers chose items themselves from a selection right on the sales floor. Soda fountains disappeared in favor of broader product selections. By the 1970s, with American suburbs in full growth, the brick-and-mortar location of choice was next to a grocery store, which the drugstores depended on to bring traffic to the shopping mall. There was no concern about competing against each other; grocery stores did not have pharmacies, and drugstores were not focused on offering grocery products.

In the 1980s, Walgreens detected the beginning of a trend that would lead it again to redefine its business model. The growth of health maintenance organizations and prescription insurance coverage for individuals through their employers meant that prescription prices were no longer as important to patients; they paid the same copayment no matter which pharmacy they went to, as long as that pharmacy accepted their insurance. Since pharmacies could not compete on price, convenience became the differentiating factor.

To increase and enhance convenience, Walgreens began experimenting with moving its stores out of shopping malls, choosing instead to place them in freestanding locations on high-visibility, high-traffic corners where it was easy for customers to drive in and out of. The freestanding locations were an unqualified success, and the growth in prescription insurance coverage impacted Walgreens just as the company had anticipated. In 1990, only 26 percent of prescriptions were paid, at least in part, by insurance programs other than government plans such as Medicaid and Medicare. By 1997, that percentage had risen dramatically to 60 percent. It reached 82 percent by 2009.

As its freestanding stores thrived, Walgreens sought other ways to make them even more successful. The company opened its first freestanding store with a drive-through pharmacy in 1991 in Minnesota. It took the concept a step further in 1992, when Walgreens marked a watershed moment by entering the Indianapolis market and opening seven new stores on the same day—all freestanding stores with drive-through pharmacies. That would be the basic store model for the rest of the decade as the company entered dozens of new markets around the country.

Using this model, the company went from opening 100 stores a year at the beginning of the 1990s to nearly 500 a year by the end of the decade, increasing its store count from 1,500 to more than 3,000. Throughout the 1990s, Walgreens perfected a model that made it the unquestioned leader in the drugstore industry.

At the beginning of the 1990s, Walgreens also was arguably the largest liquor retailer in the country, selling beer, wine and spirits in a majority of its stores. But as the 1990s progressed and the company sought to take full advantage of its ultraconvenient retail locations, liquor departments became less of a fit, for two reasons:

- Myriad local regulations governing liquor sales meant that many of the purchasing, merchandising and inventory tracking work had to be done at the local level rather than at the corporate level, which took up an inordinate and inefficient amount of store managers' time.

- Convenience food items became more important to time-starved customers.

The bottom line was that food offered a greater opportunity than liquor. By the second half of the 1990s, Walgreens decided to fully embrace convenience foods and other consumables, and eliminated most of its liquor departments. By the early 2000s, with Walgreens store count approaching 4,000, liquor departments remained in only several hundred stores in a few particularly strong liquor sales markets, mostly in Florida and Arizona.

THE 2000s—NEW CHALLENGES AND A NEW STRATEGY

In the 2000s, Walgreens faced new competition on several fronts, including the growth in Internet retailers such as drugstore.com, PlanetRx.com and Soma.com. Some viewed this as the end of brick-and-mortar drugstores— why stop at the store when your everyday needs can be delivered right to your door?

> I think that there is something structurally wrong with the drug store business and that structural problem is the Net. . . . I think (Walgreens') model and their profitability is coming under attack from the proliferation of all the vitamin and long-term drug websites. Those sites are well-capitalized and they can afford to wreak havoc with Walgreen's margins.[1]
>
> —Jim Cramer on TheStreet.com, March 27, 2000

> It seems to have escaped notice that with doorstep delivery of shampoo, foot creams, and the like from Webvan and PlanetRx.com, expensive shelf space at conventional drug stores may only gather dust.[2]
>
> —PC Computing Magazine, February 2000

The reality was quite different. Customers didn't find that it saved significant time to order personal care and household products from their desktop computer, or they couldn't wait to have it delivered days later. Online pharmacies also were slow to develop relationships with insurance payers to cover prescriptions ordered from them. All of that dramatically slowed their anticipated growth.

When the dot-com bubble burst, only drugstore.com survived to remain an independent company by providing a differentiated product selection and services to attract a loyal customer base. While drugstore.com found success through beauty, clinical skincare and other products not typically carried by community drugstores, it trailed in development of its pharmacy business. Walgreens acquired drugstore.com in 2011, bringing together its broader online product selection with Walgreens' expertise in online pharmacy services.

New competition also surfaced from other traditional competitors. In 2006, Walmart introduced a new pricing model for the industry with a selection of generic drugs that sold for just $4. And in 2007, the CVS drugstore chain announced it would purchase Caremark, a pharmacy benefit manager (PBM). PBMs design and administer prescription drug plans for employers and other groups, setting up formularies for which drugs will be covered and putting together a network of pharmacies where beneficiaries could go to have their prescriptions filled. By vertically integrating the administrator of the prescription drug program and the provider of the pharmacy services, CVS hoped to expand its business in both segments.

By 2008, Walgreens also began to see a dramatic slowdown in the growth of new generic prescription drugs entering the market. Generic drugs, although lower priced than brand name medications, are more profitable for pharmacies. But with fewer new generics hitting the market in the second half of the decade, pharmacy profitability also slowed industrywide.

All of these developments converged to lead Walgreens to dramatically change its competitive strategy near the end of the decade.

First, the company took a hard look at its expansion program. With a singular emphasis on store growth over the previous 20 years, Walgreens reached a store count of more than 7,000 and established itself in every market across the country, with a presence in all 50 states plus Washington, DC, and Puerto Rico. However, many of the company's stores were beginning to show their age and were in need of renovations. The time had come to put an emphasis on getting more production out of its core of 7,000 drugstores, rather than depending solely on new store openings to drive growth.

The company decided to slow down its store growth and use some of those resources instead to renovate its existing stores and make them more productive. In the fall of 2008, Walgreens announced a plan to slow its annual store growth rate from about 9 percent a year to 2 to 3 percent a year by fiscal 2011.

Second, Walgreens embarked on a significant program to cut costs and increase productivity, with a goal of saving $1 billion annually by 2011 over its base year of 2008.

ENHANCING THE CUSTOMER EXPERIENCE AND EMPHASIZING HEALTH CARE

And third, the company sought to enhance the customer experience in the stores while becoming a true multi-channel retailer—one that gives customers what they want, when they want it and where they want it.

As Walgreens looked at ways to enhance the customer experience, it quickly realized its stores were overwhelming the customer with too much product choice. Over the past decade, the chain had tried to offer additional convenience by widening its product selection, and the number of products available to stores eventually increased from about 17,000 to nearly 25,000. Despite the broader selection, basket size (the number of products an individual customer purchases on each shopping trip) did not increase noticeably over that time. Instead, it held steady at just over three items per customer. Streamlining the product mix would make it easier for customers to find what they were looking for, and would make it easier for store personnel to manage inventory. Walgreens quickly removed more than 4,000 items per store in about a year.

In addition to eliminating product lines, the Customer-Centric Retailing initiative converted thousands of stores to a new design that made shopping more convenient. It was more than simply redecorating. The new format changed the sightlines in the stores by reducing shelf height. As a result, when customers walked through the front door, they could see the pharmacy at the back of the store and knew they were in a healthcare retailer. The pharmacy also was redesigned to provide additional privacy for pharmacists to counsel patients face to face and administer immunizations. Clearly, the emphasis was on pharmacy, health and wellness services.

The seamless integration of brick-and-mortar stores, online shopping and mobile applications was another key part of the strategy to enhance the customer experience. As a true multichannel healthcare retailer, Walgreens allowed patients to order a prescription refill in person, on the phone, on Walgreens.com or even by scanning their prescription label using a smart phone. If customers prefer, they can get a text message on their mobile phone letting them know when their prescription is ready for pickup. For nonpharmacy shopping trips, customers would soon be able to check store inventory online before they go to the brick-and-mortar store, a capability only 22 percent of multichannel retailers offer, or order products online for in-store pickup. Company research indicated that increasing traffic to its website sends traffic to the stores: about half of the visitors to Walgreens.com said that their next action was to go to a Walgreens store, and that percentage was growing. Clearly, the convenience of online shopping does not replace the convenience of a physical store—the two complement each other. Walgreens research also showed that multichannel customers were three times more valuable than single-channel customers.

While still keeping its focus on convenience, Walgreens' new goal as part of its strategic shift was to become America's first choice for health and daily living needs, a position for which the company believed it was uniquely qualified. Its center of gravity was its more than 7,500 drugstores, with two-thirds of Americans living within 3 miles of them. These stores provided convenient access to goods and services in thousands of communities across the country—from expanded grocery offerings in urban food deserts (areas with limited or no access to fresh food) to prescription and healthcare services in medically underserved communities.

In addition to its drugstore network, Walgreens was positioned on the frontline of health care with its medical facility pharmacies, retail clinics, worksite health centers and 70,000 healthcare service providers. By adding to its pharmacy offering other health and wellness services, including acute and chronic care, health tests, flu shots and other immunization and infusion services, Walgreens sought to help its millions of patients "get well, stay well and live well."

Leading the way were Walgreens' 27,000 pharmacists, who the company increasingly sought to be viewed as a key resource in disease prevention and treatment for chronic illnesses. To that end, it has expanded the role of the pharmacist (where allowed by states) into chronic disease management, health tests such as blood pressure and blood glucose, medication therapy management and prescription drug adherence programs. In the fall of 2009, with the H1N1 flu pandemic the top health concern in the United States, Walgreens had more certified pharmacist immunizers than any other retailer and was able to offer flu shots all day, every day, in every store.

Walgreens also greatly expanded its capabilities in specialty pharmacy services for patients with such complex health conditions as HIV/AIDS, rheumatoid arthritis, cystic fibrosis, infertility or cancer. Their medications can be expensive, require completion of additional forms and are often difficult to administer. Walgreens' highly trained specialty pharmacists, nurses and patient care coordinators help patients navigate these issues, and are available 24/7 to answer questions.

Expanding its role as a pharmacy, health and wellness provider, Walgreens opened more than 700 in-store clinics and worksite health centers where nurse practitioners or physician assistants are available to test, diagnose and provide treatments for routine illnesses without an appointment.

All these changes contributed to the overall strategy to make Walgreens America's first choice for health and daily living needs. In 2010, Fast Company magazine ranked Walgreens as the sixth most innovative health care company for leadership in healthcare services.

So where do beer and wine fit into this scenario?

DECIDING TO REINTRODUCE A PRODUCT CATEGORY

In the wake of the Great Recession and economic crisis that hit with full force in 2008, Walgreens launched a major effort to cut costs and increase productivity of its core business. And like any smart business, Walgreens looked for new sources of revenue.

As it began the process of reducing its costs by $1 billion a year, one of the ideas on the revenue side of the business was to widely reintroduce beer and wine into the stores. Internal company research indicated that customers were looking for one-stop shopping experiences where they could buy a range of products at one location rather than travel, park and pay at a variety of stores. Convenience food had been a winning category for Walgreens, and the company could see that the demand for convenient beer and wine purchases was similarly strong.

Furthermore, improved information technology would make it possible for more of the administrative work involved in selling alcoholic beverages to be handled centrally, where permitted by law, taking the burden off the store managers. The company's analysis showed that offering a selection of beer and wine had tremendous potential for profit. But would it fit in with the health and wellness brand image that the company was focused on?

Walgreens weighed the potential increase in profits against the possibility of reputational harm. Its tests of a moderate selection of beer and wine at select stores in Florida were proving to be successful. Customers were receptive and didn't express significant concerns about the category appearing in their local drugstore. Also working in favor of the program was the growth of magazines and popular shows on the Food Network that focused on pairing beer and wine with food. This attention to beer and wine as central parts of a meal helped drive interest in beer and wine pairings, bringing the products further into the mainstream and in demand. In addition, Walgreens' convenient locations and its reputation as a trusted retailer made it an attractive alternative for the casual purchaser of wine and beer. Feedback from women shoppers, in particular, demonstrated the desire to purchase beer and wine from clean, well-known retailers as opposed to outlets at which they were less comfortable shopping.

With the customer feedback in hand and sales results to support the positive impact on the bottom line, company management concluded that a modest selection of beer and wine would be both appropriate and advantageous. Just as important was Walgreens decision on what not to carry. Spirits, or hard liquor, single-serve cans and fortified beers would not be part of the rollout for several reasons.

First, eliminating spirits from the product selection also eliminated some inventory and distribution complications. Second, it allowed the company to apply for a beer/wine license in municipalities that distinguished between beer/wine sales licenses and full liquor licenses. And third, it significantly reduced the risk of opposition to its applications, based on the belief that a beer/wine license would be much less controversial than a full liquor license. In municipalities that did not distinguish between beer/wine sales and full liquor sales for licensing, Walgreens was prepared to state its intentions to only sell beer and wine despite the full liquor license application.

By early 2009, not only did Walgreens decide to roll out beer and wine across more stores, the company committed to doing it as fast as possible. After excluding stores where state or local legal requirements would preclude the sale of beer and wine, the company planned to introduce this product category in about 5,500 of its 7,500 stores—in less than 24 months! Getting 5,500 stores prepared in such a short time was no small task.

The first step was to apply for the more than 5,000 beer/wine or liquor licenses that would be required, a process that could take months for each application and involve public hearings in many communities. The application process was assigned to the company's tax department, which was already familiar with obtaining local licensing and ensuring stores adhere to municipal business ordinances. Once the application process was under way, and sometimes even before that process started, a well-planned and well-executed communications program and government affairs outreach program would be essential. The rest of this chapter will focus on the communications program.

PLANNING, IMPLEMENTATION AND EVALUATION

The first step in communications planning was to identify all key stakeholders, anticipate what their concerns were likely to be, and begin to determine appropriate messages for each. In this situation, stakeholders included:

- *Customers.* They would need to know what was changing on the sales floor.

- *The communities in which the stores operated.* What would this mean for their neighborhood?

- *Government officials.* In many cases, their approval would be needed.

- *Walgreens employees.* Store management would need to know about this new product category they will be responsible for. Store employees would have new regulations to follow, and they may have concerns about selling these products. Corporate staff could be asked about Walgreens push into beer and wine by friends and family.

- *Advocacy groups and nongovernment organizations (NGOs).* Some may have concerns about additional retail outlets moving into the category.

- *Shareholders.* Some individuals may avoid investing in companies that sell these products or may question the investment into it.

- *Analysts.* What will the impact be on overall sales, and what kind of returns will it generate?

The core messages, applicable to any of these stakeholders, were summarized in a fact sheet (Appendix A) that could be shared with interested parties such as elected officials, community advocates or consumers.

PREPARING LOCAL PRESENTERS

The process for obtaining liquor licenses varies widely. In some areas, it's a simple matter of filing an application; other cities or counties require the retailer to make a presentation at a public hearing. Because of the sheer number of licenses needed, corporate staff could not handle it alone. Walgreens would rely on local staff—market vice presidents, district managers and individual store managers—to carry its message to their communities and their local government officials.

It was important that market vice presidents and their teams be adequately supported with the tools and information they needed to be effective advocates for the company's position.

In addition to the fact sheet (reproduced in Appendix A), Walgreens prepared a letter to the editor and an op-ed piece that store managers could send to their local newspapers, as well as extensive and detailed internal Q&A documents.

Yet one of the most important communications vehicles was a series of webinars with groups of 5 to 10 members of the store management team attending at a time. These were a collaborative effort by corporate communications, government affairs, store operations, legal and merchandising, and were conducted by corporate communications staff. The webinar explained what to expect at a public hearing, how to prepare, even how to dress. It told the Walgreens representative who would be likely to attend the hearing (residents, neighborhood associations, competitors), and how it is different from a court hearing (no judge, jury or witnesses). It identified potential issues or objections that might be raised, and explained in detail how to respond to each one. The role of Walgreens' representative was simple, but important: explain why the company is requesting the license; how it will handle sales safely and responsibly; how all application requirements have been met; and address any questions and concerns posed by the government officials or other speakers.

An especially important part of the webinar was the tips on how to address issues or concerns from individuals with passionate viewpoints. The strategy laid out in the webinar emphasized the importance of directing the answer to the municipality's council or committee conducting the hearing. Representatives were instructed to focus on what they were able to address factually, and answer the question simply and concisely. They also were trained not to editorialize or to respond with a range of possible solutions. Answers were reviewed that covered a range of topics, including business, moral and community questions.

With advance notice of when these public hearings would take place in communities around the country, corporate communications staff would schedule these webinars as needed, sometimes several sessions within a week, so that the presenters would be trained just before their local hearings. This way, the information would be fresh in their minds. Walgreens store management made hundreds of these presentations over the course of a year. Local management also brought back information on community issues or potential opposition, adding to what the company learned through its routine media monitoring activities.

As local management represented the company at licensing hearings, Walgreens had to decide whether to take a reactive approach to public relations surrounding the application process or to "get in front of the issue" with proactive media outreach. One factor weighing against a proactive approach was that it was difficult to get indications on where a proactive approach was needed to combat opposition. Any significant opposition in a particular community was typically unknown until after the licenses were applied for or the hearings conducted. Only then could a situation be identified where more proactive outreach would be needed (see case study below). And in those cases, outreach was made to local media that focused on clarifying any misconceptions about Walgreens' plan. In most areas, though, the application process did not become a significant issue, and it would have been a mistake to turn it into one through a proactive campaign. The idea was to make this a normal process of running a business, rather than a special initiative that required drumming up supporters and earning third-party endorsements.

CASE STUDY: OVERCOMING OBJECTIONS IN WISCONSIN

THE SITUATION

Walgreens wanted to sell beer and wine in select locations around the Milwaukee metropolitan area, where a prominent newspaper had recently raised awareness and concerns about alcohol abuse.

Wisconsin has long been known for its drinking culture, but in 2008 an award-winning investigative series in the *Milwaukee Journal-Sentinel*, "Wasted in Wisconsin,"[3] showed just how pervasive alcohol abuse was in the state. The newspaper cited government and industry data that ranked Wisconsin number one in binge drinking, percentage of drinkers in the population and driving under the influence. But it was more than dry statistics; the *Journal-Sentinel* profiled 72 people killed by drunk drivers—one for each county in Wisconsin.

Editor Martin Kaiser wrote,

> Our purpose is to increase awareness of a critical issue in our state—the abuse of alcohol and the powerful and destructive impact it has on every segment of the larger community. Awareness can trigger resolve, and resolve can lead us to voluntary steps and changes in the laws that could make Wisconsin a safer place to live.[4]

THE STAKEHOLDERS

In addition to meeting with city leaders, Walgreens decided to engage in a dialogue with the *Milwaukee Journal-Sentinel*. The influential newspaper's support—or disapproval—of its plans would have a major impact on the company's ability to obtain liquor licenses and on public opinion.

As it did in many markets, the company first requested meetings with city leaders to explain its plans in advance, and to enlist their help in determining which store locations would be appropriate for beer and wine sales and which locations would not. But even before the company had formally applied for a license, one Milwaukee alderman publicly raised concerns about Walgreens' entry into beer and wine sales. Early press coverage solicited views from various Milwaukee aldermen, many of whom expressed similar concerns.

ACTIONS TAKEN

With the media quickly engaged on the issue, Walgreens corporate communications staff moved forward with a proactive media plan. Knowing the strength and influence of the *Milwaukee Journal-Sentinel* in the city, the company attempted to frame the licensing debate through a positive editorial stance from the paper. The company was able to arrange for officials from its corporate office and local management to meet with the *Milwaukee Journal-Sentinel*'s editorial board and explain its rationale for beer and wine sales, while emphasizing its history as a responsible retailer. Among the key message points specific to Milwaukee:

- Walgreens planned to apply for licenses at fewer than half of its stores in the city.

- Due to its desire to sell wine, Walgreens would have to apply for full-package liquor licenses, but it was willing to put conditions on the licenses that would limit it from offering spirits.

- Walgreens would not offer single-serving beers, miniatures, pints or half-pints in Milwaukee, which are seen as conducive to alcohol abuse.

- Its selection would include 6-, 12-, 18- and 24-packs of beer and full-size bottles of wine to appeal to casual, moderate beer and wine customers.

- The selection would take up less than 2 percent of store shelf space, so it would not have the feel of a traditional liquor store. This setting for beer and wine sales would be very conducive to Walgreens' typical shoppers, 70 percent of whom are women.

- Walgreens has a very responsible program set up for selling beer and wine, and was currently licensed to sell beer and wine in 45 states.

- Through its pharmacy operations, Walgreens has proven it can operate in a highly regulated environment.

- Many people may not realize that Walgreens also has a long history of responsible sales of alcohol. Up until the early 1990s, most of its stores sold liquor and the company was one of the largest liquor retailers in the country.

The messages got through: an editorial[5] published June 29, 2010, came out in support of Walgreens, as long as liquor licenses were granted on a case-by-case basis. It stated, in part:

> The licensing committee also should take into consideration the benefits of a large chain like Walgreens selling beer and wine. Walgreens is more likely to police its own grounds to prevent loitering and more likely to make sure that its employees are trained in the safe practice of alcohol sales. . . . Walgreens is a trusted name, and we doubt the company will do anything to tarnish its 100-year reputation in the city.

OUTCOMES

This outreach to government officials and the news media helped Walgreens secure all three of the initial beer and wine licenses it sought in Milwaukee, and additional license applications were planned for the future. In addition, by early 2011 Walgreens had more than 30 stores selling beer and wine in the metropolitan area outside the city of Milwaukee.

RESPONSIBLE RETAILING

During the rollout of beer and wine applications across the country, Walgreens had made a point of its history as a responsible retailer. And at times it was called on to reinforce that message in debates with smaller, but very influential, groups. Walgreens communications plan included messaging to respond to these respected, professional groups. And the company ensured it responded to concerns large and small.

For example, a member of a state board of health received a newsletter that strongly criticized Walgreens' entry into beer and wine, but had many of its facts wrong. Rather than taking the newsletter at face value, the board of health member forwarded it to a market vice president he knew at Walgreens asking for clarification. With the help of corporate communications, the executive sent a strong, definitive rebuttal of the article, explaining the company's real strategy. The response from the board of health member: "Thanks for your thoughtful response on this . . . . Our concern is the same as Walgreens: keeping products that may be harmful to youth out of their hands through various safeguards."

Small actions also helped ensure that Walgreens maintained its reputation as a responsible retailer of beer and wine. When a trade publication published a photo of a Duane Reade store in New York City (Walgreens had recently acquired the Duane Reade drugstore chain) showing ping-pong balls for sale next to the beer, the company quickly responded. It realized the merchandising at that store could have been perceived as encouraging customers to play beer pong. Aware that this could create a negative image and hurt its chances of obtaining additional liquor licenses in New York, the company advised its store managers to keep ping-pong balls away from beer and monitor their signage for appropriateness.

And when the Indiana Retail Council (IRC), which had supported Walgreens' permit applications in that state, asked Walgreens to support its campaign to change Indiana law, the company had a decision to make. The IRC was working to overturn the ban on Sunday liquor sales and the ban on the sale of cold beer in drug, grocery and convenience stores (by law, only package liquor stores could sell chilled beer). When asked for advice, corporate communications recommended against displaying the IRC's posters (e.g., "It's time to change Indiana's outdated liquor laws!" and "End the cold beer monopoly") because it might be perceived as promoting alcohol sales to people under 21 who would see the signs prominently displayed at the store entrance. But the IRC's stickers, applied directly to beer and wine ("Ever wonder why you can't buy me on Sundays"), would be appropriate because they would likely only be noticed by those old enough to purchase beer and wine.

Corporate communicators are often called on to advise management about the reputational consequences of various actions, as well as to craft responses to customers, officials and advocates. Because they are in a position to know about a broad range of issues and sensitivities, they can help the company calibrate its public image. Communicators also are sensitive to how a series of small decisions can impact a company's overall image and reputation.

PROMOTING A CONTROL-BRAND BEER

Control-brand products are attractive for retailers (they appeal to value-minded shoppers), are another way to build customer loyalty and are typically more profitable than national brand products. Just as it does with over-the-counter medications and health and beauty products, Walgreens sought to introduce proprietary beer and wine brands in early 2011.

Having gone through the process of obtaining beer and wine licenses—and assuring community leaders across the country that beer and wine would be a small part of its business—Walgreens could have faced a backlash if it aggressively promoted Big Flats 1901, its new control-brand beer. On the other hand, a retailer *is* in the business of selling products and can't afford to be too shy about it.

Corporate communicators can find themselves between competing and equally valid interests. In this case, the category managers responsible for sales of the product were urging a full-scale promotional campaign, while the legal and government affairs teams urged restraint. The company needed to strike the right balance between supporting this control-brand launch and keeping a low profile on the promotion of specific beer/wine products.

Walgreens found a solution by partnering with Winery Exchange, the company that supplied Big Flats 1901 to its stores. Winery Exchange would take the lead and reach out to approximately 20 targeted beer/wine editors and bloggers, introducing Big Flats 1901 and talking about its quality and value. As an additional point of fact, they would state that the beer is available only at Walgreens. The idea was for coverage in the food/beverage trade press to get picked up by mainstream media outlets. That would allow the product to obtain widespread media attention without Walgreens having to directly promote it. To build online interest, Winery Exchange launched a Facebook page for Big Flats 1901, again, mentioning Walgreens only as the retailer that carries it.

The campaign worked exactly as planned. Stories about Big Flats 1901 appeared in more than 30 print publications in the first several weeks, including *Fortune,* the *Wall Street Journal*, the *Chicago Tribune* and the *St. Petersburg Times*. In addition, dozens of television outlets across the country aired reports on the product. It even made an appearance on *The Colbert Report*, where comedian Stephen Colbert made fun of the beer's taste and low price.

From the time the beer began appearing in Walgreens stores in mid-December 2010 until media outreach began in mid-January 2011, the biggest sales day for Big Flats 1901 was on New Year's Eve, 2010. But as soon as media stories started appearing about Big Flats 1901, sales soared. By the last week of January, daily sales of Big Flats 1901 were double their previous high achieved just a month before.

CONNECTING WITH CORPORATE SOCIAL RESPONSIBILITY

Another way Walgreens promoted itself as a responsible retailer of beer and wine was by connecting the sale of a new control-brand wine with its ongoing commitment to community outreach and corporate social responsibility. Walgreens worked with renowned Australian winemaker Daryl Groom to introduce a special wine called Colby Red.

Groom was inspired to create the wine in honor of his 12-year-old son, Colby Rex Groom, who was born with a hole in his heart and has undergone multiple surgeries to treat the defect. By selling the wine nationwide through Walgreens, Groom's intention was to raise awareness of heart disease and support the American Heart Association.

Treasury Wine Estates, parent company of Australian icon Penfolds, where Groom once served as senior red winemaker, and the Groom family pledged to donate a combined $100,000 to the American Heart Association with the first vintage. And as the wine gains acceptance in the market place, the Groom family pledged to increase contributions.

With red wine known to have benefits for heart health and the Groom family's connection with the American Heart Association, all parties involved agreed on a product launch in February 2011 to coincide with American Heart Month. As the product arrived in Walgreens stores across the country, special end-stand displays were rolled out. The product also was supported through special mention in Walgreens' Sunday newspaper insert.

Going beyond traditional paid media, Walgreens worked with Treasury Wine Estates to promote the product to media outlets. Outreach was conducted to both trade publications and mainstream media. More than 20 print outlets picked up the story, including Gannett News Service. In addition, the story was pitched to NBC's *Today Show*, which enthusiastically followed up. The show interviewed the Groom family in California and filmed the product at a local Walgreens store just after the special product display was rolled out. The Groom family also was interviewed live on the show when the story aired later that month.

During the interview, *Today Show*[6] cohost Savannah Guthrie said:

The father and son made about 50 cases of red wine together. They called their creation Colby Red. But when Daryl shared the story with one of his buyers, it turned into something more.

Daryl Groom: "When Walgreens came to us and said they wanted to sponsor us, then it became a bigger project. Our first bottling we did is 20,000 cases."

Guthrie: "The goal now, continue making Colby Red and raise funds for organizations that support heart research."

EVALUATION

Walgreens achieved its goal of developing a beer and wine offering that was acceptable to the vast majority of communities across the country, effectively communicated that offering to various stakeholders and contributed to its overall business objectives.

Over an 18-month period, Walgreens participated in hundreds of public hearings, spoke with hundreds of elected officials and community activists, responded to more than 200 media inquiries, was the subject of more than 1,200 print publication stories during the rollout period, and ultimately began selling beer and wine in more than 5,500 stores.

News coverage was generally neutral in tone, with several noteworthy positive stories, such as the editorial in the *Milwaukee Journal-Sentinel* that helped pave the way for license approvals in that city, and the *Today Show* story on Colby Red that pointed out Walgreens' community outreach efforts through its partnership with the Groom family.

Once the rollout of beer and wine was completed to the majority of stores planned to receive it, the category was credited with significantly adding to Walgreens' overall comparable store sales. In the retail industry, comparable store sales are considered a key indicator of sales growth. The metric includes only stores that have been open for at least one year, so it discounts any sales growth created by additional new locations. In the second quarter of fiscal year 2011, Walgreens front-end (or nonpharmacy) comparable store sales increased 4.3 percent. Beer and wine alone were credited with adding more than three-quarters of a percentage point to that number—a significant impact from just one product category.

Financial analysts, one of the key stakeholders identified early on in the communications plan, viewed the move into beer and wine positively. In fact, stated *the Wall Street Journal* in a June 3, 2010, article, "Credit Suisse Group analyst Edward Kelly said the company's beer and wine effort appears to be doing 'extremely well' and should have been done 'a long time ago.'"

Walgreens' Big Flats 1901 control-brand beer also was received positively by analysts. A Fortune.com article on Feb. 8, 2011, said, "BB&T Capital Markets analyst Andrew Wolf says that in addition to generating incremental sales, Big Flats 1901 will create what he calls a 'value impression' over Walgreens' whole beer category."

Looking at how the communications of Walgreens' beer and wine offering was conducted and the results that were achieved, it is important to keep in mind that even though Walgreens is ranked among the 50 largest companies on the Fortune 500 list, much of the communications took place in one-on-one or small group discussions in stores and town halls across America.

That was consistent with Walgreens focus on being a community drugstore. With two-thirds of the U.S. population within three miles of one of its stores, Walgreens emphasizes products and services that are relevant to the local community. In support of its community outreach, Walgreens created a new position in 2008 called a Community Leader—a store manager who also would be in charge of involving a handful of nearby stores in their local communities. This includes getting involved in local events and seeking out products from local vendors. In fact, Community Leaders are measured in part on the community events in which their area stores participate. The Community Leader also serves as a mentor for other store managers in the area.

As liaisons to their communities, Community Leaders were often the first ones approached to represent Walgreens at licensing hearings. The critical role of corporate communications was to give these local representatives the information and preparation they needed to represent the company to their individual communities.

LOOKING AHEAD

When considering today's social and economic trends, Walgreens is communicating to key healthcare stakeholders that it is well positioned to play an even greater role in America's health care system, while also continuing to meet the daily living needs of its customers.

Our aging population is driving growth in Walgreens' traditional prescription business. The average person over 65 years fills 31 prescriptions a year, and 3.6 million people are turning 65 each year. Some 45 percent of all Americans take some type of medication for a chronic condition. In addition, the healthcare reform law signed in 2010 will give an additional 32 million people access to care by 2014, which will stretch an already taxed primary care physician network. Walgreens can fill the gap. With its community pharmacists, nurse practitioners at worksite health centers and retail clinics, and multichannel offerings through both online and mail services, Walgreens has an integrated, national network of 70,000 healthcare service providers that is prepared to meet the challenges of healthcare reform.

One way Walgreens wants to address America's future health needs is by transforming the role of its community pharmacists. The company is providing greater opportunities for its pharmacists to interact with patients by streamlining their workload, redesigning pharmacy layouts to promote more face-to-face conversations and expanding their scope of services.

The company also is increasing its efforts at improving health outcomes and demonstrating the value of its healthcare services through sophisticated analytical information. With this data, Walgreens client service and sales organization can customize programs and capabilities to large and small employers, health plans, pharmacy benefit managers, health systems and government agencies.

Walgreens' organizational goal is to be America's first choice for health and daily living needs. As the most convenient place already to get a prescription filled, the company is expanding its wellness offerings to include vaccinations, blood pressure checks, services such as a strep throat test from a nurse practitioner and personal advice from a healthcare professional.

Preventing and managing chronic medical conditions are the biggest challenges confronting America's healthcare system. Walgreens wants to lead the way by offering innovative programs that can change how patients manage their prescriptions for conditions like diabetes and other chronic illnesses. One such program is offering 90-day supplies of medication through the patient's local Walgreens community pharmacist. This program makes it more convenient for patients to stay compliant with their prescriptions.

Through these offerings, Walgreens seeks to help millions of patients "get well, stay well and live well." And it wants to be at the top of the list for places to get daily necessities, whether that is a greeting card, a cleaning product, fresh food for that evening's dinner or a bottle of wine to go with it.

As it moves into these new product and service offerings, Walgreens must always consider the viewpoints of its stakeholders, and how they will perceive the changes. It must anticipate and overcome objections, including those from competitors threatened by Walgreens' entry into their markets and NGOs concerned about the impact on their particular cause. And it must effectively communicate its strategies through media outreach, government outreach, social media and the channel that has been and always will be the most effective—face-to-face meetings.

APPENDIX A

WALGREENS

FACT SHEET: Reintroducing Beer and Wine Sales at Walgreens

OVERVIEW

Directly responding to customer demand, Walgreens will bring back a modest selection of beer and wine for sale in stores throughout the country. Our customers want more of a one-stop shopping experience where they can buy a range of products at one location rather than having to travel, park and pay at a variety of different stores. Given our convenient locations and reputation as a trusted retailer, Walgreens is an attractive alternative for the sale of wine and beer.

Walgreens has extensive experience managing the sale of regulated products with strict controls, like our medications. We also have a strong history of serving our communities as a responsible retailer, and we look forward to upholding that commitment with the reintroduction of beer and wine.

HISTORY

Walgreens has successfully merchandised and sold alcoholic beverages since the end of Prohibition. Although profitable, many managers found the category cumbersome and time consuming to maintain, so it was discontinued in the majority of stores in the 1990s. Now, with a scaled back offering and inventory technology advancements, we have the increased ability to safely and efficiently resume beer and wine sales while maintaining our high standards for responsible retailing.

PRODUCT ASSORTMENT

Beer and wine will make up a small portion of each eligible store. Walgreens' modest selection of these products will occupy less than 2 percent of the total shelf space—one product line among thousands of other products you would expect in a drugstore. Beer and wine will make up less than 5 percent of our total sales.

- The proposed assortment has been refined to appeal to casual, moderate beer and wine drinkers as an additional Walgreens convenience.

- The beer selection will consist of 6 packs, 12 packs, 18 packs and cases only. There will be no single servings or any other variation that would be considered conducive to alcohol abuse.

- The selection will be value to mid-priced. Walgreens will also work with local beer and wine producers to customize our selection with local products. Local vendor participation will continue to grow in the future.

OPERATIONAL CONTROLS AND EMPLOYEE TRAINING

Walgreens has taken great measures to assure that any beverage containing alcohol will be sold in a responsible and appropriate manner. Detailed policies and procedures are already in place and will be strictly enforced *without exception.*

- Employees must undergo extensive training prior to beer and wine availability at each store.

- Walgreens policy states that employees must request identification for any customer attempting to purchase alcohol who appears to be under the age of 40. Register prompts ensure compliance before proceeding with the transaction.

- Underage employees will not handle the selling or stocking of alcohol products.

DISCUSSION QUESTIONS

1. Why is it important for customers to understand why a retailer is adding or discontinuing a product category? What would have happened if customers didn't think beer and wine belonged at Walgreens?
2. What are the risks and benefits of having local store management represent the company at public hearings, rather than someone from the corporate office?
3. Did Walgreens take an unnecessary risk by seeking a positive editorial from the Milwaukee newspaper? What if the editorial board wasn't convinced of the company's arguments?
4. For the most part, customers welcomed beer and wine at Walgreens; however, the company did receive occasional complaints from customers and activists. Would you respond to them, and if so, how?
5. Do you think corporate communicators should have a say in a company's business decisions, or should they be limited to communicating the decision? What do you think their role should be?
6. How do corporate communicators balance competing interests within the company?
7. With Facebook and other social media more entrenched in many peoples' daily lives today, how might you use those platforms in a similar campaign today?
8. To what extent can a company engage its employees as brand ambassadors, especially for controversial issues or crises?

NOTES

1. Jim Cramer, "An Alibi to Sneeze At," TheStreet.com, 27 March 2000.
2. "Internet Victims," *PC Computing Magazine*, February 2000.
3. Staff reporters, "Wasted in Wisconsin," *Milwaukee Journal-Sentinel*, 2008 series http://www.jsonline.com/news/30565984.html.

4. "Series Puts Focus on Excessive Drinking - JSOnline." Milwaukee Journal Sentinel - Breaking News, Sports, Business, Watchdog Journalism, Multimedia in Wisconsin. Web. 19 Nov. 2011. http://www.json line.com/news/wisconsin/31206499.html.

5. Editorial Board, "Push for Alcohol," *Milwaukee Journal-Sentinel*, 29 June 2010 http://www.jsonline.com/news/opinion/97428554.html.

6. *Today Show*, NBC, 21 February 2011.

ADDITIONAL READING

Gerzema, John, and Michael D'Antonio. *Spend Shift—How the Post-Crisis Values Revolution Is Changing the Way We Buy, Sell, and Live* (San Francisco: Jossey-Bass/A Wiley Imprint, 2011).

41

C H A P T E R

THE PHARMACEUTICAL INDUSTRY
From Promotion to Constituency Relations

Elliot S. Schreiber, Ph.D.
Clinical Professor of Marketing and Executive Director
Center for Corporate Reputation Management
Bennett S. LeBow College of Business
Drexel University

A CHANGING PHARMACEUTICAL INDUSTRY CREATES NEW CHALLENGES FOR STRATEGIC PUBLIC RELATIONS

The pharmaceutical industry is in a state of flux and is undergoing tremendous change. Much of this change is due to increased pressure to control healthcare costs in general and the cost of drugs in particular. The industry feels like it is under siege from patients, insurance companies and governmental regulators.

These pressures have created a new market environment for the industry and, with it, the need for new public relations practices. In the current environment, and particularly since the advent of the Internet, patients have increasingly become self-educated and have changed the patient–physician dynamic. In turn, the physician has been asking for more from the pharmaceutical industry and the industry has been looking for new ways to communicate, not only to retain its relationships with doctors, but also to build new relationships with patients.

Most pharmaceutical companies historically have research and development (R&D) and sales organizations. They developed a drug, patented the drug and then gave it to its sales team to "detail" to physicians, in hopes that they will prescribe it to their patients.

The pharmaceutical industry is changing, but change is difficult. Until the early part of the twenty-first century, the pharmaceutical industry was one of the most profitable of any industry. It was the "darling" of Wall Street. In the past decade, growth has slowed and companies have had to cut costs, consolidate and merge for greater efficiencies and broader pipelines. The challenge, then, for pharmaceutical public relations professionals is great, both for internal and external communications.

For decades, the route to profitability for pharmaceutical companies was to develop a so-called "blockbuster" drug, which traditionally has been a drug with sales in excess of $1 billion. This objective has become more difficult. The cost of developing such blockbusters is enormous. Lower profits have made investments in R&D more difficult, and pressures from investors to increase profitability have lead to more cost-cutting versus increased investments.

In addition, and perhaps most importantly from a public relations perspective, the entire value proposition of the industry has come under challenge. The industry had been able to explain the high cost of medications as the result of the huge investments and timeline needed to bring new drugs to market. These costs can run as high as $800 million and the time frame can be 12 years for most drugs, with many failing in their final phase of development. The risks are high; the returns had to be high.

The search for drug pipelines has moved from inside to outside. As companies have found their own pipelines insufficient and the need for organic growth more difficult, they have turned to mergers and acquisitions. Between 2005 and 2010, the industry saw a major consolidation. Some of the more noteworthy mergers included Pfizer's acquisition of Wyeth, Merck's merger with Schering-Plough and Roche's acquisition of Genentech.

With an aging population, increasingly sensitive to the costs of pharmaceuticals, that value proposition has been challenged. It is no longer as well accepted. It is shocking that an industry that does so much for society is now challenged to explain itself and is losing the confidence and trust of much of the public. In fact, the reputation of the pharmaceutical industry is among the lowest of all industries, ahead of only oil, chemicals, utilities and tobacco.

As the public has become more sensitive to the costs of pharmaceuticals, there has been an increasing interest in generic drugs. Generics had traditionally been the "bane of existence" of the pharmaceutical industry. They were viewed as "vultures" waiting in the wings for a drug to go off patent. The industry tried to convince the doctor and patient that these were lesser copies of the original, branded pharmaceutical. To enhance this argument, the Pharmaceutical Manufacturers Association (PMA) changed its name to Pharmaceutical Research Manufacturers Associations (PhRMA) in 1994. However, the costs of drugs has put pressures on insurance programs to lower the costs of health insurance, and they have become active in promoting generics, incentivizing both the patient and the pharmacist to switch the patient to a generic, if one is available.

While the diminished reputation of the industry creates a major public relations challenge, it is made more difficult by the industry's traditional branding strategies. Most of the energy and resources go toward branding individual products rather than the corporation. As a result, companies are perceived as being the same—large R&D organizations making drugs for a variety of illnesses. Even physicians know little about the individual companies because the sales people spend their time with doctors talking about the drug and not the capabilities of the company behind the drug. With relatively little communication with the general public and much of the desired communication restricted by regulations, the industry is looking for new ways to regain the confidence and trust of the public.

THE NEW CONSTITUENCY RELATIONS FOCUS

The changes in pharmaceutical public relations have been tremendous. Until the early 1990s, pharmaceutical public relations primarily supported marketing communications and direct promotion of products to doctors. However, public relations has become more complex and heavily issue-oriented as the pressures on the industry continue to grow. It must now be more strategically integrated into decision-making processes, more aligned with long-term business objectives, and able to meet the new challenges of a highly regulated and increasingly competitive healthcare marketplace. As a result, more public relations departments in pharmaceutical companies are gaining responsibility for issues management, public affairs and relationships with key opinion leaders, including trade organizations and regulatory bodies.

With the rise of managed care and healthcare reform, new challenges include designing meaningful responses to marketplace and government developments.

Pharmaceutical companies must identify the nontraditional audiences that are driving these developments and affecting business through legislation, public policy and public opinion. A company must then gain an appreciation of the needs and motivations of these audiences to ensure that messages speak directly to the values of each targeted group. This need to address new audiences has moved pharmaceutical public relations away from its marketing communications or financial relations orientation toward a more strategic constituency relations focus.

An important step in understanding pharmaceutical public relations' sharpened focus on constituency relations is to recognize that manufacturers have been thrust from a traditional business and market environment into a highly charged political environment. As the industry's environment changes, so too does the number of its constituents and the complexities of its relationships among them. As a result, many pharmaceutical companies are struggling to realign and refocus their public relations activities, focusing increasingly on public policy and public affairs.

In this new world, companies must quickly elevate the role of public relations and recognize that powerful forces—policymakers, patient and public interest advocates, managed care groups, activists and the media—are taking control and exerting greater influence on the business of selling pharmaceuticals. These groups, among others, accuse the industry of indifference toward patients, price gouging and deprivation of patients who are poor or lack insurance of the medicines their physicians prescribe.

Such scrutiny requires sensitivity toward and a complete understanding of constituency relations. Where PR professionals once used communications to help brand management increase market share, they now, like politicians, must use more targeted, interactive communications to address their constituents' needs. Whereas they sought message control in the past, they must now exchange information and ideas and establish, build and nurture relationships. Market share alone will no longer be the tool to measure leadership. Constituents will reward companies that create dialogue and consensus with the respect and trust that is essential for conducting business today. With this trust, publics will, to a certain degree, give corporations the benefit of the doubt regarding product value, marketing practices, prices and profits. Constituents will give manufacturers permission to continue in the business of selling drugs.

One of the major issues facing PR professionals in the pharmaceutical industry is the restriction on the use of social media for Food and Drug Administration (FDA)-regulated drugs that continue to handicap the industry. While patients and an increasing number of younger physicians use the Internet for search, blogging and social media for information about drugs, diseases and therapeutic treatments, companies are typically restricted by their legal departments from participating in these channels for fear of sharing information that abridges appropriate FDA drug communications. All communications about a drug are required to also carry all of the information about side effects. Fearing that the company cannot control information appropriately in social media, lawyers often prefer noncommunications. This has meant that pharmaceutical companies are unable to dialog with patients and their families in ways available to other industries.

PUTTING THINGS IN PERSPECTIVE

Until recently, the pharmaceutical industry's overall charter was to develop and market products to support its primary customer, the prescribing physician. Issues of payment were of little concern: patients and insurance companies dealt with payment, with very little involvement by doctors.

It was the industry's role to develop and manufacture drugs and educate physicians. It was the doctor's role to prescribe and counsel patients on how to use the medicine. This relationship between company and doctor continued well into the 1980s, when increasingly high profit margins brought pharmaceutical companies into the public spotlight.

In the new marketing environment, pharmaceutical companies must fundamentally change the way they communicate and do business. Companies are being forced to manage operations within a highly charged political environment that holds them accountable for the cost of care. Companies must learn how to effectively respond to widespread criticism and public policy and public opinion pressures, and learn how to leverage their responses for business advantage.

Simply put, cost sensitivity is redefining the role of pharmaceutical public relations. The cost-effectiveness of therapeutics, for example, in addition to safety and efficacy, has become key to all communications and marketing. The value of each product must now be demonstrated to a diverse group of audiences (or new customer bases) such as providers, patients and payers. Moreover, since prevention and wellness measures, as opposed to therapeutic treatment of illness, are encouraged to reduce the financial strains on the healthcare system, and more patients are being forced to take responsibility for their health, PR can no longer exclusively focus on product attributes. The human factor or human value of health care must become part of the message and communications process. In addition, the traditional value proposition for the cost of pharmaceuticals (that a typical drug takes 12 years from inception to commercialization, at a cost of about $800 million) no longer has the same weight with either the public or politicians. Unless the industry can communicate its value and the value proposition of pharmaceuticals, the reputation of the industry will continue to suffer, and with that will come calls for increased regulation.

With patients, and all constituents, pharmaceutical communications must have four strategic dimensions. PR today must: (1) involve and form relationships with audiences to demonstrate commitment; (2) redefine questions and concerns in the context of cost-effectiveness and social value; (3) share emotion and the human value of the industry; and (4) demonstrate integrity to assure all publics that the industry acts to serve the social needs of the country.

From a public relations perspective, the Internet has changed the dynamic of communications for the pharmaceutical industry, just as it has with all industries. However, the industry is more restricted in its use of social media than perhaps any other industry.

A major change influenced by the Internet is in the physician–patient relationship. Patients now visit a physician with information about their illness and the possible treatment. There is a joke among doctors that by the time a patient now sees them they already have had a second opinion from the Internet. Social communities have formed on the Internet of consumers with a variety of health interests and issues. Some of these are formed by "disease organizations" such as the American Heart Association and American Cancer Society, among others. Other sites have been formed by patients themselves looking to find a community of others who share their disease, in order to share information about treatment options. The advent of sites like WebMD has spawned others to provide medical information that previously was only available from a personal visit to a physician.

The pharmaceutical industry is hampered compared with other industries in their dealings with social media. Patients are out there looking for information but the industry is restricted from communicating with the patient about drugs by the FDA, unless they provide information that is full and complete, including all of the potential side effects and counterindications.

THE INDUSTRY RESTRUCTURES

In the early 1990s, the pharmaceutical industry began a fundamental restructuring that had already occurred in many other industries. In the year 1993 alone, the U.S.-based industry lost approximately $100 billion in market value and cut nearly 35,000 jobs. Many have blamed this on President Clinton's healthcare reforms; however, this restructuring mirrored developments in both the public and private sectors. The factor that initiated most of the restructuring was not healthcare reform—an industry does not downsize on the threat of change—but rather the growing forces of cost sensitivity on the part of the payers in the system. The patient, or the public, was not a major component of this bottom line–driven mission and method of business.

The restructuring of the industry continued through the later part of the 1990s and into the new century. Then, beginning in about 2008–2009, the industry began consolidating. This was inevitable from a market perspective, but shocking nonetheless. The pharmaceutical industry was one of the only major industries that continued to have so many players doing essentially the same thing, i.e., spending similar amounts on R&D and developing drugs, many copies of others, with little differentiation among the various companies. This changed with the mergers of many major companies, including Pfizer's acquisition of Wyeth, Merck's acquisition of Schering-Plough and Roche's acquisition of Genentech. The mergers occurred for scale, cost efficiencies and to acquire needed drug pipelines.

At the same time, the focus of many companies in the industry started to change, primarily as a result of greater cost sensitivity. The modus operandi of most large pharmaceutical companies had always been to seek a blockbuster drug, which traditionally has been defined as a drug with sales of at least $1 billion per year. Many companies began to question the wisdom of this objective in light of the large R&D budget it required. Many companies instead focused on therapeutic areas where they could make money more quickly and recoup their return on their R&D investment.

GOVERNMENT CONTROL OF HEALTHCARE SPENDING

The pressures on pharmaceuticals are a continuation of a trend begun in the 1970s, when the U.S. Congress began to consider legislation to control rising hospital spending (then, as now, the largest segment of healthcare expenditures). This led to the American Hospital Association's "Voluntary Effort to Contain Hospital Costs," which worked until congressional pressure subsided. The Congress then passed the Tax Equity and Fiscal Responsibility Act of 1982, which introduced the Prospective Payment System (PPS) into health care.

The PPS created the DRG (diagnosis-related group) method of payment. DRGs are a patient classification system used not only for reimbursement but also for quality control, budgeting and planning. Under current legislation, patients are placed in a DRG based on their primary and secondary diagnoses as determined at discharge from the hospital, and other factors including age, discharge status and surgical procedures required. Payment rates for each diagnosis are set in advance, and the hospital is paid only that amount regardless of services rendered. All costs in excess of the DRG are absorbed by the hospital. Conversely, the institution retains the full payment if costs are lower than the DRG rate.

The objective was to drive down costs sustained by the federal government, namely, those covered by Medicare, but it was also intended to be a model for the private sector to follow.

Healthcare costs as a percentage of the gross domestic product (GDP) approached 17 percent in 2010. There are economists who believe that the United States could be spending 20 percent of GDP on health care within 10 years, unless the industry is reformed. Although pharmaceuticals account for only 7 percent of the total, overall healthcare costs, there continues to be greater sensitivity about the cost of pharmaceuticals than almost any other segment of the healthcare industry. Much of this is attributable to the profits made by pharmaceutical companies, but much also stems from the fact that health insurance covers a larger percentage of the price of delivery of healthcare (e.g., doctors' visits and hospital stays) than it does for therapeutics. For example, in Canada and other countries in which there is universal health care and government controls on the cost of pharmaceutics, there is less public outcry over the cost of pharmaceuticals and more of a concern about access to doctors, medical diagnostics and treatment, since delivery is regulated and "metered" by the government.

PRIVATE SECTOR INITIATIVES

The changes that have occurred in the medical delivery system, and which are likely to continue, have been brought about more by private industry than by government. Uwe Reinhart, James Madison professor of economics at Princeton University, has suggested that the pharmaceutical industry might be better off in the long run with a heavy government hand than with megapurchasers in the private sector, simply because the government has an interest in the industry's viability as a research enterprise. He has indicated that he would rather deal with the government's Office of Management and Budget Director than with a CEO who wants to cut healthcare costs for his or her company. The same might be said for mayors and governors who are bearing the costs of increasing healthcare expenditures for public employees who are increasingly aging and retiring and straining the budgets of municipalities and states. Their aggressive actions to control costs might exceed that of the federal government.

This, of course, was not always so. Less than a decade ago, drug companies ran a fairly simple business. They discovered and marketed drugs, which they priced at a premium, and watched profits roll in. However, with the rise of managed health care in the United States, drug companies have come under increasing pressure to bring their prices down. These developments began in the early 1980s with the growth of health maintenance organizations and other managed care practices. Companies, sensitive to the effect of the escalating cost of medical benefits on the bottom line, began to change their employee benefits policies. Companies that could do so initiated healthcare benefits changes that required employees to increase their co-payment for medical treatments.

At the same time, companies in many areas began to form alliances to pressure local hospitals and doctors to control their prices. Companies began providing to their employees a list of "qualified" doctors in the local area who would perform tests, surgery or other procedures within prescribed pricing parameters. Doctors whose fees were outside of these boundaries were blacklisted.

Companies got serious about bringing down the costs of health care when the cost of medical benefits became the third-largest employee cost for many companies, trailing only salaries and vacations. The involvement by companies, in turn, began to effect changes in the system. As hospital costs were squeezed, the marketing environment changed. The purchasing agent within the hospital became the most important decision maker.

Radiologists had less involvement in the decision as to which x-ray film and equipment to buy; pathologists had less input into the decision as to which medical diagnostic system to buy. As a result, companies that had focused efforts on improving the quality of their x-ray film had to focus increasingly on cost; diagnostic companies which had fallen over one another to add more tests to their instruments to make them competitively more attractive had to think of the bottom line. Company benefits managers also began insisting that employees seek generic alternatives to ethical drugs and that second opinions be sought on elective surgeries. The focus on generics, in particular, had a dramatic impact on the industry.

The pharmaceutical and diagnostic companies were slow to change their marketing and communications activities despite these changes in the industry. Pharmaceutical salesmen, or the so-called "detail men," continued to call on physicians to tout their new drugs; diagnostic companies manufactured instruments with reagents that were exclusive to their systems and could not be interchanged with another. The industry continued until recently to see its role as developing and selling drugs. Public relations professionals within pharmaceutical companies were marketing-focused, finding new ways to attract attention to their products. All along, however, there was little attention paid to cost since, by and large, this continued to be passed on to the customer who could, in turn, pass the costs along to someone else.

THE INDUSTRY DEFENDS ITSELF

Although all of these market changes have been in place for a long time, it was during the Clinton Administration that government officials began to publicly question the primary motivation of the pharmaceutical industry. Was the industry motivated by an interest in the health of its patients or by profits? Would they sacrifice the former for the latter? By raising these questions, one could argue that administration officials were providing their own answers. President Clinton made it okay to question whether it was appropriate for the pharmaceutical industry to make money on its drugs. Some of these arguments were potentially dangerous. For example, one member of the healthcare advisory team put together by First Lady Hillary Rodham Clinton and Judith Feder of Georgetown University suggested that the pharmaceutical industry should be regulated like a public utility.

In response to the growing focus on industry profits, the pharmaceutical industry ramped up its public relations efforts, arguing that, while the public focused on the cost of drugs, pharmaceuticals actually save money since they frequently treat people outside of the hospital and are, in fact, often the reason the patient did not have to be hospitalized.

Moreover, the industry pointed out that it costs, on average, $250–800 million to bring an ethical drug to market, and even more for a genetically engineered pharmaceutical. Although drugs might be costly, the reimbursement was argued to be fair given the enormous investment and time, as much as 12 years, until a drug cleared FDA approval. Moreover, although a successful drug might bring large profits, few people recognized how much money and time the industry had lost with research efforts that did not bear fruit.

Companies engaged in research also pointed out that the companies that made generics did not have to bear these costs. Often, the greatest investment by generic companies was in patent attorneys who challenged the patents of existing drugs prior to patent expiration, sometimes successfully. These companies had little or no research investment. They only formulated and sold products at a lower price. What escaped scrutiny, however, was that these generic companies' margins often were equal to those of the research-based pharmaceutical companies.

What the entire industry failed to understand was that they were arguing facts against mounting perceptions to the contrary. As any student of marketing knows, fact and perception are one and the same in the marketplace.

The Clinton initiatives were defeated, yet the concern about pharmaceutical pricing and the value proposition of the industry remained active, even though below the surface. With the aging population, pressures started to mount on mayors and governors throughout the United States for ways to control healthcare costs. Although the administration of George W. Bush addressed changes in Medicare, it did not allow insurance companies or municipalities to challenge the costs of medicines.

In 2008, both Hillary Clinton and Barack Obama challenged each other during the presidential primaries on how drastic changes to healthcare legislation should be. The Republicans offered tax incentives, but did not want to impact the total healthcare insurance plans in the country. Shortly after Obama was elected president,

BOX 41-1 GLOBAL STRATEGY

Managed care represents about 50 percent of all U.S. pharmaceutical sales, more than double what it had been 20 years ago. As a consequence, the industry downsized its existing operations while, at the same time, going on a buying spree for multisource (i.e., generic) pharmaceutical companies. One of the largest buys was Merck's $6 billion acquisition of Medco Containment. SmithKline bought Diversified Pharmaceutical Services for $2.3 billion. Bayer Corporation chose not to purchase outright but to invest about $310 million to buy a 28 percent stake in Schein Pharmaceutical, one of the largest generic operations, with the option to purchase the company in total after seven years. The creation of Novartis AG from the merger of Ciba-Geigy and Sandoz created a two-sided company: Novartis, which is a traditional big pharmaceutical company, and Sandoz, a generic products company. At the same time, generic companies like Israel's Teva Pharmaceuticals, appear to be moving toward "the middle," that is, toward areas that were traditionally the purview of research-based pharmaceutical companies.

With the purchase of Genentech by Roche in 2008, the industry began to see what the future would look like. The traditional delineation of biotechnology, research-based pharmaceuticals and generics began to morph into a more consolidated industry. Companies recognized that from the customer perspective, it did not matter how the drug was created. What mattered is that the drug was available. In addition, the scale economics of pharmaceuticals began to unravel. The industry's traditional focus on the development of blockbuster drugs led to leaner pipelines. The money being spent to develop a blockbuster (i.e., a drug with sales in excess of $1 billion per year) drained the R&D pool to expand the pipeline. This, in turn, created concerns on Wall Street, which no longer saw the industry as a good investment.

At the same time, the nature of pharmaceutical sales began to change. The FDA began to question the meals and gifts that pharmaceutical companies gave to physicians. To steer clear of problematic issues, many teaching hospitals barred pharmaceutical sales people from calling on physicians and pharmaceutical companies volunteered to scale back the gifts given to doctors.

As 2010 came to a close, it ended a tumultuous time in the entire healthcare industry, but particularly for pharmaceutical companies. All market factors continued to point to still more turmoil to come.

European companies also were acquired. Bristol-Myers Squibb went into generics in Europe by buying 25 percent of Germany's Azupharma.

---

the Democrats passed the most sweeping change to healthcare delivery and insurance in the nation's history. About 30 million uninsured people were given health insurance; children were covered to a greater degree, and up to 26 years of age, if still covered by their parents; and it made it illegal for insurance companies to deny insurance for "preexisting conditions."

Interestingly, during the debates on healthcare legislation, it was the insurance industry and not the pharmaceutical industry that was the target of anger. The pharmaceutical industry offered its support to the president in exchange for assurances that drug prices would not be capped or challenged in the legislation. With the mid-term elections of November 2010, the healthcare legislation was one of the most hotly contested issues, particularly for Republicans who ran on promises of repealing the legislations, which they called "Obamacare." Although they had little chance of actually repealing the legislation, given the general support in the Senate and the veto ability of the president, health care once again promises to be a hot issue in the 2012 election.

Regardless of what legislation is offered, some fundamental issues remain. The aging population continues to increase concerns about the cost of drugs in the United States. Cities and states, faced with increasing numbers of Medicare/Medicaid enrollees, continue to face greater strain on already strained budgets. In addition, as the baby boomers, the largest single age cohort, began to retire, they further strained the budgets of companies and municipalities. By the early part of the new century, mayors and governors, including Mayor Bloomberg of New York City and Governor Arnold Schwarzenegger of California, began to call for importation of drugs from Canada, where pharmaceuticals are less expensive. The issue for the elected officials was the rising cost of prescription drugs for an increasingly older population, which was putting pressure on Medicare and Medicaid at the federal, state and local levels, as well as the growing ranks of retiring unionized public employees who had lucrative healthcare policies.

The industry in the United States began focusing on safety of importation, but "Pandora's box" had been opened. The AARP took up the importation issue and many on-line pharmacies began to emerge. However, the most problematic result of the Canadian drug price issue was that the mirror was turned back on the U.S. drug industry with more intense questions about why Americans pay prices so much higher than citizens of other countries. The value proposition that had served the industry for so long, i.e., cost of drug development, was unraveling further.

A number of drug company CEOs and the PhRMA, the industry's primary trade association, began a major public relations campaign arguing that the United States was actually subsidizing drug prices in other countries and that without the higher prices of U.S. drugs, the United States would no longer be the innovation center for new drugs. Although this argument had some resonance with Congress, it did little to placate the average American consumer.

In short, public relations professionals found themselves without a message that resonated with the public or with public officials equally well.

RESPONSE TO THE NEW FOCUS ON COST

It is interesting to note that the arguments of the pharmaceutical industry have continued to be the same. Usually, if someone uses an argument for more than 20 years and discovers that it still has not convinced the audience, one changes the message. That, regrettably, was not what the industry did. For much of the time, the arguments were being made to members of Congress who could not muster enough public support to force changes in the healthcare system—we do, in fact, have in the United States the world's finest system, for those who can afford it. However, the industry did not recognize that the audience had changed. The audience now was composed of corporate benefits managers, hospital purchasing agents, and others of similar background. The message of recovering research costs was no longer appropriate.

By 1994, the unique selling proposition had become cost. As a result, the industry began to go through a restructuring and downsizing as margins were squeezed. Still, the reactions by the industry have been slow, with most companies expecting that better times would return. By the year 2000, it was clear to most companies that they had to get used to a "new normal."

Acquiring generic companies was the strategic direction chosen by some research-oriented companies. In times of uncertainty and change, there are a variety of market movements and mergers. Merck set the direction for most companies through its acquisition of a generics and distribution company, Medco, whereas the giant Swiss pharmaceutical company, Roche Holdings, decided to integrate horizontally by acquiring an ethical pharmaceutical company, Syntex, for $5.3 billion. Time will tell which was the right strategy.

"What is interesting here," notes financial analyst Sam Isaly of Mehta and Isaly, "is that you have the world's largest pharmaceutical company in terms of market cap betting one way, and the world's second largest, Merck, betting the opposite view."[1]

This merger fever has involved both U.S. and foreign companies. Everyone, it seems, is responding to what financial analyst Arvind Desai of Mehta and Isaly calls a "global trend toward frugal health care."

SLOW CHANGES IN PUBLIC RELATIONS TACTICS

The shifts in the competitive environment, coupled with healthcare reform proposals, wreaked havoc on the industry. Public relations messages and marketing techniques have not kept pace. It is easy to understand why it took a while for the industry to combat its critics effectively. Unlike the chemical and oil industries that have had to deal with decades of criticism, public scrutiny and regulation, the pharmaceutical industry found it difficult to cope with the public's skepticism and distrust. Yes, some critics argued the industry needed money for research, but why so much? Why, people argued, does the industry need to grow 25 percent per year "on the backs of sick people"?

The Obama Administration's attacks on the healthcare system found the industry unprepared and disjointed in its response, unlike the chemical industry. Years of Superfund and chemical phobia had helped shape the Chemical Manufacturers Association (CMA) into an organization with strong involvement by the industry's CEOs, who spent considerable time formulating common industry positions. The CMA slowly transformed itself from a group of independent-thinking companies with only a few outward-thinking leaders like Du Pont, Dow, and Monsanto, into an organization with significant resources spent on communications and public education. In contrast, the PhRMA, formerly the PMA, remained a group of free and separately thinking executives. Little effort was given to public education; the organization was more reactionary. Whereas national meetings of the CMA concerned themselves with issues updates and trends, PhRMA's agenda was still primarily social. One might question why the industry had not changed given the fact that they had been united in fighting the Clinton Administration's attempts at health care reform in the 1990s. One reason is that the intervening years lulled the industry into complacency. Health care reform was talked about, but it never materialized in the United States.

The Obama Administration got health care reform through Congress by changing the "boogeyman" from the pharmaceutical industry to the insurance industry. Although the drug industry had some rationale for their costs, the insurance industry was much more vulnerable. As a whole, the industry has a poor reputation. In the healthcare area, the industry had made money by denying at risk people and group insurance. In other words, it insured those who were less likely to need insurance. Obama used the 30 million uninsured and underinsured, denial of preexisting conditions, and other issues to raise public outrage and get his healthcare bill approved and into law.

As of this writing at the end of 2010, the future of healthcare legislation was once again questioned. The election of a Republican Congress in the mid-term elections of 2010 raised the specter that some of the Obama healthcare initiatives could be overturned or have funding cut.

GO GLOBAL

What the Democrats in the United States have wanted to do to its healthcare system already has been done in much of the world, often to a greater degree than we in this country would likely ever contemplate. When profitability is impacted, companies often go global to find a market. The pharmaceutical industry is no exception; the industry has become much more global in recent years. Unlike the chemical industry, there cannot be the same degree of importing and exporting of products due to regulatory requirements. However, drug companies are playing on a world field like never before.

THE NEW ROLE OF PUBLIC RELATIONS

Today, the public relations function within the pharmaceutical industry is very different from what it was just 10 years ago. Then, the job was very heavily centered on marketing communications, promoting products to doctors. Today, the position is far more complex and heavily issue-oriented. Public relations in the pharmaceutical industry today needs to be far more integrated into strategic decision making by the company and more focused on how to help the company meet its long-term business objectives.

Several examples of communications by the pharmaceutical industry show signs of change and some signs of the past.

It has been suggested that all children should be vaccinated. Because millions of people are uninsured, it was suggested that the states should become the agents through which vaccines are provided free to all children. The immediate industry response was to argue that this would cut into monies needed for future research and would undermine the industry. The first time this issue was raised was during the Clinton Administration. Although the industry did fight the issue at first, public opinion forced the manufacturers of vaccines to provide the vaccines free to indigent patients.

This example shows the inability of marketing–communications-oriented public relations to identify the key issue in this situation. This was an early administration challenge to determine if the industry was focused on patients or profits. What better example to choose than to question the availability of products for children.

At the same time, there are regular calls from more liberal legislators for mandated price controls on drugs. The industry's trade groups argued that price controls did not work and that they would erode important monies needed for research. The industry argued that pharmaceuticals comprised only 7 percent of all health-care costs and that price controls would have no impact on the nation's healthcare costs.

Once again, the argument of the composition of pharmaceuticals within the total healthcare price tag missed the point. The issue was another test of the principal of profits versus health. The pharmaceutical industry was becoming a convenient target for the administration.

Instead of recognizing the issues and the options available to manage them, the industry's early reaction was to behave as it had in the past—to confront and argue with old messages.

With Merck's leadership, some things began to change. Merck was the first company to announce that it would voluntarily control prices of its drugs to the rate of inflation. Within weeks, 17 pharmaceutical companies had made the same pledge. With that offer of voluntary price controls, the threat of mandated controls was removed from the administration-proposed legislation. Still, 18 drug companies, among which were some of the largest and best known, refused to make such a pledge. Instead, these companies stuck to their original arguments about needed research dollars and the limited impact such controls would have on the nation's healthcare costs.

With an aging population and growing problems of obesity, there will be increasing need for health care in general and pharmaceuticals in particular. Diseases that were not even talked about 10 years ago like Alzheimer's disease, are creating new opportunities for the industry. Heart disease, stroke, cancer and diabetes continue to rise, since all are related to obesity. The opportunities for pharmaceutical companies to make money by addressing these diseases will increase, but at the same time so will pressures for companies to control the costs of drugs and diagnostics. So, as the industry continues to meet the challenges of the market, it will continue to find itself in controversy because its products are expensive.

CHANGING THE MESSAGES AND TACTICS TO REACH THE AUDIENCES

A pattern emerges in both of these scenarios—that is, an industry that has continued to argue the need for profits for research has a difficult time changing its message, even when this message no longer works. Pharmaceutical salesmen in the early 1970s were trained to argue against generics on the basis of needed research and development costs. In 1994, the same arguments were still being used. If, after so many years, one learns that the message has not been heard, one has two choices. One can yell the same message louder and with more vigor. Or one can try to understand why the audience is not accepting the message and attempt to change the message to address the needs of the audience. Much of the industry remains focused on the first alternative.

At the same time, the industry continues to go through fundamental structural change. Public relations activities at pharmaceutical companies are beginning to catch up to these changes as top management recognizes that it needs public relations counsel as a prelude to public relations tactics.

The key public relations activity in the pharmaceutical industry has shifted from being marketing communications or financial relations oriented, toward counseling with a view toward constituency relations. As the industry has changed, the number of constituents and the complexities of the relationship among these constituents have changed. As a result, many pharmaceutical companies are struggling with a catch-up process, trying to realign and refocus their public relations activities and to focus increasingly on public policy and public affairs.

To some practitioners in other industries, these changes may seem, in the words of Yogi Berra, like "déjà vu all over again." The practice of public relations as constituency relations emerged as a standard in the chemical, oil and other industries that came under public scrutiny and criticism years ago.

The international arena is another place in which public relations is changing. For years, pharmaceuticals were managed on a country-by-country basis. Compounds developed in one country and approved by its regulatory agencies are not easily exported. While the European Union has recognized and accepted the regulatory practices of EU countries, the United States continues to require that all drugs go through a lengthy clinical trial period prior to FDA approval. These regulations are in place regardless of whether the drug has already been approved in another country.

However, the issues of healthcare reform and cost containment are international in nature. Government and third-party pressures on medical costs are growing not only in the United States, but also in Germany, Italy, France and Japan.

In the 1950s, social psychologists Muzafer and Carolyn Sherif found that a "significant other" or reference group usually determined influence and attitude change. In the medical community, influence typically resides in the medical school from which the doctor graduated and in leading research physicians at leading teaching hospitals who help establish consensus on treatments for various disorders. The public relations practitioner is often involved in medical symposia and other meetings at which medical consensus is established. Similarly, press conferences for new product announcements usually feature leading researchers who provide the important "endorsement" of the pharmaceutical as an efficacious therapy for a particular disorder. Budgets for public relations often must reflect the need to provide counseling or spokesman fees to doctors and researchers who endorse a company's products at symposia and through presentations.

It is not just changing messages, but also the technology that has changed and will continue to affect how public relations is practiced in pharmaceutical companies. The Internet and social media have created huge changes in the way consumers get their information. When someone gets sick or thinks he has a medical problem, his first course of action is to initiate a Google search or a search on a medical website such as WebMD. The Internet search has replaced the initial call to the physician for many people. But this has also changed the way patients deal with doctors. It is not uncommon now for patients to "self-diagnose" through their Internet search and then seek treatment from the doctor. This has helped stimulate physician–patient dialogue, but at the same time it has increased the number of physician visits and a call for more drugs.

While most patients turn to the Internet, pharmaceutical companies are restricted in the realm of social media. No other industry is so constrained from communicating with the customer through preferred technology. The legal community, concerned about the FDA, has virtually "gagged" the public relations professionals in many companies, particularly when talking about prescription pharmaceuticals. The FDA guidelines state that a company cannot communicate to the public about a drug without also including full disclosure of its side effects. This restriction makes such things as Twitter, which is microblogging restricted to 140 characters, very difficult, if not impossible. In addition, even if one converses with a patient or potential patient on a neutral blog site, most companies fear that they could inadvertently step over the line of FDA guidance. As a result, public relations professionals in the pharmaceutical industry, unlike their counterparts in other industries, are unable to communicate with the various stakeholders using social media. In addition, the length of public relations messages, because there is such concern with meeting legal and regulatory guidelines, become more akin to legal messages than those one might expect from PR professionals. It is a restriction that pharmaceutical professionals learn to deal with, even if they would prefer otherwise. The industry has asked the FDA to study social media and provide new guidance on the use of social media that better reflects the times. Although the FDA promised guidance in November 2009, what was given did little to clarify the situation and more to continue to confuse what can or cannot be done.

A number of new and aggressive sales and marketing practices increased the criticism of the pharmaceutical industry and created new issues for public relations professionals to deal with. The more controversial issues are discussed next.

Direct to Consumer Marketing

As the traditional sales channels for pharmaceutical companies began to erode and sales of drugs began to stagnate, pharmaceutical companies created a new category of marketing to stimulate demand and create patient "pull" or demand. In the early part of the twenty-first century, pharmaceutical companies began using what has been called direct-to-consumer (DTC) advertising. Rather than simply "pushing" drugs through their normal channel, which entailed promoting or, in industry terms, "detailing" the product to physicians, the industry turned to "pull" techniques to encourage patients to go to their doctors for treatment. Most DTC communications is in the form of advertising. The ads spell out a disease and the symptoms and encourage the viewer to self-diagnose and see their doctor.

DTC advertising has been effective in stimulating physician visits and drug sales. In fact, it has been so effective that it has become controversial in its own right. The United States and New Zealand are now the only two countries that allow DTC advertising. The practice is banned in all other countries, since it is believed that DTC ads lead to over prescribing of medications and to increases in drug sales for unnecessary purposes.

The industry counters that DTC advertising has succeeded in getting more people to their doctor for problems that might not otherwise have been diagnosed.

Off-label Marketing

Off-label marketing is another aggressive sales techniques used by pharmaceutical companies to increase lagging sales of their drug companies. According to the FDA, companies can only market on indications that are approved. Many companies try to circumvent these approved rules and market "off label." The average off-label use of pharmaceuticals is estimated to be about 40 percent. However, in some situations, e.g., attention deficit disorder, gastrointestinal diseases, and others, off-label use approaches 90 percent. That is, about 90 percent of patients are being treated with a drug that the FDA did not license or approve for that purpose.

How does this happen? At the same time the FDA restricts pharmaceutical company marketing, there are no restrictions on how physicians can prescribe a medication. A doctor can use any drug in any way he or she feels is appropriate and for any indication. How doctors get knowledge of off-label uses of the drugs is a matter of controversy and FDA scrutiny. Many pharmaceutical companies spent a lot of time sponsoring physician meeting at which one or more physicians talk about off-label uses of drugs. Although the drug companies pay the physicians to speak, they claim that they are not encouraging the physician to say anything he or she would not want to say. Defending and explaining this practice has occupied a considerable amount of time among pharmaceutical PR people.

Declining Reputation of the Pharmaceutical Industry

The pharmaceutical industry's reputation continues to slip. In fact, by 2010, most reputation studies, including those by the Reputation Institute and Ipsos, have found that the public puts the industry only ahead of tobacco, oil and utilities in terms of negative perceptions. It is amazing that an industry that does so much good for the health and well-being of society finds itself at a level that must be considered "reputation risk"—that is, a level of negative reputation that invites greater regulation and public distrust.

Although the industry suffers reputationally, no pharmaceutical company has engaged in a major corporate reputation program to change its reputation versus others' in the industry in a meaningful way with its key stakeholders. The value that the pharmaceutical companies continue to sell is in the individual drugs that they sell. All of the marketing and public relations efforts seem to go into "pushing" the value of an individual drug during its patent life, suggesting that the value of the company can be seen in the product.

The traditional focus of the pharmaceutical industry on its individual drugs versus the value of the company that developed these drugs is something that should be a concern of public relations professionals. The sales organizations in pharmaceutical companies focus on products because that is where their compensation comes from. They argue that the average sales call with a physician is so short (about 2–3 minutes) that all they can focus on is the drug. There also is a belief in the industry that the physician does not really care about the company, but rather only about the therapeutic treatment for his or her patient.

As the market environment becomes more complex, one has to question whether this traditional view of drug over corporate reputation is the right way to go.

DISCUSSION QUESTIONS

1. What can the pharmaceutical industry do to change the discussion away from cost and toward a value proposition that the public would find more appealing?
2. What have been the major forces that have changed pharmaceutical public relations?
3. If you were a pharmaceutical public relations person, what are the three issues you would want your company to address?
4. What do you see as the challenges for public relations as a result of the mergers and acquisitions occurring in the industry?
5. Are the greatest communications challenges internal or external in the pharmaceutical industry?

6. The pharmaceutical industry has gone through tremendous change, but many of the employees of the industry have been working within their companies for many years. What challenges do you think public relations can address with regard to culture change?

7. Why do you think that the pharmaceutical industry has remained fairly silent during the healthcare debates of the Obama Administration? Was this a good public relations position?

8. The reputation of the industry has diminished. What do you think the industry as a whole can do to reverse these trends and regain public trust?

9. Should companies continue to speak as "one voice" from PhRMA, the industry trade group, or should each pharmaceutical company seek to differentiate on its own?

NOTES

1. "The Road Not Taken: How Fritz Gerber of Roche Holdings Became the Maverick of the Drug Industry," *Financial World* (July 19, 1994), 38–41.

ADDITIONAL READING

Aitken, M., and H. Frazier. "A Prescription for Direct Drug Marketing." McKinsey Quarterly, 2000, www.mckinseyquarterly.com/health/prdio00.asp.

Angell, M. (2004), "The Truth about the Drug Companies." *The New York Review of Books*, 51, (12) (July 15, 2004).

Bradley, S., and J. Weber. *The Pharmaceutical Industry: Challenges in the New Century*. Boston, MA: Harvard Business School Press, 2004, No. 9-703-489.

Congressional Budget Office. Research and Development in the Pharmaceutical Industry, 2006.

IBM Business Consulting Services. Beyond Mere Survival: Pharmaceutical Firms Adapting and Thriving through on Demand Operations, 2003.

Knowledge@Wharton. "The Prices of Progress: Can Drug Companies Make Medicines More Affordable?," 2005.

Knowledge@Wharton, "Analyzing Brand-Name and Generic Drug Costs in the U.S. and Eight Other Countries." 2003.

Piachaud, Bianca. 2002. "Challenges Facing the Pharmaceutical Industry." Contemporary Review 280, no. 1634: 152. Academic Search Premier, EBSCOhost (accessed November 20, 2011).

Rmarattan, L., and M. Szenberg. "Global Competition in the United States Pharmaceutical Industry." *American Economist* 50, 2 (2006): 65–82.

42

CHAPTER

CONSULTING, TECHNOLOGY SERVICES AND OUTSOURCING
An Integrated Approach to Marketing and Communications

Roxanne Taylor
Chief Marketing and Communications Officer
Accenture

Jayme Silverstone
Senior Director, Marketing and Communications
Accenture

INTRODUCTION

The information technology (IT) professional services industry has changed dramatically over the past decade. In 2011, it is estimated to be a $672 billion global industry[1] with hundreds of competitors, ranging from niche consulting firms to full-scale, global information technology services providers. Not surprisingly, this explosive growth has created greater opportunities for the marketing and communications function within these companies—and tested the skills and capabilities of marketing and communications professionals working in the industry.

This chapter explores how the industry has changed, and how the role of marketing and communications has evolved and expanded to become a strategic partner in the business, helping the leading companies grow and succeed.

INDUSTRY OVERVIEW

Broadly speaking, the organizations in this industry provide their clients some combination of the following services:

- Consulting—including strategy formulation, organizational design, change management, process re-engineering, process excellence, risk management and business process transformation

- Technology services—including systems design, integration and management

- Outsourcing—including managing and continuously improving an entire business function on behalf of a client

Companies—and government agencies—buy these services to meet a wide range of needs. For example, a client may engage a consulting company to help develop and achieve current or new strategic goals, enter new markets or increase revenues in existing markets—or often, all of the above. The client may seek a business partner to help improve their operational performance or deliver their products and services more effectively and efficiently. The client may want to augment capabilities they do not have in-house or, in the case of outsourcing, to turn over the running of technology applications or business processes such as finance and accounting so that the client can focus on its core competence.

In a "business-to-business" environment like this, where the focus lies on improving an organization's ability to serve its customers, and perhaps its customers' customers, the core marketing and communications challenge is to make these kinds of intangible services relevant and differentiated to the client. The provider must convince the buyer that it has the vision and expertise—often complex and specialized skills and capabilities—and the ability to deliver more value for its services than the competition. Ultimately, the company must persuade potential buyers that it is the best choice to help them achieve their most strategic business objectives.

This challenge is made all the more difficult by the fact that the industry has an incredibly wide range of competitors. This highly competitive environment needs to be factored into any marketing and communications program and includes the following types of organizations:

- Large multinational providers, including the service arms of global hardware and software technology providers

- Offshore information technology service providers in lower-cost locations, particularly in India, that offer services often at highly competitive prices

- Niche solution or service providers that compete in a specific geographic market, industry segment or service area

- A client's own internal resources

Within this industry and competitive framework, a full-service provider like Accenture is particularly well positioned. As one of the world's leading management consulting, technology services and outsourcing organizations, Accenture has more than 236,000 employees serving clients in more than 120 countries, offering a broad range of capabilities across all industries and business functions. Its mission is to help its clients—primarily *Fortune* Global 500 and *Fortune* 1000 companies, as well as government agencies—become high-performance businesses and governments.

Accenture operates globally with one common brand and business model, principles that are at the heart of its marketing and communications strategy. The company's *high performance business* strategy is directly aligned with its brand positioning of *High Performance Delivered*. We will explore the benefits of this integration in detail later in the chapter.

INDUSTRY CHANGES AND TRENDS

During the past decade, the consulting and IT services industry's leaders have had to grapple with new entrants, more sophisticated buyers, globalization, geopolitical and economic turmoil, new sources of talent, new technology and new ways to deliver services to clients. Following is an overview of the most significant changes.

Offshore Service Providers

One of the most profound shifts has been the emergence of offshore service providers in lower-cost locations, particularly in India. One of the distinctions of the offshore providers is that they are pure-play providers, meaning that IT services is their primary business. This disruption of the industry's competitive dynamics forced the established, multinational players to shift their strategy—both in terms of where they source talent and the types of services they offer.

This shift also reshaped the way services are delivered to clients to be more price competitive. The traditional consulting model leveraged deeply skilled staff who typically worked at the client's facilities. The past decade has seen the emergence of "global delivery centers," which are facilities where teams with specialized skills come together to serve a client with scalable and standardized processes, methods and tools.

Accenture made a strategic decision to develop a global delivery model, which includes the company's Global Delivery Network. This network, with currently more than 141,000 professionals, is made up of Accenture employees working at local offices and client sites around the world, as well as at more than 50 delivery centers, including in India, China, Spain, the Philippines, Mexico, the United States, Argentina and Brazil. Teams of technology, outsourcing and business-process professionals come together to use proven assets to create and deliver business and technology solutions for Accenture's clients.

Accenture's Global Delivery Network is an important capability for the company, and by virtue of its size and breadth, it is a competitive differentiator reflected in the company's marketing programs and brand positioning. In addition, the Global Delivery Network helps make the services the company provides more tangible to its clients. In fact, Accenture hosts more than 1,000 companies annually at its various network locations around the globe.

Alliance Partnerships

Another significant industry change has been the growth of alliance partnerships. Alliance partners complement a provider's capabilities—whether in a specific technology area, a specific industry or a specific geographic market. They augment the provider's knowledge of the many technology products available for meeting the client's diverse needs.

However, in this broader business environment, it is not uncommon for traditional IT services competitors to also be alliance partners in certain technology product areas. For example, a consulting provider may have a sales and delivery alliance with a hardware vendor who brings complementary products and capabilities. Yet the hardware vendor may also have its own technology consulting capability. This kind of competitive interaction is certainly challenging and highly nuanced, yet it is a characteristic of the way the industry operates today.

Developing an alliance marketing program is an important step to leveraging the full impact of this important delivery channel—and ensuring that the end customer understands the greater value offered from an alliance relationship.

Geographic Expansion

One last industry change worth highlighting is how customer demand has expanded beyond the developed economies of North America, Europe and Japan and into emerging markets in Asia, Latin America, Africa and the Middle East. As expected, service providers have shifted their strategy to build capability to meet customer demand in these markets. Likewise, marketing and communications strategy has evolved with brand-building activities to support growth in these emerging markets, as well as to target new customers.

In summary, although the industry today is considered to be mature, it is still highly competitive, fragmented and continues to grow and evolve. Given the current industry environment, an integrated approach to marketing and communications becomes paramount if a company is to successfully differentiate itself.

MARKETING AND COMMUNICATIONS CHANGES AND TRENDS

In light of the extraordinary change in the industry—and in the global business environment in general—marketing and communications professionals have raised their game proactively to earn a seat at the table and a voice in corporate strategic decision making. The marketing and communications functions of the leading companies in the industry have had to adapt to the industry trends described previously, as well as to other challenges, such as:

- More sophisticated buyers

- A proliferation of stakeholders

- Greater complexity and volume of offerings

- Lengthier sales cycle

- Digital channels, including social media

- Reduced budgets

- Corporate reputation risk

- Increased regulation

- Demand for greater transparency

Against this backdrop, marketing and communications professionals are called upon to provide counsel to senior leadership on strategic issues ranging from the competitive landscape to buyer values to new ways to reach clients through social media.

For example, consider technology and the plethora of new channels to communicate with key audiences that have emerged in only a few short years. Buyers of consulting and outsourcing services are typically the most senior-level executives of large organizations. Historically, to reach these buyers, marketing campaigns relied on traditional tactics such as targeted industry events and discussion forums, sponsorships, print advertising and direct mail of publications showcasing the company's thought leadership, to name a few examples.

However, digital communications are becoming increasingly popular even with senior-level buyers and must be considered in the overall marketing mix today. Many executives have experience with social networks and digital channels in their personal lives to access information. More and more they are turning to these channels in work-related contexts. Buyers may also have higher expectations for how an IT services provider incorporates new technologies in its marketing activities.

As a result, marketing and communications professionals have made a strategic shift to develop deep, specialized capabilities across a wide range of new technologies and tools: Internet marketing, online video, microsites, mobile applications, quick response (QR) codes, blogs and microblogs, social networking sites and so on.

These tools are now indispensable, especially given the proliferation of stakeholders that an organization engages with on any given day. For example, although the client remains at the center of every campaign and activity, there are numerous stakeholders today, such as experts who write blogs, new digital journalists, and academics, who interact with the company's brand and can influence the perception of the brand.

Consider employees. In a professional services context, the employee in many ways personifies the "product." Employees are the most visible and, frankly, effective contact with the client, often working side by side with the client's own employees at the client's facilities. As such, employees become an extremely important channel for representing the brand and personality of the company in the marketplace. This requires a well-integrated employee communication strategy to ensure that employees feel engaged, understand the company's business strategy and are able to deliver results.

Another important stakeholder is the industry analyst. Analysts in firms such as Gartner and IDC conduct extensive commercial and proprietary research and provide an objective view of the players in the industry. Buyers often turn to industry analysts for advice in selecting a service provider, given the analysts' extensive knowledge of each competitor's offerings and perceived strengths and weaknesses. Therefore, a positive industry analyst report is viewed as a credible endorsement of the provider.

Often, marketing and communications teams include industry analyst relations practitioners, as well as traditional media relations professionals, who are responsible for developing relationships with the industry analysts and providing a window into the organization. The industry analysts are important influencers and a key part of a successful marketing and communications strategy.

It is also worth highlighting that many stakeholders today have a keen interest in how the organization interacts with the community in which it operates. They expect the organization to focus on—and communicate about—such issues as corporate social responsibility and environmental responsibility, as well as other business imperatives such as diversity and business ethics.

As a result, the most successful companies have applied the principles of integrated marketing to their corporate citizenship and diversity efforts, aligning communications activities with the company's strategy and core brand positioning. This type of consistent and integrated messaging, where the company and its employees "walk the talk" as it relates to the company's values, helps build credibility with this important audience.

The box below gives the reader a feel for the many different types of stakeholders who play a role in the industry today. It is critical to develop a marketing and communications strategy that addresses this diverse, multistakeholder environment.

STAKEHOLDER MANAGEMENT

The role of marketing and communications is to use communications, channels and content as a strategic advantage to reach a wide range of stakeholders, including:

Clients/prospects (*Fortune* Global 1000 companies; government agencies)	Media (print and online journalists)
Employees (current full-time and part-time employees; contractors)	Industry analysts (e.g., Gartner, IDC)
Alumni (former employees)	Equity analysts (e.g., J.P. Morgan, Credit Suisse, Evercore Partners)
Recruits (university graduates; experienced hires)	Community members/agencies (corporate social responsibility associations)
Investors (individual and institutional shareholders)	Suppliers (technology, routine services)
	Alliance partners (software and hardware vendors)
	Government officials/entities (local, state, national)

One final point: all of these stakeholders represent diverse types of individuals who consume information in different ways. This puts even greater demands on the marketing and communications function to ensure that it has the expertise to select the right channel—with the relevant content—to reach the target audience.

Let us turn now to how to create a successful integrated marketing and communications strategy to reach all stakeholders with a consistent and positive view of the brand.

PLANNING, IMPLEMENTING AND EVALUATING A SUCCESSFUL INTEGRATED MARKETING AND COMMUNICATIONS STRATEGY

ALIGNMENT WITH THE BUSINESS STRATEGY

The most important first step in developing a successful integrated marketing plan is to align all marketing and communications activities with the strategic priorities of the business. Consider the expectations placed on the marketing and communications function. At the highest level, the function is responsible for creating a differentiated image for the company in a competitive marketplace and for creating a unifying brand positioning to ensure that the company communicates with customers, employees, recruits and other stakeholders in a consistent manner. Marketing and communications programs are designed to foster and reinforce positive attitudes among buyers, and to maintain customer mind-share as well as expand a customer's share of wallet.

These goals can be met only by implementing a strategic, integrated approach to marketing and communications. This is even truer in today's highly competitive marketplace, with most companies focused on cost efficiency and maximizing the return on their marketing investments.

Yet the concept of integrated marketing is relatively new in this industry. Consulting organizations traditionally had very separate marketing efforts—often the domain of an individual group within the organization that focused on a small number of local clients. This resulted in conflicting and inconsistent marketplace messages that often eroded trust. However, for a consulting or outsourcing buyer that is seeking a long-term partnership to help address its most strategic business needs, trust is a critical part of the decision.

One way to build that trust is through consistent behavior and messages. This means that whether the company's clients are in Boston, Buenos Aires or Bangalore, they experience the same values, methodologies, marketing messages, culture and service across the entire organization. In other words, they encounter a single, global brand.

Today, integrated marketing is a requirement, not an option or a luxury. In fact, integration now extends beyond the marketing and communications function into the broader organization. This means that the marketing and communications strategy and priorities need to be integrated with every aspect of the business and across all stakeholders. This is particularly important in the area of employee communication and retention, remember the point earlier about how employees of a professional services company are the primary embodiment of the brand.

In addition, the need for complete alignment with the business strategy has become even more pronounced over the past decade as the scope of the marketing and communications function itself has expanded—from its traditional role in brand and image building, to new responsibilities ranging from recruitment marketing to targeted sales campaigns.

But even more important today, given the emphasis on cost efficiency that is likely to remain unchanged for the foreseeable future, is measuring the value of marketing's contribution to the business. One of the best ways to do this is by aligning marketing programs with the business goals and investments the company is making to drive growth.

Accenture was an early adopter of integrated marketing, and the company continues to follow an integrated marketing model that aligns all of its *image development*, *market development* and *business development* activities to focus on the individual client or prospect. The purpose of integrated marketing is to generate profitable business for Accenture by building the company's image in the marketplace, developing new markets and creating loyal client relationships in a highly connected, synergistic way. Every marketing activity the company undertakes is designed to lead a client or prospective client toward a partnering relationship with Accenture. Integrated marketing is based on the concept that the entire organization should work together in a brand-consistent manner to drive growth in the business in the most robust and efficient way possible.

INTEGRATED PLANNING

Once the marketing activities and business goals are aligned within the context of an overall integrated marketing model, the marketing and communications team can successfully embark on integrated planning. Integrated planning is vital in a multichannel, multistakeholder environment. This ensures that plans are integrated globally across the full range of marketing and communications activities—from brand positioning, advertising, media relations, events and employee communications, to lead generation, client outreach, opportunity management and sales support.

Also critical in the planning process is using market research to guide decision making. Market research can help facilitate more effective image development, market development and business development activities. For example, research provides an objective look at buyer needs and issues, as well as the competitive dynamics of the industry. Research is also used to track the effectiveness of ongoing marketing and communications programs by measuring awareness, consideration and preference, as well as advertising effectiveness and brand equity, along with other measures such as internal communications effectiveness.

In nearly every industry, marketing and communications resources are stretched thin as a result of budget cuts and departmental downsizing. With a focus on integrated planning that leverages fact-based research, the marketing and communications team can focus on fewer, bigger things that will have the greatest impact.

Moreover, adopting an integrated model leaves room for flexibility and adaptability—two key drivers of success. In today's rapidly changing business environment, a company must be able to translate new opportunities into results with speed and agility. This applies to the marketing and communications function as well.

MARKETING AND SALES LIFE CYCLE

The integrated planning process always begins with the client or prospect. One tool to help marketing and communications professionals shape the most effective marketing activities is the marketing and sales life cycle (Figure 42.1).

The life cycle is a framework for thinking about a client's attitudes toward, beliefs about and relationship with the service provider. Marketing strategies and campaigns are determined by the client's stage within the life cycle, with the goal of moving the client along from awareness and knowledge, to consideration and preference and eventually to purchase and loyalty. Each contact with a client is a crucial opportunity to move to the next stage in the life cycle. The stages are described as follows:

- *Awareness*. The buyer is aware that the organization exists as a provider in the industry.

- *Knowledge*. The buyer knows something about the company's offerings and its key messages, and may be familiar with some offerings of competitors.

- *Consideration*. Based on specific impressions about the organization's work, the buyer puts the organization on a short list of providers.

- *Preference*. The buyer ranks the organization at the top of its short list.

- *Purchase*. The buyer hires the organization for its needs.

- *Loyalty*. The services are delivered to the buyer, and the resulting value accrued to that buyer is the first step toward a strong working relationship. Ideally, the buyer and provider develop a long-term, partnering relationship.

The graphic also shows how the integrated marketing model can be applied to the marketing and sales life cycle. For example, image development activities focus on the earlier stages of awareness and knowledge, whereas market development activities primarily achieve consideration and preference. Business development activities are intended to drive purchase and loyalty.

In addition, although the life cycle clearly places the client or prospective client at the center, it can also be successfully used across many different stakeholders, including employees. An employee engagement plan can align with the phases of the life cycle—beginning with the employee's awareness and knowledge of the company's business goals and career opportunities, moving to the employee's preference to work for the company and finally loyalty to develop a long-term career at the company.

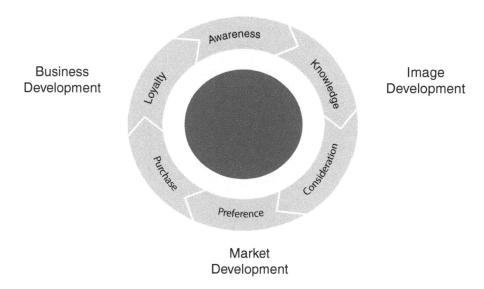

F I G U R E 42.1

Marketing and Sales Life Cycle

No matter which stakeholder is at the center, it is essential to choose the right mix of tactics for each phase to achieve the stated communications objective. The remainder of this chapter explores the core elements of integrated marketing and the marketing and sales life cycle—beginning with brand positioning.

BRAND POSITIONING

No matter what the industry, corporate branding efforts must achieve two overarching external and internal goals to be truly successful. First is to increase market share, name recognition and corporate reputation. Equally important is for the brand to become a source of pride for employees and to increase employee engagement.

In a business-to-business environment, corporate branding presents some unique challenges. For example, trust, transparency and authenticity take on even greater importance when selling intangible services. Buyers make their decisions about professional services providers based both on the capabilities and offerings, and how the buyer genuinely *feels* about the organization. The brand must identify the organization and inspire positive feelings toward the organization. These inferential qualities are so critical given the intangibility of the services provided.

In addition, every brand holds a position in the minds of its core stakeholders. This brand positioning is the distinctive net impression that people have about the organization. Positioning defines what a company does, who it does it for and the benefit and value it delivers. Positioning provides the basis on which the corporate brand is built.

For a brand to resonate with all of its audiences, the brand messages must be consistent internally and externally. Companies must educate and communicate everything that the brand stands for, widely and often, and collaborate with stakeholders to ensure that they are truly experiencing the brand, seek feedback and use stakeholder input to improve the brand regularly.

Accenture is an interesting example in that the company's strategy, high performance business, is completely aligned with its brand positioning, High Performance Delivered. Brand positioning denotes the place that any company wants to occupy in the minds of its clients, prospects, employees and future talent—in other words, what the company wants to be known for.

For Accenture, the High Performance Delivered positioning is the single theme Accenture wants people to associate with the company and the single message the company drives into the marketplace. By having a clear and singular message that permeates all aspects of its marketing and communications strategy, Accenture is able to drive even greater value and return from its marketing investments.

In 2003, the company established its High Performance Delivered branding campaign with the goal of making Accenture synonymous with high performance. The campaign was unique in aligning the advertising messages with the company's proprietary research into the defining characteristics of high-performance businesses. The campaign used a variety of tactics including print, airport and online advertising, as well as expanded efforts in direct marketing, events and thought leadership—all communicating the research findings.

In addition, as the message around high performance began to resonate with external audiences, the company realized the need to extend the brand to its employees through an extensive internal communications effort. Quite simply, the employees of Accenture exemplify high performance and practice what is promised in the company's marketing and advertising. The High Performance Delivered campaign has been refreshed several times since its launch and is the most successful campaign in the company's history. Today, the Accenture brand is fully integrated across all aspects of Accenture's business, and research shows that Accenture and High Performance Delivered are, indeed, synonymous.

In summary, a company's brand positioning is the cornerstone of its integrated marketing strategy and permeates the entire integrated marketing model. Let us now look at each component of the model, including several tactics that can be used to move a buyer through each phase of the marketing and sales life cycle.

IMAGE DEVELOPMENT

The starting point on the journey through the marketing and sales life cycle is awareness, and to drive awareness, *image advertising* can be very effective.

Image advertising is now a staple of the companies operating in this industry. But it was not always this way. At the time of the first publication of this handbook in 1997, image advertising in the industry was only about a decade old. In fact, Accenture is widely credited as the first major consulting organization to advertise at a significant level, beginning in 1989 when it was formerly known as Andersen Consulting (see Case Study: Accenture Rebranding).

In the early days of the consulting industry, advertising was used primarily to create the overall brand and image, and it still is an effective tool to put the organization's brand in front of prospective clients. But as the industry has evolved, and as differentiation among providers has gotten more difficult, more targeted, "offering-specific" advertising has emerged.

In addition, as the industry has become more global, in terms of both the scope of the services a provider offers and the worldwide nature of the client base, the most effective advertising strategies today are global. A global advertising strategy must attain the highest levels of consistency, meaning that the same image, message and brand personality traits are delivered consistently to each market. This integration and consistency contributes to the strength of the brand.

Other important image building techniques include media relations, external communications and events and sponsorships—all of which help build and enhance an organization's image by putting its name front and center with its clients.

For example, an integrated *media relations* program is used to build reputation, educate the audience and differentiate the organization in a crowded field. Successful media relations campaigns are integrated with the overall brand strategy, the overall marketing and business objectives and a solid understanding of the target audience. In this industry, media relations professionals are tasked with creating messages and communications materials that represent and promote the company's views on major global corporate, industry and economic issues. The goal is to ensure balanced and accurate coverage across the full range of media outlets globally.

Another important channel to reach stakeholders is through *external publishing programs* that present a company's unique point of view, typically through a branded publication, on a wide range of topics. This focus on thought leadership marketing has expanded significantly to bring a company's ideas and insights to the marketplace in a compelling and relevant manner. Topics can range from business trends to talent management to strategy execution to technology vision—in other words, topics that reflect the full range of capabilities the organization provides to its clients. By showcasing insights from the company's experts, the company is able to share a point of view that is relevant to the buyer and, ideally, moves the buyer around the life cycle to further engage with the company.

For Accenture, given its brand positioning of High Performance Delivered, the company offers practical insights for organizations that aspire to high performance. These insights are packaged in multiple ways to reach the company's many stakeholders. For example, on the company's website, a section called "Latest Thinking" provides access to videos, blogs, RSS feeds, podcasts and numerous research and insights. In addition, *Outlook*, the company's quarterly journal of High Performance Business, is distributed through a direct-mail program to a targeted audience of nearly 5,000 senior executives at the company's largest clients and prospects. *Outlook* journal, as well as three additional electronic titles—*Outlook* Point of View, *Outlook* Q&A and *Outlook* Case Study—are published on Accenture's website where individual articles are downloadable.

Another key element of image building includes *events* and *sponsorships*. The most successful sponsorships and event-marketing programs are client-centric: they are relevant to an executive in a particular industry, or provide access to new insights and networks across industries.

Events and sponsorships have been a cornerstone of Accenture's marketing and communications programs for decades. In fact, since 1995, more than 30,000 clients and Accenture hosts have attended approximately 300 events held in more than 20 countries on five continents. The company has focused on large, exclusive sponsorships to reach its clients and prospects, including the World Golf Championships—Accenture Match Play Championship and the Royal Shakespeare Company. In addition, Accenture hosts industry conferences, such as the Global Convergence Forum for the communications industry and the International Utilities and Energy Conference, both of which have become the leading conferences in their industries.

More recently, Accenture has developed a series of "C-suite networks" to bring together clients and prospects in similar leadership roles across different industries to participate in both virtual and in-person forums. These networks are member driven, meaning that the members set the agenda and determine the content most relevant to them. These networks provide an important opportunity for executives to connect through shared insights and leading-edge research, and to engage in a global, peer-to-peer dialogue.

Lastly, image development activities play an important role in attracting the best talent to work for the organization. There is enormous competition today for top talent, and the area of *recruitment marketing* has exploded in the past decade. For Accenture, this area is particularly important, as the company hired more than 70,000 people in fiscal 2011.

Recruitment marketing programs focus on image development, recruitment lead generation and relationship-building activities to help achieve the organization's recruitment goals. Recruitment marketing professionals develop a deep understanding of what candidates value and how they perceive the organization, and then tailor messages that ultimately differentiate the company's career experience.

MARKET DEVELOPMENT

The next area of integrated marketing—and the next stage in the marketing and sales life cycle—is market development. Market development activities build on the awareness and knowledge gained through image development investments, and move the buyer toward consideration and preference.

In other words, a focus on market development helps build client relationships and enhance differentiation. Marketing professionals are responsible for packaging the company's portfolio of offerings in a compelling way and focusing marketing investments on the highest-value, differentiated activities. Essentially, this is about creating more personalized and customized marketing programs that match the buyer's needs with the company's capabilities.

One approach Accenture has taken to drive market development is through innovation centers. For example, the Accenture Technology Labs is a research and development organization that explores new and emerging technologies. An important part of the Labs' mission is to create a vision of how technology will shape the future and invent the next wave of business solutions. From a market development standpoint, the Labs provide an opportunity to host Innovation Workshops for clients to explore emerging technologies and for the company to establish its position as a technology innovator.

Another example is the Accenture Institute for High Performance, which researches and publishes practical insights into critical management issues and global economic trends. Institute researchers around the world team with Accenture experts to conduct original research and analysis that demonstrate how organizations become and remain high performers. This research is fully aligned with the company's business strategy and brand positioning, and is therefore a powerful marketing tool in articulating what the company offers its clients.

Accenture has also expanded its *database marketing* and *data mining* capabilities to better integrate contact management, marketing campaign functionality and reporting. This has been essential to coordinating activities across thousands of clients and prospective clients. Ultimately, these efforts help marketing professionals who sit within Accenture's industry groups to align their marketing campaigns to specific sales opportunities and, ideally, help win new business.

BUSINESS DEVELOPMENT

There is a strong link between market development and business development. Looking at the marketing and sales life cycle, business development is about moving the buyer to purchase and then helping build loyalty through a long-term relationship. A subtitle for this section could even be "bringing marketing closer to sales."

During the past decade, the alignment of marketing activities with the core business strategy has required a new level of acumen and creativity from marketing and communications professionals. For example, in order to have a seat at the table with senior leadership, today's marketing and communications director needs to have a well-researched point of view about the industry, the buyer and how best to communicate the breadth—and value—of the company's offerings.

The craft of communication is still critical, and perhaps even more so, in terms of message development and writing, even bringing storytelling into the marketing mix. But equally important has been the development of a certain type of marketing and communications professional who is integral to the sales process—aligning marketing to sales, from the very first stages of lead generation and client account planning, through the final stage of presenting the proposed solution. In this industry, that process could last months or even a year.

The leading companies in the industry have raised the game in terms of how they present a value proposition to a prospective client in the most compelling and relevant way. A marketing and communications professional trained in message development is invaluable to the sales team today—able to craft a targeted message that differentiates the organization, clearly states the value to the client and is delivered creatively, with impact.

Accenture's marketing and communication function has developed some novel ways to surround the buyer. For example, a few years ago, the team pioneered "opportunity-centric marketing." With this approach, a core marketing team—with deep industry and functional experience—works side by side with a sales team to provide the buyer with differentiated messages and then customize a set of marketing tactics to reach the buyer's key decision makers. During the past year alone, this effort has contributed to several billion dollars in new sales for the company, with marketing teams participating in sales opportunities in 26 countries.

The sales process in this industry will continue to be complex. As stated earlier, buyers have a wide range of options and, in fact, are increasingly choosing multiple suppliers. The industry trend toward longer, more strategic relationships between providers and clients will also continue. Especially in an outsourcing sale, the buyer is often looking for a strategic partner to manage an entire business process and, increasingly, share in the risks and rewards of the operation.

All of this points to a more strategic role for marketing professionals to play throughout the entire sales process and in building customer loyalty.

MEASUREMENT

Measuring the effectiveness of an integrated marketing and communications program is one of the most important activities for marketing leadership to undertake, but it is often challenging to measure accurately the impact of a given campaign. This is especially true for the large, global, full-service providers in this industry, given that there are hundreds of brand touch points with a given client or prospect.

Nevertheless, the most successful marketing and communications operations track nearly every stage of the marketing and sales life cycle, measuring such areas as general awareness (by both prospective clients and prospective recruits), differentiation in the marketplace, client retention, media mentions and client satisfaction. In addition, employee communications are now measured with the same discipline, using both annual surveys and frequent "pulse" surveys to understand the internal audience's attitudes, beliefs and preferences, and their alignment with the company's business strategy.

Overall, both external and internal research can provide valuable insights into the changing needs of stakeholders so that marketing and communications strategies across the entire life cycle remain relevant and differentiated.

THE FUTURE

Making predictions is never easy, yet a few themes are emerging that will likely shape the future of the industry, and have an impact on marketing and communications in the years ahead:

- Continued globalization
- Industry consolidation
- New services and offerings
- Technology innovation
- Digital media/channel fragmentation
- Economic and geopolitical instability

- Changing regulatory environments
- Buyer sophistication
- Sourcing the best talent

In many ways, the only constants are uncertainty and unpredictability. Business strategy will continue to shift quickly, and this will require the marketing and communications function to be even more agile and flexible. For example, as a company looks to expand into new sources of revenue, marketing resources need to be able to respond, adapt, redeploy and ultimately align seamlessly with the growth strategy.

Likewise, marketing and communications professionals need to be out in front themselves—looking around corners, refreshing their skills, continually evaluating and experimenting with new technologies, tools and channels. Social media today offers the organization an incredible array of channels through which to have a dialogue among stakeholders. Companies are going to need to find the right balance between encouraging this dialogue and ensuring that their employees are using these digital tools responsibly.

Lastly, given the severe global economic disruption of the past few years, it is likely that many companies will continue to focus on cost management, increased productivity and return on investment. Marketing and communications teams can get out ahead of this trend by looking for more efficient ways to operate and to collaborate. One example is by partnering with their organization's procurement function to optimize the value of vendor relationships. Another example is through shared-service teams, often in cost-effective locations, that provide the internal marketing and communications organization with specialized expertise. Just as clients in this industry look for a provider to manage various businesses processes, the marketing function can leverage a specialized hub of experts to drive greater cost efficiency through repeatable processes.

All of these challenges can be met with a broadly integrated approach to marketing and communications. In a dynamic, complex and increasingly virtual world, integration is the cornerstone to maximizing the investment in the brand and across all marketing and communications activity. The decade ahead will be an exciting time for marketing and communications professionals with tremendous opportunity to grow and succeed in their careers.

CASE STUDY: ACCENTURE REBRANDING

The Accenture brand was launched on January 1, 2001. It is widely considered to be one of the largest and most successful rebranding campaigns in corporate history.[2] This case study describes the rebranding from its background to its successful completion, including the integrated marketing strategy the company used to reach its many stakeholders.

BACKGROUND

Accenture today is a global management consulting, technology services and outsourcing company with net revenues of US$25.5 billion for the fiscal year ended August 31, 2011. As of September 2011, the company had more than 236,000 employees serving clients in more than 120 countries.

Although the name Accenture has only existed for 10 years, the company traces its history to the 1950s with the installation of the first computer system for commercial use in the United States at General Electric. Initially called Andersen Consulting, Accenture was formally established in 1989, when a group of partners from the Consulting division of the various Arthur Andersen firms around the world formed a legally separate business unit focused on consulting and technology services. By the year 2000, the company had achieved more than a decade of tremendous growth, with net revenues exceeding US$9.5 billion and more than 70,000 professionals in 46 countries delivering to clients a broad range of consulting, technology and outsourcing services and solutions.

On January 1, 2001, the company changed its name to Accenture (from Andersen Consulting) as the result of an arbitrator's decision on August 7, 2000, that severed the contractual ties between Accenture and Andersen Worldwide Société Coopérative (AWSC). The arbitrator expressly recognized the legal separateness of Accenture from Arthur Andersen firms and AWSC. This positive outcome included an important condition: the license to use the Andersen Consulting name would expire on December 31, 2000. The company had a monumental task ahead to create, implement and introduce the world to a new name—in just 147 days.

FROM ARBITRATION DECISION TO LAUNCH

The immediate priority was to select a new name. The company engaged Landor Associates, a strategic brand consulting and design firm, to generate potential names. Their efforts were supplemented by a "brandstorming" competition held among the company's employees. The competition was an important way to bring employees into the naming process.

From the thousands of possible names generated, 550 candidates were chosen and a process of trademark and web domain availability reduced the number of potential names to 51. Those 51 names were then subjected to a series of tests, including cultural and linguistic analyses in 47 countries, legal review and testing among the target C-suite audience. The 10 surviving names were presented to the company's leadership team for final review. The name Accenture, which was proposed by Oslo based employee Kim Petersen during the brandstorming competition, was the final selection.

The new name (which rhymes with "adventure") was announced on October 26, 2000 through a global webcast to employees and a briefing with key media. The name derives from "an accent on the future," and the forward mark (">") above the "t" in the logo emphasizes the company's forward-looking approach.

After the announcement of the new name, the business was still operating as Andersen Consulting and preparing the groundwork for the name change. The company approached the challenge just as it does any client project: a program management team coordinated all efforts with a detailed task list and timeline. The effort was monumental and spanned 55 teams of nearly 2,000 employees, 178 Accenture offices and 3,500 client sites.

A teaser advertising campaign was created to generate interest in the upcoming name change. The "teaser" treatment had the corner of the Andersen Consulting logo torn away to reveal the words "Renamed. Redefined. Reborn. 01.01.01." Also, as an indication of the magnitude of the effort, the company tasked 2,000 employees globally with documenting all instances of the Andersen Consulting name on signage, stationery and databases to be ready for replacement with the new Accenture name.

LAUNCH

On January 1, 2001, the company adopted the new name and the website switched to www.accenture.com, signaling the start of a comprehensive integrated marketing campaign. The primary focus was on awareness, targeting all of Accenture's stakeholders—senior-level executives at clients and prospects, employees, recruits, media and industry analysts, among others.

Externally, on January 1, the company reached 40,000 clients and prospects as well as 1.5 million recruits with targeted marketing, and also launched a new advertising campaign introducing the Accenture brand. Internally, the company rebranded 178 offices in 47 countries. This included everything from replacing signage, to printing 7 million business cards, to changing 1,200 internal technology applications and 20,000 internal databases.

The global advertising campaign, launched on January 1, 2001, included a first phase covering television, poster, print and Internet, including high-profile TV spots during the New Year's Day U.S. college football bowl broadcasts. Traditional advertising was supplemented by local creative treatments: an office building in Paris was wrapped in the Accenture logo, taxis in London carried the Accenture brand and large billboards went up in public arenas in Italy.

Clients and prospective clients were sent a package of collateral materials, which included a letter from then chief executive officer, Joe Forehand, as well as a capabilities brochure and a copy of Accenture's *Outlook* journal, which had been rebranded and redesigned. This was an important opportunity not only to share the new name, but also to tell a bigger story about the breadth of the company's services.

Employees were invited to a global webcast on January 3, hosted by Joe Forehand from Australia, where the World Golf Championship—Accenture Match Play Championship—was being held in Melbourne. All employees also received a printed launch package, with a letter from Joe Forehand, a book describing the new brand and a special edition of the employee internal magazine. Celebration launch parties for employees were held in Accenture offices across the world, helping to make the new brand resonate at the local level. This was an important first step in ensuring that the employees personified and represented the brand to the company's clients and in the marketplace.

The second phase of advertising started on January 28, with TV spots during the U.S. Super Bowl broadcast, and later with professional soccer in Japan. The campaign built on the initial awareness exercise by using the phrase, "Now It Gets Interesting." Surprising facts about cutting-edge uses of new technology were used to position Accenture as an organization that was able to partner with businesses to help them exploit new market opportunities. By the end of March 2001, Accenture had run advertising in all 47 countries where it operated at the time, totaling some 6,000 TV spots and 1,000 print ads during its first three months.

By incorporating many of the principles of integrated marketing into the rebranding effort, Accenture ensured that all program elements were integrated globally, as well as aligned with the company's strategy and core brand positioning. Also, in order to ensure that its employees lived the brand, the company engaged its employees throughout the process and integrated the rebranding campaign with every aspect of the business. The new Accenture brand positioning became the cornerstone of the company's integrated marketing strategy.

POST–LAUNCH RESULTS/ACCENTURE TODAY

Accenture was rigorous about measuring the effectiveness of the rebranding and repositioning programs. According to several studies the company executed in the marketplace, by the end of 2001, awareness of the Accenture name in most countries was at or above levels recorded by Andersen Consulting before the name change. The company's research also showed impressive results across the stages of the marketing and sales life cycle. For example, awareness had achieved 96 percent of its previous level and consideration had increased 350 percent. The company also measured an 11 percent increase in brand equity.[3]

Fast forward 10 years, and on January 1, 2011, the company celebrated the 10th anniversary of the Accenture name. Many elements of the company's core brand positioning when it was launched are still in place today. The company is also guided by the same six core values.

Yet as the industry has grown and evolved, so has the Accenture brand. Today, the brand stands for a broader range of services, and Accenture is differentiated by the idea of "High Performance Delivered." The company's brand equity enables it to move into new market spaces with immediate credibility, and the brand helps attract the best people to join its team. Most notably, with the strength of a single, global, integrated brand, the company has been able to expand its market leadership in an increasingly competitive marketplace.

Overall, the Accenture brand was ranked 45th in Interbrand's 100 Best Global Brands for 2011, at a value of $8 billion, representing 54 percent growth since the brand debuted on the list in 2002.[4] By any measures, the Accenture brand launch can be considered to have been a remarkable success.

DISCUSSION QUESTIONS

1. How would you apply the integrated marketing model to reach customers in other industries?
2. Think about how you would adapt the marketing and sales life cycle to plan and develop internal communications campaigns to reach the company's employees. How would you define the stages and corresponding tactics?
3. When you think about the next 10 years of marketing and communications in professional services industries, what technologies and channels do you think will be most successful and relevant in reaching customers?
4. Case study question: If you had been a competitor during the time of the name change, what strategy would you have adopted to counter Accenture's rebranding campaign in the marketplace?

NOTES

1. Gartner Forecast, IT Services, 2007–2014, 1Q11 Update, March 2011.
2. Kevin Keller, "Accenture: Rebranding and Repositioning as a Global Power Brand," *Strategic Brand Management* (Upper Saddle River, NJ: Pearson Prentice Hall, 2008).
3. Kevin Keller, "Accenture: Rebranding and Repositioning as a Global Power Brand," *Strategic Brand Management* (Upper Saddle River, NJ: Pearson Prentice Hall, 2008).
4. Interbrand's 100 Best Global Brands, 2002 and 2011, www.interbrand.com.

43

C H A P T E R

THE FINANCIAL AND BANKING INDUSTRY
Investing in Our Stakeholders

Anonymous

> *The captains of finance and the public stewards of our financial system ignored warnings and failed to question, understand and manage evolving risks within a system essential to the well-being of the American public. Theirs was a big miss, not a stumble.*
>
> —The Financial Crisis Inquiry Commission Final Report,[1] January 2011

A RAPIDLY CHANGING INDUSTRY; AN URGENT NEED TO REBUILD TRUST

In the fall of 2007, Americans were feeling pretty good about the economy. Despite two wars financed solely with debt and with the federal budget surplus of 2000 a distant memory, many Americans were confident about the future and spending more than they earned. Interest rates were dropping, real estate was a sure thing and Wall Street was minting money, selling and reselling groups of debt obligations, mostly home mortgages, that received investment-grade ratings from well-respected rating agencies. Everyone, it seemed, was getting rich on paper.

Starting in early 2008, the concurrence of a growing national deficit, an overheated housing market and mounting consumer debt created the Great Recession, the most significant downturn in the U.S. economy since the Great Depression 80 years before. Unemployment more than doubled from the fall of 2007 to late 2009,[2] when it rose to over 10 percent. The Dow Jones Industrial Average fell from a high point of almost 14,000 to barely over 7,000 just 16 months later.

Nearly 8 million people lost their jobs. Millions more lost their savings, their businesses and their homes. Credit dried up, seemingly overnight. General Motors and Chrysler, traditional mainstays of the U.S. economy, were bailed out, or rescued, by the government. Major financial institutions that were not regulated banks—Merrill Lynch, Lehman Brothers, AIG, Washington Mutual, Countrywide—either failed, were acquired by other, larger institutions or were bailed out because they were deemed too big and too important to fail. No one was left untouched by the Great Recession.

Banks did not cause the Great Recession, but their actions, most of which were perfectly legal, contributed to the devastation that followed. The industry has almost regained its financial footing, but its relationship with the public is deeply scarred: the economy itself has certainly not recovered, and at the time of publication in the autumn of 2011, there is talk of a possible second recession.

Financial institutions are facing the biggest onslaught of new regulation since the Great Depression. The financial industry continues to be under siege from consumers, special interest groups, business customers, regulators, elected officials and policy makers.

The fundamental issues that triggered the financial meltdown are summarized in an official memorandum from the Office of Comptroller of the Currency, which supervises all national banks:

> The downturn in the credit cycle was precipitated by the same underlying factors witnessed in past financial crises: Liberal underwriting, high leverage, rapid growth, and concentrations.
>
> Facilitated by low interest rates, progressive deterioration in underwriting standards took place over an elongated bull market. Weak underwriting became prevalent in the banking system and among non-bank competitors in residential mortgage and home equity lending, credit cards, commercial credits . . . and commercial real estate . . . At the same time the financial system and many customers took on higher leverage (and weaker forms of capital) to enable growth. Rapid expansion in select business lines, often financed by short-term wholesale funding sources, tended to mask the build up of risk. Fragmented databases and otherwise insufficient processes to identify similar risks within and across various lines of business and legal entities . . . resulted in the failure to identify and therefore measure, monitor and control exposure concentrations.
>
> A unique factor in this downturn relates to the absence of transparency to external parties—namely funds providers, counterparties and investors. At most large banks the lack of transparency resulted in an inability of external constituents (and sometimes insiders) to comfortably understand a specific bank's risk profile and to know if they were materially exposed to a feared risk exposure (i.e., subprime lending.) Opaque financial status helped to fuel the transition from declining confidence during the early part of 2008 to outright fear in the second half of the year and through much of the first half of 2009.

A STORY WITH NO HEROES

This is a story mostly without heroes, and only a very few true villains. It evolved from a complex brew: inconsistent regulation and enforcement, government officials who continued to push for homeownership, consumers who wanted bigger American Dreams than they could afford, financial engineers who found creative ways to make quick money without regard for the consequences and the the credit ratings agencies who gave investment-grade ratings to securities based on subprime mortgages. These ratings in turn inspired a flood of global investments and subsequent losses that ran into the billions of dollars and led to the bankruptcy and failure of several well-known financial institutions.

Banks, consumers, the government and the ratings agencies all share blame for the financial crisis. Some lenders made mortgage loans to people who could not realistically afford to repay them. Many consumers, as borrowers, lived beyond their means, bought homes that were affordable only in wildly unrealistic future expectations, borrowed money they could not pay back and signed loan, credit card and checking account agreements they did not understand. Alarmingly, consumers have shown an increased willingness to simply walk away from their homes when they can no longer afford to pay the mortgage.

Now, they feel betrayed by the lending industry. They found that the rules they knew to play by were suddenly changed when the economy tumbled. Individuals got caught by things in the small print that they didn't understand or hadn't read. Small businesses that had relied on their long-term relationships with their bankers found their credit lines cut when the economy, or their business, turned sour. Individuals bought financial products from their investment advisors that neither the consumer nor many of the advisors fully understood.

As for regulators, a January 25, 2011, *New York Times* story reported,

> The government commission that investigated the crisis casts a wide net of blame, faulting two administrations, the Federal Reserve and other regulators for permitting a calamitous concoction: shoddy mortgage lending, the excessive packaging and sale of loans to investors and risky bets on securities backed by

the loans . . . [Though] the Financial Crisis Inquiry Commission accuses several financial institutions of greed, ineptitude or both, some of its gravest conclusions concern government failings, with embarrassing implications for both parties.

The financial crisis has obviously created a new environment for financial institutions and, with it, a need for public relations to reframe the discussion, which currently is based on blame, anger and misunderstanding. In fact, public perception of the banking industry is at a near all-time low. The communications crisis that came along with the financial crisis is much different than that caused by an oil spill, for example, or by a drug found to be unsafe. Those are, indeed, crises, and not small ones. But unlike those kinds of crises, the Great Recession directly affected virtually every American and, for some, in permanent, life-altering ways. People lost retirement savings, so they have had to delay their retirement. People lost their homes or found that their homes were suddenly worth less than their mortgages. Credit lines were cut. Millions of people lost their jobs and their health insurance.

The public's anger at the banking industry and at the government, as well as the nearly universal impact of the economic crisis, has fueled the grassroots movement called Occupy Wall Street. This organization's slogan is "We are the 99 percent," which refers to the great inequality between the wealthiest 1 percent of the country and everyone else.

WALL STREET VERSUS MAIN STREET BANKS

Banking today is often viewed as a highly profitable industry. But the banks that have been enormously profitable are, for the most part, the Wall Street banks, like JPMorgan Chase, Bank of America, Morgan Stanley, Citi and Goldman Sachs.[3]

These banks are global investment and money center banks, whose profits and bonuses are driven more by investment banking activities (e.g., trading, fees from debt and equity issuances, private investments and asset management) rather than the more traditional and far less profitable business of extending credit, taking deposits and managing cash for individuals, small businesses and large global corporations.

When the media and policymakers talk about the banking industry as a whole, they are focusing mostly on the biggest banks and the Wall Street bankers, as evidenced in the *New York Times* on April 14, 2011. The newspaper carried an article about a Senate committee report called "Wall Street and the Financial Crisis: Anatomy of a Financial Collapse":

[The report cites] internal documents and private communications of bank executives, credit ratings agencies and investors [describing] business practices that were rife with conflicts during the mortgage mania and reckless activities that were ignored inside the banks and among their federal regulators . . . the report focuses on an array of institutions with central roles in the mortgage crisis: Washington Mutual, an aggressive mortgage lender that collapsed in 2008; the Office of Thrift Supervision, a regulator; the credit ratings agencies Standard and Poor's and Moody's Investors Service and the investment banks Goldman Sachs and Deutsche Bank.

The report identified 19 recommendations for changes to regulatory and industry practices.

These include creating strong conflict-of-interest policies at the nation's banks and requiring that banks hold higher reserves against risky mortgages. The report also asks federal regulators to examine its findings for violations of laws. The report adds significant new evidence to previously disclosed material showing that a wide swath of the financial industry chose profits over propriety during the mortgage lending spree. It also casts a harsh light on what the report calls regulatory failures, which helped deepen the crisis. Singled out for criticism is the Office of Thrift Supervision, which oversaw some of the nation's most aggressive lenders, including Countrywide Financial, IndyMac and Washington Mutual . . .

But the crisis wasn't the Wall Street banks' alone. Mid-size and smaller banks made many of the same kinds of mistakes: lots of bad home mortgage and commercial real estate loans, inadequate capital and liquidity and a failure to follow presumptive credit and risk management processes.

As a result, at the same time that big banks were getting bigger, small and mid-size banks were struggling to remain competitive. These were the banks that used to be the bedrocks of their communities. They attracted bankers who simply wanted to make a respectable living *and* give back to their communities. These banks and their bankers supported charitable organizations, area sports teams and public schools. Bankers were civic leaders in their communities.

A BRIEF HISTORY: THE HOUSING BUBBLE

The Yale Economist Robert Shiller blames the subprime crisis on the "irrational exuberance" that drove the economy's two most recent bubbles: the first, in the 1990s was in stocks, and the second, from 2000 to 2007, was in housing.

Our focus here is the housing bubble. As housing became more and more valuable in the 90s and early 2000s, it became an ever more appealing investment. Banks, the government-sponsored enterprises (like Fannie Mae and Freddie Mac) and investors believed that the value of real estate would not diminish.

In 2004, in a Cowles Foundation Paper, Shiller and economist Karl Case wrote,

> During a housing price bubble, homebuyers think that a home that they would normally consider too expensive for them is now an acceptable purchase because they will be compensated by significant further price increases. They will not need to save as much as they otherwise might, because they expect the increased value of their home to do the saving for them. First-time homebuyers may also worry during a housing bubble that if they do not buy now, they will not be able to afford a home later. Furthermore, the expectation of large price increases may have a strong impact on demand if people think that home prices are very unlikely to fall, and certainly not likely to fall for long, so that there is little perceived risk associated with an investment in a home."

And in August 2009, Shiller wrote in the *Wall Street Journal*:

> A bubble is a self-fulfilling prophecy for a while, as successive rounds of buyers push prices higher and higher. But the willingness to pay higher and higher prices is fragile: It will end whenever buyers perceive that prices are no longer going up. Hence bubbles carry the seeds of their own destruction. Only time is needed for bubbles to end.

Until the turn of this century, homebuyers generally had to make a down payment of 10 percent or more, have a good credit score and show a steady income in order to get a mortgage. By 2002, mortgage brokers changed some of the rules and began writing mortgages with significantly lower standards, many of them to people who would never be able to keep up with the payments. In fact, between 2002 and 2007, over $3 trillion in loans were made to homeowners with poor credit and/or undocumented income.

Investment banks and brokers essentially created new types of products that packaged large numbers of nonconforming mortgages together, which would then, for a fee, be sold to investors. Those investors had the belief that home values would not go down and that these products were low risk.

Investments banks and brokers bundled the large volume of lower-quality mortgages with those that were higher quality and sold them as instruments called collateralized debt obligations (CDOs).[4] Because the investment banks bundled "good" mortgages with questionable ones, they could sell investors on CDOs by explaining that most of the mortgages were solid, so there was no need to worry about the others. Insurance companies like AIG insured CDOs with credit default swaps (CDSs).[5]

CDOs and CDSs proliferated. More and more mortgage brokers were dealing in subprime mortgages; investment bankers sliced and diced those mortgages and sold them as CDOs; insurers, betting the CDOs would not go bad, covered the CDOs with credit default swaps.

However, in 2008, throughout the country, the number of home foreclosures began to climb faster and faster. AIG had to cover its CDSs; the division at AIG that sold them ultimately incurred some $25 billion in losses, which made the company's stock price plummet. When the housing bubble collapsed, so did AIG.

Credit ratings agencies (Standard & Poor's, Moody's Investor Service and Fitch Group) assign ratings to issuers of some kinds of securities as well as the securities themselves. The ratings are based on credit worthiness, and have direct impact on the securities' interest rates.

These agencies are now under scrutiny for the part they played in the housing bubble and the crisis that followed. They gave investment-grade, "money safe" ratings for the CDOs based on subprime mortgage loans. The American economist Joseph Stiglitz has said, "I view the rating agencies as one of the key culprits. . . They . . . performed the alchemy that converted the securities from F-rated to A-rated. The banks could not have done what they did without the complicity of the rating agencies." In January 2011, the Financial Crisis Inquiry Commission reported,

> The three credit rating agencies were key enablers of the financial meltdown. The mortgage-related securities at the heart of the crisis could not have been marketed and sold without their seal of approval. Investors relied on them . . . This crisis could not have happened without the rating agencies. Their ratings helped the market soar and *their downgrades through 2007 and 2008 wreaked havoc across markets and firms.*[6]

In addition, rating agencies are paid by the investment banks and other companies that sell the securities, which has led to claims of conflicts of interest.

By September 2008, the U.S. financial system was in a free fall. In his book, *Too Big To Fail* (2009), Andrew Ross Sorkin writes,

> . . . the following days would bring a near collapse of the financial system, forcing a government rescue effort with no precedent in modern history. In less than 18 months, Wall Street had gone from celebrating its most profitable age to finding itself on the brink of an epochal devastation. Trillions of dollars in wealth had vanished, and the financial landscape was entirely reconfigured. The calamity would definitively shatter some of the most cherished principles of capitalism. The idea that financial wizards had conjured up a new era of low-risk profits, and that American-style financial engineering was the global gold standards was officially dead.

Lehman Brothers had filed for bankruptcy. Merrill Lynch sold itself to Bank of America, which also bought Countrywide (the biggest violator in the mortgage debacle). AIG became majority-owned by the U.S. government. Goldman Sachs and Morgan Stanley turned themselves into highly regulated commercial banks, in order to try to stabilize their capital and liquidity situations.

TARP: THE GOVERNMENT STEPS IN

In response, the federal government initiated the Troubled Asset Relief Program (TARP). Global credit markets were nearly at a standstill in September 2008. TARP was created to allow the U.S. Department of the Treasury to purchase some of the most illiquid and difficult-to-price securities (like CDOs) from financial companies, with the hope that this would, in turn, increase the liquidity of the secondary mortgage market. It is a broad economic relief program created by the Emergency Economic Stabilization Act signed by President George W. Bush in October 2008. It authorized the Treasury Department to purchase as much as $700 billion of troubled assets from financial institutions in order to strengthen the financial sector. It then was modified and turned into a source of capital, through the issuance of preferred equity, to rebuild confidence in, and the viability of, the entire banking sector.

Originally created to stabilize the financial sector, TARP quickly became a badge of shame for banks. It was unfairly labeled as a taxpayer bailout, only adding to the ill will directed at banks.

HEIGHTENED REGULATIONS

One significant result of the financial crisis is a wave of new regulations that govern everything from how a bank communicates with its customers to capital standards. These regulations are both complex and hotly contested.

It's not certain that they will repair the system or prevent future crises. Some of the regulations are focused on increasing fairness to the consumer; others are perceived as purely punitive to banks. Many require extensive resources—money, technology and people—for banks and the government to implement.

Many of these have not yet been fully fleshed out, so it's not clear how they will impact the industry. However, they are likely to bring great change to the business of banking.

One of the biggest concerns among American banks is that the regulations, and their associated costs, will prevent the banks from being globally competitive. Higher capital standards, trading rules, price controls and bank taxes could make American banks weaker against global competition. In today's global economy, American banks' inability to compete on a worldwide scale could further hurt the American economy.

Bankers also worry that there will be unintended consequences to the new regulations—that credit will be more expensive and harder to acquire and that the number of "unbanked" Americans, those who do their banking with payday lenders and check cashing centers, will dramatically increase as the costs of having a checking account increase.

The Dodd-Frank Act (formally named H.R. 4173, the Dodd-Frank Wall Street Reform and Consumer Protection Act) was signed into law in July 2010. At over 2,300 pages, the bill is the largest and most complex piece of financial reform since the Glass-Steagall Act of 1933, which was enacted as an emergency response to the failure of thousands of banks in the Great Depression.

The Dodd-Frank Act covers Wall Street oversight, executive compensation, mortgage reform, investment practices and more. Some consumer advocates and economists say that it reduces the chances of another crash by forcing large banking and financial institutions to have more capital to cover potential losses.

It also established a new regulatory entity, the Consumer Financial Protection Bureau.

The bill is controversial. It includes provisions that the banking industry believes will restrict the ability of traditional banks to serve their local communities. It is estimated that bankers will have an additional 5,000 pages of new regulations as a result of the bill.

It is feared that customers will end up bearing the brunt of compliance cost increases. Banks are already adding new customer fees; many banks are cancelling free checking.

THE DEBATE CONTINUES

The new regulatory entity, the Consumer Financial Protection Bureau, which was created by Dodd-Frank with the mission of making "markets for consumer financial products and services work for Americans," has the authority to examine banks, thrifts and credit unions that have more than $10 billion in assets. However, at the time of publication, the Bureau remains leaderless, hamstrung by campaign politics.

In July 2011, President Obama replaced his first controversial nominee to head the CFPB, Harvard Law Professor Elizabeth Warren, with former Ohio Attorney General Richard Cordray. A few days later, Senate Republicans said they were no more likely to confirm Cordray, a prosecutor of financial crimes and a contentious figure among bankers, than they were to confirm Warren. In October, a majority of the Senate Banking Committee voted to pass Cordray's nomination. However, he is still subject to an official vote of a divided Senate. Without a director, the CFPB can only enforce existing laws. It cannot create new rules or regulations regarding "abusive" bank practices or for mortgage brokers or payday lenders that aren't technically banks.

As the 2012 presidential election heats up, some of the Republican candidates are calling for a repeal or complete overhaul of the Dodd-Frank Act.

While the route to full economic recovery may remain uncertain, one thing is very clear: the debate about regulation and sanctions against banks and regulators is far from over.

As of Spring 2011, bank regulators and the nation's big banks were coming to an agreement focused on banks' mistreatment of borrowers in foreclosure cases. According to an April 10, 2011, op-ed in the *New York Times*, the agreement is ". . . a wrist slap at best . . . unlikely to ease the foreclosure crisis . . . All homeowners will suffer as a result. Some 6.7 million homes have already been lost in the housing bust, and another 3.3 million will be lost through 2012. The plunge in home equity—$5.6 trillion so far—hits everyone because foreclosures are a drag on all house prices . . ."

Then, in September 2011, the Federal Housing Finance Agency, which oversees Fannie Mae and Freddie Mac, filed suit against more than 12 big banks, including Bank of America, JPMorgan Chase and Goldman

Sachs, accusing them of misrepresenting the mortgage market. These suits are harsher than anything that's come before: they seek reimbursement for losses on the securities held by Fannie Mae and Freddie Mac. Together, those mortgagers lost more than $30 billion. The losses to date have been borne mostly by American taxpayers.

THE CHALLENGE OF RESTORING TRUST

According to the Rasmussen Reports, in March 2011, only 44 percent of Americans expressed confidence in the banking industry. (In February 2009, shortly after the Wall Street meltdown, the number was just 39 percent.) By contrast, just before the meltdown in July of 2008, 68 percent expressed confidence in the industry.

In a 2009 Gallup poll, only 19 percent of Americans surveyed expressed confidence in the integrity of bankers. Consumer confidence in banks' integrity is at the lowest level since Gallup began asking the question in 1976. As recently as 2005, 41 percent of Americans expressed confidence in bankers' integrity.

In April 2010, a Pew Research poll found that just 22 percent of respondents rated banks and other financial institutions as having "a positive effect on the way things are going in this country." This was lower than the ratings they gave to Congress, the federal government, big business, labor unions and the entertainment industry. Even though Americans remain skeptical about government control over the economy, an April 2010 poll conducted by Pew Research found that some 61 percent of respondents supported *more* financial regulation, virtually unchanged from the spring of 2009.

These statistics present unprecedented challenges for public relations in this industry. Once trust is lost, it is very difficult to regain: Edelman, the world's largest independent public relations firm, published its eleventh annual trust survey early in 2011. Its headline: "Trust Plunges in the United States While Resilient across the Globe—*Banks Stuck at the Bottom of Industry Rankings.*"

According to the survey, the "composite trust score" in this country—an average of public trust in business, government, nongovernmental organizations (NGOs) and media—is currently so low that the United States fell among the bottom four countries. (Three years ago, the United States was in the top four countries in terms of trust.)

The Edelman survey finds that financial services is the least trusted sector globally (50 percent), and banks are the second-least trusted (51 percent). In the United States, trust in banks collapsed, with banks dropping from the number 3 spot in 2008 (71 percent) to second from the bottom in 2011 (25 percent), tied with financial services.

CEO Richard Edelman said, "Company actions must deliver on the expectation for a collaborative approach that benefits society, not just shareholders; transparency about how it makes money; and communication in surround-sound through all forms of media."

Yet most banks have responded by doing what they did before, which is to sell complex products and services that people really do not understand, and focusing on supporting small businesses and giving back to their communities. They are ramping up overdraft fees and eliminating free checking.

The "motherhood and apple pie" message that so many banks are using—a message that suggests banks are quintessential elements in American life and valued by every American—lacks authenticity and seems terribly outdated.

What's more, the banking industry as a whole has been slow to engage effectively in social media. With a few exceptions, banks have stayed away from it, citing regulatory restrictions. While it's true that government regulations, particularly those pertaining to customer information and privacy, do impact how banks can use social media, they do not prohibit its use.

A recent report from Ovum, a market analysis firm, says that 60 percent of the world's retail banks still have no plans to use social media. Privacy and security concerns are their primary reasons for avoiding social media.

So communications professionals in the banking business will no doubt turn to traditional forms of public relations and employee engagement to win back the hearts and minds of customers, communities and investors.

NO MORE BUSINESS AS USUAL

Financial institutions have often relied on their customers' complacency and/or ignorance of the "fine print" as well as their (sometimes irrational) optimism that borrowing rates will never go up and home prices will never go down. Banks' long-held lack of transparency has worked largely in their favor because their customers allowed it to work. Since all banks were pretty much the same, customers did not have a better alternative, so they stayed put, even when they believed their bank had treated them unfairly.

However, the dire state of public opinion means that no financial institution can afford to continue business as usual.

Instead, they should forgo hidden fees, "gotcha" clauses and small print. They must be forthcoming with information and provide easy-to-understand products and services. In short, they must make it very easy for consumers, small business customers and large corporate customers alike to understand what the rules are.

They must focus on changing the dialogue, redefining community, fair banking practices and creating positive change in society. Here are specific ways that financial institutions can move forward in new ways.

Philanthropy as a Public Relations Tool

Developing an effective philanthropic strategy can help banks establish a positive identity with each of their key stakeholder groups: the public, employees, stockholders and government officials. Companies with well-defined grant criteria, used to attract or select grant requests, have the most effective corporate giving programs. Company programs that involve the company in public/private partnerships and encourage employee engagement can effect the greatest change.

Philanthropy is separate from marketing and sponsorships: the difference is where the money comes from. Charitable gifts come from a bank's profits; marketing and sponsorships generally come out of operating expenses. The IRS permits a company to give up to 10 percent of its profits to nonprofit organizations, though few companies give that much. Most are likely to give 1 to 2 percent of the pretax net income to charitable causes.

According to American Banker,

> Strapped for cash as their profits plummeted during the financial crisis, many financial institutions were forced to cut back on their charitable giving. Citigroup Inc. cut its philanthropic funds by 32% in 2009, a year in which its net losses totaled $1.6 billion.

> Charitable giving budgets were back on the upswing in 2010, but they were still below pre-crisis levels and they are expected to be flat this year. As a result, many banks have been trying to give more with less, putting more emphasis on employee volunteerism, for example, by offering perks such as paid time off to devote to organizations that the company supports.

> At the same time, banks have retooled their giving. They are providing more hands-on assistance to organizations that foster economic development and support the community, and they are buying fewer tickets to lavish fundraising events.

To create effective contributions programs, banks can determine objectives, establish measurable results and assure the budget is sufficient to achieve and quantify objectives.

Through strategic philanthropy, banks can establish a favorable reputation, associated with a good and important cause. They can create visibility for their senior executives. They can improve the quality of life in their communities in order to attract and retain employees. They can build relationships with potential customers. They can engage positively with political leaders.

Using Social Media for More Effective Communications

Social media allows the public to be heard. As noted earlier, banks as a whole have been slow to engage in social media. They've used regulatory restrictions to avoid it, though regulations do not prohibit the use of social media.

As a result, to bankers' detriment, they didn't hear the ever-louder words of discontent among consumers as the financial crisis grew. And they were blind to the coming public relations disaster.

Financial institutions could benefit in at least two ways by getting on board: social media creates virtual communities (and so allows a bank to completely redefine what community is), and it levels the playing field, allowing everyone to voice an opinion or an idea.

Recent research by Participate Systems, a Chicago-based company that provides outsourced online sales and customer support community solutions, produced the following data about the return on investment in online communities:

- Community users remain customers 50 percent longer than noncommunity users.

- 43 percent of support forums visits are in lieu of opening up a support case.

- Cost per interaction in customer support averages $12 via the contact center versus $0.25 via self-service options.

- Community users visit nine times more often than noncommunity users.

- Customers report good experiences in forums more than twice as often as they do via calls or mail.

Specifically, banks should improve their websites, insuring transparency, and making it easy for consumers not only to lodge complaints, but to get their complaints resolved. And they should institutionalize the practice of regularly engaging online with their consumers.

One banking company stands out from the rest in its sophisticated use of social media. Wells Fargo was the first U.S. bank to launch a corporate blog, in March 2006. The company now has several blogs, and employees use them to brainstorm as well as communicate with customers. (The blogs are the most-read nonbanking pages on Wells Fargo's site.) Employees also submit ideas regularly on a company wiki. Wells Fargo now has a presence on Facebook, Twitter and YouTube.

Read on, however, to learn what can happen when a company launches into social media without really understanding how transparent it is.

CASE STUDY: CHASE WADES INTO SOCIAL MEDIA

In a January 2011 article on www.socialmediatoday.com, Pam Moore wrote the "Top 12 Reasons Why Businesses Will Fail at Social Media in 2011." Her number one reason: they do not understand the ecosystem.

> Too many think if they learn the tools and technology they got it covered. They couldn't be further from the truth. The most important aspect of social media is to understand the art, the environment and how you can fit in. It doesn't work like the days of traditional advertising where you push a message and expect to change thought via a cool ad, billboard or TV commercial. Instead you must not only find a way to become part of the community, build your own community but also be able to successfully grab attention of your audiences authentically and via relationships. This is not easy for the organization only focused on tools and technology.

The 2009 experience of JPMorgan Chase & Company is a case in point. That year, the bank conducted an online contest to award a total of $5 million to 100 charities. Though contests using social media to award or raise money for charities are not uncommon, they have not been common among banks, and the Chase Community Giving contest was the largest ever mounted at the time.

The results of that contest are mixed and show how the real-time transparency of social media can mean new public relations hazards.

Chase encouraged Facebook users to sign onto Chase's fan page, where they could cast 20 votes for the nonprofits of their choice. More than a million people signed on to vote.

Three days before the contest ended, Chase stopped giving participants access to voting information. In addition, three nonprofit organizations, Justice for All (an antiabortion organization), the Marijuana Policy Project and Students for Sensible Drug Policy, accused chase of disqualifying them. Before the individual vote counts were taken down, each of these organizations had well over 1,000 votes and seemed to be in the running for a charitable gift.

In an e-mail message, a Chase spokesman wrote, "We have taken down individual charity counts with a couple of days left to build excitement among the broadest number of participants, as well as to ensure that all Facebook users learn of the 100 finalists at the same time and so we have an opportunity to notify the 100 finalists first."

Here's how contests like these usually work: a company selects a number of charities that they would give money to, and asks people to vote among them. Instead, Chase took a database of 500,000 nonprofit organizations and uploaded the information on to Facebook. (Chase specified that the charities must confirm they did not discriminate in any way, had an operating budget less than $10 million and had a mission that aligned with Chase's corporate responsibility guidelines, which are posted on its website—education, health care, housing, the environment, combating hunger, arts and culture, human services and animal welfare).

The bank allowed "crowdsourcing" to choose the winning 100 charities.

Chase did not have a leader board showing a ranking of the charities based on votes on the Chase Community Giving page on Facebook. So organizations could find out how many votes they had, and who voted for them, but did not know how their total compared with that of other organizations. Beth Kanter, who blogs about social media and nonprofits wrote,

> The biggest mistake [Chase] made was not providing a leader board, that tracked participants progress. Leader boards and dynamic vote counts help make a contestant's job of getting out the vote easier. With the Chase Bank Online Contest, the lack of a leader board created a lot of extra work for the nonprofits. They had to spend time combing through pages of other organization's voting records. Also, it doesn't make for a clear call to action message.

By not having a leader board and by pulling the vote tallies before the contest was over, Chase eliminated the perception of transparency. And, though they did give $5 million to charities, they got a lot of bad publicity, particularly when the organizations that believed they were disqualified and their supporters turned back to social media to complain broadly.

CONCLUSION

PUBLIC RELATIONS OPPORTUNITIES IN THE TWENTY-FIRST CENTURY

The banking industry will continue to evolve at a rapid pace. Continued consolidation and globalization will both decrease the number of competitors and increase the level of competition. Strategic public relations will be critical for banks' success on the competitive, ever-shifting playing field. Following are three opportunities for public relations wins today and into the future.

OPPORTUNITY NO. 1: ARTICULATE A CLEAR VISION

Successful public relations is about thought leadership—communicating a strategic vision to the public in a professional, informative, influential way. Banks need to identify their strengths and contributions to customers and communities, and articulate them clearly. Comprehensive communications efforts must be driven by overall business strategies, to cement and strengthen the critical bond between banks and their customers.

OPPORTUNITY NO. 2: CHANGE THE DIALOGUE

Most of America's bankers do not belong to the relatively small group whose actions were the largest contributors to the financial crisis. Most, like other businesspeople in this country, are committed to doing their jobs well, selling good products and providing good customer service. Public relations professionals in this industry must find a way to move beyond a defensive strategy.

OPPORTUNITY NO. 3: REDEFINE COMMUNITY

While regulators, policymakers and bankers work to find ways to avoid, going forward, what happened in 2008, public relations strategy can focus on building community with customers, inviting dialogue, making sure their banks are accessible and increasing transparency. This is made particularly challenging because the Internet, mobile banking and ATMs have made local bank branches less relevant today than they were in the twentieth century. However, the strategic use of social media is one critical and highly effective way to redefine and build new communities and enhance the relationship of banks to their stakeholders in the future.

DISCUSSION QUESTIONS

1. What have been the major forces that have changed banking public relations?
2. If you were working in public relations in the banking industry, what are the three issues you would want your company to address?
3. What are the greatest communications challenges the banking industry faces?
4. What can the banking industry do to regain public trust?
5. How could the banking industry use social media? What platforms might be used?
6. If you were a spokesperson at Chase, how would you have responded to complaints about its Facebook charity contest?

NOTES

1. The FCIC is a 10-member, government-appointed commission charged with investigating the financial crisis.
2. According to the U.S. Department of Labor, Bureau of Labor and Statistics, unemployment was over 10 percent in October 2009.
3. Morgan Stanley and Goldman Sachs were not banks until after the financial crisis.
4. CDOs are structured asset-backed securities. Their value comes from the cash flow generated by the associated pool of assets. A CDO is split into different risk categories, or tranches, with differing levels of payment seniority. Senior risk classes offer lower coupon rates, while junior risk classes, those that are riskier, offer coupon rates to compensate for additional default risk. If the CDO does not have enough cash to pay all of the investors, those in the more junior categories are the first to stop receiving payment. CDOs grew prolifically from 2004 to 2007, then, in the wake of the subprime mortgage crisis, declined precipitously— many of the assets in the CDOs had been subprime mortgages. When global investors stopped buying CDOs in 2007, they contributed to the collapse of some of the structured investments held by investment banks. This also led to the bankruptcy of several subprime lenders.
5. CDSs are forms of insurance that protect the owner if a borrower defaults.
6. Emphasis is the Author's.

ADDITIONAL READING

England, Robert Stowe. *Black Box Casino: How Wall Street's Risky Shadow Banking Crashed Global Finance.* California, CA: Praeger Publishers, 2011. Print.

Hudson, Michael. *The Monster: How a Gang of Predatory Lenders and Wall Street Bankers Fleeced America— And Spawned a Global Crisis.* New York, NY: St. Martin's Griffin, 2011. Print.

McGee, Suzanne. *Chasing Goldman Sachs: How the Masters of the Universe Melted Wall Street Down—And Why They'll Take Us to the Brink Again.* New York, NY: Crown, 2010. Print.

Morgenson, Gretchen. *Reckless Endangerment: How Outsized Ambition, Greed, and Corruption Led to Economic Armageddon.* New York, NY: Times Books, 2011. Print.

Sorkin, Andrew Ross. *Too Big to Fail: The Inside Story of How Wall Street and Washington Fought to Save the Financial System — and Themselves.* New York, NY: Penguin, 2011 (updated edition). Print.

44

C H A P T E R

THE FOOD AND BEVERAGE INDUSTRY
Catering to People's Palates

Richard L. Nelson
Vice President, Corporate Communications
ACCO Brands Corporation

Marguerite Copel
Vice President, Corporate Communications
The Dean Foods Company

A STRATEGIC APPROACH TO PUBLIC RELATIONS

When you think about it, few things are more personal—more *intimate*—than food. To begin with, it goes into our mouths and inside our bodies. It satisfies our first appetite and provides us with the longest-lasting source of human pleasure. Food is necessary for its nutritional value, but the enjoyment associated with eating brings it into another realm: consider the friendships and family ties forged and renewed over meals, the cultural signposts food provides for immigrant ethnic groups or the ways in which certain aromas can trigger the sights and sounds that accompanied them in the past. One whiff of a fresh-baked apple pie and you're instantly transported to Grandma's kitchen. The pop of a champagne cork brings you back to that once-in-a-lifetime trip to Times Square on New Year's Eve.

On a less romantic level, food and beverages long have dictated the most personal concerns of the human species: health. Ever since the Old Testament's King Og discovered that eating certain plants could cause harm—or, conversely, that swallowing an oyster whole would *not* kill him—mankind has realized the inseparable relationship between the things we eat and the way our bodies react. Today, as we stagger under the onslaught of nutritional studies, food safety concerns or issues such as sustainability or the benefits of organic versus nonorganic, the selection and preparation of food plays an increasingly large role in everyday life and health.

Eric Schlosser, in his book *Fast Food Nation*, said, "A nation's diet can be more revealing than its art or literature." And the food conversation, which began as a quiet dialogue, has grown more vociferous. A 2011 Google search for food blogs turned up more than 91 million results covering everything from recipes with hiyayakko (chilled tofu), to the pros and cons of regulation, to advice ("Wear gloves when chopping hot peppers!"). Very few food manufacturers do *not* have blogs, and you can "follow" PopChips on Twitter.

The proliferation of so-called mommy blogs continues to play a significant role in our cultural fabric; a report by eMarketer predicts there will be 4.4 million mommy bloggers by 2014. And, a new mobile food app pops up every time you start to feel hungry. You can shake your phone on Urbanspoon to find a local restaurant, and savvy restaurateurs text and tweet about hot specials to make customers feel like insiders. The massive availability of foodie information—right and wrong—makes getting through with your food or beverage message a challenge. Perhaps we need to heed the advice of Michael Pollan in his wildly successful book, *In Defense of Food: An Eater's Manifesto,* which is summed up in his opening sentence, "Eat food. Not too much. Mostly plants."

As Michelle Stacey writes in her book, *Consumed*, "Food is no longer simply food but preventive medicine, a scientific abstraction, a moral test, and, sometimes, a mortal enemy. This love/hate relationship invests food with more freight than it can carry . . ." It also opens the door to unusual abuses, such as the tendency to exaggerate a product's extranutritional values, which has led to government regulation of health claims for foods and beverages.

Stacey writes specifically about Americans, but in cultures the world over, food represents the most personal of choices. In most countries, these choices are made from a huge variety of options, multiple times each day. This fact alone distinguishes the food industry from all others and is paramount in shaping and coloring the whole mix of marketing strategies.

Within that mix, public relations plays a highly significant role. Advertising almost always creates a slight suspicion among consumers because they know the advertiser paid large sums to paint the best picture of its product. The third-party endorsements that public relations professionals seek from the press, universities, government and other influencers can ease this suspicion. Such endorsements take on a particularly important and credible role in the case of products as personal and essential as food and beverages. Also, peer-to-peer conversations hold tremendous influence: the mommy blogosphere is perhaps one of the best examples of this new influence shift. Research shows we are influenced the most by "people like me." How, then, should we promote food? The strategies and tactics employed can take as many forms as there are creative public relations specialists.

TAKING A STRATEGIC APPROACH

Successfully reaching those publics requires a strategic public relations plan that begins with a simple question. What business problem are we trying to solve? Is our product hampered by a poor reputation? Do we need to build awareness? Can we enhance its relevance? Our job is to change behavior—clear and simple. To do this, we must develop a plan that *starts* with strategy and *ends* in tactics. A press release, event in Times Square or colorful brochure is only as successful as the carefully crafted plan that will change behavior and move the needle. Most companies in most industries sell to a certain percentage of the population. But only one industry sells to the entire population. Everybody eats and drinks—24/7. As a result, the communication stakes are high in the world of food and beverage. In every case, however, the strategies must reach at least one, and preferably several, of the many relevant publics.

THE INFLUENCE OF STAKEHOLDERS

Chief among these audiences, of course, are consumers. Public relations reaches them in both direct and indirect ways. One approach uses the media to go directly to consumers, informing, engaging and influencing them through general-market press releases and news conferences, pitching individual stories to general-interest newspapers and magazines and placing qualified spokespeople on a seemingly ever-expanding array of radio and television talk shows.

An equally effective but less direct method of reaching consumers is by "influencing the influencers": developing programs to reach health professionals, retailers, trade media and other interested parties, each of whom plays a part in helping the consumer choose which food or beverage product to buy. Other influencers include the scientific community, including academic scientists, whose critiques and validations play an essential role in the efforts just described, and trade associations, which can act as third-party spokespeople on behalf of a product.

Not to be left out of the dialogue are the manufacturers themselves (as well as their shareholders, who expect to see profits and dividends from these companies); advocacy groups such as the Center for Science in the Public Interest and PETA; agricultural firms and organizations, whose interests and agendas may or may not dovetail with those of the groups already mentioned; and the elected officials and government regulators charged with safeguarding the consumer from both unhealthy food and unwarranted nutritional claims. Finally, there are the employees of food and beverage companies, one of the most important audiences of all. Without their ownership and support, an external marketing communications program becomes immeasurably harder to execute. Conversely, if an organization has 1,000 employees who feel good about the company, it has 1,000 positive brand ambassadors.

INDUSTRY CHANGES

To understand the public relations opportunities and challenges that are particular to this industry, it is important to recognize three distinct waves of influence that have affected it over the past several decades.

First, as in most industries, food and beverage companies have seen their world completely transformed by technological advances, which have led to geometric growth, an endless array of potential new products and markets and rapid changes in the manufacture and transportation of food. These technological developments in turn have spurred an equally profound series of sociological changes, from the days in which families prepared all their meals at home (and often from food grown on their own land) to the present, when many people eat out more often than in (and frequently simply heat or reheat prepreparred meals when at home). Meanwhile, the food and beverage industry in the United States, Canada and Europe, and to varying degrees throughout the world, has had to adjust to a growing network of regulatory rules and restrictions.

The technological revolution in the food industry began with the development of more efficient farming and production techniques. These include the use of agricultural chemicals to reduce losses due to insects and other pests and other chemicals to quicken the maturation of crops and livestock. The improved yields that resulted from these advances helped reduce prices for food. Due to another trend—consumers' burgeoning interest in healthy, artisanal and organic food—there is a resurging interest in closer-to-home access to farm-grown foodstuffs. Across the developed world, one sees a resurgence of farmers markets and grocery stores featuring locally grown produce, meat and dairy products.

Other technological leaps have had similar impacts on the industry, while at the same time spurring analogous sociological developments. Most important among these was the packaging revolution, which began with the invention of large-scale food canning in the nineteenth century. The canning industry made great strides during the Civil War—canned and tinned goods were used to feed both armies and at the same time became popular with civilians—and World War II provided a similar impetus to the development of the ready-to-eat foods that later caught on with the general public. Around 1920, Clarence Birdseye, an explorer and inventor, became fascinated with the way Canadian Eskimos stored their food. Birdseye developed a process for the successful quick-freezing of fresh produce, and the frozen-food industry was born.

These developments, along with advances in transportation such as refrigerated trucks, trains and air transport that permit the nationwide distribution of perishable goods, have revolutionized the ways in which Americans purchase and consume foods. A hundred years ago, Mom walked down to the corner food store and asked that nice Mr. Jones behind the counter for a pound of flour from the barrel in the back. Today we shop in supermarkets that have grown into virtual town squares of aisles, departments and subsections, carrying every variety of American, ethnic and imported foods, many of which are designed for once-undreamed-of convenience. In addition, shop-and-delivery services now proliferate. We can buy anything from paper products and drink mixes to foie gras and gourmet chocolates at Amazon.com, which began by carrying only shrink-wrapped, order-on-demand books. Online grocery services such as Peapod and NetGrocer continue to add more cities to their growing rosters.

At the same time, this craving for convenience has fostered the exponential growth of the quick-service restaurant and has exported the fast-food phenomenon throughout the world. This, too, is part of the revolution in how we eat—a revolution of sociological impact and technological achievement. Not long ago, families gathered around the dinner table in an exercise in communication and connection necessitated by the labor-intensive home-cooked meal. Today, that "quality time" is spent in the car en route to McDonald's, where we eat and then often disband to separate work, school and leisure activities. Indeed, we have created a nation of "sinkers" who eat around the kitchen sink versus the family table.

The success of quick-service restaurants would not have been possible without the availability of national advertising vehicles—magazines, national newspapers such as *USA Today,* news services and syndicates like the Los Angeles Times syndicate or Bloomberg News and network broadcasts on radio and television. These national media were important for another reason as well: earlier, they had played a major role in the development and marketing of the national-brand products that replaced the regional specialties defining America's food production. This was perhaps best seen with the rise of national brands of beer, most notably Budweiser, to replace the local beers once produced by community breweries, which are seeing a resurgence today.

With a growing consumer interest in "real" and "genuine" as opposed to mass produced, localization is increasing in popularity. Growth of the craft brewing industry in 2010 was 11 percent by volume and 12 percent by dollars compared to growth in 2009 of 7.2 percent by volume and 10.3 percent by dollars. Locavores and nonlocavores alike are gravitating toward artisanal cheeses and jams. Boutique retailers specialize in local products, and even online specialty stores are joining the trend: Fodoro.com features only gourmet food that is made by artisanal producers and farmers.

Technology not only drives sociological change, it also must respond to that change. In recent years, the food industry's vaunted technological skills have dovetailed with retailing innovations to meet changing, and even contradictory, consumer needs and desires. Thus, in the midst of the proliferation of restaurants priding themselves on huge portion sizes and quick-service chains offering "upsized" meals for a bargain price, modern America also finds itself obsessed with healthful foods and treats. From salads, yogurt, free-range turkeys and sugar-free sundaes to natural peanut butter, fat-free cookies, gourmet coffee and bottled water—all of these serve as examples of the backlash against generic uniformity. This backlash has forced, in some cases, quick-service restaurants and mega-supermarkets to market healthful choices and offer up solutions to nutrition-challenged offerings.

For example, in 2011, Walmart, the world's biggest retailer, vowed that by 2015, their suppliers needed to reformulate some packaged food items to reduce sodium by 25 percent, reduce sugar by 10 percent in others and remove all remaining industrially produced trans fats in all its packaged food products. In addition, Walmart planned to develop simple front-of-package labels that would help customers identify wiser food choices.

These changes play out against the background of government regulatory control, which has attained an increasingly higher profile as the public's concerns over health issues grow. These concerns date back more than a century and reached their first great peak in 1906, when publication of *The Jungle,* Upton Sinclair's muckraking exposé of unhygienic and unsafe practices in the meat industry, led to the passage of the Pure Food and Drug Act. Today, the federal government spends more resources than ever on issues that range from the original concerns of food safety, including the growing and manufacturing processes, to claims made in advertising, public relations materials and packaging. The reason? The proliferation of new concepts, new products and line extensions; to wit, a shelf in the supermarket soft drink aisle might hold regular, sugar-free, zero-calorie, low-sugar, caffeine-free, diet caffeine-free, flavored, "throwback" and vitamin-enhanced versions of the same brand. The dairy case across the way displays regular, reduced-cholesterol, low-fat and no-fat versions of the same brand of cheese, and a visit to the produce section reveals a square watermelon—easier to pack and store.

FOOD SAFETY

New technologies have shown that both labor and land productivity can be increased, sometimes dramatically. Yet with more advances come more hazards. Technology cannot entirely reduce the risk of salmonella from eggs, E. Coli in spinach or melamine in Chinese-made pet food and dairy products. Globalization has led to a rising number of international recalls and outbreaks such as "mad-cow" disease in the United Kingdom, United States and Japan. In 2011, the same year that Jennie-O Turkey recalled 55,000 pounds of salmonella-tainted turkey burgers, the Food and Drug Administration (FDA) unveiled a website dedicated to helping consumers search for recalled food.

Fears of bioterrorism have had global impact. On a smaller scale, locally sourced food is not without its food safety challenges. In either case, real or imagined food safety scares can impact demand and, ultimately, company profits. A number of companies have claimed bankruptcy as a result of widespread recalls. And an outbreak of a food-borne illness can do irreparable harm to the public's perception of the wholesomeness of a product or the reputation of a company that offers it.

Here are a few of the food safety issues that communications professionals managed in the last decade.

In September 2006, the FDA issued a statement warning of E. Coli bacteria in spinach. The outbreak originated on a central California farm. It eventually claimed five lives and caused 205 illnesses across 26 states. Ultimately, the industry reported a $350-million loss. The spinach industry launched a multifaceted campaign after the event to regain brand equity. They took a leadership position and asked the FDA for mandatory standards for fruits and vegetables to improve safety, they described the steps being taken to solve the problem, they reached out to consumers with a 24-hour hotline and they widely disseminated information on how to properly prepare spinach. Tom Stenzel, president of the United Fresh Produce Association, conducted a media tour to discuss further safeguards. This is a good example of crisis communication that had long-term positive effects.

In 2008, six infants died, and 300,000 people were hospitalized after consuming melamine-contaminated milk-based products in China. Melamine is generally used in the manufacture of fire-retardant plastic. But in this case, it was reported that melamine was illegally added to milk to improve the apparent protein content. Some U.K. and U.S. companies were affected when they bought milk products from China. Unlike the spinach food safety issue, the melamine issue was poorly handled. Despite the breaking international news surrounding this scandal, the Chinese government was slow to respond to questions. The news media reported that not until the Chinese Health Ministry officially confirmed that the milk powder was contaminated by melamine did the government or industry undertake any initiative to warn the public. Later, government inspections revealed that the products of 22 Chinese dairy firms were contaminated with melamine. The Chinese government did not take this lightly: on January 22, 2009, the Intermediate People's Court in Shijiazhuang, China, sentenced to death two persons accused in the tainted-milk scandal in China.

In January 2009, a U.S. peanut company, Peanut Corporation of America (PCA), issued a recall after discovering possible salmonella contamination. The recall expanded to include 2,100 products from more than 200 companies nationwide that contained its peanut products. According to the Centers for Disease Control (CDC), the salmonella contamination spread through 46 states, claiming eight lives and sickening more than 700 people. This was another example of poor food safety crisis response. It was reported that at the onset, the owner aggressively defended PCA, claiming that every safety precaution was taken. He did not express remorse, regret or empathy despite unsafe practices. The owner regretted having to take action but did not express any regret or take any responsibility for the company's role in harming consumers.

After new evidence surfaced that demonstrated the problems stemmed from an ongoing practice, it was alleged that PCA stopped virtually all communication, including communication with employees who were laid off from plants that were forced to close as a result of the contamination. PCA offered no compensation for those affected by their negligence, which, in this case, included deaths. They were accused of expressing no desire to compensate anyone for pain, suffering and anguish at being put in harm's way. PCA attempted to draw out the investigations as long as possible and resisted while claiming cooperation. PCA president Stuart Parnell refused to testify at congressional hearings. The company ultimately declared bankruptcy.

In August 2010, two Iowa farms recalled more than half a billion eggs, as a result of 1,500 cases of illness associated with salmonella. The FDA said the contamination was most likely due to a lack of cleanliness and substandard cage size. It was reported that the DeCoster family agribusiness operations, owner of the company at the center of the outbreak, was a habitual violator of health and safety laws and had been sued repeatedly over practices that included cruelty to animals.

As a result, public disclosure of food safety information—restaurant inspection reports, in-plant videos and public postings of test results—intensified and will continue to intensify. Transparency is our future.

What is the reality for communications professionals?

The food industry faces unique problems. Our culture cannot tolerate an imperfect food supply, but a perfect food supply simply is not attainable. Nevertheless, the food supply in the developed world is remarkably safe. Will it remain that way? How do communications professionals prepare for the next major issue? And what will it be?

We need to be able to see the emerging trends that will impact the food and beverage industry. The key here is *emerging*. Staying on top of the issues is not enough. To be truly effective, communications professionals need to stay *ahead* of them. Key issues will continue to be:

Laws: In 2010, the U.S. government passed the Food Safety Modernization Act, a law that would strengthen the power of the FDA to oversee the national food supply and create a food safety culture in the United States. The bill is considered a sweeping change to the food safety system, with a major focus on preventing food-borne illness.

Regulations and enforcement: About 2,700 U.S. state and local health agencies are the foundation of the food safety regulations and enforcement system. The investigative capacity of these important agencies is unlikely to increase. Companies in regulated industries must speak for themselves, but they can only do so credibly while supporting the agencies that ensure the safety of the food supply. It is in the best interest of the food and beverage industry to make certain that the regulatory regime remains robust.

Local food: In 2009, the local food movement picked up a major advocate, U.S. First Lady Michelle Obama. She used her high-profile position to encourage Americans to eat locally grown produce, emphasizing its taste and nutritional benefits as well as its positive impact on the local economy.

Childhood obesity: The U.S. Department of Agriculture (USDA) was charged in the Child Nutrition Bill with establishing nutritional standards for the nation's schools in 2011. The standards apply to all food in the school, including food and beverages supplied by vending machines. First Lady Michelle Obama, with her "Let's Move" campaign and the new Dietary Guidelines for Americans, was instrumental in promoting this change.

Food imports: In late 2009, the Department of Homeland Security opened a center to make sure food imported to the United States is safe. The center came out of the President's Food Safety Working Group. Imported food and its safety are increasingly receiving much attention.

Traceability: The forces behind traceability want to be able to drive to an agricultural farm, walk to a specific field, go down the right row and reach over and pick up whatever is causing a problem. They want a system that will prevent the financially devastating recall costs and outbreaks that make more people sick.

USES OF PUBLIC RELATIONS

In this dizzying vortex of new products, multiple brands, food safety issues, new regulations, changing consumer needs and competing health claims, a savvy, strategic and well-executed public relations campaign can have an enormous impact. By giving the consumer a specific, unadvertised reason to think well of a product, the public relations manager can create respect and sometimes even demand that will separate the product from the large and confusing pack, changing consumer behavior.

One such example is the Butterball Turkey Hotline that Swift & Company cooked up in 1981. It has become as much a part of our social fabric as eating turkey at Thanksgiving, which of course is the point. Each year, for the months of November and December, professional home economists and nutritionists answer questions about correct preparation and salvage last-minute disasters for callers to the free 1-800-Butterball line. During the hotline's first year, six home economists fielded questions from 11,000 callers. The publicity was so widespread, and consumer reaction so positive, that in 2010, the numbers had grown to 50 professional nutritionists and economists fielding more than 100,000 questions. The publicity that surrounds this service, which seems to yield a feature story in food sections of every newspaper annually, garners tremendous attention for the company. The coverage does something else: it positions the Butterball brand's makers as experts, the people who know everything there is to know about turkeys. In consumers' minds, this equates to Butterball turkeys being better than other brands.

Public relations positioning is part of an overall integrated strategic communication program and an integral component of the communication mix. It plays an integral role in helping the company to meet its business goals, in part, by projecting a calculated image. Public relations professionals always have been known as creators of the image; they also must help preserve the image. Part of that responsibility lies in PR's counseling function.

PR's role as counselor comes into play most urgently during times of crisis. (See Chapter 26 on crisis communications.) Crisis communication is its own subspecialty, due in part to the speed of information, vastness of our food supply and the greater prevalence of food contamination, and in part to increasingly sophisticated methods of packaging and food processing. The more elements and stages involved in the process, the greater the chance of something going wrong. However, sometimes a crisis occurs when, literally, nothing is amiss. On Valentine's Day in 1986, a New York woman complained of finding glass in a jar of Gerber baby food. As the company investigated the claim, local television stations and wire services picked up the story, resulting in copy-cat complaints cropping up from as far away as Florida. This occurred even as the New York health authorities gave Gerber a clean bill of health, and the FDA declared that it was unable to substantiate any claims. Yet complaints eventually occurred in 40 states and in countries as distant as Australia.

This case study is of particular importance because of the strong, uncompromising stand Gerber took against something the media urged them to do—recall the product. Still smarting from a 1984 incident in which Gerber proactively recalled baby juice that a consumer said contained pieces of glass—even though they found no glass in the product and no regulatory agency found any reason to do so—Gerber remained firm in its decision not to recall the baby food. However, much like their counterparts at Pepsi during the 1993 Diet Pepsi tampering incidents in which syringes were "found" in various cans of Diet Pepsi, Gerber executives did not let matters stand with a mere announcement of their intent. Rather, they embarked on an aggressive communications campaign with one clear objective: demonstrating Gerber's safe processing and packaging procedures to the media; the trade, federal, state and local authorities; healthcare providers; and even their own employees. They launched interviews, direct mail and other communication vehicles. The results were significant: less than a year later, Gerber had maintained and even slightly increased its market share. In both the Gerber and Diet Pepsi crises, the companies successfully and accurately portrayed themselves as victims, winning the sympathy of the public.

Not so fortunate were the Japanese dairy and vegetable industries. In 2011, an immense earthquake and tsunami caused massive damage in Japan, including the partial meltdown of several nuclear reactors. Japanese health officials said radiation levels in spinach and milk from farms near one of the plants exceeded government safety limits. The Science and Technology Ministry also said that miniscule amounts of radioactive iodine had been detected in Tokyo and neighboring prefectures and had seeped into the food chain. In response to global alarm, Japan's cabinet secretary insisted the contaminated foods "posed no immediate health risk."

Americans were skeptical of the Japanese government's claims—skepticism that turned into concern when it was announced that tainted milk and spinach were found along the west coast of the United States. Although it had been nearly 30 years since the nuclear reactor meltdown in Chernobyl, those old enough to remember also remembered the resultant increased cases of thyroid cancer. The Environmental Protection Agency (EPA) quickly issued a statement that radiation levels would have to be 5,000 times higher to reach the "intervention level" set by the FDA. This initial positioning, though accurate, was not consumer friendly. It needed to say, in no uncertain terms, "milk is safe."

Food companies, the dairy industry and trade associations acted quickly to partner with EPA, FDA, USDA and CDC, as well as state and local health departments, to help consumers understand the true risk. The result was consistent positioning, language and messaging used by industry and government alike on hotlines, websites and in response to the media. Twitter and blogs were on fire with both sides of the issue equally represented. This is a strong example of how the private and public sector can work together to reach a successful outcome. Though the issue raged over three days, quick industry partnership with government and regulatory agencies helped quell the fears of a rightly concerned public. Research fielded the weekend after the breaking news showed consumers continued to believe that milk was safe and understood the infinitesimal risk.

The benefits of building and nurturing alliances can prove most critical in times of crisis. One example involved the StarKist Company, the target of negative publicity for tuna fishing practices that resulted in dolphin deaths. As the twentieth anniversary of Earth Day approached, awareness reached a critical mass; boycotts were initiated against both StarKist and its parent, H.J. Heinz, and Congress pushed for regulation.

The company decided to take the lead in adopting a worldwide "dolphin-safe" policy that would set a standard for the industry. Critical to their strategy and success was coalition building; positive response from environmentalists and congressional leaders was needed to change consumer distrust to support. Public relations counsel worked with environmental leaders to involve StarKist in Earth Day, to be held one week after the company's announcement of its change in practices. Influential environmental leaders and members of Congress praised the company and issued statements of support. The boycott was lifted on StarKist, and the boycott leader, Earth Island Institute, took out an ad in the *New York Times* specifically thanking the company.

The change in policy gave the company a positive message; getting that message out successfully involved the thoughtful building of strategic alliances to provide influential third-party endorsements.

INTERNATIONAL ISSUES

Coalition building is a strategy employed by sophisticated public relations practitioners since the pioneering days of Edward Bernays and John Hill. But since public relations and marketing sophistication can be an elusive quality, marketers need to be especially sensitive to cultural differences when pursuing initiatives outside their traditional geographic spheres of business.

Consider the case of a U.S.-based food manufacturer seeking to market its cake mixes in Japan. The company knew that few Japanese kitchens, because of their tiny size, had an oven; they also knew that almost every Japanese household had a rice cooker. So they developed and marketed a cake mix that could be baked in a rice cooker, hoping to make great inroads into the market—without fully appreciating that, to the Japanese, rice is sacred. They eat it white and unsullied. And they certainly do not want to make it in a cooker that has leftover smells or flavors of vanilla or chocolate that remained no matter how hard they scrubbed.

Other problems can occur because of the different forms of communication and tools available (or not) to public relations professionals. In Latin America, Eastern Europe, most of Africa and much of Asia, newspaper stories are frequently bought and, just as frequently, editorial mentions will be directly linked to advertising expenditures. Companies that know this can use it to their advantage.

In the late 1970s, Kellogg's embarked on a program to promote breakfast nutrition throughout the world by placing health-oriented articles in the foreign press as is the practice in America. The company found not just its greatest success but also its only success in publications in which it advertised.

Different cultures can—unknowingly—influence product sales in unconventional ways. In the late 1960s, toothbrush sales in South Vietnam increased after the Vietcong began using them to clean their weapons. U.S. troops inadvertently caused condom companies' stock to rise when it was revealed that they were using condoms to protect rifle barrels from sand. And feminine napkin sales were higher than expected in South America; it wasn't until years later that the company learned they were being used by farmers as dust masks.

When Coca-Cola was first sold in China in 1927, its brand needed to be transliterated into Chinese characters. While the company did the research to find the right Chinese characters, a number of shopkeepers couldn't wait and made homemade signs with Chinese characters that may have sounded like Coca-Cola, but their meaning was quite another thing, including "female horse fastened with wax" and "bite the wax tadpole."

Still, advanced communications technology has brought about Marshall McLuhan's predicted "global shrinking," resulting in an increasingly sophisticated concept of marketing throughout the world. Such powerhouse global marketers as Nestlé, Pepsi and others have sought local marketing partners in other nations to help spread the word about their products with appropriate market sensitivity, and this has accelerated the acceptance and comprehension of modern marketing tools. In addition, the marketing conglomerates themselves—Omnicom, Publicis, the WPP Group, Interpublic and others—have effectively created worldwide networks of advertising and public relations agencies to support both multinational and local clients.

This gives the food and beverage industry several options when it comes to public relations suppliers in foreign markets. Manufacturers can connect with one of the global firms such as Hill & Knowlton, Burson-Marsteller, Ketchum, Fleishmann-Hillard or Edelman Public Relations worldwide to enjoy the much-touted advantage of a network of offices wired into a central headquarters. They can work with networked independent agencies, or they can construct their own networks of independent agencies, choosing from the best vendors in each individual locale whether or not these vendors are owned by or affiliated with a large multinational. Not surprisingly, each has its advantages and disadvantages.

The large-firm approach affords the client a coherent, centralized public relations strategy across all markets. It also locks in (theoretically, at least) all of the services and capabilities offered by the agency throughout its network. The client can often save time and money by dealing directly with headquarters, rather than with a series of office managers. But despite their best efforts, each large agency network has strengths and weaknesses throughout its system. Its Frankfurt office might be the standout player in all of Germany, but the Hong Kong office may lack anyone with food or beverage expertise. Some offices may be affiliates, as opposed to agency owned, diluting a possibly tenuous influence of headquarters. And finally, the local office in, for example, Buenos Aires may choose to take on a competing client and resign the multinational client; if the agency's control is weak enough, even the corporate office will not be able to prevent this from happening.

On the other hand, setting up a county-by-county network can prove daunting. Without a lot of time or a large enough staff, the public relations practitioner will be hard pressed to keep each individual regional agency briefed and up to speed on the company's products and programs. The network approach also makes it tougher to establish a coherent campaign, since each agency will want to add its own entrepreneurial touches to the well-crafted strategy—often whether or not they are on target. The practitioner may spend more money, since the minimal fees for acceptable service from all these individual offices may eclipse the package deal that could be made with a multinational. The superb service received in all markets may well offset such drawbacks, but then again, the Hong Kong market just might not be that important.

As global marketers continue to expand their reach, the vendors of global communications services seem likely to do the same. Within the next few years, several leading food and beverage brands from North American and European manufacturers may well be supported by a handful of top advertising and public relations service organizations. This trend can be seen with products such as alcoholic beverages and carbonated soft drinks, convenience and snack foods and chocolate candies, as well as the quick-service restaurant industry.

Regional products will continue to have their place, of course. Few in the United States, for example, have heard of a "squash," but in Britain, that word denotes a popular form of fruit-based soft drink. Local traditions dictate that Norwegians like their cheese one way, Italians another and Chinese not at all, with Americans among the few cultures that embalm cheese in plastic wrap and then place it in cold storage until it is consumed. Pasta, rice, tea, coffee, sauce and soups are the stuff of local preference, and they will likely resist the trend toward globalization. In addition, some products are destined to remain regional commodities due to problems with distribution or large-scale manufacturing: frozen foods, most dairy products and baked goods and fresh meats, fish, fruits and vegetables.

Whether utilizing public relations to benefit a product here or abroad, however, one thing remains clear: public relations no longer works in a vacuum. It's no more logical to think in terms of stand-alone public relations programs than it is to think of stand-alone advertising programs. The dividing lines among elements of the marketing communications mix are blurring; the public relations function is as apt to implement a direct mail program as the advertising group is to propose a contest. Also, there is an increasing number of PR practitioners working in "marketing communications," where their role is to generate publicity for the company's ad campaign. As one example, the highly successful National Milk Moustache "Got Milk?" ad campaign became the umbrella for a marketing mix of advertising, public relations and promotion. "Behind-the-scenes" interviews with celebrities on the making of the commercials, milk giveaways, spokesperson tours and even a milk scholarship worked in tandem to round out the campaign and take milk's message into areas where traditional advertising could not go.

As marketing budgets shrink and audiences for traditional forms of advertising become more fragmented, public relations plays an increasingly important role in the marketing mix. While public relations programs cannot generate brand awareness as effectively as mass-market advertising, public relations is often more effective than its marketing cousins in motivating consumer behavior, shaping consumer attitudes, deflecting criticism of a product or brand and refining the contours of brand imagery. By its very nature, public relations is a more targeted discipline, and marketers—who are finding it less attractive to spend large sums on television advertising that reaches fewer people in desirable demographic groups—are turning to public relations as a more efficient, more focused vehicle of persuasion.

Food and beverage marketers, along with most consumer product marketers, generally allocate between 10 and 20 percent of total marketing funds for public relations programming. This rule of thumb applies most often when the total marketing budget includes a substantial sum for advertising. When marketing budgets do not allow for enough advertising to achieve a threshold of effectiveness—in today's dollars, a media spend of $8 million to $10 million is considered a minimum requirement for a national campaign—publicity budgets are likely to constitute an even larger percentage of the total marketing budget.

Some companies still maintain large staffs of public relations specialists who plan and execute public relations programs that support marketing and business objectives. Increasingly, however, corporations structure the function to support the corporation's agenda as a whole. Public relations practitioners must be agile and knowledgeable in multiple aspects of their craft.

Public relations communications strategists serve a dual role—as strategists and as astute purchasers of outside services from vendors such as advertising and public relations agencies, social media specialists, promotion agencies and media-buying services.

The field of food and beverage public relations abounds with specialties that support the profession. Media-trained registered dietitians are available as temporary product spokespersons for national media tours or defensive work in a crisis. Home economists and food technicians develop recipes for public relations programs, and food stylists are available to ensure that specialist food photographers find the most attractive ways to portray the client's product for the daily newspapers' food sections. Health communications agencies, which also work for pharmaceutical clients, develop strategies for gaining third-party endorsements from healthcare professional groups for foods and food ingredients. Many generalist public relations agencies will not employ these specialists themselves but hire them on a project basis and usually mark up their costs. Some corporations explore whether a network of individual specialists or small agencies is cost effective for work on a project basis.

Because of the size of the industry, food and beverage companies, particularly those that don't want or can't afford the entire mix of services offered by public relations agencies, may hire a service that specializes in media segmentation. The company may want electronic distribution just to small-town newspapers, just to major-market newspapers, to certain magazines, to all magazines, to single-market television or to the entire industry.

A TACTICAL APPROACH TO THE INDUSTRY

As pointed out earlier, the strategies and tactics employed on behalf of a product can take as many forms as there are public relations professionals. But certain tried-and-true formats are worth noting in some detail (see Häagen-Dazs case, Figure 44.2).

Few consumers can resist, and few critics can attack, an activity of true good will. One sterling example in the food industry comes from McDonald's Corporation. Its creation of the Ronald McDonald Children's Charities begat the Ronald McDonald Houses, which provide housing and support for the families of critically ill children. McDonald's also has funded such national programs as an all-star marching band for high-school musicians and, as part of marketing efforts, the company places particular emphasis on giving back to communities through sponsorships and donations. Together, these activities become a strategy for painting a glowing picture of the entire McDonald's concept.

Other companies also focus on local communities. While Starbucks has an international program of grants and partnerships, each individual store is given a budget for community involvement.

Such actions help build consumer trust and community loyalty. While it takes time to establish faith in an institution, the rewards are great because the consumer's positive viewpoint adheres beyond specific products to the company behind them—and, by extension, to new products the company subsequently develops. This in turn creates a "trust bank," a concept pioneered by McDonald's public relations counselor Al Golin (see Preface), in which gifts to the community serve as "deposits" upon which the company can draw when needed.

When a food or beverage product reaches a milestone anniversary, one effective tactic is the use of nostalgia to evoke warm memories and positive associations. This tactic, as old as advertising itself, is especially well suited to the subtleties of public relations and is particularly useful when attempting to revive an older product or brand. Examples from recent history demonstrate the potential effectiveness of such campaigns.

In 1988, Kraft General Foods used the sixtieth anniversary of Velveeta to revive interest in the cheese, whose popularity had eroded. The company initiated a media blitz that emphasized two main points: Velveeta, a product so identified with the technologically obsessed 1950s, had in fact appeared three decades earlier in a "simpler, purer" world; and, rather than a nutritionless food product, Velveeta was actually a blend of all-natural ingredients. Different tactics, including a strong media relations program and the development and publicizing of recipe booklets, were employed, all in honor of the food that "brought back childhood memories."

In 1993, McDonald's chose to recognize the anniversary of one of its cornerstone products, the Big Mac, created by a McDonald's franchisee back in 1968. In addition to a nationwide publicity campaign, the company focused on one particular city, Pittsburgh, where the Big Mac had been created. The mayor renamed the city "Big Mac City, U.S.A." at an anniversary party featuring a marching band, the world's biggest Big Mac cake and local citizens singing the famous "Two All-Beef Patties" jingle.

Since 1902, Barnum's Animals Crackers have delighted kids of all ages. For its one-hundredth anniversary, the company wanted to bump sales by reaching out to both past and present consumers. The resulting integrated marketing campaign asked consumers to vote for one of four new animals—the koala, cobra, walrus and penguin. The winner would be permanently included in the box. Without any advertising and a small amount of point-of-sale support, its public relations campaign measurably increased sales and consumer awareness in each of its two stages—by 41 and 21 percent, respectively.

Often consumer surveys can provide interesting, relevant or otherwise newsworthy messages with which to approach the media. An ice cream manufacturer, for instance, might conclude a scientific consumer survey with the somewhat unscientific question, "When are you most in the mood for an ice cream treat?" When the public relations department later releases the news that 67 percent of respondents crave ice cream immediately following an evening of passion, it is sure to garner a few headlines and broadcast news bits.

A marketer can complement and extend an advertising campaign by piggybacking its public relations efforts. With an integrated marketing communications approach, a company can communicate one aspect of a product through advertising and another with public relations.

For example, in 2010, the leader of the free world made an off-hand remark that he might hold a "Slurpee Summit" with the new Republican House leadership. This set the Slurpee brand on a mission to make the summit a reality. What was put into motion? A completely integrated marketing communications plan. 7-Eleven put an ad in a national newspaper touting "One Slurpee Nation" and "Join the Unity Tour 2010." They reached out to the White House offering to cater a Slurpee Summit with Purple Slurpees, bringing blue and red together. And, they placed stories in traditional media and on blogs and sent tweets. Though highly successful, this campaign did have its warts. The Slurpee Summit also garnered unwanted attention when Dana Milbank, columnist for the *Washington Post*, wrote, "The first meeting between President Obama and Republican leaders since the election would be called the 'Slurpee Summit'—a thing of no nutritional value."

In 1984, Wendy's International caused a remarkable stir with its "Where's the Beef?" ad campaign, designed to tout the size advantage of Wendy's burgers over the competition. Starring an unlikely spokesperson, a septuagenarian actress named Clara Peller, the catch phrase became a national phenomenon when, in the 1984 presidential campaign, Democratic hopeful Walter Mondale adopted "Where's the Beef?" as a challenge to the ideas of one of his opponents. Wendy's took full advantage of the situation by immediately capitalizing on the enormous popularity of Clara Peller through media tours, press conferences and one-on-one interviews. Subsequent commercials featuring Clara and "Where's the Beef?" were debuted at press conferences and highlighted on *Entertainment Tonight*. Outtakes of commercials were publicized on various national and local television shows.

The advertising campaign ended in 1985, after Peller performed in a commercial for Prego Pasta sauce, saying that she "finally found" the beef. This became a public relations challenge of another sort. The media demanded to know why Wendy's fired Peller, and Wendy's responded they did no such thing, that Clara's contract had simply not been renewed.

With public relations, it's also possible to generate excitement in advance of the advertising campaign and thus help to improve viewership in an age of commercial clutter and "zapping" via remote control. The best example of this is the way in which food and beverage companies known for their imaginative commercials—Coca-Cola, Pepsi-Cola, Doritos and Anheuser-Busch, to name a few—target and

In 1994, Hormel Corporation came up with a historically themed way of redefining its canned pork and ham mix, Spam, for a new generation. Spam was patented back in 1937 but gained recognition when it became a wartime staple in Britain in 1939. Enter the fiftieth anniversary of D-Day, which provided an irresistible public relations platform and gave the company an opportunity to go to the press with an "update" message on Spam's new uses, redesigned logo and line extensions.

preannounce the Super Bowl broadcast as the nationwide debut of a new ad campaign. This influences viewers to stay tuned for that "hot new ad" with rapt anticipation—more anticipation, in the case of many Super Bowl contests, than is generated by the game itself. Another successful publicity program in this vein comes from Taster's Choice instant coffee, whose eagerly anticipated ads featuring an intriguing liaison between "that British woman and that American man" were the subject of articles in periodicals ranging from *TV Guide* to *Newsweek*—and are still watched via YouTube.

As discussed above, the examples of both Velveeta and Spam succeeded in matching a product's profile to shifting public wants or concerns. In the food industry, this has attained a pronounced importance and most often takes the form of highlighting the nutritional benefits of a product or exploiting the latest scientific research in related fields. This tactic goes back to the last century, when a young doctor named John Harvey Kellogg and his brother, William Keith Kellogg, forever changed the way Americans eat breakfast. They believed everyone, not just those on special diets, would be interested in wholesome food, as they were. They developed a flake produced with "the sweet heart of the corn." To distinguish Kellogg's Corn Flakes from other cereal products, William Kellogg put his initials, W.K., on each box, to indicate that his corn flakes were "The Original."

Recent years have seen a burgeoning of foods designed to capture a health-conscious public's attention, and public relations efforts have proved an invaluable part of the subsequent campaigns. Two of them—the NutraSweet Company's introduction of its all-natural fat substitute Simplesse and the Quaker Oats Company's exploitation of the phenomenon that surrounded early anticholesterol claims for oat bran products—depended heavily on unbiased media support and health-professional outreach. These are precisely the sorts of arenas in which public relations opens far more doors than do traditional advertising efforts.

In the early years of this century, social media entered the mix in a powerful way. There is strong evidence that social media increases traffic and sales. Twitter, Facebook and foursquare have huge populations who extol—or debunk—a product's virtues. Food companies stepped into the social media space in a big way. Gatorade's "Mission Control" center included full-time employees who monitored social media networks for Gatorade mentions and responded if necessary. Gary Hirshberg, "CE-Yo" of Stonyfield Farm, said, "Social media is a gift to our industry." His company selected nutrition bloggers and flew them to the company's farms in Vermont. They then blogged about what they learned. Hirshberg said the company generated "millions of hits" for about $10,000. Even food banks got into the act with New York's City Harvest launching viral YouTube videos on how to "rescue food."

Children are not immune to a targeted approach to health: Sesame Street and Dora the Explorer encourage kids to eat nutritionally and move around, and the Disney Channel's "The Wiggles" promotes health with songs such as "Fruit Salad, Yummy Yummy."

From a defensive standpoint, a savvy communications blitz can defend against interest-group or consumer concerns and complaints. In fact, this strategy seems tailor-made for public relations sweeps: countering such charges with a major advertising campaign would foster a Goliath-versus-David scenario in relation to the common-man imagery of those making the charges. Consider the example of the food and beverage industry's successful crusade to reverse the FDA's ban on the sugar substitute saccharin from U.S. products. In 1977, when the ban was announced, protest was coordinated through the Calorie Control Council. This group, an international consortium of food and beverage manufacturers, focused on such issues as overly cautious test analyses and called attention to the benefits of saccharin to diabetics and the morbidly obese—two groups that were greatly affected and able to generate sympathy on the part of the public.

A related tactic allows the preemption of consumer backlash against a product by taking responsible action that not only mitigates the problem but also accrues deposits in the trust bank. Most alcohol campaigns include a "drink responsibly" tagline; consider the "Know When to Say When" campaign launched by the country's largest brewer, Anheuser-Busch, to promote responsible drinking—a campaign that can be seen as advocating a *reduction* in consumption of the advertiser's own products.

Finally, many companies employ a selection of reliable strategies when introducing a new product. A recipe strategy provides the female head of household the opportunity to experience the product on her own terms. Supporting tactics include the development and effective distribution of recipe books or cards to help promote product usage, cooking demonstrations, spokesperson media tours, satellite media tours, video news releases and audio news releases, all tactics that have proven effective for the food and beverage industry. Land O'Lakes, Bays English Muffins, Sun-Maid Milk Chocolate Raisins and many other brands have recipe contests using their products. Many companies have had success by establishing a presence in national or regional conferences or cooking schools, such as the respected Southern-market cooking school developed by *Southern Living* magazine.

Whatever strategies a public relations practitioner chooses, the plain fact is that garnering publicity for a new food or beverage product (or a revitalized old product) is predicated on one thing: *is it newsworthy?* The media will generally be open to your product if the information breathes life into one of the following categories: safety, taste, functionality, cultural relevance, familiarity, convenience, seasonality, health or nutritional value, presentation (or packaging) or contemporaneity. If you have to stretch too hard to make it newsworthy, you may best be advised to save money until a more newsworthy product comes along. A smarter strategy might be leveraging social media in the right venues to drive home your message.

CASE STUDY—HÄAGEN-DAZS LOVES HONEYBEES: LET'S LICK THIS PROBLEM

In 2008, stung by a lack of relevance with consumers, the Häagen-Dazs brand was looking for a way to bring the buzz back. Market share was being threatened, consumers had little connection with the brand and price increases were hurting sales. Häagen-Dazs needed to become more contemporary and regain sales momentum.

The team created a honey of a program that engaged consumers by tapping into all aspects of the marketing mix while reinforcing a critical brand attribute—all-natural ingredients. The Häagen-Dazs brand identified an obscure and underreported problem—disappearing honeybees. Honeybees are responsible for pollinating one-third of all the foods we eat, including many of the ingredients found in Häagen-Dazs ice cream, like raspberries, strawberries and pears. It discovered that colony collapse disorder (a phenomenon in which worker bees from a colony abruptly disappear) was a real risk to U.S. agriculture and specifically Häagen-Dazs. With no bees, there would be no natural flavors. With no natural flavors, there could be no Häagen-Dazs.

They started the effort with primary and secondary research, which found that Häagen-Dazs consumers care about what they eat and where their food comes from. They pay attention to what they put in their mouths and the quality of food their families eat. They are happy and eager to do their part to contribute to a sustainable society—particularly if they can make an impact through small, enjoyable, hassle-free actions. They also are willing to support causes that are genuine and relevant and are eager to find ways to teach their children about responsible sustainable living.

Using the insights from the research, the team flew into action with the following strategies:

1. Give consumers a compelling way to engage more genuinely and frequently with the brand by educating them about the honeybee plight.

2. Leverage first-mover advantage and become the first national consumer brand to support the issue and put the cause on consumers' radar.

3. Strategically use the brand name to raise awareness and underscore the brand's "all-natural" brand essence by linking to honeybees.

The hub of the campaign was created at www.helpthehoneybees.com, a site dedicated to colony collapse disorder information (Figure 44.1). Häagen-Dazs then officially launched the "HD loves HB" campaign by announcing a $250,000 research grant to Penn State and UC Davis and setting up a board of bee experts to speak to media. In-store, a new "Vanilla Honey Bee" flavor was introduced, and all Häagen-Dazs bee-dependent flavors were branded with the "HD loves HB" logo. A print partnership with *National Geographic*, *Martha Stewart Living* and *Gourmet* created custom advertorials and the first-ever plantable, seed-embedded paper insert ads, allowing readers to literally take the cause into their hands (Figure 44.2). PR was generated with a hip-hop "Bee Dance" viral video. Online, swarming bees landed on Epicurious.com's bee-dependent ingredients, illustrating colony collapse disorder's potential impact. A bee graffiti contest on Facebook urged users to submit their best honeybee-inspired drawings.

Public relations needed to bring instant awareness and understanding to the complex plight of the disappearing honeybee, hoping the campaign would pollinate stagnating sales. It was the integrated campaign's most powerful lever (Figure 44.3). This PR strategy set the tone for the entire campaign. They formed an expert advisory board, directed significant donation funds toward meaningful research and created an avenue for consumers in mass numbers to plant bee-friendly habitats to help save the bees. They launched the *HD Loves HB Campaign: Let's Lick the Problem.*

As a result, unaided brand awareness increased from 29 to 36 percent. At launch, baseline sales of Häagen-Dazs increased 5.2 percent in April 2008. Consumers increased the Häagen-Dazs brands" donation by 16.2 percent. More significantly, the U.S. House Agricultural Subcommittee invited Häagen-Dazs to testify in June 2008 to urge congressional support for colony collapse disorder research. Representative Dennis Cardoza called the Häagen-Dazs brand's involvement "extraordinary."

THE FUTURE

The future practice of public relations will be shaped by several factors: the continual shrinking of the globe by new communications media—specifically, but not exclusively, the Internet and social media; the globalization of brands; the "tabloidization" or lowering standards of media, as well as the public's growing distrust of all institutions and the trend toward integration of marketing disciplines organized around a central strategic need.

It has been several decades since news and information—good or bad, accurate or inaccurate—could be practically confined within local or regional boundaries. The interlinking of national and international wire services, the explosion of satellite-delivered television and radio news services and, more importantly, the borderless Internet dictate that a food scare such as the 2009 swine flu outbreak, which mistakenly vilified pigs as the outbreak epicenter, can instantaneously raise concerns about the safety of pork in Germany. Just as certainly, debates in the United States about the safety of genetically modified foods can and do generate parallel

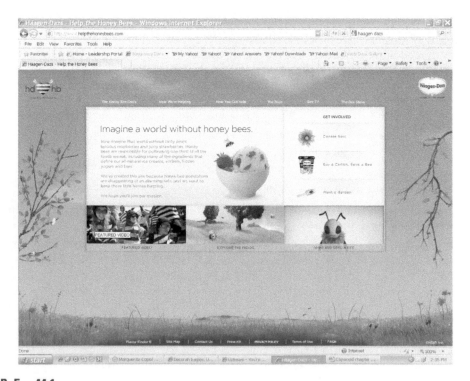

FIGURE   44.1

Häagen-Dazs Website HD Loves HB

F I G U R E 44.2

HD Love HB Ad

fears in Europe and elsewhere in the world. And the ready access to computer databases on virtually any topic means that public relations practitioners must be on constant guard to ensure that these unfiltered sources of sometimes erroneous or misleading information do not form the basis for news coverage about a marketer's company or product.

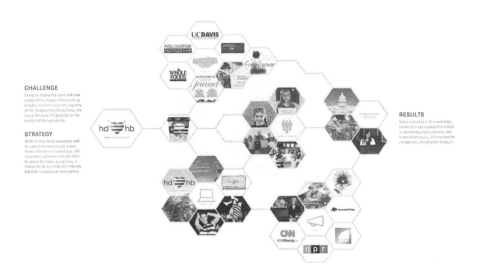

FIGURE 44.3

Multi-Faceted Honeycomb: An Integrated Plan

As brands migrate across borders, continents and hemispheres, communications practices are exported with them. This should be good news for the public relations profession since the brands that globalize generally originate in those parts of the world where public relations is practiced by competent professionals in an ethical manner.

At times, tabloid television and talk radio in the United States stretch the boundaries of truth while preying on the credulousness of viewers and listeners. "Experts" with a shingle and little else to recommend them are indiscriminately booked on talk programs to peddle their wares. They amplify these efforts by hosting charlatan blogs and posting "expert" videos on YouTube, and their claims often go unrebutted by program hosts and producers ill-equipped to sort fact from fiction. While independent groups such as the American Council on Science and Health and the food-industry-supported International Food Information Council attempt to counter this trend, they are frankly underfunded and outgunned. Food safety, nutritional value and obesity will continue to be public relations challenges. Increasing consumer education and debunking media-hyped myths will be up front for many years to come.

This challenge becomes tougher in light of the citizenry's pronounced cynicism about all institutions. It is simply not enough to say that the United States FDA, the USDA or the CDC has determined that a food is safe, organic or healthy; the public no longer believes that the government can be trusted. And who can blame them? Those same agencies have, with justification, complained for years of underfunding, which they admit affects their ability to police the food supply as well as their capacity to approve beneficial new foods, food ingredients and food technologies. Meanwhile, self-styled consumer groups position themselves as the only real protectors of the public's health, often raising spurious claims about food safety to enhance their fundraising efforts. The public ends up confused about the issues and believing no one and turns to their peers—"someone like me"—for answers.

Debunking the social media-hyped myths about the nutrition, safety and value of the food supply may be the public relations challenge of the 2010s.

No communications discipline can eradicate cynicism. In fact, traditionalists in our profession may assert that the practice of public relations and the marketing of products using public relations techniques are inimical, because marketing itself is in large measure responsible for this lack of collective faith. But there is no reason that, as public relations, advertising, promotion and other tools in the strategist arsenal partner to affect change, the principles of Arthur W. Page cannot govern even more broadly. Page, the public relations pioneer of the original AT&T, put it this way: "All business in a democratic country begins with public permission and exists by public approval."

We are all selling something. Whatever strategies we use, let us make honesty and fairness the cornerstones of our approach.

DISCUSSION QUESTIONS

1. How should PCA have managed its salmonella crisis to avoid what ultimately resulted in bankruptcy?
2. Your company is planning to launch a new snack food targeted to preteens and teens. What social media channels and tools would you use to reach those audiences directly? What are the pitfalls to avoid in marketing to children and young adults?
3. Describe three or four ways that a food manufacturer can employ philanthropic programs to enhance their corporate and brand reputations.
4. Your company markets the same drink under different brand names in 47 countries, but you are seeking a unified approach to product positioning in all markets. Which approach is better suited to your needs: hiring a global public relations agency or creating your own network of agencies in each country where you do business?
5. A so-called mommy blogger with a significant following has launched an online vendetta against your product. What strategies and tactics can you employ to blunt the impact of these attacks?
6. Your firm recently acquired a legacy brand specializing in cheeses that were well known to your grandparents but barely remembered today. What elements of your marketing plan can bridge generations and create nostalgia for the product while introducing a younger demographic to the brand?
7. Your agency represents a food ingredient that has been demonstrated to be safe by regulatory agencies around the world and yet continues to be subjected to rumors and scare campaigns that seek to undermine its reputation. What are the five most important strategies the agency can adopt to help turn this situation around?
8. You have just completed a successful media tour with a high-visibility celebrity endorser of your highly nutritious, popular artisanal bread. Two days later, he is embroiled in a sex scandal that is quickly gaining momentum with the tabloid broadcast and print media. And, tweets are starting to roll in. Now what?

ADDITIONAL READING

Cramer, Janet M., Carlnita P. Greene and Lynn Walters. *Food as Communication: Communication as Food.* New York, NY: Peter Lang, 2011. Print.

Gass, Robert H., and John S. Seiter. *Persuasion, Social Influence, and Compliance Gaining.* Pearson Education, Inc.: Boston, MA, 2010. Print.

Marchand, Charles Roland. *Creating the Corporate Soul.* Berkeley: University of California, 1998. Print.

McWilliams, James E. *Just Food: Where Locavores Get It Wrong and How We Can Truly Eat Responsibly.* New York, NY: Little, Brown, 2009. Print.

Nestle, Marion. *Safe Food: The Politics of Food Safety.* Berkeley: University of California, 2010. Print.

Pollan, Michael. *In Defense of Food: An Eater's Manifesto.* New York, NY: Penguin, 2008. Print.

Schlosser, Eric. *Fast Food Nation: The Dark Side of the All-American Meal.* Boston, MA: Houghton Mifflin, 2001. Print.

Weber, Karl. *Food, Inc.: How Industrial Food Is Making Us Sicker, Fatter and Poorer—And What You Can Do about It; A Participant Guide.* New York, NY: PublicAffairs, 2009. Print.

45
C H A P T E R

THE OIL AND NATURAL GAS INDUSTRY
Communicating in a Challenging Environment

Sam Falcona
Vice President (Retired), Communications and Public Affairs
ConocoPhillips

The use of petroleum seeps (bitumen, pitch, asphalt and tar found near the earth's surface) began well before recorded time, when ancient cultures used them for waterproofing, for road and ship building as well as for lighting. However, it was not until the nineteenth century, when improved techniques were developed to extract oil from underground and the process of refining crude oil into kerosene was invented, that the industry began its journey to become an integral part of the global economy and our everyday life. In fact, the access to oil played a major role in both World Wars and continues to shape world politics, as evidenced by the continuing conflicts in the oil-rich Middle East.

The importance and complexity of the oil and energy industry has made it one of most studied, tracked industries in history. Communications at all levels of the business has played a crucial role in understanding the industry as well as support and criticism of it. Each of the following discussions of the industry contains the seed elements of communication management issues with questions for the reader to address. The industry is a perfect example of the challenges faced by public relations professionals in high-visibility, high-risk businesses, as seen in the following cases and examples.

In 2009, according to the Energy Information Administration (EIA), the world produced approximately 84.4 million barrels of petroleum products per day. The United States alone produced approximately 9.1 million barrels per day and consumed 18.8 million barrels per day. Hence, we need to import petroleum products from abroad every day to sustain our economy and standard of living (Figure 45.1).

As the chart below indicates, net imports have generally increased since 1985, while U.S. production fell and consumption grew.

There are 2.1 million Americans who work directly in the oil and natural gas industry, and there are another 7.1 million jobs in other sectors, from logistics to manufacturing to research to retail, that are also supported by the industry.[1]

In 2009, the United States produced 11 percent of the world's petroleum and consumed 22 percent.

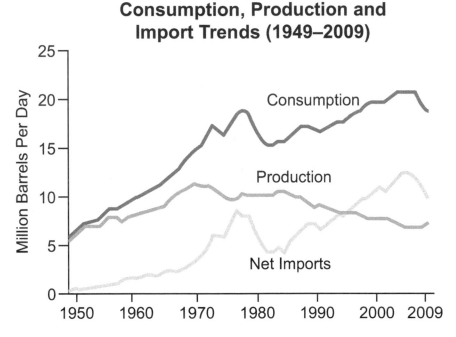

Consumption, Production and Import Trends (1949–2009)

FIGURE 45.1

Source: U.S. Energy Information Administration, Annual Energy Review 2009, Table 5.1 (August 2010)

THE BASICS OF THE INDUSTRY

Oil was formed from the remains of animals and plants (diatoms) that lived millions of years ago in a marine (water) environment before the dinosaurs. Over millions of years, the remains of these animals and plants were covered by layers of sand and silt. Heat and pressure from these layers helped the remains turn into what we today call crude oil (Figure 45.2).

After crude oil is removed from the ground, it is sent to a refinery by pipeline, ship or barge. At a refinery, different parts of the crude oil are separated into usable petroleum products. Crude oil is measured in barrels. A 42-U.S.-gallon barrel of crude oil provides slightly more than 44 gallons of petroleum products (Figure 45.3).

PETROLEUM & NATURAL GAS FORMATION

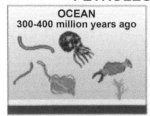

OCEAN
300-400 million years ago

Tiny see plants and animals died and were buried on the ocean floor. Over time, they were covered by layers of silt and sand.

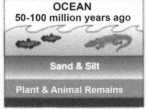

OCEAN
50-100 million years ago

Over millions of years, the remains were buried deeper and deeper. The enormous heat and pressure turned them into oil and gas.

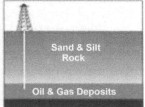

Today, we drill down through layers of sand, silt, and rock to reach the rock formations that contain oil and gas deposits.

FIGURE 45.2

Source: U.S. Energy Information Administration

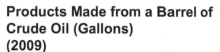

Products Made from a Barrel of Crude Oil (Gallons) (2009)

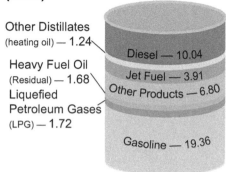

Other Distillates
(heating oil) — 1.24

Diesel — 10.04

Heavy Fuel Oil
(Residual) — 1.68

Jet Fuel — 3.91

Liquefied
Petroleum Gases
(LPG) — 1.72

Other Products — 6.80

Gasoline — 19.36

F I G U R E   45.3

Source: U.S. Energy Information Administration

WHAT IS A REFINERY?

A refinery is a high-visibility and sometimes controversial factory that takes crude oil and turns it into gasoline and many other useful petroleum products (Figure 45.4). A typical refinery costs billions of dollars to build and millions more to maintain. It runs 24 hours a day, 365 days a year and requires a large number of employees to operate it safely.

All refineries perform three basic steps: separation, conversion and treatment.

After the separation process, heavy petroleum components or "fractions" are on the bottom; light fractions are on the top. The difference in their weights allows this separation. The lightest fractions, including gasoline and liquid petroleum gas, vaporize and rise to the top of the distillation tower.

The most widely used conversion method is called *cracking* because it uses heat and pressure to "crack" heavy hydrocarbon molecules into lighter ones. A cracking unit consists of one or more tall reactors and a network of furnaces, heat exchangers and other vessels.

To make gasoline in the treatment step, refinery technicians carefully combine a variety of streams (outputs) from the processing units. Among the variables that determine the blend are octane level, vapor pressure ratings and special considerations, such as whether the gasoline will be used at high altitudes.

Both incoming crude oil and the outgoing final products need to be stored. These liquids are stored in large tanks on a tank farm near the refinery. Pipelines then carry the final products from the tank to other tanks across the country.

INDUSTRY SEGMENTS[2]

The *upstream* segment involves the exploration and production (E&P) of oil and natural gas, from cutting-edge geology to high-tech offshore drilling platforms. The United States is the world's third-largest producer, with more than 500,000 producing wells and approximately 3,800 oil and natural gas platforms operating in U.S. waters. Combined, they produce almost 2 billion barrels of oil a year.

One of the most capital-intensive operations is using drill ships to locate, evaluate and drill wells at sea up to depths of 10,000 feet. A modern drill ship may cost $600 million to build and outfit and, in some environments, costs nearly $1 million per day to operate (Figure 45.5).

The *downstream* segment includes the nation's 141 refineries, which process more than 15 million barrels of crude oil every day. This segment also includes transporting petroleum products by tanker trucks from

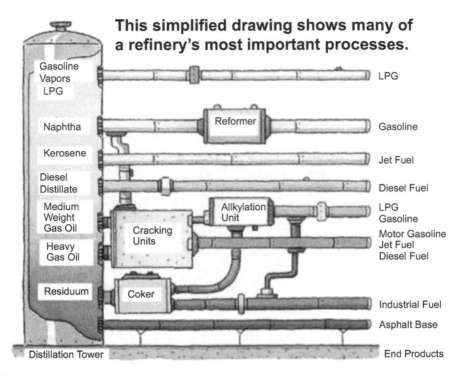

This simplified drawing shows many of a refinery's most important processes.

F I G U R E   45.4

Source: http://www.api.org/images/hurricane_map_popup_4_1.gif

thousands of local terminals to approximately 161,770 service stations across the United States and the ownership and operation of those retail outlets. Product marketing (gasoline, oils, lubricants, etc.) is also the responsibility of the downstream segment.

The *pipeline* segment comprises the nation's 165,000 miles of pipelines that move crude oil from wells on land and platforms in the oceans to refineries, and then to terminals where fuels are released to retail outlets.

Some of the pipeline infrastructure in the United States is nearly 60 years old and will eventually need to be replaced. These networks of underground product highways move the fuels for our automobiles, trucks and airplanes. When these pipelines were built, most were underground, through unpopulated areas. However, they now can be found near suburban housing developments and business areas that have been built in the last 30 years.

The *marine* segment involves all aspects of transporting petroleum and petroleum products by water, including port operations, maritime firefighting and oil spill response. Oil tankers make up a major portion of this segment.

The major integrated oil and natural gas companies have operations in all segments of the industry. Some smaller companies focus their efforts in just one or two segments.

YOUR ARE THE COMMUNICATOR

Let us imagine you are the communicator and marketer for the retail gasoline branded products. Research consistently reports that 96 percent of the consumer's selection is based upon price and location—"I like this brand because I can make a right turn on my way to work and make another right turn to get on the highway. I do not have to wait for lights or cross the highway."

What is your branding strategy, and what marketing tools would you use for your products in the United States when price and location are the drivers? Why are retail outlets such as Sam's Club, Costco and grocery chains now selling gasoline?

PIPELINE ACCIDENTS AND INCIDENTS

On September 9, 2010, a natural gas pipeline exploded in San Bruno, California. Eight deaths were reported[3], and 38

F I G U R E   45.5

houses were destroyed.[4] The 30-inch pressurized pipeline, which was laid down in 1948, ran underneath a densely populated urban area (e.g., Figures 45.6 and 45.7).

COMMUNICATIONS ORGANIZATION

There are various reporting structures for the communications function in the major integrated companies. Typically, the department is headed by a vice president or manager and is responsible for the following:

- External communications (media relations, financial communications, corporate fact book for industry analysts, crisis and issues management, etc.).
- Internal communications (employees, retirees and speechwriting).

F I G U R E   45.6

FIGURE 45.7

- Community relations (corporate, local and international, special events, historical archives and employee volunteer programs).

- Foundation or charitable giving, including special donations as part of the company's disaster relief efforts. This department works closely with the board of directors to develop and implement the company's contributions strategy and coordinates the company's relationships with nonprofits and nongovernmental organizations (NGOs). Most major donations require board approval.

- Advertising (corporate TV and print, coordination of business unit or regional advertising and coordination of industry advertising and communication efforts such as the American Petroleum Institute's [API's] programs).

- Graphics (corporate identity and logo standards, corporate printing and duplication, benefits brochures, etc.).

YOUR ARE THE COMMUNICATOR

- It is 5:15 PM, and you were planning to attend your first black-tie event representing the company when you received the call about the explosion.
- You have 20 minutes to draft a step-by-step plan to deal with the explosion in San Bruno and brief the CEO, who is returning to the office ASAP.
- Your bulleted plan should include positions, responsibilities and resources required.
- You are located 45 minutes from the site.
- The clock is ticking . . .

Communications support for the various business units (upstream, downstream, etc.) is provided by communications professionals on the corporate staff or by employees actually assigned to and located within the business unit. In some cases, communications is provided in a shared-services environment where functional costs are allocated to departments via formulas that are negotiated yearly. Shared services usually include human resources, information technology, communications and security.

Depending on the specific communications needs at the time, companies hire from all experience levels, from recent college graduates to midlevel and senior communicators. A limited number of paid college summer internships are available and are usually the best entry points into the company.

ANNUAL REPORTS

One of the most challenging and interesting projects in communications is producing the annual report. The various steps to produce an annual report, such as buying paper, indentifying a design agency and contractor, developing an outline and assigning sections to the business units, photography, adhering to Securities and Exchange Commission requirements and the chairman's message are essentially the same steps as those in major corporations.

However, in the oil industry, modified reports are developed and produced for major international locations where it is important to keep key stakeholders informed in their own languages. The process of writing reports in Russian, Norwegian, Spanish, Portuguese, Arabic, Chinese and Bahasa becomes very complicated as one navigates through host-country sensitivities. Sometimes, simple items such as photographs and even the title of the report will need to be changed in respect of local cultures and customs. Photo shoots, whether of board members or assets, require extensive coordination and flexibility. Imagine coordinating a helicopter and photographer to shoot a major asset north of the Arctic Circle and learning that the weather precluded any flights for this very expensive aerial view.

YOU ARE THE COMMUNICATOR

Who determines the theme of your annual report? How do you decide what business areas will be showcased? What role will the ever-changing financial regulations play in your report? Does your board of directors play a role? Why is the mailing of the proxy along with the report so important? While the report is being printed, you find out that one of your featured employees was accidently killed at the refinery. Do you stop the press run? What if this employee is on your cover?

INVESTOR RELATIONS AND GOVERNMENT RELATIONS

Success in business and in life can be closely linked to relationships. Two key relationships that communicators must understand and develop are those with investor relations (IR) and government relations (GR). Unless it involves an issue directly under IR's and GR's purview, the communications department is usually the "smoke detector" that goes off when there is an accident, incident or major issue. Often, communications will be the first to find out about an issue or event, probably through the news media. Your first instinct should be to include and notify the IR and GR representatives.

Here are some examples of why this is important:

- A fire and explosion in a tank farm in Oklahoma is very important to the federal and state elected officials from that state. The GR staff will make notification calls ASAP to provide these elected officials with whatever information they have at hand along with a promise to keep them updated. A call to a senator's chief of staff to inform is much better than a call from the news media to the senator's office asking for comment, especially if this is the first time he or she heard about the incident.

- The IR department works very closely with industry analysts from around the globe. These analysts are responsible for knowing their companies and predicting how various scenarios, such as supply disruptions, will impact the company's financial results. Giving the IR department a heads up lets IR evaluate the situation and prepare talking points to address analyst questions.

- Closing facilities, personnel layoffs and moving jobs from one state to another are important issues for GR. In addition to giving elected officials a heads up that a major announcement is

IMPORTANCE OF FACT BOOKS AND FACT SHEETS

In these days of trying to put all your information online, do not underestimate the importance of a wire-bound color fact book with information about your company and facilities, including production (manufacturing stats) by assets, countries and regions. The industry analysts find this tool, usually produced by the communications department, to be extremely useful, and they look forward to an updated copy every year.

From a news media standpoint, major print journalists rely on it to understand the scope and uniqueness of company operations. Often, they will reference their questions in terms of the fact book, such as, "On page 18, the fact book indicates that production at Ekofisk area is 122 million barrels per day, but your recent analyst briefing (PowerPoint) indicates it is 148 million barrels per day. Which is correct and why?"

forthcoming, there are federal and state requirements that must be followed. The Worker Adjustment and Retraining Notification Act (WARN) is an important requirement. (See the Department of Labor website for more information.)

COMMUNITY RELATIONS AND REBUILDING TRUST IN THE COMMUNITY

The Rodeo Refinery, located in Contra Costa County across the bridge from San Francisco, was built more than 100 years ago and has undergone numerous expansions and switched ownership multiple times. On August 22, 1994, when it was owned by Unocal, the refinery started releasing Catacarb, a commonly used oil-refining catalyst that can cause skin burning, shortness of breath and headaches. The leak continued for 16 days before the company told state and federal authorities. Almost 600 residents and 75 employees reported symptoms in the days following the company's disclosure. Unocal pleaded no contest to 12 criminal counts filed by the state and agreed to pay a $3 million fine. In 1997, Unocal reached an $80 million settlement with the more than 6,000 nearby residents.

Years later, a newly assigned plant manager met with local community leaders, including NGO local groups that had strengthened their opposition to the plant after the 1994 release. After he introduced himself, he showed the group his text pager and told them that this is how he is kept abreast of the status of the plant and any issues that might arise. In a spirit of transparency, he gave a similar text pager to the local community leader and elected official. This bold act went a long way toward beginning to regain community trust. Later, there was an incident at the plant and, as expected, the local news media called one of the community leaders for comment. The community leader said that he was aware of the incident and said it was no big deal.

WORKING WITH AGENCIES

There are many opportunities for agencies to work with companies and industry organizations. Most companies have an advertising agency of record and often work with general and specialized PR firms on continuing projects, one-time issues or events and on a crisis contingency basis. As mentioned earlier, the key is relationships and culture fit. Most of the oil and gas companies have unique corporate cultures, and the key to landing an assignment is culture and attitude fit.

One of the biggest hurdles is client conflict. An agency working for company A cannot work for company B. So it pays to know ahead of time who is on retainer for whom and what are the noncompete restrictions. More importantly, look for agencies with a good talent pool that understands the industry, with experience working with its issues and that know that *upstream* is one word, not two. As with any good agency search, ensure that the agency members participating during the proposal phase are also the same ones that will be working on the account.

THE IMPORTANCE OF INDUSTRY ASSOCIATIONS

The oil and natural gas industry supports 9.2 million American jobs and provides a $1 trillion lift to the U.S. economy each year. The API is the only national trade association that represents the entire oil and natural gas industry. It is located in Washington, DC, and its employees include economists, lobbyists, communicators and industry sector specialists. There are also various standing committees including legal, upstream, downstream, safety, communications and Security, headed by company executives.

One of API's major challenges is communicating the importance of the industry to the U.S. economy and the implications of governmental actions (taxes, drilling restrictions, gasoline prices, etc.) across the broad spectrum of stakeholders. One of the reasons that the United Sates lacks a long-term energy policy is that in the past, many policymakers, government officials and consumers have not been provided accurate data and future predictions regarding the energy mix and therefore have developed slanted perspectives and unreasonable expectations.

API has led the charge in the traditionally nonproactive industry to develop and implement a major communications outreach geared to educating audiences on energy realities and the real-world implications of policy proposals. By raising the level of energy literacy among key audiences, informed and intellectually honest discussions can then occur about the best course of action for energy consumers, American workers, the economy and U.S. energy security.

An example of API's education efforts includes sponsored studies assessing energy policies such as "Taxes versus Access," which shows that increased taxes actually reduce government revenue. API developed a variety of materials that government officials, the news media and other influencers can use to educate themselves and, in turn, educate others. These materials are also linked to primers on gasoline prices, energy policy and tax issues.

In 2010, due in large part to API's and the industry's education about the adverse consequences to consumers, jobs, the economy and energy security, voters in key states opposed the idea of raising taxes on the oil and natural gas industry. And while support for expanded offshore drilling was affected by the 2010 BP accident in the Gulf of Mexico (GOM), Americans do not support the idea of abandoning those resources. Making these national policy topics personally relevant to consumers (voters) has engaged them and helped shape policy decisions.

API also realized that the communication tools used are also important and that a variety of outlets should be used to reach audiences. In addition to websites such as Energy Tomorrow, Energy Nation and Energy Citizens, the industry uses Twitter, Facebook, YouTube, Flickr, Bog Talk Radio, Slideshare, Scribd, RSS and daily e-mails. For more information, go to: blog.energytomorrow.org, www.youtube.com/energy, twitter.com/EnergyTomorrow and www.facebook.com/Energy.Tomorrow.

COMMUNICATIONS ISSUES FACED BY THE INDUSTRY

The challenges and opportunities faced by industry communicators on a daily basis cover the full range of strategic and integrated communications. Imagine being the communicator in the following settings:

- You are an internal communicator at the corporate office and just became part of a confidential team that is developing the communications plan to lay off 3 percent of your workforce. Your stakeholders include not only employees but the local community, state and federal government officials, regulators, etc.

  o Your peers on the staff want to know what you are doing. What do you tell them? They suspect something is up.

  o You just found out that your best friend's department is being eliminated, and there are no transition positions. Do you tell your friend so that he or she can start looking for a job? What if your friend is about to buy a house or expensive sports car?

BP'S MACONDO WELL TRAGEDY

On April 20, 2010, an explosion occurred on BP's Deepwater Horizon rig in the GOM, which killed 11 people and caused widespread pollution in the Gulf. In the months that followed, oil began washing ashore from Texas to Florida. More than 45,000 people and 445 vessels were hired by BP to assist in the cleanup efforts. The well was successfully shut down on July 15, 2010.

TYPICAL COMMUNICATIONS ASSIGNMENTS IN THE INDUSTRY

- Corporate HQ—external, internal, community relations, advertising
- Refinery—external, internal, community relations
- Pipelines and transportation—external, internal, community relations
- Foreign office—assigned to business unit as a general communicator
- Marine operations—external, internal, community relations
- Upstream and downstream—general communicator working closely with corporate
- Joint ventures—general communicator, either short term or permanent
- Branded products—marketing, advertising, external, internal
- Industry associations (API, National Petroleum Refiners Association, etc.)—general and specialized communicators

- You are the only communicator at a refinery (not unusual) that just had an explosion, and three employees are missing. Your corporate headquarters first learned about this incident through the news media. In fact, their best initial source of information is the local TV traffic helicopter, which is streaming live video over the Internet. As the communicator onsite, you are working with local government officials to evacuate the neighborhood and ask the elementary school, which is located next to the refinery, to close all windows and shelter in place.

  o Whom do you contact first? Corporate, the news media or your sister, since one of the missing employees is your brother-in-law?

  o Do you let corporate handle the national media (CNN, Fox, etc.)? What about the local media?

  o Where do you suggest the families that were evacuated go to wait out the incident? The refinery manager told you to "take care of it."

- You are the communicator at a marine terminal, and you found out that one of your tankers is leaking oil as it enters one of the most pristine waterways in the United States. This is also the same tanker that a few days earlier had several crewmembers injured due to heavy seas after it left the Port of Valdez in Alaska and was bringing crude oil to a West Coast port.

- You are the communicator at a pipeline company that just had an underground pipeline carrying natural gas explode as a construction crew, which was building a new subdivision, accidently ruptured the line. Again, the news media is providing you with a live view of the accident site, which is 1,500 miles away.

  o What is your source of updated information? Who is going to update the news media? Your commercial airline flight will not get you into the area until tonight. What do you do now?

- You are the downstream communicator supporting the fuels distribution company that supplies 2,500 branded gasoline stations on the West Coast, and you were just informed that there is a possibility that your product is contaminated and is causing fuel injectors to clog, resulting in automobiles stalling on the road during rapid accelerations.

  o The quality department has been working on this issue for at least a week. Your gasoline or any other brand might not be the cause of the stalling. What do you do? Do you proactively reach out to the news media? Do you draft a press release? Who can assist you? What do you think the legal department will say about communications?

FIGURE   45.8

- You are responsible for communications and community relations at an international headquarters in a country that has just been hit by a devastating tsunami (Figure 45.8). Thousands are killed or missing, including some of your employees, and you are faced with communicating both externally and internally to your stakeholders. You are also tasked with asking corporate for millions of dollars in relief aid on behalf of your host country.

  o How do you communicate with your employees? Regular means of communication (cell phones) are not operating since the towers have been destroyed and much of the local infrastructure has been damaged.

  o How do you expedite your request to corporate for $3 million in disaster relief funds? How do you deal with the Foreign Corrupt Practices Act (FCPA)? How do you determine the area's immediate humanitarian need?

FCPA

The Foreign Corrupt Practices Act of 1977 was enacted for the purpose of making it unlawful for certain classes of persons and entities to make payments to foreign government officials to assist in obtaining or retaining business. The FCPA also requires companies whose securities are listed in the United States to meet its accounting provisions.[5]

THE IMPORTANCE OF THE GULF OF MEXICO

The Gulf Coast region of Louisiana, Mississippi, Alabama and Texas is the heart of the nation's oil and natural gas industry. It accounts for nearly half of the U.S. refining capacity, and the GOM accounts for about 30 percent of the oil and 13 percent of the natural gas produced in the United States. On any given day, there are as many as 30,000 industry employees and contractors working offshore.

Refineries and pipelines originating in the Gulf Coast region are major suppliers to other parts of the nation, which is why motorists in states far from Texas and Louisiana sometimes feel the price effects of a hurricane. According to the EIA, half the gasoline used on the East Coast and half the crude oil processed in refineries in the Midwest are shipped from the U.S. Gulf Coast region of the United States.

The country relies on pipelines, barges and tankers to deliver crude oil and refined petroleum products reliably to where they are needed throughout the country (Figure 45.9). In order for pipelines to move these

F I G U R E 45.9

Source: http://www.theodora.com/pipelines/united_states_pipelines_map.jpg

commodities, there must be a steady supply of product (oil or gasoline) to push forward what is already in the lines and electric power to run the pumps that move the commodities along.

HURRICANES AND STORMS IN THE GULF OF MEXICO

The 2005 hurricane season brought two back-to-back major hurricanes, Katrina and Rita. A large part of our offshore oil and natual gas infrastructure was in the direct path of the two storms. More than 100 offshore structures were destroyed during these storms; there were no injuries to offshore workers, nor were there any significant spills from offshore production facilities in spite of wind gusts reaching 200 mph in some areas.

Here are the steps taken by the offshore segment of the industry to prepare for a storm and return to operations after a storm:

- Days in advance of a tropical storm or hurricane moving toward or near their drilling operations, companies will evacuate all nonessential personnel and begin the process of shutting down production.

- As the storms gets closer, all personnel will be removed from the drilling rigs and platforms, and production will be shut down. Drill ships may relocate to a safe location.

- In areas not expected to take a direct hit from the storm, companies often choose to shut down operations as a precaution, due to the fact that storms can veer at the last minute.

- After a storm has passed and flight operations can safely resume, operators will initiate "flyovers" of offshore facilities to evaluate damage from the air. For onshore facilities, these flyovers can identify flooding, facility damage, road or other infrastructure problems and spills. Offshore flyovers can look for damaged drilling rigs, platform damage, spills and possible pipeline damage.

- Once safety concerns are addressed, operators will send assessment crews to offshore facilities to physically assess the facilities for damage.

- If facilities are undamaged, and ancillary facilities, such as pipelines that carry the oil and natural gas, are undamaged and ready to accept shipments, operators will begin resuming production. Drilling rigs will commence operations.

Electricity plays an important part in resuming operations ashore since power disruptions are quite common after a hurricane. Refinery operations can also be hampered by a lack of crude oil feedstock (product to process) if offshore production platforms or ports and pipelines have sustained damage or loss of power supply.

Most companies have sophisticated CCs that include the latest high-tech equipment (Figure 45.10). The communications department usually has its own special area with computers, printers and dedicated telephone lines to respond to news media inquiries. Most CCs have the capability for employees who are travelling to participate and watch center operations via the Internet. So an employee

MEDIA RELATIONS AND STORMS

The news media will begin calling your company once a hurricane or storm is forecasted to enter the GOM. There are stringent company policies concerning what information can be publicly disseminated at any time since it could impact the financial markets. Financial analysts are particularly interested since they use sophisticated modeling to analyze financial and stock implications. Therefore, constant coordination with your IR department is paramount.

Some of the standard news media questions include:

- What operations and number of personnel are in the projected path of the storm?
- What type and amount of production could possibly be impacted?
- When will the company make the decision to evacuate?
- Have you activated your command center (CC)?
- Can we fly out to a rig or watch from the CC?

Once the CC is activated, the communications department will usually assign representatives to sit in the CC to coordinate communication efforts. Most CCs are located at the corporate headquarters; however, sometimes a small temporary CC is set up near the accident site. Most centers are usually staffed 24/7 until normal operations have resumed.

F I G U R E   45.10

BP Command Center, Houston, TX, 2010

in Stavanger, Norway, has the capability to see and participate in center operations, listen to the latest briefings including the maps and PowerPoint presentations and actually ask questions and make recommendations.

FUTURE OF THE INDUSTRY

It is difficult to make predictions in this industry because there are so many external factors that could easily change the energy landscape. From civil conflicts and natural disasters to governmental actions (taxes, sanctions and nationalization) and new and cost-effective extraction technologies, all these are capable of having significant impact on our global economy and our energy security.

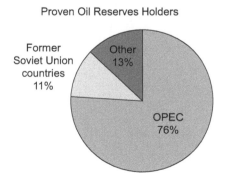

F I G U R E   45.11

OPEC member countries held over three-quarters of the world's proven oil reserves at the end of 2006

WORLD EVENTS AND THE PRICE OF CRUDE OIL

The oil and natural gas industry and the global free markets are greatly influenced by world events. The cost of oil is directly related to supply and demand around the globe, and the price of gasoline is directly related to the cost of crude oil. Companies have trading departments that operate 24/7 to buy and sell oil and refinery feedstocks. The trading floor looks very similar to a combined network news center and Wall Street trading pit where world events and market pricing are monitored on a real-time basis.

Historically, crude oil pricing is a factor of supply and demand economics. In 2007, the demand for oil in China and India increased 35 and 25 percent, respectively, while at the same time, the price of oil rose to $100 per barrel until it reached its all-time high of $145 per barrel in 2008. When the global economy went into a recession and crude oil demand from China and India decreased significantly, the price of oil dropped to just over $40 per barrel within months.

MIDDLE EAST AND PERSIAN GULF REGION

The importance of the Middle East as key oil supplier to the world cannot be underestimated. In 2011, Saudi Arabia had excess capacity and the capability to make up temporary global shortfalls. When the Libyan civil unrest began in early 2011, Saudi Arabia quickly announced to the world that they were going to increase their production to make up for the 1.8 million barrels per day that Libya was delivering to the marketplace. The question that everyone asks is how much excess capacity can Saudi Arabia or OPEC deliver in these scenarios, and how long can these efforts be sustained (Figures 45.11 and 45.12).

OPEC and Persian Gulf countries are not the same.

The Organization of the Petroleum Exporting Countries, or OPEC, was organized in 1960 for the purpose of negotiating with oil companies on matters of oil production, prices and future concession rights. Of the 12 countries currently in OPEC, only 6 of them are in the Persian Gulf.

OPEC	Persian Gulf
Iran	Iran
Iraq	Iraq
Kuwait	Kuwait
Saudi Arabia	Saudi Arabia
Qatar	Qatar
United Arab Emirates	United Arab Emirates
Algeria	Bahrain
Angola	
Ecuador	
Libya	
Nigeria	
Venezuela	

FIGURE 45.12

Source: http://www.eia.doe.gov/energyexplained/index.cfm?page=oil_imports

OIL CHOKEPOINTS

Another important factor is the world's oil transit chokepoints, which have the potential to affect both short- and long-term energy supplies. These areas are critical to our global energy security due to the high volume of oil that transits these areas. About half of the world's oil production moves over maritime routes.

The Strait of Hormuz is the world's most important chokepoint, with approximately 15.5 million barrels per day transiting the narrow strait in 2009 (Figure 45.13). Approximately 33 percent (40 percent in 2008) of all seaborne oil passed through this narrow waterway, which connects the Persian Gulf with the Gulf of Oman and the Arabian Sea. Any attempt to block or disrupt shipments in this critical area would drive energy costs upwards and would probably send world markets into a frenzy. The importance of this area to the global economy is a reason the U.S. Navy has the Fifth Fleet based in Bahrain, within close operating distance to the Strait.

CIVIL UNREST

In early 2011, civil unrest began in the Middle East and quickly spread through the region. It started in Egypt and quickly spread to Tunisia and Libya. No one knows what would happen if civil unrest should hit the Kingdom of Saudi Arabia, where there is great division between the Shiite and Sunni populations. More importantly, Iran has become a wild card whose actions cannot be predicted and which could easily provide resources and money to influence the current and future governments in the region. Any major shift in regional politics will impact global economies, but to what extent is not known.

SHALE NATURAL GAS

Perhaps the most significant energy development in the United States is shale gas, which refers to natural gas that is trapped within shale formations. Shales are fine-grained sedimentary rocks that can be rich sources of petroleum and natural gas. Over the past decade, a combination of horizontal drilling and hydraulic fracturing has allowed access to large volumes of shale gas that were previously uneconomical to produce. The production of natural gas from shale formations has rejuvenated the natural gas industry in the United States (Figure 45.14).

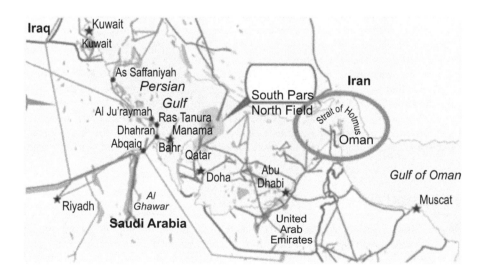

F I G U R E   45.13

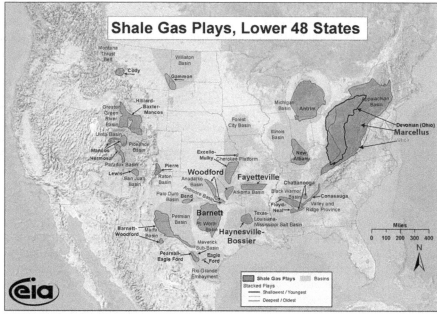

FIGURE 45.14

In 2009, the United States produced 87 percent of the natural gas consumed domestically; thus, the supply of natural gas is not dependent on non-U.S. producers as is the supply of crude oil, and the delivery system is less subject to disruption. According to the EIA, the United States now has enough natural gas to supply approximately 110 years of use based upon the 2009 consumption rate. More importantly, the Marcellus Shale in the eastern United States is a very promising area not subject to hurricanes and storms as is the GOM.

However, there are some potential environmental issues that are associated with the production of shale gas. Shale gas drilling has significant water supply issues. The drilling and fracturing of wells requires large amounts of water. In some areas of the country, significant use of water for shale gas production may affect the availability of water for other uses. Drilling and fracturing also produce large amounts of wastewater, which may contain dissolved chemicals and other contaminants that require treatment before disposal or reuse.[6]

Eventually, the United States could become a net exporter of natural gas in the form of liquefied natural gas. The March 2011 earthquake, tsunami and subsequent nuclear plant malfunctions in Japan will probably make natural gas the energy source for manufacturing and electric generation, in that country and perhaps elsewhere. As nuclear power concerns increase, more countries and industries will shift to natural gas as their energy choice.

OPERATING GLOBALLY

It has become more difficult for U.S. companies to compete with internationally owned national companies due to their local governmental support and subsidization. There is an element of risk involved when a company invests billions of dollars to explore a field, drill and develop the necessary infrastructure to transport the oil to market. In 2007, President Hugo Chavez nationalized assets of ExxonMobil and ConocoPhillips and pushed the companies out of Venezuela. According to Reuters, ConocoPhillips said it would have to knock $4.5 billion off its balance sheet after losing its assets in two Orinoco ventures.

In 2011, ConocoPhillips evacuated expatriate employees working in its Libyan operations and their families due to the civil unrest in the country. In the past, similar industry evacuations have occurred in other countries, mostly due to civil conflicts.

THE INDUSTRY IS ALWAYS LOOKING FOR GOOD COMMUNICATORS

Practicing communications in the oil and natural gas industry is both challenging and rewarding. The long hours and last-minute assignments, often in response to a crisis, can be very exhausting and, at the same time, exciting. Opportunities to live overseas in places like Singapore, Norway, Azerbaijan, Qatar and Russia provide experiences that are unique and memorable, but they are not for everyone. Personal sacrifices, including family separation and different living conditions and social customs, often make things we take for granted in the United States seem very important as they take on a new meaning overseas.

If you are interested in the industry, visit a facility or corporate headquarters, and perhaps talk to someone who is a few years out of college. Ask them about the pros and cons of working in the industry. Most who work in the industry agree that the view is worth the climb.

CASE STUDY: THE INDUSTRY FACES THE PERFECT STORM

In the late summer of 2005, a series of events began that had impact on every American and focused attention on the industry. There was extensive media coverage about gasoline shortages and the rising cost of gasoline and, eventually, probing questions about industry earnings and executive compensation. The negative consumer TV sound bites and editorials seemed to be everywhere and culminated with televised congressional hearings and calls for investigations. As a result, the industry and API reevaluated how it had been communicating to its stakeholders, conducted numerous focus groups across the country and launched a campaign to educate its key stakeholders.

LIVING OVERSEAS

- Have you ever lived in a foreign country for an extended period of time?
- What were some of the daily challenges?
- Where did you buy your groceries?
- Were you allowed to drive an automobile?
- How did social customs impact your daily life? Could you wear the same clothes you wore in the United States?
- How did you get personal mail from the United States?
- Where did children attend school?
- What about medical treatment for you and your family? What was the standard of care?
- Were there any language issues?

What are some other issues one can face living overseas?

HOW DID THIS ALL BEGIN?

Act one of the perfect storm began in August with Hurricane Katrina, followed closely behind by Hurricane Rita in September. Katrina and Rita caused massive destruction, left many people homeless and had national, state and local government officials pointing fingers at each other for any and all failures.

At that time, the oil and natural gas industry had more than 30,000 workers operating platforms in the GOM producing 30 percent of the oil and 13 percent of the natural gas in the United States. Even before the hurricanes entered the Gulf, the platforms were shut down, and employees were evacuated. These evacuations occur often during hurricane season because there are limited aviation assets (helicopters) that service the GOM, and flight operations on the platforms are limited by weather and wind conditions, so companies use an abundance of caution when making the decision to evacuate. By the time a storm is headed toward a platform, it is too late to conduct flight operations safely.

The damage to the platforms and pipelines caused by these two hurricanes was significant. Approximately 100 offshore structures were destroyed (Figure 45.15).

FIGURE 45.15

Oil Rig Washed Up on a Beach

Immediately, gasoline prices began to climb, and in some areas, there were gasoline shortages. Initially, most of the nation's attention was focused on the local situations in New Orleans and the lack of quick government response, but it quickly turned to the oil industry.

Act two began when the oil companies began reporting record 2005 earnings. This period (early February 2006) started the Washington rumblings: why was gasoline so expensive? Did the industry take advantage of the hurricanes to increase prices? The reported earnings and net income set records on Wall Street.

Act three was a *New York Times* article that appeared on April 15, 2006, and completed the perfect storm. The article entitled "For Leading Exxon to Its Riches, $144,573 a Day" highlighted the $686 million compensation that retired Exxon Chairman Lee Raymond was given during the period from 1993 to 2005, when he headed Exxon, increased the market value of the company fourfold to $375 billion and paid out $67

FIGURE 45.16

billion in total dividends to its investors. The Exxon share price also increased 13 percent per year during his tenure as head of Exxon. It is hard for someone to grasp $686 million, but everyone, especially someone that makes $65,000 a year, knows what $144,573 a day means.

It was shortly thereafter that legislators in Washington began to call for hearings and investigations, and there was even talk of windfall profits tax on the oil companies (Figure 45.16). Windfall profits tax hit the industry in the early 1980s, which severely impacted the industry and the U.S. economy, as nearly half of the industry workforce was laid off and capital investment funding was significantly reduced. The loss of technical expertise was significant, as many of the workers that were laid off at that time left the industry and never returned.

CASE STUDY DISCUSSION QUESTIONS

- What are some other tactics or tools that could have been used and why?

- How do you explain profits and rising gas prices to the average American?

- How will you know if your plan was successful?

- Should you use a national spokesman? If so, who would you suggest and why?

- Are there certain states that are openly for or against oil companies? If so, why do you think?

- Why are U.S. refineries, oil production and natural gas production platforms concentrated around the GOM?

- What do you say when a senator asks why the industry has not built or expanded refinery operations in his or her state? Do you tell the news media that the state and local community has opposed plans to expand capabilities?

AS A COMMUNICATOR, WHAT WOULD YOU DO?

You are the head of communications for a major company, and you are also the chairman of the general committee on communications at API. What do you recommend to the CEOs of the top eight companies operating in the United States as they all say, "we have to do something"?

Here's a hint: start with research and develop a communications and public affairs strategy. Who are your

HERE IS A SAMPLE LISTING OF SOME KEY INDUSTRY STAKEHOLDERS

Employees

- Full time
- Part time
- International
- Contractors
- Management/executives
- Shareholders
- Institutional
- Individual investors

Government

- Federal elected officials
- State elected officials
- Local elected officials
- Staffs of elected officials

International Governments

- Elected officials
- Regulators

Regulators

- National, state and local

News Media

- International
- National
- Local
- Point-of-view journalists

Industry Associations

- Integrated (API)
- Segment (National Petrochemical and Refiners Association, etc.)

Customers

- Commercial
- Retail
- International

Retail Marketers

- Company-owned stations
- Privately-owned stations

Labor Unions

- National
- International

Local Community

- Neighbors
- Accident/incident impacted

Nonprofits

- International
- National
- Local

NGOs

- National, state and Local
- International
- Relationship NGOs

stakeholders? The industry has a unique set of stakeholders. (See Stakeholder Box.)

As with any good plan, start with research. Find out what your stakeholders think and how they feel about your industry, including energy supplies, costs, profits, etc. Start interviewing PR firms and ask them for recommendations and proposals. Work closely with your government affairs personnel, as they are on the front lines at this point in time. Identify industry spokesmen, including key executives from the companies. Most importantly, realize that a task of this magnitude takes time and money. Keep your executives updated on your progress and even suggest they accompany you to some of the focus groups—that is usually a real eye-opener.

After six months of hard work, you are ready to implement the communications strategy/plan that developed in concert with the API staff, industry executives and your outside agencies. Here are a few of the key components of the plan:

- Conduct extensive initial and ongoing research to assess what people are thinking and how they feel about the industry.

  o Develop an educational program to educate and inform, and continuously update the program with ongoing research.

- Develop an advertising campaign (TV and print) targeted to individuals who are involved in their communities and want to learn about the issues.

- Utilize social media.

- Conduct special events such as "energy conversations" (town hall events) in the top 50 markets and arrange editorial board meetings.

The key to success is campaign flexibility. Your ongoing research, and to a certain extent, the news media coverage, will be a good indicator of how well you are moving the needle of public opinion.

Industry regulators could mean the Department of Energy, the Environmental Protection Agency or Minerals Management Service. Similarly, NGOs could mean anti-industry organizations, or it could mean groups that are sometimes aligned with companies with shared values such as protecting the environment. Every situation is different and requires good research to ensure that all key stakeholders are included in your communications strategy and plan.

DISCUSSION QUESTIONS

1. What strategies and communication tools should the industry use to tell its story? How do you coordinate industry messaging with the major integrated companies taking into consideration that the key players do not always agree on major issues (Alaska pipeline, alternative energy sources, etc.)?
2. What impact did the 2010 BP accident in the GOM have on the industry? What changes, if any, should the industry make in its communications strategy?
3. National oil companies, often owned and supported by international governments, have an advantage over U.S. companies. What can U.S. companies do to fairly compete in terms of exploration leases, projects and access? What can communications do to assist in leveling the playing field?
4. Why does the United States not have an energy policy?
5. Is it possible for the United States to end its reliance on imported oil? If so, how?
6. What steps can the industry take to communicate pipeline safety to consumers who live near pipeline infrastructure?

ADDITIONAL CLASS EXERCISES

YOU ARE THE COMMUNICATOR

- It is Sunday night, and you get a call from the *Wall Street Journal* asking for comment (not confirmation) on a major merger that involves your company.

- This merger, which will be the largest one on Wall Street this year, was to be announced at a press conference later in the week.

- Boards of both companies have not met to approve the merger, nor have specifics been finalized.

- The M&A teams are in New York finalizing agreement, and you are scheduled to travel there with the chairman later in the week

- What do you do? Whom do you call? What do you tell the *Wall Street Journal?*

In March 2006, API President and CEO Red Cavaney delivered a state-of-the-industry speech. Here are some of the key points from that speech; most are still relevant today:

- To appreciate where we are today regarding energy and where our nation needs to go, two fundamental tenets must be understood. First, the energy industry is a long-lead-time, capital-intensive industry. It cannot add capacity or flexibility overnight. And second, the energy industry cannot function effectively without a constructive partnership with government, at both the federal and state levels.

- Forty years ago, world oil reserves were largely owned by public, investor-owned oil and natural gas companies, mostly based in the United States. Today, world oil reserves are 77-percent owned by national (non-U.S.) oil companies formed during the past 30-plus years, while only 6 percent of worldwide reserves are now held by investor-owned oil and natural gas companies.

- Studies have shown that 60 percent of the cost of gasoline is attributable to the price of crude oil in the world market, where the price fluctuates with global demand, supply availability and unplanned disruptions. In the United States, the cost of crude oil is the single most important factor in determining the price of gasoline, diesel fuel, heating oil, aviation fuel and other crude products.

- The energy Americans consume today is brought to us by massive investments and reinvestments planned and made many years, or even decades, ago. Between 1992 and 2005, for example, the investor-owned oil and gas industry invested more than $1 trillion, on six continents, in a range of long-term energy projects. This trillion-dollar investment exceeded the total net income of all those companies over the same period. To succeed in reliably delivering affordable supplies of fuel to customers, the U.S. oil and natural gas industry must invest large sums of money, in both good and bad economic times. In this industry, to underinvest over time is to die a slow death.

- How can we meet these challenges here in the United States? For one thing, we cannot afford any longer to revisit energy policy only once every 10 years or so. Energy has become an every-year issue—as changes continue, as markets evolve and as new technologies come online. We must continue to address our energy policy until we get it right.

- Following Hurricanes Katrina and Rita, some people asked why our industry concentrated its facilities and operations along the hurricane-prone Gulf coast. There is a reason for this geographic concentration in a high-risk storm area. Government policies have largely limited offshore E&P to the Central and Western GOM—and our onshore facilities, including refineries, have been welcomed in communities in the region. Unfortunately, oil and natural gas development has been barred elsewhere—including the eastern half of the Gulf, the entire Atlantic and Pacific Coasts and large parts of the offshore and onshore areas of Alaska. Undiscovered, technically recoverable offshore resources could provide enough natural gas to heat 52 million homes for 120 years and enough oil to fuel 48 million cars for 60 years and heat 10 million homes for 120 years. Onshore construction in the lower 48 U.S. states has been held back by government restrictions, permitting delays and not-in-my-backyard sentiments.

- When government has interfered with markets, the result has been price volatility, supply shortages and other disruptions. In the early 1970s, many U.S. energy policymakers were "sure" that the reserves of oil and natural gas would soon be exhausted, and government policy was explicitly aimed at "guiding" the market in a smooth transition away from these fuels to new, more sustainable alternatives. Price controls, allocation schemes, limitations on natural gas, massive subsidies to synthetic fuels and other measures were funded heavily and implemented. And not one proved sustainable.

- The United States—and the world—cannot afford to leave the Age of Oil before realistic alternatives are fully in place. It is important to remember that man left the Stone Age not because he ran out of stones. And we will someday leave the Age of Oil, but not because we will have run out of oil. Yes, someday oil will be replaced, but clearly not until alternatives are found and tested —alternatives that are proven more reliable, more versatile and more cost competitive than oil.

- This does not mean that our industry is narrowly focused on oil and natural gas alone. In fact, our companies have long been pioneers in developing alternative sources of energy. For example:

  o BP is one of the world's largest producers of photovoltaic solar cells.

  o Chevron is the world's largest developer of geothermal energy.

  o Our industry is the largest producer and user of hydrogen; ExxonMobil, BP, Chevron, Shell and ConocoPhillips are key players in government/industry hydrogen fuel and vehicle partnerships.

  o Shell is one of the top players in the worldwide wind industry.

DISCUSSION QUESTIONS

- What key points above are still relevant today?

- How did the 2010 BP well accident affect drilling operations in the GOM and elsewhere?

- How do U.S. oil companies compete with state-owned national oil companies, which are subsidized by their own governments?

- What are some alternative forms of energy? Which show the most promise in coming to the marketplace in an affordable manner?

CASE STUDY: BALANCING FLUCTUATING AND FIXED COSTS (by Sam Falcona)

The price of crude oil has dramatically dropped in the last six months—from nearly $150 per barrel to below $40 per barrel. Certain exploration projects and some current projects in operation are no longer profitable due to the price of oil. A company restructuring, including layoffs, is in order.

For the purposes of this exercise, assume the following:

- The company is one of the top three U.S. integrated oil and natural gas companies.

- A small refinery that has represented (union) employees will be closed in six months.

- The company will reduce its total workforce globally by 3 percent.

- The corporate headquarters will reduce its employee headcount by 10 percent.

- The two major IT areas, presently located in two states, will be consolidated in one location.

- Severance packages will be offered to employees whose positions are being eliminated and to whom other positions are not offered. If an employee is offered the same or similar job in a different location and he or she does not want to go, then severance will not be offered.

- The company operates in more than 50 countries. Two of the foreign locations will be closed.

- Early retirement packages will not be offered.

- $10 billion of nonstrategic assets will be sold by the company.

- There will most likely be a shakeup/change in the senior management of the company.

- A state governor will file a lawsuit in an attempt to block the closing of two facilities in his state.

As the communicator, you have been tasked to develop a detailed communications plan for the restructuring. Your plan should include:

1. A contingency statement that will be used to respond to queries by the news media prior to any official announcement

2. Overall communications strategy (paragraph)

3. A proposed press release

4. A detailed set of questions and answers (Q&A) for use by management and your communications department

5. A detailed listing of all key stakeholders and the individual or department responsible for communicating with each stakeholder group (see chapter section on key industry stakeholders)

6. An updated company fact sheet incorporating the restructuring impact

7. A section developed by HR/labor relations to address represented employees

8. A detailed GR section identifying the key government and elected officials to be notified in advance of the press release

9. A section that addresses notifications and concerns that might arise outside the United States if foreign operations are impacted

10. A section developed by IR to address analyst questions and concerns, and New York Stock Exchange requirements

11. A detailed communications plan for the impacted facilities that includes:

    1. Talking points for the local management making the notifications

    2. An employee e-mail for these impacted facilities

    3. Local Q&A packet

    4. Timeline for the changes

    5. HR information

    6. Local news media communications strategy

    7. Identification of local spokesmen (for news media)

    8. Identification of B-roll (for the news media)

    9. A CEO statement that will be e-mailed to all employees after impacted facilities which have been identified for closing have been notified (in person) by their management

10. A CEO video statement (script), for internal use only

11. This communications plan could be leaked to the news media

NOTES

1. American Petroleum Institute, 2011. Web. 31 May 2011 <www.api.org>.
2. American Petroleum Institute, 2011. Web. 31 May 2011 <www.api.org>.
3. Melvin, Joshua (2010-10-28). "Death toll in San Bruno pipeline explosion climbs to eight". *San Jose Mercury News*.
4. Wildermuth, John; Fagan, Kevin; Lagos, Marisa; Van Derbeken, Jaxon (September 10, 2010). "San Bruno explosion: Some victims identified". *San Francisco Chronicle*.
5. Department of Justice, 2011. Web. 1 November 2011 <www.justice.gov>.
6. www.eia.doe.gov/energy_in_brief/about_shale_gas.cfm

ADDITIONAL READING

American Petroleum Institute, 2011. Web. 31 May 2011 <www.api.org>.
Department of Energy, 2011. Web. 31 May 2011 <www.energy.gov>.

LINKS TO SOME INDUSTRY RESTRUCTURINGS

www.chron.com/disp/story.mpl/business/energy/6692266.html
www.chron.com/disp/story.mpl/Business/6215681.html
blog.gulflive.com/mississippi-press-business/2010/03/post.html

46

CHAPTER

INTERNAL AND EXTERNAL COMMUNICATIONS IN A LAW FIRM

Mark Bain
Former Global Director of Communications
Baker & McKenzie

A growing number of law firms today are taking a more disciplined approach to internal and external communications. This trend is being driven by several factors, including macroeconomic forces in the global economy, growing competition in the legal industry and a proliferation of print and online media focusing on both the practice and business of law. These trends are converging to create a higher number and wider variety of employment opportunities in the law firms (and corporate legal departments) for communications professionals at every level.

This chapter will provide an overview of the legal industry, discuss some of the most notable trends that are reshaping it, describe some of the work that communicators in law firms are doing and suggest some trends and developments to watch during the next decade. A close reading of the first section in this chapter will significantly enhance your ability to work with the communications case at the conclusion of the chapter.

LEGAL INDUSTRY OVERVIEW

Law firms are part of the professional services sector, which includes accounting, advertising, engineering, management consulting, public relations, research and other advisory and service organizations.

While there are thousands of law firms of varying sizes, from one-person practices to global firms with more than 10,000 lawyers and staff worldwide, the global legal industry overall is quite fragmented and small, in revenue and employment terms, relative to some professional services industries.

Based on data compiled by *Legal Business* magazine, the 100 largest law firms worldwide generated a total of $74 billion in gross fee income worldwide in 2010. In sharp contrast, the "Big Four" accounting firms alone—Deloitte, Ernst & Young, KPMG and PricewaterhouseCoopers—generated nearly $94 billion in global fee income that same year. And Deloitte, the largest professional services firm in the world with 170,000 people working in 150 countries, had 2010 revenues in excess of $26 billion. Just 17 law firms reported fees in excess of $1 billion in 2010, and nine had fees of $1.5 billion or more. Only two law firms—Baker & McKenzie and Skadden, Arps, Slate, Meagher & Flom—reported global fees of $2 billion or more in 2010.[1]

According to *Legal Business*, 80 percent of the 100 largest law firms in 2010 are based in the United States, with most of the remaining 20 percent based in the United Kingdom. Fifty-four percent of the Global 100 lawyers are located in the United States.[2] Most of the 50 largest firms have offices in multiple countries, but the international presence of the second 50 firms is more limited. The American and British legal markets are especially competitive, with regional, national and international firms all vying for a slice of a legal services pie which, during the "Great Recession" of 2007–2009, shrank following seven consecutive years of robust annual growth.

Other large markets for legal services include Australia, Japan, Germany and France. The BRIC countries (Brazil, Russia, India and China), Mexico, Singapore, Malaysia and the Gulf have seen rapid growth in the legal services sector as globalization has boosted economic activity for these emerging markets.

Some large and fast-growing countries, such as South Korea and India, currently have regulations that prohibit international firms from opening offices and/or practicing law within their borders. Some international firms have formed alliances with domestic law firms in these countries, but there are regulatory limits to the degree of cooperation and legal practice allowed. On the other hand, international firms are active in providing legal support to many Korean and Indian multinational companies as they invest and grow in Asia and other countries throughout the world, in part because Korean and Indian law firms have not expanded internationally in the same manner as American and British firms.

Almost all law firms are private, not public, businesses. They are owned by the equity partners, sometimes called shareholders, who practice in the firm. Major investments and policy decisions are made by the equity partners, usually through a voting process.

This private stature also stands in contrast to other professional services industries, such as accountancy, management consulting and advertising/public relations, where the largest firms are publicly listed businesses or subsidiaries of publicly listed entities. Recent regulatory changes in Australia and the United Kingdom will permit some law firms to go public, but few firms are expected to follow this path, at least in the immediate future. While going public could provide a major injection of capital to fund their expansion, many law firms are concerned that heightened expectations from an additional and larger group of shareholders for short-term financial performance could shift an essential focus on client-service quality and satisfaction. Moreover, law firm partnerships are complex and occasionally fragile organizations, requiring a high degree of shared values and mutual trust among the equity owners of the business. Increased pressure to grow revenues and profits could undermine the client partnerships and peer-to-peer trust that binds enduring partnerships over time.

Law firms range greatly in size and scope. On one end of the spectrum, there are solo practitioners and small firms with fewer than 50 lawyers; these firms account for a large number of all lawyers in practice worldwide but generate a smaller portion of total legal revenues. Midsized firms have 50 to 500 lawyers and generate higher revenues through their work at the regional, national and even international levels. Large firms can have as many as 4,000 lawyers worldwide and may also employ as many as 6,000 additional business support staff, typically nonlawyers.

Law firms can be broadly sorted by the type of work they do. Personal injury law firms concentrate on representing individuals and groups that claim to have been injured through the negligence or action of others. The largest personal injury firms may have 50 to 100 lawyers and, to assist in marketing their work, they may have a communications professional or two on staff. Corporate law firms represent businesses of all sizes on a wide range of legal needs around their business, and while these firms can vary greatly in size, the broad nature of their business accounts for their larger size. Midsized and large firms often have one or more communications professionals on staff, and the global communications teams at the largest law firms might include 15 or more professionals whose sole focus is on internal and/or external communications.

Generally, midsized and large corporate firms present the most and, arguably, some of the best employment opportunities for communications professionals at all levels because they tend to have larger budgets, more specialized roles and job progression opportunities over the course of a career.

Law firms are organized and operated around three dimensions: geography, practice and industry.

From a geographic perspective, midsized and large law firms usually operate in multiple legal jurisdictions—countries, states (or provinces) and cities—with their own sets of laws and regulations. Midsized firms tend to do most of their business regionally or nationally. National firms have offices in many of the major business and financial centers of a country but often have little or no business beyond that country. Larger law firms have offices in several countries, and the largest international and global firms are present in 20 or more countries. Baker & McKenzie, the largest global law firm by revenues in 2010, has about 70 offices in 40 countries. Its business is relatively balanced, in revenue and headcount terms, across its four primary regions: Europe, the Middle East and Africa; North America; and Latin America and Asia Pacific.

Law firms also organize their people and work into several legal practices. These practices may be structured and labeled in slightly different ways from firm to firm, but some of the more common legal practices are antitrust and competition; banking and finance; corporate compliance; dispute resolution (including litigation); employment; environmental; financial restructuring and insolvency; intellectual property; mergers and acquisitions; and private equity, tax and securities. For each practice area, there may be several subpractices.

In addition to their geographic and practice dimensions, more law firms have, in recent years, started to organize their people and work around certain industries, including, but not limited to, agribusiness; automotive; communications; energy and mining; financial services; information technology; infrastructure; insurance, pharmaceuticals and health care; and real estate. The lawyers in these areas may specialize in a certain practice area (e.g., merger and acquisitions) and, at the same time, have extensive experience representing (as just one example) pharmaceutical companies on their mergers, acquisitions and other transactions. For highly regulated industries and the most complex legal matters, lawyers with dual specialization in certain practice and industry areas can be especially valuable to clients.

For much of the twentieth century, firms took a mostly geographic approach, but the last decade has seen firms put added emphasis on formalizing their practices and industry groups. As a result, some law firms have started to organize and operate in a more three-dimensional matrix of geography, practice and industry.

The largest law firms are typically full service, offering their clients both breadth and depth of practice and industry talent across multiple jurisdictions. By design, boutique law firms tend to have depth of talent in one or two areas of legal practice, and they are usually more geographically concentrated as well. Multinational corporations will often utilize a mix of full-service and boutique law firms around the world. This approach allows them to get most or all of the specialized legal expertise they need in each of the markets that are important to their business.

MAJOR TRENDS

The global economic, political, regulatory and social trends and forces that are now impacting business overall are also shaping law firms of all sizes.

Globalization is one of the most powerful and influential forces, particularly for the midsized and large firms. As demand for their products or services has fallen off in some developed economies, multinational companies have been turning to, and in some cases starting to rely upon, the emerging markets to deliver sales and profit growth. A 2010 research report by Standard Chartered Bank estimated that the global economy, as measured by nominal gross domestic product, could grow from $62 trillion in 2010 to $308 trillion in 2030. This includes growth in the developed economies, such as the United States, the European Union and Japan. But the report suggests that most of the future growth will come from emerging markets, resulting in a dramatic rebalancing of economic power. Standard Chartered projects that whereas the United States, Europe and Japan accounted for 60 percent of global economic activity in 2010, their share could fall to just 29 percent by 2030. China, India and Latin America, meanwhile, are forecasted to account for 43 percent of global economic activity in 2030, up from 18 percent in 2010.[3]

With globalization, there is growing economic interconnectivity between emerging markets. In the last few decades, trade and other economic activity tended to flow (in the form of goods, services, investments, acquisitions, etc.) from established to emerging economies. But in today's more integrated global economy, there is a growing volume of trade and investment activity directly from one emerging market to another. For example, Chinese state-owned enterprises are active today in acquiring assets and forming partnerships with companies in Latin America, Africa and Asia. Indian, Russian, Brazilian and Middle Eastern—corporate conglomerates are doing the same. Much of the emerging market–to–emerging market activity is centered on resources—petroleum, natural gas, coal, food and water—needed to fuel and feed economic expansion in these large, fast-growing countries.

With a larger global network to manage today, multinational companies have been seeking to improve operating simplicity and efficiency by reducing their total number of suppliers and business partners, including law firms, around the world. Many companies that once retained dozens of law firms have started to set up legal panels—essentially, a shortlist (approximately five) of leading law firms who become their preferred providers of legal services. As panel members, such law firms can capture a larger volume of their client's legal spend, but they are expected in exchange to provide more tailored legal service, often at more favorable rates. The move to consolidation is prompting many regional, national and international law firms to accelerate their expansion to new jurisdictions.

The Great Recession of 2007–2009 accentuated a related shift that had already been underway for years in the legal industry—a more concerted effort by clients to control and even reduce their expenditures on outside legal services. Many corporate legal departments today are populated with former law firm employees whose experience allows their department to bring certain legal work in-house. Moreover, these former firm lawyers are familiar with ways to reduce and better manage overall legal expenditures, including those incurred by their company's outside law firms. With intensified pressure from a range of corporate stakeholders to demonstrate greater value, in-house legal teams are keen to reduce legal costs while preserving the quality of that legal support and increasing the predictability of total legal spend.

As a result, there has been enormous pressure on law firms, magnified by the economic downturn, to reduce the fees they charge clients. To protect their own profitability, midsized and large firms are now striving to reduce their operating costs through various efforts, including outsourcing and offshoring of more commoditized legal and business support processes. Client insistence is also forcing many law firms to move away from a historical focus on the billable-hour approach to pricing work toward more flexible and predictable approaches, called alternative fee arrangements, and toward the adoption of more disciplined workflow management processes.

Against this backdrop of change, a war for top legal talent continues. Law school programs and law firm job opportunities have always been highly competitive. But with more attractive and lucrative employment opportunities in corporate legal departments, and the scramble by law firms to expand in geographic and practice terms, there is a battle to attract and keep the best and brightest young legal talent.

This war is not limited to the more junior lawyers. There is also intense competition to lure senior partners with specialized legal expertise and a large "book of business" (loyal clients who might be expected to follow the lawyer to a new firm) to switch firms. This talent war is predicated on the view that those firms with highest concentration of best people will attract the most lucrative business, and there are no signs of a ceasefire in the near future.

The war for talent is closely linked to another closely watched trend, rises in law firm profitability. Law firms use a number of metrics to track performance, and profit per (equity) partner (PPP) is one of the most common figures. In 2010, the average PPP reported at the most profitable law firm, Wachtell, Lipton, Rosen & Katz, exceeded $4 million. Interestingly, Wachtell was the fiftieth-largest firm worldwide based on revenue. In contrast, Fidal, a French firm, had an average PPP of $204,000 on revenues that were about $170 million lower than Wachtell's.[4] These are averages, and it is worth noting that the top "rainmakers" at firms can make as much as $10 million annually. Lawyers at all levels pay close attention to firm profitability because, naturally, the top performers want and expect to earn the most money.

Profitability is one of many factors impacting a law firm's brand and reputation. Indeed, brand reputation has assumed greater importance in recent years as firms seek differentiation in a cluttered, fragmented and shifting market for legal services. Law firm brands are also shaped by the specialized expertise a firm offers; perceptions of price and value; the high-profile "bet-the-business" legal work a firm does for its clients; the visibility and thought leadership of law firm partners; the conduct of a firm's lawyers and staff over time; a firm's geographic footprint; the attractiveness of a firm as a place to work; a firm's social responsibility efforts; a firm's visual identity and more. In other words, law firm brands are built—and damaged—by many of the same factors that influence corporate brands. Leading firms today realize that they must nurture, grow and differentiate their brands to help them attract, retain and engage the top talent they need to secure and serve the most-coveted clients.

It is worth noting that the long-established legal education and employment paradigms are also undergoing change. After completing a four-year undergraduate degree, the typical law student spends three additional and grueling years earning a Juris Doctor degree. She must also study intensely for and pass a difficult bar exam in the jurisdiction(s) where she wishes to practice. With significant debt (sometimes as much as $200,000) from their three years of law school and bar preparation programs, the large pool of bright and ambitious law school students must compete for a small number of the highest-paying jobs in the top law firms and corporate legal departments, positions which are often secured near the start of their third and final year of law school. Is it worth it for the aspiring attorney to get a law degree, especially if she is not attending one of the top 10 law schools and likely to finish close to the top of his class? Is there a sufficient return on the investment in a legal degree? On a purely financial level, many are starting to question the short- and long-term financial return of having a legal degree.

This brutal selection process is merely the price of entry for one's legal career. Upon joining a firm, newly minted lawyers can expect to work extremely long hours for up to a decade as they strive to make partner (become elected an equity owner of their firm), a privilege that is extended to just one in four or five firm lawyers.

No wonder that many young professionals have become disillusioned, to say the least, about their legal career and prospects. Their frustration is on full display in legal blogs, such as *Above the Law* and *Roll on Friday*. These blogs have become quite influential in raising the clamor about legal education and employment processes, and possible reforms are being hotly debated. In the meantime, disillusioned and resentful attitudes can be a significant challenge to law firms that need their people to be fully engaged if they are to provide the highest-quality service to clients and retain top talent that will be instrumental to their future success.

Finally, given all the trends noted above, law firms are adjusting their strategic plans to secure their place in an uncertain future. With their clients looking to new markets for growth, some regional firms are moving aggressively to increase their national presence, and the national firms are working just as proactively to increase their international footprint. International firms, meanwhile, are seeking to more fully integrate their offices and practices to deliver consistent, high-quality advice and service to clients around the world. Boutiques are deciding if they will remain specialized or move toward a full-service model.

It can take decades to grow a law firm organically, from the ground up, in a new location, and profits can be elusive during this extended start-up phase. Though less risky than acquisitions, organic growth takes time to build critical mass of business and talent, and success through this approach is not assured. Growth through merger or acquisition can build critical mass in locations and practice groups more quickly, but it is expensive and highly risky in law firms, due to client conflicts and possible culture clashes.

There is ample skepticism that law firms will pursue the same massive consolidation seen in the advertising and public relations industries, where in the last three decades, most of the leading firms have been snapped up by large, publicly listed holding companies for marketing services firms. And few observers envision a "big eight" or "big four" of law firms, as has happened in the accounting field. But some consolidation is occurring (e.g., the combination of Hogan & Hartson, an American firm, with Lovells, a British firm, in 2010 to form a new top-10 firm), and more megamergers are likely in the next few years. At the same time, some large and well-known law firms have been dissolving, disappearing in a matter of months when financial performance slides, partnerships become divided and departures of top talent to other, more profitable firms start to snowball.

It is a volatile time in the legal industry, where nothing seems certain—other than continued change.

OPPORTUNITIES FOR COMMUNICATIONS PROFESSIONALS IN LAW FIRMS

With so much change, the legal industry is a dynamic and challenging place for any professional to work today. It is an especially attractive option for communications professionals—particularly those with a deep interest in the corporate, financial and legal worlds, along with the skills for communicating effectively across audiences and borders to build better brands.

Law firms are intellectually rich work environments. Lawyers are, by nature and professional training, curious, diligent and hard working. They are highly analytical and extremely detail oriented. They are skilled debaters and strong writers, two essential qualities in the legal field. That is one reason why even the best legal communicators can expect to see heavy, meticulous editing of their press releases, memos and other content that is submitted to firm lawyers for review.

Legal matters are inherent to change in business and society. Ground-breaking developments in any industry often involve mergers or acquisitions, with myriad employment, intellectual property and tax implications, especially in the largest cross-border transactions. There can be antitrust questions to be resolved and various disputes to be litigated or settled. Immersion in this environment allows those in the industry to feel the pulse of business. And for those at international law firms, working across borders and cultures can be stimulating and rewarding on both a professional and personal level.

Law firms can also be frustrating places to work. Lawyers are trained to identify and manage risk, and they can quickly tell you just about everything that could possibly go wrong in any given scenario. Some lawyers have strong personalities and opinions, and when combined with the stress of their brutal workloads, a few can be impatient and downright testy at times.

Lawyers respect precedent—prior law and choices—and their willingness to embrace change and adapt to new circumstances may lag the norm for other professions. And the need to build consensus for change or action among partners, the owners of the firm, also takes time, effort and inevitably a certain amount of compromise.

Still, for many communicators and other professionals, work in a law firm can be deeply satisfying and rewarding. It's all about finding that right match of aptitude, attitude and opportunity.

PLANNING, IMPLEMENTATION AND EVALUATION

ROLE OF COMMUNICATIONS IN A LAW FIRM

Strategic priorities vary from firm to firm, but every law firm has an ongoing need to attract and retain top clients and top talent. External communications can support these priorities by raising a firm's profile to increase awareness and understanding, and internal communications can contribute to an informed and more engaged group of lawyers and staff.

Like any business, law firms have a variety of external and internal stakeholders. Existing and prospective clients are a firm's most important external stakeholders, of course. Others who matter include prospective talent in the law schools, lawyers presently working at other law firms and key influencers of stakeholder perceptions and attitudes, including legal recruiters, law school professors, legal consultants and service providers, and the media. In this regard, the disciplines of stakeholder mapping and management are just as important in a law firm as they are in a large corporation.

Internally, lawyers are primary stakeholders in any firm, and there can be differences in messaging for equity and nonequity partners, associates, paralegals and other timekeepers (those who complete time sheets and bill time to clients). Among professional staff at a firm, there are managers, subordinates and clerical staff fulfilling a wide range of business support functions, including business development, marketing, communications, finance and accounting, talent management, human resources, knowledge management, client and matter intake and information services. These staff members look after the day-to-day business of their law firm, helping the lawyers concentrate on the practice of law and client support.

Like other professional services, law firms market an intangible product—legal advice. This advice is derived from knowledge and expertise, and a fundamental role of communications is to capture and convey that knowledge and expertise in a compelling manner to all stakeholders. Advice is paired with client service that must be responsive and informed.

Relative to the marketing of other professional services, legal marketing tends to make less use of image advertising. Historical bar restrictions are a major reason for this, but even where those regulations have been relaxed, a general aversion to legal advertising persists.

Clients today expect their lawyers to be not only expert in technical legal matters but also up to speed on their specific business strategies, corporate culture, governance practices and more. Because many in-house lawyers today have a strong technical understanding of what a law or regulation says, and they are familiar with the way that law or regulation has been interpreted and applied in other situations, clients are looking to their lawyers for commercially pragmatic solutions to increasingly complex business problems. In the 24/7 world of global business, clients do not have time for a 15-page memo sent next week when two pages this afternoon will suffice. This puts the onus on law firms to think, act and behave in a fluent and client-driven manner—working across borders and practices to provide seamless and effective advice. That is a formidable challenge for any firm that has a broad global footprint and depth in multiple jurisdictions or practices.

Finally, communications in support of change management is vital in law firms that are growing quickly or shifting strategic priorities. Lawyers tend to be rational, analytical thinkers who require a compelling business case for change before they will embrace new ideas and approaches. Brief motivational videos with inspirational messages or management exhortations alone can fall flat in this environment because lawyers look closely not only at what is being said but also what is not being said.

EXTERNAL COMMUNICATIONS ACTIVITIES

Law firm communicators can be involved in a number of different external communications activities. Following are a few examples.

Publicity and media relations: The legal industry is closely followed by a large and active group of print and online media, especially in the United States and United Kingdom. Media, such as *The American Lawyer, Legal Week, The Lawyer, Legal Business, Asian Legal Business* and *Latin Lawyer,* report on the business of law—clients won and lost, major legal talent hired, industry trends and issues and firm financial performance. Other media matter as well. The business and financial press (e.g., the *Financial Times, The Economist,* the *Wall Street Journal,* etc.) report on broader trends and developments in the legal industry, and specialist media exist to follow developments in the areas of tax, intellectual property, banking and finance, mergers and acquisitions, the energy industry and more.

Thought leadership: Prominent lawyers will often convey thought leadership on legal and business developments by providing quotes for news stories and authoring opinion pieces (op-ed or bylined articles) for media outlets. While much of this will appear in legal or trade media, it's not uncommon for lawyers to appear in major business media and on television news and talk programs to provide a perspective on a wide range of business and legal topics. Lawyers can be credible third-party commentators who can bring clarity to complex developments and processes.

Events: Law firms frequently host events, forums, conferences, road shows, webinars and other gatherings to discuss the latest business, legal and regulatory developments in detail. Often, white papers, original research and other reports containing thought leadership are presented in these gatherings. Most of these events are for clients only, but sometimes media are invited to attend and report on the information shared.

Rankings and directories: Given the highly competitive nature of lawyers, legal media rank law firms on a wide range of variables, including revenues and profits, deals managed, number of lawyers by location and practice, numbers of partners by gender, total number of pro bono hours logged and much more. The growth of media following the legal industry has contributed to a corresponding increase in specialized rankings and analyses on various performance metrics in the legal press. Interestingly, even though law firms are private businesses with no legal obligation to disclose such information (except in a few jurisdictions where required by law), they voluntarily disclose it anyway to help in differentiating and distinguishing their firm to attract and retain top clients and talent.

Websites: A firm's website can be one of its most visible and heavily utilized information tools to build a law firm brand. Clients will search firm websites for information on specialized expertise, specific lawyers, thought leadership on trending topics and more. Law firms are taking greater care now to optimize their visibility on search engines, such as Google, Bing and Yahoo!.

Advertising: Bar associations and justice ministries in many countries place tight restrictions on the use of image or other advertising by law firms. Still, many firms do advertise, usually to build name awareness and image, but the practice is not as pervasive as it is in the accounting and management consulting fields. Law firms active in mergers and acquisitions and other transactional practices may also place "tombstone" ads in financial publications to spotlight their role in a major deal. In some jurisdictions, however, ads, press releases and even invitations to firm events must carry prominent disclaimers noting that the communication is "attorney advertising."

Social media: For the most part, law firms have been late adopters of social media to engage with external stakeholders. Again, bar regulations are a factor. In certain jurisdictions, attorneys cannot provide what might be seen as specific legal advice via social and other media. Today, law firms are most visible on business-oriented social media, including LinkedIn and Wikipedia. Firms may also have official pages on Facebook or dedicated channels on YouTube, and many use Twitter to broadcast firm news. But with the exception of some specialists in intellectual property law, few firms today are using blogs or other social media tools to actively engage, in a real-time and continual manner, with external audiences. Most observers expect to see this change dramatically in the next few years. At this writing, firms are starting to make greater use of legal blogs, Twitter accounts and other social media platforms.

INTERNAL COMMUNICATIONS

In a business where talent attraction and retention is central to success, engaging your existing attorneys and staff is enormously important.

Law firms, like all businesses, have their own formal communications networks and informal grapevines. And to paraphrase Mark Twain, misinformation can spread throughout a firm before management ever hears about it or can get a response out. That is why many firms today are adopting structured, proactive and interactive internal communications programs.

Such programs start with efforts to create clarity and understanding at all levels about the firm's vision, mission, values and strategy. It's important for people to have context for decisions that will impact their careers and financial well-being.

It is equally important to communicate progress against the firm strategy and goals, celebrating accomplishments and recognizing groups and individuals who were instrumental to that success. There is also an ongoing need to communicate firm policies and processes.

When new offices are opened or practices are formed, these are significant milestones in a firm's evolution, and the achievement needs to be put in a broader strategic context for all lawyers and staff. Likewise, when firms suffer setbacks—client losses, talent departures, office closings, financial underperformance—employees today expect the facts, with concrete explanations from leadership on how such setbacks will impact them and the firm.

Internal communications can also help to foster greater unity and teamwork within a firm. Again, this takes on added importance as a firm grows.

Lawyers have an affinity for the written word, so it's not uncommon for firms to use e-mail, e-newsletters and intranets to get messages out internally. The larger the firm is, however, the more voluminous and, sometimes, overwhelming these written communications can become.

Increasingly, law firms are making more use of social and digital media to communicate and engage with internal stakeholders, especially those under 35 who have been raised in a technology-rich world. Videos are great tools for telling stories and presenting people. Videoconferences can be used to present quarterly reports and urgent updates. Live "town hall" meetings are indispensable and increasingly common. Speed and authenticity assume greater importance when using these tools.

OTHER COMMUNICATIONS-RELATED ACTIVITIES

Social responsibility is increasingly important in law firms today. Lawyers have professional obligations, under the bar regulations in most countries, to lend their legal skills to disadvantaged community members who may not have access to justice. The top firms, however, have moved well beyond the mandatory obligations to develop sophisticated social responsibility programs that include not only pro bono legal work but also community events, sustainability initiatives and diversity programs. These efforts resonate with and motivate the people who work in law firms today, because most people want to make a difference and give back to society. Law firm social responsibility also matters to clients whose own companies have made this a core value and strategic priority of their own.

As law firms become more international in scope, *diversity* matters more. Cross-cultural relations take on greater practical importance, so diversity programs, with their focus on respect for people of varying backgrounds, can create more harmonious, unified, productive and innovative businesses.

Sustainability has also entered the legal lexicon. Law firms are becoming more organized and disciplined about reducing their carbon footprint. Some firms are moving to more electronic filing and document management systems and turning their offices into green workplaces where recycling, energy-efficient lighting and heating/cooling systems and other conservation measures are the norm. Some firms have formed sustainability committees responsible for raising internal awareness of environmentally responsible operating practices and for promoting an overall "greening" of their firm's operations, including the purchase of credits to offset their carbon footprint.

Finally, it is not uncommon for law firms, especially midsized and large firms, to use *public relations firms*. Quite often, law firms will retain a public relations consultant or agency to help raise the media profile of their practices and partners. Law firms want to promote their thought leadership in their prioritized areas of law, and public relations firms can help, given their familiarity with the media and trending business topics. Law firms must also interact with the print and online legal media on news about the business of law—new partners added, offices opened, financial results, lawsuits against firms and so forth—and public relations firms can help with this as well. Public relations firms can assist law firms in developing internal communications strategies and tactics, and some communications consultants provide specialized expertise in issue and crisis management at law firms (e.g., allegations of firm or partner misconduct, major defections of top partners, etc.). Public relations firms can also add value with advice on emerging communications practices, such as the use of social media in the law firm environment.

There are a number of public relations firms that specialize in working primarily with law firms, and these firms bring an intimate understanding of the legal press, litigation communications, financial communications and more. These specialists may also understand the unique culture of law firms and partnerships. Most of the larger, full-service public relations firms have worked with a law firm at one time, along with other professional services clients, and they can bring value as well.

Finally, while lawyers in some firms will occasionally retain public relations firms to work alongside them on a particular client's legal matter, there are serious client confidentiality and legal privilege risks to be carefully considered before making such an arrangement. Some firms have policies in place that prohibit such arrangements with public relations firms.

THE FUTURE OF COMMUNICATIONS IN A LAW FIRM

There is no question that globalization will remain a driving force for change in the next decade and beyond. As corporations go global, their advisors, including law firms, will try to go with them. This includes law firms that are based outside the traditional legal centers of the United States and England. Take for example King & Wood, a fast-growing Chinese law firm, which currently has more than a dozen offices in China, one office in Japan and two offices in North America. As Chinese conglomerates expand their international reach, King & Wood, along with other Chinese law firms, can be expected to rise in scale and stature.

More law firm consolidation is expected. Client conflicts will continue to make some large-scale law firm mergers impractical. But to build a critical mass to be in a position to serve multinational clients around the world, some firms are bound to pursue mergers.

The firms that are already international will look to solidify their competitive positions by broadening their platforms, especially in emerging markets, and by building greater depth of talent in all locations. As this happens, they could have an advantage over firms with small teams or just representative offices in emerging markets.

Like most companies, law firms have for decades made their offices primarily responsible for fundamental operating decisions—hiring staff, reporting revenues, distributing profits and so forth. But as firms have expanded to provide a broader range of legal services in multiple regions of the world for their multinational clients, some have started to explore more practice-driven, rather than office-centric, approaches to organizing and managing their business. As integrated financial systems make it easier to track profit and loss of practice groups, these groups will start to exert more influence over strategic decisions, including hiring, training and development and promotion of both lawyers and staff. Practices will get larger business development, marketing and communications budgets to manage, and full-service firms will be faced with the challenge of orchestrating and harmonizing their office- and practice-generated messages in the marketplace.

Under pricing pressure from clients, firms will look to lower their cost to deliver legal services through the use of outsourcing and offshoring of certain business and legal processes. There has already been a push to move contract development and review, routine intellectual property tasks and other repetitive and commoditized work off the desks of higher-priced law firm associates and onto the desks of paralegals inside the firm, in lower-cost jurisdictions and in third-party vendors in India, the Philippines, Ireland and South Africa.

Law firm brands and reputations will be built and, in some cases, destroyed. Progressive firms will move beyond superficial branding efforts loosely built around a slogan, a logo and a new graphic identity to more deeply define, through research, the unique qualities that differentiate their firm from other firms and make them more compelling to clients. With these programs will come more robust campaigns around thought leadership, using multiple tools, including social media, to connect firms with clients.

Internal communications will gain currency as firms look to create more satisfied and engaged teams of high-performing talent. These teams will be more diverse in composition, as firms become more international in scope. Change communications will help fast-growing firms move forward.

All external and internal communications will be less top-down and more interactive. Social media will help firms manage real-time, two-way dialogues with several stakeholders, and instead of controlling messages, firms will become facilitators of dialogues.

The lines between different communications disciplines—public relations, advertising, promotional events and so on—will start to blur as integrated teams develop more cohesive, comprehensive campaigns.

Legal media will continue to press for greater disclosure of financial and nonfinancial law firm information, and law firms, while still private businesses, will become more open and transparent organizations.

Finally, social responsibility will become less of a "nice to do" and more of a strategic priority for law firms, who will be more thoughtful and focused in how to use pro bono, community, sustainability and diversity initiatives to improve their communities, motivate their people and better serve their clients.

All in all, it will be an exciting time for communicators to work in the legal profession.

CASE STUDY

The fictitious law firm Beringer, Rai, Iglesias, Eto and Feingold LLP (BRIEF) was established in New York in 1962. Today, it has eight offices across the United States and Canada, which generate three quarters of its fees and about 60 percent of its profits.

During the last decade, BRIEF expanded internationally by opening four new offices in financial and legal centers—London, Paris, Mexico City and Hong Kong.

Though smaller than its domestic operations, BRIEF's international network has been growing at a much faster rate, averaging double-digit annual increases in fees and profits over the last few years, even in the downturn. Profitability in these international offices (aside from London, an expensive jurisdiction) has also been substantially higher than in North America, where the costs for talent and facilities is higher overall.

BRIEF's domestic revenues and profits had already started to plateau before the global financial crisis in 2007, but they saw significant declines during the downturn, much as they fell at most firms as overall demand for outside legal services fell faster than operating costs could be cut. Law firms have high fixed costs; long-term leases in Grade A commercial buildings are expensive and difficult to renegotiate, and firms are reluctant to reduce attorney headcount given a war for top talent in the industry.

BRIEF's international offices have grown mostly by serving the firm's long-standing U.S.-based clients as they have expanded their businesses in Europe and Asia. Encouraged by this success, BRIEF has been looking carefully at opening new international offices. Jurisdictions high on its priority list include China, Japan, Australia, Brazil, Germany, Russia and Saudi Arabia. Each prospective location offers several opportunities and challenges, and fortunately, BRIEF partners have identified some potential for the firm to get immediate work from long-standing firm clients if BRIEF enters these locations, provided it goes in with wholly owned offices (not affiliations or "best-friends" relationships with other firms) to ensure consistent quality of advice and service.

At the same time, BRIEF has had attractive opportunities to add substantially to its American practice. Several respected firms of comparable or slightly smaller size have held preliminary talks with BRIEF's managing partner over the last few years to explore a possible merger that would dramatically grow the firm's scale and capabilities in the United States, the largest—and most competitive—legal market in the world. Some of these partners have presences outside the United States, but unlike BRIEF's, these international offices are comparatively small.

BRIEF began as a firm specializing in intellectual property (IP) law. Over the years, it has diversified its practices to take advantage of opportunities by adding lawyers focusing on tax, employment, mergers and acquisitions and litigation. It now has a critical mass of talent in these practice areas, and some of its lawyers are highly rated—but none of BRIEF's practices other than intellectual property are considered "top tier" in the standard rankings of legal talent.

There has been internal pressure to add several new practices in a move toward becoming a truly full-service firm. But BRIEF leadership has yet to take any major steps in that direction.

Today, BRIEF has almost 500 lawyers worldwide. Most are located in the United States, more specifically, New York, Chicago and San Francisco. The firm bolstered its business support staff during the last decade by adding to its business development, marketing, IT and HR ranks. The marketing department has been using a PR firm for seven years to help it build the external profile of several practices in the United States, including intellectual property. However, spend on this PR firm, which was modest to begin with, dropped during the global financial downturn as part of BRIEF's broader effort to reduce costs and preserve partner profits.

BRIEF's lawyers and staff were growing uneasy and restless.

The downturn took a big bite out of partner profits, which now average $607,000 per equity partner. In 2007, PPP peaked at $798,000, the highest performance in the firm's history.

In the last two years, BRIEF lost about 15 talented partners, who jumped to other firms for various reasons, but more money was a common reason. BRIEF lost some good clients when these partners left, too. But fortunately, the negative publicity was minimal, because most of the departures involved one or two partners, and they were spread over time and across practices.

When in 2011, however, BRIEF lost a prestigious team of 15 prominent IP lawyers—7 partners and 8 associates. Included was the global chair of the IP practice group, a well-known and highly respected professional and the most senior woman in the firm. The legal press wrote extensively, and quite critically, about the exodus, given the large size of the group, the high-profile clients they represented, the firm that picked the group up and the steady drip of partner departures in recent years. Media have seen this pattern before—a slow initial erosion of talent followed by the departure of larger groups, which is usually a sure sign of greater fundamental problems at a law firm. Once such departures snowball, a firm can lose most of its talent and clients in just months, leading to "dissolution" of the firm (a total shut down) and years of legal fighting among creditors.

The 15-attorney IP team joined a fast-growing and much larger firm with a greater international platform. In the press release and news coverage surrounding the move, the former BRIEF partners noted that while they admired BRIEF and thought it was a good firm, they were attracted by the opportunity to build a global IP practice by leveraging the large and well-established global network of their new partnership. These statements were true and, of course, polite. But insiders knew that this group was part of a larger faction that was frustrated that BRIEF had not moved more aggressively to build its international capabilities. Internally, it was widely known that the IP practice group leader who led the breakaway had tried in vain to persuade BRIEF leadership and partners that their best strategic choice was to invest in international growth, rather than a merger to build their U.S. capabilities.

Professional staff in the firm were quite unsettled by the most recent departures and growing increasingly unclear and concerned about the firm's direction and future. Yet, while the senior staff was most alert to the high-level stalemate on firm strategy, midlevel, junior and clerical staff knew something was not quite right, and they were becoming more and more concerned. After taking a salary cut and seeing reduced bonuses during the downturn, a few of the firm's best staff had recently left after receiving more attractive offers from other firms.

The negative press around the IP team's departure convinced BRIEF's managing partner that he needed to add a senior communications professional to the management team immediately. They could not continue to rely on PR firms for help, so hiring a seasoned communications advisor—someone who knew legal communications—had to be an urgent priority. This new hire would need to develop an external and internal communications strategy quickly. He or she would also have to set priorities, because, initially at least, there was no budget or time to add more than one or possibly two other junior members to the communications team.

The choices were clear but difficult.

BRIEF needed to gain clarity and agreement among existing partners on its strategic direction—either faster international expansion or taking advantage of special opportunities for growth through merger or acquisition in the United States, the market responsible for three-quarters of its fees. BRIEF could not afford to do both without unacceptable financial sacrifice by the partners in their incomes over the next few years. Both choices presented attractive yet uncertain opportunities—and large risks. The future of the partnership and the future of the firm depended on this choice.

Meantime, there remain many brushfires to extinguish each day, and these smaller issues are distracting management from the broader strategic choices. The firm needs new business development staff to help the partners grow revenues now, while reinforcing and securing client relationships. New HR people are needed to address some of the training and development issues that were contributing factors in the recent loss of top talent, not to mention recruiters who can help to replace the lost talent. The firm's IT and financial systems are functional but not fully integrated, having been assembled piece by piece as the firm added new offices and practices over the years. As a result, management information is often slow to obtain and sometimes inaccurate, and this can add to borrowing costs and trim profits. As of the writing of this chapter, BRIEF is at a crossroads, and its decisions will determine its future.

DISCUSSION QUESTIONS FOR CASE STUDY

1. What is BRIEF'S best strategic choice—international expansion or a domestic merger or acquisition? Why?
2. How can communications help BRIEF? How would communications efforts differ, if at all, depending on whether the firm chooses international expansion or a domestic merger? Why?
3. If you were the new head of communications at BRIEF, what communications priorities would you set, and what major initiatives or tactics would you implement? Given the situation, what's more important—internal or external communications?
4. What skills and abilities will the new head of communications need to be successful in this role?
5. Is this an attractive communications job for a qualified and talented communications professional to take? Why or why not? What are the potential rewards and risks to this career move?

DISCUSSION QUESTIONS

1. Given the trends and developments in the global economy overall and the legal industry in particular, what is the primary role for internal and external communications in a law firm? How does communications advance a law firm's strategy?
2. In addition to communications, what other factors shape a law firm's brand reputation?
3. For law firms today, is external communications more important than internal communications, or vice versa? Why?
4. Relative to other businesses, law firms have not been early adopters of social media. Why is that the case, and what more could law firms be doing today with social media to engage with their key internal and external stakeholders?
5. What are the pros and cons of working in communications at a law firm? How would a communications career in a law firm compare with one at a comparable accountancy firm, management consulting firm or other professional services organization?
6. What issues and crises do law firms encounter? How can communications help firms manage such crises?

NOTES

1. Report: Global 100, *Legal Business*, London, July/August 2010.
2. Report: Global 100, *Legal Business*, London, July/August 2010.
3. Report: Standard Chartered Bank, *The Super-Cycle Report*, London, November 2010.
4. Report: Global 100, *Legal Business*, London, July/August 2010.

ADDITIONAL READING

Above the Law, www.abovethelaw.com (blog on legal industry topics; more of a US focus)
Everyday Public Relations for Lawyers by Gina Furia Rubel (book)
Roll on Friday, www.rollonfriday.com (blog on legal industry topics; more of a UK focus)

PRACTICAL SKILLS AND KNOWLEDGE

Writing bluntly in October of 2003, noted Chicago journalist Studs Terkel commented on Upton Sinclair's self-published book called *The Brass Check* written in 1919, 13 years after *The Jungle*.

> The brass check was the coin used in whorehouses. The customer went up to see the madam and he would pay his two bucks—this was long before inflation—and receive a brass check, which he would give to the girl. And at the end of the day the girl would cash in all her brass checks and get half a buck apiece. So Upton Sinclair took the brass check, and made it a reference to the press in those days. The journalists were pretty much brass check artists, they were like the girls in the brothel. And how much of that has changed in the past century?[1]

This metaphor is a bit strong today; however, please allow me to carefully proceed to suggest a way that the powerful symbol will not lose its value in modern parlance but contain lessons for the intelligent joining of journalism and PR.

Having learned the brass check story many years ago in my doctoral-level journalism classes, I began collecting brass checks at antique shows and in small shops in New Orleans, San Antonio and other cities with a rich history. Some are fake and easily identified as such, while others seem original. My reason for collecting them was to use the visual symbol in talks and argue against the very logic of the idea. The only time I have given a brass check to another person was as a carefully planned birthday gift for my good friend, John Ziomek, at an intimate gathering honoring his tenure at the Medill School of Journalism. John was a real journalist who did not always agree with the nonjournalists about his field at Medill, but he was also open to friends of journalism. I spoke in his class more than once on how PR and journalism might learn to cooperate and later used the parts of the same talk in Peking University's journalism and PR classes.

I have worked with journalists for most of my professional life. We share a great deal. Our respect for the written word is almost holy, and the demand for precision is shared, as the chapters in this PR skills and knowledge section will demonstrate. I watched many of my friends who were reporters move into positions in political communications and assume roles in communications at universities, corporations and government. The principal source of qualified and experienced communications professionals was, for many decades, former reporters. Today, as the PR field grows, hiring needs are met by graduating educated and trained specialists in public relations itself. We try to invoke, with knowledge, reading and interaction in the classroom, a respect for journalists that must be continued despite economic pressures on journalism. The research seems obvious to those of us immersed in an economic tumbler in the second decade of the new century. A *PR Week* (a notable trade publication) survey in 2010 reveals the pressures on journalism:

> Continuing a trend from the 2008 and 2009 surveys, over 70% of respondents in this year's survey indicate a heavier workload as compared to last year, with the majority (58%) stating that the number

of stories for which they are responsible has increased over the past two years. As in 2009, the primary cause of the increased workload is the need to contribute to online reporting. Of those surveyed, 62% are required to write for online news sections, with 39% contributing to their publication's blog. 37% of US journalists also now must maintain a Twitter feed. Canadian media are also experiencing greater demands for their time.

The survey also reported additional pressures on journalists leading to greater reliance on PR:

31% of respondents indicated that "staff cuts/layoffs" most affected their jobs over the past three years. This finding is significantly higher than 2009 (22%), which affirms that the instability and uncertainty in 2009 weighed heavily on the minds of reporters. Second to staff cuts/layoff, 29% of those surveyed stated that "tightening budgets" had the greatest impact on their work. Similar issues were recognized by Canadian journalists, with 21% pointing to staff cuts/layoffs and 33% suggesting tightening budgets.[2]

Meanwhile, according to the U.S. Bureau of Labor, jobs as "public relations specialists" are growing by 24% between 2008 and 2018.[3] *The Economist* also predicted growth in December 2010: "According to data from Veronis Suhler Stevenson (VSS), a private-equity firm, spending on public relations in America grew by more than 4% in 2008 and nearly 3% in 2009, to $3.7 billion. That is remarkable when compared with other forms of marketing. Spending on advertising contracted by nearly 3% in 2008 and by 8% in the past year. PR's position looks even rosier when word-of-mouth marketing, which includes services that PR firms often manage, such as outreach to bloggers, is included. Spending on such things increased by more than 10% in 2009."

It is true that movement from journalism to PR creates a bit of tension. As a matter of fact, the percentage of journalism graduates who actually used their professional degree training (a relatively small part of their liberal arts degree) is low. Most graduates may go to law school or other jobs with a liberal arts degree coupled with great writing and journalism training. In fact, after less than four years, the majority of journalism graduates who entered journalism posts left those demanding and sometimes low-paying posts for jobs and careers in public relations, based on an internal study at Medill.

The evidence of the need for a redefined relationship between journalists and public relations professionals was reflected in my graduate classroom recently. The interaction of the full-time journalism and PR/IMC students and their desire to tell a mutually accurate, interesting and relevant story was clearly discussed. They concluded that the old stereotypes of conflict were not necessary if they were more transparent and authentic with each other. The shortage of newspaper outlets and the demand for more content delivered on the web has compelled cooperation. One of the experienced journalism students said, "We want you to tell us as much about the issue as possible so that we can write a more interesting story." She acknowledged that most stories were not antagonistic but needed more detail to be sure their editor approved the story for publication.

Of course, there are cases (relatively few as a percentage of all news and content) in which tough investigative techniques may have to be employed by journalists. Most stories can be mutually collaborative to inform the readers. It is also true that it is difficult for PR professionals to release all the information if there are financial disclosure and timing issues (see Chapter 17). The future seems to hold the promise of PR and journalism working together to tell stories to the readers', viewers' or listeners' benefit.

In my experience, the "false bravura" of believing that journalists cannot trust PR and vice versa is an unnecessary conflict. In a world with fewer journalists, the existing and remaining newspapers are shorthanded, so it is more likely that journalists will have to learn to trust PR. While owned content controlled by nonjournalists is one alternative (see Chapter 53), the value of professional journalism as a "third-party" reporter of facts and information will always likely trump reporting by companies and NGOs, even if that reporting becomes more transparent and authentic.

This section is important to the development of a new generation of PR professionals. It illustrates with very practical chapters the most common basis of cooperation between PR, journalism and stakeholders—well-written and well-produced stories for the eye and ear. It has been an important goal in my career to be sure that the PR students in my school (and others) realize the pressure on them to be outstanding communicators. Professor Emeritus George Harmon has been a rock of professionalism and academic leadership in Medill for over 25 years. His work as a reporter, editor and educator in business reporting gave him a point of view and experience that is invaluable to all students. Companies that ask for his evaluation of the communication skills of their managers have told me they depend on George to help make decisions on who receives a promotion or who will be hired. Over the years, Professor Harmon has developed a writing test that separates the wheat from the chaff in writing and editing. In fact, the test is similar to tests given by PR, consulting and communications departments in corporations for their hiring decisions. Despite some criticism from faculty who believe students should be strong writers before they enter graduate school, the mix of international, experienced and inexperienced students has created new barriers. Giving the test as a "pretest" to all the students and even the faculty shows that we all have a lot to learn. The promise of the course that Professor Harmon and I developed over 20 years ago is that we (really, Professor Harmon) can double or triple performance scores in the final exam.

Another Harmon inspiration for this section of work on communications skills is the adage that "good writing is good thinking and good thinking is good writing." Logically, this reminds us that clear storytelling and message development is evidence of clear ideas and strategy. My argument for "putting the 'C' back in IMC" (putting communications back in integrated marketing communications) is really a cry for higher standards of writing and editing for each succeeding generation.

The chapters in this section cover the waterfront of communication management, strategies and skills: creative writing, press releases, websites, blogs, microblogs, owned content, speechwriting (writing for the ear), telling and writing stories as a powerful communications tool, learning to communicate in virtual worlds and more. In the same essay referenced above, Studs Terkel noted:

> Fortunately, we have an alternative press. The effect of the alternative press is seemingly minor, but it has a ripple-in-the-water effect. You can tell that is true when you read the letters to the editor in the *Chicago Tribune*—my barometer of what the public is thinking. But aside from alternative journals such as *In These Times*, *Bill Moyers Journal* and *The Daily Show* with Jon Stewart, Upton Sinclair's brass checks are alive and well today.[4]

With homage to Terkel, I would suggest that the whole realm of new media offers us the richness of alternative points of view—always a good thing. In the future the "brass checks" metaphor will not be needed. As prurient as it seemed, the idea will possibly fade into history when journalists and public relations professionals find a balance between goals and skills in a more transparent social media and traditional media world.

NOTES

1. www.inthesetimes.com/article/639/no_brass_check_journalists
2. multivu.prnewswire.com/mnr/prnewswire/43321
3. Lacey, T. Alan, and Benjamin Wright. Occupational employment projections to 2018. Bureau of Labor website, posted December 10, 2009, and December 22, 2010.
4. www.inthesetimes.com/article/639/no_brass_check_journalists

47

C H A P T E R

CHANGING YOUR OWN BEHAVIOR TO ENHANCE BEHAVIORAL RESULTS

Kerry D. Tucker
Chief Executive Officer
Nuffer, Smith, Tucker, Inc.

Bill Trumpfheller
President
Nuffer, Smith, Tucker, Inc.

How many times have you heard or even said: "We've got to tell *our* story to the public. We need to make *them* understand our position. If *they* could just see the 'big picture.'" The assumption is that if we can just get our target public to understand, they will do what we want them to do.

But there is a big flaw in this assumption.

For the most part, people don't care about *our* organization's problems. They've got enough of their own. And simply communicating information to obtain a desired behavior rarely works. Thirty years of research across a wide range of disciplines and issues have shown that providing information alone on an issue, a product or service will not significantly change the behaviors of a given public.

We live in a society with excess information. Literally tens of thousands of bits of information bombard us every day. Some we want; some we don't . Some of it we absorb and use; most of it never registers cognitively at all.

As communicators, we have not always succeeded in shaping our communications into information the target public wants or needs. We typically organize our information into an understandable and (what we believe to be) creative format and then blurt it out in the public arena and hope for the best. That rarely works.

No matter how motivated the communicator might be, unsolicited information rarely finds as motivated a receiver. Very few members of a given public are prepared or even willing to act to the extent we want them to on the content of a public relations communication. A simple example helps make the point.

Mike Rose opens up his crisis management and media training consulting firm just down the street from you and sends out a tasteful card and e-communication sharing his new address, e-mail and phone number. He sent that card trying to elicit action—or behavior. He wants people to call him. Do people automatically call for an appointment? Probably not. People will call him—that is, behave the way he wants them to—only if they perceive the need for counsel on how to handle a crisis or a media interview.

This chapter explores three phases of a behavioral public relations program, two of which occur before a communication is sent or other campaign tools are created: strategy development, packaging and delivery. They apply to public relations and issues management as well as marketing communication.

Included in the packaging segment of this chapter is a behavioral framework that represents one systematic way practitioners can organize writing and public relations tactics to carry out the public relations plan that taps into our knowledge of human motivation.

STRATEGY DEVELOPMENT

Successful behavioral strategy evolves from a planning process designed to help public relations practitioners carry out their fundamental responsibility: to help their organizations or clients build and maintain a hospitable business climate.[1]

Public relations is best organized when it has systems in place to anticipate issues likely to affect the organization and has plans to address the top-priority issues (both threats and opportunities) at an early stage when they are most manageable. For example, an agricultural trade group might have to face a litany of issues involving the environment and competition for natural resources. A telecommunications firm could face public concern about invasion of privacy. A governmental regulatory agency may face growing skepticism over regulations that do not make common or economic sense. Preparing for anticipated changes can often head off undesirable changes or speed up those that are positive.

One effective public relations planning process, designed by Nuffer, Smith, Tucker, Inc., includes eight steps, as shown in Figure 47.1. Once a system has been set up to anticipate and prioritize issues likely to impact the mission of an organization, plans turn to building and maintaining relationships with others affected by the issues important to your organization.

FIGURE 47.1

Public Relations Planning Process[2]

Clarifying the threat or opportunity and analyzing the other groups affected is part of the second step in this public relations planning process: *the situation analysis*. Assessing the likely perceptions, positions and behavioral inclinations of those holding a stake in the issue lays the foundation for publics identified later in the process. The situation analysis also includes an assessment of the forces working both for and against the potential threat or opportunity, and assumptions about which direction the issue appears to be headed.

The situation analysis provides a database to call upon when you begin making behavioral strategy decisions. The first decision lies with the position of the organization. The key question to ask in searching for the strategy with the highest odds for behavioral outcome is: can you take a position that is mutually beneficial to the organization, to most of the stakeholders you have identified and analyzed in your situation analysis and to the greater public good? Positions designed for mutual benefit have the most potential for eliciting widespread public support.

Once a position is decided on, the planning process turns to the publics most critical to advancing that position. Once again, the situation analysis provides the database. Of the stakeholders analyzed:

1. Who are the decision makers on the issue?

2. Who has influence on the decision makers?

3. Who is likely to support your position?

4. Who is likely not to support your position?

5. Whom can you successfully target to make the biggest difference in advancing your organization's position on the issue?

The answers to these questions led to targeted, segmented publics. Behavioral goals—the ultimate outcomes and objectives that make possible the measurement of success—represent the next step in the behavioral planning process. *The behavioral strategy is then the route taken to achieve each objective.*

Force field analysis, a situational problem-solving technique developed in the 1940s by Kurt Lewin, is extremely helpful here. The playing field is diagrammed by forces working for and against your behavioral goal(s). The visual impact gives you a sense of the complexity of the issue and the factors that will need to be addressed for behavioral results (see Figure 47.2).

The strategy development process is advanced by asking a series of questions:

- Which factors will make the biggest difference in advancing the desired behavior? Of those, which can we be successful addressing?

- Of these priority issues, how can those that restrain us be eliminated or at least minimized? How can those that support our behavioral goal be strengthened?

- Which new forces can we add to the force field to advance the desired behavior?
  The final question says it all:

- Where can we put time and resources to make the biggest difference in advancing our behavioral goal?

Communication (or education) is only one strategic option. Public relations practitioners tend to draw a line in the sand and limit themselves to the communication option. The truth is that other options are often needed to garner public support for an organization's position or a desired action. Public relations practitioners should recommend strategies beyond communication, even if they aren't the ones who carry them out. Other successful behavioral strategies[3] include:

- Changing rules or laws (for example, restricting the movement of citrus and closely related plants in and out of certain regions to limit the spread of an invasive pest and a plant disease it is known to carry)

- Making social or structural changes (such as physically redesigning campsites to make accidental fires less likely or redesigning toilets to use less water)

- Creating interpersonal support (such as organizing support groups like Weight Watchers or pulling together a formidable group of leading retail and food-service produce buyers to demand improvements in food safety standards and procedures, and applying pressure on growers, shippers and industry leaders)

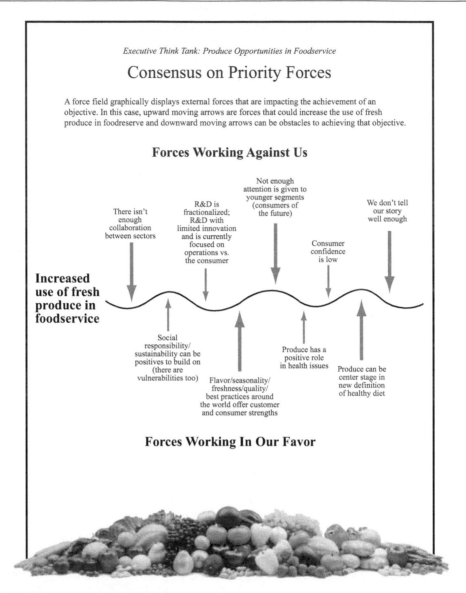

Executive Think Tank: Produce Opportunities in Foodservice

Consensus on Priority Forces

A force field graphically displays external forces that are impacting the achievement of an objective. In this case, upward moving arrows are forces that could increase the use of fresh produce in foodreserve and downward moving arrows can be obstacles to achieving that objective.

Forces Working Against Us

Not enough attention is given to younger segments (consumers of the future)

There isn't enough collaboration between sectors

R&D is fractionalized; R&D with limited innovation and is currently focused on operations vs. the consumer

We don't tell our story well enough

Consumer confidence is low

Increased use of fresh produce in foodservice

Social responsibility/ sustainability can be positives to build on (there are vulnerabilities too)

Produce has a positive role in health issues

Produce can be center stage in new definition of healthy diet

Flavor/seasonality/ freshness/quality/ best practices around the world offer customer and consumer strengths

Forces Working In Our Favor

FIGURE 47.2

Force Field Analysis of the Issues and Factors Involved in Reducing Solo Car Trips[4]

PACKAGING FOR BEHAVIORAL OUTCOMES

Messages are created to advance the behavioral goals and objectives. They are developed as part of communication strategy. A logical question to ask is: what can be said about the position that will facilitate the desired behavior? What can we say to maximize the forces working in our favor and minimize those working against us?

The goal behavior for the California Citrus Research Board is to motivate residents to visually inspect for the Asian citrus psyllid, an invasive pest that can carry a plant disease that is incurable and will wipe out citrus trees in California. Its priority messages are:

- The disease-carrying Asian citrus psyllid is a death sentence for California citrus trees that can, with your help, be stopped before it's too late.

- The disease-carrying Asian citrus psyllid is catastrophic to trees and not only threatens local farms and farmers that we count on for our fresh, healthy, locally produced citrus, but also consumers' ability to buy and grow citrus fruits in their backyards.

- If the disease-carrying Asian citrus psyllid is found, you must contact your local agriculture commission office ASAP; time is critical, and affected trees must be destroyed in order to keep the disease from spreading throughout the state.

The canned tuna industry was facing mounting pressure from NGOs over purported high levels of mercury found in fish. While what the NGOs were communicating was factually incorrect, the industry as a whole was struggling to counter the criticism. Chicken of the Sea decided to lead the industry in communication outreach to clear up the confusion and miscommunication.

Its priority messages are:

- Shelf-stable seafood is a nutrition powerhouse—one that people need to take advantage of—packed with Omega-3 fatty acids, protein and vitamin D, and low in saturated fat, cholesterol and calories. It is also convenient and affordable.

- Consumers have shied away from shelf-stable seafood, caused in part by confusion related to the health benefits it provides. Unfortunately, many people not reaping the benefits of shelf-stable seafood are America's hungry—38.2 million people (including 13.9 million children) living in food-insecure households, meaning their access to food is limited by lack of money or other resources.

- The American Heart Association, American Diabetes Association, American Medical Association and USDA/HHS dietary guidelines all say consumers should "eat at least two servings of fish each week."

While people naturally resist change, communication strategies and messages (and tactics) can be organized to increase the odds of breaking through the information clutter we all face daily. They can do so by contrasting existing behavior with the desired behavior, facilitating discomfort with existing behavior and offering help in adopting a new action.

An effective framework to apply in evaluating communications against behavioral principles is organized around four basic sets of questions:

1. *Does the communication raise a public need, concern, or interest?* Attracting California residents' attention about an invasive species that can barely be seen with the naked eye could be a daunting challenge, unless you paint a real-life scenario that draws both the attention and desired behavior. Helping these stakeholders realize they may never be able to grow and eat citrus from their own back yards elicits an emotional response to inspect homegrown citrus trees and alert authorities if there are signs of the pest.

2. *Is your desired behavior clearly and credibly packaged to meet the need, resolve the concern or satisfy the interest?* The more precise you are in packaging and presenting the desired behavior as a resolution to the need, concern or interest you have raised, the better. Food prices were rapidly increasing, and numerous reports were showing consumers might be sacrificing nutrition for cost savings. Chicken of the Sea addressed that concern by demonstrating that canned and pouched tuna contain equal amounts of much-need protein as fresh yet expensive meat options but at significantly lower prices.

3. *Have you clearly presented the benefits of action and the consequences of inaction? Have you made the strongest case you can to create discomfort with existing behavior?* The key to moving past public

resistance to change is often creating discomfort with an existing behavior pattern. Homeowners who have invested thousands of dollars to install custom natural stone surfaces in their kitchens and baths will be aghast upon learning typical household cleaners destroy both the surfaces and the consumers' investment, and plain soap and water don't do away with germs. Presenting a safe and proven alternative will bring them a level of comfort and motivation to change their behavior.

4. *Have you helped the receiver mentally rehearse the desired behavior?* Mental rehearsal is a natural process of thinking about a planned behavior—what you will do, when you will do it, where you will do it and, most importantly, how you will successfully perform the behavior. It is analogous to a dress rehearsal that all of us run through at some level or another before we try a new behavior.

Most people have difficulty transferring information to behavior without help. Focusing only on sharing information leaves the action up to the receiver. The risks are great that an individual will pass up the information, not because it isn't useful but because you haven't helped create a mental picture of how to use it.

For example, what are the steps to encourage a call or letter to members of the Public Utility Commission on behalf of the Coalition for Local Control? It may be as simple as providing a name, phone number and address. It may also mean helping individuals think of how they will answer potential questions from the commission staff. Providing individuals with tips on how to adopt the desired behavior is probably the most common mental rehearsal technique. For example, mothers being encouraged to manage their children's food choices in a less controlling way may be given the following tips: monitor what your children eat over several days rather than by food or by meal, and have plenty of healthful foods—particularly fruit and vegetable snacks—on hand.

With brochures and pamphlets, cueing phrases such as "think through," "when was the last time you," or "picture yourself" can be particularly helpful. Questions also help an individual think through the desired action. Examples include: "What is your best option for taking the action?" or "If that doesn't work, what can you do to make it work?" The key is getting people to begin thinking about incorporating the desired behavior into their own lives.

This four-element framework is helpful in organizing written content for oral presentations, web communications, collateral materials, publicity angles, public service announcements and business letters—virtually any public relations tactic. It also can serve as valuable criteria to evaluate communication content for the greatest odds of stimulating supportive behavior.

A news release written for the Citrus Pest and Disease Prevention Program responded to the coming Chinese New Year, a time upon which citrus fruit is shared among friends and relatives as symbols of good wishes for the New Year (Figure 47.3).

A concern was raised that while those celebrating the holiday would be following tradition, they could also be unwittingly spreading a dangerous citrus disease. The release laid out the consequences that Asian citrus psyllids have the potential to carry a disease that destroys production, appearance and value of citrus trees and the taste of their fruit and juice, and that once a tree is infected with the disease, there is no cure and the tree will eventually die.

Further into the release, the desired behavior was to limit the spread of the psyllids, and for rehearsal steps, there was a series of tips on what to do to avoid the possibility of sharing contaminated citrus:

- If giving oranges or other citrus fruit as gifts, make sure that there is no plant material such as leaves or stems attached to the fruit and that the fruit is washed to make sure there are no psyllids on the gift.

- Inspect your citrus trees each month for the pest. A hand lens or magnifying glass may be necessary to see the psyllid, which is the size of an aphid.

- Plant only California-grown, certified trees that are known to be free of the disease.

- Don't move plants out of the quarantined area, because they might be carrying psyllids.

- Dry out plant clippings for two weeks before putting them in green waste recycle bins, or double-bag clippings to avoid moving psyllids.

Citrus Pest & Disease Prevention Program

Contact: Katie Rowland
             Nuffer, Smith,
Tucker
             kr@nstpr.com
             619/296-0605, ext.
254

CHINESE NEW YEAR CUSTOM COULD SPREAD DANGEROUS CITRUS PEST

Jan. 21, 2011 – Giving oranges or tangerines as gifts to friends and relatives as a symbol of good wishes is a celebratory custom of the Chinese New Year, but it could have dire consequences – the gesture could spread the disease-carrying Asian citrus psyllid.

The Asian citrus psyllid – which is confirmed to be in Imperial, San Diego, Riverside, San Bernardino, Orange, Ventura and Los Angeles counties, sparking a quarantine in those areas – can be the carrier of a fatal tree disease, called Huanglongbing, also known as HLB or citrus greening disease. While not harmful to human health, HLB destroys production, appearance and value of citrus trees, and the taste of their fruit and juice. Once a tree is infected with the disease, there is no cure and the tree will eventually die.

While the psyllids in California have not been found to be carrying the disease, the Citrus Pest and Disease Prevention Program is reminding those celebrating the Chinese New Year that we all play a critical role in keeping the disease out of California. The organization, which points out that it is illegal to bring citrus trees or cuttings into California form other states or countries, offers these tips:

- If giving oranges or other citrus fruit as gifts, make sure there is no plant material such as leaves or stems attached to the fruit and the fruit is washed to make sure there are no psyllids on the gift.

- Inspect your citrus trees each month for the pest. A hand lens or magnifying glass may be necessary to see the psyllid, which is the size of an aphid.

- Plant only California-grown, certified trees that are known to be free of the disease.

- Don't move plants out of the quarantined area, because they might be carrying psyllids.

- Dry out plant clippings for two weeks before putting them in green waste recycle bins or double bag clippings to avoid moving psyllids.

"This pest and disease are dangerous," said Ted Batkin, president of the California Citrus Research Board and a participant in the Citrus Pest and Disease Prevention Program. "If the disease infects a homeowner's tree, that tree will need to be removed, and the best way to protect our citrus is to control the pest."

The California Citrus Research Board is trapping for the pest and testing for the disease in California, augmenting the programs of the county agricultural commissioners, California Department of Food and Agriculture, and the U.S. Department of Food and Agriculture. The majority of detections of the psyllids in Southern California trees have been in residential citrus trees.

For more information and to find out what to look for, visit

www.CaliforniaCitrusThreat.org. If you think you have found a psyllid, act fast.

Time is critical. Call the California Department of Food and Agriculture hotline

at 800/491-1899.

The pest and the disease have already caused devastation in Asia, India,

parts of the Middle East, and South and Central America. The pest and the

disease have been found domestically in Louisiana, South Carolina, Georgia and

Florida. In Florida, the psyllid and HLB are ravaging the citrus industry. The

insect pest, in the absence of disease, is also found in Hawaii, Texas and

California.

#

FIGURE 47.3

Press Release Illustrating the Four-Element Communications Framework[5]

THE TACTICS OF MESSAGE DELIVERY

Tactical decisions on how best to carry out each strategy are next. It is here that you decide what communication vehicles will best contribute to the desired behaviors. How can we best reach the opinion leaders and their publics?

Obviously, you need to know where your targeted publics get their information. Of equal importance is which information sources have the most behavioral clout. Which carry the greatest odds of facilitating support for your position on an issue?

Credibility is the primary selection criterion because it has the greatest impact on behavioral goals and objectives. The more personal the communication, the more important the credibility factor. The more credibility, the more likely the targeted public is to receive, accept and act on your message.

Traditional communication tactics can be segmented for credibility into five categories in order of believability:

1. Individual presentation (one on one, small group, large group)

2. Personal communication (telephone, e-mail)

3. Targeted media (specialty magazines, trade and employee media)

4. Mass media coverage

5. Advertising[6]

Because advertising is the least credible tactic in the practitioner's quiver—also frequently the least personal—this chapter will not explore it in any further detail but will focus on the new social media followed by the four traditional tactics described above.

ONLINE AND SOCIAL MEDIA

In the best-selling book, *Groundswell: Winning in a World Transformed by Social Technologies*, authors Charlene Li and Josh Bernoff call the online phenomenon a spontaneous movement of people using online tools to connect and take charge of their own experiences to get the things they want—information, support, ideas, products, bargaining power—from each other rather than traditional institutions.

In her literature review paper, "Engagement with Social Media and Outcomes for Brands: A Conceptual Framework," Camilla Bond of Monash University cites Kaplan and Haenlein describing social media as "Internet-based applications that help consumers share opinions, insights, experiences and perspectives." These applications can include collaborative projects (e.g., Wikipedia), blogs, content communities (e.g., You Tube), social networking sites (e.g., Facebook, Twitter and LinkedIn), virtual social worlds (e.g., Second Life) and virtual game worlds (e.g., World of Warcraft) (Figure 47.4).

Quite simply, social media is all about people talking to each other much like they have done since the beginning of time. Now, technology has upped the game, but it is still all about people talking to people.

The phenomenal growth of social media has revolutionized the practice of public relations and marketing worldwide. The parallel growth of mobile technology makes social media accessible 24/7 and even more powerful.

FIGURE 47.4

A Newsletter Format Featuring Brief News Capsules

The consumer-driven engagement of social media brings peer-to-peer endorsements and reviews on brands, products, services and issues to an extraordinarily higher level than ever experienced.

Recommendations by personal acquaintances and opinions posted online are the most trusted forms of communication globally, according to trendwatching.com, which cited a Nielsen survey showing that 90 percent of people having online conversations worldwide trust recommendations from people they know, while 70 percent trust consumer opinions posted online. Product reviews are wildly popular. Expect smart companies to increasingly post their apologies and solutions, preferably directly alongside reviews from unhappy customers. A quick and honest reply or solution can often defuse a damaging complaint. And if a company believes—and can prove—that a particular review is unfair, expect the occasional candid rebuttal.

All of this comes with a convergence of various forms of a rising demand for transparency. This can be prompted by activist agendas and provocative videos going viral. For example, television's *Nightline* responds to a video of animal abuse, and the video goes viral in 30 seconds, energizing a large group of consumers and the general public, where the vast majority would not have had the social networking infrastructure to view the video a couple of years ago.

"Any organization's biggest threat is a 17-year-old kid with a camera who knows how to use Google," said Peter Shankman at the second San Diego Social Media Symposium, hosted by Nuffer, Smith, Tucker, Inc. and San Diego State University.

Li argues in Information-Age.com, and in her new book, *Open Leadership*,[3] for an opportunity to use openness strategically. She draws the distinction between openness and generalized transparency. Transparency, she says, is simply about revealing information to outside parties. There is no way anyone can be completely transparent. We are not even completely transparent in our closest personal relationships.

"Openness, on the other hand, implies the greater inclusion of third parties in the operation of a business," says Li, "whether it is explaining the motivation behind key decisions, by including customers and partners in the product innovation process, or by conducting customer support in open, public forums, or any other application of social technology that encourages participation."

The real question is: "How open is open enough?" writes Dave Balter, CEO of BzzAgent in the Harvard Business Review blog, The Conversation. Where does the line get drawn?

"Committing to transparency shouldn't be confused with sharing confidential information," says Balter. "Rather, it means providing some insight into your thinking and considerations so that those around you can feel involved and empowered . . . Every business has setbacks and challenges . . . If a company recognizes their mistakes and is up front about them, most consumers are willing to show a more lenient sense of understanding."

The first step in planning the use of social media is listening. Ask yourself these questions:

- Where are the discussions about our company, our products or issues we care about taking place?

- What do those discussion entail?

- What is the tone, the tenor?

- Where can we get support?

- Where are the land mines?

- Where are the voices of influence?

- What is working for and against our participation?

In the best selling book, *The Tipping Point*, Malcolm Gladwell talks about connectors (people who know a wide variety of other people through some sort of social connection) and mavens (people who are lay experts on things that interest them—wine, fashion, cars, etc.). Bernoff and Ted Schadler in the book *Empowered* cite that 80 percent of impressions about products and services come from 6 percent of online connectors (people with lots of social network connections). That is 11 million very connected people. About 13 percent of the U.S. online community or 24 million people are considered mass mavens. They generate 80 percent of online posts (blog posts, blog comments, discussion forums and reviews). Mass connectors and mass mavens are almost twice as likely to use mobile Web as online consumers, and mobile Web users often have more influence. In summary, a small subset of online connectors and mavens account for nearly all of the influence. They are indeed mass influencers.

"Many companies approach social computing as a list of technologies to be deployed as needed—a blog here, a podcast there—to achieve a marketing goal," writes Li in Forrester Research's blog. "But a more coherent approach is to start with your target audience and determine what kind of relationship you want to build with them, based on what they are ready for."

Long before the term *social media* became part of today's culture and vernacular, Chicken of the Sea built a social media platform to engage consumers, mainly mothers and household menu decision makers, about the brand and its products. Known as the Mermaid Club, it is an online affinity club built for consumers by consumers. Rather than build a site based on what the brand thought consumers wanted, Chicken of the Sea asked what consumers wanted and built the club accordingly. The success of that approach followed an eventual redesign of the brand website and the strategies behind Chicken of the Sea's Facebook and Twitter presence (Figure 47.5).

"It's a fractured world," writes Mike Rose in the Nuffer, Smith, Tucker blog, News and Smart Talk. "If we're not listening to our audiences, we're irrelevant . . . They'll tune us out and look elsewhere for information." Says Shankman, "You don't control the direction of your company anymore—your customers and clients do. Your job is to create amazing customer experiences."

A presence on Facebook or Twitter might make sense for some organizations. But social media can also mean outreach to key bloggers. It can mean working with your most loyal "fans" or advocates to make them into your brand ambassadors and get them talking about you both on- and offline. It can also mean creating a custom community just for your brand. No matter which way you slice it, success in social media is about building meaningful relationships with your audiences by providing value and being authentic, and the best social media strategies are those that are integrated with other outreach efforts.

FIGURE 47.5

A Magazine-Style Newsletter Form[7]

BECOME A "TALKABLE" BRAND

"Give consumers a great experience and they'll share it with others," says word-of-mouth marketing consultant John Moore. Moore encourages companies to become a "talkable" brand—cultivating consumers to genuinely talk up your company's brands, products and services.

"The most trusted and recommended brands have some form of talkability attached to it or it won't translate into the sales effect," says Eileen Campbell of Millward Brown in *Brandweek*. In a Millward Brown survey of 20,000 U.S. consumers in 2010, consumers ranked Amazon.com and FedEx numbers one and two as the most trusted and recommended brands because of the high degree of trust and reliability they have come to expect from these two brands. Amazon.com ranked highest because it is not only a consistent provider of e-commerce goods, but there is also the recommendation piece of it, Campbell said, referring to one of the site's features, which recommends products to buyers. Given all of this, 90 percent of word-of-mouth communication is offline.

The priority is with the relationships, and not with the technology, say Li and Bernoff. A tool that enables relationships in new ways will catch on faster than one that does not. Faster on the Internet means weeks and months, not years. Evaluate new technologies with these questions:

1. Does it enable people to connect with each other in new ways?

2. Is it effortless to sign up for?

3. Does it shift power from institutions to people?

4. Does the community generate enough content to sustain itself?

5. Is it an open platform that invites partnerships?

EVALUATING SOCIAL MEDIA

Social media today is at the crossroads of personal communication and traditional media. While research on behavioral outcomes with social media is very limited, most of the discussion on evaluating both traditional and new media centers on building and maintaining longer relationships with the audiences you care most about. It is not as much about campaigns as it is creating lifelong value.

Camilla Bond hypothesizes from her literature review that social media consumption, social media engagement and consumer roles in social media are antecedents to brand awareness, word of mouth, purchase intention and satisfaction with social media.

The reality is that we are still on the ground floor of measuring the impact of social media.

A menu of the potential metrics in play today includes:

- Engagement

- Number of fans/followers, brand sentiment (e.g., positive, negative, neutral perceptions of a company or product)

- Number of coupons downloaded and redeemed

- Number of friends referred or links shared via social media

- Number of blog comments, volume of brand mentions versus those of competitors

- Click-through on links shared via social media (e.g., clicks to company website/offers)

- Time spent in your community

INDIVIDUAL PRESENTATION

One-on-one, eyeball-to-eyeball communication is incredibly powerful, especially if the message is delivered by a credentialed expert—an individual whose views on a subject are respected, even sought out. A respected scientist shares new research data with another scientist. The leader of a prestigious community business group shares the impact of a proposed legislative initiative with a business colleague. A physician shares the latest development in preventive treatment with a patient.

Opinion leaders are direct conduits to targeted publics. They already have the relationships you need to facilitate support for your position on an issue. If they buy into and adopt your organization's position, they can help advance it with their own constituencies, both independently and as campaign spokespersons.

The most trusted institutions in the Western world are nongovernmental organizations (NGOs), according to the 2011 Edelman Trust Barometer (see Chapter 16). Conversations with friends and peers are also powerful influences.

One-on-one communication is credible; messages can be personalized to the needs, concerns and interests of the receiver, and a case can be built for the desired behavior. The dialogue that results from this type of exchange is a powerful technique for changing behavior.

Practically speaking, one-on-one communication, facilitated by a public relations practitioner, is usually reserved for opinion leader–to–opinion leader communication. Examples include a meeting arranged for a leading scientist and decision-making bureaucrats within the Department of Health and Human Services to initiate discussion on a new direction on public policy; a meeting arranged between the "right" constituent and a state senator on a pending legislative vote; and a meeting arranged between chief executives of the two major corporations in town to recruit participation in a fundraising drive.

Building coalitions is a highly effective mechanism for one-on-one communication with opinion leaders. Coalitions bring together opinion leaders representing various interests who share a common issue. Mutually beneficial positions are facilitated through dialogue. Strategies are crafted together to advance the position.

While coalition building has long been a tactic in managing regulatory and legislative issues, its use is expanding to other areas of public relations as one-sided communication tactics are increasingly replaced with relationship-building strategies. Building relationships requires dialogue and harmony among those sharing a stake in the issues confronting organizations and industries. Coalition building is prospering because most companies and industries can no longer afford to exist alone. There is power in numbers. There is power in diversification. The collective influence of many interests is formidable. The credibility of coalition building can generate support for a desired behavior from the constituencies of opinion leaders and broader publics.

Nearly as important as one-on-one communication is the use of small-group presentations in which individuals are given opportunities to seek answers to their questions, challenge assumptions and work through the benefits and consequences of embracing the desired behaviors.

Interaction is more difficult with large-group presentations. Organizing presentations using the behavioral framework and providing adequate time for questions and answers are the most effective techniques. Sticking around after the presentation and soliciting questions and answers is also effective. Dialogue is the greatest strategy for creating discomfort with existing behaviors, which is necessary to facilitate change.

PERSONAL COMMUNICATIONS

When individuals know and respect one another, personal communication runs a close second to one-on-one, in-person communication. E-mail, texting and telephone communication becomes more difficult when the parties do not know one another. An e-mail or letter from a trusted colleague can open the doors for a public relations practitioner to make a coalition recruitment call to a targeted opinion leader. Or, a cold call can be followed up with a letter and package of materials building a case for the importance of getting on board.

Next to face-to-face communications and the telephone, direct mail—be it traditional or e-mail—is one of the most personal tactics and one of the most effective. Public relations–driven direct mail, because of its subtlety and use of credible third-party spokespersons, can be very effective.

Public relations practitioners use direct mail as a means of facilitating communications not only between an organization and its publics but also between opinion leaders and opinion leaders, as well as between opinion leaders and their constituencies. A simple letter can be a powerful tool when sent by the right person *to* the right person. Lists of opinion leaders are as important to a practitioner as media lists.

There are a few things to keep in mind when writing direct mail, e-mail, personal letters and other communications tools. Public relations writing is more than just sitting down at a word processor and writing beautiful prose or generating a hard-hitting publicity angle. Writing for public relations focuses on advancing messages to create supportive behavior from groups of people who are involved with or affected by the way an organization conducts its business. Consequently, the most effective way to write and organize techniques for public relations writing is to use knowledge about human motivation. In the end, it is not how well you have generated what you, the writer, consider to be an interesting letter or publicity angle, but rather, how well you catch the attention of targeted publics and help them work through the steps necessary to generate supportive behavior.

The four-element behavioral framework presented earlier is a guide for organizing all public relations writing. The behavioral framework can be used to package written materials with the greatest odds for reaching and motivating targeted publics to act; to build the case for an issue and to advance it with employees, opinion leaders and target publics in oral presentations, direct mail, publications, special events and publicity.

TARGETED MEDIA

Specialty newspapers, magazines, industry trade publications (virtually every industry has at least one and frequently several), websites, blogs and newsletters provide direct routes to targeted publics. Like specialty sections of newspapers, they are prescreened for the target audience and already address the appropriate needs, concerns and interests.

Specialty publications often carry more credibility with the reader than mass media because of the in-depth way in which they cover their subject. Their readers also tend to be more active seekers of information than mass media readers and, as such, more receptive to behavioral objectives. The Edelman Trust Barometer research shows that reports from industry analysts and business magazines are the most credible sources of information about a company.

Newsletters—online or print—are among the better-received controlled publications, especially when they are designed to meet targeted public interests or needs.

The purpose of newsletters is usually threefold:

1. To present special information to a special audience

2. To positively reinforce cognitions and attitudes about the sponsoring organization[8]

3. To generate supportive behavior for an organization's position on issues

Newsletters should be organized for mutual benefit of the sender and receiver. Formats vary from rapid-fire, three-dot journalism and "Kiplinger-style" news capsules (see Figure 47.4) to slick, four-color publications with photographs and illustrations (see Figure 47.6).

MASS MEDIA COVERAGE

It should be noted that mass media credibility—television, newspapers, radio—has waned in recent years as new media (online, social media) has caught fire. Today, public relations campaigns merge traditional and new media to maximize impact.

PRINT

Among the first tasks handed to a public relations practitioner is the research and writing of support materials for publicity campaigns. Position papers, backgrounders, biographies and fact sheets, query letters, advisories and news releases are among the tools researched and written by public relations professionals.

Fact sheets describe quickly and clearly in some variation the basic who, what, when, where, why and how of an issue or organization. In fact, a simple fact sheet format can reflect those very questions.

NEWS

Dairy Council *of* California®
Healthy Eating Made Easier

Annual Report Issue 2010

Dairy Council taps opportunities for shaping eating habits in schools

By Peggy Biltz, Chief Executive Officer, Dairy Council of California

Discussions inevitably turn back to the core of what we do – helping school children shape lifelong eating habits with milk and milk products as the cornerstone of food groups needed daily for health and wellness.

Dairy Council Learning Objectives
⬇
Knowledge
⬇
Skills
⬇
Dietary Attitudes
⬇
Eating Behaviors

A question we constantly challenge ourselves with, especially during difficult economic times, is how does Dairy Council of California continue to add maximum value to the dairy industry? What do we do that provides the industry with a unique advantage?

These discussions inevitably turn back to the core of what we do – helping school children shape lifelong eating habits with milk and milk products as the cornerstone of food groups needed daily for health and wellness.

A student going through the California school system can be reached by Dairy Council as many as seven times beginning at kindergarten, moving to first and second grade, third grade, fourth or fifth grade, middle school and high school. There are even preschool and after-school programs. These programs are designed to reach children at periods in their life when they are most likely to be developing their food habits and questioning their food choices. Ongoing reinforcement is the best way to ensure lifelong healthy eating habits and the impact of all of these programs are far greater than any single initiative.

Two million kids, two weeks

Two million children a year undergo Dairy Council instruction with all of the school districts in California represented. In most instances, we provide teachers 10 nutrition lessons (or two weeks of instruction) a year.

The dairy industry's 90 years of investment in school nutrition education would literally be impossible for any industry to initiate today. There's just no extra time in the classroom given the test score and economic pressures on teachers. Maintaining our dominance as school nutrition educators is a daily challenge of creativity and innovation.

Accountable to learning objectives

Dairy Council has built this educational franchise by continually pushing the behavioral envelope. That is, putting resources behind helping educators break new ground on what it takes to create learning success. In return, we've created educational models, which successfully shape daily nutritious eating habits.

From the very beginning, we sought out partners in behavioral education at leading universities and consulting firms and worked with them to help us apply behavioral theory to program development. Traditionally, educators have taught facts. Our behavioral system stresses what to do with facts – how to use them.

All of our nutrition education programs are designed and validated for very specific learning objectives. These objectives focus on improving knowledge, skills, dietary attitudes and behaviors. Generally speaking, pre- and post-instruction testing show increases in what children say they consume of milk group foods. Fruits and vegetables also show increases and there are consistent decreases in non-nutritious items like soft drinks.

The dairy industry's 90 years of investment in school nutrition education would literally be impossible for any industry to initiate today.

(continued on page four)

F I G U R E   47.6

A Media Advisory[9]

A fact sheet may describe an issue, an organization, a special event or an important change in organization policy. Fact sheets are basic, quick-read information for executives, coworkers, spokespersons, external opinion leaders and journalists.

The *backgrounder* goes into more detail than the fact sheet. The writing style continues to be brief, direct, concise and informative. The writing tone is neutral and factual.

Backgrounders are a key mechanism used to report on current issues and trends of importance to the mission of the organization. A backgrounder may be used as part of a report to shareholders or a board of directors. It may be used to train a spokesperson for a media interview. Or, it may stand on its own as a component of a press kit organized to advance a position on an issue.

A *position paper*, often referred to as a "white paper," evolves from the situation analysis. In fact, it can be considered the public version of the situation analysis. While the situation analysis provides data for management to develop its position on an issue, the position paper describes the organization's position and its rationale for that position. It clearly takes a stand on an issue and provides evidence to support its position.

Writing a *news release* provides the practitioner with basic training in what it takes to generate news; it is the training ground for generating publicity. Two additional criteria should be added to the who, what, where, when, why and how news criteria of a release. First, it is written to advance public relations objectives, and second, the release is organized to capitalize on behavioral principles, using the behavioral framework.

Publicity targeted to stimulate dialogue among opinion leaders, their peers and their constituencies can be powerful. The following two-paragraph feature lead, published in the *Wall Street Journal*,[10] raises a public's interest, provides a solution and offers some concrete imagery. Note that the spokesperson's direct quotation even uses the word *solution*:

> WASHINGTON—Does the air in your office make you nauseous? Try sitting next to a plant. Better yet, sit next to a fan pointed at a plant.
>
> The National Aeronautics and Space Administration says plants can clean up fumes from paint, furniture, and cigarettes that make office workers woozy. B. C. Wolverton, a scientist at NASA's Stennis Space Center in Bay St. Louis, Miss., calls plants a "promising, economical solution to indoor air pollution."

One of the leads used by the Associated Press strengthened the concept: thousands of Americans, attempting to become healthier, may be poisoning their bodies with huge doses of vitamin supplements that can be dangerous in large quantities, a group of scientists said Monday.[11]

The Associated Press lead raised an audience concern (that supplements may be dangerous), and the third and fourth paragraphs delivered the second part of the message verbatim from the news release:

"We in the scientific community are concerned with the increasing notion that supplements can be used to prevent serious diseases, such as cancer and osteoporosis," said Dr. David Heber, chief of clinical nutrition at the UCLA School of Medicine.

"Americans should get their nutrients from food instead of pills," Heber said. "Large supplement doses of single nutrients won't prevent diseases, but instead will upset absorption of other nutrients."[12]

The lead raises the need/concern/interest. This is followed in the body copy by the desired behavior as a solution, a description of the benefits of acting on the message and the consequences of inaction. Helping the reader think about how to adopt the desired behavior (mental rehearsal) also falls in the body of the copy.

Once the case is adequately made, preferably on one page but no more than two to three pages, the release is complete.

ELECTRONIC MEDIA

Most radio and television publicity opportunities come from interview placements on talk and news shows, secured through the *query letter*. As in news releases, content for the query letter starts with brainstorming ideas to advance your behavioral framework.

The query letter is usually a one-page description of the news angle. It forces the practitioner to organize his or her thoughts and to crystallize the most salient news angle. Reasons are presented to pique the interest of the reporter in a story idea.

When dealing in television, there is the added need for visual ideas. The query letter to television news assignment editors or talk show producers must provide suggestions for bringing the story alive for the eye. Ask yourself: What action do we want the audience to take? How can we expand the message with visuals? What visual best demonstrates our message? How can we best transfer

When a news release is completed, the writer should ask the following guiding questions:

1. Have I clearly raised a public need, concern or interest?
2. Is the desired behavior clearly presented as a believable solution?
3. Have I clearly presented the benefits of acting and the consequences of inaction? Have I made the strongest case I can to create discomfort with existing behavior?
4. Have I helped the individual mentally rehearse the desired behavior?

the message to the viewer's own real-life experiences? The first paragraph of the query letter is as important as the lead in a news release. It must grab the reader's interest. To illustrate, the following was the first paragraph of a query letter from US WEST Cellular to local newspapers:

"The stage is set. The gloves are off. The battle lines are drawn. To the victor goes dominance in Seattle's growing cellular telephone service."

Thus, you lead the query letter with a strong appeal to the needs, concerns or interests of the journalist who is charged with determining public interests.

The lead paragraph should be followed up with a series of tightly written, brief paragraphs or bulleted facts describing the news angle and why it is important to readers, listeners and/or viewers.

Advisories, like query letters, are designed to quickly pique the interest of the media gatekeeper. A mental picture of a special event such as a news conference is painted for those who make decisions regarding who gets in the newspaper or on a broadcast news or talk show.

Successful media advisories have common characteristics. First, they get attention with a hard-hitting paragraph about the nature of the event and why it should be covered. Second, they read fast (short words and sentences). Third, they are contained in one (or two) page. And fourth, they are sent to the right person.

In a media advisory for Nuffer, Smith, Tucker's second Social Media Symposium, the what, when and where were outlined with additional information raising the need, concern and interest at the top (Figure 47.7).

Writing *public service announcements* (PSAs) is another story. Public relations practitioners are called on to capitalize on time given free by radio and television stations to messages in the public interest. Quality, time-intensive, but conversational writing can be the difference for successful PSAs.

Keep the PSA simple, try to motivate the listener or viewer to one basic action step. Straightforward, clean action steps work the best.

All of these tactics are strengthened when using the behavioral packaging discussed earlier. All are strengthened when speaking through those who shape the opinions of the publics targeted: their opinion leaders.

FUTURE PUBLIC RELATIONS BEHAVIOR

Information alone rarely obtains a desired public behavior. Decades of research bear it out. Practitioners, in their guts, know it too.

As communicators, we have to do a better job of shaping our communication into information that targets publics' wants or needs. Public relations campaigns that are systematically strategized, packaged and delivered to target publics with specific, supportive behavioral outcomes at the core stand a much better chance of breaking through today's information clutter and demonstrating to the CEO that public relations *can* generate measurable, supportive behaviors, *can* make an impact and *can* move the needle.

CASE STUDY

Public concern over the use of pesticides continues to plague agriculture despite the belief of the scientific community that, by and large, the public has little to worry about. The industry believes pesticides are safe when used according to label directions and the regulatory system works effectively. At the same time, there is acknowledgment that public perceptions are genuine, that debate is not going to end, nor will the public ever be satisfied with the agricultural industry as it exists today.

Agriculture has historically invested in technology to meet the mutual needs of its industry and the public. In fact, the technology is here to produce seed genetically engineered to protect itself from insects and disease. Farmers will be able to purchase biological insecticides that have been designed to be more efficient, longer lasting and effective on a broader spectrum of pests than in the past. They will have low-dose, high-activity chemicals that biodegrade so rapidly that they will pose no threat to groundwater or the environment, and many other novel, creative, environmentally sound tools to safeguard their crops against the ravages of weeds, insects and disease.

Despite these anticipated advances to manage the pesticide issue, agriculture is faced with public anxiety about technological advances like biotechnology. So far, the scientific community has clearly failed to frame the benefits of such technology in a way that overcomes the anxieties.

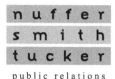

public relations

Hi John,

Social media is changing not only the way consumers communicate with each other, but also the way businesses interact with their audiences. It's impacting many things — and some would argue everything — we do. In light of this, Nuffer, Snith, Tucker and San Diego State University's Digital and Social Media Collaborative are presenting the second San Diego Social Media Symposium.

Teresa Siles, director of social media for Nuffer, Smith, Tucker, and Bill Trumpfheller, president of Nuffer, Smith, Tucker, are available for in-studio interviews to discuss the symposium and key topics, including: how to listen to the social media dialogue, how to engage audiences in conversations, how to energize loyal fans, and new technologies and trends.
Trumpfheller or Siles can also answer the following questions:
1. Why is social media so important for businesses?
2. What are some of the dos and don'ts of social media?
3. What are the pros and cons of social media?
4. How can companies get started in social media?

I will be contacting you shortly to determine your interest in scheduling an interview to take place between Jan. 10 and Jan. 25, 2011. In the meantime, feel free to visit www.sdsocialmediasymposium.com for more information on this event.

Thank you,

Katie Rowland
Nuffer, Smith, Tucker
619/296-0605, ext. 254
kr@nstpr.com

F I G U R E   47.7[13]

XYZ Crop Protection, an agricultural chemical company, is putting a public relations program in place to redirect the threat of public resistance to coming technology. The firm's vice president of corporate affairs' behavioral goal is to accelerate the product-approval process. Her target publics are regulatory and government officials and academic research scientists.

DISCUSSION QUESTIONS FOR CASE STUDY

1. Write a brief situation analysis, based on the information provided, including a force field analysis diagram.

2. Organize a behavioral framework.

3. Develop a tactical recommendation.

DISCUSSION QUESTIONS

1. Write a description of the issue-driven public relations process described in this chapter. How does this compare with your perceptions of public relations prior to reading this chapter?
2. Write a couple of paragraphs on what it takes to initiate behavior through communication using the four steps of the behavioral framework described in this chapter.
3. Why is a mutually beneficial position on an issue important to a public relations strategy?
4. Write a paragraph describing the value and use of opinion leaders—both online and offline—in advancing supportive behaviors from targeted publics.
5. Write a hypothetical situation analysis for a university or organization faced with dramatic budget cuts. What will work against the organization or university as it plans to manage the budget issue? What will work in the university's or organization's favor? Chart it on a force field analysis diagram.
6. With the answer to question 5 as a foundation, write a behavioral objective for a public relations plan for the budget-strapped university along with strategies, messages and tactics to advance the behavior strategies, messages and tactics.

NOTES

1. "A Challenge to the Calling: Public Relations Colloquium," sponsored by San Diego State University, Northwestern University, and Nuffer, Smith, Tucker, Inc., 1992.
2. Tucker, Kerry D., Doris Derelian, and Donna Rouner, *Public Relations Writing, An Issues-Driven Behavioral Approach, 2nd ed.* (Englewood Cliffs, NJ: Prentice Hall,1994), p. 9.
3. *Pr reporter* 26, no. 5 (January 31, 1983).
4. Produce Marketing Association.
5. California Citrus Research Board.
6. Center, Allen H., and Frank E. Walsh, *Public Relations Practices: Managerial Case Studies and Problems* (Englewood Cliffs, NJ: Prentice Hall, 1985), p. 17.
7. *Chicken of the Sea.*
8. Grunig and Hunt, *Managing Public Relations*, p. 455.
9. Dairy Council of California.
10. *The Wall Street Journal*, September 27, 1989, p. 1.
11. Associated Press, *Arizona Daily Star*, May 6, 1986, p. 1.
12. Associated Press, *Arizona Daily Star*, May 6, 1986, p. 1.
13. Nuffer, Smith, Tucker.

48

C H A P T E R

CREATIVITY
Powering Integrated Marketing Communications Ideas

Marty Kohr
Faculty, Department of Integrated Marketing Communications
Medill School of Journalism, Marketing and Integrated Marketing Communications
Northwestern University
Director, 4A's Institute of Advanced Advertising Studies and 4A's Seminar Committee
Leader, Powering Creativity Seminar
Former Advertising Practitioner
DDB, Y&R, Hal Riney and Leo Burnett

The "big idea" was championed by David Ogilvy throughout his hall of fame career. In today's world of ever-increasing audience fragmentation and hyperspeed acceleration of communication options, a "unifying idea" is perhaps more descriptive. At Medill Northwestern University, we teach students about the unifying power of integrated marketing communications ideas.

As an advertising practitioner for over thirty years, I am fortunate to have managed some of the most talented teams in the communications business and experienced first hand the power of creative ideas in strengthening brands. A prime example of one of these campaigns was the Budweiser "Whassup!?" campaign, created by my team at DDB Chicago. Over the past five years, I have had the opportunity to more deeply understand where effective ideas come from and how everyone across the spectrum of marketing communications, including public relations experts, can be more creative and productive in their thinking. This is the core of what I hope to communicate with you.

IDEAS

The Merriam-Webster dictionary defines *idea* as "a formulated thought or opinion, the central meaning or chief end of a particular action or situation." That is a good start, but the Wikipedia crowd takes it a step further, defining *idea* as "whatever is before the mind when one thinks . . . a representational image . . . a concept." They really hit on the essence of the meaning when they state, "The capacity to create and understand the meaning of ideas is considered to be an essential and defining feature of human beings." This understanding is critical for any successful marketing communications individual, regardless of that person's area of specialty.

BIG IDEAS

"It takes a big idea to attract the attention of consumers and get them to buy your product. Unless your advertising contains a big idea, it will pass like a ship in the night." These are well-known words of David Ogilvy in his iconic book, *Ogilvy On Advertising*. "It is horribly difficult to recognize a good idea. Research can't help you much because it cannot predict the cumulative value of an idea."[1] He offers these tips on recognizing a big idea.

- Does it make you gasp when you first see it?
- Do you wish you had thought of it yourself?
- Is it unique?
- Does it fit the strategy to perfection?
- Could it be used for 30 years?

When asked what was the best asset a person could have, Albert Lasker, one of the most astute people in advertising, replied, "Humility in the presence of a good idea."[2]

"When you reach for the stars, you may not quite get one, but you won't come up with a handful of mud either"[3] are famous words summing up Leo Burnett's advertising philosophy. I believe it's appropriate advice for anyone in the idea generation business.

THE NEED TODAY

In today's ever-accelerating world of audience fragmentation, media channel proliferation, new technologies and message bombardment, it is increasingly difficult for any one brand or communication to get noticed and draw attention in the marketplace. Well stated by Teressa Iezzi in her 2010 book, *The Idea Writers*,

> . . . today as a copywriter or other brand creativity maestro, you're not just making something that will compete with other brands and with other messages created by brands. You're making something to compete with every other piece of content, every other media experience that a person has during her waking hours. So you are charged with making something that stands on its own as a worthwhile thing for a person to engage with, brand or no brand.[4]

You not only have to develop an idea and executions to sell your brand, you also have to compete against the likes of *American Idol*, Lady Gaga, the latest YouTube video, text messages from friends, tweets from Ashton Kutcher and everything else vying for the attention of your customer and other brand participants.

VALUE OF A UNIFYING IDEA

Many communicators don't like the term *big idea*, because it conjures up images of old-fashioned advertising campaigns driven by an expensive launch on top-rated television shows and extended via magazines and other targeted media, not to mention the state of panic that can ensue when creative people are challenged to come up with a big idea.

Instead of talking *at* people, effective marketing communications today talks *with* people. It engages them in conversation. The marketer is no longer in charge. It is the consumer who has control. We must create brand communication that people want to attend to, that they seek out and share with their social circle.

Successful ideas today often evolve from a smart, strategic idea that grows to become a larger, more powerful, integrating concept. It starts with a nugget of thinking that flows out of a deep consumer insight. Others are invited and encouraged to support and build on the idea. Seth Godin calls it "Unleashing The Ideavirus." In his book by the same name, he states, "In creating an ideavirus, the advertiser creates an environment in which the idea can replicate and spread. It's the virus that does the work, not the marketer."[5]

A strong integrated marketing communications idea coordinates limited resources, rises above marketplace noise and clutter, surrounds and engages the target audience and, ultimately, builds stronger brand relationships with its consumers. While it used to be that you could run one spot on three TV networks and reach almost everyone, now you have to understand your audience, how they live, how they engage with media, how they get their information and entertainment, how they interact with friends and so on, to build a communication and experiential web that surrounds and interests them. If all this is not integrated behind one idea, you risk being too fragmented and, thus, invisible.

DOMINO'S PIZZA REINVENTION

In December 2009, Domino's Pizza issued a press release celebrating its fiftieth anniversary and announcing a revolutionary product makeover. Just before New Year's Eve, another press release announced an aggressive blend of traditional and social media to get the word out and induce trial. In January 2010, Domino's President Patrick Doyle went on TV and YouTube with documentary-style videos responding to customer dissatisfaction and introducing the reinvented Domino's. Their product was totally rebuilt from the crust to the sauce to the toppings. Crispin Porter + Bogusky created tension-filled "mea culpa" communication messages featuring dissatisfied customers and dismayed employees. Heavy television exposure rapidly generated awareness. YouTube, Facebook, Twitter and Dominos.com were used to go deeper into the story and offer trial incentives. Traditional Sunday newspaper insert coupons were used to broaden the trial. Internal communications programs were executed to stimulate employees in Ann Arbor and out in local communities and stores. While very risky, the initiative was a big success, with domestic sales growth of 9.9% in 2010. It demonstrated the power of a totally integrated idea, boldly executed internally and externally—from their chefs in the test kitchen through to their consumers' taste buds.

IDEAS CAN BE MOST ANYTHING

Ad Age Creativity writer Teressa Iezzi sums it up well:

> The Consumer Control Era has meant that creatives must make things that people want, that they seek out and share with their circle, or with the world. It has meant that the marketing end game has transcended reach, just grabbing eyeballs, and it has become a matter of engagement, of inviting a conversation and making a meaningful, ongoing connection. And, while yes, any copywriter worthy of the title strives to make better ads, now those "ads" can be most anything—a film, a TV show, a mobile app, a blog, a retail experience, a product, a song, a game, a distribution idea, a tweet, a scheme to get people to pay for tap water.[6]

THE PEPSI REFRESH PROJECT

A good example of a unique interactive marketing idea is The Pepsi Refresh Project. After more than a decade as one of the premier brands on the biggest advertising stage, the Super Bowl, Pepsi announced that the brand would not advertise in the 2010 broadcast. In place of Cindy Crawford, Michael Jackson, dancing YMCA bears and other big talent performing in big-budget television spots, Pepsi decided to tap into the growing social consciousness of the young generation. On January 13, 2010, Pepsi issued a press release announcing that www.refresheverything.com was open for Americans to cast their votes for grants totaling more than $20 million

WINNING THE PEPSI REFRESH AWARD

By Jacquelyne DenUyl
Director, Cure JM Board, and mother of a child with JM

In 2010, one of the winners of the first-place $250,000 Pepsi Refresh grant was Cure JM Foundation, an all-volunteer, nonprofit organization dedicated to finding a cure for a rare and potentially fatal disease affecting children, called juvenile myositis (JM). Jacque DenUyl explains the excitement of the voting process and the importance of the grant for research.

> Since JM affects 3 children in a million, our community is much smaller than most of the organizations we competed against. Cure JM supporters used every tactic possible to win this grant, from social media and e-mails, to writing the voting information on their cars. Teachers asked students to text their vote during class. Principals allowed entire schools to vote during morning announcements. Church ministers asked congregations to text their vote before services started. Musicians asked their audiences to vote before concerts began. Kids stood on street corners with signs to vote for Cure JM. Schools, baseball leagues, etc. sent out mass e-mails about voting for Cure JM. I saw some very creative ways of getting votes, including a college student who took a bullhorn after a fire drill and asked his classmates to vote. I also heard from a friend who texted her vote for Cure JM on the last day of voting, just after giving birth in the Labor and Delivery Room!
>
> The $250,000 grant is now half the budget of our small foundation where 90% of our donations go directly to research. It has affected the state of mind of our patients as well. The young adults, who never liked to talk about their disease before, now spread awareness and

to be awarded to consumer-generated programs supporting local communities. Traditional and nontraditional media vehicles were used to raise awareness of the Pepsi initiative and the many ways for people to get involved in refreshing their world. Press releases were constantly issued to spread the story, communicate grant winners and counter criticism of the voting process. Facebook and Twitter became important means of engagement. Community organizations vying for votes added their own grassroots communications.

While the cola wars continue between Coca-Cola and Pepsi and because Pepsi has since gone back to a mix of entertainment and social good marketing, there is little doubt of their success in reaching people and generating buzz. Keys to success include the insight that consumers like to do business with brands that do social good and that have an integration of marketing communications elements that are aligned with the way people access information.

IDEAS AND WHERE THEY COME FROM

Strong integrated marketing communications ideas stem from unique consumer insights. These insights come from studying consumer truths, trends, perceptions, actions, purchase habits, media engagement and passions.

Integrated marketing communications ideas are not taglines, logos, TV spots, banner ads, events, promotions or any other short-term tactics. Rather, they are simple concepts that communicate the foundation for brand engagement. They grow out of an illuminating human truth that, when discovered, inspires unique connections between people and brands. Examples include:

- So easy, even a cave man can do it (Geico).
- So easy, even a baby can do it (E*TRADE).
- Stop thinking about it and start actually doing it (Nike).
- For people who think differently (Apple).
- Spread happiness around the world (Coke).
- The low-cost airline (Southwest).
- Real beauty comes in many shapes, sizes and ages (Dove).

RESPONSIBILITY FOR IDEA GENERATION

Back in the heyday of Mad Men, it was the responsibility of the ad agency's creative department to generate ideas. Writers and art directors were paired up and got the big salaries and bonuses to generate the big ideas. Today, everyone employed

across the spectrum of marketing communications is accountable for ideas. This includes account executives, researchers,
account planners, media strategists, public relations professionals, media relations specialists, promotion experts, event
experts, digital planners and producers and other brand
content creators. All the people who touch a brand and its
communication have an opportunity and a responsibility to
contribute by generating new ideas or building on an existing
idea with their creative thinking.

A. G. Lafley, former chairman and CEO of Procter &
Gamble, calls them "Game Changers" in his so-named
book. A game changer is a visionary strategist who alters
the game his business plays, a creator who uses innovation
for growth, a leader who understands that the consumer is
boss instead of the CEO, an integrator who sees innovation
as a beginning-to-end process, a humanist who sees innovation as a social process.[7]

support through their social media
pages because of the Pepsi Refresh
campaign. The Pepsi grant will
be used to continue funding the
Cure JM Program of Excellence
at Children's Memorial Research
Center in Chicago, along with
an important study on cardiovascular risk in children with
JM. Remaining funding has been
earmarked for a critical genome
study. For more information,
please visit www.curejm.org.

As Leo Burnett so wisely noted, "I have learned to respect ideas, wherever they come from. Often they
come from clients. Account executives often have big creative ideas, regardless of what some writers think."[8]

Clients want strong, strategic ideas regardless of where they come from.

"It really doesn't matter to us where the idea comes from or who champions that idea. If it's the strongest
idea and we believe it meets the brand strategies and is aligned with consumer insights, that's what we are going
to execute against." This comment was by Joe Kuester, senior brand manager for consumer-goods marketer
Kimberly-Clark, about media companies taking the lead in idea generation (reported by Steve McClellen of
Advertising Age).[9]

In a well-known 2008 airline baggage mishap, United Airlines customer service employees missed numerous opportunities to adequately respond to singer/songwriter Dave Carroll's complaint that they broke his
guitar. After months of getting nowhere, he created a music video and posted it on YouTube. "United Breaks
Guitars"[10] was viewed over 1.5 million times in four days and has since gone over 10 million hits. Carroll was
interviewed on the *Today* show, CNN and *Jimmy Kimmel Live*. United responded but too late. The *London
Times* reported that negative public relations cost United shareholders over $180 million in lost stock value.
While this figure is debatable, there is no debate that someone at United should have had a better idea when
Mr. Carroll first started to complain. Brand representatives at all points of customer contact, including flight
attendants, social media monitoring experts and corporate public relations managers, are responsible for brand
building (or preserving) ideas.

EVERYONE CAN THINK MORE CREATIVELY

James Webb Young, advertising professional and professor, in 1940, wrote *A Technique for Producing Ideas*,[11]
a book lauded by one of the most famous ad men of all time, William Bernbach, chairman and worldwide chief
executive officer of Doyle Dane Bernbach Inc. States Bernbach,

> James Webb Young conveys in this little book something more valuable than the most learned and de-
> tailed texts as he writes about the creative spark, the ideas which bring spirit and life to an idea or an
> advertisement. You will be making the most of all the forces in your life and all your natural equipment
> if you follow the procedures he outlines so simply and lucidly.[12]

Young proselytized a relatively simple five-step process:

1. Gather information

2. Digestion

3. Incubation

4. Birth of idea (aha!)

5. Development of idea

James Webb Young, like many smart thinkers before and since, identified an idea as a new combination of old elements and said the capacity to bring old elements into new combinations depended on one's ability to see relationships. He further explained that the best creative people were also the most curious about all things.

The late Steve Jobs, whom Walter Isaacson, in his 2011 best-selling biography, calls "the ultimate icon of inventiveness, imagination, and sustained innovation"[13] agrees with Young on many fronts. Leander Kahney, in his 2008 book *Inside Steve's Brain*, reports the following about Jobs' beliefs. "Innovation comes from people meeting in hallways or calling each other at night with a new idea. Ask creative people how they did something, they feel a little guilty because they didn't really do it, they just saw something and connected things in new ways."[14]

A PROCESS TO DEVELOP IDEAS

It is all about gathering and connecting dots, as Steve Jobs strongly believed. So that is what I have been doing over the past five years—gathering and connecting dots on how to help anyone come up with better, more effective ideas. These ideas could be to build your client's brand, your agency's brand or your own brand. While there is no one process for every person in every situation, this offers a path of thinking that has worked for others and could work for you.

ALWAYS BE CURIOUS

Most every creative thinker will tell you: if you're not curious about life and why people do the things they do, you're in the wrong business. Leo Burnett certainly felt so: "Curiosity about life in all of its aspects . . . is still the secret of great creative people." Steve Jobs too: "Creative people have had more experiences or thought more about their experiences than other people. A lot of people haven't had very diverse experiences, so they don't have enough dots to connect and they end up with linear, lesser solutions. The broader one's understanding of the human experience, the better ideas he will have."

DEFINE THE OBJECTIVE

A well-defined problem is the foundation to a creative idea, confirms David Murray in his book, *Borrowing Brilliance*.[15] Darwin believed it was more difficult to see the problem than to come up with the solution. What are you trying to achieve? Increase sales among existing customers? Bring in new customers? Grow the category? Dominant-share brands, like Heinz Ketchup, promote recipes using their product. Challenger brands, like GEICO, try to steal share by asking you to spend 15 minutes comparing rates. Allstate created Mayhem to counter Geico's encroachment. What are you trying to accomplish? Identifying the problem often identifies the solution.

PURGE OLD PREJUDICES

Guy Kawasaki, in *Rules For Revolutionaries*, calls it purging. Dispose of old prejudices and assumptions that constrict your thinking. Start with a clean sheet of paper and a clear brain.[16]

GATHER INFORMATION

Gather all relevant information for the task at hand. Gather as many dots of information as you possibly can. Deeply understand the consumer and everything that might possibly impact his or her attitudes, behavior and purchase decisions. Understand the marketplace and your competition. Learn everything you can about your brand and its history. Review every piece of available research and data point relevant to your problem.

KNOW YOUR CONSUMER

How do they use your product? How do they view your brand? What do they like? What do they dislike? How do they differentiate you from the competition? How do they get their information? How do they make decisions? How do friends and family influence them? What are their passions?

Observing people in real-life situations to find out what makes them tick, how they interact with the brand, what confuses them, what they like and hate and what needs are not addressed is key to *The Art of Innovation*, as stated by Tom Kelly in his so-named book and practiced at his company, IDEO, the leading design firm in the United States. Go to the store, watch how they buy things, see what else they buy. Eat at their restaurant, sit at their bar, hang out with them. Walk around their home. Get permission to peek in their closets, cupboards, garage and yard.[17]

Think about your own experiences. Immerse yourself in the product experience and examine your own behavior, feelings and motivations. David Ogilvy's theory is that the best ads come from personal experience. "Some of the good ones I have done have really come out of the real experience of my life, and somehow this has come over as true and valid and persuasive."

It is not enough to see or hear what people say; you have to interpret meaning to divine underlying motivations or needs. Henry Ford said of the first car he ever built: "If I'd asked my customers what they wanted, they'd have said a faster horse."

The customer may not always know what's best for them. Steve Jobs has said the customer did not lead him to develop the Mac. "You can't just ask customers what they want and then try to give that to them. By the time you get it built, they'll want something new." Few consumers know what's possible beyond their current experiences. That's your job.

Talk to experts. Bartenders know their customers very well. The same is true for hair stylists, beauticians, personal trainers, yoga instructors, insurance agents, cab drivers, repairmen, retail sales clerks, your field sales and marketing people—anyone who interacts directly with your consumers. The experts' views of your customers are invaluable. Each discussion with an expert is equal to hundreds of individual discussions with end users and usually delves much deeper.

COLLECT DOTS

Keep a sketchbook to gather your nuggets of information and initial pieces of ideas. Look around your office or classroom for the most creative thinkers; chances are they keep a notebook or collect ideas on their iPad or some other device. Besides contributing to the task at hand, it can help you over time. The most creative folks have stacks of books that they refer back to time and time again. The most productive teams have a war room with lots of wall space to gather dots.

STUDY THE COMPETITION

Study your competition. What are they trying to accomplish? How does their product and brand compare with yours? How are their consumers similar to or different from yours? How do they engage with them? Are there vulnerabilities you can detect?

STUDY OTHER CATEGORIES

Consider other categories for inspiration. Have they faced similar problems? Have they found success that might help you? We all know that the book publishers of the world are studying the music industry to try to figure out how to handle their rapidly developing digital situation. As David Murray says in *Borrowing Brilliance*, it's smart to borrow and build on the ideas of others.

Greg Hall, visionary brewmaster of Goose Island, Chicago's top craft brewer, was looking for inspiration. While talking to a distiller, he got the idea to age his imperial stout in bourbon barrels. Goose Island's Bourbon County Stout Rare, aged for two years in 23-year-old bourbon barrels, sold out their limited batch in a few days at $45 a bottle. Goose Island also studies wine labels for design ideas for their high-end Belgian-style ales that, like wine, pair well with fine cuisine.

Award-winning Alinea chef Grant Achatz and his partner opened up a new restaurant. They adopted a business model that borrows from the theater world. To counter the "no-show" problems that plague restaurants, they require that customers make reservations online and pay a fixed price in advance for the menu, or "performance," offered. If they don't attend the scheduled event, it's the customer's problem, not the restaurant's. Also, like the theater, there is a new show (aka menu) every three months. They are even considering a subscription series for repeat customers, again based on the theater world.

It is perfectly okay to borrow ideas. It's a trait of the most successful inventors. "The secret to creativity is knowing how to hide your sources." said Albert Einstein. "I steal from every movie I've ever seen," said Quentin Tarantino.

STUDY CONSUMER TRENDS AND CULTURAL SHIFTS

What is happening in your consumer's world that could be leveraged to gain consideration for your brand? What network television and cable shows are they watching? What other content interests them? Study the many books, newspaper and magazine articles, blogs and websites on trend spotting and future forecasts. How are your consumers and your brand being affected by what is happening today and forecasts for what might happen tomorrow? Can your brand benefit from the aging population, growing concerns surrounding sustainability, increasing mobility of communications and information retrieval, privacy concerns or any other current issue or trend?

Is there a cultural issue your brand can champion or push against? Dove championed against the supermodel beauty myth with great results. Burger King rallied their most loyal super fans against metrosexuality. P&G's Dawn Dishwashing Soap couldn't have had better timing when they launched their wildlife protection campaign in 2010. Press releases on their cause marketing efforts to clean up oily birds were distributed prior to the Gulf oil spill in April.

LOOK TO OTHER WORLDS

Inspiration comes from nature for the world's greatest thinkers. The earliest Egyptian and Greek architects used the golden Fibonacci ratios as found in nautilus shells as inspiration for their iconic structural designs. The arches of tree branches influenced better bridge design. George de Mestral in 1941 observed how burrs stuck to his dog's coat and invented Velcro. Elephant trunks, chameleon tails and the patterns of swirling galaxies are studied to help create more efficient flows for water, air and electrical systems. BiomimicryInstitute.org promotes learning from and emulating natural forms, processes and ecosystems to create more sustainable and healthier human technologies and designs.

"If you're looking where everyone else is looking, you're looking in the wrong place," says a quote attributed to maverick entrepreneur, HDNet chairman and Dallas NBA team owner Mark Cuban.

Be open to finding what you are not looking for. Unexpected bacterial growth on mold led Alexander Fleming to the discovery of penicillin in 1928. Teflon, Post-it Notes and cellophane are other accidental discoveries.

Look to the past. Super Glue was rediscovered by inventor Harry Wesley Coover Jr. in 1951 when he recalled his failed research during WWII. Every idea has its own time of opportunity.

AWAKEN THE COLLABORATIVE SPIRIT

Two heads are better than one, and a team of well-directed marketing people multiplies power exponentially. In the traditional advertising business, the creative brief served for decades to focus the efforts of writers and art directors. The same type of brief can help stimulate all elements of the integrated marketing spectrum, including the public relations team.

THE INTEGRATED MARKETING COMMUNICATIONS IDEA BRIEF

The integrated marketing communications idea brief, like the more traditional creative brief, is a concise document that communicates the goal and provides guidelines for thinking. It is a means to an end—effective marketing communications. It is a simple story of truths crafted to instruct and inspire. It should tell a compelling story on one page. It should excite and motivate team members to work on the project. In short, a brief is a print ad to influence the integrated marketing team you work with.

INTEGRATED MARKETING COMMUNICATIONS IDEA BRIEF CONTENT

While there is no one format that fits all initiatives, a good communication brief should consider the following elements.

PROJECT SCOPE

A good brief starts with a succinct definition of the scope of the project. What do you want to accomplish? Are you looking for a unifying idea? Or do you need an integrated campaign to come out of an already defined idea? Or are you developing one element of a campaign, like a consumer ad or public relations initiative?

TARGET AUDIENCE

Beyond demographics, how can you best describe your target in terms of psychographics? What are the personalities, values, attitudes, interests or lifestyles of the people you want to engage?

TARGET INSIGHT

What is the key insight about the target and its intersection with the brand? (We will discuss this in more detail shortly.)

THE ONE THING

What one thing do you want them to think, feel, believe or do? Force yourself to focus on the most important thing.

WHY

Why should they think, feel, believe or do this? What one, two or three support points can be used to help persuade your target?

TONE

What is the brand character or personality that should be carried through in the tone of communications? Is the brand scrappy, fun loving, serious or full of enthusiasm?

ADDITIONAL GUIDELINES

Are there any execution guidelines that need to be adhered to? Are there specific consumer engagement vehicles to be considered? Are there budget parameters to keep ideas realistic?

MEASUREMENT

How will success be measured? Will it be by sales volume, revenue, market share, distribution gains, clicks, likes on Facebook, awareness or attitude shifts?

WRITING AND OWNING THE BRIEF

A strong brief creates a discipline for the client and agency. It promotes partnership and ownership among all brand communication stakeholders. It distills core marketing information and consumer knowledge into one key message. It is precise and logical and eliminates the unnecessary. It provides clear, simple direction. It tells a story. It should be self-explanatory. Above all, it should be brief!

There are no firm rules on who writes the brief. Usually it is the account person or planner who can most effectively and efficiently capture the best input from all experts in the process. Most importantly, everyone involved with the project, including the client, should feel a sense of contribution. Before work commences, everyone should sign off on the brief and have a strong feeling of ownership. This not only leads to the smartest brief, it also will help everyone rally around and support the resulting ideas.

CONSUMER INSIGHT

A key element of any brief is identifying a unique insight that can lead to more effective consumer engagement. Insights help capture attention and lead to stronger connections between people and brands. Insights let brands in. A good insight well used leads consumers to think, "That's just how I feel," "you know what I need," "you get me" and the ultimate "I want you as part of my world."

An insight is the power of seeing into a situation; the act of apprehending the inner nature of things or of seeing intuitively; the capacity to discern the true nature of something; an elucidating glimpse; a truth that surprises. Often it's not obvious. It is probably not top of mind with your target.

Uncovering insights involves an element of revelation or discovery. Maybe they have forgotten about something. Maybe it has always been there, below the surface, but no one has pointed it out. Or maybe they haven't seen it in quite that way before. You have tapped into the main vein when you hit on an unrecognized human truth.

MASTERCARD'S PRICELESS CAMPAIGN

MasterCard and their marketing partner, McCann Erickson, in 1997 tapped into a very powerful insight, a deep human truth that was growing in awareness and acceptance following more than a decade of conspicuous consumption. It was right at the connecting point between the consumer and the brand. The insight—the higher value of experiences over material goods—was "Priceless." The well-known tagline: "There are some things money can't buy. For everything else there's MasterCard." More than 14 years later, it is still going strong in over 108 countries and 50 languages, with hundreds of executions across the spectrum of emotional experiences, supported by myriad paid, owned and earned media and public relations. Not many campaigns run this long. Those that do are tapped into a deep consumer truth.

Barbara Werner, a strategic marketing expert at McGarryBowen, Chicago, suggests you build to a consumer insight in three steps. Identify the fact, then the accepted consumer belief (ACB) and finally, the insight. A *fact* is an observation of some reality about the consumer, category or product. An *ACB* is an idea about the product or category that the consumer currently acknowledges. An *insight* is an undiscovered or forgotten truth that surprises. Dove's Real Beauty Campaign provides a good example.

DOVE'S REAL BEAUTY INSIGHT

Fact: Only 2% of women consider themselves to be beautiful.
ACB: Feeling attractive gives women confidence.
Insight: Women resent the unrealistic beauty standards perpetuated by the beauty industry.

While neither Barbara Werner nor I worked on the campaign, we think this type of thinking resulted in the video that was at the heart of this award-winning, highly effective integrated marketing communications campaign (http://www.youtube.com/watch?v=hibyAJOSW8U).

UNCOVERING INSIGHTS

Much of what has been covered so far in this chapter should be considered to help uncover consumer insights and ideas. Always be curious. Define objectives. Purge prejudices. Talk with consumers. Talk with experts. Keenly observe what is going on with all brand participants. Study consumer trends and cultural shifts. Look to other categories, other worlds. Solicit collaboration from all team members.

CONNECTING THE DOTS

Whether you have a team of people on your side or you are going at it solo, it's up to the individual to connect the dots to formulate new ideas. James Webb Young, Steve Jobs and most every creative person admits that the secret is connecting two previously unconnected ideas. Young calls it *digestion*. Feel each fact of knowledge over. Turn it this way and that. Look at it in different lights. Bring two together and see how they fit. Look for relationships. Look for new applications. Look for new combinations. Look for evolutions.

IDENTIFY MULTIPLE CONNECTIONS

Think fluently. The light bulb, phonograph, telegraph and radio are just a few of over 1,000 U.S. patents by Thomas Edison. His goal was one minor invention every ten days and one major invention every six months. Michael Michalko talks about this and more in his very worthwhile books, *Cracking Creativity*,[18] *The Secrets of Creative Genius* and *Thinkertoys*.[19]

Think productively, not reproductively. Ask how many different ways you can look at the problem and how you can rethink it. Think about how many different ways it might be solved. Albert Einstein said if you asked the average person to find a needle in a haystack, that person would stop when he found it. He, on the other hand, would tear through the entire haystack looking for all the possible needles.

Consider novel combinations. Einstein did not invent the concepts of energy, mass or speed of light, but using what he called "combinatory play," he created something new: the theory of relativity.

Creative, right-brain thinking is not about finding just one answer; it is about uncovering all possible answers. It's why right-brainers will rule the future, according to Daniel Pink in his groundbreaking book, *A Whole New Mind*.[20]

It is about making new connections. Leonardo da Vinci is said to have been sitting in a piazza observing life, when he heard a bell ring as someone threw a pebble in a pool. As he observed the concentric ripples emanating out from where the little stone hit the water, he wondered if that is how sound traveled—in waves.

Guy Kawasaki in his book, *Rules For Revolutionaries*, refers to digestion as prodding. His tips include looking at the problem in its broadest context. Look on the opposite side of the obvious. Start at the goal and work backwards. Divide big problems into smaller ones. Look for frustrations with current products. Shake and bake.

The process is something like what takes place in a kaleidoscope, Young said.

Every turn rearranges all the little pieces of colored glass or bits of information into new relationships, revealing new combinations, new patterns—new potential ideas. However, like a kaleidoscope, at this stage there is no one clear picture. Everything is a jumble in your mind. You have reached the hopeless stage.

INCUBATION

You have now filled your conscious and unconscious mind, your left and right brain, with a lot of information and possible ideas. It is now time to let it incubate. You make absolutely no effort of a direct nature. You drop the whole subject and put the problem out of your mind as completely as you can. Turn to whatever stimulates your imagination and emotions. Listen to music; go to the theater or a movie, read poetry or a detective story. Get away from it. Stop thinking about it. Go for a long walk. Go to a different part of your brain.

LET THE IDEA EMERGE

Archimedes shouted "Eureka!" when he got in his bathtub, saw the water rise and realized a way to measure the volume of the king's gold crown. He had been thinking about the problem for a long while and was in a relaxed state when it hit. Many report that their "Aha!" moments happen in the morning shower or other times when their minds are fresh, not focused on any one problem and more open to unconventional ideas.

THE INSIGHT EXPERIENCE

Why good ideas come to us when they do is the subject of Jonah Lehrer's article that ran in the July 28, 2008, issue of the *New Yorker*, "The Eureka Hunt."[21] In trying to explain the "Aha!" moment that saved a smoke jumper years ago in Montana, he tapped into the ideas of Mark Jung-Beeman, a cognitive neuroscientist at Northwestern University, who has spent decades researching what happens inside the brain when people have an insight. According to Jung-Beeman, the insight process is an act of cognitive deliberation. The brain must be focused on the task at hand, then transformed by accidental, serendipitous connections. We must concentrate, but we must concentrate on letting the mind wander. Before there can be a breakthrough, there has to be a mental block. When the insight comes, it arrives like a revelation yet seems quite obvious. Attention has been diffused. The mind is more relaxed, in a more pleasurable state. New connections are made with all the information that has been stored deep in the right brain. You have let your mind wander to where it wants to go.

BUDWEISER'S "WHASSUP!?" CAMPAIGN

August A. Busch IV, in the business cover story in *USA Today* on September 8, 2000, observed: "In our lifetimes, we'll never see so much value created from a single idea. It makes Budweiser a brand for every culture, every demographic and every community. It makes Budweiser a younger, hipper, more contemporary brand."[22] His words were supported by sales volume, consumer attitude research and industry recognition. "Whassup!?" won every top marketing effectiveness and creative award, including the most coveted, the Grand Prix, given to the advertising campaign judged best in the world by the Cannes International Advertising Festival in 2000.

"Whassup!?" resulted from a well-defined objective, deep consumer and brand understanding, identification of a true consumer insight, one person making a critical new connection and a team effort in which everyone involved built on the idea with their own creative thinking.

DDB Chicago's creative and production teams partnered with original short film creator and director Charles Stone III to tell the story. Busch Media found unique ways to align the message with live sports, when beer drinkers make appointments with friends. Web experience creators developed ways for fans to interact online. E-mail postcards with the audio pneumonic could be sent to friends. Fans overloaded Budweiser.com for a free foreign language program to connect with friends around the world with 37 different translations of "Whassup!?" Consumers generated hundreds of parodies to virally exchange with friends. Public relations helped spread the backstory of the true friends from Philadelphia. Media relations generated guest appearances on Letterman, Oprah, Leno and many other programs. Event marketers took the guys across the United States. and across the pond to the United Kingdom. They made hundreds of sports venue appearances and even sang "Take Me Out To The Ballgame" at Wrigley Field. Point-of-sale extensions were created by retail marketing and shopping experience experts. The guys hosted Bud Bowl, via on-premise and off-premise material. Most importantly, Anheuser-Busch management aggressively supported the idea and defended the campaign against initial criticism.

It's a rare brand campaign that actually gets out in front, instead of simply mirroring or following popular culture. A short video summary of the power that can be created by a unique thought that builds with multiple contributing ideas can be viewed at the following link: http://www.youtube.com/watch?v=NB0Ho17Ja2c.

SUMMARY

In today's world of aggressive brand competition for consumer involvement that grows exponentially every day, an integrated marketing communications idea best illuminates the path to success. We are all fortunate to live in a world where the only restriction is the power of our thinking. I hope this chapter has provided you with ideas to power your own creativity. Whatever your mission or discipline, enjoy the journey.

DISCUSSION QUESTIONS

1. What was your most recent, most powerful creative idea?
2. Was it the result of a well-defined objective?
3. Did you invest time in uncovering everything possible about your audience and the task at hand?
4. Did you keep nuggets of information and thoughts in a sketchbook or notebook?
5. Did you connect multiple dots and come up with as many solutions as possible?
6. Did you allow time for your thoughts to percolate?
7. When did the creative idea hit? Where you in a more relaxed state of mind?
8. Did your idea come out of deep audience understanding and unique insight?
9. Did you share your idea with others and invite them to build on it?

NOTES

1. Ogilvy, David. *Ogilvy on Advertising*. New York: Multimedia Publications, 1983. p. 16.
2. Schultz, Arthur, and Jeffrey Cruikshank. *The Man Who Sold America, The Story of Albert Lasker*. Boston: Harvard University Press, 2010.
3. Burnett, Leo. *Communications of an Advertising Man: Selections from the Speeches, Articles, Memoranda and Writings of Leo Burnett*. Chicago: Leo Burnett Company, privately printed, 1961. p. IX.
4. Iezzi, Teressa. *The Idea Writers*. New York: Crain, Palgrave Macmillan, 2010. p. 78.
5. Godin, Seth. *Unleashing the Ideavirus*. New York: Hyperion, 2001. p. 26.
6. Iezzi, Teressa. *The Idea Writers*. New York: Crain, Palgrave Macmillan, 2010. p. 8.
7. Lafley, A.G., and Ron. Charan. *The Game Changer*. New York: Crown Business, 2008.
8. Burnett, Leo. *A Collection of Inspiring Words that Leo Burnett Wrote or Spoke*. Chicago: Leo Burnett Company, privately printed, 1971. p. 22.
9. Kuester, Joe, quoted in McClellen, Steve. Media Agencies As Content Creators, *Advertising Age Media Works*, April 24, 2011. http://adage.com/article/mediaworks/media-agencies-make-mark-content-creators/227163/.
10. United Breaks Guitars. http://en.wikipedia.org/wiki/United_Breaks_Guitars, http://travel.latimes.com/daily-deal-blog/index.php/smashed-guitar-youtu-4850/.
11. Young, James Webb. *A Technique for Producing Ideas*. Chicago: Crain Communications, 1940, 1960, 1975, 1979.
12. Bernback, William. Foreword to a *Technique For Producing Ideas*, by James Webb Young. Chicago: Crain Communications, 1979. p. h.
13. Isaacson, Walter. *Steve Jobs*. New York: Simon and Schuster. 2011. p. xxi.
14. Kahney, Leander. *Inside Steve's Brain*. New York: Portfolio, 2008.
15. Murray, David. *Borrowing Brilliance*. New York: Gotham Books. 2009.
16. Kawasaki, Guy. *Rules for Revolutionaries*. New York: Harper Business, 1999.
17. Kelly, Tom. *The Art of Innovation*. New York: Currency-Doubleday, 2001.
18. Michalko, Michael. *Cracking Creativity*. Berkeley: Ten Speed Press, 2001.
19. Michalko, Michael. *Thinkertoys*. Berkeley: Ten Speed Press, 2006.
20. Pink, Daniel. *A Whole New Mind*. New York: Riverhead Books, 2006.

21. Lehrer, Joe. The Eureka Hunt, *The New Yorker*, July 28, 2008.
22. McCarthy, Michael. Top Brewer Also Reigns as King of Marketing, *USA Today*, September 8, 2000.

ADDITIONAL READING

Godin, Seth. *Unleashing the Ideavirus*. New York, NY: Hyperion, 2001.

Iezzi, Teressa. *The Idea Writers*. New York, NY: Crain, Palgrave Macmillan, 2010.

Isaacson, Walter. *Steve Jobs*. New York, NY: Simon & Schuster, 2011. Ogilvy, David. *Ogilvy on Advertising*. New York, NY: Multimedia Publications, 1983.

Johnson, Steven. *Where Good Ideas Come From*. New York, NY: Riverhead Books, 2010.

Kawasaki, Guy. *Rules for Revolutionaries*. New York, NY: Harper Business, 1999.

Kelly, Tom. *The Art of Innovation*. New York, NY: Currency-Doubleday, 2001. Schultz, Arthur, and Cruikshank, Jeffrey. *The Man Who Sold America: The Story of Albert Lasker*. Boston, MA: Harvard University Press, 2010.

Lafley, A.G., and Charan, Ron. *The Game Changer*. New York, NY: Crown Business, 2008.

Michalko, Michael. *Cracking Creativity*. Berkeley, CA: Ten Speed Press, 2001.

Michalko, Michael. *Thinkertoys*. Berkeley, CA: Ten Speed Press, 2006.

Murray, David. *Borrowing Brilliance*. New York, NY: Gotham Books, 2009.

Ogilvy, David. *Ogilvy on Advertising*. New York, NY: Multimedia Publications, 1983.

Pink, Daniel. *A Whole New Mind*. New York, NY: Riverhead Books, 2006.

Schultz, Arthur, and Cruikshank, Jeffrey. *The Man Who Sold America: The Story of Albert Lasker*. Boston, MA: Harvard University Press, 2010.

49

C H A P T E R

WRITING FOR THE EAR
The Challenge of Effective Speechwriting

Lee W. Huebner, Ph.D.
Professor
George Washington University
Former Publisher and CEO
International Herald Tribune

It seems that human communities inevitably greet important changes in their collective life with a mixture of euphoria and hysteria. Surely this has been true of our response to breakthroughs in communication technology—they either will save us, we say, or they will ruin us.

We talk this way about the Internet today, just as earlier generations talked in similar ways about television, radio, film, the telegraph and the printing press. One can look back and find long and elaborate prognoses, both utopian and dsytopian, for each development.

It is striking to note, however, that this pattern also was evident as ancient civilization became increasingly dependent on a new technology called "writing." Socrates, in Plato's dialogue "The Phaedrus," famously worries that relying on written discourse will undermine the human capacity for genuine memory and internalized wisdom, as well as the ability to sharpen ideas in the crucible of direct, personal interaction. The rich oral culture of ancient Greece was threatened, he feared, by the recent development of the highly efficient Greek alphabet and the new reading culture that it fostered.

What Socrates was saying, among other things, is that speaking and writing are two quite different forms of communication, and that we could expect to lose a great deal if we came to depend too much on writing as our dominant means of public discourse.

In discussing the place where the two forms, speaking and writing, interact—as this essay on speechwriting seeks to do—it seems appropriate to begin by delineating these essential differences.

THE ENDURING ADVANTAGES OF "ORALITY"

It cannot be said, of course, that Socrates' argument did much to discourage the increased use of the written word in public affairs. Its profound efficiencies both for the writer and the reader, its ready transportability (over time and through space), its "fixedness" and, later on, the relative ease with which it could be duplicated all made writing a cornerstone of advancing civilization. But at the same, the unique values of what is sometimes

751

One of America's leading film critics, Roger Ebert, paid moving tribute to the communicative power of the spoken word when he appeared in the Spring of 2011 before the annual TED conference (Technology, Entertainment, Design), a leading global forum for the discussion of new ideas. Cancer of the jaw had deprived Ebert of his ability to speak—but he was not content, he insisted, simply to fall back on his skills as a writer to connect with his audience. Instead, he went to great lengths to recreate for his audience the advantages of orality. He appeared personally on the platform, sitting alongside his wife and two friends as they read aloud, on his behalf, the material he had composed for the occasion. While they spoke, he physically added a lively dose of personality to the words through vivid facial expressions and a range of vigorous gestures.

And that was not all; Ebert went on to demonstrate the capacity of a computerized voice to read his text aloud, noting the increasing availability of this technology, while also demonstrating its communicative shortcomings (in telling a joke, for example).

Finally, to highlight the demonstration, Ebert introduced a still newer technology that actually employed his own voice—recorded in his many television appearances before he became ill—to present a part of his text, digitally deconstructing and then reconstructing distinctively personal sounds to deliver the newly composed message.

Ebert's TED presentation emphatically evidenced the high premium placed, even by this prolific master of the written word, on the unique communicative power of orality.

The new voice-reconstruction technology that Ebert demonstrated is still in a relatively early stage of development. When words or phrases are broken out of old contexts and pieced together in new ways, rhythm, intonation and cadence are understandably compromised. But the technology is improving, and the day may soon arrive when any person's written words can be readily and effectively converted into his or her own spoken words—through a digital reproduction of the writer's voice—or a digitized voice of the writer's choosing.

For some time now, of course, voice recognition technology has enabled computers to capture dictation or conversation in called "orality" have by no means been neglected through the centuries.

Contemporary scholars continue to underscore the tradeoffs that come when the human voice gives way to marks on a piece of paper. They point to the enormous potential for added power when a human personality is a part of the communications equation, including the increased authority, authenticity and credibility of messages that are accompanied by what Walter Ong has called a sense of the communicator's "interiority."

These qualities have, of course, become even more salient in a time when television and the Internet can transmit the human voice and image as readily and inexpensively as the printing press and the telegraph have been able to reproduce and transport written characters.

Those who are involved in the exercise of speechwriting can argue that they are trying to have the best of two worlds, providing for a speaker the potential advantages of a written text, while allowing audiences to apprehend that text through the prism of a human personality.

The problem is that the combination does not always work out so well.

The worst speeches in the world, in fact, are, in this writer's judgment, prescripted manuscript speeches that are written to be read (not heard) and are then recited by "speakers" in ways that further drain them of personality. Better a bad, spontaneous speech, one might say, than a bad scripted one.

Think of the times when one leaves a speaking event with the comment: "He was much better in the question-and-answer period." Or "It was only after she got away from her text that the program came alive." Audiences invariably prefer the warmth and directness of a conversational style (however much it may ramble or repeat) to the numbing ordeal of sitting patiently while a lifeless reader drones stiffly through a document that could have been comprehended more easily (and more speedily) if copies had simply been passed out for everyone to read.

Most good speeches, in fact, do not use full manuscripts: most people who speak regularly for a living, especially in the political word, prefer the extemporaneous form, and for good reasons. What may be sacrificed in precision, and even occasionally in eloquence, can be more than offset when an audience senses that the message is truly unfolding from "inside" the speaker—with all of the communicative bonuses associated with orality.

An *extemporaneous* address, we should quickly remind ourselves, is something different from an impromptu speech, which is too often a seat-of-the pants, spur-of-the-moment creation, frequently collapsing into incoherence when a speaker agrees to "say a few words" without giving the assignment sufficient forethought. Good extemporaneous speeches, on the other hand, are usually well prepared, with outlines, key phrases and vital details established in advance, whether they are noted on paper or etched in the speaker's memory. And often, those who are called speechwriters are called upon to do precisely this sort of preparation—channeling their work into speech outlines, or even into an assortment of "suggested remarks," a potpourri of supportive materials that can then can be woven into an effective extemporaneous address by a capable speaker.

written form. What Ebert was describing is a reversal of that process, a digital conversion of writing back into speaking—marshalling the powers of highly personalized orality and marrying them to writing's own special efficiencies. It is a similar process, it would seem, to that of effective speechwriting.

Mark Twain, insightfully, remarked that "it takes about three weeks to prepare a really good extemporaneous speech." The observation has applied to many great "off-the-cuff" speakers, including, as his biographers now tell us, Winston Churchill, who would often rehearse through long morning deliberations the precise language of even the most informal remarks he would make that afternoon.

To cite another apt example, Raymond K. Price, who supervised the White House writing staff when this writer worked there under President Nixon, has estimated that 19 out of 20 Nixon speeches were given without the use of notes. But this did not mean they were spontaneous: they were usually well outlined by the President beforehand, and usually supplemented by staff submissions using the "suggested remarks" format.

Presidents Kennedy, Johnson and Clinton, on the other hand, liked sometimes to begin with well-prepared texts and then interlace unscripted elaborations. Martin Luther King, Jr., on the other hand, used and then reused beautifully honed speech passages, improvising eloquently within carefully prepared patterns.

President Reagan famously spoke from stacks of small note cards, interchangeable and reusable. President Obama marshals well-considered talking points, rarely using a paper manuscript, though, when necessary, making skillful use of a teleprompter.

In sum, even carefully prepared speakers will often go out of their way to appropriate the evident advantages of orality. And for some, it is important to underscore the fact that they are not "using notes." Nixon would sometimes have the lectern removed from the stage just before he walked onto it, leaving for his use a single stand-up microphone (he said he hated the teleprompter). Others (Clinton is one) have made a show of "throwing aside" a text that has ostensibly been prepared for the occasion.

This perceived appreciation for spontaneity—and the concomitant implication of authenticity—is why, in a vast majority of public speaking classes, the most common advice for students is to "speak from the heart," to "have a conversation with the audience." It is the mantra of public speaking teachers everywhere: "Just be natural. Say it in your own words. Be yourself." And, truth be told, this is normally very good advice.

And yet the manuscript speech persists as a common and honored form of public address. For if bad manuscript speeches cluster on the poor end of the quality spectrum, the best manuscript speeches are at the opposite pole—the most likely of all speeches to live in memory, and in history.

Yes, orality has unique and sometimes indispensable advantages. But there is another critical dimension to the story. A fully written speech text, whether one prepares it for oneself or engages the help of others, can, in the right circumstances, also have enormous value.

THE ADDED VALUE OF A SPEECH MANUSCRIPT

To begin with, of course, a speech manuscript can achieve a level of verbal precision that extemporaneous speaking cannot match—and which can be essential in the discussion of sensitive topics. The difference between the right word and the almost-right word, Mark Twain has said, is the difference "between lightning and the lightning bug." Whether one chooses to use the word *opponents* or *adversaries* or *enemies* or *opposite numbers* may be worth a measure of careful deliberation during the speech preparation process.

In a delicate speaking situation—President's Obama's 2009 Cairo speech to the Muslim world comes to mind—almost every sentence can present a word-selection challenge of enormous import. This challenge was compounded by Obama's decision to reject a suggested text for Cairo in which controversial issues had been muffled in a broadly staffed, risk-averse group writing process. He chose instead to use his own pen and that of speechwriter Ben Rhodes to confront, directly but adroitly, some the world's most sensitive diplomatic issues.

Similarly, a written manuscript can put together, often after an elaborate trial-and-error process, memorable and moving combinations of words—reaching rhetorical heights that the extemporaneous speech normally writes off or, at best, leaves to the inspiration of the moment.

There is also a certain symbolic value that arises out of the mere existence of a manuscript: in some situations it can be a persuasive affirmation of the importance of the occasion—and a subtle admonition that the audience should "listen to this speech as carefully as I have prepared it." The actress Cher opened her eulogy at the funeral of her former husband, Sonny Bono, by saying, "Please excuse my papers, . . . because I've had to write some of it down doesn't mean that I'm unprepared. It just means that I'm overprepared in that this is probably the most important thing I've ever done in my life."

Many of us will remember, on the other hand, some fairly dreadful, spontaneous speeches; ill-considered wedding toasts might be a common example. But we may also have been present when such remarks have been written out rather fully in advance—to everyone's enormous advantage. The manuscript strategy may seem to clash with the social intimacy of some occasions, but it can also enable a caring speaker to convey an intended meaning in the most faithful way possible.

Using a manuscript also means that the length of a speech can be precisely calculated, whether for a ceremonial occasion, when brevity is demanded, a broadcast situation where precise timing is mandatory or a conference or convention setting, where a chairman's gavel will often be employed, rigorously and vigorously, to keep speakers on schedule. More than that, a speaker can often use the time available most efficiently when phrasing can be carefully chiseled in advance, reducing the risk of unplanned verbal detours—along with the need to omit important material as time elapses.

Working with a text has the additional advantage of what we might describe as "institutionalization"—using the speechwriting and vetting process to achieve consensus and legitimacy within an organization. By asking others to review the text in advance, a speaker can not only protect against careless errors or mischievous misjudgments but can also achieve the "buy-in" of those who feel they have contributed to the final result.

Similarly, a manuscript can help expand, broadly and easily, the size of the potential audience. Releasing an advance text can significantly stimulate press coverage. A prepared text can readily be e-mailed, posted on a website or reprinted for physical distribution. Some speaking occasions are even created to legitimize what has essentially begun life as a written document; a political campaign may release a text with an indication that it was "prepared for delivery" on a given occasion—whether the delivery actually happened or not.

Finally, a fundamental advantage of the speech manuscript is that the speaker need not take the lead role in preparing it. Others can help—and they do—which is why craft of speechwriting has become a professional pursuit in its own right in recent years, performed increasingly by a specialized guild of (presumably) skilled practitioners.

The persistence of simple stage fright contributes to this phenomenon. Even the most confident of leaders can turn anxious at the thought of wandering into the public arena without the security blanket of a well-worded text. The sheer complexity of modern life also contributes to the challenge; it takes more time and greater expertise to get one's arms around many subjects these days. Almost every institution, moreover, is inextricably linked to an ever-wider range of issues, constituencies, markets and settings, which means an ever-growing range of audiences and topics. As an institution's perception of its stakeholders broadens, the challenge of addressing those stakeholders in a thoughtful and competent manner becomes ever more daunting.

At the same time, of course, busy speakers have less time to prepare for such assignments.

If all of these considerations are not reason enough to call for a speechwriter's help, we should also remember that audiences are becoming more demanding. They, too, live busier lives and are more protective of their time. They come to a speech with higher expectations and less patience than may once have been the case. Constant exposure to the most sophisticated, compelling and entertaining messages that Madison Avenue and Hollywood can fashion has undoubtedly had its own impact on public expectations.

In addition, speeches "wear out" more quickly than they once did. Media exposure and public mobility mean that the best lines and thoughts and jokes and stories—indeed, the best speeches—travel more quickly to more ears in more places than ever before. And the Internet compounds this phenomenon. The days are gone when a great orator could build a career around one or two glittering gems of rhetoric, repeated in thousands of settings. Meanwhile, speakers who are inconsistent in the way they address different audiences pay a higher, faster price for such carelessness. The whole world may be listening, which puts greater pressure on today's speakers to be original—and to be consistent.

On every side, then, stakes are rising for public speakers, complicating their preparations and amplifying expectations. And all of this is also happening at a time when writing skills are generally thought to be in decline. It is little wonder that even the most self-reliant of speakers will turn more often to a "wordsmith"—or to a stable of wordsmiths—who can help in preparing a scripted speech.

What this means, of course, is that the realistic answer to the ubiquitous problem of the deadly full-text speech is not to use texts less but to use texts better.

Preparing better texts, in turn, means heeding the distinction between written and spoken communication, which Socrates insisted upon almost two and a half millennia ago—endeavoring to write speeches that will appeal to the ear of the listener who hears them in person and not only to the eye of the reader who sees them on a screen or on paper.

The spoken word and the written word are two very different forms of communication, but we need not be forced into selecting between them, The two approaches, in fact, can be combined to important advantage in a well-crafted speech, enlisting both the power of orality and the advantages of the written document. We can, indeed, try to have the best of both worlds.

THE EAR'S THREE BIG HANDICAPS

What makes the ear so different from the eye in the way it apprehends a speech? Briefly—and very simply—we can point to three factors: the ear is slow, it is forgetful and it is passive.

To begin with, the ear is slow—or, to put it another way, the brain is stupendously fast when it takes in visual data, whether in the form of complex pictures or the plain symbols we call writing. The legendary journalist Walter Cronkite, always proud of his training as a print reporter—would often remark on how everything spoken during his half-hour newscast on network television would fall short of filling even a single page of a print newspaper. Similarly, a professor's normal 50 minute lecture—when captured on paper—could probably be read by a student in 10 or 12 minutes, were it distributed to a class in that way.

The spoken word may have many advantages over the written word as a way to engage audiences, but it is certainly a lot less efficient.

This fact may explain why good print writers are inclined to jam much more information into a speech text than the ear can possibly handle, with its slow absorption rate. And the result is that a good deal of information in a densely written speech often makes very little impact on the brain of even a careful listener, spilling over uselessly instead—much as water does when it is poured too quickly into a narrow funnel.

The ear's second great handicap is that it has a relatively poor memory. When students in a class are asked to recount a favorite childhood memory, the recollections they share are almost always visual—what someone did, how someone looked or moved, what the setting was like, who else was present. Almost never is the favorite memory an aural one.

We often say we remember things in "the mind's eye." We never say that we remember things in "the mind's ear." We say that things go in one ear and out the other. We never say that things go in one eye and out the other. Compared to the eye, the ear has a particularly poor memory.

The third handicap under which the ear labors is its passive nature. It has trouble selecting the messages to which it will pay attention. It is hard, for example, to use one's sense of hearing to focus in on one conversation when a variety of messages are coming in at the same time—at a crowded party, for example. And it is impossible for the ear actually to "rehear" something that has already been expressed—or to leap ahead to a message that has not yet been spoken. Unlike the active "reading" eye, the passive "listening" ear cannot even slow down or speed up the rate at which it absorbs information. When spoken words and the ear are involved, it is the speaker who controls the rate at which information flows. But the reverse is true when one reads what someone else has written.

The eye, of course, skips around and selects routinely—we flip back to the early pages of a novel to remember who is who and who did what. We jump around—and ahead—in reading a written piece of news. We look to see how long a magazine article, or a book chapter, will run, and whether we are likely to fall asleep before we get to the end of it.

But listeners to a speech are trapped in the immediate moment, dependent on a passive sense of hearing.

Given all of these handicaps, it may seem a wonder that we still choose, on so many important occasions, to speak rather than to write. And yet, we do so, realizing, even if we do not articulate the reasons, that orality has some unique offsetting advantages.

But how then can we best go about the task of blending both sets of advantages—preparing written texts that also come alive when they are transmitted orally?

The key consideration is to take account of the ear's built-in handicaps and, as best we can, to compensate for them. Often this will mean translating from "eye language" to "ear language"—much as one translates from English to Italian or Arabic or French. It is not too much to say that the two different writing processes do in fact draw upon differing sets of writing tactics.

WRITING FOR THE EAR: FIVE TACTICAL CONSIDERATIONS

Those tactics can, for the sake of convenience, be discussed under five headings. And, for the sake of even greater convenience (and just for fun), the five categories can all be labeled with a word beginning with the letter *P*.

1. PERSONALITY

The first of these useful labels is the word *personality*—and the case for highlighting this concern has already been made. Aristotle referenced this communicative virtue when he wrote about a communicator's "ethos"—what we today might call his or her credibility—an added persuasive element that is independent of the argument ("logos") or the emotional power ("pathos") of the language itself.

This added ingredient, the power of a living personality, is, of course, the fundamental reason for delivering a message in speech form rather than in written form in the first place! But that added power can have its full impact only if the manuscript allows the personality of the speaker to come through.

At the simplest level, this means that first-person pronouns will appear more often in good speech texts than in texts prepared for the eye. The passive voice will be used less often (or one should say, "we will use the active voice more often!"). And personal anecdotes will play a major role. In fact, one of a speechwriter's more important but sometimes more difficult challenges can be that of "interviewing" his or her speaker in advance of the speech in an effort to elicit such personal material.

Additionally, of course, the speaker's unique vocabulary, cadence, idiom, frame of reference, sense of humor—all that we might mean when we talk about someone's "voice"—are characteristics that a good speechwriter will work to incorporate into a text.

It is never easy, of course, for any person to write in another person's voice. In fact, a hurdle for some writers can be their own sense of inappropriate presumption when they try to capture someone else's expressive style.

To be sure, playwrights and screenwriters do this all the time, but they are usually inventing dialogue for a fictional figure. But speechwriters must come up with words that speakers will publicly claim as their very own, and, until the speaker/writer relationship is well established, the writer undertaking this task may naturally feel some sense of hesitation.

And yet it is important to take the plunge, knowing that even partial steps in this direction can raise significantly the quality of many manuscript speeches. One example, an important rhetorical high point of Richard Nixon's 1968 quest for the presidency, was the closing passage of his convention acceptance speech, when he spoke of the dreams of American children—and remembered how his own dreams had been inspired by the sound of distant train whistles in the night, as he fell asleep in his California home. The approach was suggested by a recently hired speechwriter who had earlier been a high school teacher, William Gavin. It illustrated the ability of a writer, even one who may not have had a close earlier relationship to a speaker, to find a helpful way to personalize a speech manuscript.

2. PACE

The second tactic beginning with a *P* is *pace*. But be careful—this admonition does not refer to the pace at which the speech is delivered. It does not call upon speakers to talk more slowly. In fact, a compelling quality of many good speakers is that they perform with high energy and often at a relatively rapid rate.

What good pacing should mean in this context is the rate at which new information is introduced to the audience—the ratio of ideas to words. And the argument here is that it takes many more words to convey meaning to the ear than it does to the eye. The ear is not only slow, but it is passive. It cannot hit a "pause button," nor can it "rewind," should it misunderstand a point or even daydream for a moment.

This is why former Reagan speechwriter Peggy Noonan urges speechwriters to incorporate "daydream" time into their texts. Speechwriting guru Jeff Scott Cook sums up the point in five magic syllables: "More words per square thought."

This advice is precisely the opposite of the classical counsel given by Professor William Strunk to his writing students a century ago and sanctified for decades in the best-selling volume, *Strunk and White's Elements of Style*. Their core advice: "Omit needless words." The speechwriter's guideline, to the contrary, would say: "Add more words—without adding more ideas." Give the ear of the audience a chance to catch up—to ponder, to question, to react.

This can be done by simple repetition of key lines or by incorporating well-chosen filler words and phrases, rhetorical questions, humanizing asides. We might call this creative verbal "padding," serving to pique interest and reinforce meaning (e.g., "What does this all add up to?" or "Doesn't that sound like a good idea?"). Musicians might call it vamping, filling time in useful ways, before introducing a new element.

Above all, proper pacing means disentangling complex passages—giving each independent element its own showcase, rather than condensing a wide array of information into a compact bundle of dependent clauses.

For example, a good journalist might write: "Last week, campus police raided Founder's Residence Hall, seizing what they called a 'soft-porn ridden laptop,' which contained sophomore Jack Smith's final project in his Art History class project."

Great lead, an editor might say. (And this fact may explain why so many fine journalists have indifferent success when they try their hand at speechwriting.)

A good speechwriter, on the other hand, might translate that material this way: "Let me tell you about an amazing thing that happened on our campus last week. It involved a laptop computer—but not just any laptop. It was loaded with what the police called 'soft-core pornography.' Yes—that's what they called it and that's why they staged a raid on Founders Hall. The student whose computer was taken is Jack Smith. He is a sophomore who is majoring in Art History. And what the police called 'pornography,' he described as a capstone class project. Now what does that tell you about our campus culture these days?"

More words per square thought—in this case, more than five times as many words, conveying precisely the same information, but with a much higher chance that it will be noted, understood and remembered by the listening ear.

Or consider this passage from a speech by former U.S. Senator Bill Bradley, describing a once-hopeful bipartisan commitment to campaign finance reform:

"And then nothing happened. Nothing happened in 1995, in '96 or '97. Nothing happened in '98 or '99. Five years have passed. Two elections have passed. Two sessions of congress have come and gone. And still nothing has happened . . . Why is that? I'll tell you . . . "

Omit needless words? No, in the speechwriting world, effective pacing through the use of a few extra words can be the name of the game.

3. PARTITIONING

The third *P* that deserves more attention in writing for the ear is what we might call *partitioning*—often described as the "structure" or "architecture" of a speech. How does the mind store and recall a variety of details? By categorizing them, and thus integrating a wide array of disparate information into simpler general patterns.

An audience-friendly speech text should ideally go out of its way to identify clearly—and even to label in advance—its most important sections and subsubsections, as it breaks larger chunks of discourse into smaller and more digestible pieces.

The mind works by compartmentalizing. If asked to name our household possessions, we probably would think about them room by room. If the subject were to be professional colleagues, we might categorize them department by department. A strong outline can be to a speech what an organization chart is to a company, helping us make sense of a large array of diverse data.

The architect I. M. Pei has described "user-friendly" buildings as places where people can relate their own location within the building to the layout of the building as a whole. A family walking through a museum, for example, should have a comfortable sense of how much they have seen and how much still lies ahead, so they can plan their time accordingly.

Good speech architecture should similarly give the listeners a clear sense of where they are in the speech, how far the speaker has moved and, roughly, how much more is coming. Readers can easily glance to see just how far along they are in a written text. But the ear, trapped in the immediate moment, cannot do this unless the speaker has provided some useful cues.

This is why it is so helpful to have a clear overall preview—a roadmap—at the start of the speech. A good roadmap, in turn, is ideally followed by useful signposts along the way, indicating just when the process is moving from one stage of the journey to another.

President George W. Bush, especially when Michael Gerson was playing a lead speechwriting role, reflected this concern with rhetorical partitions planted firmly in place throughout a text. In his first inaugural address, for example, the marker was the repeated use of the phrase "America at its best . . . " to introduce varied expositions about American character. Similarly, his 2001 address to Congress following the September 11 attacks was organized around four rhetorical questions, each one introduced by the phrase: "America is asking . . . "

Steve Jobs' reputation as a mover and shaker in the high-tech business world has been echoed by his reputation as an effective speaker—a marketer and an educator. One of his trademarks has been his identification early in his speeches of their overall structure, often involving three or four major points. A prime example (not only of skilled partitioning but also of Jobs' concern for personalizing a speech) is his highly regarded Stanford University commencement address in 2005. He began by greeting the graduates this way: "Today I want to tell you three stories from my life. That's it. No big deal. Just three stories."

Similarly, a typical Jobs opening line at his high-tech conference went simply like this: "There are four things I want to talk about today. So let's get started . . . " And when he moved from point to point, it was usually with the clearest of verbal markers, e.g., "That (the iPhone) was the second thing I wanted to talk about today. Number 3 is about iTunes."

Information and argument can be easily jumbled and lost to memory unless it is firmly anchored in clear architecture. It should not be surprising, given Jobs' extraordinary concern for product design, that his speeches were so clearly and simply structured, not at the expense of detail and nuance, sophistication and complexity, but as a user-friendly way of packaging those qualities.

The mind works better when it can fit what it hears into mental file folders. Just as a book in a library can be lost forever if it is not carefully placed on the right shelf, so even the most careful research or most creative argument can be wasted if it is not linked to a clear and compelling pattern.

Some of these mental file folders are obvious. One can organize discussions around cause and effect, or problems and solutions, or temporal categories (past, present and future) or spatial terms (east to west, top to bottom). A new speechwriting text (2010) by the Washington speechwriting veteran, Robert Lehrman, prominently resurrects the motivated sequence as an organizing tool, based on Alan Monroe's work in the 1930s, through which a speech can be divided into five psychologically relevant steps: attention, need, satisfaction, visualization and action.

Even the most arbitrary divisions can be helpful, e.g., "I want to share with you today three pieces of bad news and three pieces of good news." "I would like to talk about four steps in our crusade: the need to investigate, educate, legislate and litigate." Extended metaphors can be useful, e.g., the country is like a wilderness camper, who needs a compass (the constitution), a map (the budget) and a source of quick energy (a tax cut). And a powerful, related technique is to build a speech around a strong narrative—a story that itself progresses in compelling, memorable stages.

It has been said that the normal speech has three parts: a beginning, a muddle and an end. Turning that muddle in the middle into a memorable and coherent message is the central challenge implied under this the third *P*, what we have called partitioning.

4. PICTURES

If we begin with the premise that visual memory is more powerful than aural memory, it then follows that the ability to use sound to create pictures will be a particularly useful way to meet the speechwriting challenge. *Picturing* is the fourth *P* on our tactical list.

The inevitable truth of oral communication is that too many words do, in fact, go in one ear and out the other. But if those words—having gone in one ear—can etch a mental picture once they enter the brain, then the fact that they also go quickly out the other ear will not be a matter of such enormous consequence. The etching will persist; the mind will retain the picture.

Study upon study has shown how well audiences remember concrete language. The *Harvard Business Review* has reported on how presidential word choice correlates with presidential images. The cited study measured the proportion of image-based words used in major presidential addresses (e.g., "sweat" or "heart" or "path") as opposed to more abstract concept-based words (such as "alternative" or "commitment" or "work"). The conclusion: the higher the proportion of image-based words in their inaugural addresses, the higher the Presidents ranked in various assessments of charisma and leadership. President Carter, for example, called in his inaugural address for a "resurgent commitment to the basic principles of our nation," in contrast to President Kennedy's entreaty: "Let us explore the stars, conquer the desert, eradicate disease, tap the ocean depths and encourage the arts and commerce."

Language that "glows in the dark," or "Velcro" language, to use another appropriate term, is language that illustrates and exemplifies, communicating the abstract by citing the particular. It is often metaphorical, using imagery that can be easily recalled and that then endures to help frame an entire argument. Examples range from Churchill's "iron curtain" to Bryan's "cross of gold," from Eisenhower's reference to falling international "dominos" to Newton Minow's description of U.S. television as a "vast wasteland."

It has been said that Warren Buffett's breakthrough as a public guru, after many years of enormous but relatively quiet investment success, came in 1984, when he built a speech at Columbia University around the vivid metaphor of a national coin-flipping contest. Through the years that followed, Buffet's advice to shareholders continued to reverberate with highly visual similes that appealed to larger audiences. Taking bad investment risks was like kissing a frog and hoping it would become a prince. Lucky investors were like a duck taking credit for rising in the world after a torrential rain had lifted the level of the pond. Heedless investors were like those who insisted on staying at Cinderella's ball until the last moment before midnight, failing to note that there were no clocks in the ballroom. And of course, it is only when the tide goes out that we discover who has been swimming naked.

When Ronald Reagan died in 2004, his son most effectively evoked his father's memory when he talked about the late president's habitual use of the "thumb's up" gesture. Visual imagery, of course, had been central to President Reagan's career as "The Great Communicator," who would himself insist that his texts included challenges such as: "Mr. Gorbachev tear down this wall!" or descriptions of the United States as a "shining city on a hill."

Because visual references are so memorable, they can also be vulnerable to a kind of verbal jujitsu, when the same images are turned against their originator. Mario Cuomo's 1983 response to Reagan's "city on a hill" references, for example, described a "tale of two cities," one of them characterized by the "gutter where the glitter doesn't show." John McCain began to talk midcampaign in 2008 about "Joe the Plumber," but the tactic was blunted as the actual Plumber Joe became more visible. And if the senior President Bush, rather than saying "Read my lips. No new taxes," had instead made a more abstract fiscal commitment (as some of his aides were then urging), his later reversal of that position might not have carried quite so high a political cost.

Presidential rhetoric continues to build around visual imagery. The second President Bush closed his post–September 11 address to Congress in 2011 by reminding his listeners of the personal memories they would always carry of just what they were doing when the World Trade Center towers fell. And "I will carry this," the President concluded, as he displayed and described the police shield of an officer who died in the line of duty on the morning of the attack.

When Barack Obama declared victory on election night in 2008, he described a 106-year-old voter who had "been there for the buses in Montgomery, the hoses in Birmingham and a bridge in Selma." His inaugural address in 2009 concluded by evoking a bitter winter scene during the American Revolution (a riverside camp

In a 2010 speech to the Gates Foundation's Women Deliver conference, Melinda Gates spent her opening minutes describing in vivid detail a ceremony she had witnessed in India, focusing on a young mother, Rukmini, and her six-day-old daughter, Durga. She told of the mother's deep crimson sari, the ceremonial bathing and dressing of the infant, the courtyard where neighbors drummed and danced and sang and prayed—as the mother and child took seven ceremonial turns around the open space before the baby was held aloft, presented to the sun god, in the brilliant light of an Indian late afternoon.

The speech that followed was a long, comprehensive discussion of global challenges in the field of maternal and child health, reminding an influential audience that they, collectively, held the future in their hands. But this sometimes more abstract policy discussion took added power from the visceral impact of the opening narrative.

The time spent in sharing that narrative served, in a sense, as an investment in audience engagement. It also enabled Gates to end the speech effectively by returning to where she had started, reminding her audience, in her final sentences, of a bond uniting them with Rukmini. "For when she hugs her daughter Durga, she also holds the future in her hands."

and blood-stained snow), reinforcing his call for courage in difficult circumstances. In January of 2011, Obama's address following the Tucson shootings centered on vivid images of those who had died in that tragedy, including a 10-year-old victim of the attack now "skipping across rain puddles in heaven."

Even in less elaborate ways, the effective speechwriter will look for ways to employ concrete verbal references—to talk, for example, about Ken, who had his wrench handed to him in Hoboken last Tuesday, rather than dwelling on the "rising unemployment rate among semiskilled workers."

When T. S. Eliot wrote in the last century about the "objective correlative," as a literary theory, he was making a closely related point. The artist, he argued, can create an emotion for an audience not by describing or naming the emotion but rather by "finding an objective correlative . . . a set of objects, a chain of events, which shall be the formula of that particular emotion, such that: when the external facts are given . . . the emotion is immediately evoked."

Another twentieth-century writer, Franz Kafka, once said, "Words are like ice picks we use to break up the frozen seas within us." Finding effective "ice picks" is an increasingly difficult task in a numbed and skeptical world. But it is worth noting that such "picks" will very often involve "pictures."

5. POETRY

There is a fifth label beginning with the letter *P* that can also be a key to effective speechwriting. The word is *poetry*— and its use here refers to the communicative power of "sound" itself—the ability of qualities such as tone, cadence, rhythm, repetition and rhyme to engage the mind and to sustain memory. The sensibility involved in creating such language is essentially a musical one.

The claim was made earlier in the essay that the ear has a poor memory, and generally, that is true. But there is a significant exception to that observation: the power of musical memory. Tunes heard long ago swell up in memory even when we do not want them to; so do verbal passages that are characterized by strong cadences, not so much because of their meaning as because of their music. "Evanescent sound," Walter Ong has written, can create "mnemonically-tooled grooves," which have their own "metrical exigency," adding enormous power to the message they are transmitting.

It is central to the poet's calling to fashion words that have abiding influence because of the way they sound—a sense of "style" is often said to be at the heart of the matter. E. B. White, in his well-read essay on style, illustrated this quality by citing the immortal words: "These are the times that try men's souls." He then observantly wondered as to whether that line would have been remembered for more than two centuries if Thomas Paine had instead written, "Times like these try men's souls." Or "Men's souls are tried by times like these." Or even, "Soul wise, these are troubled times."

The example suggests that the secret of achieving poetic impact may be somewhat elusive—a matter of having an ear for language, which is similar to having an ear for music. Patrick Buchanan (who was a presidential speechwriter before he became a presidential candidate) has described the process of writing in this vein as "going iambic," massaging language until it sounds just right. "They are honed," he said of his most memorable lines, as a writer and a speaker. "You work on it and you work on it and then you get the cheer line."

It also follows from what has just been said that the best way to judge a speech text is not to read it over silently but actually to read it aloud, or, better yet, to have someone read it to you while you put yourself into the mind-set of an eventual audience. Again, a useful classroom technique for conveying this sensibility is to have students write speeches that someone else then delivers, while the writer is required to listen to his or her own words in the same way that an audience hears them, and to note how different they sound when witnessed from the audience's point of view.

In the end, the fundamental point is that a well-honed passage can often linger in the same way that a visual image can endure. One can quote rhetoricians going back to Aristotle or Cicero or Quintilian to make this point about the similarity of visual and musical memory—or one can quote Irving Berlin: "A pretty girl is like a melody / that haunts you night and day. / Just like the strain / of a haunting refrain, / she'll start upon / a marathon / and run around your brain . . . "

This list of tactical considerations—involving personality, pace, partitioning, pictures and poetry—is not intended to be either exhaustive or infallible. Most rules for writers are made to be broken, and the best test for any speech is not "Did it follow the guidelines?" but rather, "Did it work?" On the other hand, the tools described above are, at the very least, techniques of proven value, approaches to writing that have helped many speakers overcome the special challenge of reaching audiences through their ears rather than their eyes.

Used well, they can help create that magical moment when a speaker discovers that the heads before him are nodding in assent, that eyes are brightening and faces are reacting, that hearts are beating and synapses are snapping and that the message is getting through.

AND WHAT IF THE AUDIENCE IS A FAILURE?

That magic, however, happens altogether too rarely. And one sad result is an understandable but pernicious tendency for advocates these days to respond to the problem by blaming the audience.

Well—we say—we are living in a time of fear, selfishness or indifference. A malaise, we argue, has swept across the landscape. Media fragmentation means that audiences are less open minded or not on my wavelength. Or, media clutter means that my message simply got buried.

Or, on a less cosmic level, the jury was loaded against me; or, the new boss never liked me to begin with; or, you know what office politics are like.

Oscar Wilde summed up the great modern excuse when he responded, after being asked how things had gone at the opening of one of his plays in London the night before: "The play? Oh yes, the play was a great success! Unfortunately, the audience was a failure."

It is true, of course, that audiences often let us down, and that communication challenges are steeper than we would like them to be in an often unreasonable world. But we know this going in. And that is precisely what the challenge for communicators is all about—not to write a play that pleases us, or a brief, or a letter, or a press release, or a website, or a public service announcement or a speech. Our challenge, rather, is to connect with the audience we are given.

Where does effective communication really take place? On a computer screen? In the pages of a magazine? In an auditorium? Or a classroom? Or a press release? No—the place where a communication is proven to work or not—the place where it comes alive—is in the mind of an audience. If it does not happen there, it does not happen.

And we should realize from the start that this is often going to be difficult terrain. We know that the audience will often be overloaded, or exhausted, or bored, or biased or living in its own solipsistic universe with a set of preexisting convictions buzzing around their heads, as Bertrand Russell once said, like a swarming pack of flies.

Our challenge as communicators is to find a way to deal with all of that. What we need might well be called a "radically audience-oriented" philosophy of communication. Jeff Scott Cook put it well in an aphorism that might well hang over the desk of every communicator: we should, he says, focus "less attention on what it is that we want to put into the mind of an audience, and more attention on what is already there."

It is not easy to put this admonition into practice. We inevitably get so caught up in what we are thinking—"What am I going to say??"—that our focus insistently swivels back from our audience to ourselves.

Focusing on audiences involves not only knowledge of how they think but also a feeling for how they themselves communicate. It means being able to speak their language, appealing not only to their motives and values but also using images and vocabulary that have power in their own cultures and subcultures.

Understanding an audience requires an unusual ability to stand "on the other person's porch"; to view the world from a variety of perspectives; to walk around, as the old proverb puts it, "in another man's moccasins" and to fashion a speech by thinking not from the inside out but from the outside in.

Among the things that speechwriters are most inclined to forget is the fundamental fact that the audience is going to be listening with its ears, not reading with its eyes.

THE POWER OF TELLING STORIES

A useful way to gather all of these considerations together is to think briefly, and finally, about an increasingly popular way to talk about compelling communication—capsulized by the term *storytelling* (see Chapter 52).

That word has recently been in vogue in the journalism world, for example, to describe a skill that extends across various information platforms. Political observers, similarly, use the term to explain the explosive success of political figures from Barack Obama to Sarah Palin, suggesting that a striking biographical narrative can have unique power.

Similarly, the "case study" method—a staple of legal and managerial education—is coming into greater use in other disciplines, using concrete narratives to illustrate general principles.

At a time when public attention is an increasingly precious commodity, stories can not only cut through the clutter but can stick and stay in public memory, for all of the reasons that have been discussed above.

The power of stories, of course, is profoundly tied to oral communication. It was, in fact, the repetition of powerful stories over long years—in marketplaces and around campfires—that created the first literatures in human history, giving societies a sense of definition, cohesion and identity. This process continued for a long time before the stories were captured and codified and ascribed to individual writers—a Moses or Homer.

It is striking, however, that the renewed interest in storytelling in our day may result from a rather opposite cause, not the scarcity of effective information and cultural reference points but the reverse: a surfeit of communication. Words and images are multiplying in a tide so massive that we are virtually drowning in it. "Information overload," we often call it, and it results in what a recent book by Torbel Klingbert calls "the overflowing brain," where judgment and discretion fades under the assault of "too much information."

How does an effective communicator respond to this challenge? Storytelling—we think and hope—might be one way to do it.

Nicholas Kristof suggested in a 2009 *New York Times* column that the world's most powerful leaders (gathered at that moment at a global summit meeting) would be more likely to leap into a nearby pond to rescue a drowning child then they would be to fulfill humanitarian aid pledges that would save many thousands of lives. "Jumping up and down about millions of lives at stake can even be counterproductive," he contended, citing studies that show a greater public willingness to donate to one needy person than to many.

The literary power of the story of Anne Frank's childhood, *The Diary of a Young Girl*, illustrates this central point. As someone has wisely said, the horror of the Holocaust is best expressed not by saying that six million people died, but rather, that one person died—six million times.

It is a useful thought for speechwriters as they try to communicate, ever more effectively, in an ever more difficult environment, about the great issues of our times.

LINKS TO SPEECHES MENTIONED IN THE TEXT

Warren Buffett, Columbia University Speech on Superinvestors, 1984 (text) www4.gsb.columbia.edu/ null?&exclusive=filemgr.download&file_id=522

Cher at Sonny Bono's Funeral, January 9, 1998 www.youtube.com/watch?v=gdHdd5ejAeY&feature= related

George H. W. Bush, Republican Convention Speech, August 12, 1988 millercenter.org/scripps/archive/speeches/detail/5526, www.amazon.com/FiguresSpeech-Ways-TurnPhrase/productreviews/1880393026/ref=sr_1_11_cm_cr_acr_img?ie=UTF8&showViewpoints=1

George W. Bush, Inaugural Address, January 20, 2001 www.youtube.com/watch?v=rXzgMdj5urs

George W. Bush, Address to Congress Following Terrorist Attacks, September 20, 2001 www.youtube.com/watch?v=ZMj9g6WRLfQ

Mario Cuomo, Democratic Convention Speech, July 16, 1984 www.youtube.com/watch?v=kOdIqKsv624

Roger Ebert, The Act of Speaking, TED Conference, April 14, 2011 www.youtube.com/watch?v=KNXOVpN8Wgg

Melinda Gates, Address to the Women Deliver Conference, June 7, 2010 www.gatesfoundation.org/speeches-commentary/Pages/melinda-gates-2010women-deliver.aspx

Steve Jobs, Commencement Speech at Stanford University, June 14, 2005 www.youtube.com/watch?v=UF8uR6Z6KLc

Richard Nixon, 1968 Republican Convention Speech, August 8, 1968 (text) www.presidency.ucsb.edu/ws/index.php?pid=25968#axzz1NrZk5y00

Barack Obama, Tucson Memorial Service, January 12, 2011 www.youtube.com/watch?v=ztbJmXQDIGA

Barack Obama, Cairo Speech to the Muslim World, June 4, 2009 www.youtube.com/watch?v=B_889oBKkNU

Barack Obama, Election Night Remarks, November 4, 2008 www.youtube.com/watch?v=jJfGx4G8tjo

Barack Obama, Inaugural Address, January 20, 2009 www.youtube.com/watch?v=VjnygQ02aW4

Ronald Reagan, Republican Convention Speech, August 23, 1984 www.youtube.com/watch?v=-Gu-M-lF9Gs

Ron Regan, Eulogy at his Father's Burial Service, June 11, 2004 www.msnbc.msn.com/id/5235593/ns/msnbc_tv-hardball_with_chris_matthews/t/ron-reagans-eulogy-his-father/

DISCUSSION QUESTIONS

1. What is the most memorable speech you have heard recently? Why do think it has stayed with you?
2. Think about some of the least successful speeches you have listened to. Do they have any common failings?
3. What do you think that the scholar, Walter Ong, was getting at when he suggested that oral messages had the added advantage of conveying a sense of "interiority"?
4. How would you summarize the most important reasons that writing for the ear might be different from writing for the eye?
5. Your friend is debating whether to write out in full the toast he is going to give for his parents' wedding anniversary. What pros and cons would you mention for using a script as compared to speaking informally?
6. Does it take something away from the credibility of a speech if you learn that it was written by someone other than the speaker? What might the speaker or the writer have done to help minimize that risk?
7. Do you ever find yourself daydreaming and thus losing the thread of a speech or a lecture? How might a speaker best prevent that from happening?
8. How does the literary theory of the "objective correlative" apply to the art of effective speechwriting?
9. Do you often feel that you are experiencing TMI (too much information) when you hear someone speak? Do you think that others might ever react that way to a speech you are giving? What might be done to prevent such a reaction?

ADDITIONAL READING

Jeff Scott Cook, *The Elements of Speechwriting and Public Speaking* (1996).

Joan Detz, *How to Write and Give a Speech* (2002).

William F. Gavin, *Speechwright: An Insider's Take on Political Rhetoric* (2011).

Robert Lehrman, *The Political Speechwriter's Companion: A Guide for Writers and Speakers* (2009).

Peggy Noonan, *What I Saw at the Revolution* (2003).

Peggy Noonan, *On Speaking Well* (1999).

Walter J. Ong, *Orality and Literacy (New Accents)* (2002).

Arthur Quinn and Barney R. Quinn, *Figures of Speech: 60 Ways To Turn A Phrase* (1995).

William Safire, *Lend Me Your Ears: Great Speeches in History, Updated and Expanded Edition* (2004).

Robert Schlesinger, *White House Ghosts: Presidents and Their Speechwriters* (2008).

William Strunk and E. B. White, *The Elements of Style: 50th Anniversary Edition* (2008).

Maryanne Wolf, *Proust and the Squid, The Story and Science of the Reading Brain* (2007).

50 CHAPTER

WRITING FOR YOUR AUDIENCE MATTERS MORE THAN EVER

George Harmon
Professor Emeritus, Medill School of Journalism
Northwestern University

Earthquakes brought death and destruction to thousands of Japanese, and so an American comedian decided to use Twitter to poke fun at Japan.

In a twinkling, he lost a lucrative gig as the voice of an insurance commercial.

Insensitive jokes that might have worked late at night amid an audience of inebriated Americans fell flat in the sober light of tragedy.

Exit a big paycheck. It flew away in the writing. (Or maybe the self-editing.)

And nearly every week, now that we're all publishers without editors, we see the career of another prominent person destroyed by his own writing.

Big message: writing matters more than ever. Writing for your audience matters more than ever.

Bigger message: everybody needs editing.

Written messages can destroy brands and companies. They can put stock valuations in the tank. They can invade privacy. They can land journalists in libel suits. They can create inaccuracy and demolish a lifetime effort to build trust.

But wait. How can this happen? We're professionals. We were *A* students in writing in middle school. We don't need any help with our writing. How can it be that years later, much to our dismay, our work was substandard in the workplace.

Part of the problem is how we learned. We were taught to write book-length paragraphs and then term papers, with the conclusion at the end. Then we entered a world of short paragraphs with the main point at the beginning.

Part of the problem is editing. Nowhere have we received extensive instruction in editing. Yet most of the errors that occur in written material happen because of poor editing.

Part of the problem is speed. Information hasn't changed; its delivery methods have. The Revolutionary War's decisive battle of Princeton took place around New Year's, and the public learned of it in March. Civil War soldiers were killed in the South three weeks after the armistice at Appomattox. Events of the Vietnam War appeared on TV a week later. Now we see war in real time. And feeds such as Twitter instantaneously brings us news of revolutions, floods and wildfires.

Slower distribution in the past meant that editors often intruded in order to save writers from disastrous mistakes. Today, you are your own editor, instantaneously. And nobody trained you for that.

Think of three distinct and separate functions: writing, editing and rewriting. Do the first two with enough effort, and you eliminate the need for the third. Rewrites cost time, money and morale. Writers hate to be rewritten, especially when the rewriter introduces error. In my decades of working with major corporations, I have yet to see a piece of business writing that editing cannot save. Rewriting just isn't necessary. It happens because people don't want to learn to edit.

What should we do?

USE A WRITING PROCESS

Ask any published writer—someone whose living depends on words—about the toughest problems. The answer normally is organization and writer's block.

Separating your writing into distinct functions helps you stay on message, defeat writer's block, add speed and avoid error.

The writing process refined by the Poynter Institute, a journalism think tank in Florida, has five steps: idea, research, organization, rough draft and edited draft.

1. IDEA/TOPIC

Summarize your point in a single sentence. That sentence summary—what it is all about—should appear in the text in plain language. Web research tells us that readers want the main idea to be in the headline or first sentence.

2. RESEARCH/REPORT

Gather facts to support what the summary sentence says. Here is the place to invest your time.

3. ORGANIZE

Using pencil and paper, quickly create a diagram or story map that pulls together the main idea and its supporting points. One common map looks like a daisy with no more than three or four petals. Off each petal, you can add facts that back up each supporting point for the main idea. In the eye of the daisy is the key idea in three or four words: "Man bites dog."

Another map looks like a squid. Yet another resembles an octopus. Forget about those high-school outlines with roman numerals, *A, B, C, i, ii, iii.*

Ideally your three key words in the eye of the daisy are a subject, a predicate and a direct object. Who does what to whom?

Can't make it too simple? Think of it this way: suppose you had room only for a few words that you could say. Take a look at the *New York Daily News* or the *London Daily Mail* every day. And what if you're in a theater, smell smoke and see a flame licking at a curtain? One word. With an exclamation point.

But, someone might say, "My teachers told me to start with a blank page and be creative." Perhaps that works for some. But other creative professions do organize. A painter usually puts a light skeleton on the canvas to guide the paint. Ad agencies start with a storyboard. So do movie directors and web producers.

A skeleton organization usually unlocks creativity rather than stifles it.

Organization, done this way, can happen in four or five minutes. Once you've done it, set the diagram/map next to the keyboard.

Most importantly, stay on message. We all know the feeling of not being on message. As the saying goes, "An idea ran back and forward in his head like a blind man, knocking over the solid furniture" (F. Scott Fitzgerald).

4. DRAFT

Using the diagram/map, rapidly write the article in one sitting. Here is where your creativity is most useful. You need to figure out the order in which the supporting points will create a compelling story. You need to arrange facts in ways that create smooth transitions.

Best advice: just tell it. Think of Aunt Minnie and just tell her the story. Then walk away from what you have written, for an hour, for half a day. Put some space between you and your story.

5. EDIT

Here you create a final draft. Once you've been away from your story for a while, you have a better chance of returning to it in the disguise of a reader. Here's where you use our six-step editing system. (We'll come to that in a bit.)

We have said that the writing process helps you stay on message, defeat writer's block, add speed and avoid error. It allows you to break your writing into manageable chunks, making your life much easier than starting with a blank screen and pressuring yourself to be brilliant.

When you run into obstacles at any part in the process, you move back one step. That's where your problem resides: Can't organize it? Do more research. Can't write it? Reorganize it. Can't research it? Change the idea to one that's researchable.

Seems simple enough, but then why is our world of communication littered with the following phrases: "this is a nonsmoking floor," "flight attendants, disarm the doors!" "leveraging our core competencies," "please join us in the boarding process" and "this ends the audio portion of your flight."

My answer is bad editing or no editing.

Everybody needs editing. Somebody capable has edited this article, and I'm grateful for that.

The best editors make plenty of mistakes, despite having years of experience. Microsoft Word types "their" when you meant "there." Somebody has to catch it before it reaches a reader. Editors sometimes don't.

When editing your own writing, you face the dilemma of reading across six distinct categories at the same time:

- Trimming words or tightening the sentences

- Substituting for jargon or complexity that we don't need

- Grammar and punctuation

- Style: Associated Press, Yahoo!, University of Chicago or your corporation's

- Facts

- Structure and sense of the article ("storytelling")

If you are like this writer, you find it impossible to think productively about six things at once. Brain research shows that, at most, a human can keep three ideas current, often with one of them dominating the other two. Therefore we find cities passing ordinances forbidding texting while driving. Insurance companies long have been aware that so-called distracted driving is dangerous.

So it is with editing. Distracting yourself will cause trouble. Our editing system asks you to pass through the article six times, each time looking to correct one specific problem. When editing others, particularly those who write for corporations, government and academia, you should make two passes, removing excess words and substituting complicated words with accurate synonyms that are simpler, before you get to the four editing steps. If you are editing a professional writer, you should make the same two passes first, but you will need to make far fewer corrections.

A great advantage of removing and substituting words is that the article becomes easier to read and edit. Readability increases an editor's efficiency.

Removing words, repairing grammar and creating consistent style leaves you with a text that allows you to concentrate on what is most important: accurate facts and a compelling story. Inaccuracy is a source of unending woe. An intriguing story causes people to remember a message.

If we repair a piece of writing, we have done a great favor for our reader.

And *who are our readers*? Just average people: busy, distracted, sometimes using English as a second language. They are trying to do too many things at once. Multitasking probably is a modern myth; research increasingly shows that we are built to adequately perform one task at a time, not many tasks. We try anyway.

Some people disagree with that research. But writers and editors must face the truth: on screen, we are dealing with a distracted, tired reader who is fleeing the page. If you are writing a book, you might receive fewer deficits of attention, but broadband has complicated life for the writer.

Writing for the web casts a wide net for readers. No longer are we producing a brochure that will go to a specific list of people. We may think that we're writing for specific readers on the web, but information tends to wind up in strange places because of the viral way that it spreads electronically. Anything you write for the web can wind up literally anywhere. In reality, we are writing for the whole world, not specific customers. Our job becomes similar to that of the Associated Press or Reuters: communicating with all audiences at once. So it is no surprise that a savvy vice president of a pharmaceutical company once told her communications staff, assembled in one room from around the globe: "I want you all to write like the Associated Press."

(Speaking of inadvertently writing for the whole world, here's what can happen: In 2008, an airline CEO set out to reply to a passenger wanting compensation for a flight delay that caused him to miss a concert. He e-mailed an employee: "Please respond, but we owe him nothing as far as I'm concerned. Let him tell the world how bad we are. He's never flown us before anyway and will be back when we save him a penny." Unfortunately for the CEO, he hit "reply all," and the email went to many people at the company and wound up on travel blogs.)

The Associated Press and its competitors write basic English that creates revenue. They live by the written word. Wire services were global, international, worldwide before any other industry, as early as the Crimean War. They connected well when readers shifted from paper to the computer screen.

What do we know about reading on screen? It is 25 percent slower than on paper. If a reader devotes 5 minutes and reads 100 words a minute, you might need 400 words on screen where you used to write 500 for paper. You need to pare down your sentences to their essentials.[1]

So we must deal with distraction and slower reading. And here comes another obstacle: Websites as yet are not fully designed for reading. Fonts that work well on paper, such as Baskerville or Goudy or Times Roman, became Arial or Helvetica on a screen because of the poor legibility of the cathode ray tube. But eventually all of our screens will have higher resolution than the human eye can perceive. A screen might become easier to read than the printed page, making possible everything that a high-quality printing press does for the reader.

Books, along with most magazines and newspapers, employ designs that benefit the reader. Your favorite paperback novel usually has a little more than one and a half alphabets, or 40 to 50 characters, on a line of type. Depending on the width of a page, the editors achieve that goal by enlarging or reducing the height of the type. We see a lot of 9- and 10-point type (with 72 points equating an inch) in newspapers and magazines with narrow columns). We see a lot of 12- and 14-point type in books. Editors of books want us to avoid swinging our heads and eyes to read a line.

But the common width on a web page is about 80 characters in 13-point type. This is too wide for the eye, and reading slows.

All the more reason to trim words when you edit, right?

Consider the reader's knowledge. Few people know a little about a lot, plus a lot about a little. Most college graduates never again read literature after leaving school. Functional illiteracy varies from 20 to nearly 50 percent, depending on the methodology, the definitions and the sampling areas. Illiteracy is worse than ever, and the United States ranks last in literacy among industrialized nations.[2]

Some retailers believe that 90 percent of consumers' buying research now begins with a bit of research on the web.

Your reader does not know what you think she knows about your topic. The Heath brothers, authors of *Made to Stick*, warn of the "Curse of Knowledge." You know more about the topic than the reader ever will. So use writing and editing to help her.

In a way, except for the delivery system of words, nothing has changed too much. Remember the greats of advertising and public relations: Ivy Lee, Edward Bernays, Arthur Page, Albert Lasker, David Ogilvy and many more giants of communication. They used language to bring into harmony the goals of their clients with those of society. In this century, consumers now control the brands, and word-of-mouth is the most trusted selling tool. If a company's message is unclear or off-target, consumers will rewrite it before forwarding it on the web. That is not to a company's advantage.

Let's go back to the *A* we scored in high school. Whom were we writing for? The teacher alone, not a wide variety of people we wanted to absorb our ideas. And what was the teacher's mission? To help us build our vocabularies and to help us think on paper with more complexity, not to sell a product or tell the news. Our teachers weren't wrong. Their mission was not to train us for industry. They taught complex writing in order to boost vocabulary and critical thinking in hopes of getting us ready for higher learning.

Some of our schoolteachers urged us to write longer sentences containing bigger words. Some of our bosses urged us to use management-speak, in order to sound professional. For example, "we have leveraged our core competencies," or "unparalleled expertise distinguishes [insert company name] as the world's premier provider of international communications solutions to the legal industry." (The company translates legal documents.) Instead we need to keep sentences short and reduce syllables.

In a time when almost all writing is digital, we have more tools allowing us to measure readability or how difficult a passage is to read and understand.

We have reputable resources to help us determine what is correct. Is it *e-mail* or *email*? How does a *flier* differ from a *flyer*? A *hanger* from a *hangar*? A *principal* from a *principle*? For answers, most publishers rely on stylebooks. They include the *University of Chicago Manual of Style* (for books and some magazines), the *Associated Press Stylebook* (for news and for many global corporations) and the *Yahoo! Style Guide* (for digital publishing).

International English is all-important. Variations are huge between American English and British English (two nations separated by a common language, as the saying goes). Neither is identical to international English. Nor are Canadian or Australian English. All are too regional.

Yet they are converging, bit by bit. British writers who work internationally say they are watching British English slowly give way to American English minus its slang. Certainly American English established itself as the lingua franca of the World Wide Web. But it is common to see evidence of non-American editors: Al Jazeera spells it "programme," the *Wall Street Journal* uses "dreamt" in a headline. In England, a singular noun sometimes takes a plural pronoun: "PayPal set up their European headquarters here."

RETURN TO OUR EDITING SYSTEM

Print your story on paper and read it closely. You will catch more errors that way. Use a pencil with an eraser; it allows you to change your mind. Don't look for everything wrong at once. Break your editing into manageable steps and make it into a game.

EDITING STEP 1

Our first task is to trim some words. Let the computer count the words. Your job as an editor is to make it shorter and clearer. Remember, the reasons for that are to increase readability and to make the message fit within the limitations of the computer screen. And more and more people are reading on telephones. That makes trimming more and more important. Follow the advice of Abraham Lincoln: "Be careful that you write accurately rather than much."

But how do we figure out what words to cut?

Words that need trimming fall into generic categories:

Redundancy, or saying the same thing twice, or tautology. Examples: Foreign imports, located at, first priority, sum total, consensus of opinion, most unique, IRA account, HIV virus, one world, plans for the future, active participant, mutual agreement, preboarding, preexisting mutual agreement, tiny paper clip, past history, untimely death, new innovation, decide one way or another, look forward, actual experience, component parts, advance planning, advance reservations, advance warning, all meet together, armed gunman, ATM machine, autobiography of my life, awkward predicament, cease and desist, cheap price, close proximity, commute back and forth, each and every, end result, estimated roughly, filled to capacity, general public, green in color, join together, never at any time, null and void, past experience, poisonous venom, prerecorded, reason is because, regular routine, suddenly exploded, surrounded on all sides, unexpected surprise.

Oxymorons, or self-contradictions. Working vacation, exact estimate, aging yuppie, genuine imitation, incredibly real, larger half, original copy, negative income, instant classic. Cut those phrases to a single word.

Such oxymorons, William Matthews wrote in a poem of that title, "should coat our tongues with ash."

They are a vehicle for humor: Cubs highlights, jumbo shrimp, act naturally, rap music, passive aggression, same difference, elevated subway, completed research, living dead.

Attack the adjectives. If you have more than one adjective in front of a noun, you are creating a potential problem for the reader. The brain likes to think in nouns and verbs. Strings of modifiers before a noun, such as "emerging object-oriented client/server development market," make the eye hunt for meaning.

Nonsense, or language that by itself inspires confusion on a first encounter (think about the person new to English). Trust officer, debt service, assisted living, self storage. "Flight attendants, disarm the doors." "This is a nonsmoking floor."

Empty words. One rule is to take anything you have written, do a word count on your computer and then excise 10 percent of the words. Most of the time, it will read more clearly. You might be able to find 10 percent simply by removing words that add no meaning:

We take the position that; it is our opinion that; a substantial majority of employees; we held a meeting for the purpose of; during the course of our conversation; in the event that we find ourselves in disagreement; at a later date; plans for the future; located at; by virtue of the fact that; at the present time; at this point in time; this policy has been in full force and effect for the period of a year; she is currently working on; take under advisement; a substantial segment of the population; are fully cognizant of; effect the destruction of; we limited our discussion to the basic fundamentals; in this connection, the writer would like to point out the discrepancy that exists; she is a person who does an excellent job as a programmer; the main consideration is a matter of time; please plan in advance to present your recommendations when the next meeting is held; reduced demand for product; period of accelerated negative growth; workshop sessions; public opinion survey; petroleum hydrocarbons; attached hereto; loan obligation; budget forecast; dollar amounts; prompt and speedy; true facts; vitally essential; assemble together; consensus of opinion; endorse on the back; follows after; revert back; free and gratis; new beginning.

EDITING STEP 2

Our second task is to *substitute* clearer words that get rid of jargon, professional slang and obscurity. As James Thurber said, "A word to the wise is not sufficient if it doesn't make sense." Specifically we are looking for the following:

Euphemisms, which are popular ways of avoiding offense, disguising fear or being tactful. They are overused in business, either as camouflage or in laziness. It is okay to avoid mentioning the word *death* in a letter of condolence, but in fiction or factual writing, we do not write phrases such as "Hamlet passed on."

Business terminology often has an aversion to saying what it means. Business and government tend to rename things that have grown unpopular, have acquired nasty connotations or have started to feel old-fashioned. In government, torture became *enhanced interrogation*. Increasing taxes became *revenue enhancement*. A homemade bomb became an *improvised explosive device*. In business, bug killer turned into *pest control* and then *crop protection*. Stockbrokers became *account executives*, then *money managers* and *investment executives*. A stock-market slide became an *equity retreat*. Workers became *partners* and *associates*. Black-and-white TV became *television with nonmulticolor capability*, before it disappeared altogether. A death could be a *negative patient care outcome*.

Your coworker morphed into an *associate*. An explosion in a nuclear power plant became *energetic disassembly*. A life jacket became a *personal flotation device*. Billboards became *outdoor advertising*. A suicide on train tracks became *pedestrian involvement*. Infomercials became *paid programming*. Rich people became *advantaged* and then *high-net-worth individuals*.

No one is fired, laid off, pink-slipped or canned. Big executives resign "for personal reasons." When you are unemployed, you're *in an orderly transition between careers*. It might also be called restructuring, downsizing, separation, corporate leaning, slimming down, rightsizing, demassing, sending people off for opportunities to find the right fit, delayering, eliminating jobs, workforce readjustments, headcount reductions, negative employee retention, being asked to take early retirement, furloughed, requested departures, streamlining, managing our staff resources, surplussing, volume-related schedule adjustment, initiating a career alternative enhancement program, hiring permanent replacements, being given freedom to pursue new career opportunities, employee transition program, buyout, on special assignment, MIA'd (management-initiated attrition) or terminated. The word *terminate* changed quickly. In spy lingo, to assassinate was to "terminate with extreme prejudice."

The so-called political correctness of the 1980s and 1990s was a delight to linguists because of the ingenuity of its euphemisms. Short people became *height-disadvantaged*, bald men became *hair-disadvantaged* or *follicly challenged* (according to comedians), a commune became an *intentional community*. A pet became a *companion animal*, with its owner or master being *caretaker, guardian, steward* or *human companion of the nonhuman companion*. Terrorists who happen to fight on our side are freedom fighters waging wars of liberation for self-determination and human rights.

Scholars of linguistics often oppose such renaming, for research convinces them that language is separate from thought. In other words, removing the word *freedom* from the language still leaves people wanting to be free, whether or not they are allowed to use the term. Dehiring someone will not convince her that she has not been fired.

Inflated labels and titles, or industry jargon designed to enhance importance. More than six decades ago, essayist George Orwell warned in a famous essay called "Politics and the English Language" that bureaucratic language was either a lazy or a false way of presenting truth. The situation is little better today.

Corporations, unconsciously or even deliberately, obscure their messages. Building engineer (once a janitor), content generators (writers), sanitary workers (trashmen), executive assistant (secretary), maintenance engineer (building manager), outside aerial technicians (once utility linemen), delivery ambassadors (or pizza drivers), behavior transition corridor (school hallway), early learning center (nursery school), combustion indicator (fire-alarm bell), movable partition (a door), decorative fixture (a window), equipment access (a manhole), predriven (a used car), automotive inflatable restraint systems (airbags.)

A tourist glides today along the Rhine or the Danube on a flat-bottomed boat, not a barge: "Barge? I paid this kind of money to be on a barge?" *The New Yorker* magazine, which delightfully uses cartoons that lampoon businesses, once published a drawing of galley slaves rowing while their boss, bullwhip in hand, answered a cellular phone: "Human Resources."

Everywhere are business "solutions," 1.12 billion on Google. (No more is a solution a liquid we put into a test tube in chemistry class.)

- "The purpose of the site is to provide a forum for the presentation of solutions to vital concerns in the areas of health, population, development and the environment."

- "Virtualization solutions are built on the most trusted virtualization platform in the world."

- "A complete online store solution that contains both a catalog frontend and an administration tool backend which can be easily installed and configured over a web-based installation procedure."

Oh yes! Give us more solutions! Now that we have so many problems demanding solutions, we're truly in trouble.

Pomposity, which dresses an idea or an event or a product in language that is unnecessarily self-important. The title of a paper delivered to economists can be "Stylometrics: Statistical Evidence on the Decline in the Quality of Writing in the Economics Profession." A communications professor might lecture on "Cognitive Moderators of Negative Emotions: Implications for Understanding Media-Context Effects."

You run a "leading business process outsourcing company offering high-quality and cost-effective data entry solutions to businesses," but what exactly do you do? A potential customer might like to know. What's the color of your auto? Bamboo pearl.

As editors we're on the lookout for phrases such as "adaptive structuration theory" and "interaction effects." If they don't make much sense to the average person, we had better define them in plain language or find substitute words that are clearer.

For instance, "polychromic orientation" seems to be a new way of saying *multitasking*. Could it be that *multitasking* is a buzzword too often associated with teenagers?

Business slang, which works well if all of us are baseball players, MBAs or lawyers. But if we are in a roomful of baseball players, MBAs and lawyers, we soon are asking each other to translate the terminology. We all want to sound as if we are part of an inner circle. So we say bottom line, deplane, prioritize, finalize, optimize, ongoing, colorization and parameter. We no longer find information; we access it. We speak of feasibility, cost-effectiveness, funding, conferencing, partnering, dimensioning, viability, orientation, parameters and ongoing commitments to quality of interfacing that will impact or maximize solutions for our client population.

"The patient did not fulfill his wellness potential," wrote a medic, muddying the fact that the patient died, as well as placing blame firmly on the deceased.

No longer do we call or write you; we "reach out."

A site called American English Online (www.stupaul.net/aeo/now-slang.htm) delights in officespeak, a curious amalgam of sports metaphor, psychobabble and MBA patois:

"Welcome to Chicago! Mr. Johnson's expecting you, but he's not in his office right now. He's huddling with his staff. He's been looking forward to your visit. Let me page him and let him know you're here."

"In the meantime," she continues, "help yourself to some fresh Starbucks." She motions down the hall to a coffee station.

You pass the open door of a meeting room and hear loud voices. "What we've got here," an excited voice says, "is a big glitch. This is a mega account and it's my gut-feeling that we need to do something quick or heads will roll."

Speak the code or you cannot join the tribe. If you do not hit the sweet spot, you might be the fall guy. Let's hope that the customer from Europe or Asia, holding a potential for an order worth millions, can understand what our tribe is saying.

Verbs from nouns, and vice versa. We add *-ize* to a noun and turn it into a verb or a longer noun. Positivize, incentivize, corporatize. We add *-ing* to create a new gerund: multitasking, multiwindowing. "Peter Power of the Dealer Services Department will now also be officing at this address." We add *-tion* to boost a noun. An Army commander wrote a private's parents: "I am pleased to inform you that Michael has arrived safely at Fort Bliss and has begun the soldierization process."

Dictionary.reference.com calls *-ize* "a verb-forming suffix occurring originally in loanwords from Greek that have entered English through Latin or French (baptize, barbarize, catechize)."

Misused or mixed metaphors. A metaphor is a figure of speech comparing a term to represent something it does not literally apply to in order to suggest a resemblance, and it is a grand way of putting the abstract into human terms. Referring to child-worshippers and child-haters, one writer said, "The opposing emotions seem to be stitched together something like the two skins of a baseball."

Often we cannot sustain an image throughout an expression. An executive once told *American Banker* newspaper: "This is probably a watershed in our central bank policy. We've got a whole new ball of wax in monetary policy. The channels are different and we're seeing central bank policy in full light." The dean of a law school told the *New York Times:* "That fly-by-night stuff is nothing but a smoke screen, which they have used to feather the nests of the professoriate which has captured the accreditation process."

Oh my, what wisdom is therein: No one else can make me feel the colors that you bring. Players' names should be entered in numeric order. The ship of state has a difficult road ahead. There's a silver lining in all that red ink. Start at the 40,000-foot level, then drill down. One has to tidy up the loose ends so that changes will ignite our engines of growth. He's a pretty sharp cookie.

Executives in the United States have a habit of mixing metaphors from American sports: We need to move the ball down the field, because one more strike and we're out. That puzzles the international community. Tip to international writers: look for sports metaphors from soccer, horse racing and even golf.

When do we editors decide to let stand a euphemism, a redundancy or any verbal sin? Usually when we have a solid strategy for doing so.

EDITING STEP 3

What's next, now that we have edited our writing so that it will reach more people and provide a clearer message? We need to ensure that we don't have errors in *grammar and punctuation*.

Yes, many people in America have learned English without learning grammar. Fewer have done so in Great Britain. And you don't learn German, French, Spanish or Chinese without knowing your grammar. People who come to the United States using English as a second language easily notice the bad grammar of Americans' speaking and signage. Just ask them, and you will hear plenty of examples.

And, yes, many Americans believe either that punctuation is unimportant or that the rules are up to the writer. It is okay, they believe, to put the quotation marks inside the comma. But thousands of newspapers, magazines and book publishers say it is not okay. Their business models depend partly on the rules of punctuation because clarity and readability create revenue for them. Ernest Hemingway, no fool, was an advocate of standard punctuation. It helped the reader follow his stories better, and his stories earned him a lot of money.

"My attitude toward punctuation is that it ought to be as conventional as possible," Hemingway said. "The game of golf would lose a good deal if croquet mallets and billiard cues were allowed on the putting green. You ought to be able to show that you can do it a good deal better than anyone else with the regular tools before you have a license to bring in your own improvements."

Let's look for *convoluted grammar*. "Richard Dombrowski on the Midwest Stock Exchange floor married Jennifer Smith on September 19." An ad sought to find a Freeze Dried Pharmaceuticals Manager. A letter sent out by an executive search company: "Our firm has recently undertaken a search for the Provost of George Mason University." Had they tried a missing-persons bulletin?

Remove *passive voice*. "Priorities were established," "mistakes were made," "there will be a meeting," "viewer discretion is advised." The inference is that no human did these things. They just happened. Is passive voice part of a late-century American timidity, a way of sliding off the hook? If "mistakes were made," who can come around later and say, "*You* blew it, *you* goofed"? "The girl walked the dog" is always shorter and more direct than "the dog was walked by the girl." The brain thinks in the active voice ("the dog bit me," not "I was bitten by the dog"). But if you write in the passive voice, an editor must rewrite your sentence in order to make it active.

Dead constructions (or "expletives") perform no function in a sentence. They add clutter and rob a sentence of its power by placing emphasis on a weaker verb. Example: "It was their aim to stretch out the time required to take over the market." It is much more direct to write: "They hoped to stretch out the time required to take over the market."

EDITING STEP 4

Once we are done with editing for usage, punctuation and grammar, we can turn to *style*. And by style, writers don't mean Jane Austen style or Edgar Allan Poe style. They mean, "Set me a manual that makes our word usage consistent through an entire document."

Is it 12 midnight, 12:00 a.m., 12 a.m., 12 AM, 2400 or just midnight? Is it 9%, nine per cent or 9 percent? Your style guide will tell you. They are all excellent: Associated Press, Chicago Manual of Style, Yahoo!, New York Times and so on. They keep you consistent. Most corporations and public relations agencies have adopted the AP, augmented by small guides pertaining to a specific company. But Yahoo!'s digital-leaning guide may make inroads as years go on.

Check for style as you proofread, too. Microsoft Word's autotype function can introduce error by using wrong words and homonyms: *peak* for *peek*, *there* for *their*.

A style guide will help correct *overcapitalization*, or the habit of capitalizing common nouns à la the King James Bible, Thomas Jefferson and battalions of lawyers. "Please complete this Retainer Agreement." We know from surveys of readers that overcapitalization and acronyms are a barrier to readability.

And a style guide will convince us to place a long title in lower case behind the name instead of "in charge of the project is Executive Vice President and Director of Planning T. Bradford Hutchins III." Cut down on the capital letters and Mr. Big's name will jump out at the reader. This also holds true for products and brand names.

Why argue about what to capitalize when the answers are so readily available in style guides and dictionaries? Communications professionals roll their eyes in agreement when you ask whether their companies' top executives spend too much time agonizing over what to capitalize.

EDITING STEP 5

Once your style is in order, you *check the facts*. You may be sure that the Great War ended in 1919, but check it anyway. Put a small check mark above each fact, just as a fact-checker might do at *The New Yorker*.

EDITING STEP 6

Now you have reached the most important and most creative part of writing and editing: storytelling. Keep in mind that readers prefer narrative format to exposition or description. If there is a way to build part of the article into narrative ("here is how the product emerged"), help it along with a little editing to build sequence or suspense. Now, finally, you are actually working instead of playing word games. Now you are ready to sell the piece of writing to a reader.

Finally we are nearly ready to publish. We need a *headline*.

We know from Eyetrack research that the eye looking at a computer screen goes right away to the headline and the first sentence, not to the photo or the ad or the logo. That may be because we think of the Internet as an information medium. We go there to find something out. Readers' eyes travel the screen in a far different way than they read a page of a book.

Heat maps of the eye's travels show that we read the screen in a vague semblance of an *F* pattern, spending most energy on the headline and first sentence (See Figure 50.1). We also know that people average only a few seconds on any Web page they access, and that if they stay on the page, they will give you little more than four more seconds for every hundred words that you give them.

So the headline is crucial. It needs to echo the heart of the story, using just a few words. From CNN: "What Syria's neighbors are thinking." From Kraft Foods: "Budget deliciously." From a Toyota magazine ad showing workers on an auto line: "Filled with pride."

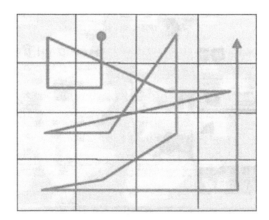

FIGURE 50.1

How the Eye Tracks on a Computer Screen. www.poynterextra.org/eyetrack2004/main.htm

It is ironic that some users of Twitter feel constricted by the limit of 140 characters, when most news organizations are able to create headlines in 35 or 40 characters that convey more information than a tweet.

Businesses ought to employ headlines that make use of the powerful marketing words, just as news organizations start with *how* or *why* if the story warrants that approach. Think about the power of these words: *you/your, health, easy, free, new, now, save, benefit, faster, money, safe, fun, only.*

What words are likely to get a press release picked up by the media? Try these: *money, fat, cancer, sex, safe, easy, secret, green, environment.* If you want regional coverage, try words of major interest locally, such as *mountains, fishing, seashore.*

WHAT IS THE PAYOFF FOR SO MUCH ATTENTION TO DETAIL?

Good writing and editing means good business. Think of the importance of high-quality writing for public relations. Consider how the shopping networks create narratives for products ("But wait . . . There's more!"). Writing alone built direct-response marketing, now a $300-billion-a-year industry.

Look at some of history's great slogans:

Have you driven a Ford lately?
BMW: The ultimate driving machine.
Single malt: unnecessarily well made.
Plop, plop, fizz, fizz, oh what a relief it is (Alka-Seltzer).
Betcha can't eat just one (Lay's Potato Chips).
Gets the red out (Visine).

All of these go to the heart of the product and make money for the corporations.

The top companies tend to communicate clearly. Among the world's most valuable brands are Apple, Microsoft, Coca-Cola, IBM, Google and McDonald's, all of which pay attention to their writing.

THE WRITING PROCESS AND THE EDITING SYSTEM CAN HELP YOUR CAREER

Being identified as a capable writer can get you a job or a raise. Over and over, surveys have shown that writing is the no. 1 skill that corporations look for. Typical of those who hire is Barry Salzberg, who became global CEO of Deloitte Touche Tohmatsu in 2011: "I look for speaking and writing skills, values and experiences . . . I like the person who has communication skills."

A study once showed that Fortune 500 CEOs were exceptionally clear writers and speakers. Dow Chemical once stated: "Our whole philosophy is that the articulate individual is promotable." Some CEOs won't read a memo longer than a page. A vice president of a large advertising firm said: "We look at how much attention a person pays to detail. Things like grammar, spelling, and mechanics mean a lot to us. We figure, if the person can't accomplish these things, how can we expect him or her to move on to the bigger job?"

Joel Raphaelson, once creative head of Ogilvy & Mather, said: "As people advance in their careers, they have to make recommendations. The recommendation may be a good idea, but if it isn't made in writing in a way that's clear, it's less likely to get acted on. There is a connection between expressing ideas well, forcibly, and clearly in writing and getting ahead."

Increasingly, corporations are testing the writing abilities of applicants. Unfortunately for some job-seekers, corporate tests tend to focus largely on editing skills: grammar, spelling, punctuation and proofreading. Someone who writes "I am flying to NYC to do final interview for biggest steal company" is probably going to be disappointed.

Less-than-careful writing and editing can get you sued. The national advertising division of the Council of Better Business Bureaus, a self-regulator for ads, says formal complaints have grown steadily since the advent of the Internet. United Parcel Service drew a lawsuit from FedEx for saying it had the "most reliable" service, because that claim relied on old data. GE had to pay $11.4 million for saying its X-ray product was safer than a competitor's.

LET'S PUBLISH

When you're done editing and headlining the piece, let the computer do a word count and a grammar/punctuation check. It should then give you readability scores. If sentences average 17 words or less, comprehension is about 85 percent.

Readership measures such as the fog index have some value. The index, or Gunning readability formula, measures the reading level, by grade. Some fog index levels: Michigan official driver's manual, 6.7; King James version of 23d Psalm, 9.3; federal income tax instructions, 9.3; instructions on a frozen turkey dinner, 10.3; *Time* magazine lead article, 12; a computer manufacturer's press release, 21.6.

You want to shoot for grade levels between 9 and 12. Why, when so many readers have college degrees? People read more slowly on screen, they might be tired or distracted or they might use English as a second language.

Many readability formulas exists: Flesch Reading Ease, Fog Scale Level and Flesch-Kincaid Grade Level, FOG, SMOG, Powers-Sumner-Kearl, FORCAST, Spache, Dale-Chall and Fry Graph. We like them all. Together they tell us that you can reach more readers by shortening sentences and using simpler words. But this is not "dumbing down." One could argue that the more complex an idea, the simpler should be its language. For illustration, see the canon of great writers whose works have survived centuries.

Go to "Tools" in Microsoft Word and run through the grammar check. If you don't get a readability formula along with the word count, go to "Preferences" and check the box under "Spelling and Grammar" to "Show readability statistics." How do you measure up?

This chapter, for instance, has an average sentence length of 14 words, 2 percent passive sentences, a Flesch reading ease score of 57 and a Flesch-Kincaid grade level of 8. Those scores are sufficient for me. If they were too weak, I could edit some more to improve them.

It's interesting to look at the statistics that Amazon provides for some of its books. James Joyce's *Ulysses* is said by all to be difficult reading, yet its grade level is 9. It's common to find books on communications that are written at grade level 22, which is so high as to be meaningless. My trouble with reading Joyce is not his sentences or his word choices; it is that the many references to mythology, history, literature and so on make the reader wish for an entire encyclopedia in his head.

Finally—excuse my digressions—your article is written, edited and ready to be "published" out there in the ether.

But first ask yourself some basic questions, or the readers will ask them for you because you have begged them to respond on your website.

Have I explained, explained, explained myself clearly enough? Ideally our 17-year-old niece should be able to understand what we are saying.

A CHECKLIST FOR THE WRITER

1. Spelling of proper names. Start at the bottom and work upward, looking at words with capital letters.
2. Clarity. Make sure that the identifications are correct for each difficult term.
3. Message. Does the piece stick to a single unifying point?
4. Sound. Find a corner to yourself and read the piece aloud.
5. Spell check, nineteenth-century version. Read sentences back to front. Or run your cursor from bottom to top. This will cause you to examine each word.
6. Fat. Find out how to use the word count function on your computer's word-processing program. Measure the piece, then cut 10 percent. If you can't, give it to a colleague to cut.
7. Directness. Search for the passive voice and remove it.
8. Distance. Remove yourself from ownership. Walk away from the piece for a while. When you come back to it, try to look at it as a reader would.

Have I cut the number of words to the minimum? It's possible to do so, and that's the secret of many immortal writers. For economy of words, we can find inspiration from people such as the great poet Christina Rossetti (1872):

In the bleak midwinter
Frosty wind made moan,
Earth stood hard as iron,
Water like a stone;

Do I understand how much the audience is likely to know, and want to know, about my topic? For instance, if I am writing about government, I must keep in mind that 61 percent don't know how long a U.S. senator serves and 29 percent don't know the name of the current vice president. We often overestimate the stock of readers' information while we underestimate their intelligence. Readers may be poorly informed about current events, but they are not stupid. They don't mind being reminded of simple facts, and they don't mind something that is easy to read.

Have I told an interesting story? After all, that is why so many mystery stories sell so well and why we watch police dramas on TV.

If I blew it completely, am I willing to take measures, such as the writing process, the editing system, the readability measurements, to make sure it does not happen next time?

Have I told the story to the reader, rather than to myself or to my boss? If we write and edit to gain approval from the boss rather than the customer, we have a problem. They should be in sync.

Clear writing is not easy. It takes practice, practice, practice. It takes trips to the dictionary and to usage books. According to the supersalesman Dale Carnegie, in *How to Win Friends and Influence People*, "It was easier to make a million dollars than to put a phrase into the English language."

Take off your business costume and meet the customer face to face. Said the late Abbie Hoffman, a wise if ineffective "revolutionary" in the 1960s: "Never impose your language on people you wish to reach."

SIX TIPS TO REMEMBER

1. Watch out for piling adjectives before the noun, because the reader has to slow down in order to avoid losing the noun.
2. Avoid using the same word twice in a sentence or a paragraph.
3. Look for new action verbs for the beginning sentence. Having your company's press releases "announce" this and "announce" that makes it seem almost as if the company doesn't do anything but proclaim.
4. Try to cut down on the passive voice. "The product engineering department has also been restructured" could be "the product engineering department also has a new structure."
5. Police the jargon. "Growing" sales and "market share" are jargon that ought to stay inside a company.
6. Avoid acronyms, overcapitalization and all-cap headlines. Many corporations are settling arguments over trivial matters by adopting the Associated Press Stylebook. Their rationale: it's logical, and it's widely accepted.

MORE QUESTIONS FOR THE WRITER

- Is the first sentence intriguing, interesting, accurate and appropriate?

- Have I put the facts in logical and readable order?

- Do my transitions eliminate jolts as the story shifts from one topic to another?

- Do any paragraphs need separating? Combining?

- Do the sounds of the sentences vary? Is the voice of the writer consistent?

- Have I slipped unnecessarily into jargon or cliché?

- Can I trim any fat?

SELF-TEST ON USAGE, STYLE, GRAMMAR AND PUNCTUATION

(Each of the following sentences contains at least one error. *You can rearrange a phrase, but don't rewrite any sentence*.)

1. William L. Peterson, chairman of Amazing.com Corp., told securities analysts Friday morning that he intends to retire "within five years, for sure".

2. A Wall Street report which gave projections of future Amazing.com Corporation earnings was criticized quite harshly last week by both of the woman that serve on the board, Peterson said.

3. As the directors scanned the report, there was a groaning noise made by one of the women.

4. Shares of the company were unchanged as the Dow Jones industrial average plunged to it's lowest point in three years as a result of the mornings' profit taking.

5. President Thomas B. Clark said that board members that attended last week's special meeting had felt badly about the company's performance.

KEY TO QUIZ ON USAGE, STYLE, GRAMMAR AND PUNCTUATION

1. (2 errors) William L. Peterson, chairman of Amazing.com Corp., told securities <u>analysts</u> Friday morning that he intends to retire "within five years, for <u>sure.</u>"
   • Typo on "analysts"
   • Quotes go outside a period or comma; do not remove quotes because it changes meaning

2. (6) A Wall Street report <u>that</u> gave projections of ~~future~~ Amazing.com <u>Corp.</u> earnings was criticized ~~quite~~ harshly last week by both of the <u>women</u> <u>who</u> serve on the board, Peterson said.
   • Restrictive clause uses "that"
   • Projections automatically look at the future; redundant
   • AP style abbreviates "corporation," although the company does not

POPULAR BOOKS FOR COMMUNICATORS

The Associated Press Stylebook and Libel Manual
It contains most of the answers you will need, briefly. (Sample entry: "adviser. Not advisor.") Also included are a punctuation guide, a libel manual and proofreaders' marks.

Bruce, Harry J., Russel K. Hirst, and Michael L. Keene, *A Short Guide to Business Writing*
An excellent guide to writing memos, reports and speeches.

Burchfield, R. W., *The New Fowler's Modern English Usage*
For more than a century, writers have turned here to settle bothersome disputes of grammar.

Dunsky, Marda, *Watch Your Words*
The longtime editing teacher at the Medill School created the shortest, cheapest and arguably the best grammar book alive. It is filled with self-tests, answers provided.

Fogarty, Mignon, *Grammar Girl's Quick and Dirty Tips for Better Writing*
She was a technical writer who began doing five-minute podcasts. Now she is an institution.

Kessler, Lauren, and Duncan McDonald, *When Words Collide: A Media Writer's Guide to Grammar and Style*
The authors provide a grammarian's bible, well indexed, with self-tests and lists of worrisome notions such as the words most commonly misspelled by journalists.

Lutz, William, *Doublespeak* and *The New Doublespeak: Why No One Knows What Anyone's Saying Anymore*
Using seeds planted half a century ago by Orwell, this Rutgers professor skewers the masters of the obtuse phrase: educators, bureaucrats and business executives.

Maggio, Rosalie, *How To Say It*
She chooses the correct word, phrase, sentence, paragraph or sample letter for 40 types of correspondence, from fundraisers to thank-yous.

Murray, Donald, *Writing for Your Readers: Notes on the Writer's Craft from the Boston Globe*
Tips and more tips on how to add "vigor, clarity and grace" to writing.

O'Conner, Patricia T., *Woe is I*
Here is the grammarphobe's guide to better English by using plain English.

Rayfield, Robert E. et al, *Public Relations Writing: Strategies and Skills*
Designed as a textbook, it provides an overview of the public-relations practitioner's duties and many practical examples. The writing chapters are solid and augmented by a grammar section.

Sabin, William, *Gregg Reference Manual*
A comprehensive guide to grammar and usage for the office worker.

Strunk Jr., William, and E.B. White, *The Elements of Style*
This old favorite, in print and popular for decades, is the benchmark for books on writing. Professor Strunk's one-time student was E.B. White, famous for writing *Charlotte's Web*.

Truss, Lynne, *Eats, Shoots & Leaves: The Zero Tolerance Approach to Punctuation*
The author had a lot of fun in writing about punctuation, and her book became a best seller in England and then the United States.

WEB WRITING

www.useit.com/papers/webwriting is a great site.

Yudkin, Marcia, *Persuading on Paper: The Complete Guide to Copy That Pulls in Business*
She helps writers of sales letters, ads and press releases.

Zinsser, William, *On Writing Well*
A hot seller for years, this guide to writing nonfiction covers business, technical, science, criticism and sports writing as well as general principles. Lively and entertaining, Zinsser issues pithy guidelines such as "Clutter is the disease of American writing" and "There's not much to be said about the period except most writers don't reach it soon enough."

Zinsser, William, *Writing to Learn*
Writing *is* thinking.

- "Quite" is a qualitative adjective that adds virtually no meaning (also "rather," "very")
- Humans are involved, so use personal pronoun
- An extra point for getting rid of passive ("drew harsh criticism from")

3. (2) As the directors scanned the report, ~~there was a groaning noise made by~~ one of the women groaned.
   - Use of "there was" constitutes a dead construction
   - The verb should not be in passive voice

4. (3) Shares of the company were unchanged as the Dow Jones industrial average plunged to its lowest point in three years as a result of the morning's profit-taking.
   - Use of "its" vs. "it's"
   - Misplaced possessive
   - Compound noun needs hyphen

5. (3) President Thomas B. Clark said ~~that~~ board members who attended last week's special meeting had felt bad about the company's performance.
   - No "that" necessary after "said," although used after a word such as "commented"
   - Personal pronoun
   - "Feeling badly" might have something to do with one's fingertips; "bad" is one's condition

NOTES

1. Jakob Neilson, http://www.useit.com/alertbox/9703b.html.
2. 2003 National Assessment of Adult Literacy, U.S. Dept. of Education, 1992 National Adult Literacy Survey, U.S. Dept. of Education, Statistical Abstract of the U.S., CIA World Fact Book.

ADDITIONAL READING

Bruce, Harry J., Russel K. Hirst, and Michael L. Keene. *A Short Guide to Business Writing*. Englewood Cliffs, NJ: Prentice Hall, 1995. Print.
Dunsky, Marda. *Watch Your Words: The Rowman & Littlefield Language-Skills Handbook for Journalists*. Lanham, MD: Rowman & Littlefield, 2003. Print.

Fogarty, Mignon. *Grammar Girl's Quick and Dirty Tips for Better Writing*. New York, NY: Henry Holt and Co., 2008. Print.

Fowler, H. W., and R. W. Burchfield. *The New Fowler's Modern English Usage*. Oxford: Clarendon, 1996. Print.

Goldstein, Norm. *The Associated Press Stylebook and Libel Manual*. Reading, MA: Perseus, 2000. Print.

Krug, Steve. *Don't Make Me Think!: A Common Sense Approach to Web Usability*. Berkeley, CA: New Riders Pub., 2006. Print.

Lutz, William. *Doublespeak* and *The New Doublespeak: Why No One Knows What Anyone's Saying Anymore* New York, NY: HarperCollins, 1996.

Maggio, Rosalie. *How to Say It: Choice Words, Phrases, Sentences & Paragraphs for Every Situation*. Paramus, NJ: Prentice Hall, 2001. Print.

McDonald, Duncan, Lauren Kessler, and Tracy Ilene Miller. *Exercises Book: When Words Collide: A Media Writer's Guide to Grammar and Style*, Eight Edition. Boston, MA: Wadworth/Cengage Learning, 2010. Print.

Murray, Donald Morison. *Writing for Your Readers: Notes on the Writer's Craft from the Boston Globe*. Old Saybrook, CT: Globe Pequot, 1992. Print.

O'Conner, Patricia T. *Woe Is I: The Grammarphobe's Guide to Better English in Plain English*. New York, NY: Riverhead, 2003. Print.

Rayfield, Robert Emmett. *Public Relations Writing: Strategies and Skills*. Dubuque, IA: Brown & Benchmark, 1995. Print.

Sabin, William A. *The Gregg Reference Manual*. Boston, MA: McGraw-Hill, 2001. Print.

Strunk, William, and E. B. White. *The Elements of Style*. Boston, MA: Allyn and Bacon, 1999. Print.

Truss, Lynne, and Bonnie Timmons. *Eats, Shoots & Leaves: Why, Commas Really Do Make a Difference!* New York, NY: G.P. Putnam's Sons, 2006. Print.

Yudkin, Marcia. *Persuading on Paper: The Complete Guide to Copy That Pulls in Business*. New York, NY: Plume, 1996. Print.

Zinsser, William Knowlton. *On Writing Well: The Classic Guide to Writing Nonfiction*. New York, NY: HarperCollins, 2006. Print.

Zinsser, William Knowlton. *Writing to Learn*. New York, NY: Harper & Row, 1988. Print.

51

C H A P T E R

STORYTELLING
All Stories are True

Emma Caywood, MLIS
Storyteller and Storytelling Consultant

One of the fundamental, yet unspoken, truths about stories is that most people find stories with lessons or morals incredibly annoying. Ask any child what he thinks of the story "The Boy Who Cried Wolf" or "The Tortoise and the Hare." For that matter, ask any adult what he thinks of *Who Moved My Cheese*. What these stories have in common is that they exist primarily to teach a lesson, rather than to connect one human being to another. Their characters are badly developed and aren't designed to make you care about them. They exist to propel the message onto the listener. This is the kind of story that bad managers will memorize and recite to help motivate their worker bees. (Once upon a time there was a bee in a hive. . .)

This is not the kind of storytelling that this chapter will be about.

There are also many storytelling business books on how stories can be used effectively in organizational storytelling and how the perfect story can be found to make your staff work harder and understand the company mission. I heard a talk about six years ago touting storytelling as the new PowerPoint presentation. That is to say that storytelling can be the new vehicle to make your talks engaging and interesting. If you want to learn more about how storytelling can create company unity, motivate change and push your company forward as an organization, I highly recommend reading *Squirrel Inc.: A Fable of Leadership through Storytelling* by Stephen Denning, once you finish this book. It will teach you the art of organizational storytelling, all wrapped within its own story about a company of squirrels making changes in their nut-gathering policies.

But this is also not the sort of storytelling detailed in this chapter.

This chapter will focus on how to use your company's or your customer's stories to better market and promote your product or service. While in organizational storytelling, you can get away with stories that have an obvious moral, because employees are being paid to listen and expect that the person has a thesis and therefore the thesis can be more thinly veiled; customers (or potential customers) have a right to walk away at any point. They need more from a story to keep listening.

And how do we find that "more"? What are we trying to get out of these stories?

STORYTELLING?

The first thing we need to do is define what we mean by storytelling. Storytelling, in my view, is the bestowing of events from one person to another with the use of words, sounds and sometimes images. Oral stories are generally made up on the spot, calling the teller to build on a basic framework with interesting details improvised during the telling. Storytelling can be used to entertain, impart wisdom and pass on values or culture. For the purposes of this chapter, we're going to look at true, and truth-inspired, events with a beginning, middle and end and characters that reflect back upon your brand culture. Storytelling is the oral or written telling of these events and characters.

Storytelling is one of the oldest art forms, along with cave paintings. Before the written word, storytellers and poets would travel across the lands to tell stories from village to village. It is the common thread that unites us. Some universal stories, like Cinderella, pop up in most cultures across the world. We are the collection of stories that we tell about ourselves, about our families and about our culture. If you make a product or perform a service that people find useful, desirable, aspirational, nostalgic or essential, chances are your company features in the self-defining stories of your customers or potential customers. This chapter will show you how to seek out customer stories, identify a good customer story, develop it and use it to create both potential profit and a feeling of goodwill toward your company.

Your story is what sets you apart from other businesses that serve the same purpose as yours. Your origin story, your customer stories and the stories that you create every day just by existing are what make your company unique. If this story can be infused into every interaction had with the public, it can personalize your business and make customers not only feel that your company is the right company to be dealing with, but also make them feel good about that interaction.

THE HISTORY OF BUSINESS STORYTELLING

Once upon a time, when you purchased something, you knew where it came from. Produce came from a certain farmer, you knew the man who owned the cows that gave you the milk, and the fabric you bought off bolts in the dry goods store were made by someone. Everyone knew his neighbor, and nothing was produced by child labor in China.

That's a nice story, isn't it? Perhaps it was true, for some people, at one point. All this was, of course, lost due to industrialization and free trade. But the stories were imbedded with the products in such a way that no storytelling consultant was needed to find the stories in the products. They just were their stories. Times change, the world became a global market and people became divorced from the producers of the physical things in their lives. Much was gained, but that connection was lost.

Some of the first companies that realized that engaging customers with the concept of story were the back-to-the-earth companies that wanted to appeal to people's desire to know their neighbors and go back to the land. Celestial Seasonings, a tea company headquartered in Boulder, Colorado, has always been a storytelling company. From the beginning, with the story of its roots (as a collective who picked free-growing herbs off the side of hills, tied them in silk pouches and sold them at farmers markets, according to the fictional story told on most of their tea boxes), Celestial Seasonings has been a company that makes their customers feel connected to them and to the land. Each of their teas has a fictional story that it tells or alludes to on the box. They continue to engage with story using social media, telling the stories of how certain teas got their names:

> While touring our tea production facility, 11-year-old Danielle Ballard—an aspiring ballerina with a passion for The Nutcracker—left her idea for a tea called "Nutcracker Sweet" in our suggestion box. It was a great idea, and we made it into a great tea. Danielle's an adult now, but the tea she inspired many years ago is still helping to make the holidays a little more special.[1]

Not only is this tea capitalizing on the story of *The Nutcracker*, but it also has its own "origin story," that of a young, aspiring ballerina who loved *The Nutcracker* and loved Celestial Seasonings Tea. Celestial Seasonings communicators were pioneers both in finding a story for every one of their products, but also in allowing the customers to join in the storytelling.

Toy companies have always been good at telling stories that will make kids want their products, but most of them never considered creating a two-way conversation. In 1986, the Pleasant Company (before selling to Mattel) created the American Girl dolls and brought the dolls to life with a whole series of short historical fiction books telling about the lives of these dolls. The clothes, furniture and other accessories (sold separately) are also all featured in the books. However, they did not just monologue stories to go with their products. In 1992, they started a magazine called *American Girl*. In addition to the short stories featuring the doll characters, they also had a "Help Wanted" section in which readers could submit stories or ideas for print.[2] They later added a "True Stories" section where customers and readers could have their stories of a challenge or interesting event from their own lives put into print.

Wheaties' marketing campaigns have relied on the stories of athletes since 1934, when Lou Gehrig was first pictured on their box to go with their marketing slogan: "The Breakfast of Champions." They have featured athletes and other heroes, and their stories, on their boxes ever since. In 1984, Wheaties sponsored a nationwide "Search For Champions," looking for sports heroes that hadn't yet made the national news. Many submitted, but Chris Spielman, a shy 16-year-old rising senior football star from Massillon, Ohio, was entered by a local booster and ended up being the first high school student to ever be on a Wheaties box.[3] Wheaties knew that the only thing better than telling the stories of a famous sports hero on the boxes of their product was telling the story of a future sports hero, a customer, on their boxes.

ALL STORIES ARE TRUE; SOME STORIES ACTUALLY HAPPENED

But before we get into customer stories, the concept of origin stories should be discussed. An origin story can be very powerful. Every employee should know how their company was founded so that they can truly understand their company's core values. This is especially true in newer companies: those whose values haven't had time to drift from the impetus for the company. Every company has its own potential marketing goldmine (or possible PR nightmare) in its origin story. The idea of the origin story can be seductive, but dangerous. If your company really has a folksy or pastoral or "by accident my product was created and wasn't that lovely" story, then it's a great way to create a feeling of loyalty in your customers. When you hear that Wheaties was created "when a Minneapolis health clinician accidentally spilled some wheat bran mixture on a hot stove, creating tasty wheat flakes,"[4] it does make you feel good inside. Is it true? If it is, then that's a great story. If not, then it's debatable whether company origin myths are good substitutions for company origin stories.

True and heartwarming stories are the best stories to tell. Inogen One is a company that makes portable oxygen concentrators. They began when one of the company's co-founders, Alison Perry, made a nine-hour trip over winter break with her grandmother Mae, right after she had been prescribed oxygen therapy. She realized that her grandmother needed a better way to travel, without worrying about when she would run out of oxygen.[5] Inogen One's website has Mae's story and picture, a story that begins with a problem, leads to the creation of the product and company and ends with Mae's life made better by the product. You can find this story at www.inogenone.com/the_story_of_mae. This is almost the perfect example of an origin story and a customer story meeting. You can't buy this sort of PR. They're lucky such a great story happened.

There's a saying in storytelling that "all stories are true; some stories actually happened." This is a lovely statement with which I agree, but we must define what we mean by that statement.

There has been much reported about the eBay creation story, and whether it is better classified as a creation myth than as a creation story. As one version of the story goes, Pierre Omidyar's fiancée Pam Wesley liked collecting Pez dispensers. They had been at a store in France, but when they got 100 miles away from it, she regretted not buying a few of the dispensers that she'd rejected. They started talking about how it would be wonderful if there could be a way to access every resale store and garage sale in the world from your home computer. This is the story that PR manager Mary Lou Song gave to the press in 1997. The press ran with it, as the press always does with a great story. In an e-mail to me, she explained that "in the early days of eBay, people would ask, How did Pierre come up with the idea? I always said that Pierre had an interest in economics and perfect markets. The first item he listed was a broken laser pen, and he was excited to discover that there could be a market for something like that. Usually, this explanation would just provoke more questions about why anyone would want to use eBay for broken things. And that's when I would share Pierre's story about Pam, Pez and France. Pam and Pez was never the sole reason that Pierre built eBay. But I believe that it was just one more proof point for him about why it would work."[6] The Pez story, though not the singular event that caused the creation of eBay, was both part of the inspiration and a good story that the press could run with. In fact, there's no such thing as a singular inspiration for any company. But we'll get to that.

FICTIONAL STORIES CAN WORK

When your faux origin story exists in lieu of a boring or nonexistent one, or is framed as a fiction, then it is serving your company. Juicy Couture's faux origin, "Once upon a time in a land far, far away called Pacoima there were two nice girls who liked stuff. Juicy Couture swept the land & they lived happily ever after," is a lot more interesting than promoting that the company began by simply making maternity pants. This story doesn't exist to cover up their real origins because it's written as a fairy tale. It works because the sort of story they choose frames the sort of company image they want to have: a girly-girl fairy tale clothing company.

Goodyear Tires' origin story is the Dickensian story of Charles Goodyear, the eventual inventor of weatherproof rubber.[7] In short, Charles Goodyear spent his whole life in and out of debtor's prison, all the while trying to create an all-weather rubber, and once he finally did, he still didn't profit much from it, since he dawdled at the European patent process and lost out on it. The whole saga can be found in a *Reader's Digest* article from 1958, reprinted on Goodyear's website as its history: www.goodyear.com/corporate/history/history_story.html. Charles Goodyear has nothing to do with the founding of the Goodyear company; it is merely named in his honor. However, the historical account of all the failures in Goodyear's life has become the company's origin story. An origin story can just be the story of its namesake. It does not need to be the story of the company. On its website, Goodyear also explains the history of the company under /history/history_overview.html, but not under "/history_story." It is a fine story, but not as interesting as Goodyear's.

The danger of faux company stories occurs when the company puts the story out with the intent to cover up a story they do not want associated with their product. Coca-Cola's incomplete origin story aims to frame their image:

> Like many people who change history, John Pemberton, an Atlanta pharmacist, was inspired by simple curiosity. One afternoon, he stirred up a fragrant, caramel-colored liquid and, when it was done, he carried it a few doors down to Jacobs' Pharmacy. Here, the mixture was combined with carbonated water and sampled by customers who all agreed—this new drink was something special. So Jacobs' Pharmacy put it on sale for five cents a glass.[8]

This version of the story leaves out the beverage's "patent medicine" history, in which Coca-Cola claimed to both energize and soothe the nerves of their consumers, due to the presence of the coca leaf in the beverage. Granted, the beverage was created before the concept of soft drinks had been developed. But Coca-Cola does not want to be associated with their actual origin story, since that is not how they want to frame their product. For a company that uses stories so successfully in most of their marketing and PR, their denial of their heritage, rather than finding a clever way to tell the story with a positive spin, is disappointing. Coca-Cola does, however, do great things with stories that I will explain in a proceeding case study later on.

YOUR ORIGIN STORY

Every company has an origin story. It might not sound pithy or interesting to you, because it is your story and you know it already, but there are ways to find the drama in every story. Most origins fall into a few common archetypes: garage startup, kid with a far-fetched dream, inspiration found by helping out loved ones, pastoral/old-timey imagery, the struggle to defy the odds and starting out trying to do one thing but ultimately doing something else instead. There are stories that are outliers, of course, but most likely, your story is one of the above, even if it doesn't feel like it. The methods described below to get customers to tell their stories can be adapted when working with your company's founders or yourself to craft a (mostly) true origin story, if your company lacks one.

Authentic personal stories are understood, at a basic human level, to be true. And truth creates a sense of personal connection between your customers and your company. So find the true story that will create customer loyalty in your customers and potential customers.

COMPANY STORIES 2.0

Why gather stories? Why not just make them up? Wouldn't it be easier to just hire a creative writing team to create the perfect story for your purposes? And fiction isn't inherently bad. If you write the perfect story and use it in a way that discloses to the public that it is a fiction, that is still interesting use of storytelling. However, don't forget that when the company tells the story, it seems self-serving: because it is. But when your customers tell your story, people will be more inclined to listen.

That is where Storytelling 2.0 comes in. When many people hear "2.0," they think of the tech industry. Really, 2.0 is simpler than that. 2.0 is about creating a dialogue, rather than a monologue. A company that only has an origin story is simply creating a monologue. You have a product or service, and you tell your customer base about it. People don't want that any more; they want to be a part of the conversation. They want to see themselves in the business transaction as more than just the people paying the money. They want to know where their products came from, and they want an opportunity to explain how the product has affected their lives.

COCA-COLA'S DIGITAL STORYTELLING PERFORMANCES

It was the Coca-Cola Company that pioneered using a new form of personal storytelling to promote their product and connect with their consumers: digital storytelling. In the early to mid-1990s, the now-late Dana Atchley developed the concept of digital storytelling in California. With the help of Denise Aungst Atchley, Joe Lambert, Nina Mullen and programmer Patrick Milligan, Atchley created a workshop-based approach, allowing "ordinary" people, from high school students to the elderly, to create short videos of personal stories, often emotional, using images, audio of the storytelling and some video.[9] What they started eventually formed the Center for Digital Storytelling in Berkeley, California.

In 1995, Douglas Ivester, then president of the Coca-Cola Company (later CEO, now retired), pushed Paul Pendergrass, head of corporate communications, to find a way to truly interact with the public as human beings. Pendergrass saw Atchley's *Next Exit* show of digital stories on tour and invited him to show these stories to top executives at Coca-Cola. At the end of the presentation, Ivester asked Atchley, "What does Coca-Cola mean to you?" Atchley was able to, on the spot, come up with two personal stories from his childhood relating to Coca-Cola. His second interview was with Deborah MacCarthy, then director of attractions at the World of Coca-Cola in Atlanta who was working on planning the Las Vegas version, and they began collaborating on creating a unique storytelling theater there.[10]

In the Las Vegas World of Coca-Cola, there are three prongs to Atchley's idea for the storytelling component: live actors in the museum area bringing Coca-Cola's history to life, an interactive theater where digital stories about Coca-Cola are shown by a live storytelling moderator and a bank of computers where the audience members can write up their own Coca-Cola memories. There is now a website where you can read these submitted stories and submit your own: www.thecocacolacompany.com/heritage/stories. Each of the 12-minute performances in the 64-seat theater shows three video stories out of the twelve available, chosen by the storyteller in charge for each showing.

One of the stories at the World of Coca-Cola tells the story of the World War II soldier who went to war with six bottles of Coca-Cola. The first he drank as soon as he got to India, the next four were shared with his fellow troops but the final bottle he kept, believing that if he drank it, "it would be like leaving home." He carried the bottle thorough the whole war, and his family still has it today; it even survived a house fire. This story can be viewed on Atchley's website: www.nextexit.com/dap/woc/truestory1.html. Another story (which can be found on the same website) is about Coca-Cola merchandise collectors who end up getting married at the World of Coca-Cola Atlanta during a convention. One of the stories collected from the computer databases was eventually made into a digital story for the show. It was about a woman who was so grateful that the protago- nist gave up his cab for her on a dark and stormy night that she handed him the only thing she had that could express how grateful she was: a bottle of Coca-Cola.

The purpose of these theaters is good storytelling, a sense of community, a sense of nostalgia and a creation of the sort of brand loyalty that translates to higher profit margins. Atchley may have been an artist by trade, but he understood the purposes of the Coca-Cola exhibit: "Any presentation has to have a dramatic arc. We wanted to create the sense of a journey, with a call to action at the end. If I give a presentation that's intended to sell, I tell a story whose call to action is 'Purchase my product.' In Las Vegas, our goal is to get people emotionally involved in the brand—so much so that they're ready to spend big bucks in the retail store downstairs."[11]

According to Atchley, storytelling is a way to solidify branding with a story's emotional component: "Companies like Coca-Cola are seeking new ways to strengthen their relationship to the consumer. One of the best ways of doing this is on an emotional level. Coca-Cola is a product that, for so many people, makes connections to life experiences and memories. I use tools to create digital stories that are designed to go past traditional product branding."[12]

If you go to Coca Cola's website, www.thecoca-colacompany.com/heritage/stories, you will find an em- barrassing wealth of these sorts of stories, inspired by the World of Coca-Cola's digital stories. Included are stories about romance, military, reminders of family, special family times, childhood memories, an affordable luxury, times with friends, a memory of home, Coca-Cola bottles, Coca-Cola collectibles, Coca-Cola employ- ees, advertising stories, new Coke stories and bottling companies stories. They are also constantly seeking more submissions through the same website. Unfortunately, to read any of these stories, you end up having to load a PDF for each type of story, only to be faced with the individual stories streaming down for pages, looking like a long essay, since none of the stories is even given a title. Some of the stories are brilliant, but some of the stories are quite dull. Coca-Cola leaves it up to their potential consumers to wade through them to find the interesting stories. The most useful thing about this gathering of stories right now is the solipsistic glee that story submitters can get when they go to the site and find their story "published." This is not to discredit the brand loyalty this must inspire in the story submitters, or the loyalty caused by the feeling of submitting such a story, especially when doing so from the computers at the exhibit. However, a better organizational method could be used, to cap off this brilliant experience.

WHAT STORIES TO GATHER

When going out into the world to find customer or consumer stories, it is important to first determine two things: what sorts of stories you want and what you plan on doing with the stories once they are gathered. Each of these things affects how stories should be gathered.

Are you looking for stories to help create a new advertising campaign based on real stories? If so, you will probably want stories with a significant change to them, or at least a very strong hook. You will want a protagonist with a plight that the potential customer can relate to. You probably want a story in which your product or service changes the person's life in a significant way, a way that viewers could see as being the change in their own lives. Citibank's "stories" campaign (stories.citi.com) works like this. For confidentiality reasons, the stories you see there or on television are not actual customer stories, but they are inspired by real stories gathered by the company based on what customers do with their reward points.[13] Although they are not truly real stories, they are so well developed that it almost doesn't matter. Though it is arguable that it might forge a more authentic connection with the customers if they were real, they do, however, feel real. And each com- mercial spot ends with a request to tell them your story, thus creating the social bonds that stories are meant to form: I tell one story, which prompts you to tell me a similar story. This is 2.0.

Are you looking for short anecdotes that will be readable at point of purchase? Those are different sorts of stories. They probably won't have as much of a change in the protagonist in them. Those stories are more vignettes, frozen pictures told in words. Cold-EEZE actively seeks out customer stories via their website, Twitter and other promos that they put on their packaging. These are short snapshots of stories: "'Whenever I feel my throat getting scratchy I start taking at least one or two Cold-EEZE a day. I've never missed a show thanks to

Cold-EEZE. My students can all boast the same results. Thanks to Cold-EEZE for helping ensure the show always goes on.'—Joelle C." They will sometimes reuse the stories on their blog, and below, the stories ask for more stories: "Thanks to all of our fans for telling us their wonderful stories! We hope you'll be inspired by these to share yours below and on our Facebook Page. How did you and Cold-EEZE first meet? Did a friend introduce you? Was it love at first sight or a slow crescendo? Now that you're hooked, are you loyal to one particular flavor?"[14] Cold-EEZE is constantly cycling through new stories, which encourages the 2.0 conversation between them and their customers.

If you are planning on having a website section devoted to stories, go beyond Coca-Cola's method. If you want every story submitted to make it to the website, create a voting-up and -down system so that readers can participate in deciding which stories are featured and which stories drift beyond the fold. There are some real gems on that site, such as one about someone's grandmother buying a bunch of glass bottles of Coke Classic to stash away when New Coke came out, and how the teller still finds the bottles today, and one about a couple who used six-ounce glass bottles of Coke instead of champagne for their wedding toast. If those could be voted upwards, more people could read them. It could be a historical archive for your company's customers that shows the best of the best of the stories gathered. Now, you can only find a collection of stories akin to your grandmother's attic: there are some great stories in there, but you have to go searching for them among the broken furniture and old tax returns.

Are you developing new marketing strategies based upon the sorts of stories you gather? This probably feels more familiar to you, since this is the sort of market research and consumer survey that are commonplace in the worlds of marketing and branding. The most important thing to remember is to honor the stories and storytellers and what they are trying to say about your product, rather than trying to bend what they are saying to fit your view of your product. Gathering stories means a loss of control, but it will help you reach a more authentic place.

Stories can do more than just create new marketing, advertising and PR campaigns. They can help you, as a company, reflect back upon what it is that you are doing, so that you can be a better company. They can give you a better sense of your own history and your own mission and help shape your vision for the future. They might even help you develop your goals and objectives to get there.

GATHERING STORIES

There are many ways to gather stories. A request for stories over e-mail, your website, social networking sites or a sign in your store would be a way to reach customers. Contests are a way to get your customers to put a lot of thought and care into the crafting of their stories, not to mention increasing the number of stories submitted. Generalized stories can be requested, but specific prompts will probably generate more stories that you can use. Explain why you want the stories. An unpromoted tab on your website called "Tell us your story" with a simple submission form or an old-fashioned "Please e-mail us your story at marketing@company.com" won't generate a lot of submissions, and the submissions that are generated won't be targeted toward your goals. A FAQ or submission guidelines will not only help the story submitter submit stories you can use, but it will also encourage them to submit, since they know the rules. A lot of companies use the buzz word *story* when using forms to collect customer data. Your customers do not want to spend a lot of time carefully crafting a story if they're just being used for customer data. Testimonials and stories are not the same thing. Make it clear that you really do want their stories, and let them know why.

If you plan on collecting stories from your customers from scratch while they are in the room with you, it's a good idea to start with a short meditation and a prompt. The prompts will probably speak to three major types of themes: persevering through hardship, reciprocity and love in friendship and family and defining moments. Obviously the prompts will be catered to your product or service, but these are the prompts I use for general storytelling workshops. They can easily be adapted and tweaked to emphasize your company's needs.

- Think of the first time you realized that you were different, but that this was a good thing.

- Think of your first day of something: your first day of elementary school, your first day of high school, your first day of work, your first day of military service. What kept you strong?

- Remember a moment of true sister/brotherhood. This could be with actual family or the family we form. What made this bond unique?

- What was a time when you felt all was right with the world? What did it take to get there, or what have you done to get that feeling back?

- Have you ever done something that you always had wanted to do?

- Tell me about someone who changed your life.

- Tell me about a special occasion during which things went wrong.

- Tell me about meeting someone who is special to you.

- What was your worst day ever? Are you glad it happened?

Here's a list of slightly more product-oriented prompts (X being the product):

- Do you lead a unique lifestyle devoted to X?

- Did you overcome personal challenges or adversity to buy your first X? Or did you have to overcome any fears to do so?

- Do you dream of owning X? Tell us about that dream.

- How did buying or using X change your life?

- Tell a funny story about X.

- Have you ever used X to make the world a better place?

Not all prompts will work for all products, but let your potential storytellers know that you're not just looking for moving testimonials; you're looking for the truth.

If you have a group of people in the room, the best way to gather stories is to literally lead them through a meditation on the prompt or collection of prompts. Get them into a comfortable position and have them close their eyes and concentrate on their breathing. Have them clear their minds of all worries and distractions. Wait until they are calm and uninfluenced by outside distractions. Then pose the prompt. Pause and wait for them to come to an idea. You'll sense the moment when most of them have the idea by the change in their posture. This is the point where you can step in and tell those who have an idea to really invest in the memory and really transport themselves back to that time and place. Tell those who don't have a memory that this is all right. Expand the prompt. They might have been thinking about the topic too narrowly. If we were using the sisterhood/brotherhood prompt, they might be stuck on the fact that they are only children. Start listing times of their life that they might have felt sisterhood with nongenetic sisters: from scouting groups, athletic teams, sororities or school. Expand outwards for a while, helping prompt the idea. When you think everyone has an idea, ask anyone who does not to raise his hand. Remember, they still have their eyes closed, so no one else will see. If someone is still without a story, tell her that it's all right; a story might not come until they split off into pairs. Sometimes you need a story to inspire another story. Allow them to keep brainstorming with the pressure off while you focus on those who have stories in mind. If a lot of your tellers are having trouble coming up with stories, the prompt is too narrow, and you need to think bigger, expanding the prompt to encompass more than one of the above ideas. Only one or two people should be without a story at this point.

This is when you ask them to picture the story in their minds. They might begin the idea with an image, with a line of dialogue or with a fluid memory. Whatever way the idea presents itself, it will exist in a context. Figure out where the story begins. All stories have a beginning. How does this one begin? Then figure out the change. How did you change in this story? Change can be little, or change can be big, but every story has change of some sort. The change will hopefully be a positive one that deals with your product or a negative one that puts them on the path to using your product. After the change comes the end, the lesson learned. Tell them to think about details, especially those that jump out at them with the initial burst of idea, but not to work too hard at the concept of details yet.

This is the point where you make them open their eyes and find a partner. It should be someone they don't know too well. If some participants don't have stories yet, make sure that they pair with someone who has a story. Groups of three are permissible, if necessary. Divide the partners into group A and group 1, neither being more important than the other. Choose A or 1 to go first. Allow them to tell the story to their partner. Allow enough time for most of the groups to get through the story, then direct the partner to ask questions of the teller. This is where the details will come out. Direct the listener to ask for the five sense details they are curious about.

The details should feed the heart of the story, not be the heart of the story. One of the problems with using the five-senses approach to getting details out of a storyteller is that after all the five-senses work is gathered, the storyteller needs to figure out which details matter and which do not. That it was raining on someone's wedding day might matter. That it is 50 degrees Fahrenheit and partly cloudy on Thanksgiving probably does not. That the bride wore a white dress does not need to be mentioned. That the bride wore a purple dress matters. That the cat is eight pounds probably doesn't change the story. If he's 25 pounds, that might matter. However, even interesting details are on a sliding scale when it comes to not overburdening a story with detail. However, the listener will automatically ask for the details that are pertinent to the story. After the interview process is done, the other partner should then tell his or her story.

As for those who made it through the meditation without finding a story of their own, tell them not to worry. Like the visitors to the World of Coca-Cola, after hearing the other teller's story, they will probably think of their own. Again, if too many people are having trouble thinking of their own stories, the prompt is too narrow.

After your participants have told their stories to each other, it is time to take volunteers to tell their stories to the whole group. However, instead of allowing the overeager participants to nominate themselves, ask for partners to nominate the other partner's story. They know when they've just heard a story that strikes a chord and that has meaning beyond the life of the teller. They'll also enjoy gently picking on each other, making the other person tell the story. This will also eliminate the awkward pause that happens when you ask a room of people to put themselves in the spotlight.

Emma Caywood Shares her Story

Let as many people tell as are nominated. Get permission to audio record this part of the session, so you can capture the oral story in the words of the participant. Most people speak more naturally and logically than they write. Storytelling is an oral medium. If you are going to get people in a room to come up with stories, do not have written-down stories be your endgame. Transcribe them later, to get that end product. If you want written-down stories, use other methods to get them. You will find that most people can tell a story better than they can write one.

As for the people who are not nominated to go, if enough time is given so that everyone can be nominated, and someone really does not want to go, allow for that. Do not force them if they don't want to and their partner doesn't make them. You probably don't need that story, anyway. If enough time is given for everyone to be nominated, however, everyone will be. So don't worry too much about that.

GLOWING TESTIMONIALS VERSUS STORIES

Perhaps the most important thing to remember when trying to find the perfect customer story is the difference between a glowing review and an interesting story. If you go to Amtrak's website, you can find a bunch of so-called stories gathered from their customers. To save you the time of reading them, they go like this: Customer (and perhaps family) decides to not fly somewhere and take the train instead. They take the Amtrak to their destination. On the way, they are amazed by the luxury, good food, friendly employees and beautiful countryside, and they meet some nice fellow passengers along the way. They vow to never fly again.

Now, to the casual marketing eye, this sounds like a perfect customer story. The customer had a flawless experience with the product and tells it with many details. However, these stories do not actually work to promote the product. At least, they do not work to promote the product in the context of company gathered and disseminated stories. If these series of glowing events were posted, unprompted, to a website such as Yelp.com, they would be brilliant. People go to Yelp expecting unbiased reviews. If they came across such a glowing list of positives about a company on Yelp, they would (mostly) trust the review, as long as it wasn't aberrant in the context of the other reviews. However, when they come to your website, look at your packaging or promotional materials or see your advertising, they expect bias. So a flawless glowing review is of little positive value, especially if it is boring in a dramatic context. Even if these series of positive events were encountered on Yelp, they would be boring to read. They would serve a purpose, but not one rooted in meaningful storytelling.

This is due to the fact that storytelling needs a crisis, not necessarily crisis in the terms described in Chapter 26. For the purposes of storytelling, crisis will be redefined as "any event or happening that takes a part of the world we have grown comfortable living with and turns it upside down."[15] Without a crisis, the "story" is a portrait of something without events. A crisis can be events such as illness, accidents, death, war, job losses, breakups or other catastrophic events, but it can also be weddings, graduations, new jobs or positive changes in lifestyle. Change is the essential element in this definition. If you look at a Hollywood movie, it is the change that happens in the protagonist's life that is the heart of the film. Without change, there is no story.

Now, one could argue that the Amtrak customer stories do have a crisis: at the end, they choose to never fly again. However, the crisis comes at the end of the long stories, rather than being given the focus. The significant crisis has to fuel the story. If the story simply ends with the crisis, your potential customers or current customers will not keep listening to the story until the end.

A simple story only needs a few elements. It needs a main character for the audience to care about, impending trouble or change, the crisis, insight leading the main character to realize what change has taken place or needs to take place and, finally, the affirmation. A more interesting version of the Amtrak narrative would start earlier. The current stories only have insight and affirmation. The crisis was implied in the insight but not told. The interesting part of the story was skipped. What about plane travel is unfulfilling? Has the customer ever had a really bad plane trip? How could this story be juxtaposed with a few corresponding details from the bogged-down current version to create impending trouble and crisis, leading to the choice to take the train? This sounds terribly negative, but it doesn't have to be. Yes, your storytellers might bring you nightmare stories of flying, and that would work better than the current stories, but negativity only sets up train travel as a less terrible alternative, rather than the fulfillment of a dream. The trouble and the crisis could stem from the desire of the protagonist, rather than external forces. The protagonist could long to see the country and always get assigned to an aisle seat. He could get a widow seat but further wonder about the details of the landscape. She could read a novel or visit Travel Town (the outdoor train museum) in Los Angeles and desire the romantic dream of train travel, and have it fulfilled. The crisis doesn't have to be negative. It just has to take the forefront in the story.

Going back to the Amtrak examples, the laundry list of glowing things about the train trip only overburdens the story. If the crisis of the story is never flying again, there had to be one thing that tipped the scales. The storyteller might not be able to figure it out right away, but if really pushed to explain what it is about, plane travel that was unfulfilling, then he could pick which details are really essential to the story. Random details are not what make a story good. Necessary details are what bring a story to life. If the time of day, the color of the sweater or the breed of the dog has no bearing on the character development or plot, all those details serve to do is bog down the listener with imagery that retards the plot development. This is not unique to business storytelling.

THE FUTURE

Considering the young people of today, who've grown up with social networking, Web 2.0 content creation and the ability to become a fan of companies on Facebook in lieu of watching the television commercials they now fast-forward through, the ability to interact with your customers in a dialogue, rather than a monologue, is fast becoming essential. Those companies that cannot allow their customers to see the story in their interactions will not develop the relationships that they need. Stories are not just for toy companies, natural companies or nostalgic brands. This chapter has covered the storytelling efforts of companies in the tea, toy, cereal, soda, medical supplies, Internet marketplace, clothing, automotive supplies, banking, over-the-counter pharmacy and transportation industries. If you google "Tell us your story," you will get further results in beauty/acne/scar care, sports supplies, pets, software, motor oil, independent film, thrift stores, colleges, dating sites, pharmaceuticals and travel industries, as well as countless libraries, human rights organizations, health care organizations, environmental groups, faith organizations and other nonprofit groups all engaging their customers to tell them their part of the story and turn the monologue into a dialogue. And that's only on the first 25 pages of Google hits, out of 4,740,000 results today, May 25, 2011. This will increase in the years to come.

It is not enough, however, to be one of those websites, one out of more than 4.7 million. Story gathering works only if the company itself knows how to tell its own story—its true or adjacent-to-true story—and knows what to do with the customer stories once it collects them. The solution for every company is different, since not only is every industry different, but every company is different. However, with the tools in this chapter, hopefully a few of the successful strategies will be worth trying, so you don't get left behind in this 2.0 world.

APPENDIX A: SCREENPLAY STRUCTURE

Now, your company isn't planning on writing a 120-page screenplay about your customers' stories. However, the timing of the structure of a movie needs to be understood to understand how the Western world wants their stories to be structured. It is not only important to hit all these plot points, but it is important to hit all the plot points with the right amount of time between them.

How to Structure Your Story like a Hollywood Movie

Pages/ Minutes	Structure Point	What That Means for the Story	In a Monster* Movie
10	Inciting Incident	Something happens that sets the protagonist on a journey.	The mad scientist discovers a new, exciting compound.
30/35	End of Act 1	The point of no return.	Someone drinks the compound and turns into a monster.
60/65	Midpoint	Something changes in the journey.	Up to this point, the scientist has been running from the monster. At this point, he realizes he must chase after it and destroy it.
90/95	End of Act 2	Low point/dark moment: All is lost.	The monster kills the scientist's girlfriend. He loses the will to live.
95/105	Gathering of Allies	Protagonist gathers all his friends and wits together for one last-ditch effort to destroy the problem.	The scientist realizes that only he can kill the monster, so he must discover the antidote!
116	Climax	Problem is destroyed! Or all is lost in a tragedy.	The scientist feeds the antidote to the monster, and he turns back into what he was before. Or it kills him.
119	Dénouement	Things resolve, as they will.	The scientist destroys his lab. Or he makes a new compound, setting up the sequel.

*The monster can be a metaphor for personal demons, as well.

People who don't think they understand film structure understand it so well that they feel the plot markers go by like breathing. A film seems long if the third act is too long, no matter how long the actual film is. Film structure is story structure, these days.

APPENDIX B: THE HERO'S JOURNEY

Joseph Campbell's *Hero of One Thousand Faces* describes the *hero's journey*, one of the best-known story structures. Campbell studied mythic structure and came up with a number of steps that are followed in a classic hero's-journey story. When reading the steps, you can think of *The Odyssey*, *The Iliad* or *King Arthur*, but you can also think of *Star Wars IV: A New Hope*, which was also written to exactly follow this structure.

A. Departure

1. The Call to Adventure
   An event happens in the life of the protagonist that will put him on a life-changing path.

2. Refusal of the Call
   The future hero rejects the call to action.

3. Supernatural Aid
   Once the hero is on the quest, his supernatural help becomes apparent.

4. The Crossing of the First Threshold
   This is when the hero leaves behind the world he knows and commits to adventure, with no thoughts of turning back.

5. The Belly of the Whale
   This is when the hero fully separates from the world he once knew. Sometimes this looks like hitting rock bottom, but it is really about the transition between worlds and selves.

B. Initiation

1. The Road of Trials
   This is a series of trials or tests that the hero must face. They often occur in threes, and some tests are failed.

2. The Meeting with the Goddess
   This point in the journey is when the hero experiences unconditional, all-encompassing love. This can be represented by a woman or a goddess, but it can take place within the self, when the hero can see himself as a whole.

3. Woman as the Temptress
   The hero is tempted to stray from his quest by a woman or by some other temptation.

4. Atonement with the Father
   The hero must confront and be initiated by a force that holds power over his life. The old view of self or the hero's character of admiration must be killed so that the hero can come to himself.

5. Apotheosis
   This is the period of rest, the time spent in literal or metaphorical heaven, before the character must face the return.

6. The Ultimate Boon
   This is when the goal is achieved, and the thing set out to find is accomplished.

C. Return

1. Refusal of the Return
   The hero has no interest in returning to normal life after the adventure.

2. The Magic Flight
   Sometimes the hero's escape from the boon is as difficult is getting into it.

3. Rescue from Without
   Sometimes the hero needs help from the outside to rescue him from the boon, especially if he has been depleted by the journey.

4. The Crossing of the Return Threshold
   The hero must retain the wisdom gained during the journey and transfer this knowledge to the earthly world.

5. Master of the Two Worlds
   The hero must have a Buddha- or Jesus-like understanding of how to exist and hold the knowledge of both realms.

6. Freedom to Live
   When the hero no longer fears death, he has the freedom to fully live.

Understanding this classic story structure can help you identify what sorts of stories will appeal to the mythic brains of your customers.

APPENDIX C: EIGHT LEVELS OF CHARACTER TRANSFORMATION

Jason Ohler, a digital storytelling expert, has outlined eight levels of character transformation that can be seen in film and other sorts of storytelling.

1. Physical/Kinesthetic: The character develops strength or dexterity.

2. Inner Strength: The character develops courage or overcomes a fear, often with great risk to herself.

3. Emotional: The character matures and thinks beyond his own needs.

4. Moral: The character develops a conscience.

5. Psychological: The character develops insight and self-awareness.

6. Social: The character accepts new responsibility with respect to family, community or a group.

7. Intellectual/Creative: The character advances intellectual/creative ability to learn or do something new.

8. Spiritual: The character has an awakening that changes his entire perspective.[16]

Sometimes the character will go through more than one of these at a time. Often it's hard to truly see yourself and know what sort of growth you went through during a story, but these are useful ways for the person collecting the story to consider the crisis in each story and the importance of the growth. One or two of these character transformation descriptions will fit your company's idea of their image or product better, so it's good to recognize the stories that sit best on your brand.

DISCUSSION QUESTIONS

1. Why does your company need a strong origin story? Do companies only have one origin story? How do you choose which to tell?

2. Why is storytelling essential to the concept of 2.0?
3. Why gather customer stories? Why not just use fiction?
4. What are digital stories, and how does Coca-Cola use them to increase sales?
5. What is the difference between a good point-of-purchase story and a story that would work in a digital storytelling video?
6. What is meant by "crisis" in a story, and how does it differ from the normal definition of crisis?
7. What is the difference between a testimonial and a story? How can Amtrak make the story section of their website more compelling?

NOTES

1. Celestial Seasonings. "The Story of Nutcracker Sweet Black Holiday Tea." 7 Dec 2010. Web log post. www.facebook.com/note.php?note_id=465880921990.
2. "American Girl Magazine." *American Girl Dolls Wiki.* 25 May 2011. Web. americangirl.wikia.com/wiki/American_Girl_Magazine.
3. Shook, Scott H. "The Boy on the Wheaties Box." *A Century of Heroes.* Massillon Memories Publishing Company, 10 Sept. 2010. Print. pp. 782–784.
4. Wheaties. "Wheaties: A Rather Humble Beginning." 25 May 2011. Web. www.wheaties.com/pdf/wheaties_history.pdf.
5. InfoChachkie. "Leverage Your Startup's Origin Story To Reinforce Your Mission & Values." 25 May 2011. Web. infochachkie.com/origin.
6. Song, Mary Lou. "Re: Getting the Facts Straight." Message to the author. 31 May 2011. E-mail.
7. Goodyear Tire & Rubber Company. "The Charles Goodyear Story." 23 May 2011. Web. www.goodyear.com/corporate/history/history_story.html.
8. "Coca-Cola History: Coca-Cola Heritage Timeline." 5 May 2011. Web. heritage.coca-cola.com.
9. Hartley, John, and Kelly McWilliam. "Computational Power Meets Human Contact." *Story Circle: Digital Storytelling around the World.* Chichester, U.K.: Wiley-Blackwell, 2009. Kindle. p. 3.
10. Beal, Tita Theodora. "Computers as Hearth." Dana Atchley Next Exit Digital Storytelling. 23 May 2011. Web. www.nextexit.com/dap/woc/hearth.html.
11. "Experience the Real Thing." *Fast Company.* 23 May 2011. Web. www.fastcompany.com/magazine/31/coke.html?page=0,1.
12. Motion Gallery—Dana Atchley. Adobe. 5 May 2011. Web. www.macromediastudio.biz/ap/motion/gallery/atchley/image6.html.
13. @Citibank. Twitter.com. 12 May 2011. Web log post.
14. Cold-EEZE. "Inventions so Crazy, You'll Forget All About Your Cold!" 20 May 2011. Web log post. cold-eeze.com/blog/cold-eeze-news/inventions-so-crazy-you%E2%80%99ll-forget-all-about-your-cold.
15. Davis, Donald. *Telling Your Own Stories: For Family and Classroom Storytelling, Public Speaking, and Personal Journaling.* Little Rock, AR: August House, 1993. Print. p. 20.
16. Ohler, Jason. *Digital Storytelling in the Classroom: New Media Pathways to Literacy, Learning, and Creativity.* Thousand Oaks, CA: Corwin, 2008. Print. p. 10.

ADDITIONAL READING

ORAL STORYTELLING

Collins, Rives and Pamela J. Cooper. *The Power of Story: Teaching through Storytelling.* Long Grove, IL: Waveland, 2005.

Davis, Donald. *Telling Your Own Stories: For Family and Classroom Storytelling, Public Speaking, and Personal Journaling*. Little Rock, AR: August House, 1993.

Lipman, Doug. *Improving Your Storytelling: Beyond the Basics for All Who Tell Stories in Work or Play*. Little Rock, AR: August House, 1999.

Maguire, Jack. *The Power of Personal Storytelling: Spinning Tales to Connect with Others*. New York, NY: J.P. Tarcher/Putnam, 1998.

Sawyer, Ruth. *The Way of the Storyteller*. New York, NY: Viking, 1942.

STORY STRUCTURE/WRITING

Campbell, Joseph. *The Hero with a Thousand Faces*. Princeton, NJ: Princeton UP, 1968.

Lamott, Anne. *Bird by Bird: Some Instructions on Writing and Life*. New York, NY: Pantheon, 1994.

McKee, Robert. *Story: Substance, Structure, Style and the Principles of Screenwriting*. New York, NY: Regan, 1997.

Ohler, Jason. *Digital Storytelling in the Classroom: New Media Pathways to Literacy, Learning, and Creativity*. Thousand Oaks, CA: Corwin, 2008.

BUSINESS STORYTELLING

Denning, Stephen. *The Leader's Guide to Storytelling: Mastering the Art and Discipline of Business Narrative*. San Francisco, CA: Jossey-Bass/A Wiley Imprint, 2005.

Denning, Stephen. *The Springboard: How Storytelling Ignites Action in Knowledge-era Organizations*. Boston, MA: Butterworth-Heinemann, 2001.

Denning, Stephen. *Squirrel Inc.: A Fable of Leadership through Storytelling*. San Francisco, CA: Jossey-Bass, 2004.

Godin, Seth. *All Marketers Are Liars: The Power of Telling Authentic Stories in a Low-Trust World*. New York, NY: Portfolio, 2005.

Simmons, Annette. *Whoever Tells the Best Story Wins: How to Use Your Own Stories to Communicate with Power and Impact*. New York, NY: Amacom, 2007.

Vincent, Laurence. *Legendary Brands: Unleashing the Power of Storytelling to Create a Winning Marketing Strategy*. Chicago, IL: Dearborn Trade, 2002.

52

CHAPTER

BRANDED CONTENT STRATEGY
Meaningful Stakeholder Interaction

Sara E. Smith, MSIMC
Business Intelligence and Content Strategy Consultant
Boulder, Colorado

Clarke L. Caywood, Ph.D.
Professor and Past Chairman
Department of Integrated Marketing Communications
Medill School of Journalism, Media, Integrated Marketing Communications
Northwestern University

> *Content includes the text, graphics, video, and audio that make up an interactive experience.*
> —Kristina Halvorson

> *Simply put, content is contextualized data.*
> —Rahel Bailie

So, what *is* content strategy as a communications-based management idea, exactly? Before we go any further, let's take a minute to clearly define terms. In the case of *content strategy*, "content" therefore becomes the "stuff" that's put out there, be it video, social media chatter, advertising campaigns and journalism that span the channels of TV, print, digital, mobile and more. Furthermore, "good content" is the stuff that is leveraged to achieve strategic and measurable business and other organizational objectives including revenue generation. Good content creates meaningful and memorable experiences that gets users talking and buzzing and keeps them coming back for more.

Daunting, isn't it? With this, content can be just about anything, from a user-uploaded video on YouTube of *Singing Babies!*,[1] to a wildly popular fashion photo blog, such as Scott Schuman's *Sartorialist*,[2] to a *New York Times*–published long-form journalistic reporting piece on life in the Sudan that can be curated in some way to, literally and figuratively, cash in.

So, why content strategy? Why now? In the digital age, anyone with an Internet connection and the ability to upload content is a potential publisher. While many of us never intended to be publishers, even the simple act of Tweeting, or posting to Facebook, is essentially Web publishing. Thus, the question has finally come: what to do with all of that content floating around on the web? Positive content that is often rich with meaning and that can be used to the benefit of your organization, client or brand is often right there, in front of us, whether it was created internally or by an unknown user. Therefore it must be managed for reuse, response or reinterpretation. If it is negative content, it should be managed as part of the crisis plan. Quick, call the content strategist!

Content strategist is a relatively new term describing an expert who is experienced in strategically marrying multimedia content to communication, business goals and end-users' needs. Content is at the center of all interactive experiences, and the content strategist plans for the creation, aggregation, governance and distribution of content (establishing strategy and guidelines): processes that add real value to the user while contributing to tangible brand goals and business objectives. The content strategist also synchronizes content strategy with the user experience design to fully realize meaningful, interactive experiences.

ISSUES BETWEEN OLD AND NEW CONTENT PROVIDERS

We use the word *content* frequently in this chapter, but the following may be helpful to your thinking on what has become content. On March 21, 2011, Bob Burch, VP of business development at AOL, posted a blog entry entitled, "Stop Calling it Content," in which he recounts the story of a so-called content generator, who, at 36, is living on his brother's floor and hasn't found financial success. In the telling of this story, Burch muses, "It occurred to me that calling it content commoditizes it and sends a message to the creative community that quality doesn't matter. It's not unique to AOL either; everyone in Silicon Valley calls it content." Burch goes on further to say:

> Journalists and reporters are also artists of a certain kind—maybe better described as passionate professionals. The business model of news distribution is changing dramatically, and we all agree that journalists need to get compensated if we want them to continue the important work they do. But I would argue that charging consumers to read news articles is not only bad for consumers, it's also bad for journalists.[3]

Although Burch's comments are clearly a reaction to the erection of the *New York Times* paywall, the implication is that new media and paid-for premium content erode journalistic freedom of expression. But they also keep the lights on at many news bureaus that would otherwise be shuttered by the explosion of citizen journalists who often lack formal journalistic training. However, these days, everything is a screen, essentially a viewing mechanism for this so-called content that we cannot seem to live without, and if history repeats itself with this one, premium content is something we are likely to pay for, both as generators and consumers.

A FEW OTHER IMPORTANT TERMS TO CONSIDER

INFORMATION ARCHITECTURE

Information Architecture is a specialized skill set that interprets information and expresses distinctions between signs and systems of signs. It originates, to some degree, in the library sciences. Many schools with library and information science departments teach information architecture.[4]

WEB WRITING

Web writing is good writing adapted to the limits of the web as a medium and the needs of users.[5]

EDITORIAL STRATEGY

The editorial strategy is the overarching approach that outlines the voice, tone, values and concerns for content lifecycles.

METADATA STRATEGY

In essence, this is the strategy for managing data about data.

TAXONOMIES

The process of classifying and cataloguing content.

SEARCH ENGINE OPTIMIZATION (SEO)

The process of managing content for keyword optimization and site-search engines.

SEARCH ENGINE MARKETING

A form of Internet marketing that seeks to promote websites by increasing their visibility in search engine result pages through the use of paid placement, contextual advertising and paid inclusion.[6]

CONTENT CHANNEL DISTRIBUTION

The process of channel planning and determining which media will best support the content and engage the intended audiences.

This is by no means meant to be an exhaustive list (courtesy, in part, of Kristina Halvorson). Rather, it is intended to lay the foundation for this chapter and to jump-start your thinking on who does what in your own organization, and to point out that, yes, many of these roles do overlap. Although this might highlight operational redundancies, such intersections are actually prime opportunities for integration. These overlaps also allow for efficiencies in smaller organizations, where time and budgetary constraints do not always permit an entire staff of content generators and evaluators.

CONTENT STRATEGY IN PRACTICE

Below is a job description of what one agency wanted from a content manager in their specific situation. Each of these tasks is addressed in this chapter and is intended to help guide your thinking about how to apply content strategy to your own work.

JOB DESCRIPTION—CONTENT STRATEGIST: PRIMARY RESPONSIBILITIES

- Develop a thorough understanding of the client's audiences, business objectives, brand strategy, content and messaging requirements.
- Collaborate closely with agency project teams (strategy, creative, experience design, tech, etc.) to build integrated, user-centric content strategy solutions and create the most engaging content that meets the project goals, target users' needs and clients' business objectives.
- Develop content strategy for complex user experiences (transactional websites, interactive videos, social networks, mobile platforms, etc.).
- Inventory, audit, analyze and organize existing content into a clear content audit matrix document; identify gaps/needs and recommend options for sourcing new content.
- Perform detailed competitive site analysis and benchmarking in content breadth, quality, organization and presentation.

- Work with strategists to set guidelines for the editorial tone, style and voice of all content.

- Work with client to create a content development plan to enhance, edit and reformat legacy and newly created content.

- Create taxonomies and metadata frameworks for grouping and tagging content.

- Establish a style guide and editorial procedures/processes for all written elements of the site.

- Ensure that content management systems (CMSs) meet publishing and maintenance requirements.

- Define research requirements and plan for content strategy.

- Author and maintain complex sets of content documentation (such as content inventory matrix, content audit matrix, taxonomy, new content matrix, keyword mapping, style guide, content strategy presentations, etc.).

Notice the recurring theme of collaboration and integration with both other teams internally as well as the clients and consumers.

Now take a look at Figure 52.1. This image, generated by IBM Customer Facing Solutions, illustrates the critical importance of content strategy as the underpinning guideline for user experience design. Yet in order to understand user experience as it relates to the content lifecycle, and therefore implement a strategically sound CMS, you must first undertake a series of steps to better understand the needs of your organization or brand and ultimately maximize the value of your content.

The first step is to ask questions. These might include:

- Do we really need a Facebook or its equivalent page?

- Will our Tweets add value or fill a need?

- Whom is this blog intended for? Who will manage and update the content?

- How long will this content be good for? Is there a set or estimated expiration date?

- Will this content possibly alienate any of our stakeholders?

- What are our competitors doing with their messages?

- Do we have the resources to support CMS?

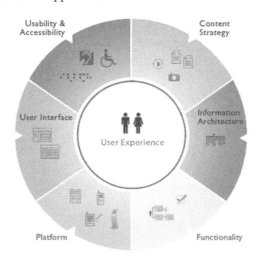

FIGURE 52.1

- Who will manage and operate the system?

- If we set priorities, what work or programs will be dropped?

- How will we measure the CMS efforts?

You will likely want to tailor the questions asked to the overall business objectives of your organization, client or brand.

Once you feel like you have gotten the answers you are looking for, the next step is to audit both the existing digital and nondigital content and devise a plan for the necessary revisions. It is important to note that, in the process of developing and managing content, you will need to constantly revise material so that your content functions in tandem with current events, corporate activities and the responses of the readers, listeners and viewers. Your audit may involve:

- Collecting all materials in a room to display your messages on the wall, on screens and so forth.

- Examining the messages and reused messages for look, feel and consistency or meeting organizational message goals.

- An inventory of past materials still used, if copies are available.

- A content analysis of the text of all digital materials to compare messages to current organizational message goals. Are you still using old messages in some parts or regions of the organization?

- A content analysis of your use of words to your competitors. Do you want to use the same or different words and content?

- A team review of all the materials to see if the work is integrated.

- Decisions to destroy some materials and highlight others and recommendations on rules for going forward with digital and non-digital content.

IMPLEMENTATION OF THE CONTENT PROGRAM

Once the audit is complete, or as complete as you feel it is ever going to be, you will want to take a hard look at your findings and continue to ask tough questions. It is important to remember that content is in many ways a deeply personal endeavor, and many of the content generators may feel an attachment to the work they have done. Like all members of an organization should, they often have a vested interest in the work they have created and will often fight to justify its existence. It is best to let the egos simmer and come prepared for a meeting that might not go according to plan. If a majority of the content needs to be reworked, pitch it as an opportunity for additional content creation. Make sure people can actually find your content. With microsites all the rage, the notion of a place within a place, or a secret garden, if you will, is romantic but ultimately meaningless if you cannot drive user traffic.

To continue the content management effort, there are six basic and key actions:

1. Identify internal and external content needs and sources.

2. Research content for its journalistic values and value to the organization's stakeholders.

3. Create or reassemble content.

4. Reuse owned and other content.

5. Eliminate continuing content not relevant to organizational and stakeholder goals.

6. Update content.

An audit of existing content (digital or otherwise) in the organization will give the content strategist a base of material including words, video and sound. The search for content should also include business partners, independent experts, associations, professional societies, journalistic outlets and trade journalism. One of the tasks of the content strategist is also to assemble content for stakeholders. Additionally, a careful review of the content from all sources is crucial. In many ways, these new sources of content are replacing traditional journalism. According to some, journalism may be dead, or dying in certain sectors, (e.g., newspapers and some magazines).[7] However, the values of journalism including factual accuracy, timeliness, newsworthiness, well-crafted writing, video or sound for the eye or ear, authenticity and transparency should not be dead to those who continue to assemble and contribute content. This moment in communications is a clear opportunity for businesses, nongovernmental organizations (NGOs) and other organizations to reestablish their credibility and build a strong positive reputation.

Creation and reuse of content must be a matter of priorities. If for no other reason, the condition of the global economy requires each manager to carefully allocate her resources to achieve the most important goals of the organization. Even more critically, the identification with stakeholders and the offer of a relationship demands more careful selection of new and reused content. Both the time of the stakeholder and the time of the content provider are valuable. As you give the stakeholder time to respond or comment, again remember that his time is valuable.

Perhaps the greatest myth attached to the creation of content of just about any kind is "build it and they will come." With a flood of information coming from numerous sources both online and off, what is important is that the information conveyed is both transparent and trustworthy. Content is essentially worthless if it comes from an unknown and untrusted source. One of the most critical factors facing content generators today is the mandate of self-identification. To fully engage with readers and users of all kinds, it is now more important than ever to say who you are, where you come from, who you represent, what your point of view is and how what you say is truthful.

Managing stale content is another critical element to effective content strategy. But, what should you do with content that has been around way past its expiration date? The answer is to archive it. Archiving can serve as a treasure box of sorts, revealing the often-rich history of an organization or brand and even serve as a timeline that suggests a tradition of thought leadership and other intangible assets. Facebook has recognized this, and in the Fall of 2011 adopted a timeline approach for arranging and presenting user profiles.

Finally, you will want to update, a lot. Keeping users, customers and other stakeholders actively engaged means offering a supply of endlessly fresh content. Updating the responses by encouraging and facilitating easy replies would be helpful. Like any other commodity, no one wants a rotting product.

CASE STUDIES: OWNED CONTENT

CASE STUDY 1: INDEPENDENT NEWS?

A Fortune 10 company was charged by a professional society with delivering content in a manner that blurred the lines between news and marketing and public relations. The company hired a journalism-trained freelance writer to write a feature article on their innovative products. They also expected him to then "pitch" the idea of such an article to a national magazine that would also pay the freelancer for writing an "independent" story. As a result of this action, the professional society created a specific clause in their value statement against this method of new content delivery. At the same time, today there are billions of words and millions of messages that are being written to fill the legitimate demand for more information on digital outlets.

What are the rules, regulations and expectations of society, business leaders, the press and critics of both for this new era of "content proliferation"? How can corporations, NGOs, government and other institutions (and the public) create a sustainable system of democratic journalistic information?

CASE STUDY 2: SPECIALIZED BRANDED INFORMATION

One company in the military equipment industry has been a credible and transparent source of information about the industry. Their website has been a trusted source for journalists, book authors, researchers, members of the government, business and media. Rather than use the site as a traditional "here are our products" location, the site contains deep information about the history of specific aircraft and related equipment. The specifications, applications and details are a fascinating one-stop source created by the engineering and public relations professionals to fill an information gap in a democratic society for important reporting and storytelling data.

What are other examples of corporate- and reader-provided content in health care for rare disease treatment, rare automobile restoration challenges, general answers to legal questions, food and dietary needs, personal and home safety solutions and career advising?

The examples are added to show the breadth and depth of this new content-provider ecosystem. One example shows some risks of providers pretending to be news outlets, and the other, more common (we hope), example is of companies filling the gap where news may not have been able to provide such specialized information.

RULES OF PRACTICE IN NEWS AND BUSINESS INSTITUTIONS

Below are two lists of possible issues to be considered to create a common understanding of the convergence of fields delivering content. The first is from the Society of Professional Journalists code (on content), and the second is from the Public Relations Society of America 2011 conference. As is the case with most lists of this nature, these are not intended to be exhaustive, but rather, serve as a guideline for strategic content creation.

SOCIETY OF PROFESSIONAL JOURNALISTS CODE (ON CONTENT)[8]

- Test the accuracy of information from all sources and exercise care to avoid inadvertent error. Deliberate distortion is never permissible.

- Diligently seek out subjects of news stories to give them the opportunity to respond to allegations of wrongdoing.

- Identify sources whenever feasible. The public is entitled to as much information as possible on sources' reliability.

- Always question sources' motives before promising anonymity. Clarify conditions attached to any promise made in exchange for information. Keep promises.

- Make certain that headlines, news teases and promotional material (photos, video, audio, graphics, sound bites and quotations) do not misrepresent. They should not oversimplify or highlight incidents out of context.

- Never distort the content of news photos or video. Image enhancement for technical clarity is always permissible. Label montages and photo illustrations.

- Avoid misleading reenactments or staged news events. If reenactment is necessary to tell a story, label it.

- Avoid undercover or other surreptitious methods of gathering information except when traditional open methods will not yield information vital to the public. Use of such methods should be explained as part of the story.

- Never plagiarize.

- Tell the story of the diversity and magnitude of the human experience boldly, even when it is unpopular to do so.

- Examine their own cultural values and avoid imposing those values on others.

- Avoid stereotyping by race, gender, age, religion, ethnicity, geography, sexual orientation, disability, physical appearance or social status.

- Support the open exchange of views, even views they find repugnant.

- Give voice to the voiceless; official and unofficial sources of information can be equally valid.

- Distinguish between advocacy and news reporting. Analysis and commentary should be labeled and not misrepresent fact or context.

- Distinguish news from advertising and shun hybrids that blur the lines between the two.

- Recognize a special obligation to ensure that the public's business is conducted in the open and that government records are open to inspection.

FROM PUBLIC RELATIONS SOCIETY OF AMERICA 2011 CODE OF ETHICS[9]

- Protect and advance the free flow of accurate and truthful information.

- Foster informed decision-making through open communication.

- Protect confidential and private information.

- Promote healthy and fair competition among professionals.

- Avoid conflicts of interest.

- Work to strengthen the public's trust in the profession.

- Be honest and accurate in all communications.

- Reveal sponsors for represented causes and interests.

- Act in the best interest of clients or employers.

- Disclose financial interests in a client's organization.

- Safeguard the confidences and privacy rights of clients and employees.

- Follow ethical hiring practices to respect free and open competition.

- Avoid conflicts between personal and professional interests.

- Decline representation of clients requiring actions contrary to the Code.

- Accurately define what public relations activities can accomplish.

- Report all ethical violations to the appropriate authority.

- Avoid anonymous Internet posting, "flogs" and viral marketing.

- Disclose payment of expert commentators.

- Be truthful in wartime communications.

- Overstate charges or compensation for work performed.

THE MARRIAGE OF SEO AND PR

While this may seem elementary, we often forget that good PR is rooted in actually being able to communicate. Because most of the content out there is search driven (save for discrete trade publications and academic journals), it must exist digitally and be optimized for mobile consumption. With this, you want to be sure to not just maximize opportunities for SEO, but also have a sound strategy in place. Failure to do so can lead to essentially meaningless content, chock full of keywords that do not actually say anything relevant to your organization or brand.

A good place to start is by brainstorming and drafting keywords as they apply to your organization and its consumers. You will then want to group these keywords and ideas around popular search terms. The free Google Adwords keyword tool[10] is an excellent resource to help guide your strategy. Once you have explored this tool, you will have a better idea of how to optimize your content for your intended audience and craft content that is, as we say, relevant and meaningful.

SOCIAL MEDIA AND CONTENT STRATEGY

Further complicating the sea of content on the web is the trivial user-generated content we wade through to get to the good stuff, that is, the kind of content that melts our hearts and that makes us want to share. And here we go with the "friend everyone, share everything" ethos that now drives much of the online user's behavioral patterns. While this may be a sweeping generalization, keep in mind the host of Tweets and Facebook posts that you've hidden from your feed.

The unfortunate reality is, there is a lot of very bad, no-good content out there. Consider these same droves of frivolous Facebook posts, Twitter updates and uploaded YouTube videos you might scour on a daily basis in search of mentions pertaining to your organization or brand. Although search processes and filters are continually improving, making sense of the mass of sentiments and opinions is a daunting task.

The bottom line is, however, if you do not own and manage your narrative, someone else will. Many agencies and client-side organizations employ community managers to corral and guide online discussions and community forums to ensure the accuracy of the information that is presented.

MONETIZING WITH CONTENT

Take, for instance, online sidebar and banner ads. You ask yourself, "Is that thing on the right really content? Really?" Okay, maybe that's a little harsh, but you get the idea, and we are sure you can relate to how frustrating it is when the distracting and irrelevant dancing monkeys appear over the recipe for tonight's dinner on a site like foodnetwork.com. Even more frustrating is when these banner ads appear across your favorite blogs, or even your trusted friend's Twitter feed. However, as mentioned above, every web experience is a screen, and that means more opportunities for advertisers to compete for share of mind with consumers who are often targeted based on his or her online behavioral data. In some cases, selling sidebar space on blogs serves as the means to keep these otherwise-unpaid bloggers up and running.

As you move forward with your own strategy for content management, it is important to ask yourself if ads such as these might be right for you or your organization. Although it is an efficient means of generating revenue, possible customer and user alienation and ensuing attrition must be considered. If your overall goal is to drive traffic, generate impressions and build long-term relationships selling your sidebar space to advertisers might not be the best idea.

COMMUNICATION THEORIES FOR A CONTENT MANAGEMENT PROGRAM

This is a list of 17 viable communication theories for rationalizing a proposal for a new program or department of content management. Each of the 17 theories of communications listed below, if explored from a content management perspective, provides intriguing ideas for discussion about how to justify a new program based on communications in a rapidly changing business and organizational environment. The theories can be examined further to determine which ones provide the managers and decision makers with a logical explanation of why a CMS might or might not fit in their organization or environment.

The value of these theories is that they provide the intellectual rationale for creating tools and tactics that can apply to professional practice. While many newer theories may not have engendered fully operational tactics, most tactics cannot be explained or defended without a theoretical framework. Ideas like the following illustrate that communication theory can indeed be applied. This list mostly examines theories and research dealing with communication in formal organizations and institutions.

As you read, you may want to consider what the dominant theoretical hypotheses are in communications. What are some likely integrated marketing communications (IMC) and owned-content creation questions that could be asked?

COMPREHENSIVE LIST OF CONTEMPORARY RESEARCH-BASED THEORIES OF COMMUNICATIONS AND POTENTIAL INTEGRATED COMMUNICATIONS APPLICATIONS[11]

1. Uses and gratifications: People use media to fill personal, political and social needs. Can the newer cable media go too far with Fox and MSNBC? Is this the new propaganda age that would be extended by owned content from companies and NGOs?

2. Agenda setting: The media do not tell people what to think; they tell them what to think about. Do audiences really want to think about Hollywood and entertainment all the time? Do stakeholders ever want to think about how you make your product and the history of your company?

3. Agenda melding: People join groups by "melding" agendas. Why is partisanship so rampant? Can we integrate business and society with common green agenda? Is it time for NGOs and corporations to share their agenda in a way that institutions can cooperate on common issues?

4. Dissonance: When confronted by new information, people experience mental discomfort, and they work to limit or reduce that discomfort. Do I buy gas from the local BP dealer? Should the dealers have used social media to bypass the corporation to make their point? Should BP have facilitated social media for their dealers? Should I give my fiancée a diamond (possibly from a conflict diamond mining source)?

5. Reinforcement: If media have any impact at all, it is in the direction of reinforcement. Which are the most effective and efficient media for which targets? Is it important to "kiss the frog" six times in this new media world? If my website attracts the most dedicated followers or users of my products or ideas, do I have to use other general media where the message may be wasted? Is social media and content management the secret answer to all my problems?

6. Parasocial relationships: People establish social relationships with media personalities. Q scores show popularity relationships with hosts from Fox, Good Morning America and microchannels. Should my owned content follow this American and human desire to know about movie stars and entertainers? Should we hire a known spokesperson or actor or try to create our own personality on our owned-content website? Should we rely on our careful truthworthy reporting of content and reuse of credible content? What is the return on investment (ROI) value of "fame"? Are trustworthiness and branding related?

7. Framing: To make sense of events, we categorize them. "Progressive is the new liberal." Who uses the term? The president is talking about stakeholders. Who defines the context of business and society?

8. Knowledge gap: The more information in the social system, the more the higher socioeconomic status groups will gain in knowledge compared to those in lower socioeconomic strata(SES). Grocery food deserts, environmental racism, hourly wages from nonunion shops: what is sustainable for whom? And, who decides?

9. Elaboration Likelihood Model: Persuasive messages can be processed using either the central (recipient is motivated) or peripheral routes (recipient is not motivated). Voting compares to which commercial purchases? Is online digital buying central? How do we process increasing numbers of messages, over increasing numbers of channels?

10. Adoption: Adopters pass through five steps—awareness, interest, evaluation, trial, adoption. Is the old model too linear, as some IMC experts claim? Is adoption even more important in a widely growing technological, entrepreneurial and innovative economy?

11. Two-step flow: Certain members of society are active consumers of media and become opinion leaders who influence others. Does this include bloggers, Tweeters, those who are linked or use re-Tweet or bitly or TinyURL?

12. Cultivation: People who are heavy viewers of TV tend to believe that the "real" world is more similar to the world seen on TV than do light viewers. What are the marketing and policy ethical issues? What about product alignment with the gullible or less cynical viewers (children, elderly, undereducated)?

13. Social learning theory: Children learn behaviors by watching them, including watching them on TV. What balance should IMC put into the system? What greater damage can advertising do to marketing? Can advertising refocus its power? Does transparent PR not gain in stature?

14. Spiral of silence: Public opinion consists of those opinions you can express in public without socially isolating yourself. Will we be allowed to blog about work? Can we be too transparent?

15. Symbolic interaction: People give meaning to symbols, and then those symbols control peoples' behavior. Why are graphics and imagery not more important in IMC? What has happened to semiotics in the classroom and research programs of IMC?

16. Mainstreaming: TV has the ability to pull people to a common understanding of an issue. Does this include freedom of speech for corporations? Politically oriented corporate messaging? How can we have a common understanding in a diverse nation? If it works in China, should we use it in the United States, and vice versa?

17. Technological determinism: Media communication and the technology it uses help shape the society in which we live. What is the real effect of a wildly popular magazine in this age, such as *People Style Watch*? What is our perception of our society? Is it the medium or the message again? How does any important issue, product or service become successful in a high-tech age?

THE FUTURE OF CONTENT STRATEGY

So what does this all mean? Again, nothing, if it is not used to achieve strategic and measurable business objectives. Science has caught up with us. Of course, this is in no way meant to be a comprehensive step-by-step for the practice of content strategy. Instead it is a place to start and jog your thoughts, and inspire further research and discussion. Please see the list of additional reading for suggested references.

In the wake of communication and stakeholder integration, the new mandate for content strategy will be enveloped in all aspects of content generation. In fact, strategic thinking, or thinking strategically, has become the new mandate for all business operations. Asking "what is the point?" has become more important now than ever, as all actions must be justified to interested and invested stakeholders.

Beyond just creating good content, the future will command the creation of good content on the go, that is, content that is designed and optimized for all mobile platforms with a current emphasis on tablet consumption.

Ever changing social, political and economic trends, innovations and inventions will define and redefine this challenging new media ecosystem. Staying ahead of, and on top of these trends will be the continuing challenge to content providers.

Could paid content and content management systems fail? Given the seeming failure of traditional journalism and media, it is not unthinkable that the newer media and structure of content creation and management may fail too.

In the past, when an agency or organization was looking to manage content, the focus was on information architecture or user experience design, two fields robust enough to stand alone on their own merits. Yet at some point over the last decade or so, as agency accountability became a more pressing concern, the specific and individually defined role of the content strategist came to be.

Of course, the natural progression is then to train and ready professionals entering the work force or retrain midlevel public relations and advertising practitioners in the field of content strategy. As universities prepare curriculums for the art and science of effective content strategy and management, it is prudent to examine and anticipate not only what is trending now, but what will be trending five or even ten years from now. We have attached a training program for your evaluation in the appendix at the end of this chapter.

APPENDIX: ILLUSTRATIVE TRAINING PROGRAM IN CONTENT MANAGEMENT FOR INDUSTRY, GOVERNMENT AND NGOS—AN IMC APPROACH TO CONTENT MANAGEMENT

Developed by Clarke L. Caywood, Ph.D., with Sara E. Smith, M.S.I.M.C., Northwestern University

Based upon the chapter, this training program is a case example to illustrate the value of content management in organizations. This training program will first explore the rapidly changing trends in a new ecosystem of news and owned content. The course looks at the delivery of a continuum of news, deliberately "fake news" and transparent branded content. The objective will be to build needed content creation and delivery programs in agencies, companies, government and NGOs. The program follows the general outline of an academic graduate class but with more practical exercises and readings in an eight-unit intensive schedule.

1. A CONTENT CONTINUUM

Goals

Identify and label examples from an online search to replace and create more content for stakeholders. Provide examples from searches to fill the continuum of content reviewed from academic publications, commercial research, books, journalism, commentary, information, edutainment, infotainment, news, fake news, news satire, earned media, owner-created news content, brand content, simulated product news.

Readings

> "Branded Content in Marketing and Public Relations," by Sara E. Smith and Clarke Caywood, Chapter 15 in *The Handbook of Corporate Public Relations and Integrated Marketing Communications*, edited by Clarke Caywood. McGraw-Hill, 2012. (This will be referred to as *Handbook*.)
> *Content Rules: How to Create Killer Blogs, Podcasts, Videos, EBooks, Webinars (and More) That Engage Customers and Ignite Your Business (New Rules Social Media Series)*, by Ann Handley, C.C. Chapman and David Meerman Scott, 2010. Read the case for content, pages 1–14, and read the content rules, pages 15–18.
> *Losing the News: The Future of the News that Feeds Democracy in the New News Media*, by Alex S. Jones. Oxford: Oxford UP, 2009. Chapter 8, pages 177–195.

2. WHO IS THE CONTENT AUDIENCE?

Goals

Create stakeholder maps and plans with teams to identify content audiences.

Interactive Exercises and Discussion

Who are the content stakeholders beyond the customer?

Readings

> *Content Rules: How to Create Killer Blogs, Podcasts, Videos, EBooks, Webinars (and More) That Engage Customers and Ignite Your Business (New Rules Social Media Series)*, by Ann Handley, C.C. Chapman and David Meerman Scott, 2010. Read "Insight, Inspiring Originality," pages 3–27.
> "The Stakeholder Concept: Empowering PR," by Clarke Caywood, Chapter 7 in *Handbook*.
> "Global Media Relations: Traditional Through 2.0," by Matt Gonring, Chapter 17 in *Handbook*.
> "Digital Communities: Social Media in Action," by Richard Edelman, Chapter 16 in *Handbook*.

3. WHAT IS JOURNALISM CONTENT, AND WHAT HAPPENED TO IT?

Goals

The goal is to understand the highest standard examples of modern content. Consider the following: What is journalism? Why is it in trouble, and will it be replaced by new forms of content delivery? Also, how has journalism been the key, credible content provider in developed and developing nations?

Exercises and Discussion

Review selected online and atomistic newspapers, magazines and broadcasts for examples of news content and content provided to journalism by content owners. Consider the current pressures on the news industry and the "death of news." Also, is journalism just for journalists?

Readings

> *Elements of Journalism (Revised): What Newspeople Should Know and The Public Should Expect*, by Bill Kovach and Tom Rosenstiel. Pages 1–112, including introduction.
> *Death and Life of American Journalism: The Media Revolution that Will Begin the World Again*, by Robert W. McChesney and John Nichols, 2010. Pages 1–56 and 121–157.
> *Can Journalism Be Saved?: Rediscovering America's Appetite for News*, by Rachel Mersey, 2010. Pages 1–34.
> *Losing the News: The Future of the News that Feeds Democracy*, by Alex S. Jones. Chapter 6, "The Curious Story of News," pages 125–150, and Chapter 9, "Saving the News," pages 196–222.

4. REVIEW OF BEST PRACTICES IN OWNED-CONTENT PRODUCTION AND REVIEW

Goals

Public relations has been the professional source of owned content from corporations and all other organizations for over a century. The section will examine the most recent award-winning and evaluated examples of owned content with the objective of understanding best practices for content management. The current substantial notebooks are confidential and not available without special cooperation.

Discussion and Exercise

How do the best practices from agencies and other organizations exist as examples of content? What are the standards and scoring methods for content? What is the range of content programs developed by public relations professionals?

Each class team will select, from a group of high-scoring entries, the strategic programs and content award for study and review. Based on discussion and self-training, each team will score the entry and then present scores and rationale to the class.

Readings

"Dynamic Digital Public Relations Research," by Clarke Caywood, Chapter 3 in *Handbook*.
Sample Anvil entries, volumes in hard copy.
Silver and Bronze Anvils: media.prsa.org/events/silver+anvil+awards.htm?utm_campaign=PRSASearch&utm_
source=PRSAWebsite&utm_medium=SSearch&utm_term=silver%20an and media.prsa.org/article_
display.cfm?article_id=1182.
Silver Anvil training materials and case study from Gronstedt and Caywood files and www.PRSA.org.

5. SOCIAL MEDIA CHOICES AND MEASUREMENT METRICS

Goal

Better understand new media choices, the social media channels and platforms that PR seems to dominate.
Know how to measure outcomes of each with both free and professional service subscription software.

Issues to Explore in Lecture and Discussion

How does the content proposal plan measure the success or failure of the media recommendations?
What existing high-cost and even lower-cost systems exist to measure the popularity, approval, use and reuse
of content?
What are the dozens of metrics that measure content?

Readings

"Dynamic Digital Public Relations Research," by Anders Gronstedt and Clarke Caywood, Chapter 3 in
Handbook.
Subscription websites for commercial content software: academic.csuohio.edu/kneuendorf/content.

6. HOW DO YOU ADVISE AN ORGANIZATION TO BUILD A NEW CONTENT-DELIVERY PROGRAM?

Goal

Identify, understand and apply an IMC planning model to be used for proposing the creation of a content-
delivery program in an organization.

Discussion and Exercises

What are the professional contributions of journalism, independent journalism, public relations and marketing
to building a new discipline of content planning, production and evaluation?
What are news organizations, independent news providers, agencies, companies and consultants providing
through news channels?
What knowledge, skills and experience are agencies and companies requesting to create and build content
programs?

Readings

Content strategist job description from Leo Burnet Chicago and other current job listings (various) for
content providers, analysts and strategists.
*Content Rules: How to Create Killer Blogs, Podcasts, Videos, Ebooks, Webinars (and More) That
Engage Customers and Ignite Your Business (New Rules Social Media Series)*, by Ann Handley, C.C.
Chapman and David Meerman Scott, 2010. Read Part 2: "How To?," pages 139–214 and "When
Singularity Is More Than a Literary Device," pages 145–159.

7. WHAT EXTERNAL PROFESSIONAL RULES AND LAWS SHAPE CONTENT PRODUCTION AND DELIVERY?

Goal

Understand and apply developing codes regulating and guiding content development and delivery. Prepare to guide other managers on standards to avoid controversy, crisis and lawsuits.

Discussion and Exercises

Understand, discuss and apply the rules and values of content production of the news and broadcasting profession (SPJ, NAB).

Understand, discuss and apply the rules and values of content production of the public relations profession (PRSA and A.W. Page Society).

Prepare or recommend a code of ethics and practice for content delivery for the client.

Readings

Content: Selected Essays on Technology, Creativity, Copyright, and the Future of the Future, by Cory Doctorow.

How Leaders Create a Culture of Candor (J-B Warren Bennis Series), by Warren Bennis, Daniel Goleman, James O'Toole and Patricia Ward Biederman (2008).

Code of Society of Professional Journalists: www.spj.org/ethicscode.asp.

Code of National Association of Broadcasters: en.allexperts.com/q/TV-Industry-2497/NAB-Code-Ethics.htm.

Code of Public Relations Society of America: www.prsa.org/AboutPRSA/Ethics.

Arthur W. Page Society code on Internet content: www.awpagesociety.com/site/about/pr_coalition_endorses.

"Broadcast Media as Broadcast PR," by Tim Larson and Craig Wirth, Chapter 15 in Handbook.

"Public Relations Law," by Karla Gower, Chapter 4 in Handbook.

8. FINAL PRESENTATION OF CONTENT PROPOSAL

Goal

Apply your ideas, research and knowledge to your proposal to gain acceptance of your ideas.

Discussion and Exercise

Present your work to the team and panel of judges.

DISCUSSION QUESTIONS

1. What strategies are you currently employing to communicate with your stakeholders? What is working and what is not?
2. Is your content integrated with the sum total of the planned user experience in mind?
3. What is your company or organization's capacity to generate content? Is it in step with your audience's appetite for consumption?
4. Does the content being produced and published add strategic value to your organization's business objectives?
5. Is the content being published transparent and trustworthy?
6. How can the communication theories discussed in this chapter be applied to your content management process?

NOTES

1. www.youtube.com/watch?v=kz7660AoH7E&feature=player_embedded#at=35.
2. thesartorialist.blogspot.com.
3. www.bobbuch.com/post/4017816296/stop-calling-it-content.
4. www.iainstitute.org/en/learn/education/schools_teaching_ia.php.
5. www.writingfortheweb.org.
6. "The State of Search Engine Marketing 2006." *Search Engine Land.* February 8, 2007.
7. Rachel D. Mersey book, 2010.
8. spj.org/ethicscode.asp.
9. www.prsa.org/AboutPRSA/Ethics.
10. adwords.google.com/o/Targeting/Explorer?__u=1000000000&__c=1000000000&ideaRequestType=KEYWORD_IDEAS#search.none.
11. Mersey, Rachael and Clarke L. Caywood, Northwestern University Internal Report 2011.

ADDITIONAL READINGS

READINGS ON BUSINESS

Bennis, Warren G., Daniel Goleman, and James O'Toole. *Transparency: How Leaders Create a Culture of Candor.* San Francisco, CA: Jossey-Bass, 2008. Print.

Burger, T. "CiteSeerX—Towards Increased Reuse: Exploiting Social and Content Related Features of Multimedia Content on the Semantic Web." Web. citeseerx.ist.psu.edu/viewdoc/summary?doi=10.1.1.143.1454. Accessed 8/15/2011.

Dionisopoulos, G.N. "Corporate Advocacy Advertising as Political Communication, in New Perspectives on Political Advertising," edited by Lynda Lee Kaid, Dan D. Nimmo, and Keith R. Sanders. Carbondale, IL: Southern Illinois UP, 1986. Print.

Heath, Robert L. "Corporate Advocacy: An Application of Speech Communication Perspectives and Skills—And More." *ERIC—World's Largest Digital Library of Education Literature.* Web. www.eric.ed.gov/ERICWebPortal/search/detailmini.jsp?_nfpb=true. Accessed 8/15/2011.

Shanley, Michael G., Matthew W. Lewis, Susan G. Straus, Jeff Rothenberg, and Lindsay Daugherly. *The Prospects for Increasing the Reuse of Digital Training Content.* Ft. Belvoir, VA: Defense Technical Information Center, 2009. Print.

READINGS ON CONTENT

Halligan, Brian, and Dharmesh Shah. *Inbound Marketing: Get Found Using Google, Social Media, and Blogs.* Hoboken, NJ: Wiley, 2010. Print.

Halvorson, Kristina. *Content Strategy for the Web.* Indianapolis, IN: New Riders, 2009. Print.

Handley, Ann, and C. C. Chapman. *Content Rules: How to Create Killer Blogs, Podcasts, Videos, Ebooks, Webinars (and More) That Engage Customers and Ignite Your Business.* Hoboken, NJ: Wiley, 2011. Print.

Jones, Colleen. *Clout: the Art and Science of Influential Web Content.* Berkeley, CA: New Riders, 2011. Print.

Kissane, Erin. *The Elements of Content Strategy.* New York, NY: Book Apart, 2011. Print.

Pulizzi, Joe, and Newt Barrett. *Get Content, Get Customers: Turn Prospects into Buyers with Content Marketing.* New York, NY: McGraw-Hill, 2009. Print.

Rosenbaum, Steven C. Curation. *Nation: How to Win in a World Where Consumers Are Creators.* New York, NY: McGraw-Hill, 2011. Print.

READINGS ON JOURNALISM

Kovach, Bill, and Tom Rosenstiel. *The Elements of Journalism: What Newspeople Should Know and the Public Should Expect.* New York, NY: Three Rivers, 2007. Print.

McChesney, Robert Waterman, and John Nichols. *The Death and Life of American Journalism: The Media Revolution That Will Begin the World Again*. Philadelphia, PA: Nation, 2010. Print.

Mersey, Rachel Davis. *Can Journalism Be Saved?: Rediscovering America's Appetite for News*. Santa Barbara, CA: Praeger, 2010. Print.

Meyers, Christopher. *Journalism Ethics: A Philosophical Approach*. New York, NY: Oxford UP, 2010. Print.

LINKS

Brain Traffic: www.braintraffic.com.

Content Princess: contentprincess.blogspot.com.

Content strategy research and ideas from Erin Kissane: incisive.nu.

Creekmore Consulting: www.lauracreekmore.com.

Endlessly Content: endlesslycontent.com.

Knol: knol.google.com/k/content strategy#.

The #contentstrategy Daily: paper.li/tag/contentstrategy.

53

C H A P T E R

IMMERSIVE 3-D VIRTUAL WORLDS
Avatars at Work

Anders Gronstedt, Ph.D.
Chief Executive Officer
The Gronstedt Group

> *Social media is a river, and virtual worlds are an island—a place you go with intent, for context, to stop, to have rich discussions and dialogue, to participate in stories.*
>
> —Dough Thompson (aka Dusan Writer)[1]

Few breakthrough ideas have ever been conceived, and no relationships or communities have ever been built while staring at the phone and talking to disembodied voices on a phone call, watching a death-by-PowerPoint webinar drone-a-thon through WebEx or participating in a TelePresence video conferencing session that brings the drama and depth of a C-SPAN program.

So, how do you build dialogue and collaborate and innovate with stakeholders who work from coffee shops, kitchen tables and cubicles around the world? One thing is for sure: conference calls, video conferencing and webinars are not the answer.

Instead, forward-looking companies wager that the future of corporate communications will not be built on flat, static web pages but rather in traversable 3-D spaces—think Facebook meets Grand Theft Auto, or a Smurf Village reduction of your conference room. The 3-D multiuser virtual world environments were originally designed for consumer entertainment but rapidly became popular with corporations and government agencies. Virtual worlds are already used by thousands of universities for everything from 3-D campus tours for prospective students and professor office hours for students to staging historical reenactments in medieval England and holding biology classes inside of a molecule, in 3-D environments that bring context to the shared experience. Every branch of the U.S. military is using virtual worlds for tasks as far-reaching as support communities for veterans and immersion in Afghan culture before deployment.[2] And, roughly 20 percent of the Fortune 1000 corporations are using these immersive 3-D meeting spaces.[3] IBM has at least 20,000 employees using virtual worlds. The National Oceanic and Atmospheric Administration (NOAA) has been a pioneer in the use of virtual world technology and has managed 14 "islands" in the popular virtual world of Second Life to support its outreach mission.[4]

After just a few minutes in a virtual-world meeting, you will see why this is heralded as one of the most disruptive technologies of our age. It is Internet in 3-D. And it takes interaction and collaboration to

F I G U R E   53.1

Example of the Gronstedt Group's weekly "Train for Success" business meetings in the 3D virtual world

unprecedented levels. Participants move their avatars, or digital alter egos (are they really alter egos? Well . . . yes . . . sort of . . . that's the best way I can think of to describe the idea that you control the avatar and appear in the world as your avatar . . .), around a 3-D world, interacting with other people through their avatars by talking straight to their computers via headset. As people move about, the sound changes direction. If you are standing to the right of the speaker with your avatar, you all hear him from the right speaker of your headset. If you walk away from avatars who are talking, their voices fade away. This is sound and sight in 3-D. Green waves radiate from the talking avatar as it starts gesturing. The immersive environment keeps participants completely focused on the task at hand (Figure 53.1).

Virtual worlds succeed where the flatland web applications of webinars failed: they engage by offering an interactive suspension of belief. If you bump into someone else with your avatar, you apologize profusely just as you would in real life. Unlike 2-D web conferencing presentations, the 3-D virtual environment offers participants the perception of being there, which keeps them focused, engaged and motivated. Instead of communications mediated by books, PowerPoint slides and voice-over narration, virtual worlds are experiential, interactive and multisensory. People are engaged in new and exciting ways. They go to a virtual destination together. People who spend time in this space don't think of it as a "virtual world," as the notions of "real" and "virtual" become interchangeable when you're immersed in this world. The difference between a traditional webinar or video conferencing and a virtual world is the difference between looking in a window and walking into a room!

Avatar-mediated communication challenges traditional notions of identity. "I wear a mask, but I'm not hiding behind it," says Ian Hughes, one of the original virtual-world evangelists at IBM, who appears as a predator robot at business meetings in Second Life. Traditional business etiquette does not apply in the virtual world. While some companies limit the range of avatar creativity, IBM takes a more liberal position. Chuck Hamilton, who heads the virtual learning strategy at the IBM Center for Advanced Learning, says, "At IBM you can come to a meeting as a fish." While he has yet to see someone show up as a fish, Hamilton himself sports a kilt as a proud expression of his Scottish heritage, one of thousands of examples of self-expression through an avatar, which serves as an effective icebreaker at meetings. That might seem frivolous, but with low productivity caused by disengaged workers at a cost to the U.S. economy of approximately $300 billion a year, it's time to shift attention to approaches that not only transfer knowledge but actually engage people.

CASE: SCHNEIDER ELECTRIC AND IBM

How do two global billion-dollar corporations co-create value without the carbon footprint of flying executives around the world to meet? That was the question facing Schneider Electric SA, a recognized leader in helping customers manage their energy. Working with large global clients like IBM Corp. often requires energy expenditure in the form of airline travel. The most recent collaborative planning session Schneider Electric held with IBM required some 15 people to fly around the world, not the best method to develop green data centers.

"Our pilot in Second Life was to see if it was possible to have a collaborative meeting/customer workshop without the travel costs/time and perhaps create a means for even more customer intimacy because we could collaborate much more often with key people," says Mike Sullivan, vice president of global strategic accounts at Schneider.

It was not hard for Schneider to convince IBM to participate in a Second Life session. With a workforce of 20,000 employees using Second Life and other virtual worlds, doing everything from recruiting and new-hire orientations to mentoring and sales role-playing, they were well experienced.

According to Sullivan,

> The virtual worlds environment created more of a "sense of team" than in previous meetings. Our customer, IBM, had seven senior managers present, and Schneider Electric had nine present: senior managers, the account team and solution specialists. With everyone represented as an avatar, it was difficult to tell the IBM team from the Schneider Electric team. As we worked closely together to brainstorm and identify key value areas around IBM's business drivers, it created a sense of one common team.

For the collaborative planning meeting, the IBM and Schneider avatars gathered in an open-air setting along a virtual tropical coastline hosted by the Gronstedt Group Inc. and facilitated by Performance Methods Inc. The goal was to identify areas where IBM and Schneider could work together to create the best value for IBM's strategic outsourcing business. The meeting began with an update by IBM. (Even avatars can't seem to be weaned off PowerPoint slides!) As team members brainstormed potential value areas, the facilitator typed the ideas on a virtual whiteboard. Then members voted by individually clicking on their three favorite entries. After tallying the votes to identify the top three value target areas, the team worked to develop action plans. (You can watch the video here: www.youtube.com/watch?v=wsYVF25jHqw.)

An IBM leader compared the Second Life meeting to last year's live meeting by saying, "The session exceeded my expectations. It took us to a new level of collaboration. Being in Second Life got people excited about trying something new and created a team group effect even though we participated remotely."

Unlike live meetings where frequently the vendor sits on one side of the table, and the client sits on the other, often with the tension palpable, virtual-world meetings tend to be more collaborative and creative.

"Second Life also enabled participation in multiple dimensions," Sullivan says. "In a typical business meeting/customer workshop with 16 people, only a few people can speak at one time. Second Life offered the additional advantage of enabling people to type in their ideas concurrently and then to rank and vote on ideas concurrently."

THE TOP 10 KILLER APPS OF VIRTUAL WORLDS FOR COMMUNICATIONS

Early success stories from organizations like IBM and the U.S. Army, each with over four years of experience using virtual worlds, suggest a number of "killer apps," or competitive advantages, of immersive 3-D virtual world communications over more traditional forms of communication.

1. MEETINGS

Virtual worlds can be used in place of many companies' existing videoconferencing and webinar activities to employees, investors, customers and other stakeholders. The benefits of such meetings over the traditional conference calls and WebExes of the world are the sense of immersion and of being in the presence of each other. Companies like IBM frequently hold meetings that involve real-world participants in a conference room interacting with the avatars of remote participants that are displayed on a screen. This sort of event is called a "mixed reality," and those who have participated in it say there is a sense that the people are all actually together.

2. MENTORING

Companies also are using virtual environments as a meeting ground for mentors and their mentees. This has the obvious benefit of eliminating distance barriers that could prohibit certain mentoring relationships. In addition, because the employees involved are not working in the same office, they can provide each other with a unique brand of insight. IBM is using Second Life for global "speed mentoring." Traditionally, mentoring relationships at IBM remained regional; for example, a European employee would likely have a European mentor. Now employees (as their avatars) can meet in the virtual world, where they are mentored by senior managers who may be continents and cultures away.

3. EVENTS

Companies are holding virtual events such as trade shows, expos, conferences and job fairs in virtual worlds. Virtual events can bring the benefits of exposure to speakers, networking with colleagues and socializing with vendors, all without ever leaving your office. A burgeoning market of "pseudo 3-D" virtual event platforms from companies like InXpo, ON24 and Unisfair offer large virtual conferences and trade shows. They can scale to tens of thousands of simultaneous users by offering participants the illusion that they are in a 3-D environment, rather than delivering a full 3-D experience. These platforms meet requirements for scale and ease of use but compromise on the immersive qualities of moving around with your own avatar in a 3-D space. However, as the pseudo 3-D platforms are becoming more immersive and the truly immersive virtual-world platforms scale up and become more user friendly, we will soon experience trade shows with thousands of participants in true virtual worlds. For instance, the Intel-backed ScienceSim grid, based on the OpenSim platform, has run demos with over 1,000 avatars in a single region.[5]

4. EXPERIENCES

The 3-D environment of many virtual worlds can be used by PR and communications professionals to illustrate technical concepts in powerful new ways. In a virtual environment, you can construct scaled representations of any structure or system. Your avatar can have many experiences that are not possible in the real world. Here are a few examples:

- The Science Library in Second Life, for instance, affords you a novel view of the placement of carbon atoms in 3-D space.

- Exploratorium, a Second Life museum, has built a scale model of the Earth and moon system. Even real-life astronomers find that walking their avatars from the Earth to the moon gives them a more immediate understanding of the sizes and distances involved.

- The University of Denver has developed a virtual nuclear power plant. They plan on contrasting the 1946 Chernobyl power plant with a state-of-the-art power plant to give hands-on training to students and inform the public.

- A University of California psychology professor's class affords students the experience of powerful virtual hallucinations. As users get closer to a poster on the wall, words change to profanities and a creepy voice tells you to "kill yourself." This experience illustrates schizophrenia in ways that listening to a lecture or reading a text simply can't match.

Einstein famously imagined himself to be a photon speeding over the earth; virtual worlds actually allow for these types of experiences.

5. GAMES AND SIMULATIONS

While the virtual worlds discussed here are not games themselves—there is not necessarily any score, no levels, no end purpose—almost any kind of game-based experience can be developed in a virtual world. Consider Microsoft Visual Studio's crafty scavenger hunt. The users must solve various logic puzzles to gain entrance to a mysterious blimp in the sky. Inside the blimp, they have a chance to win a grand prize. This game is fun for the user and promotes the Microsoft brand.

The notion of "gamification" has recently been a rallying cry for corporate professionals. Everything is a game these days. Even recycling companies give you points for every pound of recycled material and allow you to go online and see how you compare with your neighbors. Foursquare offers "mayorships" at locations such as hotels and other major national attractions. Airlines award reward points. In fact, we are always monitored and always scored.

According to Stephanie Schwab, gamification has the following advantages:

- A fun and exciting way to be part of a community

- Audiences rewarded for participation

- Pass-along and recommendations encouraged

- Loyalty and increased sales built through repeat visits and purchases

An example of how organizations are using virtual-world gaming as global public relations efforts is the United States Army (Figure 53.2). Here, a first-person shooter game was developed as an initiative to help with recruitment. The free game provided the public a virtual soldier experience and has been expanded to include versions for Xbox and Xbox 360, arcade and mobile applications, with more than 8 million players.

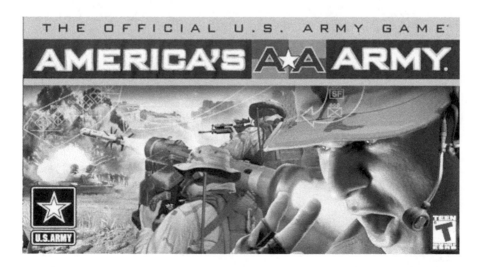

F I G U R E   53.2

The U.S. Army's "America's Army" recruitment game has been played by more than 8 million people

6. COLLABORATION

For all the razzle-dazzle of their 3-D modeling, virtual worlds are really ultimately a social networking tool. Online interaction and collaboration are taken to unprecedented levels; hierarchies are broken down; geographic boundaries are eliminated. Virtual-world meetings can be a great way to increase ease of communication across departments. A large pharmaceutical company had its research team and its sales team collaborate in a virtual world. These two teams, which notoriously worked poorly together, excelled in the virtual environment. As a result, a new drug was ready for market months ahead of time, which resulted in a substantial profit for the company.

7. ROLE-PLAYING

Virtual worlds can provide virtual rehearsals to role-play any communication skill. Consider training spokespeople through role-playing. Ample evidence implies that role-playing in a virtual world can be more effective than a live classroom-based role-play. Loyalist College in Ontario, Canada, found that Second Life role-playing increased the number of border agent students who passed a final evaluation from 56 to 93 percent when the test was moved from the classroom (Figure 53.3).[6]

"You could see the students sitting straighter in their chairs when their avatars got into a uniform," says Ken Hudson, managing director of Loyalist's Virtual World Design Centre. "They left the project with a sense of accomplishment and one of having participated in a real-world experience."

F I G U R E   53.3

Virtual world role-playing increased the number of border agent students who passed a final evaluation from 56 to 93 percent when the test was moved from the classroom

FIGURE 53.4

IBM employees step into a virtual elevator to practice their "elevator pitch" with a chief information officer

At one of IBM's islands in Second Life, employees step into a virtual elevator to practice their "elevator pitch" with a chief information officer or rehearse an important client pitch in a conference room with IBM executives playing the role of clients (Figure 53.4).

In Avaya's Virtual Rehearsal Studio in its own web.alive platform, sales reps take turns playing the role of Julia Parker, the CIO of International University, and the Avaya account rep, while other reps give feedback on the performance (Figure 53.5). There is also an opportunity to strategize on current opportunities in their pipelines. It's a social simulator where reps can practice and fail in a safe environment."

FIGURE 53.5

People can literally walk, crawl, fly and sit with their avatars inside 3-D bar charts

8. DATA VISUALIZATION

Virtual worlds can also present financial data and key performance measures in 3-D graphs. Team members can literally walk, crawl, fly and sit inside 3-D bar charts and scatter plots with members' avatars, watching patterns that aren't apparent in a 2-D PowerPoint slide (Figure 53.6).

Businesses have come a long way since the first-generation virtual conference rooms that were common in virtual worlds in the early days, around 2007. The tendency to import personal baggage from real life into the virtual world is perhaps not surprising—unimaginative repurposing has characterized the early stages of seemingly all-new media. The first cars looked like horse carriages, the first movies looked like stage shows and most corporate websites still look like basic brochures. It takes time for a new medium to develop its own character and unique vernacular. Companies that use virtual worlds to deliver the same old straight-laced meetings in a virtual boardroom have to brace for a train wreck as digital natives enter the work force. Data visualization is one great example of doing new things in new ways instead of old things in new ways.

A.

B.

FIGURE 53.6

Sales reps practice at Avaya's virtual rehearsal studio in their web.alive platform

9. 3-D PRODUCT VISUALIZATION

Products can be visualized and explored in 3-D, as well; take a car for a spin, walk across a giant computer chip or fly around a map with sales data. At the Schneider–IBM meeting's conclusion, participants were invited to teleport to IBM's green data center in Second Life to see virtual representations of how Schneider and IBM work together to achieve corporate energy efficiency. Participants were able to walk around in a 3-D virtual model of the green data center, open the server doors and watch interactive demos, such as a little trolley that whizzes about, measures the temperature around the center and delivers a 3-D thermal heat map.

10. INFORMAL COMMUNICATION

It's hard to facilitate trust and open communication on a conference call. Webinars are all about formality: you log on exactly when the meeting is scheduled to begin and start with slide one and end with the last slide, or exactly 60 minutes later, whichever comes first. Virtual worlds, on the other hand, frequently end with a live band performance and virtual libations in the martini bar! Best of all, anyone can be a great dancer in a virtual world. One of the speakers of our "Train for Success" sessions, Sarah Robbins, put it best: "No one has ever logged on to WebEx to hang out." At Gronstedt Group's "Train for Success" meetings, this informal communication can be seen in action every week: people come early and leave late to hang out and chat.

HOW TO GET STARTED

The first step to genuinely understanding virtual worlds is to get your own avatar and experience a meeting. One good place to start is at the Gronstedt Group's weekly "Train for Success" meetings. Find the schedule on the Facebook page: www.facebook.com/TrainForSuccess. You will meet some 50 business professionals and hear presentations from companies like IBM and BP and government organizations like the NOAA and the U.S. Army about how they use virtual worlds.

Next, pilot and test. Solve specific problems. Hold the next employee kickoff meeting in a virtual Las Vegas instead of the real one. Or, set up a customer visitor center with 3-D models of your products and services. Do your next product launch in a virtual world instead of flying journalists in from all over the world, and enjoy immediate feedback. Build internal success stories. Virtual worlds have to be experienced firsthand. Once you have exposed a critical mass of people to even a single meeting, you will

INFORMATION BOX: HOW TO LEAD EFFECTIVE MEETINGS IN THE VIRTUAL WORLDS

Over the four-year course of hosting our weekly "Train for Success" meetings in virtual worlds and helping a number of Fortune 500 and leading government clients with everything from executive collaboration sessions to emergency response simulations, we have accumulated a number of new competencies for virtual-world communication professionals:

1. Be a Guide-on-the-Side, Not a Sage-on-a-Stage

Virtual worlds are an empowering medium where participants can text-chat, camera-control, talk, walk and fly. Effective leaders step out of their faculty cloaks and join the conversation. Trust in all participants is also crucial, as there are some who possess knowledge and expertise that surpass anything your communication organization can hope to master. Let them teach each other. No one has better credibility than a successful peer. Use the collaborative power of virtual worlds. Use frequent breakout sessions, for instance. They can be organized in seconds; just teleport groups to different areas or erect soundproof walls between breakout groups.

2. Give Tours, Not Classes

One of the greatest sins in a virtual world is to put avatars in chairs and start lecturing to PowerPoint slides. You might as well just use WebEx. If you insist on using PowerPoint slides, put them next to each other in a poster-board session. A walking tour of poster boards will let participants linger on past slides. It gives you something to do with your avatar. And you can check that everyone is following along. Needless to say, a tour along a path with 3-D props is even better than a poster-board tour.

3. Use 3-D Props, Not 2-D

You're in a 3-D world; why drag in 2-D props like PowerPoint slides at all? Virtual worlds can be used to scale things up or down and walk inside a molecule or on top of a 3-D map. See products in 3-D, take a virtual flight in the air or walk on an oil rig. Or visualize data in 3-D and walk and crawl inside a giant 3-D bar chart; you will see patterns in the 3-D data that you never saw in a million 2-D PowerPoint bar charts.

4. Focus on Informal Communications, Not Formal

We all know that informal communications accounts for 80 to 90 percent of all actual and real communication in any organization. Virtual worlds provide an environment that approximates the informality of a water-cooler conversation—take advantage of it. Create cool lounges or beachfronts where people want to hang out and socialize. Schedule breaks and encourage people to come early and stay late for meetings, so they can interact and learn from each other.

create a groundswell of support and an army of evangelists. Think big and act bold, but start small and iterate fast. Aggregate upward and outward to generate scale and drive the organization toward enterprise-level adoption. Turn to an experienced consultant with a track record from other clients to build the pilot.

Eventually you will want a robust virtual world build-out, be it behind the firewall or in a secure hosted environment. There are a number of virtual world platforms for companies to choose from. A key criterion in selecting a platform is to pick an open technology that companies can self-host, if they so chose, with a large echo system of developers. Below are some of the top considerations for any organization that fit these criteria:

- *OpenSim*, or the OpenSim Project, is an open-source virtual-world server platform, which can be accessed with the regular Second Life viewers. While the project started as an open-source clone of Second Life, it is now capable of hosting alternative worlds with differing feature sets with multiple protocols.

- *Unity3D* is an integrated authoring tool for creating 3-D video games or virtual worlds that will run in the browser. Unity3D needs a server to operate as a multiuser platform. One such solution is ReactionGrid's Jibe platform.

- *Unreal UDK* is a video-game authoring tool, a few years older than Unity, that needs a server to operate as a multiuser platform. Avaya's web.alive represents the most viable unreal-based virtual world application on the market.

- *Kata Space* leverages the emerging WebGL/HTML5 standards to develop virtual worlds natively in any web page.

A new emerging generation of virtual worlds is browser based, which makes access a lot easier than with the heavy software downloads. By comparison, online video didn't reach broad penetration until 2005, when they could be played in the browser and no longer required separate video playing software. While Unity and web.alive run in the browser already, the next-generation virtual worlds will run natively in any web page without even a browser plug-in. The current "standards war" over which a virtual-world platform will survive will be won by the web browser, which is rapidly becoming the standard for everything.

A VISION OF THE FUTURE: VIRTUAL WORLDS MEET AUGMENTED REALITY

If virtual worlds are an *Alice in Wonderland* rabbit hole that takes us to a magical virtual place through our laptops, "augmented reality" is the lens to the world that will make the real world virtual. Most of today's smartphones, iPads and tablets are equipped with cameras, turning them into magic lenses that will provide an augmentation of the world. You can now hold up your mobile device over a bar code on a product and watch a tutorial of the product on your screen; hold it over someone's face in a crowd and a facial recognition technology will identify the person as a subject matter expert on a topic; hold it over a piece of machinery on the factory floor and quality data will be superimposed on the phone screen. GPS and compass functions in the mobile devices provide even a larger window of augmented reality. We will see eyewear with eye tracking in the next four to five years at a price point affordable to most people, turning us all into supermen who can see through buildings and identify people on the street. The technology is here already, and we are just a few years away from mass adoption. Only our own imagination will hold us back.

CASE STUDY DISCUSSION QUESTIONS

1. What was the initial motivation behind moving the meeting to the virtual world?
2. What are some of the problems with live meetings that the virtual meeting overcame?
3. What are the PR incentives and implications of a company in the energy-saving business to fly people to meetings around the world?
4. What challenges did the two companies face by holding a strategic meeting like this in a virtual world?
5. What other applications could these companies use for virtual worlds?
6. What would your avatar look like if you participated in this meeting?

NOTES

1. Thompson, Doug, "Conventional Wisdom," *Dusan Writer's Metaverse*, dusanwriter.com/index.php/2011/02/18/conventional-wisdom/#more-2722.
2. O'Hara, Colleen, "Welcome Digital Natives," *Federal Computer Week*, 2009, fcw.com/articles/2009/03/23/eric-hackathorn-noaa.aspx (4 May, 2009).
3. Linden Lab, "Open Letter to Your Boss," 2009, blogs.secondlife.com/community/workinginworld/blog/2009/08/19/open-letter-to-your-boss.
4. www.noaa.gov/features/earthobs_0508/index.html.
5. Korlov, Maria, "ScienceSim Demos 1,000 Avatars on a Sim," *Hypergrid Business*, 2010, www.hypergridbusiness.com/2010/06/sciencesim-demos-1000-avatars-on-a-sim.
6. Hudson, Ken, and Kathryn deGast-Kennedy, "Canadian Border Simulation at Loyalist College," *Journal of Virtual Worlds Research* 2, no. 1.

ADDITIONAL READING

Blascovich, Jim, and Jeremy Bailenson, *Infinite Reality: Avatars, Eternal Life, New Worlds, and the Dawn of the Virtual Revolution*, William Morrow, 2011.

Kapp, Karl M. and Tony O'Driscoll, *Learning in 3D: Adding a New Dimension to Enterprise Learning and Collaboration*, Pfeiffer, 2010.

McGonigal, Jane, *Reality Is Broken: Why Games Make Us Better and How They Can Change the World*, Penguin Press, 2011.

Reeves, Byron, and J. Leighton Read, *Total Engagement: Using Games and Virtual Worlds to Change the Way People Work and Businesses Compete*, Harvard Business School Press, 2009.

54 CHAPTER

GLOBAL PUBLIC RELATIONS NETWORKS
The Efficacy and Role of Membership Organizations in Public Relations

Gerard F. Corbett, APR, Fellow PRSA
Founder and Chief Executive Officer
Redphlag LLC

No academic examination of the public relations field can be complete without a discussion of the role and efficacy of membership organizations in the growth and progress of the public relations industry and its professionals. Today there are many global membership organizations dedicated to individual practitioners, educators, agencies and/or companies. The goal of these organizations is to advocate for the role of public relations and for the public relations professional.

The services offered by these organizations span a wide spectrum of services from accreditation, benchmarking and career coaching to professional development and networking. Many of the organizations require adherence to the ethical practice of public relations through codes of ethics, conduct, behavior and principles that define professionalism and success. Lifelong learning opportunities are also promoted by these organizations that offer curricula and learning opportunities through expert case studies, decision-making guidelines and other tips to help practitioners apply expertise to everyday tasks and challenges. The range of development opportunities includes seminars, webinars, teleseminars, boot camps and conferences on topics from social media to crisis communications.

THE EFFICACY OF MEMBERSHIP ORGANIZATIONS

In this age when knowledge and information are king and social infrastructure platforms are proliferating, professional membership organizations are becoming even more essential to the progress and professional development of public relations professionals. The fact is that the network is the currency of today's knowledge and wisdom society. A strong network has many benefits that span career advancement, benchmarking, job performance, effective crisis management, on-the-job problem solving and a myriad of other factors where it pays to have a broad and wide network of people with whom to collaborate and exchange knowledge. One other interesting fact to consider is that, in today's job market, roughly 70 percent of people who are landing jobs are doing so as a result of their networks. So it is both wise and prudent to have and maintain a network. My recommendation, therefore, is to start working on building your network as part of your job-search campaign. Here are some thoughts to consider regarding networks:

- Membership organizations are one of the best means to employ to develop a network. Join and be engaged with organizations that share your vision, career aspirations, professional affiliations and interests. This is one of the most useful ways to network and let people know who you are and to showcase your abilities.

- If you have not already done so, consider using one or more of today's social media platforms like LinkedIn or Facebook to institutionalize your network.

- Networking means both connecting and collaborating with people in person as well as through other channels, such as phone calls.

- Invite every person with whom you come in contact to join your network on your preferred platform. By institutionalizing your connections, you need never worry about updating their contact information, and you will always have a direct connection to them.

- Reach out and help someone. Networking is a two-way street. Networks operate effectively if, in fact, you use them to help others as well as to ask for help.

- Go pro bono. There are likely several nonprofits that could benefit from the experience and abilities of public relations professionals. Volunteering is also a great way to build your network.

CREDENTIALS—MARKS OF DISTINCTION

Membership organizations are also a formidable means to validate your experience and credentials. Credentials like Accredited in Public Relations (APR) and Accredited Business Communicator (ABC) are valuable to those practitioners who earn them; to the agencies, clients and organizations they represent; and, perhaps most importantly, to the public relations profession itself.

The Public Relations Society of America APR credential, established in 1964, is earned for fulfilling the profession's only national postgraduate certification program. It measures a public relations practitioner's fundamental knowledge of communications theory and its application; establishes advanced capabilities in research, strategic planning, implementation and evaluation and demonstrates a commitment to professional excellence and ethical conduct. The skills acquired through the process are applicable to any industry or practice area. Currently, more than 5,000 professionals from the agency, corporate, association and education fields hold the APR mark, Harold Burson and Daniel J. Edelman notable among them. Granting of APR is overseen by the Universal Accreditation Board. The process of earning the credential has varied benefits:

- Promotes lifelong learning. All APRs are required to complete continuing-education programs, pursue volunteer work or pursue other professional development activities to keep their skills sharp and their accredited status active.

- Aids career enhancement. Unlike other professional certifications, such as the CPA (Certified Public Accounting), accreditation in public relations is a voluntary demonstration of competency; as such, it reflects a strong commitment to the profession. Earning accreditation also provides a distinction that can set individuals apart and open doors to career advancement and higher compensation.

- Reflects positively on the field of public relations. The public relations profession is among the most misunderstood and criticized. Through their high professional and ethical standards, accredited professionals contribute to greater understanding of public relations as a vital management function and undermine those who would refer to the craft as spin, professionals as flacks and currency as misrepresentation and disinformation.

The ABC credential of the International Association of Business Communicators is another standard of professional achievement for business communicators. Accredited members practicing around the world apply the same strategic management process in all communication disciplines, across diverse cultures and in for-profit and nonprofit organizations of all sizes.

This peer-reviewed program challenges candidates to demonstrate their knowledge of strategic communication planning, implementation, measurement and ethics. Candidates who meet all requirements earn the ABC designation.

PUBLIC RELATIONS MEMBERSHIP ORGANIZATIONS

As noted earlier, there are many membership organizations globally that serve both PR practitioners and organizations. The following is a broad range of global organizations that serve the public relations industry. It is by no means a complete list but represents a good cross section of organizations that well represent the industry, professional practitioners, educators and companies and institutions.

AFRICAN PUBLIC RELATIONS ASSOCIATION

The African Public Relations Association (APRA) is the successor organization to the Federation of African Public Relations Associations (FAPRA), which was inaugurated in 1975 in Nairobi, Kenya. The primary purpose is to help in creating and enabling a professional environment for accurate perception, goodwill and understanding of necessary and effective performance of public relations practice in Africa.

Three decades after, APRA has now been registered in Nigeria in March 2008 with similar aims and objectives. They include but are not limited to the following: to be the clearinghouse for public relations information in Africa, to set standards of public relations practice through its code of ethics, to foster the establishment of national and subregional public relations associations so that the profession can flourish in the continent, to promote African unity and cooperation especially as a consultant body to the African Union and its various agencies, to publish bulletins and journals on public relations in Africa and to affiliate with all other similar international professional bodies. These aims and objectives are complemented by the Codes of Professional Conduct approved by its council.

ARTHUR W. PAGE SOCIETY

The Arthur W. Page Society is a professional association for senior public relations and corporate communications executives who seek to enrich and strengthen their profession. The membership consists primarily of chief communications officers of Fortune 500 corporations, the CEOs of the world's largest public relations agencies and leading academics from the nation's top business and communications schools who have distinguished themselves in teaching corporate communications. The Page Society has strict membership selection criteria and, consequently, has attracted the very best and brightest of the profession.

The Page Society is dedicated to strengthening the management policy role of chief public relations officers. The Page Society is upheld by management concepts, known as the Page Principles, which have been tested for more than half a century and have earned the support and respect of chief executive officers throughout the country. Since its incorporation in December 1983, the Page Society has networked together senior communications executives, representing a wide spectrum of industries. These communications professionals share an interest in helping each other and perpetuating high professional standards. The Society is named in honor of Arthur W. Page, who served as vice president of public relations for the American Telephone and Telegraph Company from 1927 to 1946. He was the first public relations executive to serve as an officer and member of the board of directors of a major public corporation. He, more than any other individual, laid the foundation for the field of corporate public relations.

BELGIAN PUBLIC RELATIONS CONSULTANTS ASSOCIATION

The Belgian Public Relations Consultants Association (BPRCA) is a not-for-profit professional association representing a group of core public relations consultancies based in Belgium. The association aims to provide standards of professionalism within the market, allow the sharing of knowledge of best practices and more broadly represent its members in Belgium. BPRCA serves as a platform for discussion on industry issues of mutual interest to the senior management of all its members. The BPRCA membership currently includes over 25 of the top consultancies in Belgium, ranging from independent, boutique agencies to international network consultancies.

The BPRCA brings together most of the consultancies in Belgium with extensive experience in providing strategic communication advice. On the basis of detailed analysis, the consultancies can implement the appropriate actions in a whole series of communication disciplines in a wide range of social, institutional and economic sectors. The BPRCA is the only professional association representing public relations consultancies in Belgium. Its members offer advice to national and multinational organizations and institutions, both within and outside of Belgium.

The BPRCA's mission is to position its members as communication specialists and to guarantee their professionalism. In addition, the association strictly monitors its members' observance of a code of ethics, indispensable in an unregulated market.

CANADIAN INVESTOR RELATIONS INSTITUTE

The Canadian Investor Relations Institute (CIRI) is a professional, not-for-profit association of executives responsible for communication between public corporations, investors and the financial community. With four chapters and 600 members across Canada, CIRI is the world's second largest society of investor relations professionals. CIRI contributes to the transparency and integrity of the Canadian capital market by advancing the practice of investor relations, the professional competency of its members and the stature of the profession. CIRI will be recognized as the Canadian authority on investor relations, committed to enabling fair and efficient capital markets. CIRI is dedicated to advancing the stature and credibility of the investor relations profession and the competency of its members.

CANADIAN PUBLIC RELATIONS SOCIETY

The Canadian Public Relations Society (CPRS) is an organization of men and women who practice public relations in Canada and abroad. Members work to maintain the highest standards and to share a uniquely Canadian experience in public relations. CPRS was founded in 1948 from two original groups—the first in Montreal and the second in Toronto. In 1953, these became associated as the Canadian Public Relations Society, and, in 1957, the organization was incorporated as a national society.

Today, CPRS is a federation of 16 member societies based in major cities or organized provincewide. All member societies adhere to the constitution of the national and member Society. In cooperation with its regional member societies and with like-minded organizations in other countries, CPRS works to advance the professional stature of public relations and regulates its practice for the benefit and protection of the public interest.

The CPRS, as a distinct Canadian association, seeks to group all public relations practitioners in Canada and to foster their professional interests; to advance the professional stature of public relations, in cooperation with its regional member societies and with like-minded organizations in other countries; to regulate its practice for the benefit and protection of the public interest; and to serve the public interest by upholding a standard of proficiency and code of ethics and by providing ongoing professional development to its members and public relations practitioners across Canada.

CHARTERED INSTITUTE OF PUBLIC RELATIONS

The Chartered Institute of Public Relations is a chartered body and is led by the president, who is the chairman of the institute and the representative of the profession in the United Kingdom. The president is elected by the members every autumn and is in post for one year. Members also elect the president-elect and honorary treasurer. CIPR is the advocate and voice of the public relations profession, a champion of professional interests, a respected partner to the broader communications community and a body that works in the public interest.

CIPR enhances the reputation and understanding of the public relations profession and the professionalism of members through the provision of world-class structures for the practice of public relations. CIPR does this by providing education, knowledge building and sharing, research, excellent governance, conduct and ethics.

Membership in the CIPR is on an individual basis. CIPR offers membership to PR practitioners at all levels in their careers and in all sectors, from those working in-house to consultancies, independent and free-lance practitioners, both nationally and internationally. There are various grades of membership (fellow, member, associate, affiliate, global affiliate, and student) spanning different levels of experience and qualifications in PR. Membership assessment is rigorous and is based on multidisciplinary experience and qualifications. Membership figures have more than doubled in the last 10 years. Approximately 55 percent of members are female; this has grown from 20 percent in 1987. Forty-five percent of members work in PR consultancy, and 55 percent work in-house. Two-thirds of CIPR members are based outside London.

COMMUNITY COLLEGE PUBLIC RELATIONS ORGANIZATION

The statewide Community College Public Relations Organization is a professional development and service organization that seeks to promote excellence in California's community college public relations and related professions. The organization serves as a central resource of information and provides counsel and assistance relating to the advancement of community colleges statewide and the professional growth of its members.

COUNCIL OF PUBLIC RELATIONS

More than 100 of the leading public relations firms in the United States are currently members of the Council of Public Relations (CPR). They represent the premier global, midsize, regional and specialty agencies across every discipline and practice area. CPR advocates for and advances the business of public relations firms by building the market and the value of firms as strategic business partners. The philosophical guidelines for the organization's activities include the following: promote excellence in the practice of public relations firms; enhance future success for member firms in a rapidly changing environment; share best practices in firm management; champion honesty, integrity and transparency; and expand and diversify the talent pool.

The council is dedicated to strengthening the recognition and role of public relations firms in corporate strategy, business performance and social education; to serving as an authoritative source of information and expert comment; and to helping set standards for the industry. The council provides its members guidelines that include the code of ethics, a statement of principles that specifically addresses transparency and disclosure.

ENTERTAINMENT PUBLICISTS PROFESSIONAL SOCIETY

Founded in 1991, the Entertainment Publicists Professional Society (EPPS) is the premiere organization for entertainment publicity and marketing professionals. With chapters in both Los Angeles and New York, its membership is diverse, representing a cross-platform of publicity, promotions and marketing executives from nearly every aspect of "traditional" and nontraditional entertainment. EPPS members represent agency, broadcast, cable TV, convergence media, crisis management, digital, feature film, gaming, home entertainment, music, nonprofit, performing arts, talent, theatrical, theme park and sports public relations professionals.

GERMAN PUBLIC RELATIONS SOCIETY

Deutsche Public Relations Gesellschaft E.V. (DPRG—the "German Public Relations Association") is a strong professional association for all communications and public relations specialists. DPRG currently has more than 3,000 members representing all the facets of the German public relations sector. Goals and objectives are setting standards, initiating an exchange of experience, sharing knowledge, ensuring quality and supporting young professionals.

DPRG was established in Cologne on December 8, 1958, as the professional association of public relations specialists in Germany. Since then, the association has informed and supported its members in professional matters. Its bylaws state that the association has set the task of improving the reputation of the profession with the general public.

Over the past 50 years or so, DPRG has developed to become a strong professional association for all communications and PR specialists. They now have more than 3,000 members representing all the facets of the communications sector in Germany, ranging from freelance PR consultants to heads of communications at DAX-30 companies. The professional profiles of their members cover all aspects of PR and communications practice.

GLOBAL ALLIANCE

The Global Alliance for Public Relations and Communication Management is the confederation of the world's major public relations and communication management associations and institutions, representing 160,000 practitioners and educators around the world. The Global Alliance's mission is to unify the public relations profession, raise professional standards all over the world, share knowledge for the benefit of its members and be the global voice for public relations in the public interest.

The Global Alliance works on the cooperative efforts of communication professionals to tackle common problems with a global perspective. By partnering with regional, national and international bodies to increase professionalism in public relations and communication management, this alliance works to enhance the influence of the industry among its constituents around the world. The Global Alliance for Public Relations and Communication Management is a nonprofit organization registered in Switzerland.

HISPANIC PUBLIC RELATIONS ASSOCIATION

The Hispanic Public Relations Association's (HPRA's) mission is to help Hispanic professional communicators enter and advance within the public relations and marketing communications fields by (1) creating an exchange of information and ideas that empower public relations practitioners to be experts in their fields; (2) promoting professional development through educational programs; (3) providing financial and internship assistance to students entering the field; and (4) advocating responsible coverage of issues and images affecting the Hispanic community.

Established in 1984, and with 250 members today, HPRA is the largest network of Hispanic public relations and marketing professionals representing agencies, government, nonprofit and corporate companies in the United States. HPRA is a resource for communications professionals and for those seeking insights into the Hispanic market by providing educational seminars and workshops focusing on the latest, up-to-date trends, issues and best practices in the field. HPRA also provides networking opportunities throughout the year.

HONG KONG PUBLIC RELATIONS PROFESSIONALS' ASSOCIATION

Established on May 1, 1995, the Hong Kong Public Relations Professionals' Association Limited (PRPA) is an independent body comprising public relations practitioners in Hong Kong. Its founding members include public relations professionals from the commercial and public sectors in Hong Kong, either working in-house or in consultancies. Since its inception, the association has been actively promoting public relations as a profession and providing regular meetings and forums to exchange views and share experiences. It is the belief of PRPA that public relations will play an increasingly significant role in organizations as well as in the development of Hong Kong's economy.

INSTITUTE FOR PUBLIC RELATIONS

The Institute for Public Relations (IPR) is a major professional organization that brings the power of research-based intelligence to public relations. As both a sponsor and catalyst, IPR delivers the evidence needed to formulate effective strategies and the methods to provide the scientifically sound measurement of results. Unlike other industry groups, IPR is an independent, not-for-profit organization. Consequently, over the years, the institute and its trustees have played a central role in elevating the entire field of public relations and continue to sharpen the ways the institute fuels this rapidly evolving field.

The institute approaches its mission like a restless activist, pursuing an aggressive agenda of research studies and peer-reviewed white papers that demonstrate the value of public relations. IPR focuses on research that matters, delivering knowledge that ultimately helps business management to achieve it goals through more effective public relations. IPR has sponsored or published more than 500 studies and papers since its founding, such as the recently published paper, "Using Public Relations to Drive Business Results."

The quality of thinking and research is possible only because at the core of IPR's mission is bridging the scientific rigor of academic leaders with the business-driven practicality of communications professionals. IPR brings educators and professionals together at global summits and regional forums. IPR also develops students—the next generation of professionals and leaders—through these forums and by encouraging professional involvement in the classroom: the subject of a recent IPR white paper, "The Professional's Guide to Guest Lecturing."

A unique strength of the institute is its dedication to actively sharing all of its knowledge. The research, best practices and thought leadership produced by the IPR is published in leading journals, discussed in their *Conversations* blog and debated at major conferences worldwide. It is also shared free online through their web-based portal for practitioners, scholars and students.

INTERNATIONAL ASSOCIATION OF BUSINESS COMMUNICATORS

The International Association of Business Communicators (IABC) is a global network of communication professionals committed to improving organizational effectiveness through strategic communication. Established in 1970, IABC serves more than 14,000 members in 85 countries. IABC members practice the disciplines of corporate communication, public relations, employee communication, marketing communication, media relations, community relations, public affairs, investor relations and government relations.

INTERNATIONAL PUBLIC RELATIONS ASSOCIATION

The International Public Relations Association (IPRA) is an association of public relations executives from all over the world. It aims at being the world's most relevant, resourceful and influential professional association for senior international public relations executives. Formed in 1955, the association aims at providing intellectual leadership in the practice of public relations globally, promoting the highest standards in the practice of public relations, providing a channel for the exchange of professional experience between practitioners engaged in public relations as well as providing opportunities for both new practitioners and students to engage in education and dialogue that will help their professional advancement.

The IPRA Council's responsibilities include nominating and electing executives of the association to manage its affairs worldwide; providing guidance and advice to the board, in particular on matters of sponsorship and marketing, IPRA events and conferences, campaigns, education and research, the association's flagship award program—Golden World Awards—and participating in the appointment of members emeritus.

INSTITUTE OF PUBLIC RELATIONS SINGAPORE

The Institute of Public Relations Singapore (IPRS), established in 1970 as a nonprofit organization, is the only accrediting body for public relations practitioners in the country. The institute's objective is to establish growth for Singapore's PR industry through knowledge acquisition, networking and exchanging of new ideas. The institute continually strives to be the leading regional PR organization that will not only project the profession but also set industry standards and increase public recognition of this profession.

INVESTOR RELATIONS SOCIETY (IR SOCIETY)

The Investor Relations Society is a professional body that improves the relationship between listed companies and investors. The Society is the U.K. member of the International Investor Relations Federation.

ISSUE MANAGEMENT COUNCIL

The Issue Management Council (IMC) is a professional membership organization for people whose work is managing issues and those who wish to advance the discipline.

NATIONAL BLACK PUBLIC RELATIONS SOCIETY

The National Black Public Relations Society (NBPRS) is the premier professional organization for African-American communicators. The NBPRS is the foremost organization for professional image makers and strategists. NBPRS has a network of 500-plus members comprised of public relations administrators, media specialists, government relations directors and communications professionals. NBPRS strives to nurture, enlighten and inform its membership about new technologies and techniques. Its goal is to empower its entrepreneurs and practitioners to network and succeed.

NATIONAL INVESTOR RELATIONS INSTITUTE

Founded in 1969, the National Investor Relations Institute (NIRI) is the professional association of corporate officers and investor relations consultants responsible for communication among corporate management, shareholders, securities analysts and other financial community constituents. The largest professional investor relations association in the world, NIRI's more than 3,500 members represent 2,000 publicly held companies and $5.4 trillion in stock market capitalization.

Investor relations is a strategic management responsibility that integrates finance, communication, marketing and securities law compliance to enable the most effective two-way communication between a company, the financial community and other constituencies: a process that ultimately contributes to a company's securities achieving fair valuation.

NATIONAL SCHOOL PUBLIC RELATIONS ASSOCIATION

Since 1935, the National School Public Relations Association (NSPRA) has been providing school communication training and services to school leaders throughout the United States, Canada and the U.S. Dependent Schools worldwide. NSPRA's mission is to advance education through responsible communication. NSPRA accomplishes that mission through a variety of diverse services to members and to other school leaders who contract with or buy from NSPRA. With over 65 years of experience, NSPRA has a reputation in the field for practical approaches to solving school district and agency communication problems.

NSPRA produces and markets communication products, maintains resource and research files, has contacts and resources within the corporate communication industry and has about 32 chapters throughout the country that provide local networking opportunities for members.

In keeping with the mission, NSPRA has provided workshop assistance to school districts, state departments of education, regional service agencies and state and national associations. For many of these groups, NSPRA has completed research-based communication audits to analyze the communication flow, targeting, content and effectiveness of their communication messages.

PUBLIC RELATIONS INSTITUTE OF NEW ZEALAND

The Public Relations Institute of New Zealand (PRINZ) is a nonprofit, incorporated society created to promote public relations and communication management in New Zealand and to serve the best interests of the people who practice it. PRINZ seeks wider recognition of the role of public relations in management; higher standards of professionalism; better qualifications for PR practitioners and an effective forum in which members can share common interests and experience.

PRINZ is a national society, has 1,100 paid members as of August 2010, is a member of the Global Alliance for Public Relations and Communication Management, organizes the annual PR conference, offers professional development courses along with regular branch and national events, organizes the annual PRINZ

Awards recognizing excellence in the industry, has an honorary national executive and has divisions in Northern, Central and Southern New Zealand.

PUBLIC RELATIONS SOCIETY OF AMERICA

Chartered in 1947, the Public Relations Society of America (PRSA) is the world's largest and foremost organization of public relations professionals. PRSA provides professional development, sets standards of excellence and upholds principles of ethics for its members and, more broadly, the multibillion-dollar global public relations profession. They also advocate for greater understanding and adoption of public relations services and act as one of the industry's leading voices on the important business and professional issues of our time.

PRSA is a community of more than 21,000 public relations and communications professionals across the United States, from recent college graduates to the leaders of the world's largest multinational firms. Its members represent nearly every practice area and professional and academic setting within the public relations field. In addition, there are more than 10,000 students who are members of the Public Relations Student Society of America at colleges and universities here and abroad.

PRSA can help extend the practitioners' network of professional contacts. The organization's 16 Professional Interest Sections put the professional in touch with other PRSA members who share particular knowledge and expertise, and offer niche conferences and learning opportunities. In addition, the 110 PRSA chapters and 10 districts connect with other local professionals in major cities and towns.

Each year, PRSA offers the chance to gain the recognition that public relations programs deserve. The Silver Anvil evening is the oldest and most prestigious industry award event, a true celebration representing the pinnacle of public relations achievement. Other PRSA awards honor individual accomplishment, tactical excellence and achievement in specialized practice areas.

PRSA's professional development programs and industry conferences were the first of their kind and continue to be imitated for their cutting-edge topics, thought-leading speakers and knowledge- and skill-building practicality. PRSA also offers the industry's only accreditation program: the Accredited in Public Relations (APR) program.

PRSA's award-winning periodicals, daily news updates and blogs help the practitioner stay on top of emerging trends and industry news. In addition, its vast, easily searchable database gives members instant access to research, articles, white papers and Silver Anvil Award–winning program case studies organized by subject, industry and business outcome.

Job seekers can enhance their job search through a career advice library, resumé guide and resumé critique service, as well as job mentoring and an "Ask the Experts" forum that offers mentoring guidance from seasoned public relations professionals. Job seekers can post their resumé for free, obtain salary advice, read career descriptions, subscribe to job feeds and job alerts and discover resume tips. PRSA Jobcenter offers employers a flat fee for any job post, as well as discounts for "niche organizations."

PUBLIC RELATIONS CONSULTANTS ASSOCIATION

Founded in 1969, the Public Relations Consultants Association (PRCA) is the professional body that represents U.K. PR consultancies, in-house communications teams and PR freelancers. The PRCA promotes all aspects of public relations and internal communications work, helping teams and individuals maximize the value they deliver to clients and organizations. The association exists to raise standards in PR and communications, providing members with industry data, facilitating the sharing of communications best practice and creating networking opportunities.

All PRCA members are bound by a professional charter and codes of conduct and benefit from exceptional training. The association also works for the greater benefit of the industry, sharing best practice and lobbying on the industry's behalf, e.g., fighting the Newspaper Licensing Agency's digital license. The PRCA represents many of the major consultancies in the United Kingdom and currently has 197 agency members from around the world, including the majority of the top 100 U.K. consultancies. Having launched in-house membership last year, it also represents 31 in-house teams, including many of Europe's leading corporations and UK public sector organizations.

PUBLIC RELATIONS INSTITUTE OF IRELAND

The Public Relations Institute of Ireland (PRII) is dedicated to promoting the professional practice of public relations in Ireland and to serving the best interests of people working in the profession.

The institute seeks wider recognition of the role of public relations in business, higher standards of professionalism, and better qualifications for PR practitioners and to be an effective forum for members to share common interests and experiences.

There are currently about 1,000 members of the PRII. They comprise public relations and communication professionals drawn from consultancies, industry, government, semi-state, voluntary and business organizations. The depth and scope of their members' backgrounds and working briefs reflect a considerable broadening of the role and responsibilities of PR professionals from the traditional media relations base and highlight its cross-functionality with a variety of disciplines including journalism, advertising, marketing, legal, financial, healthcare and commercial functions. Members of the institute subscribe to the Code of Lisbon, the Code of Athens and the PRII Code of Practice for Public Affairs and Lobbying. These codes seek to promote integrity and clear understanding in the implementation of public relations programs and closely reflect the overall objectives of the PRII itself.

PUBLIC RELATIONS INSTITUTE OF AUSTRALIA

The Public Relations Institute of Australia (PRIA) is the national industry body for public relations and communication professionals in Australia. PRIA represents and provides professional support and recognition to over 3,000 individual practitioners and more than 175 consultancies nationwide. Since 1949, it has been PRIA's role to promote and enhance the profession and its status to the broader community. PRIA enforces the highest standards of ethical practice and represents public relations practitioners in the best interests of the profession.

PRIA members are drawn from in-house and agency practice across all sectors of the industry, from corporate to government to community. Individuals are required to meet specific criteria for full professional membership. These include a PRIA-accredited tertiary qualification plus a minimum of three years' full-time practice, or a minimum of five years' full-time experience. All members are required to make a personal, written commitment to our stringent code of ethics. Consultancy members are also bound by an additional code of practice covering client relations, fees, income and general practice. To be eligible for Registered Consultancy status, the public relations agency principal must be a full professional member of PRIA.

PUBLIC RELATIONS ASSOCIATION OF AUSTRIA PUBLIC RELATIONS VERBAND AUSTRIA

The Public Relations Association of Austria Public Relations Verband Austria (PRVA) is an association of communication experts and experts in companies, agencies and organizations. Public relations is strategically planned communication management and covers all areas of organizational and business communication, such as internal relations, consumer PR, media relations, social relations, public affairs and investor relations. Through the continuous development of awareness and reputation, PR makes a lasting contribution to the achievement of the organization/company.

PUBLIC RELATIONS SOCIETY OF INDIA

The Public Relations Society of India (PRSI), a national association of PR practitioners, was established in 1958 to promote the recognition of public relations as a profession and to formulate and interpret to the public the objectives and the potentialities of public relations as a strategic management function. The society functioned as an informal body until 1966, when it was registered under the Indian Societies Act XXVI of 1961, with headquarters in Mumbai. The father figure of professional PR practitioners in India, Kali H. Mody, was the founder president of PRSI from 1966 to 1969.

PUBLIC RELATIONS CONSULTANTS ASSOCIATION OF INDIA

The Public Relations Consultants Association of India (PRCAI) is a trade association that represents India's public relations consultancy sector while providing a forum for government, public bodies, industry associations, trade and others to confer with public relations consultants as a body. The membership of PRCAI is restricted to consultancies that meet the basic criteria set out by the association.

The association provides a formal, professional mechanism, with its range of membership services and information for the PR industry to improve profitability while following a code of practice along with global benchmarks. Some of the areas that the association focuses on are: professional codes, consultancy management standards, regional networks, international information and knowledge sharing with links, referral service, job seek, guidance papers, business support, seminars and conferences, education and training and research and surveys.

PUBLIC RELATIONS SOCIETY FOR INDONESIA

The Public Relations Society for Indonesia (PRSI) is the Indonesian organization for public relations professionals, organized into chapters, representing business and industry, technology, counseling firms, government, associations, hospitals, schools, professional services firms and nonprofit organizations.

RUSSIAN ASSOCIATION OF PUBLIC RELATIONS

The Russian Association of Public Relations (RPRA) was established in 1991 as a public non-profit organization with legal personality. The founders of the RPRA include the Union of Journalists of the USSR, the Association of advertisements, Zhurfond RSFSR, United Nations Secretariat (New York, Department of Public Information), Chamber of Commerce of the RSFSR, the Russian Commodity Exchange, the Moscow Commodity Exchange, Rosvneshtorg, Vneshtorgreklama, USSR Embassy in the U.S., Office of Information Ministry of Foreign Affairs of the USSR, MGIMO, Economic News Agency and Institute of Sociology of Parliamentarism. The objectives of the RPRA include (1) building the infrastructure sector of Public Relations for a comprehensive and sustainable development of the sphere of public relations, (2) protecting the interests of the PR industry as a whole and of each subject in particular, (3) putting into practice and business turnover in the industry professional and ethical standards, and monitoring for compliance and (4) human resource development of the PR industry and improvement of higher and postgraduate education in public relations.

SHANGHAI PUBLIC RELATIONS ASSOCIATION

The Shanghai Public Relations Association (SPRA), established in 1986, is the first PR industry organization in China. The association aims to provide the platform of information exchange, communication improvement, relationship building and cooperation strengthening not only for local communities but also for multinational companies. Under the tenure of SPRA, advanced PR professional skills and theories have been brought into the local professional society.

UNIVERSAL ACCREDITATION BOARD

The Universal Accreditation Board (UAB) oversees the APR program and provides a balanced blend of backgrounds in a number of public relations specialties, with representatives from each public relations participating organization. Day-to-day operations are administered at PRSA headquarters. The UAB grants accreditation, develops the Examination for Accreditation in Public Relations and policies, and reviews appeal cases. The public relations organizations that are members of the UAB include the Agricultural Relations Council, Florida Public Relations Association, Maine Public Relations Council, NSPRA, PRSA, Religion Communicators Council, Southern Public Relations Federation, Texas Public Relations Association and Asociación de Relacionistas Profesionales de Puerto Rico (Puerto Rico Public Relations Association).

VERENIGING VAN PUBLIC RELATIONS ADVIESBUREAUS

The Vereniging Van Public Relations Adviesbureaus (VPRA) is a professional organization of public relations consultancies based in the Netherlands, formed for the purpose of looking after the interests of the members and maintaining professionalism within the public relations field.

Below is a list of the websites of the organizations and associations mentioned above.

LINKS

African Public Relations Association
www.afapr.org

Arthur W. Page Society
www.awpagesociety.com

Belgium Association of Public Relations Consultancies Association Belge des Conseils en Relations Publiques
http://www.bprca.be

Belgian Public Relations Consultants Association
www.bprca.be

Canadian Investor Relations Institute
www.ciri.org

Canadian Public Relations Society
www.cprs.ca

Chartered Institute of Public Relations
www.cipr.co.uk

Community College Public Relations Organization
ccprocalifornia.org/default.htm

Council of Public Relations
prfirms.org

Entertainment Publicists Professional Society
www.eppsonline.org

German Public Relations Society
dprg.de

Global Alliance
www.globalalliancepr.org

Hispanic Public Relations Association
hpra.camp8.org

Hong Kong Public Relations Professionals' Association
www.prpa.com.hk/eng/index.php

Institute for Public Relations
www.instituteforpr.org

International Association of Business Communicators
www.iabc.com

International Public Relations Association
www.ipra.org

Institute of Public Relations Singapore
www.iprs.org.sg

Investor Relations Society
www.ir-soc.org.uk

Issue Management Council
issuemanagement.org

National Black Public Relations Society
www.nbprs.org

National Investor Relations Institute
www.niri.org

National School Public Relations Association
nspra.org

Public Relations Institute of New Zealand
www.prinz.org.nz

Public Relations Society of America
www.prsa.org

Public Relations Consultants Association
www.prca.org.uk

Public Relations Institute of Ireland
www.prii.ie

Public Relations Institute of Australia
www.pria.com.au

Public Relations Association of Austria Public Relations Verband Austria
www.prva.at

Public Relations Society of India
prsi.co.in

Public Relations Consultants Association of India
www.prcai.org

Public Relations Society for Indonesia
www.prsociety.or.id

Russia Public Relations Association
www.raso.ru

Shanghai Public Relations Association
www.chspra.com

Universal Accreditation Board
www.praccreditation.org

Vereniging van Public Relations Adviesbureaus
www.vpra.nl

6

P A R T

CONCLUSION

55

C H A P T E R

THE FUTURE OF PUBLIC RELATIONS AND INTEGRATED MARKETING COMMUNICATIONS

Clarke L. Caywood, Ph.D.
Professor, Department of Integrated Marketing Communications
Medill School of Journalism, Media, Integrated Marketing Communications
Northwestern University

The following breaking news, released as this book went to press, suggests that the labors of the authors, editor and readers were well matched with current thinking. Based on this data, the subject of this book has a promising future:

> The international public relations (PR) consultancy sector grew bigger and stronger in 2010 and is expected to grow again in 2011, according to the latest World Report from the International Communications Consultancy Organization (ICCO). Digital and social media services are playing an increasingly important role as PR gains share against other marketing disciplines, though staffing remains a challenge. The consultancy industry saw moderate or double-digit growth in 2010 in a majority of the 24 countries surveyed.
>
> The world's two largest markets for public relations—the United States and the UK—both rebounded from a 5-percent decline in fee income in 2009 to record a double-digit recovery in 2010. U.S. consultancies posted an average 11 percent increase in overall fee revenue, while the United Kingdom saw a 13 percent increase. Both also saw improvements to profitability, the United Kingdom by an average of 30 percent.
>
> Western European countries saw more modest growth or nearly unchanged conditions (from –1 percent to +3.5 percent), though the Nordics and Central and Eastern European countries fared better, with average growth ranging from 5 percent to 12 percent for the year. Brazil and Russia pushed ahead with 23 percent and 17 percent increases in revenues respectively, supported by strong economic expansion in their countries. Australia grew by approximately 10 percent, fuelled by the increasing internationalization of public relations activities.[1]

With the continuing encouragement of such data, the primary objective of this book is to document, by example and leadership, how powerful and productive communications, as defined by the professional field of public relations, can help us lead society, industry, business, organizations and stakeholders. It seems fair to state that nearly all management teams across a wide array of fields cannot thoughtfully plan or practice without being integrated through the efforts of public relations. The chapters on stakeholders document examples and cases of how public relations brings a critical connection to all the publics, audiences and stakeholders, defining the reach of business and other organizations. We have reached a point at which managers and educators need to make sure they focus not only on the consumer, the investor and the employee, but also on the dozens, or even hundreds, of possible stakeholders. Integrated Marketing Communications (IMC) must integrate the stakeholders as well as the IMC tactics to be strategic.

Based on over 20 years of business, marketing and public relations education, as well as positions in government, business and not-for-profit management, it is my prediction that there will be no patience for men and women who want to practice their profession or craft isolated from other business and organizational functions of society. The future managers of all levels of an organization must be very much like the authors of this book, who have compiled knowledge on the best practices in their areas of expertise.

While I have practiced and taught public relations for all of my professional life, the experience I gained at Northwestern's Medill School of Journalism, Media, Integrated Marketing Communications gave me the unparalleled opportunity to work closely with the top practitioners and academics in the field throughout the world. In the last 17 years, between 1989 and 2011, six more deans have taken the place of my first Medill Dean, Ed Bassett. In the constant restructuring of the school, the field of public relations grew independently, with the field of integrated marketing communications, and even with journalism. The support for this book by leading industry experts in public relations, journalism and marketing has allowed me to help both the field and my students rise above the confusion and, sometimes, general disrespect paid to public relations. As journalism educators know, public relations has become the most sought-after second career for practicing journalists. The career move to full-time, or even freelance, writing positions for industry, NGOs and social media outlets will allow the best values of journalism to survive. Journalism is not dead, but some of the institutions of journalism, including newspapers and traditional broadcasting, are suffering. However, the values of journalism, including storytelling, confirmation of facts, balance and clear writing are thriving in social media and extensions of journalism institutions.

The traditions of the academic are often beyond the comprehension of most of my business associates. Many of them say they would like to become a professor when they retire from their lucrative corporate jobs. My gentle retort is that I would like to become the CEO or CCO of their company when I retire from the university! The real truth is that universities are wondrous institutions in the mix of extraordinarily complex organizations, created for various objectives. While I have enjoyed working in and for businesses, not-for-profits, government and universities, I prefer universities for their potential long-term view of their role in society.

At this time, it seems to me that the field of public relations as a professional education degree offers the student and participant both the widest and deepest use of his or her mind and the challenge of applying ideas into organizational action. In the 1996–1997 *Journal of Corporate Public Relations* (renamed *Journal of Integrated Communications* and finally *Journal of Integrated Marketing Communications*), I wrote about the "Renaissance" quality of the men and women in public relations. While I may have been pandering a bit to my audience, I do believe that the intellectual and practical demands made on public relations professionals require the widest knowledge of contemporary issues represented in this book. In short, the demands on the field of public relations discussed in this book are met by the authors' intellect and skill, as well as their depth of knowledge of specific issues.

I am a member of the Arthur W. Page Society, which is an organization for senior public relations and corporate communications executives, dedicated to furthering and strengthening the profession. In nearly 20 years of membership, I have never been bored or discouraged by the level of intellectual discourse at a meeting, even when I disagreed with the speakers or panel members. Our discussions have always been issues focused, with substantive ideas on the table during meetings, dinners and even in bars. I have also been stimulated by the focus of sharp minds involved in the Public Relations Society of America "Silver Anvil" judging process for more than 15 years. The generous list of other professional associations in this field discussed by Gerry Corbett in Chapter 54 may inspire you, the reader, to find the same stimulus.

The promise of public relations is the delivery of a sharper focus on the needs and interests of one or many stakeholders with relevant, important and useful messages. This pledge is reflected in the work of the many co-authors of this book, as they tell the reader how to more strategically develop efficient, effective and equitable integrated communications and management programs that accomplish the mutual goals of the organization and society.

PREDICTIONS

It seems permissible to predict some developments in the field of public relations based upon my experience and the work of the contributing authors. The challenge facing the reader will be to keep this second edition of *The Handbook* on a back shelf over the years so that it might be possible to validate these predictions. In fact, a year before this book went to press, an editor from the University of Los Andes in Santiago, Chile interviewed me during a visit to the prestigious school. His challenging assignment for me was to defend the predictions of the first edition of this book. My analysis is that the predictions held up. If your Spanish is strong enough, you can check my impressions in *Marcas y Marketing*[2] magazine.

The predictions at the end of most chapters will make it easier for future interviewers to hold us accountable. These predictions should also be fodder for discussion, training, speeches, research papers, journal articles and even books. The assertions are both micro and macro, as well as targeted to redefine communications at societal, industry, corporate/organizational, managerial and stakeholder levels.

All of the authors of this book have contributed their predictions of the future, directly or indirectly. Their ideas are rich and important, and they are best understood in the context of their subject chapters. It has been an extraordinary year working with these men and women who have generously written thousands of words to help the next generation of students and younger professionals grow in their understanding of PR and in their PR and integrated marketing communications careers. For readers who wanted to know more about how public relations relates to their careers and businesses, I am confident that you will find your work more productive and successful now that you benefit from the unique policies, strategies and tactics fostered by public relations. You may have your own predictions of how you believe communications can play a more important role in the future of your organization.

So, here are my predictions, which I hope my colleagues in China, Chile, Great Britain and the United States will reexamine in a decade or less for their wisdom and degree of accuracy.

SOCIETAL-LEVEL INTEGRATION

- Transparent relationships between companies, NGOs, individuals and governments will continue to grow, based on the contributions of communications professionals.

- Social media, in various forms, will globally redefine the relationships between various governments, between governments and their peoples, between business and government and within all relationships that are part of the broad definition of public relations.

- Shared, transparent and truthful communications about politics, the economy and social issues will be a significant vehicle for "flattening" the earth.

- Online tracking and analytical systems will follow and predict external trends and events, with greater rigor and precision, to anticipate changes relevant to products, services and stakeholders.

- The growth of newer generations of more effective media will increase the value of public relations as a communications-based field in global politics, business and society.

INDUSTRY-LEVEL INTEGRATION

- The chaos of the financial industry and loss of confidence in it during the first decade of the twenty-first century will force this industry, and others, to protect their economic standing and status with stronger self-regulation and monitoring.

- A model of cooperation for the benefit of stakeholders, rather than more unfettered competition, will flourish within and between industries, through their voluntary associations and with the encouragement of government.

- M&As and restructurings will continue at record paces at many levels to facilitate cooperation and the need for communications.

- Industries and cross-organizational associations will find a significant role for their affiliates and members to demonstrate a contribution to a society that government alone cannot moderate.

- Medical science technology such as functional Magnetic Resonance Imaging (fMRI) will produce more disciplined and rigorous stakeholder decisions.

- Testing high risk products with fMRI technology will give PR/IMC greater science credibility.

ORGANIZATIONAL- AND COMPANY-LEVEL INTEGRATION

- Organizations will be managed increasingly from the outside-in, rather than from the inside-out, with the benefit of issues management and other PR practices.

- By putting the C back in IMC, integrated marketing communications will become more integrated into the general management process, rather than be narrowly defined as a marketing subfunction.

- The barriers of traditional functional labels by educators in finance, marketing, production and other fields will be broken down by the application of communication policy, strategies and tactics.

- Greater amounts of managed global information will be used for public relations and management decision making from syndicated and proprietary databases.

- A richer mix of graduate and undergraduate educational backgrounds will be desired and demanded by organizations.

- Public relations professionals will be increasingly chosen to lead corporations and other organizations, because of their general management knowledge and their clear understanding of stakeholders.

- Global relationship building will contribute to a more significant role for public relations, using advanced communications technologies and knowledge.

- Public relations thinking and practice will permeate all levels of organizations with the ability to contribute to both long-run and short-run objectives.

- Public relations will use more "zero-based" thinking and planning to move away from incremental budgeting and implementation.

- Organizations will use more precise and fiscally measurable methods to evaluate and judge the results of integrated management and communications programs.

- Public relations will continue to grow steadily as a management function in companies and in consultancies.

- Traditional, on-site universities will have a difficult time keeping up with the demand for high-quality global communications graduates.

- Business programs will find that serving only those students whose families can afford an education will repeat the transgressions of the past, depriving the best and brightest of their place in the classroom.

STAKEHOLDER INTEGRATION

- Stakeholders will be individually traced by organizations at a global and nearly instantaneous level.

- Organizations will rely increasingly on stronger alliances with customers, suppliers and other stakeholders. In some cases, organizations will work more closely, and even collaborate, with companies that were historically viewed as the competition.

- Corporate and organizational values will align more precisely with industry and societal ethical standards.

- For graduate and eventually undergraduate students, the loss of a sensible return on investment for many costly private and even public professional degrees will increase the number of part-time degree earners and reshape the nature of learning and teaching to a working student body.

- "Renaissance men and women" with both qualitative and quantitative skills, and the hearts and minds to use these skills, will find communications an intellectually and globally challenging field of study.

In short, the organizations of the future will be fully integrated and, to a greater level, dependent upon communications, as practiced by public relations professionals, to achieve a higher level of integration. This integration, at multiple levels, will redefine public relations as an honorable and ethical leadership role for women and men to help policies, strategies and tactics that will define relationships between stakeholders as increasingly more visible, public, transparent, clear, ethical, legal, accessible and open.

As a professor in a professional field of study, I often conclude my classroom courses with career advice. First, tactical skills including research and communications will continuously improve. Second, the success of managers will also be determined by detailed knowledge of stakeholders including customers. The level of knowledge and insight should be so great that the organization cannot hold meetings, plan for the future or make decisions on issues related to the customer or stakeholder without the contribution of the PR or IMC professional in person, electronically or virtually. Such expertise will make the PR or IMC professional crucial to the success of the organization. And the success of the organization using the advanced and integrated practices of public relations will ensure the success of the field and of the professionals who lead it.

NOTES

1. "International PR Sector in Good Health with Double Digit Growth in 2010." Web log post. Public Relations Institute of Australia, 30 May 2011. www.pria.com.au/blog/id/1106.
2. *Marcas y Marketing*. www.anda.cl/PDFrevista/Revista_MyM_jun_2010.pdf.

CONTRIBUTORS

James Arnold is a management consultant who "is an unimpeachable source of judgment and counsel on matters of reputation and marketing." He advises, writes and speaks about the most valuable intangible asset of any organization, reputation: how to enhance it by optimizing opportunities for competitive advantage, or protect and defend it by mitigating risks.

He creates effective strategies, designs organizational structures and recommends operational systems and tools to measure/evaluate performance for corporations, nonprofits and government agencies. Prior to founding his own firm in 1991, he was president of a predecessor firm, Chester Burger & Co., until Mr. Burger's retirement in 1990. Before his consulting career, he had 20 years experience as a senior marketing and communications executive with political, public affairs and industry trade organizations.

With a team of senior consultants, Mr. Arnold has served more than 200 companies of the Fortune 500, as well as large government agencies and major nonprofits. He is a hands-on consultant who has counseled the top management of such diverse organizations as AOL, AARP, American Airlines, American Bar Association, American Century Investments, American Express, Accenture, Allied-Signal and AT&T—and that is just the "A's".

His specialties include: counselor for defending and enhancing reputation; identifying and mitigating reputational risks; developing strategies to create understanding, resolve conflicts and avoid crisis; positioning and branding; discovering bits and pieces of the mission in a complex organization and turning them into a memorable, well-written story; socially responsible behavior; organizational design; using research to create smart strategies that can be measured and evaluated; benchmarking and best practices.

Mr. Arnold's public affairs background includes running several state and regional political campaigns, being elected as President of Young Democrats in his home state, serving as executive director of a state democratic party, and being chief of staff to a Lt. Governor. He gained national visibility when he was named Executive Director of Legis 50/Center for Legislative Improvement, a national organization founded originally by private sector leaders to focus public attention on the Legislature as the weak link in state government, unable to fulfill its role as an equal partner to the Executive in the policymaking process. With funding from major foundations the organization conducted the Legislative Evaluation Study that resulted in a popular book, "The Sometime Governments," ranking the 50 legislatures on measurable criteria of effectiveness. Mr. Arnold directed a multi-disciplinary staff in the headquarters and state capitals that counseled legislative leaders on management issues, recommended legislative process improvements, waged public information campaigns, and conducted demonstration projects dealing with such subjects as healthcare, juvenile justice, drug abuse and alcoholism, ethics, state house reporting, economic development. lobbying regulation, streamlining legislative procedures and processes. Mr. Arnold was a consultant on the legislative article for constitutional conventions in Texas and Louisiana.

Mr. Arnold served as a trustee of the Arthur W. Page Society for 18 years. He is accredited by PRSA and elected to PRSA's College of Fellows in 1988, at that time the youngest member. He is currently an Honorary Trustee of the PRSA Foundation, a Director of the Specialty Wine Retailers Association, a member of the Executive Council of AARPNY, a founding trustee of the Museum of Public Relations, a member of the First Selectman's Committee for GCTV Ch 11, the municipally owned cable channel of Greenwich, CT, where he produces "The Word in Greenwich" a public affairs program.

Mr. Arnold was educated at Harding University, Vanderbilt University and Attingham Park College, Shropshire, England. He lives in Manhattan and Greenwich, CT. (james@jamesearnold.com)

Mark Bain was global director of communications for Baker & McKenzie, one of the world's largest law firms, from 2007–11. Prior to that, he ran his own advisory firm, upper 90 consulting, and was a senior advisor with the Reputation Institute. For more than a decade, he headed global corporate communications for Alticor Inc., and in 2005, his group was named *PR Week's* Corporate Team of the Year. Mark spent 15 years with Burson-Marsteller, the global public relations firm, in its New York, Los Angeles, Hong Kong and Tokyo offices. He is a two-time winner of the Public Relations Society of America's Silver Anvil Award, and for his contributions to building industry reputation, he received a Distinguished Service Award from the World Federation of Direct Selling Associations in 2005. Mark earned his BS degree from the University of Utah's Department of Communications in 1979.

Brent Baker has 45 years of government public affairs and educational leadership experience. He is dean emeritus at the College of Communication, Boston University. He served as dean from 1992 to 2003 and retired from BU in 2005. He was a hands-on teaching dean and professor of communication. He was a pioneer in the integration of digital technology into communications education. In 1993, he was integrating online class newsgroups and, later, class websites into his teaching. He taught government public affairs courses to both undergraduates and graduate students.

He was a Navy public affairs officer for 29 years (1963–1992), which included duty from the Vietnam War to the 1991 Gulf War (Desert Storm). He is an expert on government-media relations and, in 1984, was a member of the Government Sidle Commission on Military-Media Relations in the wake of the 1983 Grenada Invasion. The commission had the task of establishing new rules for news media covering military combat operations. In 1992, when he retired from the Navy, he was serving as the senior public affairs advisor to the secretary of the Navy and chief of Naval Operations as a rear admiral and as Navy chief of information. He was awarded the Navy Distinguished Service Medal and holds various other military awards, including the Vietnam Service Medal and Combat Action Ribbon.

He holds a BS in Radio, Television and Film from Northwestern University and an MA in Journalism from the University of Wisconsin–Madison. He also graduated with distinction from the Naval War College postgraduate program and attended the National Security Program at Harvard University's John F. Kennedy School of Government.

He is the author of various articles, book chapters and two books: *Integrated Communications in the Internet Era*, Wadsworth-Thompson Learning, Belmont, CA, 2001, and *Mass Communication: An Integrated Approach*, Thompson Publishing, Belmont, CA, 2002. He is a coauthor of the first edition of *The Handbook of Strategic Public Relations and Integrated Communications*.

Edward Barbini is vice president of external relations for IBM, overseeing all of IBM's strategies and dealings with media, analysts and key influencers worldwide, as well as being actively involved in all corporate external relations in diverse fields such as shareholder communications. He also oversees IBM's strategy and execution of social media communications.

He is an 18-year veteran of IBM and has worked in a variety of IBM's operating units, with positions including head of communications and public relations for IBM's software, systems and personal computer divisions, where he has been responsible for overseeing media relations, executive and internal communications and IT analyst relations. IBM has been honored with the top honors in communications and public relations—including the Silver Anvil and SABRE awards—during his tenure as leader of global external relations.

He is a member of IBM's Integration and Values Team, comprising IBM's top leadership, and counsels IBM's global clients on crisis communications and external relations issues.

Prior to joining IBM, Ed worked as a reporter for the Newhouse News Service and in government, where he worked in the press offices of New York City mayors, Edward I. Koch and David Dinkins, and served as press secretary to the New York State attorney general. He also oversaw the media relations efforts for the National Association of Attorneys General during his government work. He earned BA and MS degrees from Columbia University.

Jonathan D. Blum is senior vice president, chief public affairs officer for Yum! Brands, Inc. (NYSE:YUM). YUM is the world's largest restaurant company, with nearly 36,000 restaurants and 1.3 million employees in over 100 countries. YUM is the parent company of Taco Bell, Pizza Hut, KFC, Long John Silver's and A&W All-American Food.

Jonathan reports to the chairman/CEO and serves on the Partner's Council that sets the corporation's overall strategy. He also serves on the company's Compliance Oversight Committee, leads its Nutrition Policy Committee, and co-leads its Food Safety Committee and Quality Assurance Task Force. His global portfolio includes public policy issues management, internal and external communications, corporate social responsibility, community diversity, government affairs, community relations and philanthropy. Jonathan was vice president of public affairs for Taco Bell Corp. before PepsiCo spun off its restaurant companies in 1997.

Before joining the company, Jonathan served as Asia-Pacific regional director for Ogilvy & Mather Public Affairs. He also was managing director for Ogilvy's public affairs offices in Chicago, Singapore, Hong Kong and China. He held a congressional internship, served in the Carter White House and later assisted the president with his transition to the private sector.

Jonathan is an executive in residence at Northwestern University's Medill Graduate School, where he regularly lectures on integrated marketing communications and organization development. He serves as a director of Kindred Healthcare, Inc. (NYSE:KND), a leading health services company. Additionally, he serves on a number of philanthropic boards, including the Muhammad Ali Center (executive committee and past chairman), Fund for the Arts (executive committee), YUM Foundation (vice chairman) and Discovery Science Center of California (Emeritus) and is also on the board of Business Leaders in Education, Ad Council and Thornton's Inc. Advisory Board of Directors. He earned his bachelor's degree at the George Washington University (dean's list) and his Juris Doctorate at the Western New England College School of Law.

Ray Boyer is a communications consultant working with clients in the private and nonprofit sectors. He specializes in communications planning, with particular skill in media relations.

For eight years, he was head of public affairs for Williams College, followed by four years as assistant dean for external relations at Northwestern University's Kellogg School of Management. From 1991 through 2004, Ray was head of public affairs for the John D. and Catherine T. MacArthur Foundation, leaving to set up his own firm, Boyer Media.

In addition to his current work with foundations on communications planning, he designed and implemented the public relations strategy for the Chicago Innovation Awards, the Chicago region's major annual recognition of innovative new products and services. Recent work also includes projects to advance the improvement of public education and understanding of mental health. He is a communications consultant to the Kellogg School and a senior communications strategy advisor to the social science research organization

NORC at the University of Chicago. Contact: Ray Boyer, 312-330-6433, rayboyer@rboyer.com.

Keith Burton for two decades has been one of the leading industry practitioners in employee communication and change management. As president of Insidedge, he leads a global group of counselors within The Interpublic Group of Companies (IPG) who are focused exclusively on improving organizational performance by building employee trust, improving internal communication and affecting overall change at many of the world's leading corporations.

In addition to his work as a public relations industry counselor and strategist, Burton began his career as an award-winning business journalist covering the activities of major corporations in the southwestern United States for Capital Cities Communications, Inc., and A.H. Belo Corp. He also served as a Dallas correspondent to *Time* and was associate editor of *Texas Business* magazine.

Burton was an Algur H. Meadows Fellow at Southern Methodist University, where he earned a master of fine arts degree in mass communication and a bachelor of fine arts in journalism. He also served as an adjunct faculty member at SMU, and as an advisor to the Meadows School of the Arts Corporate Communications and Public Affairs (CCPA) program. He is executive-in-residence in the Integrated Marketing Communications (IMC) Program at the Medill School, Northwestern University, Evanston, Illinois.

Burton also serves on the boards of the Institute for Public Relations (IPR) and The Plank Center for Leadership in Public Relations.

Tony Calandro co-leads the sustainability practice group at VOX Global, a public affairs and strategic communications firm, where he provides strategic and account management to global companies. He specializes in working with clients to integrate social and environmental issues into a company's overall business strategies.

He also develops public/private partnerships to help clients identify innovative approaches to reducing their environmental impact or identify new market opportunities. Additionally, Mr. Calandro has contributed to a 2009 Corporate Eco-Forum published report on sustainability, titled "Show Me the Money: The Business Case for Sustainability." He also is a guest lecturer on the topic at Washington University, St. Louis University and Webster University.

Immediately prior to joining VOX, Mr. Calandro was a senior vice president and partner at Fleishman-

Hillard, an international communications firm where he co-lead the firm's Corporate Social Responsibility Specialty Practice Group. Before joining Fleishman-Hillard, Mr. Calandro spent nearly 20 years in Washington, DC, where he held several different positions, including working for U.S. Senator Edward Kennedy and U.S. Representative Terry Bruce.

Jean Cardwell is president of Cardwell Enterprises, Chicago, Illinois, a retained executive search firm that specializes in all aspects of corporate communications, investor relations, government and public affairs for corporations worldwide. Ms. Cardwell founded Cardwell Enterprises in 1984. Her first client was Exxon Corporation.

Prior to starting Cardwell Enterprises, Ms. Cardwell created a corporate communications function for J.D. Stefek, a worldwide management consulting firm where she was senior vice president of communications.

Ms. Cardwell has authored articles in the fields of corporate communications, investor relations, government and public affairs and has been a guest lecturer throughout the world. She is a coauthor of the first edition of *The Handbook of Strategic Public Relations and Integrated Communications*.

Ms. Cardwell holds a Bachelor of Arts and Sciences, a Master of Psychology and a Master of Business Administration from the University of Illinois.

Craig Carroll, Ph.D., teaches persuasion and advocacy as well as public opinion and reputation management research methods at Lipscomb University. He is department chair and associate professor. Carroll is a member of the Association for Educators in Journalism and Mass Communication (AEJMC), the National Communication Association (NCA), and the International Communication Association (ICA). He is chair of the public relations division of ICA. Professor Carroll has taught at the University of Southern California—Annenberg School and The University of North Carolina–Chapel Hill. At the latter, he was director of the Carolina Observatory on Corporate Reputation.

He is editor of *Corporate Reputation and the News Media*, featuring original research from 22 countries around the world. He was named *PR News*' "Educator of the Year" in 2008. He earned a BS from Freed-Hardeman University, an MA from Abilene Christian University and a Ph.D. from the University of Texas at Austin. His book, *The Handbook of Communication and Corporate Reputation*, will be published in 2012.

Clarke L. Caywood, Ph.D., is a full professor and member of the Integrated Marketing Communications Department in the Medill School of Journalism, Media, Integrated Marketing Communications at Northwestern University. He was one of 4 faculty members who initially created and designed the integrated marketing communications program. He is the first tenured professor of public relations to teach PR at Northwestern's Medill School of Journalism Media and Integrated Marketing Communications. Professor Caywood teaches graduate classes in public relations, marketing, social and business media, crisis management, communications management and marketing PR.

Dr. Caywood has published numerous articles and book chapters on public relations, advertising and marketing in business and political campaigns and has done research on values in contemporary advertising. Caywood is editor of the best-selling first and second editions of *The Handbook of Strategic Public Relations & Integrated Marketing Communications* (McGraw-Hill).

He was named by *PRWeek* as one of the 100 most influential PR people of the twentieth century and one of the top 10 outstanding educators in 2000. He was named Educator of the Year by the Public Relations Society of America (PRSA) and awarded the PRSA Anvil prize. He was also named the Educator of the Year by the Sales and Marketing Executives of the Chicago area. He has served as vice president of marketing for start-up company eMarketWorld. He has worked for two past governors and the attorney general of the state of Wisconsin. He ran a number of state campaigns in Wisconsin and has served as a political expert for ABC-TV Channel 7 Chicago. Since 2004, he has spoken extensively to audiences in China and Chinese business leaders in the United States. Honored as an educator, he carried the Olympic Torch in Lijiang, China. He holds a number of honorary teaching posts with Chinese universities.

He is a member of the board of Aidmatrix.org, which is a global disaster relief organization using advanced supply chain solutions. He is also a member and former trustee of the A.W. Page Society. He is founding publisher and continues as publisher of the *Journal of Integrated Marketing Communications*. He is a member of the board of the *Journal of Interactive Advertising* (University of Texas–Austin), the new *Case Research Journal* (University of North Carolina–Chapel Hill) and the *Journal of Public Relations*. He is a member of the Public Relations Society of America, the American Academy of Advertising and the American Marketing Association.

Professor Caywood received his joint doctorate in business (management) and in journalism–mass communications (advertising and public relations) from the faculty of the University of Wisconsin–Madison. He also earned a Master of Science in Public Affairs in the first class of the Lyndon B. Johnson School of Public Affairs, University of Texas–Austin, and a Bachelor of Business Administration from the University of Wisconsin–Madison.

Emma Caywood, MLIS, is a storyteller, librarian, playwright, digital storyteller and story coach. She was formerly the director of the American Accolades Screenwriting Competition and a literary manager for screenwriters at Torque Entertainment. She has studied storytelling with Rives Collins, Northwestern University, and Beth Horner, Dominican University. In addition to directing the JTE Storytellers at Northwestern, Emma has taught storytelling to integrated marketing communications students at Northwestern's Medill School. Practicing her craft, she has told stories to children, women's groups and community organizations, as well as at churches, synagogues, libraries and a chocolate shop. She has a bachelor's degree in theater and a certificate in creative writing for the media from Northwestern University and a master's degree in Library and Information Science from Dominican University.

Kevin Clark is an award-winning brand strategist, experience designer, author, and catalyst for change. He collaborates with business leaders, marketing experts, brand strategists, designers, academics, futurists, human factors scientists, and cultural anthropologists on deep wants and needs of customers, and the intersection of emerging social and technology trends. He is a sought-after global speaker about collaborative innovation and brand experience strategy.

He is president and founder of Content Evolution, a unique global federation of 40 member companies around the world, with experts in customer research, innovation, business strategy, and brand experience. Content Evolution is a collaborative federation with a focus on discovering and connecting core intentions to authentic customer experiences.

In early 2009 Kevin retired from IBM with 30 years of service. He is director emeritus, Brand and Values Experience, IBM Corporate Marketing and Communications—responsible for discovering and creating new ways for people to experience IBM, and the global IBM Brand Experience Community Leader; a community he founded in 2001. IBM is the most valuable business-to-business brand in the world valued at $60.7 billion in 2009 according to *Interbrand* and reported in *BusinessWeek*, and overall #2 brand worldwide. He received recognition from the NASA Astronaut's office in 2005 and an award from IBM as an influential executive advocate for NASA and United Space Alliance in 2006. He also received the Brand Leadership Excellence Award from the World Brand Congress in 2009. He was Brand Steward and portfolio architect of the IBM Think family of personal computer offerings, including IBM ThinkPad notebook computers (today Lenovo).

Kevin is the founder of the integral behavior school of brand experience and the author of *Brandscendence: Three Essential Elements of Enduring Brands* published by Kaplan/Dearborn in 2004, and is a contributing author to several other books. He is also coauthor of the keynote article "Unleashing the Power of Design Thinking" for the summer 2008 issue of *Design Management Review* and appearing as a chapter in *Design Thinking: Integrating Innovation, Customer Experience and Brand Value* published by Alworth Press, 2010. He is author of "Engaging and Adaptive: Beyond Ease of Use" published by *Human Computing Interaction International*, 2009. He is coauthor of "IBM's Think Strategy: melding business and brand strategy," appearing in the spring 2004 issue of Strategy and Leadership magazine, coauthor of "Experience Design That Drives Consideration" for the Winter 2006 issue of *Design Management Review*, and "How IBM Innovates" for the April 2006 issue cover story for *PDMA Visions*, journal of the Product Development Management Association.

Kevin lectures regularly at Duke University Fuqua School of Business, Yale University School of Management, University of Rochester Simon School of Business, and University of Colorado Leeds School of Business. Kevin serves on the World Brand Congress Advisory Board, is an international advisor to Human Centered Design Network of Japan, is a member of the Writers Guild of America, is a member of the Design Management Institute, and has been a senior instructor for the IBM Marketing Management Institute. He is a graduate of the University of Tulsa with a bachelor of science degree, School of Arts & Sciences, in communications, 1978.

Richard T. Cole, Ph.D., is a professor in the Department of Advertising, Public Relations, and Retailing, Michigan State University (MSU), East Lansing.

Prior to rejoining MSU in 2006, Cole was executive vice president and chief administrative officer of the nine-hospital Detroit Medical Center, which he joined after retiring as a senior vice president for the not-for-profit Blue Cross Blue Shield of Michigan in 2003, where he had been a corporate officer and had overseen a number of corporate divisions since 1991. He served on the national brand committee of the Blue Cross Blue Shield Association.

In the 1980s, Cole served in various state government roles including, deputy director of the Michigan Department of Commerce and press secretary and chief of staff to Governor James J. Blanchard. He was also president of the Michigan Education Trust, the nation's first prepaid college tuition program.

Cole currently serves on the Center for Disease Control and Prevention Child-Maltreatment Prevention Task Force and on several advisory boards. He was chairman of the Metropolitan Detroit March of Dimes (2005-2008) and of the Cranbrook Institute of Science (1998-2002), Bloomfield Hills, MI.

Cole has authored and coauthored several book chapters and articles for academic and professional publications and has participated in grants from the Kellogg Foundation, the Children's Trust Fund of Michigan and the National Institutes of Health. He is coauthor (with Derek Mehraban) of "The New Media Driver's License Resource Guide", published by Racom Communications, Chicago, 2012.

Cole received a bachelor's degree (1969) from Western Michigan University (from which he was named one of the Distinguished Alumni in 1987) and master's and doctorate degrees (1980) from Michigan State University.

Marguerite Copel, vice president of corporate communications and public affairs, serves as the chief communications strategist for Dean Foods Company, the leading dairy producer in the United States. She is also president of the Dean Foods Foundation.

As guardian of Dean Foods' corporate reputation, Marguerite leverages her 25 years in the food and beverage industry to protect the company's strong relationships with its employees, farmers, media, consumers and community partners. In addition, Marguerite manages public affairs and media relations across the country. Since joining Dean Foods in 2006, she has launched several strategic initiatives to integrate internal communications with key business objectives.

Marguerite gained her deep communications and business experience through her leadership positions at United Airlines, Ocean Spray Cranberries, Sandoz Agro, Quaker Oats, the NutraSweet Company and Burson-Marsteller. While at United Airlines in

2005, she played an instrumental role in corporate communications, employee communications and editorial services, as the company emerged from a much-publicized bankruptcy. As Ocean Spray's vice president of corporate communications and public affairs, Marguerite provided C-level communications counsel during a time of intense change in the company and across the beverage industry. In addition, she launched several award-winning public relations programs to protect the brand and increase employee engagement. She recently won a Silver Anvil for Excellence in Internal Communications.

Marguerite has spoken at numerous venues, including Georgetown University, Tufts University and Northwestern University. She also held the positions of vice president of the Arthur Page Society and president of the Chicago Nutrition Association. She has participated in Food and Drug Administration panels on food labeling, as well as on high-profile trade association teams. She graduated from the University of Wisconsin–Madison.

Gerard F. Corbett is a founder and CEO of Redphlag LLC, a strategic public relations and marketing management consulting firm, a position he has held since January 2008. He also has a coaching and mentoring practice under the "PR Job Coach" moniker and blogs as "PRJobCoach" for his own blog and as a guest blogger on several leading career management web forums.

Gerry has four decades of experience in technology, corporate communications and public relations. Prior to Redphlag, he was vice president of the Branding and Corporate Communications Group of $100-billion Hitachi, Ltd. from 1995 to 2007 and general manager of its Web Strategy Center. He previously served several leading Fortune 200 firms, including Loral Corporation, ASARCO Incorporated, Gould Inc. and International Harvester Company. He also was program manager and senior account executive with the public relations firm of Creamer Dickson Basford in Providence, RI. He launched his career in Silicon Valley as a scientific programmer at the NASA Ames Research Center.

A native of Philadelphia, Pennsylvania, Gerry has a BA in public relations from San Jose State University and an AA with a major in electronics engineering from the Community College of Philadelphia. He is accredited in public relations (APR) and a member of the College of Fellows of the Public Relations Society of America (PRSA). He serves as the 2012 Chair and CEO of PRSA and has been a member for more than 35 years. He also is a senior member of the American Institute of Aeronautics and Astronautics; a member of the board and past president of the International Advertising Association/West, and a member of the Arthur Page Society, National Investor Relations Institute, National Association of Science Writers, San Francisco PR Roundtable, New York PR Society, International Coaching Federation and Kappa Tau Alpha, the National Journalism Honor Society. For 2012 to 2013, he will serve as CEO and chairman of the PRSA.

Derek Creevey, executive vice president, corporate communications at Edelman, has 18 years of experience in corporate communications, providing corporate positioning and issues management to Edelman, as well as clients. He joined Edelman in 2001 as the firm's Director of Marketing, reporting to the CEO, Richard Edelman, became chief of staff in 2003, and served as chief administrative officer from 2009–2011.

Today, Creevey supports clients with corporate communications strategy, executive positioning, c-suite thought leadership and employee engagement. His clients include AOL and PepsiCo, where he is helping both companies engage employees to drive growth.

Over the last ten years, Creevey led Edelman's internal and external communications, helping the firm become the world's largest PR firm, up from sixth, by establishing the firm as the industry's thought, digital and creative leader worldwide. As chief administrative officer for five years, Creevey managed the firm's IT and human resource groups and several other global corporate functions.

Creevey orchestrated a number of initiatives at Edelman including the firm's employee development and training program; intranet and knowledge platforms; and orchestrating the firm's global leadership meetings. To elevate Edelman's relationship with the academic community and their students, he created an annual summit for more than 150 leading academics around the world to help them better understand how new media was advancing communications.

Creevey holds an MBA and Bachelor of Commerce from University College, Dublin, Ireland, and currently sits on the ethics advisory board of Word of Mouth Marketing Association (WOMMA).

Scott M. Cutlip was a renowned teacher in the newly developing field that he helped define at the University of Wisconsin–Madison. He spent 29 years on the faculty of the University of Wisconsin–Madison School of Journalism and Mass Communication, where he introduced the study of public relations to the undergraduate and graduate journalism school. In 1952, he cowrote *Effective Public Relations* with Allen H. Center. The tenth edition of the book was published in 2008 as Cutlip and Center's *Effective Public Relations* by Glen Broom, who had joined the original authors. The book was the number one textbook in the field for decades. At the University of Wisconsin–Madison, his grateful students named the new chapter of the Public Relations Students' Society of America for him in 1968.

Scott Cutlip was responsible for the collection of valuable papers from Arthur W. Page of Bell Telephone for the State Historical Society of Wisconsin. He was the strongest advocate of historical research and wrote the definitive history of the field of PR. His book *The Unseen Power: Public Relations: A History* was published in 1994 and forms the basis for the summary he prepared in 1996 for this his student, who is the editor of the 1997 and 2011 editions of this *Handbook*.

The Navy's graduate-level program came to the University of Wisconsin, where over many years, 165 Navy officers received advanced education and training in public information. Scott Cutlip later served as dean of the University of Georgia's Henry W. Grady College of Journalism and Mass Communication from 1976 to 1983. He received many honors, including the lifetime achievement award from the A.W. Page Society as the "Architect of Modern Army Public Relations." He passed away August 18, 2000 in Madison, Wisconsin.

Ray Day is vice president of communications for the Ford Motor Company. He leads all of the company's global external and internal communications and public relations activities. His role includes building the company's reputation globally and leading communications that reach Ford's external and internal audiences, including customers, employees, dealers, suppliers, news media, communities, governments and policy makers.

Day, 45, was appointed to his position in November 2007. He reports to Alan Mulally, Ford president and CEO.

"Ford is one of the world's most iconic and admired companies, and we have a very strong story to tell—particularly as we make progress on our plan for profitable growth around the world," says Day. "As we tell the Ford story, we are building on the fact that people see Ford as different, and we are setting ourselves apart by the great products, stronger business and better world we are creating."

Day joined Ford in 1989 and spent most of his career leading Ford's global communications and public relations activities related to the company's products, design, manufacturing, sales, marketing, brand development and corporate issues. Before being named a vice president, he served as executive director of global corporate communications and executive director of global automotive communications.

Day was based for four years in Europe, serving as head of Ford's European Product Public Affairs and living in both Germany and the United Kingdom. He led development of the communications strategy and introduction of the Ford Focus in Europe in 1998 and in North America in 1999. The Focus became one of the few cars ever to be named "Car of the Year" by automotive writers in both Europe and North America.

Early in his Ford career, Day led the company's print and television employee communications network, helping it become an internal communications benchmark throughout the industry. He was a newspaper reporter and editor in the Detroit area before joining Ford.

Day is a graduate of Wayne State University in Detroit, where he earned a bachelor's degree in mass communications. He currently serves on the boards of the Automotive Hall of Fame and Detroit Public Television. He also is a member of the organizing committee of The Seminar for public relations and a member of the Arthur W. Page Society.

Day and his wife, Debbie, and their two daughters live in Plymouth, MI.

Rob Doughty is a strategic public relations professional with a 36-year career in domestic and international corporate communications, including media relations, internal communications, marketing communications, financial, community affairs, consumer affairs and crisis communications for several Fortune 500 corporations. Doughty has provided communications counsel in the airline, food service, food processing, male grooming, biotechnology, healthcare, recycling and welding industries for both private and public companies.

Prior to starting his own firm, he served as vice president of communications for the Disneyland Resort in Anaheim, California. In this capacity, he was responsible for all communications functions including media relations, internal communications and consumer relations for the fiftieth anniversary of Disneyland.

Prior to joining Disney, Doughty served as vice president of strategic communications for Burger King Corporation and vice president of public relations for Pizza Hut, Inc. He has also served in various communications positions for The Gillette Company, United Airlines, Hill & Knowlton, Wilson Foods Corporation and Hobart Brothers Company.

While at United Airlines, Doughty was responsible for developing and implementing the crisis communications plan used following two fatal aircraft accidents. He has received numerous awards and is a published author of three books. He serves as a member of the Board of Advisors to the Journal of Corporate Public Relations published by The Medill School of Journalism at Northwestern University. He currently is vice chairman of the board of Shake-A-Leg Miami, a not-for-profit organization that provides kids and adults with physical, developmental and economic challenges through a variety of water sports, including sailing, kayaking and swimming.

Doughty received his Bachelor of Arts in Political Science from Eastern Kentucky University and earned a Master of Arts in Organizational Communications from Ohio University. He is also a member of the Arthur W. Page Society.

Jim Dudas is an organizational communication leader who turns business strategies into memorable and actionable key messages and measurable results. He has been an investigative, political and environmental journalist; director of communications for the largest global conservation organization and a public relations agency account leader for Bain & Co., the City of Chicago Bureau of Tourism, Carson Pirie Scott and the Allstate Insurance Co., for which he created and facilitated the "Allstate Forum on Public Issues."

He joined the Allstate Insurance Company's Corporate Relations Department to further develop the Allstate Forum, then moved to assignments of increasing responsibility, eventually leading communication teams in every Allstate business unit. He was on loan to the Insurance Information Institute for three months to develop and execute an industry-wide communication strategy after the costliest hurricane in the history of the insurance industry. He was Allstate's mergers and acquisitions communication leader, developing internal and external communication plans before, during and after the company's largest acquisition in its history. He ran the Allstate media relations team on four occasions. He was seconded to Allstate's Law and Regulation Department to develop public policy communication strategies. He was assigned to Allstate's marketing department to colead its integrated marketing communications efforts. He left Allstate to return to the wildlife conservation world.

His work has appeared in *The Cleveland Press*, the *Cleveland Plain Dealer*, the *Los Angeles Times*, *Journal of Higher Education*, *The Wall Street Journal* and numerous insurance trade publications.

He is a journalism graduate of Kent State University and earned his Master of Arts in Public Relations from Northern Illinois University. He has earned his Integrated Marketing Communication Certification from DePaul University.

Dudas has served as president of the Ela Area Library Board of Trustees for 12 years, during which he led a successful referendum that led to the building of one of the largest libraries in Illinois.

Richard Edelman is president and CEO of the world's largest independent public relations firm, with wholly owned offices in 54 cities and more than 4,000 employees worldwide.

Edelman has been a leader in public relations since the firm was founded in 1952. It has consistently received top industry honors, including "Top-Ranked PR Firm of the Decade" and one of the "2010 Best Places to Work in Marketing and Media" by *Advertising Age*, "2011 Large Agency of the Year" by *PRWeek*, "'09 Agency of the Year" by *Adweek* and "Agency of the Decade" and "2009 Best Large Agency to Work For" by The Holmes Report. Richard's blog, 6 A.M., which launched in September 2004, receives more than 2,000 visitors a day.

Richard was named president and CEO in September 1996. Prior to that, he served as president of Edelman's U.S. operations, regional manager of Europe and manager of the firm's New York office.

Richard has extensive experience in marketing and reputation management. He has also counseled several countries on economic development programs, including Egypt, Israel and Mexico.

Richard has a special understanding of the nongovernmental organization (NGO) movement. He has spoken on this topic at several conferences, including the Institute of Social and Ethical AccountAbility, the Conference Board and the World Economic Forum's Annual Meeting in Davos. Edelman's research on NGOs, business, government and media in the Edelman Trust Barometer has been cited by numerous publications, including the *Financial Times* and *The Wall Street Journal*.

Richard won the Silver Anvil, the highest award in the public relations industry, in 1981. He was named "Best Manager of the Year" by *Inside PR* magazine in 1995. In 2006, he was awarded "Entrepreneur of the Year 2006–NY Metropolitan Area" by Ernst & Young. Richard was named the "Most Powerful PR Executive" by *PRWeek* in October 2008, for the second year in a row, and "Agency Executive of the Year" by *Advertising Age* in January 2008. He was named one of "America's Favorite Bosses" by Glassdoor in 2010 (#8) and 2011 (#6).

He serves on the Board of Directors of the Ad Council, the Atlantic Council, the Children's Aid Society and the National Committee on U.S.-China Relations. He is also a member of the World Economic Forum, the Arthur Page Society and PR Seminar.

Richard graduated from Phillips Exeter Academy in 1972. He has a bachelor of arts degree from Harvard College (1976) and an MBA from Harvard Business School (1978). He lives in New York City with his wife, Roz, and three daughters.

Hud Englehart has more than 40 years' experience in public relations and public affairs strategy development as an agency advisor and head of communication for major corporations. He is a founding partner of Beacon Advisors, Inc., a firm that provides large and midsize businesses with corporate communications, investor relations and crisis management services.

In addition to his consulting work, Hud is an original investor in and retains a business development affiliation with Rasmussen Reports, LLC, an Internet publisher of public opinion surveys.

From 1996 to 2001, Hud was president and chief operating officer of KemperLesnik Communications in Chicago, a firm that offered integrated PR, public affairs, advertising and sports and event marketing. During his tenure, the firm operated major sports events involving the PGA Tour, NCAA basketball, and professional figure skating.

Hud spent a dozen years (1982–1988 and 1990–1996) with worldwide PR firm Hill and Knowlton, Inc., where he was on the U.S. executive committee and eventually served as managing director of the Chicago office. Clients included Navistar, Kraft General Foods, United Airlines, Gerber, Spiegel, Northern Trust Company and the *Chicago Sun-Times*. He also counseled companies in crisis working on incidents ranging from hostile takeovers, labor disputes, plant closings and industrial accidents to product recalls and contaminations, litigation and management malfeasance.

From 1988 to 1990, Hud was vice president of corporate communications for Lockheed Corporation (now Lockheed Martin), a leading U.S. defense contractor. An elected corporate officer, he was in charge of worldwide corporate communication including public affairs, financial and internal communication, advertising and media relations.

Hud began his communications career in Pittsburgh in 1969 at Mellon Bank, where he rose from staff writer to head of the Bank's first corporate communications office. At the time, Mellon was the nation's twelfth largest commercial bank.

Hud is an adjunct professor at Northwestern University's Medill School, where he teaches crisis communication to master's degree candidates. He has served on the corporate development advisory board of the University of Michigan Business School, and he is the former president of the Tony Award–winning Victory Gardens Theater in Chicago. He is a 1969 graduate of the University of Michigan.

Raymond P. Ewing is an industry leader and educational founder of the field of issues management. Mr. Ewing led the field from his post as director of strategic planning and issues management at Allstate Insurance. His work with the Allstate futurist study center provided him with leadership in the newly emerging field. Mr. Ewing also created the first course in issues management at Northwestern University as the first industry adjunct professor teaching public relations in the Medill School of Journalism. He is coeditor of the *Handbook of Communications in Corporate Restructuring and Takeovers* with Clarke L. Caywood (1992) and author of *Managing the New Bottom Line: Issues Management for Senior Executives* (1987). He is also the author of a book on his favorite author, Mark Twain—*Mark Twain's Steamboat Years: The Years of Command.* In retirement, he has taken up sculpting and shows his work frequently. His quote in a 2011 news interview about his art is a strong representation of his careers and philosophy: "We don't take ourselves seriously," he said. "But we take sculpting seriously."

Samuel F. Falcona retired as vice president, communications and public affairs, ConocoPhillips, where he was the global communications leader for this Fortune 5 company, responsible for all corporate affairs and communications—external, internal, financial, crisis, advertising, community relations, business promotion and event planning. He was also president of the $75-million ConocoPhillips Foundation.

Falcona was a career U.S. Navy officer and began his 20-year career as a carrier jet pilot and subsequently took on increased responsibilities in the media and public affairs sector. He served in the Pentagon as military assistant to the secretary and assistant

secretary of defense. His last Navy assignment was as regional director for the Navy Office of Information, Midwest, based in Chicago. After retiring from the Navy, his positions included: head of communications for Unicom/ComEd, the largest nuclear utility in the United States; director of public relations for Sears, Roebuck & Co.; vice president of corporate communications for G.E. Capital (Auto Financial Services) and executive vice president and managing director for Edelman Public Relations Worldwide.

He is a member of the Arthur W. Page Society and was the former chairman of the General Committee on Communications for the American Petroleum Institute. Previous affiliations include: PR Seminar, the Wisemen, Institute for Public Relations (board member), Bilateral U.S.-Arab Chamber of Commerce (board member) and the Houston World Affairs Council (board member).

Falcona holds a bachelor's degree in journalism from the University of Houston and a master's degree in public relations from the University of Southern California.

Rob Flaherty is president and a senior partner of Ketchum, the global public relations firm with 102 offices and affiliates worldwide. Rob serves on the agency's Worldwide Executive Committee and is responsible for the agency's Global Research Network. As a client counselor, Rob's areas of specialization are corporate positioning and issues management. He regularly facilitates sessions with client executives to develop corporate positioning and identify actions that will shape the reputation desired by a company, including some of the world's most successful technology companies. Flaherty has counseled IBM for over 10 years. On the issues management front, he has helped companies prepare for and respond to challenging situations ranging from product liability and airline accidents to data security and antitrust litigation. He serves on the board of the Institute for Public Relations and Room to Read, which focuses on literacy and girls' education in developing nations. He also serves as a senior judge in the annual Public Relations Society of America Silver Anvil competition.

Joele Frank is the founder and managing partner of Joele Frank, Wilkinson Brimmer Katcher, a leading strategic financial corporate communications firm, which has consistently ranked as one of the top M&A firms since its founding in 2000.

Ms. Frank has played a major role in more than 1,000 special situations. Noteworthy client assignments include: Airgas in its defense against the unsolicited offer and proxy contest from Air Products; Avis Budget Group with respect to its proposal to acquire Dollar Thrifty Automotive Group; PotashCorp in its defense against the unsolicited offer from BHP Billiton; Microsoft in its proposal to acquire Yahoo!; SIRIUS in its merger with XM; Merck in its merger with Schering-Plough; NRG in its defense against Exelon; Verizon in its acquisition of MCI (facing a competing proposal from Qwest); PeopleSoft in its defense against Oracle and the William R. Hewlett Trust in its opposition to the HP/Compaq merger. With respect to proxy contests and shareholder activism, Ms. Frank has advised, among others, Lionsgate in its defense against Carl Icahn, Target during its proxy contest against Pershing Square Capital Management and Motorola during its proxy contest against Carl Icahn.

Ms. Frank has been included in *PR Week*'s PR Power List and named a member of *Inside PR*'s Hall of Fame as an All-Star for Investor Relations.

Prior to founding Joele Frank, Wilkinson Brimmer Katcher, Ms. Frank was vice chairman of Abernathy MacGregor Frank, where she led the firm's mergers and acquisitions and crisis communications practices. Previously, Ms. Frank was a managing director at Ogilvy Adams & Rinehart. Ms. Frank spent seven years in AT&T's treasury department and worked closely with the investment community during the divestiture of the Bell System. She began her corporate career as a financial analyst at Allied Chemical. Before that, Ms. Frank specialized in DNA replication as a research biochemist at the State University of New York at Stony Brook.

Ms. Frank has an AB in chemistry from Mount Holyoke College and an MBA in finance from Long Island University. She is a member of the Financial Women's Association and the Economic Club of New York.

Al Golin, a veteran of over 50 years in the public relations industry, is chairman of Chicago-based GolinHarris, which has 34 offices around the world.

In addition to handling the McDonald's account for over 50 years, GolinHarris represents such companies as British Petroleum, Dow Chemical Co., Florida Department of Citrus, General Mills, GlaxoSmithKline, Kaiser Permanente, Johnson & Johnson, Nestle, Nintendo, Orange, PetSmart, Playtex, Sargento, Shire, Texas Instruments, Toyota, Unilever and Wal-Mart.

As a consultant to the U.S. Department of Commerce, Al's work centered on a major public relations awareness program for U.S. companies on the benefits of exporting to help our economy, increase employment and reduce the balance of trade deficit.

Al is a member of the board of trustees of the Goodman Theatre of Chicago and Roosevelt University, a founding board member of Ronald McDonald House Charities and public relations advisor to the National Multiple Sclerosis Society.

He is also a member of the Arthur W. Page Society, the Public Relations Seminar and the Public Relations Society of America.

He has lectured at Princeton University, Dartmouth College, Yale University, Northwestern University, New York University and the Annenberg Communication School at the University of Southern California.

Al received Lifetime Achievement Awards from the Public Relations Society of America, Publicity Club of Chicago and Inside PR magazine.

Al was named one of the 100 most influential public relations people of the twentieth century by the industry trade magazine *PR Week*, and he received the Arthur W. Page Society Hall of Fame Award for "Career Achievements and Outstanding Contributions to the Profession."

Al was honored with the prestigious Gold Anvil Award from the Public Relations Society of America. The Gold Anvil is the society's highest individual award. He was recently awarded the Alexander Hamilton Medal from the Institute for Public Relations.

His book, *Trust or Consequences*, published by Amacon Books, is currently in distribution.

Phil Gomes serves as a senior vice president with Edelman Digital, working from the agency's founding office in Chicago, IL.

Phil is responsible for crafting the online engagement policies and standards for the agency and its clients, as well as serving as an educator and counselor with regard to online communities. This expertise rolls up into business-focused social media immersion programs that educate account teams and their clients in online community principles, delivering the ability to integrate digital thinking in to day-to-day work.

While at Edelman, Phil has counseled clients within the technology, automotive, transportation, consumer packaged goods and mobile communications sectors. In this role, Phil challenges teams and companies to engage with online communities and deliver journalistic-, educational-, conversation- and entertainment-quality content.

During his near-decade in Silicon Valley prior to joining Edelman, Phil worked with such innovative companies as SRI International, Adaptec, Cornice, Matrix Semiconductor and Hitachi Semiconductor. Phil's work helped guide clients to win the Technology Pioneers Programme Award at the World Economic Forum in Davos, Switzerland. Twice.

Phil enjoys wide industry recognition as an expert on the intersection of emerging media technologies and corporate communications. As a speaker on this topic, Phil has presented to the Forbes Forum For Dynamic Mid-Sized Companies, the Public Relations Society Of America, International Association of Business Communicators and the Association of Educators in Journalism and Mass Communications, to name a few. Phil is also considered by most participants in the public relations profession to be the first in the field to start a blog—August 2001.

Phil earned a BA in communications from Saint Mary's College of California. He is also founding fellow for the Society for New Communications Research, launched in November 2005, and was conferred an award of merit for his corporate blog work for dotMobi in November 2007.

Matt Gonring is vice president of Corporate Communications at Jackson National Life Insurance Company. He oversees all corporate communications functions at Jackson, including executive communications, media relations, internal communications, community relations, financial communications and corporate advertising initiatives.

As a seasoned corporate executive, Matt has a proven record of accomplishments derived from more than 30 years of experience building and leading marketing and corporate communications teams in manufacturing, consumer goods, professional services, healthcare, and airlines businesses. He has led the functions of communications and marketing in six global enterprises over the past 24 years.

Before joining Jackson, Matt was chief communications officer at Pactiv Corporation. Until 2006, Matt was VP Global Marketing and Communications at Rockwell Automation. Prior to joining Rockwell, Matt was vice president, Corporate Communications for Baxter International and before Baxter, he spent three years as managing partner, Communications and Integrated Marketing, for Arthur Andersen. Before Andersen he spent ten years at USG Corporation as vice president, Corporate Communications. Matt held positions for eight years in the airline industry holding key headquarters communications assignments with United Airlines and Northwest Airlines. Additionally, he served in state and federal government environmental protection agencies early in his career.

Gonring has been a member of the graduate faculty at Northwestern University's Medill School of Journalism, Media and Integrated Marketing Communication's IMC program for 12 years and is also an adjunct graduate professor at George Washington University. He has written extensively for professional and business periodicals and is a frequent speaker in top-level communications and marketing forums. A board member of The Arthur W. Page Society and co-chair of The Institute for Public Relations, Matt has served on boards and as an advisor for 10 different consulting, not-for-profit and professional associations.

From American University, Washington D.C, he earned his MS in public relations. From the University of Wisconsin-Stevens Point he earned a BS in communications and political science.

Robert E. Gorman, Jr., is a communication consultant specializing in strategy development and execution. He has completed projects for organizations that include Abbott Labs, Allstate, AT&T, Verizon, the Federal Reserve Bank of Chicago, Lincoln Financial Services, Zurich Financial Services and FORTUNE China.

As an employee of Allstate Insurance prior to forming Robert E. Gorman Communication in 1995, Gorman served four chief executive officers as leader of executive communication. Prior Allstate assignments include advertising director and publisher of two consumer magazines with circulations totaling 2.6 million.

Gorman is a founding board member of the *Journal of Integrated Marketing Communication.* The journal is published by the students of the Master of Integrated Marketing Communication program at Northwestern University's Medill School. He has taught at both Northwestern University and Roosevelt University.

Gorman researched and wrote 10 articles for *Strategic Communication Management* and *Strategic HR Review* on the best practices in internal and external communications, including: "How to Connect with Employees During Change Processes," "HR's Role in Developing Brand Personality," "How to Jumpstart Your Company's Crisis Communication Process," "Communicating to Engage, Not Just to Inform" and "The Five Best Ways for Managers to Engage Employees."

He is a dean's list graduate of the University of Notre Dame and earned a Master of Science in

Marketing Communication from Roosevelt University with honors.

Other experience includes serving as public information officer of the 101st Airborne Division in Vietnam, newspaper reporter for the Hollister newspapers and public relations coordinator for Shell Oil Company.

Gorman serves on the board of directors of Emmaus House of Hospitality, a not-for-profit organization working to address hunger and homelessness in southwestern Lake County, IL.

Karla K. Gower, Ph.D., LLB, is a professor in the Department of Advertising and Public Relations and director of the Plank Center for Leadership in Public Relations at The University of Alabama.

Gower practiced law in Canada for eight years before moving to Arizona in 1992 to attend Arizona State. She worked at Blue Cross and Blue Shield of Arizona in government relations and later GateWay Community College in Phoenix where she was responsible for internal communications and media relations. At the University of North Carolina at Chapel Hill, she created collateral materials to support the development of relationships with major individual and corporate donors in the Office of University Development.

Her research focuses on legal issues affecting public relations and the history of public relations. Her publications include *The Opinions of Mankind: Racial Issues, Press, and Propaganda in the Cold War* (with R. Lentz, 2010), *Legal and Ethical Considerations for Public Relations* (2008), *PR and the Press: The Troubled Embrace* (2007), and *Liberty and Authority in Free Expression Law: The United States and Canada* (2002). She has also published articles in *Communication Law & Policy, Journalism and Mass Communication Quarterly, Journal of Public Relations Research, Public Relations Review, Journal of Communication Management, American Journalism,* and *Journalism History.* She served as editor of *American Journalism* from 2000 until 2004 and is on the editorial review boards of the *Journal of Public Relations Research* and *Journalism History.* She has contributed entries to the *Encyclopedia of Public Relations, History of the Mass Media in the United States,* and the *Historical Dictionary of Women's Press Organizations.*

She earned her doctorate in mass communication from the University of North Carolina at Chapel Hill, a master's degree in mass communication from Arizona State University, and law and bachelor's degrees from the University of Western Ontario, Canada.

John D. Graham is chairman of Fleishman-Hillard International Communications, one of the world's leading strategic communications firms. Mr. Graham, who joined Fleishman-Hillard in 1966, is credited with growing the firm from a small one-office regional public relations firm into the international powerhouse of 80 offices that it is today. During his more than 30 years at the agency's helm, Fleishman-Hillard has built a strong reputation by using strategic communications to deliver what its clients value most: meaningful, positive and measurable impact on the performance of their organizations.

During his career, Mr. Graham has personally worked in nearly all aspects of public relations, including public affairs, financial strategy, corporate strategy, investor relations, crisis situations, employee relations, strategic media placement, opinion research, issues management and general counseling. He has personally counseled CEOs of many Fortune 100 companies.

In 2000, Mr. Graham became only the third agency PR executive to be inducted into the Arthur W. Page Society Hall of Fame. In 2001, he was named PR Professional of the Year by *PR Week,* and in 2002, the University of Missouri–Columbia awarded him the Missouri Honor Medal for Distinguished Service in Journalism. In 2003, John received Public Relations Society of America's (PRSA's) Gold Anvil award for his many contributions to the public relations industry. In 2005, the International Communications Consultancy Organization named John to its International Hall of Fame. In 2008, John received the *Holmes Report*'s SABRE Award for Outstanding Individual Achievement in Public Relations and the President's Award from the International Public Relations Association. In 2009, John received PRSA's first annual Paladin Award.

Mr. Graham has authored many articles on public relations and is a frequent speaker to industry groups. He attended the University of Missouri on both an athletic and a curator's scholarship and graduated from the School of Journalism.

Stephen A. Greyser, DBA, is Richard P. Chapman Professor (Marketing/Communications) Emeritus, Harvard Business School, where he specializes in brand marketing, advertising, corporate communications, the business of sports, and nonprofit management. A graduate of Harvard College and Harvard Business School (MBA and DBA), he has been active in research and teaching at HBS since 1958. He was also an editor at the *Harvard Business Review* and later its editorial board secretary and board chairman. He is responsible for 16 books, several coedited special issue journals, numerous articles, and over 300 published HBS case studies; recent publications are *Revealing the Corporation* with John Balmer (on identity, reputation, corporate branding, etc.) and coauthored articles on "Monarchies as Corporate Brands," heritage brands (a concept he cocreated), "Aligning Identity and Strategy," and BP and ethical corporate marketing (2011). He wrote the award-winning "Corporate Brand Reputation and Brand Crisis Management" in his coedited "Corporate Marketing and Identity," a special 2009 issue of *Management Decision*.

He developed the HBS Corporate Communications elective, creating over 40 cases and articles on issues management, corporate sponsorship, relations among business-media-publics, etc. His views on corporate advertising were the subject of full-page ads in *The Wall Street Journal*'s 1996–7 advertising campaign and he spoke on corporate reputation at the House or Lords.

He created and teaches Harvard's Business of Sports course, he served on the Selection Committee for the Boston Red Sox Hall of Fame, and has authored numerous Business of Sports cases and articles. The latter include "Winners and Losers in the Olympics" (2006) and several on sponsorship, most recently a case on Bank of America's Sports Sponsorship. He has organized seminars on Fifty Years of Change in intercollegiate Athletics, the Business of the Olympics, and the Branding of China via Sports. His comments on the meaning of the Olympics for China were seen by millions in China on CCTV after the 2008 Opening Ceremonies. He received the American Marketing Association's 2010 Sports Marketing lifetime achievement award for "distinguished career contributions to the scientific understanding of sports business."

He is past executive director of the Marketing Science Institute and the charter member of its Hall of Fame, and past president and an elected Fellow of the American Academy of Advertising for career contributions to the field. He received the Institute for Public Relations 2009 special award for "lifetime contributions to public relations education and research." He twice was a public member of the National Advertising Review Boards for U.S. advertising self-regulation. He has served on numerous corporate and nonprofit boards. He was the first academic trustee of the Advertising Research Foundation and the Advertising Educational Foundation. He is a past national vice chairman of PBS and an overseer at the Museum of Fine Arts (Boston) and WGBH. He served as Alumni Association president of Boston Latin School, America's oldest school (1635), conducted its 350th and 375th Founder's Day ceremonies, and received its Distinguished Graduate Award (2005); previous honorees include Leonard Bernstein, Summer Redstone, and Theodore White.

Known as "the Cal Ripken of HBS," in over forty years of teaching he has never missed a class.

Anders Gronstedt, Ph.D., (anders@gronstedtgroup. com) is the president of Colorado-based Gronstedt Group, which helps global companies like Coldwell Banker, Deloitte, Dell, HP, Jamba Juice, Volvo Cars, Ericsson, Eli Lilly and United Healthcare and government clients like the City of New York improve performance with innovative communication and learning approaches, including next-generation digital simulations, podcasts, vodcasts, mobile learning, social media, gaming and immersive 3D virtual worlds. His articles have appeared in the *Harvard Business Review* and he is the host of the popular weekly virtual world speaking series "Train for Success" (http://www.facebook.com/TrainForSuccess).

Richard L. Hanneman is former president of the Salt Institute, a North American–based global nonprofit association of salt producers. He served as president from 1986 to 2010. Before that, he served as managing director for government and public affairs for the National Solid Wastes Association (now Environmental Industries Association). He prepared for his career in association management by serving for a decade in staff positions for state and federal elected officials. He holds an MA (history) from the University of Wisconsin–Madison and BA cum laude from Beloit College. Dick is the author of dozens of articles and is a frequent public speaker and media guest.

George Harmon is an emeritus faculty member at Northwestern University's Medill School of Journalism, where he specialized in business journalism, news writing and editing, reporting, public relations writing and liberal-arts courses offered through the Center for the Writing Arts. He currently teaches a graduate course in business communication for marketing students. For 15 years, he was Medill's news department chair.

Prior to joining Northwestern in 1980, Harmon was publisher and editor of the Chicago Daily Law Bulletin, a daily newspaper for Illinois' legal community. He joined the Law Bulletin from the *Chicago Sun-Times*, where he was financial editor. Earlier, he had been assistant managing editor for features of the *Chicago Daily News*, a 550,000-circulation evening newspaper. In 11 years at the *Daily News*, he served successively as a reporter, rewrite man, assistant city editor, financial writer, assistant financial editor, city editor, financial editor and assistant managing editor.

Since 2003, he has been a director of Paddock Publications, publisher of the *Daily Herald* (Arlington Heights, IL, 151,000 daily) and *Reflejos*. He served seven years as a director of Home News Publishing Co., which owned the Central New Jersey Home News (55,000 daily), and 15 years as board chairman of Students Publishing Co., which publishes Northwestern's daily student newspaper. As a freelance writer, he has produced articles and reviews for many newspapers and magazines and has been a part-time editorial writer for the *Chicago Sun-Times*.

As a consultant, he has trained more than 1,500 mid-level executives in communications skills and has acted as a writing coach and trainer for nearly 1,000 journalists.

His degrees are from Princeton University (AB cum laude) and Loyola University of Chicago (MBA, finance), where one year he was named the outstanding MBA alum. A veteran of the Vietnam War, Harmon served three years in the U.S. Navy as an officer.

Steven J. Harris, after a career of more than 40 years in automotive communications, is currently a senior counselor with McGinn and Company, a firm based in Arlington, VA, which specializes in crisis and litigation communications, trend analysis and issues around loyalty and risk. Prior to his affiliation with McGinn, Harris was head of global communications at General Motors (GM), where he led a team of professionals who provided a wide variety of communications services to GM's 235,000 employees and in support of GM's operations and brands in 12,000 communities and 200 countries around the globe.

In the spring of 2010, Harris also taught a graduate communications class at the University of Southern California's Annenberg School of Communications in Los Angeles.

Harris first joined GM in 1967 as a lecturer with GM's Previews of Progress educational program after graduating from the University of Southern California with a BA in Journalism.

In late 1979, he joined American Motors as head of product public relations, moving on to Chrysler as the director of corporate public relations in late 1987. He was named vice president of communications for Chrysler in January 1998. Following the merger of Chrysler and Daimler-Benz in late 1998, he was named senior vice president of communications.

In early 1999, Harris returned to GM after a 20-year absence as vice president of global communications, a post he held until the end of 2003, when he retired and opened a communications consulting practice working with two agencies and a number of top U.S. companies. He was asked to return to GM in the same role in February 2006.

Harris has served on the boards of the Arthur W. Page Society, Institute for Public Relations, Foundation for American Communications and the University of Southern California Annenberg Center for Strategic Public Relations.

On November 5, 2008, Harris received the IPR Alexander Hamilton Medal for lifetime contributions to professional public relations. In February 2008, he was one of the first recipients of the SABRE Award for Outstanding Individual Achievement in Public Relations. In 2007, he was inducted into the Arthur W. Page Society Hall of Fame and named an *Automotive News* All-Star for automotive public relations for the eighth time. The Detroit Chapter of the Public Relations Society for America named him to their Hall of Fame in 2002, and he has also received awards from *Inside PR* for crisis management and the University of Southern California's Outstanding Journalism Alumni award.

Harris was born in 1945. He and his wife, Roddie, live in Santa Fe, NM.

Mark Hass is president of Edelman China, one of China's largest PR firms with two brands – Edelman and Pegasus – and more than 220 employees. With offices in Beijing, Shanghai and Guangzhou, Edelman and Pegasus in China represent clients including HP, Oracle, BMW, RIM, MHD, The Carlyle Group, General Electric, Johnson & Johnson, Nike, PepsiCo, Pfizer, Shell, Starbucks and ADM. He also serves on the firm's global executive committee.

Hass joined Edelman in January 2010 after his independent firm, MH Group Communications, was acquired and integrated into Edelman Digital. MH Group was a New York-based consultancy that specialized in integrating traditional C-Suite corporate communications services and stakeholder engagement with the opportunities provided by emerging social networks and other digital tools.

Hass has three decades of experience as a journalist, entrepreneur and communications professional. Before launching MH Group, he was the chief executive officer of MS&L Worldwide, a leading global communications firm with offices and specialized consultancies in 27 countries. He was responsible for all aspects of the firm's performance and acted as a senior counselor to many of the world's most prestigious organizations and companies, including General Motors and Procter & Gamble.

He joined MS&L in 2002, when his public relations agency, Hass Associates, was acquired and merged into MS&L. As the founder and CEO of Hass Associates, which grew to be Michigan's largest PR firm, he was best known for his work with automakers providing strategic counsel to clients at times of risk and change, as well as for work integrating online strategies into the communications activities of global companies. Hass continues to champion innovative work with blogs, social networks and mobile technologies, as well as media and influencer strategies for building and managing reputation.

Prior to entering the public relations industry, Hass worked as a reporter and editor for 16 years at The Miami Herald, The Syracuse Post-Standard and, lastly, as assistant managing editor at The Detroit News, where his staff won the Pulitzer Prize.

Hass is a trustee of the Institute for Public Relations, an independent nonprofit dedicated to the science of PR research and measurement, and a member of the Arthur Page Society.

Hass graduated magna cum laude from the State University of New York at Buffalo with a baccalaureate degree in contemporary American and British literature, continued his education at the University of Maryland journalism masters program, and holds advanced certifications as a rescue scuba diver. He is the only American-born child of Eastern European immigrants, and was educated in New York public schools. He is married, has a 25-year-old daughter and currently lives in Beijing.

Geraldine Rosa Henderson, Ph.D., is associate professor of supply chain management and marketing sciences and associate research director of the Center for Urban Entrepreneurship and Economic Development at Rutgers Business School, Rutgers University, Newark, New Jersey. She has a Ph.D. in marketing, Northwestern University Kellogg Graduate School of Management; an MBA in marketing and organizational behavior, Northwestern University Kellogg School of Management; and in BS electrical engineering, Purdue University.

Gerri was formerly on the faculty of Duke University, Howard University, the University of Texas at Austin and Northwestern University. She has also taught at Stanford University, the University of Virginia, Thunderbird and in Executive Education at both Duke University and the University of California in Los Angeles. Courses taught include Consumer Insight, Audience Insight, Theories of Persuasion, Advertising/Marketing Communications, Marketing Management, Marketing Strategy, Consumer Behavior, Brand Management and the Global Academic Travel Experience to Southern Africa.

Gerri's primary areas of research include marketplace diversity (also known as multicultural marketing), marketplace discrimination, urban marketing and consumer networks (cognitive and social). She has published over 40 articles and has been invited to present her research throughout the world. Prior to pursuing her Ph.D., she worked for several years at IBM in relationship marketing (specializing in the healthcare, insurance and pharmaceutical industries) and briefly in brand management at Kraft Foods.

Gerri is a member of several editorial boards (including the *Journal of Public Policy & Marketing* and the *International Journal of Advertising*) and serves as an editor for a marketing communications book series and for special issues of the *Journal of Business Research* (2011) and the *Journal of Public Policy & Marketing* (2012). She also serves on several boards, including the American Marketing Association. She likes to consider herself a "doctorpreneur," since in addition to her research and teaching, she often serves as an independent consultant and focus group moderator.

Nancy A. Hobor, Ph.D., has been a senior lecturer in integrated marketing communications since retiring as senior vice president of communications and investor relations for W. W. Grainger, Inc., in 2010. She has taught at Northwestern part time since 1991. She had been responsible for Grainger's internal and external communications, community relations and investor relations since 1999.

Prior to joining Grainger, Ms. Hobor was vice president of corporate communications and investor relations for Morton International. She had previously served as director of investor relations for United Airlines. Before that, Ms. Hobor was vice president of strategic communications for Baxter Healthcare Corporation and vice president of public relations for the American Hospital Supply Corporation.

Ms. Hobor received her undergraduate and master's degrees in American history from the University of Chicago. She also received a Ph.D. in American business history from the University of Chicago, where she was a Ford Fellow. Ms. Hobor received her master's degree in business administration from Northwestern University's Kellogg School of Management.

Ms. Hobor is a member of the Visiting Committee of the Division of the Social Sciences for the University of Chicago. She served until recently as the treasurer of the Arthur W. Page Society, the leading international association of chief communication officers. She is also a former member of the boards of the Chicago Finance Exchange, the National Investor Relations Institute, and New York Stock Exchange Individual Investor Advisory Committee.

Robert Holdheim is a veteran of Edelman's Frankfurt, London and New York offices. In Frankfurt, he focused on the management of multinational accounts, including corporate positioning, business-to-business product marketing and crisis management.

In London, Rob ran the corporate, business-to-business and financial groups, spearheading the UPS and Samsung accounts across 18 European countries. He led financial marketing, positioning and crisis management programs for Commercial Union and the country of Bermuda, as well as a public affairs program for the British Department of Trade and Industry. In addition to his account and group management functions, Rob was responsible for managing Edelman's relationships and activities in Eastern Europe and coordinated Edelman Associates—an affiliate network of smaller agencies across the United Kingdom.

Prior to joining Edelman in Europe, Rob was the manager for trade and investment policy at the American Chamber of Commerce in Germany. His responsibilities included lobbying the U.S. and German governments, managing seven issue-oriented industry committees (Company Law, Finance, Trade & Investment, etc.) and supporting American companies interested in investing in Eastern Germany immediately after the collapse of the Berlin wall.

Following his initial stint with Edelman in Europe, Rob founded and ran his own company—a manufacturer/marketer of branded consumer goods. After building distribution to more than 1,000 stores nationwide, five foreign markets and several million in sales, he sold the brand to a larger company.

Rob rejoined Edelman in 2006 as head of the corporate communications group in the New York office. He now serves as managing director for India, based in Delhi and responsible for additional offices in Mumbai and Bangalore.

Rob holds a BA from Cornell University and an MA from the Johns Hopkins School of Advanced International Studies. He speaks English and German fluently and Italian and French proficiently, and has studied Arabic and Hindi.

Lee W. Huebner, Ph.D., is the Airlie Professor of Media and Public Affairs at the George Washington University. He served for 14 years as Publisher and CEO of the Paris-based *International Herald Tribune*. During this time, the *IHT*, then owned *by The New York Times* and *The Washington Post*, became the world's first newspaper with a broad global presence.

Mr. Huebner also worked as a special assistant to the President of the United States and deputy director of the White House Writing and Research Staff during the Nixon administration. He came to that position from the presidency of the Ripon Society, a political research organization that he had helped to found.

A native of Sheboygan, Wisconsin, Mr. Huebner was an undergraduate at Northwestern University, where he later taught for 12 years in the Schools of Communication and Journalism. He became director of the School of Media and Public Affairs at the George Washington University in 2006. He received his MA and Ph.D. degrees in the field of history at Harvard University. His doctoral dissertation focused on the rise of mass media and its impact on political philosophy.

A Trustee and former president of the American University of Paris, he currently chairs the Center for the Study of International Communications in Paris. He has chaired the American Chamber of Commerce in France and the European Council of American Chambers of Commerce. He has been a board member for media companies in Hong Kong and East Africa, as well as for American foundations with an international focus. He presently works in a consulting role for the Aga Khan Fund for Economic Development, and the Aga Khan University.

His teaching responsibilities have included graduate and undergraduate courses on International Media, Globalization, Speechwriting, and Political Rhetoric.

He is married to Berna Gorenstein, formerly research director to Governor Nelson Rockefeller. The Huebners have two sons, Charley and David.

Susan Croce Kelly (Kirkpatrick) is an award-winning writer and public relations executive. She is president of Kirkpatrick International, Inc., a corporate writing and publishing company with clients as varied as Shell Oil, Hearst Magazines and the American Medical Association.

In past years, she was vice president of corporate affairs for Sandoz Agro, American subsidiary of the global Swiss chemical and pharmaceutical company, and is former director of communications for Monsanto Company. While at Monsanto, she created the first-ever corporate report on Social Responsibility and was instrumental in the public introduction of agricultural biotechnology. She worked as a reporter on two metropolitan daily newspapers, is an award-winning speechwriter, author of many newspaper and magazine articles, and author of the prize-winning book, *Route 66: the Highway and its People* (photo essay by Quinta Scott), University of Oklahoma Press, 1988. In 2003 she founded *Ozarks Magazine*, a critically acclaimed bi-monthly regional magazine in one of the fastest-growing recreation and retirement areas of the United States.

A product of the American Midwest, she was graduated from Purdue University (BS Psychology), and Saint Louis University (Master of Arts, American History – Research) and the Northwestern University Kellogg School of Business Executive Management Program. She is an accredited member of PRSA and former president of the St. Louis Chapter, PRSA. Presently she is a member of the Missouri Press Association and the Sierra Club. She is a former member of the Arthur W. Page Society, IABC, Women in Communication, Golden Triangle Press Association, and Missouri Association of Publishers.

She lives with her husband, Joel Kirkpatrick, Ph.D., at the Lake of the Ozarks in Missouri. They have three children and two grandchildren. You can reach Susan at ozarksmagazine@gmail.com

Marty Kohr, after a 34-year career at DDB Chicago, Y&R, Hal Riney and Leo Burnett, Marty joined the faculty of Northwestern University's Medill Integrated Marketing Communications in September, 2008. He teaches marketing strategy and persuasive communication at the graduate and undergraduate levels, and serves as student advisor on their annual effective marketing symposium. Marty is also a director of the 4A's Institute of Advanced Advertising Studies, which is affiliated with Medill IMC, and leads 4A's seminars around the country on "Powering Creativity."

Ray Kotcher is CEO and senior partner of Ketchum, a unit of Omnicom Group and one of the world's largest public relations agencies with more than 50 offices and 50 affiliates across six continents.

Ray started at the agency in 1983. Since becoming CEO in 2000, he has overseen the expansion of the firm's global client service footprint, as well as the broadening and deepening of Ketchum's offerings. In 2009, he led one of the largest mergers in the PR industry when Ketchum and Pleon, Europe's largest strategic communications consultancy, combined operations. In 2010, he continued the firm's global expansion with major investments in the Middle East and Russia, followed by, in 2011, China and India. Ray also has helped the agency grow its range of offerings through the acquisition of five complementary businesses as well as through the creation of four specialized communications businesses, which have strengthened Ketchum's expertise in such areas as technology communications, sports and entertainment marketing and word-of-mouth marketing.

Under his leadership, Ketchum has continued its award-winning record of excellence in the PR industry, maintaining the record as the agency with the most Public Relations Society of America Silver Anvils (117). In 2011, for the third year in a row, Ketchum and its clients were recognized with the *PR Week* award (United States) for Campaign of the Year, marking an unprecedented third time an agency has received this honor.

Ray also has numerous personal and industry distinctions. He currently serves on the board of trustees of the Arthur W. Page Society. In 2008 and 2009, Ray was chair of the Council of Public Relations Firms, one of only two people to serve consecutive terms. In 2009, he was named to *PR Week*'s Power List, a ranking of 25 of the most important leaders in the PR industry and, in 2011, he received one of the Holmes Group's highest individual honors, the SABRE Individual Achievement Award.

Ray has a bachelor of arts in English from the State University of New York at Geneseo and serves as a trustee of the Geneseo Foundation board. He has a master of science in public relations from Boston University's College of Communication, has been appointed to serve on the college's executive committee and has been honored by the university as a distinguished alumnus.

John "Jack" Koten is a founding director and first president of the Arthur W. Page Society. During his career, he worked in a variety of operating, financial and corporate communications departments for Illinois Bell, AT&T, New Jersey Bell and Ameritech Corp.

At Chicago-based Ameritech Corp., one of seven telecommunications companies divested by AT&T in

1984 as the result of a federal government antitrust lawsuit, he served as senior vice president of corporate communications. He also was president of the Ameritech Foundation, which gave grants totaling $25 million annually to education, economic development and cultural institutions.

After he retired, Koten organized the Wordsworth Group, a consulting firm dedicated to assisting nonprofit organizations to improve their management practices, reputation and revenues. He has received numerous awards and honors, including honorary doctoral degrees from two institutions, and was inducted into the Arthur W. Page Society's Hall of Fame in 1995.

Charlene F. Lake, senior vice president of public affairs and chief sustainability officer, is responsible for leading AT&T's philanthropic and volunteerism endeavors, third-party advocacy program and public affairs functional support as well as coordinating signature initiatives that connect social needs with business objectives.

Ms. Lake began her career at Southwestern Bell Telephone in 1986 in Topeka, Kansas, and served in management roles in financial communications, media relations and employee communications in Kansas, Missouri and Texas. She assumed leadership over SBC's corporate advertising and sports marketing department during the mid-1990s and managed the organization through the mergers with Pacific Bell, Southern New England Telephone and Ameritech. In 2003, Ms. Lake began developing a public affairs discipline within the SBC External Affairs Department, and in 2007, she launched the development of AT&T's centralized corporate citizenship and sustainability function. A mass communication graduate of Kansas State University (KSU), she also serves on the Advisory Council at KSU's A.Q. Miller School of Journalism and Mass Communications. Ms. Lake began her professional life as a journalist, working on daily newspapers in Kansas.

Ms. Lake serves on the board of directors of the Public Affairs Council, a leading international association designed to advance the field of public affairs, and on the board of directors of America's Promise Alliance, an organization committed to preparing young people for college, work and life. Ms. Lake sits on the Corporate Advisory Board of Women Impacting Public Policy, a national bipartisan group of 500,000 women business owners who actively engage in the political process. She also serves on the Council of Advisors of the Institute for Economic Empowerment

for Women, which, among other projects, partnered with the U.S. Department of State to teach women entrepreneurs in Afghanistan and Rwanda about free enterprise and market power. For her demonstration of sustained leadership and excellence in public service, she was honored with the Iron Jawed Angel award in 2008 by the Lugar Excellence in Public Service Series in Washington, DC. Ms. Lake also serves on the Collin College Foundation Board of Directors.

A Kansas native, she is a resident of the Dallas metroplex, where she lives with her husband, Rod.

Tim Larson, Ph.D., is currently an associate professor in the Department of Communication, University of Utah, where he teaches new media, communication technology, and integrated marketing communication classes. He is the coordinator of the New Media Sequence in the Communication Department. Dr. Larson holds the following degrees: BA in psychology, Augustana College, Rock Island, IL; MS in radio-TV-film, University of Kansas; and Ph.D. in communication studies, University of Wisconsin–Madison. He has been co-director of the Integrated Marketing Communication Certificate Program at the University of Utah for the past 23 years. With co-author Craig Wirth, he is the executive producer and research director of two video documentaries on Utah radio and television history and has conducted 100 oral history interviews of Utah Broadcast pioneers, completed over the last 20 years. He and Wirth have authored a biography of Utah broadcasting pioneer Earl J. Glade, set for publication by the University of Utah Press in 2012. He is an active teacher, writer and consultant.

Stephen H. Lesnik is the cofounder, chairman and principal stockholder of KemperSports and KemperLesnik. KemperSports is a golf, hospitality and athletic facility management company operating in 27 states with more than $1 billion in assets under management. KemperLesnik is a marketing communications and public relations firm, based in Chicago. Mr. Lesnik is also chairman of the board of Career Education Corp. (NASDAQ: CECO), a postsecondary education company, with $2.0 billion in revenues.

He is the founder of the First Tee of Chicago and an honorary member of the Illinois PGA. He is ranked by *Golf, Inc.* magazine among the "most powerful people in golf." In 2009, Mr. Lesnik was inducted into the Illinois Golf Hall of Fame.

Mr. Lesnik is former chairman of the board of the Illinois Board of Higher Education, which oversees the state's universities and community colleges. He is also a former member of the board and executive committee of the Illinois Math and Science Academy.

In 2002, KemperSports/KemperLesnik was selected as Illinois Family Business of the Year by Loyola University's Family Business Center. In 2006, Mr. Lesnik was inducted into the University of Illinois at Chicago's Entrepreneurial Hall of Fame.

A former journalist, lobbyist and public relations practitioner, Mr. Lesnik is an accredited member of the Public Relations Society of America. He is also a former member of the Conference Board's Public Affairs Research Council and a past president of the Insurance Public Relations Association.

He is a graduate of Brown University and lives with his wife, Mady, and their dog, Duffy, in Winnetka, IL. Both Mr. and Mrs. Lesnik have served on a number of civic and charitable boards.

Amy Littleton leads the public relations division of KemperLesnik, an events, public relations and sports marketing agency. She focuses on creating strategic PR programs for clients, developing new client relationships and managing the day-to-day business.

While with KemperLesnik, Amy has helped to grow the agency's PR practice to include several prominent clients, such as Allstate, Aon Corporation, PGA of America, PricewaterhouseCoopers, Whirlpool Corporation and Wilson Sporting Goods. Under her leadership, the agency's PR division has thrived by providing creative yet strategic media relations, social media, reputation management, community relations and event public relations programs that produce measurable results.

Prior to joining KemperLesnik, Amy spent more than a decade working in her own PR agency business, as well as at Edelman, Slack Barshinger and General Mills, Inc. She developed and implemented strategic communications programs for, among other clients, Auntie Anne's, B2BWorks, Business Logic, Curves, iProperty.com and Illinois Power, and she assisted in managing a nationwide promotional campaign featuring the gold-medal-winning U.S. Women's Olympic Hockey Team for General Mills.

Amy holds a bachelor of science in business/marketing from The Florida State University and a master of business administration from the Graduate School of Business at Loyola University Chicago. She is an active member and past president of the Public Relations Society of America Chicago Chapter, sits on the Golf 20/20 communications committee and is a former board member of the National Association of Women Business Owners Chicago Chapter. Amy has been quoted in numerous media outlets, published many articles and received a number of awards for excellence in public relations.

Amy can be reached at amy.littleton@kemperlesnik.com, www.twitter.com/amylitt or www. linkedin.com/in/amylitt. For more information about KemperLesnik, visit www.kemperlesnik.com.

Robert P. Mark a 35-year aviation industry leader, is chief executive officer of CommAvia, an aviation industry marketing communications group that integrates emerging media into business strategies for airports and aviation businesses around the globe.

A contributing editor to *Aviation International News* and *Business Jet Traveler* magazines since 2000, Mark has twice won the coveted Airbus Aerospace Journalist of the Year award at the Paris Air Show, as well as the National Business Aviation Association's 2010 Award for Outstanding Journalism. He is the author of four McGraw-Hill books, the most recent being the second edition of the *Professional Pilot Career Guide*, published in June 2007.

Robert Mark edits the award-winning, syndicated aviation blog Jetwhine as well as cohosts and produces the weekly aviation radio show *The Airplane Geeks*. He is also a regular aviation contributor to Fox News and CNN, having appeared on both Fox's *Geraldo at Large* and CNN's *In the Arena* with Elliott Spitzer. Mark has also been featured on NBC, PBS and WGN and KFI radio. An adjunct faculty member at Northwestern University's Medill School of Journalism, he teaches marketing/public relations and communications skills/persuasive messaging, focused around emerging media.

Mark, a commercial pilot, has logged 7,000 flying hours in both the airline and business aviation environment in small training aircraft, corporate jets and even the mighty Airbus A380. Robert Mark also spent 10 years as an air traffic controller and supervisor with the Federal Aviation Administration.

He received his master of science degree from the integrated marketing communications program at Northwestern University's Medill School of Journalism. He was awarded a bachelor of arts degree in English by Northeastern Illinois University.

Contact Robert Mark at rmark@commavia. com, through his blog at www.jetwhine.com, or at 800-579-6787. You will find Rob Mark on Twitter as "Jetwhine," on LinkedIn as "Robert Mark" and on Skype as "commavia."

Scott McCallum, former governor of Wisconsin, has more than 30 years of executive experience leading organizations in the private, nonprofit and government sectors. Elected as one of the youngest State Senators in Wisconsin history, he was reelected twice, then elected four times as Lieutenant Governor prior to serving as Governor. As governor of Wisconsin, Governor McCallum was cited by *The Wall Street Journal* during the economic slowdown of 2001 as being one of the "political tough guys" for balancing the budget without raising taxes, while enacting economic reforms and creating efficiencies using technology.

Governor McCallum has taught public policy at the University of Wisconsin–Milwaukee. He has been an executive in residence instructor for Northwestern University and has taught marketing at Sun Yat-Sen University and Hunan University in China. He teaches in the School of Health and Medicine at the University of Wisconsin–Madison. He has numerous publications, most recently a chapter in *Managing Technology to Meet your Mission* and the article "How Technology Is Transforming Disaster Relief." He sits on several boards of directors. Governor McCallum received the prestigious Ernst and Young Entrepreneur of the Year award for the Texas, Arkansas, Oklahoma region. He is a coauthor of *Managing Technology to Meet Your Mission: A Strategic Guide for Nonprofit Leaders,* published by the Nonprofit Technology Network.

Governor McCallum serves as president and CEO of the Aidmatrix Foundation, the leading global nonprofit that uses information technology to create efficiencies between donors and those in need. During his tenure, Aidmatrix has grown to globally transact $1.5 billion annually with operations on six continents and with over 35,000 end-user organizations. Aidmatrix provides proven supply chain technology and Internet information systems to connect donors and those in need. Rapidly becoming the global data standard for humanitarian work, Aidmatrix IT connects the private sector, government and nonprofit organizations to achieve their missions more efficiently. Governor McCallum and Aidmatrix have received the 21st Century Achievement Award for "visionary use of information technology to promote positive social, economic and educational change" and has been called by *Computerworld Magazine* a "true hero of the information age."

Ted McDougal is principal of Jacobs + McDougal, a business communications consultancy offering PR solutions in change and reputation management. Recent assignments have included program development covering issues from acquisitions to workplace matters, including consumer marketing, corporate branding, cultural alignment and network/sales communications.

Formerly he was senior vice president and director of Ketchum's Midwest Corporate/Healthcare Practice, specializing in corporate reputation management and CEO positioning for financial services concerns, healthcare providers, manufacturers and consumer packaged goods companies.

Prior to joining Ketchum, McDougal was vice president of public relations for Sears Holdings Corporation, where he led business and financial communications for the nation's third-largest retailer. His accomplishments include successfully positioning Sears' $11-billion merger with Kmart and the $6-billion sale of the company's credit and financial products business to Citigroup, including counseling top management, building strategic consensus and coordinating investor and legal disclosures to secure favorable response from employees, customers and suppliers. In addition, he built marketing public relations programs incorporating product placement, special events, in-store promotion, online retailing and celebrity endorsement.

Before Sears, McDougal spent 17 years in financial services, spanning real estate, securities brokerage and commercial banking. He began his corporate career at Continental Bank in Chicago, where he was responsible for directing public relations, financial and marketing communications. His accomplishments include leading media relations and crisis communications during what was then the largest bank restructuring in U.S. history. He directed internal and external communication programs designed to lead changes associated with repositioning the restructured organization in the marketplace, culminating with its $1.9-billion merger with Bank of America.

A former reporter with experience in the public sector and political campaigns, McDougal earned a bachelor's degree in journalism from Purdue University.

L. James Nelson is a native of Chicago and a graduate of the University of Denver. Jim began his career in volunteer, grassroots politics early on, delivering brochures, buttons and yard signs for a wide variety of campaigns as a kid on his bicycle. Over a period of years, during and after college, Nelson has been involved in dozens of campaigns on behalf of such disparate politicos as Robert F. Kennedy, Gary Hart, Craig Barnes, Tim Wirth, Charles H. Percy, Paul

Goebel and Astronaut Jack Swigert, as well as many, many local and state campaigns.

After working in advertising and several paid political campaign positions, Nelson began his work in advocacy, government relations and public affairs with a strong emphasis in environmental matters, with the National Association of Manufacturers in Detroit, Washington, DC, and Chicago; the Farm and Industrial Equipment Institute; FMC Corporation; Waste Management Incorporated; U.S. Filter and Vivendi Environment. Between corporate assignments, Nelson served as senior group VP of corporate practice for one of Chicago's leading business-to-business public relations firms.

At various points in his career, Nelson has also consulted intensively in long-term relationships with both corporate clients, such as Safety-Kleen, Faultless Starch TRW and Kaiser Eagle Mountain, and nonprofit conservancy The Wetlands Initiative.

Nelson has served in leadership capacities with the business auxiliaries of the U.S. Conference of Mayors, National Governor's Association, National Conference of State Legislatures and State Government Affairs Council. He is a founding board member of the Illinois Chapter of the League of Conservation Voters and is a past president of the Chicago Area Public Affairs Group.

Nelson served as a delegate and presenter to the second Sino-U.S. Mayors' Conference on Urban Development, Infrastructure and Cooperation in Beijing, Suzhou and Xian.

Nelson has been drawn to adjunct work from time to time during his career at institutions of higher learning, including Medill at Northwestern University and the Kennedy School of Government at Harvard, and as lecturer on behalf of Chicago's foreign consulate community for various seminars, symposia, etc.

Jim Nelson lives in Evanston, IL, with his wife Suzanne and their large standard poodle Oscar. Their son Louis is a graduate of the school of media and public affairs at The George Washington University, is a reporter for the Washington Post and lives in Washington, DC.

Richard L. Nelson is vice president of corporate communications for ACCO Brands Corporation (NYSE:ABD), a leading global supplier of branded office products. At ACCO Brands, he is responsible for financial and corporate media relations, external communications, employee communications and corporate philanthropic programs. He joined the company in August of 2005.

In a corporate and political communications career spanning 35 years, Nelson has held senior communications and marketing posts at a number of public companies and their subsidiaries, including CNH Global N.V., First Chicago Corporation, General Motors, Monsanto Company, the NutraSweet Company, Playboy Enterprises and United Airlines. He has also counseled communications clients as an independent consultant, in addition to serving as an associate at two consulting firms, Hill & Knowlton, Inc., and the former Matha MacDonald (now Gagen MacDonald).

He began his career in Washington, DC, in a staff communications role at the Democratic National Committee and then went on to become press secretary for U.S. Representative Mark W. Hannaford and an assistant White House press secretary during the administration of President Jimmy Carter.

Nelson is a former trustee and current member of the Arthur W. Page Society and cochaired two of that organization's Spring Seminars. In addition, he is former president of the board of the AIDS Foundation of Chicago and former board president of the National Runaway Switchboard, a youth advocacy organization based in Chicago.

Until early 2008, he was also executive producer of *Listen Here!*, a public radio program that aired in nearly 70 media markets throughout North America. His firm, Miles Ahead, Inc., produced radio programs showcasing jazz music and musicians beginning in 2001.

Nelson resides in Chicago.

Michael Polzin is divisional vice president of corporate communications for Walgreen Co., the nation's largest drugstore chain and a Fortune 50 company, headquartered in Deerfield, Ill.

His proven track record in the health care and retail industries includes 20 years of experience in media relations, crisis management, labor issues, employee communications, investor relations and corporate social responsibility. Polzin joined Walgreens in 1992 as a communications specialist and was promoted to manager of media relations in 1996, director of external communications in 2005 and director of corporate communications in 2009. He was named to his current position in 2010, in which he leads Walgreens' external communications and media relations functions, including company-wide public relations activities and communications for major divisions.

Prior to joining Walgreens, he was the managing editor of the *Chicago Bear Report* and sports editor at the *Lake Geneva (Wis.) Regional News*.

He earned a BA in journalism from Marquette University, Milwaukee, in 1985. He is a member of the International Association of Business Communicators.

He and his wife, Gail, live in Buffalo Grove, IL.

Cornelius B. Pratt, Ph.D., APR, is a professor in the Department of Strategic Communication at Temple University, United States. He also teaches at Temple University Japan. He is a consultant to the African Public Relations Association. Pratt is also an honorary visiting professor of mass communication at Bingham University, New Karu, Nasarawa State, Nigeria. He served for nearly six years in the communication program of the U.S. Department of Agriculture, Washington, DC, and for 11 years on the faculty of the College of Communication Arts and Sciences at Michigan State University, the last eight years as full professor.

He serves on the editorial review boards of six academic journals, including *The South East Asian Journal of Management, Public Relations Review*, and the *Journal of Pubic Relations Research*. He is coeditor of *Case Studies in Crisis Communication: International Perspectives on Hits and Misses* (New York: Routledge, 2012). His current research interests include international and strategic communication, ethics, public relations and communication for national and regional development, particularly in emerging economies. Pratt earned his Ph.D. from the University of Minnesota at Twin Cities. He is accredited in public relations by the Public Relations Society of America.

Steve Rubel is EVP of global strategy and insights for Edelman—the world's largest independent public relations firm. In his role, Rubel works across the firm to help clients better understand how to unify their communications strategies across mainstream, new, social and owned media.

In addition, Rubel also acts as a highly visible Edelman thought leader and writer on media. He speaks dozens of times each year around the world and appears frequently in the press. In addition, he actively shares his observations and insights at steverubel.com, his monthly *Advertising Age* column and on Twitter—where he is followed by more than 50,000.

Rubel has been named to several prestigious lists, including: *PR Week*'s 40 Under 40 and the Forbes.com Web Celeb 25.

Prior to joining Edelman in 2006, Rubel worked for 15 years in a variety of marketing communications positions in corporate, nonprofit and small/midsized PR firms.

Dana Rubin is an award-winning speechwriter, ghostwriter and communications expert who helps top executives develop thought leadership platforms. She has helped leaders in the corporate, nonprofit and political sectors communicate effectively with a wide variety of key stakeholders.

Speeches she has drafted for her clients have been delivered at the Council on Foreign Relations, the United Nations, the World Bank, Chatham House, the Institute of Directors, the Windsor Leadership Trust, and many other venues. They have been quoted in the national media, including *The New York Times* and *USA Today*, and reprinted in *Vital Speeches of the Day, Executive Speeches* and elsewhere.

Ms. Rubin is the founder and director of the New York Speechwriter's Roundtable, a professional development association in New York City.

She is also a judge for the 2012 Cicero Speechwriting Awards, recognizing the year's best speeches that help leaders achieve prominence in business, politics and society.

Ms. Rubin has been the recipient of the Anson Jones, John Hancock, and Associated Press writing awards. She received her BA with honors from Yale and her MA in English Literature from the University of Texas. She lives in New York City.

Elliot S. Schrieber, Ph.D., is clinical professor of marketing and executive director of the Center for Corporate Reputation Management at the Bennett S. LeBow College of Business, Drexel University, Philadelphia, a position he has held since September 2008. He teaches courses in brand and reputation management and marketing strategy at the MBA and Executive MBA levels. He is recognized internationally as one of the most experienced and respected experts in brand and reputation management.

In addition to his teaching academic position, he also heads his own consulting firm, Brand and Reputation Management LLC, that has worked with international corporations, nonprofits and trade associations to create a holistic, integrated strategy to enhance their brand and reputation.

Schreiber is unique in having moved successfully in and out of the corporate, academic and consulting worlds during his 30-year career. He began his career as a pharmaceutical sales representative. He then went to graduate school and, after receiving his Ph.D., began his career in 1976 as a faculty member at the University of Delaware. In 1980, he moved to the corporate arena, joining the DuPont Company in Wilmington, DE, where he was on the staff of the chairman, developing strategy options for the company's move into pharmaceuticals and electronics, and later headed global marketing communications for DuPont's pharmaceutical, medical diagnostics, x-ray and electronics businesses. From 1986 to1995, he was senior vice president of corporate communications at Bayer Corporation, Pittsburgh, where he designed and built the company's North American corporate marketing and communications organization. In 1995, he moved to Toronto to become senior vice president of corporate marketing and communications at Nortel, with global responsibility for all marketing and communications functions. He was a member of the company's Executive Council and chair of the Global Marketing and Sales Council. He left Nortel in 1999 to become president and chief operating officer of Digital 4Sight, Toronto, an e-business strategy consulting and research firm. He and his partners sold the firm in 2001, and he returned to teaching and independent consulting.

He was a professor at the DeGroote School of Business, McMaster University, Hamilton, Ontario (2001-2004), and from 2004 to 2006 was a visiting professor at Penn State, Syracuse, Temple and Villanova universities. After moving back to the United States, he was senior advisor to the Reputation Institute, New York.

Schreiber holds a BA from the University of Delaware and an MA and Ph.D. from Penn State University. He is the recipient of numerous business awards and has been a featured speaker at major business and academic conferences. He is the author of a variety of articles on reputation and brand management in leading academic journals and books. His is a member of the Arthur W. Page Society and the Academic Liaison Committee of the Chief Marketing Officer Council Worldwide.

Schreiber and his wife of 41 years, Phyllis, live in Philadelphia. They have two children, Allyson, of San Francisco, and Adam, of Hoboken, NJ.

Jayme Silverstone leads marketing operations and strategy for Accenture, with responsibility for strategic planning, operations and talent management across the marketing and communications organization globally. Previously, she led executive communications, working with Accenture's chief executive officer and senior leadership team.

Ms. Silverstone joined the company in 1991. While at Accenture, she has held a variety of marketing

and communications roles in the company's technology organization and also spent several years based in both Europe and Asia Pacific overseeing thought leadership marketing activities. She is a member of the Accenture Marketing & Communications Leadership Team.

Ms. Silverstone holds a BA from Northwestern University and an MBA from the Kellogg School of Management.

Sara E. Smith, MSIMC, is an independent business intelligence and content strategy consultant based in Boulder, CO. She has worked for the Archdiocese of San Francisco, R.R. Donnelley & Sons, Euro RSCG Chicago and the Chicago for Rahm Emanuel mayoral campaign in a variety of roles in communications and strategy. She was editor-in-chief of the 2011 edition of the *Journal of Integrated Marketing Communications*.

Sara is a graduate of the Honors Program at the University of Colorado at Boulder and holds a master's degree in integrated marketing communications from the Medill School at Northwestern University.

Kurt P. Stocker serves as a director of NYSE Regulation Inc., a subsidiary of NYSE Euronext and is the chairman of the NYSE Individual Investor Advisory Board. He is a member of the Board of Governors of Financial Industry Regulatory Authority, Inc. (formerly, NASD). And has served as a member of the Advisory Committee of the U.S. Securities and Exchange Commission.

Stocker is a visiting lecturer at Northwestern University's Medill School of Journalism Integrated Marketing Communications program. Previously, he was an Associate Professor at Northwestern's Medill School of Journalism, where he served as Director of Graduate Public Relations.

From 1988–1994, Stocker was Chief Corporate Relations Officer of Continental Bank Corp. He was responsible for Continental Bank's marketing, public relations, internal communications, advertising, industry, financial communications and legislative relations programs. Prior to joining Continental, he served as Senior Vice President of Corporate Communications for United Airlines from 1985, where he was responsible for global corporate communications and customer relations.

Until 1980, he headed a number of functions at Allstate Insurance Company, including public relations, employee/labor relations, employee benefits and human resources. Stocker was a Senior Vice President for the Chicago office of Hill and Knowlton, Director of H&K's Denver office and managed its National Labor Relations and Media Training practices.

He is a past president of the Arthur W. Page Society and a member of their Hall of Fame. He served as a member of The Disclosure Advisory Board of PR Newswire Association LLC, and Ketchum's Corporate Governance Advisory Board. He was a commodore of the Chicago Yacht Club. He is a principal in Story Trading, LLC. He is also widely published in articles and books on Corporate Governance, Public Relations, Integrated Marketing and Crisis Communications. Stocker earned his BS degree in business from Marietta College in Ohio.

Roxanne Taylor is chief marketing and communications officer of Accenture. She is responsible for the company's global marketing and communications activities, including image and market development, corporate and financial communications, industry analyst and media relations, brand management, advertising and research. She leads Accenture's global team of more than 700 marketing and communications professionals and is also a member of Accenture's Global Management Committee.

Prior to being appointed to her current role in 2007, Ms. Taylor served as Accenture's managing director of corporate and financial communications. She joined the company in 1995 as director of marketing and communications for the financial services practice and was promoted to partner in 2000.

Ms. Taylor has more than 25 years of experience in marketing and corporate communications. Before joining Accenture, she held corporate communications and marketing roles for Reuters and Citicorp. She also served in a variety of product development, sales and marketing positions with Credit Suisse Bank and the Deak-Perera Group.

Ms. Taylor is a member of the Arthur W. Page Society and the Marketing 50. She also serves on the Business Committee of the Metropolitan Museum of Art and on the National Council for Research on Women's Corporate Circle Advisory Board. Ms. Taylor holds a bachelor's degree from the University of Maryland.

Bill Trumpfheller is the president of Nuffer, Smith, Tucker (NST) Public Relations and knows the true meaning of climbing the corporate ladder, as he joined NST in 1986 as an intern! An avid skier who volunteers his time for the National Ski Patrol, Bill has been a communicator and strategist since his first direct mail job at the age of 13 (stuffing envelopes for his mom's

travel agency). Bill is passionate about the community and the clients he works with, and when he's not on the slopes, he can be found serving on the boards of several local nonprofit associations and spending time with his wife and two daughters.

Kerry D. Tucker, is Chief Executive Officer, Nuffer, Smith, Tucker, Inc.

Nuffer, Smith, Tucker, Inc. (NST) is the oldest and largest public relations firm in San Diego with an office in Sacramento.

Mr. Tucker brings more than 40 years of experience to the fields of strategic planning, issue anticipation/management, public relations and coalition building. His clientele reaches deep into the national and California agri-food chain with brand marketing and healthcare forming additional areas of specialty.

Mr. Tucker has been a leader in the field of issue anticipation/management for more than a decade. In 1995, he received the Howard Chase Award from the Issue Management Council, the highest international distinction for individuals practicing issue management.

He led the creation of one of the country's first issue anticipation systems in the late 1970s and has since initiated a number of systems for clients. He led collaboration between NST and the California Institute of Food and Agricultural Research at University of California, Davis in 1993 to create Food Foresight, the first trends intelligence system exclusively for the field of food and agriculture. He also led a colloquium on the state of the art of issue management sponsored by NST, San Diego State and Northwestern universities.

Organizing multi-disciplined problem-solving teams and designing and facilitating systems to maximize their collective contributions to managing complex issues have become a point of difference for Mr. Tucker. On a parallel path, he's been instrumental in organizing and facilitating a number of national coalitions, identifying common issues and seeking consensus and commitment on mutually beneficial strategies for managing them.

Mr. Tucker's issue-driven public relations process is described in his book, Public Relations Writing: An Issue-Driven, Behavioral Approach, third edition, Prentice-Hall, 1997. He has written and spoken extensively on the subject. Under his leadership, NST was honored in as one of the country's most innovative public relations firms by a national public relations trade magazine.

John Wallis has served as global head of marketing and brand strategy since November 2008. Mr. Wallis's career with Hyatt began in 1981. Prior to his current role, Mr. Wallis served as senior vice president of product and brand development since August 2007. From 2004 through 2007, Mr. Wallis served as senior vice president of global asset management, where he was responsible for the management of more than 40 Hyatt-owned properties across North America, Latin America, Europe and Asia. He has also served in a variety of other management positions, senior vice president of marketing and sales and vice president of marketing for Hyatt International Corporation; general manager and regional vice president of Gulf states for Hyatt Regency Dubai; executive assistant manager of food and beverage for Hyatt Regency Kuwait, Hyatt Regency Fiji and Hyatt Kingsgate Sydney and various other food and beverage management positions.

Patricia Therese Whalen, Ph.D., APR, president, Whalen Communications Group, is a consultant and educator in the area of public relations and marketing communication. She is the former director of DePaul University's graduate program in public relations and advertising and served on the faculty at Northwestern University's Medill Integrated Marketing Communications (IMC) graduate program for eight years.

She has consulted for a number of consumer, healthcare, higher education, and business-to-business clients in the areas of consumer research, crisis management, strategic planning, marketing communications, and organizational change. She has also provided strategic counsel for agency clients that included Borders Books and Music; Campbell Soup Company; Koch Industries; Ball Park Franks, Medical College of Ohio, and Owens-Corning.

Pat is the author of two books: *A Marketers Guide to Public Relations in the 21st Century (Thomson, 2006)*, coauthored with Thomas L. Harris; and *Corporate Communication From A to Z—An Encyclopedia for Public Relations & Marketing Professionals (IABC, 2005)*. She authored the IABC's 2002 top-selling research study entitled, "How Communication Drives Merger Success," and contributed chapters on mergers and acquisitions for the book *Inside Corporate Communications* (Jossey-Bass, 2006 and 2010).

Prior to her academic and consulting career, Pat spent 17 years in senior corporate marketing and communication positions. She served as the top corporate communication executive for a Fortune 300 automotive manufacturing firm, where she was awarded a PRSA Silver Anvil for crisis communication. She also spent eight years with Comsat Corporation, a Washington, DC-based international telecommunications firm (subsequently acquired by Lockheed Martin) where she served as Director of Marketing and Communication.

Pat holds a doctorate in mass media from Michigan State University, a master's degree in business administration from Indiana University, and a bachelor's degree in English from the Ohio State University. She is accredited with the Public Relations Society of America and serves on its Board of Ethics and Professional Standards. ptwhalen@gmail.com, (847) 507-0626.

Craig Wirth is a very well known producer and broadcaster on network and academic television. He holds an MA from the University of Wisconsin–Madison (MA 1976) and a BA from the University of Utah–Salt Lake City (1973). He teaches communication studies, visual media, newsbreak, television journalism and visual media production. His awards include: the Quintus C. Wilson Award (1992), Nafziger Award for outstanding young alumni from the University of Wisconsin School of Journalism (1987), Emmy Award from the Academy of Television Arts and Sciences (1985) and Emmy Award from the New York Chapter of the National Academy of Television Arts and Sciences (1984). Craig.wirth@utah.edu.

INDEX

WW II and, 80–82
WWI and, 79–80
Public Relations Association of Austria (PRVA), 836
Public Relations Consultants Association (PRCA), 835
Public Relations Institute of Australia (PRIA), 836
Public Relations Institute of Ireland (PRII), 835–36
Public Relations Institute of New Zealand (PRINZ), 834
Public Relations Society for Indonesia (PRSI), 837
Public Relations Society of America (PRSA), 17, 23, 25–26, 37,
    60–61, 80, 382, 578, 803–4, 828, 835, 844
Public Relations Society of India (PRSI), 836
Public Relay, 46
Public safety, communication for, 495
Public service announcement (PSA), 248, 734
Publicists, as lobbyists, 79, 664
Publicity Bureau, U.S., 78, 85
Puerto Rico, Haitian aid by, 303
Pujo Committee, 364–65
Pulse Opinion Research, 407
Pure Food and Drug Act, 660
PWC Lodging Industry Outlook, 528

Al Qaeda, 92, 216, 232
Query letter, 733–34. *See also* Media
Quintilian, 761
Qzone, 264

Radian6, 149
Radio
    broadcasting over, 243
    deregulation of, 246–47
    as digital, 243, 246
    Rule of 7s for, 246
Radio Television Digital News Association (RTDNA), 251–53
Ragan.com, 502
Rand, Honey, 438
Random Acts of Generosity, 529–30. *See also* Hyatt Hotels
    Corporation
Rangel, Charles E., 220
Rank Group Limited, 285
Raphaelson, Joel, 775
Rasmussen Reports, 407, 411, 650
Raymond, Lee, 692
Raytheon, 496
RCRA. *See* Resource Conservation and Recovery Act (1976)
R&D. *See* Research & development
Reagan, Ronald, 89–90, 226, 753, 757, 759
Reedy, George, 87
Regulation
    of aviation, 497
    of corporations, 369
    of financial and banking industry, 646, 649–50
    for governance, 364–68
    by governments, 616
    of healthcare industry, 618–19
    of insurance industry, 518
    by IRS, 210
    of nonprofits, 291
    of pharmaceuticals, 616
    of PR speech, 61
    of PRC tobacco, 97–98, 100, 107–10, 112

stakeholders for, 5
violation of, 57
Regulation Fair Disclosure, 177
Reinhart, Uwe, 619
Relationship economy, 446–47
Relationship Economy eXpedition (REX), 446
Relationships
    brands and, 446
    communication for, 443, 502, 729
    in context, 447–48
    with customers, 529
    definition of, 4
    information through, 505
    integration of, 4
    interaction within, 4
    legal industry and, 357
    local contacts for, 8
    marketing and, 443, 638
    MPR for, 165
    by PR, 10, 581
    trust and commitment in, 581, 729
Reliance Industries, 135
Remini, Robert V., 74
Renren, 259, 264
Reputation
    of associations and organizations, 3–4, 57, 323, 350
    of brand, 134, 150, 323, 415, 474, 476, 605
    communication for, 397–98, 459–60, 469
    defamation of, 63–64
    definition of, 460, 518
    employees for, 209, 632
    expectations for, 470–71
    of financial and banking industry, 645
    governance for, 370
    image *vs.*, 518, 522
    importance of, 350, 407
    of insurance companies, 513, 518–19, 522–23, 623
    of legal industry, 57, 708
    management of, 4, 350, 390–96, 475, 518, 521
    measurement of, 518
    of organization, 3–4, 57, 323, 350
    PR and, 387
    as sensitive, 474
    stakeholders, 460, 470
Reputation, Realizing Value from the Corporate Image (Fombrun), 518
"Reputation and Reputational Risk Management" (conference), 523
Reputation Institute, 468, 512, 518
Reputation Leadership Council, 518
Reputational intelligence, 463–67
Research, system for
    for accountability, 13–14, 16, 34n4
    as analysis, 53–54
    by associations and organizations, 486
    audit for, 31–32
    budgeting for, 14
    case studies for, 26–30
    conflict of interest in, 30–31
    on consumers, 148
    content analysis for, 29–30
    for decisionmaking, 14
    firm selection for, 30–31
    focus groups for, 20–21
    as formative, 583–84

CPSIA information can be obtained
at www.ICGtesting.com
Printed in the USA
JSHW011224141219
2894JS00002BB/7